THE IDEA OF THE VERNACULAR

THE IDEA
OF THE
VERNACULAR

AN ANTHOLOGY OF
MIDDLE ENGLISH LITERARY THEORY,
1280–1520

Edited by
Jocelyn Wogan-Browne, Nicholas Watson,
Andrew Taylor, Ruth Evans

With contributions from participants in the
Cardiff Conferences on Medieval Translation:
Ian R. Johnson, Helen Phillips, Stephen Shepherd,
Alexandra Barratt, Brendan Biggs, Denis Renevey;
and with the assistance of Cynthea Masson and Patricia Sunderland

The Pennsylvania State University Press
University Park, Pennsylvania

Library of Congress Cataloging-in-Publication Data

The idea of the vernacular : an anthology of Middle English literary theory, 1280–1520 /
   edited by Jocelyn Wogan-Browne ... [et al.] ; with contributions from participants in
   the Cardiff conferences on Medieval translation, Ian Johnson ... [et al.] ; and with
   the assistance of Cynthea Masson and Patricia Sunderland.

     p.   cm.
    Includes bibliographical references (p.   ) and index.
    ISBN 0-271-01757-0 (cloth : acid-free paper)
    ISBN 0-271-01758-9 (paper : acid-free paper)
    1. English literature— Middle English, 1100–1500—History and criticism
—Theory, etc. 2. England—Intellectual life—1066–1485. 3. Criticism—England.
4. Native language.   I. Wogan-Browne, Jocelyn.
    PR255.I34   1999
    801'.95'09420902—dc21   98-19578
                                              CIP

It is the policy of The Pennsylvania State University Press to use acid-free paper for the first
printing of all clothbound books. Publications on uncoated stock satisfy the minimum requirements of American National Standard for Information Sciences—Permanence of Paper for
Printed Library Materials, ANSI Z39.48–1992.

CONTENTS

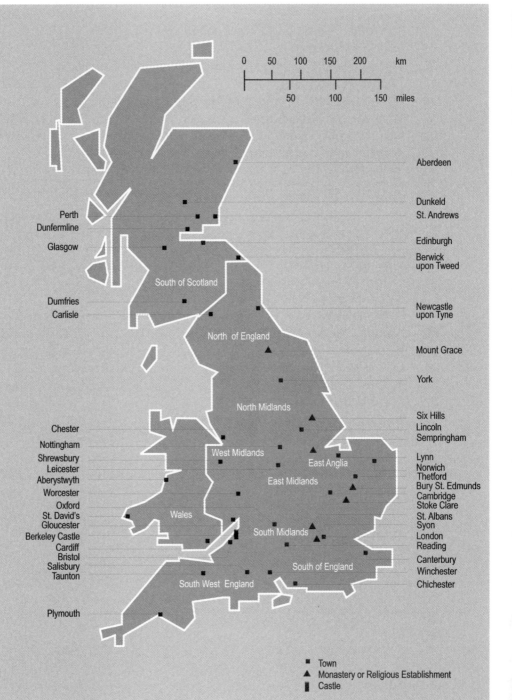

0 50 100 150 200	km
50 100 150	miles

Aberdeen

Dunkeld
St. Andrews

Perth
Dunfermline

Edinburgh

Glasgow

Berwick
upon Tweed

South of Scotland

Dumfries
Carlisle

Newcastle
upon Tyne

North of England

Mount Grace

York

North Midlands

Six Hills

Chester

Lincoln
Sempringham

Nottingham
Shrewsbury
Leicester
Aberystwyth
Worcester
Oxford
St. David's
Gloucester
Berkeley Castle
Cardiff
Bristol
Salisbury
Taunton

West Midlands

East Anglia

Lynn
Norwich
Thetford
Bury St. Edmunds
Cambridge
Stoke Clare
St. Albans
Syon
London
Reading
Canterbury
Winchester
Chichester

East Midlands

Wales

South Midlands

South of England

South West England

Plymouth

■ Town
▲ Monastery or Religious Establishment
▌ Castle

ACKNOWLEDGMENTS

The collaborations and debts of this volume are complex. The idea of examining vernacular prologues as literary theory grew directly out of the series of Cardiff International Conferences on Medieval Translation organized by Roger Ellis (one of which was co-organized by Ruth Evans). The project was developed at the instigation of Jocelyn Wogan-Browne, who invited colleagues to form an editorial committee. The project has been immeasurably enhanced by the participation of the other editors. Suggestions and discussion from many participants at the Cardiff conferences also contributed to the early stages. Although the volume was originally conceived as including Anglo-Norman and early Middle English material, and hence designed not only to acknowledge but to present something of the linguistic diversity of medieval England, it rapidly became clear that the amount of material yielded by the investigation and the complexity of its contextualization made a smaller scope necessary. Middle English written within the period 1280–1520 was then collectively adopted as the focus. In the final version, Andrew Taylor has undertaken responsibility for Part One and the Index, Ruth Evans for Part Two, and Nicholas Watson for Part Three and the Alternative Arrangements of the Excerpts, while Jocelyn Wogan-Browne has worked as general editor on all the material and contributed the Glossary, and all editors have contributed material to Part Four. Nicholas Watson and Andrew Taylor have coordinated the final stages of the book's production. We have extensively read, discussed, emended, and revised each other's material in a collaboration that, we hope, is more than the sum of its parts. We all owe a great deal to each other's work, as also to the colleagues who have contributed texts and ideas to the volume.

Ian Johnson played a major role in the initial shaping of Part One, contributing to editorial discussions and suggesting and providing first transcripts of excerpts 1.5, 1.8, 1.11, 1.12, 1.15, and 1.16 and some introductory materials. To Helen Phillips we owe excerpts 1.1 and 1.3 and introductory essays of such incisive elegance and range that we have gratefully plundered them not only in headnotes but for the framing material of the volume in Parts One and Four. Other texts were suggested and contributed by Stephen Shepherd (excerpts 2.2, 2.4, and 2.5), Alexandra Barratt (excerpts 2.6 and 3.21), Denis Renevey (excerpt 3.3), and Brendan Biggs (excerpt 2.8). These excerpts were contributed as independently edited pieces equipped with introductory material and notes, and we thank all contributors warmly for their expert work; the editors are responsible for the final form in which these excerpts appear, since contributors have graciously allowed us to adapt their materials for integration into the volume's argument as a whole.

Cynthea Masson's meticulous initial copyediting went far beyond technicalities and clarified many aspects of the work, making a significant intellectual contribution to the volume. We are grateful to Fiona Somerset for help in checking the transcriptions of excerpts 2.2 and 3.8. For further ideas and discussions, we thank Valerie Allen, Rita Copeland, Margaret Connolly, Fernando Todo, and Yoko Iyeiri. Nicholas Davis generously supplied a formulation of Wycliffite translation issues from his own work in this area, which greatly developed our account. Lynn Staley and Theresa Coletti were generous in fulfillment of their roles as Penn State Press readers and provided invaluable suggestions for the organization of the volume as well as stimulating and constructive encouragement. The anonymous readers for Exeter University Press were also very generous with specific suggestions and encouragement. We warmly thank all our readers for their work, which has contributed materially to the volume's finished shape.

Alastair Minnis, in addition to the important contribution of his pioneering work on medieval Latin theory, has played a practical role in this book's genesis. His intellectual generosity and prodigious learning was an inspiration to all who had the benefit of attending the postgraduate conferences in medieval literary theory and literary practice held alternately at Liverpool and Bristol in the mid to late 1980s. These meetings posed questions generative for this volume, and many of their participants went on to the Cardiff international translation series of conferences.

Copyediting work by Cynthea Masson and Catherine Grisé and invaluable early work on the Bibliography and Glossary by Patricia Sunderland were supported as part of several research grants to Nicholas Watson from the University of Western Ontario and the Social Sciences and Humanities Research Council of Canada, and we are grateful to the university authorities and to the SSHRC for their generosity. Further copyediting work by Stephanie Dayes, Amber Raiz, Beata Pawlowska, and Adetayo Alabi was funded by the Ontario government's "work-study" program and the University of Saskatchewan's Publication Fund. Costs associated with the book's front cover were covered in part by the Kenneth Muir Research Fund, the Department of English Language and Literature, University of Liverpool; the Research Fund, School of English, Communication, and Philosophy, Cardiff University; and the Smallman Fund, Faculty of Arts, University of Western Ontario. The other editors would like to thank Nicholas Watson for the generosity with which he has made available the research resources of his own work on vernacularity. For research support and help with research expenses, Ruth Evans thanks the School of English, Communication, and Philosophy, Cardiff University, and Andrew Taylor thanks Northern Kentucky University and the University of Saskatchewan. Jocelyn Wogan-Browne thanks the Department of English Language and Literature, University of Liverpool, for funding research assistance from her postgraduates Mary Clinton and Gwen Jones in checking her work on the Glossary. Nicholas Watson thanks Christopher Cannon for his thoughtful comments on a draft of the second essay in Part Four. We thank Peter Potter of Penn State Press for his enterprise in publishing the volume: he and his team have been among the most patient, skillful, and constructive of publishers to work with. In particular, we thank Keith Monley, our copyeditor, whose eagle eye pierced through many tangles and greatly improved the finished work.

For permission to consult and quote from manuscripts and early printed books in their care, we thank the Master and Fellows of Balliol College, Oxford; the Bibliothèque Nationale, Paris; the Bridwell Library, Southern Methodist College, Dallas, Texas; the British Library, London; the Bodleian Library, Oxford; the Syndics of Cambridge University Library; the President and Fellows of Corpus Christi College, Oxford; the Master and Fellows of Corpus Christi College, Cambridge; the Librarian of Downside Abbey; the Trustees of the National Library of Scotland, Edinburgh; the Royal College of Physicians, Edinburgh; the Department of Special Collections, Glasgow University Library; the Houghton Library, Harvard University; the Hunterian Library, Glasgow; the Huntington Library, San Marino, California; the Masters of the Bench of the Inner Temple, London; the Special Collections Librarian, Sydney Jones Library, University of Liverpool; Pembroke College, Cambridge; the Manuscripts Division, Department of Rare Books and Special Collections, Princeton University Library, Princeton, New Jersey; the Master and Fellows of Trinity College, Cambridge; the Board of Trinity College, Dublin; the Master and Fellows of University College, Oxford. For permission to reproduce the two miniatures on the cover of the paperback version of this book, we thank, in the one case, the Huntingdon Library, San Marino, California; in the other, the Dean and Chapter of Liverpool cathedral, the Sydney Jones Library, University of Liverpool, and Dr. Maureen Watry, Special Collections Librarian. For permission to reprint translations from *The Latin Verses in the "Confessio Amantis,"* translated by Siân Echard and Claire Fanger, 1991, we thank Colleagues Press, East Lansing, Michigan.

The cover of the paperback version of this book presents two unusual and contrasting donor portraits from fifteenth-century English manuscripts.

One (from Liverpool Cathedral, MS Radcliffe 6, f. 5v) is a rare presentation miniature involving two women from a Book of the *Hours of the Guardian Angel*, apparently commissioned by the wealthy gentry widow Joan Luyt between 1475 and 1483, probably for Elizabeth Woodville, queen of Edward IV. During the 1480s, Luyt became patroness of the chapel of the confraternity of All Angels, a devotional guild for women and men at Brentford, near Syon abbey (see excerpts 1.12, 3.5, 3.12), whose chapel and hospital were dedicated by Henry VI in 1433/ 1436. In the miniature she kneels, her hair decorously bound, to present the book to Woodville (whose hair is unbound, as befits a queen) with the words "wt euerlastyng ioy" (with everlasting joy), perhaps a quotation from a hymn that occurs later in the book. Although Luyt was socially Woodville's inferior and may implicitly be asking her for patronage—as the English dedicatory poem that precedes the miniature in the manuscript also suggests—these words amount to a reminder of the devout widow's influence in the spiritual realm, and hence of the interdependence between her and the queen. Luyt's profession as widow (like the confraternity she here represents) bridges the gap between active and contemplative lives. This is why she can offer not just a book but the hope of eternal salvation to England's queen, through the power of the Guardian Angel the book teaches the reader to invoke. Given the spiritual authority medieval culture also attributed to queens, perhaps Luyt can also be seen as offering this hope through Woodville to the nation as a whole. (See Sutton and Visser-Fuchs 1997 for the identifications, the dedicatory poem, and for further discussion.)

The other donor portrait (from Huntingdon Library, MS 268, f. 18r, a copy of Lydgate's *Fall of Princes* made around 1450) shows a confidently *seated* Lydgate, wearing his Benedictine habit and holding up his hand in a gesture of instruction, as he presents his book to a man wearing academic garb. The man may be Duke Humphrey of Gloucester, who commissioned the poem, and whom the miniature shows not as the poem's instrumental cause (as is usual in presentation miniatures), but as the target of its didacticism. Yet as Seth Lerer (1993: 40-44) suggests, the man may rather be Boccaccio, author of Lydgate's source text—in which case the portrait shows a translator's power over not his patron but his *auctor*. Here, again, the deferential relationship a social or cultural inferior should have toward a superior is thus both presented and complicated (see excerpt 1.7, but contrast excerpt 2.2). Luyt's kneeling stillness presents the viewer with an image of the devotional stance her book hopes to inculcate, and makes her the moral center of the *Hours of the Guardian Angel* image. Lydgate sits to the side of the *Fall of Princes* miniature, on a hard chair rather than a throne. But his thin form and black monastic clothing—traditionally associated with the virtue of humility, and far different in their austerity from what we know of the historical Lydgate—likewise give him at least equal status with his patron or *auctor*, and suggest that the relation between secular wealth and/or learning and the didactic authority of the monk-poet is also one of interdependence.

INTRODUCTION

This book provides material for a history of English literary theory and practice in the two centuries before the so-called early modern period by bringing together for the first time a wide selection of Middle English discussions of writing: its composition, cultural position, real and imagined audience, and reception. Medievalists have not always taken such discussions, in either the vernacular or Latin, seriously. Until the 1980s, when A. J. Minnis published a major study of scholastic theory, *Medieval Theory of Authorship* (1988, first published 1984), most medieval scholars paid little attention to the variety of attitudes toward language and writing found in medieval texts, the extent to which these changed over the millennium to which the term "medieval" is applied, or the interrelationships between theories of textuality and literary practice during that millennium. For all the pioneering work of Ernest Robert Curtius (1990, first published 1948/53) and, more recently, James J. Murphy (1974), Marcia Colish (1983), and others, it was widely assumed that medieval attitudes toward textual analysis consisted of nothing but a set of variations on the allegorical framework developed for biblical interpretation termed "the four senses of Scripture" (de Lubac 1959–64; Smalley 1983). This was most true of the influential Princeton school, one of whose leading exponents, D. W. Robertson (1962), argued that textual exegetics (allegorical reading leading to the revelation of a single spiritual truth) was the only valid (i.e., properly historicist) way of reading Middle English texts. Robertson's approach was from the start criticized for "interpretive determinism" (as Minnis characterizes it [1988, xv]). Yet its influence on a whole generation of medievalists (e.g., Judson Boyce Allen [1982] and R. E. Kaske [1988]) was considerable (for discussion, see Patterson 1987, 3–39; Dinshaw 1989, 28–30), not least in fostering the assumption that vernacular texts can only be understood within a frame of reference established by Latin ones. It is not surprising that historians of literary theory have often understood medievalists themselves as confirming an ancient view of the Middle Ages as a mere interregnum between the classical period and the Renaissance: a ponderous age of unreflective exegesis of the Bible and classical Latin poets such as Ovid, dominated by the authoritative pronouncements of church fathers and Latin-speaking clerics whose ideas of literature could bear no relation to a rich critical tradition thought to begin in England with Philip Sidney's *Defence of Poesy* in the 1580s (Aers 1992b; Middleton 1992).

This persistent view of medieval theory is part of an institutional marginalization of the Middle Ages (one to an extent perpetuated by medievalists themselves) that has proved resistant to challenge almost since the humanists invented the period and so constructed their own era as a renaissance, a rebirth (Vessey 1994, responding to Jardine 1993). But it can no longer be claimed to have any validity. Influenced by the growing impact of theory in other areas of literary and social studies, in the last fifteen years medieval scholars like Brian Stock (1983), Rita Copeland (1991), Martin Irvine (1994), and A. J. Minnis (1988, Minnis and Scott 1988) have shown how an array of medieval writers reflected on their activities, developing sophisticated and often still-influential traditions of thinking, not only about hermeneutics and rhetoric but about pedagogy and literacy, language, linguistics and textuality, historiography, fiction, genre, translation, and much else. At the same time, literary scholars, who had already been analyzing medieval texts within modern theoretical frameworks, have begun to set these texts alongside what we are coming to know about medieval theory, and to read each through the other so as to problematize both (for examples in a broad array of modes, see Zumthor 1972a/b; Dragonetti 1980; Dinshaw 1989; Leupin 1989; Copeland 1991; Margherita 1994; Haug 1996; Spence 1996). This move has been vital in preventing medieval or modern textual methodologies from being applied without self-conscious reflection on the political implications of any critical practice.

In recent years, coinciding with the emergence of several theoretical schools that share a common interest in the political and ideological role of literary texts (see Patterson 1987, 1990; Aers 1988, 1992a)—especially new historicism and postcolonial and cultural studies (Biddick 1993; Scanlon 1994)—there has also been new interest in the theoretical and ideological structures underlying vernacular texts. It is true that, as recently as 1992, Norman Blake claimed that "the Middle English period . . . contained almost no discussion in English about the type of language and style which might be appropriate for writings in English," so that "there is no foundation upon which one might build a theoretical approach to the literary language of the time" (1992, 502). Yet the resistance to theory implied in this (certainly incorrect) statement is no longer common. Minnis and Copeland both end their books with accounts of vernacular writers (Jean de Meun, Dante, Chaucer, and Gower) who adapted many of their practices from their Latin sources (or *auctores*); the dissemination of Latin methodologies into the vernacular literatures of late medieval Europe has been the subject of much recent research; and there is increasing evidence of the extent to which vernacular writers—and not only the high-culture writers just mentioned—had concerns of their own, products of the changing, uneasy, and complex status of vernacular writing (see, e.g., Dragonetti 1980; Lusignan 1986, 1997; or the corpus of texts translated in Shapiro 1990). The general purpose of this book is to contribute to this burgeoning awareness of theoretical writing in the vernacular by presenting one part of the surviving corpus of such writing, in the form of a neglected body of material from England and Scotland.

What is this material and why does it matter? So far as this book is concerned, much of it consists of prologues to an assortment of texts written c. 1280–c. 1520. These range from self-consciously fictional narratives to historical chronicles, theological treatises to alchemical guides, devotional meditations to public polemics, and are written in a variety of prose and poetic modes, in different dialects, and at very different lengths. We refer to these works as "literature" for two reasons: to blur the division that continues to be made between "literary" and other kinds of texts, a division whose equation of literature with the fictional prevents many Middle English texts from gaining a modern readership; and to indicate from the start that most of these prologues reflect self-consciously on a crucial medieval understanding of "literature," one that relates not to the status of the text but to that of the reader. This understanding is derived from a common distinction between *litterati* and *illiterati*—roughly "educated" and "uneducated"—whose shifting definitions along the fault line dividing Latin from vernacular (see Grundmann 1958; Clanchy 1993, chap. 7; Millett 1996; Greenblatt 1997) are a principal preoccupation of this book.

The prologues are as varied as the texts they preface, taking the form of narratives, lyrics, exhortations and prayers, formal discussions of intention and structure along academic lines, and so on. Most of the texts are translations from Latin or French, and the prologues often concern translation itself: a major cultural issue during the period, since it was often through translation that the authority of canonical Latin or vernacular texts, and of the languages themselves, was reinforced or sometimes subverted. Other prologues (and a number of passages within texts) discuss theories of authorship or language (see Part One of this book). Others address—and by addressing attempt to construct—various categories of audience (Part Two). Others try to organize readers' responses by instructing their audience in the mode of reading to be followed, or reflect more generally on the place of writing or the vernacular in secular or religious life (Part Three). (Of course, these divisions are partly arbitrary, since many prologues bridge these categories.) The intellectual background of these prologues is often to be found in Latin texts, and this use of authoritative older models is frequently made explicit. Yet on closer examination these vernacular discussions are often less dependent on these models and more distinctively concerned with issues specific to the vernacular than they pretend to be—influenced as they were by the flexibility and dialectical variety of English, a language that had yet to be standardized, bore a close relation to the spoken word, and was struggling for cultural recognition. It is for this reason that the excerpts collected in this book can be considered to constitute not just a collection of literary theory that happens to be written in Middle English, but a collection of Middle English literary theory.

The most obvious focus for such a collection might seem to be the works of Chaucer and the high-culture tradition of secular literature he represents. After all, it is Chaucer who was ascribed canonical and authoritative status in the fifteenth century, who was (and to an extent is) credited with the establishment of a distinct English literary language (Cannon 1996), and whose relations to Latin theoretical models have been analyzed most extensively (Minnis 1988; Copeland 1991). Yet although this book repeatedly invokes Chaucer in its notes and contains excerpts from a number of works in the "Chaucer tradition," its main focus is elsewhere, with some of the many other texts and writers—most of them neglected by modern scholars and readers—whose accounts of what it is to write in Middle English are not Chaucer-centered. This is in part simply because the works of Chaucer are well known and easily accessible, but mainly because the internationalist high-culture tradition he represents is less pivotal to the development of written English and of *theorizing* in and about English than is often thought. Influential as the formulation of the history of writing in English that centers on Chaucer has been, it excludes the vast bulk of Middle English writing and is only one among a number of possible accounts of what English writers understood and declared themselves to be doing. The main argument of this anthology is simply that there is such a thing as Middle English literary theory and that it needs to be taken seriously as a distinct field. (This argument is advanced in detail in the essays collected in Part Four of the book, but is implicit in the headnotes and explanatory notes to all the excerpts.) Yet one of the most striking features of the literary history of English this argument opens up—a literary history centered on the theme of the vernacular—is its capacity to place Chaucer's rightly praised achievements in context, as an important part of much larger developments. It is these larger developments in the nature and status of the written vernacular—as they are articulated, in a variety of often contradictory ways, in the prologues to Middle English texts of all kinds—that are the subject of this anthology.

USING THIS VOLUME

A Note on Conventions and Treatment of Text

Unless otherwise stated, excerpts have been edited from single manuscripts or early printed texts. Where texts survive in more than one copy or version, we have chosen representative manuscripts of particular interest for their provenance, circulation, or compilation. Where these are unknown, the earliest or fullest manuscript, or, in some cases, the one most readily available, has been chosen. Manuscript titles, incipits, and explicits are retained and, to emphasize their role as part of the texts as encountered by medieval readers, have been included *within* the lineation of our excerpts. Other conventions of transcription are as follows: abbreviations are silently expanded; þ is transcribed as *th*, ð as *y, g, s, z,* or *gh* as appropriate; consonantal *i* is transcribed as *j*, but *i/y* vocalic variation is allowed to stand; *u* is transcribed as *v* and on occasion as *w* when consonantal and as *u* when vocalic; initial *ff* is transcribed as *f* or *F*. Numerals, unless otherwise stated, have been left as lowercase Roman letters with final *j* normalized to *i,* and are clarified in notes or glosses where necessary. Scribal word division, punctuation, and paragraphing are modernized, though in several cases medieval punctuation of particular interest has been retained. Editorial emendation is signaled by square brackets and recorded in the notes. Scriptural quotations are normally identified in notes to texts where they are not identified in the texts themselves. Direct scriptural quotation is signaled by quotation marks; allusions are identified in the notes. All citations are from the Vulgate version. Citations from the Psalms also include the numbering in the Authorized Version.

In introductions, essays, notes, and headnotes, the excerpts and essays are cross-referenced by part and number in Arabic figures (thus, for example, essay 4.2 indicates the second essay in Part Four). Cross-references to specific line numbers follow excerpt numbers and are separated therefrom by a colon (e.g., excerpt 1.4: 7–10); cross-references to specific notes include an *n* (e.g., excerpt 1.12: 10–18n). References to Chaucer's works are to *The Riverside Chaucer* (Benson 1987). Shortened bibliographical references (author's surname followed by date of publication) are used throughout the book; references are given in full in the Bibliography. The latest date of publication is normally given in shortened references, with information about first date of publication supplied in the Bibliography.

0   50   100 150 200   km

50   100   150   miles

Caithness
Sutherland
Ross
Buchan
Moray
Mearns
Lochaber
Atholl
Fife

Lothian
Northumberland

Galloway

Durham
Cumberland
Westmorland
Yorkshire
Isle of Man
Staffordshire
Lancashire
Derbyshire
Cheshire
Warwickshire
Nottinghamshire
Anglesey
Lincolnshire
Flint
Leicestershire
Caernarvonshire
Rutland
Merionethshire
Norfolk
Powys
Huntingdonshire
Cardiganshire
Northamptonshire
Carmarthenshire
Suffolk
Maelienydd
Cambridgeshire
Shropshire
Bedfordshire
Worcestershire
Hertfordshire
Herefordshire
Oxfordshire
Gloucestershire
Wiltshire
Essex
Somerset
Devon
Cornwall
Kent

Middlesex

Sussex
Surrey

Dorset
Buckinghamshire
Berkshire
Hampshire
Isle of Wight

The map shows the English counties as they were prior to reorganization in the twentieth century, some of the basic geographical regions of medieval Scotland, the six counties set up in Wales by Edward I, and some of the major lordships in the Welsh marches.

PART ONE

AUTHORIZING TEXT AND WRITER

Certainly it would be worth examining how the author became individualized in a culture like ours, what status he has been given, at what moment studies of authenticity and attribution began, in what kind of system of valorization the author was involved, at what point we began to recount the lives of authors rather than of heroes, and how this fundamental category of "the-man-and-his-work criticism" began.
—Michel Foucault (1979, 141)

People compose books in four different ways. One person writes material composed by other people, adding or changing nothing; and this person is said to be merely the scribe. Another one writes material composed by others, joining them together but adding nothing of his own; and this person is said to be the compiler. Another one writes both materials composed by others and his own, but the materials composed by others are the most important materials, while his own are added for the purpose of clarifying them; and this person is said to be the commentator, not the author. Another one writes both his own materials and those composed by others, but his own are the most important materials and the materials of others are included in order to confirm his own; and this person must be called the author.
—Bonaventure (1250–52)

The increased use of English as a literary language in the fourteenth century has often been seen as inevitable, part of a natural resurgence of the language of the people and the beginning of the great tradition of English literature. What could be more natural for an English writer than to write in English? At the time, however, writing in English was not an inevitable choice. The languages of cultural prestige were Latin and, for much of the later Middle Ages, French (see essay 4.2, pages 331–34), and the role of the English writer had to be justified and defined. What now seems the predictable "triumph of English" in the fourteenth century took over a century to establish itself and was never unambiguous or complete. The excerpts edited in Part One show the persistent engagement of Middle English writers with Latin notions of authorship and authority, as also with versions of these Latin notions found in French texts. In practice, however—and despite the powerful claims, which continued to be made by some clerics, for Latin as the only language possessing true authority—the Latin-vernacular divide was far from monolithic. A writer might, for instance, be well aware of Latin conceptions of authority (*auctoritas*) in writing, but be immediately engaged in reworking a French author (Anglo-Norman *auctor, autour*) in the service of an English-speaking patron or for the benefit of an English-speaking audience (as is the case, for example, with Robert Mannyng, excerpt 1.1). Moreover, insofar as writers did defer to Latin models, their expressions of diffidence or defensiveness about the lexical and stylistic resources of English became *more* frequent in the later part of the period, at the very time when writing in English became more established. Before c.1370 (a period when French was still a serious alternative vernacular for writers and audiences), writers were less likely to express anxieties about English as a medium. They tended to present the unequal relationship of English and French primarily as a social issue rather than a stylistic one, concerned with language choice and language use: if French had superior status, it was because the upper classes spoke it. Even by the time of Mannyng's *Chronicle* (c. 1338), when translators were experimenting with widely varying proportions of Romance vocabulary, there was still little public discussion or disparagement of the lexical or stylistic resources of English. English writings and translations of this period indeed often announce their purpose specifically as service to English audiences, and the use of English becomes a way of forging communities by appealing to incipient patriotism. In fifteenth-century invocations of English literary tradition, on the other hand, luxuriantly expressed anxiety about the "dullness" of English is pervasive (Lawton 1987; and see essay 4.1, pages 320–21 below). In the polyglot culture of medieval Britain, Middle English writers' awareness of Latin and French literary authority was complex, by no means simply subservient, and fully capable of producing distinctive ideas of vernacular authorship.

The Idea of the Author

Our own categories and models for authorship do not often overlap with what can be deduced from Middle English terminology and practice. The relatively rare word *writere* in Middle English is as likely to indicate the scribe as the composer of a literary work; the term *poet* is not in widespread use before the fourteenth century (*MED: poet*); and the term for composers and compilers of narrative verse, *maker,* has not survived in any specifically literary sense. Medieval and modern English share the term "author" (Latin *auctor*), but in both Latin and vernacular use, medieval conceptions of the *auctor* differ in important ways from modern ones. Contemporary understandings of authorship often revolve around either the notion of individual genius (derived from the Romantic conception of the "artist") or that of property rights over a text (as expressed in laws governing copyright or plagiarism). Authorship in the Middle Ages was more likely to be understood as participation in an intellectually and morally authoritative tradition, within which (as Bonaventure's discussion, quoted above, makes clear)[1] a writer might fill one of several roles, copying, modifying, or translating, as well as

---

1. The epigraph is taken from Bonaventure's prologue to his commentary on the *Sentences* of Peter Lombard; this translation is adapted from Minnis 1988, 94, which also contains a useful discussion.

composing. Thus, in the prologue to Chaucer's *Legend of Good Women,* Queen Alceste defends the narrator against the God of Love's charge that writing *Troilus and Criseyde* and translating the *Roman de la rose* makes him a heretic, by arguing that the poet is probably too "nyce" (foolish) to be blameworthy, and that

He may translate a thyng in no malyce,
But for he useth bokes for to make,   **for** because; **useth** is in the habit
And taketh non hed of what matere he take,
Therfore he wrot the Rose and ek Crisseyde
Of innocence, and nyste what he seyde.   **nyste** did not know
Or hym was boden make thilke tweye   **boden make** commanded to compose
Of som persone, and durste it not withseye;   **Of** by; **withseye** refuse
For he hath write many a bok er this.   **er** before
He ne hath not don so grevously amys
To translate that olde clerkes wryte,   **that** what
As thogh that he of maleys wolde endyte   as if he wanted to write, out of malice,
Despit of love, and hadde hymself ywrought.   slander about love and had composed it by himself
(Chaucer, *The Legend of Good Women* G.341–52)

This famous account of Chaucer as a harmless compiler or translator, who is not responsible for the "matere" that he uses, since he is not the *auctor* of the books he makes, carefully minimizes his status, rendering him not worth the anger of Lord Cupid.[2] It depends on a model of authorship familiar and normative for Chaucer's culture and used in almost all the texts represented in Part One. However comically and strategically pointed, Alceste's defense assumes a model of textual production in which writers gain authority less by their originality than by their contribution to an ongoing tradition. The defense makes clear that not everyone who makes such contributions merits the title of *auctor,* which is reserved for those who reshape material in such a way as to take responsibility for it in precisely the fashion Chaucer is here said *not* to do. Yet in this model, authors are in many respects considered closer to translators, compilers, or scribes than in modern conceptions of authorship, in the sense that they do not necessarily have proprietorship of the texts on which they work, and still less of the "matere" they reshape.

As *The Legend of Good Women* implies, in practice the roles delineated by Bonaventure—scribe, compiler, commentator, author—often overlapped each other, perhaps especially in a vernacular context (see Bruns 1980). Writerly authority also remained interdependent with that of the text, since texts were often recognized as *auctores* in their own right (Lerer 1993, 12, discussing Parkes 1976, 116 n. 1). When medieval writers allude to Augustine or Ovid, the chief association that these authoritative names conjure up is not that of an inspired figure whose genius informs certain texts but that of the texts themselves. It is true that the chief location where *auctoritas* was thought to reside changed in a fundamen-

---

2. For a fine account of the complexities of this scene, see Baswell 1995, 249–55.

tally important way during the period, moving "from the divine realm to the human, and [. . .] in some measure from the past to the present" (Minnis 1988, viii; cf. Minnis 1997). Thus one of the earliest treatments of Chaucer as an *auctor*, in the lengthy prologue to Hoccleve's *Regement of Princes*, accompanies its praise of Chaucer with a picture of what he is said to have looked like (Pearsall 1994). Yet even this remarkable gesture is shot through with traditional views of authority: the poet Hoccleve shows us is an iconic figure, removed from the world of everyday contingencies as he admonishes his readers to conform to the timeless truths his verses are implied to contain. Well into the early modern period it was age, authenticity, and conformity with truth, not individual genius, that was thought to confer authority on texts and authors.

The extent to which medieval and modern notions of literary authorship differ are well illustrated in the prologue to the Middle English version of a surgical compendium, the *Cyrurgie* (excerpt 1.10), which reflects on the role of its compiler, Guy de Chauliac, and on questions of textual transmission and intellectual tradition with considerable self-consciousness and sophistication. The *Cyrurgie* is submitted to the authority of God, supreme author of the eternal life of the soul as well as of the flesh and its healing. With an attention to prose structure directly reminiscent of Latin manuals of composition, de Chauliac asks God to oversee the beginning, middle, and end of the work (11–18), which is not conceived as the creation, though it traces the activity, of its human author. The *Cyrurgie* strongly urges the value of the compendium in a culture where book ownership and reading is becoming a norm, claiming that "every man may not have alle bookes, and if he hadde, it were irkesome or noye to rede hem and goodly to holde all thing in mynde" (20–22). Yet, as a compilation, the *Cyrurgie* does not claim to be filling a lack with something new. Rather, it sees itself as constituting an addition to an authoritative tradition of medical writing that the prologue invokes by using the common rhetorical topos of deference (Curtius 1990, 83–85). Nevertheless, compilation is presented as an active process of building up and gathering in ("construcciouns and gadryng" [25–26]) that creates unity and usefulness ("onhede and profit" [20, 26]), and the famous late-twelfth-century image of contemporary writers as dwarves sitting on giants' shoulders (attributed by John of Salisbury to Bernard of Chartres) is invoked: the compiler is a child "in the nekke of a geaunt," but a child who can thereby "see als mykel [as much] as the geaunt and *somewhat more*" (24–25, emphasis added).

As a close Middle English translation of the Latin original, the *Cyrurgie* situates itself confidently in a long tradition of medical writing that stretches back as far as the Greeks, but which it might still hope to refine. A number of Middle English writers similarly find ways to align themselves with the literary traditions they seek to emulate. As Rita Copeland has pointed out, when Chaucer and Gower present their poems as part of a Latinate tradition of interpretative commentary (which they do both by extensive reference to their predecessors and by discussing the principles of interpretation that might be applied to their own work), they are not simply being self-reflexive, as we might expect a modern author to be. Rather, by strategically appropriating what Copeland calls "the discourse of [medieval Latin] academic exegesis" (1991, 179) and reusing it in their own texts, they engage in acts of "auto-exegesis" (185) that enable them to ascribe to themselves the status of *auctores* and to claim a Latinate weight of attention for their vernacular texts (a process of deference to predecessors combined with simultaneous displacement of them that Copeland calls *inventio*). At the same time, by developing vernacular ways of remaking themselves in the image of Latin *auctores,* these writers are asserting that their texts are worthy partners of the international high-culture literature most commonly associated with French courtly writing, while also distancing themselves from less exalted Middle English texts.

Much of the recent attention paid to Middle English prologues (see, e.g., Minnis 1988; Copeland 1991) has focused on these appropriations of academic Latin traditions, and the subtle ways Chaucer, Gower, and their successors deploy the trope of *translatio studii et imperii* (the transferal of learning and of empire; see further essay 4.1, pages 317–21) to make room for themselves as vernacular writers. Yet, as the *Cyrurgie*'s use of analogous strategies suggests, these "high-culture" writers are by no means unique in this regard. John Metham, for instance, even while constructing his position in relation to "my mastyr Chauncerys" and particularly to Chaucer's *Troilus* (see excerpt 1.8: 128 and 5–11), draws on romance traditions of *translatio studii* to give his *Amoryus and Cleopes* a Greek pedigree. The mysterious illuminated Greek book Metham claims as his source, which is expounded in Latin by a man just arrived in Norwich, signifies romance exoticism but is also reminiscent of the "text relics" described in hagiographic transmission narratives (see 1.8: 29–42n and compare the mixture of human and textual contact detailed in Bokenham's journey to his text, excerpt 1.11: 99–122). Saints' lives and romances in English rework their Latin and French sources in different keys, but often use strategies similar to those of literary high culture, and represent a body of convention established before the late medieval construction of the Chaucer tradition. Metham's prologue to *Amoryus and Cleopes* is very close to the fictionalized transmission story given in his treatise on palmistry,[3] and further suggests just how close and mutually influential the conventions of *Fachprosa*—"technical" prose—and more "literary" genres such as romance could be.

Over a range of genres, Middle English writers almost always do more than merely imitate or appropriate Latin conventions. The very act of aligning a text

---

3. The passage reads: "Tales [Thales] Milesias, the wyche was the fyrst phylosophyre in the citee of Atene, by the answere of god Appollo, fyrst dede wryte the syence of cyromancye in the longgage of Parce [Persia]; and mayster Arystotyll translatyd it owt of Parce into Grue [Greek]. And owt of Grue doctor Aurelyan, the wyche was born in Italy, translatyd this scyence into Latin; and owt of Latyn, John Metham, scymple scoler in phylosophy, translatyd it in-to Englyssh, the xxv wynter of hys age, prayyng all the reders of pacyence for the rude endytyng; for as myn auctor endytyth playnly in Latyn, so is my purpose pleynly to endyte in Englysshe" (Craig 1916, 85.1–11).

with a tradition to which it is said to be but a modest addition can provide an occasion for staking its claims in very specific ways. These claims can have the effect of moving the text away from the Latinate literary traditions it ostensibly "submits" to and toward a view of itself that is focused on its use of the vernacular and its difference from its predecessors. Even John Lydgate, the most Latinate writer of Middle English verse, states that the main facts about his *Troy Book* are, first, that it retells the story of the city that symbolized western European courtly values and, second, that at Prince Henry's command the text is written in *English*, so that "of the story the trouth we [the English] nat mys" (excerpt 1.7: 95). Lydgate's victory over his source, Guido delle Colonne's *Historia destructionis Troiae*, parallels the victory he anticipates Henry winning over his enemies (the French), inspired in part by Lydgate's enormously amplified reshaping of the "noble story" (91). Other writers who are equally aware of Latin definitions of *auctoritas*, like Thomas Usk, write with enough confidence in the distinctiveness of English to be indifferent to the prospect of making literary war on their French and Latin predecessors. Instead of war, Usk envisages his composition processes in *The Testament of Love* as including a literary version of theft (the kind of theft by which the English of his day was absorbing more and more French and Latin vocabulary), since "a slye servaunt in his owne helpe is often moche commended" (excerpt 1.4: 89–90). This image of a resourceful English writer learning from past *auctores* without being threatened by them depends on the idea that his or her *"dames tonge"* (29, emphasis added) is so different from other languages that to be an English writer is by definition to make meaning in a distinctive way. Although *The Testament of Love* is fundamentally indebted to at least two Latin texts, Boethius's *Consolation of Philosophy* and Anselm's *De concordia*, it thus articulates one of several arguments found in Middle English texts for the independent status of vernacular authorship. (These arguments are explored further in essay 4.1.) This independent status, moreover, comes to be seen as bound up with the particular qualities of the much-deprecated English vernacular.

A LATE MEDIEVAL IDEA OF THE VERNACULAR: "RUDE WORDES AND BOYSTOUS"

Many of the prologues edited here use an apologetic tone and express a recurrent concern for their rough and unpolished diction, or "rude wordes and boystous" (the phrase is Usk's, excerpt 1.4: 6). Chaucer claims that "ryme in Englissh hat such skarsete" that rhyming for him is "gret penaunce" (excerpt 1.3: 8–9). Walton laments his "defaute of langage and of eloquence" (excerpt 1.5: 2), while Metham apologizes for "rude endytyng" (excerpt 1.8: 23) and Ashby for "blondryng" (excerpt 1.9: 53). Bokenham apologizes because he does not draw on Geoffrey of

Vinsauf's *Poetria nova,* so that the form of his writing, "artificyal / Is in no wyse, ner poetycal" (excerpt 1.11: 83–84).

These protestations should not be taken at face value. While some writers, such as Barbour and Mannyng, self-consciously choose a simple syntax, vocabulary, and versification (see Mannyng's discussion of "strange langage" [excerpt 1.1: 33–66], and Barbour's of "suthfastnes" [excerpt 1.2: 10–20]), the work of many later writers is highly elaborate; and these are the writers who, as pointed out in the beginning of this introduction (pages 3–4), apologize most often for their rough language. If Chaucer, for instance, complains of English's rhyming capacities and his own "litel suffisaunce" in *Venus* (excerpt 1.3: 9, 4), he elsewhere affirms his confidence in the complete *sufficiency* of English to match any style (*Treatise on the Astrolabe* 28–40). The anxiety expressed in *Venus* is part of Chaucer's pervasive dramatizing of himself as a man who has trouble with his rhymes (see *The Man of Law's Tale* II [B1] 47–48, *Sir Thopas* VII 923–35 [B2 2114–25]). It is also typical of a seeming readiness to share with his readers observations of a technical interest (see, e.g., *Troilus and Criseyde* II.22–28, V.1793–99; *Sir Thopas* VII 943–66 [B2 2133–56]; *Astrolabe* 25–64; *Romaunt* 2155–62; and compare Mannyng's use of "couwee" and "baston" [excerpt 1.1: 51 and note]). This concern with language is part of Chaucer's characteristic interest in the translator's role: when he chooses to identify one of his own texts as dependent on a source, he tends to emphasize passivity, and such passages are usually attached to works that themselves have particularly passive, receptive, or suffering protagonists whose situations are mirrored in the narrator-translator's passivity, lack of free will, and powerlessness to change the preordained plot (see, in addition to *The Legend of Good Women* G.341–52, as discussed above, *Troilus and Criseyde* II.8–21, III.1324–36, V.1037–50; *Anelida and Arcite* 8–10, 20–21; *Second Nun's Tale* VIII [G] 23–25, 78–84). *Venus* is a small-scale but intense example of a concern explored most extensively in *Troilus and Criseyde.*

Both *Venus* and *Troilus and Criseyde* also exemplify a strategy of vernacular authorship Chaucer shares with other Middle English writers (Lydgate, Usk, Ashby, and many others in this volume): the author is presented as a compiler, translator, narrator, humble servant to a patron, or obeyer of a friend's or superior's wishes. Expressions of anxiety about English's stylistic resources, like other kinds of modesty topoi, may well respond to such factors as the striking extension of the English lexicon after c. 1350 by loans from French and Latin (creating a sense of insufficiency about the language's Germanic core), but they are also a good deal more. Chaucer's moves in *Venus,* for instance, find echoes in later writers (e.g., Lydgate, *Dance of Deeth* 669–72, *Pilgrimage of the Life of Man* 143–48, *Fall of Princes* II.148–61, IV.2633–5; Walton, *Boethius,* excerpt 1.5: 25–29 below), and his terms "sufficient"/"sufficiency" and "curious"/"curiosity" become regularly associated with questions of language, "copiousness," and elegance. Chaucer's tendency to imbue statements about translation with a dramatic and emotional coloring of passivity and dependency becomes a template for later writers.

Linguistic and authorial modesty topoi can function as inverted self-advertisement and also as part of a broader literary reflection on the complex position occupied by English literature (a newcomer in fifteenth-century European terms) in relation to other European vernacular literatures and to their great precursors. If these modesty topoi reflect anxiety in the face of the high cultural tradition of France—or, for fifteenth-century English writers, its great translator, Chaucer—it must be borne in mind that "anxiety" in these texts is also a *trope,* a controlled rhetorical attitude. Modesty topoi serve to establish both a poet's own achievement and that of the vernacular literary tradition in which the poet is working (Lawton 1987). Moreover, no amount of modesty prevents writers of Middle English, from the *Cyrurgie* compiler to Usk and to later writers such as Skelton and Douglas (see excerpts 3.15, 3.16), from exploring and stretching English's peculiar capacities in the service of a formidable range of literary tasks.

Textual Instability, Memory, and Vernacular Variance

Medieval textual transmission, both in Latin and in the vernaculars, is characterized by extensive borrowing and reworking. This is true not just of texts valued for their learning (which often developed as series of recompilations and commentaries), but of a broad range of other texts. As Paul Zumthor notes in an influential study of Old French (1972a, 1992), vernacular poems in the High Middle Ages exist not in a single definitive form but as a flowing series (or *mouvance*) of modifications and adaptations.[4] Scribes often contributed to this fluidity by modifying the texts they were copying. Although Bonaventure defines the scribe and the compiler as those who add nothing of their own, he classifies all four types of bookmakers, including the author, as writers, and some scribes took on the role of editor-compiler (see especially *The Book of Margery Kempe,* excerpt 1.14). Authorial and scribal reliance on memory (a faculty that was carefully developed in formal education through the use of mnemonic techniques) also affected textual stability. Clerics and vernacular reciters often knew long passages by heart and were as likely to refer to their memory as to a written book (the author of *The General Prologue to the Wycliffite Bible* [excerpt 1.15], for example, refers to a

---

4. The best example of *mouvance* in this volume is probably that of the *South English Legendary* (excerpt 2.15), versions of which are contained in over sixty manuscripts. The number and ordering of the saints' lives varies in every manuscript. Early versions of the text are distinct from later versions, combining hagiographic and other material in ways that suggest the targeting of specific local audiences (Görlach 1974). Later versions were copied into manuscript codices that may have been commissioned for particular social groups (see, e.g., Meale 1994a, 222).

number of patristic authorities, specifying the chapter or approximate place in the book, but adding, "but I have him not now" [45]).[5] Texts also varied considerably in the way they were voiced and received from one reading to another, since medieval poetry and most medieval prose was written for oral delivery.[6] Margery Kempe's *Book* (excerpt 1.14) partly presents itself as a performance of this kind, not written in the order in which the events it tells occurred but the order in which they were remembered, "for it was so long er it was wretyne that sche had forgetyn the tyme and the ordyr whan thyngys befellyn." Nonetheless, the *Book* also immediately states that "therfore sche dede nothing wryten but that sche knew rygth wel for very trewth" (114–17), defending the informal memorial practices of a vernacular *illiterata*. (Kempe herself was preoccupied with preserving her book in as "correct" a form as possible, despite the difficulties this entailed.)

Although significant areas of Latin composition and recitation (e.g., preaching, the liturgy, saints' lives) were open to reconstitution and modification, Latin offered a relatively stable language. Furthermore, while access to Latin was limited almost exclusively to male clerics, it was at least available to male clerics of any nation and any age (on this point, see Trevisa's *Dialogue,* excerpt 2.2: 15–17). In contrast, English was both unstable and highly localized. The degree of dialect variation in late medieval England meant that a poem, unless it was written in the dialect of the Oxford-London-Cambridge triangle that began to emerge as a standard in the late fourteenth century, might encounter difficulties in circulating outside its region, or at least have to be translated (in effect) from one dialect to another.[7] For a poet who hoped that his works would endure and gain wide recognition, this was a major concern, not simply in a practical sense but a symbolic one, since the vernacular came to *stand for* fluidity and instability, as against the stability of Latin. Chaucer, in *Troilus and Criseyde,* famously reflects on this linguistic fluidity:

And for ther is so gret diversite
In Englissh and in writyng of oure tonge,
So prey I God that non myswrite the,   **myswrite the** write you improperly
Ne the mysmetre for defaute of tonge.   nor fail to scan you for lack of correct speech
(Chaucer, *Troilus and Criseyde* V.1793–96)

5. As Mary J. Carruthers argues, "For us, texts only come in books, and so the distinction between the two is blurred and even lost. But, in a memorial culture, a 'book' is only one way among several to remember a 'text,' to provision and cue one's memory" (1990, 8).

6. See Coleman 1996. As Ruth Finnegan notes, an oral poem (i.e., a poem composed as well as delivered without use of writing) "has no existence or continuity apart from its performance," and often "there is considerable variation between performances, so that the literate model of a fixed correct version—*the* text of a given poem—does not necessarily apply" (1977, 28). This fluidity characterizes much medieval poetry, even if it is not oral in the stricter sense.

7. Many texts did circulate in this way, scribal semitranslation, or *Mischsprachen* or "mixed speech," often contributing to their success; see Benskin and Samuels 1981. The many works excerpted in this volume that attained something approaching a national audience are listed by region in "Alternative Arrangement of the Excerpts" below, pages 382–83.

Given the instability associated with vernacular languages, it is not surprising that it is only with the Italian poets of the Trecento, Dante (1265–1321), Petrarch (1304–74), and Boccaccio (1313–75), that concepts of extensive authorial control begin to be applied with confidence to vernacular poetry. These concepts provide an influential model for writers such as Chaucer. Chaucer's rebuke to his scribe Adam for miscopying, and concern lest *Troilus and Criseyde* be "mismetered" (V.1796) when it is copied or recited, are among the earlier clear instances of an English poet expressing a desire to exercise an enduring control over the textual dissemination of his work (Olson 1979). Yet an idea of vernacular poetry as capable of enduring is discernible at least half a century before Chaucer—for example, in Mannyng's *Chronicle,* which addresses itself to a future audience that needs to be told the name of the author and the reign in which he lived ("Robert Mannyng is my name . . . In the thrid Edwardes tyme was I" [excerpt 1.1: 74, 77]). Moreover, despite the determination with which Chaucer's successors referred to him as father or founder of written English (see Cannon 1996; and essay 4.2, pages 345–49), the notion of vernacular instability continued to be important. Nearly a century after Chaucer, William Caxton, who as a printer had strong commercial interest in the development of a broad national readership (see the final section of essay 4.3 below), laments that Englishmen are born under the influence of the ever-changing moon, so that their language varies from generation to generation, from shire to shire, and from one social group to another, and no one kind is acceptable to all: "Certaynly it is harde to playse every man bycause of dyversite and chaunge of langage" (Blake 1973, 80). Caxton is, in fact, exaggerating, possibly to dramatize his stylistic dilemma (trapped between an older ornate aureate prose style and a new, equally difficult humanist one) and to justify his solution of adopting a language "not over rude ne curyous" (the passage is quoted below on page 365). The Central Midlands dialect was in wide use as a literary standard from about 1425 on. Yet Caxton's lament does suggest the commercial and artistic difficulties in the use of the vernacular, and its capacity, even at the end of the fifteenth century, to be taken as a symbol—sometimes, as implicitly in Caxton, a female-gendered symbol—of instability: the very quality most antipathetic to Latin notions of *auctoritas.*

TRUTH AND THE OPEN TEXT

What Kempe's scribe calls the "very trewth" of a text—that is, its conformity with the moral structure of reality, its capacity to improve the reader—was often more heavily stressed in both Latin and vernacular texts than was any notion of textual stability. Usk justifies his work by an appeal to "sothe": studying God's creation will "bringen us to the ful knowlegynge [of] sothe, and to the parfyte love of the maker of hevenly thynges" (excerpt 1.4: 46–47). Lydgate criticizes his sources, especially Homer, for their partiality and—rather as does John Barbour (excerpt

1.2)—stresses the superior *moral,* as well as historical, accuracy of his version (excerpt 1.7: 132–56, 183–208). Walton prays that his rendering of Boethius may "kepe the sentence [meaning] in his trewe entent" (a prayer that is made necessary by his decision to subordinate meaning to meter, excerpt 1.5: 18–20), while Bokenham invites anyone who does not believe his stories of Saint Margaret to visit for himself the monastery devoted to her at Mount Flask (excerpt 1.11: 111–12).

So persistent is this concern with truth that vernacular writers routinely submit their works to their readers for improvement (or at least make this rhetorical gesture), envisaging the search for truth as a collaborative project that does not end with the completion of a text but simply moves into a new phase. While this is sometimes merely a topos (as, perhaps, with Lydgate, excerpt 1.7: 209–14), on other occasions it is integral to a text's meaning that it have this fluid and reciprocal relationship with the world. Julian's *Revelation of Love,* for example, while not submitting itself to be corrected by readers, presupposes that those whom the text helps to love God better than she does herself will then see further than it can, completing the text by carrying on its work in their own lives (excerpt 1.13: 52–59). This practice runs counter to the modern assumption that a work, once published, is normally beyond its author's control. For writers today, revision and correction after publication, though not uncommon in practice, are conceived as exceptions rather than expectations; the work stands alone and must speak for itself.

Medieval writers, on the other hand, often knew their intended readers personally. To the extent that they wrote to earn their living (and most did not), they were dependent not on sales to strangers but on commissions from patrons, and were thus more likely to present their work as part of an ongoing conversation.[8] It is true that by the early fourteenth century there were signs of the development of a commercial book trade in London (see essay 4.3, pages 354–55), but manuscripts more often circulated within small communities, their texts both composed and copied for known readers. Devotional texts produced for lay readers, for example, were often translated or revised and copied by the patron's personal religious adviser, who would supervise the use of the book as well its production. Writers, as much as copyists, usually directed their works in the first instance to people they knew. Walton, Lydgate, and Ashby all wrote on command (see excerpts 1.5, 1.7, 1.9); John Metham directs his "lytyl boke" to his patrons, Sir Miles and Lady Stapleton (excerpt 1.8: 116–20); the Carthusian author of the *Speculum Devotorum* (excerpt 1.12) perhaps wrote at the request of a Bridgettine nun from the neighboring house of Syon; Bokenham wrote his *Life of St. Margaret* at the request of an unnamed friend (excerpt 1.11); Usk may have written *The Testament of Love* (excerpt 1.4) to placate his political opponents; and Pecock (excerpt 1.16) evidently circulated his work among his friends, much as Chaucer and perhaps Langland did. Even texts that assume a rhetorical stance of universality,

---

8. One of the most thorough explorations of this position, Hoccleve's extraordinary adaptation and dramatization of patronage and prefatory conventions in the prologue to his *Regement of Princes,* is too long to be included here, but gives perhaps the most vividly specific and situated account of the writing of Middle English; see Furnivall 1897.

addressing the whole community of speakers of English, in practice had to make their way in the world like any other text, by slow dissemination from person to person and copy to copy. The prologue to *Speculum Devotorum* reflects well the sort of personal relations involved here; it is informal and intimate, reading more like a letter to a close friend than a message to the world at large, although the author clearly conceives that his work may circulate widely. The readership consists of both the author's "gostly [spiritual] syster" and "eny man that mygth aftyrwarde rede the boke folowynge" (excerpt 1.12: 1, 41). (On the construction of audience, see further the introduction to Part Two, pages 109–25.)

Just as one text might address several audiences, so authorship and textual authority might involve different positions, even within the same work. Writers at times claim for their work an enduring stability, and at other times insist it is provisional and subject to correction by those who are wiser, or by their social superiors (whose greater social status allegedly ensures their greater cultural refinement). These appeals to the reader to emend or complete the work are more than just polite formulas. Court poets in particular provided scripts for elaborate flirtations and could expect to have their words echoed and debated by courtly amateurs (Green 1980, chap. 4). In *Troilus and Criseyde,* Chaucer, for example, invokes both these possibilities. Near the end of the poem, after the model of classical poets such as Ovid, Chaucer consigns his work to a literary tradition, directing his "litel bok" to kiss the steps of Virgil, Ovid, Homer, Lucan, and Statius (V.1786–92). In doing so, Chaucer also follows in the steps of Dante, echoing a famous passage in canto XXI of the Purgatorio, where Statius bends to kiss the feet of Virgil (130ff.). By implication, Chaucer here claims the position of a canonical author, one whose vernacular writings, like those of Dante, can hope to be enshrined among the literary monuments of the Latin tradition. In contrast, however, the poem's initial address to young lovers presents a narrator who serves the "God of Loves servantz" and who offers his book in the hopes that it may avail the cause of some lover (I.15–21). Here, Chaucer presents himself as a court poet and his poem as a manual of seduction and courtly behavior, with an immediate social function. Similarly, when Metham (excerpt 1.8: 115–22) echoes Chaucer's address to his "litel bok" in the conclusion to his own romance *Amoryus and Cleopes,* he substitutes his patrons for the classical authors whose steps the book is to kiss, presenting himself as a courtier rather than an as author.

What Is an Author?

In the analysis of the concept of the author from which one epigraph to this introduction has been excerpted, Foucault goes on to argue that "[t]exts, books, and discourses really began to have authors . . . to the extent that the authors became subject to punishment" (1979, 148). Foucault locates the full development of authorship at "the end of the eighteenth and the beginning of the nineteenth centuries," when "a system of ownership for texts came into being" and "strict rules concerning author's rights, author-publisher relations, rights of reproduction, and related matters were enacted" (148). At this point, we have arrived at our current notion of an author as a clearly identified individual who is the sole creator of a text, has exclusive rights over it, and can be held responsible for what it says.[9] But the connection between punishment or censorship and authorship can be discerned much earlier. Reginald Pecock took great pains to ensure that his work was approved by ecclesiastical authorities and protested against the inaccurate or premature copies that he claimed had been made against his desires, yet he still was forced to surrender his books to be burned in 1447. Pecock's elaborate system of cross-references links together his long systematic work *The Reule of Crysten Religioun* and his lost work *The Afore Crier* with his short introductory *Donet* (excerpt 1.16) and its continuation *The Folower,* establishing an authorial corpus. Pecock's efforts to control the dissemination of his texts and bind them into a single interconnected corpus might be compared to those of a writer such as Gower—who commissioned presentation copies of his collected works and took pains to ensure their accurate copying (see excerpt 2.11)—and make Chaucer's failure to assemble a collection of his works all the more striking. It is true that Pecock also makes his writings subservient to his personal *intentions,* insisting in his *Donet* that if he has committed any theological errors, he will gladly correct his works, and that he should be judged on the basis not of what he has written but of what he currently believes (excerpt 1.16: 21–28). Although Pecock sees his works as a unified corpus for which he alone is responsible, he does not see this work as permanently fixed. Yet the syntactically demanding prose used by Pecock and the Lollards, as much as the aureate verse of fifteenth-century poets, was stabilizing the written English language in the fifteenth century, and thus making the concept of "vernacular authorship" plausible at the very time the notion of authorship itself was shifting in the directions Foucault traces. Perhaps, indeed, it was partly the translation of Latin *auctoritas* into English and other vernaculars that made such shifts possible.[10]

ORGANIZATION OF PART ONE

Excerpts 1.1–4: The (in)sufficiency of English. The diverse writers and genres represented in these opening extracts are concerned in various ways with the language of vernacular writings. Mannyng's early-fourteenth-century rhymed chronicle (excerpt 1.1) positions its use of English against French and against ear-

9.   This modern concept of authorship, so familiar that we now largely take it for granted, can be seen at work in the headnotes to this collection, since they endeavor to isolate a single individual as the source of what medieval writers more often present as a collaborative tradition.

10.   For further reflections on the formation of an authorial persona, see, in very different modes, de Looze 1997 and Kerby-Fulton and Justice 1997.

lier English narratives. It replays the antithesis of *litteratus* and *illiteratus* (the "lernid and the lewid") in terms of the social positions of the two vernaculars in order to claim English as the language of record, entertainment, and poetic craft, as well as a medium of wider appeal and utility than French. In excerpt 1.3, Chaucer's claim that English lacks rhymes to match French cannot easily be read as a straightforward historical account of the status and condition of English, since the poem is a bravura display of rhyming. Similarly, Usk, while describing his *Testament of Love* as "dolven with rude wordes and boystous" (dug out with simple and rough words [1.4: 9]), offers a spectacular rendering of a wide range of literary and transmission conventions into vigorous and subtle English prose. The association of English with patriotic nationalism is interestingly not the concern of these writers; only Lydgate, in a poem significantly addressed to Henry V (excerpt 1.7), makes this link. Barbour, chronicling the struggle between Robert the Bruce and the kings of England (excerpt 1.2), nevertheless writes in *Inglis* (see excerpt 1.2, headnote), and sees this as compatible with his dominant concern for the enduring and exemplary truth of his account. Despite prefacing *The Bruce* with a Latin heading, this Oxford-educated bishop finds English octosyllabic couplets (the same meter used by Mannyng) the clearest, most flexible, and most accessible medium for memorializing the deeds of recent Scottish heroes.

Excerpts 1.5–9: "Chaucerians" and authorship. These excerpts in part chart the formation of a tradition of vernacular authorship in Late Middle English, insofar as they show Walton (excerpt 1.5), Hoccleve (excerpt 1.6), and Lydgate (excerpt 1.7) explicitly positioning themselves in relation to Chaucer, and Metham (excerpt 1.8) and Ashby (excerpt 1.9) explicitly positioning themselves in relation to Lydgate, Chaucer, and Gower. These excerpts also form a repository of authorizing conventions, with antecedents and continuations in all the languages of medieval England. Claims to humility and inadequacy are among the most prolific and enduring conventions by which medieval writers align their work with authoritative textual traditions and illustrious predecessors. Walton advertises himself as a humble translator of limited abilities, lacking the intelligence, linguistic capabilities, or eloquence to perform his task (excerpt 1.5: 1–8). Nevertheless, in a number of ways he hints that he may have surpassed his predecessors both in wisdom and in eloquence. Although Walton may bow before the authority of Gower and Chaucer, he sees himself as at least a potential competitor in "makynge" (1.5: 36). Hoccleve (excerpt 1.6) laments not his inferiority to Chaucer but his inability to reestablish himself, socially and as a writer, after his lapse into insanity, generalizing his grief by seeking to link it with the sorrowing voice of the psalmist. Significantly, however, it is not Hoccleve but Lydgate (excerpt 1.7), the most lavishly deferential writer of humility topoi among the English "Chaucerian" poets, who becomes (together with Gower, see excerpt 2.11) Chaucer's recognized heir in the creation of an elevated English style, of the "aureat lycour" he claims is unavailable to his pen (excerpt 1.7: 31). Ashby refers to Gower, Chaucer, and Lydgate as the "primier poetes of this nacion" and praises them for "embellishing" the language and writing "fresshe, douce [sweet] Englisshe" (excerpt 1.9: 29, 32). Lydgate's enormous expansions of Chaucer in his *Siege of Thebes* and *Troy Book* suggest that he did not just revere Chaucer but wished to emulate and surpass him (Spearing 1984; Lawton 1987; Watson 1994). Building on Lydgate as much as on Chaucer, a group of male East Anglian writers from the mid–fifteenth century adopt poetic and moral attitudes that are sufficiently closely related for it to be possible to speak of a regional writerly self-consciousness. Metham and Bokenham (excerpt 1.11), along with their colleague Capgrave (excerpt 2.7), follow their East Anglian predecessor Lydgate's lead, adding a sobriety, dignity, and an implicitly superior morality to the central Chaucerian tradition of English *auctoritas* as an aspect of their deference. Yet while Bokenham (like Capgrave) is a serious and ambitious moral poet and Metham, too, is aware of his duty to "improve" his reader, these successors of Lydgate can assume an ironic attitude toward their own importance, while Lydgate cannot. This irony, although partly derived from Chaucer, is also self-consciously provincial. When Bokenham refers to himself not as a poet but as a Lincolnshire horse trader (the medieval equivalent of a dealer in used cars, excerpt 1.11: 217–18), he is registering in a sophisticated way his distance from the metropolis where Chaucer and Gower wrote and Lydgate was read.

Excerpts 1.10–12: Authorship and compilation. These excerpts give examples of various gestures of deference and displacement. In the *Cyrurgie* (excerpt 1.10), Bokenham's *Legendys of Hooly Wummen* (excerpt 1.11), and the *Speculum Devotorum* (excerpt 1.12), the Latin template can be seen as serving rather than as defining specific vernacular positions. Just how carefully the authorizing procedures of compilation might be deployed in specifically vernacular textual politics is suggested by the prologue to the early-fifteenth-century *Speculum Devotorum* (excerpt 1.12), a text that is concerned with the increasingly controversial matter of representing Christ's life. This prologue positions itself as much in relation to vernacular predecessors as to its Latin source material, while its claim that no single work can exhaust the narrative *matere* offered by Christ's life makes space for endless further vernacular (and Latin) retellings (1.12: 44–52). The *Cyrurgie*, on the other hand, exemplifies a less politically sensitive overlap between "high" and "low" literary culture that Voigts (1989, 1996) has argued to be distinctive of Late Middle English prose (see pages 7–8 above). In excerpt 1.11, Bokenham's explicit use of one of the most developed forms of Latin academic prologue conventions (the so-called Aristotelian *accessus ad auctores*) freights the prologue to his life of Saint Margaret with high seriousness. But its examination of the causes and means of writing also produces a vivid evocation of gossip in the provincial social circles in which this text and its *auctour* move. Here Bokenham borrows the authority of the *accessus* both dramatically and strategically.

Excerpts 1.13–14: Women as authors. For English women the problems of authority in writing were compounded by repeated injunctions to silence, and by the "tacit assumption that 'authority,' and therefore authorship, were incompatible with femininity" (Barratt 1992, 5). Some, however, seem to have turned this gendered inferiority into powerful versions of authorial humility.[11] In the short text of her *Revelation of Love* (excerpt 1.13), Julian of Norwich disavows any claim to be called a teacher—"For I am a womann, leued, febille, and freylle" (86–87)—but can, as a result of this very maneuver, claim the more convincingly to be humbly serving all her fellow Christians in the dissemination of the authoritative vision God has given her. Although relatively few women could read, the case of Margery Kempe (excerpt 1.14) reminds us still more strikingly than does Bonaventure that reading, literary composition, and the technology of writing do not have to be commanded by the same individual in order for significant texts to be created. Kempe's apparent victimization at the hands of incompetent or unwilling scribes, including the one who eventually wrote her *Book,* became matter for her book's account of the vicissitudes appropriate to Christ's spouse. These served to convince not only her priest-scribe (who apologetically added a new prologue to the *Book* to acknowledge this fact), but the spiritual cognoscenti at the Carthusian house of Mount Grace who owned its sole surviving copy in the late fifteenth century and wrote so approvingly in its margins.

Excerpts 1.15–16: Theology and the vernacular. In translating the Bible, writers reached beyond their immediate circle to a potential readership that might ultimately include the entire laity, while facing the daunting task of translating the word of God. Biblical translation had a long tradition, and various books of the Bible, such as the Psalms, were uncontroversially available to (or demanded by) the laity, but translation of the Bible as a whole, and of the New Testament in particular, became a highly charged issue at the end of the fourteenth century in England. The merits of Bible translation could still be debated openly at Oxford in 1401, but even by then the question was charged when raised in a less clerical milieu (see the section on religious writing in essay 4.2, pages 339–45). After the publication of Arundel's *Constitutions* in 1409, public debate was increasingly perilous.

   In response to this set of difficulties, the Lollard author of *The General Prologue to the Wycliffite Bible* (excerpt 1.15) elaborates (out of Augustine's treatise *On Christian Doctrine*) a defiant defense, not of Bible translation itself so much as of the unlearned reader of the Bible. In this defense, standard in Lollard accounts of Bible reading and translation (compare *The Holi Prophete David,* excerpt 2.5), charity is sufficient for any reader, however simple, to understand God's will, since charity informs the Bible through the Holy Spirit, who inspired

---

11. On the cultural achievements and influence of medieval women, often in areas that fall outside traditional masculinist constructions of power and authorship, see, among others, Bell 1988; Erler and Kowaleski 1988; Meale 1996b; McCash 1996; Ferrante 1997; Taylor 1997.

it (excerpt 1.15: 6–9, 22–23). This emphasis on charity, however, does not prevent the *General Prologue* from going on to provide a formidable array of advice and hermeneutic tools, placing much of the responsibility back on vernacular readers for the awesome task of preparing themselves properly for their direct encounter with God's word. Responding to this Lollard position (but equally confident of the fundamental competence of his vernacular audience), Reginald Pecock insists that only reason, not charity, is a sufficient guide to faith (excerpt 1.16). Given the utter reasonableness of orthodox doctrine, Pecock argues, laypeople would, through their own logical scrutiny of issues, agree with the status quo and support the church's tradition. Yet despite his fame and his status as a bishop, Pecock's trust in the laity and determination to expound orthodox theology to as wide an audience as possible led to the condemnation of his books for heresy. In fifteenth-century England, "authority"—in this case, the authority of Pecock's episcopal colleagues—was invoked to *prevent* as well as to further the emergence of vernacular traditions of writing.

1.1 ROBERT MANNYNG, *CHRONICLE:* PROLOGUE

Date and Provenance: completed 1338; east Midlands (Lincolnshire, Sixhills Priory).

Author, Sources, and Nature of Text: Robert Mannyng of Brunne (now Bourne, in southern Lincolnshire) was born c. 1265–80 (Sullens 1996, 13). He was educated at Cambridge and spent his early adult years at the Gilbertine priory of Sempringham, where in 1303 he wrote his famous manual, *Handlyng Synne.* The *Chronicle,* an account of British history from Noah's flood to the year 1307, was written later; it was, and remains, less widely known. Commissioned by Robert Malton (perhaps prior of Sixhills), this work lists its chief sources as Wace's *Roman de Brut* (c. 1160) and Piers Langtoft's Anglo-Norman *Chronicle* (c. 1310), its minor ones as the histories of Bede, Gildas, and Geoffrey of Monmouth (see 23–32 below). Despite his use of two texts written in French, one of Mannyng's themes is the oppression under which the "true" English are still said to labor almost three hundred years after the Norman Conquest. Written (like Lawman's *Brut* 150 years earlier) in what Mannyng presents as the "native" language of the country, the *Chronicle* thus offers itself as an attempt to re-

patriate a historical narrative that has too long been the property of readers of French—that is, the aristocracy (Turville-Petre 1988; Moffat 1994). (A mere generation later, however, aristocrats like Thomas, Lord Berkeley, were to present themselves as lifelong champions of *English* [see excerpt 2.2].) The prologue is highly elusive. It begins by stating that Mannyng is writing in the "symple speche" he knows for the benefit of the "lewed," offering his 25,000-line poem partly as dinner entertainment (11–12) for readers who (it would seem) lack the sophistication and status associated with those who speak French. Such topoi derive from classical literature (see Curtius 1990, 83–85), are ubiquitous in texts of the period in all languages, and can never be taken at face value (compare excerpts 1.4, 1.5, 2.1, 3.13, 3.14). Mannyng then abruptly shifts direction, indicating his political purpose to be to show "the state of the land" (14) and giving an elaborate account of the work's genesis, sources, and style: an accessible style he contrasts with the "strange Inglis" (40) used by some vernacular poets on the one hand and with the productions of professional "disours" (minstrels) and "harpours" (37–38) on the other. Mannyng says the French employs a "fayr" style, which is not possible in English. At the same time, he now presents English not as an inherently "lewd" tongue but as a language that, in poetry at least, commands a range of styles up to the most ingenious, listing elaborate verse forms he has heard used before and explaining why he chooses to avoid them.

Audience and Circulation: Mannyng says his chronicle is intended "not for the lerid bot for the lewed" (8), for a lay audience who do not understand French, envisaged as including both readers and those who are dependent on reciters. Thorlac Turville-Petre (1988) and Douglas Moffat (1994) argue that in practice this was a local audience consisting of the upper peasantry and lower gentry and clergy, who shared a belief in their status as the true English, oppressed by French-speaking aristocrats whom they thought of (in certain contexts, at least) as foreign. But Mannyng also writes with an eye to his clerical "felawes" and posterity, ending the prologue by naming himself, his patron, and both the place and the reign in which he wrote (73–82), and inscribing himself into the tradition of historical writing on which he draws. The work survives in three manuscripts: London, Inner Temple MS Petyt 511.7 (1375–1400), the sole complete copy of the work; Lambeth Palace MS 131 (1425–50); and a fragment in Oxford, Bodleian Library MS Rawlinson Misc. D.913 (1375–1400).

Bibliography: The work is edited by Idelle Sullens (1996); part 1 was also edited by F. J. Furnivall (1887), part 2 by R. P. Stepsis (1967), as well as, much earlier, by T. Hearne (1725); the Rawlinson fragment is edited by E. Kölbing (1892). The relation between the manuscripts is discussed by Edward Kennedy (1989, 2627–28), who offers a useful general account of the work and its sources. Mannyng's (and related) prologues are discussed by Turville-Petre (1996, chaps. 2–3). Mannyng's life is discussed by Ruth Crosby (1942). Turville-Petre (1988) and Moffat (1994) give contrasting accounts of the milieu in which the work was written and read; Lesley Johnson (1995) dissents from Turville-Petre's reading of the text. Derek Pearsall (1985) discusses the references to tail-rhyme romances. On the activities of *disours*, see Chesnutt 1987 and Taylor 1992. For an edition of Langtoft's chronicle, see Thiolier 1989.

Source: London, Inner Temple MS Petyt 511.7, fols. 1ra–1vb, a parchment manuscript from Lincolnshire written in double columns from the last quarter of the fourteenth century, which belonged at the end of the fifteenth century to Edmund Pymond, vicar of Laughton (Lincolnshire). Like the other two manuscripts of this text, it has a formal Latin apparatus of captions, which introduce and structure the work and even point to shifts in source in a manner that emphasizes the *Chronicle*'s serious historiographic purpose.

This excerpt was contributed by Helen Phillips.

Incipit prologus de historia Britannie transumpta per Robertum in materna lingua

[Here begins the prologue to the history of Britain translated by Robert into the mother tongue]

Lordynges, that be now here,	**Lordynges** gentlemen
If ye wille listene and lere—	**lere** learn
5 Al[l] the story of Inglande	**story** history
Als Robert Mannyng wryten it fand,	**als** as
And on Inglysch has it schewed	**schewed** interpreted
Not for the lerid bot for the lewed,	**lerid** learned; **lewed** unlearned
For tho that in this land won	**won** dwell

10 That the Latyn no Frankys con,   who know neither Latin nor French
   For to haf solace and gamen   **solace** pleasure; **gamen** entertainment
   In felawship when thai sitt samen.   **samen** together
   And it is wisdom for to wytten   **wytten** know
   The state of the land, and haf it wryten
15 What manere of folk first it wan   **wan** won
   And of what kynde it first began.   **kynde** people
   And gude it is for many thynges
   For to here the dedis of kynges,
   Whilk were foles and whilk were wyse,   **Whilk** which
20 And whilk of tham couth mast quantyse,   **couth** was capable of; **quantyse** ingenuity
   And whilk did wrong and whilk ryght
   And whilk mayntend pes and fight.   **pes and fight** peace and war

[Mannyng then outlines the plan of his Chronicle: *from Noah to Brutus, founder of
Britain, to Cadwallader, last British ruler of England; from the Anglo-Saxon conquest
to the conversion of the English; the subsequent history of the English. He notes his
sources as Wace and Piers Langtoft.]*

   And ryght as Mayster Wace says
   I telle myn Inglis the same ways;
25 For Mayster Wace the Latyn alle rymes   **rymes** versifies
   That Pers overhippis many tymes.   **overhippis** skips over
   Mayster Wace the *Brute* alle redes   **redes** presents
   And Pers tellis alle the Inglis dedes.
   Ther Mayster Wace of the *Brute* left   **Ther** where
30 Ryght begynnes Pers eft   **eft** immediately afterward
   And tellis forth the Inglis story;
   And as he says, than say I.
   Als thai haf wryten and sayd
   Haf I alle in myn Inglis layd,   **layd** composed
35 In symple speche as I couth   **couth** knew how
   That is lightest in mannes mouth.   **lightest** easiest [to recite]
   I mad noght for no disours,   **mad noght** did not compose; **disours** minstrels
   Ne for no seggers, no harpours,   **seggers** professional reciters; **harpours** harpers
   Bot for the luf of symple men
40 That strange Inglis can not ken.   **That** who
   For many it ere that strange Inglis
   In ryme wate never what it is.   **wate** know
   And bot thai wist what it mente   **bot** unless; **wist** understood
   Ellis me thoght it were alle shente.   **Ellis** otherwise; **me thoght** I would consider; **shente** ruined
45 I made it not for to be praysed
   Bot at the lewed men were aysed.   **at** so that; **aysed** helped
   If it were made in ryme couwee,
   Or in strangere, or enterlace,
   That rede Inglis it ere inowe   there are plenty who read English
50 That couthe not haf coppled a kowe,   would not have been able to link a tail rhyme
   That outhere in couwee or in baston   So either in tail rhyme or in stanzaic verse

Som suld haf ben fordon,   some people would have come to grief
So that fele men that it herde   **fele men** many men
Suld not witte howe that it ferde.   **witte** know; **it** [the narrative]; **ferde** went

[Mannyng argues that when it is a matter of reciting the narratives of Thomas of Erceldoune and Thomas of Kendale, they are never recited as composed and are much diminished thereby, something particularly exemplified by Sir Tristrem. *This text would be esteemed above "gestes" (history) if it were recited as made, but he never hears it without some part of some "copple" [either a couplet or a strophe] being omitted. The elaborate craft of these earlier makers is thus wasted: they composed in such intricate English that many people now do not understand them. He is therefore reluctant to work at "strange" rhyme, and in any case his skill is too slight to compose in such elaborate English as they used.]*

55   And men besoght me many a tyme
     To turne it bot in light ryme.   **turne** translate; **bot** only; **light** easy
     They sayd if I in strange it turn   **strange** complicated
     To here it manyon suld skurne,   **manyon** many a one; **skurne** be unwilling
     For it ere names fulle selcouth   for it uses very unfamiliar terms
60   That ere not used now in mouth.   **in mouth** in speech
     And therfore for the comonalte   **comonalte** common people
     That blythely wild listen to me,   **blythely** willingly; **wild** would
     On light lange I it began   **lange** language
     For luf of the lewed man,
65   To telle tham the chaunces bolde   **chaunces bolde** brave adventures
     That here before was don and told.   which have happened and been recorded in the past
     For this makyng I wille no mede   **makyng** composition; **wille** want; **mede** reward
     Bot gude prayere when ye it rede;   **Bot** except
     Therfore, ye lordes lewed,
70   For wham I haf this Inglis shewed: **shewed** offered
     Prayes to God he gyf me grace,   **Prayes** pray
     I travayled for your solace.   **travayled** labored; **solace** entertainment
     Of Brunne I am, if any me blame,   **Brunne** Bourne (Lincolnshire)
     Robert Mannyng is my name;
75   Blissed be he of God of heven   **of God** by God
     That me, Robert, with gude wille neven.   **neven** mentions
     In the thrid Edwardes tyme was I   I lived in the time of King Edward III
     When I wrote alle this story.   **story** history
     In the hous of Sixille I was a throwe,   **hous** [religious] house; **throwe** for a time
80   Danz Robert of Malton, that ye know,   **Danz** Dom[inus]
     Did it wryte for felawes sake   **Did it wryte** caused it to be written
     When thai wild solace make.   **solace make** to have entertainment

1   **transumpta** apparently the manuscript read-   7   **schewed** interpreted (*MED: sheuen* 8a), per-
ing, but the ink is very faint. The phrase *in materna*   haps also with a sense of "bring out, offer
lingua (2) aligns the Latin apparatus clearly on the   [entertainment]" (*MED: sheuen* 10a)
side of the English in which the text is written.   13–22   **And it is wisdom . . . fight** Mannyng's
5   **Al[l]** Sullens reads *alle*, but the second *l* is   defense of the value of history is similar to those in
very faint, and no abbreviation mark is visible.   *The Bruce* (excerpt 1.2), *The Wars of Alexander*

(excerpt 3.13), and the *Bibliotheca Historica* (excerpt 3.15).

14 **state of the land** the condition of the country: its present political and social composition, understood through an analysis of its past history

23 **Mayster Wace** Wace (d. c.1184): Jersey-born poet and writer of vernacular histories for the court of Henry II and Eleanor of Aquitaine

23–28 **And ryght . . . Inglis dedes** For the Anglo-Norman source of this passage (a copyist's comment found in one manuscript tradition of Langtoft's *Chronique*), see Thiolier 1989, 12. The prologue convention of reviewing and discussing sources as a way of acquiring and surpassing their authority in one's own work is strongly established in the vernacular by Lawman's *Brut*, the great Early Middle English adaptation of Wace, and continues throughout the period (compare Lydgate's *Troy Book*, excerpt 1.7).

26 **Pers** Piers [Peter] Langtoft (fl. 1294): canon of Bridlington in Yorkshire and author of the Anglo-Norman *Chronique* (from the founding of Britain to the end of Edward I's reign in 1307) used by Manning for the later sections of his *Chronicle*

27 **the Brute** Brut: the generic name for histories of Britain beginning with its supposed foundation by Brutus after the Trojan War ∫ **alle redes** Wace presents the whole British narrative.

28 **Inglis dedes** the deeds of the English: that is, the Angles and Saxons and the postconquest (Norman and English) inhabitants of Britain. Like his predecessor Lawman, Mannyng may have been prepared to see twelfth- and thirteenth-century traditions as both anglophone and francophone as it suited his purposes. Langtoft's *Chronique*, Mannyng's principal source for these sections, follows its *Brut* section with the history of the Saxons and Normans to the death of Henry Plantagenet (1272) and, in part three, the reign of Edward I (1272–1307).

29–30 **Ther Mayster Wace . . . Pers eft** Langtoft's account begins just where Wace's ends (in 689 with the death of Cadwallader).

34 **layd** For the past participle *layd* in the sense of "made into song," see *MED: leden* 5a).

40 **ken** understand, but perhaps also "have the capacity to recite." The problem Mannyng now goes on to outline has to do with the public reading of various verse forms as much as it does the intrinsic difficulty of their language (see "names" [59]).

41 **it ere** literally, they are. For the construction of the singular pronoun with plural verb, see *MED: hit* 4e.

47 **ryme couwee** tail rhyme, of which the basic Anglo-Norman form is a group of three lines rhyming *aab*; the third line, the "tail," is usually shorter

than the others. The form derives from Latin hymns, is rare in Continental French, but in its Anglo-Norman and English development was flexible and various. It could be doubled to form longer stanzas or mixed with other forms and was used in religious lyrics of praise as well as homiletic verse and metrical narrative romances. Some political songs in part II of the manuscript are marked by the scribe as "Couwee." For a good brief account, see Jeffrey and Levy 1990, 20–23.

48 **strangere** elaborate, *or* obscure. See Turville-Petre 1996, 36–37, and compare Usk's "straunge langage" (excerpt 1.4: 25) and Rolle's "straunge Ynglis" (excerpt 3.8: 62). The word also has overtones of "foreign, alien" (though whether this would mean Continental French or Anglo-Norman is unclear). ∫ **enterlace** entwined or crossed rhyme (*rime entrelacée, rime croisée*), rhyming *abab* in Anglo-Norman. See Jeffrey and Levy 1990, 25–26. "Enterlace" may also refer to English alliterative verse, in which, as *Sir Gawain and the Green Knight* says, "lele letteres [are] loken" (35), but there is no evidence the French term was used in this way, and Mannyng seems to be thinking of French as against English *rhymes* (see Chaucer, excerpt 1.3: 10–11).

50 **couthe not haf coppled a kowe** would not have been able to link a tail rhyme: perhaps with a pun on "tied up a cow"

51 **baston** stanzaic verse. When used as a term of prosody, Anglo-Norman and Middle English *baston* (staff, stick), like Middle English *staf* (stave), most frequently refers to a line of verse, but sometimes seems to mean a verse form, perhaps a specific stanza form (*MED: baston*) and one by implication more intricately rhymed than Mannyng's couplets. Mannyng states that he is avoiding these devices because his audience will not be able to follow if he uses them, but the very fact that he mentions them may suggest that his audience was acquainted with them. Since they are all devices associated with romance as well as lyric and homily, Mannyng may also be implying they are less suitable than his clear rhyming couplets for historical conventions of truth-telling.

67–82 **For this makyng . . . solace make** Identification of the author by name and the soliciting of the audience's goodwill and prayers at the end of a prologue is a common Anglo-Norman historical and hagiographic convention of authorial modesty (see Wogan-Browne 1994b). Mannyng's variation of it counterposes the narrator's clerkly request for prayers to the tangible rewards ("mede" [67]) demanded by minstrels.

77 **In the thrid Edwardes tyme was I** I lived in the time of [King] Edward III [1327–77]

79 **Sixille** Sixhills Priory, a Gilbertine house of nuns and canons, near Lincoln

80 **Danz Robert of Malton** Dom[inus] Robert of Malton, unidentified, but probably a Gilbertine canon from Malton, North Yorkshire, forty-five miles to the north. In the convention whereby a monastic senior is represented as commanding a composition, the writing becomes an act of obedience to a higher authority (as enjoined in the Benedictine Rule and its derivatives).

1.2 JOHN BARBOUR, *THE BRUCE:* PROLOGUE

Date and Provenance: 1375–77; east Scotland (Aberdeen). Barbour tells us he was at work on the poem in 1375 (*Bruce* XIII.709ff.), but many materials were gathered years earlier and represent the dialect and oral traditions of southwestern Scotland.

Author, Sources, and Nature of Text: John Barbour, c. 1320–95, author of the "first major Scottish work of literature written in English" (Kennedy 1989, 2681), studied in France (at Paris and perhaps Orléans) as well as at Oxford, and was archdeacon of Aberdeen by 1357 (McDiarmid and Stevenson 1980–85, 1:1–5). *The Bruce,* his only known work, is an account of the resistance of the Scots under Robert the Bruce to the invasion by Edward I of England and his son Edward II. Despite its anti-English emphasis, the poem is written in a Lowland Scots dialect "not strikingly different from northern Middle English" (Bawcutt and Riddy 1987, xv), while it is influenced stylistically by Middle English romance in four-stress couplets as much as by French romance. Its sources likewise include an English chronicle (the lost chronicle of Robert le Roy, minstrel to all three King Edwards) besides Latin chronicles and oral accounts from elderly warriors like Sir Alan of Cathcart and John Thomasson (McDiarmid and Stevenson 1980–85, 1:3–4, 38). Barbour's use of oral as well as written sources is of a piece with his poem's blending of two genres, history and chronicle, into a twenty-book historical epic focused not on the traditional subjects of medieval historiography (the matters of Troy, Britain, or Alexander) but on local and recent events. Barbour says he writes so that these events "lest ay furth in memory" (18), for the guidance of a future audience for whom his poem can have the status of a foundation narrative

comparable with the Brutus story in Mannyng's *Chronicle* (excerpt 1.1). Hence he emphasizes the "suthfastnes" of his poem (11), a word that refers to historical and moral truth at once, and so suggests an ethical purpose that places the poem in the same historiographic tradition as Lydgate's *Troy Book* or Skelton's translation of Diodorus Siculus (excerpts 1.7 and 3.15), while giving this ethical purpose a nationalistic orientation. Barbour's articulation of a desire for national "freedom" (Koht 1943, 287) uses this word in an aristocratic and chivalric, not an egalitarian, sense, portraying commoners in a positive light and appealing to the Scottish people as a whole, but identifying the interests of Scotland with those of its knightly class (Goldstein 1986) and with speakers of Scottish English, not Gaelic.

Audience and Circulation: As archdeacon and auditor of the exchequer, Barbour had regular contact with the court of Robert II (1371–90, the first Stewart king), but there is no evidence *The Bruce* was a royal commission (McDiarmid and Stevenson 1980–85, 1:10). In the late 1370s, when Robert had just come to the throne, the poem would have had a political message, flattering the king and the Douglas family and warning of the dangers of disarray among the Scottish nobility (Ebin 1971–72, 237). The poem's use of minstrel conventions aligns the audience with the groups of listeners evoked by traditional modes of poetic narrative, but its Latin heading emphasizes its clerical orientation. The poem survives in two late-fifteenth-century manuscripts: Cambridge, St. John's College MS G.23, which lacks books 1–4, and Edinburgh, National Library of Scotland MS 19.2.2. *The Bruce* has been in print in Scotland from the sixteenth to the twentieth century.

Bibliography: A detailed commentary is offered by Matthew McDiarmid and James Stevenson in their edition (1980–85); Priscilla Bawcutt and Felicity Riddy (1987) edit excerpts; A.A.M. Duncan (1997) provides a user-friendly edition with facing-page translation. For an early study of the poem as a "hymn to liberty," see Koht 1943. For a study of the poem as a response to political insecurity, see Ebin 1971–72. For its representation of class interests, see Goldstein 1986. For its critique of chivalry, see Purdon and Wasserman 1994. Other studies include Kliman 1973, 1975; Wilson 1990; Watt 1994.

Source: Edinburgh, National Library of Scotland MS 19.2.2 (formerly 1489), fol. 1ra. This cheaply produced paper manuscript is now in two volumes, the first containing *The Bruce,* the second *The Wallace,* both in the hand of John Ramsay, apparently a professional scrivener, who copied the book "hurriedly" (*raptim scriptus*) for Symon Lochmaloney, vicar of Ouchtirmunsye (Moonsie in Fife) (Skeat 1968, 1:lxiii–lxv); the writing is indeed hurried. The manuscript looks as though it may not have been bound until the outer folios had already suffered damage, and the writing is illegible in places, while parts of a Latin and English commentary that runs along the foot of many pages have been lost, perhaps when the manuscript was cropped to preserve it. The first few letters of each line of the prologue are also illegible as a result of damage, and are supplied here from McDiarmid and Stevenson (1980–85, vol. 1), who bring together a number of earlier editorial conjectures now generally accepted by scholars. In the orthography of lowland Scots, *w* appears for *v* (as in "hawe" [have] [9]) and is retained here.

Incipit liber compositus per magistrum Iohannem Barber, Archidiaconum Abyrdonensem: de gestis, bellis, et virtutibus domini Roberti de Brwyss, regis Scocie illustrissimi, et de conquestu regni Scocie per eundem, et de domino de Douglas Iacobo.

[Here begins the book composed by Master John Barber, archdeacon of Aberdeen, which is about the deeds, wars, and virtues of Sir Robert the Bruce, the famous king of Scotland, and of his conquest of the Kingdom of Scotland, and of Sir James Douglas.]

5 Storys to rede ar delitabill	delitabill pleasurable
Suppos that thai be nocht bot fabill;	**Suppos that** even if; **bot** only; **fabill** fiction
Than suld storys that suthfast wer,	**suld** should; **suthfast** truthful
And thai war said on gud maner,	**And** if; **on gud maner** well told
Hawe doubill plesance in heryng.	**Hawe** produce; **plesance** pleasure
10 The fyrst plesance is the carpyng	**carpyng** recitation
And the t'other the suthfastnes,	**t'other** the other
That schawys the thing rycht as it wes;	**rycht** exactly
And suth thyngis that ar likand	**suth** true; **likand** agreeable
Tyll mannys heryng ar plesand.	**Tyll** to
15 Tharfor I wald fayne set my will,	**fayne** gladly
Giff my wyt mycht suffice thartill,	**thartill** there to
To put in wryt a suthfast story,	**in wryt** in writing
That it lest ay furth in memory,	**lest** may last; **ay furth** for evermore
Swa that na tyme of lenth it let	**Swa** so; **tyme of lenth** long time; **let** damage
20 Na ger it haly be forget.	**Na** nor; **ger** cause; **haly** wholly
For aulde storys that men redys	

Representis to thaim the dedys
Of stalwart folk that lywyt ar,   **stalwart** sturdy; **lywyt** lived; **ar** before
Rycht as thai than in presence war.
25 And, certis, thai suld weill hawe prys   **hawe prys** be valued
That in thar tyme war wycht and wys   **That** who; **wycht** valiant
And led thar lyff in gret trawaill,   **trawaill** effort
And oft in hard stour off bataill   **stour off bataill** conflict of battle
Wan gret price off chewalry,   **price** renown
30 And war woydyt off cowardy: **woydyt** devoid
As wes king Robert off Scotland,   **king Robert** Robert [the Bruce]
That hardy wes off hart and hand;
And gud Schyr James off Douglas,
That in his tyme sa worthy was
35 That off hys price and hys bounte   **off** for; **bounte** excellence
In fer landis renownyt wes he.
Off thaim I thynk this buk to ma;   **Off** about; **ma** make
Now God gyff grace that I may swa
Tret it, and bryng it till endyng,   **Tret** handle
40 That I say nocht bot suthfast thing.

3 **Roberti de Brwyss** Robert the Bruce: King Robert I of Scotland (1306–29)

7–9 **Than suld . . . in heryng** stories that are true should therefore, if they are well told, produce double pleasure in the hearing

9 **doubill plesance** Barbour's concept of the "double pleasure" afforded by hearing a true story well told is related to a notion originating in Aristotle's *Poetics*, that an accurate representation is inherently satisfying and a source of pleasure. This idea is taken up in Horace, *Ars poetica* (333–44), in the dictum that the purpose of poetry is both to please and to instruct (see Curtius 1990, 478–79). For a discussion, see Olson 1982, chap. 1 (19–38, especially 32–33).

17–24 **To put in . . . presence war** The statement that history exists to preserve important events in the collective memory, and the following lines claiming that history has the power to reclaim the past, invoke common topoi of historical writing. Compare, for example, *Troy Book* (excerpt 1.7: 99–131) and Skelton, *Diodorus Siculus* (excerpt 3.15).

25–30 **And . . . cowardy** These lines give another common justification for writing history, that the lives of those who have performed brave deeds deserve to be commemorated. The topos recurs in *Troy Book* (excerpt 1.7: 123–31) and is critically examined in Chaucer's *House of Fame*.

33 **Schyr James off Douglas** Sir James Douglas (1286?–1330): celebrated Scottish warrior and supporter of Robert the Bruce, entrusted with taking Bruce's heart to the Holy Land (McDiarmid and Stevenson 1980–85, 1:xx and 189–248)

1.3 GEOFFREY CHAUCER, *COMPLAINT OF VENUS:* ENVOI

Date and Provenance: before 1397, perhaps 1390s; London.

Author, Sources, and Nature of Text: Chaucer's *Complaint of Venus* is based on the work of a poet probably well known to Chaucer's circle, Oton de Graunson. Graunson was a Savoyard knight who served as a retainer of John of Gaunt, Richard II, and the future Henry IV, and wrote two narrative love poems, or *dits amoreux,* and many lyrics and ballades. The *Complaint of Venus* (the title may not be Chaucer's, since some manuscripts of the work simply refer to it as a *balade*) is freely translated from three of these ballades. In the added envoi Chaucer defers to his *auctor* while presenting himself in a largely passive role—as he often does when explicitly commenting on his use of a source.

The poet's self-presentation as deferential, inadequate to the task of composition ("my litel suffisaunce" [4]), virtually incapacitated through old age, and inferior to his *auctor* draws on conventions of courtly complimenting while creating an authorial voice that matches the muted personality Chaucer gives the female speaker of his *Venus*. In tune with this association between translation and femininity, the envoi also implies that translation is secondary to original composition ("endyting" [6]) and that English is secondary to French. Yet in the very terms by which he depicts his shortcomings, Chaucer is presenting himself as a poet. The phrase "worde by worde" (10) cannot refer to literal word-by-word translation; *Venus* is far from that. Not only are many phrases omitted or changed; this notionally passive translator gives the work a wholly different unity and emotional cast by creating a female speaker where the narrative voice in Graunson's original is male. "Worde by worde" may then have a quantitative sense, "matching all the words," that is, matching all the demands made by the French rhyme scheme (despite the difficulty of doing so in English). Behind Chaucer's pose of humility thus lies a claim—perhaps half-humorous—to have demonstrated his ability, in verse written in his mother tongue, to match the skills of the "floure of hem that maken in Fraunce" (11).

Audience and Circulation: If Chaucer knew Graunson, the poem may have been presented to him, but the envoi's invocation is to "princes" (which could mean "princes" or "princess"). It is not clear whether this indicates actual or fictional court circulation; it might refer to the "princes" (judges) of a *puy*, or poets' competition. The poem survives in eight fifteenth-century manuscripts.

Bibliography: The variorum edition of Chaucer's *Minor Poems* (vol. 2), edited by Alfred David and Helen Phillips, is forthcoming; Arthur Piaget (1941) has edited the text of the French ballades. For commentary on Chaucer's poem, see Wimsatt 1991, 210–19, and Phillips 1993, a study of translation techniques and much else; see also Phillips 1994, 1997. For the way metaphors of writing are gendered, see Dinshaw 1989.

Source: Oxford, Bodleian Library MS Fairfax 16, fols. 20r–20v: a major anthology of courtly poetry of c. 1450 or earlier, containing shorter works by Chaucer, Hoccleve, and Lydgate, and poems attributed to the Earl of Suffolk, the great majority treating courtly love. The manuscript has been reproduced in facsimile, with an introduction by John Norton-Smith (1979). It consists of five distinct units, all copied by one main scribe. Booksellers often kept a stock of precopied units that could be assembled to suit a reader's taste (Pearsall 1977, 213, 217–18), and this was probably how Fairfax 16 was assembled. The reader who made the selection seems to be John Stanley (d. by 1469), usher of the chamber to Henry VI from 1450 to 1455, since his coat of arms appears on fols. 14v–15r (Norton-Smith 1979, xiii–xxiv; Boffey and Thompson 1989, 280).

This excerpt was contributed by Helen Phillips.

L'envoy

Princes, resseeyveth this compleynt in gre   **compleynt** lament; **in gre** with pleasure
Unto your excellent benignite
Directe, aftir my litel suffisaunce;   **aftir** according to; **suffisaunce** capacity
5 For elde, that in my spirit dulleth me,   **elde** old age
Hath of endyting al the subtilite   **endyting** composing poetry
Welnyghe bereft out of my remembraunce,
And eke to me hit ys a gret penaunce,
Syth ryme in Englissh hat such skarsete,   **hat such skarsete** is so scarce

10 To folowe worde by worde the curiosite   *curiosite* complexity
Of Graunson, floure of hem that maken in Fraunce.   **floure** flower; **maken** compose poetry

Here endith the Compleynt of Venus and Mars

2 **Princes** princes (or princess). Two manu-scripts copied by the fifteenth-century scribe John Shirley have "princesse," the eight other authori-ties have "princes."

3–4 **Unto . . . Directe** addressed to (frequently used in the subscription of a letter)

5 **elde** Chaucer was probably in his mid or late fifties when Graunson died in 1397, but the allusion to age may dramatize the narrator in relation to Ve-nus as unsuitable for love poetry. The excuse that age prevents one from writing well (like the excuse that youth does the same) is a topos. See Ashby's *Active Policy* (excerpt 1.9: 91–92), and, more explicitly, *Confessio Amantis* VIII.3125–31 (see excerpt 2.11).

9 **skarsete** Many English poets eschewed the more difficult French ballade stanza forms (typi-cally *ababbccb*), but Chaucer here uses an unusually prolonged rhyme scheme (*aabaabbaab*)

in a virtuoso showcase of English rhymes in a ballade form. He also orders syntax so as to focus expectancy on the rhyme words: they arrive with a sense of éclat and achievement.

10 **worde by worde** often interpreted as literal translation (as opposed to freer, sense-for-sense translation). As suggested in the headnote, it more probably here has the sense of "fully," "matching all the words" (compare *The Legend of Good Women* 1002–3). ∫ **curiosite** Although his rhyme scheme is complex, there is nothing "curious" about Graunson's style and diction, which are lu-cid and simple. Chaucer is presumably drawing on a traditional association between courtly writing in French and subtlety (compare Mannyng's account of "strangere, or enterlace," excerpt 1.1: 48).

11 **floure** flower: often used to mean finest

1.4 THOMAS USK, *THE TESTAMENT OF LOVE:* PROLOGUE (EXTRACT)

Date and Provenance: 1384–87; London.

Author, Sources, and Nature of Text: Usk, like Chaucer, was a London civil servant, but, unlike Chaucer, he became fatally involved in the factionalized world of contemporary na-tional and municipal politics. After his employer, the mayor of London, John of Northampton, was arrested in 1384 on charges of treason, Usk testified against him (his appeal against Northampton survives) and was employed by the new mayor, Nicho-las Bembre, one of Richard II's principal supporters. In November 1387 the Lords Ap-pellant, the party of lords opposing Richard, accused the king's councillors of treason. Bembre was executed on February 20, 1388, and Usk on March 4.

Usk's *Testament of Love* is a prose treatise on love, grace, and free will, whose sources include Boethius's *Consolation of Philosophy* (probably also Chaucer's *Boece*) and Anselm's treatise on predestination, the *De concordia*. Like Boethius, Usk takes imprisonment as the

starting point of an allegorical exploration of the reconciliation of human transience and di-vine compassion: as Philosophy consoles Boethius, so Love visits Usk in prison to ex-plain how he may win the favor of Margaret (the French *marguerite* means "pearl"), a fig-ure for "grace, lernyng, or wisdom of God, or els holy church" (Skeat 1897, 145.102–3). The ethical scope of the *Testament* also en-compasses Usk's political life, including his betrayal of Northampton, and this topicality has attracted more critical discussion (e.g., Strohm 1990, 1992) than the work's original-ity and accomplishment (which Chaucer and Langland may have recognized). Like Chaucer's *Venus* (excerpt 1.3), Usk's prologue mobilizes oppositions between French and English, elegance and stylistic lack, rhetoric as excess and as cultivation of meaning. Its account of these topoi, despite apparent def-erence to the usual hierarchies, asserts equal status for English and French. Usk engages with issues of language and truth and the "sentence of thynges" (7) in an argument conducted, like Langland's writing (which Usk knew), through the inexplicit as well as the overt metaphoric connections of its images. Quoting the psalmist David and Aristotle, he positions his work's discussion of ethical and philosophical issues within the metaphysical framework of the individual's search to apprehend the "privytees" (44) of a creator God hidden but knowable in part through his creation. Yet Usk's prose is hauntingly aware of the embodiedness of textual production: of the ears of listeners (1), the tongues of language users with which men speak their "poysye-mater" (19), the physicality of writing material (11–13), even the sweat shed by laboring philosophers (56). The vernacular in which these abstract and concrete polarities are embraced is labeled "boystous" (rough [6]) but is fecund in Usk's exploration, its richness speaking of the endlessness of God's "makynge" (48–49). The narrator images himself as a dwarf holding a sword: he does not pierce but is, rather, cloaked in the "cloudy cloude of unconnynge" (74), though his imagery claims that language can not only explore but enlarge the world (68). But he is also a sly servant (89–90), a gleaner of the crumbs of learning from monastic tables (82). In the creation of a narratorial presence whose understanding both voices and is contingent on "our dames tonge" (29), Usk's *Testament* seeks truth in and with language itself, in prose of an intensity and metaphoric life paralleled only in *Piers Plowman*.

Audience and Circulation: The *Testament* is known only from a printed text in Thynne's 1532 edition of Chaucer, to whom it is there attributed, as it continued to be until the late nineteenth century. While the work provides early evidence for the circulation of other works (Chaucer's *Troilus and Criseyde* and *Boece, Piers Plowman,* and perhaps *The Cloud of Unknowing*), we know little of its history in manuscript. However, Anne Middleton (1998) argues that Thynne's text was made from Usk's own copy or a near derivative. In her view, the format of the manuscript indicates how consciously Usk wrote for a circle of book producers, able to appreciate features of his art such as his division of texts into equal sections, so that each new section begins with a rubricated capital letter at the head of a new folio (see 11–16). These capitals combine to form a signature (MARGARET OF VIRTW HAVE MERCI ON THIN VSK), a form of self-naming that also suggests composition for a small circle (however, see Norton's *Ordinal of Alchemy,* excerpt 2.3, headnote).

Bibliography: The text is in Skeat's edition of Chaucer (1897, vol. 7), and in a new edition by R.A. Shoaf (1998). For Usk's appeal against Northampton, see Chambers and Daunt 1931. For his political opportunism, see Strohm 1990, 1992, opposing a philosophical reading of the *Testament,* exemplified by Sanderlin 1942 and Medcalf 1989, 1997 (see also Carlson 1993a). For the work's date, see Bressie 1928–29. Usk's rhetoric is discussed by J. D. Burnley (1985). On the prison topos, see Boffey 1991.

Source: William Thynne's 1532 edition of *The Workes of Geffray Chaucer,* printed by Thomas Godfray, London, British Library G.11623, 325r–325v, one of two copies in the British Library (*STC* 5068). This folio volume was the first attempt to produce a complete collection of Chaucer's works, and contains several other poems that were falsely attributed to him. Most of the emendations offered here are indebted to Skeat's edition. There is no surviving manuscript.

Many men there ben that, with eeres openly sprad, so moche swalowen the delyciousnesse of jestes and of ryme, by queynt knyttyng coloures, that of the goodnesse or of the badnesse of the sentence take they lytel hede, or els non.

    Sothely, dul wytte and a thoughtful soule so sore have myned and graffed in my
5 spyrites that suche craft of endytyng wol not ben of myn acqueyntaunce. And, for rude wordes and boystous percen the herte of the herer to the inrest poynte, and planten there the sentence of thynges, so that with lytel helpe it is able to spring:

this boke, that nothyng hath of the greet floode of wit ne of semelych colours, is
dolven with rude wordes and boystous, and so drawe[n] togyder, to maken the
10 catchers therof ben the more redy to hent sentence.

Some men there ben that peynten with colours ryche, and some with vers, as
with red ynke, and some with coles and chalke; and yet is there good matere to the
leude people of thilke chalky purtreyture, as hem thynketh for the tyme; and
afterwarde the syght of the better colours yeven to hem more joye for the first
15 leudenesse. So, sothly, this leude clowdy occupacion is not to prayse but by the
leude; for comenly leude leudenesse commendeth. Eke it shal yeve syght, that
other precious thynges shal be the more in reverence. In Latyn and French hath
many soverayne wyttes had gret delyte to endyte, and have many no[ble t]hynges
fulfylde. But certes, there ben some [that] speken their poysye-mater in Frenche,
20 of whiche speche the Frenchemen have as good a fantasye as we have in heryng of
Frenchemennes Englysshe. And many termes ther ben in Englysshe whiche unneth
we Englysshmen connen declare the knowlegynge. Howe shulde than a
Frencheman borne suche termes conne jumpere in his mater, but as the jay
chatereth Englyssh? Right so, trewly, the understandyng of Englysshmen wol not
25 stretche to the privy termes in Frenche, whatsoever we bosten of straunge langage.
Let than clerkes endyten in Latyn, for they have the propertie of science, and the
knowynge in that facultie; and lette Frenchmen in their Frenche also endyten their
queynt termes, for it is kyndely to their mouthes; and let us shewe our fantasyes in
suche wordes as we lerneden of our dames tonge.
30 And although this boke be lytel thankeworthy for the leudnesse in travaile, yet
suche writynges exciten men to thilke thynges that ben necessarie; for every man
therby may, as by a perpetual myrrour, sene the vyces or vertues of other, in
whiche thyng lightly may be conceyved to eschewe peryls, and necessaryes to
catche, after as aventures have fallen to other people or persons.
35 Certes, [perfeccion is] the soveraynst thing of desyre, and moste creature[s]
reasonable have, or els shulde have, ful appetyte to their perfeccion; unresonable
beestes mowen not, sythe reason hath in hem no werkyng. Than reasonable that
wol not is comparysoned to unresonable, and made lyke hem. Forsothe, the most
soverayne and fynal perfection of man is in knowyng of a sothe, withouten any
40 entent disceyvable, and in love of one very God that is inchaungeable: that is, to
knowe and love his creatour.

Nowe principally, the meane to bringe in knowlegyng and lovyng his creatour is
the consyderacion of thynges made by the creatour: wherthrough, be thylke
thynges that ben made understonding here to our wyttes, arne the unsene privytees
45 of God made to us sightful and knowyng, in our contemplacion and
understondyng. These thynges than, forsoth, moche bringen us to the ful
knowlegynge [of] sothe, and to the parfyte love of the maker of hevenly thynges.
Lo, David sayth, "thou haste delyted me in makynge," as who sayth, "to have
delyte in the tune, how God hath lent me in consyderacion of thy makynge."
50 Whereof Aristotle, in the boke *De animalibus,* saythe to naturel phylosophers:
"It is a great lykyng in love of knowynge their creatour; and also in knowynge of
causes in kyndely thynges." Consydred, forsoth, the formes of kyndly thynges and
the shap, a great kyndely love me shulde have to the werkman that hem made.
The crafte of a werkmen is shewed in the werke. Herfore, truly, the phylosophers,

55 with a lyvely studye, many noble thynges ryght precious and worthy to memory
writen; and by a great swetande travayle to us leften of causes [of] the propertyes
in natures of thynges. To whiche, therefore, phylosophers it was more joy, more
lykynge, more herty lust, in kyndely vertues and matters of reason, the perfection
by busy study to knowe, than to have had al the treasour, al the richesse, al the
60 vainglory that the passed emperours, prynces, or kynges hadden. Therefore the
names of hem, in the boke of perpetual memory, in vertue and peace arn wryten;
and in the contrarye, that is to sayne, in Stixe, the foule pytte of helle, arn thilke
pressed that suche goodnesse hated. And bycause this boke shal be of love, and
the pryme causes of sterynge in that doynge, with passyons and dyseases for
65 wantynge of desyre, I wil that this boke be cleped the *Testament of Love*.
　　But nowe, thou reder, who is thylke that wyl not in scorne laughe, to here a
dwarfe, or els halfe a man, say he wyl rende out the swerde of Hercules handes,
and also he shulde set Hercules Gades a myle yet ferther; and over that, he had
power of strengthe to pul up the spere that Alisander the noble might never
70 wagge? And that, passynge al thynge, to ben mayster of Fraunce by myght,
thereas the noble gracyous Edwarde the thyrde, for al his great prowesse in
victories, ne might yet al conquere?
　　Certes, I wote wel, there shal be made more scorne and jape of me, that I, so
unworthely clothed altogyder in the cloudy cloude of unconnynge, wyl putten me
75 in prees to speke of love, or els of the causes in that matter, sythen al the grettest
clerkes han had ynough to don, and (as who sayth) gathered up clene toforne hem,
and with theyr sharpe sythes of connyng al mowen, and made therof great rekes
and noble, ful of al plentyes, to fede me and many another. Envye, forsothe,
commendeth nought his reason that he hath in hayn, be it never so trusty. And
80 althoughe these noble repers, as good workmen and worthy theyr hyer, han al
drawe and bounde up in the sheves, and made many shockes, yet have I ensample
to gader the smale crommes and fullyn my walet of tho that fallen from the borde
among the smale houndes, notwithstandynge the travayle of the almoygner, that
hath drawe up in the cloth al the remyssayles, as trenchours and the relyef, to
85 bere to the almesse.
　　Yet also have I leve of the noble husbande Boece, although I be a straunger of
connynge, to come after his doctryne, and these great workmen, and glene my
handfuls of the shedynge after theyr handes; and, if me fayle ought of my ful, to
encrease my porcyon with that I shal drawe by privytyes out of the shocke. A slye
90 servaunt in his owne helpe is often moche commended. Knoweyng of trouth in
causes of thynges was more hardyer in the first sechers (and so sayth Aristotle),
and lyghter in us that han folowed after. For theyr passyng study han fresshed our
wyttes and our understandynge han excyted, in consideracion of trouth, by
sharpnesse of theyr reasons. Utterly these thynges be no dremes ne japes, to
95 throwe to hogges; it is lyfelyche meate for chyldren of trouthe; and as they me
betiden, whan I pilgrymaged out of my kyth in wynter; whan the weder out of
measure was boystous, and the wylde wynde Borias, as his kynde asketh, with
dryenge coldes maked the wawes of the occian-see so to aryse unkyndely over the
commune bankes, that it was in poynte to spyl al the erthe.

100 Thus endith the Prologue and hereafter foloweth the boke of the
Testament of Love

1 **eeres openly sprad** ears wide open. See *Troilus and Criseyde* IV.1422.

1–2 **swalowen . . . ryme** Usk envisages "jestes" (songs, poems) and "ryme" (narrative verse) as orally delivered. For the metaphorical association of reading, hearing, and eating, see excerpts 3.5, 3.19, and 3.20.

2 **queynt knyttyng coloures** elaborate figures of rhetoric binding the work together

3 **sentence** meaning, moral value

4–10 **Sothely . . . sentence** Like Mannyng (excerpt 1.1), Usk in a few lines passes from excusing his style on the grounds of incompetence to asserting its greater suitability for his audience.

4 **myned and graffed in** tunneled into and grafted [themselves] upon

5 **endytyng** composition

6 **boystous** rough ∫ **inrest poynte** the innermost place

7 **spring** spring up, grow

8 **semelych colours** attractive colors [of rhetoric], verbal ornament

9 **dolven** dug. The image is of the poet as a gardener. Compare excerpts 1.7: 115–18 and 3.5. ∫ **drawe[n] togyder** composed (Thynne's text reads "drawe")

10 **catchers** catchers. Since the word also has the sense "hunters," the role of the "herer" (6) may be both actively and passively conceived. ∫ **hent sentence** grasp the meaning

11 **peynten with colours ryche** describe [or narrate] with elaborate verbal ornament (with a play on painting with expensive pigments). Usk may also be alluding to Horace's celebrated phrase *ut pictura poesis* (poetry is like a picture; Horace, *Art of Poetry* 361).

12 **red ynke** perhaps a reference to the rubrication of text in manuscripts. A treatise of c. 1475 notes that "Red letter in parchemyn Maketh a chyld good and fyn Lettrys to loke and se" (*MED: red* 2a). ∫ **coles and chalke** charcoal and chalk: used in the preparation of ink and vellum and also as writing and drawing materials. Compare, for example, Pecock (see excerpt 1.16): "Write sum . . . caract with cole or chalke in the wal" (*Repressor* 166: *MED: chalk* 2). ∫ **matere** subject matter

13 **leude** unlearned ∫ **thilke chalky purtreyture** that portrayal in chalk: that is, Usk's "boystous" language (6) is but a preliminary sketch. For modesty topoi, see Curtius 1990, 83–85. ∫ **as hem thynketh for the tyme** as it seems to them at the time

14 **yeven** give ∫ **hem** them

14–15 **for the first leudenesse** because of [their] initial ignorance

15–16 **this leude clowdy occupacion . . . commendeth** this unlearned and obscure activity is

not found praiseworthy except by the unlearned, for the unlearned often praise unlearnedness

16 **Eke** moreover ∫ **syght** understanding

17–18 **In Latyn and French . . . wyttes** English writers who choose to use Latin or French. Possibly Usk is here alluding to his contemporary John Gower (see excerpt 2.11), author of *Le Mirour de l'omme* and *Vox clamantis*.

18 **endyte** compose

18–19 **no[ble t]hynges . . . [that]** The bracketed letters are missing in the copy consulted due to a hole in the paper.

19 **fulfylde** completed ∫ **poysye-mater** material for poetry

19–21 **But certes . . . Englysshe** That is, the French laugh at English writers who use their language, just as we laugh when we hear their English.

20 **fantasye** supposition (but see 28)

21 **unneth** hardly

22 **declare the knowlegynge** interpret the meaning. Usk represents English as already possessing a richness of vocabulary that stretches the comprehension even of native speakers.

23 **conne** know how to ∫ **jumpere** jumble: a word used in Chaucer, *Troilus and Criseyde* II.1037, where Pandarus tells Troilus not to "jompre . . . discordant thyng yfeere" in writing to Criseyde. The phrase is densely packed, with a further implication that, if French speakers tried to use English terms in a structured way in writing in English, they would produce "jumble."

25 **privy** recondite ∫ **whatsoever we bosten of straunge langage** however much we may boast of [our] elaborate language (compare Mannyng, excerpt 1.1: 48 and note), or knowledge of foreign language

26 **have the propertie of science** are the proprietors of knowledge

27 **facultie** field of knowledge

28 **queynt** elaborate ∫ **kyndely** natural ∫ **our fantasyes** the products of our imaginations

30 **leudnesse in travaile** crudeness of its execution

31 **necessarie** The word often implies "necessary for salvation," but here also has the ethical and philosophical sense "necessary for the good life."

32 **perpetual** eternal ∫ **myrrour** A fiction can act as an encyclopedia (the medieval encyclopedia was called a *speculum,* or mirror) of exemplary behavior to be avoided or followed. Compare, for example, the titles of excerpts 1.12, 2.17, 3.10, 3.12, and see excerpt 2.1: 67–68.

33 **lightly may be conceyved to eschewe peryls** may be easily understood how one can avoid dangers

33–34 **necessaryes to catche** to pursue necessary things. Strictures against French (e.g., 19–21) do not prevent Usk's using French-influenced syntax, as here in the inversion of object and infinitive (see also "the perfection . . . to knowe" [58–59]).

34 after as aventures have fallen to other people taking example from the events that have happened to other people. Usk is adapting a topos about "the lessons of history" (see excerpts 1.1, 1.2, and especially 3.15: 1–22) to introduce a text that philosophizes his own experience.

35 [perfeccion is] the soveraynst thing of desyre perfection is the supreme object of desire. The argument follows that of Boethius, *Consolation of Philosophy* III.pr.10–11.

37 mowen may

37–38 reasonable . . . to unresonable a reasonable being that does not wish [to make itself perfect] is compared to a creature without reason

39 a sothe one truth

40 entent disceyvable illusory understanding ∫ **very** true

42 meane means

43 wherthrough whereby ∫ **be through** ∫ **thilke** those

44 understonding intelligible ∫ **arne** are ∫ **privytees** mysteries

45 sightful visible ∫ **knowyng** capable of being known

47 sothe truth

48 makynge composition. See Ps. 91:5.

48–49 to have delyte . . . makynge how God has lent me delight in the tune in appreciation of your composing. Skeat thought this sentence corrupt and a reading of *hys* for *thy* clearer (as also would be a reading of *my* for *thy*). But Usk may be comparing David's pleasure in the creation with a compliment to a musician-poet, the syntactic difficulty stemming from the way God provides both means and object of love (as in the following Aristotelian analogy of the love of created beings for other creations and their creator).

50 Aristotle . . . De animalibus See Aristotle, *De historia animalium* 1.5.

51 lykyng pleasure. "Created things like to know their creator and the causes of natural things akin to them" (Skeat 1897, 452.64n). See Jonathan Barnes's translation of the *De historia* (1984, 1004): "nature . . . gives amazing pleasure in [the study of animals] to all who can trace links of causation and are inclined to philosophy."

52 Consydred . . . the formes a latinate (ablative absolute) construction. Usk also uses French-influenced syntactic patterns (see 33–34n).

53 shap shape ∫ **me shulde have** one should have

54–63 Herfore, truly . . . goodnesse hated Usk reworks the topos of truth's endurance in the face of worldly transmission. Compare, for example,

Lydgate on writing (excerpt 1.7: 111–31) and Skelton's defense of history writing (excerpt 3.15).

54 Herfore hence

55 lyvely living ∫ **worthy to memory** worthy of being remembered. Compare *Canterbury Tales* I (A) 3112.

56 swetande sweating ∫ **travayle** labor ∫ **of causes** about the causes ∫ **propertyes** attributes. This perhaps alludes to Bartholomaeus Anglicus, *De proprietatibus rerum,* of which there is a Middle English translation by John Trevisa.

58 lykynge delight ∫ **herty lust** hearty pleasure

60 passed bygone

61 arn are

62 Stixe the river Styx, which marked the boundary of hell ∫ **thilke** those

64 the pryme causes of sterynge in that doynge the chief causes of action in that business

64–65 with passyons and dyseases for wantynge of desyre with the passions and distresses caused by lacking [the object of] desire. The Ovidian language of the diseases and desires of love is co-opted for philosophical and theological questions of love.

65 I wil a phrase used in wills

68 Hercules Gades The island of Gades, now Cadiz, is west of the Pillars of Hercules off the coast of Spain. For Europe in the Middle Ages the pillars marked the edge of the known world. Burnley (1985, 288–89) suggests an echo of Geoffrey of Vinsauf, *Poetria nova* 56–59.

69 Alisander Alexander the Great (356–323 B.C.)

70 wagge shake ∫ **passynge** surpassing

71–72 Edwarde the thyrde, for al his great prowesse in victories Edward III (1327–77), whose victories in the Hundred Years' War included the Battle of Crécy of 1346. Usk explicitly links the exploitation of English, not French, for literary composition with conquest.

73 wote know ∫ **jape** mockery

74 the cloudy cloude of unconnynge the dark cloud of ignorance. *The Cloud of Unknowing* (? c. 1380) was not, as far as we know, in widespread circulation at this date, and Usk's possible knowledge of it and reading of Anselm's *De concordia* suggest he had access to an institutional library.

74–75 putten me in prees exert myself *or* put myself among the crowd

75–78 sythen al . . . many another Compare Chaucer, *Legend of Good Women* F.73–77.

75 sythen since

76 gathered up clene toforne hem gathered up completely before them[selves]

77 sythes scythes ∫ **connyng** ability ∫ **al mowen** mowed everything ∫ **rekes** ricks

78 **plentyes** abundances

79 **commendeth nought his reason that he hath in hayn** does not approve of the reasoning of someone he hates

80 **hyer** hire

81 **shockes** shocks: groups of sheaves placed upright for drying

81–82 **yet have I ensample . . . borde** yet I have precedent for gathering up the small crumbs and filling my bag with those that fall from the table. The reference is to Matt. 15:27, the story of the Samaritan woman who argues Jesus into helping her, but here the "crumbs" of learning are the fragments left behind both by "reaping" clerks (75–78) and the monks whose "almoygner" (83) has gathered up almost all that is left. The passage is an early example of what became a Lollard attack on the "hoarding" of knowledge by monks and clerics (compare excerpts 3.11:13–16, 3.19).

83 **almoygner** almoner: the officer of a household or monastery in charge of the formal distribution of alms

84 **the remyssayles** the scraps ∫ **trenchours** trenchers: large loaves used as plates ∫ **relyef** leavings

85 **almesse** almsgiving

86 **noble husbande** noble farmer: perhaps an intentional oxymoron ∫ **Boece** Boethius (d. 524), late classical philosopher whose writings were a major conduit through which Greek and Roman thinking entered medieval culture. Usk uses the fact that Boethius's text is itself a compilation of philosophical thought as a justification both for "gleaning" material Boethius has left out and for stealing from his "shocke" (89) where necessary.

86–87 **straunger of connynge** stranger to skill

87 **come after his doctryne** following his teaching

88 **shedynge** gleanings ∫ **if me fayle ought** if anything is lacking to me ∫ **my ful** my fill, my full [portion]

89 **by privytyes** stealthily

89–90 **A slye servaunt . . . commended** See Matt. 25:14–30.

90 **in his owne helpe** for helping himself

91 **hardyer** bolder ∫ **sechers** seekers

92 **lyghter** easier ∫ **han** have ∫ **passyng** surpassing ∫ **fresshed** refreshed

93 **in consideracion** with regard to

94 **sharpnesse** acuity ∫ **Utterly** manifestly ∫ **dremes** fancies (*MED: drem* [*n.*] 1) *or* mirth (*MED: drem* [*n.*] 2). Usk continues to develop the metaphor (active from lines 76–95) of literary activity as harvest and food: "dremes" and "japes" are trifles of knowledge and skill, rather than the food, or pearls, of truth produced by philosophical writers (with whom Usk now links himself), and are appropriately thrown to hogs (see Matt. 7:6, "do not throw your pearls before swine," quoted, for example, in *Piers Plowman* B X.9–10).

95 **lyfelyche meate** life-giving food

95–96 **me betiden** happened to me. Skeat argues that there is a lacuna at this point in the text (the product, for example, of a missing page in Thynne's exemplar), although it is possible to make sense of it as it stands, by taking "betiden" in its sense of "become of/on" (*OED: betide* 2) together with the oblique first-person pronoun *me*: "as they became for me" (that is, became life-giving food).

96 **out of my kyth** out of my native region: with perhaps a double sense of "kyth" as "knowledge" as well as "native place"

97 **Borias** Boreas, the north wind ∫ **kynde asketh** nature requires

98 **dryenge coldes** dry and cold winds ∫ **wawes** waves ∫ **occian-see** ocean (as opposed to harbor or coastal seas). The sailing of a ship is a frequent metaphor for launching a narrative, whether in poetry or prose, and is sometimes also used for exegetical and philosophical works (see Curtius 1990, 128–30, for examples). For Middle English examples, see especially *Troilus and Criseyde* II.1–4 (perhaps imitating Dante; see, e.g., *Paradiso* 2.1–18) and the conclusion of the poem *Knyghthode and Bataile* (excerpt 2.12). ∫ **unkyndely** unnaturally. Boreas's natural activity ("his kynde" [97]) has an unnatural effect on the ocean, much as Usk is pushed into philosophical reflection and a pilgrimage to truth by the extreme situation in which he finds himself (accused of treachery, that is, of breach of "troth").

99 **in poynte** at the point ∫ **spyl** destroy

1.5 JOHN WALTON, TRANSLATION OF BOETHIUS, *CONSOLATION OF PHILOSOPHY: PREFACIO TRANSLATORIS*

Date and Provenance: before 1410; southwest Midlands (Berkeley, Gloucestershire).

Author, Sources, and Nature of Text: John Walton was an Augustinian canon of Oseney,

near Oxford, whose translation of Boethius is the only work we can confidently ascribe to him. The translation is largely indebted to Chaucer's prose *Boece*, but Walton also referred to the original Latin and to a standard commentary on the work by Nicholas Trevet (1258?–1328). Walton presents himself as a humble translator of limited abilities who might never have attempted the task had not his patron (probably Elizabeth Berkeley) "do[ne] [him] violence" (4) by ordering him to write. Obedient to her command (despite the "hard and curyous" nature of Boethius's thought [11]), Walton insists on his faithfulness to the *sentence* of his source and on his obedience to God, to whom he prays as "lok and keye" of the wisdom that is the work's goal (16). By rendering Boethius poetically (in the rhyme-royal stanza made fashionable by Chaucer), he aims to surpass Chaucer and Gower, if not in the eloquence he says he lacks (57–64), then in the purity of his morality and shunning of "pagan" classicism derived from "olde poesyes derke" (42; compare Gavin Douglas, excerpt 3.16). Like other fifteenth-century writers catering to wellborn readers (including Lydgate and Metham; see excerpts 1.7 and 1.8), Walton turns the demands of his female patron into an opportunity to act as a moral purifier of the Chaucerian tradition, presented by his prologue as an active threat to those who have "receyved Cristes marke" (47) in baptism.

Audience and Circulation: According to an acrostic that appears only in an edition by Thomas Rychard, a monk of Tavistock Abbey (1525), but that has been widely credited, the work was made for Elizabeth Berkeley, daughter of Thomas, Lord Berkeley (see excerpt 2.2). There was a long tradition of translation of devotional texts and biblical commentary for and indeed by women (see, e.g., Eleanor Hull, excerpt 3.21), but the Middle English translation of philosophical works for women was not so common. It is unsurprising that none of the extant manuscripts acknowledges the hand even a highborn woman like Elizabeth Berkeley seems to have had in commissioning the work, or indeed that Walton's prologue should fail to indicate his patron's gender. Surviving in twenty-two manuscripts, with excerpts in several others, Walton's translation must have had wide circulation, considerably outstripping Chaucer's prose *Boece* in popularity.

Bibliography: The only edition is that of Mark Science (1927), who describes nineteen manuscripts (a further three are listed by Robert Raymo [1986, 2578–80]). On authorship, see Johnson 1994b and 1996. For general context, see Pearsall 1977, 224, 238–39. On Walton's self-presentation and relation to Chaucer, see Minnis 1981; Johnson 1987, 1994b; Copeland 1987; 1991, 145–49. The work has not been studied as a woman's text, but on the translation of works for and by women, see Keiser 1985; Hutchinson 1989; Tarvers 1992; Barratt 1992, 2–4. For discussion of medieval Christian treatments of pagan antiquity, see Minnis 1982a and Seznec 1953.

Source: Oxford, Balliol College MS 316 A, fols. 2r–3r, a fine fifteenth-century parchment book, written in a single column, whose colophon (fol. 109v), the fullest extant, ascribes the work to "John Walton, canon of Oseney," and dates it to 1410. The opening of the prologue and of each book has an illuminated initial and decorative frame. The manuscript was given to Balliol College by Anne Gifford in 1656; it contains only this text and (on the last leaf, fol. 110) two short devotional poems.

This excerpt was contributed by Ian R. Johnson.

Insuffishaunce of connyng and wytte,	**Insuffishaunce** lack; **connyng** ability
Defaute of langage and of eloquence	
This werke fro me schulde have be holde yytte	**holde** [with]held; **yytte** still
But that youre heste hath do me violence	**But** except; **heste** command
5 That nedis moste Y do my diligence	**nedis** of necessity; **do my diligence** make an effort
In thyng that passeth myne abilite,	
Besechyng to youre noble excellence	
That be youre help hit may amendyd be.	**be** by

This subtyle matyre of Boicius
10 Here in this *Book of Consolacyion*
So hye hit is, so hard and curyous,   **hye** abstruse
Ful fer aboven myne estimacion.   **fer** far; **estimacion** power of judgment
That hit be noght be my translacion   **be**[1] may be
Defouled ne corrupt, to God Y praye   **Defouled** defiled
15 So helpe me with hys inspiracion
That is of wysdom bothe lok and keye,

As fro the texte thast Y ne varye noght
But kepe the sentence in his trewe entent,   **sentence** [moral] meaning; **his** its
And wordes eke as nyhe as may be brought   **eke** also; **nyhe** near
20 Where lawe of metre is not resistent;   **lawe of metre** metrical rules
This matire whiche that is so excellent
And passeth both my cunnyng and my myght   **cunnyng** skill; **myght** power
So save hit Lorde in thi governement   **save** preserve; **governement** governance
That coust reforme alle thyng unto right!   **That** who; **coust** knows how to

25 I have herde speke and sumwhat have Y seyne   **seyne** seen
Of dyverse men that wonder subtilye,
In metre some and some in prose pleyne,   **metre** verse; **pleyne** full
This boke translated have sufficiently
Into Englysshe tonge, worde for worde, wel nyghe;   **wel nyghe** almost
30 Bot Y mote use the wyttes that Y have;
Thaugh Y may not do so, yete noght-for-thy   **noght-for-thy** nevertheless
Wyth helpe of God the sentence schal Y save.   **save** preserve

To Chaucere, that was floure of rethorike   **floure** flower
In Englysshe tonge and excellent poete,
35 This wot Y welle no thinge may Y do lyke,   **wot** know
Thaugh so that Y of makynge entremete,   although I meddle with versifying
And Gowere, that so craftely dothe trete   **craftely** skillfully
And in hys book of moralite: **moralite** moral matters
Thaugh I to theime in makyng am unmete,   **makyng** composing poetry; **unmete** unequal
40 Yut moste I shewe hit forth that is in me.

Noght lyketh me to laboure ne to muse   **Noght lyketh me** it does not please me
Upon these olde poesyes derke,   **olde poesyes** ancient writings; **derke** obscure
For Cristes feythe suche thynge shulde refuse;
Wytnesse upon Jerom the holy clerke.
45 Hit shuld not bene a Cristen mannes werke
Tho fals goddes names to renewe,   **fals** [pagan]; **renewe** bring to mind
For he that hath receyved Cristes marke,   **Cristes marke** the mark of baptism
Yif he do so to Criste he is untrewe.

Of tho that Criste in hevene blisse shall   **Of** among; **tho** those; **blisse** give bliss [to]
50 Suche manere werkes shuld be sette on syde;
For certanly it nedyth not at all   **it nedyth not** it is not necessary
To whette now the dartes of Cupide,   **whette** whet
Ne for to bidde Venus ben oure gyde   **gyde** guide

So that we may oure foule lustes wynne,	**wynne** gain
55 On aventure leste the same on us betyde	**On aventure** in case; **betyde** happen to
As dude on the same Venus for hire synne.	**As dude on** as happened to
And certeyns Y have tasted wonder lite	**wonder** wondrously; **lite** little
As of the welles of Calliope;	
No wondere thauh Y symply endite.	**endite** versify
60 Yut wil Y not unto Tessiphone	**Yut** yet
Ne to Aletto ne to Megare	
Besechen after crafte of eloquence,	**after** for
But pray that God of his benignite	**benignite** kindness
My spyrite enspire wit his influence;	
65 So that in shenshipe and confusion	**shenshipe** shame
Of al this foule worldely wrecchydnesse,	
He helpe me in this occupacion.	
In honoure of that sovereyn blisfulnesse	
And eke in reverence of youre worthynesse	
70 This simple werke as for an observaunce	**observaunce** act of homage
I schal begynne after my symplenesse	
In wille to do youre service and plesaunce.	**In wille** in the desire; **plesaunce** pleasure

Explicit prefacio translatoris.

Here ends the translator's preface

2 **Defaute of langage** want of words

3 **This werke fro me schulde have be holde yytte** might still have stopped me writing this work

4 **hath do me violence** a striking variation on a topos common in Latin dedicatory prologues, where writers describe themselves as coerced (*coactus*) by those who ask them to write (Curtius 1990, 85). If Elizabeth Berkeley is the addressee, there may be a hint that Walton considers his subordination to a female patron and her demand for philosophy to be acts of "violence" against the natural order. Contrast Trevisa's deference to her father in the *Dialogue*, excerpt 2.2.

9 **Boicius** Boethius (d. 524): late classical philosopher whose writings were a major conduit through which Greek and Roman thinking entered medieval culture

10 *Book of Consolacyion* the *Consolation of Philosophy*: written in 524 while Boethius was awaiting execution. For the many medieval translations, see Minnis 1987.

27 **In metre some ... prose pleyne** some in verse and some in full prose. Since the *Consolation of Philosophy* is written in alternating verses and prose passages, there is a possible ambiguity here, but the reference is probably to different translations rather than to the *prosimetrum* form of the *Consolation*. ʃ **prose pleyne** full and elucidatory

prose translation that expands and unpacks the syntax of the original. See Cropp 1987, 72–75.

37 **Gowere** John Gower (c. 1330–1408, see excerpt 2.11): also mentioned by Ashby (excerpt 1.9: 28–34)

40 **Yut moste I shewe hit forth that is in me** a variation on the topos that knowledge needs to be shared (Curtius 1990, 87). Compare *Northern Homily Cycle* (excerpt 2.1: 21–22, 40–44).

42 **these olde poesyes** that is, not Boethius's *Consolation* (which begins with a scene in which Lady Philosophy chases away the Muses of poetry), but the Roman poets (perhaps especially Ovid) from whom Chaucer and others derived their references to "pagan" gods and goddesses

44 **Jerom** Saint Jerome (c. 342–420): translator of the Vulgate Latin version of the Bible

46 **renewe** To name a god is potentially to invoke one. Compare excerpt 3.16: 55–61.

56 **As dude ... Venus** Venus, the Roman goddess of love, was trapped *in flagrante* with her lover Mars by her husband, Vulcan. See Ovid, *Metamorphoses* 4:171–89.

58 **Calliope** Muse of epic poetry and mother of Orpheus. See excerpt 1.7: 46–47.

60–61 **Tessiphone ... Aletto ... Megare** Thesiphone, Alecto, Megaera: the three Furies, called on by Chaucer's narrator in *Troilus and*

Criseyde IV.24, but interpreted as representing lust, cupidity, and anger in Trevet's commentary on the *Consolation* III.m.12. See headnote.

69 **youre worthynesse** that is, Elizabeth Berkeley: the probable dedicatee of the prologue and patron of Walton's translation. See Science 1927, xliii–xlvi.

1.6 THOMAS HOCCLEVE, *COMPLAINT:* PROLOGUE AND EXTRACT

Date and Provenance: 1421–22; London (but see Burrow [1994], who argues for 1419 as the year Hoccleve began work on the poem).

Author, Sources, and Nature of Text: Thomas Hoccleve (1368/9–c. 1426), one of the best known of the poets who set out to assume Chaucer's mantle in the fifteenth century, was also the one most closely associated with him. A clerk at the office of the Privy Seal at Westminster from 1387, he claims to have been Chaucer's pupil and acquaintance, and was part of the circle of London writers that included Usk (excerpt 1.4), Langland (excerpt 3.19), Gower (excerpt 2.11), and Henry Scogan, all of whom he could have met and whose works he knew. After an early period in which he may have written religious lyrics, his first dated work is *The Letter of Cupid* (1402), based on Christine de Pizan's *L'épistre au dieu d'amours* (1399). Over the next decade, this was followed by several poems (including the satirical autobiography *La Male Regle de T. Hoccleve* [1406]), culminating in his longest work, *The Regement of Princes,* addressed (like *Troy Book,* excerpt 1.7) to the future king Henry V. The success of this work helped make Hoccleve an official poet, commissioned to write for occasions such as Henry V's accession (1413), the translation of Richard II's bones to Westminster (1413), and the trial of the Lollard knight Sir John Oldcastle (1415). In 1416, he suffered a mental collapse from which he took five years to recover, during which the patronage network he had built up crumbled and the prolific Lydgate largely took over his public role (Burrow [1994] places Hoccleve's mental collapse earlier, in 1414). In the last period of his life, from 1421 to 1426, he returned to religious themes, intensifying the extroverted and harried persona of earlier poems into a melancholic figure who portrays himself as both anxious to regain the position he has lost and unsure if it is worth trying to do so. The *Complaint* (the first in a poetic medley now known as the *Series*) is the earliest work of this final period, in which Hoccleve poignantly describes his predicament as a man who is known to have been insane, avoided by former friends and patrons and unable to avoid the anxiety this causes him. Using a poetic language indebted to Chaucer's *Canterbury Tales* and *Troilus and Criseyde* but also to religious texts from *Piers Plowman* to Isidore of Seville's *Soliloquia* (Rigg 1970), and creating a poetic persona reminiscent of David in the Psalter or Job, Hoccleve remakes himself as poet, professional scribe, and human (born "of a womman" [34]) by setting out to prove his competence despite all. Asserting that the only way to know something is to experience it, he offers his readers a "taaste" of himself (44) through his poem, in an urgently personal gesture that shuns Chaucer's irony and associates Hoccleve with Usk, Langland, or his great female contemporaries Julian of Norwich and Margery Kempe (excerpts 1.4, 3.19, 1.13 and 3.4, 1.14 and 3.22).

Audience and Circulation: The *Series* as a whole was presented to Humphrey, duke of Gloucester (also patron of Lydgate's vast *Fall of Princes*), with at least one other presentation copy (made by Hoccleve himself and surviving as Durham, University Library MS Cosin V.III.9) being sent to Joan, countess of Westmoreland. However, while these aristocratic readers might have been expected to be moved by Hoccleve's plight and to see it in exemplary (perhaps Boethian) terms, Hoccleve must also have had an intimate audience of once and future friends in mind. The sequel to the *Complaint* is indeed a *Dialogue* *with a Friend,* about Hoccleve's career and prospects, which begins with a detailed conversation between the poet and a visiting friend about his poem and whether it is wise to publish it.

Bibliography: Edited by Furnivall (rpt. in Furnivall and Gollancz 1970, with revisions by Jerome Mitchell and A. I. Doyle; orig. pub. 1892) and by M. C. Seymour (1981), the *Complaint* has received a good deal of recent critical attention. Hoccleve's life is discussed by John Burrow (1994), who edits his life records. Still valuable is the book-length study by Jerome Mitchell (1968). Two essays on the *Regiment* discuss Hoccleve's authorial persona, Pearsall 1994 and Scanlon 1990. The

collection of essays edited by Catherine Batt (1996) has several articles touching on the *Complaint.* See also Burrow 1997.

Source: Oxford, Bodleian Library MS Arch. Selden supra 53, fols. 76–83v. This professionally copied parchment manuscript of fifteenth-century moral poetry contains Hoccleve's *Regiment of Princes* and *Dialogue* as well as short poems by Lydgate. It is carefully written, with occasional illuminated initials and blue capitals with red filigree. The Hoccleve texts in this manuscript are very close to those in Hoccleve's holograph, Durham, University Library MS Cosin V.III.9, which now lacks the quire that once contained the *Complaint* and the first part of the *Dialogue.*

Aftir that hervest inned had hise sheves,	**inned** gathered in
And that the broun sesoun of Mihelmesse	
Was come, and gan the trees robbe of her leves	**gan** began; **her** their
That grene had ben and in lusty freisshenesse,	**lusty** pleasant
5 And hem into colour of yelownesse	**hem** them
Had died, and doun thrown undir foote,	**died** dyed/caused to die
That chaunge sanke into myn herte roote.	
For freisshly broughtse it to my remembraunce	
That stablenesse in this worlde is ther noon.	**stablenesse** stability
10 Ther is no thing but chaunge and variaunce.	
Howe welthi a man be or wel begoon,	**howe** however; **wel begoon** prosperous
Endure it shal not, he shal it forgoon,	**forgoon** lose
Deeth undir foote shal him thriste adoun.	
That is every wightes conclucioun,	**wightes** person's; **conclucioun** end
15 Wiche for to weyve is in no mannes myght	**weyve** pass by
Howe riche he be, stronge, lusty, freissh and gay.	
And in the ende of Novembre, uppon a night,	
Sighynge sore as I in my bed lay	
For this and othir thoughtis wiche many a day	
20 Byforne I tooke, sleep cam noon in myn ye,	**tooke** took up
So vexid me the thoughtful maladie.	**thoughtful maladie** disease of depression
I sy wel sithin I with siknesse last	**sy** saw; **sithin** since
Was scourgid, cloudy hath bene the favour	**cloudy** dim
That shoon on me ful bright in times past.	
25 The sunne abated and the dirke shour	**dirke** dark
Hilded doun right on me and in langour	**Hilded** poured; **langour** listlessness
Me made swymme, so that my spirite	
To lyve no lust had, ne [had] no delite.	**lust** pleasure

The greef aboute myn herte so [sore] swal   *swal* swelled
30 And bolned evere to and to so sore,   *bolned* surged; **to and to** to and fro
That nedis oute I muste therwithal.   that I had to pour it out at once
I thoughte I nolde kepe it cloos no more,   *nolde* would not; **cloos** secret
Ne lete it in me for to eelde and hore.   nor leave it inside me to grow old and gray
And for to preve I cam of a womman,   *preve* prove
35 I braste oute on the morwe and thus bigan.   *braste* burst

Here endith my prolog and folwith my compleinte

[*Hoccleve describes his illness, when "the substaunce of my memorie / Wente to pleie as for a certein space" (stanza 8) five years earlier. Ever since that time, many of his friends and patrons have avoided him, arguing that "'Whanne passinge hete is [i.e., when it is very hot] [. . .] trustith this, / Assaile him wole agein that maladie'" (stanza 14), and he has been unable to shake their suspicions, despite obsessive attention to the way he looks and behaves in company. This has led to anxiety and depression: "O lorde, so my spirit was resteles! I soughte reste and I not it fonde, / But ay was trouble redy at myn honde" (stanza 28).*]

I may not lette a man to ymagine   *lette* prevent
For above the mone if that him liste.   *For* far; **mone** moon; **him liste** it pleases him
Therby the sothe he may [not] determine,   *Therby* by doing that; **sothe** truth
40 But by the preef ben thingis knowen and wiste.   *preef* proof; **wiste** understood
Many a doom is wrappid in the myste.   *doom* fate
Man bi hise dedis and not by hise lookes
Shal knowen be, as it is writen in bookes.

Bi taaste of fruit men may wel wite and knowe   *taaste* taste
45 What that it is. Othir preef is ther noon.   **What that it is** what [fruit] it is
Every man woote wel that, as that I trowe.   *woote* knows; **trowe** believe
Right so, thei that deemen my wit is goon,   *deemen* judge
As yit this day ther deemeth many oon   **yit this day** even to this day
I am not wel, may as I by hem goo   **by hem goo** walk past them
50 Taaste and assay if it be so or noo.   *assay* experience (*v.*)

Uppon a look is harde men hem to grounde   *grounde* establish
What a man is; therby the sothe is hid.
Whethir hise wittis seek bene or sounde   *seek* sick
By countynaunce is it not wist ne kid.   *countynaunce* external appearance; **kid** made known
55 Though a man harde have oones been bitid,   though a man have bad fortune once
God shilde it shulde on him contynue alway.   *shilde* forbid
By communynge is the beste assay.   *communynge* keeping company

I mene to commune of thingis mene,   *of* with; **mene** low
For I am but right lewide douteles   *lewide* uneducated
60 And ignoraunt. My kunnynge is ful lene.   *kunnynge* knowledge
Yit homely resoun knowe I neverethelees.   *homely* ordinary; **knowe** i.e., possess
Not hope I founden be so resounlees
As men deemen. Marie, Crist forbede!
I can no more. Preve may the dede.   **Preve may the dede** may my actions prove my case

1–7 **Aftir . . . roote** The first stanza, written in the rhyme-royal form made famous by *Troilus and Criseyde,* is possibly an autumnal variation on the spring opening of *The Canterbury Tales;* the passage personifies the "broun sesoun" (2) after "hervest" (1) as life's destroyer in the same way Chaucer personifies April as its renewer. Compare Usk's use of a similar seasonal setting (excerpt 1.4: 95–99).

2 **Mihelmesse** the feast of St. Michael and All Angels (September 29). The first three stanzas move gradually through the autumn to "the ende of Novembre" (17).

6 **died** The pun on "dye" and "cause to die" here is resolved through the word "yelownesse" (5), which refers literally to leaves but is also associated with melancholy and the pallor of death.

7 **That chaunge** that is, the change from life to death in the first six lines. "Chaunge" is the subject of the main clause here, while the poet is made the object of a process ("sanke into myn herte roote") over which he has no control.

13 **Deeth undir foote** A stanza of truisms reminiscent of Chaucer's *Fortune* is sharply focused around an image that (by way of the repetition of "undir foote" from line 6) retrospectively makes the "leves" (3) of the opening stanza into people trodden down by death. Compare *Troilus and Criseyde* IV.225–31, where Chaucer describes the collapse of Troilus's hopes, and the sources of Chaucer's image, Dante, *Inferno* 3.112–14, and Virgil, *Aeneid* 6.309–12.

20 **sleep cam noon in myn ye** that is, I could not sleep. The personification of sleep (like the "broun sesoun" [2]) intensifies Hoccleve's picture of himself as beset by outside forces, giving the topos of the sleepless poet (see *The Book of the Duchess* and *The Kingis Quair,* excerpt 3.23) new energy.

23 **favour** a word with complex referents in this stanza, alluding not only to divine favor but to literary patronage, professional preferment in Hoccleve's career as a scribe and civil servant, and to the affection of friends. It is characteristic of this poem to refuse to separate these levels.

28 **[had]** added above the line by the scribe

29 **[sore]** added above the line by the scribe

29–35 **The greef . . . bigan** Although this sounds reminiscent of descriptions of grief in *Troilus and Criseyde,* it is also a free paraphrase of Ps. 38:1–4, AV 39, a complaint about the brevity of life that describes how the speaker's vow to guard his mouth is overcome by renewed grief burning hot in his heart. Unlike the dreamer in *Pearl* ("Thagh kynde of Kryst me comfort kenned / My wreched wylle in wo ay wraghte" [55–56]) or Julian of Norwich ("mournynge and sorowe I made . . . with outyn

resone and dyscrecionn of fulle grete pryde" [Short Text, chap. 13]; see excerpt 1.13), Hoccleve makes no moral judgment on his inability to resign himself to his predicament.

32 **kepe it cloos** In the *Dialogue* that follows the *Complaint,* Hoccleve's friend ironically begs him to keep the poem that has "braste oute" of Hoccleve (35) "cloos for thyn honours sake" (stanza 5), because everyone has long forgotten his madness.

34 **to preve I cam of a womman** an ambiguous phrase that presumably means "to prove I am properly human," that is, sane, but that may also be linked (by way of the allusion to childbirth) to the line "That nedis oute I muste therwithal" (31), as well as to "braste oute" in the following line (35). Hoccleve's poem bursts out of him to prove that he is properly human, born of a woman. There could also be reference to the misogynistic commonplace that women are garrulous (realized most famously in *The Wife of Bath's Prologue*), and thus the implication could be that Hoccleve's complaining speech is in some fashion "womanly."

36 **compleinte** A formal and rhetorically elaborate expression of grief, the *complaint* (or *planctus*) was a common medieval poetic genre in all languages and in both secular and religious contexts. ∫ **my prolog . . . my compleinte** Hoccleve's unusual use of personal pronouns in this rubric identifies him with the poem whose project is his renewal as poet and human being. Contrast Bokenham's attempt to detach his own reputation from that of his poem (excerpt 1.11), but see also *Speculum Devotorum* (excerpt 1.12: 18–40).

37–38 **I may not lette . . . liste** That is, I cannot stop someone imagining any kind of absurdity if he wants to.

38 **mone** may allude to Hoccleve's putative status as a "lunatic." But the stargazer in these lines resembles Nicholas in Chaucer's *Miller's Tale,* who "sat evere capyng upright, / As he had kiked on the newe moone" (I [A] 3444–45).

39 **[not]** added above the line by the scribe ∫ **determine** discover or decide: one of several legal or debating terms in the passage (see also "preef" [40], "doom" [41], "deemen" [47]). Hoccleve invokes the authority of this terminology, but the kind of knowledge he wishes to convey is not in fact attainable by argument (see 44), and all these words are used in nonlegal senses: "preef" (40), for example, meaning "experience," not "proof"; "doom" (41) "fate," rather than "judgment."

42–43 **Man bi hise dedis . . . knowen be** an allusion to Matt. 7:16, "By their fruits you shall know them." The next lines (44–45) take up the image of "fruit," also alluding to Luke 6:44, "every tree is known by its fruit."

44–57 **Bi taaste . . . assay** a remarkable passage in which Hoccleve pits two discourses against one another to insist that close acquaintance with him will convince people of his sanity. One involves a tradition of reading character through the "science" of physiognomy (alluded to in 50–51), in which outward "tokens," or physical manifestations, are interpreted as signs of character traits; see, for example, *Secreta secretorum* (Manzalaoui 1977, 89–113), or the *Physiognomy* of John Metham (see excerpt 1.8). The other is the eucharistic language of taste and "communynge" (57), behind which lies an old distinction between head-knowledge (*scientia*) and heart-knowledge, or wisdom (*sapientia*), which must be based on experience ("preef" [45]). Thus the poem offers the reader a "taaste" (44, rather than merely a "look" [51]) of Hoccleve (compare accounts of reading as eating in

excerpts 3.19 and 3.20), one akin to the close reading of the body of Christ attainable in Passion meditation (see excerpt 1.13). On reading as tasting, see *The Orchard of Syon* (excerpt 3.5: 42–44).

50 **Taaste and assay** perhaps alludes to Ps. 33:9, AV 34:8: "taste and see how sweet is the Lord," although Hoccleve substitutes "assay" for "see." Compare excerpt 3.5: 22–23.

58 **I mene to commune of thingis mene** I am talking about communing with lowly things. This line retreats from the more elevated implications of the devotional language Hoccleve has used to urge familiarity with himself through "taaste" (50). The humility topoi here, omnipresent in fifteenth-century writing (compare excerpts 1.3, 1.9, 1.11, 1.12, 2.10, 2.11, 3.5, etc.), also make explicit his conception of the *Complaint* itself as offering "communynge" (57).

1.7 JOHN LYDGATE, *TROY BOOK:* PROLOGUE (EXTRACT)

Date and Provenance: 1412–20 (according to the work itself); East Anglia (Bury St. Edmunds).

Author, Sources, and Nature of Text: John Lydgate (c. 1370–1449?), monk of the wealthy Benedictine abbey of Bury St. Edmunds, was one of the most prolific and influential of fifteenth-century English writers; some 145,000 lines of verse are attributed to him. He came to Bury as a boy and was ordained as a priest in 1397, attending Gloucester College, Oxford (at least from 1406–8), and developing close connections with the royal court. Besides *Troy Book,* written for the future Henry V, he received commissions from Henry VI, the dowager queen Katherine, wife of Henry V, and Humphrey, duke of Gloucester, among others. After the success of *Troy Book* and the *Siege of Thebes,* Lydgate became in effect a poet laureate (Pearsall 1970, 160), and later writers refer to him as part of a triumvirate of founding poetic fathers with Gower and Chaucer (see, e.g., Ashby's *Active Policy,* excerpt 1.9: 28). Lydgate's main source for the *Troy Book* was Guido delle Colonne's *Historia destructionis Troiae* (1287), a Latin prose translation of Benoît de Sainte-Maure's French *Roman de Troie* (c. 1160). The

Historia represents itself as based on accounts by Dares and Dictys, two soldiers who fought at Troy (see 186n) and claims to be the truest relation of the Troy story, superior to Homer, Virgil, Ovid, and others. The work was popular well into the early modern period. Lydgate's translation amplifies Guido's voluminous work but also restructures its twenty-four books into five (probably on the model of Chaucer's *Troilus and Criseyde,* a poem with which *Troy Book* has an interestingly conflicted relationship; Watson 1994). The prologue begins with an invocation to Mars and others (1–68) and an account of the future Henry V commissioning the poem (in 1412) so that the "noble story" can be read in English "as in Latyn and in Frensche" (91–94). This passage claims royal authorization and an important political function for *Troy Book,* as Henry prepares his renewal of the Hundred Years' War with France, and summons the resources of a new vernacular literary tradition to Lydgate's aid in "refresch[ing] newe" (118) Europe's most important foundation narrative. In tune with this serious purpose, much of the prologue consists of a defense of history (99–131), an attack on poets whose fictional versions of the Troy story hide their "galle" under corrupt "sugred wordes" (150–51), and a demonstration of the superiority of Lydgate's source to other named histories (140ff.). The topos that poets are liars, while historians tell truth, is common (compare excerpt 3.15), but Lydgate may use it to mark the same important divide Walton tries to establish (see excerpt 1.5) between his ethical histories and Chaucer's fictions.

Audience and Circulation: Alain Renoir (1967) lists twenty-three manuscripts (more than survive for Chaucer's *Troilus and Criseyde*). Most of these are deluxe manuscripts intended for wealthy and politically powerful patrons; Lydgate, however, asserts that prince Henry intended the work for "hyghe and lowe" (90). Pynson printed the *Troy Book* in 1513, Marshe in 1555.

Bibliography: The text is edited by Henry Bergen (1906–35); Guido's *Historia* is edited by Nathanial Griffin (1970) and translated by Mary Elizabeth Meek (1974). Studies of Lydgate's works include Schirmer 1961; Renoir 1967; Pearsall 1970; Ebin 1985. On

dating, see Parr 1952. On Lydgate's life, see Pearsall 1997. Studies of Lydgate's relation to the Chaucerian tradition include Lawton 1987; Lerer 1993; and, with particular reference to *Troy Book,* Benson 1980; Torti 1989; Watson 1994; Baswell 1997. The promotion of English by the Lancastrians is discussed by John Fisher (1992b), Pearsall (1994), and Alan Ambrisco and Paul Strohm (1995), Lydgate's part in the construction of a unified English identity by Lee Patterson (1993a). *Troy Book* and other Lydgate manuscripts are discussed by A.S.G. Edwards and Pearsall (1989). Christopher Baswell (1995) offers a major study of the Troy story in Britain.

Source: London, British Library MS Cotton Augustus A.IV, fols. 1r–[2]r. This luxury folio manuscript, which contains only *Troy Book,* has a presentation miniature showing the author offering his book to Henry V (fol. 1r) and includes the arms of Sir Thomas Chatworth (d. 1458) and his second wife, Isabella de Ailesbury (Bergen 1935, 2–3).

O myghty Mars, that wyth thy sterne lyght	
In armys hast the power and the myght	
And named art from est til occident	**named** called; **art** are
The myghty lorde, the god armypotent,	**armypotent** all powerful in arms
5 That, wyth schynyng of thy stremes rede,	
By influence dost the brydel lede	**brydel** bridle
Of chevalry, as sovereyn and patrown,	
Ful hoot and drye of complexioun,	
Irows and wood and malencolyk	**Irows** wrathful; **wood** furious
10 And of nature brent and coleryk,	**brent** burnt; **coleryk** choleric
Of colour schewyng lyche the fyre glede,	**fyre glede** fire's ember
Whos feerce lokes ben as ful of drede	**drede** dread
As the levene that alyghteth lowe	**levene** lightning flash
Down by the skye from Jubiteris bowe:	
15 Thy stremes ben so passyng despitous,	**stremes** beams; **passyng** exceptionally; **despitous** pitiless
To loke upon, inly furious,	**inly** very
And causer art wyth thy fery bemys	**art** [you] are; **fery** fiery
Of werre and stryf in many sondry rewmys;	**rewmys** realms
Whos lordschype is most in Caprycorn,	**Caprycorn** Capricorn
20 But in the Bole is thy power lorn;	**lorn** lost
And causer art of contek and of strif;	**contek** conflict
Now for the love of Wlcanus wyf,	**Wlcanus wyf** Vulcan's wife (i.e., Venus)
Wyth whom whylom thou wer at meschef take,	**whylom** formerly; **take** caught
So helpe me now, only for hyr sake;	

25 And for the love of thy Bellona,
   That wyth the dwellyth byyownd Cirrea   That who; the you; **Cirrea** Syria
   In Lebye-londe upon the sondes rede,   **Lebye-londe** Libya
   So be myn helpe in this grete nede
   To do socour my stile to directe,   **do socour** help
30 And of my penne the tracys to correcte,
   Whyche bareyn is of aureat lycour,   **aureat** golden; **lycour** liquid
   But in thi grace I fynde som favour   **But** unless
   For to conveye it wyth thyn influence,   **conveye** accompany
   That stumbleth ay for faute of eloquence   That which; **faute** want
35 For to reherse or writen any word.   **reherse** utter
   Now help, o Mars, that art of knyghthod lord,
   And hast of manhod the magnificence!
   And Othea, goddesse of prudence,
   This wirke t'exsplyte that ye nat refuse,   **t'exsplyte** speed
40 But maketh Clyo for to ben my muse,
   Wyth hir sustren that on Pernasa dwelle   **Pernasa** Parnassus
   In Cirrea by Elicon the welle,   **Elicon** Helicon
   Rennyng ful clere wyth st[r]emys cristallyn,
   And callyd is the welle Caballyn   **welle** spring
45 That sprang by touche of the Pegasee.
   And helpe also, O thou Calliope,
   That were moder unto Orpheus,
   Whos dites wern so mellodyus   **dites** songs; **wern** were
   That the werbles of his resownyng harpe   **werbles** melodies
50 Appese dyde the bitter Wyrdys scharpe   **Wyrdys** Fates
   Bothe of Parchas and Furies infernal,
   And Cerberus so cruel founde at al;   **so cruel founde at al** always so fierce
   He coyede also best[e], foule, and tree;   **coyede** stilled; **foule** bird
   Now of thy grace be helpyng unto me,
55 And of thy golde dewe lat the lycour wete
   My dulled brest, that wyth thyn hony swete   that [you] who
   Sugrest tongis of rethoricyens,   **Sugrest** sugar
   And maistresse art to musicyens:
   Now be myn help t'enlumyne with this wirk,   **t'enlumyne** to illuminate
60 Whyche am beset with cloudis dym and dirk   **Whyche** [I] who; **dirk** dark
   Of ygnoraunce, in makyng to procede,   **makyng** composing poetry
   To be lusty to hem that schal it rede.   **lusty** pleasing; **hem** them
   Also in hert I am so ful of drede,
   Whan prudent lysters herto schal take hede,   **lysters** listeners
65 That in makyng more skylle can than I,   **can** know
   To whom I preie, ful benignely
   Of her goodnesse to have compassioun   **her** their
   Wher as I erre in my translacioun: **Wher as** whenever
   For God I take hyghly to wyttenesse
70 That I this wirk of hertly lowe humblesse   **hertly** heartfelt
   Toke upon me of entencioun
   Devoyde of pride and presumpcioun,

For to obeie withoute variaunce   **variaunce** divergence
My lordes byddyng fully and plesaunce,   **byddyng** command; **plesaunce** pleasure
75 Whiche hath desire, sothly for to seyn,
Of verray knyghthod to remembre ageyn   **verray** true
The worthynes, yif I schal nat lye,
And the prowesse of olde chivalrie,
Bycause he hath joye and gret deynte   **deynte** delight
80 To rede in bokys of antiquite,
To fynde only vertu for to swe   **swe** follow
Be example of hem, and also for to eschewe   **eschewe** avoid
The cursyd vice of slouthe and ydelnesse.

*[Henry, Prince of Wales, the future King Henry V, is praised. He is as vigorous in
practicing martial arts as his father from whom he will inherit the succession of
"Albion" (Britain), founded by Brutus after the sack of Troy.]*

[. . .] Whyche me comaunded the drery pitus fate
85 Of hem of Troye in Englysche to translate,   **hem of Troye** the Trojans
The sege also and the destruccioun,
Lyche as the Latyn maketh mencioun,   **Lyche as** just as
For to compyle, and after Guydo make,   **compyle** translate; **make** compose
So as I coude, and write it for his sake,
90 Bycause he wolde that to hyghe and lowe
The noble story openly wer knowe
In oure tonge, aboute in every age,
And ywriten as wel in oure langage
As in Latyn and in Frensche it is;
95 That of the story the trouth we nat mys:
This was the fyn of his entencioun.   **fyn** purpose
The whyche emprise anoon I gynne schal   **emprise** undertaking; **gynne** begin
In his worship for a memorial.   **memorial** remembrance

*[There follow regnal and astrological details that date the beginning of the work to
October 1412.]*

[. . .] Whyche tyme I gan the prolog to beholde
100 Of Troye Boke, imade be dayes olde,   **imade** composed; **be** in
Wher was remembrid, of au[c]tors us beforn,   **au[c]tors** authors
Of the dede of the verreie trewe corn,   **dede** deed (see n.); **corn** grain
So as it fil severid from the chaf;
For in her honde they hilde for a staf   **her** their [the authors']
105 The trouthe only, whyche thei han compyled
Unto this fyn, that we wer nat begyled   **fyn** purpose
Of necligence thorugh forgetilnesse;   **Of** by; **forgetilnesse** forgetfulness
The whiche serpent of age by processe   **by processe** in the course of time
Engendred is fersly us t'assaile,
110 Of the trouth to make us for to faille.   **faille** lack
For ner writers, al wer out of mynde,   **ner** if there were not; **wer** would be

Nat story only, but of nature and kynde   **story** history

The trewe knowyng schulde have gone to wrak,   **wrak** destruction

And from science our wittes put abak,   **science** knowledge

115 Ne hadde oure elderis cerched out and sought **elderis** predecessors; **cerched** searched

The sothefast pyth, to ympe it in oure thought, **sothefast** true; **pyth** pith; **ympe** graft

Of thinges passed, fordirked of her hewe,   **fordirked** darkened

But thorugh writyng thei be refresched newe,

Of oure auncetrys left to us byhynde;

120 To make a merour only to oure mynde,

To seen eche thing trewly as it was,

More bryght and clere than in any glas.

For ner her writyng nowe memorial,   **ner** were not; **memorial** a record

Dethe with his swerde schulde have slayn al,

125 And ydymmed with his sodeyn schoures   **sodeyn** sudden; **schoures** attacks

The gret prowes of thise conquerouris,

And dirk[ed] eke the brightnesse of her fame,   **dirk[ed]** darkened

That schyneth yet by report of her name;

For unto us her bokes represent

130 Without feynynge the weie that thei went   **feynynge** fictionalizing

In her daies, whan thei wer alyve.

[Lydgate stresses the moral function of poets and their role in preserving the reputation of great men. Everyone should live virtuously, since after death poets will not fear to write truth. Writers lock up deeds in their books with "the keye of remembraunce" (see Chaucer, Legend of Good Women *F 26), just as Statius did for the siege of Thebes, and others have for the siege of Troy.]*

[. . .]Albe that somme han the trouth spared   **Albe** albeit; **spared** avoided

In her writyng, and pleynly not declared   **pleynly** fully

So as it was, nor tolde out feithfully,

135 But it transformed in her poysy   **poysy** poetry

Thorugh veyn fables, whiche of entencioun   **of entencioun** deliberately

They han contreved by false transumpcioun

To hyde trouthe falsely under cloude,

And the sothe of malys for to schroude: **sothe** truth; **of** out of

140 As Omer dide, the whiche in his writyng

Ifeyned hathe ful many divers thyng   **Ifeyned** fictionalized

That never was, as Guydo lyst devise,   **lyst** [it] pleases

And thingys done in another wyse

He hathe transformed than the trouthe was,

145 And feyned falsly that goddis in this caas   **feyned** told fictions

The worthi Grekis holpen to werreye   **werreye** battle

Ageyn Troyens, and how that thei wer sey[n]e

Lyche lyfly men amonge hem day by day.   **lyfly** living

And in his dites, that were so fresche and gay   **dites** poems

150 With sugred wordes under hony soote,   **soote** sweet

His galle is hidde lowe by the rote,   **galle** poison; **rote** root

That it may nought outewarde ben espied.   **That** so that

And al for he with Grekis was allied,   for because
Therfor he was to hem favourable
155 In myche thing, whiche is nought commendable
Of hem that lyst to demen after ryght;   Of by; lyst pleases; demen to judge

[Ovid, Virgil, Lollius, Dares Phrygius, Dictys Cretensis, and Cornelius, nephew of Sallust, are reviewed as historians of Troy. Ovid mingles truth and falsehood, Virgil sometimes follows the unreliable Homer, Lollius also writes of the siege, but most important are Dares and Dictys, who were eye witnesses. Their texts were brought from Troy and Greece to Athens, where Cornelius translated them, but in the attempt to be brief omitted too much. The omissions are now listed.]

[. . .] The firste mevyng and cause original,   firste mevyng beginning
What was the gynnyng and rote in special,   gynnyng beginning
Ne how thei come by lond or by navie,
160 How firste the sparke was kyndeled of envie
Atwyxe Grekis and hem of Troye town,   Atwyxe between
Of whiche Cornelye maketh no mencioun:
Of her schippes nor of her vitaille,   vitaille food
Nor how that Grece is called Gret Ytaille,   Gret Ytaille Greater Italy
165 And the Lasse, as bokys verrefye,   Lasse Lesser
Is named now the londe of Romanye;   Romanye Italy
What noumbre of kynges and of dukes went
Towarde the sege, al of oon assent,   oon assent one opinion
To wynne worschip and for excersise
170 Of armys only, in ful knyghtly wyse,
Abydyng there to sen the versioun   versioun fall
Of the cite and noble Yllyoun;   Yllyoun Ilium [Troy]
Nor what the maner was of her armure,   armure equipment
Nor at the sege who dide lengest endure;
175 In what wyse eche other did assaile,
Nor how often thei metten in bataille;
How mony worthi loste ther his lyf   worthi worthy [man]
Thorough olde hatrede wrought up with newe strif
Nor of her dethe he dateth nat the yere,
180 For his writyng was particuler;   particuler partial
Withoute frute he was compendious,   frute fruit; compendious concise
This forseyde Romeyne, this Cornelius.
Wherefore but late in comparisoun,
Ther was an auctour of ful highe renoun
185 That besied hym the tracys for to swe   besied hym busied him[self]
Of Dite and Dares and cast hym nat transmwe   cast hym set himself; transmwe transform
In al the story a worde as in sentence,   as in with regard to; sentence meaning
But folweth hem by swyche convenience,   convenience accord
That in effecte the substaunce is the same;
190 And of Columpna Guydo was his name,   Columpna Colonne
Whiche had in writyng passyng excellence.   passyng surpassing
For he enlumyneth by crafte and cadence   crafte skill; cadence meter

This noble story with many fresche colour
Of rethorik; and many riche flour
195 Of eloquence, to make it sownde bet,
He in the story hathe ymped in and set,   **ymped** grafted
That in good feythe I trowe he hath no pere,   **pere** peer
To rekne alle that write of this matere,   **rekne** consider
As in his boke ye may byholde and se.
200 To whom I seie, knelyng on my knee:
Laude and honour and excellence of fame,
O Guydo maister, be unto thi name,
That excelle[s]t by sovereinte of stile
Alle that writen this mater to compile;
205 Whom I schal folwe as nyghe as ever I may,
That God me graunt it be unto the pay   **unto** to; **pay** pleasure
Of hym for whom I have undertake
So as I can this story for to make: **make** compose
Preynge to alle that schal it rede or se,
210 Wher as I erre for to amenden me,
Of humble herte and lowe entencioun
Commyttyng al to her correccioun;
And therof thanke my wille is that thei wynne,   **wynne** gain
For thorugh her support thus I wil begynne.   **support** indulgence

1–24 O myghty Mars . . . sake For the main verb of this long sentence, see "So helpe me now" (24). The delaying of a main clause is characteristic of epic style (compare the first stanza of *Troilus and Criseyde*, imitated at the opening of *Amoryus and Cleopes*, excerpt 1.8).

4 armypotent See Chaucer's use of this word to describe Mars in *The Knight's Tale* (I [A] 1982).

5 stremes rede red beams [of light]. Mars is both the god of war and the planet: red rays of light from Mars constitute his planetary influence.

9–10 malencolyk . . . brent In medieval physiological theory, body heat can dry up the blood and vital spirits, producing black bile and melancholia (9): "brennyng bredith blacnes" (see *MED: brent* 7[d]). All the qualities listed here are associated with Mars. Like the accounts of Mars in Chaucer's *Knight's Tale* (I [A] 1982–2050), Lydgate's account is both forceful and intensely ambivalent about the powers evoked: *Troy Book* begins by invoking the god of war but ends with an appeal for peace.

11 fyre Bergen (1906–35) emends to *fyry*.

14 Jubiteris bowe Jupiter is god of thunder and, as here, of lightning, as well as leader of the gods.

19 Whos lordschype is most in Caprycorn Mars rules in Capricorn because in this sign of the zodiac his astrological influence is strongest.

20 Bole the Bull: that is, the sign of Taurus, in which the influence of Mars is weakest

23 at meschef take that is, caught in adulterous love. See excerpt 1.5: 56n.

25 Bellona the Roman goddess of war

38 Othea goddess of prudence and, in Christine de Pizan's *Epître d'Othéa* (c. 1400), author of a letter of instruction to the Greek hero Hector, whose failure to heed her instructions about prudent action leads to his death and the subsequent fall of Troy. Lydgate uses the *Epître* for his account of this episode at the climax of *Troy Book* (the end of book III), and the invocation to this obscure goddess at the outset suggests not only the work's careful organization but its *moralitas* (one fit for a prince): even in battle, Mars's anger must be balanced by Othea's prudence.

40–41 Clyo . . . on Pernasa Clio: Muse of history, supposed as dwelling with her sisters, the other Muses, on Mount Parnassus by the well of Helicon

42 Cirrea The second reference to this place (compare 26) is puzzling, since Mount Parnassus is in Greece.

44–45 Caballyn . . . Pegasee Pegasus: the winged horse trapped by Bellerophon with the help of Athena. The spring of "Caballyn" is supposed to flow from the indentation left by his hoof.

46 Calliope the same Muse of epic poetry Walton refuses to invoke as a pagan goddess (see excerpt 1.5: 58). The joint invocation of Calliope and Clio (see 40) is common in epic.

51 Parchas The Parcae, or Fates, are also alluded to in *Troilus and Criseyde* V.3.

52 Cerberus three-headed hound and guardian of the classical underworld

55–56 golde dewe . . . hony swete Rhetorical skill is seen as grace and eloquence here, but is later presented as worthless when sundered from truth, as in the denunciation of Homer (140–56 and note).

60–61 cloudis dym and dirk / Of ygnoraunce Compare Usk's "cloudy cloude of unconnynge" (excerpt 1.4: 74).

73–74 For to obeie withoute variaunce / My lordes byddyng that is, Henry, prince of Wales, the future Henry V. Lydgate's obedience is that of the loyal subject and also, perhaps, the Benedictine monk (who vowed obedience to monastic superiors), and has its counterpart in his claim to follow his source "as nyghe as ever I may" (205).

81–83 To fynde only vertu . . . ydelnesse gives two standard reasons for reading (and writing) historical works. For other instances of this defense, see, for example, Curtius 1990, 88–89.

84–96 Whyche me comaunded . . . entencioun See Fisher 1992b for the importance of these lines as evidence for a "Lancastrian language policy" on Henry V's part.

88 Guydo Guido [delle Colonne]. See headnote, under "Source."

92 aboute in every age that is, available for all time. Lydgate makes a claim to write for posterity through paraphrasing his patron's wishes.

98 memorial Although the ending of *Troy Book* represents itself as being written in 1421, this line may suggest that Henry V was already dead and that the passage was added after 1422, when his son, Henry VI, came to the throne.

99 Whyche tyme . . . beholde Lydgate begins his expansive paraphrase of Guido's prologue.

101 au[c]tors MS *auntours*

101–2 Wher . . . corn This seems to mean "in which (i.e., Guido's prologue) was called to mind, through earlier authors (Guido's sources), things concerning the true, authentic wheat (of the truth) about the noble deeds (of Troy) or (since *dede* [102] is ambiguous) about the dead."

104 staf the stick of truth with which the "au[c]tors us beforn" (101) beat the wheat of history and so divide the chaff and the grain

111 ner writers . . . out of mynde if there were not writers, all would be forgotten. See excerpt 1.2: 15–20; also Chaucer, *The Legend of Good Women* F.25–6. The following passage (111–31) initiates a response to the ironic treatment of worldly fame found in Chaucer's *House of Fame* (and culminating in Gavin Douglas's *Palice of Honour*) by

insisting that good reputation is not random but a reliable and just reward for good behavior.

112 Nat story only . . . kynde not only of history but of the natural world and nature

115–24 Ne hadde . . . slayn al a complex mixed metaphor (the Latin rhetorical term is *catachresis*) in which good historical and informational writing is seen as a "merour" (120), but also as the pith of a branch that earlier writers have helped to graft ("ympe" [116]) into the minds of moderns in order to renew the past and help the living. For the "mirror" analogy, see Torti 1989, 74–75, and compare, for example, *The Mirror of Our Lady* (excerpt 3.12). For other examples of the writer-as-gardener analogy, see Usk's similarly mixed metaphor (excerpt 1.4: 4–10) and *The Orchard of Syon,* excerpt 3.5.

123 ner . . . memorial did not their writing now serve as a record

135 poysy This deliberately condescending term for poetry (associating it with a "posy" of flowers) opens what will become a wholesale condemnation of Homer's poetry as poison hidden by sugary diction (135–56).

137 false transumpcioun false alteration: from Latin *transumptio,* an elaborate form of metaphor in which the metaphorical "vehicle" is itself referred to in figurative terms (also *metalepsis*). See Quintilian, *Institutes* VIII.6.37–38.

140 Omer Homer: known only indirectly to Lydgate through his sources

147 sey[n]e MS *seye*

156 Of hem . . . after ryght by them whom it pleases to judge according to what is right

157 firste mevyng and cause original first moving: in the Aristotelian cosmology the original motion that initiated all others and was the original cause of the world. The phrasing echoes a speech by Theseus in Chaucer, *Knight's Tale* (I [A] 2987), itself based on Boethius, *Consolation of Philosophy* II.m.8.

162, 182 Cornelye, Cornelius the poet Gaius Cornelius Gallus (69–26 B.C.), famous for his love poetry, which does not survive

181 Withoute frute he was compendious That is, he was uselessly concise, rather than draw things together with the profitable concision that characterizes a good compilation. Compare the *Cyrurgie's* praise of its own compendiousness, excerpt 1.10: 19–29.

186 Dite and Dares Guido delle Colonne and his actual source, Benoît de Sainte-Maure, both claim to base their account of the Trojan War on the eyewitness accounts of two Greeks, Dictys Cretensis and Dares Phrygius.

190 of Columpna Guydo See 88n above.

193–94 **colour / Of rethorik** ornament of speech

196 **ymped in** Compare the use of this metaphor at 116 (although here it is rhetorical "flowers," not historical truth, that are grafted).

203 **excelle[s]t** MS *excellent*

205 **Whom I schal folwe as nyghe as ever I may** Lydgate may seem disingenuous here, since he does much more than merely translate Guido. But his understanding of what it means to "folwe" an author such as Guido apparently includes imitating

Guido's practice of expanding his source by rhetorical elaboration and didactic digression, giving his own stamp to a poem that becomes, in effect, an independent composition. Compare Chaucer, *Legend of Good Women* F.73–7.

209 **rede or se** read or see. There is no clear distinction, but it is noteworthy that Lydgate does not use the older formula "hear or see," with its evocation of oral delivery as an alternative to reading.

213 **And therof . . . thei wynne** I hope they gain thanks for it (i.e., for correcting my errors).

1.8 JOHN METHAM, *AMORYUS AND CLEOPES:* PROLOGUE AND ENDING

Date and Provenance: 1448–49; East Anglia (Norfolk). Metham states that the poem was written in the twenty-seventh year of the reign of Henry VI (below, 115). He probably worked at or near Ingham, the seat of his patrons, Sir Miles (d. 1466) and Lady Stapleton.

Author, Sources, and Nature of Text: John Metham is the least well known of the trio of mid-fifteenth-century East Anglian poets who inherited Lydgate's mantle, a trio whose other members are Bokenham and Capgrave (see excerpts 1.11 and 2.7), both of whom, like Metham, studied at Cambridge. Besides *Amoryus and Cleopes,* Metham wrote four works in prose (including a treatise on palmistry and a *Physiognomy*), all of which share with his poetic romance an interest in occult themes with a supposedly Eastern origin. In the prologue to this work, Metham claims to have found the story in a Greek manuscript that he deciphered with the help of a Greek man riding through Norwich (29–42): an anecdote of exotic origins congruent with a poem whose narrative presents, only to Christianize, many kinds of "pagan" material with all the enthusiasm of *Mandeville's Travels.* The poem is a romance version of the tale of Pyramus and Thisbe whose sources are unknown (although it uses material associated with the Alexander legend and borrows both from Metham's own treatises and from *Troilus and Criseyde*). Where the tale of Pyramus and Thisbe ends in the lovers' death, Metham introduces a Christian hermit who discovers their corpses and prays for them to be returned to life. Romance

modulates into the Miracles of the Virgin when Mary resuscitates them to convert the capital city of Persia. Thus Metham, closer here to Walton and Lydgate than to Chaucer, displaces the worldly and "pagan" discourses of love after first evoking these in an entertainingly exotic setting.

The poem's envoi, "Go now, lytyl boke" (116), alludes to the end of *Troilus and Criseyde* (V.1786), but where Chaucer's book is commanded to kiss the steps of classical poets, Metham's is made subject to his patrons. The deeds of Sir Miles Stapleton are said to have been narrated elsewhere by Metham (in "the story that I endyght off kyng Cassyon" [77], a work now lost) and are compared to the achievements of Alexander the Great, the ancient histories of Josephus, and the biblical narrative of Joshua; Lady Stapleton is compared to the beautiful women of the classical past. For Metham's patrons, romance and biblical epic speak to the concerns of Henry VI's magnates in a reign where "prudent port off governans" (56) was much needed in this life and careful account taken of the next. Metham indeed presents the poem as a kind of verbal chantry chapel for Lady Stapleton in its closing stanzas (95–108).

Audience and Circulation: Most of Metham's surviving works are in a single manuscript that appears to be a presentation copy to his patrons Sir Miles and Lady Stapleton. Sir Miles was a distinguished figure in the Norfolk of his time, as well as a soldier; he is named by Johannes de Caritate as patron of his translation of the *Secreta secretorum,* called *The Privyte of Privyteis* (Manzalaoui 1977, 114). The Metham and Stapleton families were related (it is possible Metham was a poor relation trying to win favor). Lady Stapleton's relative the duke of Suffolk (murdered in 1450 on his way to exile) and Stapleton were frequently on the Commission for the Peace (Moore 1912–13, 27:196–202; Craig 1916, vii–xiii; Beadle 1991, 105–6).

Bibliography: Edited by Hardin Craig (1916), the work is discussed by Beadle (1991), Lee Ramsey (1983), and Stephen Page (1996), the first with special reference to the literary culture of East Anglia. Samuel Moore (1912–13) and Russell Rutter (1987, 446–49) discuss Metham's patrons and East Anglian patronage networks. On the importance of patronage, see Harris 1989. For the literary and political implications of "council," see Barnes 1993. On the reading of fifteenth-century gentry families such as the Stapletons, see Riddy 1987, chap. 1, and Meale 1996a; on their attitude toward chivalry and violence, see Maddern 1992. For an account of Metham's interest in lay reading, especially the "reading" of images, see Evans 1998.

Source: Princeton, University Library MS Garrett 141, fols. 17r, 17v–18r, 54v–56v: an elegant presentation copy, also containing treatises on palmistry, physiognomy, and the phases of the moon and a set of prognostications for the year, all copied by a single hand. Both the first and second items, the treatise on palmistry and *Amoryus and Cleopes,* begin with decorated capitals containing the Stapleton coat of arms, so the book itself must have been intended for them. The text has been carefully corrected, with many interlinear additions, often by the original hand.

This excerpt was contributed by Ian R. Johnson.

a. Prologue

Thys ys the story off a knyght, howe he dyd many wurthy dedys be the help off a lady, the qwyche taught hym to overcome a mervulus dragon, the qwyche was a .c. fote longe. And this knyght was clepyd Amoryus, the lady Cleopes.

5	The chauns of love and eke the peyn of Amoryus, the knyght,	**chauns** fortune; **peyn** pain
	For Cleopes sake, and eke how bothe in fere	**in fere** together
	Lovyd and aftyr deyd, my purpos ys to endyght.	**aftyr** afterward; **endyght** tell poetically
	And now, O goddes, I the beseche off kunnyng, that Lanyfyca hyght!	
	Help me to adornne ther chauns in sqwyche manere	**adornne** adorn [with eloquence]
10	So that, qwere this matere dotht yt reqwyre,	**qwere** where; **dotht** does
	Bothe ther lovys I may compleyne to loverrys dysyre.	**compleyne** lament; **to** according to
	In May, that modyr ys off monthys glade,	
	Qwan flourys sprede, the qwyche within the rote	**Qwan** when; **qwyche** which; **rote** root
	In wyntyr were clos, that than with floure and blade	**clos** closed; **that** which; **blade** leaf
15	For Phebus exaltyng, with sundry hwys smellyd sote;	
	And byrdys amonge the levys grcne her myrthys made,	**her** their
	Qwan Nero Asy gan to subdwe to the empyre,	**Asy** Asia; **gan** began; **empyre** empire
	And besegyd the emperoure off Perse, kyng Camsyre [. . .]	

[Camsyre is killed in battle, Persia conquered, and two Roman lords, Palamedon and Dydas, are chosen by council of "alle erlys and baronys" and afterward "for

prudent part and gouernans" crowned kings in Albynest, the chief city of Persia.
Amoryus and Cleopes are their children, according to Metham's "autor, Fyrage,"
who commemorates . . .]

[. . .] the love and eke the adversyte

20 Off Amoryus and Cleopes, that were the chyldyr dere   **chyldyr** children; **dere** dear
Off thise lordys, how thei lovyd and dyid in fere.

And the sempyl wryter besechyth off supportacion   **sempyl** simple; **supportacion** indulgence
For the rude endytyng off this story,   **rude** crude; **endytyng** composition
But every word ys wrytyn undyr correcion

25 Off them that laboure in this syens contynwally.   **syens** branch of knowledge or art
For fulle herd yt ys, I knowe yt veryly,   **fulle** very; **veryly** truly
To plese the pepyl: but the sqwete frute schewyth the gentil tre
And the mowth the hert; yt wyl none odyr be.   **none odyr be** be no other way

But cause qwy that I this boke endyght   **cause qwy** the reason why
30 Is that noqwere in Latyne, ner Englysch, I coude yt aspye;   **noqwere** nowhere;
But in Grwe Y had yt wrytyn lymynyd bryght   **Grwe** Greek; **lymynyd** illuminated
Wyth lettyrrys off gold, that gay were wrowght to the ye,
That causyd me to mervel that yt so gloryusly
Was adornyd, and offten I enqwyryd of letteryd clerkys   **letteryd** learned (in Latin)
35 Qwat yt myght be that poyntyd was with so merwulus werkys.   **werkys** workmanship

But alle thei seyd that yt was, be supposyng,   **be supposyng** they supposed
Grwe, but qwat yt ment, thei nyst ryght noght at alle.   **qwat** what; **nyst** did not know
And as yt fortunyd, ther come rydyng
To Norwyche a Greke, to home I schewyd, in specyal,   **home** whom
40 Thys forsayd boke; and he iche word, bothe gret and smal,   **iche** each
In Latyne yt expugnyd. And thus, be hys infformacion,   **expugnyd** expounded
I had the trwe grownd and very conclusyon.

b. The Ending

[. . .] and thus this story I owte lede,   **owte lede** complete [lead out]
Mervelyng gretly that noght nowe, as in held tyme,   **held tyme** olden times
45 Men do noght wryte knyghtys dedys; nowdyr in prose ner ryme.

But qwedyr encresyng off vexacion yt causyth onlye   **qwedyr** whether
Or defaute off cunnyng, with odyr causys moo,   **defaute** lack; **moo** further
I can noght deme; but I trowe, yff men ther wyttys lyst to applye,   **deme** judge
They myght in Englond, and odyr cuntreys mo also,
50 As notabyl storyis off manhod and chyvalrye
Off knyghtys now lyvyng as off them beffore a .cii. yere;   **a .cii. yere** 102 years ago
And rather thei schuld fayle endytyng than matere.

And in Englond many notabyl knyghtys ther be
In sundry placys; but off one I make remembrauns,   **make remembrauns** commemorate

55 The qwyche lyvyd in my days in gret prosperyte   **The qwyche** who
    In este Ynglond; the qwyche for prudent port off governans   **este** eastern
    And knyghtely behavyng in Marcyis chauns   **Marcyis chauns** the fortunes of Mars, i.e., war
    Wurthy ys in the world to be preysyd, withowten ende,
    Off wryter and endyter, for oblyvyon off mend.   **endyter** poet

60 But trwth yt ys, that a gret rootyd tre
    Durabyl frute beryth: off this knyght I mene, nobyl off lynnage,   **Durabyl** enduring
    The qwyche decendyth off a gretyd aunsetre   **gretyd** honored; **aunsetre** ancestry
    Off nobyl werryourrys that successyvely, be veray maryage,   **veray** true
    The to and fyffty knyght ys computate to hys age,
65 Home God hath induyd with alle maner off suffycyauns,   **Home** whom
    So dyscrete therwith, that abyl he ys an hole reme to have in governauns. **reme** realm

    Wysdam ever settyng in yche werk beffore,
    As Salomon in Sapyens makyth remembrauns;   **Sapyens** the Book of Wisdom
    Prudens hys frend and systyr he namyd evermore,
70 With hos counsel he so demenyd hys governauns,   **hos** whose; **demenyd** conducted
    That iche wyse creature hym lovyd with hertely affyauns;   **affyauns** allegiance
    Ever as a wurthy werryur in every necessyte,
    Hym qwyt for hys kynge, bothe on lond and see;   **Hym qwyt** he acquitted himself

    As at Waxham, qwere Gyldenerys londyd to brenne the cuntre,
75 Thys excellent knyght bare hym as a champyon;   **bare** conducted
    And the hole matere, that lyste to rede and see,   **hole** whole; **that** who[ever]; **lyste** [it] pleases
    Rede the story that I endyght off kyng Cassyon,   **kyng Cassyon** Cassiel [?]
    And in the ende ye may yt fynde, affter the destruccion
    Off Corbellyon, qwere I alle hys notabyl dedys bryng to remembrauns,
80 Done wurthyly off hym in Englond and Frauns.   **off** by

    And ye that this story can noght fynde
    Seke them in the begynnyng off Alexander Macedo,   **them** [Stapleton's deeds]
    Or in Josue, or Josepus; for in thise storyis I brynge to mende
    The knyght, Mylys Stapylton, and hys lady bothe to,   **bothe to** both [of the] two [of them]
85 Now here I spare yow that yt be so.   **spare yow** refrain [from doing so] for you
    I have off hys dedys many to wryte;   **dedys** deeds
    I purpose in odyr placys in specyall them endyghte.   **in specyall** in particular

    But this knyght despousyd had a lady,   **despousyd** married
    Havyng decens be ryght lynage   **ryght lynage** direct lineage
90 Off that wurthy and excellent stok lyneally,
    That Poolys men clepe, to duke Wylyam as be cosynnage   **clepe** call; **cosynnage** blood
    Ryght nece, that off Suffolk fyrst successyvely   **Ryght** the very
    Was bothe fyrst markeys and duke; and be this remembrauns   **markeys** marquis
    Ye may noght fayl, qwat kyng had than Englond in governauns.

95 And fore that thei, the qwyche be nowe onborne,   **fore** in order; **onborne** unborn
    Qwan this lady ys pasyd, schal rede this story,   **ys pasyd** has passed away

That thei for her schal pray on evyn and morne,   **on evyn** at evening
In alle the storyis that I endyght I wryght this memory,   **memory** commemoration
That be her lyve thus sche was namyd communly,   **communly** publicly
100 Modyr off norture, in her behavyng usyng alle gentylnes,   **norture** breeding
Ever redy to help them that were in troubyl and hevynes;   **hevynes** sadness

So beuteus eke and so benyngn, that yche creature   **benyngn** benign; **yche** each
Here gretly magnyfyid, commendyng her womanhede   **magnyfyid** praised
In alle her behavyngys, ireprehensybyl and demure,   **ireprehensybyl** beyond reproach
105 And moste to commende, that off thoughte sche toke gret heede
To the necessyteys off the pore, relevyng them at every nede.
Off her beute and vertuys here I sese; for yt ys so,   **sese** cease
I hem declare in Crysaunt, and odyr placys mo.   **Crysaunt** Chrysantza [?]

And yff I the trwthe schuld here wryght,
110 As gret a style I schuld make in every degre,   **style** composition; **degre** way
As Chauncerys off qwene Eleyne, or Cresseyd, doht endyght;
Or off Polyxchene, Grysyld, or Penelope;
As beuteus, as womanly, as pacyent, as thei were wunt to be,   **wunt** wont
Thys lady was, qwan I endytyd this story,
115 Floryschyng the sevyn and twenty yere of the sext kyng Henry.

Go now, lytyl boke, and wyth alle obeychauns,   **obeychauns** obedience
Enterly me comende to my lord and mastyr eke,   **Enterly** wholly
And to hys ryght reverend lady, with alle plesauns,   **plesauns** pleasantness
Enfformyng them how feythffully I hem beseke   **hem** them; **beseke** beseech
120 Off supportacion of the rude endytyng owte of Greke;   **Off** for; **supportacion** indulgence
For alle this wrytyng ys sayd undyr correcion,
Bothe off thi rymyng and eke off thi translacion.   **thi** thy, i.e., the book's

For thei that greyheryd be, afftyr folkys estymacion,   **that** who; **grayheryd** gray-haired
Nedys must more cunne, be kendly nature,   **Nedys** necessarily; **cunne** know
125 In yche syens, qwerein thei have ther operacion,   **qwerein** wherein
Sythyn that crafft comyth be contynwauns into every creature
Than he that late begynnyth, as be demonstracion,   **as be** by way of
My mastyr Chauncerys, I mene, that longe dyd endure
In practyk off rymyng, qwerffore proffoundely   **qwerffore** wherefore

130 With many proverbys hys bokys he rymyd naturally.   **naturally** by natural ability
Eke Jon Lydgate, sumtyme monke off Byry,   **Byry** Bury
Hys bokys endytyd with termys off retoryk   **termys off retoryk** rhetorical figures
And halff-chongyd Latyne, with conseytys off poetry   **halff-chongyd** half-changed
And craffty imagynacionys off thingys fantastyk;   **imagynacionys** imaginings
135 But eke hys qwyght her schewyd, and hys late werk,   **eke** also; **qwyght** white; **her** hair
How that hys contynwauns made hym both a poyet and a clerk.   **poyet** poet

But nowe thei bothe be pasyd, and affter schal I,   **bothe be pasyd** are both dead
Qwerffor I make this schort orysun: **orysun** prayer

O welle off mercy, Jesu! that I be freelnes and foly   freelnes weakness
140 Have the offendyd in dede or in ony imagynacion,   ony imagynacion any thought
Fully off foryeffnes I the beseche, with my hertys hole entencion,   foryeffnes forgiveness
Purposyng to amende alle that I have done amys;   amys amiss
To me, Jesu, now thi mercy, ful necessary ys.

And thei that my sympyl wrytyng schal rede,
145 Off storyis off elde tyme, yff thei lyste, off ther godenes,   elde tyme olden times; lyste wish
Qwere thei Jon Metham in bokes fynde, pray for hym to spede   spede prosper
In vertuys; for he off rymyng toke the besynes   toke the besynes took on the work
To comfforte them that schuld falle in hevynes.
For tyme onocupyid, qwan folk have lytyl to do,
150 On haly dayis to rede, me thynk yt best so.

Here endyth the story of Amoryus the knyght and off Cleopes the lady.

3 **.c. fote** one hundred feet

5–11 **The chauns . . . dysyre** an imitation of *Troilus and Criseyde* I.1–7

8 **And now . . . hyght** and now, O goddess who is called Lanifica, I beg you for skill. Lanifica is one of the three Fates, or Parcae. Compare Chaucer's invocation of the Fury Thesiphone (*Troilus and Criseyde* I.6–9, IV.22–24).

12–18 **In May . . . Camsyre** Compare Chaucer, *Canterbury Tales, General Prologue* I (A) 1–12.

15 **For Phebus . . . sote** smelled sweetly, in different colors, because Phoebus [the sun] was higher in the sky

17 **Qwan . . . empyre** when Nero subdued Asia to the [Roman] empire. Metham's account of Nero's campaign is almost entirely legendary. See the account of Nero's actual campaigns against the Armenians and Parthians in Anderson 1963, 758–80.

24 **undyr correcion** Compare Lydgate's appeal for the "correction" of all readers of *Troy Book* (excerpt 1.7: 212). For the humility topos Metham uses here, see Lawton 1987. Metham's verse line lengths vary more than fifteenth-century prosody (as we understand it) approved, but it is not clear how much this mattered to Metham or to his early readers; the poem reads aloud with proper fluency.

27 **the sqwete frute schewyth the gentil tre** sweet fruit reveals the noble tree ∫ **sqwete** MS *qwete*

29–42 **But cause . . . conclusyon** Elaborate transmission narratives feature in many genres as an aspect of the cultural politics of *translatio studii* (see above, pages 7–8, and the section "Vernacular Theory and Translation" in essay 4.1). The associated topos of the book as treasure, a contact relic for its own narrative, is frequent in saints' lives and medical and other instructive prose (see

Wogan-Browne 1994a), as in treatises on "governaunce" such as the *Secreta secretorum* (Manzalaoui 1977, 205). The bright illumination of Metham's "Greek" codex (30–34) signals worth as well as ornament. Providential interpretation (as in 37–40) is also a frequent motif. For a striking East Anglian analogy, see the prologue to Capgrave's *Life of St. Katherine* (Horstmann 1893, 44–235).

32 **that gay were wrowght to the ye** that were beautifully fashioned to the eye

35 **poyntyd** decorated: used of narrative to mean "described in detail." See Burrow 1971, 69–78.

42 **I had . . . conclusyon** I had the firm foundation and the true solution

45 **nowdyr . . . ner** neither . . . nor

46 **encresyng off vexacion** increased troubles: perhaps a reference to the disastrous English campaigns in France, leading to Henry VI's surrender of Maine in 1448

48 **yff men ther wyttys lyst to applye** if men wished to exercise their ingenuity

52 **And rather . . . matere** and they would sooner run out of opportunities for composition than out of subject matter

56 **prudent port off governans** prudent bearing in his conduct

59 **for oblyvyon off mend** to prevent forgetting

64 **The to and fyffty knyght ys computate to hys age** reckoned to be of a line of fifty-two knights down to his day (MS *to .ij. and fyffty .l.*)

65 **induyd with alle maner off suffycyauns** endowed with all kinds of abilities

67 **Wysdam ever settyng in yche werk beffore** wisdom always sitting in the forefront of his deeds. The line turns into a brief personification allegory.

68 Salomon in Sapyens perhaps Wisd. 6:14 or 7:12

74 Waxham town on the coast northeast of Norwich. One of Margaret Paston's letters (dated 1444–45) refers to 1,100 Flemings landing at Waxham, of whom some 800 were killed or drowned (Davis 1971–76, 1:215). Sir Miles played a significant role in this success. ∫ **Gyldenerys** a nickname for the Flemings: perhaps derived from gilders, the common coin of the Low Countries

77 Cassyon According to Louis-Fernand Flutre (1962, s.v. *Cassiel le Baudrain*), this name would appear to be a variant name of a character in the French romances *Les Voeux du Paon* and *Perceforest*.

79 Corbellyon probably Corbeil: a city in France (Craig 1916, 163) ∫ **bryng to remembrauns** bring to mind

82 Alexander Macedo Alexander the Great (356–323 B.C.) of Macedon: conqueror of an immense empire stretching to India, and the subject of romances in French and English; celebrated in medieval "mirrors for princes" and in the *Secreta secretorum* tradition as a pupil of Aristotle

83 Josue historical book of Joshua in the Bible, which deals with the key theme of the promised land ∫ **Josepus** Josephus (A.D. 37–95): Latin historian who wrote the important *History of the Jews* ∫ **I brynge to mende** Metham may be suggesting merely that Stapleton's deeds are analogous to those of Alexander, Joshua, or the deeds recorded by Josephus, but he is probably alluding to other works in poetry or prose in which he celebrates the Stapletons. Hoccleve's *To Sir John Oldcastle* (1416) also suggests the story of Joshua as one among a number fitting for a knight (stanza 26; see Furnivall and Gollancz 1970, 14). If Metham is listing his previous works here, before promising more to come (86–87), he is working in a Middle English poetic tradition that goes back to Chaucer's lists of his own poems in *The Legend of Good Women* G.402–31 and the prologue to *The Man of Law's Tale* II (B) 45–76.

84 to MS *to .ij.*

91–92 Poolys . . . Wylyam . . . Suffolk William de la Pole (1396–1450): fourth earl and first duke

of Suffolk, influential councillor of Henry VI

93–94 be this remembrauns . . . governauns with this reminder you cannot go wrong [about] which king then governed England. Note that here Metham is addressing a future audience, for whom he is commemorating Lady Stapleton's virtues (see 95–98).

98 In MS *I*

100–101 Modyr off norture . . . Ever redy standard commendations of pious laywomen. On their practices, see Ward 1992, chap. 8.

108 Crysaunt another lost work of Metham's, apparently involving a Greek protagonist named Crysaunt, and perhaps based on the medieval Greek romance *Vélthandos and Chrysántza* (Beaton 1989, 109–10, 118–22; Agapitos and Smith 1992)

110 degre MS *dregre*

111–12 Eleyne Helen of Troy ∫ **Cresseyd** Criseyde ∫ **Polyxchene** Polixena: the sister of Troilus. All three are represented as part of Trojan high society in Chaucer's *Troilus and Criseyde*.

112 Grysyld Griselda: as in Chaucer's *Clerk's Tale*, a legendary example of patience ∫ **Penelope** wife of Ulysses, who faithfully and cunningly fended off wooers while her husband was on his epic travels

115 the sevyn and twenty . . . kyng Henry that is, 1448–49. Henry reigned 1422–1470. ∫ **sevyn and twenty** MS *sevyn and twenty .xxvij.*

116 Go now, lytyl boke Compare the envoi in *Troilus and Criseyde* V.1786–92.

126 Sythyn . . . creature since every creature acquires that skill only by practice

130 proverbys sayings: valued as *sententiae*, sayings of moral or other intensified thematic value

131 Jon Lydgate John Lydgate (1370–1449?; see excerpt 1.7)

133 halff-chongyd Lydgate has been criticized by modern critics for his heavily Latinate vocabulary, a common feature of fifteenth-century aureate style, but here Metham is complimentary, not pejorative.

146 Jon Metham Metham names himself in the middle of an appeal for the reader's prayer, a common, but not invariable, hagiographic convention. Compare Bokenham's witty refusal to allow his name to be recorded (excerpt 1.11: 212–25).

1.9 GEORGE ASHBY, *ACTIVE POLICY OF A PRINCE:* PROLOGUE

Date and Provenance: 1460s–70s, possibly 1470–71 (see Kekewich 1990, 533, and Scattergood, 1990); London.

Author, Sources, and Nature of Text: George Ashby (d. 1475) was a clerk of the sig-

net to Henry VI and later Queen Margaret of Anjou, a position roughly equivalent to that of a modern administrative assistant. These Lancastrian associations were probably responsible for his year's imprisonment in 1463 under the Yorkists (Boffey 1991, 88), which is the subject of his poem known as "A Prisoner's Reflections." The *Active Policy of a Prince* is one of two other extant works by Ashby, both based on the well-known *Liber de dictis philosophorum antiquorum* (Book of the sayings of the ancient philosophers), a thirteenth-century Latin translation of an eleventh-century Arabic collection of political wisdom. Despite its claim to stay close to the source's "intential substance" (66), the *Active Policy* combines compilation from other Late Middle English writings (including the fifteenth-century allegory *The Court of Sapience*: Harvey 1984, xxiii–xxiv) with a great deal of Ashby's own composition. The work takes a conventional view of history as a source of moral exempla and makes no explicit links between past and present, but if Margaret Kekewich is correct in arguing that Ashby wrote during the Lancastrian restoration from October 1470 to May 1471, then his timing would have given the work immediate political relevance (compare Barbour, excerpt 1.2, and Lydgate, excerpt 1.7). Ashby uses Latin for a long preliminary rubric about the work's serious political and ethical purpose, then switches to English rhyme-royal stanzas for a prologue that is a copybook example of the rhetorical gestures made by later-fifteenth-century poets. The prologue invokes Gower, Chaucer, and Lydgate, who were regarded, by the 1450s, as a definitive pantheon of founding literary fathers, although Langland, for instance, was as widely read and Ashby's own "Prisoner's Reflections" has passages closer to Hoccleve than to the Chaucerian and Boethian traditions on which it primarily draws. In terms that recall Metham (excerpt 1.8: 121–30), Ashby contrasts the "fresshe, douce Englisshe" of which these poets were the "finders" (31–32) with his own inexperienced use of English verse, and insists at length (in a manner fitting a professional and poetic giver of counsel) on his detemination not to exceed his competence.

Audience and Circulation: The poem was written for Edward, prince of Wales (1453–71), son of Henry VI and Queen Margaret, Ashby's immediate patron, and was intended to provide the prince with historical and philosophical guidance on how to rule his subjects (1–27). The survival of only a single manuscript suggests that the work did not enjoy broad circulation, but this manuscript is by no means a luxurious one, and the section containing the *Active Policy* shows signs of having circulated as an independent leaflet, which could be purchased cheaply. Such booklets were popular with a wide range of readers, including members of the gentry and urban elites. (Much of Lydgate's poetry circulated in this way: see Boffey and Thompson 1989, especially 290–91.)

Bibliography: Ashby's known works are edited by Mary Bateson (1899) and discussed by Kekewich (1990), Curt Bühler (1950), and Ruth Harvey (1984). On the tradition of books of advice to princes, see Ferster 1996. The best guide to the complexities of English administrative history is still Tout 1920–33.

Source: Cambridge University Library MS Mm.4.42, fols. 2r–4r: a slim parchment booklet, containing only Ashby's *Active Policy* and his *Dicta philosophorum*, carefully copied by a single hand and generously spaced. The opening page, with the Latin dedication to Prince Edward, is heavily rubbed and faded and illegible in many places.

[P]resens Libellus compilatus, extractus, et anglicatus in Balade per Georgium Asshby, nuper Clericum Signeti Supreme domine nostre Margarete, dei gratia Regine Anglie, etc. ex bona voluntate, Amore et cordiali affeccione, quos ipse naturali iure
5 gerit, tam erga celsitudinem et regiam maiestatem suam et prepotissimum et excellentissimum dominum suum Edwardum, eadem gratia suppremi domini nostri Regis Henrici et eiusdem regine Consortis filium progenitum, principem Wallie, ducem

Cornubie, et comitem Cestrie, pro cuius amore et complacencia
fit ista compilacio. [. . .] suum nobilem sanguinem, sub quo ipse a
10 iuventute sua hucusque, et nunquam tota vita sua in alio servicio
fuit tentus, nutritus. Dividitur in tribus temporibus, videlicet
in tempore preterito, presenti, et futuro. Tempus preteritum
exortatur, sepius memin[iss]e de rebus preteritis, ita bene in
legendo sacram scripturam et Cronica, sicut alias sp[e]culaciones
15 et experiencias [. . .] Ipse potest perfecte cond[er]e bonorum
factorum bonitatem et opini[onem] librorum. Et miserimam
ruinam malefactorum et miserorum, [. . .] nde se sapienter et
feliciter gubernare. Tempus presens f[ac]it quomodo se gerriet in
sapiencia et pollecia deo place[ntibus] et populis suis et pro suimet
20 ipsius securitate. Temp[us] futurum providet discrete et prudenter
pro rebus futuris [. . .] diendo se in honore beata fama et bona
gubern[itate] et evitando dampna vituperia et inconveniencia [. . .]
etiam fore activum in pollecia et sapiencia [. . .] subditorum securitate
et bona custodia sub debita [et fideli] obediencia per advisamenta
25 edicta et opiniones diversorum Philosophorum, quorum no[mina]
[. . .] in tractatu breviter subscribuntur.

[The remainder is illegible.]
*[This little book has been compiled, extracted, and turned into English verse by
George Ashby, lately clerk of the signet of our supreme lady Margaret, by grace of
God, Queen of England, etc., because of the goodwill, love, and cordial affection
that he naturally bears both toward her Highness and Royal Majesty and toward the
most mighty and excellent lord her Edward, by the same grace firstborn son of our
supreme lord King Henry and of the same queen his royal consort, prince of Wales,
duke of Cornwall, and earl of Chester, for whose love and goodwill he made this
compilation [. . .] his noble blood, under which he, from his youth was raised up to
this time and never placed in all his life in other's service. It is divided into three
times: namely past, present, and future. Time past urges us often to remember things
past, both by reading sacred Scripture and chronicles, and other accounts and
retellings. [. . .] He [the prince] can draw together the good done by good actions
and the judgment of books, and the misery and ruin of evil and unhappy men, from
which he [can] rule himself wisely and happily. Time present shows how he should
conduct himself with wisdom and policy with actions that are pleasing to God and
his nation and for his own security. Time future shows how he should conduct himself with foresight, discretion, and prudence with regard to things to come. . . .
[directing] himself in honor, good reputation, and wise government and avoiding
scandal and discord. . . . and furthermore to be active in government and prudence.
. . . for the safety and good stewardship of those subjects under due and faithful
obedience through the well-advised counsels and opinions of various philosophers,
whose names . . . are briefly noted in the treatise.]*

Maisters Gower, Chaucer and Lydgate,
Primier poetes of this nacion,   **Primier** first
30 Embelysshing oure Englisshe tendure algate,   **tendure** tender; **algate** in all respects
Firste finders to our consolacioun   **finders** [poetic] inventors; **to** for
Off fresshe, douce Englisshe and formacioun   **douce** sweet; **formacioun** the making
Of newe balades not used before,
By whome we all may have lernyng and lore.

35 Alas! saufe Goddes wille and his plesaunce,   **saufe** saving; **plesaunce** pleasure
That ever ye shulde dye and chaunge this lyffe,
Untyl tyme that by youre wise pourvennce   **pourvennce** foresight
Ye had lafte to us sum remembratife   **remembratife** remembrance
Of a personne, lerned and inventif,   **inventif** creative
40 Disposed aftur youre condicioun,   **Disposed** inclined; **condicioun** ability
Of fresshe makyng to oure instruccioun.   **makyng** poetic composition

But sithe we all be dedly and mortal   **sithe** since
And no man may eschewe this egressioun,   **eschewe** avoid; **egressioun** exit from life
I beseche almyghty God eternal
45 To pardonn you all youre transgressioun,
That ye may dwelle in hevenly mansioun
In recompense of many a scripture   **many a scripture** many writings
That ye have Englisshede without lesure.   **Englisshede** translated into English; **lesure** rest

So I, George Asshby, not comparisoun
50 Making to your excellent enditing,   **enditing** writing
With right humble prayer and orisoun   **orisoun** prayer
Pray God that by you I may have lernyng   **by** through
And, as a blynde man in the wey blondryng,   **blondryng** blundering
As I can, I shall nowe lerne and practise
55 Not as a master but as a prentise;   **prentise** apprentice

Besechyng almyghti God of support,
That thorough his gracious instrucioun
I may confourme me aftur the report   **confourme me aftur** follow; **report** reported example
Of vertuous and sad construccioun   **sad** sober; **construccioun** composition
60 Without minisshyng or addicioun,
Principally in th'entent and substance   **entent** import
Of my matere, with all the observance.   **matere** subject matter; **observance** care

And thaugh all thynges be nat made perfyte
Nor swetely Englisshed to youre plesance,
65 I byseche you hertely to excuse it
So that I kepe intential substance,   **intential substance** essence of the intended meaning
While I have of makynge none assurance   **assurance** confidence
Nor of balades have experience,
Acceptyng my goode wille and diligence.

70 Some personnes peraventure woll thenke
    That it myght be saide better thus or thus.   *peraventure* perhaps
    For I cannat swym, I stand on the brynk,   *For* because
    Wadyng no forther but as Crist Jesus
    Sendith me konnyng, showing unto us   *konnyng* ability
75 That a litle childe may natt so well bere   *bere* bear
    A grete burthen as a man withoute dere.   *dere* injury

    Right so though I have not seien scripture   *seien* seen; *scripture* writing
    Of many bookes right sentenciall,   *sentenciall* filled with wisdom
    In especial of the gloses sure,   *gloses sure* reliable commentaries
80 I woll therefor kepe true menyng formal,
    Nor right meche delatyng the rehersall   *delatyng* expanding; *rehersall* recounting
    Thaugh I do nat so wele as thei before,   *do nat* do not [do]
    Ostendyng my benevolence and lore,   *Ostendyng* showing; *lore* learning

    By protestacioun that my menyng
85 Shall not be wilfully for to displease   *wilfully* deliberately
    Any creatures to my konnyng,   *to my konnyng* as far as I am able
    Principally suche as I aught to please,
    Ner their estat in no wyse to displease,   *Ner* nor; *estat* rank
    But to my pore power it to magnifie,   *to* according to; *magnifie* praise
90 And in al my service it to multiplie.

    Thaugh I be fallen in decrepit age
    Right nygh at mony yeres of foure score,   *foure score* [i.e., nearly eighty]
    I pray God that in my wytt I ne rage   *ne rage* do not go wild
    But that I may wryte aftur Goddes lore,   *aftur* according to; *lore* teaching
95 Encrecyng vertuous liffe more and more,
    As myne entente is and also shal be,   *As* since
    To Goddes plesance and to my dutie.

    Under a support and benevolence,
    With a favorable directioun
100 I woll put to my peine and diligence,   *put to* add
    After the simplesse of mine opinion,   *After* according to; *opinion* judgment
    To my cunnyng and erudicioun;
    This matier is finisshe to the pleasance   *finisshe* finished
    Of almyghty Jesu and his suffrance.   *suffrance* mercy

105 In the name of almyghty Lorde Jesu,
    To whom heven, erth and helle [incl]yne,
    Whiche is the grete name higheste in vertue
    And in all gracious goodenes doth shyne,
    Whom I biseche me for to illumyne
110 That in my mater I may so procede
    Without offense and therin not t'excede.   *t'excede* to exceed, to err or offend

3 **Margarete . . . Regine Anglie** Margaret of   6–8 **Edwardum . . . principem Wallie** Edward,
Anjou, married to Henry VI in 1445   son of Henry VI and Margaret of Anjou, never suc-

ceeded to the kingship for which Ashby's treatise is intended to offer guidance. He died in 1471, ten years after Edward, duke of York, was crowned as Edward IV.

13–27 Tempus . . . subscribuntur Wise regard for time present, past, and future is an attribute of personified Prudence, traditionally envisaged as three-eyed (see *Troilus and Criseyde* V.744–49). The topos of discreet and prudent government is important in fifteenth-century writings of "counsel." See excerpt 1.8: 67–71 above, and compare Lydgate's invocation of Othea in excerpt 1.7: 38–39.

28–34 Maisters . . . lore Ashby invokes Gower, Chaucer, and Lydgate as a trinity of founding poetic "Maisters" (28). "Primier" (29) implies first in time and quality. The stanza focuses on these poets' contributions to language (32), but also their "lernyng and lore" (34): the "consolacioun" (31) they offer is not merely aesthetic.

33 balades formal, stanzaic poems

35–41 Alas . . . instruccioun Alas! to think that, but for God's will and pleasure, you might have died before leaving us some remembrance, by your wise foresight, of a learned and creative person inclined to write fresh poetry by your abilities. "Pourvennce" ascribes to the poets a foresight normally reserved for God (see *The Knight's Tale* I [A] 3011) and, according to the Latin prologue (10ff.), to be acquired by the prince. If historians memorialize the deeds of the great, these poets, according to Ashby, have memorialized themselves.

48 Englisshede Ashby conforms Gower, Chaucer, and Lydgate to the model of literature as the translation of worthy matter.

53 as a blynde man in the wey blondryng Compare *Troilus and Criseyde* II.21, "A blynd man kan nat juggen wel in hewis."

55 Not as a master but as a prentise alludes to 20. Ashby is his predecessors' apprentice.

60 minisshyng or addicioun reduction or amplification. *Abbrevatio* and *amplificatio* are the two principal methods of "artificial" poetic composi-

tion, as outlined in Geoffrey of Vinsauf's famous school text, the *Poetria nova* 203–694 (*amplificatio*) and 695–741 (*abbrevatio*) (Gallo 1971, 24–50, 50–53). Compare Bokenham, excerpt 1.11: 95–96. Ashby declares his inability to work in such modes and preference for virtuous and sober composition (59).

66 intential substance Ashby draws on the terminology of academic prologues, insisting that he will respect the essential purpose of his source text, even if his technical performance as poet (and later, 77–83, as scholar) is "nat made perfyte" (63).

68 balades Although in the hands of Gower, Chaucer, and Lydgate balades (see 33n above) are a source of "lernyng and lore" (34), they are distorted in the course of Ashby's prologue into a form of poetic composition that can be *opposed* to fidelity and sobriety in the treatment of texts.

75 a litle childe Compare the prologue of Chaucer's Prioress, spoken "as a child of twelf month oold, or lesse" (*Canterbury Tales* VII 484 [B2*1674]).

77–80 Right so . . . formal even so, because I have not seen the text of many books filled with wisdom, especially of reliable commentaries [presumably on his source], I will therefore keep to the strict formal meaning. Ashby declines, on grounds of insufficient reading, to add to his text (perhaps by adding his own "gloses sure" [79]), although in practice he does exactly that.

83 Ostendyng my benevolence and lore Compare Walton's "Yut moste I shewe hit forth that is in me" (excerpt 1.5: 40).

91–93 decrepit age . . . ne rage The figure of the aged and foolish narrator (*senex narrans*) has an illustrious precedent in Gower's *Confessio Amantis* (see excerpt 2.11).

98–102 Under . . . erudicioun under indulgence and goodwill, with well-disposed guidance, I will add my effort and diligence, according to the simplicity of my judgment, to my knowledge and learning

106 [incl]yne MS *yne* (the line is smudged)

1.10 GUY DE CHAULIAC, *CYRURGIE:* PROLOGUE (EXTRACT)

Date and Provenance: Guy (more often known as Guido) de Chauliac completed his Latin text, known as the *Chirurgia magna* (The great book on surgery) in 1363. This anonymous English translation dates from the fifteenth century (possibly the second quarter) and is from the southeast Midlands.

Author, Sources, and Nature of Text: Guido de Chauliac came from a peasant family near Lyons and attended the universities of Montpellier, Paris, and Bologna (supported in his studies by the lords of nearby Mercoeur), where he studied anatomy. He settled in Avignon in 1345, serving as the personal physician to three of the Avignon popes, including Clement VI, whom he served during the great plague of 1348. De Chauliac remained in Avignon during the plague, partly, he says, for fear of public censure, and he provides an eye-witness account of its horrors (text in Ogden 1971, 155–57; discussion in Amundsen 1977). The *Chirurgia* covers not only what is now termed surgery but medical treatments for most possible ailments. De Chauliac drew on a wide range of sources for the *Chirurgia,* notably the Greek physician Galen (129–c. 199), the Arabic philosopher Avicenna (980–1037), and more recent authorities such as William of Saliceto (c. 1210–75) and Lanfranc of Milan (d. c. 1315), as well as on his own experience as a surgeon. In the *Chirurgia* itself de Chauliac often depicts medical practice as an art rather than a science (O'Boyle 1994, 175) and criticizes his predecessors for relying solely on tradition. In his prologue, however, he minimizes any suggestion that his work was based on personal experience and instead insists on its scholarly credentials, in a passage that (as noted in the introduction to this part, page 6) gives a classic account of the medieval compilation, or *florilegium* (a collection that gathers highlights, or "flowers," from the works of others), stressing the "onhede and profit" (20, i.e., unity and intellectual advantage) of his work. By uniting different texts, one produces a unified truth (*unio* in the Latin text). The writer of the anonymous Middle English translation seems reluctant to deviate from the wording of the Latin. The syntax is not always completely idiomatic, and the vocabulary includes such rare coinages as "compendiosite" (33). However, in the context of fifteenth-century manuscript medical collections (often prestigious and, like this one, long-consulted) and given the long-standing tradition of Anglo-Norman and English vernacularization of medical and other *Fachprosa* (see Voigts 1989), this caution may indicate a concern to render the text carefully as specialized knowledge, arguing less for anxiety about the vernacular than acceptance of it as a wide-ranging medium of thought, and readiness (compare Usk, excerpt 1.4, Skelton, excerpt 3.15, and Douglas, excerpt 3.16) to explore and extend it.

Audience and Circulation: De Chauliac's Latin text was addressed directly to the doctors (here translated as "lordes leches" [30]) of Montpellier, Bologna, and Paris, three of the leading medical faculties in Europe at the time, and to the doctors and clerks of the papal court. The work circulated widely. Ogden (1971, v) identifies thirty-three Latin manuscripts. The *Chirurgia* was translated into most European languages, and there were at least three translations into Middle English, each drawing on slightly different Latin texts (Kuhn 1968). The text continued to be used into the sixteenth century and was printed on numerous occasions.

Bibliography: The Latin text has been edited by E. Nicaise (1890) and by Michael McVaugh (1997), and the edition printed in Loudin in 1585 has been reproduced in facsimile (Keil 1976). Margaret Ogden (1971) printed the complete text of the Paris manuscript, but never published her notes. Translated excerpts by James Bruce Ross are published in Grant 1974, 791–95. Other Middle English versions have been edited by Björn Wallner (1964, 1969, 1971, 1979, 1982–84, 1988, 1995–96). On de Chauliac's life, see Bullough 1971. On his contribution to medicine and the extent to which he deferred to authority or drew on practical experience, see Thorndike 1934, 3:518–19; Gordon 1959, 353–55; Ackerknecht 1968, 90. On the history of the profession, see Bullough 1966 and Siraisi 1990. On the social role of medicine, see Park 1992. For the situation in England during this period, see Gottfried 1986. The relation between Christian doctrine and medicine is examined by Darrel Amundsen (1996). For the growth of medical and utilitarian writing in Late Middle English, see Voigts 1989, 1996.

Source: Paris, Bibliothèque Nationale MS anglais 25, fols. 2r–2v. This is a large handsome volume, with elegant flourished borders and illuminations and diagrams of surgical instruments that are decorative but convey little medical information (see d'Avril and Stirneman 1981, 176, no. 218, for a description; on the diagrams, see Wallner 1965). On the flyleaves at the front and back are short notes, in what appear to be sixteenth-century hands (fols. 1r, 192v, 194v), on the effect of the phases of the moon on the duration of illness, and several fragmentary recipes for potions and ointments, one dated 1560. The implication is that this copy of the *Cyrurgie* was still being used by medical practitioners of some kind. The scribe is also the scribe of manuscripts of Trevisa's translation of the *Polychronicon* (see excerpt 2.2), Gower's *Confessio Amantis* (excerpt 2.11), and Love's *Mirror* (excerpt 3.10) (Voigts 1989, 384) and in the body of the text has carefully omitted difficult words rather, it would seem, than simply guess at them.

In Godes Name. Here begynneth the Inventarie or Gadryng Togedre of Medecyne in the Partye of Cyrurgie, compilede and fulfilled in the yere of oure Loord 1363 by Guydo de Cauliaco, Cirurgene and Doctour of Phisik in the full clere studye of
5 Mountpylerz.

After that I schall firste geve thonkynges to God, gevynge everlastynge lif of soules and helthe of bodyes and helynge grete sikenesses by the grace whiche he offrede to all fleisshe, gevynge the crafte of medecyne to be understonde of vertues kepynge the helthe and defendyng fro sekenesse or sorwe, I schal geve a besynesse
10 to hye and hardy understondynge men to expowne and to take the witte of helthe. Firste forsothe assailynge an exposicioun or a gadryng togedre of the crafte of cirurgye, I geve thonkynges to levynge God and trewe, that geveth alle thinges beynge, withoute the whiche no bygynnyng is custumably founded, turnynge ageyne moste devoutly to hym with all the strengthes of my herte, prayeng that in
15 this werk and all other he sende to me help of Holy Chirche and defende me, gevynge an happy bygynnyng and gevyng me a more happy myddel or mene in governynge and commaunde he to fulfille that it be made profitable, ledynge to the beste ende.
The resoun of this exposicioun or gadryng togedre was noght defaute of bookes,
20 but rather onhede and profit. Every man may not have alle bookes, and if he hadde, it were irkesome or noye to rede hem and goodly to holde all thing in mynde. And in construcciouns alway bettre thinges cometh. Conynges forsothe beth imade by puttyng to. It is not forsothe possible to begynne the same and ende it. We bene forsothe children in the nekke of a geaunt; neverthelatter we may see
25 als mykel as the geaunt and somewhat more. Therefore there is in construcciouns and gadryng onhede and profit. And sothe for, as the noble Plato saith, tho that beth writen schorter than it spedith beeth made over litel and derke, thoo forsothe that beeth writen to longe noyen to reders. Unnethe forsothe is ther eny booke that fleeth reproof. And therfore to the salace of myn aage and to exercice of my
30 mynde, to yow my lordes leches of Mountpyler, of Boloyne, of Parise, of Avyoun, and nameliche to the Popes clerkes, the whiche felischeped me in the service of the Pope with the whiche I was norrished in herynge, redynge, and worchyng, I schal streyne with a measurable compendiosite, kepyng menehede, the principal sawes of wise men, the whiche thei have treted in volumes of dyverse bookes of
35 cirurgie. For the whiche this book schal be cleped the *Inventarie or Gadrynge Togidre of Cirurgye*. Ne of myn owne I putte noght therto, but if it be ful fewe, the whiche by the menhede of my witt I hopede profitable. Nevertheless, if ther be oght therin unperfit, doutouse, or over mykel and derk, I submyt it to youre correccioun, and I praye that forgevenesse be graunted to my litil pore connynge.

2 **in the Partye of** concerning the subject of

4 **Cirurgene** surgeon. Because they drew blood, surgeons could not be in major religious orders and at a later period lost status, often becoming associated with barbers. ∫ **Doctour of Phisik** medical doctor. The title implied a university degree in medicine. ∫ **clere** famous ∫ **studye** university. Montpellier was a *studium generale,* or university, and also offered degrees in the arts and law. It began to surpass the medical school at Salerno in the thirteenth century, reached its peak in the first half of the fourteenth, and then began to lose ground to Bologna (Bullough 1966, 52–60).

8 **gevynge the crafte of medecyne to be understonde of vertues** God gave the craft of medicine to understand the virtues

9 **kepynge the helthe** which maintain health ∫ **defendyng** protecting (translate "which protect")

9–10 **geve a besynesse to** occupy myself on behalf of

10 **hye and hardy understondynge men** men of high and sophisticated understanding ∫ **take the witte** understand

11 **assailynge** attempting

11–18 **Firste forsothe . . . beste ende** Compare Geoffrey of Vinsauf, *Poetria nova* 71–76 (Gallo 1971, 18).

12 **to levynge God and trewe** to the true and living God

13 **custumably** normally

16 **mene** mean (*n.*)

19 **defaute** lack

20 **onhede and profit** unity and intellectual advantage

21 **noye** annoying

21–22 **and goodly to holde all thing in mynde** useful to [be able to] remember everything (the implication is that this is easier with compilations)

22 **construccions** compilations

22–23 **Conynges forsothe beth imade by puttyng to** knowledge is acquired by putting things together

24 **children in the nekke of a geaunt** children sitting on the shoulder of a giant. The image, which offers a modest explanation of why more recent

scholars can see further than their more distinguished predecessors, was a commonplace in the Middle Ages. It was attributed to Bernard of Chartres (Chancellor of Chartres, c. 1119–26) by John of Salisbury (Southern 1953, 203).

26 **as the noble Plato saith** as the noble Plato says. Guido's reference is probably based on some intermediary source. The Greek philosopher Plato (c. 429–347 B.C.) has little to say in favor of writing, although he does insist repeatedly that philosophical discussion can only be conducted properly if it is accorded sufficient time. Of Plato's texts, only the *Timaeus* circulated widely during the Middle Ages, although there were twelfth-century translations of the *Phaedo* and *Meno,* and Plato was often known through references in Cicero and Augustine.

27 **than it spedith** than is profitable ∫ **over litel and derke** diminished and obscure

28 **noyen** become tedious ∫ **Unnethe** scarcely

29 **fleeth** avoids ∫ **the salace of myn aage** the solace of my [old] age: a traditional justification for writing

30 **lordes leches** doctors: so called because of the medical practice of using leeches to draw blood ∫ **Mountpyler . . . Parise** Montpellier, Bologna, and Paris, whose universities, together with that at Padua, were the major centers for academic medical training (Bullough 1966, chaps. 3–4; Siraisi 1990, chap. 3; Park 1992) ∫ **Avyoun** Avignon

31 **nameliche** in particular ∫ **Popes clerkes** clerics working at the papal court in Avignon ∫ **felischeped** befriended

32 **worchyng** practice

33 **a measurable compendiosite** a reasonable brevity. The word "compendiosite" appears to be rare; it is not attested in the *OED,* and the *MED* provides this as the sole example. ∫ **menehede** moderation

34 **sawes** sayings

36 **but if it be ful fewe** unless it be a very few

37 **by the menehede of my witt** according to my limited understanding

38 **unperfit** imperfect ∫ **doutouse** doubtful ∫ **over mykel and derk** too complex and obscure

39 **connynge** knowledge

1.11 OSBERN BOKENHAM, *LEGENDYS OF HOOLY WUMMEN: PROLOGUS*

Date and Provenance: 1443–47; East Anglia (Stoke Clare).

Author, Sources, and Nature of Text: Osbern Bokenham (1393–1464 or later), Au-

gustinian friar of the priory of Stoke Clare, compiled his collection of female saints' lives from various sources, principally from the major Latin hagiographic collection, the *Legenda aurea,* or *Golden Legend,* made by the Dominican Jacobus de Voragine (1230–98). Bokenham may have been influenced by Lydgate's *Lyf of Our Lady* and Capgrave's *Life of St. Katherine,* both of which he knew, while the title of his collection possibly alludes to Chaucer's *Legend of Good Women* (Delany 1992). If so, we can see Bokenham's narratives of female virgin holiness as opposed to pagan seduction and betrayal as yet another example of the corrective imitation of Chaucer evident in Walton's translation of Boethius, Lydgate's *Troy Book,* and Metham's *Amoryus and Cleopes* (excerpts 1.5, 1.7, 1.8). Here, "correction" proceeds from Bokenham's adaptation of scholastic and hagiographic prologue conventions. After defining the materials and purpose of his work by invoking the scholastic structure of the Aristotelian "four causes" (see also excerpt 3.8), he moves to an account of his own experiences of Saint Margaret's power, and his travels to shrines where the stories of her miracles are preserved. This shift of mode allows a story of personal devotion to complement the scholastic language with which he assures us of the seriousness of his project. But perhaps the text is also tilting at pilgrim narrators who tell tales rather than hagiographies: unlike Chaucer's, these stories do not "sownen into synne" (*Canterbury Tales* X [I] 1085), and where Chaucer's epic ends by kissing "the steppes" of Statius and other classical predecessors (*Troilus and Criseyde* V.1791), Bokenham's pilgrim-narrator kisses the foot of Saint Margaret in launching his work. Bokenham also "corrects" Geoffrey of Vinsauf's school text, the *Poetria nova,* which he invokes in order to manufacture a claim to textual fidelity rather than rhetorical ornament as the merit of his (highly rhetorical) text. Whereas Walton and Lydgate maneuver in all earnestness, however, the tone of this prologue is partly comic, as though Bokenham is aware of writing not for a national audience but for provincial coteries, and as though vernacular writing may not be taken too seriously by his Cambridge contemporaries. Where Lydgate sees himself as the renewer of the past (excerpt 1.7: 115–18), Bokenham ends his prologue by asking his dedicatee, Thomas Burgh, to pass him off not as a Cambridge intellectual but as a horse dealer (217–18).

Audience and Circulation: Like *The Canterbury Tales,* the *Legendys* seems to have been reordered during its composition as a result of external stimulus as well as an evolving internal logic (Edwards 1994). Bokenham composed many of the legends at the request of named aristocratic and gentry women patrons, while the prologue's mock anxieties about what Cambridge wits will make of the work is directed at an Augustinian friar, Thomas Burgh (at whose request Bokenham perhaps composed the life of Margaret in the *Legendys,* and who gave the sole surviving copy of the collection to a convent of nuns). The *Legendys* thus moves between (and offers appropriate authorizing strategies to) at least three inscribed audiences: a Latinate clerical peer group figured by Burgh; female lay patrons; and professed women religious (for a comparable circulation, see excerpt 2.7). The *Legendys* survives uniquely in London, British Library MS Arundel 327, fols. 1–193r, and its only other known manuscript witness is a fragment from the beginning of the *Life of St. Dorothy* (London, British Library MS Addit. 39683, fol. 305r).

Bibliography: The *Legendys* is edited by Mary Serjeantson (1938) and translated and discussed by Sheila Delany (1992, 1996, 1998). On the production and circulation of Bokenham's work, see Edwards 1994; on Bokenham and literary authority, Johnson 1994a. For Bokenham's patrons, see Moore 1912–13. On the translation of relics and *translatio* narratives, see Geary 1978. For the relations of clerkly narrators and saints' devotional communities, see Stock 1983, 64–73, and Wogan-Browne 1994a. On devotion to the saints, see Thomas 1973 and Duffy 1992, 155–205, especially 175–76. Gail Gibson (1989) discusses devotional practice in East Anglia.

Source: London, British Library MS Arundel 327, fols. 1r–5r, a small parchment volume of the mid–fifteenth century with simple decoration and some passages underlined in a possibly contemporary hand. The manuscript contains only the *Legendys.* A note on fol. 193r suggests that the copy was made for Thomas Burgh.

This excerpt was contributed by Ian R. Johnson.

Two thyngys owyth every clerk   **owyth** ought
To advertysyn, begynnyng a werk,   **advertysyn** make manifest
If he procedyn wyl ordeneelly: **ordeneelly** in the proper order
The fyrste is "what," the secunde is "why."
5 In wych two wurdys, as it semyth me,
The foure causys comprehendyd be,   **comprehendyd** contained
Wych, as philosofyrs us do teche,
In the begynnyng men owe to seche   **owe** ought; **seche** seek
Of every book, and aftyr there entent.   **aftyr** afterward; **there** their; **entent** intention
10 The fyrst is clepyd cause efficyent,   **clepyd** called
The secunde they clepe cause materyal,
Formal the thrydde, the fourte fynal.
The efficyent cause is the auctour,
Wych aftyr hys cunnyng doth hys labour   **cunnyng** skill
15 To acomplyse the begunne matere,   **acomplyse** finish; **begunne** [once] begun
Wych cause is secunde; and the more clere
That it maye be, the formal cause
Settyth in dew ordre clause be clause.
And these thre thyngys longyn to "what":   **longyn** pertain
20 Auctour, matere, and forme ordinat.
The fynal cause declaryth pleynly   **pleynly** fully
Of the werk begunne the cause why;
That is to seyne, what was the entent
Of the auctour fynally, and what he ment.   **fynally** ultimately
25 Lo! thus ye seen mown compendyously   **mown** may; **compendyously** fully
How in these two wurdys "what" and "why"
Of eche werk the foure causys aspye   **aspye** descry
Men mown, requyryd be philosophye.
But to oure purpoos: if be "what" or "why"   **be** by
30 Be questyounn maad of thys tretyhs pleynly   **of** concerning; **pleynly** specifically
As for the fyrste, who so lyste to here,   **lyste** wishes
Certeyn the auctour was an Austyn frere,
Whos name as now I ne wyl expresse,   **expresse** declare
Ne hap that the unwurthynesse   **Ne hap that** in case
35 Bothe of hys persone and eek hys name
Myht make the werk to be put in blame,
And so, for hate of hym and eek despyht,   **eek** also
Peraventure fewe shuld have delyht
It to redyn, and for thys chesoun   **chesoun** reason
40 Throwyn it in the angle of oblyvyoun.
And yet me thinkyth it were pete   **pete** [a] pity
That my werk were hatyd for me.   **for me** for my sake
For this, I suppose, alle men weel knowe:
No man the rose awey doth throwe
45 Althow it growe upon a thorn.
Who is so nyce that wil good corn   **nyce** foolish
Awey caste for it growyth in chaf?   **for** because
Men also drynkyn ale and lef the draf,   **draf** lees
Albe it that ale thorgh draf dede ren.   **dede ren** ran

50 Gold eek, as knowe weel alle wyse men,
 In foul blak erthe hath hys growyng.
 And yet is gold as a precyous thyng
 Streyhtly beschet in many a cophyr.   **Streyhtly** narrowly; **beschet** fastened; **cophyr** coffer
 A margerye perle, aftyr the Phylosophyr,
55 Growyth on a shelle of lytle pryhs,   **pryhs** value
 Yet it is precyous; and no man whyhs   **whyhs** wise
 The verteuous crepaude despyse lest,   **crepaude** toadstone
 Thow a todys crowne were hys fyrst nest.   **todys** toad's; **crowne** head; **hys** its
 And to thys manyfold of nature   **manyfold** multiplicity
60 Exaunplys acordyth weel Scrypture;
 For, as the Old Testament beryth wytnesse,
 The sone hys fadrys wykkydnesse   **fadrys** father's
 Shal not bere, but if he it sewe;   **but if** unless; **sewe** follow
 And if he do, thanne is it dewe   **dewe** proper
65 That he be partenere in peyne   **peyne** punishment
 As he was in blame, thys is certeyne.
 Wherfore, if my werk be sure,   **sure** reliable
 Lete not disdeyn it disfigure
 Of the auctor, I lowly beseche;   **lowly** humbly
70 For sekyr that were a symple wreche   **sekyr** certainly; **symple** foolish; **wreche** vengeance
 As a lytyl toforn now here seyd is,   **toforn** before
 To slee the chyld for the fadrys mys.   **mys** misdeed
 The matere wych I wil of wryte,
 Althow but rudely I kun endyte,   although I can only compose awkwardly
75 Is the lyf of blyssyd Margarete,
 Virgyne and martyr, whom did hete   **hete** heat
 The love of Ihesu in hyr tendyr age
 So fervently, that for al the rage
 Of fers Olibrius, and his tyrannye,   **fers** fierce
80 Than Cryst forsaken she had levere dye,   **forsaken** to forsake; **levere** rather
 As pleynly declaryth hyr legende,
 As they shal heryn wych lyst attende.   **wych** whom
 The forme of procedyng artificyal   **artificyal** according to art
 Is in no wyse, ner poetycal   **in no wyse** not at all; **ner** nor
85 After the scole of the crafty clerk   **crafty** skilled
 Galfryd of Ynglond, in hys newe work
 Entytlyd thus, as I can aspye,
 Galfridus Anglicus, in hys *Newe Poetrye*.
 Enbelshyd wyth colours of rethoryk   **Enbelshyd** embellished; **colours** figures
90 So plenteuously, that fully it lyk
 In May was nevere no medewe sene   **no** any
 Motleyd wyth flours on hys verdure grene.   **hys** its
 For neythyr Tullius, prynce of oure eloquence,
 Ner Demostenes of Grece more affluence
95 Nevere had in rethoryk, as it semyth me,
 Than had this Galfryd in hys degre.
 But for-as-meche as I nevere dede muse   **muse** study
 In thylk crafty werk, I it now refuse.

And wil declaryn evene by and by   *declaryn* relate
100 Of seynt Margrete, aftyr the story,   *aftyr* according to; **story** history
     The byrthe, the fostryng, and how she cam
     Fyrst to the feyth and sythe to martyrdam   *sythe* afterward
     As ny as my wyt it kan devyse   *ny* closely
     Aftyr the legende; and sythe what wyse
105 Be whom and how oftyn she translatyd was
     And where now she restyth, and in what plas,   *plas* place
     As I dede lerne wythowte fayle
     The laste tyme I was in Itayle
     Bothe be scripture and eek be mowthe;   *be* from; **scripture** writings
110 Wych story is nothyng unkowthe   **unkowthe** unknown
     At Mownt Flask—who me not leve   *leve* believe
     Lete hym go thedyr and he shal it preve—   *thedyr* thither; **preve** ascertain
     On thys half Rome ful fyfty myle   **half** side
     Or ellys more, where men begyle   **begyle** lure
115 The wery pylgrymys kun ful well   **kun** know how to
     Wyth Trybyan in stede of Muskadel,   **Trybyan** tribian; **Muskadel** muscadel
     Where from Rome homward ageyn
     Whil I was taryed with greth reyn   *taryed* delayed; **greth reyn** heavy rain
     Thys blyssyd virgyne I dede visyte,
120 And al the processe I dede owt wryte   *processe* narrative; **wryte** copy
     Wych I purpose now to declare   *declare* relate
     On Ynglysh, and it brout wyth me to Clare.
     But who-so wyl aske me fynally
     Of thys translacyoun the cause why
125 Into oure language, I sey causys two
     Most pryncypally me mevyd therto.   **mevyd** moved
     The fyrst cause is for to excyte
     Mennys affeccyoun to have delyte
     Thys blyssyd virgyne to love and serve,
130 From alle myschevys hem to preserve,   **hem** them
     Aftyr the entent of hyr preyere   **entent** intention; **hyr** her
     Beforn hyr deth, as ye aftyr shul here.
     And no man wundyr thow I diligence   **I diligence** [do] exert myself
     Do to plesyn the wurthy excellence
135 Of thys holy maydyn, for evene by   **evene** right
     Wher I was born, in an old pryory
     Of blake chanons hyr oo foot is,   **blake** black; **chanons** canons; **oo** one
     Bothe flesh and boon, I dare seyn this,
     Where thorgh a cristal bryht and pure
140 Men may beho[l]den eche feture
     Therof, saf the greth too only   **saf** except; **too** toe
     And the hele, wych in a nunry
     Been, Redyng clepyd, as they there seyn.   **Been** are
     But as for the foot, this is certeyn,
145 Many a myracle hath ther be shewyd

Bothe on lernyd and eek on lewyd.   lernyd learned [people]; lewyd uneducated
And specyally if wyth broche or ryng
The foot men towche at here partyng   here their; partyng departure
Upon the bare, and with hem it bere,   bare bare [skin]; bere carry
150 If they ben in ony dreed or fere
The myschevyn, lete hem behete   myschevyn have had fortune; behete promise
Thedyr to bere and there to lete   Thedyr thither; lete leave
The same thyng that towchyd the fote,
And they shul sone han helthe and bote,   bote healing
155 If they it doo wyth good devocyounn.
Thys is fully myn opynyounn.
For treuly, upon my conscyence,
I had herof good experyence
Not mykyl past, yerys fyve,   mykyl a great deal
160 Whan lytyl from Venyse me dede dryve   lytyl from not far from; Venyse Venice
A cruel tyraunth into a fen
Owt of a barge, and fyve mo men;
Wher I supposyd to have myschevyd,   supposyd anticipated
Had not me the grace relevyd   relevyd saved
165 Of God, be the blyssyd medyacyoun
Of thys virgyne, aftyr myn estimacyoun.   estimacyoun judgment
For sone aftyr I had behyht the ryng,   behyht promised
Wyth wych I towchyd at my partyng
Hyr foot bare, to bryngyn ageyn,   ageyn back again
170 I was relevyd ryht sone certeyn.   ryht sone immediately
Now blissyd mote be that holy virgyne   mote may
Wych to synful preyers lyst her ere enclyne!   Wych who; lyst chooses; enclyne bend
And thys is oo skyl why I am steryd the more   oo one; skyl reason; steryd moved
Hyr lyf to translate, as I seyde tofore.   tofore before
175 Anothyr cause wych that mevyd me
To make thys legende, as ye shal se,   legende saint's life
Was the inportune and besy preyere   inportune persistent
Of oon whom I love wyth herte entere
Wych that hath a synguler devocyoun   Wych that who; synguler personal
180 To thys virgyne of pure affeccyoun.
He me requyryd wyth humble entent   requyryd asked
Whos request to me is a comaundement
That yif I hym lovyd I wold it doo.   yif if
I durst not hastyly assente hym to
185 (Weel knowyng myn owyn infyrmyte)
Tyl I had a whyle weel avysyd me.   avysyd reflected
And thanne the yeer of grace a thowsend treuly
Foure hundryd and also thre and fourty,
In the vigylye of the Natyvyte   vigylye vigil
190 Of hyr that is gemme of virgynyte,
The sevenete day evene of Septembre
Whan I gan inwardly to remembre   gan began

Hys request growndyd in pete,   **pete** piety
Me thowt it were ageyn cheryte   **ageyn** against
195 Hys desyr lengere for to denye.   **lengere** longer
And yet I sore feryd me of envye,
Wych is evere besy and eek diligent
To deprave privyly others trewe entent;   **deprave** disparage; **privyly** covertly
Wherfore, hyr malyhs to represse,   **malyhs** malice
200 My name I wil not here expresse,
As toforn is seyd; wherfore I preye   **toforn** before
And requere eek, if I it dare seye,   **eek** also
Yow, sone and fadyr, to whom I dyrecte   **dyrecte** address
This symple tretyhs, that ye detecte   **detecte** expose
205 It in no wyse wher that vylany   **vylany** ignominy
It myht have, and pryncypally
At hoom at Caunbrygge in your hows,   **Caunbrygge** Cambridge
Where wyttys be manye ryht capcyows   **capcyows** argumentative
And subtyl, wych sone my lewydnesse   **lewydnesse** lack of learning
210 Shuld aspye; wherfore, of jentylnesse,   **aspye** discern; **jentylnesse** kindness
Kepyth it as cloos as ye best kan   **cloos** concealed
A lytyl whyle; and not-for-than   **not-for-than** nevertheless
If ye algate shul it owth lete go,   **algate** at any rate; **shul** out; **owth** must
Be not aknowe whom it comyth fro,   **Be not aknowe** do not acknowledge
215 But seyth, as ye doon undyrstand,
It was you sent owt of Ageland   **you** [to] you; **of** from
From a frend of yourys that usyth to selle   **usyth** is accustomed
Goode hors at feyrys, and doth dwelle   **hors** horses; **feyrys** fairs
A lytyl fro the Castel of Bolyngbrok,   **Bolyngbrok** Bolingbroke
220 In a good town wher ye fyrst tok
The name of Thomas, and clepyd is Borgh
In al that cuntre evene thorgh and thorgh;   **thorgh and thorgh** throughout
And thus ye shul me weel excuse,
And make that men shul not muse   **muse** think
225 To have of me ony suspycyoun.
But, for to drawe to a conclusyoun
Of thys long tale now fynally,
I you beseche, frend, ryht enterly,   **enterly** wholeheartedly
That ye vouchesaf for me to preye
230 Onto thys virgyne, that ere I deye   **ere** before
Thorgh hyr merytys I may purchase
Of my mislevyng a pardounn of grace,   **mislevyng** faulty living
And of myn old and newe transgressyoun
That I may have a plener remyssyoun   **plener** full; **remyssyoun** forgiveness
235 And aftyr the ende of thys owtlawrye   **owtlawrye** [earthly] exile
Wyth hyre above for to magnyfye   **magnyfye** praise
God in hys blysful eternyte,
Where nevere shal ende felycyte.
In wych place us bothe to dwelle,
240 The lord us graunte that harwyd helle. Amen.   **that** who; **harwyd** harrowed

1–3 Two . . . ordeneelly Bokenham announces his status as a "clerk" and asserts his intention of proceeding "ordeneely," according to scholarly convention—although the prologue goes on to complicate both the way these conventions work and Bokenham's status as writer (215–19).

7–9 Wych . . . entent which people ought to search out at the beginning of every book, as philosophers teach us, and afterward [they should search out] the book's intention

10–12 cause efficyent . . . fynal the Aristotelian schema of the four causes as used in formal academic prologues from the thirteenth century and later. The terms are further explained in 13–24. The *efficient cause* is the author; the *material cause* is the subject matter or sources; the *formal cause* the structure, style, and literary procedures; and the *final cause* the purpose of the work (see further Minnis 1988, 28–29). The first three causes are comprehended in the "what," and the fourth cause in the "why," of Bokenham's opening lines (4–6; see also 26–28).

15 the begunne matere the subject matter the writer has started to treat (i.e., the *material cause*)

20 forme ordinat the form by which the subject matter is ordered (i.e., the *formal cause*)

32 Austyn frere Augustinian friar: not the older order of Augustinian canons, but a thirteenth-century order, originally the Italian "hermits of St. Augustine," which adapted Dominican constitutions and settled in Suffolk c. 1242 and founded thirty-five houses in the East and Northeast (Knowles and Hadcock 1971, 36)

33 Whos name . . . expresse Hagiographic narrators frequently adopt a humble stance of simple utility in providing the service of translation for the benefit of the saint's devotees: their name is mentioned only to solicit the prayers of their readers or the intercession of the saint. Bokenham's self-effacement is spectacular and develops the convention beyond the bounds of hagiographic humility topoi into a more inquiring account of the generation of poetry and the relation of first and second cause, poet and matter (see 62–72 below). By detaching the function of "auctour" (32) from issues of moral worth or even reputation ("name" [35]), Bokenham also steps outside much of the framework of fifteenth-century "Chaucerian" poetry, with its much-paraded deference to the founding fathers Gower, Chaucer, and Lydgate (see excerpt 1.9: 28), making room for a judgment of his poem not based on a myth of secondariness to these writers but solely on its particular value.

40 angle of oblyvyoun oblivion's corner: possibly synonymous with a dead angle, "a term applied in old books on fortification to the ground before an angle in a wall that can be neither seen nor defended from the parapet" (Brewer 1989, 36), or just a forgotten corner. Bokenham uses the phrase later in the *Legendys* (Serjeantson 1938, 129.4726).

44–45 the rose . . . a thorn a commonplace, but perhaps here more specifically taken from Saint Jerome's *Letter to Eustochium* on virginity (*Epistolae* 22.20), where it is accompanied by images of gold (see 50–53 below) and pearl (54–56)

54 margerye perle, aftyr the Phylosophyr a pearl [Latin *margarita*], according to the philosopher [Aristotle]. The image of the pearl produced within the oyster shell is present in Jerome (*Epistolae* 22.20; see 44–45n above), but "the Philosopher" more usually alludes to Aristotle.

57 The verteuous crepaude despyse lest wishes to despise the powerful toadstone (a jewel supposed to be found in a toad's forehead)

59–60 And to thys . . . acordyth weel Scrypture and to this multiplicity of nature, Scripture offers precisely compatible exempla

62–72 The sone hys fadrys wykkydnesse Ezek. 18:20: "the son shall not bear the iniquity of the father." As well as being an unworthy medium for his subject (33–34), Bokenham (aged nearly fifty at the time, according to line 248 of his prologue to the *Margaret* legend) is its progenitor. The work (the child) is not to be held responsible ("slain" [72]) for its father/author's inadequacies ("misdeed" [72]). See Bokenham's terminology for his colleague Thomas Burgh (203 below).

75 Margarete Margaret of Antioch: purportedly martyred in the fourth century, and the subject of the first life in Bokenham's *Legendys* as well as an important figure in this general prologue to the collection

79 Olibrius in Margaret's legend, the name of the prefect of Antioch who has the saint tortured and executed

81 legende legend: a written account of the life and/or martyrdom of a saint

83–84 forme of procedyng artificyal / Is in no wyse, ner poetycal the manner of proceeding is in no sense artificial or poetic. Bokenham combines references to two literary traditions: the "form of proceeding" is the Aristotelian formal cause, while the terms "artificyal" (not following "natural" or chronological order) and "poetycal" belong to the realm of rhetorical theory (see next note).

86–88 Galfryd of Ynglond . . . Galfridus Anglicus Geoffrey of Vinsauf (or Geoffrey of England): early-thirteenth-century author of an influential rhetorical manual, *Poetria nova* (the *"Newe Poetrye"* of line 88). Bokenham's "refusal" to follow this work (98) is not to be interpreted as a simple confession of incapacity, but a declaration that he is writing in a different "scole" (85), or tradition.

93 **Tullius** Marcus Tullius Cicero (106–43 B.C.): Roman rhetorician and famous orator

94 **Demostenes** Demosthenes (c. 384–322 B.C.): Greek orator (known only as a name in this period)

105 **translatyd** alludes not only to the translation of Margaret's Latin legend into the vernaculars (as in "translacyoun" [124]) but to the moving of her relics. A detailed account of how her body came from Antioch to Italy concludes Bokenham's retelling of her legend (Serjeantson 1938, 26–38).

111 **Mownt Flask** Montefiascone: a pilgrimage hospice near Lake Bolsena, about fifty miles north of Rome

116 **Trybyan . . . Muskadel** *Trebbiano* (the Italian name for the grape varietal *ugni blanc*) gives a dry white wine rather than the sweet wine produced from the *muscatel* grape.

122 **Clare** Bokenham's Augustinian friary of Stoke Clare. The manuscript has "Redyng" underlined in black (Serjeantson 1938, 4 n. 2). See further 143 below.

123 **fynally** in the end: with reference to the fourth cause, the *cause fynal*—see 12 and 21 above—and the *cause why* of 124. Bokenham has also called this cause the author's "entent" (9, 23).

131 **the entent of hyr preyere** In the legend, Margaret's last prayers before her execution are for her devotees to be granted repentance, safe childbirth, and remedy in misfortune (Serjeantson 1938, 23.834–37). Thus part of Bokenham's "entent" is to fulfill Margaret's "entent."

136–37 **Wher I was born . . . blake chanons** Serjeantson (1938, xiv) suggests that Bokenham may have come from Old Buckenham in southern Norfolk, where there was a priory of Augustinian "black" canons and which is close enough to Suffolk to be compatible with Bokenham's "Suthfolk speche" (Serjeantson 1938, 111.4064).

139 **cristal** a case or box of crystal, a reliquary

140 **beho[l]den** MS *behoden*

142–43 **a nunry . . . Redyng clepyd** a nunnery . . . called Reading. "Nunry" is puzzling, as Reading Abbey was an all-male Cluniac house, with women only in some of its outlying dependencies. A Reading inventory of 1558 includes "Bones of saynt Margarett" (Serjeantson 1938, xiv).

158 **experyence** To the *auctoritee* of his Aristotelian learning, Bokenham adds information about his personal experience of and devotion to saints, which in hagiographic convention underlines the writer's role as a channel of transmission and contact between saint and audience.

161 **A cruel tyraunth** perhaps Francesco Foscari, doge of Venice, 1423–57. The reasons for Bokenham's presence in Venice are unknown, but see Delany 1992, x–xi. The marshes around Venice were breeding grounds of diseases that killed many visitors, not least the poet Dante.

178 **herte entere** [my] entire heart. The friend is not identified but may be Thomas Burgh (221).

182 **comaundement** Hagiographic narratives frequently justify their composition by stating that they are written at the request of a monastic superior, since such a request was taken as a command (compare also excerpt 1.1: 80 and note). Bokenham performs an affective variation on this topos by insisting that his friend's request demands the same obedience from him.

189 **vigylye of the Natyvyte** the eve of the feast of the nativity of the Virgin Mary (the "gem of virginity" of 190). In the manuscript, lines 189–93 have been copied by the scribe in the order 191, 192, 189, 190, 193: corrections in the margin in an apparently contemporary hand indicate the order adopted in our text.

194 **ageyn cheryte** "Charity compels me to write" is a common topos of medieval religious literature, as is Bokenham's fear of "envye" (196). Compare, for example, Margery Kempe (excerpt 1.14: 7–9, 90–109) and Rolle's *English Psalter* (3.8: 66–69), which similarly oppose the urgings of charity and fear of malicious detractors. For charity as a reason for writing, see also Julian of Norwich (excerpt 1.13: 88–90), the *Northern Homily Cycle* (excerpt 2.1: 58), *The Cloud of Unknowing* (excerpt 3.3: 8n), *The Orchard of Syon* (excerpt 3.5: 8), and Eleanor Hull's *Penitential Psalms* (3.21: 43–45).

197–98 **Wych . . . entent** Bokenham returns to the earlier theme of his need for anonymity, showing his awareness of the possible gap between his formal "intention" as an author (as he has defined this in 123–95) and his personal intention, which the "malyhs" (199) of others may construe as the lust for fame or career advancement. Both are inappropriate in a monk and religious writer. Compare the related anxiety about the gap between what is meant and what is understood expressed by Ashby (excerpt 1.9: 84–90) and Pecock (excerpt 1.16: 11–35). Contrast *Speculum Devotorum*, excerpt 1.12: 53–55.

203 **sone and fadyr** Bokenham's terms for Thomas Burgh reflect monastic usage for senior and junior monks and for priests. Burgh is presumably Bokenham's junior as a monk, but has the title "fadyr" because he has the rank of a priest (which many monks and friars did not).

207 **at Caunbrygge in your hows** Burgh was an Augustinian friar living in Cambridge.

216 **Ageland** a district in Lindsey, Lincolnshire. See Serjeantson 1938, 291.216n.

221 **Borgh** Burgh le Marsh, Lincolnshire

1.12 SPECULUM DEVOTORUM (MYROWRE TO DEVOUT PEPLE): PREFACYON (EXTRACT)

Date and Provenance: probably c. 1415–25; London area (Middlesex, the Carthusian monastery at Sheen, near Richmond, west of London).

Author, Sources, and Nature of Text: The *Speculum Devotorum,* or *Myrowre to Devout Peple,* is a meditative prose life of Christ written (soon after the monastery's foundation by Henry V in 1413) by a Carthusian of Sheen for his "gostly [spiritual] syster" (1). She may have been a Bridgettine nun at the monastery's sister house of Syon on the other side of the Thames (see excerpts 3.5 and 3.12). The Carthusians were an order of hermits, rather than monks, and writing and copying books were a major part of their lives: activities laid down in their rule (the *Consuetudines* of Guigo II) as equivalent to preaching (see Sargent 1976; Doyle 1989). The title's term "myrowre" (*speculum*) is associated with works of comprehensive moral instruction and signals the writer's decision to expand his original project of writing a Passion meditation into an entire life of Christ in thirty-three chapters, one for each year of Christ's life (7–12). This decision aligns the work with a common late medieval shift from "passions" to *vitae,* but may have been a response to local events: the dissemination of the first full New Testament in English as part of the *Wycliffite Bible* (from the 1390s on), and the publication c. 1409 of Love's translation of the famous *Meditationes vitae Christi* attributed to Bonaventure, *The Mirror of the Blessed Life of Jesus Christ* (excerpt 3.10). The *Speculum* writer states that, after reading Love's book (a quasi-canonical text from the moment of its publication), he almost gave up his own, until his prior encouraged him to continue (24–40). However, behind this story of authorial humility the writer seems uneasy with Love's project and eager to do better. Where Love relies wholly on a set of meditations that are explicit about their partial fictiveness and that (in his version) leave out most of Christ's teaching, this writer offers as his sources two authoritative biblical commentators (Peter Comestor and Nicholas of

Lyre, see 68n, 69–70n) and the revelations of "approvyd wymmen" such as Bridget of Sweden (74 and note), and goes to considerable lengths to explain his reluctance to include the kind of "ymagynacyons" used by Love (76–80). Opposing "reason" to Love's focus on "devotion," he stresses that, as a compiler, he adds nothing of his own except what is determined by reason and a good conscience (74–76). His text is thus triply valorized by his purity of intent, his recourse to exegetical tradition, and the value of his subject. Behind this careful introduction lies a continuing debate in early-fifteenth-century England over how Christ's life should be represented in the vernacular and what kind of understanding it was proper to elicit.

Audience and Circulation: There are two manuscripts extant, Cambridge University Library MS Gg.1.6, and a manuscript kept at Beeleigh Abbey in Suffolk (both fifteenth-century). Like many devotional texts, the work was in the first instance written for a single female reader (the "gostly syster" [of Syon?] mentioned above), but the title, *"Myrowre to Devout Peple"* (59), also addresses a more general audience, suggesting that the differences noted here between the *Speculum* and Love's *Mirror* may not be entirely reducible to a difference in intended readership. The writer's chapter divisions and use of a "tabyl [of contents]" (9) was common by the early fifteenth century but could be related to the practice of *The Orchard of Syon* (excerpt 3.5), which also gives similar instructions for reading.

Bibliography: For an edition of the first two-thirds of the text, see Hogg 1973–74 (the editors thank James Hogg for access to his unpublished introduction to this edition); there are full editions in two unpublished dissertations, Wilsher 1956 and Banks 1959. For bibliography to 1992, see Lagorio and Sargent 1993, 3107–8. There has been very little work on this text, but on the author as translator, see Johnson 1989 and 1997. On the relation between the *Speculum* and the *Mirror,* see Sargent 1995. On the *Meditationes vitae Christi* and associated texts in

England in general terms, see Salter 1974 and Sargent 1984. William A. Pantin (1955) discusses the genre of the devotional mirror. For the Carthusians' role in disseminating spiritual writings, see Sargent 1976 and Gillespie 1984, and on male clerics writing for women, Keiser 1985. On the foundation of Sheen and Syon, see Catto 1985.

Source: Cambridge University Library MS Gg.1.6, fols. 1r–4v, a fifteenth-century paper volume in a single column containing only this item, a supplementary account of Saint John the Evangelist, and a short prayer in Latin and English. There is a note on one of the opening flyleaves—"*Speculum Devotorum*: et est liber domus Jhesu de Bethleem ordinis cartusiensis de shene et nomen scriptoris Willelmus plenus amoris" (*A Mirror to Devout People*: and the book belongs to the house of Jesus of Bethlehem at Sheen, and the name of the scribe is William Full-of-Love)—with a call for prayer, and several other names.

This excerpt was contributed by Ian R. Johnson.

Here begynnyth a prefacyon to the boke folowynge.

Gostly syster in Jhesu Cryste I trowe hyt be not yytt fro youre mynde that whenne we spake laste togyderys I behette yow a medytacyon of the Passyon of oure Lorde, the whyche promysse I have not putte fro my mynde but be dyverse tymys
5 be the grace of God I have parformyd hyt as I mygthe. Oure Lorde graunte hyt be to hym pleseable and to yow profytable, or to eny othyr devot servant of God. But I do yow to wyte that be conseyle I have put to myche more thanne I behette yow, to more encresynge of youre love to God and vertuys, or eny othyr that mygth be grace of God profyte be the same, as ye maye see schortly in the tabyl
10 folowynge thys prefacyon. For I have dyvydyd the boke folowynge in thre and thyrty chapetelys to the worschype of the thre and thryty yere that oure Savyoure lyvyde in erthe; and I have sette the tytyllys of hem alle in a tabyl aftyr thys prefacyon afore the boke that hosoevere lykyth to rede hyt maye see schortly there alle the matere of the boke folowynge and rede where hym lykyth best,
15 and that he mygthte the sonnyr fynde that he desyryth moste, and the bettyr kepe hyt in mynde, and also redylokyr fynde hyt yf hym lyste to see hyt agen; notwythstondynge hyt were best, hoso mygth have tyme and laysyr therto, to rede hyt alle as hyt ys sette. Also I have be steryd ofte tymys to have lefte thys bysynesse bothe for my unworthynesse and also for Bonaventure, a cardynal and a
20 worthy clerke, made a boke of the same matere the whyche ys callyd *Vita Christi*, and most of alle whenne I herde telle that a man of oure ordyr of Charturhowse had i-turnyd the same boke into Englyische. But er I began thys occupacyon I askede conseyil of spiritual and goode men and hope and leve of my pryoure. And yytt aftyrward whenne I was moste in dowte of alle and hadde purposyd to
25 have lefte alle togyderys and no more uttyrly to have do therto, yytt I thowgth I wolde aske conseyil of my pryoure, the whyche I specyally lovyde and truste myche to, and I trowe I tolde hym what mevyde me. And he ful charytably confortyde me to parforme hyt wyth sueche wordys as cam to hys mynde for the tyme. And so, on the mercy of God trustynge to whom ys no thynge
30 unpossyble, wyth drede of my unkunnynge and unworthynesse; also sumwhat bore up be the conseyil of goostly fadrys and the merytys of hem that be the mercy of God mowe be profytyd be my sympyl traveyle: in sueche tymys as I mygth traveyle

be my conscyence, wythoute lettynge of othyr excercysys and othyr dyverse
occupacyonys and lettyngys that mygth falle in dyverse wysys, I thowgth be the
35 grace of God to make an ende therof; and so att the laste oure Lorde of hys
mercy yaf me [grace, as] I hope, to parforme hyt. In the whyche, yf ye or eny
othyr devout servant of God fynde enythynge profytable or edificatyf, hyt ys to be
redressyd to the mercy of God and the merytys of hem that mowen be profytyd
therby. And yf enythynge be founde the contrarye hyt ys to be redressyd fully to
40 my unabylnesse and unkunnynge.
    Ferthyrmore, lest eny man that mygth aftyrwarde rede the boke folowynge
schulde conseyve temptacyon that a sympyl man schulde do sueche a werke aftyr
so worthy a man as Bonaventure was, sygth he wrote of the same matere, hyt
mygth be ansueryd to the satysfaccyon of hys conscyence thus. Ther ben foure
45 Evangelyst that wryten of the manhede of oure lorde Jhesu Cryste, and yytt alle
wryten wel and trewly, and that one levyth anothyr supplyeth. Also the doctorys
of Holy Chyrche exponen the same Evangelyis that they wrote diverse wysys to the
conforte of Crystyn peple, and yytt alle ys goode to Crysten peple and necessarye
and profytable. And so, thowgth he that wrote fyrste the medytacyonys
50 folowynge were but a sympyl man and of no reputacyon in comparyson of so
worthy a clerke as Bonaventure was, yytt the medytacyonys be the grace of God
mowe be ful goode and profytable to devout Crystyn soulys. And therfore I hope
ther wole none meke and devot servaunt of God conseyve mysly therof. For
thowgth the werke be but symple, yytt the entent of hym that dede hyt was ful
55 goode, and therfore hoso cunne not escuse the werke, lete hym escuse the entent.
    And for the entent of hym that dede hyt was to sympyl and devout soulys that
cunne not or lytyl undyrstonde Latyn, and also for the devout thynkynge of oure
Lordys Passyon and manhede ys the grounde and the weye to alle trewe devocyon,
thys boke may be callyd *A Myrowre to Devout Peple* [. . .]

*[Diligent meditation on Christ's humanity ("manhede") is a true path to spiritual
knowledge and true loving of God as is declared in [Henry Suso's]* Orologium
Sapientiae (The Hourglass of Wisdom). *It makes unlearned people learned and simple
people masters not of knowledge ("sciens") but of charity: it provides comfort,
spiritual health, a perfect model beyond even those of the saints and holy fathers,
and the promise of endless joy.]*

60   Also the medytacyonys folowynge be not to be red negligently and wyth
hastynesse, but dylygently and wyth a goode avysement that the redare maye have
the more profyte therof. For hyt ys bettyr to rede oo chapetele dylygently and
wyth a goode delyberacyon thenne thre wyth negligence and hastynesse, for ye
schul not consydere how myche ye rede, but how wel.
65   Ferthyrmore, gostly syster, ye schal undyrstande that the grounde of the boke
folowynge ys the gospel and the doctorys goynge therupon. And specyally I have
folowyd in thys werke tueyne doctorys, of the whyche that one ys comunely called
the Maystyr of Storyis and hys boke in Englyisch the *Scole Storye;* that othyr
Maystyr Nycholas of Lyre, the whyche was a worthy doctur of dyvynytee and
70 glosyde alle the Byble as to the lettural undyrstandynge. And therfore I take these
tueyne doctorys most specyally as to thys werke, for they goo neryste to the storye
and to the lettural undyrstandynge of eny doctorys that I have red.

Notwythstandynge, I have browgth inne othyr doctorys in diverse placys as to the
moral vertuys, and also sum revelacyonys of approvyd wymmen, and I have put
75 nothynge too of myne owen wytt but that I hope maye trewly be conseyvyd be
opyn resun and goode conscyence, for that I holde the sykyrest. For thowgth ther
mygth have be put to sum ymagynacyonys that haply mygth have be delectable to
carnal soulys, yytt that that ys doo aftyr conscyence ys sykerest thowgth the
medytacyonys mygth have be, be sueche ymagynacyonys, haply more confortable
80 to some carnal folke.

Also I have prayde yow in the fyrste chapetele of the boke folowynge, or
eny othyr devout servaunt of God that maye aftyrwarde be the grace of God rede
the boke folowynge, to seye thre *Pater Noster,* thre *Aveys,* and a *Crede* to the
worschype of the Holy Trynytee, the whyche ys oo verry God, of oure Lady, and
85 of alle seyintys and for grace that ys necessarye in redynge of the sympyl
medytacyonys folowynge, and also for the foryevenesse of the synnys of the fyrste
wrytare of hem. And the same prayere I have askyd agen abowte the myddyl,
afore the Passyon, and also in the laste ende, in betokenynge that the Holy
Trynytee ys the begynnynge, the mydyl, and the ende of alle goode werkys, to
90 whom be alle worschype joye and preysynge now and wythoute endynge, Amen.

1–5 Gostly . . . God Books for religious women
frequently begin by asserting that they are written
on request. Compare, for example, Capgrave's *Life
of St. Gilbert,* excerpt 2.7, and *The Amesbury Letter,* excerpt 2.9, as well as *Ancrene Wisse* (Savage
and Watson 1991, 47) and book I of Walter Hilton's
Scale of Perfection. The tone cultivated is one of
spiritual friendship, or *amicitia,* in which a learned
male writes for an ostensibly unlearned woman
whose professional religious status is equal to his
own. See Bartlett 1995, 86–114, for discussion of
this mode.

1   **prefacyon** preface ∫ **Gostly** spiritual
2   **trowe** believe ∫ **yytt** yet
3   **behette** promised
4   **be dyverse tymys** at various times
5   **parformyd hyt** carried it out
6   **pleseable** pleasing
7   **do yow to wyte** let you know ∫ **conseyle** advice ∫ **put to** added
8   **to more** for the greater ∫ **eny othyr** any other
[reader]
10–18 For . . . sette Compare the instructions
on reading that introduce the "kalender," or table
of contents, in *The Orchard of Syon* (excerpt 3.5),
written at almost the same time as the *Speculum*
and perhaps also at Sheen. Regarding the author's
preference that his book be read in its entirety
rather than in extract, compare excerpts 3.3–5.
11   **chapetelys** chapters ∫ **to the worschype** in the
honor
12   **tytyllys** titles ∫ **hem alle** them all
13   **afore** in the front of ∫ **hosoevere lykyth to**

rede hyt anyone whom it pleases to read it
14   **hym lykyth best** it best pleases him. The "inclusive" use of masculine pronouns is common in
texts addressing female readers. Compare, for example, excerpt 2.8.
15   **sonnyr** sooner
16   **redylokyr** more readily ∫ **hym lyste** it pleases
him
17   **hoso** whoever
18   **sette** set down ∫ **steryd** moved: a technical
devotional term for inner compulsion. Compare
excerpts 1.13: 43, 63; 1.14: 12; 3.12: 38, and so
forth.
19   **Bonaventure** (1221–74): Franciscan theologian, cardinal, and saint (canonized in 1482)
20   **Vita Christi** that is, the *Meditationes vitae
Christi:* an early-fourteenth-century life of Christ
by Johannes de Caulibus attributed to Bonaventure
21   **a man of oure ordyr** Nicholas Love completed his translation of *The Mirror of the Blessed
Life of Jesus Christ* shortly after becoming prior of
the Carthusian monastery of Mount Grace, Yorkshire, c.1409 (see excerpt 3.10).
22–23 er I began . . . pryoure In deciding to
write, the author says he took the advice of his prior
(to whom he owes obedience, although the prior
gives not only "leve" [23], but "conseyil" [26]) and
of "spiritual and goode men" [23]. Here he draws
(appropriately, for a Carthusian) on a topos of writing for hermits and anchoresses, who are often
enjoined to refer decisions not only to formal superiors but to anyone they trust: the tradition derives
from the *Vitae patrum* (an early collection of lives

and sayings of the desert fathers), and surfaces, for example, in *Ancrene Wisse* (part II; Savage and Watson 1991, 73).

22 i-turnyd translated ∫ **er** before

25 uttyrly at all

27–29 he ful charytably . . . tyme The prior of Sheen Charterhouse here gives his blessing to a literary project that is apparently in direct competition with a recent work by the prior of Mount Grace. See headnote and 21n above.

27 myche greatly ∫ **trowe** believe ∫ **mevyde** motivated ∫ **charytably** lovingly

28 parforme hyt do it ∫ **sueche** such

30 drede fear ∫ **unkunnynge** lack of skill

31 hem them ∫ **be** by

32 profytyd benefited ∫ **traveyle** work

33 be my conscyence in [good] conscience ∫ **wythoute lettynge of othyr excercysys** without hindering other [devotional] excercises. The Carthusian day contained a formidable number of hours of liturgical and private prayer, and the author may have had duties as a copyist of other works while writing his own. See headnote and 22–23n above.

34 lettyngys interruptions ∫ **falle** happen ∫ **thowgth** thought

35 make an ende MS *make ande ende*

36–40 In the whyche . . . unkunnynge The formal humility expressed here is in marked contrast to the tone taken by Love's *Mirror* (excerpt 3.10), which makes no allusion to its author's unworthiness.

36 yaf gave ∫ [grace, as] not in MS, but the sense seems to require these words.

37 edificatyf edifying

38 redressyd attributed

40 unabylnesse inability

42 conseyve temptacyon see it [as a case of] spiritual danger ∫ **aftyr** in emulation of

43 sygth inasmuch as

44–55 Ther ben . . . escuse the entent The author's defense of his project is that since no one book, even a Gospel, can say all there is to say about Christ (compare John 21:25), there is no competition between versions of his life: an argument that echoes Love's *Mirror* (Sargent 1992, 10.41–42) but would have been anathema to his Wycliffite contemporaries (compare the *Wycliffite Bible,* excerpt 1.15, and *The Holi Prophete David,* excerpt 2.5). Here the author treats the existence of *Meditationes vitae Christi* as a potential threat, instead of, as one might expect, citing the work as a major source and insisting his role is merely that of translator. The author's assertion that his "entent" was "ful goode" (54–55) is comparable to those made or

implied by Ashby, Bokenham, and Pecock (excerpts 1.9: 84–90, 1.11: 198, 1.16: 11–35).

45 manhede humanity or manhood (often opposed to "godhede," the divinity of Christ)

46 levyth leaves out

47 exponen expound ∫ **they** [the Evangelists] ∫ **diverse wysys** in different ways

49 thowgth although

51 be by

52 mowe may ∫ **ful** very

53 conseyve mysly understand [the translation] as wrongdoing

54 hyt it

56 for because ∫ **to** for

57 cunne not do not know ∫ **thynkynge** reflection

60–64 Also . . . how wel probably related to the influential prologue to Anselm's *Prayers and Meditations* (pages 212–13 and excerpts 3.1–3)

61 wyth a goode avysement with proper deliberation

62 oo one

63 wyth a good delyberacyon carefully

65–76 Ferthyrmore . . . sykyrest The author cites his sources but omits mention of the *Meditationes* as well as his use of *The Three Kings of Cologne, The Gospel of Nicodemus,* and *Mandeville's Travels* (Lagorio and Sargent 1993, 3107). The effect is to emphasize the scholarly nature of his project, although he does refer to his focus on the "lettural undyrstandynge" (70), the literal level of Scripture thought most appropriate (like the "manhood" [45] of Christ) for the uneducated. For the contentious nature of this association, see Watson 1995a, 840–46, and Love's *Mirror,* excerpt 3.10.

66 doctorys doctors [of theology] ∫ **goynge** commenting

67 tueyne two

68 Maystyr of Storyis Master of Histories: Peter Comestor, died c. 1179, whose history from the Creation to the end of the Acts of the Apostles gained him the title Magister Historiarum ∫ **hys boke in Englyisch** his book [is called] in English ∫ the *Scole Storye* the *Scholastic History* (Comestor's *Historia scholastica*)

69–70 Maystyr Nycholas of Lyre . . . lettural undyrstandynge Nicholas of Lyre (c. 1270–c. 1349): a Franciscan who taught theology at the University of Paris. His commentaries on the literal senses of the Bible, set forth in his *Postillae perpetuae sive brevia commentaria in universa biblica* (1322–30), formed the core of late medieval biblical commentary.

69 dyvynytee divinity

70 **glosyde** glossed ʃ **lettural** literal ʃ
undyrstandynge meaning

71 **neryste** closest

73 **Notwythstandynge** nevertheless

74 **approvyd wymmen** women visionaries. The
Speculum quotes from the works of Bridget of Sweden (1303–73), Catherine of Siena (see excerpt 3.5),
and Mechtild of Hackeborn (see excerpt 3.20), but the
formal sense in which these writers were "approvyd"
in the early fifteenth century is not clear, although
Bridget had been canonized in 1391. The author is
presumably alluding to the growing body of Latin and
English writing concerned with *discretio spirituum*,
the discernment of the spiritual value of visionary and
other religious experience, discussed at length in texts
such as *The Chastising of God's Children* (on *discretio
spirituum*, see Voaden 1996c). Clearly, a canon of
approved texts by women was already partly established when he wrote. See also Margery Kempe's
account of her reading, which includes many of the
items alluded to here, excerpt 3.22: 33–35.

74–75 **put nothynge too** added nothing

75 **wytt** understanding ʃ **but** except ʃ **that** what
ʃ **conseyvyd** comprehended

75–76 **be opyn resun** by clear reasoning

76 **for that I holde the sykyrest** because I consider that the surest

76–80 **For thowgth ther mygth . . . carnal folke**
an indirect but clear criticism of Love's *Mirror*,
which describes its policy of adding, for the benefit
of "carnal" readers, "ymagynacyonys" of events
that did not occur (Sargent 1992, 10.31–11.4)

77 **mygth have be put to** might have been added
ʃ **ymagynacyonys** pious imaginings (opposed to
"opyn resun" [76]) ʃ **haply** perhaps

78 **carnal soulys** worldly people ʃ **doo** done ʃ
aftyr according to ʃ **thowgth** [even] though

79 **be** been ʃ **be** through

83 **thre** *Pater Noster,* **thre** *Aveys,* **and a** *Crede*
the prayers beginning "Our Father" and "Hail
Mary" and the Creed, which formed the basis of
common devotional practice

84 **verry** true

85 **seyintys** saints

87 **agen** again ʃ **abowte the myddyl** in the
middle [of the book]

88 **in the laste ende** at the very end ʃ **in
betokenynge** to symbolize

1.13 JULIAN OF NORWICH, *A REVELATION OF LOVE* (SHORT TEXT): PROLOGUE AND CHAPTER 6

Date and Provenance: probably c. 1382–88;
East Anglia (Norwich). The illness and visions
described in the text took place in early May
1373.

Author, Sources, and Nature of Text:
Julian of Norwich (1342–after 1416) wrote
two versions of this ambitious theological treatise, both based on a series of visions she
received in 1373 during an illness. The visions
center on Christ's Passion and the fate of humanity, especially Christ's reassurance that
"all shall be well" (a statement Julian wants to
endorse, but cannot for a long time see how to
take as a promise that all humanity will be
saved). The first version is the earliest surviving work in English known to be written by a
woman. It may have been finished while Julian
was a laywoman, before she became an
anchoress in Norwich (where she was enclosed
in a cell adjoining the Church of St. Julian by
1393 and where the revised Long Text was

written). Probably a member of a gentry family either from East Anglia or from the
Northeast of England (there are traces of
Northern dialect in her texts), Julian was
highly educated (in French and possibly Latin
as well as English) and perhaps had access to
Norwich's libraries. By the early fifteenth century she was sufficiently well known as a
spiritual adviser for a chapter of Kempe's *Book*
(see excerpt 1.14: 59n) to describe a visit to her.

The prologue to the Short Text (somewhat
modified in the Long Text) constructs a careful picture of the genesis of Julian's visions as
proceeding from devotion to Christ, a desire
to suffer with him, and reverence for one of
her (legendary) predecessors who did so, the
martyr Saint Cecilia. Writing within an English context where (by contrast with
continental Europe) visions like hers were
rare, Julian stresses the orthodoxy and con-
ventionality of her reasons for wanting a

vision, and conceals the theological questionings that, she later admits (chap. 13), were also part of the background to her experience. Behind this, however, lies a more assertive stance: Julian's humility (85–87, removed in the Long Text) has the effect of broadening the implications of her personal experience and her book, so that it becomes "common and generale" (64), authoritative not only for her but for everyone. Saint Cecilia survived the "three wounds" of her execution (41–43) to preach for three days and make many converts (see Chaucer, *Second Nun's Tale* VIII [G] 533–39): Julian survives her illness to become, despite her disclaimer, a teacher.

Audience and Circulation: The Short Text was written for an indistinctly defined audience of devout people (lay or professed) and in a wider sense for all Julian's "evynn-Cristene" (50), that is, all believers. However, while it may have had some local celebrity, there is no evidence it circulated widely in practice, and Julian (like her contemporary Margery Kempe) never became one of the group of "approvyd wymmen" alluded to in *Speculum Devotorum* (excerpt 1.12: 74). The Short Text survives in one manuscript, London, British Library MS Addit. 37790 (see excerpt 3.4 for Long Text manuscripts), whose text is a copy of one made in 1413, in Julian's lifetime (below, 2).

Bibliography: Editions of the Short Text are by Frances Beer (1978) and Edmund Colledge and James Walsh (1978); see corrections and commentary by Marion Glasscoe (1989) and further bibliography in excerpt 3.4. On the work's date, see Watson 1993. For a full bibliography to 1991 (little of it relating to the Short Text in particular), see Bradley 1993, 3438–44. Christina von Nolcken (1986) discusses Julian's prose style. B. A. Windeatt (1977) compares the two versions of the text, while Julian's approach to literary authority is discussed by Lynn Staley Johnson (1991). See Warren 1985 for recluses and their patrons and Tanner 1984 for religious life in medieval Norwich. For the devotional milieu in which Julian's work may have been read, see Riddy 1996b.

Source: London, British Library MS Addit. 37790, fols. 97r–97v, 100r–101r: a large collection of theological treatises, written by one scribe, that include a Middle English version of Marguerite Porete's *Mirror of Simple Souls*, various works by Rolle, and much else. The manuscript is a Carthusian production, related to a manuscript (Somerset, Downside Abbey MS 26542, see excerpt 3.6) that belonged to the convent of Dartford. There are numerous corrections in the text, probably not in the scribe's own hand, most of which are adopted here, since they appear well informed.

a. Prologue

There es a visioun schewed be the goodenes of God to a devoute womann and hir name es Julyan that is recluse atte Norwyche and yitt ys onn lyfe *anno domini millesimo CCCCxiii,* in the whilke visyoun er fulle many comfortabylle wordes and gretly styrrande to alle thaye that desyres to be Crystes looverse.

5   I desyrede thre graces be the gyfte of God. The fyrst was to have mynde of Cryste es Passion, the secounde was bodelye syekenes, and the thryd was to have of Goddys gyfte thre woundys. For the fyrste, come to my mynde with devocyon: me thought I hadde grete felynge in the Passyoun of Cryste, botte yitte I desyrede to have mare be the grace of God. Me thought I wolde have bene that tyme with

10   Mary Mawdeleyne and with othere that were Crystes loverse, that I myght have sene bodylye the Passioun of oure Lorde that he sufferede for me, that I myght have sufferede with hym as othere dyd that lovyd him. Notwithstandynge that, I leevyd sadlye alle the peynes of Cryste as Halye Kyrke schewys and techys, and

also the payntyngys of crucyfexes that er made be the grace of God aftere the
15 techynge of Haly Kyrke to the lyknes of Crystes Passyoun, als farfurthe as man ys
witte maye reche.

  And noughtwithstondynge alle this trewe beleve, I desyrede a bodylye syght
whareyn Y myght have more knawynge of bodelye paynes of our Lorde oure
Savyoure, and of the compassyoun of oure Ladye and of alle his trewe loverse that
20 were belevande his paynes that tyme and sythene; for I wolde have beene one of
thame and suffrede with thame. Othere syght of Gode ne schewynge desyrede I
nevere none tylle atte the sawlle were departyd frome the bodye, for I trayste
sothfastlye that I schulde be safe, and this was my menynge; for I wolde aftyr,
becawse of that schewynge, have the more trewe mynde in the Passion of Cryste.

25 For the seconnde, come to my mynde with contricioun, frelye withowtyn any
sekynge, a wylfulle desyre to hafe of goddys gyfte a bodelye syekenes. And I
wolde that this bodylye syekenes myght have beene so harde as to the dede, so that
I myght in the sekenes take alle my ryghtynges of Halye Kyrke, wenande myselfe
that I schulde dye; and that alle creatures that sawe me myght wene the same, for I
30 wolde hafe no comforth of no fleschlye nothere erthelye lyfe. In this sekenes I
desyrede to hafe alle maner of paynes bodelye and gastelye that I schulde have yf I
schulde dye, alle the dredes and tempestes of feyndys and alle manere of thayre
paynes, [safe] of the owgte passynge of the sawlle; for I hope[d] that it mygt be to
me a spede when I schulde dye, for I desyred sone to be with my God.

35 This two desyres of the Passyoun and of the seekenes I desyrede thame with a
condicion, for me thought that it passede the comene course of prayers. And
therfore I sayde, "Lorde, thowe woote whate I wolde. Yf it be thy wille that I
have itt, grawnte itt me. And yf it be nougt thy wille, good Lorde, be nought
dysplesede, for I wille nought botte as thowe wille." This sekenes desyred I yn my
40 thought that Y myght have it whene I were threttye yeere eelde.

  For the thirde, I harde a man telle of Halye Kyrke of the storye of *Saynte
Cecylle*, in the whilke schewynge I undyrstode that sche hadde thre woundys with
a swerde in the nekke, with the whilke sche pynede to the dede. By the styrrynge
of this I conseyvede a myghty desyre, prayande oure Lorde God that he wolde
45 grawnte me three woundys in my lyfe tyme, that es to saye the woundys of
contricyoun, the wounde of compassyoun, [and] the wounde of wylfulle langgynge
to God. Ryght as I askede the othere two with a condyscion, [so] I askyd the
thyrde withowtyn any condyscyoun. This two desyres beforesayde passed fro my
mynde, and the thyrde dwellyd contynuelye.

b. Chapter VI

50 Alle that I sawe of myselfe I meene in the personne of myne evynn-Cristene, for
I am lernede in the gastelye schewynge of oure Lorde that he meenys so. And
therfore I praye yowe alle for Goddys sake, and cownsayle yowe for yowre awne
profyt, that ye leve the behaldynge of the wrechid worlde[s] synfulle creature that
was schewyd unto and that ye myghtlye, wyselye, lovandlye, and mekelye behalde
55 God, that of his curtays love and of his endless goodnes walde schewe generalye
this visyoun in comforthe of us alle. And ye that hyerys and sees this visioun and
this techynge that is of Jhesu Cryste to edificacyon of youre saule, it is Goddys
wille and my desyre that ye take it with als grete joye and lykynge as Jhesu
hadde schewyd it yowe as he did to me.

60   For the schewynge I am not goode but yif Y love God the better; and so may
and so schulde ylke mann do that sees it and heres it with goode wille and trewe
menynge. And so ys my desyre that it schulde be to every ilke manne the same
profytte that I desyrede to myselfe, and therto was styrryd of God in the fyrste
tyme when I sawe itte. For yt [is] common and generale, as we ar alle ane, and I
65   am sekere I sawe it for the profytte of many oder. For sothly it was nought
schewyd unto me for that God loves me bettere than the leste sawlle that is in
grace, for I am sekere thare ys fulle many that nevere hadde schewynge ne syght
botte of the commoun techynge of Haly Kyrke that loves God better than I. For yf
I loke syngulerlye to myselfe I am ryght nought. Botte in generalle, I am in
70   anehede of charyte with all myne evynn-Cristende, for in this anehede of charyte
standes the lyfe of alle mankynde that schalle be safe. For God ys alle that ys
goode and God has made alle that ys made and God loves alle that he has made.
And yyf anye man or womann departe his love fra any of his evynn-Crystenn,
he loves ryght nought, for he loves nought alle; and so that tyme he is nought safe,
75   for he is nought in pees. And he that generaly looves his evynn-Crystynn, he loves
alle that es. For in mankynde that schalle be saffe is comprehende alle that ys: alle
that ys made, and the makere of alle. For yn manne ys God and so in man ys alle.
And he that thus generalye loves alle his evyn-Crystene, he loves alle; and he that
loves thus, he is safe. And thus wille I love, and thus I love, and thus am I safe
80   (for Y mene, in the pesonn of myne evyn-Crystene). And the more I love of this
lovynge whiles I am here, the mare I am lyke to the blysse that I schalle have in
hevene withowten ende—that is, God, that of his endeles love wolde become
owre brothere and suffer for us. And I am sekere that he that behaldes it thus he
schalle be trewly taught and myghttelye comforthtede [if] hym nede comforthe.
85   Botte God forbede that ye schulde saye or take it so that I am a techere, for I
meene nought soo, no I mente nevere so. For I am a womann, leued, febille, and
freylle. Botte I wate wele this that I saye. I hafe it of the schewynge of hym tha[t]
es soverayne techare. Botte sothelye, charyte styrres me to telle yowe it, for I
wolde God ware knawenn and mynn eveynn-Crystenne spede, as I wolde be
90   myselfe, to the mare hatynge of synne and lovynge of God.
       Botte for I am a womann, schulde I therfore leve that I schulde nought telle
yowe the goodenes of God, syne that I sawe in that same tyme that is his wille that
it be knawen? And that schalle ye welle see in the same matere that folowes aftyr,
[if] itte be welle and trewlye takynn. Thane schalle ye sone forgette me that am a
95   wrecche, and dose so that I lette yowe not, and behalde Jhesu that ys techare of
alle. I speke of thame that schalle be safe, for in this tyme God schewyd me non
othere. Bot in alle thynge I lyeve as Haly Kyrke techis, for in alle thynge this
blyssede schewynge of oure Lorde I behelde it as ane in God syght, and I
undyrstode never nathynge thereyn that stonez me no lettes me of the trewe
100 techynge of Halye Kyrke.

2   **yitt** still ∫ **onn lyfe** alive
2–3 *anno domini millesimo CCCCxiii* the year
of our Lord 1413
3   **whilke** which ∫ **er** are ∫ **comfortabylle** comforting. The word is often used by Julian for the
effect her revelation and book are meant to have
(see 56, 84), perhaps in preference to words that
convey a more specific didactic intent and thus a

firmer claim to teaching authority; see the Glossary
for other instances of this word.
4   **styrrande** inspiring ∫ **thaye that** those who ∫
Crystes looverse Christ's lovers (see also 10). Julian
seems to envisage a more or less elite group of
Christians with a special devotion to the humanity
of Jesus. Compare excerpt 1.12: 56–59. For the
devotional assumptions that lie behind this passage

(although it carefully goes beyond them), see, for example, the Middle English versions of Aelred's *De institutione inclusarum,* Bodley MS, chap. 14, or Vernon MS, chaps. 14–17, two translations of one of the earliest Passion meditations in which the reader is instructed to "see" the events of Christ's life and death take place (Ayto and Barratt 1984, 17–22, 39–51). For Passion meditation in general, see Gillespie 1984 and 1987.

5   **I desyrede** The manuscript has a large rubricated capital *S* before "I," presumably anticipating *she* and possibly pointing to a form of the text in which *she* was actually used.

6   **Cryste es** Christ's

7   **come** which came

8   **me thought** it seemed to me

9   **mare** more ∫ **wolde** wished ∫ **that tyme** at that time: the time of the Passion, when Christ's followers saw his pains (18–19). Julian wishes to enter this scene not, as Passion meditation frequently enjoined, in her imagination but in "reality" (in the special sense described in 20n).

10   **Mary Mawdeleyne** Mary Magdalene: the repentant prostitute who became one of Christ's followers and was a frequent image both of the penitent sinner and the ardent lover

11   **bodylye** in the flesh. For Julian, Christ's fleshly suffering needs to be experienced in the flesh.

13   **leevyd** believed ∫ **sadlye** seriously ∫ **Haly Kyrke** holy church: sometimes almost a personified figure in Julian's thought

14   **payntyngys of crucyfexes** painted images (e.g., wall paintings or freestanding sculptures) of the Crucifixion. For the controversy over images, see Aston 1988; for one aspect of its importance here, see Watson 1993.

15   **to the lyknes of** in the image of ∫ **als farfurthe** as far

15–16   **man ys witte** man's wit, that is, human skill. Julian emphasizes that images are made by human beings, implying that this is what makes them unsuitable for her purpose, which is to reach closer to the reality than they can.

17   **noughtwithstondynge** despite

18   **whareyn** in which

20   **were belevande** were believing. Julian imagines the Passion not as occurring at a moment in the past but as perpetually available to Christ's lovers, if they can enter the necessary state of "belevande." This perception of time as cyclic as well as linear is hard to comprehend in our era, where a fiction involving time travel would be the nearest equivalent to her experience. ∫ **sythene** since

21   **thame** them ∫ **schewynge** revelation (a technical term, for Julian)

22   **tylle atte** until ∫ **trayste** trusted

23   **sothfastlye** truly. Julian's trust in her own salvation is interestingly presented here as a sign of her orthodoxy, although formally "hope" in salvation was often distinguished from the certainty implied by "trayste," which was regarded as liable to lead to spiritual pride. ∫ **safe** saved

24   **have the more trewe mynde** have better recollection: that is, in meditation on Christ's death after her religious experience. Julian presents her desire for a "schewynge" as limited in its ambitions, leading directly back to the devotional practices from which it emerges.

26   **wylfulle desyre** an urgent wish: a wish proceeding directly from her will, or *affectus,* the part of her soul or mind that in much late medieval contemplative theory longs for union with God. For the role of the *affectus* in contemplative theory, see Gillespie 1982.

27   **so harde as to the dede** severe to the point of death

28   **ryghtynges** last rites: final confession followed by the adminstration of holy oil, or extreme unction ∫ **wenande** believing

29   **creatures** people, or, literally, all created beings: possibly including the demons who come to tempt Julian and the guardian angel whose job it is to console her

30–34   **In this sekenes . . . God** Julian's desire for an experience akin to death includes the desire to be tempted by devils and suffer the fears associated with dying, often anatomized in religious writings in the *disce mori* (learn to die) tradition. The most widely disseminated example is the *Boke of Craft of Dying,* translated c. 1410 from Gerson's *Ars moriendi* (described by Raymo [1986, 2361–64]), which includes many of the topoi concerning death Julian would have known.

33   **[safe]** except (added by the corrector and arguably unnecessary) ∫ **owgte passynge of the sawlle** the soul's departure [from the body] ∫ **hope[d]** *d* added by corrector (and arguably unnecessary)

34   **spede** help

36   **it passede the comene course of prayers** it went beyond the usual path taken by prayers. Here Julian is acknowledging that to request a vision is, indeed, unusual, but is also finding a way to stress (37–39) that her vision was given by God's grace, not manufactured.

37   **woote whate I wolde** know what I want

39   **I wille nought botte as thowe wille** I only want what [literally, according to what] you want

40   **thought** Long Text manuscripts read *youth* here, which may be correct. ∫ **threttye yeere eelde** Christ's age when he began his ministry, according to

medieval belief (see excerpt 1.12: 10–12, for Christ's thirty-three years of life). Julian's illness is important to her as the beginning of a closer approach to Christ's Passion, rather than as the end of her life.

41 I harde a man telle of Halye Kyrke Julian emphasizes her dependence on oral instruction (despite her obvious learning) as part of her self-presentation as "a womann, leued, febille, and freylle" (86–87).

41–42 *Saynte Cecylle* Saint Cecilia: one of the most popular of the apocryphal virgin martyrs of the early church. See the entry under her name in Farmer 1978; compare excerpt 3.10: 23–30. Her story is told in Chaucer's *Second Nun's Tale*. The Long Text removes this reference.

42–43 thre woundys with a swerde in the nekke Cecilia is killed with a sword, but her executioner fails to dispatch her after three blows, and she preaches for three days, converting many, before she dies. The allegorization of the wounds given here (43–47) is not known elsewhere. Julian does not make the connection, but perhaps this story lay behind her desire to survive her sickness.

46–47 contricyoun . . . compassyoun . . . wylfulle langgynge to God sorrow for sin, compassion for Christ's suffering, and desire for union with God. The catalogue is structured as a spiritual "ladder" to heaven. In calling these feelings "woundys" (45), Julian draws on a tradition of applying erotic language to religious experience, which derives from allegorical interpretations of the Song of Songs and from religious applications of "Ovidian" poetry. ʃ **[and], [so]** added by corrector

50 Alle that I sawe of myselfe I meene in the personne of myne evynn-Cristene (a corrector has added *alle* before "myne" above the line in the MS) In this passage, Julian asks her readers to look beyond her and to understand her use of first-person pronouns as referring by extension to every Christian. "In the personne of" translates Latin *in persona*, often used in biblical exegesis to point out that (e.g.) David or Job is speaking "on behalf of" a larger group. ʃ **for** because

51 lernede taught ʃ **gastelye schewynge** spiritual revelation. In the chapter after this (chap. 7), Julian distinguishes three kinds of revelation: bodily, "ghostly" (spiritual), and verbal.

52 cownsayle (MS *cownsayles*) Julian is about to insist that she is not a "techere" (85), so her use of a word that applies to advice given between equals is calculated.

53 leve the behaldynge stop giving attention to

53–54 wrechid worlde[s] synfulle creature that was schewyd unto In the manuscript, a hand not the scribe's has added *worme,* apparently correcting "worlde," and added *it* before "was schewyd."

55 curtays courteous (i.e., noble, courtly). Julian regularly describes God as a courtly lover, but also emphasizes that his courtliness is not grandly distant but intimate, or "homely." ʃ **walde schewe generalye** wants to reveal publicly. The vision is first shown to Julian but needs to be passed on to her fellow Christians. Although the context of this explanation of God's purposes is a passage emphasizing Julian's desire to fade from the reader's view, it also operates as an authorizing strategy that implicitly equates her book with the revelation she has received.

56 hyerys and sees The phrase anticipates both hearers and viewers of the book.

57 this techynge that is of Jhesu Cryste The book contains teaching, but it is Christ's, not Julian's.

58 desyre MS *desyrere* ʃ **als** as ʃ **as** as if

60 For because of ʃ **but** except

61 ylke each

61–62 trewe menynge honest intention

62 to every ilke for each and every

63 styrryd moved

64 [is] not in MS ʃ **common and generale, as we ar alle ane** The revelation is not secret but consists of material that needs to be publicly proclaimed. Julian here identifies herself not as a privileged member of the group of "Crystes looverse" (4) but as a representative of common Christian humanity. ʃ **ane** one

65 sekere certain ʃ **oder** others ʃ **sothly** truly

66 for that because ʃ **leste sawlle** least soul

66–67 in grace in a state of grace

68 botte except

69 syngulerlye exclusively ʃ **Botte** but

70 anehede oneness ʃ **evynn-Cristende** fellow Christians

71 standes depends ʃ **safe** saved

73–84 And yyf . . . comforthe The passage continues to build an imagined audience of all Christians, who are joined in charity, so that Julian is not entitled to exclude anyone from her revelation, while no Christian of "trewe menynge" (61–62) is entitled to exclude her by refusing to hear her. The invocation of spiritual *amicitia* here is similar to that in texts like *Speculum Devotorum* (excerpt 1.12; see 1–5n), but Julian applies the language of equality more broadly than that text.

73 yyf if ʃ **departe** withdraw ʃ **fra** from

74 safe assured of salvation

80 for Y mene . . . evyn-Crystene for I mean as the representative of my fellow Christians

81 mare I am lyke to the blysse the closer I come to experiencing the bliss ʃ MS repeats *that I*

82 that is, God That is, the "blysse" of heaven is God.

83 sekere certain ʃ **behaldes** beholds

84 **[if]** added on line by corrector

85–87 **Botte God forbede . . . freylle** Julian's assertion that she is not a "techere" is striking, since all Christians were expected to teach, even though pastoral theorists sometimes tried to confine the teaching role of women to other women (see Gillespie 1980). The Long Text removes this passage, including the references to Julian's supposedly "womanly" frailty.

86 **leued** ignorant

87 **freylle** frail ∫ **wate** know ∫ **tha[t]** MS *thas*

88 **soverayne** chief ∫ **charyte styrres me** charity moves me. Compare, for example, Bokenham's use of the same topos, excerpt 1.11: 194–95 and note. ∫ **yowe** [to] you

89 **ware knawenn** were known ∫ **spede** helped

90 **mare** greater ∫ **hatynge** hating

91 **leve** believe

92 **syne** since

92–93 **sawe in that same tyme that is his wille that it be knawen** Julian never specifies how, and at what point in her vision ("the same matere that folowes aftyr" [93]), God declared to her his desire that it be made public, and this absence of a prophetic commission evidently constituted a problem for her. It is also unusual, for most women visionaries give clear accounts of God's instructing them to write. See, for example, *The Book of Margery Kempe*, excerpt 1.14: 73–75, and Voaden 1996c.

94 **[if]** added above the line by a hand not the scribe's ∫ **welle and trewlye takynn** properly received

95 **wrecche** wretched [creature] ∫ **dose so** do so ∫ **that I lette yowe not** [in such a manner] that I do not impede you

96–97 **non othere** no others

99 **stonez** dismays ∫ **no** nor ∫ **lettes** hinders ∫ **of** in

1.14 MARGERY KEMPE, *THE BOOK OF MARGERY KEMPE:* TWO PROLOGUES

Date and Provenance: The *Book* was written during the 1430s in King's Lynn (then called Bishop's Lynn) in East Anglia, when the author was in her sixties.

Author, Sources, and Nature of Text: One of the two great original Middle English works certainly by women, *The Book of Margery Kempe* is often described as the first autobiography in English—although "autohagiography" would be more accurate. The book is an account of the religious life of a woman from a wealthy merchant-class background who, in her late thirties, underwent a conversion in which she dedicated her life to Christ, while remaining a married lay member of her community. Parts of the book concern her conversations with Christ and religious education (see excerpt 3.22); parts recount her journeys both within England and across Europe to Jerusalem, Rome, Compostella, and Prussia; and much of it is concerned with her many difficulties in gaining acceptance for her career as an unenclosed woman. The work was rediscovered in the 1930s and has been controversial ever since, sometimes evoking scorn for its protagonist reminiscent of the scorn she appears to have aroused in some of her contemporaries. How-

ever, the view that the *Book* is a planned and executed account, rather than the mere effusion it seemed to its first modern readers, has been steadily gaining ground (see, e.g., Staley 1994).

The *Book* has two prologues, the longer of them (placed first but by its own account composed last) apparently by Kempe's second scribe, a priest friend. This prologue is partly a confession by the priest of his role in delaying the book's composition for four years, written after he has finally forced himself to read an earlier scribe's almost illegible manuscript and has recopied a portion of it. As such, it gives a detailed account of the *Book*'s tortuous genesis, an account that tells us a good deal about the difficulties an illiterate layperson could have in gaining entry into the world of writing and about the conflicting impulses the prospect of writing a book aroused in Kempe and her supporters. But the prologue should also be read as the priest's tribute to the importance of the book he is copying and his attempt to provide it with what he and perhaps Kempe think a fitting opening, sprinkled with biblical allusions and written in an appropriately formal (and syntactically extended) style. The second prologue (copied second in the manuscript though presented as written earlier) is a much balder statement of textual origins and authorizations, a template whose every element is greatly expanded in the more elaborate opening prologue. Whether or not the origins and writers of the two prologues are semifictionalized by Kempe (Staley Johnson 1991), their coexistence provides good evidence for contemporary understandings of the function and nature of the prologue as literary form. Given the increasing conservatism of English spirituality in the decades between the *Book*'s genesis and its completion (see 76–77n), the creation of the more elaborate prologue may have been a response to a perceived need for still greater authorization. Presented as the growth of confidence in the project on the part of both amanuensis and visionary, the increased specificity of the first prologue in relation to the shorter version is gained through intensified application and development of prologue conventions.

Audience and Circulation: The book survives in a single manuscript that was owned at one time by the Carthusian house of Mount Grace in Yorkshire, where it was extensively annotated and evidently carefully read. There is no other evidence of the text's medieval circulation in its full form, and it is unlikely to have been read widely. Like that of Julian of Norwich (excerpts 1.13 and 3.4), Kempe's reception in late medieval England seems confined in comparison with the circulation and status of Continental writers such as Bridget of Sweden and Mechtild of Hackeborn (see excerpt 3.20). Excerpts from the work were printed by Wynkyn de Worde around 1501 as "a short treatyse of contemplacyon taught by our lorde Jhesu Cryste, or taken out of the boke of Margerie kempe of lynn" (in the 1521 reprint by Henry Pepwell, this last phrase reads "Margerie kempe *ancresse* of lynn"), and it was in this reduced and conventionalized form that Kempe's book was most widely read before modern times.

Bibliography: The text is edited by Sanford Brown Meech and Hope Emily Allen (1940) and by Staley (1996); Alexandra Barratt (1992, 177–204) edits excerpts. The text has been much discussed, especially in the last two decades: for a bibliography to 1992, see Lagorio and Sargent 1993, 3444–45. For a collection of essays on Kempe, see McEntire 1992. On Kempe and authority, see Lochrie 1986 and 1991; Beckwith 1992a; Lawton 1992; Watt 1997. On the role of the second scribe, see Hirsh 1975, opposed by Staley Johnson (1991, developed in Staley 1994). For further bibliography, see excerpt 3.22.

Source: London, British Library MS Addit. 61823, fols. 1r–3v. This tidy paper manuscript from the mid–fifteenth century contains only the *Book*. The scribe names himself Salthows (fol. 123r), the name of a Norfolk village, and his dialect and orthography were probably close to that of Kempe's priest-scribe, from whose copy he may have worked (note the characteristic East Anglian *x* for *sh*). The text has many marginal comments, some of them by Carthusian readers, many pertaining to Kempe's religious experiences and suggesting parallels (see Lochrie 1991, chap. 6; Staley 1996).

a. Prologue 1

Liber Montis Gracie. This boke is of MounteGrace

Here begynnythe a schort tretys and a comfortabyl fore synful wrecchys, wherein thei may have gret solas and comfort to hem, and undyrstondyne the hy and unspecabyl mercy of owere sovereyne Savyowre, Cryst Jhesu, whos name be
5 worschepd and magnyfyed wythowten ende, that now in owere days to us unworthy deyneth to exercysene hys nobeley and hys goodnesse.
Alle the werkys of owere Saviowre ben for owere exampyl and instruccyone, and what grace that he werkyth in any creature is owere profyth, yf lak of charyte be

not owere hynderawnce. And therfore, be the leve of owere mercyful lord Cryst
10 Jhesu, to the magnyfying of hys holy name, Jhesu, this lytyl tretys schal tretyn
sumdeel in parcel of hys wonderful werkys: how mercyfully, how benyngly, and
how charytefully he meved and stered a synful caytyf unto hys love, wheche synful
caytyf many yerys was in wyl and in purpose thorw steryng of the Holy Gost to
folwyne [owre] Savyowr, makyng gret behestys of fastyngys wythe many other
15 dedys of penawns. And evyr sche was turned ayen abak in tyme of temptacyone
leche unto the reedspyre wheche boweche wythe every wynd and nevyr is stable, les
than no wynd bloweth; unto the tyme that owere mercyfulle lord, Cryst Jhesu,
havyng pety and compassyon of hys handwerke and hys creature, turnyd helthe
into sekenesse, prosperyte into adversyte, worshep into repref, and love into
20 hatered. Thus alle this thyngys turnyng up-so-downe, this creature, whych many
yerys had gon wyl and evyr bene unstable, was parfythly drawene and steryd to
entren the wey of hy perfeccyone, wheche parfythe wey Cryst, owere Savyowre, in
hys propyre persoone examplyd. Sadly he trad it and dewly he went it beforne.
         Than this creature, of whom thys tretys thorw the mercy of Jhesu schal
25 schewene in party the leyvyng, towched be the hand of owyre Lord wyth grett
bodyly sekenesse, wherethorw sche lost resone and here wyttes a long tyme tyl
owere Lord be grace restoryde here ageyne, as it schal more openly be schewed
aftyrward. Here werdly goodys, wheche were plentyuows and abundawnt at that
day, in lytyl whyle aftere were ful bareyne and bare. Than was pompe and pryde
30 cast downe and leyd on syde. Thei that beforne had worshepd here sythene
ful scharply reprevyd here; here kynred and thei that had ben frendys were nowe
hyre most enmys.
         Than sche, consyderyng this wondyrful chawngyng, sekyng socowr undyr the
wengys of hyre gostly modyre Holy Cherche, went and obeyd hyre to hyre gostly
35 fadyr, accusyng hyreself of here mysdedys, and sythene ded gret bodyly penawns.
And in schort tyme owere mercyful Lord vysytyd this creature wyth plentyouws
teerys of contricyone day be day, in so meche that sum men seydene sche mygthe
wepene whane sche wolde, and slawndered the werk of God. Sche was so usyd to
be slawndred and repreved, to be chedene and rebuked of the world, for grace and
40 vertu wyth wheche sche was indued thorw the strengthe of the Holy Gost, that it
was to here in a manyr of solas and comfort whan sche sufferyd any dysese for the
lofe of God and for the grace that God wrowht in hyre. For evyr the more
slawndere and repref that sche sufferyd, the more sche incresyd in grace and in
devocyone of holy medytacyone, of hy contemplacyon, and of wonderful spechys
45 and dalyawns whech owr Lord spak and dalyid to hyre sowle, techyng hyre how
sche schuld be despysed for hys lofe, how sche schuld hane pacyens, settyng alle
hyre trost, alle hyre lofe, and alle hyre affeccyon in hym only. Sche knew and
undyrstod many secret and prevy thyngys wheche schuld beffallen aftyrward, be
inspiracyone of the Holy Gost. And oftenetymes, whel sche was kept wyth swech
50 holy spechys and dalyawns, sche schuld so wepyne and sobbyne that many men
were gretly a-wondyr, for thei wystene ful lytyl how homly owere Lord was in
hyre sowle. Ne hyreself cowd nevyr telle the grace that sche felt, it was so hevenly,
so hy aboven hyre resone and hyre bodyly wyttys, and hyre body so febyl in tyme
of the presens of grace that sche mythe nevyr expressyn it wyth here word lyche as
55 sche felt it in hyre sowle.
         Than had this creature meche drede for illusyons and deceytys of hyre gostly
enmys. Than went sche be the byddynge of the Holy Gost to many worshepful

clerkys, bothe archebysshopys and bysshoppys, doctowrs of dyvynyte and
bachelers also. Sche spak also wyth many ankrys, and schewed hem hyre maner of
60 levyng and sweche grace as the Holy Gost of hys goodnesse wrowt in hyre mende
and in hyre sowle, as here wytt wold serven hyre to expressyn it. And thei alle
that sche schewed hyre secretys unto seyd sche was meche bownde to loven owere
Lord for the grace that he schewyd unto hyre, and cownseld hyre to folwyne hyre
mevynggys and hyre steringgys and trustly belevyne it werene of the Holy Gost
65 and of noone evyl spyryt. Summe of these worthy and worshepful clerkys tokyne
it in perel of here sowle, and as thei wold answere to God, that this creature was
inspyred wyth the Holy Gost, and bodyne hyr that sche schuld don hem wrytene
and makyne a booke of hyre felyngys and hire revelacyons. Sum proferyd hire to
wrytyn hyr felyngys wyth here owen handys, and sche wold not consentyn in no
70 wey, for sche was comawndyd in hire sowle that sche schuld not wrytyne so soone.
And so it was xx yere and more fro that tym this creature had fyrst felyngys and
revelacyons er than sche dede any wryten.

Aftyrward, whan it plesyd owere Lord, he comawnded hyre and chargyd hire
that sche xuld don wrytene hyre felyngys and revelacyons and the forme of here
75 levyng, that hys goodnesse mythe be knowyne to alle the world. Than had the
creature no wrytyr that wold fulfyllyne hyre desyre ne yeve credens to hire
felingys, unto the tyme that a man dwellyng in Dewchelond wheche was an
Englyschman in hys byrthe and sythene weddyd in Dewchland and had there bothe
a wyf and a chyld, havyng good knowlache of this creature and of hire desyre,
80 meved I trost thorw the Holy Gost, cam into Yngland wyth hys wyfe and hys
goodys and dwellyd wyth the forseyd creature, tyl he had wretyne as meche as sche
wold tellyn hyme for the tyme that thei were togyddere. And sythene he deyd.

Than was ther a prest wheche this creature had great affeccyone to, and so sche
comownd wyth hym of this mater and browte hyme the boke to redyne. The booke
85 was so evel wretyne that he cowd lytyl skylle theron, for it was neithyr good
Englysche ne Dewche, ne the lettyr was not schapyne ne formyd as other letters
bene. Therfore the prest leved fully ther schuld nevyr man redyn it, but it were
special grace. Nevyrthelesse, he behyte hire that if he cowd redyne it he wolde
copyn it owt and wrytyn it betyr wyth good wulle.
90 Thane was ther so evel spekyng of this creature and of hire wepyng that the
prest durst not for cowardyse speke wyth here but seldom, ne not wold wrytene as
he had behestyd unto the forseyd creature. And so he voyded and deferryd the
wrytyng of this boke wel onto a iiii yere or ellys more, notwythstandyng the
creature cryed oftene one hyme therfore. At the last he seyd onto hire that he
95 cowd not redyne it, wherfore he wold not do it: he wold not, he seyd, put hyme in
perel therof. Thane he cownseld hire to gone to a good man wheche had ben
meche conversawnt wyth hym that wrot fyrst the booke, supposyng that he schuld
cun best rede the booke, for he had sumtym red letters of the other mannys
wrytyng sent fro beyondene the see, whyl he was in Dewchland. And so sche went
100 to that man, preyng hym to wrytyn this booke and nevyr to bewreyn it as long as
sche leved, grawntyng hyme a grett summe of good for his labowr. And this good
man wrot abowt a leef, and yet it was lytyl to the purpose, for he cowd not
wel fare therewythe, the boke was so evel sett and so unresonably wretyn.

Than the prest was vexyd in his consciens, for he had behestyd hyre to wrytyn
105 this boke, yyf he mygth com to the redyng therof, and dede not hys part as wel as
he myght a do, and preyd this creature to getyn ageyn the boke yf sche myth

goodly. Than sche gat ageyn the book and browt it to the preste wyth rygthe glad
chere, preyng hym to do hys good wyl, and sche schuld prey to God for hym and
purchasyn hym grace to reden it and wrytyn it also. The preste, trustyng in hire
110   prayers, began to redyn this booke, and it was myche more esy, as hym thowt,
than it was beforne tyme. And so he red it ovyr beforne this creature every word,
sche sumtym helpyng where ony difficulte was.

    Thys boke is not wretyn in ordyr, every thyng aftyr other as it were done, but
lyche as the matere cam to the creature in mend whan it schuld be wretyne, for it
115   was so long er it was wretyne that sche had forgetyn the tyme and the ordyr whan
thyngys befellyn. And therfore sche dede nothing wryten but that sche knew rygth
wel for very trewth. Whan the prest began fyrst to wryten on this booke, hys eyn
myssyd so that he mygth not se to make hys lettyr ne mygth not se to mend hys
penne. Alle other thyng he mygth se wel anow. He sett a peyr of spectacles on hys
120   nose, and thane wast wel wers than it was before. He compleyned to the creature
of hys dysese. Sche seyd hys enmy had envye at hys good dede and wold lett hym
yf he mygth, and bad hym do as wel as God wold yeve hym grace and not levyne.
Whan he cam ageyn to hys booke, he myth se as wel, hym thowt, as evyr he dede
before, be day-lyth and be candel-lygth bothe. And for this cause, whan he had
125   wretyn a qwayre, he addyd a leef therto, and than wrot he this proym to expressyn
more openly than doth the next folwynge, wheche was wretyn er than this. *Anno*
domini mlo.cccc.xxxvi

b. Prologue 2

A schort tretys of a creature sett in grett pompe and pride of the world, wheche
sythen was drawyn to owere Lord be gret poverte, sekenes, schamis, and gret
130   reprevys in many divers contres and places, of wheche tribulacyons sum schal ben
schewed aftyr, not in ordyr as it fellyn but as the creature cowd han mend of hem
whan it were wretyne, for it was xx yere and more fro tyme this creature had
forsake the world and besyly clef onto ower Lord or this boke was wretyne,
notwythestondynge this creature had greet cownsel for to done wrytene hire
135   tribulacyons and hire felingys, and a Whyte Frere proferyd hire to wryten frely yf
sche wold. And sche was warnyd in hyre spyrit that sche xuld not wryte so sone.
And many yerys aftyr sche was bodyn in hyre spyrit for to wrytyne. And than yet
it was wretyn fyrst be a man wheche cowd neithyr wel wryten Englysche ne
Duche, so it was unable for to be red but only be specyal grace, for ther was so
140   meche obloquie and slawndyre of this creature that ther wold fewe men beleve this
creature. And so at the last a preste was sore mevyd for to wrytin this tretys, and
he cowd not wel redyn it of a iiii yere togedyre. And sythen be the request of this
creature and compellyng of hys owyne consciens he asayd agayne for to rede it,
and it was meche more esy than it was aforetyme. And so he gan to wryten in the
145   yere of owre Lord a m.cccc.xxxvi on the day next aftyr Mary Maudelyne, aftyr the
informacyone of this creature.

---

1   Mount Grace was a Carthusian monastery
in Yorkshire, among whose priors was Nicholas
Love (see excerpt 3.10). This indication of ownership is written on the flyleaf of the manuscript,
before fol. 1r, on which the text itself begins.

2   **a schort tretys and a comfortabyl** a short and
comforting treatise
3   **to hem** for themselves
5   **that who ∫ in owere days** in our time. It is a
topos of saints' lives that saints are a channel be-

tween the earthly and heavenly life of Christ and what is usually seen as a corrupt and enfeebled present. See also Heb. 1:1–2.

6 **deyneth** condescends ∫ **nobeley** nobility

7 **Alle the werkys . . . instruccyone** an adaptation of 2 Tim. 3:16, where, however, it is the Scriptures (not Christ's works as such) that are so described. The verse opens Nicholas Love's *Mirror of the Blessed Life of Jesus Christ* (excerpt 3.10), which Margery Kempe probably knew, where it is applied to reading the life of Christ.

8–9 **yf lak of charyte be not owere hynderawnce** if we are not prevented by lack of charity. The implication is that those who fail to see Christ's work in the *Book* do so through their own fault. Compare Julian of Norwich, excerpt 1.13: 73–84.

9 **leve** permission

10–11 **tretyn sumdeel in parcel of** describe in some small part

12 **caytyf** wretch. The term is current in religious works of the period. Compare excerpt 3.6: 2, a work named after the phrase the author uses to describe himself, "pore caityf."

13 **in wyl and in purpose** in desire and intention ∫ **steryng** inner impulse

14 **[owre]** added in red above the line by the scribe ∫ **behestys** vows

16 **leche unto the reedspyre** like the reed. See James 1:6.

16–17 **les than** unless

19 **worshep into repref** honor into humiliation

20 **up-so-downe** upside down

21 **gon wyl** been wayward

22 **the wey of hy perfeccyone** the road to high perfection: an image for a life fully dedicated to the imitation of Christ, as distinct from the life of common Christians

22–23 **in hys propyre persoone examplyd** exemplified in his own life

23 **Sadly he trad it and dewly he went it beforne** soberly he trod it and dutifully he traveled it before

24–28 **Than this creature . . . aftyrward** This sentence has no main clause. The passage that it introduces conflates more than a decade of Kempe's life into a single incident, and pays much more attention than the main narrative does to the role of "hyre gostly modyre Holy Cherche" (34).

25 **the leyvyng** the manner of life

27 **more openly be schewed** be more fully revealed

28 **werdly** earthly

29 **bareyne** reduced

30 **on syde** aside ∫ **worshepd** honored ∫ **sythene** afterward

31 **reprevyd** rebuked

32 **most** greatest

33 **socowr** help

34 **wengys** wings ∫ **gostly** spiritual ∫ **obeyd hyre** humbled herself. The parallel mention of the church as "gostly modyre" and a confessor as "gostly fadyr" had become a commonplace by the fifteenth century. In the main narrative (chap. 1), it is Kempe's madness, not its healing, that is caused by her confessor, while her conversion to Christ is presented (chap. 2) as independent of ecclesiastical involvement.

36–37 **plentyouws teerys of contricyone** Before and especially after her pilgrimage to Jerusalem, Kempe was much given to tears and sometimes "roaring," manifestations of devotion that have parallels elsewhere but were often thought, even by Kempe herself, to be in excess of anything legitimized by those parallels. See McEntire 1990.

37 **in so meche that** to the extent that

38 **whane sche wolde** whenever she wanted to

39 **chedene** chided

40 **indued** imbued

40–41 **it was to here . . . dysese** she experienced it, in a way, as reassurance and comfort when she suffered any distress: an adaptation of James 1:2–3

42 **wrowht** made

43–44 **in devocyone . . . contemplacyon** in the devotional practices of holy meditation, of high contemplation. The theoretical distinction between devotion and contemplation is not in practice maintained through most of the *Book*.

45 **dalyawns** amorous talk or spiritual conversation. Christ's conversation with Kempe is repeatedly referred to as a love dalliance throughout the *Book*. The image is found in England from the early-thirteenth-century *Ancrene Wisse* onward and derives from the Song of Songs.

46 **hane** have

47–48 **Sche knew . . . aftyrward** Kempe's prophetic knowledge of the future distinguished her sharply from Julian of Norwich, who consistently insists on the impossibility of such knowledge.

49 **whel sche was kept wyth** while she was experiencing

50 **schuld** "would" or "had to." Many sections of *The Book of Margery Kempe* are concerned to establish the involuntary (i.e., divinely inspired) nature of Kempe's weeping.

51 **wystene** knew ∫ **homly** intimate: a word also used by Julian of Norwich for God's dealings with the soul

53 **bodyly wyttys** bodily senses: an allusion to the distinction between the bodily and the spiritual senses, the latter having access to experience the former cannot grasp or describe

53–54 **in tyme of the presens of grace** in the time when grace was present: that is, when Kempe's religious experiences were actually in progress. The allusion is to spiritual "ravishment," which is frequently said, in English and Continental mystical texts, to weaken those who experience it. A literary influence for the topos is Song of Songs 2:5, *Quia amore langueo* (because I languish for love).

56–57 illusyons and deceytys of hyre gostly enmys illusions and tricks of her spiritual enemies. Kempe's fear of being deceived by the devil is amply demonstrated in the *Book* and is traditionally thought of (as here) as a proof of spiritual authenticity.

57–61 Than went sche . . . expressyn it Kempe's various journeys to parts of England to consult with experts on the validity of her experience take up much of the first part of the *Book*.

59 bachelers those who have taken the lowest degree (here, in divinity) conferred by a university ∫ **ankrys** anchorites. These include Julian of Norwich, with whom Kempe talked over a period of several days on a visit to Norwich, c. 1415 (*Book*, chap. 17).

59–60 maner of levyng like "forme of . . . levyng" (74–75) below, a technical phrase for the particular way Kempe lives the godly life and her dealings with the divine

63–64 hyre mevynggys and hyre steringgys her [spiritual] promptings and impulses

65–68 Summe of these worthy and worshepful clerkys . . . makyne a booke Compare the second prologue (128–46), on which this prologue is probably drawing, where only one clerk, a White Friar, is mentioned.

66 here their

67 bodyne bade ("commanded," not "asked")

67–68 don hem wrytene and makyne a booke get them to write and make a book. The phrasing leaves the initiative for writing and the authority of the resulting text in Kempe's hands.

69–70 sche wold not consentyn . . . not wrytyne so soone The authority conferred in the command of churchmen ("bodyne" [67]) is superseded by the authority of God, the source of commands to the soul.

72 dede any wryten had any [of her revelations] written down. Again, the phrase makes Kempe the source of her own book, as the subsequent narrative emphasizes.

74–75 forme of . . . levyng alludes to a genre of the prescriptive and exemplary treatise. Compare *The Form of Living* written, together with the *English Psalter* (excerpt 3.8), for Margaret Kirkeby by Richard Rolle (compare 13n above).

76–77 fulfyllyne hyre desyre . . . felingys fulfill her wish [to have her revelations written down] or

give credence to her spiritual sensations: a clause that makes it clear that Kempe's problem, once she came to write, was not lack of contact with potential scribes as such but lack of scribes who believed in her. Between c. 1415, when the initial offers to write her book seem to have been made, and the mid-1430s, when the *Book* was actually written, her own local status seems to have declined (as later chapters make clear), while English spirituality grew more conservative.

77 Dewchelond Germany: probably specifically the area around Danzig, now Gdansk in Poland

77–78 an Englyschman This seems to be Kempe's oldest son.

84 comownd wyth hym spoke intently with him. "Comownd" is the modern "communed."

84–85 The booke . . . skylle theron the book was so badly written that he was able to reach little understanding of it. Kempe's son was a merchant who probably used writing strictly for business matters and whose script may have been influenced by his time abroad (probably in Prussia).

86 Dewche German

87–88 nevyr man redyn . . . special grace Yet again poor literacy is understood not merely as a problem but as an opportunity to insist upon a text's divine authorization.

88 behyte promised

89 copyn it owt and wrytyn it betyr Note that the priest's offer is only to make a fair copy of Kempe's own book, not (as John Hirsh [1975] suggests) to rewrite it.

92 behestyd promised ∫ **voyded** avoided

94 cryed oftene one hyme therfore often begged him for it

95–96 he wold not, he seyd, put hym in perel therof he would not, he said, put himself in danger on account of it

97 conversawnt intimate

98 cun best rede best know how to read

100 nevyr to bewreyn it never to reveal it. Many saintly narratives express a desire that the book be hidden during the author's lifetime.

103 evel sett and so unresonably wretyn badly set down and written quite without reason

106–7 yf sche myth goodly if she could tactfully manage to do it

109 purchasyn win

110 hym thowt it seemed to him

112 sche sumtym helpyng where ony difficulte was with her helping sometimes where there was any difficulty. This may suggest that Kempe herself could partly read her son's handwriting (thus, that she could, after all, read, if not write), and implies that as much of her *Book* as her son was able to transcribe was already in finished form.

113–17 Thys boke is not wretyn in ordyr . . . very trewth Parts of the book are in fact in chronological order, and although much is not, this account of the process by which Kempe wrote what came "in mend" should not be taken to imply that the process of composition was casual or haphazard. Though couched as a modesty or inadequacy topos (compare, e.g., Bokenham, excerpt 1.11: 33), this is a strong claim to authority.

116 dede nothing wryten had nothing written ∫ **but** except ∫ **that** what

118 myssyd failed

120 wast wel wers it was even worse

121 hys enmy that is, the devil ∫ **lett** hinder

122 not levyne not give up

124 day-lyth daylight

125 qwayre a quire: probably a gathering of eight leaves, to which the priest has now added a preliminary first leaf for his new prologue. Interestingly, if the first prologue indeed took up a single leaf, the first quire would originally have ended around the place where Kempe is commended by Archbishop Arundel (chap. 16, fol. 18 of the surviving manuscript). Perhaps it was the copying of this scene that gave the priest the impetus to add the new prologue. ∫ **proym** prologue (from medieval Latin, *prohemium*) ∫ **expressyn** explain

126–27 Anno domini mlo.cccc.xxxvi the year of our Lord 1436

130 reprevys reproaches ∫ **divers contres** different regions

131 han mend remember

133 clef cleaved ∫ **or** before

135 a Whyte Frere the Carmelite friar Alan of Lynn: author of numerous (apparently lost) theological and exegetical works in Latin, who may have died in 1421: Kempe's confessor and most distinguished long-term friend and supporter

137 bodyn in hyre spyrit commanded in her spirit

140 obloquie scorn

142 sythen afterward

143 asayd tried

145 the day next aftyr Mary Maudelyne the day after the feast of Mary Magdalene [July 22], that is, July 23 ∫ **aftyr** according to

1.15 THE GENERAL PROLOGUE TO THE WYCLIFFITE BIBLE: CHAPTER 12 (EXTRACT)

Date and Provenance: probably 1390s; probably Oxford (the author's remark that a number of books are not available to him [42–47] may suggest the prologue was written elsewhere, away from a library: the translation itself was almost certainly made in Oxford).

Author, Sources, and Nature of Text: The *Wycliffite Bible* was the first complete translation of the Bible into English. Work on it probably began in Oxford during the 1380s and continued for at least a decade, comprising the translation itself (made from the standard Latin, or Vulgate, translation by Jerome), much work on the Latin text, and systematic reference to the best biblical scholarship available. Two complete versions survive: the Early Version and the more idiomatic and widely circulated Late Version (there are also intermediate copies). While Wyclif himself favored such a translation, there is no evidence that he had a hand in its making, although one of his associates, such as Nicholas Hereford, may well have helped set the project up; as Anne Hudson argues (1988, chap. 5), the two versions must have been the work of a team. If so, we need not assume that the project was entirely driven by a single ideology of church reform, or that all the collaborators could even have been characterized as Wycliffite. Certainly, numerous prologues to the translation circulated, and although the so-called *General Prologue* to the Late Version extracted here was written (after the Late Version was done) by a member of the translation team, it should perhaps be taken as a polemical interpretation of the project, not a definitive statement of its aims. The *General Prologue* as a whole covers a wide range of topics, including a summary of the biblical narrative and its account of God's dealing with his people. The twelfth chapter, extracted here, offers a summary of exegetical theory, with special attention to the problems of figurative interpretation, and praises the truths to be found in close attention to God's word. (It was claimed by opponents of biblical translation that figurative meanings did not survive in translation and were incomprehensible to the uneducated.) Chapter 12 emphasizes the primacy of the literal sense of the Bible and claims that a competent reading demands of the reader charity alone (compare excerpts 1.13: 73–84, 1.14: 7–15, 2.5): a claim whose radical implications for the clergy's role as guardians of truth—since the vernacular Bible is open to all readers who live virtuously, learned or unlearned—are only partly tempered by the passage's focus on the need to study.

Audience and Circulation: Two hundred and fifty copies of the Wycliffite Bible in one version or another survive, and while many of these are now incomplete and most never contained more than selections, this is a huge number, representing much the most ambitious attempt to ensure the broad distribution of any Middle English text. Almost all these manuscripts were professional productions, copied in a standard Midland dialect by scribes working in organized groups, with a degree of systematization that anticipates the print era. They were owned both by individual laypeople, such as Thomas, duke of Gloucester (who wrote his name in a Late Version copy as early as 1397), and by Lollard groups (Hudson 1988, 232–34), as well as by secular priests and others. The text was banned after Arundel's *Constitutions* of 1409, but how far it was thought of as "Wycliffite" by most of its readers is unclear. By the early sixteenth century, Thomas More could believe that this translation was made

as an episcopally approved alternative to Wyclif's version (Deanesly 1920, 1–10). The *General Prologue*, on the other hand, is less common than its modern title suggests, surviving in only eleven manuscripts, usually in abbreviated form.

Bibliography: On the Wycliffite Bible in general, see Deanesly 1920 and Hudson 1985, 67–84, 85–110, and 1986. On textual problems, see Fristedt 1953. The Early Version of the Old Testament in Oxford, Bodleian Library MS Bodley 959, is edited by Conrad Lindberg (1959–97); the Late Version (using only a few of the manuscripts), by Josiah Forshall and Frederic Madden (1850); selections from the *General Prologue* and both versions are edited by Hudson (1978). For the manuscripts, see Lindberg 1970; for the text's orthodox circulation, Krochalis 1988. On Nicholas Hereford, see Hudson 1978, 163, and Fowler 1960. F. C. Burkitt (1967) has edited the rules of Tyconius. On Wyclif's position on the literal sense, see Copeland 1993, 1–23. On Arundel's *Constitutions* and the controversy over Bible translation, see Watson 1995a.

Source: London, British Library MS Harley 1666, fols. 92v–93v, 96v–98v: a pocket-sized parchment manuscript. Although the presentation is plain and the writing much rubbed and faded, the text has been carefully corrected, with missing words supplied in the margin.

This excerpt was contributed by Ian R. Johnson.

[The chapter begins by explaining the traditional "four senses" of Scripture: the literal sense (what the text literally means on the surface, "literally" being defined so as to include figurative language), the allegorical sense (what the text can be taken to say about Christian doctrine or the church), the tropological (or moral) sense, and the anagogical sense (what the text can be taken to say about the future of this world and the next). The literal level is given clear primacy, and a long passage defines the word "figurative," drawing on Augustine's On Christian Doctrine.*]*

And whanne not oo thing aloone but tweyne either mo ben feelid either undirstonden bi the same wordis of Scripture, though that it is hid that he undirstond that wroot, it is no perel, if it may be prevyd bi other placis of Hooly Scripture that ech of tho thingis acordith with treuthe. And in hap the autour of
5 Scripture seith thilke sentense in the same wordis which [we] wolen undirstonde;

and certys the Spirit of God, that wroughte these thingis bi the autour of Scripture,
bifore sigh withoute doute that thilke sentense schulde come to the redere either to
the herere; yhe, the Holy Goost purveyde that thilke sentence, for it is groundid on
trewthe, schulde come to the redere either to the herere. For whi, what myghte be
10 purveyed of God largiliere and plentyuousliere in Goddis spechis than that the
same wordis be undirstonden in manye maners?—whiche maners either wordis of
God, that ben not of lesse autorite, maken to be preved. (Austin in iii. book of
Cristen Teching seith al this, and myche more, in the bigynnyng therof.)

    Also, he whos herte is ful of charite conprehendith, withouten eny errour, the
15 manyfoold abundaunce and largest teching of Goddis scripturis: for whi Poul seith,
"The fulnesse of lawe is charite," and in another place, "The ende of lawe" (that
is, the perfeccioun either filling of the lawe) "is charite of clene herte, and of good
conscience, and of feith not feyned." And Jhesu Crist seith, "Thou schalt love thi
Lord God of al thin herte, and of al thi soule, and of al thi mynde, and thi
20 neighebore as thi self, for in these twey comaundementis hangith al the lawe
and prophetis." And as "the roote of all yvels is coveitise," so the roote of alle
goodis is charitee. Charite, bi which we loven God and the neighebore, holdith
sykirly al the greetnesse and largnesse of Goddis spechis.

    Therfore if it is not leisir to seeke alle Holy Scriptures—to expounne alle the
25 wlappingis of wordis, to perse alle the prevytes of Scripturis—holde thou charite,
where alle thingis hangen, so thou schalt holde that that [thou] lernydist there.
Also thou schalt holde that that thou lernedist not: for if thou knowist charite,
thou knowist sum thing wheronne also that hangith that in hap thou knowist not.
And in that that thou undirstondist in Scripturis, charite is opin, and in that that
30 thou undirstondist not, charite is hid. Therfore he that hooldith charite, in vertues
either in goode condiscouns, hooldith bothe that that is opyn and that [that] is hid
in Goddis wordis. (Austyn seith al this and myche more in a sermoun of the
preysing of charite.)

*[The author now reviews the seven Tyconian rules, which sought to clarify ambigu-
ities or apparent contradictions in the Bible by explaining the range of figural meanings of its language.]*

    Also, thei that have lykinge for to studie in Holy Writ schulen be chargid that
35 thei kunne the kyndes and maners of spekingis in Holy Scriptures, and [that thei]
perseyve diligently and holde wel in mynde hou a thing is wont to be seid in Holy
Scripturis. Also—that is sovereyn help and moost nedful—preie thei that God
yeve to hem the veri undirstonding of Holy Scripture, for the[i] reden in tho
Scripturis aboute whiche the[i] ben studiouse, that God yeveth wisdom, and
40 kunnyng, and undirstonding of his face, that is, gifte and grace. Also, if her stodie
is don with meeknesse and love of Cristen lore it is of God. (Austyn writith al this
in the iii. book of *Cristen Teching*, aboute the myddil and in the ende. Isidre, in
the i. book of *Sovereyn Good*, touchith these reulis schortliere, but I have hym not
now, and Lyre, in the bigynnyng of the Bible, touchith more opinly these reulis,
45 but I have him not now, and Ardmacan in the bigynnyng of his book *De
questionibus armenorum* yeveth many goode groundis to undirstonde Holy
Scripture to the lettre and goostly undirstonding also, but I have him not now.)

    Also, nothing maye seme to be wiisere, nothing of more eloquence than is
Hooly Scripture and the autours therof, that weren enspiirid of God. And thei

epistles

50 oughten not to speke in other manere than thei diden, and the prophetis (and moost Amos) weren ful eloquent, and Seint Poul was ful eloquent in his pistlis. Also, the autoris of Hooly Scripture spaken derkly that the prevyteis therof ben hid fro unfeithful men and goode men ben exercisid either ocupied, and that in expounnynge Hooly Scripture thei have a newe grace, diverse fro the first autouris

55 (Austin, in the bigynnyng of the iiii. book of *Cristen Teching*). Also, as the litle richessis of Jewis whiche thei baren awey fro Egipt weren, in comparisoun of richessis which thei hadden aftirward in Jerusalem in the tyme of Salomon, so greet is the prophitable kunnynge of filosoferis bookis, if it is comparisouned to the kunnynge of Hooly Scripturis; for whi, what ever thing a man lernith

60 withouten Hooly Writ, if the thing lerned is veyn it is dampned in Holy Writ, if it is profitable it is foundid there. And whanne a man fyndith theere alle thingis whiche he lernyde profitably in other place, he schal fynde myche more plenteuously tho thingis in Hooly Scripture, whiche he lernede nevere in other place but ben lerned oonly in the wondirful highnesse and in the wondirful

65 meeknesse of Hooly Scripturis. (Austin seith this in the ende of ii. book of *Cristen Teching*.)

importance of scripture

   Also, Hooly Scripture conteyneth al prophitable treuthe and alle othere sciencis prevyly in the vertu of wittis either undirstondingis, as wynes ben conteyned in grapis, as ripe corn is conteyned in the seed, as bowis ben conteyned in the rootis,

70 and as trees ben conteyned in the kernels (Grostede, in a sermoun *Premonitus a venerabili patre*). Also Hooly Scripture wlatith sofymys and seith "He that spekith sofisticaly either bi sofymys schal be hatful and he schal be defraudid in ech thing," as the wiise man seith in xxxvii. c. of *Ecclesiastici*. If filosoferis, and moost the disciplis of Plato, seiden eny treuthis and prophitable to oure feith, not

almost parable-like

75 oonly tho treuthis owen not to be dred, but also tho schulen be calengid into oure us eithir profiit fro hem, as fro unjust possessouris. And as Jewis token bi autorite of God the gold, and sylver, and clothis of Egipcyans, so Cristene men owen to take the trewe seyingis of filosoveris for to worschipe oo God, and of techingis of vertues, whiche treuthis the filosoveris founden not but diggeden out of the metals

80 of Goddis purvyaunce, which is sched everywhere. So dide Ciprian, the swettest doctour and moost blessid martir, so diden Lactancius, Victorinus, and Illarie, and Greekis withoute noumbre (Austin in ii. book of *Cristen Teching*).

   Bi these reulis of Austin and bi iiii. undirstondingis of Hooly Scripture and bi wiis knowing of figuratiif spechis, with good lyvynge and meeknesse and stodyinge

85 of the Bible, symple men moun sumdel undirstonde the text of Holy Writ and edefie myche hemself and other men. But for Goddis love, ye symple men, bewar of pride, and veyn jangling and chyding in wordis ayens proude clerkis of scole and veyn religious, and answere yee mekely and prudently to enemyes of Goddis lawe, and preie ye hertly for hem, that God of his greet mercy yeve to hem very

90 knowing of scripturis and meekenesse and charite. And evere be ye redy, whatever man techith eny treuthe of God, to take that meekely and with greet thankingis to God; and if eny man in erthe either aungel of hevene techith you the contrarie of Holy Writ either enything ayens resoun and charite, fle fro him in that as fro the foul devel of helle, and holde ye stedfastly to liif and deeth the treuthe and

warning against false doctrine

95 freedom of the Hooly Gospel of Jhesu Crist, and take ye mekely mennis seyingis and lawis onely in as myche as thei acorden with Holy Writ and good conscience and noo ferthere, for liif neither for deth.

1–13 And whanne . . . therof This paragraph continues to draw on Augustine (see 12–13n). The problem of ambiguity is raised and resolved by the argument that most ambiguities are clarified elsewhere in the Bible, that they are foreseen by God (even if they were not by the human author), and that density of meaning is an appropriate characteristic of divine speech and should not be regarded as a problem.

1 oo one ∫ **tweyne** two ∫ **either** or

1–2 feelid either undirstonden perceived or meant

2–3 though that it is hid that he undirstond that wroot though it is unclear what he who wrote it understood by it

3 it is no perel there is no danger ∫ **prevyd** ascertained ∫ **bi** from

4–9 And in hap . . . to the herere and perhaps the author of Scripture sees the same meaning [i.e., the meaning of which the reader is in doubt] in the very words we seek to understand; and certainly, the Spirit of God, who wrought all these things through the author of Scripture, without doubt saw beforehand that this meaning must occur to the reader or the hearer; indeed, the Holy Spirit ordained it so that this meaning, because it is grounded on truth, should occur to the reader or the hearer ("to the herere" [7–9] is the translator's addition)

5 [we] wolen MS *wolen*

9–12 For whi . . . to be preved for indeed, what might be more generously and copiously ordained by God in God's speeches than that the same words should be understood in many ways?—of which ways other words of God, which are of no less authority, give proof

12–13 Austin in iii. book of *Cristen Teching* Augustine (354–430), *On Christian Doctrine* III.27.38 (Robertson 1958, 102)

15 largest most extensive ∫ **for whi** for which reason ∫ **Poul** Paul the Apostle

16 The fulnesse of lawe is charite Rom. 13:10

16–18 The ende of lawe . . . feith not feyned 1 Tim. 1:5

17 filling fulfilling

18–21 Thou schalt love . . . prophetis Matt. 22:37–40

21 the roote of all yvels is coveitise covetousness is the root of all evil: 1 Tim. 6:10

23 sykirly surely

24 largnesse range

24–33 Therfore . . . preysing of charite This alliterative passage attempts to reconcile the demand for careful study of the Bible implied at the beginning of the excerpt with the foundational Lollard

belief that the Bible, "God's law," is for everyone. Charity is presented as the sole interpretive tool necessary for understanding Scripture, a tool that does not depend on education and that can submit to its own failure to comprehend everything in the Bible by acknowledging the Bible's truth nonetheless. Compare Julian of Norwich, excerpt 1.13b:60–84, and *The Holi Prophete David,* excerpt 2.5; contrast Pecock, excerpt 1.16.

24 leisir opportune

25 wlappingis convolutions ∫ **perse** look through ∫ **prevytes** secrets ∫ **holde thou** if you keep

25–26 charite, where alle thingis hangen charity, on which all things depend. Compare *Piers Plowman* B V.606–7: "Thow shalt see in thiselve Truthe sitte in thyn herte / In a cheyne of charite."

26 so thou schalt holde that that [thou] lernydist there then you will keep all those things that you learn there [in Scripture]: possibly another allusion to Rom. 13:10, "love is the fulfillment of the law"

27–28 if thou knowist charite . . . knowist not if you know charity, then you know something on which a thing you perhaps do not know depends as well

29 that that that which

30 hid hidden

30–31 in vertues either in goode condiscouns through virtuous behavior or through good qualities: that is, whether your charity is being expressed through works or is an inner state

31 that [that] MS *that*

32–33 Austyn . . . charite Augustine, *Sermo* CCCL, *De charitate* II (*PL* 39:1533–35)

34–47 Also thei . . . have him not now The prologue continues to alternate between instructions that suggest the study of Scripture is a specialist activity and assertions that it requires only "meeknesse" (41). Several times the writer cites texts he does not have available to him (42–47), perhaps in part to excuse his heavy reliance on Augustine's *On Christian Doctrine.* The difficulty in obtaining books was a topos of Lollard satire (see, e.g., *Sermon of Dead Men,* excerpt 3.11: 13–16, 19–20), and may be intended to reinforce the points being made here about love as better than learning, but may reflect the actual circumstances in which the *General Prologue* was written.

34 chargid required

35 kunne know ∫ **[that thei]** MS *thei that*

37 that what ∫ **sovereyn** chief

38 hem them ∫ **veri** true

40 kunnyng knowledge ∫ **her** their

41 lore teaching

41–42 Austyn . . . book of *Cristen Teching* On

Christian Doctrine III.10.56 (Robertson 1958, 117)

42–43 Isidre, in the i. book of *Sovereyn Good* Isidore, bishop of Seville (560–633), whose most influential work was a vast encyclopedia of matters sacred and profane, the *Etymologiae*. William Rusch (1977, 199) points out that selections from this work circulated as independent texts in the Middle Ages and that *Sovereyn Good* may be a name given to one such text.

43 schortliere more briefly ∫ **I have hym not** I do not have the book with me

44 Lyre Nicholas of Lyre (c. 1270–c. 1349), a Franciscan who taught theology at the University of Paris. His commentaries on the literal senses of the Bible, set forth in his *Postillae perpetuae sive brevia commentaria in universa Biblica* (1322–30), formed the core of late medieval versions of the *Glossa ordinaria,* the standard biblical commentary. The reference is to the prologue to his commentary, which is translated closely later in the *General Prologue* (chap. 14), after the author was able to obtain a copy (see Minnis and Scott 1988, 198–200, 266–76).

45–46 Ardmacan . . . *De questionibus armenorum* Richard Fitzralph (c. 1295–1360): archbishop of Armagh from 1347 and a leading intellectual. His *Summa de questionibus Armenorum,* as well as his approach to the literal sense, seems to have influenced this prologue more than Wyclif's more abstruse account of divine authorship of the Bible (see Copeland 1993).

48–66 Also . . . *Teching* After asserting that anyone who has charity can understand the Bible, for all the importance given to learning, the author turns to give reasons (again from Augustine) why Bible reading is of supreme value (compare *The Holi Prophete David,* excerpt 2.5). The Bible is eloquent, obscure only to deter evil people and "exercise" good ones (see 53), and contains in itself all knowledge in compressed form (55–65), although it is profitable to use knowledge gained from the study of pagan or secular sciences to interpret the Bible (67–82). In its Middle English context (as distinct from its original context in Augustine), the passage stresses the primacy of Bible study to lay readers, whose interests might range widely, while also asserting the value of scholarship.

51 moost especially ∫ **Amos** Old Testament prophet ∫ **Seint Poul** Paul the Apostle ∫ **pistlis** epistles

52 that so that ∫ **prevyteis** mysteries

54 diverse differing from

55 Austin . . . *Cristen Teching* *On Christian Doctrine* (not book IV but II.6.7; Robertson 1958, 37–38; also Mark 4:12) ∫ **litle** small

56 baren carried ∫ **fro** from ∫ **Egipt** Egypt. For the topos of Egyptian gold (symbolizing pagan or, in this case, philosophical learning, which can be adapted for Christian use but is nonetheless worth little set beside the wisdom discernible in the Bible), see Augustine, *On Christian Doctrine* II.40.61 (Robertson 1958, 75–76, after Exod. 3:22, 11:2, 12:35; and see 76–82 below).

57 Salomon Solomon, the Old Testament king, famed for wealth as well as wisdom

58 filosoferis that is, pagan philosophers such as Plato and Aristotle ∫ **comparisouned** compared

60 withouten outside ∫ **dampned** condemned

61 foundid established, supported

63 tho those

64 highnesse sublimity

65–66 Austin . . . book of *Cristen Teching* *On Christian Doctrine* II.42.63 (Robertson 1958, 78)

67–70 Hooly Scripture conteyneth . . . kernels For the view that Scripture contains all knowledge *in potentia,* see the discussions of scriptural signification collected by Alastair J. Minnis and A. B. Scott (1988, chap. 6).

67 sciencis branches of learning or knowledge

68 prevyly secretly or potentially ∫ **in the vertu of wittis either undirstondingis** by means of the power of people's intelligence or understanding

70–71 Grostede Robert Grosseteste, bishop of Lincoln (1235–53): scholar and leading intellectual, much favored by Wyclif and his followers ∫ ***Premonitus a venerabili patre*** admonished by the venerable father (the first words of the sermon; see Thomson 1940, 173)

71 wlatith abhors ∫ **sofymys** sophistries

72 hatful hateful ∫ **defrauid** deprived

73 man seith MS *seith man* ∫ ***Ecclesiastici*** Ecclus. 37:23

74 moost especially

75 tho treuthis owen not to be dred those truths ought not be feared ∫ **tho** those [truths] ∫ **calengid** changed

76–82 And . . . *Teching* See 56n above.

76 us use ∫ **token** symbolize

78 for to in order to ∫ **oo** one

79 founden discovered [for themselves] ∫ **diggeden** dug

80 purvyaunce provision ∫ **sched** poured

80–81 Ciprian . . . Illarie all fathers of the church: cited by "Austin" (82), that is, Augustine, *On Christian Doctrine* II.40.61 (Robertson 1958, 75–76)

80 Ciprian Saint Cyprian (220–58)

81 Lactancius Lucius Caecilius Firmianus Lactantius (c. 240–c. 320) ∫ **Victorinus** Gaius Marius Victorinus, who converted to Christianity in 355 ∫ **Illarie** Saint Hilary: fourth-century bishop of Poitiers

83–97 **Bi these reulis . . . neither for deth** The conclusion of the chapter appeals directly to the "symple men" (85), who have been the implied subject throughout, attempting to balance the various attitudes it has taken toward learning, the learned, and the use of charity as an interpretive device. Simple readers must "bewar of pride" (86–87) in opposing the learned when they are "enemyes of Goddis lawe" (88–89), and instead should use meekness as a weapon; yet if the learned preach "eny treuthe of God" (91), meekness must be used rather to accept what is heard. The tension in this advice—between a view of the "symple" reader as awaiting instruction and one in which he or she is already informed about the faith and can withstand its opponents—perhaps helps generate the bold but conceptually vague peroration, which denounces even an angel if he "techith you the contrarie of Holy Writ" (92–93).

83 **bi iiii. undirstondingis of Hooly Scripture** by the four levels of meaning of Holy Scripture: that is, literal, allegorical, tropological, and anagogical (see the summary of the opening passage of this chapter above). For discussion, see Smalley 1983, vii–xi and chap. 1. For Augustine's influence, see Robertson 1958, ix–xx.

84 **figuratiif** figurative or metaphorical
85 **moun** may ∫ **sumdel** somewhat
87 **jangling** chattering ∫ **proude clerkis of scole** proud university scholars
88 **veyn religious** proud men of religion
89 **yeve** give
89–90 **very knowing** true knowledge
90 **whatever** whatever [kind of]
94 **to liif and deeth** throughout your life and at your death

1.16 REGINALD PECOCK, *PROLOGUE TO THE DONET* AND *THE REPRESSOR OF OVER MUCH BLAMING OF THE CLERGY* (EXTRACTS)

Date and Provenance: 1443–55; London. Surviving copies of Pecock's treatises may be revisions of earlier texts; their allusions to each other suggest he worked on them simultaneously.

Author, Sources, and Nature of Text: Reginald Pecock (c. 1392–1460), bishop of St. Asaph (1444–50) and later Chichester (1450–58), was a controversial figure who narrowly escaped being burned at the stake. A crusader against Lollard doctrines, Pecock devoted much of his life to a program of theological writing (mainly in English) that extended and explicated the standard body of truths and doctrines "necessary for all to know" by placing it in a scholastic theological system of his own devising. Throughout his work, he stresses obedience to the church—and, in 1457, was forced to demonstrate this obedience by handing over his works to be burned before a crowd allegedly of twenty thousand people. Yet believing that the faculty of reason was given to everyone as the principal means to knowledge of God, Pecock saw it as his duty to provide material for attaining this knowledge, despite ecclesiastical policies discouraging intellectual speculation. As a result, while he took issue

with the Lollard emphasis on Scripture, and on charity, not reason, as the main tool for understanding it (see the *Wycliffite Bible*, excerpt 1.15, and *The Holi Prophete David*, excerpt 2.5), his belief in lay education was in many ways similar to theirs, and it is not surprising that his project—the last sustained attempt to create a vernacular corpus of theological writing before Tyndale's Bible in the 1520s—was condemned.

Six English works by Pecock survive: *The Folower, The Book of Faith, The Rule of Christian Religion, The Poor Men's Mirror,* and the two excerpted here. The first excerpt is from the prologue to Pecock's *Donet* (named after Donatus, the fourth-century Roman author of the standard preparatory Latin grammar book), a work that Pecock claims provides a "key" to his much longer *Rule of Christian Religion* and to Christianity itself (1–5). The *Donet*, written as a dialogue, describes the relation of will, reason, and the human soul, recodifying in four tables the whole moral law of Christianity (incorporating the Ten Commandments, the Seven Deadly Sins, etc.). Pecock uses academic conventions for systematizing knowledge and claims that his tables are more complete, economical, and memorable than the "lose gibilettis" hitherto "oute of dewe processe to gider clumprid" (Hitchcock 1921, 146, 147) of earlier compendia. The prologue explains the work's function and defends its orthodoxy in terms suggesting the passage was reworked after Pecock had come under suspicion. It shows an interesting degree of doubt about the efficacy of written language as an instrument for conveying truth (paralleled by *The Cloud of Unknowing*, excerpt 3.3, and *Reynard*, excerpt 3.17).

The second passage is from Pecock's defense of the ecclesiastical status quo, the *Repressor* (pt. I, chap. 6). This work attacks the Lollard belief that any meek Christian will come to an understanding of the biblical text (pt. I), and defends images and pilgrimages (pt. II), the proper use of church revenues (pt. III), the church hierarchy (pt. IV), and the religious orders (pt. V)—all, from the 1380s, objects of Lollard criticism. In this brief extract, Pecock gives an "ensaumple" to back up his contention that reason, hidden in the heart, not the Bible, provides the fundamental test of truth, since the Bible gives only versions of truths whose essential ground is elsewhere.

Audience and Circulation: None of Pecock's works survives in more than one manuscript, and some are lost. Pecock's claim in the prologue to the *Donet* that unfinished versions of his works circulated without permission (86–94) is written with ecclesiastical censors in mind, but suggests he had achieved an audience of London readers as well as the crowds he drew for his sermons. He was also read in Oxford, and as late as 1476 Edward IV denounced him, his books, and his Oxford disciples (Babington 1860, lx). His theoretical audience incorporates the whole Christian people of England, and his works seek to address that audience at various levels of complexity.

Bibliography: *The Repressor* is edited by Churchill Babington (1860); the *Donet* and *Folower,* by Elsie Vaughan Hitchcock (1921, 1924); *The Book of Faith,* by J. L. Morison (1909); and *The Rule of Christian Religion,* by William Cabell Greet (1927). For studies of Pecock and his London milieu, see Scase 1992 and 1996.

Source: (a) Oxford, Bodleian Library MS Bodley 916, fols. 1v–4r, the unique surviving copy, a late-fifteenth-century manuscript of good-quality parchment, written by a single scribe, with corrections and marginalia in English and Latin. It contains only the *Donet.* The manuscript appears to have belonged in the sixteenth century to Jamys Ryllsey (possibly of York, fol. 64v).

(b) Cambridge University Library MS Kk.4.26, fols. 12v–13r: a late-fifteenth-century parchment manuscript, containing only *The Repressor.* The text has been corrected, and there are numerous glosses, *nota bene* marks, and underlining: the manuscript has been used by generations of readers.

This excerpt was contributed by Ian R. Johnson.

a. *from the* Prologue to the Donet

And sithen it is so, that this book berith himsilf toward the hool ful kunnyng
of Goddis lawe, even as the comoun *Donet* in Latyn berith himsilf toward the hool
ful kunnyng of grammer (as it is wel knowun of clerkis in Latyn), therfore this
present dialog myghte wel and convenientli be clepid the *Donet* or "key" of
5 Goddis lawe, or ellis the *Donet* or "key" of Cristen religioun.

If enye man wole wite whi Y make this book and othire bokis in the common
peplis langage, turne he into the v first chapitris of the book clepid *Afore Crier* and
into the first prolog of the book clepid *Cristen Religioun*, and there he mai see
therof the causis, whiche, as Y trust, ben of God and of eche man allowable and
10 preisable.

Ferthirmore, Y make protestacioun that it is not myn entent for to holde, defende, or favoure—in this book or in enye othire bi me writun or to be writun, in Latyn or in the comoun peplis langage—enye erroure or heresie or enye co[n]clusioun whiche schulde be ayens the feith or the lawe of oure Lord God.

15 And if enye such it happe me to write—or offre, or purpose, or holde, defende, or favour, bi enye unavisednes, hastynes, or ignoraunce, or bi enye othire maner—Y schal be redi it to leeve, forsake and retrete, mekely and devoutli, at the assignementis of myn ordinaries, fadris of the Chirche. In contrarye manere to this governaunce Y was nevere yit hidirto disposid, Y thank my Lord God; and Y
20 purpose nevere in contrarie wise othir to be, however it happe over hasty and undiscreet awaiters and bacbiters in othir wise of me feel or diffame. Ferthirmore, sithen an errour or heresye is not the ynke writen neithir the voice spokun, but it is the meenyng or the undirstonding of the writer or speker signified bi thilk ynke writen or bi thilk voice spokun, and also nevere into this daie was enye man holde
25 jugid or condempnid for an errer or an heretyk but if it were founde that his meenyng and undirstonding whiche he had in his writyng or in his speking were errour or heresie; therfore Y desire and aske, for charite, that noon harder or hastier holding or juging be made anentis me. And to knowe what myn undirstonding and meenyng is and schal be in wordis of my writingis, Englische
30 and Latyn, certis, oon ful goode weie is to attende to the circumstauncis in the processis whiche Y make there bifore and aftir, and whiche Y make in othire placis of my writingis. For bi this weie Seynt Austyn leerned what was the right meenyng in the wordis of Holi Scripture, as he seith in his *Book of 83 Questiouns*, the [lii] questioun. And if this weie be not for alle placis of my writingis sufficient,
35 recours may be had to my persoon for to aske of me while Y am in this liif.

If Y schulde have kunnyng and power for to so bisette my wordis that no chalenge myghte be made ayens hem, and that noon untrouthe myghte be dryve oute of hem bi argument, though al biside my meenyng and undirstonding whiche Y had in tho wordis where and whanne Y hem there wroot, certis, it were wondir
40 me to have this singuler gift, whiche nevere writer had yitt sithen Crist stighed into hevene. And therfore God send to be reders in my bokis suche men as wolen gladli aspie aftir my meenyng in my wordis and save and defende me ayens alle othire in contrarie maner disposid reders or heerers. Amen.

If enye man kan nowe, or schal kunne bettir fynde than Y have founde and
45 schal bi Goddis grace fynde, wherbi he may amende the doctryne whiche Y am aboute to write in my Englisch bokis and in my Latyn bokis into soulis profite, Y schal not lette him, but Y schal therfore thanke him. For God knowith that for helthe of Cristen peplis soulis, and for noon victorie to be wonne bi me in my side, neithir for enye glorie or rewarde to be had a this side God, Y sette me into the
50 labour of my bokis makyng.

Ferthirmore, wite alle men, bothe clerkis and othire, that the labour of my bokis making is not withoute hardnes, firste in hem conceyving in suche foorme as thei ben; and Y wote not who in lyve cowde suche a noumbre and suche a foorme fynde and dispose, and therwith pretende him in no poynt therinne faile.
55 Wherfore of every wel-disposid man my bokis schulden the more favorabili be receyved, as manye bokis bifore my daies ma[a]d ben received in grete favour for the good and profitable trouthis whiche ben in hem, though manye defautis be therwith founde in hem, for to noon it is yovun for to knowe al. For this and for

alle othir Goddis giftis, to him be preising and thanking, honour and glory, his
60   plesaunt service to him fulfilling and paiyng of al his peple, treuly, dewly, devoutly
and fully. Amen.
     And, forasmoche as over long it were me to declare now and heere how hard it
is to knowe treuthis in this liif and how litil surete is in the knowing of trouthis in
this liif—and yitt that nevertheles bettir it is a man leerne hem so than to lack al,
65   and bettir it is a man for to write and teche what and how he kan fynde into
profityng than for to leve alle suche thingis unwritun and untaught, for ellis manye
ful profitable bokis schulde we into these daies have lackid; and, forasmoche as
whanne in a mater ben dyvers opyniouns and mowe be mo opyniouns, it is honest
ynough a man to speke and write aftir oon of tho opyniouns and anothire tyme to
70   uttre the othire opinioun; and also, forasmoche as over long it were for to parfitli
denounce and notifie undir what entent Y seie and write al what Y have, or schal
seie or write, and how Y wole and entende that it be take of the heerers and
reders; and also, forasmoche as nevere man yitt wroote enye notable book whiche
couthe so suerli sett his wordis that noon inpugnacioun couthe be made there
75   ayens, as in a litil tretice Y so lenger teche: therfore Y have made *A Litil Book To
Be a Declarative* of these pointis and of mo, ayens envie and detraccioun and
malice, whiche peraventure myght rise into summe heerers or reders, being moche
redier for to suche writingis lette and distroie than for to enye suche bi her owne
laboure fynde, make, and multiplie into good occupacioun for Cristen laymen—
80   that thei bi reeding therinne dissevere hemsilf the more fro the worlde and the
fleisch, and the nygher and the oftir and the sweetlier knytte hem and couple hem
to God and to his wel willingis, as for to be a bilowe to blowe and puffe up the fier
of devoucioun in her soule into banysching aweie the coolde of undevocioun and
of uncharite, whiche coolde is modir of moche myslyving, as the contrarye heet is
85   modir of moche good lyving.
     The Donet of Cristen Religioun and *The Book of Cristen Religioun* and othire
suche of doctrine and of officiyng whiche, bifore the devyce and setting of this
present book, ben runne abrood and copied ayens my wil and myn entent, as Y
have openli prechid at Poulis, and that bi uncurtesie and undiscrecioun of freendis
90   into whos singuler sight Y lousid tho writingis to go, and for to not have go ferthir
into tyme thei were bettir examyned of me and approvid of my lordis and fadris of
the Churche, Y wole to be as noon of myn; but in as moche as in me is, Y wole
thei be rendrid up ayen and bettir formes of the same be to hem delivered whanne
dewe deliveraunce therof schal be made.
95   Bettir am not Y than was holy Seynt Gregory (wolde God Y were a quartir so
good) whiche, not withstonding hise holy ententis and hise kunnyng, founde so
moche mysdisposid men for to lette and diffame and distroie his bokis than for to
make a quartir so moche of writing into chering of Cristen soulis, that he wolde
not that eny of his bokis schulde be publischid bifore his deeth, as it is write in his
100 liif. Yhe, and aftir his deeth, summe of this bokis were bi suche now seide men
brent, and mo schulde of hise bokis be brend if help of God had not be providid.
And yit Y wote weel that if bisy and sutil inpugnaciouns schulden be made ayens
hise bokis, or ayens Austyns, or eny othire holy seintis bokis, scant ynough oon
leef schulde stonde unprovid or colowrabily unrebukid. But what were this
105 thanne? For to provoke that no writing were had, or rad, or occupied into goostli
feeding and edifiyng of Cristen soulis? A symple and a litil leerned man in

carpentrie kanne and may fynde a defaute in a kingis palice made to the kingis
worschip and eese, whiche is not able to make a pore coote for the eese and the
chering of a begger. Thus moche herof as now. More is seid in the *Litil Book*
110 bifore spokun.

Sithen Seint Jerom had manye detractouris and inpugners of hise writingis, as he
himsilf witnessith, what merveyle is if Y so have? And sithen ful manye famose
doctouris writingis ben had in greet deynte and in greet profite in the Chirche of
God, and ben wel and profitabli suffrid to be red and occupied, not withstonding
115 that (here and there among) thei fallen fro it that myght be bettir seid and whiche
thei myghten not at the fulle comprehende—what merveile were it though it so
falle by me, whiche entende not for to even me to hem but for to be a profitable
procutoure to laymen, into whoos leerning and edifiyng, as to me semeth, over
litil writing into this tyme hath be devysid?
120 Alle inpugners whiche laboren bi gile and wiile to make her inpugnacioun seme
good bifore the multitude of laymen, and at temperal lordis eeris, and at
multitude of clerkis not scolid in dyvynite, or not profundeli endewid in dyvynite,
how ever it be of her degree in scole, or state in the Chirche; and alle tho whiche bi
detraccioun and diffame, pride, sturdy herte, and envie sp[e]ken and writen, in
125 stide of clergie, God amende, for charite.

Here eendith the prolog of this book. And here bigynnith
the first chapitre of this present book.

b. *from* The Repressor of Over Much Blaming of the Clergy

Also, in caas a greet clerk wolde go into a librarie and over studie there a long
proces of feith writun in the Bible, and wolde aftirward reporte and reherce the
130 sentence of the same proces to the peple at Poulis Cros in a sermoun, or wolde
write it in a pistle or lettre to hise freendis under entent of reporting the sentence
of the seid proces: schulde the heere[r]s of thilk reportyng and remembring seie
that thilk sentence were foundid and groundid in the seid reporter, or in his
preching, or in his pistle writen? Goddis forbode! For open it is that thei oughten
135 seie and feele rathir that thilk sentence is groundid in the seid book ligging in the
librarie. And, in caas that this clerk, reporting the seid sentence or proces, spake
or wrote in othere wordis thilk sentence than ben the wordis under which thilk
sentence is writen in the seid book, thei oughten seie and feele that hise
wordis and his writingis oughten be glosid and be expowned and be brought in to
140 accordaunce with the seid book in the librarie, and the seid book in thilk proces
oughte not be expowned and be brought and wrestid into accordaunce with the
seid clerkis wordris and writingis. Yhe, though Crist and hise Apostlis wolden
entende and do the same as this clerk dooth, the peple oughte in noon other wise
than which is now seid bere hem anentis Crist and his Apostlis in this case, as it
145 is opene ynough. And sithen it is so, that alle the trouthis of lawe of kinde whiche
Crist and hise Apostlis taughten and wroten weren bifor her teching and writing
and weren writen bifore in thilk solempnest inward book or inward writing of
resounis doom, passing alle outward bookis in profite to men for to serve God (of
which inward book or inward writing miche thing is seid in the book clepid *The*
150 *Just Aprising of Holi Scripture* and of which Jeremye spekith in his xxxi^e^. c. and

Poul in his epistle Hebr. viiie. c): it muste needis folewe that noon of the seid treuthis is groundid in the wordis or writingis of Crist or of the Apostlis, but in the seid inward preciose book and writing buried in mannis soule, out of which inward book and writing mowe be taken bi labour and studiyng of clerkis mo
155 conclusiouns and treuthis and governauncis of lawe of kinde and Goddis moral lawe and service than myghten be writen in so manie bokis whiche schulden fille the greet chirche of Seint Poul in Londoun.

1–5 **And sithen . . . religioun** The opening sentence of the excerpt concludes part of Pecock's formal introduction to his work by naming it and explaining the appropriateness of the title: a common scholastic procedure also found, for example, in Richard Rolle's adaptation of Peter Lombard's prologue to his commentary on the Psalter (excerpt 3.8: 26–29).

1 **sithen** since ∫ **berith himsilf** directs itself ∫ **hool** whole ∫ **kunnyng** knowledge

2 *Donet* **in Latyn** the fourth-century *Ars grammatica* of Aelius Donatus: in the Middle Ages the basic Latin grammar and hence often a term for any basic textbook

4 **dialog** The dialogue form is often used for basic (catechetical) instruction. Compare, for example, *Dives and Pauper* (excerpt 3.9).

6 **wole** wishes ∫ **wite** to know

7 *Afore Crier* one of several lost books Pecock mentions in his surviving writings (see also 75–76, 149–50)

8 **clepid** called ∫ *Cristen Religioun* that is, *The Rule of Christian Religion*

10 **preisable** praiseworthy

11 **protestacioun** a formal defense of a writer's good intentions, the language of which is often, as here, highly legalistic

14 **ayens** against

15 **happe** befall ∫ **purpose** intend

16 **unavisednes** lack of forethought

17 **retrete** withdraw

18 **assignementis of myn ordinaries** commands of Pecock's superiors (with jurisdiction over him). Although a bishop, Pecock was subject to the authority of the archbishop of Canterbury and to ecclesiastical councils, such as that summoned to judge his works in 1457.

19 **governaunce** direction

20 **othir** different ∫ **however it happe** however it may be that

21 **undiscreet** injudicious (MS adds *li*, then marks for deletion) ∫ **awaiters** liers in wait ∫ **bacbiters** backstabbers ∫ **feel** perceive ∫ **diffame** unjustly accuse

21–27 **Ferthirmore . . . heresie** Pecock is correct in asserting that heresy is formally defined not as

an incorrect theological statement or form of words but as inner adherence to erroneous beliefs once these have been defined as incorrect by the ecclesiastical authorities. Thus it is not theoretically proper under most circumstances to say that a statement "is" heretical, only that it is erroneous or that it tends to (or might give rise to) heresy. The statement is of a piece with the emphasis both passages excerpted here lay on truth as *anterior* to language, even the language of the Scriptures.

24 **thilk** the same

24–25 **holde jugid** decided to be already judged

25 **errer** one who errs ∫ **but** unless

27 **for charite** out of charity

27–28 **noon harder or hastier holding** no more rigorous or speedy decision [i.e., than is applied to anyone else]

28 **anentis** against ∫ **to** A corrector has added *for* before this word in the MS.

30 **ful** very ∫ **to** MS *forto* with *for* in the corrector's hand

30–31 **circumstauncis in the processis** contexts of the arguments. For this insistence that individual remarks need to be contextualized, see the previous excerpt's discussion of how to deal with biblical ambiguity (*General Prologue to the Wycliffite Bible*, excerpt 1.15: 1–13), and excerpts 3.3 (*The Cloud of Unknowing*) and 3.4 (Julian's *Revelation of Love*).

32–33 **Seynt Austyn . . . Book of 83 Questiouns** Augustine's *De diversis questionibus* (*CCSL* XLIVa, 1975), which discusses a variety of questions on Christian teaching and exegesis

32 **right** true

34 **[lii]** The chapter number is omitted in the manuscript, probably because Pecock himself left the number out, intending to fill it in later, in his autograph.

36 **kunnyng** ability ∫ **bisette** employ

37 **dryve** forced

38 **hem** them ∫ **al biside** entirely different from

40 **stighed** ascended

42 **aspie aftir** search out

44 **kan** knows ∫ **schal kunne** is able to ∫ **fynde** discover

45 **wherbi he may amende the doctryne** by which he can improve the teaching. The appeal to

readers to correct and improve is a topos of prologues to many kinds of work, used, for example,
by Lydgate in *Troy Book* (excerpt 1.7: 209–14).

47 **lette** hinder

48 **bi me in my side** on my part

49 **a this side God** on this side of God, that is, in
this earthly life. Pecock hopes for heavenly reward,
not earthly fame or wealth, for writing as he does,
alluding to a topos about the reasons for writing
also found, for example, in Mannyng's *Chronicle*
(excerpt 1.1: 67–68).

51 **wite** may know

51–52 **my bokis making** the making of my
books

52 **hem conceyving** planning them. All Pecock's
works are structured with care.

53 **wote** know ʃ **in lyve** alive

53–54 **cowde suche a noumbre and suche a
foorme fynde and dispose** would be capable of in-
venting and organizing such a large number and
such a structure [of writings]

54 **pretende him** claim himself ʃ **in no poynt
therinne faile** to fail at no point in it

55 **of** by

56 **ma[a]d** a hand not the scribe's corrects the
MS reading *maed*

57 **defautis** faults

58 **yovun** given

60 **fulfilling** performing ʃ **paiyng** pleasing ʃ **of**
from ʃ **dewly** duly

62–85 **And, forasmoche . . . lyving** This passage
is a single sentence, the main clause introduced by
"therfore" (75), as Pecock explains why the difficulty of explaining everything clearly has caused
him to write a book (75–76), now lost, that focuses
on the contentious points in his teaching. There is a
disparity between the insistence that truth cannot
be fully stated in words and the number of words
Pecock generates to say this (see 145–57 and note).

62 **over too** ʃ **me** [for] me

63 **surete** certainty

65–66 **into profityng** by way of usefulness

68–70 **whanne in a mater . . . opinioun** That is,
when there are several legitimate interpretations of
an issue, it is not improper for someone to give one
interpretation on one occasion, another on another.

68 **mowe** may ʃ **mo** more

68–69 **honest ynough** sufficiently honorable

69 **a man** [for] a man ʃ **aftir** according to

71 **denounce and notifie** announce and proclaim ʃ **what** that

72 **Y wole** I wish ʃ **take of** understood by

73 **whiche** who

74 **couthe** knew how to ʃ **suerli** surely ʃ **sett** fix ʃ
inpugnacioun criticism

75 **lenger** at greater length ʃ **teche** explain

76 ***Declarative*** [more explicit] declaration.
Pecock's *Litil Book* is lost.

76–79 **ayens envie . . . laymen** For the anxiety
generated by the "envious" (a topos of many prologues), see also *The Mirror of Our Lady* (excerpt
3.12: 78–84), which bears close comparison with
this passage, and Bokenham's meditation on envy,
authorship, and intention (excerpt 1.11, especially
196–201).

77 **rise into** arise in

78 **for to** in order to ʃ **lette** to hinder ʃ **her** their

80–85 **that thei by reeding . . . good lyving**
Pecock here aligns his project with the aims of much
devotional writing, suggesting that the purpose of
his books is to inspire readers to the love of God.

80 **dissevere hemsilf** may sever themselves

81 **nygher** nearer ʃ **oftir** more often

82 **his wel willingis** that is, those with a good
will toward God ʃ **bilowe** bellows

83 **her** their

83–84 **undevocioun and . . . uncharite** lack of
devotion and charity

84 **myslyving** ill living

86 ***Book of Cristen Religioun*** that is, *The Rule
of Christian Religion*

87 **officiyng** ecclesiastical organization (presumably a reference to Pecock's *Repressor*) ʃ **devyce
and setting** devising and final revision

88 **ben runne abrood and copied** have been
publicly circulated and copied. It is unclear whether
Pecock's claim that his books were read and copied
before being properly finished is true, or whether
this passage was aimed at those investigating his
orthodoxy.

89 **Poulis** that is, Paul's Cross, London, used for
delivering major public sermons, and the site of
Pecock's most notable successes, since he was a celebrated and controversial preacher

90 **into whos singuler sight Y lousid** for whose
eyes only I released

92 **Y wole** according to my will ʃ **to be as noon
of myn** they are in no way mine. The implied parallel is between the early drafts of Pecock's books and
illegitimate children (compare Bokenham, excerpt
1.11: 61–72).

93 **rendrid up ayen** recomposed ʃ **formes** versions

94 **dewe** rightful ʃ **deliveraunce** release

95–119 **Bettir am not Y . . . devysid** In this extraordinary passage, Pecock lays bare for his
vernacular readers the roots of medieval learned
culture's dependence on a notion of *auctoritas* that
canonizes certain venerable writers and texts and
affords them a completely different kind of reading

from what Pecock can expect for his own work. Any text, even one written by a saint, *can be read* as heretical and must be approached in a proper frame of mind if it is to profit the reader; why, then, cannot Pecock's works be read in the same spirit? The passage does not claim equality with Gregory, Augustine, and Jerome, but it does contextualize their texts by noting that these too were controversial when written (indeed, Pecock's complaints against the envious echo Jerome's similar complaints [111–12]).

95 **Seynt Gregory** Saint Gregory (c. 540–604): consecrated pope in 590, an influential pastoral writer and homilist

96 **whiche** who ∫ **ententis** intentions

98 **into** for ∫ **chering** solace

99 **write** written

100 **suche now seide men** such men as [those] mentioned

101 **brent** burnt ∫ **mo** more

102 **inpugnaciouns** criticisms

103 **Austyns** Augustine's (see 32–33n) ∫ **scant ynough** scarcely

104 **unprovid** unchallenged. A note in the margin reads *De libriis compilatis a sancto Gregorio* (about the books compiled by Saint Gregory), referring to the previous passage. ∫ **colowrabily** plausibly

105 **provoke** bring [it] about ∫ **rad** read ∫ **occupied** employed ∫ **goostli** spiritual

106–9 **A symple . . . begger** That is, someone incapable of building the meanest hut can find fault with the joinery that goes into making the finest palace. The implied image here of Pecock as a craftsman building his books to the glory of God is suggestive of his success in aligning himself with London merchants and guildsmen, who seem to have formed his following.

107 **defaute** fault

108 **whiche** who ∫ **coote** hut

109 *Litil Book* that is, the *Declarative* (75–76)

111 **Seint Jerom** Saint Jerome (c. 342–420): church father, exegete, and translator of the Vulgate

113 **deynte** regard

114 **occupied** taken up

115 **thei fallen fro it that myght be bettir seid** they fall away from what might be better said ∫ **whiche** who

116 **myghten not** could not ∫ **at the fulle** fully

117 **even me** compare myself

118 **procutoure** steward

118–19 **lay men, into whoos leerning . . . over litil writing into this tyme hath be devysid** laypeople from whose learning and instruction too little writing has so far been composed, it seems to me. This

may seem an odd judgment, but Pecock presumably excludes Lollard writings, devotional prose written for the laity, and catechetical texts that teach only the most simple version of the faith. The religious texts in English left once these exclusions are made are indeed few.

120 **inpugners** critics ∫ **wiile** cunning

121 **temperal** secular

122 **scolid** schooled ∫ **endewid** endowed

123 **her** their ∫ **degree in scole** university degree ∫ **state** position

123–25 **alle tho . . . in stide of clergie** all who as learned men ("in stide of clergie") speak and write out of the desire to belittle or out of contempt, pride, obstinacy of heart, and envy

124 **diffame** evil report ∫ **sturdy** stubborn ∫ **sp[e]ken** MS *spoken*

128 **in caas** if ∫ **over studie** pore over

129 **proces** discussion

130 **sentence** meaning

131 **pistle** letter ∫ **under entent** with the intent ∫ **sentence** contents

132 **thilk** that

134 **pistle writen** written text of [his] letter ∫ **Goddis forbode** God forbid ∫ **open** obvious

135 **thilk** that ∫ **ligging** lying

137 **thilk** the same ∫ **ben** are

139 **glosid** glossed ∫ **expowned** explained, commented upon

140 **in thilk proces** on that passage

141 **wrestid** altered

142–45 **Yhe . . . ynough** Even Christ and the Apostles are no exception to the rule just explained, that if someone alters the meaning of a text in expounding it, it is their words that need to be brought into conformity with the text, not the other way about: a characteristically provocative argument, despite its reliance on the claim (Matt. 5:17) that Christ fulfills the old law instead of changing it.

143 **entende** intend

143–44 **noon other wise than which is now seid** in no other circumstances than these given now

144 **bere hem** conduct themselves

145–57 **And sithen . . . Londoun** The "book" expounded by the "greet clerk" (128), which is originally the "Bible" (129), now proves to be rather the "trouthis of lawe of kinde" (145) written in the human heart (124), which underlies and gives authority to the teaching even of Christ and his Apostles. (This understanding of the status of Scripture, which runs the risk of depriving it of its special authority, is at the heart of Pecock's attack on Lollard biblicism but was found heretical by his peers.) From this inner book, using the educated reason Pecock regards as the highest faculty, "clerkis" can produce a near infinite number of true books. The passage imaginatively justifies Pecock's prolixity while describing the richness of the "inner" book in terms reminiscent of Augustine's account of God's endlessly meaningful speech, paraphrased in *The General Prologue to the Wycliffite Bible* (excerpt 1.15: 9–12). For the topos of the "book of the heart," found not only in Pecock and the Lollard texts he attacks but in Usk (see excerpt 1.4) and Langland (see excerpt 3.19), and probably underlying any reference to a writer's need to "shewe hit forth that is in me" (Walton, excerpt 1.5: 40), see Jager 1996.

145 **kinde** nature

146 **wroten** written

147 **weren** existed ∫ **solempnest** most sacred ∫ **inward** internal

148 **resounis doom** reason's judgment ∫ **passing** surpassing

149–50 *The Just Aprising of Holi Scripture* This book is not extant.

150 **Jeremye spekith** See Jer. 31:33–34. ∫ **c.** chapter (Latin *capitulum*)

151 **Poul in his epistle** Heb. 8:10–12, commonly attributed to Paul

154 **mowe** may

155 **governauncis** ordinances

PART TWO

ADDRESSING AND POSITIONING THE AUDIENCE

The reader is the space on which all the quotations that make up a writing are inscribed without any of them being lost; a text's unity lies not in its origin but in its destination. . . . Classic criticism has never paid any attention to the reader; for it, the writer is the only person in literature.

—Roland Barthes (1977, 148)

READERS/AUDIENCES/TEXTS

"Reading" and the "reader" are not terms that speak for themselves or float free of history.[1] In the modern Western world, reading is often assumed to be a solitary and private activity. But most late medieval readers did not read in this way. Despite the spread of the practice of silent reading (Saenger 1982, 1997) and the growth of lay literacy, most people encountered texts through hearing them read aloud (Coleman 1996). Nonetheless, whether individuals were literate or not, the imagined societies and actual social systems of late medieval England and Scotland were dependent on reading communities and on public forms of textual transmission at all levels. Brian Stock's model of the diffusion of literacy through social performance theorizes how the *illiterati* were able to participate in literate culture. By a process that was only initially dependent on written texts, the written word could act on its audiences in politically transformative ways: "[T]extual communities were not entirely composed of literates. The minimal requirement was just one literate, the *interpres* [scholarly interpreter], who understood a set of texts and was able to pass his message on verbally to others. By a process of absorption and reflection the behavioural norms of the group's other members were eventually altered" (Stock 1983, 23). From a historicist point of view, "audience" is thus often a more satisfactory term than "reader" for the period 1280–1520, embracing, as it does, more of the range of participants in textual culture. In any case, given the volatile status of the vernacular throughout the period, the importance of patronage, and the often highly specific social matrices in and for which

---

1.   The shift of attention proclaimed by Barthes has taken place across a variety of critical and disciplinary perspectives: phenomenological, sociological, ethnographic, poststructuralist. In medieval studies, the mid-nineteenth-century philological approach to literature sidelined inquiry into audience and reception (for critiques of "origins" in medieval studies, see Frantzen 1990; Patterson 1987; Margherita 1994). As Michael Camille observes of the discipline of Old French, "Because early text editors were obsessed with origins and establishing the personality of an author, they tend[ed] to be unconcerned with audience, with the reception and reading of texts" (1996, 392–93). However, Camille is concerned with nineteenth-century traditions of Old French philology, which are not coterminous with Middle English traditions. Arguably, interest in the question of textual reception among Middle English scholars goes back to the 1930s; see Bennet 1937.

texts were composed (see the introduction to Part One, pages 11–12), readers and audiences were in practice as important as authors in the production of English texts and translations. In Caxton's translation of the *Book of the Knight of the Tower* (excerpt 2.16), for instance, a miniature biography of the aristocratic insti- gator of the text is given, in which the remembrance of a chivalric youth spent addressing "songes, layes, roundels, balades, vyrelayes and newe songes" (16–17) to the beloved from within a cynical male peer group is represented as provoking the compilation of a new book (though one with royal precedent [26–27]) for the knight's daughters. The compositional process fictionalizes lay and aristocratic command of further literate and literary resources (compare also Trevisa's "lord" in excerpt 2.2): priests and clerks read chronicles, histories, and the Bible aloud to the knight for him to make his selection of examples for his daughters. The con- sumption and production of texts is here represented as an overlapping process, in which there are roles for a range of reading and audience activities, neither strictly demarcated as between author and audience or as between the literate and those without Latin.

The attempt to recover medieval audiences and to consider what roles they played in producing, responding to, and using texts, and through what modes of textual address these processes occurred, is crucial for an understanding of the language politics of the period. But "audience" itself is not a single or stable term. As pointed out in the introduction to Part One (pages 10–11), the question of au- dience during this period is closely connected to the phenomenon of textual instability, and medieval texts were highly unstable, being re-created over and over again (a process Zumthor [1972a, 1992] calls *mouvance*) as they were adapted to different audiences at different periods.[2] This multiplicity of historical audiences is further complicated by the multifarious inscription of audiences in texts. Part Three of this volume examines more closely some of the reading models and pro- cesses by which texts seek to construct their audiences' responses; here in Part Two the focus is on the construction of audience itself.

ADDRESSING THE AUDIENCE

By their very nature, prologues tend to call upon their audiences directly. The re- covery of actual medieval audiences is fundamental to this volume's insistence on historicity, but there is an important sense in which "audiences" do not preexist the texts that are addressed to them but are called into being by them: in Louis

---

2. This textual transmission might be considered roughly analogous to that described by Derrida in *The Post Card* (1987). The medieval manuscript functions like the postman (*facteur*), the material sup- port for written communication. The *facteur* enters the circuit of the letter but has to go on looking for the right person to whom to deliver the message.

Althusser's terms, audiences and readers are "hailed" or "interpellated" as ideological subjects by texts.[3] Those texts inform, persuade, coerce, convince, entertain, or seduce their readers. They produce positions for their listeners from which what they say appears most intelligible (and therefore "natural" or incontrovertible). Their prologues are thus not transparent sources of knowledge about medieval audiences but locations of power, representation, difference, and desire (Belsey 1988, 405). Those who are explicitly addressed are not always those whose interests are at stake in the production of the text. Importantly, however, historically real and implied audiences are not always easily distinguished (Green 1983, 146; Zumthor 1979). "Audiences" are born (and reborn) somewhere between authorial desire, the desires of actual historical audiences, and the cultural and linguistic possibilities that shape acts of reading.[4]

Much of the evidence for actual audiences is lacking or has to be reconstructed from codicological research and close textual investigation. The company a text keeps in its "manuscript matrix" and the fortunes of that manuscript can provide evidence of probable audiences.[5] Sometimes this evidence is surprising. For example, the tract *The Holi Prophete David Seith* (excerpt 2.5) contains no internal reference to its intended audience but argues a Lollard position on the importance of vernacular biblical translation. Yet this text survives in a single manuscript that we know to have circulated in London as a "common-profit book," among devout readers of the mercantile sector, several of whom can be linked to the anti-Lollard reformer Reginald Pecock (Scase 1992). Codicological evidence testifies to the diverse social—often politically opposed—groups for whom Bible translation was a keen issue. (Compare Ashby's *Active Policy of a Prince*, excerpt 1.9, written for a royal reader but surviving only in a relatively cheaply produced booklet format.)

3.   In Althusser's words, *"all ideology hails or interpellates concrete individuals as concrete subjects"* (1971, 162). Like all texts, medieval translators' and compilers' prologues are ideological, and address, or "hail," readers through making the text intelligible, setting up positions from which they seize the meaning of the text: in other words, the text itself creates readers by constructing subject positions for them. Althusser's reading is, however, tied to an economic determinism that, although it, famously, is determination "in the last instance," is nevertheless based in capitalism, and is therefore problematic in its application to a differently structured, premodern market economy. But there is a dimension of Althusser's notion of the interpellation of an ideological subject that is potentially valuable for medievalists: its introduction, via the invocation of Lacan's mirror-stage, of the idea of seduction—of an identity that involves misrecognition, that is not wholly determined, and that is therefore predicated on incomplete desires. "Interpellation" is also useful because it does not claim that subjects are victims or that ideology is orchestrated by knowing manipulators: interpellation is a more rigorous and theoretically anchored form of the argument that readers are "constructed by various writers' own positions and preoccupations" (Crane 1992, 201).

4.   Part Two is concerned especially with the following questions about texts: what possible subject positions are inscribed in them? what meanings and what contests for meaning do they display? See Belsey 1988, 405; her list of questions one can ask of texts is adapted from Foucault 1977.

5.   The phrase "manuscript matrix" is borrowed from Stephen Nichols, via Camille (1996, esp. 386 and n. 52).

Readers and Listeners

Who was reading vernacular texts in the Middle Ages? The excerpts presented in this part do not, of course, enable us to answer this question in an empirically satisfactory way. For that we must turn to other kinds of evidence: wills; bequests; marginal manuscript annotations and signatures of ownership (such as those in the Findern, Vernon, and Auchinleck anthologies);[6] inventory citations (mention of the possession of books in the detailed lists of a person's goods drawn up on their death); information about patronage, book copying and borrowing; data from guild and civic records about dramatic performances; and evidence from heresy trials. This evidence is partial and fragmentary, and thus poses interpretive problems (see Pearsall 1985; Griffiths and Pearsall 1989; Meale 1994a).[7] No general study of late medieval English and Scottish audiences has yet been written. While knowing something about who owned books does not necessarily tell us who *read* them, it does establish that readerships existed in various social groupings and occupations, not only among clerics, monks, ecclesiastics (and, to a lesser extent, nuns). Lay book owners included the aristocracy and upper and lower gentry, squires, courtiers, lawyers, administrators and men of affairs, military leaders, wealthy merchants and their wives, students, well-off urban artisans, and at least a few urban and rural laborers.[8] By the fifteenth century the readership of works in the English vernacular was made up of an increasingly broad spectrum of social groups.

6. The Findern MS is Cambridge University Library MS Ff.1.6: see Barratt 1992, 268–74; Harris 1983; Boffey 1996. The Auchinleck MS is Edinburgh, National Library of Scotland MS Advocates 19.2.1: see Meale 1994a, 212, for the divergent scholarly views on its audience.

7. See Hudson 1985 and 1988 on the ownership and dissemination of Lollard manuscripts; Bell 1988, Riddy 1996b, and Meale 1996a on laywomen and their books; Rosenthal 1982 on aristocratic patronage and book bequests; Scase 1992 on "common-profit" books; Bell 1995 on book ownership in medieval nunneries; Ker 1964, Watson 1987, and Bell 1992 on books in English monastic houses; Doyle 1974, 1983a, 1989, and 1990 on the production and dissemination of anthologies and individual texts. Studies of individual manuscripts by Richard Beadle and A.E.B. Owen (1977) and Derek Pearsall (1990) include discussion of readers. Griffiths and Pearsall 1989, Pearsall 1983, and Carley and Tite 1997 include studies of book ownership, as does Meale 1996c. McCash 1996 contains essays on women's literary patronage in England. On private and institutional ownership, see the detailed entries in Sandler 1986; Kauffmann 1975; Morgan 1988. For more general surveys, see Harthan 1982; Calkins 1983; de Hamel 1994; Manion and Muir 1991. Cavanaugh 1984 is a major study of book bequests. The British Academy publishes medieval library catalogues (Bell 1992; Rouse and Rouse 1991), which are informative about medieval book ownership. There is no single place where ownership of foreign-produced manuscripts is catalogued. Ruth Evans and Lesley Johnson (1991) briefly discuss fifteenth-century female lay literacy in the context of courtly poetry.

8. Until recently, evidence of identifiable female readers from the mercantile sector has been lacking. Felicity Riddy is currently researching this area: for notice of her work in progress, see Meale 1994a, 212. There are very few studies, apart from Scase 1992, that deal specifically with urban audiences. Evidence for book ownership or reading among urban and rural laborers can sometimes be inferred from heresy trials (see Hudson 1988, chap. 9; McSheffrey 1995a). For a discussion of the social stratification of late medieval English society, see Dyer 1989, 10–26.

Those who were listening to English texts were similarly diverse.[9] Many laypeople had books read aloud to them (see, e.g., Caxton's *Book of the Knight,* excerpt 2.16, and *The Book of Margery Kempe,* excerpt 3.22). Arguing for the use of English in preaching, the prologue to the early-fourteenth-century *Northern Homily Cycle* (excerpt 2.1) urges that "laued men havis mar mister, / Godes word for to *her,* / Than klerkes that . . . sees hou thai sal lif on bokes" (laypeople/ uneducated people have a greater need to hear God's word than clerks, who . . . can see how they ought to live in books) (65–68; emphasis added). Yet, as Joyce Coleman (1990, 1996) points out, many *literate* audiences still preferred to gather in groups to hear texts read aloud, like Chaucer's aristocratic Criseyde, who listened to a romance with her company of women (*Troilus and Criseyde* II.81–86).[10] Reading, then, was not just a private affair. It was a performance mode that persisted throughout the fifteenth century, even when people could read for themselves. Such a practice of shared recreational "literacy" among an educated elite is suggested by the fifteenth-century *Liber niger* (c. 1471) of Edward IV, one of the fullest surviving accounts of a late medieval household: "[The king's esquires] be acustumed, wynter and somer, in after nonys and in euenynges, to drawe to lordez chambrez within courte, there to kepe honest company aftyr theyre cunyng [abilities], in talkyng of cronycles of kinges and of other polycyez [public affairs], or in pypyng, or harpyng, synging, other actez marciablez [chivalric deeds], to help ocupy the court and acompany straungers" (Myers 1969, 129).[11] As Coleman remarks, the implication of "talkyng of cronycles" is that for this actual elite social group "prelection [hearing works read] and discussion consti-

---

9.   Several studies have explored medieval reading as a social practice. Using mainly literary evidence, Janet Coleman (1981) discusses the sociopolitical meanings of book ownership, patronage, and the growth of lay literacy for the period 1350–1400. Paul Strohm reconstructs Chaucer's fifteenth-century (1982) and contemporary (1977, 1989) audiences (see also Green 1983). Susan Schibanoff (1988, 1994) probes the implications of gender difference for the historical reception of Chaucer and later medieval writers, including Caxton. Women as readers are studied in Tarvers 1992 and Smith and Taylor 1995. The audience for Middle English romances (a group that included both women and the mercantile elite) are mapped by Carol M. Meale (1992, 1994b), Derek Pearsall (1985), Stephen Knight (1986), and Peter Coss (1985). The huge corpus of information collected by REED (Records of Early English Drama) concerns the production and reception of early dramatic performances, though there is scant empirical evidence about their actual audiences: for analyses of the project, see Emmerson 1988 and Coletti 1990 and 1991.

10.   Borrowing from a medieval distinction found in John of Salisbury, Coleman (1990, 126) distinguishes between *lectio* (private reading) and *praelectio* (reading aloud to a group of listeners). Coleman also points out that where medieval writers express anxiety about reception, this has to do with language difficulties and not with mode of performance: the problem is not whether audiences can read privately but whether the choice of language will provide difficulty—a question, then, of lack of education not lack of private reading skills (128). Her argument challenges the influential work of Paul Saenger (1982) on silent reading among the late medieval laity (see also Coleman 1996, 21–23, 122–23).

11.   *Marciable* is difficult to translate: under *marciable* the *MED* gives the meaning "martial," which fits the context poorly, but the related *marcial* can mean "valiant," as well as "martial," a meaning that shades toward "chivalric," which better fits the context (cf. "factis merciall," *Spektakle of Luf,* excerpt 2.17: 32). Under *marciable* the *OED* gives "compassionate" (from a different etymology). The context here suggests a term close to "gentil," carrying strongly approbatory class and behavioral meanings.

tuted one seamless, stimulating activity" (1996, 96).[12] Recreational literacy was by no means confined to the court or to secular material. Texts like the *South English Legendary* (excerpt 2.15), as well as drama like the sensationalist *Croxton Play of the Sacrament* (excerpt 2.14), were also clearly designed to entertain as well as instruct. The audiences that made up the broad and immensely socially varied "audiate" culture that lay behind many such Middle English texts could not have been passive consumers. Whether or not they could read, they had to be sophisticated and active listeners.

Although not central to this anthology's concern with writing, it is also worth remembering that the various kinds of visual literacies involved in the "reading" of images are a significant part of the medieval relationship between text and reader (see *Dives and Pauper*, excerpt 3.9). This is true not only of civic pageants (such as the one in which the prologue to *Knyghthode and Bataile* [excerpt 2.12] is set) and plays like the *Croxton Play* (excerpt 2.14), in which spectacle may have taken precedence over the word (Runnalls 1994). The copy of Norton's *Alchemy* (excerpt 2.3) in the British Library Additional manuscript and many manuscripts of Gower's *Confessio Amantis* (excerpt 2.11) contain illuminations that are integral to the meaning of the text.[13]

Divergent and Nonconsensual Responses

One problem with the term "community" in modern critical accounts of medieval audiences and readers is that it often implies or is subtended by a mythical notion of medieval *communitas*, underplaying the extent to which collective readings are in tension with individual readings or, indeed, with one another. Textual communities, like Stock's twelfth-century heretical Waldensians, are not necessarily homogeneous, nor do they have homogeneous agendas, especially over time; they can be shifting and transitory phenomena. As Susan Crane (1992, 203) observes of Stock's apparently democratizing model of shared textual use, "[Social] stratification was not thereby eradicated." In his translation of the Benedictine Rule (excerpt 2.8), for example, Bishop Fox momentarily elides the problematic social and gendered distribution of literacy and illiteracy when he claims to have translated the Rule into "oure moder's tongue, commune, playne, rounde Englisshe" (33–34). But his predominant stance, referring to himself throughout his preface as "we" and addressing his audience of nuns in the third person, reinforces a paternalistic distinction between those who know Latin and those who

12. Strohm (1989, 22) considers this account "burnished with the mellow glow of old custom" and "anachronistic in the fifteenth-century"; Coleman (1996, chap. 5) refutes his argument.

13. For discussion of the importance of the relationship between text and image in a medieval manuscript, see Camille (1996), whose work challenges the traditional split between "discourse" and "figure," reading and seeing, in which vision is relegated to lower status (Lyotard 1971).

do not (compare Capgrave, *Life of St. Gilbert,* excerpt 2.7, and *The Amesbury Letter,* excerpt 2.9). By inviting the nuns to think of English as natural and universal, shared by all alike, Fox gives neither them nor the broader audience his prologue also implicitly addresses any room to question whether the benefits of learning Latin might not perhaps be extended to the nuns as well, or whether social and sexual divisions might not in fact be perpetuated by his translation. Nevertheless, whatever the containment strategies operative in texts for women, the possibilities of resistant readers and the social history of women's reading both argue for slippage between the ambitions and the effects of such texts. Riddy's alternative scene of female textual reception suggests that women's reading during the later Middle Ages was not entirely under male clerical control. Her delineation of a late medieval "subculture" of nuns and devout laywomen argues for a distinctively feminine approach to religious issues, such as that which shapes and supports the work of Julian of Norwich (Riddy 1996b; excerpts 1.13 and 3.4).

Stock's concept of the textual community implies that meanings evolve in social groups united at some level through literacy. But once we look hard at the use of the vernacular by textual communities, it becomes evident that the vernacular, whose use is initially a necessity, also provides the means for consensus to break down. Or, more accurately—since consensus probably never existed—use of the vernacular exposes the gaps in supposedly united communities by demonstrating the crucial nonunitary meaning of texts now opened up to diverse constituencies and therefore capable of generating divergent readings. The kind of "textual community" imagined in the prologue to *Woman's Kind in Childing* (excerpt 2.6) is one of "lettyrde" (able to read *English*) women reading the work out loud to "unlettyrd" women to "help hem and conceyle [counsel] hem in here maledyes" (2.6: 17). But the translator acknowledges that a man might read it with an altogether different agenda, to put women down: "yf hit fall any man to rede hit, I pray hym . . . that he rede hit not in no dyspyte ne sclaundure of no woman" (2.6: 19–20). The question of theorizing audience response in the Middle Ages has been largely neglected (although see Sponsler 1992), but we need to keep in mind the possibility that medieval readerly identities were dispersed and disseminated in ways that escape their apparent ideological containment in these prologues or their construction by modern critics as unified social collectives.

Addressees and Audiences

Bearing in mind Althusser's argument that audiences are called into being, "interpellated," by texts and do not simply preexist them, it is worth briefly summarizing the varieties of audience represented in the prologues in Part Two. Paul Strohm's discussion of Chaucer's audiences (1983) provides a useful, if somewhat ad hoc, taxonomy. First, there is the actual audience, both contemporary (primary) and later (secondary), about which we can sometimes, but not invariably or reliably, know. Second, there is the fictional (inscribed) audience, imagined in the text, like Chaucer's pilgrims or the "squire" addressed by his "father" in the *Spektakle of Luf* (excerpt 2.17). Third, there is the intended audience, sometimes identified by dedications and addresses to patrons, such as Gower's dedication of the *Confessio Amantis* (excerpt 2.11) first to Richard II and then to Henry of Lancaster. And last, there is the implied audience: the text's "ideal reader," anticipated or constructed by statements in the text with which he or she is encouraged to agree.[14]

Audiences represented by the excerpts in Part Two include a number in Strohm's first category. These "actual" audiences are named readers, including aristocratic patrons and dedicatees: the master of the Gilbertine convent at Sempringham (excerpt 2.7); "My dear susterys Mary and Anne" in *The Amesbury Letter* (excerpt 2.9: 1); Richard II and then Henry of Lancaster in the two versions of Gower's prologue to the *Confessio Amantis* (excerpt 2.11); Henry VI in *Knyghthode and Bataile* (excerpt 2.12); the "Duches of Bokengham" (*The Nightingale,* excerpt 2.13: 16); and the daughters of the knight Geoffroy de la Tour-Landry (excerpt 2.16). Other excerpts address more general audiences: laymen and clerics (*Northern Homily Cycle,* excerpt 2.1: 69–70, 75–80; *Ordinal of Alchemy,* excerpt 2.3: 3–4), an urban audience of all social ranks ("bothe leste and moste") at Croxton (the *Play of the Sacrament,* excerpt 2.14: 3). Still others address specific constituencies, such as women who can read English in *The Knowing of Woman's Kind in Childing* (excerpt 2.6). Most of these audiences are also the "intended" audiences of Strohm's third category, but may nonetheless have constituted, at some point, actual audiences.

Other prologues offer, as in Strohm's second category, a fictional, or inscribed, audience: a wise older knight addressing the "young squyer his sone" (*Spektakle of Luf,* excerpt 2.17: 4–5); the parson of Calais presenting his book to "my lord Beaumont" in the scripted drama of *Knyghthode and Bataile* (excerpt 2.12: 54–71). And in others the audience is not directly addressed but implied (that is, "ideal"). Trevisa's implied audience (excerpt 2.2) is all those who agree that English translation should be made available. The *South English Legendary* (excerpt 2.15) addresses no particular audience, but its use of "we" positions both author and audience as members of the constituency of Christian believers ("Wel aghte we lovie Cristendom · that is dure iboght" [2.15: 57]); *On Translating the Bible into English* (excerpt 2.4) does not name its audience, but it assumes that they have a strong interest in having the Bible in English.

Real, inscribed, intended, and implied audiences sometimes coexist, and sometimes match up—or not. The excerpts in this part illustrate some of these complexities from the wide range of Middle English theorizations of audience.

---

14. As Meale points out (1994a, 210), following Ong, "the implied audience is always in some measure a fiction."

ORGANIZATION OF PART TWO

Excerpts 2.1–3: Universal access. The first three extracts ostensibly address universal audiences under the rubric of "openness." The anonymous clerical author of the early-fourteenth-century *Northern Homily Cycle* (excerpt 2.1) claims to use English in order to make God's gifts accessible to everyone (49–64). But who are the "alle" (63) for whom these verse sermons are intended? Although, as noted below (page 125), the *Northern Homily Cycle* presents a case for freeing God's word from exclusive clerical stewardship in order to give laypeople access to the Scriptures, the prologue does not advocate that laymen read for themselves. Despite its benign rhetoric of humble service and social leveling (e.g., 75–78), it firmly positions its audience of uneducated (i.e., non-Latin-literate) laity in a hierarchical order, constructing and maintaining a major social division between lay ("laued folk") and clergy ("lered men") (33–44). It valorizes clerisy by emphasizing the value of clerical learning, and it partly does so by equating "laued" with all laypeople, "lered" with all clerics. (In practice many religious were not well educated, and one of the *Northern Homily Cycle*'s main audiences may have been secular priests.)

In Trevisa's *Dialogue* and *Epistle to Berkeley* (excerpt 2.2) the lay/clerical distinction is still important (the roles are here apportioned to the fictional "lord" and "clerk"), but the issue of accessibility is framed within the context of secular patronage. Inscribing a feudal author-patron relationship, the *Epistle* locates the desire for the text in Trevisa's actual patron, Lord Berkeley. The plucky figure of "John Trevysa" (2.2: 133) (who cannot be precisely identified either with the author or with *Clericus*) is figured as a mere servant, braving a torrent of spite to carry out his patron's will (138–40). The *Dialogue* constructs Berkeley as broker for translations in the vernacular, redistributing the intellectual capital of translated works (like the prestigious *Polychronicon*) with the largesse befitting his social rank (Somerset 1998, chap. 3). It is clear in the debate that readers are meant to side with the lord, not with the rather mean-minded clerk (see further essay 4.1, pages 323–25).

But the implied audience is not limited to the patron. By making the lord an apologist for the vernacular—a lord, moreover, who can "speke and rede and understonde Latyn" (38, 40–41)—the text implicitly engages a wider audience with potentially varied interests in the promulgation of the vernacular. The dialogue form is crucial in offering multiple viewpoints. The intention is less to arouse controversy or ambiguity than to engage the audience as active participants. Their assent to the text's liberal position on translation is secured seductively, not through coercion.

Although there is nothing obviously Lollard about the text, it was written at the height of late-fourteenth-century cultural debates about the politics of vernacular translation, so it is hardly surprising that it implies something of alternative discursive formations in which pro-translation arguments carry heretical meanings. These more controversial meanings may be implicit in Trevisa's choice of dialogue form, an effective means of both raising critique and neutralizing it. The emphasis on the need for "lewde" men to have access to English translations is also present in Lollard polemic, as is the view in the *Epistle* that access to the truth enshrined in the text will necessitate changing some of the terms (excerpt 2.2: 142–48). Contemporary audiences looking to Trevisa to bolster their political causes might have appropriated his detailed and informed arguments in favor of Bible translation (*Dialogue,* 72–90, 94–113, 116–19).

More complex subject positions for the audience are implied in the text's attitude toward the task of the translator: not just to fulfill a lay demand for the Bible in English but to empower audiences with awareness of their ignorance, and thus to stimulate their self-education. The lord mimics this position of "enlightened ignorance" when he says that there is much Latin in the chronicles that even he cannot understand "without studiyng and avisement and loking of other bokes" (42–43). The lord alludes to this task of the translator when, to the clerk's charge that the *illiterati* can ask those who do know (59–60), he replies that "the lewde man wote not what he shuld axe . . . nether . . . of whom he shuld axe" (61–63). On the other hand, it is also the lord who offers a realistic analysis of the practical difficulties people face in educating themselves (46–48). His socioeconomic analysis constructs the unlettered as more sophisticated and discriminating than does the *Northern Homily Cycle,* where they are positioned as "naturally" fixed in their ignorance.

A hundred years later, Norton's late-fifteenth-century *Ordinal of Alchemy* (excerpt 2.3) exploits the rubric of accessibility to promote an arcane work of alchemy. Norton's extended and creative use of medieval social satire (18–44) calls on his audience to accept as self-evident that every social group makes use of alchemy, uneducated laymen as well as clerks (3–4), and that its benefits should therefore be spread to all. Its educated author is the one best placed to pass this knowledge on: "For truly he that is not a grete clerke / Is nyse and lewde to medle with that werke" (50–51). Thus, despite his avowed democratizing claims, Norton invokes the conventional opposition between *litteratus* and *illiteratus,* reinforcing the hierarchy by punningly naming the work an "ordinal," as though it were a priest's manual of services. His arguments are strikingly similar to those used in favor of English translation for pastoral purposes, showing how authors could rework the existing discourse of "openness" in a variety of generic contexts and for a variety of audiences. Norton claims, for example, that "he that shuld al commyn peple teche, / . . . most for theym use playne and comon speche" (58–59). But intelligibility here is less about "open access" than about giving alchemy a stamp of respectability. One of the work's implied audiences, therefore, consists of those who might be doubtful of the benefits of alchemy (with reason, given its contemporary associations with counterfeiting). The rhetoric of plain talking constructs a readership of no-nonsense men of all social classes, but this is belied by Norton's polished elegance and erudite allusions, his hinting at the mysteries of "holi alchymye" (55). One of the attractions of this prologue may be its inclusive claim to speak to all, while signaling linguistically that its arcane knowledge is really intended for a specialized intellectual elite.

Excerpts 2.4–5: Access for all to the Scriptures. The next two excerpts argue specifically for vernacular translation of the Bible. *On Translating the Bible* (excerpt 2.4) and *The Holi Prophete David Seith* (excerpt 2.5) circulated among freethinking groups of devout laypeople. However, because they were written at a time when Bible translation was furiously debated, they participate in a highly charged discursive realm within which they must define their audiences most carefully. Concern about sailing too close to the heretical wind may account for the sarcastic assertion that "we fynden in Latyne mo heretikes than of ale other langagis" (*On Translating the Bible,* excerpt 2.4: 21–22), as well as for the text's argument about the mother tongue, which powerfully constructs *all* people as wishing for translation, not just heretics. The implied audience for *On Translating the Bible* is educated, even if not Latin-literate, or may know Latin but have strong political reasons for wishing to wrest scriptural knowledge from the clergy. This is suggested by the clever mobilization of a "relativist" argument that resignifies the languages in which the Bible was written so that they are no longer ranged in a hierarchy, with Latin at the top. Instead, Latin's high status is destabilized by depriving the word "grammaticalliche" (29) of its magic scholastic aura, one that traditionally guaranteed the "truth" of the Latin Bible, and its referent becomes simply the "abite of right spekyng and right pronounsyng and right wryty[n]ge" (34–35: compare Dante's *De vulgari eloquentia;* see essay 4.1, pages 318–21). This also brings about a sense of lay superiority to the clergy. Like Trevisa, the author refers to a tradition of Bible translation (2.4: 1–10). *On Translating the Bible* invokes the topos of the mother tongue to connote universality, so that the implied reader is given a distinct sense of belonging to the English "nation." The use of the vernacular links the reader to "English" history and origins by invoking a genealogy of insular Bible translation that goes back to the historian Bede's account of the seventh-century King Oswald's sponsorship of Bishop Aidan's preaching to the people in English (excerpt 2.4: 7–10).

In *The Holi Prophete* (excerpt 2.5), the destabilization of clerical authority takes a more polemical bent. Seeking to arouse from its probable audience of devout merchants antagonism toward clerics, it represents certain clergy as "veyn men" (7) who "do goos[t]li avoutrie [spiritual adultery] with the word of God" (20). Far from being tamed by clerkly authority, its ideal audience is goaded to remedy its own lack of access to the Scriptures, an attitude produced in part through the text's manipulation of anticlericalism to make lay readers feel superior. The audience is drawn to agree with the anticlerical stereotype that "thise clerkis ben grete folis that with sich lyvynge [i.e., hypocritical lives] prechyn opynli the lawe of God" (56). Clear differentiation between social levels *within* the laity is suggested by the way that the text distances its implied audience from the "symple men" (those who do not know Latin, as opposed to "thise proud clerkis," who do) (124–26) whose interests are, perhaps somewhat patronizingly, defended against those of "clerkis." Nevertheless, like Trevisa's lord (excerpt 2.2), the author of *The Holi Prophete* does not just accept the ignorance of "symple men" but offers a socioeconomic explanation for their inability to read the Bible in Latin: "thei hawe not tyme and leiser to turne and turne agen the bokis of Goddis lawe to cunne the lettere therof" (2.5: 129–30). The representation of the word of God as sustaining food and drink (138–56) relies on the audience's knowledge of dominant cultural models of reading as eating (see excerpts 3.19–20). This representation thus commands the audience's assent to the work's political project and its condemnation of those priests who would withhold "goostli mete" (spiritual food) (148) from the populace.

Excerpts 2.6–9: Gender and positioning. If the topos of "openness" posits a mythical world in which social difference and division is swept away by universal access to English, the following four excerpts identify a specific, female market for translation: the anonymous *Knowing of Woman's Kind in Childing*, Capgrave's *Life of St. Gilbert*, Bishop Fox's translation of *The Rule of Seynt Benet*, and the anonymous *Amesbury Letter*. The last three of these concern knowledge aimed solely at audiences of enclosed women; the first addresses women of childbearing status and those who might attend them. In actuality, many women in the fourteenth and fifteenth centuries did not know Latin (Millett 1996; Barratt 1992, 2–4). But while this fact enters several of these texts as a pretext for their translation into English, this rhetorical commonplace is not necessarily to be taken at face value as a sign of male concern to alleviate female ignorance. As excerpt 2.1 suggests, clerics usually address the laity and women—the classic *illiterati*—as those for whom English translation is most necessary, but this audience can sometimes be little more than a pretext for the production of the text in English, a production that may serve other interests.

Capgrave invokes this commonplace when offering his translation of the life of Saint Gilbert "for the solitarye women of youre religioun whech unneth can undyrstande Latyn" (17–18), while addressing his text (and hence presenting his pastoral activity as a translator) in the first place to Nicholas Reysby, master of the Gilbertine Order of Sempringham (1–4). The Amesbury author (excerpt 2.9), on the other hand, addresses his female audience directly, and does so in a particularly intimate way, as "Mary and Anne" (1), presenting his work as part of the genre of the intimate personal letter or the informal epistolary rule. Nevertheless, even here a male cleric's appeal to a female audience in part allows him to institutionalize a version of himself through the publication of a text in which he functions as pastoral adviser and superior. This does not preclude his expressing respect and affection for his readers (compare Savage 1994)—the Amesbury cleric claims his female addressees are more "deply groundyd" (11–12) than he is in the spiritual practice of *imitatio Christi*—but such deference in turn does not make his text serve exclusively the interests of his named audience. This is not to level a charge of sexism against those male spiritual directors who fashioned themselves as authors writing for the women in their charge. Rather it is to point out that the men concerned could not have seen their works as alleviating the problem of ignorance, since they were mortgaged to a structural misogyny in which female illiteracy was represented not as a cultural but as a biological fact.

If excerpts 2.7–9 smooth over the social divisions between male clerics and their subordinate, unlettered female audiences, presenting female ignorance as a "natural" state of affairs, the translator of *The Knowing of Woman's Kind in Childing* (excerpt 2.6) demonstrates an awareness that "universal access" can work against certain groups. The text offers women practical knowledge of their bodies. It is assumed that the intended female audience will bring to bear on the text their knowledge of the Galenic commonplace that "whomen ben more febull and colde be nature than men been" (8; see Cadden 1993). Even women who do not take such a negative view of their bodily makeup will have to draw on this shared cultural knowledge about female feebleness in order to accept as "natural" the text's view that women suffer from more illnesses than men. Structural misogyny constructs and naturalizes the problems of women imagined here, but a counterposition is implied in the text's desire to limit the possible effects of misogyny.[15]

The recurrence of the topos of women's ignorance of Latin as a legitimation of the translation project in these four excerpts (excerpts 2.6–9) suggests a possible connection between the vernacular and the feminine/female. In some cases this is reinforced by the use of the "mother tongue" topos, as in the prologue to the *Knowing*: "whomen of oure tonge cunne bettyre rede and undyrstande thys langage than eny other" (women who are native speakers of English [or English women] are better able to read and understand this language [i.e., English] than any other) (excerpt 2.6: 15–16). Even when the "mother tongue" is used to connote universality, the link with the mother and the deployment of the topos in ostensible addresses to a female audience (see, e.g., excerpt 2.8: 33–35) suggest strong affinities between the vernacular and the female. And whereas on the one hand these men derive social advantage by drawing on female spirituality (Bolton 1981; Coakley 1991; Biddick 1993), on the other hand the women they are writing for are not wholly contained by this strategy but haunt the use of the vernacular as the very condition of its possibility. If women are targeted as a special group that "needs" works in English, the vernacular may have the potential to feminize its male audience by

15. See Schibanoff's argument (1994) that Caxton, in his epilogue to the *Dictis and Sayings of the Philosopheris*, has misunderstood Earl Rivers's excision of misogyny from the text, or rather has shown himself incapable of imagining a man resistant to misogyny. Male resistance to misogyny is of course not straightforward, for all the reasons that make gallantry—taking the woman's side—problematic: see Gallop 1982.

aligning them with non-Latin-literate women. In fact, Vincent Gillespie claims that "the laity, for all their pragmatic literacy . . . came to occupy a position in the educational hierarchy similar to that which had long been occupied by women religious" (1984, 4; for the earlier position of women, see Millett 1996).

Excerpts 2.10–13: Relations of patronage and courtly identity. The link between women and the vernacular is pursued in Caxton's translation of Christine de Pizan's manual of military strategy, *Book of Fayttes of Armes and of Chyvalrye* (excerpt 2.10), but Caxton, in ventriloquizing de Pizan's book on behalf of Henry VII, appropriates the feminine to construct a *masculine* courtly identity for himself and his implied audience (see also excerpt 3.24: 1–28). This is a text that might conceivably have been the subject of the "talkyng of cronycles of kinges and of other polycyez" mentioned in Edward IV's household book (see page 113 above). Caxton's faithful reproduction of de Pizan's elaborate "style clergial" (Barratt 1992, 139) raises interesting questions about authorial and patronal self-fashioning. It has been assumed that de Pizan's ironic pose of humility disadvantaged her fourteenth-century audience of military men (Barratt 1992) by putting a distance between herself and them: "they that been excersyng and experte in th'arte of chyvalrye be not comunely clerkys ne instructe in science of langage" (those who are practiced and expert in the art of chivalry are not usually clerks or instructed in the arts of rhetoric) (2.10: 24–26). But Caxton's appropriation of this archness might have functioned quite differently, "producing" its audience of "bourgeois" (London?) gentlemen by deliberately distancing them from clerks. The implied audience may even have savored Caxton's performance, much as Chaucer's "knowing" audience savored his self-fashioning in such ventriloquizations as the *Wife of Bath's Prologue*.

Like Caxton's work, Gower's *Confessio Amantis* (excerpt 2.11) is also ostensibly addressed to a king. Anne Middleton has suggested that there is an incongruity between its intended audience (signaled by the dedication to Richard II and then Henry of Lancaster) and its implied readers, claiming that its tone "is not a matter of deferential politeness to a ruler, but of rising to sufficient largeness of mind and of reference for a public occasion, and a broad common appeal. The king is not the main imagined audience, but an occasion for gathering and formulating what is on the common mind" (1978, 107). Certainly the community addressed in this book, made "for Engelondes sake" (31) to remedy the scarcity of books in "oure Englissh" (30), seems partly constructed as an entire polity. Yet, given the Latin apparatus with which (for all the proclaimed stylistic choice of "the middel weie" [24]) the poem is presented, it also seems to be one with a coterie or, at least, elite scholarly aspirations. At the same time, especially in the earlier version of the prologue, the intimacies as well as the broader politics of court culture are vividly dramatized (see 2.11: 130–41).

Knyghthode and Bataile (excerpt 2.12) is a verse adaptation of the same chivalric text of military strategy drawn on by de Pizan and translated by Caxton (excerpt 2.10), and like Caxton's and Gower's works, it is intended for a king: Henry VI. Unlike the *Confessio* prologue, its (excessively) deferential tone suggests that the king was more immediately its actual intended audience (though not, of course, its only one). The language is unabashedly aureate: "tryumphatour," "prosperaunce," "celsitude." It makes extensive use of rhetorical "colors," such as the *compar* (balanced clauses) of "Thei hem by lond, thei hem by see asseyle" (93), or the numerous instances of *apostrophe*: "Hail, halyday devout!," "Lo, Souverayn Lord" (8, 80). The dialogue between the fictionalized author, a "preste" of Calais, and the inscribed reader, "my lord Beaumont" (54–71), uses the idea of "audience" to enact the ritualized codes of etiquette found at court, with appropriate forms of the second-person pronoun ("ye" from inferior to superior, "thou" from superior to inferior) and formal syntactic structures, such as the use of future, conditional, and modal verbs in interrogative clauses ("wil your advyse / Suppose that the kyng heryn pleasier / May have?" [66–68]). The work's implied audience is evidently courtly and leisured: like Caxton's, consumers of literature for entertainment, not rough-and-ready fighting men. This is an audience for whom military strategy is a noble art—men of the officer class. Yet the versification of Vegetius's classic manual suggests a text that is not wholly intended as a set of practical techniques, but one written for a court audience, mostly composed of men, who are concerned with the quintessentially gentlemanly ideal of honorableness ("the right honorable offyce of armes and of chyvalrye," excerpt 2.10: 17–18).

The Nightingale (excerpt 2.13), on the other hand, though dedicated to a noble lady, Anne, duchess of Buckingham, bears witness to the tastes of a very different kind of "courtly" audience: possibly entirely female and interested in devotional and romance material, as is suggested by aspects of the manuscript context. The proem itself uses the device of addressing the book ("Go, lityll qu[ay]ere" [13]; see the epilogue of Chaucer's *Troilus and Criseyde* V.1786) to inscribe its aristocratic dedicatee as a feudal lord and the book as feudal subject. Assigned its proper place within her retinue (19), it produces for her the subject position of a feudal patron of the arts as well as an arbiter of chaste love.

Excerpts 2.14–15: Constructing Christian, local, and national identity. Excerpts 2.14 and 2.15 are concerned with producing Christian subjects who feel themselves to be part of an all-inclusive English community. In neither text (unlike, for example, Mannyng's *Chronicle,* excerpt 1.1, or *Cursor Mundi,* excerpt 3.14) is the use of English made an issue. The late-thirteenth-century *South English Legendary* (excerpt 2.15) is presumably written in English for much the same reasons as the *Northern Homily Cycle* (excerpt 2.1)—to fulfill pastoral aims—but its address to an English, Christian audience is made not by an appeal to the English language as a uniting bond but by the inclusion of national and local saints. But the implied audience of its prologue is clearly called upon to adopt the view that the "fight" for Christianity is right, since its aim is to bring mankind to "is kunde eritage [its natural heritage]" (2). The statement commands absolute assent to the "naturalness" of Christian redemption. Unlike the *Northern Homily Cycle* (which hints at the possibility that mankind might not find it so obviously easy to follow Christ's teachings, excerpt 2.1: 31–34), the *Legendary* does not deliberately construct an ideological division between laity and clergy to legitimate the clergy's position as gatekeepers of the word of God. Nevertheless, the use of the inclusive "we" (57) is just as ideologically motivated in its effacement of the role of the clergy in promulgating the text in English.

In the later, fifteenth-century *Croxton Play of the Sacrament* (excerpt 2.14), the dramatized testing by the Jews of the efficacious powers of a little cake of bread appears as an abomination in nature rather than a legitimate process of skeptical philosophical or theological investigation. This is achieved through exploiting the dramatic devices typical of much late medieval public, performative culture—second-person exhortations to confession, the practice that consummately marked one out as a Christian ("Unto youer gostly father shewe your synne" [66]); inclusion of the whole audience to produce a strong identification with the Christian sentiments of the banns and *Play,* and with the democratizing ideals of Christianity ("all thes semely, bothe leste and moste" [3])—at the same time flagging that audience's difference from its other, the Jews. This is done not only by presenting the Jews as capable of psychopathic behavior (torturing Christ in an oven) but through third-person narrative, which works to differentiate Jews from the Christians, who are addressed in the banns in the second person. Ironically, of course, the Jews within the *Play* become members of that Christian group through conversion. The *Play* offers its Christian audience a double satisfaction, producing their identification as Christians through their difference from Jews and, paradoxically, through their sense that Christianity is all-inclusive (see Chaucer's *Prioress's Tale* and the *South English Legendary,* 2.15: 57). And, by drawing attention to the place where the play will take place—Croxton, in East Anglia—the banns also produce for their audience a sense of local identity, of belonging to a specific urban community, not just a Christian one.

Excerpts 2.16–17: Constructing "bourgeois" masculine identity. The final two excerpts are both examples of the late medieval genre of courtesy literature. Caxton's translation of the *Book of the Knight* (excerpt 2.16) most probably circulated among London urban elites. It is unfortunate that so little is known about the unique copy of the *Spektakle of Luf* (excerpt 2.17), the only item in the Scottish Asloan manuscript not in Asloan's sixteenth-century hand (Lyall 1988, 170) and therefore impossible to place in any late-fifteenth-century manuscript context. The milieus of its circulation are unknown. The fictional scene of reception in the *Spektakle of Luf*—a knight addressing his son—conforms to an expected generic pattern: most courtesy literature from the twelfth century on is addressed to boys and men (Riddy 1996b, 69). Despite taking over the knight's address of his work to his daughters, Caxton's reasons for translating the work into English might have had less to do with providing instruction for actual fathers to give to their daughters than with catering to the tastes of the "bourgeois" elite who desired courtly material.[16] Caxton's implied audience might have looked less to the work's practical advice than to the possibilities it offered for mirroring and legitimating their own paternalistic household roles. Both texts, then, are concerned with producing specific masculine, urban elite identities. However, whereas Caxton's text produces "gallant" subjects, anxious to defend women and to uphold their honor (2.16: 29–47), the *Spektakle of Luf* works off just the opposite assumption: it is misogyny that produces for the "young squyer" an appropriately "gentle" masculine identity. Both texts of course depend on a shared assumption, inherent in their choice of the "courtesy literature" form: that women's sexual behavior renders them dangerous and requires policing, but is also constitutive of elite bourgeois masculine subjectivity.

2.1 *NORTHERN HOMILY CYCLE:* PROLOGUE

Date and Provenance: c. 1315; the north of England (Yorkshire).

Author, Sources, and Nature of Text: The *Northern Homily Cycle* was probably written by an Augustinian canon or canons in or near York (Heffernan 1990, 81). The text is a collection of sermons in verse, apparently based on the Anglo-Norman *Miroir des Evangiles* by Robert of Greatham (written c. 1250–1300 for the wife of his patron; see Deanesly 1920, 149; Sinclair 1992) and largely consisting of paraphrases of the Sunday gospels for the church year. The sermons in the collection may have been read out to congregations after regular services were over. The *Cycle* is one of several long pastoral works written in English in response to the drive to educate the laity (exemplified most importantly by Archbishop John Pecham's *Syllabus* of 1281), works that also include *Cursor Mundi* (excerpt 3.14), William of Nassington's *Speculum Vitae* (see essay 4.2, pages 336–37), and Robert Mannyng's *Handlyng Synne*. The prologue envisages the text as "opening up" the Scriptures to everyone, lay as well as clerical, through being written in English rather than in learned Latin

or "courtly" French (69–74). Translation into the vernacular is conceptualized as serving both an educational and a salvific purpose for the laity. Laypeople, it is claimed, have greater need than learned clerics for better access to God's word. In recommending that the clergy make "Godes gift" of the Scriptures accessible and "open" to all, the translator takes up the position of someone concerned about the ignorance of the laity, a position consistent with much orthodox thinking in the late thirteenth and early fourteenth centuries about the pastoral role of translations. Despite its concern with open access, however, the prologue creates a clerical/lay hierarchy through its recommendations that learned clerics should take it upon themselves to educate the illiterate (39–54), partly belying the prologue's apparently democratizing aims (e.g., 99–108). Even so, much of what is stated here would come to seem radical by the end of the fourteenth century, as the language of openness and accessibility came to be associated ever more closely with the Lollards (see excerpts 2.4 and 2.5).

Audience and Circulation: The *Northern Homily Cycle* was widely circulated: there are

---

16.   On the problematic nature of the term "'bourgeois' elite," see Riddy 1996a, 67.

twenty extant manuscripts, comprising at least three major recensions and two versions ("unexpanded" and "expanded") of the full text. From the late 1380s to 1440 many copies of the *Cycle* in its expanded form were produced, apparently as part of a concerted effort supervised by a religious order and possibly as a counterresponse to Lollard translation programs (see excerpts 2.4 and 2.5, and the section "Religious Writing, 1380–1520" in essay 4.2). Significantly, the later versions of the *Cycle* omit the prologue, which stresses the value of writing in the English vernacular in a fashion that by the fifteenth century might have seemed to align the text with Lollardy. Although the collection originated in, and was disseminated throughout, the North of England (presumably to both parish priests and nonaristocratic lay congregations), by the later fourteenth century it seems to have been read in other parts of Britain: one manuscript has an Anglo-Irish provenance.

Bibliography: The "expanded" version of the whole text is critically edited by Saara Nevanlinna (1972–84) from the Harley and Cotton Tiberius manuscripts. John Small (1973) edits the "unexpanded" version, which contains the prologue edited here. On the *Cycle*'s authorship and relation to the Vernon manuscript, see Heffernan 1985a and 1990. On the pastoral legislation that may have been a factor in the work's composition, see Gillespie 1994 and Powell 1994.

Source: Edinburgh, Royal College of Physicians MS Anonima 11, fols. 16r–v: a relatively plain parchment manuscript that contains the earliest copy of the text (only the prologue and first thirteen homilies), with a copy of *Cursor Mundi* (see excerpt 3.14). Written in two columns with empty spaces for illuminated capitals, which were never added, the text may have been a preacher's compilation; it is badly discolored and often illegible. For a description, see Ker (1969–83, 2:539–40).

This excerpt, among the earliest included in this volume, presents a number of minor difficulties, and a full translation is therefore supplied.

Fader and Sun and Haligast,	*Father and Son and Holy Ghost,*
That anfald God es, ay stedfast,	*Who is singular God, always steadfast*
Worthi Driht in Trinite,	*Worthy Lord in Trinity*
A God, a miht in persons iii,	*One God, one power in three persons*
5 Withouten end and bigin[n]i[n]g,	*Without end and beginning,*
Rihtwis Lauerd and mihti king,	*Righteous Lord and mighty king,*
That mad of riht noht alle thing,	*Who made everything out of absolutely nothing*
And geres the erthe froit forth bring,	*And who causes the earth to bring forth fruit,*
Witouten the nan froit mai spring,	*Without you no fruit is able to grow*
10 For al es loken in thi welding.	*For everything is secured in your governance.*
Thou ert Lauerd, that worthi drihte,	*You are the Lord, that worthy ruler,*
That al ophaldes wiht thi mihte.	*Who upholds all with your power.*
Thou that al craftes kanne,	*You who know all skills,*
Of erthe and lam thou made manne,	*You made man of earth and loam*
15 And gaf him gast of schilwisnes	*And gave the gift of discernment to him* [see note]
That thou mad efter thi liknes.	*Whom you made according to your likeness.*
Thou filde thi[s] gaste sa ful of witte,	*You filled this spirit so full of intelligence,*
Sa quaynt and crafti mad thou itte,	*So well fashioned and skillful you made it*
That al bestes er red for man:	*That all creatures are under man's control:*
20 Sa mani wyle and wrenk he can.	*He knows so many wiles and tricks.*
Forthi suld man in thi servis	*Therefore man should in your service*
Despend his witte and his quaintis,	*Expend his wit and his cunning*

	For thu gaf man skil and insiht,	*Because you gave man reason and insight*
	And hevenis blis thou haves him hiht,	*And you have promised him heaven's bliss*
25	To kovenand that he serve riht,	*As a covenant, as long as he serves [you] properly*
	And se and knau thi mikel miht.	*And sees and acknowledges your great power.*
	One the bird be his mast thouht,	*On you must be his principal thought,*
	That ses quat thou for him has wroht,	*Who sees what you have created for him,*
	And fra quat bale thou him broht,	*And from what torment you have brought him,*
30	Quen thou fra helle on rode him boht.	*When you redeemed him from hell on the cross.*
	An unkind man es he,	*He is an unnatural man*
	That turnes alle his thoht fra the.	*Who turns his thoughts utterly away from you.*
	And wel bird everilke man,	*And well behooves it each man*
	Lof God after that he kan:	*To worship God in whatever way he can:*
35	Lered men wit rihtwis lare,	*Learned men with righteous learning*
	And laued folk wit rihtwis fare,	*And uneducated folk with righteous behavior,*
	Prestes wit matines and wit messe,	*Priests with matins and mass*
	And laud men wiht rihtwisnes,	*And laymen with righteousness,*
	Clerk wit lar of Godes worde	*A cleric with the knowledge of God's word*
40	(For he haves in him Godes horde	*(For he has within him God's store*
	Of wisdom and of gastlic lare,	*Of wisdom and of spiritual teaching*
	That he ne an noht for to spare,	*So that he ought not to spare a single bit of it*
	Bot scheu it forthe til laued menne,	*But reveal it to laymen*
	And thaim the wai til hevin kenne):	*And make known to them the way to heaven):*
45	For [all than] sal we yeld acount,	*For we all shall then give a reckoning*
	Quat that wisdom mai amount,	*Of what that wisdom may be worth*
	That God havis given us for to spend,	*Which God has given us to expend*
	In god oys til our lives end.	*In good use until our lives' end.*
	Forthi suld ilke precheour schau,	*Therefore should each preacher reveal*
50	The god that Godd havis gert him knau,	*The good that God has caused him to know:*
	For qua-sa hides Godes gift,	*For whosoever hides God's gift,*
	God mai chalange him of thift.	*God can accuse him of theft.*
	In al thinge es he nouht lele,	*He is not in every way loyal*
	That Godes gift fra man wil sele.	*Who wishes to hide God's gift from men.*
55	Forthi the litel that I kanne,	*Therefore what little I am able*
	Wil I schau til ilke manne,	*I will show to each man*
	Yf I kan mar god than he,	*If I know more good than he does,*
	For than lif Ic in charite,	*Because then I live in charity,*
	For Godes wisdom that es kid,	*On account of God's wisdom, which is renowned,*
60	And na thing worthe quen it es hid.	*And not at all valued when it is hidden.*
	Forthi will I of my povert	*Therefore I will, from my state of poverty,*
	Schau sum thing that Ik haf in hert,	*Reveal something of what I have in my heart*
	On Ingelis tong that alle may	*In the English tongue, so that everyone can*
	Understand quat I wil say.	*Understand what I wish to say.*
65	For laued men havis mar mister,	*For laymen have a greater need*
	Godes word for to her,	*To hear God's word*
	Than klerkes that thair mirour lokes,	*Than clerics who look in their mirror*
	And sees hou thai sal lif on bokes.	*And see from books how they ought to live.*
	And bathe klerk and laued man	*And both cleric and layman*
70	Englis understand kan	*Are able to understand English*

That was born in Ingeland,   *Each one who was born in England*
And lang haves ben tharin wonand.   *And has been living there a long time,*
Bot al men can noht, i-wis,   *But not all men are able, certainly,*
Understand Latin and Frankis.   *To understand Latin and French.*
75 Forthi me think almous it isse   *Therefore I consider it an act of charity*
To wirke sum god thing on Inglisse,   *To create something of benefit in English*
That mai ken lered and laued bathe,   *That may instruct both learned and laymen*
Hou thai mai yem thaim fra schathe,   *How they can protect themselves from evil*
And stithe stand igain the fend,   *And stand firm against the devil*
80 And til the blis of heven wend.   *And journey to the bliss of heaven.*
Mi speche haf I mint to drawe,   *I intend to take as my subject*
Of Cristes dedes and his sau.   *Christ's deeds and words.*
On him mai I best found mi werke,   *On him can I best found my work,*
And of his dedes tac mi merke,   *And take his deeds as my object,*
85 That maked al this werd of noht,   *He, who made this world from nothing,*
And der mankind on rode boht.   *And redeemed mankind dearly on the cross.*
The faur godspellers us schawes   *The four evangelists show us*
Cristes dedes and his sawes.   *Christ's deeds and his sayings.*
Al faur a talle thay telle,   *All four tell the same tale*
90 Bot seer saues er in thair spelle,   *But the wording in their gospels varies*
And of thair spel in kirk at messe,   *And from their gospels in the church at mass*
Er leszouns red, bathe mar and lesse.   *Lessons are read, both long and short.*
For at everilke messe we rede   *For at every mass we read*
Of Cristes wordes and his dede: *About Christ's words and his deeds:*
95 Forthi tha godspells that always   *Therefore the gospels that always*
Er red in kirc on Sundays   *Are read in church on Sundays*
Opon Inglis wil ic undo,   *I will expound in English*
Yef [God] wil gif me grace tharto.   *If God will give me the grace to do it.*
For namlic on the Sunenday   *For especially on Sundays*
100 Comes lawed men thair bede to say   *Come laymen, to say their prayers*
To the kirc, an for to lere   *To the church, and in order to learn*
Gastlic lare that thar thai here: *Spiritual teaching, which they hear there:*
For als gret mister haf thay   *For they have as great a need*
To wit quat the godspel wil say   *To know what the gospel is going to say*
105 Als lered men, for bathe er bouht   *As learned men, for both are redeemed*
Wit Cristes blod, and sal be broht   *With Christ's blood, and shall be brought*
Til hevenes blis ful menskelie,   *To the bliss of heaven, very graciously,*
Yef thai lef her rihtwislie.   *If they live here [on earth] righteously.*
For [thi] wil Ic on Inglis schau,   *Therefore I intend to show in English*
110 And ger our laued brether knawe,   *And bring it about that our lay brothers know*
Quat alle tha godspelles saies,   *What all the gospel [readings] say*
That falles tille the Sunnendayes,   *That fall on Sundays,*
That thai mai her and hald in hert   *So that they can hear and keep in their hearts*
Thinge that thaim til God mai ert,   *The things that may urge them toward God.*
115 And forthi at our biginninge,   *And therefore at our beginning*
Pray we God of hevine kinge,   *Let us pray to God the king of heaven*
That he help us for to bringe   *That he may help us to bring*
This ilke werk to god endinge,   *This same work to a good conclusion,*

And gif me grace sua make
120 This werk for laued mennes sake,
That I mai haf for my mede,
Hevenrik blis quen I am dede,
And our werc be worschipe
To God, and to the fend sendschipe
125 And joy til halwe and till angel,
And Cresten folk til sauel hel,
That it be sua says inwardlye,
Pater noster, Ave Marie, Pater noster, etc.

And give me grace so to compose
This work for laymen's sake,
That I can have as my reward
Heavenly bliss when I am dead,
And that our work be a form of worship
Of God, and destruction to the devil,
And joy to saints and to angels,
And to Christian folk a healing of their souls
That it may be so, say inwardly
"Our Father . . . ," "Ave Maria . . . ,"
"Our Father . . . etc."

1–26 Fader . . . miht The opening invocation to a Trinitarian God immediately introduces one of the main doctrines—that of the Trinity—that distinguish Christianity from other religions (e.g., Islam or Judaism) and that the authors of texts written for the laity often assumed lay people would find especially difficult. God is then addressed in his capacity as creator of the world, whose role as a craftsman all must imitate in fulfillment of their nature as humans made (unlike the rest of creation) in God's image (16). The emphasis on craft as a special human attribute (an emphasis that would make good sense in a city like York, where the cycle may have been written, with its multiplicity of craftsmen organized into guilds) prepares the way for the poet's justification of his project as a responsible use of the skill he has been given (55–60).

15 gast of schilwisnes gift of discernment. "Schilwisnes" (intelligence, discretion) is a spiritual gift from God, *MED: gost (n.)* 4.

17 thi[s] gaste MS *thi gaste*

27, 33 bird must: third-person (he, she, it) present tense of the verb *biren,* a Northern and North Midlands usage (see *MED: biren*). In Middle English this verb, a synonym of *bihoven* (to have to do), occurs almost exclusively in the North Midlands and the North, and only in the third person.

35–36 Lered men wit rihtwis lare, / And laued folk wit rihtwis fare After first stressing the unity of humanity in its possession of intelligence and responsibility to serve God, the text distinguishes two kinds of people, whose service takes contrasting forms. The terms "lered" and "laued" literally mean "learned" and "uneducated," but "laued" also refers to the lay status of all who are not priests, monks, nuns, or other professional religious. Lines 37–39 similarly associate the "lered" with "prestes" (37)—not all of whom would have been "learned" in practice—and the status of "clerk" (39). The underlying point is that the poet's way of serving God is to show others how they are meant to do the

same: a formulation that allows for the equality of all people before God, while asserting the particular institutional power of the learned and hence the authority of the text over its audience.

45 [all than] MS omits

49–54 Forthi . . . wil sele This passage alludes to Matt. 25:14–30, the parable of the talents. The poet later modestly assumes the role of the servant with a single talent ("the litel that I kanne" [55]; "of my povert" [61]), but insists that he must not behave as this servant does in the parable, burying his gift in the ground (51) instead of seeking to use it to the full. Use of this parable in justifying the composition of a religious work was a familiar topos (see Curtius 1990, 87–88).

61–74 Forthi . . . Frankis Compare the passage from William of Nassington's *Speculum Vitae* quoted in essay 4.2 (pages 336–37).

61 povert probably poverty of ability or knowledge (a modesty topos) rather than economic poverty (see 49–54n above)

67 mirour mirror. The reference here is to the genre of clerical, often pastoral books, containing basic instruction in the faith, with the title of "Mirror" or (if in Latin) *Speculum,* such as the *Mirrour to Lewede Men and Women, Speculum Christiani, Speculum Sacerdotale, Speculum Historiale.* For two other examples, see excerpts 1.12 and 3.10.

84 tac mi merke *MED: marke)n v.*(1), 11a, citing this phrase, defines the verb "merke" as "observe, consider" (hence, take [Christ's deeds] as my object [of observation and emulation]). A pun on *marke* (sense 5a) ("craftsman's trademark") is also possible.

90 seer saues different wordings: "seer," differing, various; "saues," sayings, saws

109 For [thi] MS *For*

114 ert the shortened form of the infinitive (dependent on the verb "mai") "erten," to urge, admonish, incite: to be distinguished from the second-person present singular of the verb "to be" (you "are"), often spelt *art* or *ert*

121 **haf** The scribe originally wrote *hafo* and has erased the final letter.

127 **says** Northern form of the imperative "say"

128 *Pater noster* the Lord's Prayer, referred to by its opening words in Latin, "Our Father [that art in heaven]" ∫ *Ave Marie* the "Hail Mary," also

known as "The Angelic Salutation": a form of devotional prayer to the Virgin Mary based on the greetings of Gabriel and Elizabeth in Luke 1:28, 42. These two texts, together with the Creed, made up an essential part of the indispensable minimum each Christian was supposed to know.

2.2 JOHN TREVISA, *DIALOGUE BETWEEN THE LORD AND THE CLERK ON TRANSLATION* (EXTRACT) AND *EPISTLE TO THOMAS, LORD BERKELEY,* ON THE TRANSLATION OF HIGDEN'S *POLYCHRONICON*

Date and Provenance: 1387; southwest Midlands (Berkeley Castle, Gloucestershire).

Author, Sources, and Nature of Text: John Trevisa (c. 1342–c. 1402) was a priest, chaplain to Thomas, fourth Lord Berkeley (his patron), for whom he translated six heterogeneous Latin texts, including the apocryphal *Gospel of Nicodemus;* Bartholomeus Anglicus's vast encyclopedia, the *De proprietatibus rerum* (On the nature of things); and Giles of Rome's *De regimine principum* (On the government of princes). The *Dialogue* and *Epistle* are his original works. Trevisa's life is unusually well documented, yet there are no grounds for long-standing scholarly claims that Trevisa was responsible for translating the *Wycliffite Bible* or that he participated in the project (see Perry 1925, cxv–cxxvi; Fowler 1960), even though at Oxford he may have known Wyclif and Nicholas Hereford, one of the probable translators (see excerpt 1.15, headnote). The defense of translation into English in the *Dialogue* and *Epistle,* as well as the use of the dialogue form common in Lollard polemic, invites speculation about both Trevisa's and Berkeley's Lollard sympathies (see pages 117–18 above). The texts might be read as demonstrating what Hudson (1988, 394–98) calls Trevisa's "vernacular Wycliffism," in that they concern the dissemination to the laity of a generalized "kunnyng, informacioun and lore" (26–27) rather than of theology. One might also deduce from the clerk's adoption of the position *against* English translation in the *Dialogue*

that Trevisa was hoping to deflect censure as a Wycliffite supporter. Yet the texts he translated were uncontroversial, and his anticlericalism was shared by many, including the author of *Piers Plowman.*

The two pieces edited here preface Trevisa's translation of the *Polychronicon* in five of its fourteen extant manuscripts, always with the *Epistle* directly following the *Dialogue.* The *Polychronicon,* by the Benedictine monk Ranulph Higden (d. c. 1360), is an encyclopedic history of Creation and the world compiled from various chronicle sources. Despite the profuse amount of information it offers, the prefatory *Dialogue* and *Epistle* offer few recommendations about how its projected lay audience might make use of it. Trevisa's clerk objects to the lord's argument about "open access" to the text by arguing that Latin is the *lingua franca* of all of Europe, English only of England (29–34). The lord, on the other hand, shows himself an adept at manipulating clerical arguments to refute this position (see especially 50–58 and 94–113) and to identify a potential audience for English translation (46–48): those lacking leisure, the old, stupid, poor, and those without the financial support of friends—much of the laity in fact. Yet there is a discrepancy between the lord's advocacy of translation and the *kinds* of texts Berkeley sponsored. There *was* no particular need for Trevisa to translate the texts he did. They were already available to clerics and some nobles (the lord apparently understands Latin anyway [38–39], not to mention French) and were improbable sources of information for the broad target audience the lord mentions. This discrepancy suggests that the ideological work of the *Dialogue* and *Epistle* might not have been strictly the promotion of lay learning. Rather, the texts bear witness to the appropriation of learning—and, at the same time, of the English language—as a status symbol by the lay aristocracy (Copeland 1991, 224) and to the importance of Berkeley's relation of patronage with Trevisa (Somerset 1998, 65–66, and see page 117 above). The *Epistle* makes it clear that the translation is the result of Berkeley's will, to which Trevisa's is subordinate ("youre prest and youre bedman [beadsman] obedient and buxom to worche youre wille" [133–34]; "Comfort Y have . . . that it is youre wille" [140–41]). Yet it would be wrong to conclude that Berkeley had no interest in a broad target audience. Mirrors for princes, and encyclopedias, had many gentry readers (Ferster 1996), and Trevisa's gesture of subordination may also be an elaborate posture of humility. It does not preclude his interests also being represented in the text.

Audience and Circulation: Trevisa's translation of the *Polychronicon* survives in fourteen manuscripts and several early printed editions. Despite the *Dialogue*'s orientation of the work to the lowest of the laity, its principal audience (given Berkeley's patronage and the Benedictine connections of Higden's compilation) would have been the clergy, gentry, and nobility. The pieces edited here continued to be read throughout the fifteenth and early sixteenth centuries: they appear in the first printed edition of Trevisa's translation of the *Polychronicon*, produced by Caxton in 1482 and in print until 1527. The Huntington manuscript used here also includes Trevisa's translations of Pseudo-Ockham's *Dialogue*

Between a Knight and a Clerk and Richard Fitzralph's sermon *Defensio curatorum* (Dutschke 1989, 683–84).

Bibliography: For the *Polychronicon* and Trevisa's translation, see the edition by Churchill Babington and Joseph Rawson Lumby (1865–86). The *Dialogue* has been edited from London, British Library MS Cotton Tiberius D VII, by R. Waldron (1996). On Trevisa and medieval translation, see Waldron 1988; Ellis 1982a; Lawler 1983; Copeland 1991, 225–26. On Trevisa's relationship to biblical and Lollard translation programs, see Fowler 1960, 1994, 1995; Hudson 1988, especially chap. 9. On Berkeley's patronage, see Hanna 1989b. Fiona Somerset (1998, chap. 3) discusses the ideological bases of Trevisa and Berkeley's translation project. Further discussion of these texts can be found in the section "The Distinctiveness of Vernacular Theory" in essay 4.1 (pages 321–29).

Source: San Marino, Calif., Huntington Library MS HM 28561 (the "Burghley *Polychronicon*"), fols. 41ra–42rb: a very large presentation volume, at one point owned by William Cecil, Baron Burghley (1520–98), written in two columns with many illuminated capitals and decorated borders, but with decoration unfinished in places. The text has been collated with a printed edition by Wynkyn de Worde, *Polycronicon*, Westminster, 1495 (a reprint of Caxton's 1482 edition), in the Bridwell Library, Southern Methodist University, Dallas (Bridwell Special Collections 06352). All bracketed additions and corrections in the text that follows are taken from this edition.

This excerpt was contributed by Stephen Shepherd.

a. Dialogue

DOMINUS Siththe that Babel was ybuld, men spekith diverse tonges so that diverse men beth straunge to other and knoweth nought of her speche. Speche is not iknowe but if hit be lerned. Commyn lernyng of speche is by heryng; and so alwey deef is alweye dome, for he may not here speche for to lerne. So men of fer
5   countrayes and londes that haveth diverse speches, yef neither of hem hath lerned

otheres langage, neither of hem wote what other meneth, though thei mete and have grete nede of informacioun and of lore, of talking and of speche. Be the nede never so greet, neither of hem understondeth otheres speche no more than gageling of gees. For jangle that oon never so fast, the other is never the wiser, though he

10 shrewe him in stede of "gode morowe."

This is a grete mischef that folewith now mankinde. But God of his mercy and grace hath ordeyned double remedie. Oon is that somme man lerneth and knowith many diverse speches; and so bitwix straunge men, of the whiche neither understondeth others speche, siche a man may be mene and telle either what other

15 wole mene. That other remedye is that oon langage is ylerned and iused and iknowe in meny naciouns and londes; and so Latyn is ilerned, yknowe, and yused, specialliche a this half Grece in alle the nacions and londes of Europa. Therefore clerkes of her godenesse and curtesie makith and writeth her bokes in Latyn, for hir writing and bokes shuld be understonde in diverse naciouns and londes.

20 And so Ranulph monke of Chestre wrote in Latyn his bokes of cronycles that discreveth the world about in lengthe and in brede and makith mencion and mynde of doynges and of dedes, of mervails and of wondres, and rekeneth the yeres to his last dawes from the first making of heven and of erthe; and therinne is noble and greet informacioun and lore to hem that can therein rede and understonde.

25 Therefore I wolde have the thees bokes of cronicles translated out of Latyn into Englisshe, for the moo men shuld hem understonde and have thereof kunnyng, informacioun and lore.

CLERICUS Theose bokes of cronicles bith ywrite in Latyn, and Latyn is iused and understonde a this half Grece in alle the naciouns and londes of Europa. And

30 comynliche Englisshe is not so wide understonde, iused, and iknowe, and the Englisshe translacioun shuld no men understonde but Englisshe men al oon; than how shuld mo men understonde the cronicles though thei were translated out of Latyn, that is so wide iused and iknowe, into Englisshe that is nought iused and iknowe but of Englisshe men al oon?

35 DOMINUS This questioun and doute is easy to assoyle, for if this cronicles were translated out of Latyn into Englisshe, than by so meny the moo men shuld understonde hem as al thoe that understonde Englisshe and no Latyn.

CLERICUS Ye kunneth speke and rede and understonde Latyn; than it nedeth not to have siche an Englisshe translacioun.

40 DOMINUS I denye this argument; for though I can speke and rede and understonde Latyn, ther is myche Latyn in thes bokes of cronicles that I can nought understonde, neither thou, without studiyng and avisement and loking of other bokes. Also, though it were not nedeful for me, it is nedeful for other men that understondeth no Latyn.

45 CLERICUS Men that under[ston]deth no Latyn may lerne and understonde.

DOMINUS Nought alle, for somme may nought for other maner bisynes, somme for elde, somme for defaute of witte, somme for defaute of catel other of frendes to fynde hem to scole, and somme for other diverse defautes and lettes.

CLERICUS Hit nedith not that alle siche know the cronicles.

50 DOMINUS Speke not to straitliche of thing that nedeth. For streitliche to speke of thing that nedith, onliche thing that is, and may not faile, nedith to be—and so hit nedith that God be, for God is and may nought faile. And so for to speke no man nedith to knowe the cronicles, for hit myght and may be that no man hem

knowith. Otherwise to speke of thing that nedith, somwhat nedith for to susteyne
55 other to have other thinges therby—and so mete and drinke nedith for kepyng and
sustynaunce of lyf—and so for to speke no man nedith to knowe the cronicles. But,
in the thrid maner to speke of thing that nedith, al that is profitable nedith, and so
for to speke alle men nedith to knowe the cronicles.
CLERICUS Than they that understondith no Latyn may axe and be enformed and
60 itaught of hem that understondith Latyn.
DOMINUS Thou spekist wonderlich, for the lewde man wote not what he shuld
axe—and nameliche of loore of dedes that come never in his mynde—nether wote
comynliche of whom he shuld axe. Also, nought alle men that understondith Latyn
haveth siche bokes to enforme lewde men. Also, somme kunneth nought and
65 somme mowe nought have while, and hit nedith to have an Englisshe translacioun.
CLERICUS The Latyn is bothe gode and fayre, therefore hit nedith not to have an
Englisshe translacioun.
DOMINUS This resoun is worthi to be plonged in a plodde and leyde in powder of
lewdenesse and of shame! Hit myght wel be that thou makist this resoun oonliche
70 in myrth and in game.
CLERICUS The resoun mot stond but hit be assoyled.
DOMINUS A blere-eyghed man, but he were al blynde of wit, myght se the
solucioun of this resoun, and though he were blynd he myght grope the solucioun
but yif his felyng him fayled! For if this resoun were ought worth, by syche maner
75 arguyng me myght preve that the thre score and ten, and Aquila, Symachus,
Theodocioun and Origenes were lewdeliche occupied whanne they translated holy
writ out of Ebru into Grue, and also that Seynt Jerom was lewdeliche occupied
whan he translated holy writ out of Ebru into Latyn—for the Ebru is bothe gode
and fayre and iwrite by inspiracioun of the Holy Ghost. And alle these for her
80 translaciouns bith highliche ypreysed of al Holy Chyrche. Thanne the foresaid
lewde resoun ys worthi to be poudred and laide a watir and ysowsed!
    Also, holy writ in Latyn is bothe gode and fayre, and yet for to make a sermoun
of holy writ al in Latyn to men that kunneth Englisshe and no Latyn, hit were a
lewde dede, for they bith never the wiser for the Latyn but it be told hem an
85 Englisshe what hit is to mene. And hit may not be told an Englisshe what the Latyn
is to mene without translacioun out of Latyn into Englisshe. Than hit nedith to
have an Englisshe translacioun. And for to kepe hit in mynde that hit be nought
foryete, hit is better that siche a translacioun be made and iwrite, than iseide and
nought iwrite. And so this foresaid lewde resoun shuld meve no man that hath eny
90 witt to leve the making of Englisshe translacioun.
CLERICUS A grete dele of these bokes stondith myche by holy writ, by holy
doctours, and by philosophie; than these bokes shuld not be translated into
Englisshe.
DOMINUS Hit is wonder that thou makist so feble argumentis and hast igo so longe
95 to scole! Aristotils bokes and other bokes also of logik and of philosophy were
translatid out of Grue into Latyn. Also, atte praiyng of King Charles, John Scot
translated Denys bokes out of Grue into Latyn. [Also holy writ was translated out
of Ebru into Grue and out of Grue into Latyn], and than out [of] Latyn into
Frensshe, than what hath Englisshe trespassed that hit myght not be translated into
100 Englisshe? Also, Kyng Alvrede, that founded the Universite of Oxenforde, translated the best lawes into Englisshe tonge, and a grete del of the Sauter out of Latyn

into Englisshe, and made Wyrefrith, Bysshop of Wyrce[s]tir, translate Seynt
Gregories bokes *Dialoges* out of Latyn into Saxoun. Also, Cedmoun of Whiteby
was enspired of the Holy Gost and made [wonde]r poysies in Englisshe neigh of
105   alle the stories of holy writte. Also, the holy man Beda translated Seynt Jone
Gospel out of Latyn into Englisshe. Also, thou wost whare the *Apocalips* is ywrite
in the walles and roof of a chapel bothe in Latyn and in Frensshe. Also, the gospel
and the prophecie and the right fey of Holy Chirche mot be taught and ypreched to
Englisshe men that kunneth no Latyn. Thanne the gospel and prophecie and the
110   right fey of Holy Chirche mot be told hem in Englisshe; and that is not ydo but by
Englisshe translacioun, for siche Englisshe preching ys verey Englisshe
translacioun. And siche Englisshe prechyng is gode and nedeful; thanne Englisshe
translacioun is gode and nedeful.
   CLERICUS Yf a translacioun were imade that myght be amended in eny poynt,
115   somme men hit wold blame.
   DOMINUS Yif men blameth that is not worthy to be blamed than they bith to
blame. Clerkis knowith wel ynowgh that no synful man doth so wel that he ne
myght do better, nether makith so gode a translacioun that he ne myght make a
better. Therefore Origenes made twey translaciouns and Jerom translated thries the
120   Sauter. I desire not translacioun of these bokes the best that myght be, for that
were an ydel desire for any man that now is here alyve. But I wold have a skilfulle
translacioun that myght be knowe and understond.
   CLERICUS Whether is yow lever have a translacioun of these cronicles in ryme other
in prose?
125   *DOMINUS* In prose, for comynliche prose is more clere than ryme, more easy and
more pleyn to knowe and understonde.
   CLERICUS Than God graunte us grace graithely to gynne, wit and wisdom wiseliche
to worche, myght and mynde of right menyng to make translacioun trusty and
trowe, plesyng to the Trinite, thre persones and oon God in mageste, that ever was
130   and ever shal be [. . .]

Explicit Dialogus

b. Epistle

Welthe and worshipe to my worthy and worshipful lord Sir Thomas, Lord of
Berkley. I, John Trevysa, youre prest and youre bedman obedient and buxom to
worche youre wille, holde in hert and thenke in thought and mene in mynde youre
135   medeful menyng and speche that ye spake and seide that ye wold have Englissh
translacioun of Ranulph of Chestres bokes and cronycles: therefore Y wolde
fonnde to take that travail and make Englissh translacion of the same bokes as
God grauntith me grace. For blame of bakbiters wol Y not blynne, for envye of
enemyes, for evel spighting and speche of evel spekers wol Y nought leve to do this
140   dede, for travayle Y wol nought spare. Comfort Y have in medeful makyng and
plesing to God, and in wityng that Y wote that it is youre wille.
   For to make this translacioun cleer and pleyne to be knowe and understonde, in
somme place Y shal sette worde for worde, and actif for actif, and passif for
passif, arewe right as thei stondeth, without chaunging of the ordre of wordes. But
145   in somme place Y mot chaunge the rewe and the ordre of wordes, and sett the actif

for the passif, and ayenward. And in somme place Y mot sett a resoun for a worde
and telle what it meneth. But for alle siche chaunging, the menyng shal stonde and
nought be ychaunged. But somme wordes and names—of cuntreys, of londes, of
citees, of watris, of ryvers, of mounteyns and hilles, of persons and of places—mot
150 be ysett and stonde for hemself in her owne kynde (as *Asia, Europa, Affrica,* and
Siria; Mount Athlas, Syna and *Oreb; Marach, Jordan,* and *Arnon; Beethlem,
Nazareth, Jerusalem,* and *Damascus; Hanibal, Risyn, Assuerus* and *Cirus* and
many siche wordes and names).

Yif eny man makith of these bokes of cronicles a bett Englissh translacioun and
155 more profitable, God do his mede. And for ye makith me do this medeful dede, he
that quiteth alle gode dedes quite youre mede in the blisse of heven in welth and
likyng with alle the holy seyntis of mankynde, and the nine ordres of angels—
angels, archaungels, *principates, potestates, virtutes, dominaciones,* [thrones],
cherubyn and seraphyn—to se God on his blisful face, in joy without eny ende.
160 Amen

Explicit Epistola

1 **Siththe that Babel was ybuld** [ever] since Babel was built. God's punishment for the building of
the Tower of Babel after the flood was the division of
languages, the whole world having previously been
"of one tongue" (Gen. 11:1–9). ∫ **diverse** various

1–27 **men spekith . . . lore** The lord here defines
a distinctively vernacular version of "universality."
Recognizing that the aftereffect of Babel is the fragmentation of language (1–10) and that Latin can
function as a *lingua franca* (15–19), the lord nevertheless rejects by implication the role of clerics as
mediators—which would leave the hierarchy of
languages intact—proposing instead that vernacular translation as sponsored by the lord can open
up a world of knowledge to everyone (25–27).

2 **beth** are ∫ **straunge** foreign ∫ **nought** nothing
∫ **her** their

3 **iknowe** known ∫ **but** unless ∫ **hit** it ∫ **Commyn
lernyng of speche is by heryng** speech is usually
learned through hearing

4 **deef** [someone who is] deaf ∫ **dome** dumb ∫
for to in order to ∫ **fer** distant

5 **londes** lands ∫ **speches** languages ∫ **yef** if

6 **wote** knows

7 **lore** learning

8 **no more** any more ∫ **gageling** cackling

9 **For jangle that oon never so fast** for no matter how intently one of them gabbles

10 **shrewe** curse ∫ **in stede of** instead of [saying]

11 **folewith** pursues

12 **somme** one

13 **straunge men** [men who are] foreigners [to
each other]

14 **siche** such ∫ **mene** mediator, interpreter

15 **wole mene** means ∫ **other** second

17 **specialliche** especially ∫ **a this half Grece** on
this side of Greece: that is, as far as Constantinople

20 **Ranulph monke of Chestre** Ranulph Higden
(c. 1315–c. 1360), whose translation of the
Polychronicon is prefaced by this *Dialogue*

21 **discreveth** describe ∫ **brede** breadth ∫ **mynde**
recollection

22 **doynges** feats ∫ **rekeneth** gives a reckoning
of, an account of ∫ **his** its (i.e., the world's)

23 **dawes** days

24 **hem** those

25 **I wolde have the thees bokes of cronicles
translated** I want you to arrange to have these
books of chronicles translated. The lord uses the
familiar singular form "the" with his clerk.

26 **moo** more ∫ **kunnyng** knowledge

28 **Theose** these ∫ **ywrite** written

30 **wide** widely

31 **al oon** alone

32 **mo** more

34 **but of** except by

35 **assoyle** resolve ∫ **this** these

36–37 **than by so meny the moo men shuld
understonde hem as al thoe that understonde
Englisshe and no Latyn** then men would understand them in a correspondingly greater proportion
as there are those who understand English but not
Latin

38 **Ye** you. The clerk uses the polite plural pronoun in addressing his lord. ∫ **kunneth** know how to

40 **denye** refute. The phrase "I denye" belongs
to the technical terminology of academic argument.

41 **myche** much ∫ **nought** not

42 neither thou nor [can] you ∫ **avisement** deliberation ∫ **loking** consultation

46 for other maner because of [their involvement in] other kinds of

47 elde old age ∫ **defaute** lack ∫ **catel** property ∫ **other** or ∫ **frendes** probably used here in the sense of "relatives" (Waldron 1996, 218.56n)

47–48 to fynde hem to scole to maintain them at school

48 lettes hindrances

49 Hit nedith not it is not necessary

50–58 Speke not . . . cronicles The lord's reply is couched in terms of scholastic disputation, skillfully distinguishing the senses of "need" to argue for the appropriate sense in which all men "need" to know the chronicles: "Do not speak too strictly of what is necessary. For to speak strictly of what is necessary, only something that exists and cannot fail exists necessarily—and so it is necessary that God exists, for God exists and cannot fail. And in this sense ["so for to speke" (56)], then, it is not necessary for anyone to know the chronicles, for it might be and can be that no one knows them. [Yet] to speak of that which is necessary in a second sense, [one can posit] a thing that is necessary in order to provide sustenance or by which one can obtain other things—and so food and drink are necessary for the maintenance and support of life—and in this sense it is not necessary for anyone to know the chronicles. However, according to a third understanding of what is necessary, everything that offers edification or advantage is necessary, and in that sense it is necessary for everyone to know the chronicles."

59 axe ask

60 of by

61 wonderlich amazingly ∫ **lewde** unlearned

62 nameliche especially ∫ **of** concerning ∫ **loore** knowledge ∫ **come** came

62–63 nether wote comynliche of whom he shuld axe nor does he usually know whom to ask

64 kunneth nought are not able

65 mowe nought have while may not have the time

68 plodde puddle ∫ **leyde in powder** laid in [the] dust (or perhaps, as in 81 below, pulverized)

69 resoun argument

70 game jest

71 mot must ∫ **but hit be assoyled** unless it can be refuted

72 blere-eyghed bleary-eyed ∫ **al** completely ∫ **blynde of wit** devoid of intelligence (with play on *blynde*) ∫ **se** see

73 though even if ∫ **grope** find out by feeling

74 but yif his felyng him fayled unless he lacked his sense of touch ∫ **ought worth** worth anything

75–90 myght preve . . . translacioun The lord's argument here, and at 94–113, deploys familiar examples from the received medieval history of translation and shows knowledge of the academic debates surrounding it.

75 me myght preve it could be proved ∫ **thre score and ten** Seventy translators were believed to have been employed (by Ptolemy Philadelphus, 285–246 B.C.) on the most influential early Greek translation (and adaptation) of the Hebrew Old Testament, the Septuagint, or *LXX*. See also *On Translating the Bible,* excerpt 2.4: 1. ∫ **Aquila** (fl. c. 140) was responsible for a literal translation of the Old Testament, meant to replace the Septuagint; he finished his translation c. 140. ∫ **Symachus** Symmachus, second-century translator of the Old Testament

76 Theodocioun Theodotion: another second-century translator of the Old Testament, produced a translation very close to that of the Septuagint ∫ **Origenes** Origen (c. 185–c. 254): Alexandrian biblical scholar, known (*inter alia*) for a formidable edition (c. 245) of the Old Testament, the Hexapla (Greek for "sixfold"), set out in six parallel columns that contained, respectively, the Hebrew text, the same text transliterated with the Greek alphabet, Aquila's translation, Symmachus's translation, the Septuagint, and the translation by Theodotion

77 Ebru Hebrew ∫ **Grue** Greek ∫ **Seynt Jerom** Saint Jerome (c. 342–420): translator, in 382 (at the request of Pope Damasus), of most of the Bible from Hebrew into Latin, a translation now known as the Vulgate ∫ **lewdeliche** foolishly

80 ypreysed esteemed

81 poudred crushed ∫ **a watir** in water, that is, dissolved into nothing ∫ **ysowsed** drenched

85–86 hit may not be told an Englisshe what the Latyn is to mene the meaning of the Latin cannot be expressed in English

88 foryete forgotten

88–89 iseide and nought iwrite spoken rather than written. That is, a spontaneous oral translation is not enough. It is necessary that the English version be written down.

89 meve persuade

90 leve abandon

91 dele part ∫ **stondith myche by** largely consist of

92 than therefore

94 igo gone ∫ **so longe** for such a long time

94–113 Hit is wonder . . . gode and nedeful For a parallel argument about traditions of Bible translation, see *On Translating the Bible* (excerpt 2.4: 1–12).

95 scole university ∫ **Aristotils bokes** The writings of Aristotle (384–322 B.C.) were reintroduced to the West in the twelfth century in Latin translations (mainly via Arabic intermediaries).

96 **praiyng** request ∫ **King Charles** Charles the Bald: king of the Franks (840–77) ∫ **John Scot** John Scotus Erigena (before 810–c. 877): Irish philosopher and head of Charles the Bald's palace school at Laon

97 **Denys bokes** Dionysius's books: works by an anonymous fifth-century, probably Syrian theologian, now known as Pseudo-Dionysius, who in the Middle Ages was identified with Dionysius the Areopagite (mentioned in Acts 17:34 as a convert of Paul's in Athens). Pseudo-Dionysius's synthesis of Christian dogma and Neoplatonic thought was influential throughout the later Middle Ages. See excerpt 3.3, *The Cloud of Unknowing,* for an example of a work influenced by the Pseudo-Dionysian tradition.

99 **Frensshe** French and Anglo-Norman translations of some books of the Bible were available in the thirteenth century. A full, so-called Paris Bible was available in French in the fourteenth century. ∫ **trespassed** offended

100 **Kyng Alvrede** King Alfred. The belief that Alfred the Great (849–99) founded the University of Oxford can be traced to the many early printed versions (beginning with Caxton's) of this very text. Trevisa tells the story twice, repeating what he found in Higden. Earlier insular traditions associate Alfred with wisdom literature (as with Marie de France's ascription, in her *Fables,* of an Aesop to him). Alfred encouraged programs of translation and was himself a notable translator of some of the major church fathers and of the Psalter.

101 **Sauter** Psalter

102 **Wyrefrith** Werfrith (bishop of Worcester, 873–915) translated Gregory's *Dialogues,* a collection of saints' lives, at the behest of King Alfred, probably some time after 890. ∫ **Wyrce[s]tir** MS *Wyrcetir*

102–3 **Seynt Gregories bokes** *Dialoges* the *Dialogues* of Saint Gregory (the Great) (c. 540–604; pope, 590–604)

103 **Saxoun** Anglo-Saxon ∫ **Cedmoun of Whiteby** According to Bede (see 105 below), Cædmon (d. c. 680) was an illiterate laborer at the monastery at Whitby who, through the miraculous agency of a dream vision, was given the ability to transform biblical stories into Anglo-Saxon poetry.

104 **poysies** poems ∫ **neigh of** of nearly

105 **Beda** Bede (the Venerable, c. 673–735): monk, historian, and biblical scholar ∫ **Seynt Jone** Saint John's. It is not known whether Bede actually translated John's Gospel into English.

106 **wost** know ∫ **whare** where ∫ *Apocalips* Apocalypse, the biblical book also known as the Book of Revelation

107 **chapel . . . Frensshe** the chapel of St. Mary at Berkeley Castle in Gloucestershire, where Trevisa was chaplain and where some fragmentary Anglo-Norman text still survives

107–113 **Also . . . nedeful** The lord uses a syllogistic argument, characteristic of academic disputation, to make his point that just as preaching in English is good and needful, so is translation into English. Here, the argument is that the gospel must be preached in English to the laity who do not know Latin, that such English preaching is both good and needful, and therefore that translation from Latin to English must also be good and needful (compare the *determinatio* of excerpt 2.4: see headnote).

108 **right fey** true faith

114 **amended** improved ∫ **poynt** detail

115 **blame** censure

116 **that** that which ∫ **is not worthy** does not deserve

117–18 **ne myght do** could not do

119 **Origenes** Origen (see 76n above) ∫ **twey translaciouns** The two translations are most likely Origen's transliteration into Greek letters and the translation proper into Greek found in the Hexapla (see 76n).

119–20 **Jerom translated thries the Sauter** According to Jerome (see 77n), his first translation of the Psalms was from the text of the Septuagint. This may be the translation now known as the Roman Psalter, though Jerome's connection with it cannot be established. His second translation from the Septuagint, as found in the Hexapla (c. 392), is known as the Galician Psalter. His third translation was done c. 400 from the Hebrew (the Hebrew Psalter).

121 **ydel** empty, vain ∫ **skilfulle** reasonable

123 **Whether is yow lever** would you prefer ∫ **other** or

125–26 **In prose . . . understonde** The lord's preference for prose, which is not given prominence in the text, is nevertheless remarkable, given that the majority of fourteenth-century English didactic texts were produced in verse. Although writers like Mannyng and Norton (excerpts 1.1, 2.3) point out the *difficulty* of some kinds of verse in the context of arguments about access, they still choose to write poetry. The ideological reasons for the choice of poetry and prose are varied, but it is important to note that the lord's patronage of translation does not depend on the use of elevated poetry. Perhaps Berkeley or Trevisa was influenced by the Wycliffite emphasis on close translation and rejected verse as suitable only for paraphrase or original composition.

127 **graithely** readily ∫ **gynne** begin

128 **myght and mynde of right menyng** skill and knowledge of the proper meaning

130 **shal be** A valedictory prayer based on the Creed follows, omitted in this edition. Waldron (1996, 221.149–78n) suggests that the prayer's inclusion of biblical events constitutes an example of the scriptural translation argued for by the lord.

132–41 **Welthe and worshipe . . . youre wille** As in the closing of the *Dialogue* (127–30), the opening of the *Epistle* makes heavy use of alliterative doublets.

133 **bedman** beadsman, that is, one who prays and/or says prayers on behalf of another ∫ **buxom** yielding

134 **worche** carry out ∫ **holde** keep ∫ **mene in mynde** keep in mind, am mindful of

135 **medeful** meritorious ∫ **menyng** purpose ∫ **wold have** wished to have

137 **fonnde** try ∫ **take** undertake ∫ **travail** work

138 **blame** reproaching ∫ **bakbiters** detractors ∫ **wol** will ∫ **blynne** cease, leave off

139 **spighting** incitement ∫ **leve to do** cease from carrying out

140 **travayle** labor ∫ **spare** refrain ∫ **makyng** composition

141 **wityng** knowing ∫ **wote** know

142–48 **For to make . . . ychaunged** Argument about the relationship between clarity and meaning, and the role of grammar and syntax, is highly charged during this period. See further *On Translating the Bible* and *The General Prologue to the Wycliffite Bible* (excerpts 2.4: 27–35, 1.15: 34–97), the second of which emphasizes, *contra* Trevisa's "pragmatics," the special role of charity in understanding meaning.

142 **For** in order

142–43 **in somme place** in one place

143 **sette** translate ∫ **actif** active (tense)

144 **arewe** in order, in due succession (*MED: aroue* [*adv.*] 2a) ∫ **right** just ∫ **stondeth** stand (i.e., in the Latin text) ∫ **ordre of wordes** word order

145 **in somme place** in another place ∫ **rewe** sequence

146 **ayenward** vice versa ∫ **sett** give ∫ **resoun** explanation

147 **telle what it meneth** gloss its meaning ∫ **for** despite

149 **watris** [bodies of] water

150 **ysett** given ∫ **hemself** themselves ∫ **kynde** that is, original form. Most of the examples that follow are of biblical origin, but all are taken more immediately from the translation of the *Polychronicon*.

151 *Syna* Mt. Sinai ∫ **Oreb** Mt. Oreb (Judg. 7:25, 8:3) ∫ **Marach** [the river] Marah (Exod. 15:23) ∫ **Arnon** [the river] Arnon (see, e.g., Num. 21:13–14)

152 *Hanibal* Hannibal (247–182 B.C.): Carthaginian leader against Rome in the Second Punic War ∫ *Risyn* Resen: king of Syria (see Gen. 10:12) ∫ *Assuerus* Ahasuerus: king of the Medes and Persians (see Esther 1:1) or Assur, son of Shem (see Gen. 10:22) ∫ *Cirus* Cyrus: king of Persia (see 2 Chron. 36:22)

155 **God do his mede** may God reward him ∫ **ye** that is, Lord Berkeley ∫ **makith** cause

155–56 **he that quiteth** may he who rewards

156 **quite youre mede** may he reward your merit ∫ **welth** well-being

157 **likyng** pleasure ∫ **the nine ordres of angels** The New Testament alludes to seven orders of angels (thrones, dominions, virtues, powers, principalities, archangels, and angels), organized into a hierarchy by early Christian theologians. In *The Celestial* (or *Angelic*) *Hierarchy* (c. 500), Pseudo-Dionysius (97n) added two orders mentioned in the Old Testament, the cherubim and seraphim. According to this revised angelology, the highest of the nine orders were the seraphim, cherubim, and thrones. The hierarchy established by Pseudo-Dionysius was most influentially disseminated to the later Middle Ages by Hugh of St. Victor (1096–1141) and by Saint Thomas Aquinas (1225–74) in his *Summa theologica* (1266–73).

159 **to se God on his blisful face** to look on the blissful face of God

2.3 THOMAS NORTON, *ORDINAL OF ALCHEMY*: PROHEMIUM

Date and Provenance: c. 1477; southwest England (Bristol).

Author, Sources, and Nature of Text: Thomas Norton (c. 1433–1513/14), esquire, of a well-known Bristol family, wrote the *Ordinal* (apparently his only work) while a senior civil servant in Bristol, working, like Chaucer, as a customs controller. He also refers to himself as a member of Edward IV's household, and may have been employed by the king to help with the recall and reissue of the English coinage in 1466, a task especially suitable to an alchemist. Norton's treatise sets out to offer a practical guide to alchemy, rather than an allegorical interpretation, as was the case with some other contemporary compilations.

Claiming, in the manner of Chaucer's Franklin, to avoid the niceties of rhetoric ("I may not curyously endite" [57]) and to employ "playne and comon speche" (59; compare excerpts 1.8 and 1.9), Norton aims to teach the secrets of alchemy to "al commyn peple" (58, a group, however, that was probably never meant to include women). Although these gestures of inclusiveness are partly modeled on the ideals of social harmony of medieval estates theory (18–39), the estates material is treated satirically (for antimercantile sentiments, see 28–29), and the often elaborate vocabulary, puns, and other rhetorical devices of the prologue in fact serve to construct its audience in fairly narrow terms. Alchemy was often associated in the later Middle Ages with criminal practices such as poisoning and counterfeiting money (see Chaucer's *Canon's Yeoman's Prologue* VIII [G] 668–79), an association that accounts for Norton's concern to define the "good" alchemist (a blend of chivalric and religious ideals) and for his stress on the democratizing benefits of alchemy.

In the treatise itself, he tells several stories about fraudulent alchemical practices in contemporary England, contrasting the activities of alchemical quacks with the solemn mission to reform English piety and economics to which true practitioners are called. A prophetic passage at the opening of part V implies that he is himself the bringer of the true benefits of alchemy to England and that his life will "Honour alle Englishe grounde" (Reidy 1975, 45.1400). Despite its practical orientation, in many ways the *Ordinal* becomes a defense of true alchemy, a defense whose purpose is to establish the respectability of the practice while warning most people away from attempting it.

Toward the end of the prologue Norton engages with contemporary debates about the status of the vernacular and problems of textual transmission, demanding that no one should change his "writyng," and arguing that to change "som oone sillable" (174) would be to destroy the essential value of the work for the wise men who are able to find in it a "selcouth privyte" (marvelous secret

[173]). Here the value of the signifiers is stressed in a manner that parallels some of the late-fourteenth-century arguments about Bible translation, for example, that found in Wyclif's *De ecclesia* (Hudson 1988, 244). But Norton's thinking here is alchemical as much as literary, associating his text's words with the ingredients of the formulas it describes, which cannot be altered in any detail without disaster, and with the "trowth" he insists must guide the practitioner (110). His presentation of his text is extraordinarily ambitious, arguing that its special quality of comprehensibility (associated with his use of the vernacular; see essay 4.1, pages 325–26) makes it a "standarde perpetualle" (129) of alchemical excellence and an "Ordinalle" (130–35) that synthesizes all previous thought on the subject (compare the *Cyrurgie,* excerpt 1.10).

Audience and Circulation: There are thirty-one extant manuscripts, many of them costly, ranging from the fifteenth to the seventeenth centuries. The *Ordinal* also appears in several seventeenth-century printed editions, including those of a translation of the work into Latin, which was reprinted in the eighteenth century in Geneva (J. J. Mauget, 1702, 1716). Little has been done on the medieval readership of this text or of alchemical and occult writings in general (see Braswell 1986, 349, 355), but Norton's name was well known in Tudor and Stuart England, kept alive in part by his great-grandson, Samuel Norton, another distinguished alchemist, who seems to have had access to a revised version of the *Ordinal,* now lost, and whose *Key of Alchimie* (1577) mentions Thomas as one of the seven great English alchemists of Edward IV's time. Ascham's *Scholemaster* (1567) mentions Norton as a poet alongside Chaucer, Wyatt, and Surrey; a copy of the *Ordinal* was owned by the mathematician John Dee; and Ashmole included Norton's *Ordinal* as the first work in his 1652 anthology of English alchemical writings, the *Theatrum Chemicum Britannicum* (see Holmyard 1928 for a facsimile and Debus 1967 for a reprint). Both Ashmole and the bibliophile Francis Thynne were interested enough in the text to note that, despite

Norton's claim to prefer anonymity (14–16), the first syllable of the proem and first six books, plus the first line of book seven, together make the couplet "Thomas Norton of Briseto, / A parfet master ye maie him trowe" (Reidy 1975, xlii; compare Usk's method of signing *The Testament of Love,* excerpt 1.4). A Middle English translation of Norton's Latin prologue to the *Ordinal* occurs in three sixteenth- and seventeenth- century manuscripts owned by Ashmole (Robbins and Cutler 1965, 401), suggesting that the translation of the work's Latin prologue had a career of its own, separate from that of the Middle English *Ordinal.*

Bibliography: The text is critically edited by John Reidy (1975), who provides a reconstruction of Norton's life and a useful introduction to the history of alchemy. There is only one study, by M. Nierenstein and P. F. Chapman (1932); see also E. J. Holmyard's introduction to his edition (1928). Lynn Thorndike (1934, 4:352) comments briefly. On the cultural meanings of alchemy, see Delany 1990, 1–18, and Obrist 1982; in relation to Chaucer, see Duncan 1968. On alchemy as a site where modernizing values could originate, see Patterson 1993b.

Source: London, British Library MS Addit. 10302, fols. 2r–6r (the forty-line Latin prologue on fol.1, which provides an appropriate aura of dignity for this vernacular work but adds little not found in the prohemium, has here been omitted for reasons of space). The manuscript contains only the *Ordinal,* up to the end of chapter V. It is a very small pocket book, and although not a luxury volume, it has some illuminated capitals, an illuminated full-page frontispiece, and full- or three-quarter-size illuminations on fols. 6v, 32v, and 67v. The end of every line of verse has been carefully filled in with colored lines. There are no signatures of ownership.

Prohemium

Prohemium prologue

	To the honour of God oon in persones three	**oon** one
	This boke is made that laymen shuld it se,	**that** so that; **se** see
	And clerkis also aftir my decese,	**clerkis** scholars; **decese** death
5	Wherbi al laymen which puttith them in prese	through which all laymen who exert themselves
	To seche bi alchymy grete riches to wynne	**seche** seek; **grete** great
	May fynde goode concelle ar thei such werk bigyn,	**concelle** counsel; **ar** before
	And grete deceptis thei may herbie eschew,	**deceptis** frauds; **herbie** hereby; **eschew** avoid
	And bi this doctryne know fals men fro the trewe.	**doctryne** instruction; **know** distinguish
10	Nethirles clerkis grete secretis here may leere,	**Nethirles** nevertheless; **leere** learn
	But al laymen shal fynde here cause to feere	**feere** mistrust
	And to be ware fals illusions	
	Which multipliers worch with theyre conclusyons.	
	But for that I desire not wordly fame	**for that** because; **wordly** worldly
15	But your gode preyers unknowe shal be my name,	**But** except for; **unknowe** unknown
	That no man shuld theraftir serche ne looke,	**looke** look for it
	But wisely consydire the flowris of thise booke.	**flowris** valued points
	Of every state which is within mankynde	**Of every state** from every estate
	If ye make serche, moche peple ye may fynde	**moche** many
20	Which to alchymy theire corage doth addresse	**Which** who; **corage** desire
	Only for appetite of lucour and richesse;	**for** out of; **lucour** lucre
	As popis with cardynales of dignitee,	**As** such as; **with** together with; **dignitee** nobility
	Archbissopis and bissopis of hye degree,	**degree** rank
	With abbottis and priours of religion,	**priours** priors

25 With freris, heremites and prestis many on,	with many a friar, hermit, and priest
And kingis, with princis and lordis grete of blode,	**grete of blode** of great lineage
For every estate desirith after goode;	**estate** social rank; **goode** material wealth
And merchantis also which dwelle in fyre	
Of brennyng covetise have therto desire;	**brennyng** burning; **covetise** covetousness
30 And comon workmen wil not be owt lafte,	**owt lafte** left out
For as wel as lordis thei love this noble craft,	
As goldsmythis whom we shuld leest repreve,	**leest** least; **repreve** blame
For sightis in theire craft movith hem to bileve.	**sightis** observations; **movith** cause
But wondir is that wevers dele with suche werkis,	**wondir is** it is a marvel; **wevers** weavers
35 Fremasons and tanners with pore parish clerkis;	**Fremasons** stoneworkers; **with** as well as
Staynours and glasiers wil not therof cese,	**Staynours** painters; **glasiers** glaziers
And yet sely tynkers wille put theyme in prese	**yet** even; **sely** simple
With grete presumpcion, but yet som colour was	**yet** still; **colour** excuse
For alle suche men as gife tyncture to glas.	**gife** give; **tyncture** color
40 But many artificers have be over swifte	**artificers** craftsmen
With hasty credence to fume awai theire thrifte,	**credence** credulity; **fume** burn away
And alle be it that losse made them to smerte,	**alle be it** although; **smerte** smart (*v.*)
Yet ever in hope continuede theire herte,	
Trustyng somtyme to spede right welle.	**spede** be successful
45 Of many such truli I can telle	**Of** about; **truli** truly
Which in such hope contynued al there lyfe,	**there** their
Wherbi thei were pore and made to unthryfe.	**Wherbi** by which; **unthryfe** lose money
It had be good for theym to have left of	**of** off
In seson, for noght thei fownde but a scoffe;	**noght** nothing; **scoffe** jibe
50 For truly he that is not a grete clerke	
Is nyse and lewde to medle with that werke.	**nyse** foolish; **lewde** ignorant
Ye may trust wel it is no smale engyne	**engyne** skill
To know al secretis perteynyng to the myne,	
For it is most profunde philosophie,	
55 The subtile science of holi alchymye;	
Of which science here I entende to write,	
How be it I may not curyously endite,	**How be it** although; **curyously** elegantly
For he that shuld al commyn peple teche,	**that** who; **shuld** intends to
He most for theym use playne and comon speche.	**most** must
60 Thogh that I write in playn and homely wise,	
No good man shulde suche writyng despyce.	**despyce** despise
Al mastirs which write of this soleyne werke,	**soleyne** serious; **werke** discipline
Thei made theire bokis to many men ful derk,	**derk** obscure
In poyses, parabols, and in methaphoris alleso,	**poyses** poems; **alleso** also
65 Which to scolers causith peyne and wo;	
For in theire practice when thei wold it assay,	**wold** wanted; **assay** try out
Theie leys their costis as men see al day.	**leys** lose; **costis** outlay; **al day** commonly
Hermes, Rasis, Gebere, and Avycenn,	
Merlyn, Ortolane, Democrite, and Morien,	
70 Bacon, and Raymonde, with many auctours mo	**auctours** authorities
Write undir covert, and Aristotille alleso;	**undir covert** secretly
For whate herof thei wrote with theire penne,	**herof** about [alchemy]

Theire clowdy causis dullid many men.   **clowdy** obscure; **causis** arguments; **dullid** bored

Fro laymen, fro clerkis and so fro every man,

75 Thei hidde this arte that no man fynde it can

Bi theire bokis, thofe thei shew reson fayre,   **Bi** from; **thofe** though; **reson** ground for belief

Wherby moche peple be broght into despeyre.

Yet Anaxagoras wrote playnyst of theym al,   **playnyst** most clearly

In his Boke of Convercions Naturalle.

80 Of al the olde faders that ever I fownde   **olde faders** forefathers

He moste disclosid of this sciens the grownde.   **grownde** basis

Wherof Aristotille hadde grete envye,

And him rebukith unrightfullye   **unrightfullye** improperly

In many placis, as I can welle reporte,

85 Entending that men to him shulde not resorte.   **Entending** intending; **men** one

For he was large of his connynge and love,   **large** generous; **connynge** knowledge

God have his sowle in blys with hym above.

And such as sowide envyous seed,   **sowide** sowed

God forgife theym theire mysdede,

90 As the monke which a boke dide write

Of a Ml. receptis in malice for despite;   **Ml. receptis** 1000 formulas

Which be copied in many a place,

Wherbi hath be made pale many a face,

And many gownys hath be made bare of hue,   **hue** color

95 And men made fals which biforetyme were true.   **biforetyme** previously

Wherfore my pitee doith me constrayne

To shew the trouth in few wordis and playne,

So that ye may fro fals doctryne flee,   **doctryne** instruction

If ye geve credence to this boke and to me.

100 Avoide youre bokis writen of receytis,   **Avoide** do away with; **receytis** formulas

For al such receptis be ful of deceytis;   **deceytis** fraudulent claims

Truste not such receptis, and lern wel this clause: **clause** sentence

Nothing is wroght but bi his propre cause;   **his** its; **propre** own; **cause** reason

Wherfore practice fallith ferre behynde   **ferre** far

105 Where knowlich of the cause is not in mynd:

Wherfore remembre evyrmore wisely,

To werch nothing but ye know how and whi.   **but** unless

Also he that wold in this arte procede,

To eschew falshode he hath grete nede;

110 For trowth is good which this arte most gyde,   **trowth** truth

Wherfore to falshode ye may nevyr slyde;

But stedfastly your myndes most be sett

Fals colorid metalle nevir to conterfett;   **Fals** falsely; **colorid** gilded

As thei that seche blanchers or citrinacions

115 Which wil not abyde alle examynacions,   **alle examynacions** any close inspection

Wherewith fals plate thei make as thei can,   **plate** metals

Or monay to begile som good trew man.   **monay** coins

But God hath made that of his blessid arte

Al that be fals shal have therof no parte.

120 He must have grace that wold for this arte sewe,   **wold** wishes; **sewe** petition

Therfore of right hym nedith to be trewe.   **hym nedith** it is necessary for him

Also he may not be trowbled in his mynde
With owtward chargis, which this arte wold fynde;
And he that wold have his entent
125 He must have riches sufficient.
In many wayis he may not loke,   he cannot look in many different places
But only pursue the ordire of this boke,   **But only persue** but only [needs to] follow
Namyd of Alchymye the Ordinalle,
The *crede michi*, the standarde perpetualle;   *crede michi* "believe me"
130 For like as the Ordinalle to prestis settith owte   **Ordinalle** ordinal; **to** for
The servyce of the dayes as thei go abowte,   **go abowte** change [through the year]
So of al the bokis unorderide in alchymye   **unorderide** unarranged
Th'effectis be here set owte ordirlye.   **effectis** essentials
Therfore this boke to an alchymystre wise   **alchymystre** alchemist
135 Is a boke of incomperable price,   **price** value
Whose trowth shal nevir be defilede,
Thofe it appere in homly wise compiled.   **homly** unpretentious
And as I hadde this arte bi grace fro hevyn,
I geve you the same here in chapiters sevyn,
140 As larglie as I bi my foialte may,   **larglie** generously; **foialte** trustworthiness
Bi licence of the dredful Juge of Domysdai.   **dredful** fearsome; **juge** judge
The first chapitere shal al men teche
Whate maner peple may this science reche,   **maner** kind [of]; **reche** attain
And whi the trew science of alchymye
145 Is of olde faders callid blessid and holye.   **olde faders** forefathers [of the science]
In the seconde chapiter may be sayne   **sayne** seen
The nyce joys therof with the grete peyne.   **peyne** pain
The thrid chapiter for the love of oone   **oone** one
Shalle truly disclose the maters of oure stone,   **maters** properties; **stone** alchemists' stone
150 Which the Arabies doyn Elixer calle,   **Arabies** Arabs; **doyn** do
Wherof is it there undirstond ye shalle.   **Wherof is it** what it is made of
The iiii.th chapiter techeth the grose werke,   **iiii.th** fourth
A fowle laboure not kyndly for a clerke,   **fowle** dirty; **kyndly** suited to
In which is fownde ful grete travayle,   **ful grete** very great; **travayle** labor
155 With many perilis and many a fayle.   **fayle** failure
The v.th chapiter is of the subtile werke   **v.th** fifth
Which God ordeynyde only for a clerke,
But ful few clerkis can it comprehende,
Therfore to few men is this science sende.   **sende** sent
160 The vi.te chapiter is of concorde and love   **vi.te** sixth
Bitwene low naturis and hevynly spere above,   **spere** sphere
Wherof tru knowlige avauncith gretly clerkis
And causith fortherance in our wondre werkis.   **fortherance** progress; **wondre** wondrous
The vii.th chapiter truly teche yow shalle   **vii.th** seventh
165 The doutfulle regymentis of your firys alle.   **doutfulle** difficult; **regymentis** regulation
Now soverayn Lord God me gyde and spede   **gyde** guide; **spede** prosper
For to my maters as now I wil procede,   **maters** subject matters
Prayng al men which this boke shal fynde,
With devowte prayers to have my soule in mynd;   **mynd** remembrance
170 And that no man for better ne for wors

Change my writyng, for drede of Goddis curs;   drede fear
For where quyck sentence shal seme not to be,   quyck intelligible; sentence meaning
There may wise men fynd selcouth privyte;   selcouth marvelous; privyte secret of nature
And changing of som oone sillable
175 May make this boke unprofitable.
Therfore trust not to oon reding or tweyne,   tweyne two
But xx. tymes it wolde be oversayne;   xx. twenty; wolde be needs to be; oversayne studied
For it conteyneth ful ponderose sentence,   ponderose weighty
Al be it that it fawte forme of eloquence.   it fawte it lacks
180 But the best thing that ye do shalle
Is to rede many bokis, and then this withalle.   withalle in addition

13 **Which . . . conclusyons** which false coiners bring about with their results. Concerning "multipliers," see Chaucer, *Canon's Yeoman's Tale* VIII (G) 1391. The exact meaning of "conclusyons" here is difficult to determine; it may refer to the outcome of counterfeiting practices (i.e., the coins produced as a result), or it may be metaphorical (implying some kind of sleight of hand) or technical: "An inference or conclusion, whether drawn from premises or observations" (*MED: conclusioun* 3).

14–17 **But for that . . . thise booke** Compare Bokenham's discussion of the purposes of anonymity (excerpt 1.11: 196–225).

17 **flowris** This can mean both the "moral and spiritual virtues [of this book]" and its "rhetorical embellishments" (*MED: flour* [*n.*] 1, nos. 2c and 2e).

18–51 **Of every state . . . werke** The list of those who will benefit from alchemy is modeled on the traditional tripartite social division derived from medieval political science and already redundant (in actual social terms) by the fourteenth century. To the traditional "three estates"—spiritual leaders, landholders, and workmen—Norton adds a fourth category, merchants (28), as Chaucer does in *The Canterbury Tales* and Langland in *Piers Plowman*. Norton invokes estates theory at least partly to satirize certain of its categories. Thus all social groups, from high-ranking ecclesiastics to simple tinkers, are derided for turning to alchemy out of a desire for what Norton ironically terms "goode" (material wealth).

34–39 **But wondir . . . glas** But it is a marvel that weavers deal in such works, [as well as] stoneworkers and tanners and poor parish clerks. Painters and glaziers will not abandon the practice of it, and even simple tinkers will be avid [to practice alchemy] with great presumption, even though there would be some excuse for all men whose job involves tinting glass [i.e., since their job involves chemical processes related to alchemy].

38 **but yet som colour was** presumably a pun on the two meanings of "color" suggested by the context: the tinctures used by glass stainers, and the colors of alchemy, to which were attached an elaborate scheme of allegorical significances as well as practical scientific properties in indicating the stages of chemical and physical changes in materials. Compare 94n below.

44 **somtyme . . . welle** to be very successful in the future

48–49 **It had be . . . a scoffe** it would have been better for them to have stopped in time, for they found nothing but a jibe

53 **myne** mine, that is, the mining of minerals

64 **poyses** *MED: poesi* 1b gives the meaning as "a poem, a passage of poetry," but sense 1a, "figurative language," would also fit the context. ∫ **parabols** allegorical narratives, parables ∫ **methaphoris** figures

67 **their** MS *theie*, last three letters rubbed

68 **Hermes** Hermes Trismegistus: supposedly the discoverer of alchemy and author of the *Tractatus aureus*. In the sixteenth and seventeenth centuries alchemy was known as the Hermetic art. ∫ **Rasis** al-Razi (c. 850–925): Arabic chemist, known to the Latin world as Rasis or Rhases ∫ **Gebere** Geber, which may correspond to the Arabic writer Jabir ibn-Haiyan. To "Geber" was attributed the authorship of a major thirteenth-century alchemical treatise, the *Summa perfectionis* (Sum of perfection). ∫ **Avycenn** ibn-Sīnā, or Avicenna (980–1037): one of the best-known philosophers and physicians of the Arabic world

69 **Merlyn** The medieval Merlin is a mythical conflation of a historical figure (a poet of the late fifth century) with later literary representations of him as the enchanter of Arthurian romance, skilled in necromancy. ∫ **Ortolane** Ortolanus or Hortulanus (fl. 1358): a shadowy figure who may have been a Dominican friar, often grouped with Arnauld de Villanova (see 90–91n), Ramón Lull (see 70n), and Albertus Magnus as chief among the renovators of alchemy ∫ **Democrite** Pseudo-Democritus: the author of what was considered to

be the earliest known Greek alchemical text, the *Physika kai mystika* ∫ **Morien** Morienus Romanus: author of an Arabic alchemical work, *Liber de compositione,* a Latin translation of which was made by Robert of Chester in 1144

70 **Bacon** Roger Bacon (1214–92): Franciscan philosopher and reputedly the author of an alchemical treatise, *The Mirror of Alchemy*. He compiled an annotated redaction of the pseudo-Aristotelian *Secretum secretorum* that, among other things, explains the alchemical synthesis of gold. Bacon defended the *Secretum* against conservatives who attacked parts of the book as magic. ∫ **Raymonde** Ramón Lull (c. 1232–c. 1314): Catalan mystic, Christian missionary among Muslims (to which end he learned Arabic), and writer of over 250 courtly, philosophical, mystical, and scientific works, including the *Book of the Order of Chivalry* and the *Ars generalis ultima*. An alchemical treatise attributed to him, the *Codicillus,* is not in fact his.

71 **Aristotille** Aristotle (384–322 B.C.). His study of natural science, the *Meteorology,* provided the basis for the alchemical ideas developed by Avicenna, and many of his works were drawn on by medieval alchemists. In the late-fifteenth-century alchemical treatise the *Book of Quinte Essence,* Aristotle is cited as the author of the *Boke of Secretis* (Furnivall 1866, 10).

78 **Anaxagoras** mid-fifth-century B.C. Greek philosopher whose name often lends authority to medieval alchemical treatises (e.g., the influential *Turba philosophorum*), along with those of Socrates, Plato, Pythagoras, and Cicero

79 **Boke of Convercions Naturale** This work is unknown, suggesting that Anaxagoras may function for Norton rather as "Lollius" does for Chaucer in *Troilus and Criseyde*.

81 **disclosid** with the first *s* added above the line with a caret

85 **men** with *n* added above the line with a caret

86 **he was large** The reference is to Anaxagoras (see 78 above).

90–91 **As the monke . . . for despite** A thirteenth-century treatise, *De secretis nature* attributed to Arnauld de Villanova, warns against trust in formulas (receipts), citing the exemplum of a monk "who had labored hard in the art for twenty-two years and knew nothing. Then, desperate, he made a book which he entitled *The Flower of Paradise,* which contained more than 100,000 receipts, and allowed that book to be copied. And thus he deceived both the people and himself because he was altogether without hope" (quoted in Duncan 1968, 650). Presumably Norton's reference is to this story, which must have had a certain currency.

91 **Ml.** [*mille*] thousand

94 **many gownys . . . bare of hue** clerks have

been made pale with fear. There is a possible play here on rhetorical "colors" (see also 38n above).

95 **men** with *ny* inserted above with a caret, to read *menny,* in a nonscribal hand

114 **blanchers** whitening powders or reagents (alchemical and cosmetic) ∫ **citrinacions** an alchemical term meaning "yellowing agents": "Of metal: the process of turning yellow (the final stage in transmutation [of base metals into gold])" (*MED*).

120 **He must have grace** Here, and at 138, Norton stresses the operations of grace both for him as author (138) and for the practitioners of alchemy. While this is of a piece with Norton's quasi-clerical presentation of the text as an *ordinal* (see essay 4.1, page 326, for discussion), it is also an implicit denial of earthly sources of knowledge and understanding. The passage offers a mystification of the art of alchemy that casts doubt on Norton's avowed aim of "accessibility."

122–23 **Also he . . . which this arte wold fynde** also the man who would attain this art cannot have his mind troubled by external responsibilities ["owtward chargis"]

128 **Ordinalle** a book setting out the order of church services, that is, setting out rules

138 **And as I hadde this arte bi grace fro hevyn** See 120n.

140 **foialte** an unusual form, apparently combining the elements of *foi* (faith) and *lealtie* (loyalty), and clearly related to *fealte*. The other manuscript witnesses show that scribes had trouble with the form, writing *fryaltee* (?frailty) or *fealtie* (Reidy 1975, 9).

148 **the love of oone** the love of unity, the love of the one God (the phrase is perhaps deliberately cryptic). Norton aligns alchemy with Christian purposes, already anticipated in the work's punning title, *Ordinal* (128). He may well be thinking here of the structure of the text itself, with the first three chapters constituting some kind of threefold mystical ascent. Since "one" in later alchemical tradition can refer to the king (Reidy 1975, xxxix–xl), it is just possible that there is a further encrypted meaning here.

152 **grose werke** gross work: the purification and preparation of metals (Reidy 1975, lx and glossary)

156 **subtile werke** subtle work: the skillful combination of pure natures of substances obtained through distillation (Reidy 1975, lx and glossary)

160–61 **of concorde . . . spere above** The division between earth and heaven—between mortal bodies ("low naturis") and the transcendent, immortal realm of God—is potentially healed by alchemy's transforming power, in a manner analogous to that of the doctrine of the Incarnation. There is an interesting congruence between Norton's pro-alchemy arguments and some of the late medieval debates around transubstantiation and the nature of the Eucharist (on which, see Rubin 1991).

165 **regymentis of your firys** Several illuminations in the British Library manuscript of the *Ordinal* show alchemists at work, tending small furnaces. The heating of materials in order to produce other elements is fundamental to alchemical processes. Chaucer's Canon's Yeoman, a practicing alchemist, admits to facial disfigurement from having so often "blown" his fire to encourage its flames (*Canon's Yeoman's Prologue* VIII [G] 666–7).

2.4 ON TRANSLATING THE BIBLE INTO ENGLISH (EXTRACT)

Date and Provenance: c. 1401–7; south Midlands (probably Oxford).

Author, Sources, and Nature of Text: The text is anonymous, though formerly attributed, without clear justification, to the Wycliffite John Purvey, a possible supervisor of the Late Version of the *Wycliffite Bible* (see excerpt 1.15). The author may, however, have been a Lollard. The piece is a paraphrase of parts of a Latin *determinatio* (the resolving of a question in a scholastic disputation) of 1401, by the Oxford theologian Richard Ullerston (d. 1423), in favor of English translation. It was written as a contribution to the so-called Oxford debate on Bible translation. Ullerston is better known as the author of official attacks on Lollard heterodoxy; his advocacy of biblical translation (from a self-consciously orthodox position) exemplifies how "many opinions later identified with Lollardy could be questions of neutrality in the early years of the movement" (Hudson 1985, 83); indeed, there are obvious continuities between Ullerston's position (even in its polemical English form) and the stance of the *Northern Homily Cycle* (excerpt 2.1). The title *The Compendyous Treatise* sometimes given to this piece is found only in a printed edition from 1530 and is not in any of the medieval manuscripts. This text takes up the defense of English biblical translation by noting the precedent offered by other vernacular translations of the Bible and by citing a number of historical authorities. Though not made explicit here, at stake in this argument is the question of which social and religious groupings will attain, or retain, the power conferred by access to the Scriptures. The argument that the "truth" of Scripture would be construed as heretical by the untutored "people" through a grammatically literal translation into English (as the opponents of translation would have it) is countered by the bold contention that "we fynden in Latyne mo heretikes than of ale other langagis" (21–22) and that "grammatical" accuracy is nothing more than the "right" way of communicating, not solely the province of learned clerks.

Audience and Circulation: The Middle English text survives, not always complete, in nine manuscripts copied betwen the early fifteenth and early seventeenth centuries, in all of which it is anonymous and undated; it is also preserved in at least two early printed editions (in one case as part of the 1563 edition of Foxe's famous *Actes and Monuments* [see *STC* 3021]).

Bibliography: Editions have been printed by Bühler (1938) and Deanesly (1920, 437–45). For context, see Hudson 1985, 1988, and Watson 1995a; for manuscripts and bibliography, see Talbert and Thomson 1970, 529, corrected by Hudson 1985, 249–52.

Source: Cambridge, Trinity College MS B.14.50, fols. 27r–29v: a small, unadorned paper book from the fifteenth century. The manuscript is in two parts, the first containing short entries in English and Latin on a variety of religious topics, including the sacrament, tithes, and the Lord's Prayer. The second part has longer pieces, again in English and Latin, with Lollard sympathies, including the *Sixteen Points Brought Against the Lollards* (edited in Hudson 1978).

This excerpt was contributed by Stephen Shepherd.

Also seventi doctoris, withouten mo, byfore the Incarnacioun translatiden the
Bibile into Greek ought of Ebrew. And after the Ascencoun many translatiden al
the Byble, summe into Greek and summe into Latyne. But Seint Jerom translatide
it out of Ebrew into Latine; wos translacioun we usen most. And so it was
5 translatid into Spaynesche tunge, Frensche tunge, and Almayne. And other londes
also han the Bibel in ther moder tunge, as Italie hath it in Latyn, for that is ther
moder tonge, and be many yeeris han had. Worschipful Bede in his first boke *De
gestis Angulorum* tellith that Seint Oswold, kyng of Northehumberlond, axide of
the Scottys an holi pischop, Aydan, to preche his puple, and the kynge of hymself
10 interpreted it on Engliche to the puple. If this blessid dede be aloued to the kynge
of al hooli chirche, how not now as wel aughte it to be alowed a man to rede the
gospel on Engliche and do therafter?

But ther ben summe that seien if the gospel were on Engliche, men myghten
lightly erre therinne. But wel touchith this holi man Richa[r]d Hampol suche men,
15 expownyng this tixte, *Ne auferas de ore meo verbum veritatis usquequaque*, ther
he seith thus: "Ther ben not fewe but many that wolen sustene a worde of falsenes
for God, not willing to beleve to kenynge and better than thei ben." Thei ben liche
to the frendes of Jobe, that wiles thei enforsiden hem to defende God, they
offendeden grevosly in hym. And though suche ben slayne and done myracles, thei
20 nevertheles ben stynkyng martirs. And to hem that seien that the gospel on
Engliche wolde make men to erre, wyte wele that we fynden in Latyne mo
heretikes than of ale other langagis; for the *Decres* rehersith sixti Latyn eretikes.
Also the hooli evaungelistis writen the gospelle in diverse langages, as Matheu in
Judee, Marke in Ytalie, Luck in the partyes of Achaie, and John in Asie after he
25 hadde writen the *Apocalips* in the yle of Pathomos—and al thes writen in the
langage of the same cuntre, as seith Ardmakan.

And the Grekis, wiche ben nobel men, han al this in ther owne langage. But yit
adversaries of trewith seien, wane men rehersen that Grekis and Latyns han al in
ther owne langage, the clerkis of hem speiken grammaticalliche and the puple
30 understo[n]dth it not. Witte thei that, though a clerke or another man thus lerned
can sette his wordis on Engliche better than a rewde man, it foloweth not herof
that oure langage schuld be destried. It were al on to sei this, and to kitte oute the
tunges of hem that can not speke thus curiosly. But thei schulde understande that
"grammaticaliche" is not ellis but abite of right spekyng and right pronounsyng
35 and right wryty[n]ge.

[Margin note: Bible into other languages; how come not into English?]

[Margin note: more hereliss in Latin than other lang.]

1–12 **Also seventi . . . and do therafter** For similar arguments about the tradition of biblical
translation, see Trevisa's *Dialogue* (excerpt 2.2).

1 **doctoris** learned men ∫ **withouten mo** only,
alone

1–2 **translatiden the Bibile . . . ought of Ebrew**
that is, the Septuagint, or *LXX*: the most influential early Greek translation (and adaptation) of the
Hebrew Old Testament, which was believed to have
been the work of seventy translators employed by
Ptolemy Philadelphus (285–246 B.C.). See also excerpt 2.2: 75n.

2 **ought** out ∫ **Ebrew** Hebrew ∫ **Ascensoun** Ascension

3 **Seint Jerom** Saint Jerome (c. 342–420) is
best known for translating the Bible into Latin in
382, at the request of Pope Damasus. His translation provided most of the Latin Vulgate version of
the Bible in its conventional form.

4 **wos** whose

5 **Almayne** German ∫ **londes** countries

6 **han** have ∫ **moder** mother

7 **be** for ∫ **yeeris** years ∫ **Bede in his first boke**
See Bede, *Historia ecclesiastica gentis Anglorum*

(Ecclesiastical history of the English people) III.3, finished in 731.

7–8 *De gestis Angulorum* The deeds of the English (i.e., the *Historia ecclesiastica*)

8   **Oswold** Oswald (c. 605–42), a convert to Christianity, was instrumental in the conversion of much of his kingdom. ∫ **axide** asked

9   **pischop** bishop ∫ **Aydan** Saint Aidan (d. 651) based his missionary work in the newly founded see of Lindisfarne, of which he was consecrated the first bishop in 635. ∫ **preche** preach to ∫ **puple** people ∫ **of hymself** himself

10   **interpreted** translated (from [according to Bede, see 7n above] Aidan's Scottish) ∫ **on** in ∫ **aloued** permitted

11   **aughte** ought

12   **do therafter** continue to do so

13   **ben** are ∫ **seien** say

14   **lightly** easily ∫ **therinne** in [understanding] it ∫ **touchith** that is, answers ∫ **Richa[r]d Hampol** Richard Rolle of Hampole (c.1300/1305–49) (MS *Richad*): hermit and author of numerous theological and devotional writings in Latin and English, cited as an English holy man of exemplary orthodoxy who approves of biblical translation. The specific reference is to his *Latin Psalter* (for Rolle's *English Psalter,* see excerpt 3.8): *nonnulli pro deo . . . quamuis melius literatis* (Faber 1536, fol. 69v; Porter 1929, 559). ∫ **suche men** that is, those who complain about the Englishing of the gospel

15   **expownyng** expounding ∫ *Ne auferas . . . usquequaque* take not the word of truth utterly from my mouth (Ps. 118:43, AV 119) ∫ **ther** where

16   **wolen** will, wish to ∫ **sustene** maintain ∫ **a worde of falsenes** a lie

17   **to beleve . . . than thei ben** to believe in the understanding and [in the existence of those who are] better than they are ∫ **liche** like

18   **Jobe** Job (Job 16:2) ∫ **wiles** while, as long as ∫ **enforsiden hem** exerted themselves

19   **offendeden . . . in** offended against ∫ **done** do (*v. pl.*)

19–20 **And though suche . . . stynkyng martirs** After interpolating the comparison with Job (18), the author returns to Rolle's *Latin Psalter* (see 14n above) for this sentence (*si occidantur . . . foetentes martyres*) (Faber 1536, fol. 69v; Porter 1929, 559). Read: "Even if such people die for their cause and perform miracles after death, they may be martyrs but they'll still stink."

21   **wyte** [let them] know (*imp.*) ∫ **mo** more

22   *Decres* The *Decreta* (Decrees), also known as the *Decretum Gratiani* (c. 1140), is the authoritative compendium of canon law compiled by the Italian monk Gratian (d. before 1159) as a comprehensive body of ecclesiastical rules or laws in matters of faith, morals, and discipline that could in principle be imposed on all Christians by authority of the church. ∫ **rehersith** gives the story of ∫ **eretikes** heretics

23–25 **Also the hooli evaungelistis . . . Pathomos** Compare Trevisa's list of Bible versions not originally written in Latin, excerpt 2.2: 97–107.

23   **as** namely

24   **Judee** Judea ∫ **Ytalie** Italy ∫ **Luck** Luke ∫ **partyes** parts ∫ **Achaie** Achaea ∫ **Asie** Asia (i.e., Asia Minor)

25   *Apocalips* Apocalypse, or Book of Revelation: the last book of the Bible, often attributed in the Middle Ages to John the Evangelist ∫ **yle** isle ∫ **Pathomos** Patmos

26   **Ardmakan** Richard Fitzralph (c. 1295–1360): archbishop of Armagh [Ardmachanus] from 1347. The reference is to his *Summa . . . in questionibus Armenorum,* a criticism of certain policies in the Greek and Armenian churches of the time. Fitzralph's writings influenced Wyclif and are frequently cited in English tracts advocating biblical translation (see excerpt 1.15: 45–46 and note). He was something of a hero to Wycliffites and other reformers in fourteenth-century England (see Kerby-Fulton 1990).

27   **yit** still

28   **trewith** truth ∫ **wane** when ∫ **rehersen** repeat the argument

29   **the clerkis of hem** their learned men ∫ **speiken grammacalliche** speak in a learned, or obscure, fashion (perhaps using Latin syntax while speaking in English)

30   **Witte** [let them] know (*imp.*)

31   **sette** render ∫ **on** into ∫ **rewde** common ∫ **herof** from this

32   **destried** destroyed ∫ **al on . . . and** as much to say this as ∫ **kitte** cut

33   **thus curiosly** in such an elaborate or refined manner

34–35 **"grammaticaliche" is not ellis . . . right wryty[n]ge** "grammatically" is nothing more than using correct speech, correct pronunciation, and correct writing. There seems to be a deliberate echo here of the scholastic insistence on correctness in the learning of grammar. See the definition of grammar as "the skilful art of speaking and writing correctly," cited in many twelfth-century grammar-school texts, such as Peter Helias's *Summa super Priscianum* (see Reynolds 1996, 18). The author thus mobilizes arguments considered quite proper to the fundamental discipline of the *trivium* in the service of a less orthodox aim.

2.5 THE HOLI PROPHETE DAVID SEITH (THREE EXTRACTS)

Date and Provenance: 1380s–1420s; probably east Midlands.

Author, Sources, and Nature of Text: *The Holi Prophete David Seith* (for the context of this phrase, see 132–36 below) is one of a large number of vernacular and Latin discussions of Bible reading written around the production of the *Wycliffite Bible* (see excerpt 1.15) during the period of the Lollard controversy (c. 1380–c. 1415). Like the other vernacular discussions, it is anonymous. Its author may have known Wyclif's *De veritate sacre scripturae* (On the truth of Holy Scripture), with which it has some similarities, but Margaret Deanesly's claim that Wyclif himself wrote *The Holi Prophete* is unlikely (1920, 268–71). Although many of its themes are prominent in Lollard antiecclesiastical polemic (e.g., Hudson 1978, 75–83), it may in fact be wrong to think of this as a Lollard work at all, at least in any narrow sectarian sense. The text's defense of lay Bible reading and attacks on the clergy often recall reformist vernacular texts such as *Piers Plowman* (excerpt 3.19) and *Dives and Pauper* (excerpt 3.9), or *The Cloud of Unknowing* (excerpt 3.3), all of which have a similar attitude toward the danger of overeducation, and the surviving manuscript (see below) did not circulate in Lollard circles. The treatise is a defense of the place of the Bible and Bible reading in the life of the church and the individual lay Christian. Its opening (not given here) extrapolates its case from Ps. 118:103, AV 119, "How swete ben thi spechis to my chekis," interpreting the word "chekis" (cheeks) as "myn undirstondyng and love" to argue (as does excerpt 2.4) the interdependence of good living and Bible study in the lives of Christians: an interdependence that allows virtuous laypeople to prefer their own understanding to that of patently corrupt members of the clergy. The passages extracted here amount to about a third of the treatise and summarize its main arguments, as well as exemplify the connections between those arguments and a strain of anticlerical satire that seems designed to lead lay readers to think that their status makes them intrinsically superior to most of the clergy. The first passage attacks the clergy and the improper use of knowledge; the second provides the lay reader with six "weies" to come to knowledge of the Bible, which comprise a mixture of intellectual study and *imitatio Christi;* the third is a defense of lay Bible reading and an attack on those who oppose it.

Audience and Circulation: The work survives in one manuscript, Cambridge University Library MS Ff.6.31 (pt. 2, fols. 1–16), where it is followed by four more tracts that quote the Bible from the Wycliffite Early Version; *The Holi Prophete* itself makes its own translations. For a study of the London circulation of this manuscript as a "common-profit book" circulating among devout readers of the merchant class (several of whom can be linked to the anti-Lollard reformer Reginald Pecock; see excerpt 1.16), see Scase 1992. This form of lay testamentary charity was modeled as a pattern in use among the humbler secular clergy (Scase 1992, 265). For other common-profit books that circulated in the same milieu and contained a variety of texts from *Pore Caityf* (excerpt 3.6) to Walter Hilton's *Scale of Perfection* and *Eight Chapters on Perfection* (both of these exemplary in their orthodoxy), see Sargent 1983, and essay 4.3, pages 358, 360–61.

Bibliography: The text is edited by Deanesly (1920, 445–56, with 446–49, 451–53, 454–55, corresponding to the passages edited here), whose analysis of the milieu in which such works circulated is supplemented by Hudson (1988, chap. 9). For a bibliographic guide to vernacular Lollard texts, see Talbert and Thomson 1970, 354–80, corrected by Hudson 1985, 249–52. For the circulation of this text, see Scase 1992. Simon Hunt (1994) edits a set of tracts in favor of Bible translation in Cambridge University Library MS Ii.6.26.

Source: Cambridge University Library MS Ff.6.31, pt. 2, fols. 2r–3r, 5r–6v, 9r–12v, 13r–

14v. The common-profit inscription in the volume is on the last page (fol. 100): "This booke was made of the goodis of Johnn Collopp for a comyn profite that that persoone that hath this booke committed to him of the persoone that hath power to committe it have the use therof the terme of his liif prayng for the soule of the seid Johnn, and that he that hath the forseid use of commyssioun, whanne he occupieth it not, leene it for a tyme to sum other persoone. Also that persoone to whom it was committid for the terme of liif under the forseid condiciouns delyvere it to another persoone the terme of his liif: and so be it delyvered and committed fro persoone to persoone man or womman as longe as this booke endureth." (For other manuscripts with this inscription but with different donors, see Scase 1992, 261.) Biblical quotations are usually identified by abbreviated Latin book titles and chapter numbers in the text in this manuscript; in this transcription, verse numbers are added and the names of biblical books and chapter numbers are recorded in the modern English format used elsewhere in this volume.

This excerpt was contributed by Stephen Shepherd.

a. [On clerkly misappropriation of scripture]

Sum men of good wille redin besili the text of Holi Writ, for to kunne it and kepe it in here lyvynge and teche it to othere men bi hooli ensample. And for the staat that thei stondyn ynne, and for this werk, thei han the blissyng of God, as he seith in the Gospel (Luke 11:28), "Blessid ben thei that heryn the word of God and
5   kepin it." And in the first chapter of *Apocalips* Seynt Joon seith "he is blessid that heerith and redith the wordis of this prophecie and kepith tho thyngis that ben writen therynne." But othere veyn men besie hem faste to studie to kunne the lettre of Goddis lawe and thei bisi hem nat treuli to kepe the sentence therof. And therfore thei disceyven hemself and in maner sclaundren the lawe of God.
10   First thei schulde studie to kunne wel the trewe sentence of Goddis lawe, aftirward to kepe it in werk, and thanne to speke therof mekeli and charitabli to the edificacion of othere men. For if thei jangelyn oonli of this blessid lawe to schewe here cunnynge abowe othere men, and kepe not it opynli in here werkis but doon opynli the contrarie, thei ben contrarie to hemsilf. And this cunniynge turnyth hem
15   to more dampnacion. For Crist seith in the Gospel (Luke 12:47), "A servaunt that knowith the wille of his lord and dooth it not schal be betyn with many betyngis." James seith in the iiii c[hapetre], it is synne to hym "that can good and dooth it not." And Poul seith, "Kunnynge makith a man proud"—that is, nakid kunnynge withoute goode werkis, whanne it is medlid with pride, veynglorie, and boost. Sich
20   men semen to do goos[t]li avoutrie with the word of God. For there thei schulde take of the Hooli Goost trewe undirstandyng of Hooli Writ, bi gret meknesse and hooli praier, to brynge forth very charite and goode werkis, thei takyn the nakid undirstondynge bi presumcion of mannes witt, and bryngen forght pride, veynglorie, and boost, to coloure here synnes and disceive sutilli here neghebours.
25   Siche maner of peple schulden takyn hede what Poul comaundith, "to kunne no more than nedith to kunne, but to kunne to sobirnesse"—that is, as moche as perteyneth to salvacion of thin owene sowle, eithir to edificacion to othere mennes.

[The author discusses the various manners of knowing, warning especially against the danger of seeking knowledge simply for the sake of vanity.]

Cristene men wondren moche on the weiwarnesse of divers clerkis that bosten
30 that thei han passynly the cunnynge of Hooli Writ, sithyn thei makyn hemself
most unable therto. For thei feynen to studie, kunne, and preche Hooli Writ for
pride of the word, for covetise of ertheli goodis, and for wombe-joie, to lewe in
delices, bodeli ese, and ydilnesse. Agenes hem seith God (Prov. 12:11), "He
that suyth ydilness is most fool," and the Lord Ihesu seith (Matt. 11:25),
35 "Fadir, Lord of hevene and of herthe, and knoweleche to the"—that is, "I herie
the"—"for thou hast hid thise thyngis—that is, prevites of Hooli Writ—"fro wise
men and prudennt of the world, and thow hast schewid tho to meke men." And
Crisostom seith that good levynge is a lanterne to brynge men to veri
undirstondyng of Holi Writ, and withoute good lyvyng and the drede of God no
40 man is wise. And the wise man seith (Wisd. 1:4), "Wisdom schal not entre into
an yvel-willid soule nether schal duelle in a bodi suget to synnes," sithen these
grete synnes biforeseid makyn the dewel to dwelle and to regne in the sowle of
siche veyn clerkis. No wondir though he brynge hem to gostli blindnesse and fals
undirstondyng of Hooli Writ. These men semen grete foolis, that poisone hemself
45 bi the mystakynge and undirstondynge of the hoolsum mete of Hooli Writ; and
thei bind hemsilf bi ropis of deedli sinnes, and betake hem prisoneris to the devyl,
and bryngen the chayn of deedli synne abowte here nekk wherbi thei schollen ben
hangid in helle. And therfore Hooli Writ seith (Prov. 5:22), "The wikkidnesses
of an yvel man takyn him, and ech is streigtli bounden with the ropis of hise
50 sinnes." Thise men ben grete foolis in alle maner, for if thei han verili the
undirstondyng of Holi Writ, and doon wetyngli and custumabli theragenes, thei
goon lyvynge doun to helle, as Seynt Austin seith on this word on the salm,
"*Descendant in infernum viventes.*" And if thei han not the trew undirstondung of
Hooli Writ and bosten that thei han it passande alle othere men, thanne be thei
55 open foolis, fouli disseyved of the devel, the world, and of there fleisch. Pryncipali
thise clerkis ben grete folis that with sich lyvynge prechyn opynli the lawe of God.
For as Crisostom seith on Matt. 5:13–14—on that word "*Vos estis sal
terre, vos estis lux mundi*"—he that lyveth yvele opynli in knowyng of the peple,
and prechith treuli the lawe of God, dampnyth hymself, sclandrith othere men, and
60 blasfemeth God.

b. [Six points on reading scripture for oneself]

But leve we alle thise cursidenessis biforeseid, and comforte we Cristine peple to
take trustili and deyutously the text of Hooly Writ and the trewe undirstondyng
therof. Cristene men schulden preye devoutli to God, auctor of al wisdom and
kunnynge, that he give to hem trewe undirstondyng of Hooli Writ. Thus seith the
65 wyse man, "Lord, give thou to me wysdoom that stondith aboute thi setis," that I
wete what failith to me and what is plesant befor thee in al tyme. The secunde
tyme, thei schulde meke hemsilf to God in doynge penaunce that God opene to
hem the trewe undirstondyng of his lawe, as he openede witt to hise apostolis to
undirstonde Hooli Scripture. The thridde, thei schulden sugette hemself to the

70 wille of God, and bileve stidfastly that his lawe is trewe, and truste feithfuli in
    Goddis help; and for this thei schullen have the blissyng of God and the blesse of
    hewene, and schullen graciousli be herd in here preier. For God dispicith not the
    praier of meke men, and he herith the desire of pore men that knowen verili that
    thei have no good but of God. The fourthe tyme, thei schulden meke hemself to
75 here bretheren, and enquere mekeli of every lerned man—and speciali of wel-
    wellid men, and weel-lyvynge—the trewe undirstondyng of Hooli Writ; and be thei
    not obstinat in ther owne wit but gyve stede and credence to wisere men that han
    the sperit of wisdom and of grace. The fifthe tyme, rede thei besili the text of the
    Newe Testament and take thei ensample of the hooly liyf of Crist and of hise
80 apostilis, and truste thei fulli to the goodnesse of the Hooli Goost, which is spesial
    techere of wel-willid men. For Crist seith in the Gospel to hise disciplis, "The
    Hooli Goost schal teche you al treuthe that is necessarie to helthe of soulis." And
    Joon seith in his epistil, "That anoyntyng"—that is, grace of the Hooli Goost—
    "techith yow of alle thingis that perteyneth to helthe of sowle." The sixte tyme,
85 thei schulden see and studie the trewe and opyn exposicioun of hooli doctours and
    othere wise men as thei may eseli and goodli come therto.
        Lat Cristene men travaile feithfulli in thise vi weies, and be not to moche aferid
    of objectiouns of enemyes seyynge that "the lettere sleeth." Thise enemyes menyn
    thus: that the letere of Hooli Writ is harmful to men, and fals and reprevable,
90 sithen that it sleeth men by deeth of synne. But sekirli thei mystaken the wordis of
    Hooly Writ, and here mystakyng and weiward menynge, and here wickide lyvynge,
    bryngen in deeth of soule; that is synne. But agens here fals menynge Crist seith in
    the Gospel of Joon (John 6:63), "The wordis wiche I have spoken to you ben
    sperit and liyf," and in the same chapetre Seynt Peter seith to Crist, "Lord, thou
95 hast wordis of everlastyng liyf." Poul seith (2 Thess. 2:8), that the Lord
    Ihesu "bi the spirit of his mouth"—that is, his hooli and trewe wordis—"schal sle
    Anticrist," and the prophete Isaie seith (Isa. 11:4), that "God by the spirit of his
    lippis schal sle the wickid man"—that is, Anticrist. Thanne sithen the wordis of
    Crist ben wordis of everlastyng liyf—that is, brynge trewe men to everlastyng
100 blisse—and sithen thise wordis schulyn sle Anticrist, the wordis of Crist been ful
    hooly and ful mighty and ful profitable to trewe men. But Poul menyth thus, by
    auctorite of the Hooly Goost, whanne he seyth "the lettere sleeth," that
    cerymonyes eithir sacrifices of the elde law, withoutyn goostli undirstondyng of
    the newe lawe, sleeth men bi errour of mysbileve. For if men holden that bodeli
105 circumcisioun is nedful now as it was in the Elde Testament, it is errour and
    mysbileve agens the treuthe of the Gospel. Also, if men holden that the sacrifice of
    bestes is nedful now as it was bifore Cristis passioun, it is errour and mysbeleve
    agens Crist and his Gospel. Therfore, this lettere, undirstonden thus fleischli,
    sleeth the mysundirstonders. Therfore Poul seith, "the sperit quekeneth"—that is,
110 goostli undirstondyng of ceremonyes and sacrifices of Moises lawe quekeneth men
    of right bileve that now, in stede of bodeli circumsisioun, takyn baptym taught and
    comaundid of Crist, and, in stede of sacrifices of bestis in the elde lawe, takyn
    now Crist and his passioun and hopyn to be sawid therbi with His mercy and here
    owene good lyvynge. Also, the lettere of the Newe Testament sleeth rebel men that
115 lyven theragens custumabli withouttyn amendyng in this lif. For Crist in the
    Gospel seith to sich a rebel man, "The word wich I have spoke schal deme hym"—
    that is, dampne hym—"in the laste day." Also God seith "I schal sle false men and

rebel agens my lawe and I schal make to lywe feithful men that kepyn my lawe."
Thanne though the letere sleeth in maner beforseid, it sueth not therfore that the
120 lettere is fals and harmful to men, as it suith not that God is fals and harmful in
his kynde, though he sleeth justli bi deeth of bodi and of soule hem that rebellen
fynaly agens his lawe. Also this sentence, "the lettere sleeth", schulde more make
aferid proude clerkis, that undirstonden the trewethe of Goddis lawe and lyven
custummabli theragens, than symple men of witt that litil undirstonden the lawe of
125 Crist and bisie hem to lywe weel in charite to God and man. For thise proud
clerkis, the more thei cunne Cristis lawe the more they make hemself dampnable
for here high cunnyng and here wickid lyvynge; and the symple men for here lytyl
cunnyng groundyn hemsilf the more in meknesse, and bisie hem to lerne the wei of
salvacioun. Thus, though thei hawe not tyme and leiser to turne and turne agen
130 the bokis of Goddis lawe to cunne the lettere therof, thei han and kepyn the fruit
and the veri sentence of al the lawe of God thourgh kepyng of duble charite—as
seynt Austyn seith in a sermoun of the preisyng of charite. And of ech sich symple
man the hooli prophete David seith thus: "Blessid is the man whom, Lord, thow
hast taught, and hast enformyd hym of thi lawe"—that is, charite; and in
135 Deuteronomye it is seid that "a lawe of fier"—that is, charite—"is in the rigt
ho[n]d of God."

c. [God's word as the audience's food]

. . . oure Lord Ihesu seith to hise apostlis (Mark 16:15), "Preche ye the Gospel to
everi creature"—that is, to every staat of men. And God comaundith in Moises
lawe that tho bestis that chewe not code be demed unclene—that is, that alle thei
140 that tretyn not and thinke not and speke not of the lawe of God aftir that thei han
herd it ben unclene bi Goddis doom and unable to blisse. Therfore David seith "I
schal blesse the Lord in al time: his heriynge schal be evere in my mouth." It is of
fendes weiwardnesse to forbede Cristene men to fede here soulis on Goddis word.
For God seith (Deut. 8:3), "A man livith not in bred alone, but in ech word
145 that cometh forth of Goddis mouth;" and the same sentense is co[n]fermid bi
Crist Ihesu in the Gospel (Matt. 4:4). Thanne sithen Ihesu Crist ordayneth his
word to be sustynaunce of mennys sowlis, it is a fendis condicion to refreine
Cristene men fro this goostli mete, sithen withoutyn it thei mowe not liven in grace
neither comen to bliss. Also God seith (Amos 8:11), "I schal sende hungyr on the
150 herthe; not hungir of breed neithir thourst of watir, but to heere the word of God."
As it were a gret cruelte to withholde bodeli mete and drynk fro hungri men and
thoursti (and tho withholderis schulde ben gelti of bodeli deeth of the same men)
so it is a moche grettere cruelte to withholde goostli mete—that is, Goddis word—
fro Cristene men that hungryn and thoursten therafter—that is, desiren it gretli to
155 kunne and to kepe it and to teche it othere men for the staat that thei stonden
inne. And thise witholders ben cursid of God and been sleeris of mennys soulis.
For God seith (Prov. 11:26), "He that hedeth whete schal be cursid among the
peple." But skilefulli Cristene men reden and stodien Hooli Writ to cunne it and
kepe it, for Crist seith in the Gospel (Matt. 22:4), "I have maad redi my mete,
160 my bolis and my volatilis ben slayn and alle thyngis ben redi: come ye to the
weddyngis"—wheron Crisostom writeth thus: Whatevere thyng is sought to helthe
of soule now, al is [ful]fillid in [s]cripturis; he that is unkunnynge schal fynde there

that that he owith to lerne; he that is rebellour and synnere schal fynde there the scourgis of doom to comynge, whiche he owith to drede; he that trawailith schal
165 fynde there the glorie of biheste of everlastynge liyf, and while he etith this scripture—that is, bileveth, kepith, and holdeth in mynde—he schal be more sterid to good werk; he that is of litil corage and sike in his soule schal fynde there mene metis of rightwisnesse, and though thise mene metis makyn not the soule fat—that is, parfit in goostli lyvynge—natheles tho suffre not the soule to die; he that is of
170 grett corage and feithful schal fynde there goostli metis of more continent liyf— that is, mor parfit liyf—and thise metis bryngyn him nigh to the kynde of angels; he that [is] smetyn of the devil and woundid with synnes schal fynde there medicinable metis that schullen reparaile hym to goostli helthe bi penaunce. Nothyng faylith in this feste that is nedful to helthe of mankynde, that is, Hooli Scripture.

1 redin read ∫ besili diligently ∫ kunne know
2 here their ∫ lyvynge way of life ∫ ensample example
3 staat spiritual condition ∫ stondyn stand ∫ ynne in ∫ han have ∫ blissyng blessing
4 ben are ∫ heryn hear
5 kepin keep, enact ∫ Apocalips Revelation 1 ∫ Seynt Joon Saint John: putative author of the Book of Revelation; before modern times, generally identified with Saint John the Evangelist
5–7 he is blessed . . . writen therynne Rev. 1:3
6 tho those
7 veyn foolish ∫ besie busy ∫ hem themselves ∫ faste vigorously
8 lettre literal word (i.e., the Latin text) ∫ sentence meaning
9 disceyven deceive ∫ in maner in this way ∫ sclaundren slander
11 in werk in [their] actions ∫ mekeli meekly
12 jangelyn chatter ∫ to schewe in order to exhibit
13 cunnynge knowledge ∫ opynli publicly ∫ werkis deeds ∫ doon do
14 contrarie to hemsilf inconsistent in themselves (i.e., hypocrites) ∫ turnyth leads
16 dooth does ∫ betyn beaten ∫ betyngis beatings
17 c[hapetre] MS c
17–18 that can . . . dooth it not James 4:17 ∫ can knows
18 Kunnynge makith . . . proud 1 Cor. 8:1 ∫ that is a convention of Latin biblical exegesis (see also 26, 35, 83, 96, 98, etc.) ∫ nakid mere
19 medlid mixed ∫ veynglorie foolish pride ∫ boost boasting
20–24 goos[t]li avoutrie . . . veynglorie, and boost This metaphor depends, at a remove, on the the common scholastic equation of the letter of God's word with the carnal and mortal. True understanding is, like marriage, a productive coupling of text and reader and brings forth "charite" and "goode werkis," but mere knowledge is like adul-

tery and produces [bastard] spiritual fruits of pride, vainglory, and boasting. This image is among the pervasive analogies in Piers Plowman; see especially Do-wel as "trewe wedded libbynge folke" (B X.108ff.).
20 semen seem ∫ goos[t]li spiritual ∫ avoutrie adultery ∫ there where
21 take of take from ∫ bi through
22 to brynge forth in order to bring forth ∫ very true ∫ nakid literal
23 undirstondynge meaning ∫ bi presumcion of mannes witt that is, presuming human intelligence to be sufficient ∫ forght forth: a typical East Anglian back-spelling. The scribe may be copying from an East Anglian exemplar.
24 coloure disguise: see MED: coloure 5b. The word has been identified as a possible item of "Lollard sect vocabulary" (Hudson 1985, 165–80). ∫ sutilli subtly
25 hede heed ∫ Poul the apostle Paul
25–26 kunne no more . . . to sobirnesse Rom. 12:3
26 to sobirnesse in moderation
27 eithir or ∫ to edificacion to to the edification of
29 wondren wonder ∫ on at ∫ weiwarnesse waywardness
30 passynly surpassingly ∫ sithyn since
31 unable unfitting ∫ therto for it ∫ feynen pretend
32 covetise covetousness ∫ wombe-joie gluttony. Compare the portrait of the doctor of divinity in Piers Plowman, excerpt 3.19. ∫ lewe live
33 delices fleshly pleasures ∫ ese ease ∫ Agenes against
34 suyth pursues ∫ most fool greatest fool. The Vulgate's reading, stultissimus est, suggests that "fool" is an adjective, foolish, but in this Middle English phrase it is more probably a noun.
35 herthe earth ∫ knoweleche to the that is, I acknowledge you ∫ herie praise

36 **previites** secrets

37 **schewid** shown ∫ **tho** those (i.e., the secrets of Scripture)

38 **Crisostom** Saint John Chrysostom (c. 347–407): bishop of Constantinople from 398 to 404 and one of the great preachers of the early church. The reference here is to his *De sacerdotia* (Concerning the priest; Nairn 1906). ∫ **levynge** living

40–41 **Wisdom schal not . . . suget to synnes** The Old Testament Book of Wisdom is regarded as apocryphal by the modern reformed churches but accepted as canonical by the Roman Catholic Church, as it was by the medieval Catholic Church.

41 **yvel-willid** evil-willed ∫ **nether** nor ∫ **duelle** dwell ∫ **suget** subject

43 **siche** such ∫ **No wondir though** it is no wonder that ∫ **he** that is, the devil

45 **undirstondynge** that is, misunderstanding ∫ **hoolsum** wholesome ∫ **mete** food

46 **bi** with ∫ **deedli** mortal ∫ **betake hem** deliver themselves

47 **aboute** around ∫ **schollen** shall

49 **takyn** captures ∫ **streigtli** tightly

50 **in alle maner** in every way

51 **doon** act ∫ **wetyngli** knowingly ∫ **custumabli** regularly ∫ **theragenes** against it

52 **lyvynge** alive ∫ **Seynt Austin** Saint Augustine of Hippo (354–430): one of the most influential of early Christian theologians ∫ **salm** psalm: Psalm 54 in Augustine's *Enarrationes in psalmos* (Expositions on the Book of Psalms) (*PL* 36:639)

53 *Descendant in infernum viventes* let them go down living into hell: Ps. 54:16, AV 55:15

54 **bosten** boast ∫ **passande** surpassing

55 **fouli** foully ∫ **disseyved** deceived ∫ **of** by

56 **lyvynge** way of life

57–60 **Crisostom seith . . . and blasfemeth God** Chrysostom, *De sacerdotia* 4.4 (see 38n above)

57 **on that word** concerning the text

57–58 *Vos estis sal terre . . . vos estis lux mundi* you are the salt of the earth; you are the light of the world

58 **yvele** sinfully ∫ **in knowyng of the peple** with the people's knowledge

59 **treuli** accurately ∫ **dampnyth** condemns ∫ **sclandrith** treats with contempt

61 **leve we** let us leave aside ∫ **cursidenessis** wicked practices ∫ **biforeseid** previously mentioned ∫ **comforte we Cristine peple** let us take comfort as Christian people

62 **deyutously** dutifully

63 **schulden** should ∫ **auctor** author, source

64–65 **the wyse man** that is, Solomon: supposed author of the Old Testament Book of Wisdom

65 **Lord, give thou . . . thi setis** Wisd. 9:4 ∫ **that** who ∫ **setis** thrones

66 **wete** know ∫ **what failith to me** what I am lacking ∫ **befor** to ∫ **al tyme** always, in all points

66–67 **The secunde tyme** that is, the second point (following the first point, in 61–66 above)

67 **meke** humble (*v.*) ∫ **opene** may reveal

68 **as he openede witt to hise apostolis** as he revealed understanding to his apostles

69 **thridde** third (i.e., the third point) ∫ **sugette** subject (*v.*)

74 **but** except

75–76 **wel-wellid . . . weel-lyvynge** men of good will and leading a good life

77 **wit** intelligence ∫ **gyve** grant ∫ **stede** status

78 **rede thei** let them read ∫ **besili** diligently

80 **spesial** [the] special

81–82 **The Hooli Goost . . . helthe of soulis** John 16:13

83 **Joon** Saint John the Evangelist ∫ **anoyntyng** blessing

83–84 **That anoyntyng . . . helthe of sowle** 1 John 2:27

86 **goodli** virtuously

87–90 **Lat Cristene men . . . synne** This discussion of Saint Paul's well-known statement that "the letter kills" again alludes to the common scholastic view that the letter, or literal meaning, is equated with the carnal and mortal (see 20–24n above). The opposition here is with the "spirit," or meaning, hidden within or behind the letter. Opponents of biblical translation claimed that access to the letter alone was dangerous, in an effort to protect the claims of the clergy to be the only mediators of the "spirit," or true meaning.

87 **to** too ∫ **aferid** afraid

88 **the lettere sleeth** 2 Cor. 3.6 ∫ **lettere** literal meaning ∫ **sleeth** kills ∫ **menyn** intend

90 **sithen that** since ∫ **by deeth of synne** by [leading them into] mortal sin ∫ **sekirli** certainly

94–95 **Lord, thou hast wordis of everlastyng liyf** John 6:68

97 **Anticrist** Christ's chief enemy, referred to in 1 John 2:18, 22, 4:3, and 2 John 7; often identified with the beasts in Revelation. The Chester Corpus Christi play has a pageant of "Anticrist." ∫ **Isaie** Isaiah

101 **trewe men** This phrase is another possible item of Lollard "sect vocabulary" (Hudson 1985, 165–80), but the context here may suggest no more than that "true men" are those who understand the word of God and whose lives reflect that understanding by being virtuous.

103 **elde law** that is, the Old Testament

104 **newe lawe** that is, the New Testament ∫ **bi errour** through the error ∫ **mysbileve** false belief

104–14 **For if men holden . . . good lyvynge** The reference is to the sacrament of baptism, whereby the literal marking of the body by circumcision, the practice that marked the Jews as God's people in the old law ("Elde Testament," 105, means both "Old Testament" and "old law"), is converted to a symbolic marking, the sign of the cross made in water on the forehead, a practice that marks the Christians of the new law. Following Paul, the writer rejects a belief in the literal practices of the Old Testament (such as circumcision). The argument offers an analogy with reading Scripture that bolsters the writer's arguments about access to the word of God: that lay readers, offered such access, would not only understood the text literally but apprehend the spiritual meaning.

106 **holden** hold

108 **lettere** text ∫ **fleischli** that is, literally or materialistically (see 87–90n)

109 **the sperit quekeneth** 2 Cor. 3:6 ∫ **quekeneth** revives

110 **Moises** Moses'

111 **right** true ∫ **takyn** receive ∫ **baptym** baptism

112–13 **takyn now Crist** that is, receive Christ's body in the Eucharist

113 **sawid** saved

114 **rebel** disobedient

115 **custumabli** habitually ∫ **amendyng** correction

116 **deme** judge

116–17 **The word . . . in the laste day** John 12:48.

117 **dampne** condemn ∫ **in the laste day** at the end of his life (or at the Day of Judgment) ∫ **sle** slay

117–18 **I schal sle . . . kepyn my law** a paraphrase of Bar. 4:1, an Old Testament book thought apocryphal by modern reformed churches but accepted by the medieval Catholic Church

118 **I schal make to lywe feithful men** I shall cause faithful men to live

119 **sueth** follows

121 **kynde** nature ∫ **justli** justly

124 **theragens** against it ∫ **symple men of witt** men of untrained intelligence

127 **high cunnyng** erudition

128 **groundyn** establish

129–30 **turne and turne agen the bokis** turn repeatedly [the pages of] the books

132 **seynt Austyn** Augustine (see 52n) ∫ **in a sermoun** perhaps *PL* 39:1533–35 (*Charitatis laus . . .*) or *PL* Supplementum II:449–52. Saint Augustine's teachings on charity, the greatest of the theological virtues, were highly influential throughout the Middle Ages, especially in biblical exegesis. The "duble charite" (131) is the motion of the soul toward God and also toward oneself and one's neighbor for God's sake. ∫ **ech sich** every such

133 **the hooli prophete David** King David: reputedly author of the Psalms, which were

sometimes, but not always, categorized as "prophecy" in the Middle Ages

133–34 **Blessid is the man . . . thi lawe** Ps. 93:12, AV 94

134 **enformyd** informed, instructed ∫ **of** about ∫ **and** that is, and in

135–36 **a lawe of fier . . . rigt ho[n]d of God** Deut. 33:2

138 **staat** estate (i.e., social or occupational class)

139 **tho bestis . . . unclene** those beasts who do not chew the cud should be judged unclean (Lev. 11:3)

140 **tretyn** concern themselves ∫ **aftir that** as

141 **unable** that is, ineligible ∫ **to blisse** to achieve the state of bliss, that is, go to heaven

141–74 **Therfore David . . . Hooli Scripture** For other uses of this argument about spiritual eating, see *Piers Plowman* (excerpt 3.19) and Mechtild of Hackeborn's *Book of Ghostly Grace* (excerpt 3.20).

141–42 **I schal blesse . . . in my mouth** Ps. 33:2, AV 34:1

142 **heriynge** praise

142–43 **of fendes** devilish

143 **weiwardnesse** perversity ∫ **forbede** forbid

145 **sentense** statement

147 **fendis** fiend's (i.e., evil) ∫ **refreine** discourage

150 **herthe** earth ∫ **breed** bread

152 **tho** those ∫ **schulde** would ∫ **gelti** guilty

154 **therafter** for it

154–55 **desiren it gretli to kunne** desire greatly to know it

155 **for the staat** because of the [spiritual] condition ∫ **stonden** stand

156 **sleeris** killers

158 **skilefulli** with reason ∫ **stodien** study

160 **bolis** bulls ∫ **volatilis** fowl

161 **Crisostom** See 38n above.

161–73 **Whatevere thyng . . . helthe bi penaunce** See *In Matthaeum homilia xli,* in Montfaucon 1835–39, 6:914.

163 **that that** that which ∫ **owith** ought ∫ **rebellour** rebellious

164 **to comynge** approaching ∫ **owith** ought ∫ **trawailith** labors

165 **biheste** promise ∫ **etith** eats

166 **sterid** prompted

167 **sike** sick ∫ **mene** humble, lean

168 **metis** foods, dishes

169 **natheles** nevertheless ∫ **tho** those [foods] ∫ **suffre** allow

170 **grett** great ∫ **continent** abstemious

171 **nigh** close

172 **smetyn** struck ∫ **of** by

173 **medicinable** healing ∫ **reparaile** restore

174 **faylith** is lacking ∫ **feste** feast

2.6 THE KNOWING OF WOMAN'S KIND IN CHILDING: TRANSLATOR'S PROLOGUE

Date and Provenance: uncertain, though probably 1380s–1420s; ?northeast Midlands.

Author, Sources, and Nature of Text: An anonymous translation, *The Knowing of Woman's Kind in Childing* is a gynecological text derived in part from a French translation of a Latin compilation, the *Cum auctor* (sometimes known as the *Trotula major*). The Latin source circulated widely in Europe in the fourteenth and fifteenth centuries, and was attributed to Trotula, a woman doctor who practiced in Salerno, southern Italy, in the later eleventh or early twelfth century. Trotula's name was associated with several Latin treatises that were translated into various European vernaculars from the thirteenth century onward. However, only one text is known for certain to have been written by her, the twelfth-century *Practica secundum Trotam* (Practice according to Trota [Trotula]), which was never translated from the Latin. Chaucer's inclusion of Trotula in Jankyn's "Book of Wicked Wives" (*Wife of Bath's Prologue* III [D] 677) may suggest that the text circulating under her name was a byword for a particularly wayward or even dangerous femininity. While it seems in one sense obvious and "natural" to present knowledge about the female reproductive system under the rubric of a woman's name, it is of course extremely rare to find a woman as *auctor*, given that the prevailing tradition (both late classical and medieval clerical) of authorship and authority was almost entirely masculine.

Audience and Circulation: The text survives in five fifteenth-century manuscripts and seems often to have circulated with other medical treatises and collections of medicinal recipes (though the manuscript edited here contains only this text). Although it draws on the medieval commonplace that women did not know Latin and therefore required translations, the prologue is unusually explicit about women's practical need for this sort of intimate text. However, the female audience is not defined in specific terms other than by their degree of literacy. In proposing the work as a manual whereby literate women (namely, those with an ability to read English) might instruct illiterate women, the prologue is nevertheless conscious that its readership might include men, and warns against their reading the text from misogynist positions (19–24).

Bibliography: Barratt (1992) edits excerpts and provides contextual discussion. For an edition of the complete text, edited from London, British Library MS Addit. 12195, see Howarth 1996. For further information on Trotula and medieval gynecology, see Benton 1985; Green 1989 and 1992; Baird-Lange 1985; Rowland 1981. Monica Green is currently preparing a translation of the so-called Trotula texts.

Source: Oxford, Bodleian Library MS Douce 37, fols. 1r–2r: a small parchment manuscript of the first half of the fifteenth century with a writing area approximately 4 x 3 inches. It contains only this text, and is perhaps a pocket book, designed to be carried around for regular consultation rather than be kept in a library. There are some later marginalia, and the first folio is stained and rubbed.

This excerpt was contributed by Alexandra Barratt.

[O]ure lorde God, whan he had storid the worlde, of all creaturis he made manne
and woman, [a] resonabull creature, and badde hem wexe and multiply, and ordend
that of them ii schulde cume the thurde and that of the man, that is made of
hote and drye mature, schulde come the sede and that the woman, that ys made of
5 cold matyre and moyste, schulde receyve the sede, so that [of] the tempure of hote
and colde, moyste and dry, the chylde schulde [be] engendy[r]de, ryht as we seen
treys, cornys and herbys mou not growe withoute resonabyll tempure of the iiii.

And forasmoche as whomen ben more febull and colde be nature than men been
and have grete travell in chyldynge, ther fall oftyn to hem mo diverse sykenes than
10 to men, and namly to the membrys that ben longynge to gendrynge. Wherfore, in
the worschyp of oure Lady and of all sayntys, I thynke to do myn ententyffe
bysynes for to drau oute of Latyn into Englysch dyverse causis of here maladyes,
the synes that they schall knou hem by, and the curys helpynge to hem, afture the
tretys of dyverse mastrys that have translatyde hem oute of Grek into Latyn. And
15 because whomen of oure tonge cunne bettyre rede and undyrstande thys langage
than eny other, [that] every whoman lettyrde [may] rede hit to other unlettyrd and
help hem and conceyle hem in here maledyes withowtyn scheuynge here dysese to
man, I have thys drawyn and wryttyn in Englysch.
And yf hit fall any man to rede hit, I pray hym and scharge hym in oure Lady
20 behalve that he rede hit not in no dyspyte ne sclaundure of no woman, ne for no
cause but for the hele and helpe of hem, dredynge that vengauns myht fall to hym
as hit hath do to other that have scheuyd here prevytees in sclaundyr of hem;
undyrstondynge in certeyne that they have no other evylys that nou be alyve than
thoo women hade that nou be seyntys in hevyn.

1 [O]ure MS *ure* with smudged space for *o* ∫
storid supplied, stocked ∫ of with
2 [a] MS rubbed and illegible ∫ resonabull having the faculty of reason ∫ wexe increase, that is, give
birth (see Gen. 1:28)∫ ordend decreed
3 of from ∫ them those ∫ ii two
4–6 hote and drye . . . moyste and dry Following a tradition that went back to the Greek writers
Aristotle and Galen, medieval physiology held that
the heat and dryness of man's body enable production of sperm, whereas the cold and moisture of a
woman's body produce menstrual fluid but not semen; this fluid is coagulated by the semen to form
the body of the offspring (see Blamires 1992, 38–
42; Cadden 1993).
4 mature matter ∫ sede seed, semen
5 that [of] the MS *that the* ∫ tempure propor-
tionate mixture
6 [be] MS rubbed and illegible ∫ engendy[r]de
conceived ∫ ryht just
7 treys trees ∫ cornys grains ∫ herbys plants ∫
mou not cannot ∫ the iiii that is, the four elements of
heat, cold, moisture, and dryness. Following the
ancient Greek scientific traditions of Aristotle and
Galen, it was a medieval commonplace that the
material world was constituted of varying balances
of these four elements, by analogy with the bodily
"humors" of blood (hot), choler (dry), melancholy
(cold), and phlegm (moist). The correct balance of
these humors in the human body maintained health.
8 forasmoche as in that ∫ whomen women ∫
more febull weaker. Women's cold, moist nature
was held to make them intellectually inferior.
9 travell labor ∫ chyldynge giving birth ∫ mo diverse sykenes more varied complaints

10 namly in particular ∫ membrys that ben
longynge to gendrynge the reproductive system
10–12 in the worschyp . . . Latyn The
translator's claim to have Englished the work in
honor of Mary ("oure Lady"), a claim interpolated
by this translator and not present in the original
text, presumably depends on the Virgin's special
appropriateness as most blessed of mothers.
11–12 do myn ententyffe bysynes exert myself
diligently
12 for to to ∫ drau translate ∫ here their
13 synes symptoms ∫ afture according to
14 tretys treatments ∫ dyverse mastrys various
authorities. The source text draws partly on the
early-second-century Greek medical writers
Muscio and Seranus. ∫ hem them
15 whomen of oure tonge English-speaking
women ∫ cunne know how to
16 [that] every in order that every (MS *euery*) ∫
lettyrde literate: that is, able to read English ∫ [may]
rede MS *rede* ∫ unlettyrd illiterate
17 conceyle advise ∫ maledyes maladies ∫
scheuynge showing
18 drawyn translated
19 yf hit fall any man to rede hit if it should happen that any man read it ∫ pray request ∫ scharge
enjoin
19–20 in oure Lady behalve on our Lady's behalf
20 not in no dyspyte ne sclaundure of no
woman not out of any malice toward or in order to
defame any woman
20–21 ne for no cause nor for any reason
21 but except ∫ hele healing ∫ dredynge fearing ∫
vengauns punishment

22 **do done** ∫ **other that** others who ∫ **scheuyd** revealed ∫ **here prevytees** their secrets (i.e., women's secrets) ∫ **in sclaundyr of hem** to slander them (i.e., women)

23 **in certeyne** certainly ∫ **they** that is, women

23–24 **they have no other evylys . . . seyntys in hevyn** That is, women alive today have the same troubles [i.e., diseases] as those women had who are now saints in heaven. This reference may derive from the increased devotion in the later medieval period to married women saints—Angela of Foligno, Bridget of Sweden, Elizabeth of Hungary, Dorothy of Montau—and to the cult of Saint Anne, mother of the Virgin (Duffy 1992, 181–82). Malory's Queen Guenevere defends her conduct in similar terms (Vinaver 1971, 720.22–23).

2.7 JOHN CAPGRAVE, *LIFE OF ST. GILBERT:* PROLOGUE

Date and Provenance: 1451; East Anglia (Lynn, Norfolk).

Author, Sources, and Nature of Text: John Capgrave (1393–1464) was an Augustinian friar who spent most of his life in Lynn, Norfolk, where he was prior and, after 1453, prior provincial. He was the most distinguished and prolific of the trio of East Anglian poets (including John Metham and Osbern Bokenham, see excerpts 1.8 and 1.11) who saw themselves as the disciples of Chaucer and Lydgate, and is the author of a large corpus of Latin and English works, including a *Life of St. Katharine* in five books, which is as long and ambitious as *Troilus and Criseyde* or Lydgate's *Life of Our Lady. The Life of St. Gilbert* purports to be a translation of an older Latin life of Saint Gilbert (c. 1083–1189), who founded his order in 1137 after establishing seven women followers in a cloister at Sempringham (Foreville and Keir 1987). That source is not now known, although it has always been wrongly identified as the standard Latin version extant in three manuscripts (Fredeman 1972, 114). One probable source was the Office (i.e., the religious services) in honor of Gilbert that the nuns would have said on his annual feast day. Despite the work's avowed pastoral and exemplary purpose, it seems that Capgrave was also interested in issues of genealogy and national identity, since he added an account of Gilbert's hybrid parentage, Norman on his father's side and English on his mother's (Munro 1910, 63). The choice of the founder's life as an exemplary text for those in religious orders is entirely standard, as is the lengthy etymology of Gilbert's name (22–42).

Audience and Circulation: The text was written for the nuns of Sempringham, Norfolk, "whech unneth can undyrstande Latyn" (18), as Capgrave claims, but is addressed to Nicholas Reysby, master of the Gilbertine Order of Sempringham, who already knew Capgrave's *Life of St. Augustine.* A further address to men in the audience (8–12) suggests that Capgrave anticipated a plural reading community (compare excerpts 1.11, 2.6, 2.8, 2.9); despite the mention of "solitarye women" (17), the translation is intended for wider publication. Capgrave's address to a female audience may explain one interesting alteration to the established narrative: the story of Gilbert's being tempted by his host's daughter is replaced by an abstract discussion of his chastity (Fredeman 1972, 123). Many of Capgrave's Latin texts are lost, and his works were probably not widely read (Lucas 1983, xxiv), although his achievements were acknowledged by Bokenham (*Legendys of Hooly Wummen* 6354–60: see excerpt 1.11). Many of his surviving works are extant in a small number of manuscripts, either holographs—that is, texts written out by the author in his or her own hand (like the source of the text printed here)—or texts whose copying was closely supervised by Capgrave himself. On the other hand, although the *Life* is preserved only in two manuscripts (the source below and the fragmentary British Library MS Cotton Vitellius D.XV, of which only seven small fragments survive from the Cotton fire), it probably circulated outside the convent, as various signatures of ownership in the one complete manuscript suggest.

Bibliography: The *Life* is edited by J. J. Munro (1910). The most recent substantial critical discussion, chiefly concerned to disprove Capgrave's dependence on the only known Latin version of Gilbert's life, is that by Jane Cowan Fredeman (1972). For incidental remarks on Capgrave's translation practices in this text, see Ellis 1982a. There is a chronological table of Capgrave's life and an account of the author and his works in Lucas 1983, xv–xxix. See also Lucas 1982 for discussion of Capgrave in the context of English literary patronage. For a full-length study of Gilbert's life and of the Gilbertine order, see Golding 1995. On Capgrave as an author, see Seymour 1996b. Capgrave's vernacular hagiography is discussed by Derek Pearsall (1975) and Karen Winstead (1991) in their studies of his *St. Katharine*. On Capgrave's relation to Chaucer, see Winstead 1996.

Source: London, British Library MS Addit. 36704, fols. 46r–47r (apparently a holograph). This small and attractive manuscript is carefully rubricated but not a luxury production. It contains both the *Lives* of Augustine and Gilbert and a treatise on Augustinian rule, taken from a sermon Capgrave delivered at Cambridge in 1422 (see 8–12). Signatures of ownership suggest that the manuscript belonged to an East Anglian nonaristocratic family in the later fifteenth century. Typical East Anglian spellings used by Capgrave include "whech" (with *e* for *i* [24]) and the unusual "who" (for *how* [20]) and "rith" (for *right* [44]).

To my wel-beloved in oure Lord God maystir of the ordere of Sempyngham, whech ordre is entytled onto the name of Seynt Gilbert, I, ffrere J. C., amongis doctouris lest, send reverens as to swech dignyte, desiring clennesse to youre soule and helth to youre body.

5   Now withinne fewe dayes was notyfied onto me that the lyf of oure fader Seynt Augustyn, whech that I translat into oure tunge at instauns of a certeyn woman, was browt to youre presens, whech lykyd yow wel as it is told, save ye wold I schul adde therto alle thoo relygyous that lyve undyr his reule. But to this I answere that it was not my charge, but if men like for to knowe this matere
10 diffusely thei may lerne it in a sermon that I seid at Cambrige the yere before myn opposicioun, whech sermon uphap I wil sette in Englisch in the last ende of this werk.

Than aftir ye had red this lyf of Seynt Augustyn ye sayde to on of my frendes that ye desired gretly the lyf of Seynt Gilbert schuld be translat in the same forme.
15 Thus mad he instaunce to me, and I graunted both your petycioun, this for I wold not frustrate him of his mediacioun. To the honoure of God and of alle seyntis than wil we begynne this tretys, namelych for the solitarye women of youre religioun whech unneth can undyrstande Latyn, that thei may at vacaunt tymes red in this book the grete vertues of here maystyr. For here may thei loke as in a
20 glasse, who thei schal transfigure here soules lych onto that exemplary in whech thei schul loke.

Of the interpretacioun of his name, what it schuld mene in Englisch (for we have it not redily in oure bokes of interpretaciones) we wil speke in swech maner as auctouris whech dyvyde names in partes. "*Gyla*," thei sey, is a word of Hebrew,
25 as mech to sey as "he that passeth fro o cuntre to anothir." And "*ber*" is a welle, or a pitte, eke deryved fro the Ebrewe tunge. "*Tus*" is a Lateyn word, in Englisch "a swete gumme," whech we throwe in oure encenseris whan we schal doo a special honoure to God. Thanne soundith his name thus onto oure heryng: "This holy man was a walkere here in erde that passed fro the welle onto the swete
30 savour." The welle clepe I the holy baptem in whech he was wasch fro Adam his

synne. The swete savour name I the holy opynyoun of this man whech savoured
so swetely in this land that it mad many men to selle al that thei had and folow the
steppes of poverte. Of this savour spak the blissed apostel whan he saide: "We be
the good odour of oure Lord Crist in every place, both to hem that schul be saved
35 and eke to hem that schul perisch. To summe be we savoure of lyf and to summe
savoure of deth." So semyth it that the clene lyf of Seynt Poule, and the
devoute preching of hym, was onto hem whech were chose to be saved a savoure
of evyrlasting lyf, and to hem that were reprobat a savour of everlastyng peyne.
Alle this is seid to acording of Seynt Gilbertis name, that al his lif from his baptem
40 onto his deth ran in swech a swete savoure that yet at these dayes the devoute
virgines of his ordre beren witnesse that of the rote of his doctrine sprange alle
these fayre flouris of virginite.

     This is the preamble or elles the prologe of Seynt Gilbertis lif, whech lyf I have
take on hand to translate out of Latyn rith as I fynde before me, save sum
45 addicionis wil I put thertoo whech men of that ordre have told me, and eke othir
thingis that schul falle to my mynde in the writyng whech be pertinent to the
matere.

1 **maystir** In the margin is written *M[agister].
Nicholas Reysby* ∫ **Sempyngham** MS *simpyngham*
with *i* subpuncted for erasure and *e* written above

2 **entytled onto the name of Seynt Gilbert**
which takes its name from Saint Gilbert ∫ **ffrere** friar
∫ **J. C.** that is, John [Iohannes] Capgrave. In the margin a later hand has written *Johannis Capgrave*.

2–3 **amongis doctouris lest** the least important
of learned men

3 **clennesse** moral purity

5 **was notyfied** [it] was notified ∫ **onto** to

5–6 **the lyf of oure fader Seynt Augustyn**
Capgrave's *Life of St. Augustine* was written sometime before 1451. Augustine's monastic rule of c.
397 became the basis of the Augustinian order of
canons, as of other religious communities, male and
female (van Bavel and Canning 1996, 3–6).

6 **whech that I translat** which I translated (MS
transalat, with the middle *a* subpuncted for erasure)
∫ **instauns** instigation ∫ **a certeyn woman** The identity of this woman is unknown: in the *Life of St.
Augustine,* which precedes this *Life* in the MS, she is
called a "gentille woman" (fol. 5r).

7 **lykyd yow wel** pleased you well ∫ **save** except
∫ **wold** wished

8 **thoo relygyous** those religious [orders] (see
10n)

9 **charge** responsibility ∫ **for to** to

10 **diffusely** at length ∫ **a sermon that I seid at
Cambrige** (*I* inserted above the line with a caret) In
1422, Capgrave was appointed by the prior general
to study at Cambridge, where he delivered a sermon
on the twelve orders living under the Augustinian
Rule (Lucas 1983, xx). A version or abstract of this

sermon is printed by Munro (1910, 145–48) (MS
fols. 116r–19r).

10–11 **myn opposicioun** formal oral examination. Capgrave took his Bachelor of Theology
degree at Cambridge in 1423.

11 **uphap** possibly. The form of the word in the
MS is unusual. The MS clearly reads *vnphap,* and if
the MS is a holograph, it is possible this is an authentic form, which could be transcribed with a double
initial vowel (*uuphap*). ∫ **sette** compose ∫ **last ende**
very end

15 **mad he instaunce to me** he entreated me ∫
both your petycioun both your requests ∫ **this** added
in margin

17 **than** then ∫ **tretys** treatise ∫ **namelych** especially ∫ **solitarye** living apart from the world

18 **unneth** scarcely ∫ **at vacaunt tymes** that is,
hours not occupied by saying the Office and other
duties. Most conventual regimes allowed time (usually in the afternoons) for reading devotional
literature and saints' lives (Hutchinson 1989).
Compare *The Orchard of Syon,* excerpt 3.5: 17–20.

19 **here** their ∫ **maystyr** master, that is, Saint Gilbert

20 **glasse** mirror. The metaphor of the mirror
used here is a common medieval one; the object
(here, a book) as mirror offers readers not a reflection of themselves but an example to be gazed on for
edification or imitation (see, e.g., excerpt 3.12). ∫
who how (i.e., so they may discover how) ∫ **lych onto**
like ∫ **exemplary** an exemplar, a pattern of conduct

22–42 **Of the interpretacioun . . . virginite** The
elaborate etymology of the saint's name is a standard hagiographical procedure, and derives from

the practice in the popular *Legenda aurea,* a widely disseminated collection of Latin legends. See, for example, Chaucer, *Second Nun's Prologue* VIII (G) 85–119. The mode is also common in Latin scholastic prologues, especially under the standard heading of "the title of the work" in the so-called Type C prologue (Minnis 1988, 19–20).

23 **bokes of interpretaciones** works of etymology (*MED: interpretacioun* 11a). The *Etymologiae* of Bishop Isidore of Seville (c. 560–636) was one of the most widely used of such works. ∫ **in swech maner** after the manner of

24 **auctouris** *auctores,* authoritative writers or texts from the past ∫ **a word of Hebrew** a word from Hebrew

25 **o** one

26 **eke** also ∫ *Tus* MS *Thus,* with *u* subpuncted; *tus* in red in the margin

27 **encenseris** censers, containers used in church or chapel to disperse incense ∫ **doo** perform

28 **soundith his name thus onto oure heryng** his name conveys the following meaning to our ears (i.e., when it is broken up into its constituent units of sound)

29 **in erde** on earth ∫ **onto** unto, toward (MS *on,* with *to* added in red above the line)

30 **savour** smell ∫ **clepe** call ∫ **baptem** baptism

30–31 **wasch fro Adam his synne** washed [clean] of Adam's sin

32 **thei** MS *i* is added above the line with a caret ∫ **and folow** *2 Cor 2* (2 Cor. 2) added in red in the margin

33 **the blissed apostel** Saint Paul

33–36 **We be the good odour . . . savoure of deth** 2 Cor. 2:15–16

36 **semyth it** it appears ∫ **clene** pure, impeccable

38 **reprobat** damned

39 **to acording of** in accordance with

40 **ran** took its course ∫ **at these dayes** in these present times

41–42 **of the rote . . . flouris of virginite** The metaphor probably alludes to the iconography of the tree or rod (Latin *virga*) of Jesse (associated not only with Christ's lineage from the Virgin Mary but with consecrated virginity in general).

44 **take on hand** undertaken ∫ **rith** just ∫ **save** except that

46 **falle to my mynde** come into my mind ∫ **be** are

47 **matere** subject matter (i.e., Gilbert's life)

2.8 BISHOP FOX, *THE RULE OF SEYNT BENET:* PREFATORY LETTER

Date and Provenance: 1517; the south of England.

Author, Sources, and Nature of Text: Richard Fox (c. 1448–1528), created bishop of Exeter and lord privy seal by Henry VII in 1487, and bishop of Winchester from 1501 until his death, was a friend of Erasmus and was the founder, in 1517, of Corpus Christi College, Oxford, for the education of secular clergy. Fox's translation of the Rule of St. Benedict ("Benet"), undertaken at the request of the heads of the four religious houses for women in his Winchester diocese (Romsey, Wherwell, St. Mary's, Winchester, and Wintney), was a major contribution to vernacular religious culture in the early sixteenth century. One year earlier, Erasmus had published his edition of the Greek New Testament, with its preface urging access to the Scriptures for all. The Benedictine Rule is the foundational text of Western monasticism. Compiled c. 540 for the monks of Monte Cassino, it sets out the principles along which

life in the monastic community should be ordered, and a portion of it was read daily in every Benedictine house and provided the model for many other orders. Gregory the Great relates that Saint Benedict's sister, Saint Scholastica, presided over a community of religious women. Fox's careful translation (unlike some earlier English versions, a rendering of the complete Rule) explicitly aims to produce a vernacular version for nuns in late medieval England, a rationale for which is provided by the familiar topos of women's insufficient command of Latin (see pages 120–22). The pastoral aims of Fox's translation also serve to legitimate his own position as a self-conscious *auctor.* Like Capgrave and the Amesbury writer (excerpts 2.7 and 2.9), Fox inserts himself into a triangular structure, where the bond between male spiritual director and male auditor (perhaps implied, for example, in the masculine pronouns of 1–5 or the legal tone of 10–13) is underwritten by the group of women in that director's charge. Importantly, however, the text itself envisages a reading situation that takes place among women alone and out of male jurisdiction (11–17; compare Riddy 1996b).

Audience and Circulation: Fox adapts the text for his intended female audience, often adding short explanatory phrases and consistently referring to "mynchyns" (i.e., nuns) and "susters" where the original Rule has *monachi* and *fratres*. In a few passages concerning such matters as absence from the monastery and the receiving of guests, Fox retains the male terms, explaining that he considers this material inappropriate for nuns because such activities would expose them to temptation by bringing them into contact with men. Little is known of the text's circulation. In addition to furnishing the nuns with manuscript copies of his translation (37; none of these manuscripts survive), Fox had it printed by Richard Pynson, ostensibly for the purpose of making further copies available "amongis them" (36), but presumably also for public circulation. Although it can be inferred that this prefatory letter was added to the printed version, we otherwise have no way of knowing whether the manuscript and printed versions of the translation were the same. Despite the way the text presents itself as an intimate address to enclosed women, in its printed form it is also in part a public demonstration of responsible episcopal care (as well as responsible scholarly translation), directed not to the work's intended recipients but to the wider public, who were becoming increasingly interested in ecclesiastical reform and government. On the other hand, only two printed copies survive, and its actual readership outside the four

Benedictine houses for women in Fox's diocese may have been limited. Twenty or so years after its composition (i.e., in the 1530s), all religious houses in England were "dissolved" by Henry VIII, rendering the translation to all intents and purposes obsolete.

Bibliography: The prefatory letter is edited by P. S. Allen and H. M. Allen (1929). Justin McCann (1952) provides an edition and translation of the Latin Benedictine Rule. On Fox's pastoral concerns, see Greatrex 1990. On the nunneries for whom Fox's translation was designed, see Coldicott 1989.

Source: Oxford, Bodleian Library Arch.A.d.15, Aiir–Aiiv (*STC* 1859), collated with the other early printed copy in the British Library, G.10245; no variants were found. The text was printed in 1517 in London by Richard Pynson, with a title page that reads *Here begynneth the Rule of seynt Benet* and has two woodcuts, one of nine clergy carrying a casket in procession, the other of a pelican wounding herself (Fox's personal device, see 41n). On the back of the title page, the pelican is depicted again, this time beside a shield, crozier, and miter (emblems of Fox's episcopal office). The initial *F* at the beginning of the letter (1) is a further small woodcut, depicting a bishop with crozier (presumably Fox himself), and a similar figure appears yet again at the beginning of the main text. There are corrections to the text in more than one sixteenth-century hand. According to an inscription on the last page of text, the book belonged to Dame Margaret Stanburne, prioress of the Benedictine Priory of St. Michael, Stamford.

This excerpt was contributed by Brendan Biggs.

Forasmoche as every persone ought to know the thyng that he is bounde to kepe or accomplisshe, and ignorance of the thynge that he is bounde to do cannot nor may not excuse him; and forasmoche also as the reding of the thynge that a persone is bounde to do and execute, except he understande it, is to the executinge
5 therof nothyng vailliable, but only thyng inutile, travell in vayne, and tyme loste:
    We, therfore, Richarde, by the permission and suffrance of our Lorde God Bisshope of Winchester, revolvinge in our mynde that certayne devoute and religiouse women, beinge within our diocese and under our pastorall charge and cure, have not only professed them to th'observance of the Rule of the holy

10 confessoure Seinte Benet, but also be bounde to rede, lerne, and understond the
same, when they be novices and before they be professed; and also after their
profession they shulde nat onely in themselfe kepe, observe, execute, and practice
the sayd Rule, but also teche other their sisters the same; insomoche that for the
same intente they daily rede and cause to be red somme part of the sayd Rule by
15 one of the sayd sisters amonges themselfe, as well in their chapiterhowse after the
redinge of the Martyrologe as sommetyme in their fraitur in tyme of refeccions
and collacions: al the which redingis is alwayes don in the Latin tonge, wherof
they have no knowlege nor understondinge, but be utterly ignorant of the same;
whereby they do nat only lese their tyme but also renne into the evident daunger
20 and perill of the perdicion of their soules:

We, the sayd Bisshope, knowing and consideringe the premisses, and
rememberyng that we may not without like peryll of our sowlle suffer the sayd
religious wemen, of whose sowles we have the cure, to continue in their sayde
blindenesse and ignorance of the sayd Rule, to the knowlege and observance
25 wherof they be professed; and specially to th'entent that the yonge novices may
first knowe and understande the sayde Rule before they professe them to it, so
that none of them shall mowe afterward probably say that she wyste nat what she
professed, as we knowe by experience that somme of them have sayd in tyme
passed:

30 For these causes, and specially at th'instant requeste of our ryght dere and
welbeloved doughters in oure Lorde Iesu th'abbasses of the monasteris of Rumsay,
Wharwel, Seynt Marie's within the citie of Winchester, and the prioresse of
Wintnay, our right religious diocesans, we have translated the sayde rule into oure
moders tonge, commune, playne, rounde Englisshe, easy and redy to be
35 understande by the sayde devoute religiouse women:

And bycause we wolde not that there shulde be any lacke amongis them of the
bokis of this sayd translation, we have therfore, above and besyde certayne bokes
therof which we have yeven to the sayde monasteris, caused it to be emprinted by
our welbeloved Richarde Pynson of London, printer, the xxii day of the monethe
40 of January, the yere of oure Lorde MCCCCCXVI, and the viii yere of the reigne of
our soverayne lorde Kynge Henry the VIII, and of our translacion the xvi.

4 **except** unless
4–5 **to the executinge therof nothyng vailliable** of no use in performing it
5 **inutile** useless ∫ **travell** work
7 **revolvinge** considering
9 **cure** spiritual care ∫ **professed** vowed ∫ **them** themselves
10 **Seinte Benet** Benedict of Nursia (c. 480–c. 550), regarded as the founder of monasticism in the West
10–11 **the same** the language of formal legal deposition or affidavit (compare the repeated use of *the sayde*: see 13, 14, 22, 23, 28, 33, 35)
11 **before they be professed** before they have taken their religious vows
13 **other their** their other
13–14 **for the same intente** for that purpose [of teaching the other nuns]

14 **cause to be red** that is, have read aloud (on this practice, called "prelection" by Coleman [1996], see the Introduction to Part Two, pages 113–14)
15 **chapiterhowse** chapter house, the room used in a religious house for a formal assembly
16 **Martyrologe** martyrology: a collection of lives of Christian martyrs arranged according to the calendar. The appropriate section was read at the daily meeting in the chapter house. ∫ **fraitur** refectory
16–17 **refeccions and collacions** meals. For the custom of mealtime reading in nunneries, see Hutchinson 1989; see also *The Mirror of Our Lady*, excerpt 3.12: 126–30.
17 **al the which redingis** Since vernacular martyrologies and saints' lives were read in late medieval nunnery refectories, Fox may here mean the Benedictine Rule specifically.

19 **lese** waste ∫ **renne** run
21 **premisses** points made above
27 **shall mowe afterward probably say** will plausibly be able to say afterward ∫ **wyste** knew
28 **we knowe by experience** Fox was very concerned with enforcing enclosure. In 1506, at Romsey Abbey, Fox removed the subprioress and felt it appropriate to "administer severe censures" (Doubleday et al. 1900–14, 2:131). However, reports of scandalous conduct by the nuns at Romsey, as elsewhere, may owe much to stereotypical perceptions and fears regarding the unruly feminine. In a letter to Wolsey of January 18, 1528, Fox responded to a criticism that he had dealt too harshly with the nuns in his diocese, and acknowledged that he did not permit the nuns to leave their monasteries, adding, "and yet soo much libertie appereth some tyme to muche"; without strict enclosure there "can be noo surtie of th'observance of good religion" (Allen and Allen 1929, 150). Another attempt by Fox to make sure the keeping of enclosure was internalized by novices was his presentation of a text of the order of consecration of nuns (now Cambridge University Library MS Mm.3.13) to the Abbey of St. Mary's, Winchester, with the words to be spoken in Latin by the participants in the ceremony and the directions translated into English (for text, see Maskell 1970, 2:307–31).
30 **instant** urgent
31–33 **Rumsay ... Wintnay** Fox refers here to the heads of the four religious houses for women in the diocese of Winchester; all were in Hampshire. The abbess of the Benedictine abbey at Romsey was Anne Westbrook; that of the Benedictine abbey at Wherwell, south of Andover, was Maud Rowse; that of the Benedictine Abbey of St. Mary, Winchester (Nunnaminster), was Joan Leigh; Anne Thomas

became prioress of the Cistercian priory at Wintney (i.e., Harley Wintney) in 1497 (Doubleday et al. 1900–14, 2:126, 132, 137, 151).
34 **moders tonge** For the topos of the mother tongue (used here as an index of its communicative abilities as well as affective qualities), see Usk's *Testament of Love* (excerpt 1.4: 29) and excerpts 2.4: 7, and 2.17: 27. ∫ **rounde** honest
37–38 **above and besyde certayne bokes therof** in addition to manuscript copies of it (see headnote)
38 **yeven** given
39 **Richarde Pynson** (d. 1530) was one of the most important early London printers.
39–40 **xxii ... MCCCCCXVI** that is, January 22, 1517 (from the late twelfth to the mid–eighteenth century in England the year was generally considered to begin on March 25, the feast of the Annunciation). Henry VIII came to the throne in 1509; Fox was translated to Winchester in 1501.
41 **translacion** translation. Bishops who move up the implied hierarchy of dioceses, from one see to another, are described as "translated," rather than "appointed," to their new sees, a word also used of the movement of sacred relics from one place to another. Fox stresses his formal authority by paralleling his sixteen-year reign at Winchester with Henry VIII's eight years as king of England. As bishop, his personal symbol was the pelican piercing its breast to feed its children with drops of its own blood (a common medieval belief about the pelican, which was often taken as a natural symbol for Christ and his self-giving love). His pelicans still adorn the roof bosses in the choir (the area in front of the high altar) of Winchester cathedral: a powerful symbol at once of formal episcopal authority and the maternal relationship he believed bishops should have with their spiritual charges.

2.9 *THE AMESBURY LETTER:* PROLOGUE

Date and Provenance: c. 1510–19; the south of England (the convent at Amesbury, Wiltshire). The prioress "Cristina" mentioned in the *Rule* is probably Christine Fauntleroy, prioress from at least 1510 to c. 1519 (possibly from as early as 1507 to as late as 1530), and the only Christine in the list of all the known Amesbury prioresses given in the Victoria County History of Wiltshire (Crittall and Pugh 1956, 242–59). The text was not actually written at Amesbury (24), and its dialect has some East Anglian features as well as others more characteristic of South West Middle English.

Author, Sources, and Nature of Text: The text was written by an anonymous religious, possibly a priest, chaplain, or clerk, but not necessarily attached to the nunnery (see 24n below). *The Amesbury Letter* is, as the prologue states, a basic instruction book for nuns in the precepts of the enclosed life, and a manual of "right living." It explicates the three major commitments of religious profession (obedience, poverty, chastity), with special emphasis on chastity—spiritual virginity rather than physical "intactness" being especially valued. Standard authorities on virginity and chastity (Augustine, Jerome, Aldhelm, Bernard) are invoked: cited from Seneca is the awful warning of the vestal virgin who thought longingly of marriage and was deemed to be no longer a virgin as a result; the Song of Songs and its *hortus conclusus* (enclosed garden) provides imagery of double enclosure, physical and mental. Readers are reminded of the professions they have signed with "your owne hond . . . or yf ye cannott ynsted therof ye make a crosse" (fol. 28r) before the bishop of Salisbury and their prioress, Cristina. Saint John's and Daniel's visions are mentioned among the signs and rewards of purity, but no reference is made to women's visions, even though both the tradition and contemporary examples of holy women were relatively well established in England by the early sixteenth century (Voaden 1996b). Like many of its predecessors (such as Aelred of Rievaulx's treatise on the enclosed life for his sister, or the continuingly influential thirteenth-century guide for recluses *Ancrene Wisse*) *The Amesbury Letter* presents itself as an informal and personal communication. It is not an official manual such as the Benedictine Rule (see excerpt 2.8). Intimacy as a topos in these letters assists writers as well as readers, enabling them to explore their own humility (e.g., 8–12) and desire to offer service to those who "take the payne" (54) to read them. Although the *Letter* is extant only in a modest and plain manuscript, Amesbury was a great nunnery of royal foundation and continuing royal patronage, a history perhaps alluded to in the late medieval tradition that Queen Guenevere died there (Benson 1986, 100–104, 111).

Audience and Circulation: The text is addressed to two nuns, Mary and Anne, and was probably intended for private reading. That the sole copy remained at Amesbury suggests that its readers were from within the convent. This does not preclude its having been copied and read elsewhere, although no other copies survive and the dissolution of religious houses under Henry VIII in the 1530s (perhaps within the lifetimes of the text's recipients) probably cut its useful life short.

Bibliography: On religious life at Amesbury, see Parrey 1994. For women's use of and access to religious literature, see Meale 1996a and Dutton 1995. For the manuscript, see Ker 1964; Watson 1987; Jolliffe 1974. On Amesbury's books, see Morgan 1988 and Bell 1995. On the spatial arrangements for women and clergy at Amesbury, see Gilchrist 1994, 94, 103.

Source: Oxford, Bodleian Library MS Bodley Addit.A.42, fols. 1r–4r; the unique manuscript of *The Amesbury Letter*, which contains only this text (incomplete at the end and with a quire missing in the middle), is extensively damaged by damp, making it illegible in parts. It is a small and unadorned book, perhaps a pocket book designed for private reading or reading aloud in small groups. In this transcription, scribal flourishes are treated as flourishes and not transcribed as final *e*. The prologue is edited here for the first time.

My dear susterys Mary and Anne, wyth all the other devoghth dyscyples of the scole of Cryste in your monastery of Amysbury, be grace and the blessyng of oure Lorde evyrlastyng. Amen.

    Remembryng and consyderyng your good and relygyouse desyres to have hadde
5 sum goostly conforte and sum maner off instructyon of me nowe att the tyme of
your professyon, and specyally apon the wordes of the same and the
substancyallis, wherby as ye thowghth yow myghth wyth Goddys helpe be the
more apte and abylle to the performans of the same professyon, how be hyt Y am
but a young dyscyple in that scole myselfe, and therfore hit were more meet and
10 convenyant for me to lerne to use perfectyon yn my owyne person then to take on
me to teche hit to other, and namely to suche as peradventure be more deply
groundyd theryn then I am. Yet notwythstondyng, for bycause oure master Cryste

seyth in the gospell, "*Omni petenti te tribue*," and many other lyke sentens we
have in scripture wych sowneth all that to every good and cherytabyll desyre
15 concernynge mannys goostly welth every man sholde gladly condescende and
graunte. Rememberyng also in the other parte the harde wordes
of Almyghty God by hys prophet Davyth; *Psalmorum lxxv*, "*Terribile et ei qui
aufert spiritum*," wyche is to sey, "Hit is a ferful thyng ony man to refuse or to
putt awey the good mocyons of the Hooly Goost."
20   Consyderyng youre both desyres to be cherytabyll and also, as I thynke, to
cumme of the instincte and movyng of the Hooly Goost, wych ys the wel of all
goodnes, thes both thynges compellyth me (unabyll thowghe Y be after the poore
dyscrecyon God hath lentt to me) to doo what I kan for the accomplyshment of
your desyres, and whereas I can nott cum to doo hit personally, to doo hyt wyth
25 my pen, wych may better abyde wyth you then thowghe Y had spoken it wyth my
mowghthe.
      And forasmyche as after the mynd off Seynt Gregory that oure master Cryste
cambe ynto thys worllde nott only to redeme man by the merytys of hys passyon
(wyche he myghth ryghth sone have done yff hit hade so pleasyd hym), but was
30 heer also conversant amongyst men contynually by the space of xxxiii yers and
half one, to the en[ten]t that hys good and virtuose lyfe and conversacion sholld be
a sufficyent, directe and [me]k example for us to order oure levyng therafter. And
nott only that, but also wyth his good and hollsum doctrine ful dilygently and full
effectually he movyd and exortyd every man wyth hys wordes to leve theyr
35 voluptuose lyvynge and to lyve perfyghtly and welle, wherby they myghth atteyne
to the lyfe everlastyng, as ful playnly apperyth in dyvers places of holy scripture.
      Therfore as to this poore exortacion wych I entend to make to you, I thynke Y
can nott take a more convenyent ground then is thys seynge of oure master Cryst
wych is w[rytyn] yn the goospelle of Seynte Luke, "*Habebis thesaurum in celcis;
40 veni sequere me*"; wych wordes may be englyshyd in this maner, "Thowe shalle
have a tresure or rewarde yn hevyn; cum and folow me." In wych wordes to oure
conforte fyrst he promysith a rewarde, and after he shewyth what we shall doo to
deserve it. But forasmyche as noo man can have ne convenyantly axe a rewarde
tyll he have deservyd it, or doon sumwhat for hyt, and for bycause thes bysynes of
45 laboure belonge to us, and the gevyng of reward to hym, I entende in thys symple
processe to wryt[yn bysyly] of such thing as belonge[s] us to doo, and soo to shew
after my symple abylyte, both by auctorytes and examples of scripture, sumwhat
of the maner of lyvynge that Criste callyth every relygiouse person to. And also
how that yn the wordes of your professyon ye pro[my]ce and bynde yourselfe to
50 the same, wych that ye may so observe and kepe that ye may atteyne to the
rewarde wych he hath promysyd to all that be his trew dyscypllis and folowars, hit
is necessary that ye dayly make devote prayers to God, whom Y now beseche to
assyst and to order me yn thys mater, that I may write suche thyngis as may be to
[your] pleasure and sumwhatt profytabyll to you wych shall take the payne to rede
55 hit. Amen.

1–3 **My dear susterys . . . Amen** The informal
epistolary opening announces that the text is a personal letter rather than an official manual (contrast
Fox's address to his readers, excerpt 2.8). For late
medieval epistolary styles, see Davis 1971–76.

1   **susterys** sisters, female members of a religious order, professed nuns (i.e., as opposed to
novices). This is a standard form of address for
women religious, whether related to the writer or
not. ∫ **Mary and Anne** These two nuns have not been

identified. The address here suggests intimacy, although this may be part of the topos of informality and spiritual friendship. ∫ **devoghth** devout

1–2 dyscyples of the scole of Cryste followers of Christ's teaching

2   monastery convent ∫ **be** let there be [to you]

4   consyderyng taking into account ∫ **good** proper, (morally) good

5   goostly spiritual ∫ **conforte** comfort: often given as the motive or desired end of a religious work. See the Glossary; compare, e.g., excerpt 1.14:2–3. ∫ **off** of ∫ **of** from

6   professyon making the vow for entering a religious order. The nuns at Amesbury lived under the Benedictine Rule (excerpt 2.8) and the statutes of Fontevrault, of which Amesbury had been refounded (by Henry II) as a daughter house during the twelfth century (several centuries into its long history). ∫ **apon** concerning ∫ **the wordes of the same** the words of your vow

6–7 the substancyallis its essentials

7   wherby as ye thowghth yow myghth with which [instruction] you thought that you might ∫ **yow** followed by erasure [. . .]

8   abylle suited, fitted ∫ **how be hyt** albeit, even though

9   but only ∫ **scole** that is, in the school of Christ (2), as a follower of Christ's teaching ∫ **meet** fitting

10 convenyant appropriate, proper ∫ **to use perfectyon yn** to apply the principles of perfection to

10–11 then to take on me than to take it upon myself

11 namely to suche as especially to those who ∫ **peradventure** perhaps (MS *peraventure,* with *d* inserted above the line with a caret)

11–12 be more deply groundyd theryn then I am have a greater knowledge of its basic principles than I have. In spite of their supervisory roles regarding the women they address (see previous two excerpts), it is not uncommon for male clergy spiritual directors of women to represent themselves as spiritually inferior to their female pastoral charges.

12 notwythstondyng in spite of this ∫ **for bycause** because

13 *Omni . . . tribue* give to all those who ask from you (Luke 6:30) ∫ **many other like sentens** many other similar wise sayings

14 wych sowneth all that all of which touch on the fact that ∫ **cherytabyll** charitable (i.e., characterized by charity [*caritas*], the love of God)

15 mannys goostly welth the spiritual well-being [of others]

16 in the other parte that is, of the Bible, namely, the Old Testament ∫ **harde** severe

17 by conveyed by

17–18 *Terribile . . . spiritum* it is dreadful for the man who cuts off the spirit (Ps. 75:12–13, AV 76). Authorship of the Psalms was often attributed in the Middle Ages, as since, to the Old Testament king David.

18 ferful terrible ∫ **ony man** for anyone

19 putt awey reject ∫ **mocyons** promptings

20 youre both desyres the desires of both of you

21 cumme of [your desires] come from ∫ **instincte** impulse ∫ **movyng** stirring ∫ **wel** source

22 thes both thynges both of these things ∫ **unabyll thowghe Y be** although I am unable ∫ **after** according to

23 dyscrecyon discernment ∫ **lentt** granted ∫ **accomplyshment** fulfillment

24 whereas I can nott cum to doo hit personally since I am not able to come and do it in person. The writer was therefore probably not attached to the nunnery.

24–25 to doo hyt wyth my pen to do it with my pen (i.e., to write you a letter)

25 wych may better abyde wyth you which may remain with you better. There may be a pun here on "abyde": the written text will remain in their possession but it will also be better adhered to. ∫ **then thowghe** than if

27 as added later above the line with a caret, perhaps by a corrector ∫ **mynd** opinion

27–32 the mynd off Seynt Gregory . . . to order oure levyng therafter The precise reference here in the works of Gregory the Great (Saint Gregory) (c. 540–604) has not been located. However, compare the following commentary by Gregory on 1 Pet. 2:21 ("Christ suffered for us, leaving us an example, that we might follow in his footsteps"): "And therefore to this end God appeared in flesh, that he might stir human life into action by admonishing, kindle it by offering examples, redeem it by dying, make amends for it by his resurrection . . . let the mediator of God and men appear, so that I may know him by his form of living and that I may truly be simple" (translated from *Moralium in Job* XXI.xxxi, *PL* 76:196). The Amesbury writer recommends to the nuns a particular form of *imitatio Christi* (imitation of Christ), not one concerned exclusively with the Passion of Christ but following the pattern of virtue and obedience the *Letter* elaborates.

29 ryghth sone immediately

29–30 was heer also conversant also lived and had his being here [on earth]

30 by for

30–31 and half one and a half; canceled in a later hand, with *mo*[?]*e* added above the line

31 en[ten]t purpose (MS *en[. . .]t* with heavy smudging)

32 **sufficyent** adequate ∫ **directe** unmediated ∫ [me]k meek (editorial conjecture: only the *k* is legible) ∫ **order oure levyng therafter** direct our own way of life according to it

33 **and full** MS *and [. . .] full,* with *and* followed by an erasure

34 **effectually** earnestly ∫ **movyd** stirred ∫ **leve** abandon

35 **voluptuose** sensual and indulgent

36 **as ful playnly apperyth** as is very clearly seen ∫ **dyvers** various

38 **convenyent** suitable ∫ **ground** foundation, that is, biblical text

39 **w[rytyn]** written (editorial conjecture: only the *w* is legible in the MS)

39–40 *Habebis . . . me* you shall have a treasure in the heavens; come and follow me (Luke 18:22) (the Vulgate has the singular form *in cælo* [in heaven]). The translation "tresure or rewarde" (41) for *thesaurum* is a typical instance of a Middle English doublet (the linking of two synonyms with *or*), common in many texts as well as in translations. See "to refuse or to putt awey" (18–19), and compare especially *The Mirror of Our Lady,* excerpt 3.12 passim.

40 **englyshyd** Englished, translated into English

42 **shall doo** must do

43 **forasmyche as** insofar as ∫ **axe** ask

44 **tyll he have** until he has ∫ **sumwhat** something ∫ **bysynes** duties, industry (MS *bysynes,* with *ses* added in the margin in a later hand to read *bysynesses*)

45 **to us** that is, to all of us mortal and sinful human beings

46 **processe** account ∫ **to** MS *to [. . .]* with erasure ∫ **wryt[yn bysyly]** write industriously(?). The phrase is badly smudged in the manuscript. ∫ **as belonge[s] us to doo** which it is our duty to do (MS *belonge[s]* with final *s* not clearly legible in the MS)

47 **auctorytes** *auctoritates,* written authorities

49 **how that** seeing that. This phrase introduces a long subordinate clause; the main clause begins "hit is" (51–52). ∫ **pro[my]ce** promise (editorial conjecture; only the *pro* and *ce* are legible in the MS)

49–50 **to the same** to that same thing: the form of living to which Christ calls the religious

53 **order** regulate

54 **[your]** editorial conjecture: not legible in MS ∫ **wych** who ∫ **the payne** the pains

54–55 **to rede hit** "Reading" here may embrace private reading and reading aloud. See Millett 1996; Riddy 1996b; Coleman 1996.

2.10 WILLIAM CAXTON, TRANSLATION OF CHRISTINE DE PIZAN'S *BOOK OF FAYTTES OF ARMES AND OF CHYVALRYE:* PROLOGUE

Date and Provenance: 1489; ?Westminster (near London) (or possibly Bruges).

Author, Sources, and Nature of Text: This is one of many prologues translated by William Caxton (c. 1422–91), printer and translator. The *Book* is a comprehensive manual of military strategy and chivalry, a translation of *Le livre des fais d'armes et de chevalerie* (1412) by Christine de Pizan (c. 1365–c. 1434), the French (originally Italian [58–59]) writer, some of whose works were known in English court circles in the fifteenth century (see *The Book of the City of Ladies,* excerpt 3.24). At least four copies of the French original are in British libraries. De Pizan's sources were various treatises on the art of war, both contemporary and of late antiquity, including Fulvius Vegetius Renatus's fourth-century work, *De re militari* (About

military matters, also known as the *Epitoma rei militaris,* The military institutions [of the Romans]). Vegetius was translated into various European vernaculars, including Anglo-Norman; there is a French version by Jean de Meun and numerous Middle English versions (see excerpt 2.12). Little is known about the circumstances in which de Pizan's text was written; it may have been intended for the dauphin Louis de Guyenne (Teague 1991, 28). Mindful of the English threat to France in the fifteenth century, de Pizan makes uncomplimentary references to England, some of them cut by Caxton (Teague 1991, 29). Caxton's translation, made at the request of the powerful monarch Henry VII, was possibly intended in part to legitimate Henry's position as a chivalric king and to be of use to him in England's wars with France (Teague 1991, 36–37).

Audience and Circulation: Caxton produced only one edition, but twenty copies are extant. Concerned to establish an English market for literature that was fashionable at the Burgundian court (Meale 1992, 294), Caxton had also translated (in 1484) Ramón Lull's *Book of the Order of Chivalry* (c. 1250), one of the most important late medieval chivalric manuals. The *Book of Fayttes of Armes* probably had an audience of knights, esquires, and gentlemen.

Bibliography: Caxton's text is edited by A.T.P. Byles (1937), the prologue by Barratt (1992, 158–62), to whose edition the version given here is indebted and who offers useful comment on de Pizan's "style clergial" and use of humility topoi; the French source is edited, with valuable critical discussion, from Paris, Bibliothèque Nationale MS 603, by Christine Moneera Laennec (1988). For critical studies of de Pizan's French text, see Willard 1970 and Teague 1991. On de Pizan's patrons, see Laidlaw 1982; Rutter 1987; Meale 1992. For a tradition of female militancy that may have influenced de Pizan, see Solterer 1991. The standard accounts of Caxton's life and works are Blake 1976 and 1996. (For further bibliography and discussion of de Pizan, see excerpt 3.24.)

Source: London, British Library IB.55131, Ai–Aii (*STC* 7269), one of three copies in the British Library: a folio book, printed by William Caxton in Westminster, January 14, 1489. This copy may have belonged to Sir John Lumley in the sixteenth century. Byles notes that in its use of signatures, even spacing, paragraph marks, and wood initials, this edition is "a fine example of [Caxton's] art in its maturity" (1937, xxx).

Here begynneth the Book of Fayttes of Armes and of Chyvalrye. And the first chapytre is the Prologue, in whiche Chrystyne of Pyse excuseth hirself to have dar enterpryse to speke of so hye matere as is conteyned in this sayd book.

5 ## Capitulum Primum

Bycause that hardynes is so moche necessarye to entrepryse hye thynges whiche without that shold never be enpryse[d], that same is covenable to me at this present werke to put it forth without other thyng, seen the lytylhed of my persone, whiche I knowe not digne ne worthy to treate of so hye matere,
10 ne durst not only thynke what blame hardynes causeth whan she is folyssh. I thenne, nothyng moeved by arrogaunce in folyssh presumpcion but admonested of veray affeccion and good desyre of noblemen in th'offyce of armes, am exorted after myne other escriptures passed (lyke as he that hath toforn beten doun many strong edyfices is more hardy to charge hymself
15 defye or to bete doun a castell or forteresse whan he feleth hymself garnysshed of covenable stuffe therto necessarye) thenne to entrepryse to speke in this present book of the right honorable offyce of armes and of chyvalrye, as wel in thynges whiche th[e]rto ben convenyent, as in droytes whyche therto be appertenaunt, lyke as the lawes and dyverse auctours
20 declaren it.

To the purpoos, I have assembled the maters and gadred in dyverse bokes for to produce myne entencion in this present volume. But as it apperteyneth this matere to be more executed by fayt of dylygence and witte

than by subtyltees of wordes polisshed, and also considered that they that
25 been excersyng and experte in th'arte of chyvalrye be not comunely clerkys
ne instructe in science of langage, I entende not to treate but to the most
playn and entendible langage that I shal mowe, to that ende that the
doctryne gyven by many auctors, whiche by the helpe of God I purpose to
declare in this present boke, may be to alle men clere and entendible. And
30 bycause that this is thyng not accustomed and out of usage to wymen
(whiche comynly do not entremete but to spynne on the distaf and ocupie
theim in thynges of houshold) I supplye humbly to the said right hie offyce
and noble state of chyvalrye that in contemplacion of theyr lady Mynerve,
born of the contre of Grece, whome the auncyents for hir grete connyng
35 reputeden a goddesse (the whiche fonde, lyke as olde wrytyngis sayen and as
I have other tymes sayd, and also the poete Bo[cace] recyteth in his Boke of
Clere and Noble Wimmen, and semblably recyten many other, the arte and
manere to make harnoys of yron and steel), whiche wyl not have ne take it
for none evyl yf I, a woman, charge myself to treate of so lyke a matere but
40 wyl ensewe th'enseignement and techyng of Seneke, whiche saith, 'Retche
the not what they saye, soo that the wordes be good.' And therfore and to
purpos in manere poetyke it plaiseth me t'adresse suche a prayer to the
foresayd lady:

"O Mynerve, goddesse of armes and of chyvalrye, whiche by vertue of hye
45 entendement above alle other wymen fondest and institutest (emonge th'other
noble artes and sciences whiche of the toke their begynnyng) th'usage to forge of
yron and steel armours and harnois propice and covenable to covure and targe the
body of man agaynst the strokes of dartes, noyous shotte and speres in bataylle;
fayttes of armes, helmes, sheldes, targes and other harnoys defensable fro the first
50 comen, institutest and gavest manere and ordre to arenge batailles and t'assaille
and fight in manere. Adoured Lady and hie Goddesse, be thou not displeased that
I, symple and lytyl woman, lyke as nothyng unto the gretenes of thy renommee in
cunnyng, dare presently compryse to speke of so magnyfike an offyce as is th'office
of armes, of whiche fyrst, in the said renomed contree of Grece, thou gavest
55 th'usage. And insomoche it may plaise the to be to me favorable, that I may be
somwhat consonaunt in the nacyon where thou was born, whiche as thenne was
named the Grete Grece, the contree beyonde the Alpes or montaygnes, whiche now
is sayd Puylle and Calabre in Ytalye where thou were born, and I am, as thou
were, a woman Ytalien."

---

1 **Fayttes** deeds
2–3 **Chrystyne of Pyse** Christine de Pizan
(Pezano or Pizano, the town in northern Italy from
which de Pizan's father originally came)
3 **excuseth** justifies ∫ **to have dar enterpryse** for
having dared to undertake ∫ **hye** elevated
4 **matere** subject matter
5 **Capitulum Primum** chapter one
6–10 **Bycause that . . . whan she is folyssh** The
sentence is awkward because the translation omits
several lines of French after "thynke." Translate:
"Because courage is so necessary in order to under-

take important projects that without it would never
be taken on, it befits me in this present work to display that same quality of courage with no other
justification, since the insignificance of my person,
which I know to be neither important nor worthy
to deal with such an elevated subject matter, dared
only think about what censure courage brings when
she is foolish." The justification of the authorial
project in terms of sexual difference contains an
ironic double reference: boldness is needed, firstly,
following the convention of the modesty topos, to
overcome the inability to deal adequately with

noble subject matter but, secondarily (and ironically), to outbrave the censure that women traditionally incur for bold behavior.

7   **enpryse[d]** undertaken (text has *enpryses*)

10–20 **I thenne ... declaren it** I then, not at all motivated by the arrogance of foolish presumption but urged by the true affection and worthy petition of noble warriors, am thus urged on by my previous writings—just as a man who has previously destroyed many strong buildings is bolder to undertake to declare war on or destroy a castle or fortress when he feels he is equipped with the appropriate materials necessary for that—to undertake to speak in the present book of the very honorable office of arms and chivalry, as well as of the [other] matters that are relevant to it, such as the legal rights that apply to it, just as law and various authorities expound it

18 **th[e]rto** text has *thrto*

19 **auctours** authorities

21 **To the purpoos** on that subject ∫ **gadred in** collected from

22 **for to** in order to ∫ **produce** bring about

22–23 **it apperteyneth** it suits

23 **by fayt** through ∫ **dyligence** care ∫ **witte** intelligence

24 **considered** given

24–25 **they that been** those who are

25 **excersyng** practiced ∫ **be not comunely** are not generally ∫ **clerkys** learned men

26 **instructe** instructed ∫ **science of langage** the study of language, rhetoric (one of the seven liberal sciences or arts) ∫ **I entende not to treate but to** I intend to use only

27 **entendible** intelligible ∫ **that I shal mowe** that I am able [to use] ∫ **to that ende** with the purpose

28 **doctryne** instruction

29 **declare** expound

30 **thyng** matter ∫ **out of usage to wymen** unusual among women

31 **entremete** engage in any activity

31–32 **ocupie theim** busy themselves

32 **in** with ∫ **supplye** supplicate, beg ∫ **said right hie** previously mentioned very lofty ∫ **offyce** service (of arms)

33 **state** rank ∫ **Mynerve** Minerva

34 **connyng** wisdom

35 **reputeden** considered ∫ **the whiche** who (i.e., Minerva) ∫ **fonde** invented ∫ **lyke as** as

36 **other tymes** at other times ∫ **Bo[cace]** Boccaccio. Caxton prints "Boece" [Boethius] but the manuscripts of de Pizan's French text have "Bocace," and the reference is certainly to Boccaccio (1313–75). His *De claris mulieribus*

(Concerning famous women, i.e., the "Boke of Clere and Noble Wimmen" [36–37]) was one of de Pizan's sources for her *Othéa* and her *Book of the City of Ladies*. See excerpt 3.24. ∫ **recyteth** relates

37 **Clere** famous ∫ **semblably** in a similar maner ∫ **recyten many other** many others relate

38 **harnoys** armor (and military equipment in general)

38–39 **whiche wyl not have ne take it for none evyl** which [i.e., the lofty service of arms] will not receive or consider it any harm

39 **charge myself** take it upon myself ∫ **so lyke** such

40 **ensewe** follow ∫ **Seneke** Seneca (c. 3 B.C.–c. A.D. 65): Roman philosopher, dramatist, and statesman. Barratt (1992, 160) suggests that the quotation is possibly from the *Ad serenum de tranquillitate animi* XI.8, which de Pizan also used in *The Body of Policy:* "I shall never be ashamed to quote a bad author if what he says is good."

40–41 **Retche the not ... wordes be good** do not heed what people say as long as your words are good (that is, as long as you know that the words themselves have probity)

41–42 **to purpos** to that end

43 **foresayd** previously mentioned

44–51 **O Mynerve ... fight in manere** This long sentence, in which the main verbs appear very late, after a series of dense subordinate clauses, is difficult to punctuate in order to make good sense. The best sense seems to be "O Minerva, goddess of arms and of chivalry, who, endowed beyond all other women with an elevated purpose, invented and established (among the other noble arts and sciences that took their origins from you) the practice of forging from iron and steel armor and military equipment advantageous and suitable to cover and shield the human body from the piercing of arrows, harmful throwing of weapons and spears in battle: deeds of arms, helmets, shields, bucklers, and other protective equipment having originated first with you, you instituted and established the use and rules to draw up battles and to attack and fight in the proper way."

52 **lyke as nothyng unto** as nothing compared with ∫ **renommee** fame

53 **compryse** conceive ∫ **offyce** service

54 **renomed** renowned

56 **consonaunt in** in harmony with ∫ **as thenne** at that time

57 **the Grete Grece** Grece Magna Græcia (Sicily and the cities of southern Italy)

58 **sayd** called ∫ **Puylle** Apulia ∫ **Calabre** Calabria

59 **a woman Ytalien** an Italian woman

2.11 JOHN GOWER, *CONFESSIO AMANTIS:* PROLOGUE, TWO VERSIONS (EXTRACTS)

Date and Provenance: Early Version: c. 1390; Later Version c. 1393 or later (internally dated as the sixteenth year of Richard II's reign, that is, 1392: see 32 and note). London (Southwark).

    Author, Sources, and Nature of Text: John Gower (1330–1408), Chaucer's "moral Gower" (*Troilus and Criseyde* V.1856), enjoyed a reputation as a writer second only to Chaucer and Lydgate for more than a century after his death. He is known to have been closely acquainted with Chaucer (Chaucer gave him power of attorney in 1378). Born into a well-off family with aristocratic connections, he was employed in Kent and Suffolk, possibly in a legal or civil capacity, until 1377, when he moved to the Priory of St. Mary Overys, near the Tabard Inn in Southwark, London. Having formed close connections with Richard II, to whom the *Confessio Amantis* is dedicated in the first instance (see excerpt b), he later rejected Richard, transferring his allegiance to Henry of Lancaster (later Henry IV), to whom he dedicated the final recension of his poem (excerpt a). For the Later Version, Gower rewrote part of the prologue (see 32n) and also a passage of 144 lines at the end of the poem, in which he had generously praised Richard.

    Gower is one of the few late medieval authors whom we know to have written in all three major languages of England. His *Vox clamantis* (c. 1386) is in Latin, and his *Mirour de l'omme* (1378) in French. The choice of English for the *Confessio Amantis* is linked to the presentation of the poem as powerfully patriotic: "for that fewe men endite / In oure Englissh, I thenke make / A bok for Engelondes sake" (29–31). The *Confessio* is a series of dialogues between Amans (the lover) and Genius (a priest of Venus) on the subject of love, structured, rather in the manner of a medieval penitential manual, according to the schema of the seven deadly sins. Most of the text consists of exempla, stories illustrating Genius's arguments, and in this sense the text can also be seen as a story collection parallel-

ing Chaucer's *Canterbury Tales* and *Legend of Good Women.* Gower's poem is as much concerned with ethical and political questions as *amor* (book VII, for example, contains a minitreatise in the "mirror for princes" genre), situating love in a sapiential context that appears to be in some sense related to the tradition of affective piety found in works such as *Piers Plowman* (compare Usk's *Testament of Love,* excerpt 1.4).

    The prologue addresses a multiplicity of themes and audiences. Its opening evocation, in Latin verse, of the Trojan diaspora provides one frame for notions of Englishness (and a "father" of the English tongue in the shape of the Anglo-Saxon invader, Hengest) for the benefit of rulers and inhabitants of "New Troy" (London, see 125). The stylistic choice of "the middel weie" (24) and "oure Englissh" (30) invokes wider audiences— courtly, lay, civic, and gentry—than the royal dedicatee, audiences polarized not linguistically but according to their desire for pleasure or instruction ("of lust . . . of lore" [26]). At the same time as it renders themes of the aging world out of Anglo-Norman and Latin into English (35–38, 59–67), the poem also offers a scholastic apparatus of Latin prose summaries (19n, 117n) and densely allusive riddling Latin verses at the beginning of each book and chapter. It invokes the Latin-literate (or those who could command the services of clerks) as audiences within the polity of "oure Englissh" as well.

    The two versions of the prologue (they diverge at 32) are different in their effects, for all their overlap. The earlier prologue makes serious play on, among other things, the topos of feudal service as desire and as compulsion (foreshadowing the narrator's self-presentation as a lover in the rest of the poem). This prologue's vividly conversational tone nonetheless stages a lively intimacy with its various Ricardian audiences, extending to the narrator's comic parody of Brutus (where Brutus sails an ocean, the narrator finds himself rowing, by chance, on the Thames,

123–30), and his own translation into his king's barge (compare excerpt 2.12). In the revised version for Henry IV, a more formal and bookish address to Lancastrian seriousness prevails, and temporal instability and the translation of powers and wisdom are more strongly thematized.

Audience and Circulation: There are forty extant manuscripts, suggesting a wide circulation. Many of these include Latin prose summaries of the English text, which, since they appear even in early manuscripts, point to Gower's having personally supervised the work (Minnis 1988, 275). Their presence may indicate that Gower intended the poem to circulate among an educated and literate (in Latin) audience, but this apparatus of *auctoritas* was probably welcomed and expected by a wider range of medieval readers in a major ethical work (Minnis 1988, 177–90). Printed by Caxton in 1483, the poem also appeared in sixteenth-century editions and was acclaimed as an important English work throughout the early modern period: Gower appears as the narrator in Shakespeare's *Pericles* (c. 1610), which is based on a story in the *Confessio*.

Bibliography: The *Confessio,* including both versions of the prologue, is edited by G. C. Macaulay (1900–1901); Russell Peck (1980) edits selections; Siân Echard and Claire Fanger (1991) translate the Latin verses; and Echard (1998) discusses Gower's treatment of Latin authorities in the *Confessio*. Echard and Robert F. Yeager are currently preparing a new edition. Minnis (1988, 177–90) discusses the prologue in terms of its debts to Latin scholasticism. Minnis (1983) and Peter Nicholson (1991) edit essays on the *Confessio*: Nicholson's are reprints, representing the scope of the critical field from Macaulay to the present. Yeager (1990) offers a biographical reading of the poem, Fisher (1964) a critical biography of

Gower. On the topic of wisdom in Gower's works, see Minnis 1980 and Simpson 1995. On the poem's exempla, see Scanlon 1994, 245–97. For an account of Richard II's spectral haunting of the Lancastrian regime, see Strohm 1996b. On "Lancastrian Gower," see Strohm 1992 and Grady 1995. On Gower as political writer, see Coleman 1981, 126–56. For a sociohistorical reading of the *Confessio*, see Strohm 1979. On the promotion of literature at Richard's court, see Bennett 1992.

Source: (a) Oxford, Bodleian Library MS Fairfax 3, fols. 2r–2v (Later Version): a careful, though not elaborate, late-fourteenth-century manuscript that is a large-format anthology of three works by Gower in three languages: *Confessio Amantis,* the *Traitié,* and the *Carmen de mulipliciorum pestilencia*. It contains some illuminated initials and two miniatures. As Macaulay points out, the first leaf of the manuscript, containing the dedication to Henry of Lancaster, is a replacement (in a scribal hand different from the rest) of a leaf that presumably contained the Early Version of the prologue, with the dedication to Richard II. In the late sixteenth century, the manuscript was owned by Lady Isabel Fairfax (her signature appears on fol. 2r, top col. b).

(b) Oxford, Bodleian Library MS Bodley 294, fols. 1r–1v (Early Version): an early-fifteenth-century Gower anthology with the same contents as the Fairfax manuscript and the same two miniatures. A highly professionally planned and carefully executed text, it was owned by a certain Edwarde Fletewoode in the sixteenth century.

There are several "intermediate" stages of the *Confessio,* although only two major forms of the prologue. Only the passage that Gower changed has been represented in both forms here. Translations of the Latin verses are from Echard and Fanger 1991.

a. Later Version

Torpor, ebes sensus, scola parva labor minimusque
Causant quo minimus ipse minora canam:
Qua tamen Engisti lingua canit Insula Bruti

Anglica Carmente metra iuvante loquar.
5 Ossibus ergo carens que conterit ossa loquelis
Absit, et interpres stet procul oro malus.

[Dull wit, slight schooling, labor less,
Make slight the themes I, least of poets, sing.
Let me, in Hengist's tongue, in Brut's isle sung,
With Carmen's help, tell forth my English verse.
Far hence the boneless one whose speech grinds bones,
Far hence be he who reads my verses ill.]

Incipit Prologus

here begins the prologue

Off hem that writen ous tofore
 Off of; **hem** those; **ous tofore** before us
The bokes duelle, and we therfore
 duelle remain
10 Ben tawht of that was write tho:
 are instructed by what was written then
Forthi good is that we also
 Forthi therefore; **good is** it is good
In oure tyme among ous hiere
 hiere here
Do wryte of newe som matiere,
 Do wryte [that we] write; **of newe** in a new way
Essampled of these olde wyse
 Essampled of modeled on; **wyse** wise (books or men)
15 So that it myhte in such a wyse,
 wyse manner
Whan we ben dede and elleswhere,
Beleve to the worldes eere
 Beleve to survive for; **eere** ear
In tyme comende after this.
 comende coming
Bot for men sein, and soth it is,
 for men sein because people say; **soth** true
20 That who that al of wisdom write
 who that whoever; **al** entirely
It dulleth ofte a mannes wit
To him that schal it aldai rede,
 To him for the person; **schal** must; **aldai** all day
For thilke cause, if that ye rede,
 thilke the same; **if that ye rede** if you advise this
I wolde go the middel weie
 the middel weie the middle path (of style)
25 And wryte a bok betwen the tweie,
 tweie two (extremes)
Somwhat of lust, somwhat of lore,
 Somwhat partly; **lust** pleasure; **lore** learning
That of the lasse or of the more
 That so that; **lasse** lesser (i.e., pleasure)
Som man mai lyke of that I wryte:
 lyke of take pleasure in
And for that fewe men endite
 for that because; **endite** write
30 In oure Englissh, I thenke make
A bok for Engelondes sake,
The yer sextenthe of kyng Richard.
 the sixteenth year of King Richard's reign
What schal befalle hierafterward
 hierafterward in the future
God wot, for now upon this tyde
 wot knows; **tyde** moment
35 Men se the world on every syde
 se see
In sondry wyse so diversed,
 sondry wyse various ways; **diversed** changed
That it welnyh stant al reversed,
 that it is nearly completely turned upside down
As for to speke of tyme ago.
 compared to how it used to be
The cause whi it changeth so
40 It needeth nought to specifie,
 nought not
The thing so open is at ye
 so open is at ye is so plain to see
That every man it mai beholde:

And natheles be daies olde,   **natheles** nevertheless; **be** in
Whan that the bokes weren levere,   **levere** more precious
45 Wrytinge was beloved evere
Of hem that weren vertuous;   **Of** by
For hier in erthe amonges ous,
If noman write hou that it stode,   **noman** nobody; **hou that it stode** how things were
The pris of hem that weren goode   **pris** worth
50 Scholde, as who seith, a gret partie   **as who seith** so to speak; **a gret partie** in large part
Be lost: so for to magnifie   **for to** in order to; **magnifie** spread the fame of
The worthi princes that tho were,   **tho** then (in earlier times)
The bokes schewen hiere and there,   **schewen** set forth
Wherof the world ensampled is;   **Wherof** through which; **ensampled** instructed
55 And tho that deden thanne amis   **deden** did; **amis** wrong
Thurgh tirannie and crualte,
Right as thei stoden in degre,   **Right** according to; **in degre** in social status
So was the wrytinge of here werk.   **here** their
Thus I, which am a burel clerk,   **burel clerk** clerk of simple learning
60 Purpose for to wryte a bok   **Purpose** intend
After the world that whilom tok   **After** about; **whilom tok** once existed
Long tyme in olde daies passed:
Bot for men sein it is now lassed,   And because people see it is now degenerated
In worse plit than it was tho,
65 I thenke for to touche also   **thenke** intend; **touche** deal with
The world which neweth every dai,   **neweth** renews itself
So as I can, so as I mai.   so far as is in my power, so I will do it
Thogh I seknesse have upon honde   **upon honde** i.e., to deal with
And longe have had, yit woll [I] fonde   **fonde** try
70 To wryte and do my bisinesse,   **do my bisinesse** exert myself
That in som part, so as I gesse,
The wyse man mai ben avised.   **avised** counseled
For this prologe is so assised   **so assised** composed in such a way
That it to wisdom al belongeth:
75 What wysman that it underfongeth,   **What** whichever; **underfongeth** receives
He schal drawe into remembrance   he shall take into his memory
The fortune of this worldes chance,   **fortune** vicissitudes
The which noman in his persone   **in his persone** in himself
Mai knowe, bot the God al one.   **al one** alone
80 Whan the prologe is so despended,   **so despended** has thus come to an end
This bok schal afterward ben ended   **ben ended** continue to the end
Of love, which doth many a wonder
And many a wys man hath put under.   **put under** subdued
And in this wyse I thenke trete   **wyse** way; **trete** direct my discourse
85 Towardes hem that now be grete,   **grete** powerful
Betwen the vertu and the vice
Which longeth unto this [office].   **longeth unto** are the hallmark of
Bot for my wittes ben to smale   **ben to** are too
To tellen every man his tale,
90 This bok, upon amendement   **upon amendement** to be amended

To stonde at his commandement,   *according to his commandment*
With whom myn herte is of accord,   **of accord** *in agreement*
I sende unto myn oghne lord,   **oghne** *own*
Which of Lancastre is Henri named:
95 The hyhe God him hath proclamed
Ful of knyhthode and alle grace.   **knyhthode** *chivalry*
So woll I now this werk embrace   **embrace** *undertake*
With hol trust and with hol believe;   **hol** *entire*
God grante I mot it wel achieve.   **mot** *may*

100 ii. Tempus preteritum presens fortuna beatum
Linquit, et antiquas vertit in orbe vias.
Progenuit veterem concors dileccio pacem
Dum facies hominis nuncia mentis erat:
Legibus unicolor tunc temporis aura refulsit,
105 Iusticie plane tuncque fuere vie.
Nunc que latens odium vultum depingit amoris,
Pace que sub ficta tempus ad arma tegit;
Instar et ex variis mutabile Cameliontis
Lex gerit, et regnis sunt nova iura novis:
110 Climata que fuerant solidissima sic que per orbem
Solvuntur, nec eo centra quietis habent.

[Now fortune leaves the blessed time of yore,
And turns the antique customs on her wheel.
Harmonious love begat the ancient peace,
When yet man's face was herald of his mind:
The air of that age shone, one-hued, with laws;
The paths of justice then were plain and smooth.
Now hidden hatred paints a loving face,
The law, chameleon-like, transforms and shifts:
And hides a time of war beneath feigned peace.
In novel realms, new laws; and regions that
Were strong, through Fortune's wheel are rendered weak,
Nor there a hub of quiet do they find.]

b. Early Version

. . . A book for king Richardes sake,
To whom bilongeth my ligeance   **ligeance** *allegiance*
With al myn hertes obeissance   **obeissance** *humble respect*
115 In al that ever a liege man   **liege man** *subject*
Unto his king may doon or can: **may doon or can** *is allowed or able to do*
So ferforth I me recomaunde   **So ferforth** *to that extent*
To him which al me may comaunde,   **which** *who;* **al** *entirely*
Prayend unto the hihe regne   **Prayend** *praying;* **hihe regne** *high throne (of God)*

120 Which causeth every king to regne,
That his corone longe stonde,   longe stonde may endure for a long time
I thenke and have it understonde.   thenke consider
As it bifel upon a tyde,   As it bifel as it happened
As thing which scholde tho bityde—   as something that was meant to happen when it did
125 Under the toun of newe Troye,
Which took of Brut his ferste joye,   of from
In Temse whan it was flowende   In Temse on the Thames
As I by bote cam rowende,   by bote in a boat
So as Fortune hir tyme sette,   So as just as; hir tyme sette established her influence
130 My liege lord par chaunce I mette;   par chaunce by chance
And so bifel, as I cam neigh,   neigh near
Out of my bot, whan he me seigh,   seigh saw
He bad me come into his barge.   bad ordered
And whan I was with him at large,   at large in the open
135 Amonges othre thinges seyde   as part of a range of things we spoke about
He hath this charge upon me leyde,   charge duty
And bad me doo my busynesse
That to his hihe worthinesse
Som newe thing I scholde booke,   booke put in a book
140 That he himself it mighte looke   looke peruse
After the forme of my writynge.   After according to; forme style
And thus upon his comaundyng
Myn hert is wel the more glad   wel the more glad much gladder
To write so as he me bad;
145 And eek my fere is wel the lasse   eek also
That non envye schal compasse   compasse decide
Without a resonable wite   wite cause
To feyne and blame that I write.   feyne lie about; blame slander
A gentil herte his tunge stilleth,   someone of noble heart silences his tongue
150 That it malice noon distilleth,   so that he does not utter any words of slander
But preyseth that is to be preised;   that what
But he that hath his word unpeysed   unpeysed unweighed
And handeleth [onwrong every] thing,   handeleth [onwrong] misrepresents
I pray unto the heven king
155 Fro suche tunges he me schilde.   Fro from; he me schilde may he shield me
And natheles this world is wilde   wilde desolate
Of such jangling, and what bifalle,   jangling evil talk
My kinges heste schal nought falle,   heste command
That I, in hope to deserve   in hope to deserve hoping to deserve
160 His thonk, ne schal his wil observe;   thonk gratitude; ne schal shall not [fail]
And elles were I nought excused,   elles otherwise
For that thing may nought be refused
[Which] that a kyng himselve byt.   byt commands
Forthy the symplesce of my wit   symplesce simplicity
165 I thenke, if that it [myhte] avayle,   avayle be of use
In his service to travaile: travaile labor
Though I seknesse have upon honde,

And long have had, yit wol I fonde,   fonde try
So as I made my byheste,   byheste promise
170 To make a book after his heste,
And write in such a maner wise,
Which may be wisdom to the wise
And pley to hem that lust to pleye.   pley delight; **that lust** whom it please
But in proverbe I have herd seye   **in proverbe** in a proverb
175 That who that wel his werk bygynneth   **who that** whoever
The rather a good ende he wynneth;   **rather** sooner; **wynneth** obtains
And thus the prologe of my book
After the world that whilom took,   **After** concerning; **took** existed
And eek somdel after the newe,   **somdel** somewhat
180 I wol bygynne for to newe.   **for to newe** to compose

3 **Engisti lingua** Hengist's tongue. Hengist was a fifth-century Anglo-Saxon leader who agreed to cease raiding and to settle in England, where he became the founder of the Kentish royal line (Bede, *Historia ecclesiastica* 1:15). In Geoffrey of Monmouth's twelfth-century legendary history, he becomes a figure of treachery, instigating the "night of the long knives" (*Historia regum Britanniae* 4:16). As with the *Gawain* poet's treatment of Aeneas in the opening scene of *Sir Gawain and the Green Knight,* it is unclear how ambivalent a figure of English's ancestry Hengest is here. ∫ **Insula Bruti** Brutus's Island. Brutus, according to Geoffrey of Monmouth and others, was the anonymous founder of Britain after the end of the Trojan War. His name accordingly invokes a tradition of noble legendary genealogy.

4 **Carmente** Carmentis, legendary Arcadian prophetess and inventor of the Latin alphabet

5 **Ossibus . . . loquelis** a notable crux, providing several difficulties of interpretation. "Ossibus . . . carens" (lacking bones) is a periphrasis for "tongue": see Echard and Fanger (1991, 2 n. 2), who suggest Ecclus. 28:21 as a possible source. The force of the phrase "que conterit ossa" (that grinds down bones) is perhaps an ironic acknowledgment of the power of a reader's—or interpreter's—words to wrest meaning away from authorial intention.

6 **oro** [my] gold: a reference to the worth of Gower's work, an encrypted allusion to the figure of buried riches

8–10 **Off hem . . . write tho** The word order is inverted in this concise opening, but is perfectly good Middle English: "The books of those who wrote before us are still in existence ["duelle"], and we are therefore instructed by what was written then [in the past]."

8–18 **Off hem . . . after this** The allusion is to the topos of the authority (*auctoritas*) of old books and

their role in preserving the wisdom of the past. See the prologue to Chaucer's *Legend of Good Women* G.17–28 and Lydgate's *Troy Book* (excerpt 1.7: 99–131). Gower's reworking of the topos does not so much assert that present writers continue that tradition, humbly following past authority, as make the bold claim that they can contribute to it by injecting new material. Here, the present is not simply that time which is informed by the past but that which will become the future past and which will thus stand in the same relation to tomorrow's present as ancient wisdom does to contemporary authors.

14–15 **wyse . . . wyse** an example of *rime riche,* a particularly prized form of medieval rhyming on homonyms: in effect, a kind of pun (Zumthor 1979). The rhyme words are morphologically identical (or nearly identical) but semantically distinct. See Chaucer's general prologue to *The Canterbury Tales* I (A) 17–18: "The hooly blisful martir for to seke, / That hem hath holpen whan that they were seeke," and 119–20 below (Early Version). The use of *rime riche* often signals an elevated style.

19 **Bot for men sein** By this line in the margin of Fairfax 3 appears the following Latin prose commentary: "Hic in principio declarat qualiter in anno Regis Ricardi secundi sexto decimo Iohannes Gower presentem libellum composuit et finaliter compleuit, quem strenuissimo domino suo domino Henrico de Lancastria tunc Derbeie Comiti cum omni reuerencia specialiter destinauit" (In the beginning this declares how, in the sixteenth year of King Richard II, John Gower composed and eventually completed the present little book, which is especially directed with all reverence to his most valiant lord, Lord Henry of Lancaster, then count of Derby).

19–21 **Bot . . . mannes wit** The narrator's fear of dulling the reader's wit through offering too much indigestible wisdom is a version of the traditional humility topos. Compare Chaucer's *Complaint of Venus* (excerpt 1.3: 5–7), where it is "elde" (old age) that dulls the poet's wit. See also Ashby, *Active Policy of a Prince* (excerpt 1.9: 91).

24 **the middel weie** Medieval style is traditionally divided into three: high, middle, and low. For the distinctions, see John of Garland (c. 1195–c. 1272), the *Parisiana poetria* (c. 1233), quoted in Miller 1977, 71: "There are . . . three styles, corresponding to the three estates of men. The low style suits the pastoral life; the middle style, farmers; the high style, eminent personages." Implied in Gower's reference to style may be an allusion to the "estates" topos, with the choice of the middle way a gesture toward harmonizing social differences, which may link to the explicit use of the vernacular as a vehicle for addressing an inclusive English audience.

26 **Somwhat of lust, somwhat of lore** The poem's potential audience is defined not in terms of an opposition between "lered" and "lewed" (as in *Northern Homily Cycle*, excerpt 2.1) but between those who delight in wisdom and those who want something more entertaining (compare "sentence" and "solaas" in *The Canterbury Tales* I [A] 798). The poet's aim to strike a balance between didacticism and entertainment is reminiscent of Horace's famous dictum about pleasure leading to instruction (*Ars poetica* 333–44; see excerpt 1.2: 9n). For the theme of readerly choice, see excerpts 3.13–16.

29–31 **And . . . sake** It is unclear what the narrator means by his claim that he is writing for England's sake. This may be a deferential gesture to the poem's dedicatee, Henry of Lancaster (93–94), or a self-conscious attempt to articulate the importance of the vernacular. Nevertheless, the statement presents the work's status as that of an "English classic" (Minnis 1988, 177).

32 From this line onward, the earlier and later versions of the prologue diverge. ∫ **kyng Richard** Richard II (1367–1400): his reign was dominated by struggles between the king and the barons, who wanted to curb his power. After confiscating the Lancastrian estates after John of Gaunt's death, he was deposed in 1399 by Henry Bolingbroke of the house of Lancaster, who succeeded him as Henry IV and to whom Gower shifted his allegiance (93–94). The sixteenth year of Richard's s reign was 1392; it is possible that this represents a "backdating" of the revised version of the poem, meant to suggest that Gower publicly shifted his allegiance earlier than he in fact did: the replacement of Early Version prologues by Later Version ones in manuscripts such as Fairfax 3 (see headnote, "Source") suggests a desire on his part to imply that the *Confessio* had always

been intended for Henry. Gower's later public attitude toward Richard is exemplified in his *Cronica tripertita* (c. 1400), where he speaks of "hateful Richard" (Coleman 1981, 133; for further discussion, see Strohm 1996b).

33–42 **What schal . . . beholde** These themes—of the world's decline and the political evils of Richard's reign—had already been pursued in detail by Gower in the first book of his Latin poem *Vox clamantis,* a response to the English rebellion of 1381.

43–54 **And natheles . . . ensampled is** Compare this defense of the value of "wrytinge" with Barbour's *Bruce* (excerpt 1.2: 15–24).

55–58 **And tho . . . werk** and those who at that time did wrong through their tyranny and cruelty, according to their social status, so the narrative of their deeds represented them

59 **a burel clerk** "Burel" is a kind of coarse cloth, so this phrase is an oxymoron. Compare Chaucer's *Franklin's Prologue* V (F) 716: "by cause I am a burel man." Just as the Franklin's humble self-presentation is belied by his highly rhetorical style, so the simplicity of Gower's narrator is here belied by the deployment of elaborate Latin commentaries and verses. Protestations of lack of rhetorical skill become common in fifteenth-century prologues. See Walton's translation of Boethius (excerpt 1.5: 1–2) and *Speculum Devotorum* (excerpt 1.12: 39–40).

68–69 **Thogh . . . fonde** Although Gower was in ill health at the time of writing the poem, the narrator's illness functions as a fictional representation of his troubled psychological state, presenting on a micro level the prologue's macro concerns with the world's degeneration. It also anticipates the poem's conclusion, in which the narrator rejects *amor* because of old age. Compare the use of the topos of psychological disturbance in the opening lines of Chaucer, *Book of the Duchess* 1–15, and Hoccleve's *Complaint* (excerpt 1.6); and for the topos of old age, see also Chaucer, *Boece* 1, m.1. Contrast the use of the topos of authorial illness in Julian of Norwich, where it functions as a desired and necessary pretext for writing (excerpt 1.13: 6).

74 **it to wisdom al belongeth** every part of it concerns wisdom

80–83 **Whan . . . under** The prologue, which has insisted on the topic of wisdom, nevertheless prefaces a treatise on the apparently frivolous subject of love. The link is elegantly achieved through the topos of love defeating many a wise man.

84–87 **And in . . . [office]** MS *officie.* Following Macaulay 1900–1901, these difficult lines might be interpreted thus: "And in this manner I intend to direct my discourse to those who are powerful, steering a middle line between the virtues and the vices that are the hallmark of their office [taking into account the fact that those in power will necessarily exhibit virtues and vices]." Peck (1980, 495 n. 4) suggests that "in this wyse" (84) may mean "in the mode of courtly romance."

94 Which of Lancastre is Henri named who is called Henry of Lancaster [later Henry IV]

100–111 *Tempus . . . quietis habent* As Echard and Fanger (1991, 4) point out, the metaphor of Fortune's wheel is only implicit in the Latin's references to "turning in a circle" (*vertit in orbe* [101]) "throughout the world" (*per orbem* [110]). The verse alludes to many topoi of the world's degeneration after the golden age: for an explication of some of its wordplay, which may move between English and Latin (and perhaps French), see Echard and Fanger 1991, 4–7 and notes.

112–16 A book . . . can Gower's self-presentation as feudal subject is signaled by the distinctive vocabulary: "ligeance," "obeissance," "a liege man." Though part of the poem's dedication to Richard, this can also be read as a version of the humility topos. For a similar stance as loyal subject, see Lydgate's act of submission to Henry, prince of Wales (*Troy Book*, excerpt 1.7: 73–74).

117 In the margin of MS Bodley 294 appears the following Latin prose commentary: "Hic declarat in primis qualiter ob reuerenciam serenissimi principis domini sui regis Anglie Ricardi secundi totus suus humilis Iohannes Gower, licet graui infirmitate a diu multipliciter fatigatus, huius opusculi labores suscipere non recusauit set tanquam fatuum ex variis floribus recollectum presentem libellum ex variis cronicis, historiis, poetarum philosophorumque dictis, quatenus sibi infirmitas permisit, studiosissime compilauit" (At the outset this declares how, out of reverence for his most fair prince and lord, King Richard II of England, his humble subject John Gower, although for a long time exhausted by repeated serious illness, did not refuse to undertake the labors of this little work; but he very studiously compiled the present book, however foolish the compilation, from various choice extracts: from various chronicles, histories, and sayings of the poets and philosophers, as far as his illness allowed him).

117–24 a bravura sequence of *rime riche* (see 14–15n above)

119–20 Prayend . . . regne The reference is to the divine right of kings, which authorizes through God the right of the monarch to reign.

125–26 newe Troye . . . joye Trinovant, or New Troy, was the name given to London by Geoffrey of Monmouth (in his twelfth-century legendary history of Britain; see 3n above) in a legendary genealogy that traced the ancestry of the British back to the Trojan hero Aeneas (who came from Troy to Rome) via the hero Brutus (who came to Britain from Rome), from whom the British were supposed to have derived their name. The model of transmission in the legend of the founding of Britain is a version of the topos of *translatio imperii* (see essay 4.1, pages 317–21).

127 In Temse The mise-en-scène of the poem's genesis on the Thames alludes complexly to the romantic-historical themes of Troy (see previous note). In addition to its parodic elements (see headnote), it may signal the optimism (and social conservatism) of a romantic fashioning of the present ("newe Troye" [125]) in the image of the past.

146–48 That . . . write so that no instance of hostility [i.e., anyone who feels hostile] could contrive to tell lies about what I write and slander it without a reasonable cause

152–55 But he . . . schilde but as for the man who uses injudicious words and misrepresents everything, I pray to the King of Heaven that he may shield me from such [malicious] tongues. The metaphor of the "word unpeysed" suggests a juridical process of weighing up meanings and consequences.

153 [onwrong every] The scribe has had difficulty here: MS *outkrong eny*. All MS variants agree in making *onurong* a single word (not an adverbial phrase) deriving, presumably, from the Middle English *wringen*, to wring, twist.

156–57 And natheles . . . jangling and nevertheless this world has been made desolate through such evil talk

157–60 and what bifalle . . . his wil observe and whatever may happen, my king's command shall not come to nothing, nor shall I, hoping to deserve his gratitude, fail to carry out his desire

163 [Which] MS *What*

164–66 Forthy . . . travaile therefore if the simplicity of my intellect can be of any use, I intend to labor in his service

165 [myhte] MS *may*

167 seknesse See 68–69n above.

178–79 After . . . newe Gower significantly extends the topos of *auctoritas,* insofar as the narrator draws his inspiration equally from the conventional, revered past and from the newly dignified present (see 8–18n above).

2.12 *KNYGHTHODE AND BATAILE:* PROEM

Date and Provenance: c. 1457–60; probably London.

Author, Sources, and Nature of Text: This work claims to have been written by a parson of Calais, possibly Robert Parker, sometime in the household of Humphrey of Gloucester and later a priest of Calais (Pearsall 1977, 240). The text is a versification of Fulvius Vegetius Renatus's well-known fourth-century military treatise, *De re militari* (also known as the *Epitoma rei militaris,* The military institutions [of the Romans]). Vegetius is mentioned (59); however, this version is apparently quite independent of other medieval translations of Vegetius, such as Christine de Pizan's early-fifteenth-century *Livre des fais d'armes et de chevalrye* (the source of Caxton's translation, the *Book of Fayttes of Armes and of Chyvalrye,* excerpt 2.10) or the translation of 1408 commissioned by Thomas Berkeley, Trevisa's patron (see excerpt 2.2). An occasional poem that celebrates a (real or fictitious) royal entry of King Henry VI (1421–71) and his queen into London, the text may have been commissioned by a patron (perhaps "my lord Beaumont" [54]) or written in order to secure patronage. Yet the poem seems also to have the more specific aim either of reminding Henry of his duty as king to protect Calais, which, since the end of the Hundred Years' War in 1453, had been the only part of France in England's hands, or of urging him to fight off the threats to his rule from the Yorkist party, the Lancastrians' great rivals in the fifteenth-century civil war known as the Wars of the Roses. In 1458 Calais was a Yorkist stronghold (Harriss 1960). Henry was a disastrously bad warrior who squandered all the gains his father, Henry V, had made in the long war with France and who had only the most tenuous hold on power in England during his long reign (Griffiths 1981, 533). But he was famous for his religious devotion. The parson's strategy—whether or not the defense of Calais is his object—is thus to emphasize Christ's role as conqueror and to fuse this role with Henry's duties as a king in an attempt to present warfare as a devotional exercise. Indeed, in the latter part of this difficult proem, it is sometimes hard to tell if Henry or Christ is the subject. The proem is written in self-consciously aureate language that is typical of much fifteenth-century courtly poetry (e.g., 12, 37, 70) and owes as much to Lydgate as Chaucer. It names its own verse form as that of the "balade" (60) (for a balade by Chaucer, see excerpt 1.3). The proem is remarkable for its vivid dramatization of patronage and presentation. Like a presentation miniature come to life, the poem's account of the leading knight of the day (see 54n) vowing to study the poem as if it were his Psalter is designed to produce the very effect it represents.

Audience and Circulation: The poem's editors, R. Dyboski and Z. M. Arend (1936, xxiii), suggest that the poem was presented to King Henry VI in 1458 in a partially finished state, and then completed in 1459, but there is no evidence for this. Possibly it was written for the "love-day," or temporary reconciliation, between the houses of York and Lancaster in 1458 (Heffernan 1975). Its implied readers and very likely its actual ones, are courtly and lay. The fact that this handbook of military strategy, which de Pizan—and Caxton—render in prose (excerpt 2.10), is here rendered in verse may indicate that it was written to entertain, impress, or persuade, rather than to be put to military use (although Vegetius was regarded as an important guide to military strategy). The Middle English text is extant in only three manuscripts, but this suggests that it had some currency within court circles apart from its status as a presentation work. The two later manuscripts, in a careful update, replace mention of King Henry VI with mention of the Yorkist king Edward IV.

Bibliography: The text is critically edited by Dyboski and Arend (1936), using the Cambridge manuscript as base text; for an edition and discussion of a text written for a comparable occasion, see Heffernan 1975. For a detailed account of the poem's political and propagandistic context, see Scase forthcoming. On Vegetius in late medieval England, see Lester 1988, 15–17. On royal entries, see Withington 1918; Kantorowicz 1944; Kipling

1977, 1990; Stevens 1987, 52ff.; Fradenburg 1991. A new standard work on royal entries is Kipling 1998. On late medieval civic triumph, with reference to the representations of the coming of a sovereign as analogous to the advent of a savior figure, see Kipling 1984. On the problems of Henry VI's reign, see Griffiths 1981 and Watts 1996. On the Yorkist control of Calais, see Harriss 1960 and Lander 1980, 199–200. For the town's strategic importance, see Warner 1926.

Source: Cambridge, Pembroke College MS 243, fols. 1r–2v (the proem is distinguished from the body of the poem by its separate foliation): a fifteenth-century parchment booklet containing only this text (carefully rubricated), bound together with other, originally separate, booklets. The earliest extant manuscript, it names Henry VI ("Harry . . . . of Fraunce / And England" [121]) as the king. Like the other two extant manuscripts, it has Vegetian side notes in Latin.

Proemium

Proem

Salve, festa dies
.i. martis!
Mavortis avete
5 Kalende! Qua Deus
ad celum sublevat
ire David.

Hail, holy day
of the 1st of March!
Welcome the calends of March!
when God
lifted David up to heaven

Hail, halyday devout! Alhail, Kalende
Of Marche, wheryn David the Confessour
10 Commaunded is his kyngis court ascende.
Emanuel, Jhesus the conquerour,
This same day, as a tryumphatour,
Sette in a chaire and throne of majestee,
To London is comyn. O Saviour,
15 Welcome a thousandfold to thi citee!

halyday holy day; **Kalende** calends (i.e., 1st)
wheryn on which; **Confessour** believer
is commanded to ascend to his king's court

tryumphatour conqueror
chaire triumphal car; **majestee** majesty
is comyn has come
Welcome a thousandfold a thousand times welcome

And she, thi modir (blessed mot she be),
That cometh eke, and angelys an ende,
Wel wynged and wel horsed, hidir fle,
Thousendys on this goode approche attende;
20 And ordir aftir ordir thei commende,
As Seraphin, as Cherubyn, as Throne,
As Domynaunce, and Princys hidir sende;
And, at o woord, right welcom everychone!

thi modir thy mother (Mary); **mot** may
That cometh eke who also comes; **an ende** last of all
hidir fle may you fly here
may thousands attend this fair procession
and may they command order upon order of angels
As namely; **Throne** thrones (an angelic order)
Domynaunce dominions; **Princys** principalities
at o woord in brief; **everychone** everyone

But Kyng Henry the Sexte, as Goddes sone
25 Or th'emperour, or kyng Emanuel,
To London, welcomer be noo persone;
O souverayn Lord, welcom! Nowwel, Nowwel!
Te Deum to be songenn, wil do wel,
And *Benedicta Sancta Trinitas!*
30 Now prosperaunce and peax perpetuel
Shal growe—and why? For here is *Unitas.*

as who appears like, represents

welcomer be noo persone no one is more welcome
Nowwel hurrah
Te Deum praise you God; **wil do wel** will serve well
Benedicta Sancta Trinitas blessed holy Trinity
prosperaunce prosperity; **peax** peace
Unitas unity

Therof to the Unitee *Deo gracias*
    Deo gracias thanks be to God (i.e., let it be sung)
In Trinitee! The Clergys and Knyghthode
And Comynaltee better accorded nas
    and the commons have never agreed better
35 Never then now. Now nys ther noon abode,
    Now nys ther noon abode now there's no delay
But out on hem that fordoon Goddes forbode,
Perjurous ar, rebell[you]s and atteynte,
    who are perjurers, rebellious and convicted
So forfaytinge her lyif and lyvelode,
    forfaytinge forfeiting; **lyvelode** livelihood
Although Ypocrisie her faytys peynte.
    her faytys peynte paints their deeds (to look good)

40 Now, person of Caleys, pray every seynte
    person parson; **Caleys** Calais; **pray** pray to
In hevenys and in erth of help th'availe.
    of help th'availe for the benefit of help
It is, that in this werk nothing ne feynte,
    It is namely; **ne feynte** be defective
But that beforn good wynde it go ful sayle;
    but that it may sail on a good wind
And that not oonly prayer but travaile
    and so that not only prayer but effort
45 Heron be sette, enserche and faste inquere,
    may be applied to it, seek and earnestly inquire
Thi litil book, *Of Knyghthode and Bataile*,
    Knyghthode chivalry
What chivaler is best, on it be were.
    Whoever is the best of knights, may he heed it

Whil *Te Deum Laudamus* up goth there
    up goth there is sung there
At Paulis, up to Westmynster go thee;
    Paulis St. Paul's cathedral
50 The Kyng comyng, *Honor, Virtus* the Quene,
So glad goth up that blisse it is to see.
    So glad goth up is sung so gladly
Thi bille unto the Kyng is red; and he
    Thi bille your petition
Content withal, and wil it not foryete.
    Content withal is happy with it; **foryete** forget
What seith my lord Beaumont? "Preste, unto me
    Preste priest; **unto me** to me
55 Welcom." Here is t'assay, entre to gete.
    Welcom you are welcome

"Of knyghthode and bataile, my lord, as trete
    trete deal with
The bookys olde, a werk is made now late,
    bookys olde ancient books; **late** recently
And if it please you, it may be gete."
    gete obtained
"What werk is it?" "*Vegetius,* translate
    translate translated
60 Into balade." "O preste, I pray the, late
    balade verse; **late** let
Me se that werk." "Therto wil I you wise:
    Therto wil I you wise I will show it to you
Lo, here it is!" Anon he gan therate
    Anon he gan therate at once he began at that point
To rede, thus: *Sumtyme it was the gise*—
    rede read; *Sumtyme* once; *gise* custom

And red therof a part. "For my servyse
    For my servyse in my devotions
65 Heer wil I rede," he seith, "as o psaultier."
    as o psaultier as though on the Psalter
"It pleaseth you right wel; wil your advyse
    wil your advyse is it your opinion to
Suppose that the kyng heryn pleasier
    heryn i.e., in this book; **pleasier** pleasure
May have?" "I wil considir the matier;
    May have may find; **matier** subject matter
I fynde it is right good and pertynente
    pertynente appropriate
70 Unto the kyng; his celsitude is hier;
    Unto for; **celsitude** sublimity; **hier** here
I halde it wel doon hym therwith presente."
    I consider it right to present him with it

Almyghti Maker of the firmament,
O mervailous in every creature,
    O how marvelous you appear in every living thing
So singular in this most excellent
    So singular taking such unique form
75 Persone, our Souverayn Lord! Of what stature
    Persone person; **Souverayn** sovereign

Is he, what visagynge, how fair feture,   visagynge face; **fair feture** beautiful of features
How myghti mad, and how strong in travaile!   **mad** formed; **in travaile** in working
In oonly God and hym it is t'assure   one can rely on the one God and on him
As in a might, that noo wight dar assaile.   for strength, he whom no one dares attack

80 Lo, Souverayn Lord, *Of knyghthode and bataile,*
    This litil werk, your humble oratour,   **oratour** petitioner
    Ye, therwithal your chivalers, t'availe,   to help you, your knights as well
    Inwith your hert to Crist the conquerour   **Inwith your hert** within your heart
    Offreth for ye. Ther, y[ev]eth him thonour;   **for ye** on your behalf; **him** (i.e., Christ)
85 His true thought, accepte it, he besecheth,
    Accepte; it is to this tryumphatour   **to this tryumphatour** for this supreme conqueror
    That myghti werre exemplifying techeth.   that mighty war teaches by example

    He redeth, and fro poynt to poynt he secheth,   **fro poynt to poynt** item by item; **secheth** scans
    How hath be doon, and what is now to done;
90 His providence on aftirward he strecheth,   he extends his providence according to this
    By see and lond; he wil provide sone   **he wil provide** he will make adequate preparations
    To chace his adversaryes everychone,   to chase every one of his adversaries
    Thei hem by lond, thei hem by see asseyle.   they attack them by land, they by sea
    The Kyng his oratoure, God graunt his bone,   God grant the king's petitioner his prayer
95 Ay to prevaile in knyghthode and bataile.

    Amen.

3–10 *.i. martis* . . . **ascende** March 1 is Saint David's Day. *Pace* Dyboski and Arend (1936), the David referred to in these lines is not primarily the Old Testament king (1 Sam. 16; 2 Sam. 2) but the Welsh saint (c. 520–89). Saint David was best known to the late Middle Ages as having established the see of St. David's in Pembroke, West Wales, but there was a tradition of Saint David's royal or noble birth (Williams 1979, 110). It is unclear whether there is also any nationalist significance in the allusion to a Welsh saint. Henry's son Edward, prince of Wales (b. 1453), was still an infant at the date of the poem.

8 **Kalende** Despite the explicit classical reference here, "kalende" can also mean "beginning" in Middle English. See *Troilus and Criseyde* II.7 and excerpt 2.13: 37.

9 **Confessour** one who makes a public witness to Christian belief: together with martyrs and virgins, one of the principal categories of medieval saints

11 **Emanuel** a name found in both the Old and New Testaments. In Isa. 7:14 and 8:8 it has been interpreted by Christian commentators as a title for the Messiah (it means "God is with us"); in Matt. 1:23 it is unambiguously applied to Christ. It designates the messianic aspect of Christ and is used

appropriately here in the context of Christ as triumphant conqueror.

11–12 **Emanuel . . . tryumphatour** On the image of Christ as militant king and chivalric hero, compare *Piers Plowman* B XIX, in which Will sees Christ as "conquerour of cristene" (14) and is instructed by Conscience that "knyght, kyng, conquerour may be o persone" (knight, king, and conqueror may exist in one person) (27). Christ's arrival in London (with Mary and all the angels attending, 16–24) is really Henry's; as king, Henry represents Christ, and his court represents that of heaven.

19 **on** MS *or*

20–22 **And ordir . . . sende** On the orders of angels, see excerpt 2.2: 157n.

25 **kyng Emanuel** See 11n above.

28 *Te Deum* a Latin liturgical hymn to the Father and Son, in rhythmical prose, used in the Office of Matins

31–35 *Unitas* . . . **now** Continuing the presentation of Henry as Christ's representative, this passage conflates the peace and unity existing within the Holy Trinity with the peace Henry is said to have brought to the three estates of English society, the clerks, knights, and commons (33–34). In practice, Henry's long reign was remarkable for one of the most persistent civil wars in English history, the so-called Wars of the Roses.

36 But out . . . forbode but out with them who destroy God's commandment

37 rebell[you]s The *you* is an editorial conjecture, since the letters are illegible in the MS.

40 Caleys Calais (an important city on the northeast coast of France, at the narrowest point of the English Channel) was held by the English from 1347 to 1558. England gave up all her other possessions in France at the end of the Hundred Years' War in 1453.

40–47 Now, person of Caleys . . . on it be were The author (the "person of Caleys") prays to all the saints for help, so that his book will not be found defective and may prosper in its aim (43), but says he must back his prayer up with hard work by searching out the best of knights in order to show him his book: the best of knights proves to be "my lord Beaumont" (54). From 44 to 54, the narrator admonishes himself, presenting himself as an eager petitioner for royal favor trying to work his way up the social ladder so that he can present his book directly to the king. For the phrase "litil book," see excerpts 1.8: 116 (*Amoryus and Cleopes*) and 2.13: 13 (*The Nightingale*).

42–43 that in this werk . . . go ful sayle The metaphor of the book as ship may derive from *Troilus and Criseyde* II.1–7, in which the narrator imagines his "connyng" (faculty for writing poetry) as a boat laboring in the "tempestous matere (subject matter) / Of disespeir that Troilus was inne." The figure was a prominent literary topos for narration in fifteenth-century poetry.

50 The Kyng . . . the Quene at the king's coming "honor," at the queen's "virtue"

52 Thi bille unto the Kyng is red The parson has submitted a petition to the king in advance, one that perhaps enables him to gain admission to the court at Westminster (where the procession goes, after the service at St. Paul's).

54 my lord Beaumont Viscount Beaumont was appointed Chamberlain (the official charged with attendance upon the king) in the place of the duke of Suffolk in 1450. He died in the Battle of Northampton in 1460. ∫ **unto me** with *After my mastre* in the right-hand margin of the MS

55 Here is t'assay, entre to gete this is the moment to try to gain an entry

63 Sumtyme it was the gise This is, in fact, the opening line of the poem proper.

65 as o psaultier Psalters had become daily reading for the secular nobility and—increasingly in the fifteenth century—for the middle classes (see Barratt 1975, 264; also excerpt 3.21, Eleanor Hull's *Commentary on the Penitential Psalms*). The unusual link made here between the Psalms and this translation of Vegetius—which Beaumont says he will use *instead of* the Psalms in his devotions—continues the proem's conflation of warfare with religious devotion.

74–75 this most excellent / Persone, our Souverayn Lord could refer equally to Christ or to Henry as Christ's representative. At 80 the phrase "Souverayn Lord" seems to refer only to Henry.

80–91 Lo . . . lond a difficult passage. Translate: "Lo, sovereign lord [Henry], on your behalf your humble petitioner offers this little work to Christ the conqueror, [who dwells] within your heart, to help you and also your knights. There [within your heart] give him [i.e., not me] honor for it. Accept his true thought [i.e., as conveyed by this book], he begs you; [for] mighty war teaches by example [i.e., even] this supreme conqueror. He analyzes ["redeth," i.e., reads] and scans item by item the things that have been done and are about to be done, and according [to what he sees] he extends his providence by sea and land." This passage further reinforces the analogy between Henry and Christ and presents Christ "reading" the world as the narrator urges Henry to read the book, deriving lessons from what he sees that enable him to guide the future course of events. The parson gives the book not to Henry but to Christ in Henry's heart, and having done this is able rhetorically to identify the book's contents with Christ's will. Henry is thus urged not simply by Vegetius but by God himself to learn how to make war, and so practice the imitation of Christ in this respect, as he already does in others.

84 y[ev]eth The *ev* is an editorial conjecture, since the letters are illegible in the MS.

95 At to prevaile that he [the king] will always prevail

2.13 *THE NIGHTINGALE*: PROSE INTRODUCTION AND PROEM

Date and Provenance: 1446; ?southwest Midlands.

Author, Sources, and Nature of Text: This anonymous poem was once attributed to

Lydgate, but this cannot be proved (Meale 1996a, 157). The source, stated within the text to be a Latin poem, has not been identified (although the reference may be to

Archbishop Pecham's Latin poem *Philomena,* also made for a royal female reader, Eleanor, queen of Edward I). In poetry indebted to classical Latin writers such as Ovid, nightingales were often associated with the tragic story of Philomela (or Philomena), brutally raped by her brother-in-law Tereus and changed into a nightingale (see *Troilus and Criseyde* II.64–69, drawing on Ovid's *Metamorphoses*). But in the late Middle Ages, another tradition, derived from Christian Latin poetry, was equally important. This tradition, represented by this text and by Pecham's *Philomena* (as well as more loosely by another *Philomena* poem by John of Hoveden, and by passages of Richard Rolle: Rigg 1992, 208–26; Watson 1991, 121–22), associated the song of the bird at five of the canonical hours with five meditations on the life of Christ (Burrow 1986, 60 n.12, and 3–11 below). This Christlike nightingale features regularly in the English and French reading of aristocratic women, and illustrates a continuity in women's religious reading between the thirteenth and fifteenth centuries. Other, secular, poems link the nightingale with spring and the pleasures of romantic love (Shippey 1970; *Troilus and Criseyde* II.918–22), and nightingales are also participants in several Middle English bird-debate poems, such as Sir John Clanvowe's fourteenth-century *Boke of Cupide* (Patterson 1992, 9), and two fifteenth-century satires about women, both entitled *The Clerk and the Nightingale* (Robbins 1955, 176–79). Nightingales therefore featured in a number of generic traditions and gave rise to different gendered and class-based meanings and responses, depending on context. This poem's verse dedication alludes to secular, romantic, and erotic meanings (21–27), but its prose introduction places the poem in a spiritual tradition, firmly displacing the erotic. The prose introduction, however, is not quite an accurate guide to the following fifty-nine-stanza poem (Glauning 1900, xl), which pairs episodes from the Old and New Testament for each of the five "hours."

Audience and Circulation: The dedicatory proem (certainly not by Lydgate) is addressed to Anne, duchess of Buckingham (d. 1480), a vigorous and cultivated woman who left not only a book of hours, a primer, and French and English devotional books but a French version of Lucan to her daugher-in-law, Margaret Beaufort (Jones and Underwood, 1992, 142–43, 173). Margaret may have been the work's patron. There are two manuscript versions extant: Oxford, Corpus Christi College MS 203, from which the text here is edited and in which the poem appears with Chaucer's *Truth* (called in the manuscript *Proverbium Scogan*) and a short poem, "Se meche sey lytyll and lerne to suffre in tyme" (*Proverbium R. Stokes,* according to the manuscript: see *Index of Middle English Verse,* no. 3083); and London, British Library MS Cotton Caligula A.II (from the second half of the fifteenth century), which is a compilation of romances and domestic, didactic, and religious works (including a *Charter of Christ* and some Carthusian material; Guddat-Figge 1976, 169–72). The manuscript context for this poem suggests aristocratic lay readers—particularly, but not necessarily exclusively, women readers.

Bibliography: The poem is edited by Otto Glauning (1900). On nightingale traditions in general, see Shippey 1970; Pfeffer 1985; Williams 1997. Chapter 3 of Williams 1997 focuses on medieval representations, with particular attention to courtly poems from the thirteenth to the fifteenth centuries. On the courtly associations of nightingales, see Patterson 1992. On "prymers" (books of devotions based on the canonical hours), see Barratt 1975. Joseph Baird and John Kane (1978) edit other English and French nightingale poems in this devotional tradition. For Pecham's *Philomena,* see the editions by G. M. Dreves, Clemens Blume, and H. M. Banister (1886–1922, 50:602), by Blume (1930), and by William Dobell (1924), which has a facing-page English translation. For discussion, see Raby 1953, 425–29. For John of Hoveden's Latin *Philomena,* see Blume 1930; see also Raby 1935 and 1953, 389–95, for further Hoveden texts and comment. For Hoveden's Anglo-Norman translation of the poem, see Stone 1947. For a Middle English paraphrase, see d'Evelyn 1921 and Raby 1935. The best discussion of the Anglo-Latin literary context in which *Philomena* poems were written is Rigg 1992, 157–239.

Source: Oxford, Corpus Christi College MS 203 [C], fols. 1r–2r, with variant readings from British Library MS Cotton Caligula A.II, fol. 59r (the first two stanzas and prose introduction are omitted in the British Library MS). The Corpus manuscript is a small booklet made up of a single quire with twelve leaves. The pages (a mixture of parchment and vellum) are ruled and the hand neat and careful, but despite the text's evocation of and dedication to an aristocratic audience, this is far from a luxury production. Above the opening of the prose introduction, in the scribe's hand, are the words *Assit principio s[ancta] maria meo* (May Saint Mary help me in beginning this).

a. Prose Introduction

It is seyd that the nyghtyngale of hure nature hathe a knowleche of hure deth. And lyke as the swan syngeth afore his deth, so sche, in the day of hure deth, assendyth into the top of the tre and syngeth *in hora matutina* [a] lame[n]table note. And so aftyre, by mene degrees avalynge lowere, *hora prima, hora tercia, hora sexta, et*
5 *hora nona,* tyll sche com doun into the myddys of the tre. And there, *in hora nona,* sche dyeth. This ys moral[y]syd unto Cryste an[d] into every crystyn sowle, that schuld remembre the ourys of Cristys passyoun. And allso by *hora matutina* ys undurstonden the begynnynge of the world, and the gret fall of owre fadure Adam and the naty[vi]te of every [man] and [p]*atris sapiencia* declared. And in like wyse
10 *hora p[rim]a, Crucifige, hora sexta,* and *hora nona* declared wyth the Ages of the Worlde in tyme of Noe and of Abraham. And so forthe brefly t[ouc]hed the Resurecion, the Ascensyone, Pentecost, and Corpus Cristi Day, et cetera.

b. Proem: The Dedication

Go, lityll qu[ay]ere, and swyft thy prynses dresse,   **prynses** princess; **dresse** address
Offringe [thy]selfe wyth humble reverence
15 Unto the ryghte hyghe and myghty pryncesse,
The Duches of Bokengham, and of hur excellence   **Bokengham** Buckingham; **hur** her
Besechinge hyre that of hure pacyence
Sche wold the take, of hure noble grace   **take** accept
Amonge hyre bokys for the asygne a place,   **for the asygne a place** assign a place for you

20 Unto the tyme hyr ladyly goodnesse   **Unto** until; **hyr ladyly goodnesse** her noble goodness
Luste for to call unto hyr highe presence   **Luste for to call** it pleased [her] to summon
Suche of hyre peple that are in lustynesse   **lustynesse** a time of pleasure
Fresschly encoragyt, as galantus in prime tens,   **galantus** gallants; **prime tens** springtime
Desyrous for to here the amerouse sentensce   **amerouse** amorous; **sentensce** opinion
25 Of the nyghtyngale, and in there mynde enbrace,   **there** their
Who favoure moste schall fynde in loves grace,   **Who** whoever; **favoure moste** most favor

Commandyng them to here wyth tendernesse   **here** hear
Of this youre nyghtingale the gostely sensce,   **gostely** spiritual
Whos songe and deth declaryd [is] expresse   **declaryd [is] expresse** is expressly declared
30 Yn Englysh here, ryghte bare of eloquence,   **ryghte** completely
But notheless, consydred the sentence,   **consydred the sentence** having pondered its meaning

All love unlaufle, y hope, hit wyll deface   **unlaufle** forbidden; **deface** obliterate
And fleschly luste oute of theyre hertis chace,   **fleschly luste** sexual gratification

Meved of corage be vertu of the sesone,   [their] hearts stirred through the power of the season
35 In prime tens renoveled yere by yere,   renewed every year in spring
Gladyng every hart of veray resone,   gladdening every heart with absolute propriety
When fresch May in kalendis can apere,   **kalendis** i.e., beginning of the month
Phebus ascendyng, clere schynyng in his spere,   **Phebus** i.e., the sun; **clere** brightly; **spere** sphere
By whom the colde of wyntyre is exylyde
40 And lusty sesone th[u]s newly reconcylede.   **reconcylede** [is] restored to favor [from exile]

To speke of sclepe, hyt nedys moste be had   **sclepe** sleep
Unto the noresyng of every creature   **noresyng** nurturing
(Wythoute whych braynes moste be madd,
Outragesly wakynge oute of mesure),   from immoderately and excessively staying awake
45 Except thoo that kyndely nature   **thoo that** those whom
Mevethe to wache, as the nyghtyngale,   **Mevethe to wache** urges to keep awake
Whych in hire sesone by sclepe sett no tale.   Who does not care to sleep in her mating season

—So sche, of kynde, all the someres nyght   **of kynde** by her nature
Ne secyth not wyth mony a lusty note,   **Ne secyth not** does not cease
50 Whedyre hit be dry or wete, derke or lyght,   **Whedyre** whether
Redyly rehersyng hure lessone ay by rote   willingly going over and over her lesson by rote
(Gret merevell hit is the enduring of hyre throte)   it is a great marvel her throat endures it
That hyr to here hit is a secunde heven,   **hyr to here** to hear her
So melodyouse and [mery] ys hure steven.

1 **of hure nature** by her very nature. The references in 1–3 to the nightingale's foreknowledge of its death and to the piteous lament it sings in death are medieval commonplaces, derived from Pliny's *Natural History* (Shippey 1970, 49). Religious nightingale poetry (partly influenced by the *Planctus*, or complaint, a genre in which Christ, the Virgin, or another religious or secular figure laments his or her lot in life) identifies the nightingale with Christ but also with "every crystyn sowle" (6), who shares vicariously in Christ's suffering (compare excerpt 1.13). As lines 20–33 make clear, the passionate allegorical nightingale of this religious tradition is a deliberate counterpart to other literary nightingales, who stand for erotic, not religious, love.

2 **lyke as** just as ∫ **syngeth** the g badly rubbed but still legible in the MS ∫ **afore** before

3 *in hora matutina* at the hour of matins: that is, the Office (daily public prayer performed at fixed hours) that took place, according to the Benedictine Rule, at 2 A.M. and was generally considered to be the first Office, or hour (*hora*), of the day: hence the allegorical position of the nightingale at the top of the tree. The subsequent *horae* (prime, terce, sext,

and none) are associated, according to a traditional scheme of meditations on the life of Christ, with hours of Christ's Passion, from prime until his death at none (Barratt 1975, 266–67, and for a good Anglo-Norman example, see Jeffrey and Levy 1990, 181–85), and are here paralleled by the allegorical progress of the nightingale through the branches of the tree. ∫ [a] not visible because buried in a crease ∫ **lame[n]table** pitiful (MS *lametable*)

4 **aftyre** subsequently ∫ **mene** intermediate ∫ **avalynge** going down ∫ *hora prima* the Office of prime (i.e., 6 A.M.) ∫ *tercia* terce ∫ *sexta* sext

5 *nona* none. As the names suggest, terce, sext, and none were appointed to be said at the third, sixth, and ninth hours respectively (i.e., 9.00 A.M., 12 P.M., and 3.00 P.M.). Together with prime they make up the so-called Little Hours of the Office.

6 **moral[y]syd unto** given a moral interpretation corresponding to (MS *moral.syd*)

7 **ourys** hours (i.e., the hours [of the Passion] on Good Friday)

8 **undurstonden** signified ∫ **fadure** father

9 **naty[vi]te** badly smudged in MS ∫ **[man]** MS has a series of minims and an indeterminate middle let-

ter. ∫ [p]atris MS atris, a very smudged and preceded by an illegible smudged letter ∫ [p]atris sapiencia literally, the wisdom of the Father: a designation of Christ. In 1 Cor. 1:24, Paul speaks of Christ as "the power of God and the wisdom of God"; see also 1 Cor. 8:5–6; Col. 1:15–17.

10 *Crucifige* "Crucify": the crowd's demand to Pontius Pilate that Jesus be crucified. The incident is found in all the Gospels (Matt. 27:15–26; Mark 15:6–15; Luke 23:13–25; John 18:28–19:16).

10–11 **Ages of the Worlde** Christian authors divided biblical history into *ætates mundi* (the ages of the world). The most influential scheme, proposed by Saint Augustine, defined six ages, corresponding to those of an individual: "an *infantia* from Adam to Noah, a *pueritia* from Noah to Abraham, an *adolescentia* from Abraham to David, a *juventus* from David until the Babylonian captivity, a *gravitas* from the captivity until the coming of the Lord, and the present *senectus* which will last until the end of time" (Burrow 1986, 80). The Christian could look forward to a seventh age of everlasting rest. These "ages" were also often linked to different schemes of hours, or *horae*, as in this passage.

11 **Noe** Noah, saved by God from the Flood through building the ark. His era, the second age of the world, is signified by prime in the poem (Glauning 1900, 8, 200–204). ∫ **Abraham** one of the great Old Testament patriarchs, father of Isaac, whose era is represented by terce (Glauning 1900, 11, 274–80) ∫ **t[ouc]hed** middle letters badly smudged in MS C

12 **Resurecion** the Resurrection of Christ from death on Easter Sunday, the principal Christian festival ∫ **Ascensyone** the Ascension of Christ into heaven ∫ **Pentecost** also known as Whitsunday or Whitsun because it was an especially favored day for baptism, for which white clothes were worn: the day when the Holy Spirit was given to the Apostles as the first Christians, symbolizing the completion

of the redemptive act of Good Friday and Easter. Pentecost was second only to Easter as a Christian festival. ∫ **Corpus Cristi Day** The movable feast of Corpus Christi (celebrating, as the Latin suggests, "the body of Christ") was inaugurated in 1264, following a campaign by the Liège holy woman Juliana of Mont Cornillon (1193–1258). It was finally instituted in 1311 as an official celebration of the doctrine of transubstantiation, the belief that the wafer of the Mass was transformed into the body of Christ. The dates of the feast fall within the period May 21–June 24.

13 **qu[ay]ere** book (MS qu[. . .]ere); reading supplied from British Library Cotton Caligula MS

14 **[thy]selfe** MS [. . .]selfe; reading supplied from British Library Cotton Caligula MS

16 **The Duches of Bokengham** Anne, duchess of Buckingham (d. 1480): daughter of Ralph Neville, first earl of Westmoreland, and of Joan Beaufort, daughter of John of Gaunt and Katherine Roet (and a dedicatee of Hoccleve's poetry). Anne Neville was married (before 1424) to Humphrey Stafford, first duke of Buckingham (d. 1460). In 1467, when she was over sixty, she married the Yorkist Walter Blount (Jones and Underwood 1992, 206).

36 **hart** not clearly legible in MS C; reading confirmed from British Library Cotton Caligula MS

37 **kalendis** See excerpt 2.12: 8n.

40 **th[u]s** MS C *this.* "Thus," which makes better sense, is supplied from British Library Cotton Caligula MS.

43 **Wythoute** *oute* added above the line in the same hand

45 **kyndely nature** literally, natural nature: that is, nature by its very nature

51 **lessone** lesson: an excerpt from the Bible or other sacred writing, read aloud (often in church)

54 **[mery]** omitted in MS C; reading supplied from British Library Cotton Caligula MS

2.14 *THE CROXTON PLAY OF THE SACRAMENT:* BANNS

Date and Provenance: c. 1461; East Anglia (possibly from the Thetford, Norfolk, or Bury St. Edmunds, Suffolk, areas; Davis 1970, lxxxiv–lxxxv; Beckwith 1992b, 70); for skepticism about the Bury St. Edmunds connection (about which most scholars agree), see Lerer 1996, 60.

Author, Sources, and Nature of Text: This anonymous play is a dramatization of one of

the well-known anti-Semitic host-desecration myths that were common (often in visual or dramatic form) in northern Europe from the fourteenth century onward (Davis 1970, lxxiii–lxxiv; Langmuir 1990a, 209–89; Dundas 1991; Biddick 1993). *Croxton* is the only extant play of its kind in Middle English. Unlike all other surviving examples of medieval English religious drama (except for moralities like *Everyman* or *Wisdom*), it is neither biblical narrative nor saint's life. It relates the story of a Jew who buys the host—the consecrated wafer that, in orthodox late medieval Latin Christian theology, did not simply represent but actually was the body of Christ—from a Christian merchant. The Jew then tortures it with his fellow Jews and cooks it in an oven, from which a bloodied Christ appears, bringing about the repentance and absolution of the merchant, and the conversion of the Jews to Christianity. Its performance was probably not tied to a particular occasion, such as the feast of Corpus Christi or Midsummer, as was the case with the biblical dramas produced in many large northern cities from the fourteenth to the fifteenth centuries by the urban trade guilds (groups of workers in particular trades, such as masons or goldsmiths). Although the nature of this proclamation (the play's so-called "banns") could imply that it was performed by a professional or semiprofessional touring company (Lerer 1996, 47), rather than by a guild, there are no records of payments, hiring, or accounts to confirm this possibility. However, the sensationalist elements of the play may be designed to appeal to a paying audience and thus to ensure a profit for an itinerant company (Coldewey 1994, 206). The unique mid-sixteenth-century copy (in three different scribal hands), which existed separately before it was bound into its current manuscript, may have been intended as a performance copy or may be a copy of a late-fifteenth-century performance copy: a stage direction at the end, following a cast list, reads "IX may play yt at ease" (it can easily be performed by nine actors). The play's intensely visual and spectacular form erases the boundary between staged performance and religious ritual—as is implied in the banns, where, in a deliberate attempt to control the audience's reaction, the spectacle of conversion is offered as an incitement to a sense of contrition in spectators (65–68). According to Lerer (1996, 51), a set of punning legal references in the play (10, 75) invite the audience not only to watch a play but to bear witness to a legal action involving extreme punishment, thus constructing that audience as active participants in its juridical processes.

Audience and Circulation: Unknown. The manuscript contains various sixteenth- and seventeenth-century texts unrelated to the play. The book belonged to John Madden, president of the Royal College of Physicians of Ireland, who died in 1703 (Davis 1970, lxx). Norfolk place-names in the play suggest that audiences would have recognized these local references (Coldewey 1994, 197). The dialect has some East Anglian features: note, for example, the characteristic spelling of *dowghtys* (68, 69) (Davis 1970, lxxxiii–lxxxiv). The existence of the play testifies to the often-remarked importance of East Anglia as a site of dramatic activity in the Middle Ages (see Coldewey 1994; Gibson 1989, 34–35). That the play only survives in a Tudor transcription suggests *Croxton*'s relevance to the later period's own concerns with heresy and iconoclastic debates (Lerer 1996, 53; Duffy 1992, 81).

Bibliography: Edited by Norman Davis (1970) and David Bevington (1975), the play has often been read as a piece of anti-Lollard propaganda (Cutts 1944), but some recent studies have emphasized the play's orthodox piety (Maltman 1974; Homan 1986–87; Nichols 1988–89). Eamon Duffy (1992, 105–9) considers the play's representation of aspects of late-fifteenth-century English culture. Sarah Beckwith (1992b) offers a political reading of its symbolism, and Seth Lerer (1996) discusses it as a spectacle of torture. For discussion of staging, see Grantley 1983. On the nature and formation of medieval anti-Semitism, see Langmuir 1990a; on anti-Semitism as a problem for historians, see Langmuir 1990b.

Source: Dublin, Trinity College MS F.4.20, Catalogue no. 652, fols. 338r–339r. The play is in a small unbound paper booklet now kept separate from the rest of the manuscript (but still foliated fols. 338–57). A facsimile of the unique manuscript is reproduced and analyzed by Davis (1979). The *dramatis personae* and stage directions are rubricated in yellow. There are many difficult readings, where the manuscript is nearly illegible or the scribe appears mistaken, and the transcription offered here differs in some details from that of Davis. The basic form of the verse is four four-stress lines, sometimes linked to form eight-line stanzas.

PRIMUS VEXILLATOR. Now the Father and the Sune and the Holy Goste,

That all this wyde worlde hat wrowght,   **hat wrowght** has made

Save all thes semely, bothe leste and moste,

And bryne yow to the blysse that he hath yow to bowght!

5 We be ful purposed with hart and with thowght   **We be ful purposed** we fully intend

Off our mater to tell the entent,   to tell the import of our subject

Off the marvellys that wer wondursely wrowght   **wondursely wrowght** wondrously done

Off the holi and blyssed sacrament.

SECUNDUS [VEXILLATOR]. S[o]vereyns, and yt lyke yow to here the purpoos
     of this play

10 That [ys] representyd now in yower syght,   **representyd** presented

Whych in Aragon was doon, the sothe to saye,   **Aragon** Aragon, Spain; **sothe** truth

In Eraclea, that famous cyte, aryght.   **Eraclea** a city in Aragon (unidentified); **aryght** indeed

Therin wonneth a merchaunte off mekyll myght,   **wonneth** lives; **mekyll myght** great power

Syr Arystorye was called hys name,   **Arystorye** Aristorius

15 Kend full fere with mani a wyght,   known far and wide to many a person

Full fer in the worlde sprong hys fame.   **sprong** extended

PRIMUS. Anon to hym ther cam a Jewe,   **Anon** soon

With grete rychesse for the nonys,   **for the nonys** for the nonce

And wonneth in the syte of Surrey—this full trewe—

20 The wyche hade gret plente off precyous stonys.   **gret plente** large amounts

Off this Cristen merchaunte he freyned sore,   **he freyned sore** he asked earnestly

Wane he wolde have had hys entente.   when he would have had his desire

Twenti pownd and merchaundyse mor   **merchaundyse mor** a greater amount of goods

He proferyd for the Holy Sacrament.   **proferyd** offered

25 *SECUNDUS.* But the Cristen marchaunte theroff sed nay,

Because his profer was of so lityll valewe;   because his offer was worth so little

An hundder pownd but he wolde pay   but if he would pay a hundred pounds

No lenger theron he shuld pursewe.   then he wouldn't have to ask any longer

But mor off ther purpos they gunne speke,   but began to speak more about their business

30 The Holi Sacramente for to bey;   **for to bey** in order to buy

And all for the[y] wolde be wreke,   and all because they wanted to be avenged

A gret sume off gold begune down ley.   **begune down ley** he began to put down

PRIMUS. Thys Crysten merchante consentyd, the sothe to sey,

And in the nyght afftter made hym delyveraunce.   the real night handed it over to him

35 Thes Jewes all grete joye made they;

But off thys betyde a straunger chaunce: but as a result a stranger event happened

They grevid our Lord gretly on growND,   **grevid** harmed; **on grownd** there

And put hym to a new passyoun;   and subjected him to a second Passion

With daggers goven hym many a grevyos wound;   **goven hym** gave him; **grevyos** grievous

40 Nayled hym to a pyller, with pynsons plukked hym doune.   **pyller** pillar; **pynsons** pincers

SECUNDUS. And sythe thay toke that blysed brede so sownde   *sythe* then; **brede** bread
And in a cawdron they ded hym boyle.   *And they had it boiled in a cauldron*
In a clothe full just they yt wounde,   **full just** tightly fitting; **wounde** wrapped
And so they ded hym sethe in oyle;   *and caused it to be boiled in oil*

45 And than thay putt hym to a new turmentry,   **turmentry** torture
In an hoote ovyn speryd hym fast.   *shut it firmly in a hot oven*
There he appyred with woundys blody;   **appyred** appeared
The ovyn rofe asondre and all tobrast.
PRIMUS. Thus in our lawe they wer made stedfast;
50 The Holy Sacrament sheuyd them grette favour;   **sheuyd** showed
In contrycyon thyr hertys wer cast
And went and shewyd ther lyves to a confesour.   **shewyd ther lyves** made their confession

Thus be maracle off the kyng of hevyn,   **be maracle** by a miracle
And by myght and power govyn to the prestys mowthe,   **govyn** given
55 In an howshold wer convertyd J[e]wys elevyn.   *in one household eleven Jews were converted*
At Rome this myracle ys knowen welle kowthe.

SECUNDUS. Thys marycle at Rome was presented, forsothe,
Yn the yere of our Lord, a thowsand fowr hundder sixty and on,   **on** one
That the Jewes with Holy Sa[c]rament dyd woth,   **dyd woth** did injury [to], harmed
60 In the forest seyd of Aragon.   *in the aforesaid forest of Aragon*

Loo, thus God at a tyme shouyd hym there,   **shouyd hym** showed himself
Thorwhe hys mercy and hys mekyll myght;   **Thorwhe** through; **myght** great power
Unto the Jewes he gan appere   **he gan appere** he did appear
That thei shuld nat lesse hys hevenly lyght.   **lesse** lose
65 PRIMUS. Therfor, frendys, with all your myght
Unto youer gostly father shewe your synne;   **gostly father** spiritual father [i.e., confessor]
Beth in no wanhope daye nor nyght.   *do not despair, either by day or night*
No maner off dowghtys that Lord put in.   *do not call that Lord into any kind of doubt*

For that the dowghtys the Jewys than in stode   *for the doubts the Jews had then*
70 As ye shall se pleyd, both more and lesse,   *as you shall see performed, in every detail*
Was yff the Sacrament were flessche and blode;   **yff** whether
Therfor they put yt to suche dystresse.   **put yt** subjected it
SECUNDUS. And yt place yow, thys gaderyng that here ys,
At Croxston on Monday yt shall be sen;   **Croxston** Croxton
75 To see the conclusyon of this lytell processe   **processe** performance
Hertely welcum shall yow bene.

Now Jhesu yow sawe from trey and tene;   **sawe** save; **tene** suffering and pain
He send us hys hyhe joyes of hevyne;   **He send us** may he send us
There myght ys withouton mynd to mene.
80 Now, mynstrell, blow up with a mery stevyn.

Explicit   **Explicit** end

1   *PRIMUS VEXILLATOR* first banner-bearer

3   **Save . . . moste** may he save all these worthy people, both the humblest and the greatest ∫ **all** inserted above the line with a caret

4   **bryne** bring. This may be a genuine form or a scribal error (Davis 1970, lxxix). ∫ **hath yow to bowght** has bought for you

7   **wrowght** The *ro* is above the line, replacing two illegible letters crossed through.

7–8 **Off the marvellys . . . sacrament** Late medieval lay devotion to the Sacrament of the Mass (which was vigorously promoted by the church, especially after the introduction of the feast of Corpus Christi in the late thirteenth century) brought with it many accounts of miracles associated with the host (see, e.g., Rubin 1991, 108–29; Bynum 1987). These emphasized both the reality of the Sacrament and the need to show it reverence. For the church's attempts to protect the host and wine and impose uniformity in how they were produced, consecrated, and guarded, see Rubin 1991, chaps. 1–2.

8   **blyssed** MS *blbyssed,* with second *b* blotted

9   **Sovereyns, and yt** sirs, if it (MS *Svereyns*)

10 **ys** editorial addition; not in MS ∫ **representyd** This refers not only to the staging of a play but may have a legal connotation: to take an offender or prisoner into legal custody (*MED: representen* 16; see Lerer 1996, 50). Perhaps the audience is invited to think of the play as staging a legal action to which they will be witnesses.

11 **Aragon** Medieval Europe's most deeply entrenched Jewish community was in Spain, where Jews lived alongside Muslims and Arabs until they were expelled in 1492 (Chazan 1980, 319). Although it is the merchant, not the Jew, who comes from Aragon, it is probable that Spain provided a mythically appropriate setting for the play's representation of Jewish "heresy."

12 **Eraclea** There are apparently no other medieval examples of this name. One possibility is that the name was derived from the emperor Heraclius, whose statue features in a tale of Christian origin concerning the differing significance of representation for Christians and Muslims (Camille 1989, 150). The associations of Heraclius's name may have been considered appropriate for a play concerned to define the meaning of the central Christian image of "corpus Christi."

16 **fer** inserted above the line with a caret

17 **hym** HS *hyn*

18 **for the nonys** The phrase "for the nonce," like "aryght" (12) or "on grownd" (37), is conventionally known as a tag, a common feature in a variety of late medieval verse texts. Apparently used to fulfill alliterative, metrical, or rhyming requirements, tags have sometimes been explained as

empty clichés. However, their use not only signals a particular mode of address to the audience (they are typical of "oral" or "popular" styles of poetry), but can also convey specific meanings or be exploited for ironic effect (see 37n for an example).

19 **the syte of Surrey** the city of Syria. Compare the use of "Surrye" (Syria) as a typically "Oriental" location in Chaucer's *Man of Law's Tale* II (B) 134, where it is associated (as in *Croxton*) with the exotic and the "other," a place of fabulous wealth and home of the Saracens. In Chaucer's text the Muslim "Sowdan" (sultan) lives there. Camille notes, however, that in the later Middle Ages "Jews and Muslims were inextricably linked together in the consciousness of Christians" (Camille 1989, 164); this might explain why the Jew in *Croxton* is represented as coming from a Muslim country. ∫ **this full trewe** this is the honest truth

20 **The wyche hade gret plente** written above the line, where the scribe had originally written, and then crossed through, the first four words of the next line, that is, "Off this Cristen merchaunte"

21 **freyned** MS *freynend*

23 **Twenti pownd** MS *xxti. li*

27 **hundder pownd** MS *cf.li* (the *f* is clearly an error). The expansion given here is based on the written-out occurrence of the phrase at 58.

30 **bey** MS *bye*

31 **the[y]** MS *thei*. The plural pronoun refers to the Jews in general, of whom the Syrian Jew is a representative. ∫ **wolde** MS *woldr*

33 **the sothe to sey** to tell the truth

34 **the** MS with illegible letter above *th*, crossed through ∫ **made hym delyveraunce** Although the primary meaning here is that the merchant hands over the Sacrament to the Jew (*MED: maken deliveraunce: deliveraunce* 4[a]), there may also be a pun on "redemption" (*MED: deliveraunce* 1[a]), anticipating the role of the Sacrament later in the play in redeeming and converting the Jews.

35 **made** the *d* written over a previous *y*

37 **on grownd** perhaps an ironic reference to the Jews' inability to conceptualize Christ's body except as a material object "on the earth" or to the practice, most vividly presented in the York *Crucifixion* pageant, of torturing Christ while he lay stretched out on the ground on the cross

38 **new** MS *nell* ∫ **new passyoun** The Jews make Christ suffer again, repeating the torments heaped upon him by their ancestors. The play offers a spectacle of Christ's second Passion in a spirit not simply of anti-Semitism (although anti-Semitism is assumed as the correct attitude for Christians throughout the play) but of devotion: compare, for example, Julian of Norwich's desire to be present at the Passion (excerpt 1.13a), or the exercises in

which Christ's sufferings are made real for the meditator described in *Speculum Devotorum* or Nicholas Love's *Mirror* (excerpts 1.12, 3.10).

39 hym The first scribal hands ends.

41 sownde whole, unbroken. Davis (1970) glosses this as "salutary," but the meaning "unbroken," attested by the *MED*, would seem to fit the context better, since what is principally at stake in the Jews' torture is the ability of the bread/body of Christ to remain whole, whatever is done to it.

42 boyle MS *boylde*

46 ovyn MS *ob ovyn*

48 rofe asondre shattered in pieces ∫ **all tobrast** burst apart completely

49 our lawe our religion, that is, the Christian religion, as opposed to the Jewish faith. The latter is also described, by one of the Jews, as "owr law" later in the play (415). ∫ **stedfast** firm in belief

55 convertyd MS reading is difficult. Davis reads *counteryd*, which is just possible. ∫ **J[e]wys elevyn** MS *J wyll wys xj*, with *wyll* partially crossed through. Davis's emended reading is *iwys*.

56 At Rome ... kowthe this story of a miracle is very well known at Rome [that is, it has been formally confirmed by the church] ∫ **this** MS *th this*

57 presented formally reported ∫ **forsothe** indeed

58 our MS *your* ∫ **thowsand fowr hundder sixty and on** MS *Mlcccc.c.lxj*, with the fifth *c* subpuncted for erasure

59 woth MS abbreviation for *with*

61 Loo MS *be* (crossed through) *loo thy*

63 gan MS *gayn*

65 Therfor MS *th* (crossed through) *therfor*

73 And yt place yow if it shall please you ∫ **gaderyng** audience

74 Croxston There are numerous Croxtons in East Anglia: several in Norfolk, on the border with Suffolk, and others in Lincolnshire and Cambridgeshire (Davis 1970, lxxxiv–lxxxv). As a likely origin for the play Davis suggests the Thetford area, which also has connections with the important market town of Bury St. Edmunds (Beckwith 1992b, 70).

75 processe generally a narrative, but here it seems to have the more specific sense of a "play" or "performance" (*MED: proces* 4). Lerer (1996, 50) draws attention to the word's legal connotations: the proceedings of a legal action or a suit (see 10). "Conclusyon" also has a legal sense: judgment, or the outcome of a legal action (on the theatrics of lawcourts, see Enders 1992).

77 from MS *fron* ∫ **trey** MS *treyn* ∫ **trey and tene** a set alliterative phrase

78 hyhe joyes of hevyne written above the line, where the scribe had originally written, and then crossed through, the last four words of the next line, that is, "withouton mynd to mene"

79 There ... mene where there is might that is beyond the power of the intellect to utter ∫ **ys** MS *ys* (crossed through) *ys*

80 blow up with a mery stevyn sound your instrument with a merry sound ∫ **up** MS *p* (crossed through) *up*

2.15 SOUTH ENGLISH LEGENDARY: PROLOGUE

Date and Provenance: c. 1270–85; southwest Midlands (possibly Worcester).

Author, Sources, and Nature of Text: The *South English Legendary* is an anonymous encyclopedic compilation of short narratives of saints' lives arranged according to the order in which their feast days occur during the church year. The genre to which it belongs is known as the *sanctorale* (i.e., sermons on saints), although in its scope the *Legendary* far exceeds homiletic *sanctorale* compilations such as John Mirk's *Festial* (1390s). The *Legendary* also includes scriptural material and narratives of the life of Christ (i.e., the *temporale*). The text draws material from many sources, including the *Legenda aurea* (Golden legend) of the Dominican Jacobus de Voragine (c.

1228–98). Written as both a Christian and a nationalist enterprise, the text includes a number of specifically English saints (e.g., Thomas à Becket of Canterbury, Kenelm of Mercia, Frideswide of Oxford, and Edward the Confessor). The proportion of native English saints rises in fifteenth-century manuscripts of the *Legendary*, suggesting not only that the material could be varied to suit local cults of saints but that the text continued to be a focus for nationalist, as well as devotional, impulses. The *Legendary* thus shares concerns with other medieval "historical" narratives that deal with lineage, transmission, nationalist regeneration, and community identities. For example, it has been suggested that it shows affinities with romance (Speed 1994, 143), while its account of Christian history as the continuous growth of a plant nurtured by the triumphant evangelism of the saints somewhat resembles secular narratives based on the topos of *translatio imperii* (the transferal of empire; see, e.g., excerpt 1.7, Lydgate's *Troy Book,* and the discussion of this topos in the section "The Distinctiveness of Vernacular Theory" in essay 4.1, pages 317–20). Its high proportion of retellings of anti-Semitic stories perhaps registers anxieties during the period immediately preceding the expulsion of Jews from England in 1290 (for documentation of the event, see Chazan 1980, 317–18). Though the image of Christ as knight is a topos of religious writing, the crusades may also resonate in the prologue's representation of the historical extension of the empire of Christendom as a military campaign led by Christ and his saints. The poem is written in septenary rhyming couplets, usually with four and three stresses on either side of the caesura (which is marked in some manuscripts by a point [*punctum* or *punctus elevatus*]). There is a freely distributed and variable number of unstressed syllables (so that the lines may be as short as nine and as long as fifteen syllables). The stressed syllables are not normally highlighted by any pattern of alliteration: the *South English Legendary* uses alliterative phrases sporadically for rhetorical emphasis, but not as a constituent element of its verse. This meter is a flexible narrative form, open in performance to a great deal of variety and emphasis, and one widely distributed and long used in medieval England.

Audience and Circulation: The *Legendary* was probably written for a broadly conceived audience that included secular readers and listeners, female religious, and others. Unlike other large-scale Middle English religious works from the early fourteenth century (such as the *Northern Homily Cycle* and *Cursor Mundi,* excerpts 2.1, 3.14), it contains no discussion of its audience, purpose, or language. Sixty-two manuscript copies of the collection survive in a variety of dialects, most of them dating from the fourteenth century, indicating a remarkably wide diffusion for a vernacular text (see Görlach 1974; Speed 1994, 143); there are also many fragments, selections, and adap-

tations. Indeed, the *Legendary* seems to have been the most widely distributed Middle English work before *The Prick of Conscience* (c. 1350; see excerpt 3.7) and Langland's *Piers Plowman* (1370s–80s; see excerpt 3.19) and must in some sense have been an officially promoted text, widely used to aid in the celebration of the feasts of the saints and as an instrument of lay education. The Cambridge manuscript from which the prologue is edited here has annotations in a sixteenth-century hand, which may be that of Archbishop Parker, a leading figure in the English Reformation, who presented the manuscript to Corpus Christi College. The prologue, which sometimes precedes and sometimes follows other material from the *Legendary,* is found only in the early-fourteenth-century manuscripts, some of which entitle it *Banna Sanctorum* (The banns of the saints), as if it were the proclamation of a play (see previous excerpt), or a procession. Thomas Liszka (1985, 1992) has argued that the prologue was originally written as a transition from *temporale* to *sanctorale* sections of the *Legendary,* with the complete work structured as a Rogationtide procession of God's earthly army (the church militant) into battle alongside "Christ's knights" (the saints, otherwise known as the church triumphant). For an account of the contents of *South English Legendary* manuscripts, see Manfred Görlach's important study (1974).

Bibliography: The text is edited by Carl Horstmann (1887) and by Charlotte d'Evelyn and Anne Mill (1956), with notes in a separate volume by d'Evelyn (1959). Various critical studies, chiefly literary-historical, include Braswell 1964, Pickering 1996, Görlach 1974, Samson 1986, and Jankofsky 1992. There are brief but useful comments in Speed 1994.

Source: Cambridge, Corpus Christi College MS 145, fols. 1r–1v: a decorated, clearly written, and carefully corrected early-fourteenth-century parchment book. An inscription on fol. 1v–2r suggests that the book belonged to the priory of Augustinian canons at Southwick, Hampshire, in the late fourteenth or early fifteenth century and was the gift of John Kateryngton, a canon there. In the manuscript the verse lines are divided by a raised point, reproduced here.

Nou blouweth the niwe frut · that late bygan to springe,
That to is kunde eritage · mankunne schel bringe.
This nyuwe frut of wan ich speke · is oure Cristendom
That late was an eorthe ysouwe · and later forth it com.
5 So hard and luther was the lond · on wan it ssolde sprynge,
That wel unnethe eny more · me myghte theron bringe.
God him was the gardiner · that gan ferst the sed souwe,
That was Jesus, Godes sone, · that tharefore alyghte louwe.
They he seuwe that sed himsulf, · so hard was mannes thoght
10 That ar it were with reyn ysprengd · hit ne might morie noght.
With a swete reines deu · he sprengde this harde more
With is swete herte blod · and yaf is lyf therfore.
Derworthe was the swete blod · that it was with ysprengd;
Atte laste with is herte blod · ther com out water ymengd.
15 Tho bigan this nyuwe sed · somdel to cacche more,
Ac yute after this many man · his blod ssadde thervore.
Verst the martir Seinte Stevene · and the appostles that were ded,
That hare blod and hare lyf yaf · to norisschi that swete sed
And this other martirs ek · that oure Louerdes knyghtes were
20 That schadde hare blod for Cristendom, · that it yperissed nere.
The bataille was strang inou · that oure swete Louerd nom,
And his deciples suththe abrod · to hold up Cristendom.
Wanne a kyng wole bataille nyme · to holde up is righte,
He ordeineth verst is ost · and yarketh hem to fighte.
25 Byvore he set is alblasters · and is archers also,
Is trompours to scheuwe wat he is, · and is baner therto.
And if the kyng thanne aredy is, · mid the veorste he wole be[o]
Vorto hardie al is men · that non ne scholde fle.
Thanne mot in the rerewarde · hardy knightes wende
30 Hare louerdes right to holde up · and the bataille bringe to ende.
And if hi beoth couwardes in hare dede, · the bataille is al ilore.
In this manere oure swete Louerd · an eorthe was ibore
For to byginne Cristendom, · and sette ferst the more.
His trompours and is alblasters · he sette verst byvore,
35 The prophetes and is patriarks · that longe byvore hym wende,
To telle men that he wolde come, · here stat for to amende.
Therof hadde here vomen hoker · and to busmare ham louwe
And tormentede ham swuthe stronge · and to gronde ham slowe
Suththe oure swete Louerd himsulf · to this bataille alyghte
40 And nam mannes fleyss and blod · in wan he wolde fighte.
This bataille nolde he noght byginne, · ne is baner arere,
Ar he hadde fleissis strengthe · and ar he fol woxe were.
He was nyne and twenty yer · ar he armede hym therto,
Ar he bygonne [for] Cristendom · this bataille for to do.
45 Tho let he ym army feorst · tho he was vol woxe man,
Tho he aveng oure Cristendom · in the flum Jordan.
His cosyn Sein Jon the Baptist · armed hym tho there,
Anon as an hardy kyng · his baner lette arere.

Sein Jon was is baneour, · and is baner bar byvore
50 And faste faght as an hardy knight · forte is lif was ilore.
Tho the baneour was aslauwe, · the kyng ne dradde noght;
In this bataille he wende anon · vorte he to dethe was ibroght.
And yute, for al is strange deth, · ilore he hadde is righte
Yif is knightes of the rerewarde · the strengore [ne] couthe fighte.
55 Of here louerd ensample inome, · and flecchi nolde hi noght,
The apostles ne the martirs, · ar hy were to dethe ibroght.
Wel aghte we lovie Cristendom · that is dure iboght
With oure Louerd is heorte blod · that the sper hath ysoght.
Men wilneth muche to hure telle · of bataille of kynge
60 And of knyghtes that hardy were, · that muchedel is lesynge.
Woso wilneth muche to hure · tales of suche thinge,
Hardi batailles he may hure here, · that nis no lesinge,
Of apostles and martirs · that hardy knightes were
That studevast were in batailles · and ne fleide noght for fere,
65 That soffrede that luther men · al quik hare lymes to tere.
Telle ichelle bi reuwe of ham · as hare dai valth in the yere.
Verst bygynneth at Yeres day, · for that is the verste feste
And fram onto other so areng, · the wile the yer wol leste.

1–2 On manuscript titles for the prologue, see Liszka 1985, 408. ∫ **Nou blouweth . . . schel bringe** now the new fruit that recently started to grow is flowering ["blouweth"], that fruit which will bring humanity ["mankunne"] to its natural heritage. The "new fruit" is glossed in line 3 as "Cristendom," but it might equally refer to Christ himself. The image of the redemptive Christ as a symbol of spring and of the renewal of the natural world is a medieval commonplace, as in the well-known lyric "I sing of a maiden" (Brown and Robbins 1943, no. 1367) and the prologue to the *Northern Homily Cycle* (excerpt 2.1: 3–10). Where the *Northern Homily Cycle* praises God's creation, and humanity as a supreme example of that creation, the *South English Legendary* focuses on the redemption of sinful humanity (8–12), an introductory move that perhaps aligns the vernacular with narratives of inclusive salvation (see Watson 1997b for an exploration of this theme in other texts).

3 **of wan ich speke** of which I speak

4 **That late . . . forth it com** which was recently sown here on earth and more recently it bloomed

5 **luther** evil ∫ **on wan it ssolde sprynge** on which it had to grow

6 **That wel . . . bringe** that one could scarcely succeed in getting any root to take hold in it

7 **God him was the gardiner** For the topos of God as gardener, see especially Julian of Norwich, *Revelation of Love* Long Text chap. 51 (excerpt 3.4), and Langland, *Piers Plowman* B XVI (both conceivably influenced by this passage). For the preacher as a gardener, see *The Orchard of Syon*

(excerpt 3.5). The topos has roots in various biblical passages, including John 15:1–11 (the true vine) and Matt. 13:1–9 (the parable of the sower). ∫ **that gan ferst the sed souwe** who first sowed the seed

8 **That was Jesus** which was Jesus ∫ **alyghte louwe** came down to earth

9 **They he seuwe that sed himsulf** although he sowed that seed himself ∫ **hard** obdurate

10 **ar it were . . . morie noght** until it had been sprinkled ["ysprengd"] with rain, it could not take root

11 **deu** dew ∫ **harde more** hard root

12 **is his** ∫ **herte blod** heart's blood ∫ **yaf is lyf therfore** gave his life for it

13 **Derworthe** precious ∫ **that it was with ysprengd** that it was sprinkled with

14 **Atte laste** finally ∫ **blod . . . water ymengd** blood mingled with water. See John 19:34 (also 58 below). Here, unusually, the water John describes as flowing from Christ's side with his blood is treated as the more important of the two liquids, whose dispersal into the world is indeed the climax of Christ's redemptive mission, since water is essential for any plant's survival.

15 **Tho bigan . . . more** then this new seed began a little to take root

16 **Ac** but ∫ **yute** still ∫ **many man · his blod ssadde thervore** many a man shed his blood for it. That is, many a Christian martyr gave his or her life for the sake of Christ.

17 **Verst** first ∫ **Seinte Stevene** Saint Stephen: the first Christian martyr, whose death by stoning is re-

corded in Acts 7:54–60 ∫ that were ded who died

18 That hare blod . . . sed who gave their blood and their life to nourish that sweet seed

19 this these ∫ ek also ∫ that oure Louerdes who were our Lord's

20 schadde shed ∫ that it yperissed nere so that it would never die

21 The bataille was strang inou the battle was fierce enough. On Christ's death on the cross as a battle, a topos that goes back at least as far as the Old English *Dream of the Rood*, see *Piers Plowman* B XVIII. ∫ nom engaged in

22 suththe afterward ∫ abrod [journeyed] widely

23 bataille nyme engage in battle ∫ holde up is righte uphold his right

24 He ordeineth . . . fighte he first arranges his troops in battle formation and prepares them for fighting

25 Byvore . . . archers also in the front line he places his soldiers armed with crossbows ["alblasters": bowmen] and his archers too

26 Is trompours . . . therto his trumpet blowers to show what kind of person he is, and his standard also

27 And if the kyng . . . wole be[o] and if the king is then ready, he will be among the first ["veorste"], that is, in the front line (MS be[erasure])

28 Vorto hardie . . . fle to make all his men bold so that none of them should flee

29 Thanne mot then must ∫ rerewarde rearguard ∫ wende go

30 Hare louerdes right to holde up to uphold their lord's right

31 hi beoth couwardes they are cowards ∫ hare dede their deeds ∫ ilore lost

32 an eorthe was ibore on earth was born

33 For to byginne in order to establish ∫ sette ferst the more first set the root

34 His trompours . . . byvore he placed his trumpet blowers and his crossbowmen first in the front

35 The prophetes . . . hym wende who were the prophets and his patriarchs who long ago went before him. The Old Testament prophets and patriarchs, such as Isaiah, are imagined as corresponding to the men placed in the front line of an army.

36 here stat for to amende to make their condition better

37 Therof hadde . . . louwe for that reason their enemies ["vomen"] had contempt ["hoker"] and degraded them in shame ["to busmare"]

38 swuthe stronge very harshly ∫ to gronde ham slowe struck them down

39 alyghte entered into

40 And nam mannes fleyss For the treatment of the doctrine of the Incarnation as Christ arming

himself with human flesh and blood, see Bozon's "Coment le fiz Deu fu armé" (Jeffrey and Levy 1990, 186–91) and the extraordinarily dynamic account in *Piers Plowman* B XVI–XVIII. ∫ nam took ∫ in wan he wolde in which he wanted to

41 nolde he noght he would not ∫ ne is baner arere nor raise up his banner

42 Ar before ∫ fleissis strengthe bodily strength ∫ fol woxe fully grown

43 He was nyne . . . therto he was twenty-nine years old before he armed himself for it

44 Ar he bygonne before he began ∫ [for] Cristendom MS *Cristendom* ∫ this bataille for to do to fight this battle

45 Tho let . . . woxe man then he allowed himself to be first armed when he was a fully grown man

46 aveng received ∫ flum river

47 armed hym tho there then armed him there

48 Anon . . . arere at once like a bold king he had his standard raised

49 is baneour his standard-bearer ∫ bar byvore carried ahead of him

50 faste faght fiercely fought ∫ forte is lif was ilore until his life was lost

51 Tho when ∫ was aslauwe was slain ∫ ne dradde noght was not afraid

52 wende anon · vorte he to dethe was ibroght entered soon before he was killed

53 And yute . . . righte and yet, for all his hard death, he would have lost his right

54 Yif is knightes . . . couthe fighte if his knights on the rear guard had not been able to fight more strongly ∫ [ne] couthe MS *couthe*

55 Of here louerd . . . noght they [i.e., the apostles and martyrs of 56] followed the example of their lord, and would not waver ["flecchi"] ∫ inome taken (perhaps in error for *thei nome*: "they took") (MS *Inome*)

56 ne nor ∫ ar hy were to dethe ibroght before they met their death

57 Wel aghte . . . iboght well ought we to love Christendom that is dearly bought

58 Louerd is heorte blod Lord's heart blood ∫ the sper See John 19:34, the basis of the legend of the blind centurian Longinus alluded to here and dramatized in *Piers Plowman* B XVIII.78.ff. ∫ hath ysoght had reached

59 Men wilneth . . . bataille people desire greatly to hear tell of battle ∫ Men wilneth impersonal: "one desires"

60 that muchedel is lesynge the greater part of which is fictitious

61 Woso wilneth muche to hure whoever wishes greatly to hear

62 Hardi batailles . . . no lesinge he may hear bold battles here, and that's no lie

63 **that hardy knightes were** who were bold knights

64 **That studevast . . . for fere** who were steadfast in battles and did not flee from fear

65 **That soffrede that luther men · al quik hare lymes to tere** who allowed evil men to tear apart their limbs while alive ["quik"]

66 **ichelle** I will ∫ **bi reuwe** in order ∫ **hare dai valth** their day occurs

67 **Verst bygynneth . . . verste feste** first it begins at New Year's Day, for that is the first feast day

68 **And fram . . . yer wol leste** and so on, one following another, throughout the whole year; "areng" is an adverb meaning "in a row, one after the other." The choice of this adverb (which is related to *arengen:* "to draw up in ranks or a line of battle") suggests a link between Christ's action of drawing up his soldiers in battle order and the arrangement of saints' lives in this *sanctorale* collection. Implicitly, this prologue constructs the book itself as an arrangement of fighting men.

2.16 WILLIAM CAXTON, TRANSLATION OF GEOFFROY DE LA TOUR-LANDRY, *BOOK OF THE KNIGHT OF THE TOWER:* PROLOGUE

Date and Provenance: 1484; Westminster (near London).

Author, Sources, and Nature of Text: The *Book of the Knight of the Tower* is Caxton's translation of a French deportment book written in 1371–72 by a knight, the fourth Geoffroy de la Tour-Landry, for his daughters. It belongs to the popular late medieval genre of "courtesy literature": handbooks of practical and morally edifying advice about social behavior. The knight's French text and Caxton's English translation are unusual: most didactic literature of this period written and read in England, whether in Latin, French, or English, is addressed to boys and men (Riddy 1996a). Addressed to the knight's daughters, the *Book*'s exempla are of good and bad women, largely drawn from the Bible. Although the knight refers (78) to a book he has made for his sons, this volume (if it was ever written) has not yet come to light (Offord 1971, 197). The popularity and wide European circulation of the knight's book throughout the medieval period and up to the nineteenth century is attested by the twenty-one extant manuscripts, together with one manuscript of an anonymous English translation (1422–61) made during the reign of Henry VI (Wright 1868) and also a German version, *Der Ritter vom Turn,* first published in Basle in 1493 and reprinted many times up to 1850. There are also French printed versions from 1514. Although Caxton did not always perfectly understand the French he was translating, he did sometimes deliberately intervene to abridge or shape the material. The text's domestic ethos, couched in the form of a knight's advice to his daughter, suggests that the work might have appealed to an English gentry and bourgeois audience (both male and female) on two levels: to their social aspirations and to their desire to control not only daughters but servant girls within the regime of the household (Riddy 1996a).

Audience and Circulation: Six copies and one fragment of Caxton's translation survive. There is no specific dedicatee of the translation, and its late-fifteenth-century readership is uncertain (Belyea 1981), although Caxton's reading public to a considerable extent consisted of London urban elites for whom the household ideology of this text would have been particularly suitable. The reasons for Caxton's choice of this text for translation are unknown, although it is reasonable to assume that, as with his translation of de Pizan's *Book of Fayttes and Armes* (see excerpt 2.10), he was setting out to create a market in England for texts that were fashionable at the Burgundian court.

Bibliography: The *Book* is edited by M. Y. Offord (1971). On the French sources, see Grigsby 1963. Roberta Krueger (1993) offers a feminist analysis of la Tour-Landry's text. For discussion of medieval courtesy literature, see Nicholls 1985, 7–74; for that directed at women, see Hull 1982; Bornstein 1983; Ashley 1987; Riddy 1996a. For other editions of deportment literature, see Power 1928 and Furnivall 1868. On Caxton as author, see Blake 1986 and 1996. For the reading programs for women advocated by the Knight of the Tower, see Meale 1996c, 1–2.

Source: London, British Library IB.55085, Air–Aiir (*STC* 15296), compared with another copy of the same edition, Oxford, Bodleian Library Arch.G.d.13 (3), fols. 118r–19v. The Oxford copy is substantially the same as the British Library one, but has several additional final *es* (e.g., *whiche*). This folio volume was printed (with somewhat irregular spacing) by William Caxton in Westminster, January 31, 1484. The book is described by Offord (1971, xi–xv); it also contains a *Distychs of Cato*, Chaucer's *Boece* followed by a Latin epitaph for Chaucer, and *Aesop's Fables*.

Here begynneth the book whiche the Knyght of the Toure made, and speketh of many fayre ensamples and th'ensygnementys and techyng of his doughters.

Prologue

5 [I]n the yere of oure Lord a M thre honderd lxxi, as I was in a gardyn under a shadowe, as it were, in th'yssue of Aprylle all moornyng and pensyf, but a lytel I rejoysed me in the sowne and songe of the fowles sauvage whiche songe in theyr langage, as the merle, the mavys, the thrustell, and the nyghtyngale whiche were gay and lusty. This swete songe enlustyed me and made myn herte all t'enjoye, so that thenne I wente remembryng of the tyme passed in my youthe, how Love hadde holde me in that tyme in his servyce by grete distresse in which I was many an houre gladde and joyeful, and many another tyme sorowful, lyke as it doth to many a lover. But alle myn evylles have rewarded me sythe that the fayre and good hath gyven to me, whiche hath knowleche of alle honoure, alle good and fayre mayntenyng. And of alle good she semed me the best and the floure, in whome I so moche me delyted. For in that tyme I made songes, layes, roundels, balades, vyrelayes, and newe songes, in the mooste best wyse I coude.

But the deth whiche spareth none hath taken her for whome I have receyved many sorowes and hevynesscs, in suche wyse that I have passed my lyf more than twenty yere hevy and sorowful. For the very herte of a trewe lover shall never in ony tyme ne day forgete good love but evermore shal remember it. And thus in that tyme as I was in a grete pensyfnes and thought, I behelde in the way and sawe my doughters comyng, of whome I hadde grete desyre that they shold torne to honoure above alle other thyng. For they ben yong and litil and dysgarnysshed of al wytte and reson, wherfor they ought at begynnyng to be taught and chastysed curtoisly by good ensamples and doctrynes as dide a quene—I suppose she was Quene of Hongry—whiche fayre and swetely chastysed her doughters and them endoctryned, as is conteyned in her book.

And therfor when I saw them come toward me I remembryd me of the tyme when I was yong and roode with my felauship and companyes in Poytou and in other places. And I remembre me moche wel of the fayttes and sayenges that they told of suche thynges as they fond with the ladyes and damoyselles that they requyred and prayd of love. And yf one wolde not entende to theyr prayer, yet

another wold requyre withoute abydyng. And though so were that they had good
35 or evyll answers, of al that they rought not. For they had neyther drede ne shame,
so moche were they endurate and acustomed, and were moche wel bespoken and
had fayre langage, for many tymes they wold have overal deduyte. And thus they
doo nothyng but deceyve good ladyes and damoysellys, and bere overall the
tydynges, somme trewe and somme lesynges, wherof there happed many tymes
40 injuryes and many vylaynous diffames withoute cause and withoute reason. And in
alle the world is no gretter treson than for to deceyve gentyll wymmen ne to
encrece ony vylaynous blame. For many ben deceyved by the grete othes that
they use, wherof I debate me oftyme with them, and saye to them, "Ye over-false
men, how may the goddes suffre yow to lyve that soo oftymes ye perjure and
45 forswere youreself, for ye hold no feythe?" But none putt hit in araye bycause they
be so moche and so ful of disaraye. And bycause I saw that tyme soo ledde and
disposed, yet I doute me that somme ben suche in this tyme present.

Therfore I concluded that I wold doo make a lytel booke wherin I wold doo be
wreton the good maners and good dedes of good ladyes and wymmen and of theyr
50 lyves, soo that for theyr vertues and bountees they ben honoured, and that after
theyr dethe ben renommed and preysed and shal be unto the ende of the worlde,
for to take of them good ensample and contenaunce. And also by the contrarye I
shall doo wryte and set in a book the myshappe and vyces of evylle wymmen
whiche have usyd theyr lyf and now have blame, to the ende that the evylle maye
55 bee eschewed by whiche they myght erre whiche yet ben blamed, shamed and
dyffamed.

And for this cause that I have here sayd, I have thought on my wel-bylovyd
doughters, whome I see so lytel, to make to them a litil book for to lerne to rede,
to th'ende that they maye lerne and studye and understonde the good and evylle
60 that is passyd, for to kepe them fro hym whiche is yet to come. For suche ther be
that lawgheth tofore yow whiche after youre back goo mockyng and lyeng,
wherfor it is an hard thyng to knowe the world that is now present.

And for these resons, as I have sayd, I went oute of the gardyn and fond in my
weye two preestes and two clerkes that I hadde, and tolde to them that I wolde
65 make a book and an examplayre for my doughters to lerne to rede and
understonde how they ought to governe themself and to kepe them from evylle.
And thenne I made them to come and rede before me the book of the Byble, the
gestes of the kynges, the cronycles of Fraunce and of Englond, and many other
straunge historyes, and made them to rede every book, and dyde doo make of
70 them this book, whiche I wold not set in ryme but al along in prose for to abredge
and also for the better to be understonden, and also for the grete love that I have
to my doughters whom I love as a fader ought to love them. And thenne myn herte
shal have parfyte joye yf they torne to good and to honoure, that is, to serve and
love God and to have the love and the grace of their neyghbours and of the world.
75 And bycause every fader and moder after God and nature ought to teche and
enforme their children, and to distourne them fro the evyll waye and to shewe to
them the right weye and true pathe, as wel for the savacion of theyr sowles as for
th'onoure of the body erthely, I have made two bookes: that one for my sonnes,
and that other for my doughters, for to lerne to rede. And thus in lernynge hit
80 shalle not be but that they shalle reteyne somme good ensample, or for to flee the

evylle and reteyne the good, for it may not be but in somtyme they shal remembre somme good ensample or som good lore after that hit shalle falle and come to theyr mynde in spekyng upon this matere.

Thus endeth the prologue.

2   **speketh** it tells ∫ **fayre** pleasing ∫ **ensamples** exempla, illustrative cases ∫ **ensygnementys** precepts

5   **[I]n** space for an illuminated capital ∫ **a M thre honderd lxxi** 1371

5–6   **under a shadowe** in a shady spot (but the figurative sense of "shadow" is also present: "in gloom, with a shadow over me")

5–7   **as I was in a gardyn . . . but a lytel I rejoysed me** If "but" is an adversative conjunction here, as it is in the French source, and not the adverb "only," then the sentence changes construction after "as I was in a gardyn." Anacolutha (inconsistent grammatical constructions or syntax within a sentence) are not uncommon in Middle English (see especially excerpt 3.14), which anyway has a less fixed grammatical structure than Modern English.

6   **in th'yssue of** toward the end of ∫ **moornyng** sorrowful ∫ **a lytel** somewhat

7   **rejoysed me** delighted ∫ **sowne** sound ∫ **sauvage** wild ∫ **songe** sang

8   **as** namely ∫ **merle** blackbird ∫ **mavys** song thrush ∫ **thrustell** throstle

9   **lusty** merry ∫ **enlustyed** cheered ∫ **t'enjoye** to rejoice

10   **I wente remembryng of** I happened to remember. The French has *Il me va souvenir*: "the remembrance comes to me."

10–11   **how Love hadde holde me in that tyme in his servyce by grete distresse** how Love had kept me during that time in his service under great duress

12   **lyke as it doth** just as it [Love] does

13–15   **alle myn evylles . . . mayntenyng** all my sufferings have repaid me since the fair and good lady, who has knowledge of all honor, has bestowed on me a wholly good and fair demeanor. As Offord points out, this sentence is awkward and does not correspond exactly to the French source. If "the fayre and good" is the subject and "alle good and fayre mayntenyng" the object, the sentence makes good sense as a statement of the archetypal situation of the courtly lover, suffering the pains of love and idealizing his lady but finally rewarded for his service when she looks on him kindly.

14   **whiche** who

15   **mayntenyng** bearing ∫ **semed me** seemed to me

15–16   **in whome I so moche me delyted** she in whom I took so much delight

16   **in that tyme** at that time ∫ **layes** lays, short narrative poems ∫ **roundels** rondeaux: poems consisting of ten or thirteen lines, having only two rhymes throughout, and with the opening words used twice as a refrain ∫ **balades** ballades: poems consisting of triplets of seven-lined stanzas, each ending with the same line as the refrain and usually an envoi

17   **vyrelayes** virelays: short songs arranged in stanzas with only two rhymes, the end rhyme of one stanza being the chief one of the next ∫ **in the mooste best wyse I coude** as best I could. Compare Chaucer's Black Knight, *Book of the Duchess* 471–86, 1156–59.

18   **whiche spareth none** who spares nobody

19   **hevynesses** griefs ∫ **in suche wyse** in such a manner

20   **very** true

20–21   **in ony tyme ne day** at any time or on any day

22   **pensyfnes** state of thoughtfulness ∫ **behelde in the way** looked along the path

23   **of whome** for whom ∫ **torne** turn

24   **alle other thyng** everything else ∫ **ben** are ∫ **dysgarnysshed of** lacking in

25   **wytte** good sense ∫ **at begynnyng** from the beginning ∫ **chastysed** disciplined

26   **curtoisly** in a courteous manner ∫ **suppose** believe

27   **Quene of Hongry** This queen has not been firmly identified. She might have been Elizabeth of Bosnia (d. 1382), wife of Louis I of Hungary and Poland, who was known to have composed a deportment book for her daughters (Offord 1971, 195.11/31–32n) ∫ **whiche** who ∫ **fayre** pleasantly

27–28   **them endoctryned** instructed them

29   **remembryd me of** remembered. The verb is reflexive; compare French *je me souviens de.*

30   **felauship** comrades ∫ **companyes** [military] companies ∫ **Poytou** Poitou (Aquitaine, France): a place particularly associated in the Middle Ages with romantic love: see Bloch 1991.

31   **remembre me moche wel** remember very well ∫ **fayttes** deeds, behavior ∫ **sayenges** adages

32   **of** about ∫ **fond** experienced ∫ **damoyselles** young ladies (unmarried and aristocratic)

33 **requyred** importuned ∫ **prayd of** begged for ∫ **entende** pay attention to

33–34 **yet another wold requyre** yet another man would importune her

34 **abydyng** delay ∫ **though so were that** whether ∫ **good** favorable

35 **evyll** negative ∫ **of al that they rought not** they did not care about all that

36 **endurate** hardened ∫ **acustomed** used to it ∫ **moche wel bespoken** very eloquent

37 **wold** wished to ∫ **overal** above everything else (or perhaps "everywhere": Caxton's intended meaning is not clear) ∫ **deduyte** pleasure

38 **good** honest

38–39 **bere overall the tydynges** carry the gossip everywhere

39 **lesynges** lies ∫ **happed** arose

40 **injuryes** insults ∫ **vylaynous** despicable ∫ **diffames** slanders

41 **gentyll** aristocratic

41–42 **ne to encrece** or to add to

43 **wherof** for which reason ∫ **I debate me oftyme** I often argue. The imperfect tense in some versions of the French source suggests that the knight may be quoting what he said to his comrades. ∫ **over-false** exceedingly false

44 **goddes** that is, the pagan classical gods (associated with courtly love) ∫ **suffre** allow ∫ **that soo oftymes ye** you who so often

44–45 **perjure and forswere youreself** perjure and abjure yourselves

45 **ye hold no feythe** you are not loyal ∫ **putt hit in araye** put it in order, made amends for it ∫ **they** It is unclear whether this refers to the false men or their oaths.

46 **moche** many ∫ **disaraye** unmannerly behavior

46–47 **I saw that tyme soo ledde and disposed** I saw [such men] at that time so inclined and disposed [to that behavior]

47 **I doute me** I suspect ∫ **ben suche** are like that

48 **I wold doo make** I would have made

50 **soo that** how: renders French *si comme* ∫ **bountees** good qualities

51 **renommed** renowned

52 **for to take of them good ensample and contenaunce** in order that they might serve as a good example and pattern of conduct ∫ **by the contrarye** in opposition to this

53 **set in a book** For a work of the kind envisaged by the knight, see excerpt 2.17. ∫ **myshappe** wrongdoings

54 **usyd** misspent ∫ **have blame** receive censure

55 **eschewed** avoided

55–56 **by whiche they myght . . . shamed and dyffamed** in the paths of which [evil] those women

who are nevertheless censured, shamed, and slandered might err. That is, those who are pure but who nevertheless get censured may be able to avoid evil. The clause translates "ou l'en pourrait erre come celles qui encore sont blasmees" (Offord 1971, 196.12/33–34n).

57 **cause** reason ∫ **that I have here sayd** which I have just spoken about ∫ **thought on** carefully thought about

58 **whome I see so lytel** who appear to me so small ∫ **for to lerne to rede** to learn to read (i.e., the deportment book will also serve as a primer)

60 **fro hym** from that

60–61 **suche ther be that** there are men who

61 **lawgheth tofore yow** laugh pleasantly in your presence ∫ **after** behind

62 **the world that is now present** the current state of the world

63–72 **And for these resons . . . to love them** A semidramatized vernacular account of compilation and its contributory agents and processes authorizes the knight's text. Compare the account of Bonaventure, cited in the Introduction to Part One, page 3, and that of Bokenham, excerpt 1.11: 1–24. See also the *Cyrurgie*, excerpt 1.10.

63–64 **fond in my weye** came across

64 **two preestes and two clerkes that I hadde** two priests and two scholars that were in my household ∫ **tolde to them** explained to them

65 **examplayre** exemplar: a book containing examples to learn from and follow

67 **them** that is, the priests and scholars ∫ **before me** in my presence ∫ **the book of the Byble** Various books of the Bible circulated in French versions, but the reference here is probably to a collection of exempla, the *Miroir des bonnes femmes,* drawn from the Bible and other sources (Offord 1971, xxxix–xl).

68 **gestes** deeds

69–70 **dyde doo make of them this book** had them [the priests] make this book. It is unclear whether "of" should be read as "by" or "from" here: if the latter, the phrase would mean "had [them] make this book from them [the source books]."

70 **set in ryme** compose in verse ∫ **al along in prose** in prose throughout. The remark that the book proper will be composed in prose may be explained by the fact that there are traces of rhyming couplets in the French (Offord 1971, 197.13/11n), suggesting that most of the prologue was originally written in verse. ∫ **for to abredge** in order to condense it

73 **torne** turn

74 **to have** to gain ∫ **grace** goodwill

75 **after** in accordance with

76 **enforme** instruct ∫ **distourne them** turn them
aside
77 **as wel for** as much for ∫ **savacion** salvation
78 **erthely** mortal
78–79 **that one . . . that other** the one . . . the
other
79–80 **hit shalle not be but** that is, it must come
to pass
80 **reteyne** remember ∫ **or for to flee** or that they
may flee from

81 **for it may not be but** for it can only happen
that ∫ **in somtyme** within a period of time
82 **lore** teaching
82–83 **after that hit shalle . . . matere** As Offord
notes, Caxton's version differs from the French
source here; the sense as he has translated it means
something like "if it should so happen that such
things should come to mind when they come to be
speaking about this matter."

2.17 *SPEKTAKLE OF LUF:* PROLOGUE

Date and Provenance: 1492; southeast Scotland, perhaps St. Andrews: the text refers to
Sandris as the place of its composition (fol.
150), although this could refer to the diocese
of St. Andrews, which contained other towns
and cities, including Edinburgh.

Author, Sources, and Nature of Text: The
Spektakle of Luf purports to be a translation of
an unidentified Latin text. At its conclusion, the
translator is presented (in the manner of
Gower's Amans in the *Confessio Amantis,* excerpt 2.11) as a superannuated clerk and
beadsman of Venus's court no longer able to
perform "the service that I had bene accustomyd
to do" (Craigie 1923, 297). Like the previous
excerpt (2.16), this is an example of didactic
courtesy literature, and its address to a boy is
the most common one for this genre (Riddy
1996a). Taking the familiar form of a knight's
advice to "a young squyer his sone," the text is
related to the "mirror for princes" tradition
(Ferster 1996). However, as the chapter headings given here show, it is partially structured as
a penitential, listing various forbidden acts—
such as "the delectatioun of luf with uther
mennis wyffis" (13–14)—and offering caution-
ary exempla. For all its apologies to women (see
39–41n below), the text is highly misogynist;
like the book read to the Wife of Bath by her
clerical husband, Jankyn, or the book envisaged
by the Knight of the Tower (see excerpt 2.16:
52–56), the *Spektakle* is little more than a catalogue of dangerous "wicked wives" and
"wicked women" who lure men into commit-
ting acts of "delectation." For the generic
context, see Blamires 1992, which amply demonstrates both the extensiveness of misogynist

material in medieval literature and the extent to
which this material tended to become contested
once it entered the vernacular, the "matarnall
toung" (27), in which it was available to women
and married men as well as to clerics.

Audience and Circulation: The "G. Myll"
whose name is given at the end of this translation (if indeed it is a translation, which seems
open to question; see 25n) may be the scribe and
not the author or translator (we are indebted to
Priscilla Bawcutt for this information). Nothing is known about the circulation of the text
before its inclusion in Asloan's early-sixteenth-
century anthology. John Asloan (or Sloane), a
notary public active in Edinburgh between
1497 and 1530, copied out this manuscript (ex-
cepting the *Spektakle*) and one other, Oxford,
Bodleian Library MS Douce 148 (a copy of
Lydgate's *Troy Book,* see excerpt 1.7; van
Buuren-Veenenbos 1982, 26). Asloan's anthology is a miscellany, containing devotional and
penitential prose treatises, a portion of Trevisa's
translation of Higden's *Polychronicon* (see excerpt 2.2), English and Scottish chronicles in
verse, and numerous shorter verses or extracts,
including items by Dunbar and Lydgate as well
as some of Henryson's *Fables* (see excerpt 3.18);
thirty-four items listed by Asloan have not survived. It appears to have been largely, but not
exclusively, a consciously nationalist compilation, reflecting Scottish interests and authors;
some of the pieces (especially the prose items)
survive only in this manuscript.

Bibliography: Edited by W. A. Craigie
(1923), the text has attracted little scholarly attention. For a description of the manuscript,
see van Buuren-Veenenbos 1982, 5–12, and for

its contents and the dates of all extant items, van Buuren-Veenenbos 1982, 414–19. An unpublished typescript catalogue in the National Library of Scotland provides much additional information. For further accounts of Asloan and his manuscript, see Cunningham 1994 and van Buuren 1996. For sexuality and satire in Middle Scots, see Newlyn 1991 and 1992. On the text's inclusion of narratives of "the

harlot's progress," see Riddy 1997, 241–42.

Source: The Asloan manuscript (Edinburgh, National Library of Scotland MS Asloan 16500 [formerly NLS 4233], fols. 137r–137v). This large manuscript appears to be a household commonplace book. The *Spektakle* is the only part of the manuscript not in Asloan's hand (van Buuren-Veenenbos 1982, 21–26; Lyall 1988, 170).

Heir begynnis the lytill buk entitillit and callit the *Spektakle of Luf* or *Delectatioun of Luf of Wemen*, quhilk is devydit in viii partis.

Titulo

The first part schawis how a gud ald knycht and wyss arressonit with a young
5   squyer his sone that was to mekle amoruss tuiching the delectatioun of wemen.

Capitulo primo

The secund part schawis the dictis or sayngis of haly doctouris and of the ald philosophouris that he allegis agane the delectatioun of luf.   *Capitulo secundo*
The thrid part schawis the famouss histouriis and noble examplis in tymes by-
10 passit by the quhilk men suld eschew the delectatioun of luf.   *Capitulo tercio*
The fourt part schawis quhy men suld eschew the delectatioun of damesellis or young wemen.   *Capitulo quarto*
The fyft part schawis that men suld eschew the delectatioun of luf with uther mennis wyffis quhilk is adultre, with diverss examplis allegit thareapon.
15   *Capitulo quinto*
The sext part schawis quhy men suld eschew the delectatioun of wedowis and agit wemen.   *Capitulo sexto*
The sevynt part schawis that men suld forbeir the delectatioun of wemen of religioun as nunnis or utheris, with gret examplis allegit thareapon.
20   *Capitulo septimo*
The [eight] part schawis the conclusioun of this lytill buk with the excuss of the translatour.   *Capitulo octavo*
As I was musing upone the restles besynes of [this] translatory warld, quhilkis thochtis and fantesyes trubblit my spreit, and for to devoyd me of sic
25 ymagynationis I tuk a lytill buk in Latyn to pass mye tyme. The quhilk as I had red and consederit, me thocht the mater gud and proffitable to be had into our wulgar and matarnall toung, for to causs folkis to mair eschew the delectatioun of the flesche, quhilk is the moder of all vicis. Tharfor be the sufferans of God I purpois to endure me to the translatioun of the samyn, becauss of the gud and proffitable
30 mater it treitis of, that was how a gud, anceant knycht, that in his youthheid had frequentit his body in the deidis of chevalrye to the encressing of his name to honour, nochtwithstanding his gret besynes in the factis merciall, in lyk wyss he had occupiit himself in the study of naturall philosophy, to the end that he suld eschew vice.
35   The quhilk gud ald knycht opnyt and declarit unto a young squyar, his sone, that was to gretly amoruss, the evillis and myshappis that men cummys to, throw

the gret plesans thai haif in wemen be the delectatioun of the flesche, except the
luf quhilk is detfully usit in the haly band of matermoney, tuiching the quhilk I
will nocht speik in my sempill translatioun, beseking all ladyes and gentillwemen
40 quhar it is said in ony poynt to thare displesour, thai put nocht the blaim thairof
to me bot to myn auctor, that was the fyrst compylar of this buk, the quhilk is
intitillit and callit *The Spectakle of Luf.* For in it apperis and schawis sum evillis
and myshappis that cummys to men thairthrow, as the filth or [sp]ottis of the face
schawis in the myrrour of glas.

45 Her endis the prolouig, how the gud knycht arresson[nit] his sone.

1   **Heir** here ∫ **buk** book ∫ **entitillit** entitled ∫
Spektakle an unusual translation of the common
generic Latin term *Speculum* (mirror or exemplar).
However, "spektakle" can also mean the exhibition
of a specified vice. As the translator declares (39–
44), the book is intended to act as a mirror, not by
reflecting a good example but by exhibiting the
vices of "luf" (sexual or adulterous love).

2   **Delectatioun** sensual enjoyment ∫ **Wemen**
women ∫ **quhilk** which

3   **devydit** divided ∫ **in** into ∫ **titulo** title

4   **schawis** shows ∫ **ald** venerable (by virtue of
his age) ∫ **wyss** wise ∫ **arressonit with** rebuke

5   **squyer** the son of a knight ∫ **to mekle** too
greatly ∫ **amoruss** amorous ∫ **tuiching** in the matter
of, concerning

7   **dictis** sayings ∫ **sayngis** quoted words ∫
doctouris learned men

8   **allegis agane** adduces as proof against

9–10 **by-passit** former

11   **quhy** why ∫ **suld** should ∫ **eschew** avoid ∫
damesellis unmarried women (especially those of a
noble or good family)

13   **uther** other

14   **with diverss examplis allegit thareapon** with
various examples adduced in proof

16   **wedowis** widows

18   **forbeir** refrain from

19   **as** such as ∫ **utheris** other kinds [of religious
women] ∫ **gret** important

21   **[eight]** MS *viii* ∫ **excuss** apology: that is, a conventional way of ending a literary work by excusing
one's efforts

23   **besynes** activity ∫ **[this]** MS added in a modern hand to replace an illegible word ∫ **translatory**
characterized by movement from one state to another. The OED does not list an occurrence of this
word before 1727, and in this sense not before
1849; there is no entry in the MED.

23–24 **quhilkis thochtis** thoughts of which

24   **trubblit** troubled ∫ **spreit** mind ∫ **for to** in order to ∫ **devoyd me** rid myself ∫ **sic** such

25 **ymagynationis** thoughts ∫ **I tuk a lytill buk in
Latyn to pass mye tyme** a conventional account of
the genesis of a translation. Compare Christine de
Pizan's reading of *The Lamentations of Matheolus,*
which precipitates the writing of *The Book of the
City of Ladies;* see excerpt 3.24. There is no reason
to think that this passage indicates a single Latin
source for the *Spektakle,* although it may do so.
Vernacular works often claim a nonexistent source,
as with Henryson's *Testament of Cresseid* or
Chaucer's *Troilus and Criseyde,* which claims to be
based on the works of Lollius. The author may be
indicating a general dependence on a literary tradition (reflections on the evils supposedly brought
into the world by women) associated with Latin,
and may also be anxious to avoid taking direct responsibility for sentiments profoundly unpopular
with women themselves. See 37–41 below; see also
The Wife of Bath's Prologue for a well-known fic-
tionalization of one woman's response to
misogynist material. ∫ **as I had red** when I had read it

26 **consederit** thought about ∫ **me thocht the
mater gud** the subject matter seemed to me to be
worthy. The construction "me thocht" is impersonal. ∫ **to be had** to be translated ∫ **wulgar** common,
vernacular

27 **for to causs** in order to make ∫ **folkis** people
∫ **to mair eschew** to avoid even more

28 **moder** mother ∫ **be the sufferans of God** with
God's will ∫ **purpois** intend

29 **endure me** apply myself ∫ **the samyn** the same
∫ **gud** respectable

30 **anceant** venerable ∫ **youthheid** youth

31 **frequentit his body** subjected his body to
[regular military drill], busied himself physically ∫
encressing augmenting

32 **besynes** activity ∫ **the factis merciall** martial
deeds ∫ **in lyk wyss** similarly

33 **naturall philosophy** natural science/natural
law (as an embodiment of divine law)

35 **opnyt** revealed

36 **to** too ∫ **cummys to** arrive at ∫ **throw** through

37 **plesans** sexual gratification ∫ **haif** have ∫ **be** in

38 **detfully usit** paid according to the debt: that is, according to the church's standard teaching on the proper role of sexual intercourse within marriage, namely, for the procreation of children, to avoid the sin of lechery, and in order to render the marriage debt, the obligation of the partners to "pay" each other with their bodies. See Miller 1977, 371–72, and Chaucer, *Parson's Tale* X (I) 914–20. ∫ **band** bond ∫ **matermoney** matrimony

39 **nocht** not ∫ **sempill** simple, blameless

39–41 **besekyng all ladyes . . . to myn auctor** beseeching all ladies and gentlewomen that where what is said is in any particular to their displeasure, they do not blame me for it, but my author. A conventional apology (see, e.g., *Troilus and Criseyde* V.1772–76). It is repeated at the text's conclusion, with the addition that only those women will object who are "of the condicionis of thire ladyes that

is before wrytene" (Craigie 1923, 297–98; on apologies to women, see Mann 1990).

41 **auctor** the writer of the source text

42 **sum** a number of

43 **thairthrow** through it (i.e., through amorous exploits)

43–44 **as the filth or [sp]ottis . . . myrrour of glas** just as the stains or marks of sin that appear on the face are seen in a mirror. Rather than an exemplary "mirror," or "speculum," projecting an ideal model of behavior (see excerpts 1.4: 28–31, 2.7: 16–18), "of glas" suggests a looking glass and physical marks (perhaps with a further meaning of disease, as in the "spottis blak" visited on Henryson's Cresseid) as the sign of sexual transgression.

43 **[sp]ottis** bracketed letters added in a modern hand to replace letters missing through manuscript damage

45 **arresso[nit]** bracketed letters added as above

MODELS AND IMAGES
OF THE
READING PROCESS

Part Two of this anthology explores how vernacular texts construct images of readers or reading situations, showing how such images almost never have the straightforward relationship they often claim with their actual audience. Part Three addresses the related matter of how texts describe reading itself. The excerpts collected here focus on the efforts vernacular writers and translators made to orchestrate the reading their works would receive or to find models and images for the reading experience. Written over a period of two centuries during which questions about who should read, what should be available for them to read, and what the motives for reading should be were asked with special urgency, these excerpts can be seen as a series of attempts to address these questions and argue their implications. Issues of gender, social class, profession, religion, or nationalism thus all influence how a work asks its readers to understand it.

The excerpts are organized in groups that represent the variety of reading models available in the period, the relations between these models, and the uses to which they were put. Reading could be thought of as a form of meditation that opens a door into the soul or as a source of information about the world; it could be a means to arouse feeling, or involve disciplined exercise of the power of reason; it could be serious or frivolous, undertaken to save the soul or to avoid boredom; it could be practiced alone, even silently, or (much more commonly) in small or large groups, gathered together for collective instruction or amusement (Coleman 1996). All of these types of reading or reading occasion have their literary topoi or models, and most of these have a long history of (usually) Latin use that precedes their adoption in vernacular texts. This history is sometimes invoked by writers to show readers that their encounter with a text is also one with a cultural tradition. Poggio Bracciolini's prologue to his translation of a historical compendium by Diodorus Siculus, an ancient Greek historian, begins with assertions about how historical writing acts as a bridge between past and present that readers can use to situate themselves, culturally and ethically, in relation to all that has gone before (see Skelton's translation, excerpt 3.15). Diodorus preserves a millennium of Mediterranean history; Poggio bridges two millennia by rendering him into Latin; and Skelton renders Poggio into English, so that readers learn, not only about the past, but about tradition itself as historical writing represents it. In different contexts, Nicholas Love's account of Saint Cecilia's constant meditation on Christ's Passion lends authority to a mode of reading in which devout feeling takes the place of a more intellectual response to the Gospels (Love's *Mirror*, excerpt 3.10); Henryson's appeal to almost all the topoi ever used to justify fiction gives notice that the *Fables* (excerpt 3.18) reevaluate the whole relation of poetic form and meaning; and King James I of Scotland's invocation of Boethius's *Consolation of Philosophy* at the opening of *The Kingis Quair* (excerpt 3.23) asserts his competence to act as a reader of his own experience and thus to contribute to the genre in which he is working, the aristocratic dream poem.

Yet even the most apparently direct rendering of a set of conventions from Latin, French, or (once) Dutch into English involves rethinking, as models are adapted to fit new circumstances and as material originally written for an educated elite is made available to those whom clerics, throughout the period, still thought of as *illiterati,* people whose ability and willingness to understand what they should from their reading was a source of anxiety. The texts excerpted in this part, and elsewhere in this book, provide ample evidence of the strength of late medieval vernacular literary culture in England and Scotland, and of the competence and sophistication not only of writers but also of a wide variety of readers. Yet in many ways and with different implications, the readers of most of the works excerpted here were still required to see themselves as *vernacular* readers whose status was (or could at any moment become) a matter for special concern. It is as though the very concept of the vernacular reader (like that of vernacular writing) was problematic and needed constantly to be redefined and redefended. The self-consciousness that could accompany the act of reading a vernacular text as a result of this complex of attitudes is one of the main themes of this part.

ORGANIZATION OF PART THREE

Excerpts 3.1–5: Religious reading models (1): meditative and contextual models. Part Three begins with five contrasting responses to a model of meditative reading whose early roots were in the monasteries and hermitages of the ancient world but that was redefined for the late Middle Ages in the prologue to Anselm of Canterbury's *Prayers and Meditations.*[1] This collection of private, nonliturgical prayers (prayers that do not form part of a church service) was written in Latin in the late eleventh century (1070–1104) and was copied and imitated in many languages for centuries following.[2] The collection opens with the following instructions:

> The prayers and meditations written below, since they are intended to excite the reader's mind to the love or fear of God and are uttered in conversation with him, are not to be read where there is noise but in quiet,

1. For an account of Anselm's *Prayers and Meditations* and its background, see Richard Southern (1990, 91–118), who describes the relation between "meditation" in Anselm's sense and earlier meanings of the word (e.g., in the Benedictine Rule) and stresses the link between meditative reading and psalm singing; Southern (1990, 67–87) also treats the importance of the rest of the Bible, and the influence on Anselm of Augustine. Southern draws on the pioneering research of André Wilmart (1971, orig. pub. 1932).

2. For a study and edition of a particular collection of "Anselmian" prayers and meditations, see Bestul 1987, whose introduction gives a good account of the genre and its development.

nor superficially and at speed but slowly, with intense and profound meditation. Nor is a reader to think to read any of them all the way through,
but only as much as, with God's help, will do to kindle a longing for prayer,
or as much as is satisfying. Nor need anyone always begin at the beginning but wherever suits best. For this reason, the prayers are subdivided
into paragraphs, so that one may begin or end where one chooses, in case
too many words or frequent repetition of the same section should lead to
boredom. Let the reader take from them instead what they were meant to
provide, the warmth of devotion. (Translated from Schmitt 1946–61, 3.3)

In this careful statement of the need to subordinate reading (*lectio*) to the needs of
meditation and prayer (*meditatio* and *oratio*), the reader is told, on the one hand,
to absorb the text as deeply as possible, on the other, to read affectively and selec-
tively, rather than with a rationalizing eye trained on the whole. Anselm
emphasizes the control readers must exercise over their experience of his text,
which he presents as a means to a devotional end (not, for example, as a series of
authoritative prescriptions for proper behavior). As always, however, his instructions do not provide a transparent view of how the *Prayers and Meditations* ask
to be read. First, for all Anselm's understanding of meditation as a mode involving
the whole person, his account leaves unexpressed much of the intellectual work
his text performs—one of the meditations, for example, is a treatise on the redemption. Second, that Anselm must preserve a pose of humility before God and the
reader means that the prologue cannot address one of the text's most important
functions: to impose Anselm's intense persona on the reader, inviting her or him to
become Anselm by speaking to God in his voice. As a founding text of late medieval "affective spirituality," some of whose early copies were dedicated to
highborn women,[3] the *Prayers and Meditations* provided an important model for
vernacular religious reading in Anglo-Norman and Middle English. Yet in light of
these complexities, it is not surprising that in most of the contexts in which the
prologue reappears it should again provide only a partial view of the reading
model it claims to represent.

At least five excerpts edited here imitate or respond to this model of devotional
reading, two of them (*A Talking of the Love of God*, excerpt 3.1, and the *Pseudo-
Augustinian Soliloquies*, excerpt 3.2) by direct paraphrase, two (*The Cloud of
Unknowing*, excerpt 3.3, and *A Revelation of Love*, excerpt 3.4) by careful reversal, and one (*The Orchard of Syon*, excerpt 3.5) by interpretative re-creation. The
paraphrases provide interesting evidence of the extent to which even texts whose

---

3. "Affective spirituality" is a general term describing the religious culture of western Europe between the twelfth and fifteenth centuries, in particular that culture's emphasis on emotion and the will (the
Latin word *affectus* refers to both). See, for example, Bynum 1982 and 1987. Southern (1990, 91–93)
describes the role of aristocratic women in the production of Anselm's book and of another important
collection of prayers, those of Jean de Fécamp.

ostensible focus was on the inner life were influenced by religious politics, especially the controversies over the vernacular reader's capacity to understand
theology, which came to a head around 1400 (see essay 4.2, pages 339–45). *A
Talking* (excerpt 3.1) is all about the meditator's decision to remove herself from
the world in spiritual marriage to Christ, the bridegroom, and sets out in part to
give readers a sensual verbal equivalent of the experience of spiritual marriage.
Yet the text survives in two manuscripts whose huge size suggests to some scholars that they were made as bastions against Lollard vernacular theology (Pearsall
1990). In its manuscript context, the world from which the text removes the reader,
and the act of helping her to leave that world, may thus be politicized in ways the
text's original compiler did not envisage. The *Soliloquies* (excerpt 3.2), written
somewhat later than *A Talking,* is more explicitly embroiled in the world it ex-
horts the reader to leave behind. This text begins (at least, in one of its two
surviving versions) by paraphrasing Anselm's prologue (1–14), then shifts to a
discussion of the confusion the translator says could result from the text's address
to God in the plural (on the model of its French source's use of the polite plural,
vous [15–35]). Yet the meditations this prologue introduces are much too theologically complex and *argued* to be read piecemeal, especially once the translator
has added explanatory digressions that engage the reader with some of the most
controversial issues of the day. The nuns for whom this version of the *Soliloquies*
was done can hardly have lacked the education to take its use of plural pronouns
in their stride. In light of the text's contents, the prologue looks very like an attempt to package an intellectually demanding vernacular work as though it were
a purely affective text like *A Talking,* by addressing its readers as though they fit
a stereotype of the ignorant nun (see Capgrave, *Life of St. Gilbert,* excerpt 2.7:
17–18; Fox, *The Rule of Seynt Benet,* excerpt 2.8: 17–18) the translator knew
was a fiction. Self-aware readers of this text must have sensed the constraints under
which it reached them, since it invites them to internalize an image of themselves
the text also implicitly admits does not correspond to reality.

At least the second of these excerpts is thus, in aim, less different than it seems
from those in which the authors of the *Cloud* (excerpt 3.3) and the explicit to the
Revelation (excerpt 3.4) acknowledge the intellectual complexities of their texts
by working *against* Anselm's reading model, stressing that these texts must be read
as a whole and only by properly prepared people. The topos these excerpts employ has its own history as a variation on the common plea that a text be kept
whole and have nothing added to or subtracted from it. Outside a vernacular
devotional milieu, these passages might not have evoked the Anselmian model at
all.[4] But in this context, the selective reading a meditative text requires—which
assumes that verbal truth is seamless, the whole mirrored in all its parts—is seen
as a threat to the theological balancing act the works perform. Very much as the

---

4. See, for example, Rev. 22:19, which threatens damnation to those who take anything away from
the book, or, for a secular example, Chaucer's plea at the end of *Troilus and Criseyde* (quoted above, page
11 of the Introduction to Part One).

translators of the *Wycliffite Bible* (see excerpt 1.15) and other religious texts reveal an anxious care not to deviate from the closest possible rendering of the original, so these passages demand a fidelity from their readers that imposes a responsibility on them quite different from that of the Anselmian model: a responsibility to defer to a text by rigorous determination to understand it and unflinching trust in its orthodoxy.[5] At the same time, this demand shows a nervous awareness on the part of the authors that it is readers, not they, who control the process by which what they say is understood, and that they can do no more than persuade readers to exercise a care they cannot impose.

Last in this group, *The Orchard* (excerpt 3.5) provides the subtlest account of the play between author, translator, text, and reader, introducing the nuns of Syon Abbey to Catherine of Siena's *Dialogo* by elaborating an image of the book as an orchard divided into the formal alleys of an aristocratic garden, like those Criseyde walks in with her women (see *Troilus and Criseyde* II.813–23). This image may partly be designed to deflect attention from the text's complexity, as seems to be one purpose of the *Soliloquies* prologue. Yet this prologue's deference to its reader's ability to gather "fruyt or herbis" (15) as she wishes from her reading also shows a trust in a specific (if privileged) vernacular audience that is in sharp contrast to the suspicion evident in the *Cloud*. Here the emphasis on choice characteristic of the meditative reading model is allowed an explicit place in the way readers approach a text that is intellectually demanding.

Excerpts 3.6–12: Religious reading models (2): self-transformation and knowledge. The next excerpts exemplify other reading models found in religious texts, models that share a common concern with readerly access to knowledge, and address the relationship of reading to spiritual and intellectual development more directly than the first group of excerpts. First are three fourteenth-century works that offer encyclopedic coverage of the truths considered necessary for salvation, *Pore Caityf* (excerpt 3.6), *The Prick of Conscience* (excerpt 3.7), and Rolle's *English Psalter* (excerpt 3.8). Two of these are organized as what *Pore Caityf* calls a "laddir of dyverse runges" (19), the structure of the text corresponding to a process of transformation readers are supposed to undergo as a result of reading it. This structuring principle is often found in texts concerned with mystical ascent, but is here applied to two bodies of general didactic material that seem to imply very different views of the capacity of readers to manage their spiritual lives.[6] Where *Pore Caityf* addresses readers as equals, assuming their willingness to reform once

5. For the controversy over Bible translation, see Watson 1995a. See also the emphasis on responsible Bible reading in *The General Prologue to the Wycliffite Bible* (excerpt 1.15) and *The Holi Prophete David Seith* (excerpt 2.5). For the care taken by Middle English translators, see Ellis 1982a; a pertinent example is provided by the translator of the *Soliloquies* (excerpt 3.2), who will not change a plural pronoun (*vous*) in the French to a singular one (*thou*) in the English, despite the confusion he asserts this may cause.

6. The two most famous examples of mystical works structured around the process of ascent they describe are Pseudo-Dionysius's *Mystical Theology* (c. 400) and Bonaventure's *Itinerarium mentis in Deum* (The mind's journey into God) (c. 1270).

the text has put the ladder to heaven in place, the *Prick of Conscience* claims to have been written for sluggish souls who must be terrified into virtue, most of it consisting of accounts of the vileness of the body, the Day of Judgment, and the punishments of purgatory and hell. Again, however, things are more complex than they seem, for this work is so up-to-date in its presentation of the otherworld that one of its purposes must have been as a cosmic atlas, meant for study by readers whose interest was as much in the information it provides as in the spiritual transformation it offers. Like the *English Psalter* (excerpt 3.8)—which offers readers a careful commentary on a book that it calls the Bible in miniature (37–39), and whose prologue is a brilliant combination of affective and intellectual approaches to the Psalms—the *Prick of Conscience* appears to have a confidence similar to that of *Pore Caityf* and many other fourteenth-century texts about the unequivocally benign effects of theological knowledge on vernacular readers.

This confidence becomes controversial in the four fifteenth-century texts excerpted in the second half of this group, written under the shadow of Arundel's *Constitutions* of 1409 (see essay 4.2, pages 343–44): *Dives and Pauper* (excerpt 3.9), Nicholas Love's *Mirror of the Blessed Life of Jesus Christ* (excerpt 3.10), *Sermon of Dead Men* (excerpt 3.11), and *The Mirror of Our Lady* (excerpt 3.12). In *Dives and Pauper* we find a clear Middle English statement of a millennium-old topos (deriving from the sixth-century pope Gregory the Great) that religious images (sculptures, paintings, stained glass) are "books" for the uneducated that they can learn to read as an alternative to the more abstract written texts to which they have no access (6–7). The passage defends images against the attacks of Lollards, who held that translation could make texts (especially Scripture) available to all. At the same time, however, the work reveals common ground with Lollard views, simply by holding the traditional practice of venerating images up to scrutiny in this vernacular context, implying that the "uneducated" can no longer be equated with those who do not know Latin and that, for at least many laypeople, images are not enough. In Love's *Mirror* (excerpt 3.10), on the other hand, the topos of the image as a book is reversed, as Love presents a written life of Christ as an image—a vernacular substitute for the Bible, whose English translation Arundel had recently banned and which Love argues needs to be permanently kept away from "lewed men and wommen" (3). Here, devout meditation on Christ's life and death is explicitly aimed at preempting detailed and intellectually demanding study, and even at inviting readers to internalize a view of themselves as inherently incapable of such study (7–22)—so alarmed has the conservative orthodoxy this text represents become by the prospect of a laity able to read, quote, and question Scripture.

Finally, the peroration to *Sermon of Dead Men* (excerpt 3.11) and the extensive extracts from another Syon text, *The Mirror of Our Lady* (excerpt 3.12), offer respectively a protest and a cautiously pragmatic response to Love's influential reading model. The *Sermon* comforts readers for the way learning has become all but impossible for the mass of English people, by describing the vision of God in heaven as an eternity of reading in the book of life, threatening clerics like Love with eternal exclusion from the only library that really matters (8–16). *The Mirror of Our Lady,* written for nuns who had access to unusual numbers of vernacular and Latin texts in the royal abbey of Syon (see also *The Orchard of Syon,* excerpt 3.5), is more positive, giving a description of reading that is as clear an account as we have of how different kinds of religious texts were intended to function, while explaining its own purpose with exemplary care (98–166). What is also interesting about this work's elaborate introductory apparatus, however, is that it was necessary at all, given the exclusive status of the institution for which it was written. In the early fifteenth century, there were seemingly no milieus in which the reading of vernacular religious texts was uncontroversial.

Excerpts 3.13–18: Reading as self-improvement and the idea of taste. Most of the religious texts in Part Three imply (or else refute) a dichotomy between learned Latinate clerical writers and ignorant vernacular lay and/or women readers, focusing on questions of access to knowledge, readerly capacity, and responsibility, and the relations between vernacular texts and various kinds of religious truth. But controversies over religious reading were by no means the only consequence of the spread of vernacular literacy and the rising prestige of English from 1300 on. Issues arising from secular literature were also important, as readerly interest in an array of narratives and in historical, philosophical, and practical issues created a body of English texts (most of them translations) to accommodate it. As explored in more detail in essay 4.2, one reason for the creation of this body of writing was nationalistic, as the upper levels of English society strove to keep up with Continental, especially French, conceptions of what a properly cultivated vernacular literature ought to contain and what an educated gentleman or -woman should have read, at a time when the French language was slowly falling out of large-scale insular use. Yet although the writings that resulted were often suffused with aristocratic values and imagery, they only rarely fit the notion of "courtly" literature that twentieth-century critics have derived from a relatively narrow tradition of fiction that begins with the *Roman de la rose* and culminates (for readers of English) in Chaucer and his successors. Whereas texts in this tradition sometimes present their sole purpose as pleasure—as if they were written for the "idle" reader symbolized by the porter Oiseuse in the *Roman de la rose*—most Middle English secular writing is consciously serious, written rather for the reader wishing to use leisure time (*otium* as distinct from *otiositas,* idleness) for self-improvement in a tradition stretching back to classical Rome. The appeal of most of these works is pragmatic, ethical, or informational, pleasure (in the famous topos derived from Horace) leading to instruction (Curtius 1990, 88–89; Olson 1982). On the rare occasions this is not so, pleasure often emerges as morally suspect. Indeed, the didactic emphasis is so strong that our distinction between secular and religious writing sometimes corresponds to no clear-cut difference in the nature of the material or in the audiences or reading occasions it seeks. Rather as modern "escape" literature (such as science fiction or fantasy) sometimes seeks to overcome its relatively low prestige by unremitting didacticism and defensiveness about its cultural value, so medieval secular writing is generally concerned to emphasize the high seriousness of its purpose.

Most excerpts in this section thus focus on the instruction to be gained from reading and on its relation to pleasure, often asserting their own usefulness by disparaging other modes of secular writing they see as competitors. The alliterative *Wars of Alexander* (excerpt 3.13), for example, positions itself within an array of stories, arguing that only the "wild-hedid" like foolish tales (12) and that a taste for the imperial history it offers is a sign of wisdom. The emphasis on readerly choice might seem to align this type of prologue with the Anselmian reading model. Here, however, the audience the poem addresses (a group of like-minded readers or hearers that perhaps originally consisted of members of a gentry or aristocratic household) is seen, with some flattery, as leisured, discerning, and broadly educated, comprising people with many kinds of text to hand who can be relied upon, with gentle prompting, to select what is most beneficial. In this model, history matters more than fiction and is read for its exemplary impact on the reader in the fashion of a saint's life. Yet the text that follows actually provides not only the improvement that the prologue promises but many of the kinds of information and entertainment it rejects: Alexander's journeys are full of exotic marvels. Despite the didactic imperatives that govern the prologue, it anticipates the beginning of a process that, in the sixteenth and seventeenth centuries, would lead to the cabinet of curiosities, the grand tour, and the idea of a "gentlemanly education."

A revealingly triumphalist application of the same topoi is found in the prologue to *Cursor Mundi* (excerpt 3.14), an encyclopedic history of the world (written c. 1300, up to a hundred and fifty years before *The Wars of Alexander*) that in practice deals almost exclusively with sacred history: a fact that enables it to declare itself not as one of a number of useful stories but as "the best boke of alle" (1). *Cursor Mundi* aims to trump the merely secular historical narratives whose form it imitates by giving superior models for imitation and a more important past than histories of Troy, Thebes, the rise and fall of Rome and Camelot, or the life of Alexander can claim. Indeed, it comes close to consigning these histories to the rubbish bin of fictions only a fool would take seriously (22)—undermining the very idea of readerly taste and discretion on which it is purportedly based. Can serious vernacular readers legitimately choose secular stories to entertain and inform themselves? Despite the continuing importance of Troy and Camelot and the eminence of twelfth-century English historiography (Lawman, Wace, Geoffrey of Monmouth, Benoît de Sainte-Maure), it seems that in some parts of fourteenth-century England such a question could still be in doubt.

The other excerpts in this group, from the late fifteenth or early sixteenth century, might be taken to demonstrate how much more solid the answer to this

question had become—how much more firmly the notion of serious secular vernacular reading was established—at the end of the period covered in this book.
Yet scrutiny reveals a less clear-cut picture. In Skelton's translation of the
Bibliotheca historica (excerpt 3.15), for example, historians are equated with divine providence in their ability to bring the whole world under a single scrutiny
(their own or the reader's), as well as to commend virtue, expose vice, and teach
truth to everyone—everyone, that is, who can manage Skelton's prose (13–22).
Yet here, too, the place of history must be defended against competitors, its philosophical, rhetorical, and moral value strenuously asserted, and its potential pitfalls
ignored. In the prologue to book V of Gavin Douglas's superb translation of
Virgil's *Aeneid* into Middle Scots (excerpt 3.16), there is defensiveness again, this
time in relation to the idea that reading can be a form of play, not always moral in
its intention but sometimes, at least, a source of unmoralized aesthetic pleasure.
Douglas's poem, with its long original prologues and high sense of the role of his
translation in the establishment of an eminent Scottish literature and language, is
itself a kind of epic of reading, and this prologue includes one of his many detailed
appreciations of Virgil's skill (28–45). The *Aeneid,* it seems, is special because it
has something for everyone, no matter what their taste, whether for earnest morality or for games and sports (46–54). But even to state that "myrthis and myrry
plays" (especially involving pagan deities [55–57]) have their place in a work of
serious literature generates anxiety, and the prologue ends by praying that nobody
will forget that earthly pleasure can lead to sorrow (62–63). Pleasure can never
escape from instruction for long.

   Only in the last excerpts of the section, from Caxton's *Reynard the Fox* (excerpt 3.17) and Henryson's *Fables* (excerpt 3.18), is there serious challenge to this
view, in two accounts of a work's moral usefulness that beg to be read in part ironically. *Reynard* is about deception and warns readers that it may itself be deceptive,
needing to be carefully read several times (like *The Cloud of Unknowing,* excerpt
3.3) before it can be understood. But when the prologue insists that the work's
intent is lofty, teaching the reader to avoid, not practice, the vices by *seeing through*
them rather than learning to appreciate their skill and comic appeal, we are confronted with a dilemma that precisely points up the questionable place of fiction
as a mediator of truth in medieval thought: for how is the reader to know where
moral sentiment ends and deception begins? Similarly, when Henryson insists that
the whole purpose of his beast fables resides in the *moralitates* that follow them,
many of which seem to bear little relation to the stories they explain, we are left
with reading instructions that can neither be straightforwardly used to interpret
the text nor rejected. The *moralitates* are, after all, written with a fine sense of the
rhetorical possibilities of denunciation and are highly effective short sermons. The
text Henryson describes as "ane maner of translatioun" from Latin (32) uses the
ambiguity inherent in any serious vernacular literary project to collapse the whole
distinction between instruction and pleasure, rhetoric and truth. In what might
seem a modern way but that has roots in ancient and medieval notions of *imitatio*

such as those that organize the *Bibliotheca historica* (excerpt 3.15), the *Fables* suggest that virtue is itself rhetorical, performed by its practitioners, not natural to them.

Excerpts 3.19–24: Accounts of the reading experience. The final group of six excerpts moves away from formal reading models to focus on accounts of the reading experience itself, some fictional, one practical, others autobiographical. Although these, too, are texts needing interpretation, such accounts provide us with the most detailed evidence we have for how medieval people responded to their reading. The six excerpts in this group suggest that though their authors believed that a book could provide readers with untrammeled access to the experience it describes—that the world of the text and that of the reader could be continuous—they also recognized the gap between reader and text, actual and desired effect. Three excerpts deal directly with readerly resistance to and misappropriation of texts, a theme one might have thought confined to the ironic world of Chaucer's dream poetry.

Excerpt 3.19, part of passus XV of the C text of William Langland's *Piers Plowman*, and excerpt 3.20, from *The Book of Ghostly Grace* (a translation of Mechtild of Hackeborn's *Liber specialis gratiae*), employ the image of reading as eating. This image derives from a monastic reading practice called *ruminatio* (literally, chewing the cud), described in Jean Leclercq's classic study *The Love of Learning and the Desire for God* (1961). *The Book of Ghostly Grace* (excerpt 3.20) recounts a dream that reveals the importance of Mechtild's book to its compiler years before the book is composed. In a eucharistic gesture, Mechtild offers her sisters and the narrator honeycomb from a chalice (16–19): an image of the power and immediacy with which her visionary book conveys God's grace to readers. Eating words also symbolizes access to wisdom in *Piers Plowman* (excerpt 3.19). But here such eating is a penitential activity that demands abstention from real (or, at least, rich) food. It is contrasted with the different mode of knowing-through-reading practiced by the doctor with whom the narrator, Will, and Patience are dining. For the doctor, knowledge is so divorced from experience that he cannot understand anything he reads, and has used his knowledge only to gain a position in which he can gobble rich food in stomach-churning quantities (22–24, 46–47). Yet the passage is saved from the anti-intellectualism of a text like Love's *Mirror* (excerpt 3.10) by Will's righteous anger at the doctor, who could be using his rich and varied knowledge to good effect by humbly sharing it. It is academic elitism, not learning itself, that is Langland's target.

The other four passages involve individual experiences of reading particular texts. The *Commentary on the Penitential Psalms* (excerpt 3.21), Eleanor Hull's translation of an unlocated French text, provides a detailed exemplification of what *ruminatio* involved. Hull's *Commentary* masticates every phrase of Psalm 50 with the help of Gregory, Augustine, and a battery of techniques for allegorical exegesis, and makes considerable intellectual demands, although the end at which the text aims is clearly devotional. In a different vein, King James I of Scotland, in his autobiographical *Kingis Quair* (excerpt 3.23), recounts how he whiled away a long night with Boethius's *Consolation of Philosophy* and was then inspired to describe his own encounters with Fortune and their happy resolution. James derives the topos of the book at bedtime from Chaucer's *Book of the Duchess* and *Parliament of Fowls,* with the variation that here the book leads to a waking recollection of his past, not to a dream. This easy continuity between the narrator and his reading of Boethius is most suggestive of how fifteenth-century readers turned to ancient texts confident that they could provide keys to contemporary life. If Boethius's view of Fortune is recast in the process—James views her as a benign power, where Boethius turns away from her altogether—this is not, apparently, a problem.

Such a gap between source text and reader becomes, however, a major focus in two of these excerpts, from *The Book of Margery Kempe* (excerpt 3.22) and Brian Anslay's translation of Christine de Pizan's *Book of the City of Ladies* (excerpt 3.24), for here both writers find that they do not like what is in the books they have worked so hard for the privilege of knowing. After a chapter (chap. 57, not included here) that describes her desire for the salvation of the whole world, Kempe recounts how her prayer to find someone to read to her is answered by the arrival of an unbeneficed priest, who introduces both her and himself to a cross-section of theological writings, to the satisfaction and benefit of both (34–36, 44–45). Yet the idyllic tone is broken when (51–60) Kempe returns to the issue of salvation, to find that in her conversations with God he now insists on the reality of damnation, even allowing the devil to show her obscene visions until she relents (70–77). After her introduction to formal theology, Kempe is no longer able to believe in the God she wants, one who always answers her prayers to elevate mercy over justice. Here, book-learning proves debilitating as well as enabling. In the early-sixteenth-century English translation of *The Book of the City of Ladies* (excerpt 3.24), the book's printer, Henry Pepwell, has little trouble in reading Anslay's translation of de Pizan as a tribute to male cultural prowess (despite his brief hesitation about printing the book [12–13]). But the text's narrator has a different experience. Christine de Pizan takes time off from her serious study to read a misogynist poem, *The Lamentations of Matheolus,* only to find herself faced with the realization that the attitudes revealed in this poem are typical of the comments about women she has noted in her reading as a whole. Yet rather as Kempe's contemporary, Julian of Norwich, counterattacks on the issue of the church's stance over salvation and damnation, so de Pizan turns the despair she describes into the springboard of her extraordinary attempt to rewrite Western literature's account of women. This personal account of an experience that was and remains common to many—in which the reader temporarily capitulates to a text and a view of herself she ought to withstand—concludes this part with a final demonstration of the sophistication and flexibility of medieval thinking about the nature of texts, their meanings, and how they impinge upon their readers.[7]

3.1 *A TALKING OF THE LOVE OF GOD*: PROLOGUE

Date and Provenance: 1330s–70s (?); probably the west Midlands.

Author, Sources, and Nature of Text: This lengthy meditation consists of a series of prayers to, and evocations of, the crucified Christ, who is here the object of fear, grief, compassion, erotic reflection, and gratitude; it may have been written to be read in front of a painting or sculpture of the Passion. The text is largely an expansion and conflation of two earlier meditations, *An Orison of God Almighty* and *The Wooing of Our Lord*, written for anchoresses (women living as hermits in cells adjoining churches) in the west Midlands around 1250 and closely related to the famous *Ancrene Wisse*. *A Talking* brings these works up to date with more accounts of Christ's pain, in the graphic mode of later medieval devotion (perhaps using material from James of Milan's *Stimulus amoris*), and adds this prologue, adapted from the prologue to Anselm's *Prayers and Meditations* (quoted above, pages 212–13) but emphasizing the specifically emotional content of the text that follows. Elsewhere, the author adapts other passages from the same work, once mentioning Anselm by name as the source of some especially fine sentiments. As the prologue states, the text is in a rhythmic and partly rhymed prose well suited to its status as a religious soliloquy that dwells passionately on the details of Christ's suffering and the reasons he alone, not any merely earthly man, is a worthy bridegroom to the soul. The text is carefully punctuated, in both surviving manuscripts, to bring out its affective qualities.

Audience and Circulation: The text survives in two manuscripts, known as the Vernon and Simeon manuscripts, which were compiled together in northern Worcestershire around 1390 and contain large numbers of religious works, including the *South English Legendary* (excerpt 2.15), the *Northern Homily Cycle* (excerpt 2.1), *The Prick of Conscience* (excerpt 3.7), and the A text of *Piers Plowman* (excerpt 3.19). Vernon is connected with the aristocratic Bohun family and may have been compiled for an aristocratic or monastic readership, perhaps for nuns (see Meale 1990, 135). *A Talking* itself seems also to have been originally written for nuns, since the meditator refers to her "holy ordre" and the occasion of her "trouthe plighting" when she was married to Christ.

Bibliography: Edited by Salvina Westra (1950), the work has been discussed largely in relation to its style. R. W. Chambers (1932) claims it as evidence for the "continuity of English prose" between the Old and Middle English periods; Margery Morgan (1952a/b) discusses it as an example of the use of the Latin prose *cursus* in a vernacular text. Lois Smedick (1975) challenges Morgan's findings, and Chambers's more sweeping conclusions, originally published in the early 1930s, are no longer accepted. Benedicta Ward (1983) provides a rather disparaging comparison of the work to Anselm's meditations. For further bibliography, see Lagorio and Sargent 1993, 3451. For translations of the work's main sources, see Savage and Watson 1991, 245–57, 322–24. For the

---

7. Not included here, for reasons of space, are examples of the practical aids given late medieval readers, in the apparatus of tables of contents, chapter divisions, rubrics, and other formal and conceptual structures that became standard features of many types of books in the two hundred years before printing. Many of the texts presented here (e.g., *The Orchard of Syon*, excerpt 3.5, and Love's *Mirror*, excerpt 3.10) contain apparatuses of this kind. The classic study is by M. B. Parkes (1976); for a recent study of textual division in Middle English manuscripts, see Keiser 1995.

manuscript context, see Pearsall 1990. On the suffering Christ as object of meditation, see Aers and Staley 1996, chaps. 1 and 3.

Source: Oxford, Bodleian Library MS Eng. poet.a.1 (Vernon MS), fol. 367vb. The Vernon manuscript is arguably the most important collection of vernacular religious texts of the late fourteenth century: a huge and expensive manuscript that gathers together a broad array of devotional and vernacular theological writing in a manner that in some ways parallels, in others may have been intended to oppose, Lollard book production. *A Talking*

is one of a number of prose texts, originally written for contemplatives, in part 4 of the manuscript, including works by Rolle and Hilton as well as a late version of *Ancrene Wisse*. For a facsimile of the manuscript, see Doyle 1987. In this excerpt, manuscript punctuation and capitalization have been retained.

Some of the terms translated below are used here in a technical sense that is rare elsewhere. As with many medieval texts the punctuation gives performance instructions on pauses in reading rather than on interpreting syntax.

Heer Is A tretys. A talkyng of the love of God.

This tretys. Is a talkyng of the love of God. And is mad for to sturen. hem that hit reden; to loven him the more. And to fynde lykyng. and tast in his love. Hit falleth for to reden hit. esyliche and softe. So as men may mest in Inward felyng. and
5 deplich thenkyng. savour fynden. And that not beo dene. But biginnen and leten in what paas so men seoth. that may for the tyme yiven mest lykynge. And whon men hath conceyved. the maters with redyng. Inward thenkyng. and deoplich sechyng. withouten eny redyng uppon the selve maters. and of such othere that God wol senden. hose wole sechen. schal given inward sight and felyng in soule.
10 And swetnes wonderful, yif preyere folwe. But hose wole in meditacion swete fruit fynden; hit mot be taken in wone. with threo poyntes that folewen. Affyaunce. And continuaunce. And louh herte and clene. that he truste sikerliche to fynden that he secheth. And that his thought beo harde iset. And ful bisyliche i-kept. And holden himself unworth. out of Godes yifte. And wlate on himselven. thorw
15 siht of his fulthe.
Men schal fynden lihtliche this tretys in cadence. After the bigynninge. yif hit beo riht poynted; and rymed in sum stude. To beo more lovesum. to hem that hit reden. God yive us grace so for to rede; that we mowen have hevene to ure mede. Amen.

---

1   **talkyng of** soliloquy about: the work entitles itself and names its own genre at the outset, a "tretys" that is also a *soliloquium* (see excerpt 3.2), an address by the speaker to herself and God
2   **mad for to sturen** written so as to move: the work describes its *intention* ∫ **hem that** those who
3   **lykyng** pleasure ∫ **tast** taste (see excerpt 1.6: 44)
3–4 **Hit falleth for** it is necessary
4   **esyliche** slowly ∫ **softe** quietly (note that it is assumed the text will be read aloud, even if privately) ∫ **mest** most
5   **deplich thenkyng** concentrated meditation ∫ **savour fynden** find spiritual profit. "Savour" is a

technical term in the language of devotion, derived from Latin *sapere* (to taste) and the abstract noun *sapientia* (wisdom); it means something like "affective recognition of the truth." See Ward 1983 for an analysis of the prologue's sensualization of Anselm's more abstract terminology. ∫ **beo dene** completely (*MED: bidene*)
5–6 **And that . . . mest lykynge** And not all the way through. But begin and leave off at whatever place people may find gives most pleasure at that time.
7   **conceyved. the maters** internalized (or become impregnated with) the subject matter: a process of carefully re-creating the work's accounts

of Christ's life and death internally in an attempt to precipitate "inward sight" and "swetnes" (9, 10), using the "spiritual senses" as opposed to the physical ones. For Julian of Norwich's impatience with the limitations of this exercise, see excerpt 1.13a.

7–8 **deoplich sechyng** profound examination. The movement is from reading, through meditation and rumination, to prayer (see "yif preyere folwe" [10]).

8   **selve maters** same subjects

9   **hose** whoever ∫ **wole sechen** desires to look for it ∫ **schal given** shall be given

11 **in wone** in abundance. Meditation must be prolonged and frequent if it is to work. ∫ **poyntes** items ∫ **Affyaunce** trust

12 **continuaunce** perseverance ∫ **louh** humble ∫ **clene** pure ∫ **he** Masculine pronouns are often used and/or retained, even in compilations specifically for women. Their use does not preclude inscribed or intended female audiences. See also excerpt 3.2: 3n (*Soliloquies*) and the explicit discussion in *The Mirror of Our Lady* (excerpt 3.12: 14–19n). ∫ **sikerliche** confidently

13 **beo harde iset** be concentrated completely upon it ∫ **bisyliche** diligently ∫ **i-kept** sustained

14 **unworth** worthless ∫ **out of Godes yifte** except for God's grace. Despite the earlier assurance that this is an exercise that works (8–9), any spiritual "fruit" (10) that results from it must in correct theology be attributed to God's actions, not those of the meditator. ∫ **wlat on** loathe

15 **siht** sight ∫ **his fulthe** his own filth (i.e., sin)

16 **lihtliche** easily ∫ **cadence** meter or regular rhythm. See Smedick 1975 for an analysis.

17 **riht poynted** properly punctuated (or correctly read aloud) ∫ **sum stude** certain places ∫ **lovesum** love-inspiring

18 **to ure mede** for our reward

3.2 *PSEUDO-AUGUSTINIAN SOLILOQUIES:* PROLOGUE AND DIGRESSION

Date and Provenance: perhaps 1390–1420; perhaps east Midlands.

Author, Sources and Nature of Text: The *Soliloquies* are a set of theologically complex but also highly emotional meditations that were attributed to Augustine and contain material by him but that actually originated in Latin in the thirteenth century and include material by other writers, notably the twelfth-century theologian Hugh of St. Victor. They were read in many languages until well beyond the end of the Middle Ages and contributed to an image of Augustine (based in large part on his *Confessions*) as a strenuously inquiring and self-reflexive thinker that has had a profound impact on the Western sense of the self from at least the time of Anselm onward. The Middle English version was translated from an unknown French version by an anonymous, probably clerical writer. His translation was subsequently revised by a second writer, who constructed a prologue by combining a passage from Anselm's prologue to his *Prayers and Meditations* (see pages 212–13 above) with the first version's self-conscious epilogue on the need to adapt the translation to make it more read-able and on the use of plural pronouns to address God. This prologue is edited as (a) below. The original translator added several lengthy digressions and shorter passages (omitted by the reviser) that explain difficult points and address current issues and anxieties, particularly to do with the Lollard heresy. The digression on the topic of idolatry, edited here as (b), is a case in point, motivated by the need to distinguish what the text says about idols from Lollard attacks on the veneration of images, attacks that made belief in the worth of such images a litmus test of orthodoxy in early-fifteenth-century England. The writer's defense is skillful, encouraging orthodox reading practices that submit to, rather than challenge, established interpretations of biblical passages. However, the digression moves far outside what would usually be considered a meditative reading mode and raises interesting questions about the extent to which a theologically sophisticated text like this was designed to be read in the ruminative devotional manner recommended in the prologue to the revised translation, the extent it was actually written for the kind of concentrated intellectual study the text certainly requires in order to be understood. Nuns were typically instructed by clerics to feel, not think, but in this case (as, perhaps, with *The Orchard of Syon*, excerpt 3.5) the instruction may have been partly a topos, designed to conceal or normalize the work's more ambitious and unusual purpose.

Audience and Circulation: The text is in two fifteenth-century manuscripts, Cambridge, Mass., Harvard University MS Houghton Richardson 22, which preserves what must be the original version of the translation addressed to an audience of nuns, and London, British Library MS Cotton Titus C.xix, whose text has been revised to address a less specific audience. Cotton Titus omits the digressions and other controversial passages, omits most chapter numbers, and adds passages at the ends of chapters (some of them adapted from the writings of Richard Rolle) to turn them into distinct meditations with a more affective emphasis.

Bibliography: The only studies of the Middle English *Soliloquies* are by Robert

Sturges (1985, 1995), who is preparing an edition of the text. For the Latin text of the *Soliloquies* and its sources, see *PL* 40:863–98. For the contexts in which the work was read, see the discussion of women's reading by Riddy (1996b) and the study of books owned by female religious houses by David Bell (1995). For the debate over images, see *Dives and Pauper* (excerpt 3.9).

Source: (a) London, British Library MS Cotton Titus C.XIX, fols. 3r–4v (the prologue): a richly produced fifteenth-century manuscript, in which the text appears with Rolle's *Passion Meditations;* (b) Cambridge, Mass., Harvard University, Houghton Library MS Houghton Richardson 22, fols. 43v–46v (the digression). This is a careful but less expensive manuscript of the first quarter of the fifteenth century, now incomplete at the beginning. The text appears with the Middle English version of the *Benjamin* treatise attributed to the *Cloud* author (see excerpt 3.3 below), various prayers, and other brief pieces (see Voigts 1985, 56–60).

a. Prologue

These meditacyons or prayers that bene writen within this boke suwyng bene made to exite and stere the mynde of the reder to the drede of God and to the love of God, and to verey knowyng of hymsilfe. And therfor thei be not to be radde in grete hast and in grete tumultuosite but in quyetnesse; not wyth gret swithenesse
5 and hastenesse but moderatly and easely and with amorouse and a wise entent and abydyng meditacion. Ne the [redere] schalle not entende that he rede eche of hem alle over, but as muche as he may or kan goostly feele; or so muche that he may througli Goddes grace and helpe avayle, and inflawme his affeccions to prayer or to swete meditacions; or els as moche as for the tyme may be delyte hym to stere
10 his soule to the love of God. Ne allwey it is not nede to begynne at the begynnyng, but where it plesith hym best. And therfor every chapeter is distincte wyth paraphes, that where it lyketh hym he may begynne and also ende, ne lest often repeticion of one thing schulde make hevenesse. But rather he schulde gader sum swetnesse of his redyng. For that entent thei where made.
15   And ye schalle undurstonde that I have nought writen alwey as it stondith in the boke wher after I wrote. For in translatyng of one langage to another, some wordes mosten be chaunged and in some places moo wordes mosten be seyde. For Englysche is so boystous of itsilfe, that elles it wille be fulle unsavery for to rede. Therfor, as me semeth, is moste lysable. And I have writen in the spekyng to God,
20 for reverence, "ye" and "youres"—and so I fynde in the Frenche booke that I wrote after, "vous" and "vostre," that is to sey, "ye" and "yours." But some

replyen ther agenste, for it is seyde that it is plurye. And so schulde thei not done: for oure lorde God, thonked mot he ever be, taketh hede principally to a mannes entent more than to the wordes. Also oure lord God, or he made man, seyde

25 *Faciamus hominem ad ymaginem et similitudinem nostram*—"Make we man after oure ymage and after oure lyknes." Ther he spake in plurie, the Fader to the Sonne, so may we speke to the Fader and to the Sonne and to the Holy Goste in plurie of personis and only one God in thre persones. But, be it man or be it woman, as they feelen hem best disposed or most devoutly steride to sey, be it

30 "yowe," be it "the" or "yee," let hem sey: for both is good, and plesyth welle God. For oure lorde God, worschipped and praysed be he allewey, he is so mercyfulle and benyngne that he taketh after mannes entent, as I sey befor. For many man and woman seith here *Pater noster, Ave,* and a *Crede* full overthowartly, and no worde lyke as it was made; yit God of his grete mercy and goodnesse resceyve here

35 good wille and here good entent.

Now that mercyfull God and man, Crist Jhesu, graunte us grace continualy to thinke and to do and also to sey as most may be to his worschip and plesyng, and oure perpetualle salvacion. Amen.

b. Digression

Here seynt Austyn despysyth fals ydolys that were som tyme. For in olde tyme

40 men made many goddys and ymagys of hem. Some pepel helde the sonne for here god, and some the mone, som the other planetis, somm the elementys; and some helde for here god what thing they sawgh first aday, hound or catte or other thynge. Some pepel bylevyd in Mahounde and into Termagaunt; some heldyn and bylevedyn in Berith and in Astarot—and in many suche other moo, that I reherse

45 nat here. And of these they had ymagys of golde and sylver and of other metal and of stones and tree i-made to the worschyp of hem, and honouryd hem as here goddys, the whiche were feendes, some of hem. And in doynge of this they synnyd dedly, bothe in thouht and in dede; for they bylevyd in feendes, and forsokyn God her maker that made alle thynge of nauht.

50 Also the childryn of Israel they had a calfe of golde wrouhte by the feendes craft, the whech they worschippid and helde for her god. And after, whan it was destruyed, they had another that hyht Belfagor, that was prince of ydoles amonge the Sarasynnys, the wheche they worschepyd and helde it here god. And moo other they had afterwarde, as it is writen in storyes. And therfor oure lord God,

55 that sawe and knew her hertes and here grete ignoraunce and bestialte, defendid hem, and comaundyd hem that they schuld nat make ymages ne similitudis of no thinge that is in hevyn ne in erthe; for they were that tyme so blynde derkyd in synne that they wold anone have made it here god.

But now, thankyd be God, the pepyl have more discressioun than they had that

60 tyme. Therfor sith that owre lord Criste Jhesu—worschippid mote he evermore be!—toke flesshe and blode of the gloriouse virgyn owre lady seynt Mary, the pepyl with ful feyth in the Trynyte they have ymagis and do make ymages to the worschip of God as for a love tokyn. And this they done for to have hym the more in remembraunce and in devocioun. And this is wel done, for it is a gode booke to

65 the lewid peple that are unlettryd and also for other, to renew the more here mynde in God, and in the passioun of his manhode. And riht as lordis and ladyes done

reverens to the kynges token or letter whan they seen it, and to the preente of his
seele—they wote wel that the preente ys but wexe, yit for reverence of the kynge
they done of here hodis therto—riht so the trewe Cristen pepill they wote wel that
70 ymages are nat goddys but figuris i-made to the likenes of God and of owre lady
and of seyntys. Therfore they done worship and reverence therto in entente to
worschip and plese God and owre ladi and the seyntis that they are made after.
And with trewe love and feyth in God they do thus.

Hit is a grete differens of the opynyon and the entent of these Cristen pepyll and
75 of the opynnyon of hem that weren in olde tyme, that bylevyd on fals goddis.
Therfor I saye as seynt Austyn sayth: alle soche fals goddis that are nat lyke to God
despisid ben they in hevyn and in erthe. Seynt Austyn ys a worthi seynt that
bylevyd perfihtly in God Crist Jhesu and in alle his wordis and werkys. And who
that bylevyth perfitely in God Crist Jhesu and in alle his wordis and werkys, they
80 byleve verreyly in the sacrament of the awter and in alle the poyntis that Holy
Chirche techith.

This mater I me[v]e for some personys have mystake thoo wordis of seint
Austyn, ther he spekyth of ymages and of fals goddis. They take his menyng
upsodowne, and turnyth it alle in another kynde than he thouhte. And so they fall
85 into erroure and evel opynyonys, and schende hemselfe in folwyng the feendys
counsayle by mystakyng of scripturis. Therfor whan any creature hath suche
conseytes or dowtys in redynge of scriptures, or by ymagynacions or temptacioun,
they schuld anone take counsayle of clerkys and do by here doctrinis. For Seynt
Gregory seyth that scripture withowte expowninge is deeth. Certis it makyth many
90 to erre, lacke of gode clergy. Clergy is moche worth for it is trewe leder to the riht
wey of trowth, ther grace is ther amonge.

*[There follows a passage demonstrating the value of learning from the life of Dionysius
the Areopagite, converted by Paul in Athens after reasoning his way to belief in the
existence of one God from the eclipse and earthquake that accompanied Christ's
Passion.]*

But allas, allas! for the pepyl that holden opynyons ayenst Holy Chirche wele
nat take ensaumple of this worthi seynt, ne of alle other seyntys that weren and
have been here byforn, that were so trewe lovynge to oure lord God, and stabel in
95 the feyth and in good lyvynge. God for his endles mercy have pyte on hem that
stant in the contrary wyse and withdrawe the feendis power that blyndyth hem so
gretly, and graunt hem grace of amendement, and us all! Amen.

And now I turne ayeen to the meditacions of seynt Austyn.

1 **boke suwyng** following book
2 **exite** excite ∫ **stere** move ∫ **reder** reader. This
text (like *A Talking,* excerpt 3.1) anticipates a single
reader reading aloud to herself at a pace only she
can set (as lines 3–6 make clear). ∫ **drede** fear
3 **verey** true ∫ **hymsilfe** The use of masculine
pronouns does not preclude a text's addressing or
even being specifically designed for women readers.
Compare *A Talking,* excerpt 3.1: 12 and note, and
The Rule of Seynt Benet, excerpt 2.8: 1–4; see also

the discussion of this issue in *The Mirror of Our
Lady,* excerpt 3.12: 14–19n.
4 **tumultuosite** confusion ∫ **swithenesse** intensity
5 **moderatly and easely** in a relaxed and mod-
erately paced way ∫ **amorouse** loving
6 **abydyng** lasting ∫ [**redere**] MS *rathere* ∫
entende that intend to ∫ **hem** them
7 **goostly feele** respond to in spirit
8 **througli Goddes grace and helpe** avayle fully
attain God's help and grace. For the theological

point here, compare excerpt 3.1: 14 and note. ∫ **inflawme** kindle

9 **may be delyte hym to stere** may give [enough] pleasure to arouse

10 **nede** necessary

11–12 **distincte wyth paraphes** divided into paragraphs

12 **that** so that ∫ **where it lyketh hym** where it pleases him ∫ **ne lest** lest ∫ **often** frequent

13 **schulde make hevenesse** should cause boredom

14 **entent** intent (the author's intention; see 5 for the reader's intention) ∫ **where** were

15–19 **And ye schalle . . . is moste lysable** The translator defends the policy of changing words to make his text more readable.

15–38 **And ye schalle . . . perpetualle saluacion. Amen** This passage also occurs as an epilogue to the original version of this translation in MS Houghton Richardson 22, fols. 53v–54r.

16 **wher after I wrote** from which I translated ∫ **of** from

18 **boystous** crude. For the topos that English is inferior to French, see, for example, Chaucer's *Complaint* (excerpt 1.3). For an attack on the topos, see Usk's *Testament* (excerpt 1.4: 11–29). ∫ **elles** otherwise ∫ **unsavery** unpleasant

19 **Therfor** that is, this policy ∫ **as me semeth** it seems to me ∫ **lysable** readable ∫ **in the spekyng to God** in addressing God

19–28 **I have writen . . . in thre persones** Having defended his policy of changing words to make his text more "lysable" (19), the translator now defends what may seem an excessive literalism with which he follows the French practice of addressing God with plural forms, not the usual Middle English practice of using singular ones ("thee" and "thou").

21 **wrote after** translated

22 **replyen ther agenste** argue against this ∫ **plurye** plural

23–24 **taketh hede principally to a mannes entent** takes notice principally of a person's intention

24 **or** before

25 *Faciamus . . . similitudinem nostram* Gen. 1:26, where, in the Latin text, God refers to himself in the plural (*faciamus*)

27–28 **in plurie of personis** as a plurality of persons. The Trinity can be addressed in the plural, as three persons (Father, Son, and Holy Spirit), or the singular, as one God.

29 **steride** moved

32 **befor** that is, in lines 23–24

33 *Pater noster, Ave . . . Crede* the Lord's Prayer, the Ave Maria, and the Creed: part of the indispensable minimum each Christian was sup-

posed to know ∫ **overthowartly** mistakenly: the analogy is with people incorrectly speaking Latin words they do not fully understand, and the author adopts the canonically approved attitude that the intention of devout but uneducated people matters more than comprehension and grammar (compare the "povere commune laborers" who "percen with a Paternoster the paleys of hevene" in *Piers Plowman* B XI.457–59). For an example of a situation in which lay difficulties with Latin are potentially urgent—the case of midwives of mothers who need to baptize babies in danger of death—see the careful account in John Mirk's *Instructions for Parish Priests* (c. 1390), discussed in Shaw 1985, 53–54.

34 **here** their

39 **Here** that is, in the passage of the pseudo-Augustinian *Soliloquies* immediately preceding this digression ∫ **seynt Austyn** Saint Augustine (354–430), bishop of Hippo in northern Africa and the most influential Latin theologian of the early church ∫ **som tyme** at one time ∫ **in olde tyme** The translator attempts to neutralize Augustine's contempt for idols by historicizing it, distinguishing between pagan idols (which are seen as a problem long past) and Christian images. As he later admits, however (82–84), attacks on idols were readily translatable into attacks on images, and at least one Lollard text, *The Lanterne of Light* (Swinburn 1917, 85), cites Augustine in support of its opposition to the veneration of images. However, the translator's ploy here was a common one in orthodox defenses of images; compare, for example, Walter Hilton's *De adoracione ymaginum,* which likewise explains that God forbade the ancient Israelites to worship idols but did not mean the prohibition to apply to the church (Clark and Taylor 1987, 370–99).

40–41 **helde the sonne for here god** considered the sun their god. The source of much of this passage is apparently Mandeville's *Travels,* whose portrait of the Terre de Foy (land of faith) describes the "diuerse loy" (diverse law) of a people some of whom worship the sun, some the fire, some trees, some snakes, or the first thing they meet in the morning ("qar ascuns adorient le solail, et ascuns le feu, ascuns arbries, ascuns serpentz. ou la primere chose qils encontrent la matyne" [Warner 1889, 82]). Mandeville's approval of these people (who live in his present, not the distant past evoked by the *Soliloquies* translator) is in sharp contrast to the disapproval expressed here. For another religious text that uses Mandeville's *Travels,* see *Speculum Devotorum,* excerpt 1.12, headnote.

42 **what** whatever ∫ **aday** in the morning

43–44 **Mahounde, Termagaunt, Berith, Astarot**

traditional names for "heathen" deities or devils

43 **heldyn** trusted

44 **moo** more

46 **tree** wood ∫ **i-made to the worschyp of hem** made in their honor

47 **feendes** devils (believed to inhabit pagan images; see Camille 1989, 57–72)

48 **dedly** mortally ∫ **forsokyn** forsook

49 **of nauht** from nothing

50–53 **calfe of golde . . . helde it here god** See Exodus 32: the story of the golden calf made by the Israelites during their desert wanderings.

50 **wrouhte** made

52 **hyht** was called ∫ **Belfagor** Belphegar in the Latin Vulgate; see Num. 25:3, 5; Deut. 4:3.

53 **Sarasynnys** Arabs, a generic term for non-Christians/non-Jews (also "heathens," "pagans") ∫ **here** their

53–54 **moo other** others

54 **storyes** histories. The author has in mind works like Peter Comestor's *Historia scholastica,* Vincent of Beauvais's *Speculum historiale,* or the Middle English *Cursor Mundi* (excerpt 3.14), which recount the Israelites' experiments with idols.

55 **bestialte** stupidity ∫ **defendid** forbade

56 **similitudis** likenesses. See Exod. 20:4.

56–57 **no thinge** anything

57 **blynde derkyd** blindly darkened

58 **anone** at once

59–63 **But now . . . love tokyn** The translator's defense of images takes the unusual form of an assertion that they are a sign of intellectual and spiritual advance on the part of "the pepyl" (59), rather than a concession to lay ignorance (compare *Dives and Pauper,* excerpt 3.9: 6–7). Implicit too is the idea that Christ's Incarnation (his appearance as a living image) cancels the Old Testament's prohibition against idols.

60 **sith** since ∫ **mote** may

62 **do make** cause to be made

64–65 **gode booke to the lewid peple** The description of images as books for the unlettered derives from a letter of Gregory the Great (c. 540–604) (see Aston 1984, 115) and, like the defense of images that follows, is omnipresent in early-fifteenth-century discussions of image veneration; compare *Dives and Pauper* (excerpt 3.9).

65 **mynde** memory

66 **passioun of his manhode** the suffering he underwent in his human nature

67–68 **preente of his seele** imprint of his seal

68 **wote wel** know well. The comparison of those who worship images with aristocratic recipients of the king's seal again suggests that veneration is a sign of intimacy with, not distance from, God.

The author's confidence in the "pepyl" (59, 62) here is in marked contrast to his anxiety about the confusion plural pronouns may cause (19–35). ∫ **wexe** wax

69 **they done of here hodis** they take off their hoods

70 **figuris** copies

71 **in entente to** with the intention of

74–75 **Hit is . . . fals goddis** there is a great difference of opinion and intent between these Christian people and the opinion of those who lived in ancient times, who believed in false gods

76–77 **as seynt Austyn sayth . . . in erthe** In the passage immediately preceding the digression edited here, "seynt Austyn" is credited with an anathema on false gods ("alle godys that be nat lyke to you [God], perysshe mote they in hevyn and in erthe").

77 **despisid ben they** let them be despised

78–79 **who that** whoever

80 **verreyly** truly ∫ **sacrament of the awter** sacrament of the altar, that is, the Mass ∫ **poyntis** that is, doctrinal details. A belief that the bread and wine are "verreyly" (or *substantially*) Christ's body and blood was a litmus test of early-fifteenth-century anti-Lollard orthodoxy.

82 **mater** topic ∫ **me[v]e raise** (MS *mene*) ∫ **for** because

83 **ther** where (see 39n above)

84 **upsodowne** upside down ∫ **another kynde than he thouhte** a sense other than that he intended

85 **schende** injure

86 **by mystakyng** through misinterpreting ∫ **scripturis** authoritative writings

86–91 **Therfor . . . amonge** This passage apparently defends the translator's practice of interpolating expositions into his "scripture" (89), insisting that learning is a barrier against heresy, not a cause. For the controversial context of the passage, see Watson 1995a, 840–46.

87 **conseytes** impulses ∫ **dowtys** doubts ∫ **ymagynacions** speculations

88 **do by** follow ∫ **doctrinis** teachings

88–89 **Seynt Gregory** Gregory the Great (see 64–65n above): an unidentified quotation, probably from the *Cura pastoralis.* The translator may intend a riposte to Lollard attacks on "glosing" (overinterpreting) the Gospels.

89 **expowninge** interpretation

90 **clergy** learning. Compare *Piers Plowman* C XV (excerpt 3.19). ∫ **leder** guide

96 **stant in the contrary wyse** hold to the opposite opinion

97 **amendement** forgiveness

3.3 *THE CLOUD OF UNKNOWING:* PROLOGUE

Date and Provenance: probably 1370s–80s; east Midlands.

Author, Sources, and Nature of Text: This treatise is the longest work by the anonymous author of several rather specialized discussions of prayer and the contemplative life, including a sequel, *The Book of Privy Counsel.* These works describe a form of silent prayer that, they claim, leads to moments of mystical union, as "the cloud of unknowing," concealing God, is pierced by darts of longing love. The theological background to the work is the "negative," or apophatic, mysticism developed from the works of Pseudo-Dionysius, a Christian Neoplatonist of the fifth century who was adulated in academic circles through the late Middle Ages but whose influence in vernacular texts (like Eckhart's *German Sermons* [1320s] or Ruusbroec's Dutch *Spiritual Espousals* [1370s]) was seen by many ecclesiastics as dangerous. The *Cloud* author (one of whose works is actually a paraphrase of Pseudo-Dionysius's *Mystical Theology,* entitled *Denis Hid Divinite*) is anxiously aware of such suspicions and hopes to circumvent them by attempting to restrict his audience and by going on the offensive against those who, as he claims, willfully misunderstand him through pride, envy, or a sense of intellectual superiority. Indeed, this difficult text is full of attacks on the learned. It claims to view too much learning as a more serious hindrance to understanding than too little. Despite this claim, however, the prologue reverses the pattern found in the topoi taken from Anselm's *Prayers and Meditations* (see excerpts 3.1 and 3.2) by insisting that this text requires not piecemeal devotional reading but concentrated intellectual study, so that the exercise it describes can be properly understood and practiced. Like many vernacular religious texts of the period, its attitude toward learning and its audience's needs seems somewhat unresolved.

Audience and Circulation: The *Cloud* was apparently written for a young male contemplative (probably a newly enclosed hermit) but also anticipates reaching a broader readership of men and women, religious and lay, not all of whom will necessarily be fit as an audience (since the work's ideal reader is ostensibly not defined by external status but inner quality). The text has come down to us in seventeen copies, some fragments, and two Latin translations. Most of these originate from, and seem mainly to have circulated within, monastic communities (most frequently Carthusian), but this may be partly a matter of chance or a result of the restrictive nature of fifteenth-century intellectual culture. Book II of Walter Hilton's popular *Scale of Perfection* borrows the *Cloud*'s language (albeit to its own, rather different theological ends), introducing a version of its ideas to a wider audience, and the work was still being read in the sixteenth and seventeenth centuries.

Bibliography: Edited by Phyllis Hodgson (1944), the text has been much translated and commented upon, often by Christian writers on the spiritual life. For a bibliography to 1991, see Lagorio and Sargent 1993, 3425–29. For an analytic bibliography, see Minnis 1986. For comments on the work's construction of a model of vernacular readership and the ideology that underlies this, see Watson 1998. For literary studies, see Burrow 1977 and Ellis 1980. For the work's sources, see Clark 1980 and Minnis 1982b. The work's author was at one time thought to be Walter Hilton, but John Clark (1978) discredits this theory. For a translation of Pseudo-Dionysius, see Luibheid 1987; for his influence, McGinn 1991; Louth 1981 and 1989.

Source: London, British Library MS Harley 674, fols. 17v–18v. This fifteenth-century collection of all the works now attributed to the *Cloud* author was used as the basis of Hodgson's edition. It is a middle-size and very neat parchment manuscript, carefully produced, rubricated, and corrected, with extensive Latin marginal glosses (sometimes amounting almost to a commentary or translation). It has all the appearance of a would-be definitive text of the corpus.

This excerpt was contributed by Denis Renevey.

Here biginneth the preyer on the prologe.

God, unto whom alle hertes ben open, and unto whom alle wille spekith, and unto
whom no prive thing is hid, I beseche thee so for to clense the entent of myn hert
with the unspekable yift of thi grace, that I may parfiteliche love thee and
5 worthilich preise thee. Amen.

Here biginneth the prologe.

In the name of the Fader and of the Sone and of the Holy Goost, I charge thee and
I beseche thee with as moche power and vertewe as the bonde of charite is
sufficient to suffre, whatsoever thou be that this book schalt have in
10 possession—outher bi propirte outher by keping, by bering as messenger or elles
bi borowing—that in as moche as in thee is by wille and avisement neither thou
rede it, ne write it, ne speke it ne yit suffre it be red, wretyn or spokyn of any or
to any bot yif it be of soche one or to soche one that hath bi thi supposing in a
trewe wille and by an hole entent purposed him to be a parfite folower of Criste—
15 not only in actyve levyng bot in the sovereinnest pointe of contemplatife leving the
whiche is possible by grace for to be comen to in this present liif of a parfite soule
yit abiding in this deedly body—and therto that doth that in him is, and bi thi
supposing hath do longe tyme before, for to able him to contemplative levyng by
the vertuous menes of active levyng. For elles it acordeth nothing to him.
20   And over this, I charge thee and I beseche thee bi the autorite of charite that yif
any soche schal rede it, write it or speke it, or elles here it be red or spokin, that
thou charge hem as I do thee for to take hem tyme to rede it, speke it, write it, or
here it al over. For paraventure ther is som mater therin, in the beginnyng or in
the middel, the whiche is hanging and not fully declared ther it stondeth—and yif
25 it be not there, it is sone after or elles in the ende. Wherfore yif a man saw o
mater and not another, paraventure he might lightly be led into errour. And
therfore, in eschewing of this errour bothe in thiself and in alle other I preye thee
par charite do as I sey thee.
       Fleschely janglers, opyn preisers and blamers of hemself or of any other, tithing
30 tellers, rouners and tutilers of tales and alle maner of pinchers, kept I never that
thei sawe this book; for myn entent was never to write soche thing unto hem.
And therfore I wolde that thei medel not therwith, neither thei ne any off thees
corious lettred or lewed men. Ye, though al that thei be ful good men of active
levyng, yit this mater acordeth nothing to hem, bot yif it be to thoo men the
35 whiche, though al thei stonde in actyvete bi outward forme of levyng, nevertheles
yit bi inward stering after the prive sperit of God (whos domes ben hid) thei ben
ful graciously disposid—not contynowely as it is propre to verrey contemplatyves,
bot than and than—to be parceners in the hieyst pointe of this contemplative acte.
Yif soche men might se it, thei schuld by the grace of God be greetly counforted
40 therby.
       This book is distyngwid in seventy chapitres and five. Of the whiche chapitres,
the last chapitres of alle techeth som certeyn tokens by the whiche a soule may
verrely preve whether he be clepid of God to be a worcher in this werk or none.

2–5 **God . . . Amen** The opening invocation is from the prayer at the beginning of the Mass. It is, oddly, rare for Middle English religious texts to open with authorial prayers (they are more often placed at the end, not the beginning, of prologues). The arrangement here emphasizes both the essential equality linking writer and reader as servants of God and the purity and mystery of what follows.

2   **wille spekith** desires are known

3   **prive** secret

4   **unspekable** ineffable: a favorite concept in a text that argues that God is indescribable

7–23 **In the name . . . al over** This opening warning to readers is couched in the legal language used for excommunications and exorcisms, attempting to make what can only be a request into a conjuration that performs the exclusion it describes. Religious texts that seek to limit their own circulation are relatively rare, but compare the *approbatio* that circulated with copies of Marguerite Porete's *Mirror of Simple Souls* (c. 1305), including the Middle English version (Watson 1996). There is a suggestive analogy with magic books, where exhortations to secrecy, insistence on the esoteric nature of the material, and warnings about copying are more common; see, for example, the *Sworn Book* of Honorius of Thebes (described in Kieckhefer 1989, 170–71).

8   **vertewe** force ∫ **bonde of charite** the bond that holds writer and reader together as Christians (see Julian of Norwich's use of a similar concept, excerpt 1.13b)

9   **sufficient to suffre** is able to bear ∫ **whatsoever** whatever, that is, of whatever profession (see 15n below)

10 **bi propirte outher by keping** whether as your property or as your responsibility. The term "keping" probably alludes to the situation of a librarian with responsibility for lending books in a monastic or university context, although it could refer to the type of circulation associated with "common-profit" books, which were passed from hand to hand (see excerpt 2.5; Scase 1992). ∫ **bering** carrying

11 **by wille and avisement** by intention and advice

12 **rede it, ne write it, ne speke it** read it, nor copy it, nor expound it: the three possible ways medieval texts could be "published" (compare the use of these terms in 21–23) ∫ **suffre** allow ∫ **of any** by anyone

13 **bot yif it be** unless it is ∫ **bi thi supposing** in your judgment

14 **hole** whole, that is, sound, wholehearted ∫ **purposed him** undertaken

15 **actyve levyng . . . contemplatife leving** the traditional division of Christian modes of living into the active life of the layperson or secular priest and the contemplative one of a monk, hermit, or

nun. The terms also refer here to the spiritual states associated with these ranks. *The Cloud* is written primarily for an audience of contemplatives (although see 33–38), whereas the sequel, *The Book of Privy Counsel*, addresses a broader audience of all Christian believers.

17 **abiding in this deedly body** dwelling in this mortal body ∫ **doth that in him is** does what he is capable of. The phrase alludes to a fourteenth-century Latin tag associated with the Oxford theologian Robert Holcot and common in Middle English texts: God will not deny grace to those who do what they are capable of (*facere quod in se est*).

18 **for to** in order to ∫ **able him** prepare himself

19 **menes** habits (also implying ways to an end), that is, the works of charity associated with the active life ∫ **elles** otherwise ∫ **acordeth nothing to him** is in no way relevant to him

20 **the autorite of charite** As a specialist on the inner life, the author has little use for formal authority as designated by ecclesiastical rank, although, since "charite" is frequently associated with the Holy Spirit, the phrase implies a privileged knowledge of the truth on the author's part.

21–23 **rede it, write it . . . here it al over** See 12n above.

22 **take hem** take for themselves

23 **al over** right through ∫ **paraventure** perhaps

24 **hanging** incomplete ∫ **declared** explained ∫ **ther it stondeth** where the "mater" (23) is discussed. *The Cloud* circles round and round a small body of "mater," much of which consists of further warnings against the danger of misunderstanding, without ever finishing a discussion in the way this phrase implies: hence the need for a sequel, *The Book of Privy Counsel*.

25 **in the ende** by the end of the book ∫ **o** one

26 **lightly** easily ∫ **errour** the spiritual and intellectual condition of heretics

27 **eschewing** shunning

28 **par charite** for love's sake (a French phrase naturalized into Middle English)

29–33 **Fleschely janglers . . . lewed men** The author's attempt to warn specific kinds of readers (from chatterboxes to gossipers, to carping critics, to the merely curious) off his book employs a version of the topoi used by some poets to distinguish their efforts from the productions of mere minstrels and to insist that they do not write for fame. Compare, for example, Robert Mannyng, excerpt 1.1: 37–38.

29 **Fleschely janglers** unspiritual chatterboxes

29–30 **tithing tellers** gossipers

30 **rouners and tutilers of tales** whisperers and rumormongers ∫ **pinchers** faultfinders

30–31 **kept I never that thei sawe this book** I never cared that they should see this book.

31 **unto** for

33 **corious** inquisitive. The word has a powerful negative force throughout *The Cloud* as the work's major term for an improper reading attitude. ∫ **lettred or lewed** educated or uneducated ∫ **though al that** even though

34 **acordeth nothing** is not suitable ∫ **bot yif** unless

35 **stonde in actyvete bi outward forme of levyng** remain in the active life so far as their external state is concerned

36 **stering** urging ∫ **after** according to ∫ **domes** judgments

37 **verrey** true

38 **than and than** now and then ∫ **parceners** sharers

39 **counforted** uplifted, spiritually encouraged. For the term "comfort" as the expected reaction to a work of spiritual instruction, see the Glossary.

41 **distyngwid** divided

42 **som certeyn tokens** a number of signs—not "certeyn" in the modern sense of "sure." Because God's "domes ben hid" (36), full knowledge of his will is impossible for the *Cloud* author to attain.

43 **clepid** called ∫ **worcher** worker

3.4 JULIAN OF NORWICH, *A REVELATION OF LOVE* (LONG TEXT): EXPLICIT

Date and Provenance: after 1393–c. 1415; East Anglia (Norwich). Integral to the Long Text is a revelation dated 1393, so serious work on the text as we have it is unlikely to have begun earlier.

Author, Sources, and Nature of Text: The Long Text of Julian of Norwich's *Revelation* is a theologically speculative expansion of her earlier account (perhaps completed c. 1388; see Watson 1993) of a vision that took place in 1373, when the author was thirty (see the passages from Julian's Short Text in excerpt 1.13). We know almost nothing of Julian herself apart from what she tells us, not even her real name, but it is clear that by 1393 she had become an anchoress at the Church of St. Julian's, Conesford (in Norwich), where she was still enclosed around 1415, when she was visited by Margery Kempe (see excerpts 1.14 and 3.22). Her book is among the most ambitious works of theological speculation in Middle English. It argues, all but explicitly, that at the Day of Judgment all humanity will be saved, implying that certain of the church's teachings, in particular about God's anger at sinners, are true in a relative, not an absolute, sense. In an age when harsh attacks on ecclesiastics (whether from Lollards or other reformist writers) were common, it also manages to combine this argument with a carefully maintained deference to the church. The explicit (a final address to the reader) given in two manuscripts may be scribal but probably originates from Julian's circle. In insisting on a contextualized reading of each part of the book (in a manner that suggests nervousness regarding how some of Julian's ideas will be received), the explicit parallels the prologue to *The Cloud of Unknowing* (excerpt 3.3) and, like the *Cloud*, distances the text from the Anselmian reading model, with its emphasis on feeling, not thought, and its willingness to allow the reader to select (see excerpts 3.1 and 3.2).

Audience and Circulation: The book was written for "al myn even Christen" but did not circulate widely in the Middle Ages. Its long version survives in full form only in three seventeenth-century manuscripts copied by English Benedictine nuns in France, and in a printed edition (made by Serenus Cressy) from 1670; the Short Text is in one fifteenth-century manuscript, while excerpts from the Long Text survive as part of a devotional treatise in a Westminster cathedral treasury manuscript dated c. 1500. However, it is clear from Margery Kempe's visit to Julian, and from the regularity with which her name occurs in wills from 1393 on, that she was something of a celebrity in early-fifteenth-century Norwich, and her book, too, may have been better known than present evidence suggests, at least in East Anglia.

Bibliography: The Long Text is edited by Glasscoe (1993), Colledge and Walsh (1978), and Georgia Ronan Crampton (1994). The *Revelation* has been much translated, excerpted, and discussed. For a bibliography to

1991, see Bradley 1993, 3438–44; von Nolcken 1986 offers an analytic bibliography to 1984. The chapter headings and other apparatus are discussed by Staley Johnson (1991), who thinks them to be authorial. Windeatt (1977) compares the Long and Short Texts of the *Revelation*. For a study of the work's composition, see Watson 1993. For its devotional milieu, see Riddy 1996b. For its theology of salvation, see Watson 1997a/b. For the work's political and social context, see Aers and Staley 1996, chaps. 4–5. The best general study is Baker 1994. Ann Warren (1985) discusses recluses and their patrons. On medieval Norwich, see Tanner 1984. For a new collection of essays on Julian, see McEntire 1998.

Source: London, British Library MS Sloane 2499, fol. 57r (1600–1650). Julian's *Revelation* is the only text in this manuscript, a careful (if irregularly written) early-seventeenth-century copy of a fifteenth-century manuscript; some of the spellings seem to have been modernized. Colledge and Walsh (1978, 8) suggest the copyist may have been Clementina Cary (d. 1671), founder of the English Benedictine convent at Paris; the copy was almost certainly made in France by a nun.

I pray almyty God that this booke com not but to the hands of them that will be his faithfull lovers, and to those that will submitt them to the feith of Holy Church and obey the holesom understondyng and teching of the men that be of vertuous life, sadde age and profound lerning. For this revelation is hey divinitye and hey
5 wisdam; wherfor it may not dwelle with him that is thrall to synne and to the devill. And beware thu take not on thing after thy affection and liking and leve another, for that is the condition of an heretique. But take every thing with other. And trewly understonden, all is according to Holy Scripture and growndid in the same—and that, Jhesus our very love, light and truth shall shew to all clen soules
10 that with mekenes aske perseverantly this wisdom of hym. And thou to whome this booke shall come, thanke heyley and hartily our savior Crist Jhesu, that he made these shewings and revelations for the and to the of his endles love, mercy and goodnes, for thine and our save guide and conduct to everlestyng bliss—the which Jhesus mot grant us. Amen.

2 **faithfull lovers** Compare "Crystes looverse" at the opening of the Short Text (excerpt 1.13: 4 and note). ∫ **feith** orthodox belief

3–4 **obey . . . lerning** The reader must submit both to the church in a formal sense and to the authority of wise Christians with the virtue, age, and learning to understand the book in full; the latter group seem not to be writers but what would later be termed "spiritual directors," such as the various people Margery Kempe consulted on her spiritual needs and desires. For the topos involved here and its ultimate source, see the process of consultation the author of *Speculum Devotorum* says he went through before undertaking his book (excerpt 1.12: 22–23 and note).

3 **holesom** wholesome

4 **sadde age** mature years ∫ **this revelation** As the sentence makes clear, the phrase conflates Julian's "booke" (1) with the revelation it describes, and presupposes the argument for the book's project, found in excerpt 1.13b (the Long Text re-produces and expands most of this part of the Short Text), that the revelation is intended for, and can be apprehended by, everyone (excerpt 1.13: 55 and note). ∫ **hey divinitye** sublime theology

5 **dwelle with** remain with (here the "revelation" is personified)

6 **on one** ∫ **after thy affection and liking** according to your preference and pleasure

7 **condition** attribute ∫ **every thing with other** everything with everything else

8–9 **all is according to Holy Scripture and growndid in the same** everything in the book is in agreement with the Bible, and grounded in it. The Bible becomes the third source of authority cited in the explicit (after "Holy Church" and "men . . . of vertuous life" [2, 3–4]). Actual citations of Scripture in the text are rare.

9 **that** that is, the orthodoxy of the revelation "growndid" (8) in Holy Scripture ∫ **very** true ∫ **clen** pure

9–10 **Jhesus . . . shall shew to all clen soules that . . . aske . . . of hym** The reader's prayerful approach to the "booke" (11) must replicate Julian's approach to her revelation, and will be helped by Jesus; "shew" and "shewing" (12) are technical terms in the *Revelation* for moments of divinely inspired vision. The force of the sentence is that with understanding of the book's "wisdom" comes assur- ance of its orthodoxy, so that anyone suspicious of the work's orthodoxy has not understood the book.

10 **perseverantly** perserveringly

12 **for the and to the** for you and to you

13 **save guide and conduct** The emphasis on the text's safety as a guide acts as a final assurance of its orthodoxy.

14 **mot** may

3.5 *THE ORCHARD OF SYON:* PROLOGUE

Date and Provenance: written 1420–40; London area (Middlesex, at or near Syon Abbey).

Author, Sources, and Nature of Text: The *Orchard* was written for the nuns of the richly endowed Bridgettine convent at Syon (founded by Henry V in 1415–20, reputedly in expiation of his father's sins). The writer was perhaps a priest at Syon or a Carthusian at the twin foundation of Sheen (see excerpts 1.12, 3.12, and, for a text translated by a gentlewoman associated with Syon, 3.21). The *Orchard* is a translation of Cristafono Guidini's Latin version of Catherine of Siena's Italian *Dialogo della divina providenzza* (Dialogue concerning divine providence). The *Dialogo* itself is a prolonged theological discourse supposedly dictated in a state of ecstasy by Catherine to various scribes shortly before her death from self-starvation in 1378 (although the text's actual origins are more complex than this). It was one of the most celebrated of the books written by visionary women in the late Middle Ages, and one of a small number translated into Middle English. The conceit of the orchard that structures the text is the translator's, offering the work as a moral entertainment whose purpose is as much refreshment as improvement. Gardens and orchards in aristocratic estates and convents were designed for leisurely walking; at Syon there must have been much laying out and planting in the early years to parallel the translator's metaphoric labors. As the work's "gardener," the translator takes some responsibility for the text's effects but stresses readerly choice. Indeed, his division of the work into sections, itemized in a "kalender" at the beginning of the work, gives readers as much information as possible in approaching the work. Yet as with the *Pseudo-Augustinian Soliloquies* (excerpt 3.2), it needs asking to what extent the emphasis on feeling, not thought, and on the subordinate role the text ostensibly serves is a convenient fiction behind which the work's readers can engage in serious theological study of a kind theoretically "unsuitable" for women religious (see excerpts 2.7, 2.8, 2.9).

Audience and Circulation: The text survives in three fifteenth-century manuscripts, a printed edition by Wynkyn de Worde from 1519, and several sets of excerpts. Like Bridget of Sweden's *Liber celestis* and Mechtild of Hackeborn's *Book of Ghostly Grace* (see excerpt 3.20), parts of it were staple reading for devout aristocratic laywomen as well as nuns. Not surprisingly, however, in view of its title and opening lines, the work remained closely identified with Syon Abbey, which functioned as a kind of icon of devotional practice for many late medieval English women.

Bibliography: The work is edited by Phyllis Hodgson and Gabriel Liegey (1966). It has been discussed by Mary Denise (1958), Hodgson (1964), and most recently Denise Despres (1996). Barratt (1992, 95–107) edits excerpts. Riddy (1996b) gives a useful picture of the reading milieu in which it and other similar texts circulated. For Syon and the Bridgettines, see Catto 1985; Beckett 1993; Hutchinson 1993 and 1995; Rhodes 1993. For a translation of the *Dialogo* with bibliography and discussion of Catherine, see Noffke 1980. For the topos of literature as refreshment, see Olson 1982.

Source: London, British Library MS Harley 3432, fols. 2r–2v and 7r–7v. This is a clear, expensively produced early-fifteenth-century parchment manuscript that must have been copied shortly after the work was finished, perhaps from a fair copy of the translator's autograph. The manuscript, which contains only the *Orchard,* is the base text for Hodgson and Liegey's edition.

Religyous modir and devoute sustren clepid and chosen bisily to laboure at the hous of Syon in the blessid vyneyerd of oure holy Saveour, his parfite rewle which hymsilf enditide to kepe contynuly to youre lyves eende undir the governaunce of oure blessid Lady, hir servise oonli to rede and to synge as hir special servauntis
5 and doughtren, and sche youre moost sovereyne lady and cheef abbes of hir holy covent: I, synfulle, unworthi to bere ony name, to the worschip of that holy Saveour and at the reverence of his glorious modir, to youre goostly recreacioun with help of youre praieris, compellid by charite for goostly affeccioun, purpose to wryte to you aftir my symple felyng the revelaciouns of oure Lord to his chosen
10 mayde, Kateryn of Sene. This book of revelaciouns, as for youre goostly cumfort, to you I clepe it a fruytful orcherd. This orcherd by Goddis grace my wil is to devyde into sevene parties and ech party into fyve chapitres as ye mowe se and rede in the kalender folowynge.

In this orcherd, whanne ye wolen be conforted, ye mowe walke and se bothe
15 fruyt and herbis. And albeit that sum fruyt or herbis seeme to summe scharpe, hard or bitter, yit to purgynge of the soule thei ben ful speedful and profitable, whanne thei ben discreetly take and resceyved by counceil. Therfore, religiouse sustren, in this goostli orcherd at resonable tyme ordeyned I wole that ye disporte you and walke aboute where ye wolen with youre mynde and resoun in what aleye
20 you lyke, a[nd] namely there ye savouren best as ye ben disposid. Ye mowe chese if ye wole of xxxv aleyes where ye wolen walke, that is to seye of xxxv chapitres, o tyme in oon, anothir tyme in anothir. But first my counceil is clerely to assaye and serche the hool orcherd and taste of sich fruyt and herbis resonably aftir youre affeccioun, and what you liketh best, aftirward chewe it wel and ete thereof for
25 heelthe of youre soule.

And now, sustren, I ceesse of this prolog, and in maner of a kalender here I wole schewe you now the ordenaunce of this orcherd in tyme comynge by Goddis grace, as hym lust of his mercy to graunte me bodily hele and tyme of liif to plante it and sette it with sich fruyt and herbis as oure Lord schewide to the forseid
30 mayde in hir contemplacioun whanne hir soule was raveschid fro al bodily feelyng, as witnesseth hir clerkis and alle hir disciplis. And for as myche as I seid tofore this book schulde be devydid into vii parties and ech partie into v chapitres, here therfore I bigynne the kalender and comende me to youre prayeris.

[A lengthy table of contents follows.]

Lo sustren, I have schewid you what ympis and trees I have founde and gaderid
35 to plaunte and to sette in youre goostly orcherd. The aleyes of youre orcherd ben ful longe and brode, whereynne ben manye walkynge pathis whiche schulen lede you truly to what fruyt where you lust to feede you, in what partye thei ben sett or plauntid. But, sustren, lyke it to you to knowe that in gaderynge delitable fruyt I foond ful bittire wedis—bittir and soure thei ben to taaste but profitable to

40　knowe. Siche wedis I purpose to sette among good fruyt, not for feedynge but to
　　youre knowing. Tasteth hem and knoweth hem that ye mowe beware of eny gostli
　　enemye when thei profre you suche wedis. Savoureth hem not for ful fedynge, for
　　perilously thei worche and ful ofte to the dethe, but bi grace souner it be
　　remedied.
45　　　But sustren, though my herbis be gaderid, yit a tyme I must have of settynge
　　and of plantynge sometyme amonge in my tyme of pleienge. Grete laborer was I
　　never, bodili ne gostli. I had never grete strengthe myghtli to laboure with spade
　　ne with schovel. Therfore now, devoute sustern, helpeth me with preiers, for me
　　lackith kunnynge, ayens my grete febelnes. Strengthe me with youre pite. And
50　have me recommendid in youre gostli exercise to oure blessid Lady. And salewith
　　her in my name with devoute *Aves*, havynge sometyme mynde on her V Joies and
　　sometyme on her V Sorowes whiche she had in erthe. With this laboure I charge
　　you not but as youre charite stirith in you. With that vertu helpeth me forthe, for
　　hastly I go to laboure, in purpose to performe this gostli orchard as it plesith
55　almyghti God to lightne my soule with trewe felynge and clere sight. Whiche
　　Jhesu Crist for his moders love graunte only to his worschip and to youre gostly
　　lernynge and confortable recreacion. Amen.

1　**modir…sustren** respectively the abbess and
the nuns ∫ **clepid and chosen** called and chosen.
Syon was initially filled by recruiting anchoresses
for the foundation. The doubling of synonyms is
common in Middle English translations but especially characteristic of this particular writer.

1–2 **laboure…vyneyerd** See Matt. 20:1–16, the
parable of the vineyard paraphrased in the *Gawain*
poet's *Pearl*, perhaps here with further reference to
the account of the beloved as vineyard in Song of
Songs 8:11–12.

2　**the blessid vyneyerd of oure holy Saveour** is
both the world (as in the parable) and, more specifically, Syon Abbey. Other texts written for Syon also
begin with a discussion of the meanings of the name
"Syon" (see, e.g., *The Mirror of Our Lady*, excerpt
3.12: 13–19). Syon's Rule (see 2–3n below) starts
with Christ's declared intention of planting himself a
new vineyard, the Bridgettine order. ∫ **parfite** perfect

2–3 **which hymsilf enditide** which he himself
dictated. The Bridgettine Rule was said to have
been dictated to Saint Bridget of Sweden (d. 1373)
by Christ. Syon was dedicated to Christ and the
Virgin, who are invoked in this opening as, respectively, its patron (since the "vyneyerd" [2] is his)
and its abbess (6–7 below).

4　**hir servise oonli** As well as the Bridgettine
Breviary, the nuns of Syon used the *Mirror of Our
Lady* (excerpt 3.12) and were encouraged to use
Rolle's *English Psalter* (excerpt 3.8). On the Offices
at Syon, see Hutchinson 1989, 219–23.

6　**unworthi to bere ony name** The translator
explains his decision to remain anonymous as a

gesture of humility (although the first readers must
have known quite well who he was); compare
Bokenham's discussion of the uses of anonymity
(excerpt 1.11: 32–72).

7　**at the reverence of** out of reverence toward ∫
goostly recreacioun spiritual refreshment. The
book is intended for private reading (alone or in
small groups) during the time not occupied by the
liturgy or other formal duties; in practice, this confined reading of the work to afternoons, the only
substantial leisure time in the monastic day.

8　**compellid by charite for goostly affeccioun**
compelled by love because of spiritual affection
(i.e., love of God as well as benevolence toward sisters in religion): a reason often invoked for
undertaking devotional writing (see excerpt 1.11:
194–95 and 194n) ∫ **purpose** intend

9　**symple felyng** humble skills

10　**Kateryn of Sene** Catherine of Siena (d. 1378),
prolific writer of letters as well as author of a theological treatise, the *Dialogo*: one of the medieval
church's "approvyd wymmen" (as the *Speculum
Devotorum* has it, excerpt 1.12: 74) and, since
1970, one of two women doctors of the Roman
Catholic Church ∫ **goostli cumfort** spiritual support

11　**to you I clepe it** for your benefit, I name it.
The translator's role in structuring, introducing,
and, here, renaming the work is given unusual
prominence. This may suggest that he acted as pastoral director to the nuns, but is also of a piece with
the highly responsible mediative role the translator
of another major Syon text, *The Mirror of Our
Lady* (excerpt 3.12), accords himself. From the

outset, the translation of this text is justified by its specific usefulness in a specific context.

12–13 sevene parties . . . folowynge Compare the division of *Speculum Devotorum* (another text from a milieu closely related to *The Orchard* and *The Mirror of Our Lady*) into thirty-three chapters with an accompanying table (excerpt 1.12: 10–18 and elsewhere).

12 mowe may

13 kalender table of contents

14 conforted uplifted (see 10n above, and compare Julian of Norwich's use of this term, excerpt 1.13: 83–84)

16 to purgynge for purging. The metaphor is medicinal. Compare the penitential food eaten by Will and Patience in *Piers Plowman* C 15, excerpt 3.19. ∫ **speedful** helpful

17 discreetly take and resceyved by counceil when they are taken with discretion and received with care: an allusion to the crucial monastic and eremitic ideal of *discretio*, the principle of moderation, which should govern individual and collective decisions regarding the conduct of life, especially in relation to ascetic practices and (as in the metaphor here) medicine or food

18 resonable tyme ordeyned See 7n above.

18–19 disporte you and walke an image of recreation common (as noted in the introduction to Part Three, page 215 above) to secular and religious milieus (compare *Troilus and Criseyde* II.813–931).

20 a[nd] namely there ye savouren best and especially where you find most enjoyment. "Savouren" is a technical term in devotional language (see 3.1: 5n) and here perhaps alludes to the prologue to Anselm's *Prayers and Meditations*, quoted above (pages 212–13). ∫ **a[nd]** MS *a*

21 xxxv aleyes thirty-five paths

22 clerely completely ∫ **assaye** try out

23–24 aftir youre affeccioun according to your preference

24 chewe it wel an allusion to *ruminatio*, the meditative reading associated with monasteries

27 ordenaunce structure (as in Latin, *ordinatio*)

28 hym lust as he wills ∫ **hele** health ∫ **tyme of liif** time to live

29–30 the forseid mayde that is, Catherine of Siena

30 hir soule was raveschid fro al bodily feelyng Absence of "bodily feelyng" is part of the technical definition of the mystical state of being "raveschid" (Latin, *raptus*, "snatched").

31 tofore before

34 ympis grafts or slips: an allusion to the practice of grafting branches from one variety of fruit tree onto another. In practice the literary equivalent of grafting (i.e., compiling chapters or sections out

of several passages in the original) is not in evidence in the treatise. For another literary use of the metaphor, see Lydgate's *Troy Book* (excerpt 1.7: 116).

37 what fruyt where you lust to feede you whichever fruit you want to feed yourself with

38 lyke it to you may it please you

39–40 bittire wedis . . . profitable to knowe doctrines (such as that of eternal damnation) that must not be meditated upon too deeply (in case they drive the reader to despair or to question God's justice) but must be understood (compare excerpt 3.22: 46–77, *The Book of Margery Kempe*)

42 Savoureth See 20n above.

43–44 but bi grace souner it be remedied unless it is quickly remedied by grace

45 though my herbis be gaderid that is, though I have organized my material ∫ **settynge** sowing

45–55 But sustren . . . sight This passage, which asks for prayers to help the work along (49–54), seems to suggest that, despite the instructions to read it in its entirety, the translation was made available to the nuns as it was written (see also "in tyme comynge" [27]) and thus that it was made at or near Syon itself (see 48–49n below). It also implies that the translator's "ordenaunce" (27 and note) was initially devised in the copy of the Latin text he used for his translation, and thus that the entire project was carefully thought through before any of the work was written.

45–46 a tyme I must have . . . of pleienge That is, the translation will absorb much of the writer's available leisure time and may go slowly.

47–48 I had never grete strengthe myghtli to laboure with spade ne with schovel Unlike the Syon nuns who "bisily . . . laboure" (1), the translator is too weak to work hard. The primary reference is, of course, to the labor of writing, but the sentence could be an indication that the translator was a Carthusian, rather than from Syon (see headnote). The Carthusian Rule (the *Consuetudines*) excuses the brothers from manual labor of the kind at least ostensibly performed by members of some other religious orders and commands the writing of books instead. If the translator was a Carthusian, the humility topos used here would thus have particular point.

49 kunnynge ability

50 gostli exercise spiritual exercises ∫ **salewith** salute

51–52 Aves . . . V Sorowes The Ave Maria and the five joys and sorrows that Mary is said to have enjoyed and suffered during her life are omnipresent in Marian devotion.

51 mynde remembrance of

53 but except

57 confortable recreacion spiritual refreshment (see 10n above)

3.6 *PORE CAITYF*: PROLOGUE

Date and Provenance: c. 1380s; possibly central Midlands.

Author, Sources, and Nature of Text: This work is an unusually careful compilation from several devotional and pastoral sources: the works of Richard Rolle, *Ancrene Wisse,* various treatises on the Commandments and the Creed, and other works, not all of them yet identified. It was made by an anonymous, presumably clerical writer (probably a Franciscan) at about the time the early Lollards were beginning to propagate their program of universal vernacular education. As a systematic attempt to lead uneducated readers to the knowledge of God without invoking formal priestly authority, it is a good example of "reformist," but not Lollard, attitudes toward the laity before the battle lines between orthodox and heretic hardened (compare, e.g., *The Holi Prophete David,* excerpt 2.5). That is, the author believes in the need to educate his readers, at least in the truths necessary for salvation, but does not subscribe to Lollard positions about those truths, although he does share with Lollard writers the ambitious desire to reach an audience that includes all English-speaking people. By comparison with some works, notably *The Prick of Conscience* (excerpt 3.7), the work also has a benign sense of what these necessary truths are, depending more on the goodwill of readers than its own capacity to frighten them with threats of damnation or exhortations to penance. The prologue sets out the rationale for the work and its structure as an integrated ladder to heaven, beginning with basic catechetical instruction (the early parts of the work may be modeled on Pecham's *Syllabus* of 1281; see the section "Middle English Writing, 1300–1380," in essay 4.2, pages 334–39), continuing with more affective material (Passion meditation, passages of Rolle, and so forth), and concluding with a treatise on virginity that is presumably intended to complete the lay reader's imaginative translation from the "active" to the "contemplative" life.

Audience and Circulation: *Pore Caityf* survives in almost fifty manuscripts, most of them (despite the prologue's emphasis on the work's integration) containing only extracts of the full treatise, sometimes reworked into new compilations (such as the short compendium found in Manchester, John Rylands Library MS English 85). Many of the manuscripts were expensively produced and were probably owned by priests or wealthy laypeople (or else by nuns, as was the manuscript edited here). Yet the work also featured in trials of suspected Lollards of lower rank; indeed, copies apparently interpolated by Lollard or Lollard-leaning scribes survive (see Hudson 1988, 425), and both its appeal to the "simple" and its composition in sections made it suitable for booklet copying for a poorer readership, whose cheap copies of the text would have been unlikely to survive. For a relatively plain copy originally owned by a London merchant, which circulated as a "common-profit book" (London, British Library MS Harley 2336), see Scase 1992.

Bibliography: The sole edition of the work (only available as a Ph.D. dissertation) and most of the studies are by Mary Teresa Brady. For the edition, see Brady 1954a; for general studies, see Brady 1954b and 1980. Other studies are cited by Lagorio and Sargent 1993, 3470–71, who give a summary of the work's contents (3135–36). For a contextual discussion, see Hudson 1988, chap. 9, and Watson 1995a, 848–49. For the work's pastoral ideology, see Watson 1997a. For an analysis of the circulation of religious compilations, see Gillespie 1989.

Source: Somerset, Downside Abbey MS 26542, fol. 94r. This is a fifteenth-century parchment manuscript that (besides some short English and Latin pieces) also contains *The Prickynge of Love,* a translation (perhaps by Walter Hilton) of a treatise on the spiritual life called *Stimulus amoris,* by James of Milan, and some short items (for a description, see Watkin 1941). It is a carefully produced manuscript with systematic capitalization in red and blue pointing the structure of its texts, and with more elaborate illumination and borders for *The Prickynge of Love.* The manuscript's handwriting and layout associate it with London, British Library MS Addit. 37790 (which contains the sole surviving copy of the Short Text of Julian of Norwich's *Revelation of Love;* see excerpt 1.13). In the early sixteenth century it belonged to Beatrice Chamber, a nun at Dartford Abbey in Kent (see Bell 1995, s.v. "Dartford") and later to Yorkshire families.

On its initial blank leaf is an inscription, "Ave Maria Amen. This boke is youe to Betryce Chaumbir. And aftir hir decese to sistir Emme Wynter, and to sister Denyse Caston, nonnes of Dertforthe. And so to abide in the saam hous of the nonnes of Dertforthe for euer. To pray for hem that yeue it."

This tretyse suffisith to eche Cristen man and womman

This tretyse, compiled of a pore caityf and nedy of gostly help of al cristen peple, by the gret mercy and help of God shal teche simple men and wymmen of gode wille the right way to hevene, yf thei wille besye hem to have it in mynde and to
5 worche therafter, withouten multiplicacion of many bokes. And as a child willing to ben a clerk begynneth first atte grounde, that is his a.b.c., so he, this desiring to spede the betir, begynneth atte grounde of helthe, that is Cristen mennes bileve. For withouten bileve it is impossible, as Seint Poule seith, that any man plese God (Hebr. xi ca). But for bileve is nat sufficiant bi it self to mannes salvacion
10 withoute gode workes of charite, as Crist seith by his apostle Seint Jame, therfor he purposith with Goddis help suyngly to telle the Commaundementes of God, in whiche the charitable werkes ben contened that longen to bileve. And for it is hard to purchase ought of God in prayer til man verraily bileve and lyve after his hestes, as he seith himself in the Gospel—"wherto seien ye to me Lord, Lord, and
15 don nat tho thinges that I seie?"—therfor, foluyng after the Hestes, he thinkith with the help and mercy of God, to shewe shortly the praier that Jhesu Crist taughte his disciples, that is the *Pater Noster;* and after these, somme short sentences, exciting men to hevenly desir. For thus it bihovith to stye up, as by a laddir of dyverse runges, fro the grounde of bileve in to the keping of Goddis
20 commaundementes and so up fro vertu into vertu, til to he se God of Syon regnyng in everlasting blis, the whiche to us alle graunte, he that lyveth and regnith withouten ende, merciful God. Amen.

1 **suffisith** The work begins by advertising its own compendiousness.

2 **of a pore caityf and nedy of gostly help of al cristen peple** by a poor wretch who needs spiritual help from all Christian people. For another use of the term "caityf," see excerpt 1.14: 13. The compiler of *Pore Caityf* presents himself as the equal of his readers, rather than claim any authority over them as preacher or cleric. "Pore" may be an allusion to the Franciscan order.

3 **simple** unlearned, unpretentious. Like "caityf," the word was much in vogue in the late fourteenth and early fifteenth centuries to describe a correct devout attitude. For Lollard equivalents to these terms, see Hudson 1985, 165–80.

4 **besye hem** busy themselves ∫ **have it in mynde** remember it The book needs to be thor-

oughly internalized as well as acted upon ("worche therafter" [5]) if it is to be useful.

5 **multiplicacion of many** that is, too many. As a compendium, the work will both save readers expense and protect their "simple" natures by avoiding unnecessary learning. Compare *The Cyrurgie*, excerpt 1.10: 19–26. ∫ **willing** wanting

5–6 **as a child . . . so he** The metaphor applies to the reader, who can become a "clerk" in a spiritual sense by studying the book, but, taken literally, applies to the writer educating himself through his labors.

6 **atte grounde** at the foundation. Grammar (the first discipline in the *trivium* of grammar, rhetoric, logic) is the ground of learning, and the alphabet is in turn the ground of grammar.

7 **bileve** belief or Creed. The first section of the work is an exposition of the Apostles's Creed.

9 (Hebr. xi ca.) that is, Heb. 11:6 ∫ **But for** but because

10 **as Crist seith by his apostle Seinte Jame** See James 2:24 ("faith without works is dead").

11 **he purposith** he [the author] intends ∫ **with Goddis help** with God's help. The phrase may seem formulaic, but acts as a counterweight to any impression the prologue gives that it is offering a method for Christian living that *automatically* brings results. Compare "with the help and mercy of God" (16), and see excerpts 3.1:14n and 3.2:8n. ∫ **suyngly** following this ∫ **telle** that is, list ∫ **Commaundementes of God** that is, the Ten Commandments, the subject of the second section

11–12 **in whiche the charitable werkes ben contened that longen to bileve** in which are contained the charitable works that follow from belief

13 **purchace** acquire ∫ **ought of** anything from ∫ **after** according to

14 **Hestes** Commandments ∫ **as he seith himself in the Gospel** See Luke 6:46.

15 **foluyng after the Hestes** following the section on the Commandments

16 **shewe shortly** briefly expound

17 *Pater Noster* the Lord's Prayer: the subject of the third section of the work

17–18 **somme short sentences** In practice, there are several substantial further sections, so "sentence" is probably to be taken in its meaning of "summary, compendium," or "passage of prose, written work" (see *MED: sentence* 5d, 5c).

18 **it bihovith** it is necessary ∫ **stye up** climb up

18–19 **a laddir of dyverse runges** a ladder with different rungs: a common image for spiritual ascent in medieval religious texts. The author may have had in mind another work in the style of a compilation, Richard Rolle's *Emendatio vitae*, on which he draws later in the treatise and whose chapter 10 describes the previous nine chapters as the *gradus* (rungs) by which one attains purity of heart (Watson 1995b, 10.1–2). One source of the image is the ladder Jacob saw in a dream, reaching from earth to heaven, on which the angels ascended and descended (Gen. 28:12). The Benedictine Rule (see excerpt 2.8) uses the image in its seventh chapter, "On Humility"; Saint Bernard of Clairvaux (1091–1153) reworks it in his influential treatise on loving God (*De diligendo Deo, PL* 182:974–99).

20 **til to he se God** until he sees God ∫ **Syon** the biblical Zion

21 **the whiche to us alle graunte** may he grant it [this sight] to us all

3.7 *THE PRICK OF CONSCIENCE:* PROLOGUE (EXTRACT)

Date and Provenance: c. 1350; the north of England.

Author, Sources, and Nature of Text: This lengthy anonymous poem on the body, sin, death, the Judgment, and the shape of the otherworld used to be attributed to Richard Rolle. The work claims to be a simple tract for unlettered readers whose ignorance is so complete that they have not even learned to fear God, let alone love him. Yet its picture of hell, heaven, and purgatory draws on Anselm, Honorius of Autun, and other authorities on the topic with unusual attention to up-to-date theological detail, in a field of thinking that was changing rapidly. Moreover, many manuscript copies of the poem come with an elaborate Latin commentary, while a full Latin translation of the work also survives in multiple copies. All this, not to mention the poem's sheer length, suggests that its true purpose was informative, even scholarly, as much as evangelistic; this is perhaps why it describes itself as a "tretice" (2). The prologue elaborates a

reading model somewhat comparable to that found in *Pore Caityf* (excerpt 3.6), and the work can be seen as a theological compendium in the style of that work, but written in verse, not too long before prose became the fashionable medium for such projects (see excerpt 2.2: 123–26, for an early comment on the greater suitability of prose). But the intellectual traditions on which the two works draw are different. Here readers must put themselves through a grueling stage-by-stage process that is indebted not to the devotional texts on which *Pore Caityf* depends but to the ascetic meditations of the early thirteenth century, especially Innocent III's *De miseria condicionis humanae* (On the wretchedness of the human condition) and the pseudo-Bernardine *Meditationes piissime* (Devout meditations), texts that begin by inculcating self-disgust and fear and only gradually introduce the possibility of hope in the prospect of heavenly joy.

Audience and Circulation: Surviving in over a hundred manuscripts and in every major English dialect, the *Prick* was much the most widely circulated Middle English poem and almost the only work in Middle English whose circulation was comparable with that of the *Wycliffite Bible* (of which there are still some 250 partial or complete copies). Copies associated with most classes of the laity, secular priests, monks, nuns, and others survive or are recorded, and despite its length the work is often found complete, rather than in extract. Yet as Hudson (1988, 485–87) makes clear, the text, though it was regarded as orthodox, was owned by various suspected Lollards and in the atmosphere of anxiety that surrounded the movement was sometimes held suspect itself. Furthermore, like many other Middle English religious works (including *Pore Caityf,* excerpt 3.6, and Rolle's *English Psalter,* excerpt 3.8), it was periodically interpolated with passages of anticlerical satire.

Bibliography: Edited from a single manuscript by Richard Morris (reprinted 1973) and given a number of stylistic appraisals as part of the oeuvre of Richard Rolle in late-nineteenth-century German dissertations, the work has been given little attention since Hope Emily Allen (1910) disproved the theory of Rolle's authorship. There is now a guide to the manuscripts (Lewis and McIntosh 1982) and a number of detailed studies of individual manuscripts or passages (listed in Raymo 1986, 2490–91, along with the German dissertations), but nothing by way of literary analysis or source study: a remarkable circumstance, given the work's importance. On Anglo-Norman sources, see Relihan 1978. Rather different examples of otherworld description in vernacular visionary writing are found in Easting 1989; the work's salvation theology is briefly considered in Watson 1997b.

Source: Cambridge University Library MS Dd.11.89, fols. 14r–14v: a small book, on parchment, with several other religious items, including *The Abbey of the Holy Ghost,* all in fifteenth-century hands. Robert Lewis and Angus McIntosh (1982, 42–43) list this copy as MV10 and show that it is written in a mixture of (mainly Southern) dialects that are suggestive of the complexities of the poem's circulation history and its popularity well outside the areas of original composition.

[Summary of 1–327: Hail God, the Trinity, maker of all, who made all and at the end will destroy all but heaven and hell, as those who read this book through will see. Humanity is the summit of God's creation, and has dominion over it and power to reason and choose, and to come to heaven or be condemned to hell. Humanity is in the image of God, has been ransomed by God, and owes him love, obedience, and meekness: to gain which one must know God, his works, and first oneself. But some who are capable of this knowledge do not have it; these need to learn it from those who know more, if they are to save their souls, since lack of knowledge is no excuse, and without it they will go astray. Yet there are many obstacles in the way of gaining this learning: pride and worldly glory, which make one incapable of knowledge and blind to one's own dire predicament. Those in this condition cannot even fear God.]

Bot ho so can naught drede may lere,	**ho so** whoever; **lere** learn [to fear]
That this tretice wol rede or here,	
Yif thay rede or here to the ende	
The maters that er tharein contenyd,	
5 And undurstand hem alle and trowe,	**hem** them; **trowe** believe
Parchance there hertes suld abowe,	**Parchance** perhaps; **abowe** bow down
Thoru drede that thay suld conseyve tharby,	**conseyve** experience
To werk god werkes and fle foly.	**god** good
Tharefor this bok ys in Englis drawe,	**drawe** translated

10 Of fele maters that ar unknawe   **fele** many; **unknawe** unknown
    To lewed men that er unconna[n]d,   **lewed** uneducated; **unconna[n]d** uninformed
    That can no Latyn undurstand:
    To mak hemself frust to knowe   to make them know themselves first
    And from synne and vanites hem drawe,   **hem drawe** withdraw themselves
15 And for to stere hem to ryght drede,   **stere** move; **ryght drede** proper fear
    Whan this tretes here or rede,   **Whan** when [they]
    That prik here concience wythinne,   **prik** may prick; **here** their
    Ande of that drede may a ful bygyng   **ful** fool; **bygyng** begin
    Thoru confort of joyes of hevene sere,   **sere** various
20 That men may afterward rede here.
    Thys bok, as hit self bereth wyttenesse,
    In seven partes divised isse.   **divised** divided
    The frust part to knowe and have in mynde
    Is of the wrechenesse of mannus kynde.   **mannus kynde** human nature
25 The secund ys of the condicions sere
    And of unstabelnesse of thys world here.   **sere** various
    The thryd parte is in thys bok to rede
    Of the deth and wich he is to drede.   about death and why it is to be feared
    The ferth part of purgatori,
30 Ware souls ben glensed of here foly.   **glensed** cleansed
    The fythe is of the day of dome,   **day of dome** Day of Judgment
    And of the tokenes that byfore schal come.
    The syxt ys of paynes of helle
    Thar dampned schal ever dwelle.   **Thar** where
35 The seved ys of the joyes of hevene.   **seved** seventh
    These ar the partes of this bok sevene,
    And of alle parte fynd men may
    Fele maters in this bok to say.
    Go we to that parti that frust ys,
40 That spekes of manes wrechenes—
    For alle that ywrite ys bifor to luke,   for everything you see written before this
    This het an ontre of this bok.   is called a prologue to this book

2 **rede or here** read to oneself or hear. "Here" alludes to the public reading of texts that Coleman (1996) argues was widely practiced until the end of the Middle Ages (see also 16).

9 **ys in Englis drawe** This suggests that the poem is a translation from Latin, which is not strictly true, although its purpose is to convey Latin theological thinking into the vernacular. The work lacks the elaborate defense of the use of English found in other major religious poems of the first half of the fourteenth century—*The Northern Homily Cycle* (excerpt 2.1), *Cursor Mundi* (excerpt 3.14), and *Speculum Vitae* (pages 336–37 below)—and offers more theological elaboration than these texts. The passive construction used here avoids the neces-

sity for the author to refer to himself as "I" or "we," which seems a particular concern in this text, whose authority ostensibly derives not from a preacher or cleric but from the extent to which its elaborately detailed depiction of the cosmos is coterminous with reality (see "fele maters" [10 and 38, and 21n]).

11 **unconna[n]d** MS *unconnad*

13 Compare the opening line of the pseudo-Bernardine *Meditationes piissime*, proverbial by the fourteenth century, "Multi multa sciunt sed seipsos nesciunt" (Many people know many things but do not know themselves); the line is quoted in *Piers Plowman* B XI.3.

16 **Whan this tretes here or rede** when [they] hear or read this treatise (see 2n above)

17 **prik** is a vernacular version of Latin *compunctio,* or compunction: the state of sorrow at sin and fear of its punishment, often considered by theorists of the pastoral life as an essential first stage in any legitimate process of reform. See McEntire 1990.

18 **of that drede may a ful bygyng** out of that fear [even] a fool may begin [to reform]. On the basis of the readings in other manuscripts, the proper reading here is probably "may a love begin" (i.e., fear of God leads to love), but the text makes good sense as it stands.

21 **as hit self bereth wyttenesse** as it bears witness itself. The *Prick* insistently points to its own formal characteristics (see also 41–42). The phrase might seem a filler but would have a purpose in a public reading of the work (see 2n above). The division of a text or book into appropriate parts (see "divided" [22]) was a task of the preacher or lecturer. By insisting that the book divides itself, the author of the *Prick* removes from the public reader

the aura of authority that goes with making such divisions and restores it to the book itself.

26 **unstabelnesse** instability: the commonest medieval complaint against this world, found both in religious contexts and in texts like Boethius's *Consolation of Philosophy,* Chaucer's *Troilus and Criseyde,* or Malory's *Morte d'Arthure.* Compare Hoccleve's *Complaint* (excerpt 1.6: 8–10).

29–30 **The ferth part . . . foly** The doctrine of purgatory as a third destination for the dead, distinct from hell and heaven, came to be widely accepted in the Western church only during the twelfth and thirteenth centuries (Le Goff 1984). This poem is one of the earlier descriptions in English to acknowledge purgatory's separate existence and thus to present an up-to-date topography of the otherworld.

32 **tokenes** signs heralding the Judgment: much invoked in medieval texts for the hope they held out that the end of the world could be predicted

3.8 RICHARD ROLLE, *THE ENGLISH PSALTER:* PROLOGUE

Date and Provenance: c. 1345; northeast England (Yorkshire).

Author, Sources, and Nature of Text: Richard Rolle (d. 1349), hermit, mystic, and prolific author of ecstatic writings in Latin and English, was one of the most widely read English writers of the late Middle Ages. His works survive in almost five hundred manuscripts (including about one hundred vernacular manuscripts). This abbreviated (though still lengthy) version of Peter Lombard's standard Psalter commentary (with many characteristic Rollean additions) was probably made in the first instance with a single reader in mind (see below), albeit with a view to a larger audience as well. Given its date, the commentary is remarkable for the demands it is willing to make on its readers and for its assumption that direct knowledge of the biblical text—in a form of English as close as possible to the Latin—is desirable. Thus, in the body of the work, each verse is quoted in Latin, translated word for word so that the original can be understood (as is made clear in the prologue [62–64]), then paraphrased more loosely with a brief interpretation: a structure suited for highly

motivated readers, with some (but not perfect) Latin, who are capable of concentrated study. In its ambition, the text parallels the contemporary *Prick of Conscience* (excerpt 3.7) and anticipates later Lollard and reformist attitudes toward the vernacular, although the language the prologue uses to praise the Psalms is affective, emphasizing their value for individuals more than for the church as a whole. The work's prologue is in three parts: an evocation of the benefits of singing the Psalms (much of it from Augustine and Cassiodorus); a version of Peter Lombard's prologue, a formal exercise in identifying the Psalter's title, subject, structure, and intent known as a "type C" prologue (Minnis 1988, 9–39), which gives a number of reasons for the centrality of the Psalms in church life and liturgy; and a comment on Rolle's project, its policies, and purpose.

Audience and Circulation: The *English Psalter* seems to have been written for Margaret Kirkeby, who was a nun at Hampole Priory in Yorkshire and, from 1348, an anchoress and for whom Rolle also wrote a treatise called *The Form of Living.* A verse prologue to Oxford, Bodleian Library MS

Laud Misc. 286, states that the Psalter was composed "at a worthy recluse prayer, cald dame Merget kyrkyby" (Bramley 1884, 2), and, since all Rolle's other English works are occasional pieces, this is likely to be true. The text circulated widely and survives in forty manuscripts, many of which contain revised and amplified versions of the text: one of them a massive revision made by a Lollard scribe in the 1390s. By this time the work was read and copied in the South of England, as well as in the North, and from the early fifteenth century it became a standard text in convent and monastic libraries in addition to being copied for secular priests and devout laypeople. It was considered a pioneering attempt to vernacularize the theological genre of the biblical commentary. Defenders of Bible translation cite it as one of the major vernacular precedents for the Wycliffite Bible (see Hudson 1985, 154, for examples).

Bibliography: Edited by H. R. Bramley (1884) from a Northern manuscript, the work was given its first careful analysis by Dorothy Everett (1922–23), who listed the manuscripts and versions and whose work is indispensable; a series of editions of parts of the text in Fordham University theses has never been completed (see Lagorio and Sargent 1993, 3415–16, for references). For a study of the work in the context of Rolle's career, see Watson 1991, 242–48, which has further bibliography. For a study of Psalter commentaries as a genre, see Minnis 1988. For the Psalms in medieval England, with material on Rolle, see Kuczynski 1995. For a stylistic analysis of Middle English versions of the Psalms, especially the *Middle English Glossed Prose Psalter,* see St.-Jacques 1989. For Rolle's translation practices, see Ellis 1982a. Rolle's *Latin Psalter,* which is sometimes a source for the *English Psalter,* is available in an early printed edition (Faber 1536) and a dissertation that transcribes that edition (Porter 1929).

Source: Oxford University College MS 64, fols. 3r–3v. This manuscript, used in Bramley's edition, is a good late-fourteenth-century text in a consistent dialect close to Rolle's own; probably a monastic production, it contains only this work. The manuscript has several refoliations and signs of continued use, perhaps into the sixteenth century, when it was owned by William Wraye (fol. 7r).

Grete haboundance of gastly comfort and joy in God comes in the hertes of thaim
at says or synges devotly the psalmes in lovynge of Jhesu Crist. Thai drope
swetnes in mannys saule and hellis delite in thaire thoghtis, and kyndils thaire
willes with the fyre of luf, makand thaim hate and brennand withinen and faire
5 and lufly in Cristis eghen. And thaim that lastes in thaire devocioun thai rays
thaim in til contemplatyf lyf and oft sith in til soun and myrth of heven. The sange
of psalmes chases fendis, excites aungels til oure help; it does away synne, it
quemes God, it so enformes perfytnes, it dos away and distroys noy and angire of
saule and makes pees itwix body and saule; it bryngs desire of heven and despite of
10 erthly thynge. Sothly this shynand boke is a chosen sange byfor God, als laumpe
lyghtnand oure lyf, hele of a seke hert, huny til a bittire saule, dignyte of gastly
persons, tonge of prive vertus: the whilke heldes the proud til meknes, and kynges
til pore men makes undireloute, fosterand barnes with hamlynes. In thaim is so
mykill fayrhed of undirstandynge and medicyne of wordes that this boke is cald
15 garthen closed, wel enseled, paradyse ful of all appils. Now with halesome lare
drovyd and stormy saules [it] bryngis in til clere and pesful lyf, now amonestand to
fordo synne with teris, now hyghtand joy til ryghtwismen, now manassand hell til
wyckyd. The sange that delites the heres and lerese the saule is made a voice of
syngand, and with aungels whaim we may noght here we menge wordis of lovynge,
20 sa that worthily he may trow him aliene fra verray lyf wha sa has noght the
dilatabilte of this gyft. O wondirful suetnes, the whilk waxis noght soure thurgh

the corupciouns of this warld bot, ay lastand in the dignyte of it, in grace of purest
softnes is waxand! All gladnes and delite of erth wanys and at the last wytes til
noght; bot it, the langere tyme it has, the mare it is, and aldiremast agayns man
25   ded, when luf is perfitest.

This boke is cald the Psautere, the whilk nam it has of an instrument of musyke
that in Ebru is "nablum," in Grek "psautery," of "psallm" (that in Inglis is "to
touche"); and it is of ten cordis and gifes the soun fra the overere, thurgh
touchynge of hend. Alswa this boke leres to kepe the Ten Comaundments and to
30   wyrk noght for erthly thynge bot fore heven that is aboven; and swa we gif soun
fra upward at the touchynge of oure hend, when all that we wele doe is for Goddis
luf. Alswa this boke is distyngid in thris fyfty psalmes, in the whilk thre statis of
Cristin mannys religion is sygnifyd: the first in penance, the tother in rightwisnes,
the thrid in lovynge of endles lyfe. The first fifty is endyd in *Miserere mei Deus,*
35   the tother in *Misericordiam et iudicium cantabo,* the thrid at *Omnis spiritus laudet
dominum.*

This boke, of all haly writ, is mast oysed in Haly Kyrke servys, forthi that in it
is perfeccioun of dyvyne pagyne, for it conteyns all that other bokes draghes
langly: that is, the lare of the Ald Testament and of the New. Tharein is discryved
40   the medes of goed men, the pynes of ill men, the disciplyne of penaunce, the
waxynge in rightwise lif, the perfeccioun of haly men the whilk passis til heven,
the lyf of actyf men, the meditacioun of contemplatifs and the joy of
contemplacioun, the heghest that may be in man lifand in body and feland; alswa
what synne reves fra mannys saule and what penaunce restores—it is na ned to tell
45   ilkan here, fore thurgh the grace of God thou sall fynd thaim oppynd in thaire
stedis.

This scripture is cald "boke of ympnes of Crist." Ympne is lovynge of God
with sange. Til an ympne falles thre thyngs: lovynge of God; joiynge of hert or
thoght; affectuouse thynkynge of Goddis luf. Sange is a gret gladnes of thoght of
50   lastand thynge and endles joy, brestand in voice of lovynge. Wel than is it sayd
"boke of ympnes," for it leris us to love God with [g]lad chere and myrth and
softnes in saule—noght anly in hert bot alswa with voice lovand, and kennand
thaim that are unconand.

The matere of this boke is Crist and his spouse, that is Haly Kyrke, or ilk
55   ryghtwise mannys saule. The entent is, to confourme men that ere filyd in Adam
til Crist in newnes of lyf.

The maner of lare is swilke: umstunt he spekis of Crist in his godhed, umstunt
in his manhed, umstunt in that at he oises the voice of his servauntes. Alswa he
spekis of Haly Kyrke in thre maners: umwhile in the person of perfite men,
60   somtyme of unperfite men, som tyme of ill men whilk er in Hali Kyrke by body
noght by thoght, by name noght by ded, in noumbire noght in merit.

In this werke, I seke na straunge Ynglis, bot lyghtest and comonest and swilk
that is mast lyke til the Latyn, swa that thai that knawes noght Latyn by the Ynglis
may com til mony Latyn wordis. In the translacioun I folow the lettere als mykyll
65   as I may; and thare I fynd na propire Ynglis, I folow the wit of the worde, swa that
thai that sall red it thaim thare noght dred errynge. In expounynge, I fologh haly
doctours, for it may come in some envyous man hand that knawes noght what he
sould say, that wil say that I wist noght what I sayd, and swa doe harme til hym
and til othere, if he dispise the werke that is profytabile for hym and othere.

1 **haboundance** abundance, a word that, as the opening makes clear, sums up the Psalter's aesthetic and devotional richness in the eyes of medieval users ∫ **gastly** spiritual

2 **at** that: a Northern form. See also 58 below. ∫ **says or synges** probably distinguishes between private recitation of the Psalms and public singing in a liturgical context (i.e., in a church service). ∫ **lovynge** praising. Rolle distinguishes between love, or "lof/lov" (praise), and "luf" (love).

2–3 **Thai drope swetnes** The first section of the prologue emphasizes the power of the Psalms by describing their effect as automatic, as though they are capable of overpowering any readerly resistance. The need for concentrated study of the Psalter is only introduced after this point is established.

3 **mannys saule** the human soul ∫ **hellis** pour

4 **hate** hot ∫ **brennand** burning

5 **eghen** eyes

5–6 **And thaim . . . contemplatyf lyf** and those who continue in their devotion, they [i.e., the psalms] raise them up into the contemplative life

6 **oft sith in til soun and myrth of heven** often into the song and mirth of heaven. Here, as later, Rolle touches on one of his main themes, the ineffable heavenly song to which contemplatives can attain, of which he sees the Psalms as a verbal translation. See Watson 1991, chap. 2. ∫ **oft sith** often

6–21 **The sange of psalmes . . . of this gyft** This passage translates excerpts from the Psalter prologues of Augustine (*PL* 36:64) and Cassiodorus (*PL* 70:10), both of whose commentaries (like Rolle's) begin by imitating the Psalms' own distinctive mode—praise—in elaborate praise of the Psalter itself. The singing of the Psalms ("The sange of psalmes") is described as an especially potent form of prayer, useful for every aspect of the religious life.

8 **quemes** pleases ∫ **enformes perfytnes** shapes perfection ∫ **noy** disturbance

9 **itwix** between ∫ **despite** contempt

10 **Sothly** truly ∫ **shynand** shining ∫ **als** like

11 **hele of a seke hert** the remedy for a sick heart

11–12 **dignyte of gastly persons** the nobility of spiritual people

12 **tonge of prive vertus** the voice of secret virtues ∫ **whilke** which ∫ **heldes** constrains ∫ **til** to

13 **undireloute** bow down ∫ **fosterand barnes with hamlynes** nurturing children in gentleness. Although powerful enough to subdue kings, the Psalms are tender enough to nurture children.

14 **mykill** much ∫ **fayrhed** beauty ∫ **medicyne of wordes** For another example of this metaphor, see excerpt 3.5: 15–17.

15 **garthen closed, wel enseled, paradyse ful of all appils** an enclosed garden, a sealed well, paradise full of all apples: phrases from Song of Songs 4:12–13, where they refer to the bride

15–16 **Now with halesome lare . . . pesful lyf** sometimes [the Psalter], with its wholesome teaching, brings anguished and stormy souls into a pure and peaceful life

16 **drovyd** tormented ∫ [**it**] MS omits ∫ **amonestand** admonishing ∫ **to** in order to

17 **fordo** destroy ∫ **hyghtand** promising ∫ **ryghtwismen** righteous people

17–18 **manassand hell til wyckyd** threatening the wicked with hell

18 **heres** hearers (although other manuscripts read "hertes") ∫ **lerese** teaches

18–19 **made a voice of syngand** becomes the voice with which we, too, sing. The Psalms, from being merely delightful words, become the singer's voice as they are internalized and as the singer joins the ranks of the angels and saved souls praising God in heaven.

19 **whaim** whom ∫ **menge** mingle

20 **worthily** truly ∫ **trow him** believe himself ∫ **aliene** estranged ∫ **verray** true ∫ **wha sa** whoever

21–23 **O wondiful . . . whilk waxis . . . warld . . . waxand . . . wanys . . . wytes** Alliteration, principally on "w" and "s," heightens the rhetorical effect in this passage of praise.

21 **dilatabilte** delectation ∫ **suetnes** sweetness

22 **ay** eternally ∫ **the dignyte of it** that is, its own nobility

22–23 **in grace of purest softnes is waxand** is always growing in the delight of clearest pleasure

23 **wanys** wanes ∫ **wytes** fades

24 **mare** greater

24–25 **aldiremast agayns man ded** and most of all at the point of a person's death

26 **This boke is cald the Psautere** The abrupt change of tone here is the result of a change of source, from Cassiodorus (*PL* 70:10) to Peter Lombard. For a translation of the equivalent passage of the Lombard's Latin, see Minnis and Scott 1988, 105–12, the notes to which explain many points passed over silently here. The next passage expounds, in fixed order, the Psalter's name (26–29), structure (29–36), use (37–39), contents (39–46), formal title (47–53), subject matter (54–55), intention (55–56), and manner of teaching (57–61): for a poetic example of the "type C" prologue to which this structure belongs, see excerpt 1.11. ∫ **of** from

28 **overere** upper part

29 **hend** hand ∫ **Alswa** also ∫ **leres** teaches

29–36 **Alswa . . . *dominum*** The tripartite division of the Psalter was traditional, going back at least to Augustine. Rolle omits much detail found in Peter Lombard, who offers various arrangements and numerological comments. The Latin phrases are the titles and first phrases of Psalms 50, AV 51 ("Have mercy on me, O God"), and 100, AV 101 ("I will sing of mercy and judgment"), and the last words of Psalm 150 ("Let everything that has breath praise the Lord").

31 **fra upward** from our highest nature

32 **distyngid** divided ∫ **thris** thrice

37 **oysed** used ∫ **forthi that** because

38 **dyvyne pagyne** the divine page (Latin *divina pagina,* a common term for Scripture)

38–39 **conteyns all that other bokes draghes langly** sums up everything the rest of the Bible expounds at length. The notion that the Psalter contains the whole Bible in microcosm was a medieval commonplace (see, e.g., Minnis 1988, 42–58). For comparable praise of the compendium or compilation as a literary form preferable to texts that "draghe langly," compare excerpts 1.10: 19–24, and 3.6: 2–5.

39 **lare** teaching ∫ **discryved** described

40 **medes** rewards ∫ **pynes** punishments

40–41 **the waxynge** the process of growing

41 **the whilk passis til heven** who are on their way to heaven

43 **the heghest that may be in man lifand in body and feland** of the highest kind someone can have in a living, feeling body. The summit of contemplative joy is reserved for heaven, but the Psalter offers the closest earthly equivalent.

44 **what synne reves fra mannys saule** what sin steals from the human soul

44–45 **it is na ned to tell ilkan here** there is no need to explain all of them here. This signals another series of omissions from Peter Lombard's commentary.

45 **oppynd** declared

46 **stedis** places

47 **ympnes** hymnes

47–48 **Ympne is lovynge of God with sange** a hymn is the praise of God through song: a formal definition of the hymn

48 **joiynge** rejoicing

49 **affectuouse** passionate

49–50 **of lastand thynge** about eternal things

50 **brestand** bursting ∫ **in** into

51 **[g]lad** MS *clad*

52 **softnes** pleasure ∫ **anly** only ∫ **alswa** also

52–53 **kennand thaim that are unconand** teaching those who are unlearned. Singing the Psalms becomes a pastoral or evangelistic activity, a metaphor for the lived Christian life.

54–55 **matere** and **entent** translate the Latin technical terms *materia* (a work's subject matter)

and *intentio* (a work's purpose) ∫ **ilk ryghtwise mannys saule** every righteous person's soul

55–56 **to confourme . . . lyf** to conform to Christ in newness of life people who are defiled in Adam (i.e., by Adam's sin)

57 **maner of lare** translates the technical Latin *modus tractandi* (method of teaching). ∫ **umstunt** sometimes

57–58 **he spekis of Crist . . . of his servauntes** That is, some passages of the Psalms refer to Christ as God, some to Christ in his incarnate humanity, some to Christ as the power of the Holy Spirit working in his servants.

58 **oises** uses

59 **umwhile** sometimes

59–60 **perfite . . . ill men** the three traditional categories of Christian: perfect, imperfect, and wicked

60–61 **whilk er . . . noght in merit** who are members of holy church in body, not thought, in name, not deed, by number [i.e., formally speaking] but not in merit

62 **In this werke, I seke na straunge Ynglis** in this book I am not striving after elaborate English. Compare Mannyng's similar rejection of "strange Inglis" (excerpt 1.1: 40). Rolle turns from translating portions of Peter Lombard to address the reader in his own voice. ∫ **lyghtest** easiest

63 **mast lyke til the Latyn** closest to the Latin. Rolle does not acknowledge the tension between his two stated aims, to be idiomatic and to be faithful to the original. To some extent the tension is overcome by the strategic use of synonyms (e.g., translating into doublets, with a Latin-derived word accompanied and glossed by one derived from Old English), but in practice, fidelity to the original generally wins out in the body of the translation.

64 **com til** come to [understand] ∫ **follow the lettere** translate word for word (i.e., follow Latin word order and syntax), or follow the literal sense (rather than any of the passage's allegorical meanings)

65 **thare** where ∫ **propire** suitable ∫ **the wit of the worde** the meaning of the sentence

66 **thaim thare noght dred errynge** there is no need for them to fear falling into error ∫ **thare** need (*v. imper.*) ∫ **expounynge** [my] exposition

66–67 **I fologh haly doctours** Rolle excuses his dependence on sources (on which he generally prefers not to rely), not by stating that they have expounded the Psalter better than he can (an admission that would perhaps undermine the previous account of the Psalter's continuing power), but by citing the need to reassure readers of the authority of the exposition. Compare *Speculum Devotorum* (excerpt 1.12: 73–76), and, for other invocations of the "envoys" to justify literary strategies, excerpt 1.11: 196–98 (Bokenham), and the extended discussion in 1.16: 62–85 (Pecock).

68 **wist noght what I sayd** did not know what I was talking about (i.e., both "did not understand the text" and "had not experienced what I claimed to have experienced")

3.9 *DIVES AND PAUPER:* PART ONE, CHAPTERS 1–3 (EXTRACT)

Date and Provenance: 1405 or 1410; probably southwest England (perhaps Bristol).

Author, Sources, and Nature of Text: *Dives and Pauper* is a lengthy treatise on the Ten Commandments, written in the fashionable early-fifteenth-century form of dialogue. It was written by an anonymous friar, also author of a later work called the *Longleat Sermons,* which outspokenly opposes the recent imposition of Arundel's *Constitutions* of 1409, insisting on the continuing duty of all knowledgeable Christians to preach and teach God's law (Hudson and Spencer 1984). The text consists of a slightly one-sided conversation between Dives, the representative of the intended reader (who is wellborn, earnest, and male), and Pauper, the representative of the author (who is fictionalized as a poor wandering preacher). After a first section ostensibly dealing with the topic of poverty but in fact explaining how a life of virtue is consistent with the possession of wealth, it covers each of the Commandments in turn, dealing with various practical aspects of the Christian faith, generally from a social, or sometimes legal, perspective, and introducing a number of more abstract theological topics. These include some of the more controversial issues of the day, like the value of images and pilgrimage or the meaning of the Eucharist, all of which are discussed frankly, from the perspective of the "reasonable" educated layman, and with no apparent fear of persecution. The work's sources, which include a number of canon-law texts, reveal author's and reader's interest in secular and ecclesiastical government and the public, rather than devotional, life of a wellborn layperson: a life that is seen as independent of priestly control to the extent that Pauper almost never invokes his authority to convince Dives of a position but depends solely on persuasion, treating Dives as an equal. (See Trevisa's *Dialogue,* excerpt 2.2, for a text in which the clerkly writer is clearly subordinate to his aristocratic patron.) The passage here is untypical of the work as a whole, in that it deals with the affective topic of venerating images by "reading" them in the manner of a devotional biography: by 1410 a controversial subject (compare excerpt 3.2b), on which the work develops a position that is orthodox in outline, if not always in detail. Yet this subject too is dealt with in an objective, not affective, tone, conceding to the reader the right to think independently and rationally about his or her devotions.

Audience and Circulation: The work survives in eleven manuscripts (eight complete), some owned by the wealthy laypeople for whom it was written, others by monasteries and university colleges. It was printed three times before the Reformation (1493, 1496, and 1536). Like other works, it also filtered down to readers well below the governing classes and featured in at least one heresy trial (see Hudson 1988, 417–20, for examples and a discussion).

Bibliography: The work is edited by Priscilla Barnum (1976–80), but has received little commentary beyond discussion of its date. Barnum's volume of introduction and notes has never appeared, although a brief introduction to her first volume (1976–80, 1:ix–xvii) gives some account of the issues surrounding the work, with further bibliographic references. For the work's ambiguous status as a "reformist" text verging on Lollard positions, see Hudson 1988, 417–20; Hudson and Spencer 1984; Watson 1995a, 849, 854–56. For the controversy over images, see Aston 1984 and 1988. For lay devotion in the fifteenth century, see Duffy 1992. On "reading" Christ's body, see Gillespie 1984 and Aers and Staley 1996, chapters 1–2.

Source: Glasgow University Library MS Hunterian 270, fols. 21r–22v: a handsome and carefully corrected fifteenth-century parchment volume containing only this work, written in one column with many rubrics and occasional marginal glosses. Its appearance is typical of the surviving manuscripts of this work, most of which exhibit similar care. The manuscript belonged to Henry Parker (d. 1470), a Carmelite of Doncaster. It is the base text used by Barnum for her edition.

[Dives attacks images as contrary to the first commandment and is slowly convinced of error.]

DIVES. Qherof servyn these ymagys? I wolde they weryn brent everychon!
PAUPER. They servyn of thre thynggys. For they been ordeynyd to steryn manys mende to thynkyn of Cristys incarnacioun and of his passioun and of holye seyntys lyvys. Also they been ordeynyd to steryn mannys affeccioun and his herte
5 to devocioun, for often man is more steryd be syghte than be heryng or redyngge. Also they been ordeynyd to been a tokene and a book to the lewyd peple, that they moun redyn in ymagerye and peynture that clerkys redyn in boke. [. . .]
DIVES. How shulde I rede in the book of peynture and of ymagerye?
PAUPER. Qhanne thu seeist the ymage of the crucifix, thynke on hym that deyid
10 on the cros for thin synne and thi sake, and thanke hym of his endeles charite that he wolde suffryn so mechil for the. Take heid be the ymage how his head was corownyd wyth the garlond of thornys tyle they wentyn into the brayn and the blod brast out on every syde for to dystroyghe the heye synne of pryde that shewyt hym most in mannys hed and wommanys—and make an ende of thi pryde. Take
15 heid also be the ymage how hese armys weryn spred abrod and drawyn wol streyte upon the tree tyl the senuys and the veynys crakyddyn, and how hese hondys weryn naylid to the cros and stremedyn on blode for to dystroyghe the synne that Adam and Eve dedyn wyth here hondys qhanne they tokyn the appyl agens Godys forbode. [. . .]

[Pauper works his way through the seven deadly sins and different aspects of Christ's suffering in this fashion.]

20 And, as Seynt Bernard byddyght, take heid be the ymage how his heid is bowyd doun to the, redy to kyssyn the and comyn at on wyth the. See how hese armys and hese hondys been spred abrod on the tree in tokene that he is redy to fangyn the and halsyn the and kyssyn the and takyn the to his mercy. See how his syde was openyd and his herte clovyn on too, in tokene that his herte is alwey opyn to
25 the, redy to lovyn the and to forgevyn the alle trespas yyf thu wylt amende the and askyn mercy. Take heid also how hese feet weryn naylyd wol harde to the tree in tokene that he wyl nought flein awey from the but abydyn wyth the and duellyn wyth the wythouten ende. On this maner, I preye the, rede thin book and falle doun to grounnde and thanke thin God that wolde doon so mechil for the, and
30 wurshepe hym abovyn alle thyngge—nought the ymage, nought the stok, stoon ne tree, but hym that deyid on the tree for thin synne and for thin sake [. . .] For yyf thu doo it for the ymage or to the ymage, thu doist ydolatrye. [. . .]

[Dives points out that people have trouble with this distinction, and Pauper underlines its importance.]

DIVES. How myghte they doon al this aforn the ymage and thow nought wurshepyn the ymage?

35 PAUPER. Often thu seeist that the preist in chirche hatz his book aforn hym on the deske. He knelyst, he staryst, he lokyst on his book, he heldyst up hese hondys, and for devocioun, in caas, he wepyst and makyst devowte preyerys—to qhom, wenyst thu, the prest doth al this wurshepe?

DIVES. To God and nought to the book.

40 PAUPER. On the same maner shulde the lewyd man usyn his book, that is, ymagerye and peynture, and thynkyn that he wurshepyst nought his book, ymagerye and peynture, but that he wurshepyst God abovyn alle thyngge and seyntys in here degre, and that al the wurshepe that he doth aforn the ymage he doth it nought to the ymage but to hym that the ymage representyst hym.

1 **Qherof servyn these ymagys?** What is the use of these images? ∫ **brent** burnt. Images were occasionally burned by Lollard sympathizers from perhaps the mid-1380s on, and threats to burn them were common (see Hudson 1988, 303, for examples). By alluding to burning, the text is able to raise the specter of Lollardy (which, by 1405–10, was falling out of favor among most of the upper and merchant classes) and thus covertly urge readers toward conformity with what had become a key position in the anti-Lollard stance. Compare excerpt 3.2b.

2 **ordeynyd** established ∫ **steryn** move

6 **tokene** symbol ∫ **a book to the lewyd peple** a book for uneducated people: the standard defense of images, deriving from Gregory the Great's letter to Bishop Serenus of Marseilles and endlessly cited during the image controversy between 1390 and 1410 (see Aston 1984, 115, 138)

6–7 **that they moun redyn . . . in boke** so that they can read by means of sculptures and paintings [the things] clerks read in books. *Dives and Pauper* does not address the fact that it is also a book, one written not for "clerkys" but for a notionally "uneducated" lay readership, and thus avoids what for Lollard writers was an inevitable opposition between images and vernacular books.

8 **How shulde I rede** For accounts of the devotional "reading" of Christ's body this phrase alludes to, see Gillespie 1984.

9 **Qhanne** when

11 **mechil** much ∫ **the** thee ∫ **Take heid** observe ∫ **be** in

13 **brast** burst ∫ **for to** in order to

15 **drawyn wol streyte** extended very forcibly

16 **senuys** sinews

18 **here** their

18–19 **agens Godys forbode** against God's commandment

20 **byddyght** exhorted. For this passage, see Bernard of Clairvaux (d. 1153), *Sermon on the Song of Songs* 20, a famous account of devotion to the Passion.

21 **comyn at on wyth the** be united with you

22 **fangyn** seize

23 **halsyn** embrace

24 **on too** in two

25 **amende the** make amends

26 **wol harde** very hard

29 **that wolde** who wished ∫ **doon** to do

30–31 **stok, stoon ne tree** stump, stone, nor tree (or wood). Phrases such as this are commonly used in negative descriptions of images, especially pagan idols (compare excerpt 3.2: 45–47). The kind of veneration of images encouraged here, in which the image is a "token" of what it represents, not something worthy of veneration in its own right, was theoretically unorthodox by 1410, when anti-Lollard theorists had established a strong position (much influenced by eucharistic theory) on the importance of offering adoration (*latria*) to the actual object and venerating it as more than a mere memorial. But the position taken here seems to have been de facto acceptable, similar to that implied in the *Pseudo-Augustinian Soliloquies* (excerpt 3.2: 59–73) and by later writers like Pecock (see excerpt 1.16).

33 **aforn** before ∫ **thow** yet

35–38 **Often thu seeist . . . wurshepe** an interesting description of the gestural rhetoric that might accompany an act of public reading (whether the priest is reading his "book" to himself, before or after a church service, or aloud to his congregation)

37 **in caas** sometimes
40 **lewyd** unlearned

40–41 **his book, that is, ymagerye and peynture** That is, sculpture and painting are to the unlearned as books are to clerics.

43 **in here degre** according to their rank
44 **that** whom ∫ **representyst hym** represents to him

3.10 NICHOLAS LOVE, *THE MIRROR OF THE BLESSED LIFE OF JESUS CHRIST*: PROLOGUE (EXTRACT)

Date and Provenance: c. 1409; northeast England (Yorkshire), at Mount Grace Charterhouse.

Author, Sources, and Nature of Text: This work is a version of the important *Meditationes vitae Christi.* The *Meditationes,* a retelling of the Gospels (with much additional material) was attributed to the Franciscan theologian Bonaventure (d. 1274), though actually composed by a slightly later and less famous Franciscan, Johannes de Caulibus (early fourteenth century). This version was made by Nicholas Love—the newly elected prior of England's newest Carthusian house, who earlier in his career may have been an Augustinian friar (see Sargent 1992, xxii–xxiii)—and rapidly established itself as one of the most important Middle English religious texts of its era. Written specifically to counter Lollard teachings and in particular as an orthodox substitute for the Wycliffite Bible, the *Mirror* was submitted to Archbishop Arundel at the time his *Constitutions* were being published (1409) and received his enthusiastic approbation as a model of devout writing for the uneducated. Many manuscripts of the work include a memorandum recording Arundel's approval, stating that he read the book over several days and "commended it, ordering it to be published for the edification of the faithful and the confutation of heretics and Lollards" (translated from Sargent 1992, 7). At the work's publication, Arundel was admitted to the confraternity of Mount Grace, and a few years later a holiday in his honor was declared throughout the order, a rare privilege that is suggestive of the close ties he had established with Mount Grace, perhaps as a result of the *Mirror.* The work

elaborates an affective doctrine of unremitting meditation on the life and death of Christ, which it proposes as a substitute for Bible reading and the asking of doctrinal questions. Most of it consists of a devotional biography of Christ that draws together the gospel accounts (shorn of much of Christ's actual teaching) with stories from other sources, as well as prayers, exhortations, and an anti-Lollard treatise on the Sacrament. The prologue is one of the best discussions in Middle English of the internal visualizing of sacred history, which formed so important a part of devout lay reading practice and of one ideology that underlies that practice.

Audience and Circulation: Like the Wycliffite Bible, the *Mirror* was copied systematically and in a single, broadly comprehensible dialect (that of the Central Midlands) and was soon distributed to convents, parish churches, and lay owners. There are nearly sixty manuscripts in existence, and the work was one of the bestsellers of the early print era, with nine editions between 1484 and 1530. For an early, worried, but perhaps resisting response to the work, see another text derived in part from the *Meditationes, Speculum Devotorum* (excerpt 1.12). For what may be an attempt to refute the work's conservative model of instruction, see the prologue to an unedited work by the author of *Dives and Pauper* (excerpt 3.9), the *Longleat Sermons* (Hudson and Spencer 1984; Watson 1995a, 855–56).

Bibliography: The work is edited by Michael Sargent (1992), who provides an indispensable introductory discussion of its context, and a full bibliography. For further discussion, see Salter 1974 on the devotional background; Gillespie 1984, 1987, and Watson 1997a on Passion meditation. For a sociological study, see Beckwith 1993. On political context, see Watson 1995a, 851–55. Sargent 1995, and Oguro, Beadle, and Sargent 1997 give more information on the manuscripts, sources, and early forms of the text.

Source: Cambridge University Library MS Addit. 6686, pp. 4–7 (this manuscript is paginated, not foliated). This is an early-fifteenth-century parchment manuscript that also contains the *Contemplations on the Love and Dread of God* and book I of Walter Hilton's *Scale of Perfection*. The text is closely related to that found in a manuscript kept at Mount Grace during the fifteenth century (Cambridge University Library MS Addit. 6578), which may have been the copy submitted to Arundel (see Sargent 1992, lxxii–lxxvi, for a full account). The prologue, which begins with the rubric "The byginnyng, the proheme of the boke that is clepede *The Mirroure of the Blessede Lif of Jhesu Criste*" (p. 1), contains an elaborate table of contents similar to that in *The Orchard* (excerpt 3.5) and *Speculum Devotorum* (excerpt 1.12).

[All that is written is written for our doctrine, says Saint Paul, and this is true of the stories of lives of holy people and preeminently of anything written about our lord Jesus Christ, and the life he lived in his human nature. Saint Augustine states that Christ is so great a medicine that every human sin may be healed by reflecting on his virtues.]

And for this hope and to this entent with holy writt also bene writen diverse bokes and tretees of devout men, not onlich to clerkes in Latyne bot also in Englishe to lewed men and wommen and hem that bene of symple undurstandyng. Amonge the whech bethe writen devoute meditacions of Cristes life more pleynly in
5 certayne parties then is expressede in the gospelle of the foure Evangelistes. And as it is seide, the devoute man and worthi clerke Bonaventure wrote hem to a religiouse woman in Latyne: the which scripture and writyng for the fructuose matire therof stiryng specialy to the luf of Jhesu and also for the pleyn sentence to comune understandyng semeth amonge other sovereynli edifiyng to symples
10 creatures the weche as childrene haven nede to be fedde with mylk of lyght doctrine, and not with sadde mete of gret clergie and of hye contemplacion. Wherfore at the instaunce and prayer of summe devoute soules to edificacion of seche men or wommen is this drawynge oute of the forseide boke of Cristes life writen in Englishe—with more put to in certayne parties and also with drawyng of
15 diverse auctoritees and matires as it semeth to the writere hereof moste spedful and edifiynge to hem that bene of symple understandyng. To the whech symple soules, as seynt Bernard seith, contemplacion of the manhede of Criste is more likyng, more spedeful and more siker than is hie contemplacion of the godhede. And therfore to hem is principaly to be set in mynde the ymage of Cristes
20 Incarnacion, Passion and Resurreccion, so that a symple soule that can not thenke bot bodies or bodily thinges mowe have sumwhat acordyng to his affeccion wher with he may fede and stire his devocion.

[There follows a discussion of how meditations can appropriately embellish the gospel narrative and add edifying pictures of things even if they may not have happened. The "Mirror" of the book's title is explained, and the following passage from the Latin Meditationes is introduced as "Bonaventure's" prologue.]

Amonge other virtuese comendynges of the holi virgyne Cecile it is writen that
she bare alwey the gospel of Criste hidde in her breste—that mai be undirstande
25 that of the blessed life of our lord Jhesu Criste writen in the gospelle she chace
certayne parties moste devoute—in the which she set hir meditacion and her
thouht nyght and day with a clene and hole herte. And when she had so fully al the
manner of his life overgonn, she began ayeyne. And so with a liking and swete
taste, gostly schewyng in that manere the gospell of Criste, she set and bare it ever
30 in the privete of her breste. In the same I counseil that thou do. For amonge al
gostly exercyses I leve that this is moste necessarye and moste profitable, and that
may bringe to the hyest degre of gude livyng, that stant specialy in perfite
despisyng of the worlde, in pacience suffryng of adversites and in encrese and
getyng of vertues. For sotheli thou schalt never finde wher man may so perfiteli be
35 taght—firste fort[o] stable his herte ayeyns vanites and deceyvable likynges of the
worlde, also to strengh him amongst tribulacions and adversitees and forthemore
to be kept fro vices and to getyng of virtues—as in the blessed life of oure lord
Jhesu, the which was ever withoute defaute most perfit.

First I say that besi meditacion and customable of the blessede life of Jhesu
40 stableth the saule and the hert ayeyns vanitees and deceyvable likinges of the
worlde. This is opunli schewede in the blessed virgine Cecile befor nemede, when
she fillede so fully her hert of the life of Criste that vanitees of the worlde might
not entre into her. For in al the grete pompe of wedding where so many vanitees
bene usede, when the organes blewene and songene, she set hir hert stably in God,
45 seiyng and preying, "Lord, be my herte and my bodi clene and not defilede, so that
I be not confoundet!" Also as to the secounde: whereof haven martires here
strengh ayens diverse tormentees bot, as seynt Bernarde seith, in that thei setten al
here herte and devocion in the passione and the woundes of Criste?

[This and other benefits of Passion meditation are elaborated further.]

Wherefore thou that coveitest to fele trewli the fruyt of this boke, thou most
50 with al thi thought and al thin entent in that maner make the in thi soule present
to thoo thinges that bene here writen, seyd, or done of oure lord Jhesu, and that
bisily, likyngly, and abidyngly as thei thou herdest hem with thi bodily eres, or sey
thaim with thin eyen doun, puttyng awey for the tyme and levyng al othere
occupacions and bisynesses. [. . .]

1–3 **And for this hope . . . symple undurstandyng**
Devotional books are seen here supplementing the
Bible (an idea abhorrent to Lollards), although, in
what follows, this quickly shifts to Love's real point,
which is that such books should *replace* the Bible for
"lewed men and wommen."
   2   **onlich** only
   3   **lewed** unlearned ∫ **hem that** those who
   4   **more pleynly** more fully and/or more simply.
Love is explaining how the *Meditationes* on which
the *Mirror* is based give details of Christ's life not
found in the Gospels, but also how they omit material (especially teaching material) from the Gospels.

6   **Bonaventure** See headnote.
   7–11 **the whiche . . . contemplacion** Note Love's
use of an impersonal voice that conceals the processes by which the *Meditationes* have achieved the
status he describes, or by which certain readers are
defined as "needing" spiritual "mylk," not meat
(10–11), even though these very issues were deeply
controversial when he wrote. It is a large part of the
skill of this prologue to present the *Mirror* and its
translator's authority as absolute without giving
any reasons for this.
   7–8 **fructuose matire** fruitful subject matter
   8   **stiryng** moving

8–10 **also for the pleyn sentence . . . to symples creatures** and also because the [book's] plainness of meaning to the common understanding seems, in comparison with other writings, particularly helpful to simple people ["creatures"]

10–11 **mylk . . . mete** See 1 Cor. 3:2. Only spiritual milk is suitable for beginners.

11 **sadde** serious ∫ **clergie** learning

12 **at the instaunce and prayer of summe devoute soules** For the devotional topos that a work is written on request, compare excerpt 1.12 (*Speculum Devotorum*). Unusually, the "devoute soules" said to have asked for the book are distinguished from the "men or wommen" (13) it is written for, the implication perhaps being that Love writes as representative of devout *clerics*.

13 **seche** such ∫ **drawynge oute** translation

14–16 **with more put to . . . understandyng** Love is careful to explain his alterations of his source.

14 **put to** added ∫ **drawyng of** drawing on

16–18 **To the whech . . . godhede** paraphrased from William of St. Thierry's *Golden Epistle*, a text often attributed to William's more famous colleague, Bernard of Clairvaux (d. 1153). Meditation on Christ's humanity is appropriate for the simple, whereas meditation on the more abstract subject of Christ's divine nature should be reserved for the educated and spiritually mature.

18 **likyng** attractive ∫ **spedeful** profitable∫ **siker** secure

20–21 **can not thenke bot bodies** can think only about bodies

21 **acordyng to his affeccion** appropriate to his emotions

23 **comendynges** commendations ∫ **Cecile** Saint Cecilia, one of the most popular of the apocryphal virgin martyrs of the early church (see the entry under her name in Farmer 1978). Love here draws not only on the *Meditationes* but on the life of Cecilia in Jacobus de Voragine's *Legenda aurea*, the most famous medieval collection of saints' lives (which he paraphrases in 23–30), making Cecilia into a figure for a privatized and silent devotion whose mode is affective and repetitive, not progressive. For a very different understanding of the moral

to be drawn from Cecilia's life and death, see Julian of Norwich, *Revelation of Love,* excerpt 1.13a.

25 **chace** chose

28 **overgonn** worked her way through ∫ **liking** pleasing

29 **gostly schewyng** revealing (or visualizing) in her spirit ∫ **bare** carried

30 **private** secrecy

31 **leve** believe

31–32 **that may bringe** one that may bring

32 **stant specialy** especially consists

34 **sotheli** truly

34–35 **thou schalt never finde . . . taght** you shall find no place where someone can be taught so well. The phrase introduces a series of three items—stabilizing the heart, strengthening against adversity, protecting against vice (35–37)—which are then further discussed. This structure, where the meaning of a text (or, in this case, a life) is subdivided for detailed discussion, is standard in late medieval sermons and treats Cecilia's life as though it were a verse of Scripture.

35 **stable** steady (*v.*) ∫ **deceyvable** deceptive ∫ **likynges** pleasures

36 **forthemore** for the more

39 **besi** intense ∫ **customable** habitual

40 **stableth** steadies

46 **confoundet** ruined

46–48 **whereof haven martires . . . woundes of Criste.** The passage is translated from Bernard of Clairvaux's *Sermons on the Song of Songs* 61 (*PL* 183:1073–74): martyrs flee the world by hiding, in their imaginations, within the wounds of the crucified Christ, so wrapping their bodies with his body.

46–47 **here strengh** their strength

47 **bot** except ∫ **in that** insofar as

49–54 **Wherefore . . . bisynesses** For the advice to "make the in thi soule present" (50) to the events of Christ's life, see excerpt 1.13a and notes (Julian of Norwich, *Revelation*).

50 **the** yourself

52 **bisily, likyngly, and abidyngly** intently, willingly, and constantly ∫ **as thei** as though

53 **levyng** leaving

3.11 *SERMON OF DEAD MEN:* PERORATION

Date and Provenance: c. 1400; (?) west Midlands; the dialect is "Central Midlands Standard," but there are very few pointers regarding the place or the date of composition.

Author, Sources, and Nature of Text: This lengthy anonymous funeral sermon is linked in the manuscripts with parts of what is now a fragmentary sermon cycle, consisting of this work plus seventeen sermons on the gospel passages prescribed to be read on approximately a quarter of the Sundays of the year, as well as a few feast days like Christmas (for the organizing principle, see the *Northern Homily Cycle,* excerpt 2.1). Whether the cycle was ever complete, and whether the *Sermon of Dead Men* was specifically composed as part of it, is not known. Like the cycle as a whole, the sermon belongs in the large category of Middle English works that seem Lollard in attitude without being definitively so in doctrine (see excerpt 2.4 and headnote). In its peroration, the work's treatment of death and the Last Things (heaven, hell, and the Day of Judgment) does omit all mention of purgatory (whose existence was denied by many Lollard writers) but does not set out to refute the doctrine, while the rest of its discussion is theologically comparable with texts like *The Prick of Conscience* (excerpt 3.7). The text's antagonism to monks and clerics is equally ambiguous, reproducing a common Lollard complaint that the learned deny the unlearned access to saving knowledge, but in a way that could align it with a text like *Pore Caityf* (excerpt 3.6) as easily as with more obviously radical works. What is clear is that the work registers a protest against the kind of attitude toward the unlearned eloquently displayed in the previous excerpt (3.10, Love's *Mirror*), describing the vision of God in heaven as an eternal opportunity to read from the source of all knowledge and promising that "deynous doctouris" (15) who refuse to give the unedu-

cated access to learning in this life will be unable even to read God's "book" in the next.

Audience and Circulation: The work survives in two manuscripts and may have been meant for private reading as well as for actual preaching. This is suggested not only by the work's length but by cross-references elsewhere in the sermon cycle—for example, sermon 15, "Whoso wole se more of this mater, he may fynde in the sermoun of Deed Men" (Cigman 1989, 194)—that imply address to a reader, not a listening audience. On the other hand, the passage below is highly alliterative and is clearly meant to be read aloud, whether as a formal sermon or within a small group of hearers.

Bibliography: The work is edited by Gloria Cigman (1989), but has generated little discussion, though Cigman provides some analysis (1989, xlii–li; 1996). See Hudson 1988, chap. 9, for the milieu in which the text circulated, and Spencer 1993 for a study of preaching in late medieval England.

Source: Oxford, Bodleian Library MS Rawlinson C.751, fols. 25r–25v. This is a small early-fifteenth-century parchment manuscript written in a single column by a single scribe. The text appears with ten other sermons from the cycle as well as five tracts from *Pore Caityf* (excerpt 3.6). In the manuscript's present form, *Sermon of Dead Men* is incomplete at the beginning. For a description of the manuscript, see the introduction to Cigman 1989 by Jeremy Griffiths (xxi–xxix).

The fourthe good thing in whiche prinsepaly that blisse shal stonde inne shal be the glorious sight of the Trinite, bothe in his godhed and in his manhed, of whiche spekith Crist in the gospel of Jon, seying thus: *Hec est vita eterna ut cognoscant, etc.*—that is, "This is the liif that ever shal last, that thei know thee, verrey God in
5 Trinite, and whom thou sendist, Jesus Crist." This sight of God in his godhed and manhed togider the aungels desiren ever to biholde therin, as the apostil Peter witnessith in his pistil.

This is the Book of Liif that Jon spekith of in the *Apocalipse*. This boke makith man that lokith [ther]inne so kunnyng of the first day that he knowith al clergy
10 and kunnyng of craftis and al wit hathe at his wille of what he wole desire. Alle myraclis and merveylis, the most that ever God made, whiche were wonderful to her wit while thei wandrid here, shal be to hem light ynow that loken on this

book. The lewidest knave of the kychyn here shal be there clerke, and take dignite
of degre in dyvinite at the first lesson that he lokith in this boke, when alle
15 deynous doctouris shullen drawe there abacke that now letten suche lewid men to
lerne her Lordis lawe. For what persoone that plesith God most perfitly in this
worlde, be he clerke, knyght or knave, when he thider comyth, shal be most made
of and next the mageste.

This boke shal never be claspid up ne closid in no cloyster, but as opun to one
20 as to another, for that is oure Lordis ordre. This boke is so bright and so breme to
hem alle that he nedith never other light of launterne ne of laumpe, as large as the
plase is, to loke in her lesson. The lovely loking on her lesson shal like hem so wel
that thei shal ever wake and never winke, withouten ony werines, and ever fast
withouten feding of ony worldly fode: for the feire sight of his face shal fully feest
25 hem alle. Now blessid is that blessid place and alle the peple therein, and blessid
is that bright body that bryngith hem al that witt!

Lorde, for the blode that thou bleddist to bye man with so dere, gyve us grace
to have in mynde these foure last thingis, that we mow se with thi seyntis the sight
of thi face. Amen. Amen.

1   **The fourthe good thing** The preceding three
are the city of God, the joy each individual will feel,
and the communal joy the saved will feel. Each is
carefully subdivided. ∫ **prinsepaly** principally

2   **bothe in his godhed and in his manhed** The
formulation is derived from the doctrine of the Incarnation and is frequently applied to Christ but is
rare in discussions of the Trinity.

3   *Hec . . . cognoscant* John 17:3. The Middle
English translation adds a phrase, "in Trinite," not
in the original (4–5).

7   **pistil** epistle. See 1 Pet. 1:12. The phrase "in
his godhed and manhed togider" (5–6) has no
equivalent in the original.

8   **Book of Liif** See, for example, Rev. 3:5. In
describing the vision of God as a book (designed,
as the following passage implies) for "looking" as
much as for reading, the *Sermon* author may be
alluding to the illustrated Apocalypses produced
for devout lay reading especially from the thirteenth century onward (books that would have
been unaffordable as personal books for much of
the *Sermon*'s intended audience). See Lewis 1991
and 1995, for discussion of these books, and excerpt 2.2: 106–7 (Trevisa's *Dialogue*), for an
example of an Apocalypse mural.

9   **[ther]inne** MS *inne* ∫ **clergy** learning

10   **kunnyng of craftis** knowledge of skills ∫ **al
wit hathe at his wille of what he wole desire** understands whatever he wants at will. Compare *Sawles
Warde*, where the blessed "witen of al thet is ant
wes ant eaver schal iwurthen, hwet hit beo, hwi and
hwerto, and hwerof hit bigunne" (know about everything that is and was and ever shall be, what it

is, why, and for what end, and where it began from)
(Millett and Wogan-Browne 1992, 104.1–2).

10–13   **and al wit . . . book** This passage rewrites
in explicit class terms a common topos that details
the bodily and spiritual rewards given the blessed in
heaven: the *dotes corporis* and *dotes animae*, elaborated in Anselm's *Similitudines*, which make an early
appearance in Middle English in *Sawles Warde*. See
Savage and Watson 1991, 219–20. The *dotes* include radiance, security, swiftness, and wisdom.

11   **most** greatest

11–12   **wonderful to her wit** incomprehensible
to their intelligence

12   **hem** them ∫ **light ynow** simple enough ∫ **loken
on** look at

13   **lewidest** least educated ∫ **here . . . there** common synonyms for "in this life" and "in the next"

13–14   **take dignite of degre in dyvinite** attain
the dignity of a degree in divinity. This account of
the reversal of status between high and low is reminiscent of *Piers Plowman* C XV (excerpt 3.19).

15   **deynous** disdainful ∫ **drawe . . . abacke** hesi-
tate ∫ **that** who ∫ **letten** prevent

16   **her** their

16–18   **For what persoone . . . mageste** This
statement of the doctrine that heavenly reward is
commensurate with earthly virtue rather than rank
is quite orthodox (frequently found, e.g., in Rolle),
although its use here is obviously anticlerical.

18   **next the mageste** that is, closest to God

19   **claspid up** an allusion either to the chained
and locked books of medieval institutional libraries or to the locked chests in which books were often
kept (compare Justice 1994, 67–73)

20 **ordre** a pun on "religious order" and "rule" ∫ **breme** splendid

21 **he nedeth** it [i.e., the book] needs ∫ **he nedith never other light of launterne ne of laumpe** See Rev. 21:23 and compare *Pearl* 1044–47: "Hem nedde nawther sunne ne mone . . . / The self God watz her lombe-lygt, / The lombe her lantyrne, wythouten drede."

21–22 **as large as the plase is** despite the size of the place

22 **loke in her lesson** to look over their reading (*lectio*) ∫ **like** please

23 **winke** sleep. The ascetic but exclusive ideals of the clerical life will be open to all in heaven.

24 **feest** feast (*v.*)

26 **bryngith hem al that witt** In contrast to Love's *Mirror* (excerpt 3.10), the body of Christ, as it is contemplated, here bestows "witt," knowledge, more than it does devout feeling.

27 **dere** precious

3.12 *THE MIRROR OF OUR LADY:* THREE PROLOGUES

Date and Provenance: 1420–50; London area (Middlesex), at or near Syon Abbey.

Author, Sources, Nature of Text: This tripartite work is mostly a commentary on, and in part a translation of, the Bridgettine Office (or order of service) used daily by the nuns of Syon. Like the Bridgettine Rule, the Office was claimed to have been dictated to Bridget by God in her vernacular (Swedish) but then given a definitive Latin translation by a panel of clerics, an act of translation from a less to a more authoritative language that *The Mirror of Our Lady* rather anxiously reverses. In commenting on the Office, the anonymous author exercises a care and stylistic expansiveness that are typical of works written for Syon during its early years (such as *The Orchard of Syon,* excerpt 3.5, and the translation of the Bridgettine Rule, *The Rewyll of Seynt Savioure*). Such qualities may in part suggest that these works were translated by the same man: a reference in the *Mirror's* second prologue to "this boke, or eny other of oure drawyng" (78–79), shows that the author of this work had written, or expected to write, more. They may equally suggest that the *Orchard, The Mirror of Our Lady,* and *The Rewyll of Seynt Savioure,* at least, were written as parts of a coherent program of vernacular writing for the Syon nuns, who had special needs as members of the only Bridgettine house in England, as well as special privileges as members of a well-endowed royal foundation. But the caution the author elaborately shows in introducing his book also suggests the difficulties of writing a religious work in English after Arundel's *Constitutions*

(see the section "Religious Writing, 1380–1520," in essay 4.2, pages 339–45), even for so privileged an audience as the Syon nuns. The confident account of the place of reading at Syon given in the prologue to book II of the work ([b] below)—which lists five things to be kept in mind while reading, while giving an interesting account of the range of religious texts available to the nuns and the purposes each theoretically served—thus needs to be read in light of the less assured prologues with which the work begins. The first of these prologues, to book I, is a defense of the need for the nuns to understand what they read and sing; the second, a defense of the work itself against detractors and a careful account of the translation policy followed in the work and the difficulty of avoiding ambiguity (with which compare especially Trevisa's *Dialogue* and *Epistle,* excerpt 2.2, and the account of scriptural ambiguity in *The General Prologue to the Wycliffite Bible,* excerpt 1.15).

Audience and Circulation: The work survives in a single (now divided) manuscript of the later fifteenth century (Aberdeen University Library MS 134 and Oxford, Bodleian Library MS Rawlinson C.941) and an edition printed in 1530 by Richard Fawkes. This edition seems to have been made in the hope of reaching a wider audience than the small community of Bridgettines at Syon, as part of a program of self-advertisement by the Syon community; there are signs that this program was undertaken as a rearguard action against the reforms under way in the English church that, during the 1530s, led to the dissolution of English religious houses (see Hutchinson 1995).

Bibliography: Edited from Fawkes's 1530 edition by John Henry Blunt (1873), the text has been analyzed by Roger Ellis (1984, 115–23) and Ann Hutchinson (1989, 1993, 1995), who is preparing a new edition. For bibliography relating to Syon, see *The Orchard of Syon* (excerpt 3.5). For later texts that serve a similar function and also employ the topos about the inability of nuns to understand Latin but that do not share the nervousness evident in this fifteenth-century text, see Bishop Fox's translation of *The Rule of Seynt Benet* for the nuns of the Winchester diocese (excerpt 2.8) and *The Amesbury Letter* (excerpt 2.9). On the popularity of Bridget of Sweden and the English

circulation of her revelations, see Ellis 1982b.

Source: London, British Library C.11.b.8, Aii–Bi, Giii–Gv (*STC* 17542): one of at least seven surviving copies of this handsome folio volume, which was printed by Richard Fawkes in London, November 4, 1530. Fawkes printed only the first two of the work's three parts. An opening woodcut shows Saint Bridget writing her order's Office to the dictation of the Holy Spirit (here part of a Trinitarian pietà, balanced by the Virgin and newborn child, as the Father holds the dead Son). The equivalent illustration in the manuscript, in contrast, shows a bleeding, dolorous Christ (see Blunt 1873, lxi, lxii, for reproductions).

a. Prologues to Book I

Here begynneth the Prologue of thys presente boke folowynge, which is called *Oure Ladyes Myroure*.

Viderunt eam filie Syon, et beatissimam predicaverunt. These wordes are writen in Holy Scripture and are thus to say in Englyshe: "The doughtres of Syon have sene
5 hyr" (that is to say, oure Lady), "and they have shewed hyr moost blessyd." In whiche wordes, the Holy Goste sayth thre thinges that longe to the praysynge of oure mooste blessed Lady: fyrste, who they be that prayse hyr (whan he sayeth "the doughters of Syon"); the seconde, what they doo or they begynne to prayse hyr (whan he sayeth that they "have sene hyr"); the thyrde, the maner of hyr
10 praysynge (whan he sayeth "and they have shewed hyr mooste blessed"). Therfore, he sayeth "The doughtres of Syon have sene hyr and they have shewed hyr most blessed."

    Fyrste, the Holy Goste tellyth who they be that prayse our Lady, for he callyth them "doughtres of Syon." But though all Chrysten soulles that treuly lyve in
15 Chrysten fayth may be called "doughtres of Syon," that is to say, of Holy Chyrche, yet more properly ye ar called "doughters of Syon." For not onely ye ar doughtres of Holy Chyrche by Chrysten byleve, as other Chrysten people ys, but also ye are doughtres of this holy relygion, which as a mother noryssheth youre soulles in grace, in this monastery that ys named Syon. [. . .]
20   The seconde thynge that the Holy Goste tellyth in these wordes ys that ye ought to doo or ye begynne to prayse oure Lady: and that ys that ye oughte to "se her." For ye wote well that no man ne may well shewe the worthynes or the propertyes of any thynge to the praysynge therof but yf he have fyrste som syght and knowlege of the same thinge by one meane or other. How shall ye then condewly
25 shewe by outwarde praysyng the excellent hyghnes and worthynes of the moste blyssed hevenly quene, oure reverente Lady, as yt is full fayre expressed in al youre holy servyce, but yf ye have fyrste syght therof by inwarde understandinge?

    But for asmoche as many of you, thoughe ye can synge and rede, yet ye can not se what the meanynge therof ys; therefore to the onely worshyp and praysyng of

30 oure lorde Jesu Chryste, and of hys moste mercyfull mother oure Lady, and to the
gostly comforte and profyte of youre soules, I have drawen youre legende and all
youre servyce in to Englyshe, that ye shulde se by the understondyng therof how
worthy and holy praysynge of oure gloryous Lady is contente therin, and the more
devoutely and knowyngly synge yt and rede yt and say yt to her worshyp. [. . .]
35   And for as moche as ye may se in this boke as in a myrroure the praysynges and
worthines of oure moste excellente Lady, therfore I name it, *Oure Ladyes
Myroure*—not that oure Lady shulde se herselfe therin, but that ye shulde se her
therin as in a myroure, and so be styred the more devoutly to prayse her, and to
knowe where ye fayle in her praysinges, and to amende, tyll ye may come there ye
40 may se her face to face wythouten eny myrroure.
     And therfore now, moste dere and devoute systres, ye that ar the spouses of
oure lorde Jesu Chryste and the specyall chosen maydens and doughtres of his
moste reverende mother, lyfte up the eyen of your soulles towarde youre soverayne
lady, and often and bysely loke and study in this her myrroure, and not lyghtely
45 but contynually, not hastynge to rede moche atones but labouryng to knowe what
you rede, that ye may se and understonde her holy service and how ye may serve
her therwyth to her most plesaunce, that lyke as it goyth dayly thorughe your
mouthes, so let yt synke and savoure contynually in youre hartes. [. . .]

*[There follows a series of subjects for meditation on the life of Mary for each day of
the week.]*

     The thyrde thynge that the Holy Gooste shewyth in the sayde wordes is the
50 maner how ye shall prayse oure mooste reverende and gloryous Lady: and that ys
openly, mekely and devoutly. For openly ye owghte to prayse her and dystynctely,
that other folke may understonde youre praysyng to theyr edyfycacyon. And
therfore he sayeth, "they have shewyd": for a thyng that is shewyd is made open
to other folkes knowlege. Ye ought also to prayse her mekely, so that in the open
55 shewynge of her praysynge, ye seke her worshyp and not youre owne. And
therfore he saythe, "They have shewyd *her*," and not hymselfe. Devoutly also
ye ought to prayse her, beholdinge in youre mynde in tyme of youre praysynge by
inwarde love and devocyon, how glorious, how excellente, and how blyssyd she ys
above all creatures whome ye prayse. And therfore he saythe, "They have shewyd
60 her moste blessyd." [. . .]

Here endyth the fyrste prologue and begynneth the seconde.

Yt is not lyght for every man to drawe eny longe thyng from Latyn into oure
Englyshe tongue. For there ys many wordes in Latyn that we have no propre
Englyssh accordynge therto, and then suche wordes muste be turnyd as the
65 sentence may beste be understondyd. And therfore, though I laboure to kepe bothe
the wordes and the sentence in this boke as farre as oure language wyll well
assente, yet some tyme I folowe the sentence and not the wordes as the mater
asketh. There is also many wordes that have dyverse understondynges, and some
tyme they ar taken in one wyse, some tyme in an other, and som tyme they may be

70 taken in dyverse wyse in one reson or clause. Dyverse wordes also in dyverse
scryptures ar set and understonde some tyme other wyse then auctoures of gramer
tell or speke of. Oure language is also so dyverse in yt selfe that the commen
maner of spekyng in Englysshe of some contre can skante be understondid in some
other contre of the same londe. And for these causes and suche other, yf any
75 persones there be that holde themselfe connyng—as some do, that whan they can
onely a lytell gramer or a lytel Latyn, and scarcely that wel—they ar more bolde to
catche at a mannes saynge or at hys wrytynge then wolde many wyse clerkes that
be. Therfore yf eny suche parsone happen to se this boke, or eny other of oure
drawyng, and fynde eny thynge therin not drawen to hys entente and therfore is
80 redy to blame yt and to say yt is wronge, I counsell you that in symplenes seke
your soulles fode, and to take lytell hede at hys saynges: wyttynge well that the
wyser that eny man ys, the better wyll he be advysed or he blame an other mannes
studdy, and the lesse good that he can, the more presumptuous wyll he be to fynde
defaulte and to deprave, ye, often tymes tho thynges that he understondyth not.
85 And therfore they that holde them selfe so wyse may be contente wyth theyr owne
wysdome, for I began thys werke nothynge for them, but for the edyfycacyon of
you that fele symplely in your owne wyttes and love to be enformyd. I am not
wyser then was Seint Hierome, that in the drawyng of Holy Scripture from other
langage in to Latyn sayth how he was compellyd at eche boke to answere to the
90 bakbyt[in]ge of them that depraved hys laboure.
　　But for that I knowe myne owne feoblenes, as well in connyng as in verteu,
therefore I wyll neyther seke defaulte in other ne maynteyne myne owne. But
lowely I submyt me and all oure wrytynges and other werkes to the correccyon of
oure mother Holy Chyrche, and of the prelates and fathers therof, and of all that
95 are wyser and can fele better—besechynge you all way mooste dere and devoute
systres to praye that bothe thys and all other dedes be ever rewlyd to oure Lordes
worshyp. Amen.

b. Prologue to Book II

Devoute redyng of holy bokes ys called one of the partes of contemplacyon, for yt
causyth moche grace and comforte to the soulle yf yt be well and dyscretely used.
100 And moche holy redynge is ofte loste for lacke of dylygence that yt is not entended
as yt oughte to be. Therfore yf ye wyll profyte in redynge ye nede to kepe these
fyve thynges.
　　Fyrste, ye oughte to take hede what ye rede that yt be suche thynge as ys
spedefull for you to rede and convenyente to the degre that ye stonde in. For ye
105 oughte to rede no worldley matters, ne worldely bokes, namely suche as ar
wythout reason of gostly edyfycacyone and longe not to the nede of the howse; ye
oughte also to rede no bokes that speke of vanytyes or tryfels and moche lesse no
bokes of yvel or occasyon to yvel. For syth youre holy rewle forbydeth you all
vayne and ydel wordes in all tymes and places, by the same yt forbyddeth you
110 redynge of all vayne and ydel thynges. For redynge is a maner of spekeynge.
　　The seconde: whan ye begynne to rede or to here suche bokes of gostly fruyte as
accordeth for you to rede or to here, that then ye dyspose you therto with meke
reverence and devocyon. For lyke as in prayer man spekyth to God, so in redynge

God spekyth to man; and therfore he oughte reverently to be herde. And also
115 meke reverence had to the worde causeth grace and lyghte of understandynge to
enter in to the soulle, wherby the soulle seyth and feleth more openly the trouth of
the worde and hathe the more comforte and edyfycacyon therof. [. . .]

The thyrde: that ye laboure to understande the same thynge that ye rede. For
Caton taughte his sonne to rede so hys preceptes that he understande them. For yt
120 is, he sayth, "grete neglygence to rede and not to understande." And therfore
when ye rede by yourself alone, ye oughte not to be hasty to rede moche at ones,
but ye oughte to abyde therupon, and som tyme rede a thynge ageyne twyes, or
thryes, or oftener, tyl ye understonde yt clerely. For saynt Austyn sayeth that no
man shulde wene to understonde a thynge syffycyently in eny wyse by ones
125 redynge. And yf ye cannot understonde what ye rede, aske of other that can teche
you; and they that can oughte not to be lothe to teche others. [. . .] They also that
rede in the Covente ought so bysely to overse theyr lesson before and to
understonde yt that they may poynte yt as it oughte to be poynted and rede yt
savourly and openly to the understondinge of the heres. And that may they not
130 doe but yf they understonde yt and savoure yt fyrste themselfe.

The iiii thing that is to be kepte in redyng is that ye dresse so your entente that
your redyng and study be not only for to be connynge or for to can speke yt
fourthe to other, but pryncypally to enforme yourselfe and to set yt awarke in
youre owne lyvynge. [. . .]
135 The fyfte thyng ys dyscressyon, so that after the matter ys, therafter ye dresse
you in the redyng. For ye shall understonde that dyverse bokes speke in dyverse
wyses. For some bokes ar made to enforme the understondynge and to tel how
spiritual persones oughte to be governed in all theyr lyvynge that they may knowe
what they shall leve and what they shall do, how they shulde laboure in clensyng
140 of theyr conscyence and in gettyng of vertewes, how they shulde withstonde
temptacyons and suffer trybulacyons, and how they shall pray and occupy them in
gostly excercyse, with many suche other full holy doctrynes. And when ye rede
in eny suche bokes, ye oughte to beholde in yourselfe sadly whether ye lyve and do
as ye rede or no, and what wyl and desyre ye have therto. [. . .]
145 Other bokes ther be that ar made to quyken and to sturre up the affeccyons of
the soule, as som that tel of the sorowes and dredes of dethe, and of dome and of
paynes, to sturre up the affeccyons of drede and of sorow for synne. Som tel of
the grete benefites of our lorde Gode, how he made us and boughte us and what
love and mercy he shewyth contynewaly to us, to sturre up oure affeccyons of love
150 and of hope in to hym. Somme telle of the joyes of heven, to sturre up the
affeccions of joye to desyre thyderwarde; and some telle of the foulnes and
wretchednesse of syn, to sturre up the affeccyons of hate and lothynge ther agenst.
When ye rede these bokes, ye oughte to laboure in yourselfe inwardly, to sturre up
your affeccions accordingly to the matter that ye rede—as when ye rede maters of
155 drede ye ought to set you to conceyve a drede in yourselfe; and when ye rede
maters of hope ye oughte to sturre up yourselfe to fele comforte of the same hope,
and so fourth of other. Netheles yt is expediente that eche persone use to rede and
to study in this maner of bokes suche matters as be moste convenyente to hym for
the tyme. For yf eny were drawen downe in bytternes of temptacyon or of
160 trybulacyon yt were not spedefull to hym for that tyme to study in bokes of

hevynes and of drede, though he felte hymselfe wyllyng therto, but rather in suche
bokes as mighte sturre up hys affeccyons to comforte and to hope. [. . .]

There be also some bokes that treate bothe of maters to enforme the
understondyng and also of matters to sturre up the affeccions, somtyme of the
165 tone and some tyme of the tother. And in redynge of suche bokes ye oughte to
dyspose you to bothe as the matter asketh, and as I have now sayde before. [. . .]

3   *Viderunt . . . predicaverunt* Song of Songs
6:8. Much of the first prologue consists of an exposition of this verse, which is divided (5–10) and
expounded in the manner of a sermon about the
meaning and justification of the book. The author
avoids translating *"predicaverunt"* as "have
preached," which might dangerously imply (at least
to church authorities ignorant of the Bridgettine
Rule) that the nuns of Syon have a preaching mission rather than a duty to "shew" truth by their
lives. He may also add "Syon" to his text, a word
that is not in modern editions of the Vulgate Bible.

5   **shewed** could mean "declared" but is interpreted in the first prologue rather as "witnessed."

6   **longe to** belong to, that is, are relevant to

8   **or** before

14–19 **But though . . . Syon** All Christians are
"doughtres of Syon" in a certain sense, but the nuns
of Syon Abbey can claim a special relation to the
term. The presentation of Syon nuns as simultaneously representative of all Christians and as
specially privileged seems characteristic of texts
written for them. In their prayer to the Virgin the
nuns are reminded that "ye saye not *gratas* and
quas [Latin feminine endings] that myghte be sayde
onely of you, but ye say *gratos* and *quos* [masculine
endings] that whyle ye knytte *nos* therto [i.e., while
you say prayers that appropriate these masculine
endings to yourselves] muste nedes be understonde
bothe of men and wymen" (Blunt 1873, 93).

17 **by Chrysten byleve** by virtue of [your] Christian faith

18 **this holy relygion** this holy religious house,
that is, Syon Abbey

20–27 **The seconde thynge . . . inwarde
understandinge** The general moral point that praise
requires knowledge of what is praised is particular-
ized so as to justify the author's literary project, to
give sight or "inwarde understandinge" to the nuns
by translating their service.

22 **wote** know

23 **to the praysynge therof** in order to praise it ∫
but yf unless

24 **condewly** duly

25 **hyghnes** majesty

26 **full fayre** most beautifully

27 **fyrste** beforehand ∫ **by** through

28 **for asmoche as** because ∫ **synge and rede** that
is, as choir nuns

28–29 **yet ye can not se what the meanynge
therof ys** that is, yet you do not understand the
meaning of the words. The topos that nuns did not
understand Latin recurs, for example, in Fox's
translation of *The Rule of Seynt Benet* (excerpt
2.8), but its relation to reality was no doubt variable (Bell 1995, chap. 3).

29 **onely** singular

31 **gostly** spiritual ∫ **drawen** translated ∫ **legende**
lessons, that is, the readings accompanying the service

33 **contente** contained

34 **knowyngly** intelligently

35–40 **And for as moche . . . myrroure** With this
explanation of the work's title (which is unusually
precise in its account of the meaning of the common
"speculum" image), compare, for example, excerpts 1.4: 63–65 (Usk's *Testament*), 1.12: 56–59
(*Speculum Devotorum*), 2.17: 1–2 and 1n
(*Spektakle of Luf*). Mirrors were commonly held to
be not only reflective but exemplary, and to show
patterns of what one should be, rather than simply
reflect what one was.

38 **styred** moved

39 **there** where

41–42 **spouses . . . maydens . . . doughtres** As
"professed" virgins, the Syon nuns are Christ's
spouses and wear (like other nuns) his wedding ring,
and are the Virgin's servants and daughters, since
she is the preeminent example of professed virginity
as well as the mother of the bridegroom. However,
since Syon was dedicated to Christ and the Virgin,
this language again has a more particular reference;
compare excerpt 3.5: 1–6 (*Orchard of Syon*).

43 **eyen of your soulles** spiritual eyes

44 **bysely** earnestly ∫ **lyghtely** casually

45 **hastynge** rushing ∫ **atones** at once

46 **that** so that

47 **her most plesaunce** her greatest pleasure

47–48 **that lyke . . . youre hartes** so that just as
it daily goes through your mouth, so let it enter and
be tasted continually in your hearts. On "savoure"
(48), see 3.1: 5n (*A Talking*).

51 **openly** publicly ∫ **mekely** humbly

52 **that other folke may understonde youre praysyng to theyr edyfycacyon** Since the Syon nuns were strictly enclosed, it is unclear how they were supposed to "edify" "other folke," but the reference may be to the devout lay gentlewomen who found various informal types of association with the foundation (such as Eleanor Hull, see excerpt 3.21). Alternatively, the passage may anticipate a wider audience for *The Mirror of Our Lady* itself, as a text that represents the nuns to the world.

56 **hymselfe** themselves

62 **lyght** easy

63–64 **that we have no propre Englyssh accordynge therto** to which there are no corresponding English words (compare Rolle on the same problem, excerpt 3.8: 64–66)

64 **turnyd** translated

65 **sentence** meaning

67 **assente** agree

68 **asketh** requires: a standard apology for having to retreat from word-for-word into sense-for-sense translation ∫ **understondynges** meanings

68–74 **There is also many wordes . . . same londe** Latin words need to be translated according to their meaning in a given context, which often differs from dictionary meaning, and English words mean different things in different dialects (compare *Troilus and Criseyde* V.1793–94). This linking of what might be considered two separate language problems has the effect of deprivileging Latin and Latin learning, in preparation for the defensive passage that follows.

70 **reson** sentence

71 **scryptures** writings ∫ **set** ordered ∫ **auctoures of gramer** authorities on grammar

73 **skante** hardly

74 **contre** region

75 **connyng** learned

75–76 **that whan they can onely a lytell gramer or a lytel Latyn** who when they understand only a little grammar or a little Latin

78 **yf eny suche parsone happen to se this boke** The figure of the male critic imagined here as a reader of the text is partly a topos of defensive passages but also suggests uncertainties about the work's actual circulation, or perhaps about its reception either by nuns who know more Latin than they are said to (see 28–29n) or by their priests. For the topos that makes any criticism of a text into a sign of the critic's lack of charity, see, for example, excerpt 1.14: 8–9 (Margery Kempe), and Julian of Norwich's theological elaboration in excerpt 1.13b: 60–84.

79 **not drawen to hys entente** not translated according to his understanding

80–81 **in symplenes seke your soulles fode** seek your soul's food in humility

81 **hys saynges** that is, the way things are said

82 **the better wyll he be advysed** the more prudent will he be ∫ **or** before

83 **can** is capable of

84 **deprave** condemn

86 **nothynge** in no way

87 **symplely** humbly ∫ **enformyd** instructed

88 **Hierome** Jerome (c. 342–420), late-fourth-century translator of the Vulgate Latin version of the Bible. Pecock alludes to Jerome's critics in similar terms (excerpt 1.16: 111–12).

90 **bakbyt[in]ge** slanderous attacks. Fawkes's text reads *bakbytge*.

91 **connyng** learning

92 **maynteyne** persist in

92–95 **But lowely . . . fele better** For this double submission, see excerpt 3.4: 1–4 (Julian's *Revelation*) and notes.

93 **lowely** humbly

95 **fele** understand

96 **rewlyd** directed

98 **partes of contemplacyon** reading, meditation, and prayer (*lectio, meditatio, oratio*): a triad traditionally invoked in both monastic and devotional texts (compare *A Talking*, excerpt 3.1)

100 **entended** understood

104 **spedefull** profitable ∫ **convenyente** appropriate

106 **wythout reason of gostly edyfycacyone** not intended for spiritual edification ∫ **longe not to the nede of the howse** do not belong among the house's [i.e., convent's] requirements. Note the emphasis on communal responsibility even in the choice of private reading, for the reason given in 110 ("redynge is a maner of spekeynge": even private reading is not silent).

111 **gostly fruyte** spiritual fruition

112 **accordeth** are suitable

113–14 **as in prayer man spekyth to God, so in redynge God spekyth to man** a standard definition, perhaps taken from Richard Rolle's *Emendatio vitae*, chap. 9 (see Watson 1995b, 54–55)

119 **Caton** either Cato the Censor, 234–149 B.C., or his great-grandson Cato Uticensis, 95–46 B.C. The following lines paraphrase the opening of the *Distichs of Cato*, a popular medieval book of proverbs and moral commonplaces said to have been taught by Cato to his son.

122 **abyde** dwell

123 **saynt Austyn** Saint Augustine (A.D. 354–430) (exact source unidentified). The instruction to read a text several times is a topos; compare Caxton's *Reynard* (excerpt 3.17).

124 **wene** presume

127 **in the Covente** The reference is to reading in the refectory while the nuns eat.

128 **poynte yt** punctuate it or pronounce it with correct emphases (compare excerpt 3.1: 16–17, *A Talking*)

129 **savourly** with feeling ∫ **heres** hearers

132–33 **can speke yt fourthe to other** know how to tell others about it

133 **set yt awarke** set it working

135–36 **after the matter ys, therafter ye dresse you in the redyng** you conform your attitude in reading a book to the nature of its subject matter. The author then gives a breakdown of several kinds of spiritual reading: rules for living (137–44), treatises on the Last Things (145–47), on the Creation and Passion (147–50), the joys of heaven (150–51), human sin (151–52). All these topics need to be apprehended by the reader in quite different ways. Compare the advice given in *The Orchard* not to "savour" too deeply the "bittire wedis" mingled among Catherine's "delitable fruyt" (excerpt 3.5: 39–45), and its warning that spiritual death can follow from doing this. For a list of books known to have been available to Syon nuns (which includes items in all of the religious genres alluded to here, but also includes more secular material), see Bell 1995.

138 **that** so that

139 **what they shall leve** what they must avoid

143 **sadly** seriously

145 **affeccyons** emotions

146 **dome** judgment

147 **drede** fear

149, 151 **affeccyons, affeccions** Fawkes's text twice reads *afffeccions*

157 **Netheles yt is expediente** Despite telling a reader to conform her attitude to what she reads, her choice of book must also be according to what is most appropriate for her at the time.

159 **eny were drawen downe** if anyone were dragged down

160 **spedefull** profitable

160–61 **bokes of hevynes and of drede** books concerning grave and fearful matters

165 **tone . . . tother** the one . . . the other

166 **as the matter asketh** as the subject matter requires

3.13 *THE WARS OF ALEXANDER:* OPENING

Date and Provenance: c. 1360–1450; northwest Midlands or the north of England (? Lancashire), although the huge spread in possible dates of composition puts any localization in question.

Author, Sources, and Nature of Text: This poem (of which only the first twenty-five passus, almost six thousand lines, survive) is one of the longest and most accomplished works of the so-called "alliterative revival." The poem is largely a translation of a Latin life of Alexander, based on Leo of Naples's tenth-century *Nativitas et victoria Alexandri magni*, perhaps the most important of the many medieval sources for the conqueror's exploits, which is itself a translation of a Greek romance by Pseudo-Callisthenes (see Duggan and Turville-Petre 1989, xiii–xvii). As one of the "nine worthies," a pupil of Aristotle, founder of Europe's first "world" empire, traveler to exotic lands, and mighty example of the operations of Fortune's wheel, Alexander occupied a place in the minds of medieval English people comparable to that of Arthur or the Troy legend. Besides *The Wars of Alexander,* there is a Middle English prose version of the Latin life, a rhymed romance *Alisaunder,* and no fewer than nine translations of the *Secreta secretorum* (a letter of instruction supposedly written to Alexander by Aristotle) to testify to his importance. This work is typical of a number of alliterative poems in its concern with the meaning of history, and in particular with the founding stories of Western or English civilization. Even a very different poem, *Sir Gawain and the Green Knight* (with which the *Wars* has a close but elusive relationship), displays many of the same preoccupations, despite its lightheartedness and self-conscious fictionality. Other examples include *The Destruction of Troy* and the alliterative *Morte Arthure,* both of which also share most of the topoi about the importance of choosing what to read or hear during times of leisure, the same topoi with which the *Wars* opens, inviting readers to make use of their time to learn something useful, rather than listen to "wanton werkis" (12). For variations on these themes, see the next three excerpts (3.14–16) and the opening of *The Orchard of Syon* (excerpt 3.5).

Audience and Circulation: The poem survives incomplete in two fifteenth-century manuscripts, both from the county of Durham in northeastern England. One of these, Dublin, Trinity College MS 213, may have been owned and copied at Durham Priory, possibly for use in teaching. As with many alliterative poems, and despite the strong evocation of a listening occasion with which the work opens, we have little concrete idea of the uses to which the *Wars* was put or the audiences it reached. However, two other alliterative poems, *The Destruction of Troy* and *William of Palerne*, are known to have been written by clerical poets for, respectively, a Lancashire knight and the earl of Hereford, Humphrey de Bohun, and the *Wars* may well have a similar origin.

Bibliography: The poem has been edited by Hoyt Duggan and Thorlac Turville-Petre (1989), who provide a full bibliography (lii–lvii), including a list of their own stylistic and literary studies. Turville-Petre also edits extensive excerpts in his anthology of alliterative verse (1989). For a general analysis of the alliterative revival, see Turville-Petre 1977; for

some exploratory essays, Lawton 1982; a good literary study of the poem is Lawton 1981. For background discussion of medieval views of Alexander, see Cary 1956; for the *Secreta secretorum* (purportedly Aristotle's advice to the young Alexander), see Manzalaoui 1977.

Source: Oxford, Bodleian Library MS Ashmole 44, fol. 1r. This is a paper manuscript of the mid–fifteenth century, incomplete at the end, that contains only the *Wars*. It is written in single columns, with careful corrections and marginal annotations, either by the manuscript's one scribe or a later hand (Duggan and Turville-Petre 1989, ix–x). In the manuscript, the poem is untitled, although it does contain passus headings (in Latin), which refer to the work simply as "Alexander." Neither manuscript of the *Wars* marks half lines in the verse—compare excerpts 2.15 (*South English Legendary*), 3.19 (*Piers Plowman*), 3.24 (Henry Pepwell's introductory stanzas to *The Book of the City of Ladies*)—but we have added raised points at the half-line for ease of reading here.

When folk ere festid and fed · fayn wald thai here	festid feasted; fayn gladly
Sum farand thinge eftir fode · to fayn thare hertis,	farand pleasant; fayn cheer
Or thai ware fourmed on fold · or thaire fadirs othir	Or before; on fold on earth; othir either
Sum is leve to lythe · the lesing of sayntis	leve happy; lythe hear
5 That lete thaire lifis be lorne · for oure Lord sake,	lorne lost
And sum has langinge · of lufe lays to herken,	lufe lays love songs
How ledis for thaire lemans · has langor endured;	
Sum covettis and has comforth · to carpe and to lestyn	carpe speak
Of curtaissy, of knyghthode, · of craftis of armys,	craftis feats
10 Of kyngis at has conquirid · and ovircomyn landis;	at that
Sum of wirschip, iwis, · slike as tham wyse lattis,	
And sum of wanton werkis, · tha that ere wild-hedid.	wanton werkis foolish deeds
Bot if thai wald on many wyse · a wondire ware it els,	
For as thaire wittis ere within · so thaire will folowis.	
15 And I forwith yow all · ettillis to schewe	forwith before; ettillis intend
Of ane emperoure the aghefullest · that evir armys hauntid;	
That was the athill Alexsandire, · as the buke tellis,	athill noble
That aghte evyn as his awyn · all the werd ovire;	who ruled the whole world as his own
For he recoverd quills he regnyd · the regions all clene,	recoverd conquered; quills until
20 And all rialme and the riches · into the rede est.	the rede est the red East
I sall rehers—and ye will, renkis, · rekyn your tongis—	and if; renkis knights; rekyn guard
A remnant of his rialte · and rist quen us likis.	

1 **When folk ere festid** For the public reading that seems to be alluded to here, see Coleman 1996.

3 **Or thai ware fourmed on fold · or thaire fadirs othir** of events that happened before they, and their fathers as well, came into being on this earth

4 **lesing** redemption (see *MED: lesen* [*v.*] 5, and *OED: leesing* [*vbl. sb.*] 2)

7 **How ledis for thaire lemans · has langor endured** how youths have endured sorrow for their lovers. Compare *Sir Gawain and the Green Knight:* "How ledez for her lele luf hor lyvez han auntered / Endured for her drury dulful stounde" (1516–17). From this line onward, this prologue is divisible into groups of four lines, each alliterating on a single sound. As Duggan and Turville-Petre point out (1989, 182), this suggests that two lines have been lost between 4–7 and 7–11.

11 **Sum of wirschip, iwis, · slike as tham wyse lattis** some, truly, of honor, who think themselves wise

13 **Bot if thai wald on many wyse · a wondire ware it els** it would be a wonder if people did not desire in different ways. Compare excerpt 3.12:

157–59 (*The Mirror of Our Lady*), and the next three excerpts.

14 **For as thaire wittis ere within · so thaire will folowis** for as their temperaments are within, so their desire follows. "Wit" and "will" are a pair often meaning "reason" and "passion," but here "wit" is generalized to a concept close to "taste."

16 **Of ane . . . hauntid** of the most awesome emperor who ever practiced arms

17 **Alexsandire** Alexander the Great (d. 323 B.C.): throughout the Middle Ages the most famous historical hero of ancient Greece

21 **rekyn your tongis** that is, be silent

22 **remnant** fragment. The word implies a rich tradition of medieval moralizing about the relative impermanence of the exploits of even the most famous worldly conqueror and carries as well the customary implication of a large and diverse literary subject matter beyond the text in hand. **ʃ and rist quen us likis** and we can rest when we like: a statement of the need to divide a reading of the poem into more than one occasion, which reinforces the idea of readerly choice thematized by the whole prologue

3.14 *CURSOR MUNDI:* PROLOGUE (EXTRACT)

Date and Provenance: c. 1300; the north of England; updated at least twice within the following 150 years, once in a distinct Southern adaptation.

Author, Sources, and Nature of Text: This anonymous work is, as its title (The courser of the world; see 2n below) suggests, a history of the world from Creation to Doomsday, with a firm focus on religious history. It is one of a number of encyclopedic religious poems in Middle English written between c. 1270–85 (the date of the *South English Legendary,* excerpt 2.15) and 1350, including Robert Mannyng's *Handlyng Synne,* the *Northern Homily Cycle* (excerpt 2.1), *The Prick of Conscience* (excerpt 3.7), and *Speculum Vitae* (see essay 4.2, pages 336–37): works whose scope and scale in some ways anticipates the program of writing in prose undertaken by Lollards and others from the late fourteenth century on. The sources of *Cursor Mundi* are many and various, differing somewhat from version to version, but include a historical compendium, the *Historia scholastica* by Peter Comestor, and

a theological treatise, the *Elucidarium* by Honorius of Autun, two authoritative twelfth-century works whose synthetic pedagogical projects the *Cursor Mundi* author is concerned to emulate in the vernacular. Like the *Northern Homily Cycle* and *The Prick of Conscience,* the poem is in octosyllabic couplets, a meter Mannyng refers to as "light ryme," contrasting it with elaborate ("strange") verse forms that are too difficult for an audience to hear or a reciter to remember (excerpt 1.1: 56, 40); "light ryme" seems to have been the meter of choice for instructive and historical writing in the period. The prologue describes the array of possible stories and "Sa[ng]es sere of selcouthe rime" (the many beautifully rhymed songs [17]) available to the audience in three languages, but insists that only the story of salvation that it tells is worth hearing, and only English (the language of the "commune" [78]) worth writing (see essay 4.2, pages 334–35, for further discussion). Much of this is presumably to be understood as a response to the topoi about reading and choice in texts like *The Wars of Alexander* (excerpt 3.13), although this prologue also seems to be among the earliest texts written in English to contain these topoi.

Audience and Circulation: Nine relatively complete manuscripts survive, widely dispersed in dialect, date, and ownership. As late as the 1440s, for example, a nun of Syon Abbey owned a copy, and another was made by the fifteenth-century Yorkshire bibliophile Robert Thornton (Thompson 1994a). The poem's tendency to accumulate further passages on other subjects (from devotions to the Virgin to the practical apothegms of the *Distichs of Cato*) suggests that it was not viewed as a solely theological work but as a one-volume library of useful knowledge (compare excerpt 1.10). This is, indeed, much the claim the prologue makes for the poem in its original form.

Bibliography: For a parallel-text edition of four manuscripts, with extensive notes, see Morris 1874–93. A thorough analysis of the work and its sources was made by Sarah Horrall, who published her results in articles and a collaborative edition of the Southern Version (Horrall 1978–90). For a full bibliography to 1985, see Raymo 1986, 2503–7. The work's pedagogical use of the vernacular is discussed in Thompson 1994b. On its construction of Englishness, see Turville-Petre 1996. On its "Frenchness," see Thompson 1997.

Source: Oxford, Bodleian Library MS Fairfax 14, fols. 4r–5r, a parchment copy of the work made in Lancashire in the late fourteenth century; *Cursor Mundi* is the sole text. The text is written in two columns with few adornments (although occasional rubrication) and has many notes of ownership on the flyleaves (e.g., by Thomas and Robert Belyngham, dated c. 1500). Unusually, the scribe identifies both himself and the person for whom the copy was made: "Stokyngbrig scripsit istum librum Willelmo Kervour de Lanc" (William Carver of Lancashire) (fol. 123v). Due to rubbing of the parchment some letters are no longer visible, but the text can readily be reconstructed. The excerpt from the prologue edited here compresses Fairfax's 270 lines to just under a hundred.

This is the best boke of alle
The cours of the werlde men dos hit calle.

Men covettes rimes for to here	
And romance rede of mony maner:	**rede** [to] read
5 Of Alisander the Conquerour,	
Of July Cesar the emperour,	
Of Grece and Troy the grete strife	
Ther mony thousande lost thaire life,	**Ther** where
Of Brute that was bolde of hande	
10 First conquerour of Ingelande,	
Of king Arthorow that was rike,	**rike** powerful
In his tyme was nane hym like,	
Of ferles [th]at ther kynges felle,	of marvels that befell that king
Of mony aunters I here of telle	**aunters** adventures
15 Of Wawen, Cay, and other stabil	**stabil** firm
For til kepe the rounde tabil. [. . .]	[*eight lines omitted*]
Sa[ng]es sere of selcouthe rime	many beautifully rhymed songs
I[ng]eles, Frenche, and Latine.	**I[ng]eles** English
To [r]ede and here ilkan ys prest	**ilkan ys prest** each one is eager
20 [The thin]ges that ham likes best.	**ham likes** please them
The [wy]se mon wil of wisdome here	
The fole him drawes to foly nere.	**fole** fool; **nere** nearer

The wrang to here of right ys [la]the   **[la]the** reluctant
The proude wit buxomnes is wrath.   **buxomnes** humility
25 Bot by the frute men may see
Of wat vertue ys ilka tree [. . .]   **ilka** every [*fourteen lines omitted*]
Ensaumple now by ham I say: **ham** them
That ledes thaire life in riot ay,   **ay** always
In riot and in ricolage,   **ricolage** ribaldry
30 Of al thaire life spende thai the stage.   they waste away their entire life
For now ys nane halden in cours   **in cours** in repute
Bot qua con love paramours,   **Bot** except; **qua** those who; **con** know how to
That foly love, that vanite   **foly** foolish
Ham likes now na other gle: **gle** game
35 Hit ys bot fantum soth to say,   **fantum** a delusion
To day hit ys, to morne away [. . .]   here today, gone tomorrow [*ten lines omitted*]
Forthi blesse I that paramour   **Forthi** therefore
Quen I have nede me dose socour   who looks after me when I am in need
That saves me in erthe fra synne,
40 And holpes me heyven to wynne. [. . .]   **holpes** helps [*four lines omitted*]
Suche in erthe ys funden nane,   **funden** found
For ho ys moder and maydane,   **ho** she
Moder and mayden neyverthelesse   a mother yet nevertheless a virgin
Forthi of hir toke Criste his flesse;
45 Qua truly lovys ay this lemman,   **Qua** whoever; **ay** always; **lemman** beloved
This ys the love sal never began;   **began** deceive
For in this life ho falis never,
And in the tother ho lastes ever.   **tother** the other [life]
Of suche an sulde men mater tak[e]   **an** a one
50 Ye crafty that con rimes make,   **crafty** skillful [people]
Of hir to make bath rime and sange
And love hir squete sone amange.   and love her sweet son also
Quat bote ys to sette travayle   what use is it to undertake a labor
Aboute thinge wil noght avayle?
55 That ys bot fantum of this wer[l]de,
Als ye haf oft sene and herde [. . .]   [*six lines omitted*]
Lavedy ho ys of lavedis alle   **Lavedy** lady
Mylde and meke witouten galle [. . .]   **galle** bitterness [*eight lines omitted*]
In hir worshepe walde I begyn
60 A lastande werk apon to myn;   **apon to myn** i.e., for people to remember
For myche worshepe ho con us wyn   **worshepe** honor
Fayne I walde men knew hir kyn.   **kyn** nature
Ther-fore sum gestes wil I shawe
That done ware in the alde lawe,   **alde lawe** Old Testament
65 By-twix the alde lagh and the newe
How Cristes birth began to brewe.   **began to brewe** began to come about
I sal shew you verrament   **verrament** truly
Shortly of a[i]thur testament;   **a[i]thur** both
Al this werlde or that I blyn   **or that I blyn** before I stop
70 Wit Cristes help I sal overryn

And tel sum gestes principale
For al may na mon have in tale [. . .]   for nobody can tell everything

[There follows 104 lines listing the "gestes" to be told]

Ofter haly kirkis state   following the church's statute
This ilk boke ys translate   **ilk** same
75 Until Ingeles tonge to rede   **Until Ingeles tonge** into the English language
For the love of Englis lede,   **lede** people
Englis lede of Engelande
The commune for til understande.   so the commons will understand
French rimes here I rede   I hear French rhymes being read
80 Communely in iche a stede   **in iche a stede** everywhere
That mast ys worth for Frenche man.   **worth** useful
Quat ys worth for him nane can?   What use is it to someone who knows none?
Of Engeland nacioun
Ys Englis man thar-in commoun,   are all the English people together
85 The speche that man with sone may spede   **man** someone; **spede** prosper
Mast tharwit to speke ware nede.   **Mast** most; **tharwit** therewith
Selden was for any chaunce
Englis tong praysed in Fraunce!
Gif we ilkane thaire langage   **Gif we** let us give; **ilkane** each one
90 Me think then we do nane outrage.   **outrage** disgrace
To lewet and Englis men I tel   **lewet** uneducated
That understandes quat I spel [...]   **quat** what [*fourteen lines omitted*]
Now of this proloug wel I blyn   **blyn** cease
In Cristes name my boke begynne.
95 *Cursor of the Werlde* I wil hit cal,
For almast hit overrynnys al.
Take we our begynnyng than
Of him that al this werlde began.

1–12 **This . . . like** The work begins by dismissively evoking the "matters" of Troy, Greece, Rome, and Britain, which made up the staple of secular historical romance. Like other themes used here (such as the passage of time and the need to use it wisely [27–36, 53–55]), this rejection of secular matter is a frequent Anglo-Norman prologue topos in a range of genres: in Denis Piramus' tilting at Marie de France in his prologue to the life of King Edmund, for instance, but also in less "literary" genres such as versified calendars and Sunday readings. On Anglo-Norman prologues, see Wogan-Browne 1994b.

2 **cours of the werlde** translates *cursor mundi*, the title usually given the work in the manuscripts

5 **Alisander the Conquerour** Alexander the Great (d. 323 B.C.): the most famous historical hero of ancient Greece throughout the Middle Ages, and

the subject of a body of Middle English poetry (see excerpt 3.13, headnote)

6 **July Cesar the emperour** Julius Caesar (d. 44 B.C.): Roman general, dictator, and historian, whose life and death led to the transformation of the Roman republic into an empire; not, in practice, a common subject of Middle English poetry

9 **Brute** Brutus: a son of King Priam of Troy and the mythical founder of Britain; eponymous hero of Lawman's epic *Brut* (early thirteenth century) and other Middle English and Anglo-Norman works

11 **king Arthorow** King Arthur: the most famous (though mythical) early English king, whose court at Camelot provided a setting for much Middle English, Anglo-French, and Celtic poetry and prose from the mid–twelfth century onward

13 **[th]at** Here and in the next lines the parchment has become scrubbed and the letters illegible.

15 **Wawen, Cay** Gawain and Kay: two of Arthur's best-known knights

19–22 **To [r]ede . . . nere** For a similar statement of readerly choice, compare *Wars of Alexander,* excerpt 3.13: 11–14.

24 **The proude wit buxomnes is wrath** the proud person is made angry by songs about humility

25–26 **Bot by the frute . . . tree** See Matt. 7:16: "by their fruits you shall know them."

30 **Of al thaire life spende thai the stage** perhaps an allusion to the parable of the prodigal son ∫ **stage** a period of time

31–32 **For now . . . love paramours** for nowadays no one is considered reputable except those who know how to love as lovers (i.e., practice "refined" love)

31–36 **For . . . away** This is a common complaint against *amour courtois* (here parodied as "foly love" [33]) in religious writings. Is is given extra point here by the poem's use of English, a language that in 1300 was not as closely associated as it was to become with the literature of aristocratic love.

34 **Ham likes now na other gle** no other game now pleases them

49–50 **Of suche an . . . rimes make** you skillful people who know how to write poetry should take one like her as a subject. Poems to the Virgin often consciously compete with secular love poetry.

55 **wer[l]de** MS *werde*

59–60 **In hir worshepe walde I begyn / A lastande werk apon to myn** The poet intends to honor the Virgin by adding to the canon of "lastande" (enduring) literary works. For other examples of this interest in posterity in pre-Chaucerian writing, see excerpts 1.1: 76–78 (Mannyng's *Chronicle*), and 1.2: 17–20 (Barbour's *Bruce*).

63 **gestes** deeds. The word may be deliberately reminiscent of the vocabulary of secular romances.

68 **a[i]thur** MS *arthur*

70 **overryn** relate, also "run around" (the poem circumnavigates all human history)

73–92 **Ofter haly kirkis state . . . quat I spel** For an analysis of this discussion of English, see the section "Middle English Writing, 1300–1380" in essay 4.2, pages 334–39.

96 **For almast hit overrynnys al** for it tells nearly all, for it is longer than almost anything

3.15 JOHN SKELTON, TRANSLATION OF POGGIO BRACCIOLINI, *BIBLIOTHECA HISTORICA OF DIODORUS SICULUS*: PROLOGUE (EXTRACT)

Date and Provenance: 1488; London.

Author, Sources, and Nature of Text: The *Bibliotheca* is a lengthy historical compilation by a Greek writer of the first century B.C., a compendium of the work of earlier historians that deals with the civilizations of the eastern Mediterranean during the first millenium B.C. The work was translated into Latin before 1449 by the humanist scholar and bibliophile Poggio Bracciolini, whose translation was printed three times between 1472 and 1485 and became well known in England in the late fifteenth and sixteenth centuries. Its prologue, for example, was adapted by Caxton for his 1482 edition of John Trevisa's translation of Higden's *Polychronicon* (see excerpt 2.2). John Skelton finished his version of the *Bibliotheca* in 1488, the year he left Oxford (with a brilliant reputation as orator and classicist) to enter the royal service, and his work seems to be an exercise in elaborate rhe-

torical prose. It is quite different from the satirical poetry for which he was to become famous, although it demonstrates a similar flair and perhaps a similar tendency toward extremes. The point of the exercise seems to have been to exploit the resources of the English vernacular to and beyond their limits, in an attempt to meet the challenge of the humanist Latin style emanating from Italy. Skelton employs a huge vocabulary, packed with neologisms, and his syntax is far too complex to be parsed by modern or any other system of punctuation. But the translation is also close to the point of crabbedness, as if the English language has to be racked in order to make it carry the scholarly burden Skelton is placing upon it. Like the previous two excerpts (from *The Wars of Alexander* and *Cursor Mundi*, 3.13 and 3.14), although far more elaborately, Poggio's prologue extols the genre in which the work is written—in this case, historical prose—at the expense of all other genres, especially poetry, which is here made synonymous with "fiction" and "lies." As the next excerpt (*Eneados,* 3.16) makes clear, the prologue is a notable example of the appropriation and re-appropriation of topoi characteristic of the endless war between history and fiction, a war that flared up famously in England a century later with Sidney's *Defence of Poesy.* Many of the claims Poggio makes for history are actually derived from standard accounts of the uses of poetry, such as those given in Boccaccio's *De genealogia deorum gentilium,* book XIV. (Compare also the prologues to Barbour's *Bruce* and Lydgate's *Troy Book,* excerpts 1.2 and 1.7.)

Audience and Circulation: The translation is so tortuous, and often so dependent on a reader's knowledge of the Latin original, that it cannot have been meant for a large audience. It was never printed and now survives incomplete in a single manuscript. However, Caxton's prologue to *Eneydos* (further discussed and quoted in essay 4.3, pages 364–65 below) mentions the work as evidence of Skelton's brilliance, in asking the laureate to "oversee" his own much more carefully comprehensible translation: "For [Skelton] hath late translated the *Epystlys* of Tulle [Cicero], and the *Boke of Dyodorus Syculus,* and diverse other werkes, oute of Latyn into Englysshe, not in rude and olde langage but in polysshed and ornate termes craftely, as he that hath redde Vyrgyle, Ovyde, Tullye and all the other noble poetes and oratours to me

unknowen" (Blake 1973, 80). Poggio's intended audience was notionally universal, but was in practice always meant to be similarly confined to an intellectual elite, as its use not only of Latin but of a self-consciously elevated style indicates. The "universal reader" of both original and translation is the early modern humanist intellectual.

Bibliography: Edited by F. M. Salter and H.L.R. Edwards (1956, 1957), Skelton's English translation has attracted even less comment than Poggio's Latin one. For a bibliography of Skelton studies, see Kinsman 1979, updated by Staub 1990. For Skelton's humanist milieu, see Carlson 1993b. For a negative assessment of Skelton's contributions to English vocabulary, see Stevens 1992.

Source: Cambridge, Corpus Christi College MS 357, fols. 3r–5r. This paper book, carefully written in a single column, was owned by Robert Pen, a gentleman of the chapel under Henry VII and Henry VIII (d. 1538). The last one and a half books of Skelton's translation, the sole text in the manuscript, are now missing. The prologue, which has been abbreviated here (although its main arguments have been retained), is prefaced by the rubric, "The prohemy of diodorus th'auctor."

Punctuation of this passage has proved extremely difficult, since Skelton's English often owes more to Latin than vernacular idioms. There are also a number of puns that only make sense in Latin.

Men ar hyghly bounde of a congruence unto these wrytars of maters and histories that by their laborious estudye have pourchaced hye enprowmentes unto the lyf of man. They manyfeste unto theym that lyste to rede, by exemplifyenge of those that ben passed, what we ought to coveyte and desyre and what we ought to
5   avoyde and eschewe. For thoo thynges and fayttis that we rede, by experymentis of many maters with many folde laborious travaylles and jeopardies whereas we ourself be fer fro the daunger, they gyve to us specyal informacion what best may helpe our lyf t'endure. Wherfore he is of noblys in wysedome most soverayn acounted whiche, many tymes enurid with adversite, hath behold and seen many
10   cytees and townes and the maner of the world, the cognycion of straunge thynges apperceyved as wel in welthe as in adversite, hath in hym contened the doctryne that bareyne is and voyde of all perylous adventures.

Forthermore, alle erthely men lyvynge, joyned as it were by one collaterall
allyaunce (hou be it by ferre distaunce of yeres and contrees they be ensondred),
15 yet these wryters conveye theym as it were to one aspecte, so as eche of other may
have contemplacion: ensiewynge Goddes devyne provydence whyche,
comprehendynge as wel th'ornacye of heven as the dyversyfied natures of men—
comprysed as it were in an ordre in commyn for evermore, enryched with his
hevenly rewarde as it is sittynge and metely unto every man—in lyke wyse these
20 wryters behave theymself that in theyr werkis have regystred the fayttes and gestes
of alle the world envyron, as it were of one cyte, have by conscripcion compacte
theym to gydre unto a parfyght and wele encomyne.

Therfore it is with honeste procedynge, by th'advertysement of other mennes
errours with circumspecte guydynge, the bettre to ordre our present lyf—and not
25 t'enserche what other men have doon, but what thynge demened theym into the
beste, and it to leye tofore the eye of our remembraunce, consequently ensiewynge
the same in effecte. Of olde faders whome longe contynuaunce of yeres illumyned
with prudence, theyr advys and sadde directions of yonge persones hyghly be
commended. And so longe tofore theym processe hystoryal was had in
30 memoryal—as ye see, contynuance and lengthe of yeres compryseth moo examplis
of maters than doth the brief age and lyf of man. So that processe historyal is to
be acompted most avayllable for th'ordynary institucion of mannes lyf: as well for
yonge persones (whome the lecture or redynge of dyverse maters maketh peregal
with theyr oldres in prudence) as to aged persones to whome longe contynuance of
35 yeris hath mynystred notable experyence of manyfold maters.

And beyond thys, mater historyal hath avaunced persones ful symple of havoir
and comen of baas and lowe progenye unto emperyal resydence and royal
domynyon. It couragith noble pryncis t'enterprise valyaunt prowesse and
marcyall fayttis, to th'encreace of their glorye inmortall. It encyteth coragious
40 knyghtes to have a famous brute whiche foloweth and endurith after this temporal
deth. It maketh theym more quyck and prompte to entrepryse alle jeopardies for
the deffence of theyr countreye. It puttyth dastardis unto grievous abasshement
of their male talente ony thynge to doo of shrewdnes, for drede of sclaunderous
reporte.
45   And somme thurgh the motyf of litterature—whiche maketh a due probate and
testymonye moeved—have as wel edefyed famous cytees, as they have assigned
laudable decrees and grounded lawes unto the behoef of mannes temporal lyf.
And somme by crafty invencion of new faittes and doctryne have founde
beneficyal pollicyes for the wele in comyn. But the singular laude and
50 commendacion in especyall of alle maters wher thurgh worldly welth may be
enjoyed, and the most chief and soverayn causatyf therof, ought to be ascribid
unto historyal processe. It is the sure garnyson of alle suche thyngis that by vertue
be wrought and perfourmed, offrynge hymself in testimonial unto mysguyded and
undisposed persones, exhibytynge hymselfe bounteuous toward alle maner of
55 people. Thenne, sith it is soo that suche thynges as be recounted and indede of
fables and tryphlis reportynge of the paynful jewesse and dedely woo of helle
hugely procure the myndes of peple unto compassion and to observe justyce and
equyte, of a more forcyble apparence it is to be extemed that historyal mater,
which is the very assured maistresse of trouthe, as the very tendre moder
60 of philosophie, frameth us unto maners and to vertue addressith. Alle people

welnyh, thurgh the inconstaunt frayelte of nature, contynue the most parte of their
lyf in slumbrynge slouthe and sluggysshenes—whos maner of lyvynge here and
fynall departynge out of this lyf present is rasyd with oblyvyon oute of
remembraunce, so as of their dedely conversacion ensieweth after their deth noo
65 famous memorial. But the noble fayttes of vertue be inmortally registred in
the courte of fame, specially whan the bounte of mater historyal cometh in place
and is admytted to make reporte. [. . .]
    Moreover it soveraynly assistith lusty eloquence, whiche is of so hye excellence
that no thynge may be founde more famous than it is. By her, Grekes have a
70 preferrement byfore alle other nacions of Barbary. By her, men of litterature have
a precellence beyonde alle other that bareyn be and naked of doctryne. Thenne,
syth vertue historyall is onely suche a maistresse by whome men emonge theym
self alle other excelle, thenne it semeth it is thynge as precyous and of so grete
valewe as ever was the florysshynge courage and polisshed eloquence of lusty
75 utteraunce. And surely we suppose that persones of noble conversacion be digne
and worthy to be enhaunced with laudable commendacion as the persones whiche
unto us have shewed the presedentis of vertue; but, where as it is that somme have
unto theym another way chosen, poemys after myn oppynyon delyten the mynde
of man with wanton pleasure rather than it prouffyteth. And thees sanxiouns,
80 decreis, and lawes of the world by alle apparence in them contene penal correction
rather than ony doctryne delectable. And so of alle other facultees, they nothynge
inferre of prosperous welthe; the prouffyte that in theym resteth hath a
commyxtion with noyous dommage. Somme of these facultees gyve informacion
craftely, a lesynge to cloke by collusion and colour of trouthe; but onely historyal
85 processe, representynge the wordes equyvalent unto the dedes, in her compryseth
all convenable avauntage. For it incyteth a man unto alle that upon honeste is
grounded, and hugely abhorreth alle vices detestable. She bryngeth manerly
persones unto avaunsement. Alle haskardes she shaketh theym out of conceyte.
And, in conclusion, by experyence of the thynges whiche she descrybeth, hyghly
90 she profyteth in conductynge us unto the strayt way of sensyble understondynge.

1 **ar hyghly bounde of a congruence** collectively much indebted ∫ **maters and histories** the first example of a doubling of terms that occurs throughout. They can usually be taken as synonyms.

2 **enprowmentes** improvements. Compare Usk's praise of earlier writers who have made the task of living easier and are worthy of commemoration as a result (excerpt 1.4: 54–63).

3 **lyste** desire ∫ **exemplifyenge** telling exemplary stories

5 **fayttis** exploits ∫ **by experymentis** that is, by giving [us] experience

6 **jeopardies** dangers

7 **specyal** excellent ∫ **what** that is, about those things that

8 **endure** last

8–9 **Wherfore he is . . . with adversite** for he is considered most superior in excellence of wisdom

who, many times inured to adversity

10–11 **the cognycion . . . adversite** and, having investigated unfamiliar matters both in health and in adversity: translates a Latin ablative absolute clause

11 **welthe** well-being ∫ **contened the doctryne** absorbed the teaching

12 **bareyne . . . and voyde** bare and devoid. The clause refers to the "doctryne," which is free from danger itself, despite being learned (except by readers of histories) through danger.

13–14 **collaterall allyaunce** mutual alliance

14 **ensondred** separated

15 **aspecte** view. That is, historians make all time and place available to the individual reader: notice the mercantile image implied by "conveye" at the same time as the text is claiming to view history through time and space *sub speciae aeternitatis*.

16 **ensiewynge** imitating

17 **ornacye** intricacy. The clause is a concessive statement: God's providence has wider scope than human history making.

18 **in an ordre in commyn for evermore** in a single eternal and communal order. Humanity is an order, as are the orders of angels, and God sees them now as he always will, according to the rewards he will mete out to them.

19 **sittynge and metely** appropriate and suitable

19–20 **in lyke wyse these wryters behave theymself** in this same way [following divine providence] these writers behave

21 **envyron** around ∫ **as it were of one cyte** as though they were members of a single city (a literary version of God's New Jerusalem) ∫ **conscripcion** puns on "conscription" and its root sense (from Latin *conscribere*, "to write down together"). The historian creates community by writing it. The idea gains force from the common image of the "book of life" in which everyone's deeds are recorded in heaven. For parallel praise of the compendium, see excerpt 1.10: 19–26 (Guy de Chauliac's *Cyrurgie*). ∫ **compacte** (*v.*) compiled

22 **encomyne** puns on "community" and "encomium": the praise that the historian metes out differently to different people, depending on their desert, in a manner paralleling divine reward

23–27 **Therfore it is . . . in effecte** and so history, by displaying (with circumspect judgment) the errors of other people, the better to order our present life, proceeds honorably—not prying into what other people have done but what urged them to the best, and laying this before the eye of our memory, causing us to imitate this in our own lives [syntax rationalized]. That is, history is not about the exposure of others or the facts of their lives but about the exemplary possibilities of the past.

25 **demened** impelled (*MED: demeinen* [*v.*] 16)

27 **olde faders** elders

28 **sadde** steadfast

29 **tofore** before ∫ **processe hystoryal** historical narrative

30 **memoryal** the memory. Historical writing underpins even the wisdom of the ancients, since history resides in the memory and is, in a sense, the same as the memory on a collective level.

32 **institucion** organizing

33 **lecture** reading aloud ∫ **peregal** equal

36 **havoir** behavior. The list of the benefits of reading history becomes more specific: history has raised the lowborn to greatness and (38–39) encouraged princes to deeds of valor.

37 **comen** descended ∫ **baas** base

39 **marcyall fayttis** martial deeds

40 **brute** renown

41 **entrepryse** undertake ∫ **jeopardies** risk

42–44 **It puttyth dastardis . . . reporte** history makes villains deeply embarrassed to do anything wicked in their ill will, for fear of having bad things said of them

45–46 **And somme . . . moeved** and some, moved by the promptings of literature, which renders a just testimony and report [i.e., of someone's deeds]. This sentence and the next are concessive, admitting that other types of writing besides history can move people to useful tasks. "But the singular laude . . ." (49) returns to the theme that history is the preeminent literary genre.

46 **edefyed famous cytees** built famous cities ∫ **assigned** instituted

47 **unto the behoef** to the benefit

48 **crafty invencion** skillful discovery ∫ **faittes** activities

49 **wele in comyn** that is, the commonwealth, common well-being

51 **causatyf** cause

52 **garnyson** harvesting

54 **undisposed** ill-ordered

55–58 **sith it is soo . . . equyte** since the things that are told and written in fables and idle tales ["tryphlis"] of the painful duress and mortal sorrow of hell greatly move people's minds to compassion and the observance of justice and equity. This may be a slighting allusion by Poggio to Dante's *Inferno*.

55 **indede** indeed

56 **jewesse** duress

58 **of a more forcyble apparence it is to be extemed** it is far more likely

59 **as** as [it is]

60 **frameth** fashions. That is, history, which is about truth, is much more likely to improve us morally than fiction, which is not.

63 **rasyd** erased. Most people are not remembered by history, since their lives, lived in sloth, are of no import. This assertion that history remembers only the famous may seem at odds with the earlier statement that history brings together the experiences of everybody, but the underlying assumption is that the famous, while not typical, are normative, and thus represent everyone.

64 **dedely** mortal ∫ **conversacion** manner of living ∫ **ensieweth** there follows

65 **memorial** remembrance

66 **courte of fame** Compare Chaucer's *House of Fame*. ∫ **cometh in place** makes an appearance

68 **lusty eloquence** fine rhetoric. This paragraph undertakes the task of praising rhetoric while dispraising poetry, again by reference to history's grounding in "truth," not mere pleasure.

69 **her** that is, eloquence

70 **preferrement** status ∫ **Barbary** an allusion to the ancient Greeks' term for all foreigners, "barbarians." Through Herodotus, Thucydides, and Diodorus Siculus, the Greeks pioneered the tradition of historical writing within which Poggio wishes to position his own translation.

71 **precellence** preeminence ∫ **doctryne** teaching

71–73 **Thenne, syth vertue . . . alle other excelle** since eloquence gives status to particular groups ["Grekes" (69), "men of litterature" (70)], historical achievement, the only mistress through whom men can excel all others, ought to be valued. The omitted paragraph (after 67) argues that where "scrowes [scrolls] enscribled" may decay, historical renown is increased, not wasted, by time's passage.

74 **courage** spirit

75–77 **And surely we suppose . . . presedentis of vertue** and indeed we might suppose that people who talk well [i.e., rhetorically] are as worthy to be glorified with praise as people who have shown us how to live well. The next sentences then go on to deny this, by denigrating those who like or write poetry (77–79), law (79–81), and so forth.

77 **presedentis** axioms

79 **rather than it prouffyteth** more than it is profitable ∫ **sanxiouns** laws. The study of law is the opposite of that of poetry in containing no pleasure, only "penal correction" (80), but is still not as good as history.

81 **doctryne delectable** pleasurable teaching ∫ **facultees** literally, university faculties; metonymically, the subjects studied in them

83 **commyxtion** mixture ∫ **noyous dommage** destructive harm

84 **craftely** deceitfully ∫ **lesynge** falsehood. The reference is to disciplines that employ allegory: literature and theology (although the latter, the single discipline history could not challenge directly, even in fifteenth-century Italy, is, significantly, not mentioned). Compare Henryson's account of allegory and fable, excerpt 3.18. ∫ **collusion** illusion

85 **representynge the wordes equyvalent unto the dedes** that is, in which words take the shape of the deeds they describe. Compare Barbour's notion of the "double pleasure" of words that are at once beautiful and true (excerpt 1.2).

86 **convenable avauntage** good benefit

86–87 **upon honeste is grounded** is grounded in integrity. History's claim to represent the truth literally now becomes a basis for arguing that only literal representation can carry moral integrity, so that only history can "ground" the reader in morality.

87 **manerly** virtuous

88 **avaunsement** prosperity ∫ **haskardes** fools

90 **the strayt way of sensyble understondynge** the narrow path of affective understanding: that is, knowledge imbued with feeling, *sapientia*

3.16 GAVIN DOUGLAS, *ENEADOS:* BOOK V, PROLOGUE

Date and Provenance: 1513; the south of Scotland.

Author, Sources, and Nature of Text: This remarkable translation of Virgil's *Aeneid* into Middle Scots is one of three major poems written by the aristocratic bishop of Dunkeld, Gavin Douglas, during his relatively short life (?1475–1522). The others are *King Hart* and *The Palice of Honour,* a response to *The House of Fame* much concerned to repudiate Chaucer's ironic picture of the chanciness of earthly fame and to argue that "honor" is a reliable basis on which to build civil and aesthetic systems of value. Such an argument is also implicit in the *Eneados.* Completed a few months before the Battle of Flodden Field (where James IV and much of the Scottish aristocracy were killed) and constituting the earliest attempt to render the entirety of one of the great classical epics into a dialect of English, the poem is notable for its self-consciousness about the translator's art and duty. The poem's claim—laid out in the prologue to the whole work, repeated and refined in the prologues to each of its thirteen books—is that, in translating one of the foundational works of Western culture in a style worthy of the original, Douglas is performing a cultural service equivalent to that performed by Virgil, founding Scottish letters by creating a Scottish language worthy to act as a vehicle for Virgil's poem. The act of translation itself thus becomes part of the poem's epic subject. Book V of the *Aeneid* is mainly about the games and sacrifices organized by Acestes to celebrate Aeneas's arrival in Sicily. Douglas's prologue evokes the book's mood of joy, defending "plesance and joy" (19) while extolling Virgil's moral strategies in what is almost a reply to the arguments made in the previous excerpt. Yet the final stanzas of the prologue qualify this optimism about play and reading, conceding the dangers inherent in fiction in a way comparable to that of Chaucer's "retractions" at the end of *Troilus and Criseyde* and *The Canterbury Tales*.

Audience and Circulation: Douglas ended his life in exile in London and, despite his insistence that he intends to make a contribution to Scottish, not English, literature, his work was read south of the border as much as it was in Scotland. Douglas knew humanist intellectuals like Polydore Virgil and John Major (Bawcutt 1976, chap. 2), and wrote for them as much as for an audience without access to the original. This is, indeed, one of the reasons the *Eneados* is so self-conscious about its status as a translation. The work was extensively used a generation later by Surrey for his own version of Virgil, and survives in seven manuscripts, the latest from the early seventeenth century. It was printed in London in 1553 but had to wait until 1710 for its first Scottish edition.

Bibliography: Edited by D.F.C. Coldwell (1957–64), the work has been much discussed, especially in connection with its supposedly "transitional" status between medieval and Renaissance periods. For bibliography to 1985, see Scheps and Looney 1986. For an appraisal of Douglas's career, see Bawcutt 1976. More recent studies include Blyth 1987, a book-length study of the *Eneados;* Canitz 1990, on Douglas's prologue to the poem, and Canitz 1991, on Douglas as a translator; Pinti 1995, on Douglas's construction of vernacular literary authority. Jack 1988 provides a general history of Middle Scots literature. Medieval and early modern adaptations of the *Aeneid* are discussed in Singerman 1986, while Virgil's impact on insular vernacular literature is analyzed at length by Baswell (1995). For the topos of literature as recreation, see Olson 1982.

Source: Cambridge, Trinity College MS O.3.12, fols. 78r–78v. The text in this small and neatly copied paper-folio volume, in which *Eneados* is the sole work, was made by Matthew Geddes, Douglas's secretary, and is the earliest of the seven that survive. Containing a number of marginal notes in Latin, it may have been made under Douglas's personal direction.

In Middle Scots spelling, modern English *wh* is usually represented *quh* ("what" is "quhat," "who" "quho," and so on), while *ght* is often represented as *cht* ("thocht" for "thought").

Gladys the grond the tendir florist greynn	**greynn** field
Byrdys the bewys and thir schawys scheynn,	**schawys scheynn** shining groves
The wery huntar to fynd hys happy pray,	**happy** chance
The falconeyr rych ryver onto fleyn;	
5 The clerk rejosys hys bukis our to seyn,	**our to seyn** to read
The luffar to behald hys lady gay;	
Yonng folk thame schurtis with gamm, solace, and play;	**schurtis** amuse
Quhat maist delytyth or lykis every wight,	**Quhat** whatever; **lykis** pleases
Tharto steris thar curage day and nycht.	**steris** moves; **curage** heart
10 Knychtis delytis to assay sterand stedys,	**assay** test; **sterand stedys** lively horses
Wantoun gallandis to trayl in sumptuus wedis;	**wedis** clothes
Ladeys desyris to behald and be seyn;	
Quha wald be thrifty courtyouris says few credis;	**thrifty** prosperous; **credis** creeds
Sum plesance takis in romans that he redis,	**Sum** this one
15 And sum hess lust to that wes nevir seynn;	**hess lust** takes pleasure

Quhou mony hedis als feil consatis beynn.
Twa appetitis oneth accordis with othir: oneth scarcely; othir each other
This lykis the, perchance, and not thi brothir.   lykis the pleases you

Plesance and joy richt hailsum and perfyte is,   hailsum wholesome
20 So that the wyss tharof in proverb wrytis,   wyss wise
"A blith spreit makis greyn and floryst age."
Myne author eyk in *Bucolykis* endytis: endytis writes
"The yonng enfant fyrst with lauchtir delytis
To knaw hys moder, quhen he is litil page.   page boy
25 Quha lauchis not," quod he, "in thar barnage,   barnage childhood
Genyus the god delytyth not thar tabill,
Nor Juno thame to kepe in bed is habill."

The hie wysdomme and maist profund engyne   engyne talent
Of mynne author Virgile, poete dyvyne,   mynne my
30 To comprehend makis me almaist forvay,   forvay lose my way
So crafty wrocht hys wark is, lyne by lyne.   crafty wrocht skillfully worked
Tharon aucht na mann irk, compleyn nor quhryne,   irk go dull; quhryne grumble
For quhy? He altyrris hys style sa mony way,
Now dreid, now stryfe, now lufe, now wa, now play,   wa sorrow
35 Lanngeir in murnnyng, now in melody,   Lanngeir before
To satyfy ilk wightis fantasy: ilk wightis each person's; fantasy fancy

Lyke as he had of every thynng a feill   Lyke as as if; feill understanding
And the willys of every wight dyd feill.   willys desires; feill understand
And tharto eyk so wysly writis he
40 Twichinng the proffyte of the commonn weill,   Twichinng regarding
Hys sawys beynn full of sentencis, every deill   sawys sayings; sentencis meanings
Of moral doctryne, that menn suld vycis fle.
Bot gyf he be nocht joyus, now lat se!
For quha so lyst seyr glaidsum gemmys leyr,   seyr many; gemmys games; leyr learn about
45 Ful mony myrry abaytmentis followis heir.   abaytmentis recreations

Now harkis sportis, myrthis, and myrry plays,   harkis listen to
Ful gudly pastans on mony syndry ways,   pastans pastimes
Endyte by Virgil, and heir by me translate,
Quhilk William Caxton knew nevir al hys days,
50 For, as I sayd tofor, that mann forvays: forvays goes astray
Hys febil proyss beynn mank and mutulate,   proyss prose; mank weak
Bot my propyne comm fromm the press fute hait,   propyne lines
Onforlatit, not iawyn fra tunn to tunn,   Onforlatit undecanted; iawyn splashed
In fresch sapour new from the berry runn.   sapour taste

55 Bachus of glaidness, and funeral Proserpyne,
And goddes of triumphe, clepyt Victorie,
Sal I you call as your namme war dyvyne?   call invoke; as since; war used to be
Na, na, it syffysyt of you ful smal memorie:
I byd nothir of your turmentis nor your glorie;   byd take heed of

60 Bot he quhilk may ws glaid perpetualy,

    glaid gladden

To brynng us tyll hys blyss on hym I cry.

    tyll to

Sen erdly plesour endis oft with sorow, we se,

    Sen since; **erdly** earthly

As in this buke nane exemplys ye want,

Lord, our prottectour to all trastis in the,

    to all trastis to all who trust

65 Bot quham na thinng is worthy nor pyssant,

    Bot without; **pyssant** powerful

To us thy grace and als gret mercy grant,

    als as

So for to wend by temporal blythness

    wend pass; **temporal** worldly

That our eternale joy be nocht the less!

    be may be

Here endys the proheymm and begynnys the fift buke.

1 **Gladys . . . greynn** the soft flowery field gladdens the ground. "Gladys" is assumed in each of the subsequent three lines. The various items listed mostly belong within the world of courtly fiction symbolized by *The Romance of the Rose*.

2 **Byrdys . . . scheynn** birds [gladden] boughs and shining groves

4 **The falconeyr . . . fleyn** the falconer [is glad] to fly his hawk by a noble river

8–9 **Quhat maist . . . day and nycht** people's hearts are moved day and night by whatever most delights them. Compare Chaucer, *General Prologue* I (A) 11; see also excerpts 3.13–15.

11 **Wantoun . . . wedis** lively young fellows love going around in expensive clothes

13 **Quha wald . . . credis** courtiers on the make don't say many prayers. This line is the first sign in the prologue that the beauty it evokes has its morally suspect side.

15 **And sum . . . seynn** and this person longs for what was never seen. Perhaps this is a reader of travel literature and the marvelous.

16 **Quhou . . . beynn** there are as many fantasies as there are heads. See Chaucer, *Squire's Tale* V (F) 202–3: "Diverse folk diversely they demed; / As many heddes, as manye wittes ther been." ∫ **Quhou mony** however many ∫ **feil** many

21 **A blith . . . age** a happy spirit makes age green and flourishing. See Prov. 17:22.

26–27 **Genyus . . . habill** Genius the god cannot please them at board, nor Juno in bed. That is, nothing can give them pleasure. For this passage, see Virgil, *Eclogues* IV.60–63. Genius was a generic name for the attendant spirit of an individual or household in Roman mythology. Juno was the wife of Jupiter, the chief god of the Roman pantheon, often associated with the sexual lives of women.

28–45 **The hie wysdomme . . . followis heir** an evocation of the close reading of Virgil that Douglas insists is the foundation of his translation. See the general prologue to *Eneados,* especially 297–310, and Douglas's discussions of Caxton (138–262) and Chaucer (339–414) (Coldwell 1957–64, 2:7–15).

29 **mynne author Virgile** Virgil (d. 19 B.C.): Roman poet, author of a set of *Eclogues*, the *Bucolics*, and his epic (dedicated to the emperor Augustus), the *Aeneid*. As Dante's choice of Virgil as his guide in *The Divine Comedy* shows, Virgil was regarded as the serious classical poet *par excellence*. Poets as late as Milton sought to model their careers on his.

37–38 **Lyke as . . . feill** as though he had intimate understanding of everything and understood the desire of everyone

40 **commonn weill** commonwealth. The line evokes the notion of "common profit" in Chaucer's *Parliament of Fowls* (see also excerpt 3.15).

43 **Bot . . . se!** but see here if Virgil is not also capable of being joyous!

44 **For quha . . . leyr** for whoever wants to hear about many delightful games

49–50 **Quhilk William Caxton . . . forvays** These lines are part of a running battle Douglas fights with William Caxton (d. 1492) and his *Eneydos* (1490), a prose romance loosely based on a French reworking of Virgil's epic that figures in Douglas's poem as a symbol of inadequate (because enfeebling) vernacularization. For Caxton's account of his translation policy in this work, see essay 4.3, page 365 below.

52 **Bot . . . hait** but my verse comes from the press hotfoot (with a pun on "foot" as "verse foot," and another on "press" as "winepress" and "printing press"). Douglas translates Virgil directly, but Caxton via at least one intermediary.

53 **Onforlatit . . . tunn** undecanted, not splashed about from vessel to vessel

55 **Bachus of glaidness** Bacchus, Roman god of mirth ∫ **funeral Proserpyne** funereal Proserpine: queen of the underworld

56 **Victorie** Roman goddess of military conquest

57 **Sal I . . . dyvyne?** shall I invoke you, since you had the name of divinities? Douglas begins to distance himself from Virgil by refusing to invoke the deities who are presiding patrons of this book of the *Aeneid*. Compare Walton's anxieties about pagan gods (excerpt 1.5). The shift of mood is ostensibly in rejection of Virgil's theology, but is also made into a complex act of homage, an imitation of what Douglas has just praised as the unique way he "altyrris hys style" (33).

58 **Na, na . . . memorie** no, no, a very faint memory of you would be enough
60–61 **Bot he . . . I cry** Douglas invokes the Christian God instead.
63 **As in . . . want** as you cannot lack for examples in this book
67 **blythness** happiness
68 **nocht the less** not lessened

3.17 WILLIAM CAXTON, *REYNARD THE FOX*: PROLOGUE

Date and Provenance: 1481; Westminster (near London).

Author, Sources, and Nature of Text: This prose rendering of stories from the ever popular Reynard cycle (known generically as the *Roman de Renard*) is Caxton's translation of a Dutch original, which he issued in 1481 and again eight years later. The Reynard cycle has rather the same subversive relationship with the genre of beast fable that fabliau (such as *The Miller's Tale*) has with the protagonists of serious romance narratives. Reynard at once represents and exemplifies deceitfulness, and since the effect of deceitfulness is precisely to corrode moral behavior by recasting it as *posture,* this quality is hard to contain within the moral structures of fable, with its dependence on a stable system of allegorical correspondences. With their comic attitude toward the predicament into which successful deceitfulness throws human society and human systems of representation, Reynard stories often serve as a place where radical doubts about the stability of moral structures and the capacity of language to express truth can be raised in a safely lighthearted manner. These stories, of which Caxton provides a sizable collection, thus contain some of the most comically ironic reflections in literature on the gap between what is said and what is meant. Where Douglas's *Eneados* (excerpt 3.16) fiercely denies the correspondence—drawn by historians like Poggio (see excerpt 3.15)—between poetry or fiction and lies, stories in the Reynard tradition rejoice in that correspondence (compare Chaucer's *Nun's Priest's Tale,* which draws on this tradition). It is notable that Caxton even omits the moralizing

epilogue with which his source for *Reynard* ends, denying the resolution his original insists upon.

Audience and Circulation: Caxton's market for a small and relatively inexpensive book such as this was potentially broad and not limited to the lay audience the prologue invokes. Unlike some of his books, *Reynard* was not published under the ostensible protection of an aristocratic patron, but this may have more to do with the work's genre than with any expectations Caxton had about the class of his readers (perhaps because any dedicatee of *Reynard* would run a risk of being identified with the work's protagonist). Little is known about the circulation of this work, which has survived in relatively few copies (the 1489 edition in only one). Its rarity now, however, should be taken not as a sign that the book was not popular—that Caxton reprinted it shows that it was—but as an indication of the slim chances of survival for any medieval book cheaply produced in a plain format for a wide array of readers.

Bibliography: The text has been edited by Blake (1970). For Caxton, see Blake's many studies, most recently Blake 1991, especially 231–58, 259–74, and, for further bibliography, Blake 1986 and 1996. For the *Roman de Renard* and its complex history, see Best 1983 and the annual journal *Reinardus: Yearbook of the International Reynard Society* (1991–).

Source: 1481 edition, London, British Library C.11.c.3 A3v (*STC* 20919). One of at least six surviving copies of this small folio, printed by William Caxton in Westminster, January 6, 1481. For a more detailed description, see Blake 1970, lix–lxi.

Hyer begynneth th'ystorye of Reynard the foxe.

In this historye ben wreton the parables, goode lerynge, and dyverse poyntes to be
merkyd, by whiche poyntes men maye lerne to come to the subtyl knoweleche of
suche thynges as dayly ben used and had in the counseyllys of lordes and prelates
gostly and worldly, and also emonge marchantes and other comone peple. And
5 this booke is maad for nede and prouffyte of alle god folke, as fer as they in
redynge or heeryng of it shal mowe understande and fele the forsayd subtyl
deceytes that dayly ben used in the worlde: not to th'entente that men shold use
them, but that every man shold eschewe and kepe hym from the subtyl false
shrewis, that they be not deceyvyd. Thenne who that wyll have the very
10 understandyng of this mater, he muste ofte and many tymes rede in thys boke, and
ernestly and diligently marke wel that he redeth—for it is sette subtylly, lyke as ye
shal see in redyng of it—and not ones to rede it. For a man shal not wyth ones
over redyng fynde the ryght understandyng ne comprise it wel, but oftymes to rede
it shal cause it wel to be understande. And for them that understandeth it it shall
15 be ryght joyous, playsant and prouffitable.

---

1 **th'ystorye** narrative, though the word also
makes a comic claim for seriousness (see also
"historye" [2])

2 **lerynge** instruction ∫ **poyntes** details, but also
"strategies"

3 **merkyd** noted

4–5 **lordes and prelates gostly and worldly**
ecclesiastical and secular lords and prelates. The
work pretends to offer men and women knowledge
of the deceitfulness of those in power, as well as of
"marchantes and other comone peple" (5): an unusual pose in Caxton's oeuvre.

6 **for nede and prouffyte of** for the necessity
and the benefit of

7 **shal mowe** shall be able ∫ **fele** perceive, comprehend

9 **eschewe** avoid

10 **shrewis** evil persons ∫ **who that** whoever ∫
very true

12 **that he redeth** what he reads ∫ **sette subtylly**
subtly put

13 **not ones to rede it** not read it over [only]
once. As noted in the introduction to Part Three
(pages 219–20), these tonally ambiguous exhortations to readers to study the story of Reynard
seriously and diligently can be compared with instructions to readers of *The Cloud of Unknowing*
(excerpt 3.3). See also Julian's *Revelation* (excerpt
3.4) and the advice the translator of *The Mirror of
Our Lady* derives from Augustine about the need
to read texts several times (excerpt 3.12: 120–25).

13–14 **ones over redyng** reading through once

14 **comprise** understand

3.18 ROBERT HENRYSON, *FABLES:* PROLOGUE

Date and Provenance: c. 1450–1500; the
south of Scotland (perhaps Dumfrerline).
   Author, Sources, and Nature of Text: Little
is known of the life of Robert Henryson. He
was admitted to the University of Glasgow in
1462, when he was already a mature man,
spent his later years as teacher and perhaps
notary at the grammar school at Dumfermline,
and died before 1505 (Fox 1981, xiii–xix). Besides the *Fables,* he wrote a dozen short poems,
Orpheus and Eurydice, and a sequel to
Chaucer's *Troilus and Criseyde, The Testa-*

ment of Cresseid, which was finished by 1492;
when these poems were written is unclear, as is
much about their audience and interpretation.
The *Fables,* Henryson's longest work, is a collection of thirteen beast fables in rhyme royal,
each followed by a poetic *moralitas* explaining
the fable's meaning. The fables are partly based
on the Latin collection of Aesopic tales made
by Gualterius Anglicus (c. 1175), whose own
source is the so-called Romulus collection (Fox
1981, xliv–lv); other sources include the *Roman de Renard* in some version (see excerpt

3.17), Chaucer's *Nun's Priest's Tale*, and Lydgate's *Isopes Fables*. Chaucer's influence is also felt in Henryson's versification and vocabulary, although how far this justifies labeling Henryson a "Scottish Chaucerian" is controversial. Fables were a staple of the grammar-school curriculum, and the Aesopic collections were popular throughout the Middle Ages and well into the early modern period, highly regarded as vehicles of moral teaching, even if they were also criticized for their fictionality by historians like Poggio Bracciolini (excerpt 3.15). Henryson's prologue, which is loosely based on Gualterius's twelve-line prologue, is a compact compendium of the topoi associated with the beast fable and other literary prologues, systematically evoking the various current theories about the relation between form and meaning, vehicle and tenor, pleasure and instruction. As with all his writing, its tone is impenetrably deadpan, refusing to decide between the reading possibilities it raises, often suggesting irony, but never lapsing into parody or renouncing the didacticism integral to the Aesopic mode. Like the *moralitates* at the end of many of the fables, which patently fail to account for the meaning of the story they are supposed to explain but insist on their adequacy, the prologue is a conundrum that apparently sets out to confront its readers with an irresolvably ambiguous statement about the purpose of literary fiction.

Audience and Circulation: The prologue claims the *Fables* were written "be requeist and precept of ane lord" (34), but it is unclear if this is true. Henryson must have written for readers with a good knowledge of vernacular courtly poetry, but who these were is unknown; he does not seem to have had the international contacts of his contemporary Douglas (excerpt 3.16). Henryson is included in the list of dead Scottish poets in Dunbar's *Lament for the Makeris* (1505); before 1530, many of his poems were copied by John Asloan into the "Asloan" manuscript, and the *Fables* were included in the mid-sixteenth-century "Bannatyne" manuscript; by 1532, *The Testament* was in England, where Thynne printed the poem as a work by Chaucer; in the 1570s, two editions of the *Fables* were printed in Edinburgh, one by Henry Charteris, one by Thomas Bassandyne.

Bibliography: The works of Henryson are edited by Denton Fox (1981), who provides invaluable analyses and bibliography; a selection from the *Fables* is edited by Bawcutt and Riddy (1987). For a survey of scholarship, see Fradenburg 1984. For an analysis of Henryson's poetic career, see Fox 1984. Critical analyses of the *Fables* include Gray 1979 and Powell 1983, carefully historicized interpretative studies, and Greentree 1993, a study of Henryson's narrator.

Source: Edinburgh, National Library of Scotland F.5.b.48, A2–A3: the only known surviving copy of this slim and tiny octavo volume, printed by Thomas Bassandyne in Edinburgh in 1571, and itself derived from a lost earlier edition. It was formerly in the library at York Minster. The fables are set in *Civilité* type, which is based on medieval cursive script, making the print resemble handwriting; the poetic *moralitates* are set in roman script, setting them off visually from the texts on which they comment. The edition has two woodcuts, one depicting Aesop, the other the Cock and the Jasp.

Thocht feinyeit fabils of ald poetre   **feinyeit** imagined; **ald** old
Be not al grunded upon truth, yit than   **al** altogether; **yit than** even so
Thair polite termes of sweit rhetore   **polite** polished; **termes** language
Richt plesand ar unto the eir of man;
5 And als the caus that thay first began   **als** also; **began** i.e., to be written
Wes to repreif the haill misleving   **repreif** reprove; **haill** entire; **misleving** sinful living
Off man, be figure of ane uther thing.   **be figure** using the image

In lyke maner as throw the bustious eird,   **bustious eird** rough ground
Swa it be laubourit with grit diligence,   **Swa** if; **grit** great

10 Springis the flouris and the corne abreird,   **the corne abreird** the first shoots of corn
   Hailsum and gude to mannis sustenence;   **Hailsum** wholesome
   Sa dois spring ane morall sweit sentence,   **morall sweit sentence** a sweet moral meaning
   Oute of the subtell dyte of poetry,   **dyte** writing
   To gude purpois, quha culd it weill apply.   **To gude purpois** to useful effect

15 The nuttis schell, thocht it be hard and teuch,   **teuch** tough
   Aldis the kirnell, and is delectabill;   **Aldis** encloses; **kirnell** kernel
   Sa lyis thair ane doctrine wyse aneuch   **doctrine** moral lesson; **wyse aneuch** wise enough
   And full of frute, under ane fenyeit fabill;
   And clerkis sayis, it is richt profitabill
20 Amangis ernist to ming ane merie sport   **ernist** serious pursuits; **ming** mingle
   To light the spreit and gar the tyme be schort.   **light** lighten; **spreit** spirit; **gar** make

   Forther mair, ane bow that is ay bent   **ay** always
   Worthis unsmart and dullis on the string;   **Worthis** becomes; **unsmart** limp
   Sa dois the mynd that is ay diligent
25 In ernistfull thochtis and in studying.
   With sad materis sum merines to ming   **sad** serious
   Accordis weill: thus Esope said, I wis,   **Accordis** harmonizes; **I wis** truly
   Dulcius arrident seria picta iocis.

   Of this authour, my maisteris, with your leif,   **leif** permission
30 Submitting me in your correctioun,
   In mother toung of Latyng I wald preif   **of** from; **preif** attempt
   To mak ane maner of translatioun,
   Nocht of my self for vane presumptioun   **of** by; **for** out of
   Bot be requeist and precept of ane lord   **precept** command
35 Of quhome the name it neidis not record.   **it neidis not** there is no need to

   In hamelie language and in termes rude   **hamelie** homely
   Me neidis wryte, for quhy of eloquence   **Me neidis wryte** I have to write
   Nor rethorike I never understude;
   Thairfoir meiklie I pray your reverence,
40 Gif that ye find it throw my negligence
   Be deminute, or yit superfluous,   **deminute** lacking; **yit** also
   Correct it at your willis gratious.   **willis gratious** gracious pleasure

   My author in his fabillis tellis how
   That brutal beistis spak, and understude   **brutal** brutish
45 Into gude purpois dispute, and argow   **Into gude purpois** sensibly; **dispute** disputations
   Ane sillogisme, propone and eik conclude;   **propone** propound; **eik** also; **conclude** round off
   Put in exempill and in similitude   signifying by parable and by analogy
   How mony men in operatioun   **in operatioun** in their deeds
   Ar like to beistis in conditioun.   **like to** similar to

50 Na mervell is ane man be lyke ane beist
   Quhilk lufis ay carnall and foull delyte,   who constantly loves fleshly and foul pleasure
   That schame can not him renye nor arreist   **That** so that; **renye** shame; **arreist** stop
   Bot takis all the lust and appetyte,   **takis** gathers

And that throw custum and daylie ryte	ryte habit
55 Syne in thair myndis sa fast is radicate	Syne thereafter; radicate rooted
That thay in brutal beistis ar transformate.	transformate transformed

This nobill clerk, Esope, as I haif tauld,	
In gay metir and as poete lawriate	gay handsome
Be figure wrait his buke, for he nocht wald	for because; nocht wald did not want to
60 Lak the disdane off hie nor low estate;	Lak the disdane off suppress [his] scorn for
And to begin, first of ane cok he wrate,	
Seikand his meit, quhilk fand ane jolie stone,	meit food
Of quhome the fabill ye sall heir anone.	anone at once

1–2 **Thocht . . . truth** although imagined fables [found] in old poetry are not completely grounded in the truth. "Feinyeit" also means "lying," so Henryson raises at once the problematic status of the fable in relation to the truth. The stanza argues that, despite this problem, fables are pleasurable and improving, stating the work's goal to be "repreif" (6) of folly, thus announcing its mode as satirical.

7 **be figure of ane uther thing** that is, using the vehicle of something other than direct description of their subject, human "misleving" (6)

8–14 **In lyke maner . . . weill apply** The lines are expanded from Gualterius but may also allude to Chaucer, *Parliament of Fowls* 22–25. Henryson's lines emphasize the difficulty of poetic creation or interpretation (it is unclear whether the stanza's subject is poet or reader) and the intractable quality of the soil that is to be worked.

14 **quha culd it weill apply** for anyone who knows how to put it to use

15–16 **The nuttis schell . . . delectabill** The topos of the nut and kernel was a very common way of describing the relation between pleasure and instruction in allegory, associated with the image of rhetoric as a "veil" modestly concealing but also revealing the truth; for discussion of the topos, see Robertson and Huppé 1963. Henryson juxtaposes this model for reading with the very different one in the previous stanza, where the flower of meaning *grows out* of the textual plant and pleasure does not need to be discarded in apprehending the "sentence."

19–21 **it is richt profitabill . . . gar the tyme be schort** The topos that writing poetry is a defense against idleness is common, found in the *Distichs of Cato* 3:6 (Boas and Botschuyer 1952); see also Olson 1982, chap. 2.

28 *Dulcius . . . iocis* serious things have a sweeter face when they are adorned with pleasures

29–30 **my maisteris . . . correctioun** It is possible that a particular audience is being invoked, but these gestures of deference, like those to the anonymous "lord" below (34), may be invoked largely to show Henryson's mastery, in an astonishingly small space, of all the necessary conventions.

32 **ane maner of translatioun** a kind of translation. The *Fables* are indeed only a translation in "ane maner," and Henryson, with a striking lack of the usual deference to his source, acknowledges this rather than hide behind the fiction of rigid adherence to an authoritative Latin text. Contrast the very different articulation of the source/text relationship in Douglas's *Eneados* (excerpt 3.16).

36–42 **In hamelie language . . . gratious** For further examples of these modesty topoi, see excerpts 1.8: 116–43 (Metham's *Amoryus and Cleopes*) and 1.9: 49–69 (Ashby's *Active Policy of a Prince*).

44 **brutal beistis spak, and understude** In medieval thought, humans were often distinguished from "beistis" by their capacity to reason. The speaking beast (especially one who can "sillogisme, propone" [46]) is thus a contradiction in terms: suitably so, given what these beasts represent (see 50–56).

56 **thay in brutal beistis ar transformate** Circe turns people into beasts in Ovid's *Metamorphoses,* but in this preacherly stanza humans achieve this transformation by themselves.

57 **Esope** Aesop: the ancient Greek fabulist who was credited with most of the vast numbers of beast fables produced in ancient and medieval times

58 **gay metir** a reference to the Latin elegiacs employed by Gualterius. Henryson endorses the use of a mannered and artificial verse form. Contrast Mannyng's concern about the use of "strange" rhymes for the historical writing of the *Chronicle* (excerpt 1.1: 55–64 and notes). ∫ **as poete lawriate** Fox (1981, 5) emends to *in facound purpurate,* the reading found in the Bannatyne manuscript (National Library of Scotland Advocates' MS 1.1.6).

61 **first of ane cok he wrate** Henryson pretends to be translating tale by tale from his source. The first poem in the *Fables* is *The Cock and the Jasp*, part of whose plot is summarized here.

3.19 WILLIAM LANGLAND, *PIERS PLOWMAN*: C TEXT, PASSUS XV (EXTRACT)

Date and Provenance: c. 1385–87 (or perhaps later); southwest Midlands (Worcestershire) and/or London.

Author, Sources, and Nature of Text: The final version of William Langland's *Piers Plowman* seems, in part, to have been a worried response to the revolt of 1381, in which the name of his protagonist, Piers, had been used as a rallying cry by the rebels. This version of the poem seems to have occupied him until his death (in 1387 or, as has recently been suggested, some years later; see, e.g., Hanna 1994, Kerby-Fulton and Justice 1997) and may not, even so, have been finished. The scene from which this passage is taken occurs immediately after the first phase of Will's search for Dowel is complete and the gains and losses of his conversations with Wit, Study, Clergy, Scripture, and others have been summed up by Imaginatif, who stresses above all Will's need to learn the virtue of patience. Here, Will accordingly finds himself as Patience's humble dinner companion at a meal given by Clergy, part of whose purpose is to reconcile Will to Reason, whom Will has insulted two passus earlier. As it happens (in the C version of this scene, though not the earlier B-text version), Reason runs off in passionate pursuit of Piers Plowman before the meal is over, as Patience, Will, and Conscience take their leave of Clergy to go on pilgrimage: a turn of events that throws Imaginatif's carefully balanced assurances regarding the value of learning, and even the centrality of patience, into some question. The passage hence concerns the place of learning in the spiritual life, opposing the gluttony of the learned doctor (Clergy's favored guest) with the penitential food eaten by Patience (who is here compared with Piers), while associating Patience's mode of eating with a mode of reading reminiscent of the Anselmian reading model of several earlier excerpts (e.g., 3.1,

3.2, 3.5). However, another strand of thought may critique the same reading model, by validating not only Patience's patience with the poor food he and Will receive but also Will's anger at the doctor's greed and at being offered food the doctor would disdain. In echoing Will's judgment on the doctor, the poem suggests that a satirical response to intellectual elitism may be as appropriate as a patient one, protesting against the exclusiveness associated with learning, in a fashion comparable to Lollard and reformist texts like the *Sermon of Dead Men* (excerpt 3.11) or *The Holi Prophete David* (excerpt 2.5; see also excerpts 1.13 and 1.14).

Audience and Circulation: A *succès de scandale* from the time of its composition—to the point that Langland never seems to have had the chance to finish any version of the poem before parts of it began to be copied—*Piers Plowman* continued to be read in all its versions until well into the sixteenth century, and survives in some fifty manuscripts. The textual relationships between the surviving manuscripts suggest that at least three hundred copies of the work must have been in circulation by 1400, a huge number for a vernacular text at the time (Hanna 1994). Though its largest audience was perhaps members of the clerisy—monks, secular priests, and university students—the text circulated widely among an impressive range of social classes for some two hundred years.

Bibliography: Many editions exist, the most user-friendly of which are Schmidt 1995b (B text) and Pearsall 1978 (C text); references in the notes are to Pearsall's edition. The standard critical edition of the C text is now Russell and Kane 1997. Schmidt 1995a provides a parallel edition of the A, B, C, and so-called Z texts (volume 2 of this edition, containing the apparatus and notes, is yet to appear). Hoyt Duggan (1994) runs an extensive and growing electronic archive of all the manuscripts. A good guide to the poem and the bulky scholarship it has generated is Alford 1988. A good interpretive study, designed for student use, is Simpson 1990. For Langland's biography, see Hanna 1994. For connections with the revolt of 1381, see Justice 1994. The symbolism of food in this passage is explored by Jill Mann (1979) and Anne Savage (1993). On the relations between Latin and English in the poem, see Machan 1994. A year-by-year bibliography is published by *The Yearbook of Langland Studies*.

Source: Cambridge University Library MS Addit. 4325, fols. 50v–51r. This manuscript contains only *Piers Plowman*; it is carefully written and laid-out, in a single column, with each line divided by spaces and, usually, punctuation by virgules or stops. Passus divisions are marked out with Latin incipits and explicits; personal names, technical terms (such as "Adjectyf"), and Latin words are underlined, and omitted lines are added clearly and carefully in the margin, with each verse preserved as a separate line. Apart from a flourished border on fol.1r, the manuscript is undecorated. It probably belonged to Thomas Tyrrwhit (1730–86), early editor of Chaucer and clerk of the commons. This transcription follows the manuscript spacing and punctuation (here by raised points) that divide Langland's long alliterative line in two and also follows the manuscript in highlighting proper names. Comparison with Pearsall's edition of the C text will show something of the degree of variation found in *Piers* manuscripts.

Thenne cam *Conciense,* · and *Clergye* aftur,
And beden me ryse and rome, · for with *Reson* scholde I dyne.
And I aros and romed forth, · with *Reson* we mette.
We reverenced *Reson,* · and romede forth softelye   softelye gently
5 And metten with a maystur, · a man ilyk a frere.   maystur scholar; ilyk like; frere friar
Conciense knew hym, · and welcomed hym fayre;
Thei wescheden and wypeden, · and wenten to the dyner.
Paciense as a pore thyng cam, · and prede mete for charyte,   prede mete begged food
Ilyk to *Perus plowman,* · a palmere as he were,   Ilyk like; palmere pilgrim
10 Cravede and cryede, · for *Cristus* love of hevene,
A melus mete for a pore man, · or money, yf the[i] hadden.   melus mete food for a meal
Conciense knew him wel, · and welcomede hem alle,
Wesschen and wypeden, · and wenten and seten.
The maystur was mad to sytten furst, · as for the most werthi;   furst in the first place
15 *Reson* stod and stihlede, · as for stywarde of halle.   stihlede served
Pacience and I, · were put to be mettus,   mettus table companions
And seten by ous selve, · at a syd table.   ous selve ourselves
Clergye called aftur mete, · and thenne cam *Scripture*   called aftur mete summoned dinner
And served heom thus sone, · of sondry metus menye,   sondry metus different foods
20 Of *Austyn,* of *Ambrosye,* · of alle the fower evangelius,
Edentes et bybentes que apud illos sunt
Ac of these metus the maystre · myghte nat wel schewe;   schewe chew
Forthi he hyght mete of more cost, · mortrewes and potagus.   hyght ordered
Of that that men myswonne, · thei made hem wel at ese;   that that that which

25 Ac her saus was oversour, · and onsaverly igrounde   onsaverly unpleasantly
    In a morter, *post mortem*, · of meny bytter peynus   peynus pains
    But yef hy synge for the soulus, · and wepe salte terus.   But yef unless; hy they; the i.e., their
    Vos qui peccata homini comeditis nisi pro eis lacrimas
    effudertis ea que delitiis comeditis in tormentis [evometis]
30 Thenne *Reson* radde, · ryght anoon aftur,   radde advised
    That *Conciense* comaunde scholde, · to do come *Scripture*   do come make come
    And brynge bred for *Paciense*, · bytynge apartye,   bytynge eating; apartye on one side
    And to me that was hys mette tho, · and other mete bothe.
    He sette a sour lof, and seyde, · "*Agyte penitenciam*,"
35 And syththe he drow ous drynke, · *diu perseverans*,   syththe then; drow poured
    "As longe," quath he, "as the lyf, · and lykame may duyre."   lykame body; duyre endure
    "This ys a semely service," · seyde *Pacience*.   semely gracious
    Thenne cam *Contricion*, · that hadde koked for heom alle,   koked cooked
    And brought forth a pytaunce, was *Pro hac orabit omnis sanctus in tempore optimo.*
40 *Conciense* comforted ous bothe, · *Clergye* and *Scripture*,
    And seyden, "*Cor contritum et humiliatum, Deus, non despicies.*"
    Pacience was wel apayed · of this propre servyce   apayed of satisfied with
    And made myrthe with this mete; · ac I mornede evere   mornede grumbled
    For a doctour atte hye deys, · drank wyn faste—   hye deys high table
45 *Ve vobis qui potentes estis ad bibendum vinum*—
    And eet mony sondry metus, · mortrewes and poddyngus,   mortrewes stews
    Braun and blood of the goos, · bakon and colhopus.   bakon and colhopus bacon and eggs

2 **And beden me ryse and rome** and told me to get up and walk ∫ **for** with *Reson* **scholde I dyne** In the B text, Will and Patience dine with Conscience, with Reason as a guest. Here, Reason is the steward in charge of a household of which Conscience and his wife, Scripture, are in the position of lord and lady, with Clergy as a third master of the household. This unusual social arrangement breaks down during the passus (see 24n).

8–9 *Paciense . . .* **a palmere as he were** Patience's first appearance in the poem associates him at once with poverty (the phrase "patient poverty" has often been used by this point), but also with Piers in one of his manifestations in the first part of the poem, dressed as a "palmere" (VIII.56–64).

16 *Pacience . . .* **mettus** Patience and I were seated as tablemates. Will is seated with the virtue he needs to acquire, and below a representative of some of the abuses he needs to learn to "suffer" rather than outspokenly criticize (see headnote).

17 **syd table** The doctor sits at a raised table (high table) and is given food suitable for someone who is the social equal or superior of his host, while Patience and Will are fed at a side table and given

the less expensive food that might also be given the household servants.

20 *Austyn . . . Ambrosye* Augustine of Hippo (d. 430) and Ambrose of Milan (d. 397), two of the so-called fathers of the church

21 *Edentes . . . sunt* eating and drinking such things as they have: Luke 10:7

23 **mortrewes and potagus** stews and soups

24 **thei made hem wel at ese** In the B text, the plural pronouns here refer to the master and his man (B XIII.40–42). Here, the man is absent, and "they" can only refer to the master, Clergy, and Conscience himself, who will decide later in the passus that the compromises Clergy makes in order to associate with the likes of the friar mean that he must temporarily be left behind. Thus Will's "impatience," which bursts through in this description and elsewhere, is strongly endorsed by Conscience himself, despite its moral questionability. For a different explanation, see Pearsall (1978, 249.48n), who argues that "they" is a relic from the B text but may have a reference to friars in general here in the C text.

26 **a morter**, *post mortem* rich eating in this life will lead to suffering in purgatory or hell after death

28–29 *Vos . . . [evometis]* you who feast upon the sins of men, unless you pour out tears for them, you shall vomit up amid torments the food you now feast on amid pleasures (MS *etcetera*). The source has not been identified.

32–33 **brynge bred . . . and other mete** bring bread and other food to Patience, eating on one side, and to me, his table companion

34 *Agyte penitenciam* do penance: Matt. 3:2

35 *diu perseverans* long persevering: Matt. 10:22

39 **pytaunce** pittance. In Middle English the word already means "small amount," but its more technical meaning is probably intended here. A pittance was a charitable gift of food or money given

to hermits, anchorites, monks, nuns, or, in this case, pilgrims. ʃ *Pro hac orabit . . . optimo* for this [forgiveness] shall all the saints pray to you in the best time: Ps. 31:6, AV 32

41 *Cor contritum . . . despicies* a contrite and humbled heart, God, you will not despise: Ps. 50:19, AV 51:17

45 *Ve vobis . . . vinum* woe to you who are mighty to drink wine! Isa. 5:22

46–47 **mortrewes . . . colhopus** The nature of the doctor's food (intensely processed, intensely carnivorous, intensely greasy) adds an appropriately visceral quality that supports Will's disgust. See further Savage 1993. ʃ **bakon and colhopus** bacon and eggs

3.20 MECHTILD OF HACKEBORN, *THE BOOK OF GHOSTLY GRACE:* EPILOGUE (EXTRACT)

Date and Provenance: c. 1400–1440; provenance unknown. Both manuscript copies are in versions of the Central Midlands dialect that became a literary standard during the fifteenth century, but there are signs the text was originally in a Northern dialect.

Author, Sources, and Nature of Text: *The Book of Spiritual Graces,* also known as *The Book of Special Graces,* is an account of the visions of the nun Mechtild of Hackeborn (1241–99) and was written in Latin at the end of the thirteenth century at Helfta, a Cistercian convent in Saxony (northwestern Germany), where Mechtild was choir mistress (*domina cantrix*). The work is one of three lengthy visionary texts produced there between 1270 and 1300. The others are *The Flowing Light of the Godhead,* by the exiled Beguine Mechtild of Magdeburg, who seems to have retired to Helfta to complete the work, and a collaborative work, *The Herald of Divine Love,* partly by and partly about the nun Gertrude the Great (1256–1301), Helfta's most learned writer, who was also the author of a set of Latin *Spiritual Exercises* and other, lost writings, some of them in German. Gertrude was probably also the main writer of this work, which was begun without Mechtild's knowledge, although much of it is based on Mechtild's oral accounts of her experiences. The *Book* is the sole Helfta text to have been rendered into Middle English, from

an abridged version of the Latin text (Halligan 1979, 10–14), by a translator who assumed the work's narrator to be male. It was one of several Continental mystical works rendered into English during the period (several of them apparently by Carthusian monks). They include the *Liber Celestis* of Bridget of Sweden, Catherine of Siena's *Dialogo* (see excerpt 3.5), the *Revelations* of Elizabeth of Hungary, Marguerite Porete's *Mirror of Simple Souls,* Suso's *Horologium sapientiae,* and Ruusbroec's *Spiritual Espousals* (part of which is used in the compilation *The Chastizing of God's Children*).

Audience and Circulation: The full translation survives in only two manuscripts, but there are fragments of Latin copies and many other partial English versions of "Maud's Book" (as it was called) to testify to Mechtild's importance both to male monastics and to female religious and secular readers. An extract was incorporated into the *Speculum Devotorum* (excerpt 1.12), and the text is mentioned in *The Mirror of Our Lady* (see excerpt 3.12), as well as the Latin *Speculum spiritualium,* an important Latin compilation of devotional writings made around 1400 by English monks (Halligan 1979, 47–51). Mechtild may have been a "second-tier" woman visionary, less well known than Bridget of Sweden, Catherine of Siena, and Elizabeth of Hungary but often quoted in the prayer books and other works circulating in women's religious houses and aristocratic households in the fifteenth century. Yet her book must have been of great interest, for it made its way without the advantages shared by these other women, all of whom were beatified or canonized and who were known through *vitae* (saintly biographies) as well as through their writings. English users of "Maud's Book" knew nothing of its protagonist except what it tells.

Bibliography: The text has been edited by Theresa Halligan (1979), who provides a full introduction and description of the manuscripts; Barratt (1992, 49–60) edits and discusses excerpts. For Gertrude's *Spiritual Exercises,* see Lewis and Lewis 1989. For the nuns of Helfta, see Finnegan 1962 and Bynum

1982, as well as Newman 1995. For bibliography since 1979, see Lagorio and Sargent 1993, 3458. For an account of the text's English circulation, see Voaden 1996a. For the milieu in which the Middle English text was read, see Riddy 1996b. For a study of the metaphor of food and its importance to women religious, see Bynum 1987.

Source: London, British Library MS Egerton 2006, fol. 212r, the base manuscript for Halligan's edition. This is a neat and careful copy of the mid–fifteenth century, with a number of signatures indicating ownership, including a fifteenth-century signature by a certain Marg[ar]et Thorpe (fol. 127r). Halligan (1979, 22) suggests it may have been made at the Carthusian house of Axholme (on the Lincolnshire-Yorkshire border).

Offe the visioun whiche the wrytere of this booke hadde iii yeere before he wrate itt. And howe this booke was kepte privye, ande whate gostelye comforth some of here sustrene felydde when thaye redde thareyn privelye or itt was knawene. 16ᵐ

5   Before in the same boke, itt es schewede in this manere that this booke come
     verrelye of God ande be his grace itt es writtene ande that itt es namenede of God
     The Booke of Spyritualle Grace. For that same persone whiche wrote itt—some
     thareof be inpartey of here owne tellynge to whome this was schewede of God,
     ande some thareof be partye be tellynge of thame that were famyliare with here—
10   sawe, thre yeere before or he wrate, this vysioun in his slepe:
         Itt semede to hym that this holy maydene of whome we speke was devoutelye
     comwnede, ande when sche schulde come agayne from comwnynge, sche begane to
     synge with a hye voyce: *Domine, quinque talenta et c.,* that es to say: "Lorde,
     thowe gaffe me fyve besauntes or fyve pens to spende; I haffe wonne overe that
15   othere fyve." And aftere that, sche sayde: "Who wille haffe of the honye of
     hevenlye Jerusalem?" Ande anone hym thowght sche profryde a honycombe, owte
     of a vesselle that sche hadde, to alle the sustrene in the qweere whiche come to
     here. Ande that same persone that sawe as by vysioun [went] to here also, als hym
     thought, ande sche gaffe hym a gobette of brede owte fro the honye. Ande while
20   sche helde that breede in here handdys, wonderfullye that gobette of breede with
     the honye both togydders bygane to wexe owte into a loofe, so that the gobette of
     breede wexe owte in a hoole loofe, ande the honycombe persede the lofe withyn
     and withowte, and thorowe here handdis. Whilys sche helde that loofe, itt
     droppede in so moche plenteuosnes ande habundaunce that itt wette alle here
25   lappe, ande so ranne forth ande moystede alle the erth abowte them.
         Also another tokynne of this booke thare was, that while this booke was kepte
     fulle warlye of certayne persones whiche wrote itt, itt happede that on a holyedaye
     one of here sustrene walde reede thareon, ande when sche hadde unnethis openede

the booke, come anothere sustrene ande with a stronge spyritte sayde to here that
30 openede the booke: "A, sustere, whate goodenesse ande frewte es in this booke!
For the furste tyme that evere I lokede thareopoun, my herte felte suche a
wonderfulle ande a luffynge styrrynge, that itt wente thoroweowte alle the partyes
of my bodye."

Tharefore this booke worthelye hadde [and] hath the name *The Booke of*
35 *Spyrytualle Grace*, that suche a thynge was schewede in the fygour of swa swete a
lykoure, also that itt peersede so lyghtlye ande so softelye thare hertys that lokede
thareopoun. Thare es nothynge swettere than the comforth of Goddis grace, ande
thare es nothynge that so informeth ande lyghttenes a sawlle als his grace; for that
grace herteth ande comforteth a sawlle to alle goodenes.

1–4 Offe the visioun . . . knawene This chapter of the epilogue deals with two signs ("tokynne" [26]) of the book's special status: a visionary anticipation of its composition (1–25), and an instance of the book's ability to give "comforth" even before being read (26–33). The notion of a book or text having its own inherent power and functioning like a contact relic is common in saints' lives and related contexts. See Wogan-Browne 1994b.

2 he he, that is, Gertrude the Great, who does not name herself in the course of recounting her fellow nun's visionary life and whom—in spite of the feminine pronoun "here" (3), which refers to Mechtild—the translator takes to be a man ∫ **privye** secret

3 gostelye comfort spiritual comfort

3–4 when thaye redde thareyn privelye or itt was knawene when they secretly read it [*or* parts of it] before it was known

4 16ᵐ 16 *capitulum* (chapter)

5 Before in the same boke This epilogue repeats material from earlier in the work, once more affirming the veracity and authority of the text.

6 verrelye truly

7 *The Booke of Spyritualle Grace* Different manuscripts of the Latin original render this title either as *Liber spiritualis gracie*, as here, or as *Liber specialis gracie*, its proper title. Latin abbreviation practice would make the two titles virtually indistinguishable.

7–9 some thareof be . . . here some of it without a medium ["be inpartey," i.e., through sharing] from her own report, to whom this [revelation] was showed by God, and some part of it at the report of those who were familiar with her

11–12 was devoutelye comwnede was taking communion devoutly. The vision's scene is set at Mass.

13 *Domine, quinque talenta et c.* Lord, five talents, etc. See Matt. 25:15.

14 thowe gaffe me fyve besauntes you gave me five pennies ∫ **overe that** in addition to that.

Mechtild is the good servant in Jesus' parable who, given great gifts by his lord, turns them to good account and so is praised and rewarded.

16 hym thowght it seemed to him ∫ **sche profryde a honycombe** Mechtild's preeminence as a servant of God enables her to enact a special sacrament, like Mass but involving honey instead of bread and wine. Convents are often compared to beehives in didactic texts for nuns; see, for example, Rolle's *Bee* (Allen 1931, 54–56).

17 qweere choir (where the sisters would sing Mass)

18 [went] MS omits

18–19 als hym thought as it seemed to him

19 gaffe gave ∫ **gobette** piece ∫ **owte fro the honye** from out of that honey

19–25 Ande while . . . abowte them The moment Gertrude, the text's scribe/compiler, communes with Mechtild, honey gives birth to bread, which grows into a loaf. Thus Gertrude portrays herself as a crucial catalyst for the book (honey, like yeast, is an ancient fermenting agent: see Wilson 1991, 327, 360). Allegorical precision is not to be looked for here, but the bread is perhaps the book that both women (or, in this translation, Maud and her male scribe) will write, which acts as a vehicle for Mechtild's honey without being able to contain it (19–23). The "Eucharist" in which she dispenses divine grace can thus have an effect outside the convent walls and beyond the visionary occasion Gertrude is recounting.

21 wexe owte expand outward

22 persede infused (perhaps also "pierced," as an allusion to Christ's nailing on the cross)

23 itt that is, the honey

26 tokynne of this booke that is, sign of this book's divine inspiration

27 warlye carefully ∫ **of** by

28 here her ∫ **walde reede thareon** wanted to read in it ∫ **unnethis** scarcely

29 sustrene sisters: probably an error for the singular form, *sustere*

30 **frewte** fruit

34 **[and]** MS reads *yn itt*, and there is possibly some confusion here

35–36 **in the fygour of swa swete a lykoure** in the emblem of such a sweet liquid (the book is now

the honeycomb, not the bread). "Fygour" is a version of Latin *figura*, an allegorical image.

36 **lyghtlye** easily

39 **herteth** heartens

3.21 ELEANOR HULL, *A COMMENTARY ON THE PENITENTIAL PSALMS:* PSALM 50 (SELECTIONS)

Date and Provenance: 1440s; south Midlands (Hertfordshire), St. Albans (perhaps the Benedictine priory of Sopwell).

Author, Sources, and Nature of Text: Dame Eleanor Hull (born Eleanor Mallet) was born of a gentry family, probably in Somersetshire, around 1395 and died a widow in 1460 (her husband, Sir John Hull, died c. 1420). Connected via both her father and her husband to the Lancastrian court, and in her own right a pensioner and household servant of Henry IV's second wife, Joan of Navarre, she may have played a role in the foundation of Syon Abbey by Henry V (see excerpt 3.5, *The Orchard of Syon,* and 3.12, *The Mirror of Our Lady*): a St. Alban's chronicle records that she was one of those who brought to Henry's notice the hermit-priest Thomas Fishbourne, the first confessor general at Syon. The surviving records of her life give a good picture of a devout gentrywoman's existence between court and monastery. She had close relations with the important Benedictine abbey of St. Albans, and retired to the nearby priory of Sopwell after her husband's death. It was probably at Sopwell that she translated from French two devotional works, *A Commentary on the Penitential Psalms* and *Meditations on the Seven Days of the Week.* The *Commentary,* which is based on an untraced thirteenth-century French original, is a long exegetical reading of the seven psalms said to have been written by the penitent King David. Recitation of these psalms was often prescribed as a penance by confessors, and the translation could possibly have been similarly prescribed. The work's ultimate sources include several of the classic commentaries on the Psalter, especially those of Augustine and Peter Lombard, as well as works by Gregory (the *Moralia in Job* and *Homiliae in Hezechielem*) and others. With its use of sometimes elaborate allegorical interpretation and exegetical techniques such as the division of a verse into parts and the distinction of several meanings for the same phrase, it is a good example of how a really detailed (if, by 1400, also somewhat old-fashioned) reading of a biblical text might work. Its exegesis of King David as sprinkled with hot oil and fried like a fritter in the heat of charity (51–56) is thus closer than chronology alone would suggest to the preoccupations with food and transformative reading exemplified in excerpts 3.19 and 3.20. Here, however, the text, so to speak, consumes the reader: through meditative absorption of the Psalter (regarded as containing in itself the whole of Old and New Testament teaching in miniature), the penitent, like David, is, in a single intense movement of thought, reincorporated into the house of God (21) and becomes part of a salvation history recapitulated in the concluding prayer (92–118). The commentary provides a good example of the way in which the disciplined and demanding reading of biblical texts such as the Psalter, originally associated with professional religious (see, e.g., *A Talking of the Love of God,* excerpt 3.1, and Rolle's *English Psalter,* excerpt 3.8), was being adopted by increasing numbers of devout gentlewomen and -men in the decades after the Lollard controversy.

Audience and Circulation: The work survives in one manuscript, Cambridge University Library MS Kk.1.6, which was in part written by Richard Fox (a layman in the service of St. Albans who was an amateur scribe and book collector) before 1454, perhaps for his own use. There are no indications that the text was meant for circulation. Vernacular versions of Scripture were not being written for wide dispersal at this time, three decades after Arundel's *Constitutions* (which sought to ban such translations) in 1409. Its composition may have been undertaken as a personal exercise and meant to be seen only by intimate friends. It is notable that, unlike Rolle's *English Psalter* (excerpt 3.8), the text has no translator's prologue describing its purpose and audience.

Bibliography: The text has been edited by Barratt (1995), who gives a full discussion of Eleanor Hull's life (for which, see also Barratt 1989) as well as of the text, the manuscript, and its scribes; an excerpt has also been edited by Barratt (1992). For the piety of late medieval gentlewomen, see Riddy 1996b, and on late medieval private reading in England, Taylor 1996. For the exegetical techniques used here, see Alford 1973.

Source: Cambridge University Library MS Kk.1.6, fols. 82r–108r (excerpts). This is a large paper and parchment volume with 247 folios, containing not only Eleanor Hull's two works but a prose treatise on the Passion and several religious poems by or attributed to Lydgate. The Latin biblical quotations embedded in the text (which Hull must have taken from her source but clearly understood in detail) have been badly mangled, probably by the scribe (not, in this part of the manuscript, Richard Fox), who may not have understood the standard abbreviation marks Hull used (although it is possible that the problems originated with Hull herself or her source). The errors in the Latin are left uncorrected in the transcription but mentioned in the notes.

This excerpt was contributed by Alexandra Barratt.

This tytyl seythe, "in the end, of the psalmis of David." Here byfore, ye have herd what a tytyl ys: the tytyl ys the entre of the techyng for to undyrstond the psalme. Psalme, he seythe, ys the preysyng of God with song that is browht forthe by suetnes of the everlastyng joye. And for that David had foryete the preysyng of
5   God almyghty for the veyne plesance of his flessche, he made this psalme, wherof the tytyl sownyth, "in the end, of the psalmis of David." And hit sownyth as moche as therof he seyd, "Y have be wykkid and wrecchyd al my lyfe unto now, but now schal Y drawe towardys hym that is the ende of al evelys; and in this proffytable ende, that is the begynnyng of al goodnes that ever were and ever schal
10   be, Y schal begynne my presysyng, besechyng the Almyghty that he make me worthy to preyse hym aftyr his gret mercy, and that he foryeve me my mysdedys. And therfor with gret repentance Y seye, and with fervent dezyre of myn hert: *Miserere mei Deus secundum magnam misericordiam tuam.*" [. . .]

[There follows an exposition of this and subsequent verses of Psalm 50, beginning with a free translation of the passage from the second Book of Samuel (chapters 11–12), which recounts the narrative traditionally supposed to lie behind the writing of this psalm: the tale of David's adultery with Bathsheba, his assassination of her husband Uriah, his marriage to Bathsheba, and repentance of his sin under the goading of the prophet Nathan, sent by God to reprove him.]

Docebo vias etc. "I schal teche," he seythe, "the wrongful thy weyes, and the
15   wykkyd schal be convertyd to the." This repentant yeveth ous gret hope of the pytous mercy of God. Fyrst he wept his synnys, and then he behyhtyth to be a meystre, and seythe that he wyl teche the wykkyd the wey of God. For he undyrstode wel and knew that no sacryfyce ys more plesant to God almyghty and mercyful then ys an holy jelosye that man hathe to save soulis, aftyr the scripture
20   that seythe: *Nullum quippe deo tale est sacrificium qualis est zelus animarum.*

(Of this holy jelosye seythe David in another place: *Zelus domus tue commedit me,*
"The gelosye of thyn house etyth me.") And therfor he drewe hym for to fulfyl the
spirytuel cence of the comandement that was don in the olde lawe in makyng of a
sacryfyce to God. Now undyrstond, for this is the lettre. They toke pure floure
25 that ys callyd *simile,* and put hit in a pan, and sprengyd oyle theron, and fryed hyt.
And that prest that by erytage had the offyce of his fader schold offre hyt to our
Lord al hote in swete smellyng. Seynt Gregoyre expounyth wel this lettre, that ofte
tymys had felt that fryyng. The floure of *simile* that ys fryed is the clene hert and
wyl of the ryghtyws man, that oftyn tymys ys tormentyd and fryed by the
30 afflyccyon of holy jelosye and by the traveylous werke of drawyng mani soulys to
God. And then ys the clene soule sprengyd with oyle and fryed in the pan, when
sche brennyth with holy jelosye in the chastysyng of them that withdrowe hemselfe
from God.

And notwithstondyng he [chastysyth] hem, so that the rygour of his chastysyng
35 was medled with the suetnes of mercy, then schynyth he bryht byfore God that
hathe suche gelosye in wynnyng of soulys to the use of God. For hym he
undyrtakyth most egrely that he lovyth moost charytably, and when he reprevyth
and offendyth tho that he lovyth and to whom he awyht moost, then offryth he to
God the fruture, al hote sprenggyd with the oyle of love and fryed in the
40 charytable panne of his ryghtwysnesse. The prest that by erytage schold offre the
fruture hote: that ys, he that by good werkys and by nobles of vertuys schewyth
hymselfe for to be certeynly the sone of the Almyghty and gothe not oute of
kynrede from the wyl of his Fadre by the wylte of his evel lyfe. And yf a man
withdrawe hym from al fowle werkys erdly, and by charyte of holy jelosye
45 enforcyth hym to teche other, he offryth al the floure fryed in his auter. He offryth
not to his Fadre al the fruture [hote] but yf he brenne in parfyt desyre for to
torne his neyhbor to God.

In this wyse dyde holy David: he offryd to God a clene hert and a ryght speryt
and in the grace of the Holy Goost he was al confermyd so as he requeryd here
50 byfore: *Et spiritu principali confirma me,* that ys of God the verrey Fader, of whom
and by whom he wold be asuryd of al the goodes that he requeryd of hym. And
aftyr the confermyng of his propre helthe, he schewyth that he was sprengyd with
the oyle of mercy and fryed in the gret hete of charyte for to teche his neyhbors,
and seyd to God, his Fadre, to whom he wold offre [hote] al the fruture and fyrst
55 brenne in hym and then in another: *Docebo iniquos vias tuas et impii ad
te convertentur.*

Ye schul undyrstond that ther ys dyfference betuene *iniquos et impios. Iniqui,*
tho ben the false Crystyn people and contrarye to the wyl of God, *et impii* ben the
paynemys, the worchyppers of ydolys that knowyn not the weyes of God, of
60 whiche ben many convertyd by the holy predycacyon of the prophecye of David
and by the swete melodye of the holy psalmys of the Sauter. And wetyth vereyly
that he that this seyd to our Lord, "Y schal teche the froward your weyes *et impii
ad te convertentur,*" hyt was not seyd by noon elacyon but by true provydence, for
by his holy wordis many that erryn schal be asoylyd of ther synnys. And
65 notwithstondyng, with al that he wyst wel that a fowle and a perylous thyng hit is
for to repreve another of evel and [withholdyn] the same evel within hymselfe.
And therfor he seyd, as to the almyghty God: *Libera me de sanguinibus Deus,
Deus salutis mee, et exultabit linguam meam iusticiam tuam.*

Libera me etc. "Delyvere me from blode, good God myn hele, and my tonge
70 schal enhance thy justyce." Hyt semyth as he wold sey, "O God and kyng, large
yever of the helthe that y desyre for myselfe and to come to other by me; and that
hit may be parformyd, delyvere me fro blodes." We knowyn wel that in Latyn
declineson we sey not *sanguines* ne *sanguina;* but the Grekys put hit in plurel
nombre, as he had fyrst found hyt in the langgage of Ebrew. And the interpretor
75 had lever sey lasse aftyr the Latyn then for to withdrawe anythyng fro the
propryete. For theras David seythe *Libera me de sanguinibus,* therin he undyrstod
hys many synnys that his flessche and his blode has causyd hym, *ad ipsa peccate
respiciens apostelis* that camyn of the flessche and of the blode of man; and seythe
in ther reprevyng: *Caro et sanguinis regnum dei non possidebunt.* "Flessche and
80 blode" he callyth the synnys that comyn of our corupcyon, in the company of
whiche we may not come to the kyngdom of God. And therfor prayeht the good
psalmystre, "*Libera me de sanguinibus,* of the blode of Urie that y schad, and of
the blode of avoutrie that by that blode y went to have covered; and of thes
delyvere me, Lord, *ab omni corupcione pene et culpe.* For ye be God almyghty *et*
85 *Deus dator salutis mee que salus erit [in] incorupcione cum mortalis homo induet
inmortalitatem.* Then schal myn hele be parfyt when this dedly corupcyon schal be
clothyd with everlastyng lyfe, and we schal see the ryght as thou art. Then schal
my tonge be gladyd in thy justyce, that ys, that Y schal with joye anounce to the
synful and the wykyd the worthy schorgys of my synnys and the grace and the
90 grete mercy that Y fele. And so thou schalt be drad in thy justyce and lyfte up by
preysyng of thy pyte and mercy: *Et sic exultabit lingua mea in iusticiam tuam.*" [. . .]

*[This and subsequent verses are expounded, in a discussion that includes an analysis
of sacrifices made under the "Old Law" (i.e., the ritual laws given in the Pentateuch,
which were considered no longer binding on Christians) and their spiritual meaning,
and the meanings of the city Jerusalem. The exposition ends by applying the lessons
of the psalm to the reader in a prayer that works its way again through the entire
psalm in abbreviated form:]*

Now requere we to the almyghty God that by the conseyl of his gret pyte, that he
make ous verrey repentant as he dyd the good David, and by his gret mercy he
foryeve ous al our synnys and purge ous and clense ous of al our wikkydnys aftir
95 the grete benygnyte of al his mercyes; so that, by the knowleche of our synfulnes
wherby we have offendyd hym, that he yeve ous to know the trowthe and to have
undyrstondyng of the hyd thyngys of his sciens, and that he yeve ous grace to kepe
the whytnes and the clennys of our baptem, and that he yeve ous joye and gladnys
wher no delyt fyndyth trespas, and that he torne his face from al our synnys and
100 make ous so ryghtfulle in al goodnys that never for our old malyce he withdrawe
his holy speryt from ous, but that he yeve ous that gladnys that ys our only helthe;
and that he wyl conferme ous by his pryncipalyte that we may folowe his weyes by
true confescyon and, as he ys almyghty God and only yever of al helthe, he
delyvere ous from our synnys that our hertys and our mouthes mowyn worthyly
105 anounce your preysyng, and with our bodyes and with our hertys, that we maye
make to hym a plesaunt sacryfyce, so that with troublyd hertys in verrey
repentance and mekyd by the werkys of penance, he joyne ous in the edyfyyng of
the wallys of hevenly Jherusalem, wherinne he lyvyth and regnyth as God,

syngulerly gode and myghty: wher he resceyvyd acceptably for to parforme our
110 helthe *sacrificium iusticie*, that ys, the holy body of his dere Sone, that for ous he
soffryd to be tredyd and offryd into the hondys of synful men, by whom God
resceyvyth our werkys in erthe, so that we mow come to the parfeccyon of the
ryghtwysse that purly and holy offryd hemselfe body and soule, lyfe and dethe; and
therfor they regnyn with God and schal regne with God in the lond of lyvyng men,
115 wher God by his grete mercy yeve ous his gloryous felawschip where soffycanse ys
of al goodnes and joye that never takyth ende; *quod nobis et vobis prestare
dignetur per Jhesum Christum dominum nostrum, qui cum deo patre et spiritu
sancto vivit et regnat deus per omnia secula seculorum. Amen.*

---

1 **This tytyl seythe** The title given Psalm 50 in the Vulgate (Septuagint version) is "In finem. Psalmus David, cum venit ad eum Nathan propheta quando intravit ad Bethsabee" (Ps. 50:1, AV 51): "In the end: a psalm of David when Nathan the prophet came to him after he had gone in to Bathsheba." The first sentences of the commentary expound this title. ∫ **Here byfore** that is, at the beginning of the treatise, commenting on Ps. 6:1 (Barratt 1995, 3.5–12 and note).

2 **the entre of the techyng** the introduction to the teaching: a formal definition of a title ∫ **for to** in order to

3 **Psalme . . . with song** a psalm, he says, is the praise of God by means of song: taken from Peter Lombard's Psalter commentary, which is itself borrowing from Augustine (Barratt 1995, 3.14–15 and note). Compare Rolle's definition of "ympne" in the *English Psalter* prologue, using the same sources (excerpt 3.8: 47–48).

4 **for that** because ∫ **foryete** forgotten

5–6 **wherof the tytyl sownyth** whose title signifies

6–7 **as moche as therof he seyd** as though in these words he was saying. There follows a paraphrase of the title (6–11) that extrapolates its moral meaning (see Alford 1973 for this standard exegetical method).

8 **drawe towardys** approach

13 *Miserere mei Deus . . . .tuam* have mercy upon me, God, according to your great mercy: Ps. 50:3, AV 51:1

14 *Docebo vias etc.* I shall teach your ways, etc.: Ps. 50:15, AV 51:13

15 **repentant** penitent (i.e., David). On the great penitents, see Collins 1985.

16 **behyhtyth** promises

17 **meystre** master, that is, teacher. David passes from being a penitent sinner to being a teacher. Although Hull's French source may have been written for women, nowhere in the discussion that follows

are the problems associated with women and teaching authority, so evident in Julian of Norwich's *Revelation* and *The Mirror of Our Lady* (excerpts 1.13 and 3.12), raised.

19 **then** than ∫ **jelosye** zeal ∫ **scripture** writing

20 *Nullum quippe . . . animarum* certainly, there is no sacrifice to God like a zeal for souls: Gregory, *In Hiezech*. I, Hom. XII, 578–79 (*CCSL* CXLII, 1971)

21 *Zelus domus tue commedit me* Ps. 68:10, AV 69:9 ∫ **commedit** Read "comedit."

22 **etyth** consumes ∫ **drewe hym** set himself

23 **spirytuel cence of the comandement that was don in the olde lawe** the figurative sense of the commandment made in the Old Law (Lev. 2:1 and 6:20–22). Allegorical interpretation of Jewish ritual practice was a staple of medieval exegesis and often, as here, relied on the great sixth-century exegete, Gregory (for the next passage, see his *In Hiezech*. I, Hom. XII, 586–97 [*CCSL* CXLII, 1971]). The strange (to modern eyes) metaphorical texture of the passage that follows, in which people's hearts are flour sprinkled with oil and fried with the heat of charity, finds many counterparts in medieval literary allegories, as it does in the later conceits of metaphysical poetry.

24 **this is the lettre** this is the literal meaning of the passage

25 *simile* ["simila"] flour ∫ **sprengyd** sprinkled

26 **by erytage** by hereditary right ∫ **schold offre hyt** had to offer it

27 **expounyth** expounds

27–28 **that ofte tymys had felt that fryyng** who had often felt that frying: that is, in the allegorical sense the text now expounds (an assertion that Gregory knows what he writes about)

30 **traveylous werke** laborious work ∫ **drawyng** converting (see "drewe hym" [22] and "withdrowe" [32])

34 **notwithstondyng** although ∫ **he [chastysyth] hem** MS *chatysyth* ∫ **so that** as long as

35 **medled** mingled

35–36 **then schynyth . . . use of God** then he who has such zeal in winning souls to God's use shines bright before God ∫ **gelosye** zeal

36–37 **hym he undyrtakyth most egrely that he lovyth moost charytably** perhaps "the righteous man reproves most fiercely the person he loves most charitably," or "God reproves . . ." As often in Middle English, the pronoun reference is ambiguous.

38 **awyht** owes

39 **fruture** fritter (i.e., the flour called *"simile,"* simila [25])

42 **certeynly** in truth

42–43 **gothe not oute of kynrede from the wyl of his Fadre** does not turn away from his kinship against his father's will (an allusion to the parable of the prodigal son)

43 **wylte** willfulness

44 **fowle werkys erdly** disgusting worldly deeds

45 **enforcyth hym** pains himself ∫ **auter** altar

46 **[hote]** MS *hoe* ∫ **but yf** unless

49 **requeryd** requested

50 *Et spiritu principali confirma me* and strengthen me with your principle spirit: Ps. 50:14, AV 51:12 (in the sense here expounded, where *"spiritu principali"* is taken to refer to God the Father) ∫ **verrey Fader** true father ∫ **of whom** from whom

51 **goodes** good things

52 **confermyng of his propre helthe** strengthening of his own health

54 **[hote]** MS *hole*

54–55 **fyrst brenne in hym and then in another** first burn in himself and then in another (i.e., by converting someone else)

55–56 *Docebo iniquos vias tuas et impii ad te convertentur* I will teach the wicked your ways, and the impious will be converted to you: Ps. 50:15, AV 51:13

57–64 **ther ys dyfference . . . of ther synnys** The psalm is here read as distinguishing between wicked Christians and pagans (the *"impii"*), whose conversion the psalm truly prophecies, since David's words have indeed converted many (61–64). For the identification of pagans and idol worship, see excerpt 3.2b (*Soliloquies*).

59 **paynemys** pagans

60 **predycacyon** preaching

61 **wetyth vereyly** know truly

63 **elacyon** arrogance ∫ **provydence** foresight

64 **erryn** are in error (i.e., theological error) ∫ **asoylyd** absolved

65 **wyst** knew

66 **[withholdyn]** keep (MS *withholdyth*)

67–68 *Libera me . . . tuam* deliver me from the bloods, O God, O God of my salvation, and my tongue will exalt your justice: Ps. 50:16, AV 51:14, literally translated (read "lingua mea" for "linguam meam")

69 **hele** salvation

70 **enhance** exalt ∫ **Hyt semyth as he wold sey** it seems as though he would say: a standard way of introducing a paraphrase of a verse in order to expound it

70–71 **large yever** generous giver

71 **to come to other by me** to come to other people through me

71–72 **and that it may be parformyd** and in order that it may come to pass

72–76 **We knowyn wel . . . propryete** Augustine, *Enarrationes in Psalmum L* 19:3–7 (*CCSL* XLVII, 1956)

72–73 **in Latyn declineson** in the Latin declension

73 **the Grekys** As Barratt (1995, 244.1103n) points out, "Grekys" must be singular here (following *graecus* in the commentary's source and spelling Latin *-us* by Middle English *-ys*) and refers to the Greek translator of the Septuagint version of the Bible.

73–74 **in plurel nombre** that is, in the plural

74 **as he had fyrst found hyt** as he first encountered it

74–76 **And the interpretor . . . propryete** That is, and the translator preferred to show less respect for the rules of Latin grammar than to lose anything of the correct meaning. This translation policy is also the one adopted by Rolle (despite his avowal that he uses simple English) in *The English Psalter* (excerpt 3.8: 64–66) and the translators of the Early Version of the *Wycliffite Bible* (excerpt 1.15).

76 **theras** where ∫ **therin** that is, implied in those words

77–78 *ad ipsa peccate respiciens apostelis* (read "peccata" and "apostolus") the apostle regarding the same sins

79 *Caro et sanguinis regnum dei non possidebunt* (read "sanguis") flesh and blood will not possess the kingdom of heaven (1 Cor. 15:50, here interpreted to mean "fleshly sin will not possess . . ."). This passage is from Augustine, *Enarrationes in Psalmum L* 19:7–12 (*CCSL* XLVIII, 1956) and may also make use of Peter Lombard's commentary on the Psalms (*PL* 191:491A).

83 **avoutrie** adultery ∫ **went** thought ∫ **covered** concealed

84 *ab omni corupcione pene et culpe* from every corruption of pain and guilt

84–86 *et Deus dator . . . inmortalitatem* and God, giver of my salvation, which will be whole and incorruptible when the mortal person takes on immortality (from Peter Lombard's commentary on the Psalms, *PL* 191:491A–B)

86 **dedly corupcyon** mortal corruption

88 **gladyd in** gladdened by

89 **worthy schorgys** rightful punishment

90 **drad** feared

91 *Et sic exultabit . . . tuam* (Ps. 50:16, AV 51:14) and so my tongue will exalt your justice

92 **conseyl** urging

93 **verrey** truly

94 **aftir** according to

95 **benygnyte** benevolence

96 **yeve** may give

97 **sciens** knowledge

98 **whytnes** whiteness, that is, purity

99 **trespas** offense

100 **for our old malyce** because of our former sinfulness

102 **conferme ous by his pryncipalyte** make us steadfast by exercising his kingship

105 **your preysyng** (*sic* MS) that is, the praise of God

107 **mekyd** made humble ∫ **joyne** unite ∫ **edyfyyng** building

110 *sacrificium iusticie* (Ps. 50:21, AV 51:19) the sacrifice of righteousness

111 **tredyd** cruelly treated. Christ's Passion is often figured by the image of the wine press, following Isa. 63:2–3.

115 **soffycanse** sufficiency

116–18 *quod nobis . . . Amen* which may God deign to bestow on us and you, through Jesus Christ our Lord, who with God the Father and the Holy Spirit lives and reigns, God through every age, Amen: a standard formula for ending a sermon

3.22 MARGERY KEMPE, *THE BOOK OF MARGERY KEMPE:* BOOK I, CHAPTERS 58–59 (EXTRACT)

Date and Provenance; Author, Sources, and Nature of Text; Audience and Circulation; Source: See excerpt 1.14, where the second scribe's prologues to *The Book of Margery Kempe* are edited. In the passage from the middle of the *Book* given here, Kempe describes how she gained access to a group of theological classics, despite her apparent inability to read. But we also learn about the cost of her self-education, for the description of the books she heard is followed by an account of a sharp lesson in orthodoxy as she is obliged to accept for the first time the doctrine of eternal damnation.

Bibliography: In addition to the references given in excerpt 1.14, see Ellis 1990, on Kempe and books; for arguments regarding Kempe's self-consciousness as a writer, Staley 1994; on relations between Kempe and her spiritual advisers, Dillon 1996. Other studies include Goodman 1981, Wallace 1984, Partner 1991; a discussion of this excerpt is in Watson 1997b.

On a tyme, as the forseyd creature was in hire contemplacyone, sche hungryd rythe sore aftyr Goddys word and seyd, "Alas, Lord, as many clerkys as thu hast in this world, that thu ne woldyst sendyn me on of hem that mythe fulfillyn my sowle wyth thi word and wyth redyng of holy scripture, for alle the clerkys that prechyn may
5   not fulfillyn [it], for me thynkythe that my sowle is evyr alyche hungry. Gyf I had gold inow, I wolde yevyn every day a nobyl for to have every day a sermowne, for thi word is more worthy to me than alle the good in this werld. And therfore, blyssed Lord, rewe on me, for thu hast takyn awey the ankyr fro me whech was to me synguler solas and comforte, and many tymes refreschyd me wyth thin holy
10 worde." Than answeryd owre Lord Jhesu Cryst in hire sowle, seying, "Ther xal come on fro fer [contre] that xal fulfillyn thi desyre."

So, many day aftyr this answere, ther cam a preste newly to Lynne, whech had
never knowyn hire beforne, and, whan he sey hire gon in the stretys, he was gretly
mevyd to speke wyth hire and speryd of other folke what maner woman sche was.
15 Thei seydyn thei trustyd to God that sche was a ryth good woman. Aftyrward the
preyst sent for hire, preyng hire to come and spekyn wyth hym and wyth hys
modyr, for he had hiryd a chawmbyre for hys modyr and for hym, and so they
dwellyd togedyre. Than the sayd creature cam to wetyn hys wille, and spak
wyth hys modyr and wyth hym, and had rythe good chere of hem bothyn. Than
20 the preyste toke a boke and red therin how owre Lord, seyng the cite of Jerusalem,
wept therupone, rehersyng the myschevys and sorwys that xulde comyn therto, for
sche knew not the tyme of hyre visitacyone. Whan the sayd creature herd redyn
how owre Lord wept, than wept sche sore and cryed lowde, the preyste ne hys
modyr knowyng no cawse of hyr wepyng. Whan hire crying and hire wepyng was
25 cesyd, thei joyyd and were rythe mery in owre Lord. Sithyn sche toke hire leve
and partyd fro hem at that tyme.
      Whan sche was gone, the preste seyd to hys modyr, "Me merveylythe meche of
this woman why sche wepithe and cryithe so. Nevertheles me thynkythe sche is a
good woman, and I desyre gretly to spekyn more wyth hire." Hys modyr was wel
30 plesyd and cownselyd that he xulde done so. And aftyrwardys the same preyste
lovyd hire and trustyd hire ful meche and blissed the tyme that evyr he knew hire,
for he fond gret gostly comfort in hire, and cawsyd hym to lokyn meche good
scripture and many a good docto[wr] whech he wolde not a lokyd at that tyme had
sche ne be. He red to hire many a good boke of hy contemplacyone, and other
35 bokys, as the Bybyl wyth doctowrys therupon, Seynt Brydys boke, Hylton's boke,
Boneventure, *Stimulus amoris, Incendium amoris*, and swech other. And than wist
sche that it was a spirit sent of God wheche seyd to hire, as is wretyn a lityl
beforne, whan sche compleynyd for defawte of redyng, these wordys, "Ther schal
come on fro fer [contre] that xal fulfillyn thi desyre." And thus sche knewe be
40 experiens that it was a rythe trewe spiryt.
      The forseyd preste red hire bokys the most part of vii yere er viii yere, to gret
encres of hys cunnyng and of hys meryte, and he suffryd many an evyl worde for
hyre lofe, inasmeche as he red hire so many bokys and supportyd hire in hire
wepyng and hire crying. Aftyrwardys he wex benefysyd and had gret cure of
45 sowle, and than lykyd hym ful wel that he had redde so meche beforne.

Capitulum 59 Thus, thorw heryng of holy bokys and thorw heryng of holy
sermownys sche evyr encresyd in contemplacyone and holy meditacyone. It were
in maner unpossibyl to writyn al the holy thowtys, holy spechys, and the hy
revelacyons whech owre Lord schewyd unto hire, bothyn of hireselfe and of other
50 men and women, also of many sowlys, sum for to ben savyd and sum for to ben
dampnyd, and was to hire a gret ponyschyng and a scharp chastisyng. For to
knowyn of tho that xulde be savyde, she was ful glad and joyful, for sche desyred,
in as meche as sche durst, alle men to be savyd. And whane owre Lord schewyd to
hyre of any that xulde be dampnyd, sche had gret peyn. Sche wolde not heryn it
55 ne belevyn that it was God that schewyd hire sweche thyngys and put it owt of hire
mende as meche as sche myth. Owre Lord blamyd hire therfore and badde hire
belevyn that it was hys hy mercy and hys goodnesse to schewyn hire hys prevy
cownselys, seying to hire mende, "Dowtyr, thu must as wel heryn of the dampnyd

as of the savyd." Sche wolde yevyn no credens to the cownsel of God but rathar
60 levyd it was sum evyl spiryt for to deceyvyn hire.

Than for hire frowardnes and hire unbeleve owre Lord drow fro hire alle good
thowtys and alle good mendys of holy spechys and dalyawns and the hy
contemplacyone whech sche had ben usyd to beforetyme, and suffyrd hire to have
as many evyl thowtys as sche had beforne of good thowtys. And this vexacyone
65 enduryd xii days togedyr, and, lyche as beforetyme sche had iiii owrys of the
forenoon in holy spechys and dalyawns wyth owre Lord, so had sche now as many
owrys of fowle thowtys and fowle mendys of letchery and alle unclennes, as thow
sche xulde a be comowne to al maner of pepyl. And so the Devyl bar hyre on
hande, dalying unto hire wyth cursyd thowtys liche as owre Lord dalyid to hire
70 befornetyme with holy thowtys. And, as sche beforne had many gloryows visyonys
and hy contemplacyone in the manhod of owre Lord, in owre Lady, and in many
other holy seyntys, rythe evyn so had sche now horybyl syghtys and abhominabyl
(for anythyng that sche cowde do) of beheldyng of mennys membrys and sweche
other abhominacyons. Sche sey as hire thowt veryly dyvers men of religyone,
75 preystys, and many other, bothyn hethyn and Cristen, comyn before hire syght that
sche mythe not enchewyn hem ne puttyn hem owt of hire syght, schewyng here bare
membrys unto hire. [. . .]

Than sche seyd, "Alas, Lord, thu hast seyd beforetyme that thu schuldyst nevyr
forsake me. Wher is now the sothfastnes of thy word?" And anon aftyr cam hire
80 good awngel unto hire, seying, "Dowtyr, God hathe not forsakyn the ne nevyr
schal forsake the, as he hathe behyte the, but, for thu belevyst not that it is the
spiryt of God that spekythe in thi sowle and schewyth the hys prevy cowneslys of
summe that xul ben savyd and summe that xal ben dampnyd, therfore God
chastisyd the on this wyse and maner, and this chastisyng schal enduryn xii days tyl
85 thu wyl belevyn that it is God whech spekyth to the and no devyl."

---

1 **forseyd creature** that is, the narrational figure of Margery Kempe in the text, invariably
referred to in this way

5 **[it]** added in the margin of the manuscript as
a correction ∫ **alyche** alike

6 **nobyl** noble (a gold coin)

8 **rewe** have pity ∫ **ankyr** an anchorite who at an
earlier stage had been Kempe's spiritual adviser (the
pun on "anchor" is often exploited in Middle English;
see e.g., Savage and Watson 1991, 101 and n. 39)

10 **xal** that is, shall. *X* for *sh* is characteristic of
fifteenth-century East Anglian orthography.

11 **[contre]** (correction added in the margin of
the manuscript) region. The priest has arrived in
town, apparently jobless, from far away.

14 **speryd of** asked about. The priest's interest
in Kempe is taken to be divinely ordained, but it is
apparently precipitated by his immediate impression of her difference from other people: hence his
question, "what maner woman sche was," and its
studiedly ambiguous response.

15–18 **Aftyrward . . . togedyre** one of the many
seemingly verbatim reminiscences of a message or
episode that crowd many parts of *The Book*. The

priest presumably mentions his mother to make it
clear that Kempe will have a proper chaperone for
her meetings in his rooms.

18 **wetyn** know

20–22 **how owre Lord . . . wept . . . visitacyone**
See Matt. 23:37 and Luke 19:41–44. The priest's
choice of topic is interesting—whether he is reading directly from the Gospels here or from a sermon
or *vita Christi*—for in Matthew's version, Christ
here presents himself in explicitly feminized terms
as a mother hen wishing to give refuge to her chicks,
who will not take it. It is possible the priest is to be
seen as already responding to Kempe's prophetic
persona, which aligns her passionately with Christ.

21 **myschevys** mischances

22 **sche** she, that is, Jerusalem

23 **wept sche sore and cryed lowde** Kempe's
weeping was a prominent part of her devotion and
caused her much embarrassment and difficulty. For
a study of the doctrine of compunction, which in
some sense underlies this devotional practice, see
McEntire 1990. For studies of her weeping in relation to Continental visionary practice, see Wallace
1984 and Dillon 1996.

25 **Sithyn** afterward

26 **hem** them

30 **xulde** should

30–45 **And aftyrwardys . . . meche beforne** Kempe's education by means of this priest is presented from the first as an account of his education also. She acts as a catalyst to encourage his reading, as well as giving him counsel. What might have been understood as a hierarchical relationship, with him acting as her spiritual instructor, is an equal one whose benefits are mutual. This version of their relationship is carefully foreshadowed in the priest's conversation with his mother about their recent visitor (27–30), in which he is seen consulting her and taking her advice.

32 **gostly** spiritual

33 **docto[wr]** that is, of the church, theologian (MS *doctoa*)

34 **ne be** not been

34–36 **He red to hire . . . swech other** The books in question are the Bible, presumably with an accompanying gloss ("doctowrys therupon"); Bridget of Sweden (d. 1373), probably her *Liber celestis* or, possibly, a *vita;* Walter Hilton (d. 1396), *The Scale of Perfection* (or possibly *Mixed Life*); the Middle English version of James of Milan's *Stimulus amoris,* known as *The Prickynge of Love,* attributed to Bonaventure; and Richard Rolle (d. 1349), *Incendium amoris.* Whether the priest read all these books or also had to translate some of them (e.g., Rolle's, which we do not know to have been translated until the 1460s) is not clear (for Kempe's "honorary Latinity," see Lawton 1992). Nor is it clear where he acquired these books, although it is likely Kempe brought them to him herself: she calls him her "lystere," or reader (Meech and Allen 1940, 147.2), as though she hired him (which she earlier says she wants to do [5–7]), and the priest is presented as happy to have been exposed to books he otherwise would not have known (44–45). The last two books are cited by the priest-scribe in his defense of Kempe's weeping (Meech and Allen 1940, 153.37–154.13).

38 **defawte** lack

39 **[contre]** correction added in the margin of the manuscript

42 **cunnyng** learning

43 **lofe** love

44 **wex benefysyd** acquired a benefice: that is, was given (probably) a parish to run, after his long wait. Clerical underemployment was a serious problem in the early fifteenth century.

45 **lykyd hym ful wel** he was very pleased.

49–50 **bothyn of hireselfe and of other men and women** concerning both herself and others

51–54 **For to knowyn . . . gret peyn** Kempe is troubled not only by the notion of damnation but by revelations concerning the coming or past damnation of actual individuals. Her anxiety about such revelations might be seen as justifiable, since all revelatory experiences were supposed to be held in suspicion. She may, indeed, have learned this lesson from several of the books the priest read to her. However, it is one of the major themes of her book that the spirits who speak to her are true (see 40), and her distrust of her experiences here proves to be nearly disastrous.

57–58 **prevy cownselys** hidden counsels. This phrase was much used at this time of God's secrets, as it was (with very different implications) by Julian of Norwich.

59 **credens** credence

60 **levyd** believed

61 **frowardnes** obstinacy ∫ **unbeleve** lack of faith ∫ **drow** withdrew

62 **mendys** recollections ∫ **dalyawns** love talk

68 **comowne** that is, a prostitute

68–69 **bar hyre on hande** kept her under his thumb

73 **mennys membrys** men's penises

74 **sey** saw ∫ **as hire thowt** as it seemed to her

76 **enchewyn** avoid ∫ **here** their

78–79 **thu hast seyd beforetyme that thu schuldyst nevyr forsake me** probably an allusion to Deut. 31:6, 8

79 **sothfastnes** truthfulness

80 **the** you

81 **behyte** promised ∫ **for** because

3.23 KING JAMES I OF SCOTLAND, *THE KINGIS QUAIR:* OPENING

Date and Provenance: 1424–37; the south of Scotland.

Author, Sources, and Nature of Text: *The Kingis Quair* is a love allegory in which Fortune—as depicted in Boethius's fifth-century *Consolation of Philosophy* (perhaps in Walton's translation, see excerpt 1.5) and in

more recent works such as Chaucer's *Troilus and Criseyde* and Lydgate's *Temple of Glass*—appears in the unusual role of a fairy godmother who helps the narrator to win his love. The poem is almost certainly a genuine work by the king of Scotland, dealing in part with his years of imprisonment in England

(1406–24) and the rise of his fortunes toward the end of this period, culminating in his release and marriage to Joan Beaufort in 1424 (thirteen years before he was assassinated). The work is in the cosmopolitan style of fifteenth-century court writing that evolved from Chaucer's early works and was given a more imitable articulation by Lydgate. Like another aristocratic prisoner who spent a good deal of his exile in England writing Middle English poetry, Charles d'Orléans, James must have read widely while under house arrest in the south of England. He may have been one of the conduits through which the poetry of Chaucer, Lydgate, and others reached Scotland, to form a base on which was built the distinctively Scottish poetic tradition of courtly writing initiated by Henryson (see excerpt 3.18), Dunbar, and Douglas (see excerpt 3.16) later in the century. The poem's opening draws on a long tradition in which dream poems begin with accounts of reading (compare, e.g., *The Book of the Duchess* and *The Parliament of Fowls*). It is in tune with the work's optimism that the book James reads (Boethius's *Consolation*) does not make him dream but reminisce about a past from which he has no need to hide in sleep, since it has brought him happiness.

Audience and Circulation: The poem survives in a single manuscript and may not have been well known outside a small circle. It does not seem to have influenced later Scottish poets such as Henryson and Dunbar, and was not printed until 1783. Despite its quality it was never attributed to Chaucer (unlike many similar poems and prose works, including rarities such as Usk's *Testament of Love*, excerpt 1.4), suggesting it was also little known in England.

Bibliography: Edited by Norton-Smith (1971) and McDiarmid (1973), the work has attracted a great deal of commentary, much of it concerned with the question of authorship, which no longer seems in doubt. For a bibliography to 1985, see Scheps and Looney 1986. Recent studies include James 1993, on the lover figure; Carretta 1981, on James I and Boethius; Quinn 1981, on the role of memory; Boffey 1991, on the topos of imprisonment in fifteenth-century poetry; and Mapstone 1997.

Source: Oxford, Bodleian Library MS Seld. Arch. B 24, fols. 192r–193r. This paper manuscript dates from c. 1490 and may have been commissioned by Henry Sinclair, third earl of Orkney; the scribe, James Gray, was his protégé, and his arms appear in the manuscript. Besides the *Kingis Quair*, it contains Chaucer's *Troilus and Criseyde, The Parliament of Fowls,* and *The Legend of Good Women,* and, after the *Quair* (which occupies fols. 192r–211r), some shorter poems, at least one of which, *The Quare of Jelousy,* is also Scottish. On the page before the text (fol. 191v), a sixteenth-century note reads, "herefter followis the quair maid be king james of Scotland the ferst callid the kingis quair and maid quhen his ma. [= majesty] was in England." Although scholars differ from the author of this note regarding where the poem was written, it provides most of the information we have about the poem's origins. For a description of the manuscript, see Seymour 1995, 73–75.

In Middle Scots spelling modern English *wh* is usually represented *quh* ("what" is "quhat," "who" "quho," and so on), while *ght* is often represented as *cht* ("thocht" for "thought").

Heigh in the hevynis figure circulere	
The rody sterres twynklyng as the fyre,	**rody** fiery
And in Aquary Citherea the clere	**Aquary** Aquarius
Rynsid hir tressis like the goldin wyre,	
5 That late tofore, in fair and fresche atyre,	**That** who; **late tofore** recently before
Through Capricorn heved hir hornis bright;	**heved** lifted up
North northward approchit the myd nyght:	
Quhen, as I lay in bed allone, waking,	**Quhen** when
New partit out of slepe a lyte tofore,	**a lyte tofore** a little time before

10   Fell me to mynd of many diverse thing,
      Off this and that: can I noght say quharfor,   **quharfor** why
      Bot slepe for craft in erth myght I no more;   **for craft in erth** by no means
      For quhich as tho coude I no better wyle,   **as tho** at that time; **coude** knew; **wyle** trick
      Bot toke a boke to rede apon a quhile.

15   Off quhich the name is clepit properly   **clepit** called
      Boece, eftere him that was the compiloure,   **Boece** Boethius
      Schewing counsele of philosophye
      Compilit by that noble senatoure
      Off Rome, quhilom that was the warldis floure,   **quhilom** at one time
20   And from estate by Fortune a quhile   **from estate** from high estate
      Forjugit was to povert in exile.   **Forjugit** condemned; **povert** poverty

      And there, to here this worthy lord and clerk,
      His metir suete, full of moralitee,   **metir** verse
      His flourit pen so fair he set awerk,   **flourit** ornate
25   Discryving first of his prosperitee
      And out of that his infelicitee: **out of that** after that
      And than how he, in his poetly report
      In philosophy can him to confort.   **can** learned; **him** himself

      For quhich, though I in purpose at my boke
30   To borowe a slepe at thilke tyme began,
      Or ever I stent, my best was more to loke   **stent** stopped; **best** best [pleasure]
      Upon the writing of this noble man,
      That in himself the full recover wan   **recover** recovery; **wan** won
      Off his infortune, poverte, and distresse,   **infortune** misfortune
35   And in tham set his verray sekernesse.   **sekernesse** security

      And so the vertew of his youth before
      Was in his age the ground of his delytis:
      Fortune the bak him turnyt, and therfore   **the bak** i.e., her back
      He makith joye and confort that he quit is
40   Off their unsekir warldis appetitis;   **unsekir** insecure
      And so aworth he takith his penance,   **aworth** worthily
      And of his vertew maid it suffisance.   **of** through; **suffisance** enough

      With mony a noble resoun, as him likit,   **resoun** argument; **as him likit** as it pleased him
      Enditing in his fair Latyne tong,   **Enditing** writing
45   So full of fruyte, and rethorikly pykit,   **rethorikly pykit** full of rhetorical figures
      Quhich to declare my scole is over yong: **scole** schooling
      Therfore I lat him pas, and in my tong
      Procede I will agayn to my sentence   **sentence** meaning
      Of my mater, and leve all incidence.   **all incidence** everything not relevant

50   The long nyght beholding, as I saide,
      Myn eyne gan to smert for studying,   **eyne** eyes; **smert** smart
      My buke I schet, and at my hede it laide;
      And doun I lay bot ony tarying,   **bot** without
      This matere new in my mynd rolling: **rolling** revolving

55 This is to seyne, how that eche estate,   **estate** social group
    As Fortune lykith, thame will translate.   **translate** transfer

    For sothe it is that on hir tolter quhele   **tolter quhele** unstable wheel
    Every wight cleverith in his stage   **wight** person; **cleverith** clambers
    And failyng foting oft quhen hir lest rele,   **hir lest rele** it pleases her to roll
60 Sum up, sum dounn, is nonn estate nor age
    Ensured more, the prynce than the page: **Ensured** assured; **more** more than another
    So uncouthly hir werdes sche dividith,   **werdes** destinies
    Namly in youth, that seildin ought providith.   **Namly** especially: **providith** foresees

    Among thir thoughtis rolling to and fro,   **thir** these
65 Fell me to mynd of my fortune and ure;   **ure** luck
    In tender youth how sche was first my fo,
    And eft my frende, and how I gat recure   **eft** afterward; **gat recure** gained redress
    Off my distresse; and all myn aventure
    I gan ovre hayle, that langer slepe ne rest   **ovre hayle** go over
70 Ne myght I nat, so were my wittis wrest.   **wrest** struggling

    Forwakit and forwalowit, thus musing,   **forwalowit** tossing and turning
    Wery, forlyin, I lestnyt sodaynlye,   **forlyin** tired out
    And sone I herd the bell to matynns ryng,
    And up I rase, no langer wald I lye:
75 Bot now, how trowe ye? suich a fantasye   **how trowe ye?** can you believe it?
    Fell me to mynd, that ay me thoght the bell
    Said to me, "Tell on, man, quhat the befell."

1 **Heigh in . . . circulere** high in the sky (literally, high in the heaven's circular shape): the language is deliberately arcane, and the astrological references need to be worked out like a crossword puzzle. James is probably imitating Lydgate, perhaps *The Temple of Glass*.

3 **Citherea the clere** Citherea the fair [one] (here the moon, hence "horns" [6]; usually Venus), which is in the sign of Aquarius in January or February. The poem moves from winter into spring.

4 **goldin wyre** a conventional comparison of hair to fine gold thread

7 **North . . . myd nyght** the midnight approached from the north (probably, though Citherea [3] could also be the subject). The repetition ("North northward") acts as an intensifier.

11–12 **can I noght say . . . myght I no more** Compare Chaucer, *Parliament of Fowls* 106.

13 **For . . . wyle** for which reason I could then think of no better plan

16 **Boece** Boethius (d. 524): late classical philosopher whose writings were a major conduit through which Greek and Roman thinking entered medieval culture ∫ **compiloure** See also "compilit" (18). Boethius is twice referred to as the compiler of the "counsele of philosophye" (i.e., *The Consola-*

tion of Philosophy) and once as the composer ("Enditing" [44]), but not as the *auctor,* which could suggest that James has considerable knowledge of Boethius's highly synthetic work. Compare Usk's picture of Boethius as a reaper (excerpt 1.4: 86n).

19–21 **quhilom . . . povert in exile** James here draws on a tradition that the *Consolation* was a work not of Boethius's final years, awaiting execution, but of an earlier period of disgrace: a tradition he needs to invoke to further his own presentation of Fortune as a benign figure.

23 **metir** could, as with "poetly" (27), suggest that James consulted Walton's verse translation (since Boethius actually wrote in a combination of verse and prose). But compare 43–49, which implies that James knows the Latin as well.

29 **though** MS *thought*. This is a possible reading, but makes for grammatical difficulties later in the stanza.

29–30 **For quhich . . . began** for that purpose, though I began my book with the intent to obtain some rest at that time (i.e., to read until I fell asleep)

33 **full recover** James understands Boethius as having recovered not only in the sense that he learned how to overcome Fortune (see 36–42) but also in the material sense that he regained his worldly prosper-

ity. It is the delicate equipoise between these meanings that allows the poem and its optimistic narrative of worldly recovery to come into being.

44–47 Latyne tong . . . my tong Unless "Latyne" is simply a synonym for *elaborate,* these lines turn on a contrast between Latin and vernacular and suggest that James's experience as a vernacular writer (his "scole" [46]), or the vernacular itself, is inadequate ("over yong" [46]) to express Boethius's true meaning. By the end of the stanza, however, the details of Boethius's thought are dismissed as "incidence" (49), suggesting that the anxiety here is a topos whose real purpose is to admit the different levels of seriousness between Boethius's philosophical explorations and James's poem.

55–56 how that eche . . . translate how Fortune will alter the condition of each estate as she pleases

59 And failyng foting oft quhen hir lest rele and [their] footing failing often when it pleases her to roll [the wheel]

62 So uncouthly hir werdes sche dividith she divides the destinies she metes out so churlishly

63 seildin ought providith seldom foresees anything

64–68 Among thir thoughtis . . . Off my distresse refers to James's early years, when he was imprisoned for ransom in England after being captured as the result of a shipwreck. Much later he was restored to Scotland and married.

77 Tell on, man, quhat the befell speak on, man, of what happened to you

3.24 BRIAN ANSLAY, TRANSLATION OF CHRISTINE DE PIZAN'S *BOOK OF THE CITY OF LADIES:* CHAPTER 1, WITH DEDICATORY VERSES BY HENRY PEPWELL

Date and Provenance: 1521; London (de Pizan's French text was completed near Paris c. 1405).

Author, Sources, and Nature of Text: *The Book of the City of Ladies* is a relatively early work by the great French woman of letters Christine de Pizan (c. 1365–1434). *The Book of the City,* from 1405, was written not long after de Pizan's celebrated intervention in the controversy over the *Romance of the Rose,* as part of a self-conscious attempt to rethink the position of women in Western literary tradition and culture and to combat misogyny. In the *Book,* a trinity of female figures—Reason, Rectitude, and Justice—dictate to the narrator three sets of exemplary stories, demonstrating the virtue and strength of women and refuting misogynistic interpretations of the same stories. In retelling them, de Pizan represents herself as building a city that is to be a place of refuge and community for the women who live in it by following the prescriptions for female behavior set forth by Reason and her companions. The stories are from many sources, especially Boccaccio's fourteenth-century *De claris mulieribus* (On famous women), and the book alludes to many other texts, including the Bible, the *Ro-*

mance of the Rose, and the *Divine Comedy.* In the prologue, Christine is represented as encountering an explicitly misogynist text, the *Lamentations of Matheolus,* for the first time and finding herself convinced, not by the book itself, but by the apparent agreement between its attacks on women and the views found in more authoritative books. For a long moment, the entire tradition of literature, philosophy, and theology in which she has felt privileged to be educated appears posited on the single tenet of opposition to women and all they stand for.

We know little more about Brian Anslay, the English translator of the work, than the dedicatory stanzas of the printer, Henry Pepwell, tell us: that Anslay was a member of the lower gentry who was attached to the court of Henry VIII. Pepwell himself (d. 1540) is a relatively shadowy figure, whose first book, Stephen Hawes's *Castell of Pleasaunce* (1518), was issued three years before he printed *The Book of the City.* He inherited his business (a shop in St. Paul's Churchyard) from another stationer, Henry Jacobi; is mentioned in the will of Wynkyn de Worde, Caxton's successor (1534); and was warden of the Company of Stationers from 1525 on.

Only about a dozen editions bearing his name have survived. Despite his account of acquiring Anslay's translation and only then approaching the Earl of Kent to act as the book's guarantor, the translation may have been commissioned by the earl, either through Pepwell or directly. Richard Grey, third earl of Kent, was a nephew of Anthony Woodville, who owned a sumptuous de Pizan manuscript (now London, British Library MS Harley 4431) originally made for Isabelle of Bavaria (Bornstein 1977, 32; Willard 1984, 214). Woodville may have left it to his sister, Anne, at his execution in 1483 (Curnow 1975, 340–42). In 1478 Caxton published Woodville's translation of *The Moral Proverbs of Christine* (in which de Pizan is called an "auctouresse"), and it seems Grey inherited his uncle's interest in de Pizan along with his books. Pepwell's rhyme-royal stanzas pay small attention to Anslay (who may have been no more than a hired hand) and elevate Grey to the role of champion of women, which the text itself gives de Pizan. The stanzas point back to a century of courtly controversy in England and France about women and the duty of gentlemen to protect them: the so-called *querelle des dames*, which perhaps lies behind Chaucer's *Legend of Good Women*, Hoccleve's de Pizan translation, *The Letter of Cupid*, and *The Flower and the Leaf* and *The Assembly of Ladies*. They also point forward to an Elizabethan fascination with male gentility, whose literary expressions include Sidney's *Arcadia* and Spenser's *Fairy Queen*.

Audience and Circulation: In practice, de Pizan's original was written for a small circle of courtly *litterati*, some of them the aristocratic and royal women for whom she made presentation copies like the one owned by Isabel. In theory, however, the work aims to reach all women. The structure the of book's sequel, *The Treasury of the City of Ladies*, makes this universal appeal more explicit: it is a set of addresses to women from each social class. De Pizan's works were well known in England, despite her political opposition to the English. One of de Pizan's sons lived in England, and *The Book of the City* was read there within a decade of its composition, soon

after Hoccleve translated de Pizan's *Epitre d'amour* as *The Letter of Cupid* (c. 1402) and at about the time Lydgate was using sections of her *Epitre d'Othéa* to shape the central scenes of *Troy Book* (c. 1415; see excerpt 1.7). Later, the whole *Epistle of Othea* was translated by Stephen Scrope (c. 1440), and Caxton published both Woodville's translation of the *Moral Proverbs* and his own translation of *Le livre des fais d'armes et de chevalerie* (*Book of Fayttes of Armes and of Chyvalrye*, 1489; see excerpt 2.10). Pepwell's dedicatory stanzas ignore de Pizan's address to women and suggest instead that the aim of his book (that is, Grey's aim) is "Of ladyes (abrode) to sprede theyr royall fame" (20): a formulation de Pizan herself might have approved of, but that omits the instructive and consolatory functions the book was also intended to fulfill.

Bibliography: For a facsimile of Pepwell's edition, see Bornstein 1978; for a modern English translation of *The Book of the City*, see Richards 1982; the original French is still available only in a thesis edition (Curnow 1975). For a literary study of the work, see Quilligan 1991. For a biographical study of de Pizan, see Willard 1984. For bibliography on de Pizan, see Kennedy 1984 and 1994 and the annual Christine de Pizan Society newsletter. For excerpts and discussion of Middle English versions of de Pizan's works, see Barratt 1992, 137–62, and Campbell 1925. For the *Lamentations* and its context, see Blumenfeld-Kosinski 1994 and Blamires 1992 and 1997. On readers of de Pizan's French *Cité* in late medieval England, see Meale 1996a.

Source: London, British Library C.13.a.18 Bbir–Bbiiir (*STC* 7271). This translation by Brian Anslay was printed in quarto format by Henry Pepwell at the Sign of the Trinity in St. Paul's Churchyard, London, October 26, 1521. The text has several woodblocks evidently made specially for this edition. One shows Reason, Rectitude, and Justice visiting Christine in her study, another Reason showing Christine the city. There are marginal notes in a sixteenth-century hand. In this edition, Pepwell's marking of the caesura in all but one line of his verses is retained.

The kyndly entente / of every gentylman   *kyndly entente* natural goal
Is the furtheraunce / of all gentylnesse,
And to procure / in all that ever he can   *procure* take care
For to renewe / all noble worthynesse;
5 This dayly is sene / at our eye expresse   *at our eye expresse* by our own eyes
Of noble men / that do endyte and rede   *Of* i.e., concerning
In bokes olde / theyr worthy myndes to fede.

So nowe of late / came in my custodye
This foresayd boke / by Bryan Anslay,
10 Yoman of the seller / with the eyght kynge Henry,   *Yoman* yeoman; *seller* cellar
Of gentylwomen / the excellence to say,
The whiche I lyked / but yet I made delay
It to impresse; / for that it is the guyse   *impresse* print
Of people lewde / theyr prowesse to dyspyse.   *theyr* i.e., women's; *prowesse* worth

15 But then I shewed / the foresayd boke
Unto my lorde / the gentyll Erle of Kente
And hym requyred / theron to loke   *requyred* requested
With his counsayle / to put it in to prente;   *With his counsayle* and give his advice
And he forthwith, / as ever dylygente
20 Of ladyes (abrode) to sprede theyr royall fame,
Exhorted me / to prynte it in his name.

And I obeyenge gladly his instaunce   *instaunce* desire
Have done my devoyre / of it to make an ende   *devoyre* duty
Prayenge his lordshyp, / with others that shall chaunce
25 On it to rede, / the fautes for to amende
If ony be, / for I do fayne intende
Gladly to please, and wylfully remytte   *remytte* relinquish
This ordre rude/ to them that have fresshe wytte.   *ordre* composition

Thus endeth the prologue.

Here begynneth the fyrste chapytre whiche telleth howe and by whome the Cyte of Ladyes was fyrst begon to buylde.

Capitulo primo. After the maner that I have moche in usage, and to that thynge whiche the excercyse of my lyfe is moost dysposed—that is, to knowe in the hauntynge of studye—on a day, as I was syttynge in my lytell cell, dyvers bokes of
35 dyvers matters aboute me (myne entente was at that tyme to travayle and to gather in to my consayte the wayenge of dyvers sentences of dyvers auctours by my longe tyme before studyed), I dressed my vysage towarde those foresayd bokes: thynkynge as for the tyme to leve in peas subtyll thynges, and to dysporte me for to loke upon some pleasaunt boke of the wrytynge of some poetes.
40   And as I was in this entente, I serched aboute me after some praty boke. And of adventure came a straunge boke in to my handes that was taken to me to kepe. I opened this boke and I sawe by the intytulacyon that it called him "Matheolus." Then, in laughynge—bycause I had not sene hym, and often tymes I had herde

speke of hym, that he sholde not speke well of the reverence of women—I thought
45 that in maner of solace I wolde vysyte hym. And yet I had not loked longe on hym
but that my good moder that bare me called me to the refeccyon of souper, wherof
the houre was come. Purposynge to se hym in the mornynge, I lefte hym at
that tyme.
    And in the morowe folowynge, I sate me agayne to my study, as I dyde of
50 custome. I forgate it not in put[tyng] my wyll to effecte that came to me the nyght
before, to vysyte the foresayd boke of Matheolus; and then I began to rede and to
prosede in hym. But as me semed the matter was not ryght pleasaunt to people
that delyted them not in evyll sayenge, nor it was of no profyte to ony edyfyenge
of vertue—seynge the wordes and the matters dyshonest of whiche it touched—
55 vysytynge here and there, and so came to the ende, I lefte hym, and toke
hede of more hygher matters, and of more profyte.
    Yet the syght of this foresayd boke (howe be it that he was of none auctoryte),
it engendred in me a newe thought, whiche made grete mervayle to growe in my
courage and thynkynge: what myght be the cause and wherof it myght come that
60 so many dyvers men, clerkes and others, have ben and ben enclyned to say (by
mouthe, and in theyr treatyse and wrytynges) so many slaundres and blames of
women and of theyr condycyons. And not onely one or twayne, nor this
Matheolus (whiche amonge others hath no maner of reputacyon and treateth in
maner of scorne), but generally in all treatyses of phylosphres, poetes and all
65 rethorycyens (whiche sholde be longe to reherce all theyr names) speketh as it were
by one mouthe and accordeth all in semble conclusyon, determynynge that the
condycyons of women ben fully enclyned to all vyces.
    These thynges thynkynge in me ryght depely, I began to examyne myselfe and
my condycyons as a woman naturall, and in lyke wyse I dyscuted of other women
70 whos companye I haunted—as well of pryncesses and of grete ladyes as of meane
gentyll women ryght grete plentye, whiche of theyr graces have tolde me theyr
pryvytees and strayte thoughtes—to knowe by my jugement, in conscyence and
without favoure, yf it myght be trewe that so many notable men of one and other
wytnesseth; yet notwithstandynge that, for thynges that I myght knowe (as longe
75 as I have sought and serched), I coude not perceyve that suche jugementes myght
be trewe agaynst the naturall condycyons or maners of women.
    I argued strongly agaynst these women, sayenge that it sholde be to grete a
thynge that so many famous men, so solempne clarkes of soo hyghe and grete
understandynge, so clerely seynge in all thynges, as it semed, that sholde have
80 spoken or wryten lyengly—and in so many places that of payne I found ony morall
volume, what so ever the auctoure were, that or I had redde it to the ende but
some chapytres or certayne clauses were of blamynge of theym. This onely shorte
reason made me to conclude that myne understandynge, for his symplenesse
and ygnoraunce, ne coude not knowe my grete defautes—and semblably of other
85 women, that alwaye it accorded that it was so, truely. And soo I reported me more
to the jugement of other then to that I felte or knowe of myselfe.
    Thus in this thought was I as a persone halfe from hymselfe; and there came
before me ryght grete foyson of dyttyes and proverbes of many dyvers auctours to
this purpose that I remembred in myselfe one after another, as it were a welle
90 spryngynge. And in conclusyon of all, I determyned that God made a foule thynge
when he fourmed woman, in mervayllynge howe soo worshypfull a werkeman

deyned ever to make one soo abhomynable werke, whiche is the vessell—as by
sayenge of them—and the draught and herbegage of al evyll and of all vyces.

Then, I beynge in this thought, there sprange in me a grete dyspleasaunce and
95 sorowe of courage in dyspraysynge myself and all womenkynde, so as yf yt sholde
be shewed in nature. And I sayd suche wordes in my complayntes:

"Ha, lorde God, howe may that be, for if I arre not in thy fayth, I ought not
doubt that thyne infynyte wysdome and veray parfyte goodnesse had nothynge
made but that all were good. And fourmest not thou thyselfe woman ryght
100 syngulerly? And then thou gave her all suche inclynacyons that pleased the that
she sholde have. And howe maye yt be, that thou sholde have fayled in ony
thynge? And alway se here so many grete occasyons, thus juged, determyned and
concluded ayenst them. I cannot understande this repugnaunce. And yf it be
so, good lorde God, that it be true that womankynde habundeth in so many
105 abhomynacyons as many men wytnesseth—and thou sayest thyself that "the
wytnesse of many is for to byleve," by the whiche I ought not doubte but that it
sholde be true—alas! good Lorde, why haddest thou not made me to be borne in
to this worlde in the masculyne kynde?—To that entente that myne enclynacyons
myght have ben al to have served the the better, and that I sholde not have arred
110 in ony thynge, and myght have ben of so grete perfeccyon as they say that men be.

"Yet syth it is so that thy debonayrnesse stretcheth not so moche towarde me,
then spare my neglygence in thy servyce, good lorde God, and be not dyspleased:
for that servaunt that receyveth leest rewardes of his lorde leest is bounde to his
servyce." Suche wordes and mo ynowe I sayd ryght longe in my sorowfull thought
115 to God and in my lamentacyon so, as she that by my foly helde me ryght evyll
contente of that that God made me to be borne in to this worlde in kynde of
woman.

1–7 **The kyndly entente . . . fede** With these reflections on gentility and reading, contrast, for
example, *Cursor Mundi* (excerpt 3.14). In
Pepwell's verses gentility is seen as a natural quality
associated with a specific social class (see the debate
on this issue in Chaucer's *Wife of Bath's Tale*), but
is also a quality that has to be "renewed" or sustained by the activity of reading. (For the
connection between reading and gentility, see further essay 4.3, pages 362–65 below.)

11 **Of gentylwomen / the excellence to say** that
is, whose purpose is to declare the excellence of
gentlewomen. "Gentylwomen" translates de
Pizan's *dames* but narrows the application of this
word by implying that the book is entirely about
women of "gentle" (i.e., high) birth, which is not so.

12–14 **The whiche I lyked . . . dyspyse** Pepwell
represents himself as held back from publishing de
Pizan's book by popular misogyny, but this is likely
to be a formulaic, rather than real, statement of
anxiety, whose purpose is to elevate the book's patron and guarantor, the earl of Kent.

22–28 **And I obeyenge . . . wytte** Compare the
end of the prologue to Lydgate's *Troy Book* (ex-

cerpt 1.7: 206–14). In apologizing for his work,
referring presumably to typesetting errors and
other blemishes his edition may contain, Pepwell
adapts the topos many authors use.

33 **excercyse** activity ∫ **dysposed** directed ∫ **to
knowe** to attain knowledge

34 **hauntynge** exercise ∫ **studye** scholarly reading. Christine's reading is self-consciously different
from the kinds of reading considered normal for
aristocratic women, both in range and intensity and
in its private character.

35–37 **gather in to my consayte the wayenge of
dyvers sentences . . . studyed** bring together into my
understanding [my] judgments of various statements
made by various authorities I had studied a long time
earlier. Christine is represented as gathering together
in her mind *sententiae* from various sources to make
a compilation, or *florilegium*, out of them, but also
as judging ("wayenge" [36]) what she has read. This
is the first sign in the book that Christine is preparing not simply to accept the *auctoritates* she reads but
to intervene in the tradition they represent.

37 **dressed my vysage** turned my attention
(away from the "sentences" she is "wayenge" [36])

38 **to leve in peas subtyll thynges** to let profound matters alone ∫ **dysporte** entertain

40 **in this entente** about this intention ∫ **praty** pretty, that is, entertaining

41 **of adventure** by chance ∫ **taken to me to kepe** given to me to take care of

42 **intytulacyon** title ∫ **Matheolus** This is the *Lamentations of Matheolus,* a well-known misogynistic poem, possibly in the fourteenth-century French translation by Jean le Fèvre. Christine's laughter suggests that she at first feels no threat from a poem so comically extreme.

45 **in maner of solace** for fun ∫ **vysyte hym** spend time with his book

46 **refeccyon** refreshment

50–51 **put[tyng] my wyll to effecte that came to me the nyght before** fulfilling my intention that I formed the night before. The book is already more than a mere break from Christine's studies ("put[tyng]": Pepwell prints *put*).

51–52 **to prosede in hym** to work my way through his book

52–56 **But as me semed . . . of more profyte** This is one sentence in the French and has been translated without full syntactic concord by Anslay (who may have taken *verse* for *venue* in his "came to the ende" [55]).

52 **as me semed** as it seemed to me

54 **seynge** seeing

56 **hygher** reputable

57 **howe be it that he was of none auctoryte** That is, the book is not part of the tradition of serious writers regarded as authoritative. In the Middle Ages, explicitly misogynistic writing often had an air of raffish marginality, a self-conscious sense of its own extremity. In the next lines, however, Christine realizes (or comes to believe) that this is merely a pose, and that the attitudes found in such writings are in fact characteristic of those implied by far more authoritative texts.

58 **engendred** engendered. Christine becomes pregnant by Matheolus's text and, over the next lines, draws together into a monstrous birth all the remarks against women she has heard or read—using the same process of recollection she is engaged in at the beginning (35–37), but now the victim of the process, not its controller. ∫ **mervayle** astonishment

58–59 **in my courage** in my heart

61 **slaundres** false accusations ∫ **blames** reproaches

62 **condycyons** essential nature

63–64 **treateth in maner of scorne** writes as in mockery

66 **semble** a single ∫ **determynynge** deciding

68 **in me** within myself

69 **a woman naturall** a woman by nature ∫ **dyscuted of** considered

70 **haunted** frequented

70–71 **as well of pryncesses . . . grete plentye** a very large number of princesses and great ladies as well as gentlewomen of lesser rank

72 **pryvytees** secrets ∫ **strayte thoughtes** confidential thoughts. As Christine weighs experience against authority, the intimate talk of aristocratic and other women seems unable to stand on its own against the combined weight of written and authorized misogynist thought.

73 **favoure** partiality

73–74 **yf it . . . wytnesseth** if what so many notable men testify to concerning one or another [woman] could be true ("yf it": Pepwell prints *yf it it*)

76, 77 **agaynst** concerning

80 **lyengly** deceptively ∫ **of payne** with difficulty

80–81 **morall volume** work of morality

81 **or** before

82 **blamynge of** slander against

82–83 **This onely shorte reason** this small cause alone

83 **his symplenesse** its ignorance (i.e., that of Christine's understanding)

84 **defautes** faults. Christine argues herself into the view that her experience of herself and other women is of less authority than what she has read, and so cannot be true. ∫ **semblably** similarly

85 **that alwaye . . . was so** so that it was entirely fitting that this was the case ∫ **reported me** entrusted myself

86 **that** that which

87 **halfe from hymselfe** that is, half mad, condemned to judge her own "essential" nature

88 **grete foyson** a large multitude ∫ **dyttyes** sayings

88–89 **to this purpose** on this subject

89–90 **a welle spryngynge** Without realizing it Christine has remembered large numbers of sayings and proverbs against women that she thought she had been able to dismiss as irrelevant.

91 **worshypfull** honorable

92–93 **as by sayenge of them** according to what they say

93 **draught and herbegage** wellspring and home

95 **dyspraysynge** belittling

95–96 **so as yf yt sholde be shewed in nature** as if it were a natural thing

97 **I arre not in thy fayth** I do not err in your faith (i.e., orthodox Christian belief). The phrase anticipates the later charge that misogyny is heresy, invoking Christianity on the side of women.

100 **syngulerly** uniquely: here with the sense "in a special way"

102 **And alway se here so many grete occasyons** and all the time see here so many powerful causes ∫ **determyned** decided

103 **repugnaunce** inconsistency

104 **haboundeth** possesses in abundance

105–6 **the wytnesse of many is for to byleve** See John 8:17.

108 **kynde** gender

109 **the the** you the

111 **debonayrnesse** kindness ∫ **stretcheth not so moche** does not extend so far

112 **spare** be lenient toward

114 **mo ynowe** others enough ∫ **ryght longe** for a long time

115 **lamentacyon** Matheolus's *Lamentations* call forth an answering lamentation from Christine, which both temporarily concurs with and protests against its source.

116 **that that** the fact that

PART FOUR

FIVE ESSAYS

The Middle English prologues and other materials edited and introduced in Parts One, Two, and Three are not solely a contemporary critical guide to the vernacular, they also contain information relevant to medieval literary and social history, theology, historiography, philosophy, medicine and alchemy, and much else. Although our presentation of these texts tries always to make clear why they are included in a volume focusing on "the idea of the vernacular" (and the introduction to each part gives more connected analysis about the theoretical insights offered by the texts), we also attempt to be responsive to the variety of their concerns, as well as the equal variety of questions modern readers may bring to them. To an extent, this collection of excerpts thus invites treatment as an anthology of Middle English texts open to plural uses and readings, one that happens to focus especially on a rich tradition of prologue writing.

Yet this book does advance a set of arguments. They have to do with the importance of the theme of vernacularity in Middle English texts, the extent to which Middle English prologues articulate theoretical analyses both of this theme and of other literary concerns, and the extent to which these analyses are different from the theoretical apparatuses found in Latin texts, especially because of what we call their "situatedness" in a complex social or cultural context. In this final part of the book, we approach aspects of these arguments directly, drawing on the prologues in the previous three parts for most of our evidence. The five essays below take very different approaches to the vernacular and the prologues that describe it, ranging from a sketch of a literary history of Middle English focusing on the vernacular (essay 4.2) to a reflection on Middle English prologues as prologues (essay 4.5), or from an empirical discussion of late medieval developments in book production and the mechanisms of literary patronage (essay 4.3) to an analysis of the cultural roles of Middle English that orients its subject in relation to postcolonial studies and translation theory (essay 4.4). These essays are not in any sense intended to be exhaustive; obviously, many other approaches could be taken. But they do focus on what have seemed to us the most pressing issues to be addressed in delineating the field of vernacular literary theory. Moreover, the first essay in the part depicts and defends this field with arguments that underpin the whole book. Here, more than anywhere else, we have attempted to show as clearly as possible why we need the concept of vernacular theory and why this concept matters.

4.1

THE NOTION OF VERNACULAR THEORY

RUTH EVANS, ANDREW TAYLOR,
NICHOLAS WATSON, AND JOCELYN WOGAN-BROWNE

LATIN AND VERNACULAR LITERARY THEORY

The term "theory" cannot be used in relation to Middle English literature—and to the excerpts collected in this volume in particular—without considerable historical and critical negotiation. The term "medieval literary theory" is a modern one, and the appearance of Minnis and Scott's book of that title (1988) coincided with the rise within the academy of a strong interest in something called literary theory. The authors rightly insist on the contribution of the Middle Ages to the history of literary theory and criticism (1988, 11). However, although there is now a consensus that Latin scholastic culture of the Middle Ages had a body of writings that can be grouped under the rubric of "medieval literary theory," it must be understood that the category, as well as the term, is modern, not medieval. One effect of the field's focus on an exclusively Latin textual corpus has been the delineation of a theoretical field rooted in academic origins and spheres of influence.

Rita Copeland's survey of "medieval theory and criticism" (1994) subdivides the field into four areas, all derived from antiquity or the early church and all having their institutional homes in the Latin schools of the Middle Ages: Neoplatonism, the reception of Aristotle, prescriptive poetics, and textual exegesis. Neoplatonism gave the Middle Ages a theory of figurative meaning: textual signifiers (the letters themselves or the *sensus litteralis* [literal meaning]) are considered to be an allegorical veil hiding a spiritual or philosophical truth—a transcendent signified—that is articulated beyond or behind the accidents of the text; this allegorical mode of reading especially influenced medieval traditions of biblical exegesis. The study of Aristotle provided the material for a systematic science of logic, with wide-reaching effects on the teaching of language, drama, semantics, and language theory in medieval schools—although an association of poetry with ethics, also deriving from Aristotle, was of comparable importance. Prescriptive poetics offered guidance to the production of new texts rather than the criticism of existing ones, in the form of rhetorical handbooks such as Geoffrey of Vinsauf's *Poetria nova* (c. 1200), the *artes praedicandi* (arts of preaching), and *artes dictaminis* (arts of letter writing); these are loosely related to more generalized treatises on poetics like Dante's *De vulgari eloquentia* (1304–9) and Boccaccio's *De genealogia deorum gentilium* (On the genealogy of the pagan gods), book XIV (c. 1350–70). Finally, textual exegesis consisted of a huge variety of glosses and commentary on secular and sacred texts; the focus of these tended to shift during the late Middle Ages away from allegorical and toward literal modes of reading, as interest grew in the human authors of the books that make up the Bible, and the site of meaning came to be associated with the textual "surface," not the allegorical "depth" hypothesized by Neoplatonic models of reading (Smalley 1983; Minnis 1988). Relative to contemporary literary theory, the borderlines of medieval theory are thus at present fairly fixed: the bibliography is so much smaller than in the field of modern theory, the exact definition of which remains an uncertainty, perhaps even an impossibility (de Man 1986). This does not mean, however, that there are no continuities between medieval and modern ways of reading. Arguably, modern theory's break with Kantian aesthetics—that is, with the tradition of objective aesthetic judgment and Kant's ideal of "disinterested contemplation"—brings it closer to pre-Kantian medieval literary theory (Lentricchia 1980, 19). It is now becoming clear that the Middle Ages had also developed, albeit in very different forms, an extensive critical investigation into the ways in which language conveys meaning and all the uncertainties and indeterminacies this involves (see, e.g., Colish 1983; Koerner 1980; Koerner, Niederehe, and Robins 1980). This wider field of medieval theory forms an important and neglected chapter in a literary history that often skips from Aristotle's *Poetics* to Sidney's *Defence of Poesy*.

In Middle English writings, admittedly, the sustained analysis of texts and language found in Latin theoretical discussions and in vernacular texts from the sixteenth century is rare. While the impact of each of Copeland's areas of medieval Latin theory is felt in Middle English texts, these offer little as substantial or ambitious as Sidney's *Defence* or the treatises of Boccaccio and Dante. Formal analyses of exegetical issues do occur in Lollard discussions of the Bible, and there are prolonged and explicit analyses not of poetics but of the vernacular itself in the body of writing that arose out of the fierce controversies over biblical translation (see excerpts 1.15–16, 2.4–5). Yet even this material is characterized by a topical urgency that places it at a far remove from the more generalized critical and theoretical concerns articulated by Latin treatises on poetics or by writers like Sidney. Most of the other texts excerpted here address in the first instance their immediate audience or patron, rather than raise any general theoretical questions; as prologues to literary works, written in a language whose capacity for addressing serious intellectual issues was still sometimes questioned and whose status was uncertain, their theoretical components are self-evidently included for local and strategic purposes. Any theoretical analysis, however apparently disinterested and in whatever language it is written, is, of course, inseparable from an ideological and cultural context—and in this respect (as in many others) cannot in the end be distinguished from literary practice. Yet this is true of Middle English discussions of literature (as it is of vernacular discussions in other medieval languages) in an especially explicit sense. These discussions are so heavily situated—not only in the texts in which they occur but also in the social and ideological issues evoked by those texts and their use of the vernacular—that they require to be read in quantity, in careful relation to their cultural situation and, above all, with a sense of their strategic function, if their theoretical implications are to be teased out of them.

This may seem a disadvantage to readers hoping to use vernacular prologues as a simple key to the texts they introduce (let alone a key to other texts), and may seem to compromise any attempt to treat these prologues as "theory," even accepting a formalist definition of that term. Yet it is precisely the situatedness of Middle English discussions of language and of writing in a complex cultural context—and the pressing awareness of that context on the part of their writers and audiences—that gives these discussions their distinctiveness and makes the analysis of their theoretical implications potentially important. This book treats vernacular prologues as a body of theory in its own right because, for all the importance of the Latin terminology and frames of reference to which these prologues allude, Latin theorizing is often too far removed from the situation in which vernacular texts came into being to provide a satisfactory governing template for understanding these prologues or the texts they introduce.

VERNACULAR THEORY AND TRANSLATION

Modern analysis of vernacular prologues, and more generally of the implications of writing in the vernacular, has largely focused on the topic of translation. Prologues to many Middle English translations discuss strategies for rendering Latin or French texts and suggest the existence of a number of recognized translation practices that imply varying views on what constitutes "literal" translation and on what translation policy was thought to be appropriate for different kinds of text (Ellis 1982a). Discussion of Middle English translation until recently tended to be confined to analyses of the translation practices of a given text or group of texts that might or might not use the linguistic terminology of "source" and "target" languages (Bassnett-McGuire 1991) and might or might not acknowledge the different status of the (usually Latin or French) original and its Middle English translation (see further Evans 1994). "Literary" translations, such as most of Chaucer's oeuvre and Middle English romances with French sources, were discussed within a slightly different framework, one that acknowledged the translator's "craft" as a technician but tended to emphasize the originality and distinctiveness of the end product. Several volumes of essays focusing on Middle English translation, most of which adopt versions of these approaches, have been published in the last ten years (see Ellis 1989, 1991a/b; Ellis and Evans 1994; Ellis and Tixier 1996; Beer 1989; Beer and Lloyd-Jones 1995; Beer 1997), and Alastair Minnis's (1988) account of the use of academic theoretical structures by Chaucer and Gower is also related to this ongoing scholarly tradition.

This empirical approach to medieval translation has been powerfully supplemented in the last decade by a body of scholarship newly informed by medieval intellectual history, which is less concerned with translation as a pragmatic or creative practice than a site where cultural relations of dominance and subservience might be played out. In medieval Latin, the word *translatio* (translation) was often taken to be synonymous with *expositio* (interpretation) (Minnis and Scott 1988, 374). If this equation is taken seriously, it provides a justification for understanding vernacular translations not simply as attempts to transfer meaning unchanged from one language to another but as *readings* of source texts, part of whose purpose may indeed lie in their difference from those texts. Minnis's work was again important in pointing the way here (e.g., Minnis 1988). But Rita Copeland's study *Rhetoric, Hermeneutics, and Translation in the Middle Ages* (1991) provided a crucial underpinning to this approach, by showing how medieval translation practice was pulled both toward and away from the equation of *translatio* with *expositio,* as part of a millennium-long battle between opposed methods of scholastic analysis. *Enarratio* (exegesis), part of the discipline of grammar, emphasized carefully subordinated service to a source text; *inventio* (invention), part of the discipline of rhetoric, emphasized aggressive displacement of that text. Within this framework, Copeland reads the poetry of Chaucer and Gower (focusing on *The Legend of Good Women* and *Confessio Amantis*) as "secondary translations" that thematize their displacement of the classical *auctores* they use, asserting their independence as vernacular authors and implicitly claiming equal status with their sources (Copeland 1991, chap. 7).

Part of Copeland's achievement has been to recognize the intimate connection between the centrality of translation as a medieval literary practice and the embracing Latin theoretical concept of *translatio studii et imperii* (the transferal of learning and empire), a concept that was of basic importance to medieval reflections on the relationship between present and past cultures, and on the means by which cultural value and authority was transmitted from one period to another. The concept comprises two parts, one having to do with the translation of political power—as Curtius says, "the renewal of the Empire by Charlemagne could be regarded as a transferal of the Roman *imperium* to another people" (Curtius 1990, 29)—the other with the transferal of literary texts and structures of thought through commentary, translation, and the creation of new literatures that take their authority from "classical" precedents. The northern French writer Chrétien de Troyes, for example, in the prologue to his romance *Cligés* (c. 1170–82), describes how chivalry and learning moved from Greece to Rome and now, in his own time, to France (quoted in Curtius 1990, 384–85; see Kelly 1978; Freeman 1979; Patterson 1987, chaps. 5–6). Like translation practice itself (according to Copeland), this grand narrative of cultural and political translation can be understood either as an endorsement of the authority of the past as a model and source for the present or, conversely, as an account of how "modern" culture seeks to displace the past. *Translatio studii et imperii* both describes and denies change. As such, it offered medieval vernacular writers an inevitable model—a structure so deeply written into literary culture that writers might not even have registered it consciously—for articulating their double sense of dependence on and difference from Latin thought and literature.

The significance of this model for thinking about vernacularity is clearly recognized in the most famous medieval attempt to theorize the vernacular, Dante's *De vulgari eloquentia* (On eloquence in the vernacular), a treatise on poetics whose argument touches on or skirts around so many of the issues facing Middle English writers that it is worth detailed discussion. Written in Latin about the time Dante was embarking on his great Italian poem, *The Divine Comedy* (c. 1300), the *De vulgari eloquentia* represents a sustained attempt to articulate "the political or ideological issues at stake in its own project" (Copeland 1991, 180). Dante's determination to hunt down (to invent in the sense "find out") a form of Italian that is "illustrious, cardinal, royal and courtly" (Welliver 1981, 81) is also a determination to bring it into being (as an invention, something new), and involves him in an argument that must at once admit and deny the primacy of Latin. This argument depends on a discussion of vernacular dialects, whose value is judged phonaesthetically (by an aesthetic and culturally determined response to how they *sound*) and which first seem unworthy of comparison to Latin. While some are "hirsute and hispid," others are effeminate, and yet others are "crude" or "monstrous" (Welliver 1981, 75, 69); together they make up the "din of the Latin vernacular" (67; *Latin* vernacular because the Italian and other Romance dialects Dante is discussing are derived from Latin). The metaphor "din" equates the vernacular with the spoken, rather than the written, language and also—by evoking the disorder of Babel—emphasizes the fallen state of all vernaculars, whose very existence is a reminder of the loss of the unitary language spoken by Adam.

From this apparently negative picture of the vernacular grows a treatise that elevates Dante's chosen vernacular to the status of Latin and his chosen genre—the humble *canzone*—to that of the noblest poetry. Latin, a language that has its own claim to be unitary or universal, split up into three vernaculars (Provençal, French, and Italian) in which the forms of affirmation are *oc*, *oïl*, and *sì*. Italian—

the *sì*—is most prestigious because of its proximity to Latin (whose word for "yes" is *sic*) (63). But being a language "we learn without any rules by imitating a nurse" (43), it can still be sharply differentiated from a "grammatical" (rule-governed) language like Latin. The relationship between Latin and vernacular here is similar to the one the language theorist Ferdinand de Saussure (1983) describes between *langue,* the set of ideal rules and structures that make up a language, and *parole,* the actual individual speech utterances those structures make possible. However, after rejecting all the various Italian dialects as inadequate and as failing to embody "the most beautiful and illustrious Italian speech" (Welliver 1981, 67), Dante's text performs a shift in its perception of the vernacular as ruleless. Having redefined grammar as "nothing but an immutable sameness of language in diverse times and places" (63), he redeploys this notion of immutability to claim that there is, after all, an ideal grammatical form of Italian, corresponding to no individual dialect but comprehensible to all: "I proclaim an illustrious, cardinal, royal and courtly vernacular in Italy, which is of every Latin city and seems to be of none, and by which all the municipal vernaculars of Latin are measured and weighed and compared" (81). Even though it is said only to exist in the poetry of Dante and other recent writers, this literary language—written, not spoken, and corresponding to Saussure's abstract system of *langue,* rather than the concrete manifestation of *parole*—at a stroke replaces but also parallels Latin as a measure of the linguistic ideal. Uniting all the scattered Italian dialects, as Latin unites the languages of Europe, Dante's "illustrious" Italian repositions the vernacular within the myth of unity and of unitary language, redefining it not as a mutating reminder of the confusion of Babel but as a partial return to the harmony Babel destroyed.

Dante's treatise is rightly regarded as an important attempt to shift the relations of power governing Latin and the European vernaculars: using the framework of *translatio studii et imperii* to construct an argument that displaces Latin in favor of a vernacular that, Dante asserts, can be of comparable prestige to Latin and share many of its characteristics. But while this treatise is unusually explicit in setting out its argument for the "*de facto* ascendancy of vernacular culture" (Copeland 1991, 180), it is not the only text to grapple with these issues. Like writers in other vernacular languages (such as French, Provençal, Catalan, and German), certain Middle English writers were also aware of the implications of *translatio studii et imperii* for the emergence of a literary tradition in their vernacular. For reasons described in the next essay, however, English writers did not appear as self-conscious proponents of their language as a new literary vernacular until the last years of the fourteenth century, fifty years after Dante. Writing in a Germanic language that was less closely related to Latin than Italian and had long been subordinated to Anglo-Norman, these writers also adopted a less aggressive and more varied approach than Dante's.

Yet at least two bodies of Middle English writing engage in a deliberate (if not necessarily systematic) effort to assimilate and displace Latin, French, and occasionally Italian hegemony: the alliterative poetry of the West Midlands, such as

The Wars of Alexander (excerpt 3.13) or *Sir Gawain and the Green Knight,* which often stresses the unbroken line of descent connecting Troy and England (through Priam's son Brutus and, in some cases, the imperial reign of King Arthur); and the tradition stemming from the London poets Chaucer and Gower, incorporating Hoccleve, the East Anglian poet Lydgate, and some others. It is, of course, this second body of writing that established itself as England's answer to Latin and the high-culture vernaculars and that is taken as the mythic point of origin for the English literary tradition to this day. The major long poems in this tradition were almost all modeled on prestigious literary antecedents (written during the fourteen hundred years between poets such as Ovid and the fourteenth-century Frenchman Guillaume de Machaut) and, at least in a general sense, can be seen as parts of a collective attempt to render the literary achievements of the past into a new vernacular idiom. Written in a variety of English whose elaborate French vocabulary distinguished it from any particular spoken dialect and that gradually established itself as a literary "standard," these poems are English equivalents of Dante's ennobled *canzone,* since the aureate language they use is equivalent to Dante's illustrious vernacular.

The theoretical commentary Chaucer and his successors articulate in underpinning their creation of a literary language largely consists of gestures of apology for their "belatedness" and for the "unworthiness" of English as a whole or of their particular command of English. These gestures need to be read with a careful eye to their textual and cultural situatedness. When Chaucer states that "ryme in Englissh hat such skarsete" (*Complaint of Venus,* excerpt 1.3: 9) or directs *Troilus and Criseyde* to humble itself before the epic texts he imitates ("But litel book, no makyng thow n'envie, / But subgit be to alle poesye" [V.1789–90]), modern critics have had no difficulty detecting the layers of irony and concealed assertion involved. But when Lydgate or other fifteenth-century poets apologize in much this way, insisting on their dullness and lack of craft, critics have until recently tended to take them at face value, failing to see their gestures as strategic and specific inversions of the *translatio studii* motif. The prologue to Lydgate's *Troy Book* (excerpt 1.7), for example, ends by praising his *auctor,* Guido delle Colonne, and submitting his work to the judgment of readers, protesting his "humble herte and lowe entencioun" (211), just as later in the poem he protests his unwillingness to say anything to contradict his master Chaucer. As is suggested in the introduction to Part One (pages 7–8), while deference may seem merely appropriate to a translator responding to a commission from the heir to the English throne, it paradoxically forms part of a larger strategy of cultural aggrandizement. Since Guido's is the canonical account of the Trojan War, his book needs to exist in an English version (84–96); yet since the *assimilation* of the story into English is Lydgate's goal, paralleling Henry's intended reconquest of France, Lydgate aggressively reshapes his source, using the five-book structure Chaucer used in *Troilus and Criseyde* (a poem Lydgate also overwrites; Watson 1994, Baswell 1997) to create a poem three times the length of Guido's book and even more ornate. It is this that he submits to his readers in a gesture of humility that is also a virtuoso rhetorical exercise. This gesture thus both generalizes and theorizes Lydgate's position as a representative vernacular writer, situated between authoritative sources and authoritative patrons whose demands pull him in such different directions that he has to assume a double attitude of simultaneous deference and assertiveness. Implicitly, the prologue also attributes this contradictory attitude to the English language as it invents itself through *translatio studii*.

Lydgate's characteristic deference (part of his persona as a translator who is also a monk) has equivalents in other fifteenth-century writers excerpted in this volume: Walton (excerpt 1.5), Hoccleve (excerpt 1.6), Metham (excerpt 1.8), Ashby (excerpt 1.9), Bokenham (excerpt 1.11), Caxton (excerpt 2.10), and even Douglas (excerpt 3.16). These writers have their own distinctive concerns and should also be seen as conducting a complex discussion about the shaping of English as a literary language, and not as mechanically repeating gestures learned from their predecessors. This discussion had a decisive influence on the development of English and Scottish literature until the early seventeenth century. Despite the indirect form that this flexible and sophisticated discussion took and the effort required in teasing out its implications, even these few examples should suffice to suggest that it can provide as interesting an analysis as the *De vulgari eloquentia* of the relations between *translatio studii* and the processes of vernacularization—and hence that it deserves to be read with equal attention to its theoretical and cultural implications.

The Distinctiveness of Vernacular Theory

Copeland's discussion of translation practice as a combination of deference and displacement modeled on *translatio studii* makes available valuable insights into how vernacular writers theorized their projects, and offers a seductively all-inclusive narrative about the "rise" of European vernacular languages and literatures. Yet as Copeland was herself the first to recognize (1991, 221–29; also Evans 1994), the model has clear limitations, whether it is being used by medieval writers to theorize their projects or by modern scholars to analyze these theories. The model's sphere of influence is restricted to texts produced as self-conscious contributions to high literary culture, texts such as those just described, which seem preoccupied with their role in creating an "illustrious" vernacular idiom, removed—like Latin—from common speech. Moreover, the competitiveness inherent in *translatio studii*—whether this is competitiveness between the vernacular and Latin or between different vernaculars—focuses the discussions that arise from the model on a narrow range of issues to do with language and *prestige*. In annexing Latin's cultural authority, vernacular literatures demonstrate their ability to do anything Latin can do, while marking their difference from Latin; asserting the prestige of Latin texts and *auctores,* they also seek to assimilate that prestige, in an endless shuttling between gestures of deference and gestures of displacement whose most obvious effect is to tie the theory and practice of vernacular writing permanently to the question of its status in relation to Latin. The bonds are all the tighter inasmuch as the model itself derives from classical Latin, so that texts structured by it are already working within a field established by Latin (as Copeland's book brilliantly demonstrates). Dante perhaps acknowledges as much by writing the *De vulgari eloquentia* in Latin, not Italian.

However much it mattered, status was not, in fact, the one thing at stake in the emergence of Middle English or other vernacular literatures, or even in the high-culture texts just described; nor is status itself always defined according to the *translatio studii* model and in relation to Latin. Middle English writers were concerned with a range of more detailed theoretical issues, having to do not simply with authority but with reading and audience, instruction, pleasure and truth in history and fiction, and theories of meaning. In exploring these and other matters, they drew on a wide range of sources—wider than the intellectual traditions that make up Latin literary theory as currently conceived, and far wider than the ambit of the *translatio studii* model—often in a manner that was neither derivative nor competitive but pragmatic. As suggested in the introduction to Part Two (pages 110–16), Middle English writers often seem to have been more concerned with the projected audience of a text—with the kind of *community* that writing in English could make or sustain—than with the furthering of English literature. Many of the religious texts whose prologues are excerpted here offer learning to vernacular readers or theorize what it means to make such an offer by discussing the capacity of their audience and their own role as mediators of knowledge. The question of who should be able to read what is pivotally important to the vernacular politics of late medieval England and is inseparable from contentious issues of gender, class, education, and community (these issues are explored in more detail in essay 4.2 and essay 4.3, pages 331–65, below). Nicholas Love's restrictive model of lay access to knowledge, in the prologue to his *Mirror of the Blessed Life of Jesus Christ* (excerpt 3.10)—in which a holy woman's repetitive meditation on Christ's life is proposed as a pattern for all laypeople to imitate—is a riposte to Lollard and other proposals that everyone, even the "lewidest knave of the kychyn," should learn God's law directly from the Bible (*Sermon of Dead Men,* excerpt 3.11: 13; see also *On Translating the Bible into English,* excerpt 2.4, and *The Holi Prophete David Seith,* excerpt 2.5). This model is in turn criticized by Reginald Pecock (excerpt 1.16), who holds that the London laity for whom he writes are fully able to understand academic theology, and by the anonymous author of *Speculum Devotorum* (excerpt 1.12), whose exploratory account of Christ's life, written for a nun and based on the same source as the *Mirror,* questions Love's assumption that all vernacular readers have the same childlike spiritual needs. All these texts are situated not only in the complex history of the Lollard movement but in a cultural debate about vernacular readers and the role of written English in the construction of a national Christian community. This debate can be traced at least as far back as the *Northern Homily Cycle* (c. 1315, excerpt 2.1), as well as other texts, from *The Cloud of Unknowing* (excerpt 3.3) and Julian's *Revelation of Love* (excerpts 1.13 and 3.4) to the *South English Legendary* (excerpt 2.15), *Piers Plowman* (excerpt 3.19), *Pore Caityf* (excerpt 3.6), and *Dives and Pauper* (excerpt 3.9). And this debate is itself part of an even wider discussion of the relationship between language and audience that includes secular texts as well as religious ones: texts such as *The Knowing of Woman's Kind in Childing* (excerpt 2.6), which explicitly asks men not to read it or to do so sympathetically, or Christine de Pizan's *Book of the City of Ladies* (excerpt 3.24), whose unsettling portrayal of the consequences when a woman gains access to texts usually read by men was only translated into English more than a century after its composition and was even then firmly presented by its printer (Henry Pepwell) as proof not of women's qualities or its *auctoresse*'s courage and skill but of its patron's gallantry (1–28). The politics of access are at least as important to English literary history as the process by which English literature invents itself through *translatio studii*.

The importance of the theme of access and the way it differs from the theme of status is well illustrated in John Trevisa's *Dialogue Between the Lord and the Clerk* (excerpt 2.2). As one of the most explicit discussions of the English vernacular in this book—a discussion that comes down firmly on the side of open access to learning—the argument of the *Dialogue* offers an interesting contrast with that of the *De vulgari eloquentia,* as well as with those of more restrictive Middle English texts like Nicholas Love's. Like Dante, Trevisa's lord alludes to the myth of Babel as the origin of linguistic diversity. But where Dante reads the myth as a depiction of a fall from unitary meaning into a linguistic chaos that even the illustrious vernacular can only partly reverse, the lord treats it as merely a practical impediment to communication (1–10). In his utilitarian view, Babel is not a sign of the reduced status of language in general or the vernacular in particular, and the prestige of any language is barely an issue. Latin is an ideologically neutral, if partial, resolution of the problems occasioned by the aftermath of Babel, especially useful for its ability to transcend national linguistic barriers to communication. While it suffers from one disadvantage, that it is, for the most part, understood only by clerks (17–19), this problem can be overcome by the translation into English of texts like the one (Higden's *Polychronicon*) to which the *Dialogue* forms a prologue. This will disseminate knowledge to greater numbers of people (26–27) and so in a small way help undo the damage done by Babel. The lord plays his part in furthering this good work by overcoming the reluctance of the clerk (Trevisa's textual alter ego) to part with his Latin learning, arguing him into acting as a mediator between Latin and vernacular, knowledge and the English people.

Trevisa's *Dialogue* was written in the 1380s, before the Lollard controversy had made the discussion of these issues as complex as they later became; neither Gower's presentation of Babel as a figure for the disunity of the English (*Confessio Amantis*, prologue, 1017–30; 1390s; see excerpt 2.11) nor the more elaborate discussions of Babel in the Oxford translation debate (c. 1401) is imaginable as Trevisa writes (see pages 339–45 below). Yet despite its confidence—the lord's certainty of victory is in a social sense based simply on the fact that he is a lord—Trevisa's argument is not a simple one. Not only does it touch on a number of important subsidiary questions—whether Latin or the vernacular has the better claim to be considered "universal," how the concept of "necessary" knowledge is to be defined, and in what sense the inevitability of error is a reason not to translate—but a major part of its argument works by implication, rather than direct statement. One effect of the dialogue form in which the argument is cast is to engage its audience in an understanding of learning and vernacular translation as *embodied*. Although the lord partly views meaning as an entity whose independence of any given language makes it readily transmissible between languages (Copeland 1991, 225–26), his presentation of the process of understanding meaning is social. Language barriers reduce speech to the "gageling of gees" (excerpt 2.2: 8–9), so that a curse can be misunderstood as a greeting. Reading Latin requires hours of studying and poring over books ("ther is myche Latyn in thes bokes of cronicles that I can nought understonde, neither thou, without studiyng and avisement and loking of other bokes" [41–43]), while learning the language is impeded not by abstract considerations but frankly material ones: pressure of other commitments, age, lack of ability or money or patronage (46–48). On the other hand, the clerk's feeble reasons for disapproving of translation are "worthi to be plonged in a plodde," and evoke "lewdenesse and . . . shame" to anyone who can think practically; even a "blere-eyghed man" could see through them if he had his wits (68, 69, 72). The lord's colorful use of language, in combination with his mastery of the conventions of academic argumentation, has the effect of casting the issue of vernacular translation and the politics of access as a social contest, in which different groups of people struggle for control. The lord wins not only because his argument is formally superior to his opponent's, but because he is better at harnessing the rhetorical resources of the language in which the argument is cast and which it concerns. The kind of "theory" Trevisa presents us with here—and it has to be spelled out because it is implicit rather than explicit, despite the text's apparent explicitness—is one that focuses less on meaning than on the social arenas and power relations in which translation takes place. By drawing on the resources of the vernacular—drama, idiom, situated language, wit, irony—Trevisa's *Dialogue* does something that the *De vulgari eloquentia*, being in Latin, could not do and that aligns it rather with Dante's very different discussion of the vernacular in the *Convivio* (Copeland 1991, 182–84). The *Dialogue* represents itself as embodying the very principles of the primary nature of the vernacular as

Dante describes it in the *De vulgari*: not as noble and illustrious but as a language "we learn without any rules by imitating a nurse," a language of "the common people," to which "the common people" are said by Trevisa's lord to be able to respond with a sense of immediacy and familiarity.

The *Dialogue*'s deliberate lack of interest in *translatio studii* has its own Latin roots (Copeland 1991, 226). Latin structures of thought are less in evidence, however, in discussions of a theme related to, but different from, the theme of access: that of vernacular *distinctiveness*. Again and again these prologues present English as in some way distinct, presenting this distinctiveness in at least three different ways. Some prologues join Trevisa's *Dialogue* in representing English as an open language, or "common tongue," one of a network of vernaculars whose audience, if all vernaculars are taken together, is potentially universal. Others represent English as the language of a particular people, with its own distinct sphere of operation. Still others conceptualize English as a *melting pot* in which themes and concepts from Latin and other authoritative languages find new meanings in their new vernacular home. These forms derive from different understandings of what the vernacular symbolizes.

The first understanding, related to the notion of English as a "common tongue," assumes that the vernacular (sometimes also known as the "vulgar tongue") is marked by a certain crudity. But it is also the "mother" or "kynde [natural] tongue" (see the Glossary), a language with immediate access to people's feelings and easily comprehensible—as Latin is not, even to those who can understand it. Writing in English can thus do rather more than provide a practical vernacular means of access to knowledge; it can *signify* clarity and open access and do so even in texts whose projected audience is relatively narrow. For all his apparent emphasis on practicality, the lord is thinking symbolically in describing Trevisa's project as opening Higden's *Polychronicon* to all English speakers, for so lengthy and expensive a text could never have been accessible to the vast majority of people until more than a century into the print era (see Somerset 1998, chap. 3). The same is true of the massive texts produced by the Lollards, despite the assertions these texts make to the contrary. In a different sense, Langland's and Julian of Norwich's addresses to their fellow Christians also rest on a strong association between English and universality, one that may indeed have a determining influence on their theological speculations (see excerpts 3.19 and 1.13/3.4; Watson 1997a/b).

However, the symbolic openness of English is most explicitly theorized in Thomas Norton's highly successful *Ordinal of Alchemy* (excerpt 2.3), written in seven books of rhyming couplets around 1477. This text, written for "laymen . . . [a]nd clerkis also" (3–4), describes its project as an attempt to synthesize a complex subject in plain language and so open it up for everyone; as with Trevisa's *Dialogue,* this is clearly in part a rhetorical stance. According to Norton, most Latin writers on alchemy have "made theire bokis . . . ful derk / In poyses, parabols, and in methaphoris alleso" (63–64), so that even scholars cannot follow them.

Norton's book corrects his predecessors by using "playne and comon [i.e., un-adorned and vernacular] speche" (59), which can "shew the trouth" (97) and teach readers to flee "fals doctryne . . . / If ye geve credence to this boke and to me" (98–99). Alchemy, according to Norton, is an art dogged by "fals illusions" (12) and "deceytis" (101) and can only be practiced by those who are both highly in-telligent ("a grete clerke" [50]) and prepared to "eschew falshode" (109) (that is, despite Norton's assertions to the contrary, it is a specialized and elite practice). Because his book teaches and embodies the truth of alchemy, it transcends all pre-vious treatments of the subject and so deserves the name of alchemy's "Ordinalle" (an ordinal is a compendium of the official services of the church), its "standarde perpetualle" (128–29): "Therfore this boke to an alchymystre wise / Is a boke of incomperable price, / Whose trowth shal nevir be defiled, / Thofe it appere in homly wise compiled" (134–37). In this distinctly radical (and distinctly self-in-terested) discussion of meaning and truth in language, Norton's Latin sources are thus equated with falsehood (on account of their elaborateness and indirection), while his "plain" English corresponds to the truth, given him—as he says, implic-itly denying any dependence on earlier writers—"bi grace fro hevyn" (138). English is the base metal alchemy turns into gold and the best medium for describ-ing the process. Although this structure partly corresponds to that of *translatio studii*, Norton's rejection of Latin *auctores* (only the Greek Anaxagoras is praised [78–87]), as well as adoption of an approach that purports to owe them nothing thematically or stylistically, comes close to suggesting that Latin and vernacular are incommensurable: that English can learn nothing from Latin, whose commit-ment to obscurity is such that the language has few obvious uses. This is as strong a statement as any in Middle English of Latin's difference from the vernacular as a "common" and comprehensible language.

Middle English is also conceptualized not as one of a network of vernaculars whose audience is everyone but, rather, as the language of a particular people that makes meaning in a unique fashion. This understanding partly emerges from the complex situation in which Middle English was placed in relation to Anglo-Norman, Continental French and Latin, not to mention Welsh, Cornish, and Gaelic (see essay 4.2, pages 331–34). It can permeate even texts that appear to be constructed within the *translatio studii* tradition, moving these texts away from the sphere of cultural authority—in which Latin predominates—by allowing vernacular writers to reflect on the specific kinds of signification their language allows.

Thomas Usk, for example, presents himself in humble terms as one who gath-ers "the smale crommes . . . that fallen from the borde" (excerpt 1.4: 82), and his book, *The Testament of Love,* as no more than a compilation of scraps left by Boethius and other "noble repers," who "han al drawe and bounde up in the sheves" (80–81; who have drawn and bound together everything in sheaves). On one level, this is merely rhetorical humility of the kind Lydgate was to specialize in. But the physical density of Usk's language—which combines a bewildering mixture of topoi and images, many of them drawn from Latin, into a prose style that is self-consciously different from that of Latin and French—suggests that there is more to it than this. Despite his apparent deference to the usual hierarchy that placed English below both French and Latin (17–29), all three languages are ultimately of equivalent stature for Usk: French's "privy termes" (25) and the "propertie of science" (26) that pertains to Latin are matched by English words "whiche unneth we Englysshmen connen declare the knowlegynge" (21–22; which we English can scarcely explain how to understand); and "suche wordes as we lerneden of our dames tonge" form the proper language for the English to "shewe our fantasyes" (28–29). What interests Usk is not the status of Latin or French but their valence or tone: the academic authority conveyed by Latin, the "queynt" (curious or elaborate) words that the French find "kyndely to their mouthes" (28). For it is by characterizing these languages that he arrives at a depiction of the uniqueness of English. As for Trevisa (writing at the same time), and in a related way for Norton, this uniqueness again resides in the language's embodiedness, a quality that is prosaic and somewhat crude but gives the language an immediacy unmatched by Latin or French: "And, for rude wordes and boystous [crude] percen the herte of the herer to the inrest [inmost] poynte, and planten there the sentence of thynges . . . this boke, that nothyng hath of the greet floode of wit ne of semelych colours [as a French book would possess], is dolven [dug] with rude wordes and boystous, and so drawe[n] togyder, to maken the catchers therof ben the more redy to hent sentence [seize the meaning]" (5–10). Once he has established immediacy as peculiarly characteristic of English, Usk can also justify his use of a vocabulary widely dependent on French and Latin and very different from what most actual English people "lerneden of our dames tonge," as he seeks to shape a forceful written English in which "chyldren of trouthe" can taste their "lyfelyche meate" (95; life-giving food). Although from one point of view English is belated, a dwarf trying to "rende out the swerde of Hercules handes" [67–68]), in another sense it has its own qualities and can develop its own literary language. This language (for which Usk perhaps owed as much to Langland as to Chaucer) does seek to displace French (70–72) but is defined along lines that acknowledge neither indebtedness nor competition between the two languages, each of which has its own sphere of operations and characteristic tone.

A third understanding of the symbolic distinctiveness of the English vernacular is visible in the ways writers adapt Latin theoretical terminology to their own ends. If these adaptations again reveal English writers to be preoccupied with the immediacy of their texts—as if writing in English were more like *speaking* than writing—English is here a *melting pot,* in which Latin terminology, stripped of the institutional framework that gave it a clear meaning, is rendered into shapes that allow it to be used for new purposes. Usk is aware of this process (one resisted by advocates of pragmatic translation such as Trevisa), but it can best be demonstrated by analyzing how the term "entent" is used in these prologues. (Readers

are invited to use the Glossary to examine the flexible use of other literary terms.)
"Entent" is an Englishing of the Latin rhetorical term *intentio*, or *intentio auctoris*
(authorial intention), the category deployed in the scholastic "commentary tradition" as a statement of a work's meaning and structure (Minnis 1988, 20–21;
Copeland 1991, 76–83). Rather than be concerned with an author's individual
aims, *intentio*, a prescriptive category, indicates the abstract truth behind a text;
in a sense, it thus most closely corresponds not to an inherent property of a work
but to a reading practice. When Rolle writes, in *The English Psalter* (excerpt 3.8),
that the "entent [of the Psalms] is, to confourme men that ere filyd [defiled] in
Adam til Crist in newnes of lyf" (55–56), he is not defining what the Psalms are
about so much as offering a hermeneutic guide to readers, so that they discover
the proper meaning in the text.

Copeland argues that for Chaucer, Gower, and some other vernacular writers,
the category of *intentio* is taken over in precisely these exegetical terms and with
a full awareness of its history. Chaucer uses the term to identify "vernacular writing with the language of official culture" (Copeland 1991, 186), claiming for
himself the status of *auctor* whose texts have a unified structure and a formal ulterior meaning (187–88). But this may or may not be the whole story, for when we
turn to the use of "entent" in four of the texts edited here, its meaning is far from
this clear-cut. The verse prologue to Ashby's *Active Policy of a Prince* (excerpt
1.9) offers an elaborate justification for his work (a text in the "mirrors for
princes" tradition) that appears at first sight to mime the exegetical moves of the
scholastic commentary tradition by claiming to follow the "intential substance"
(66; the substance of the intent, i.e., the moral and structural principles) of its
source. Ashby alerts the audience to his allegiance to this ulterior meaning several
times (61, 84–97). Yet the work is not a translation at all but largely Ashby's own
invention: there is in fact no transcendent source that provides "entent." In other
words, "entent" functions here not as a pointer toward the learned *auctoritas* of
a source, but as a sign of the work's autonomy and the vulnerability that follows
from this; Ashby thinks of *himself* as providing the work's "entent and substance."
This is why he is so concerned that his meaning not displease readers (84–90). By
taking responsibility for the work's "entent," he alters its terms, drawing into its
orbit questions of taste and approval, authorial anxiety and readerly competence,
that have more to do with the exigencies of literary patronage than the authority
signified by *intentio*. The difference is that between a disembodied, transcendent
notion of the meaning of the text and a socially interactive one—and this difference is clearly *marked* by a text well aware of the implications of its vernacular
status. Despite apparent deference to Latin terminology, Ashby's prologue stands
on a threshold between Latin theory and the emergence of vernacular theorizing,
translating *intentio* into a vernacular context in which notions of formal meaning
and rhetorical appropriation play little part in authorial self-fashioning.

In a similar vein, Bokenham's "vernacularizing" of the so-called Aristotelian
prologue to his collection of female saints' legends (explicating how the work is

structured according to the "four causes"; see excerpt 1.11) also focuses on the issue of the work's "entent," or "final cause" (9, 23–24, 198). Like Ashby, Bokenham is concerned that others might misunderstand his "trewe entent" (excerpt 1.11: 198). The text is thought of as social, as acting on an audience; not only does it elicit from them a reaction, but this reaction is unpredictable or unstable, if only because the text's authority, and that of Bokenham himself, is also unstable. Similarly, the anonymous author of the *Speculum Devotorum* (excerpt 1.12) defends his project by asserting that "the entent of hym that dede hyt was ful goode" (54–55), thus shifting "entent" from the work to the mind of the author; while Pecock (excerpt 1.16) also justifies his project by pointing to the orthodoxy of his "entent" (11–35), arrogating to himself the power to authorize "entent" rather than deploying it, as Copeland argues Chaucer does, as a structuring or authorizing principle. The specific and *local* context in which these writers frame their projects—their personal address to known readers who are aware of them not as *auctores* but as colleagues, employees, or friends—causes them to combine the scholastic meaning of *intentio* with a different one in which the word refers to personal motivation (the true meaning of the word when Criseyde writes, with unintended irony, "th'entente is al, and nat the lettres space" [*Troilus and Criseyde* V.1630]). In the resulting amalgam, authors are mediators of an "entent" that is situated somewhere between their minds and their texts, whose attempts to express "entent" are inherently vulnerable. In all these texts, "entent" fragments: dispersing and disseminating its Latin meanings, acquiring a whole new set of vernacular contexts their authors actively evoke, insisting on the *difference*, rather than the common ground, between their projects and authoritative Latin texts. Moreover, as with Norton and Usk, this is not a difference to be denied or deployed in an aggressive attempt to displace Latin, but is there to be *explored* as a discursive system in its own right. These writers claim for their texts not "the official discourses of academic culture" (Copeland 1991, 223) but a place within a vigorous new vernacular tradition in which negotiations between authors, audiences, and meanings are the very stuff of composition.

CONCLUSION

If Middle English theory is heavily situated in its vernacular cultural and textual context (as was claimed above), it seems, then, that this "situatedness" is itself one of its major concerns. Vernacular writers do not only see themselves as engaged in an attempt to make their language the equal of Latin; they are acutely aware, in a broad variety of ways, of the differences between languages and the need to theorize their own projects in light of those differences. In some cases, such theorizations revolve around the politics of access, exploring the implications of the vernacular's special ability to communicate across the range of professions and social classes, whether to restrict that ability or to exploit it to the full. In other cases, a writer's concern is with this ability in a more mythical than political sense. Here the vernacular is a sign of the natural, of truth, plainness, and emotional directness, of the physical or embodied and the socially situated itself, and can function as such even in texts whose use of English is technical, abstract, and far from plain. This set of associations—which are explored with particular attention to their historical context in the following essay (4.2)—can be an obstacle to our seeing "vernacular theory" as theory at all: inasmuch as the word "theory" is generally associated with a set of abstract structuring principles that determine textual interpretation. The metaphoric density of Usk's language and the slippage in the word "entent" as used by Ashby and Bokenham are not informed by this kind of overarching theoretical grid and are perhaps better seen as local and strategic adaptations of terms drawn from Latin theory but cut free from their originary theoretical foundations and thus capable of utterly transfiguring or calling into question that same foundational "theory." Yet taking vernacular theory seriously—as theory—enables us to see how Middle English writers constructed an idea of the vernacular, one informed by and informing its actual cultural situation, that had a wider range and was far less derivative than any approach derived from *translatio studii,* however flexible, can grasp. It allows us to begin our investigation of Middle English uses of Latin and French source material and theoretical terminology from *within* the vernacular, by concentrating on its distinctive language and its multiple cultural situations: to see vernacular writers *reaching* for Latin strategies within a vernacular field and not simply being shaped by structures they passively borrowed or actively appropriated. Finally, it helps us respect the aims and strategies of a host of "minor" writers who are often overlooked but whose sophisticated reflections on their situation as vernacular authors undercuts any notion that Chaucer and Gower are separate and superior, most like ourselves, or like originary Latin cultural authority.

The range of these writers' relationships to Latin, as to French, culture is remarkable, and is most productively thought of as a reshaping of those cultural traditions in accord with their own interests. Vicente Rafael, writing about Tagalog culture in the Philippines under Spanish rule, claims that "for the Tagalogs, translation was a process less of internalizing colonial-Christian conventions than of evading their totalizing grip by repeatedly marking the differences between their language and interests and those of the Spaniards" (Rafael 1988, 211). *Mutatis mutandis,* the same can be said of many Middle English writers in their encounters with Latin and French.

4.2

THE POLITICS OF
MIDDLE ENGLISH WRITING

Nicholas Watson

The previous essay provides a sketch of the field of vernacular theory and argues that two of the main features of vernacular theory are its cultural and textual situatedness and its preoccupation with the status or particular qualities of different languages. The present essay (like the essay on book production and literary patronage that follows it, essay 4.3) looks at these issues in more depth, using the texts excerpted in this book to sketch a chronological history of the written language—or at least of contemporary *attitudes* toward the written language. Middle English writing was and went on being much preoccupied with its own legitimacy and status, while the use of written English, both in England itself and in Scotland, was highly politically charged throughout the period, albeit not always in the same ways. Writing in English raised large questions about national/cultural identity and about the consequences of the spread of literacy and learning both down the social scale and across the gender divide. These questions are mirrored in complex ways not only in the explicit discussion they receive but in every feature of the vernacular literature of the period, including a writer's choice of genre, length, vocabulary, syntax, and poetic or prose style. The brief history of attitudes toward the written vernacular given here thus doubles as a general literary history of Middle English, one whose focus is sociopolitical and linguistic, rather than formal or aesthetic.

LANGUAGE CHANGE

Between 1300 and 1550, the relationships between the three main literary languages of England—Latin, Anglo-Norman, and English—shifted in a number of ways.[1] Since the late twelfth century, Middle English in all its dialectal variety had been the first language of most of those who did not grow up speaking Welsh, Gaelic, or Cornish (in the western and far northern parts of the island) or else Hebrew (the language of the Jews, expelled from England in 1290). Anglo-Norman was widely used in aristocratic writing and conversation, as well as in official business in the lawcourts, the guilds, and both royal and municipal administration. But even if it remained a birth tongue for a few people, by 1300 it had long been kept in a position of prestige largely by the conscious efforts of people whose first language was English. The same was true in a different sense of Latin, the language preferred for intellectual exchange in church and university, for the liturgy (the church's religious rites), and for ecclesiastical, international, and municipal record keeping (when this was not done in French). While the language situation both before and after 1300 was fluid, the weighty presence of these two prestigious languages militated against the social or intellectual advancement of those whose only language was English. It likewise militated against the emergence of other than locally standardized written or spoken forms of the language, or indeed the development of the common technical terminologies and syntactic structures needed for wider than local discussion of legal, theological, courtly, or philosophical matters. It is true that the English writings that survive from the period 1200–1330 do not easily fit any single model of the language's status or capacity, and include texts as sophisticated as any of their French counterparts— just as they are frequently found in manuscripts alongside Anglo-Norman and Latin texts without any necessary implication that their status is inferior to these texts. Sophisticated Early Middle English writings range from Lawman's alliterative *Brut* (c. 1200) to debate poems (*The Owl and the Nightingale*, c. 1200) and lyrics like the famous *Harley Lyrics* (c. 1320), or from specialized religious prose texts like *Ancrene Wisse* (c. 1230) to verse hagiography (the *South English Legendary*, c. 1280), chronicles, world histories, homilies (the *Ormulum*, c. 1170), and more. But while the situation of course varied from generation to generation and region to region, it is not surprising that English writing from this period is relatively rare and that it seems on the whole to have been more the product of local efforts to create an English literary style from the ground up than the expression of a continuous, if largely lost, tradition.[2]

1. This sketch of the language situation in later medieval England is based on several sources. For a carefully contextualized survey of the entire field, see Clanchy 1993. For French and English in the thirteenth century, see Wilson 1943; Berndt 1969 and 1976; Rothwell 1976; Short 1980; Lodge 1991. For Latin in the thirteenth and early fourteenth centuries, see Hunt 1991; for literary Latin, see Rigg 1992. For aspects of the history of Anglo-Norman in the fourteenth and fifteenth centuries (more often referred to as Anglo-French in studies of this later period), see Rothwell 1983, 1993a/b, and 1994; Wright 1992 and 1996. Still useful for the history of English is Strang 1970. For a bibliography of further studies, see Burnley and Matsuji 1994. A useful recent survey of research into developments in written English in the late Middle Ages is provided by Voigts 1996. For Hebrew in medieval England, see Hyams 1974.

2. For the "lost tradition" view, see especially Chambers 1932. For local attempts to create a standardized written dialect in thirteenth-century England, see, for example, the AB language of *Ancrene Wisse*

Between 1300 and 1420, the position of English writing within this trilingual literary culture became much more important. It is not that Latin and French lost prestige. Latin kept most of its functions until the religious reformation of the 1530s, when the dissolution of the monasteries and the translation of the liturgy into English narrowed its uses to formal disputation in school and university and to academic writing. Lawcourts and the keepers of municipal and guild records also used Anglo-Norman very much as before, and literary texts in Anglo-Norman and Parisian French were being written and copied well into the fifteenth century and continued to have a fundamental influence on much Middle English writing (Calin 1994). While Anglo-Norman apparently came to seem parochial beside its prestigious Continental counterpart as the situations in which it was used grew narrower, Parisian French, not English, apparently became the main language of Richard II's court (Rothwell 1994). As late as the 1370s, however, the poet and moralist John Gower chose to write his first long poem, the *Mirour de l'omme* (Mirror of humanity), in Anglo-Norman, perhaps as the most appropriate language for a member of the gentry such as himself to address his peers.[3] But written English texts of all kinds also appeared in far greater quantities than previously, gathering to themselves a new sense of their importance and undergoing a degree of standardization, as writers tried both to articulate their growing consciousness of the distinctiveness and coherence of English language and culture and to give the language a status closer to that of French or Latin. Fifty years before Caxton set up the first English printing press at Westminster, English had attained much of the standardization and prestige that made his success possible.

Exactly why and how this happened is not clear: the more so since contemporary explanations of the phenomenon, such as the comments on language change in prologues to Middle English and Anglo-Norman texts, always need to be read as official versions of a far more complex actual situation. The myth of an inevitable "triumph of English" told in linguistic histories (e.g., Jones 1966; Baugh and Cable 1993, 209–18) and given a literary twist by those who ascribe to Chaucer a central role (Fisher 1992a, 29, 106; for more examples, see Cannon 1996, 646–48) is unworkable just because it reads these explanations too literally. As a result, it replicates, rather than analyzes, the ideological assumptions that underlie these prologues, giving little sense of the tensions that accompany language change or of its complexity (which is such as to doom any attempt to tell a single story to

and the *Katherine* group (Tolkien 1929; d'Ardenne 1961; but see also Smith 1992), or the orthography of the *Ormulum* (Bennett and Smithers 1974, xxiiiff.). For an exploration of what is apparently an attempt to re-create Old English versification in the *Brut*, see Moffat 1995. For accounts of the literary history of the earlier period, see Johnson and Wogan-Browne 1998 and Hahn 1998.

3. Note, however, that the upper gentry were publicly using English in written form some time before Gower wrote the *Miroir*. For an especially early example, see the inscription painted in a window at Elsing Church, Norfolk, for Sir Hugh Hasting before his death in 1347: "Pray to thi son made Marye in whose worchipe yis chirche ha[th] wrowt huwe ye hastyng Margorie my wyf Ledi forgit us nowt" (Pray to your son, maid Mary, in whose worship Hugh the Hasting [and] Margery my wife have constructed this church; lady, do not forget us) (Woodforde 1950, 6).

oversimplification). Even if it is possible to point to factors that were important—from the Hundred Years' War against France to the emergence of a new readership for vernacular theology—no account of a phenomenon as big as language change can explain everything. Yet Middle English texts do tell stories about the status of the language in which they are written, often implicitly, sometimes in competition with other stories. And if these are read as ideological constructs as well as direct reflections of actual processes, they can yield information about the changing place of the English vernacular in the culture of the period, which can in turn be useful in throwing light on the conditions under which those texts came into being and circulated and on the theoretical consciousnesses they articulate. The rest of this essay thus pieces together some of these stories, mainly from the texts excerpted in this book, in an account of the literary history of the period whose focus is the centrality of language issues to Middle English literary culture.

MIDDLE ENGLISH WRITING, 1300–1380

Fourteenth-century English texts often refer to the language in which they are written, giving various reasons for using English. *Cursor Mundi* (excerpt 3.14), for example, an encyclopedic religious poem of about 1300, appeals both to "haly kirkis state" and "the love of Englis lede, / Englis lede of Engelande" (the love of the English people, English people from England) as reasons for not writing in "French rimes": the verse the poet says he usually hears read ("French rimes here I rede / Communely in iche a stede") and whose language enjoys most prestige ("Selden was for any chaunce / Englis tong praysed in Fraunce!"). "Gif we ilkane thaire langage / Me think then we do nane outrage" (if we give everyone their own language, it seems to me we thus do no harm), the passage concludes (73–90). Recent work by Thorlac Turville-Petre and Douglas Moffat argues that statements like this should be placed in the context of English racial disharmony, in which language was taken as a marker of Saxon or Norman origin and texts like Robert Mannyng's *Chronicle* (excerpt 1.1, c. 1338) forge an *ethnic* identity for English-speaking readers by giving polemical accounts of the history of their "servitude."[4] *Cursor Mundi* is less directly divisive than Mannyng, but the poem's insistence that French is a *foreign* tongue may serve a similar agenda. Thus the phrase "Englis lede of Engelande," which may seem redundant, is actually pivotal, controversially linking the English nation and the English language by appealing to the

4. See Turville-Petre 1988 and 1996 and Moffat's response (1994), which takes issue with a number of points; John J. Thompson (1994b) deals directly with this passage of *Cursor Mundi*, but disagrees with the reading offered here. Mannyng persistently uses the language of servitude: for example, "Now ere [the English] in servage fulle fele that or was fre. / Our fredom that day for ever toke the leve" (quoted in Moffat 1994, 147). For the view that Mannyng also emphasizes continuity between Anglo-Norman and English reading communities, see Johnson 1995.

similarity of the phrase "Englis lede" and the word "Engelande" (Speed 1994; Donoghue 1990; Johnson 1995). The "Englis lede" constituted by *Cursor Mundi* and other texts is a fiction, of course: a single community, devoid of differences of dialect, social status, or gender. Moreover, the extent to which this community is textually constructed—comes into being only in, or as a result of, these texts—is concealed, since English is seen as a natural language of a natural community, not something whose meaning is *assigned*. What makes the forms of this community found in Middle English texts important, despite the way its meanings change, is the extent to which these ideas of "naturalness," of the affinity of language, people, and land—and of language's capacity to unite people and land—continue to be central to thinking about the "mother tongue."

Mannyng's *Chronicle* and similar texts create a sense of English linguistic community by at once implying that the degraded status of the language is a token of forced servitude and that it is as flexible a medium as its rivals (variations on this combination of humility and assertiveness run right through Middle English literature). But any attempt to accept Mannyng's view literally by portraying Middle English as an underdog, fighting a war of resistance against a powerful enemy, badly oversimplifies the issues. The theme of oppression became most prominent in English at just the moment (in the first half of the fourteenth century) when use of the language was no longer reliable as a genuine marker of social status, let alone racial origin. By no later than 1300, written English—a language that was much influenced by Anglo-Norman—was being promoted vigorously, at least on a regional level, as an instrument of the church's education program. This is clear from the appearance, at much the same time as *Cursor Mundi* (written in northern England), of other long religious works that attained wide circulation: Mannyng's confession manual, *Handlyng Synne* (c. 1310), written in Lincolnshire (eastern Midlands), whose source is an Anglo-Norman treatise by William of Waddington; the *Northern Homily Cycle* (excerpt 2.1, c. 1315), perhaps written by an Augustinian canon near York (northern England); and the *South English Legendary* (excerpt 2.15, c. 1270–85), which survives in more than sixty manuscripts and may derive from Worcester (southwestern Midlands). *Cursor Mundi* itself indeed appeals to "haly kirkis state" as one reason this "ilke boke ys translate" (74), a line that may allude to the legislation that developed from the Fourth Lateran Council of 1215, culminating in England in Archbishop John Pecham's *Syllabus, Ignorantia sacerdotum* of 1281.[5] The *Syllabus* set out a minimum every Christian should know and a catechetical method (English sermons, preached four times a year) by which secular clergy should convey it to their parishioners; and much writing over the next century responds to this initiative. *Cursor Mundi* is a

---

5. For the growth of pastoral theology after the Fourth Lateran Council, see Boyle 1985; for an analysis of the twelfth-century background of later medieval pastoral literature, see Goering 1992. The context of Pecham's decree is described in Gillespie 1994, 96–101. For an extended discussion of *Cursor Mundi* and pastoral theology, see Thompson 1994b.

narrative, not catechetical, text. But by aligning itself with an official program of education, it declares its language choice in terms that make its appeal to "Englis lede" a pastoral, as well as political, strategy.

Two religious texts from the middle of the fourteenth century show growing ecclesiastical support of English, though they also imply that the language's relatively low prestige and broad accessibility gave promoters pause. One is a piece of legislation, the 1357 *Injunctions* of John Thoresby, archbishop of York, issued to the province's archdeacons and outlining much the same program as Pecham's *Syllabus*. The *Injunctions* mark a turning point in ecclesiastical attitudes toward English at the archdiocesan level, for, unlike earlier legislation, they were issued both in Latin and in a stylized English paraphrase made by a Benedictine monk (John of Catterick or Gaytryge) at Thoresby's orders (Swanson 1991; Powell 1994). This work (*The Lay Folks' Catechism*) was widely copied, and on one level represents a simple recognition that, to do business, an institution with a universal mandate must have a language understood by everyone. Yet its composition was more than routine, as is clear from the detailed information that survives about its production and circulation. Unusually, not only do many manuscripts of this brief work give Gaytryge's name, but Thoresby's register (the record of his activities as archbishop) contains a full copy of the English text; a letter survives from Thoresby to Gaytryge telling him to work quickly, and the register even indicates that the two men met to discuss the matter. Fifty years later, Gaytryge's commission was still cited as evidence for ecclesiastical support of English, by contributors to the Oxford debate on Bible translation (Watson 1995a, 844). Clearly, Thoresby and Gaytryge saw themselves as innovators; perhaps they were also seen as proponents of a mode of official communication that was controversial.

The other text that shows growing ecclesiastical interest in the use of English is a lengthy catechetical poem, the *Speculum Vitae*, probably by William of Nassington, whose career as an ecclesiastical administrator in York and southwestern England covers the years 1328–59 (Peterson 1986). This poem, which may have been written close in time and place to Thoresby's *Injunctions*—and if so provides further testimony to the key role played by the clergy of York in promoting the vernacular (Hughes 1988)—gives a version of the defense of English worth quoting at length:

In Inglysche toung I sall you telle	**sall** shall
And ye sa lang wyth me wyll dwell,	**And ye** if you
Na Latyn I wylle speke na waste	**na waste** nor waste
Bot Inglysche that men uses maste.	**men uses maste** people mostly use
For that es oure kynde langage	**kynde langage** natural language
That we have here maste of usage,	
That canne ilk a man understand	**canne** is able; **ilk** each
That es bornne in Inglande.	
For that langage es maste schewed	**maste schewed** best understood
Als wele i-mang lered als lewed.	**i-mang** among; **lewed** uneducated

Latyn, als I trow, canne nane — **canne** knows
Bot thase that it of scole haves tane, — except those who learned it at school
Som canne Frankes and na Latyn
That haves used courte and dwelled ther-in, — **used** spent time at
And some canne o Latyn a perty — **a perty** in part
That canne Frankes bot febely — **bot febely** only slightly
And some understandes in Inglysce
That canne nother Latyn na Frankes.
Bot lered and lewed, alde and yonnge
All understandes Inglysche tonng.
Thare-fore I halde it maste syker than — **syker** safe, prudent
To schew that langage that ilk a man kanne, — **schew** use
And for all lewed men namely, — **namely** especially
That canne na maner of clergy — who do not have any religious learning
To kenne thaime what ware maste nede. — to teach them what they most need
For clerkes canne bathe se and rede — **bathe** both
In sere bokes of haly writt — **sere** various
How thai sall lyf, if thai loke it. — **sall** should
Thare-fore I wyll me haly halde
To that langage that Inglysche es calde.[6]

Although written within two decades of Mannyng's *Chronicle* (excerpt 1.1) and sharing its commitment to the use of written English, this passage implies a picture of the linguistic situation quite different from that of Mannyng. Here, far from being identified with a threatened community, English is accepted as an important language even by clerics (the "lered") and is the only language in which a "mixed" audience can be addressed. Where *Cursor Mundi* (excerpt 3.14) excludes French speakers, *Speculum Vitae* addresses an audience that potentially includes everyone in England, appealing to English as "oure kynde langage," the language of the whole country ("oure" including French speakers, who speak English too). Strikingly, while "clerkes" are taken to have access to religious knowledge from Latin books, English is represented as a resource even for them (and the poem was used by members of the clergy as a vernacular confession manual: Hughes 1988, 148–49). The Christian community of England—again represented without dialect or gender boundaries—is seen not only as a linguistic unity but as constituted by that unity. The poem goes out of its way to suggest that it is simply responding pragmatically to the linguistic realities it describes. But the length of its account, its use of the emotive "kynde langage," and its careful description of how English is "maste syker" (most prudent) suggest that things are not as simple as it states. When we reflect that in 1384, less than thirty years after its author's death, the orthodoxy of *Speculum Vitae* was the subject of a brief inquiry at Cambridge

6. University of Liverpool, Cohen Bequest, Rylands MS F.4.9, fols. 2v–3r. This text has not been edited, but the prologue is discussed in Baugh and Cable 1993, 141. For a later prose version of the text, see Nelson 1981.

(Gillespie 1989, 332–33)—an inquiry whose main concern must have been the vernacular language of this doctrinally mainstream text—it seems likely that the work may be suppressing a certain tension about its place in the institutionalization of English.

Just what this tension—if this is the right word—signified before the advent of the Lollard heresy in the 1380s is not quite clear, and may not have been clear at the time. Texts written in the period 1340–80 display an increasing confidence about what materials can suitably be treated in English. For example, Richard Rolle's *English Psalter* (excerpt 3.8, the earliest long English biblical commentary, c. 1345) and *The Prick of Conscience* (excerpt 3.7, a poetic treatise on sin, judgment, and the otherworld, c. 1350) provide far more theological detail than earlier English texts. These works are not written in the sermon mode of *Cursor Mundi* (excerpt 3.14) or the *Northern Homily Cycle* (excerpt 2.1) but as guides to individuals seeking knowledge and self-reform. Like many religious texts of the period, they originated in the North—where the influence of Anglo-Norman was less strong, and where the potential of written English for religious instruction seems to have been recognized rather earlier than it was in the South—but invited and found a national audience, bearing out their claim to be appropriate for any Christian reader. Yet these works both assume that their readers require not only the basic information offered by *Speculum Vitae* but the tools to study a range of theological and ethical matters and to think for themselves about them. Anglo-Norman texts such as Edmund Rich's *Mirror of Holy Church* (c. 1220), translated into English at this time, treat their elite readerships with this respect, and the same is true of certain earlier English works for nuns or anchoresses (especially *Ancrene Wisse*). Rolle's English writings (such as *The English Psalter* and the treatise *The Form of Living*, both written for the anchoress Margaret Kirkeby) are outgrowths of this tradition; his works are typical of a number of affective religious writings in English that extrapolate from the spiritual and intellectual needs of nuns and anchoresses to those of laypeople of either sex. But whatever its sources, the assumption in *The English Psalter* and *The Prick of Conscience* that members of the laity should be allowed to investigate their faith in detail—that the information these texts provide should be open to the whole community defined by the use of English—suggests an important extension of the program outlined by Pecham and Thoresby.

The relations between traditions of individual and collective reform are a major theme of the most immediately influential work of the later fourteenth century, Langland's *Piers Plowman* (excerpt 3.19, 1370–85, or later), probably written (like the *South English Legendary,* excerpt 2.15) partly in Worcestershire (southwest Midlands), as well as in London (Hanna 1994). This poem at once uses and critiques the catechetical method of Pecham's *Syllabus,* which lists the material all Christians need to know—such as the Creed, the Ten Commandments, the names of the seven sins, the Our Father and Hail Mary—in a way that, from Langland's viewpoint, cannot avoid the risk of implying that the Christian faith can be learned by rote: that knowing and following a mere list can be sufficient for salvation.

Piers Plowman is thus one of the first works to argue in English against the formalism of authoritative structures developed in Latin. Drawing on a tradition of affective theology going back to the twelfth century that gave new importance to *sapientia* as distinct from *scientia*—heart knowledge, not head knowledge (Simpson 1986; Savage 1994; Rudd 1994; Watson 1997a)—Langland, like Rolle, found explicit ways to think of the religious life of the "lewed" as possessing the potential for growth long associated with professional religious. *Sapientia,* which did not require formal theological training (though it benefited from the material provided by texts like *The English Psalter* or *Piers Plowman* itself) was available to all. Associated with the body, the emotions, women, and Christ's human nature (a grouping that comes together clearly in Passion meditations for women such as *A Talking of the Love of God,* excerpt 3.1), *sapientia* was also figured by the mother tongue and its audience; this is implied in Julian's *Revelation of Love* (excerpts 1.13 and 3.4, c. 1382–after 1393). For Langland, writing in English entails thinking not just about the national Christian community, but also about how reform of this collectivity is *in tension* with individual reform. The latter is based on going beyond the morality catechesis seeks to enforce, in order to ask harder questions of oneself, of God, or of language in the process of gaining *sapientia.* One could see Langland's work in conservative terms, as part of the long process endorsed by ecclesiastics and pursued by a burgeoning nation-state in which the laity assumed ever greater importance in church affairs (Duffy 1992). But much of the energy of *Piers Plowman* and the excitement it caused lies in its desire to explore both the necessity and the divisiveness of a situation to which the poem itself contributes, where the religious knowledge circulating ever more freely in English for the benefit of individual readers was coming to be at odds with the communal concerns of pastoral theology. In *Piers Plowman* we have both a demonstration of the moment at which English, notionally the language of the "lewed," challenges this definition of its role, and an analysis of the consequences.

Religious Writing, 1380–1520

By the 1380s several ideas of the vernacular and its growing community of readers were thus circulating in a rapidly expanding body of writing. English was the language of the "commons," the heterogeneous group who took part in the rising of 1381, uniting against the oppressions of aristocratic and monastic landowners; Steven Justice's analysis of the "acts of assertive literacy" constituted by the rebels' famous letters, which pointedly declare their peasant origins, suggests continuity between this view and Mannyng's earlier association of English with servitude (Justice 1994, 4). But English could also be claimed as the language of the nation, a powerful patriotic bond uniting commons, aristocracy, and crown against enemies from abroad. The first explicit assertion of this view may be the prologue to

Lydgate's *Troy Book* (excerpt 1.7, c. 1412). But the unifying force of English also underwrites John Trevisa's *Dialogue Between the Lord and the Clerk* (excerpt 2.2, 1387) and other works that annex the affective sense of community associated with English—given aesthetic focus in Usk's *Testament of Love* (excerpt 1.4)—to the interests of a ruling class. The *Dialogue* in particular strongly suggests that the ecclesiastical developments outlined above were to some extent paralleled by a reappraisal of the usefulness of English on the part of the country's secular leaders. Conversely, English was the language of catechesis, in which educated priests instructed laity in the simple truths of the faith: a structure in which the laity and their language were conceptualized as "carnal" and illiterate, the flesh waiting to be animated by the spirit. But it was also the language of *sapientia,* whose status as the "kynde langage" of the laity, whom Christ came to save, gave it a potentially radical role in constituting a body of the faithful defined not hierarchically but according to inner rectitude. *Piers Plowman* (excerpt 3.19, an English poem with many Latin quotations and material in French) is an early expression of this view, but the idea of the church as a community of the faithful, not a hierarchical institution, is there in Rolle's *English Psalter* (excerpt 3.8) and is basic to many texts from the 1380s and 1390s (see *Pore Caityf,* excerpt 3.6; *The Cloud of Unknowing,* excerpt 3.3; Julian's *Revelation,* excerpt 1.13; and the *Wycliffite Bible,* excerpt 1.15). The link between this definition of the church and language politics is made most directly in *Book to a Mother* (West Midlands, 1370s), written by a priest to his widowed mother. The *Book* justifies its use of English to castigate the sins of the clergy by stating: "Latin is a langage, as Walsh and Englisch; but though a man kunne speke muche Walsch, he is never the grettur clerk but he kepe Godis hestis; so thei bi the same skile, though thei kunne speke muche Latin, but thei live wel thei ben nevere the gretter clerkes" (McCarthy 1981, 79.24–80.4). All these definitions of the role and meaning of the vernacular need to be read in light of the pragmatic developments in the use of English by institutions such as Chancery, which seem to have been of real importance from about this time (although Chancery itself may have been a less important instrument of language standardization than is generally claimed, for example, by Fisher [1984]). But however we assess these developments, and for all the ideological gaps between the different views of English sketched here, it is clear that long before the standardization of much written English in the early fifteenth century—and long before Chaucer became a well-known literary figure even in London—an idea of the language as a single entity, constituting a single community, was established in a number of very different contexts.

From 1380 on, these and other ideas about the English language (its readers, its capacity, the ways it ought to be used) came into violent collision, and over the next decades were forced into a long process of systematization, in which almost all concerned eventually had to take sides as proponents or opponents of the vernacular's capacity to provide theoretically universal access to religious knowledge (see Somerset 1998). This process was partly initiated by the Oxford theologian John Wyclif, who (during the 1370s, under the protection of the duke of Lancaster, John of Gaunt) articulated a series of radical positions about church, state, sacraments, and scripture. These gradually fused with a number of existing dissenting traditions (some academic, others more popular) to form a movement that eventually acquired a label (Lollardy, at first a term of abuse) and a program coherent enough that the movement can be thought of as a religious sect. From 1382, when many of Wyclif's views were condemned at the Blackfriars Council in London, adherents of those views were subject to growing persecution—though this too took until after 1400 to become systematic, and similar views were sometimes expressed by other, "orthodox" writers without reprisal.

At the root of Wyclif's system (see further Hudson 1988) lie propositions that have large implications for thinking about authority, language, and writing; some of these we have already met in "orthodox" texts, a sign that the divide between Lollard and non-Lollard was not always clear-cut. As the Lollards understood it, Wyclif held that a priest was a priest by virtue of inner worth, not formal status, and analogously that the Mass (the consecration of bread and wine into the body and blood of Christ) was efficacious only for those worthy to receive it, in whose hearts Christ, not the bread itself, was manifest. It followed that (i) unworthy priests could not perform the sacraments; (ii) any worthy person was a priest and could preach or perform the sacraments (some Lollards, like the learned West Midlands farmer Walter Brut, conceded that this included women; Blamires 1992, 250–60); (iii) laypeople had the same responsibilities and so needed the same opportunities to learn about God's law as clerics. Thus a huge translation project, which included the whole Bible, commentaries on the Gospels and other books, and much else, absorbed the energies of academic Lollards from the 1380s on, a project that pointed to texts like Rolle's *English Psalter,* excerpt 3.8, as precedents but was of a different order of scholarly exactitude (for defenses of this project, see the *Wycliffite Bible,* excerpt 1.15; *On Translating the Bible Into English,* excerpt 2.4; *The Holi Prophete David Seith,* excerpt 2.5). Since the church's role was to be confined to spiritual matters, not temporal ones like property, the responsibility of the king, it also followed that (iv) the king could oversee the church's use of temporal property, even to disendow the church (in practice, this was an attack on the monastic orders in particular); (v) criticism of the church by the laity, and in writings meant for the laity, was to be encouraged. Much of the writing emanating from circles associated with Lollardy (and its opponents) is thus satirical; vernacular critiques of church and sometimes state introduced a new vocabulary of dissent (related to, but distinct from, the "estates" satire tradition drawn on by Langland and Chaucer) into English. Finally, since the laity needed to learn in the same way as the clergy, and since it was the Bible, not tales of saints, that was the basis of the faith, it was argued (vi) that images of the saints (referred to as "books for the unlearned"; see *Dives and Pauper,* excerpt 3.9, 1405 or 1410) should not be venerated and (vii) that pilgrimages and religious plays were abuses. In association with this rethinking of the roles of church, state, and the laity, written English was both radicalized and transformed over the next few decades, acquiring new lexis and tighter syntactic patterns, as an energetic group of reformers used it as a tool for the dissemination of religious information on a grand scale, and as writers not associated with the Lollard movement (from Thomas Usk and John Gower to Julian of Norwich and the author of *Dives and Pauper*) added their own, equally opinionated voices.[7]

The events of the period 1380–1410 are too complex to summarize here, although some of them are described in the headnotes to individual excerpts (for further reflections, see also Aers and Staley 1996). The period is one of intense literary activity, in London and Oxford and elsewhere, comprising not only Lollard writing but the poetry of Langland, Chaucer, Gower, and the *Gawain* poet; a great deal of other religious prose, much of it written in the first instance for or by women religious; and secular didactic texts like the prose translations of Trevisa (excerpt 2.2), Chaucer's *Melibee*, alliterative poems (see, e.g., *The Wars of Alexander,* excerpt 3.13), or Usk's *Testament* (excerpt 1.4, c. 1385). The Lollard texts were produced and copied systematically, in a dialect chosen to be as widely comprehensible as possible. This is the Central Midlands Standard dialect, which by 1400 was itself increasingly similar to the dialect of London used by Chaucer (Samuels 1963; Fisher 1984; Hudson 1985, 181–91) and, as the first widely dispersed standard written English since the eleventh century, represents the practical culmination of a century of reflection on the meanings of the vernacular. The writers were educated clerics, their backers members of the gentry (although after the so-called rebellion of Sir John Oldcastle in 1413 the future of the movement lay further down the social scale).[8] But while these texts articulate an ideology of universal access to learning, it is unclear how far Lollard vernacular writers ever really created anything resembling the reading community they projected, in which the populism that comes to the fore in later Lollard texts made common cause with the plans of wealthier lay Lollards. Images of community related to this Lollard vision haunt the literature of the period: not only in *The Canterbury Tales* (where low- and highborn mix freely) and other high-culture works such as *Cleanness* (where the lord calls both rich and poor to his banquet), but in didactic texts like *Pore Caityf* (excerpt 3.6) and the *Sermon of Dead Men* (excerpt 3.11), as well as in the opposite form of pictures of a nation torn apart from within (as in Gower's *Confessio Amantis,* excerpt 2.11). Yet in practice the difficulty of Lollard texts, their use of a Latinate language different from anything most people would have spoken, not to mention their expense, suggests that the classless reading community they project remained an ideal more than a reality: that written English, as the Lollards developed it, remained a language that was more symbolically than actually capable of reaching a national audience.

---

7. For an anthology of representative Lollard texts in Middle English, see Hudson 1978. For a discussion of the fluid boundaries between Lollard and "orthodox" Middle English writing, see Watson 1995a, 847–59. There is increasing evidence of a body of reformist writing not directly associated with the Lollards but sharing certain of their preoccupations; see, for example, Fletcher 1994.

8. On how the "rebellion" of 1413 was staged by the Lancastrian government, see Strohm 1997.

It took longer for responses to Lollardy to become systematic. The first programmatically anti-Lollard vernacular text is Nicholas Love's *Mirror of the Blessed Life of Jesus Christ* (excerpt 3.10), written around 1409 and copied in the Central Midlands dialect used by Lollard scribes. As a translation of a Latin work written for a nun (Johannes de Caulibus's *Meditationes vitae Christi*), this text is perhaps the most striking example of the tendency to equate women religious and the laity as target audiences, and to think of both the laity and the vernacular as symbolically female in consequence. Earlier works ignore Lollardy (while raising many common issues) or engage with it indirectly—like Hilton's *Scale of Perfection, The Chastizing of God's Children,* or the *Pseudo-Augustinian Soliloquies* (excerpt 3.2, ?before 1410)—and it is often more useful to see these works as part of the same movement of vernacularization as Lollardy, rather than as a reaction against it. Admittedly, the very fact that anti-Lollard writing is mostly in Latin may reflect recognition of how far the movement had shown up the radical potential of English. Such a recognition is explicit in two attacks on Bible translation, written near or in Oxford by William Butler and Thomas Palmer, from the early 1400s. These present a wholly negative view of the capacity of English or its speakers to comprehend theology. Claiming that English lacked grammar, that clumsiness made it an improper medium for God's word, that the carnality of English and its speakers made impossible the abstraction necessary to understand God's meaning (often conveyed through allegory), Butler and Palmer advocated a program of repression similar to the one carried out by Archbishop Arundel in his *Constitutions* of 1409. Yet Butler and Palmer wrote not as the mouthpieces of official policy but as academics, stating views colleagues found extreme. One, Richard Ullerston, wrote a defense of Bible translation and the vernacular that appeals to Rolle's *English Psalter,* the *Lay Folk's Catechism,* and Pecham's *Syllabus* as evidence that use of English had always been endorsed by the church (see *On Translating the Bible into English,* excerpt 2.4; Watson 1995a, 840–46). Despite the efforts by crown and church to repress Lollardy and restrict circulation of Lollard texts, culminating in the parliamentary act *De heretico comburendo* (1401), it proved remarkably difficult for the anti-Lollard part of the establishment to articulate any coherent policy governing the use of the vernacular. And this must in part have been because the views espoused by Ullerston were widely held. In the teeth of the evidence, prominent ecclesiastics were for thirty years unprepared to accept any automatic association between vernacular writing and the propagation of heresy.

Much of this changed with Arundel's promulgation of the *Constitutions* in 1409: an important act of censorship whose aim was control of all writing, academic debate, preaching, and even talk about religious topics in Latin or English throughout the archdiocese of Canterbury, in the name of an orthodoxy more narrowly defined than was imaginable thirty years earlier. The legislation prohibited Bible translation and unauthorized vernacular quotation from the Bible, forbade public criticism of the clergy, and limited discussion of theological ideas; all this made writing any complex religious work in English difficult, especially for professional religious (Watson 1995a, 825–30). It was some years before the *Constitutions* (and their counterparts in the archdiocese of York) took hold, and they were partly unenforceable. Yet they seem to have been successful in limiting the quantity and scope of fifteenth-century English religious writing, or at least in keeping its ambitions and circulation local. Many of the works that did get written thus never reached, and were not meant to reach, the wide public who were still reading the great fourteenth-century classics such as *The Prick of Conscience* (excerpt 3.7) and the *Wycliffite Bible* (excerpt 1.15).

East Anglian writers of the 1430s–50s, such as Osbern Bokenham (excerpt 1.11), John Capgrave (excerpt 2.7), and Margery Kempe (excerpts 1.14 and 3.22), found regional audiences, while Eleanor Hull's translations from French (excerpt 3.21, 1440s) survive in a copy partly made by a friend. Yet if two works of c. 1420–50 written for the privileged royal foundation of Syon Abbey, *The Orchard of Syon* (excerpt 3.5) and *The Mirror of Our Lady* (excerpt 3.12), were later printed, others associated with the same milieu, the *Speculum Devotorum* (excerpt 1.12, 1415–25) or the complete translation of Mechtild of Hackeborn's *Book of Ghostly Grace* (excerpt 3.20), remained rarities. The same is true of *The Amesbury Letter* (excerpt 2.9, early sixteenth century), which evokes a tradition of writing for individual religious women so carefully that it could have been written any time after the twelfth century. And even Bishop Fox's scholarly translation of *The Rule of St. Benet* (excerpt 2.8, 1517), written by a prominent ecclesiastic, still ostensibly claims a local target audience and purpose, for all the ambition that lies just behind its humanist translation agenda. There are ambitious theological works from the period, even apart from sixteenth-century reformist writing (which it is unfortunately not possible to consider here). One of these, Love's *Mirror* (excerpt 3.10), enjoyed prestige as an official vernacular theology—as an embodiment of the beliefs and devotional practices held suitable for vernacular readers—while a few other texts, including the *Seven Points of Everlasting Wisdom* (written, like Love's *Mirror,* at Mount Grace) and the many versions of Jean Gerson's *Ars moriendi* (Art of dying) circulated widely. There is also one major body of material that apparently remained unaffected by the *Constitutions*, perhaps because it was performed (not read), predated 1409, and was a civic, as well as ecclesiastical, product: the biblical drama associated with the feast of Corpus Christi (Rubin 1991, 243–87). These plays—the York and Chester cycles and the plays associated with Wakefield—were produced by urban craft guilds, mainly in northern England; another collection, "N-Town," can be localized in East Anglia (like *Croxton,* excerpt 2.14), and was probably not performed by a craft guild but testifies to the importance of urban dramatized spectacle throughout the period. Yet, despite these and other evidences of continuing interest in religious writing and performance, of the two most individual religious projects written between 1420 and 1500, Reginald Pecock's vast attempt at an English systematic theology (comprising the *Donet, The Folower,* and other works, 1440s–50s; see excerpt 1.16) and *The Book of Margery Kempe* (excerpts 1.14 and 3.22, 1430s), the author of the first was found guilty of heresy, while the second survives in a single manuscript and was nearly not written.

Despite the evidence of deep interest in theological and ecclesiastical matters by fifteenth-century readers of English (like the owners of some two hundred and fifty surviving manuscripts of all or part of the *Wycliffite Bible*, excerpt 1.15), writers of vernacular theological works in this period were thus in retreat from the radicalism of the late fourteenth century, and seem mostly to have accepted—or to have pretended to accept—a view of the capacity of English and its readers less bold than the one held by Langland, Rolle, or even William of Nassington. This is the view presented in Love's *Mirror* (excerpt 3.10, effectively endorsing the conservative position taken by Butler and Palmer described above), in which readers of English cannot aspire to understand theological abstractions or confront the scriptures directly, since they are only "symples creatures the wheche as childrene haven nede to be fedde with mylk of lyght doctrine, and not with sadde [serious] mete of gret clergie and of hye contemplacion" (9–11). Admittedly, there are few signs that the church tried to impose this view directly on gentry or aristocratic lay readers of vernacular texts; vernacular theologies from the fourteenth century (such as Hilton's *Scale of Perfection*) were indeed copied by Carthusian and other monks partly for lay consumption (see further pages 359–62 below). But this hierarchical model of the relation between clerical and lay, Latin and vernacular, remained the official line and could be applied with rigor outside the circle of privilege comprising aristocracy, gentry, and urban merchant classes. Records of heresy trials through the century provide testimony to the sacrifices people made to obtain books, but also show how suspicious the authorities could be, despite Pecham's *Syllabus* or Thoresby's *Injunctions*, of any sign of literacy or religious knowledge among peasants and artisans. At this level of society, not only Lollard books but texts like *Pore Caityf* (excerpt 3.6) or even *The Canterbury Tales* could not be read without provoking suspicion of heresy (see Hudson 1985, 142; 1988, 417–20, 485). The frequent reprintings of catechetical texts like the *Primer* from the last decades of the fifteenth century on (Duffy 1992) show that religious authorities believed in education. But they did so in a context in which the written vernacular was always liable to be seen as a dangerous instrument that needed to be corralled by any mechanism available. Tudor attempts at censorship, like Tudor heresy trials, grew out of a long tradition of ecclesiastical and state attempts to control written English.

Chaucer and the Idea of English as a Literary Language

This account has so far omitted all but occasional mention of the figure who, from just after his death until the present, has regularly been ascribed a central role in the rise of written English, Chaucer. This is not because Chaucer's career and the history of the English vernacular described above are not intimately interconnected. On the contrary, his literary career was decisively shaped by this history, just as he posthumously became an important factor in its future course. *The Book of the Duchess* (c. 1369), written for Wyclif's patron John of Gaunt, is one of the earlier datable works in English to be composed for a member of the upper aristocracy. Chaucer's sources here are determinedly French, and his later works come to borrow from Italian and Latin texts but never acknowledge a debt to English ones (unless in the parodic romance stanzas of *Sir Thopas*). Yet behind his writing lies careful reading of English texts, many of them produced in London; texts similar to those in the Auchinleck manuscript (1330–40s, including *Sir Orfeo;* Pearsall 1992, 73–77) and *Piers Plowman* (excerpt 3.19; Grady 1996) are the best attested examples, as well as (later) the *Confessio Amantis* (excerpt 2.11) and *The Testament of Love* (excerpt 1.4). Both these last were written by two poets he knew, as he may have known Langland. Living in London, and associated with prominent early Lollard sympathizers (including the poet Sir John Clanvowe and others of Richard II's chamber knights; Pearsall 1992, 181–85), Chaucer, in his works, also shows awareness of the religious controversies of the day, especially in *The Parson's Prologue* and *Tale, The Wife of Bath's Prologue* and *Tale,* and the G prologue to *The Legend of Good Women* (all 1390s). These suggest detailed interest in the theological, social, and linguistic positions advanced by the Lollards. In the G prologue, which announces the work as an abbreviated paraphrase of classical narratives by promising "The naked text in English to declare / Of many a story" (*PLGW* G 86–87), Chaucer may even be suggesting an ironic parallel between a view of himself as a *"grant translateur"* of Western secular literary culture and the Lollard translation project.[9]

Chaucer was an important technical innovator: the first to use the decasyllabic couplet for narrative poetry; the first English writer influenced by the Italian literary renaissance heralded by Dante's *De vulgari eloquentia;* the first to attempt a long narrative poem, *Troilus and Criseyde,* that asks to be compared (however humbly) with the poetry of "Virgile, Ovide, Omer, Lucan, and Stace" (V.1792). Importing numerous words into English while also worrying over the "gret diversite / In English and in writyng of oure tonge" (V.1793–94), he helped create an artificial mode of written English that influenced the course of English poetry as decisively as Lollard vernacular writings—equally innovative in their syntax and use of neologisms—sought to influence that of its religious prose. Yet, as is true too of the Lollards, most of his literary attitudes had English antecedents. As Christopher Cannon (1996) has noted, the percentage of neologisms borrowed from French and Latin in his works is no larger than is typical of fourteenth-century writers from Robert Mannyng (excerpt 1.1) on, who typically use neologisms

---

9. The phrase "naked text" perhaps deliberately critiques the Lollard emphasis on the literal sense (the "nakid wordes") of Scripture: see Delany 1994, soon to be corrected by Andrew Cole. For the phrase *grant translateur,* used of Chaucer by his friend Deschamps, see Wimsatt 1991, 242–72.

both for practical purposes and to create an elevation or internationalization of their idiom. In this regard it is Langland (who progressively rids his style of its specialized alliterative vocabulary and tends to avoid linguistic innovation) who is exceptional. Nor was Chaucer the single fourteenth-century English writer to be preoccupied with the canonical status of his texts or to express an interest in their stability. He was less practical in his concern for his poetry than his colleague Gower, who retained careful control of the copying and distribution of his works (excerpt 2.11)—whereas Chaucer left several of his major poems unfinished and never fixed the order of his last long work, *The Canterbury Tales*. Historians like Mannyng (excerpt 1.1) and the Scots poet John Barbour (excerpt 1.2), who see themselves as memorialists of the past, are also concerned that their work endure so that it can do its job, while *Sir Gawain and the Green Knight,* for all its emphasis on oral tale-telling, presents itself as the written form of a story whose cohesion and fidelity to traditional language ensures its survival: "I shal telle hit astit as I in toun herde / With tonge, / As it is stad and stoken / In stori stif and stronge / With lel letteres loken / In londe so hatz ben longe" (31–36: I shall tell it now as I heard it told aloud in town, as it is established and fixed in a firm and strong story, locked in with trustworthy words long used in this land). Other poems in the alliterative tradition, such as *The Wars of Alexander* (excerpt 3.13) and *The Destruction of Troy,* show an interest equal to Chaucer's in translating the major historical "matters" (the grand narratives) of western Europe into English. *The Canterbury Tales* is not the earliest story collection in English—Chaucer may have known two predecessors, the *South English Legendary* (excerpt 2.15) and *Handlyng Synne.* Other bodies of poetry are as technically innovative as Chaucer's; an outstanding example is the tradition of fourteenth-century lyric writing (whose history is traced in Fein 1997), whose most famous manifestations are the *Harley Lyrics* (c. 1320s) and *Pearl* (c. 1380s). And even the celebrated Chaucerian irony and self-deprecation—which importantly extends to deprecation of the English vernacular (as in the *Complaint of Venus,* excerpt 1.3: 8–11)—is suggestively similar to the narratorial tone taken by Langland, who might himself have been influenced by Rolle.

What made Chaucer so important to English literary history may have had less to do with any belief he had in himself as the founder of a self-conscious vernacular poetic tradition than with his *invention* as a founding figure, shortly after his death, by poets such as Hoccleve and Lydgate (on whom, see excerpts 1.6 and 1.7). These poets cultivated a relationship of dependence on Chaucer by depicting him as a poet worth citing and imitating, as Chaucer cited and imitated the classical *auctores,* Virgil and Ovid (but not overtly his English predecessors). In doing so, they announced the arrival of English as a vernacular of a value comparable to that of French or Italian (which had their own founding texts, *The Romance of the Rose* and *The Divine Comedy*). They brushed aside the achievements of earlier writers as mere prehistory (a still influential view), transforming Chaucer's fluid attitude toward English vocabulary by systematically reusing his coinages, so that they became fixed features of the language (Cannon 1996). In the wake of Hoccleve and Lydgate, a large number of fifteenth-century poets took care to identify their work as belonging to this tradition, adopting Chaucer's verse forms (especially the *Troilus* stanza, rhyme royal), taking over his vocabulary (which they amplified with further aureate borrowings from Latin, following Lydgate), and declaring their inevitable inferiority to him. The examples in the present volume (not even counting the excerpts from Middle Scots, discussed below) suggest the variety of materials treated in this "Chaucerian" way: philosophy (Walton's translation of Boethius, excerpt 1.5), romance (Metham's *Amoryus and Cleopes,* excerpt 1.8), advice literature (Ashby's *Active Policy of a Prince,* excerpt 1.9), saints' lives (Bokenham's *Legendys of Hooly Wummen,* excerpt 1.11), military treatises (*Knyghthode and Bataile,* excerpt 2.12), devotional verse (the pseudo-Lydgatian *Nightingale,* excerpt 2.13). Thus, at the same time that the composition of vernacular theological writings was coming under intense pressure from Arundel's *Constitutions,* a new verse tradition was gathering the momentum to dominate much of the fifteenth century. Interestingly, the poet announced as the founder of that tradition—a man who shared a patron (John of Gaunt) with Wyclif, as he shared many of his interests with some of Wyclif's followers—was part of the same fourteenth-century literary scene that included the authors of the religious texts Arundel sought to suppress.

A good deal of attention has recently been paid to the politics of Chaucer's canonization as "founder" of English letters and the part this canonization played in legitimating the Lancastrian dynasty founded by Henry IV after his overthrow and murder of Richard II in 1399 (see Strohm 1982, 1992; Lawton 1987; Fisher 1992b; Pearsall 1994). Particular stress is laid on the role of Henry's son, the future Henry V, who commissioned Lydgate's *Troy Book* (excerpt 1.7) and Hoccleve's *Regement of Princes* and who may have consciously cultivated a nationalistic "language policy" as part of a broad attempt to unify the most powerful elements in English political life around the new regime. The most widely read English poet in 1400 was almost certainly not Chaucer but Langland, whose poem, written in an alliterative plain style well adapted for circulation among different social classes across the country, aroused intense interest. *Piers Plowman* (see excerpt 3.19), its hero an English laborer, its main topic the need to reunite English society in service to God, was a truly national work, and it is likely that Hoccleve studied it closely. Yet the poem's vision of society from the bottom up, its similarities to Lollard thinking, its free use of satire and preoccupation with contemporary concerns, all made it an impossible choice as the founding work of a literature whose interests were inevitably to be those of the governing classes.[10] (Despite the satirical tradition that stemmed from it, the poem does not aspire to

---

10. For the early circulation of *Piers Plowman,* see Hanna 1994. For editions of several late-fourteenth- and early-fifteenth-century poems influenced by *Piers Plowman,* all of them satirical, see Barr 1993.

found a literary "school," or show any great interest in the concept of a literary tradition in the way Chaucer does.) Despite his early shift of allegiance to the Lancastrians, Gower's English poetry was also unsuitable, at least on its own: the *Confessio Amantis* (excerpt 2.11) makes its own use of social complaint and satire and addresses its elite audience from the perspective not of the crown or nobility but that of the "commons," offering advice to church and crown with a freedom that fifteenth-century literature was not encouraged to emulate. Chaucer's poems, on the other hand, emanated from close to the court of Henry IV's predecessor and were written in an international style based on French verse forms and making learned use of Latin and Italian sources. Unlike Langland or Gower, Chaucer was not a spokesman for a particular part of society; indeed, despite allusions to contemporary controversies in his poems, he was unusual among late-fourteenth-century English writers in the degree to which he avoided direct discussion of his times. For the Lancastrians, promoting Chaucer could thus symbolize their continuity with at least the best elements of Ricardian court culture and their determination to assert the stature of England on the international stage, while allowing them to endorse a literary mode apparently distanced from social or political radicalism. "Chaucerian" literature, elegantly removed from the language of the English peasantry by its use of French loanwords, could help to unite crown, aristocracy, gentry, urban elites, and church in a common culture that was at once distinct from and equal to the culture of its major international rival, France.

It is true that elements of Chaucer's works needed downplaying in the morally serious and submissive culture Henry V especially hoped to generate: the eroticism, obscenity, lack of didactic aim, and freethinking philosophical range of some of his poetry could not easily be found a place in the new national order. But this was no disadvantage, since it gave Chaucer's successors a role as purifiers, as well as continuers, of his work, just as Henry saw himself as a purifier of the English crown, corrupted by Richard's moral turpitude. Although their goal was the creation of a literary tradition, not its suppression, in this sense Hoccleve and especially Lydgate performed a role that paralleled the one played by Arundel, moving court poetry away from satire and moral ambiguity toward a more generalized didacticism and concern for the national interest (Strohm 1982). And if Hoccleve's career bespeaks some disillusion with this project (see his *Complaint*, excerpt 1.6), Lydgate's huge oeuvre was more than enough to fill the gap, providing amplified, aureate English versions of text after text in a career devoted to the aggrandizement of the literary culture he represented. By midcentury, Lydgate and Gower (a monk and a member of the gentry) had joined Chaucer (the crowned laureate) as members of a triumvirate of literary "fathers" (see Ashby, *Active Policy of a Prince*, excerpt 1.9: 28–41) paralleling the alliance of crown, church, and gentry on which society was ostensibly founded.

Fifteenth-century secular literature is thus strikingly different from the writing it takes as its notional source, despite its repeated assertions of imitativeness, belatedness, and dullness (Lerer 1993). Yet it is also varied, not only in the subject matter it deals with but in the relationships writers negotiate with the literary language and its history. It has regional manifestations, such as the East Anglian "school" of Capgrave (excerpt 2.7), Bokenham (excerpt 1.11), and Metham (excerpt 1.8), who adapted Lydgatian language to suit their situation as writers whose audience was the local gentry and members of religious houses. Its public was broad enough to allow the emergence of a large body of specialized scientific and utilitarian works, represented in this book by excerpts from a gynecological treatise (*The Knowing of Woman's Kind in Childing,* excerpt 2.6), a medical compendium (Guy de Chauliac's *Cyrurgie,* excerpt 1.10), and a guide to alchemy ambitiously aimed at a national audience (Thomas Norton's *Ordinal of Alchemy,* excerpt 2.3) (Voigts 1996). While texts were increasingly copied in a single dialect, the "standard" English of London or the Central Midlands, there was a compensating breadth of stylistic register even among writers who claimed to occupy the seat of high culture. Caxton's conception of himself as a popularizer of the works he translated or introduced (see *The Book of Fayttes of Armes and of Chyvalrye,* excerpt 2.10; *The Book of the Knight of the Tower,* excerpt 2.16; *Reynard the Fox,* excerpt 3.17) becomes clear if his prose is compared with Skelton's attempt to create a learned English equivalent to humanist Latin, his *Bibliotheca Historica of Diodorus Siculus* (excerpt 3.15); indeed, the prologue to Caxton's *Eneydos* makes this view of his role (and Skelton's) explicit (see essay 4.3, pages 364–65 below). Despite the relative cultural confidence of an English language whose users are aware of this array of registers, the prestige of French literature is omnipresent, notably again in Caxton's publications, which often take French texts as the arbiter of good taste and polite behavior (Green 1980; see also Anslay's 1521 version of Christine de Pizan's *Book of the City of Ladies,* excerpt 3.24). Yet French sources can serve a national project, as with Malory's *Morte d'Arthur,* in the form printed by Caxton. This cycle of Arthurian stories, which moves out from a rendering of an English alliterative poem (the *Morte Arthure*) to encompass in abbreviated form many of the narratives found in French thirteenth-century prose romances and English historiographical genres, evokes a regionally and stylistically varied world of gentry romances that had developed along their own lines for centuries. This tradition probably owed less to Chaucer than it did to works like *Mandeville's Travels.* The composition of such a cycle by a knight— like that of the *Ordinal of Alchemy* (excerpt 2.3) by a Bristol customs controller, the *Commentary on the Penitential Psalms* (excerpt 3.21) by a gentlewoman, or the survival of the substantial collection of letters by members of the Paston family (Davis 1971–76)—is another sign of the heterogeneity of fifteenth-century literature and the extent to which writing in English had become a relatively ordinary activity among people of privilege (see Riddy 1987).

More is said about fifteenth-century literary culture, especially its gentry readers, in the next essay. This is not the place to describe the developments of the early sixteenth century: the continuing deference of English literature to the cultures of

France, Italy, and Spain; the revival of satire in verse (the poetry of Skelton) and prose (the polemics of More); the renewal of religious controversies similar to those of the late fourteenth century on an international stage (symbolized in England by Tyndale's New Testament translation), which led to the reformation of the English church and the acceptance of English as the language of worship, Bible reading, and theological discussion; the role of printing in breaking down the barriers it initially helped to strengthen, by making books so inexpensive that they were impossible to keep out of the hands of even the least privileged people; and the rise of systematic, savage but often ineffective censorship in response to the flood of subversive new writing that became available in consequence.[11] The relations between these developments and the literary culture of late medieval England that formed their backdrop are intricate but also underexplored, mostly thanks to institutional imperatives that make the year 1500 a seemingly unbridgeable divide between scholars of medieval English literature and those of early modern English literature; and, for all their relevance to the history of the English vernacular, no clear account of these relationships is possible until more work is done.

Something should be said in closing this essay, however, about the literature of Scotland, represented in this book by one excerpt from a fourteenth-century text (Barbour's *Bruce*, excerpt 1.2, c. 1375), one excerpt from a text written in the early fifteenth century (James I's *Kingis Quair*, excerpt 3.23, c. 1430), and three from the late fifteenth and early sixteenth centuries (Henryson's *Fables*, excerpt 3.18, 1450–1500; the *Spektakle of Luf*, excerpt 2.17, 1492; Douglas's *Eneados*, excerpt 3.16, 1513).[12] These are survivals from a literature much of which is lost (remarkably, *The Bruce* is the earliest datable Scots poem) and almost all of which remains only in sixteenth-century printed editions and manuscripts. Throughout the period, Scotland was divided between a Gaelic-speaking "highland" population in the North and an English-speaking "lowland" one in the South, whose dialect in the fourteenth century was similar to that of northern England; thus *The Bruce*, a patriotic poem about heroic resistance to English invaders, was written in a language not dissimilar to that of *Cursor Mundi* or *The Prick of Conscience*. Our excerpts show how, by the early sixteenth century, written Scots had attained its own standard dialect, different from the standard English of the London-Oxford-Cambridge triangle and suitable as a vehicle for a national literature that was at once intimately aware of and independent from English poetry and prose. If *The Kingis Quair* (excerpt 3.23) is influenced by Chaucer and Lydgate to the point

11. For studies of these developments, which are of particular interest for the themes presented in this volume, see, for example, Helgerson 1992; Hadfield 1994 (Tudor vernacular literature and national identity); King 1982 (literature of the Reformation); Fox 1989; Jansen 1991 (literature and politics); Bristol 1985 (theater and social class); Boureau 1989 (print culture); Crane 1993 (education and humanism).

12. For studies and anthologies of Middle Scots literature to contextualize the brief comments offered here, see Aitken 1971; Agutter 1988 (the written language); Lyall and Riddy 1981; Jack 1988; McClure and Spiller 1989 (essays on literary texts); Kratzmann 1980 (Anglo-Scottish literary relations); Bawcutt and Riddy 1987 (anthology of longer poems).

that it seems Scots only in dialect, Dunbar's *Lament for the Makeris* (1505)—which mourns the deaths of Chaucer, Lydgate, and Gower at the head of a list of otherwise Scottish poets—clearly articulates this intricate double relationship (in some ways comparable to the one between fifteenth-century English and French). When Scottish poetry marks its awareness of its position on the margins of Europe and the irony of its indebtedness to the literature of its chief enemy, England, it often does so indirectly: through conventional depictions of spring marred by cold northern weather, despite being set in June, not April; or by writing (like Henryson's) whose evocation of the literary heritage of Europe is dense with learning, yet studiedly ironic. In Douglas's *Eneados* (excerpt 3.16), however, finished only months before the disastrous Battle of Flodden Field—in which James IV of Scotland and much of the Scottish aristocracy were killed fighting the English (1513)—the status of the Scots language is confronted head on. The *Eneados* is a scholarly rendering of Virgil's *Aeneid* into a vernacular that Douglas asserts is fully adequate to the task he sets it. Writing both as an aristocratic Scottish bishop and as one of a self-consciously internationalist group of humanists, Douglas upstages both Lydgate and Chaucer by being the first to apply the new scholarly standards to the English translation of a classical epic. Singling out Caxton's *Eneydos* (1490) as a paradigmatic example of enfeebled vernacularization (see excerpt 3.16: 50–51, and essay 4.3, pages 364–65 below), he transforms England into the parochial neighbor of a cosmopolitan Scotland that has little to learn from its literature. Douglas's achievement can serve as a reminder of the continuing importance of language politics into the sixteenth century and beyond (Crawford 1998).

4.3

AUTHORS, SCRIBES, PATRONS AND BOOKS

ANDREW TAYLOR

Readers of Middle English often have to use editions that, in the nature of the case, cannot effectively represent the plethora of versions and physical formats in which medieval texts circulated. The standard edition of Chaucer's works, *The Riverside Chaucer* (Benson 1987), for instance, presents all Chaucer's texts in a uniform layout. It confines manuscript information to brief notes on textual variants and places these notes in a section of their own at the back of the volume, allowing no doubts about the authority of the texts themselves to penetrate to the pages on which they are printed. During the last twenty years, however, there has been increased attention to the physical contexts in which Middle English texts were read. Manuscripts are increasingly being seen as a means to integrate "our knowledge of medieval literature with the understanding of its contemporaneous conditions" (Doyle 1983b, 145; see also Pearsall 1983, 1–2, and Nichols and Wenzel 1996). After all, medieval books were unique objects, many of them made of a material (parchment) whose variations in size, texture, and quality in itself demanded that a book's scribes and decorators (none of whose styles were quite alike either) deal with every project in a slightly different way. Books were extremely expensive, highly prized, and very often personalized, valued as gifts, individually commissioned, and specially bequeathed to others after an owner's death; books, as well as the texts they contained, played a vital role in society.[1] This essay gives an account of the social role of manuscripts and early printed books and the processes by which they were made, processes that changed greatly during the period. If (as the first essay in Part Four argues) Middle English texts and their theoretical pro-

---

1. The growing interest in the literary implications of manuscript study parallels the renewed interest among Old French scholars in the fluidity of medieval texts (Zumthor 1972a/b, 1992; Cerquiglini 1989), as well as the more general shift toward readers discussed in the introduction to Part Two.

logues need to be read with a full sense of their "situatedness," the medieval books
in which they survive—each of them different and each of them differently interesting—must be given proper attention.

BOOK PRODUCTION AND OWNERSHIP

One of the most enduring images of medieval culture is that of the great monastic
scriptorium, where copyists, rubricators, and illuminators joined together in pious labor, meticulously copying the word of God. For modern writers, the
scriptorium often becomes a symbol of a lost social and religious unity. The media
theorist Marshall McLuhan, for example, asserted thirty years ago that "medieval corporate experience" was transformed into "modern individualism" by the
print revolution, that is, the mass dissemination of commercially printed books
(1962, 1). McLuhan's millenarian vision of a society transformed by a single new
technology is now widely challenged, but the simplistic periodization that sees the
Middle Ages as devoid of social tension and medieval people as devoid of psychological complexity or commercial motivation has not entirely disappeared, and
the image of the tranquil monastic scribe cut off from worldly cares epitomizes
this view of the Middle Ages.[2]

In fact, not all medieval books were copied by monks, and most monasteries
did not even have a special room set aside for writing; St. Albans was one of the
few in England that did. For the most part monks set up their desks in the cloister
(Knowles 1950, 522). A monastic scriptorium meant a group of writers, not a
single room or building (Ker 1960, 3–11; Knowles 1950, 520; Eisenstein 1979,
1:14–15). More important, from as early as the eleventh century, many English
monasteries also hired professional scriveners. By the thirteenth century, the monasteries were no longer the only major centers for copying, for professional
scriveners were well established in towns and universities (Doyle 1990, 1; Clanchy
1993, chap. 2). In Oxford, and probably also in Cambridge, the needs of the university led to the development of a small book industry. The booksellers, working
for a mixed market, provided both exemplars (known as *peciae*), which students
might rent and copy as a cheap way of acquiring textbooks, and books of hours,
designed for the devotion of prosperous laypeople (Pollard 1964 and 1978a, 336–
44; Donovan 1991). Many of these books appear to have been collaborative
efforts, made by several artisans working under some form of supervision. By the
early fourteenth century, if not before, scribes and booksellers in London were
also producing collaborative work. The famous Auchinleck manuscript, for ex-

----

2. The most influential argument that print brought a decisive cultural break is Eisenstein 1979.
The argument has been widely challenged; see, for example, Hindman 1991. Aers 1992b offers a telling critique of the persistent characterization of the Middle Ages as a period of simple faith and social
harmony.

ample, a large miscellaneous collection of romances and religious verse dating from c. 1330–40, was the work of six scribes, one of whom coordinated the work of the others (Pearsall and Cunningham 1977, introduction; Shonk 1985). It was once supposed that these books were produced in workshops that united several scribes under one roof, but it now seems more likely that the books were produced by the loose association of artisans working in the same area.[3] The artisans who worked in the book trade in thirteenth-century Oxford were clustered in the area on Catte Street, close to what is now the Radcliffe Camera, while those in four-teenth-century London were gathered in the area immediately north of St. Paul's. If a scribe landed a job that required assistance, he simply had to walk a few steps down the road. This kind of ad hoc collaboration is a long way from the scale of production of the later print shops, which often employed a score of artisans and produced print runs of several hundred copies, but it is a form of commercial pro-duction, although a limited one (Doyle and Parkes 1978, 200), and it is equally far from the image of the cloistered monastic scribe. The divide between the late medieval manuscript book trade and the trade in printed books is, then, less sharp than is often supposed.

As the later medieval book trade developed, monastic copying neither died out nor remained unaffected by external commercial developments. The statutes of the Benedictines in 1343 and 1444 called on superiors to set their monks to writ-ing, correcting, illuminating, and binding (Pantin 1931–33, 1:38, 74; 2:51, 205, 228; cited in Doyle 1990, 3). The contemplative order of the Carthusians was also active in the dissemination of manuscripts both to readers in orders and to pros-perous laypeople (Sargent 1976 and 1989; Doyle 1989, 113–14), and played an important role in the fifteenth-century dissemination of vernacular devotional writing. Doyle notes in English monasteries a pattern of production by "compe-tent monastic scribes, domestic employees, and occasional outsiders" that continued into the sixteenth century (1990, 12). At the same time, some monas-teries appear to have become centers for commercial book distribution. Bury St. Edmunds, for example, was a center for the copying of texts by Lydgate, although the exact relation between the monastery itself and the teams of scribes, probably paid professionals who worked in the vicinity, has still not been fully determined (Doyle 1990, 6–7; Scott 1982; Rogers 1987). Although, according to the eleventh-century abbot Abbo of Fleury, copying a book "was, like prayer and fasting, a means for correcting one's unruly passions" (Leclercq 1961, 154), for the most part copying books in the late Middle Ages was a business.

Books in the Middle Ages were not all great illuminated treasures, but they were still precious and expensive; many were handed down carefully in wills—indeed

---

3. Laura Hibbard Loomis (1942), who first noticed the collaboration in the Auchinleck manuscript (Edinburgh, National Library of Scotland MS Advocates 19.2.1), attributed it to shops, small ateliers in which six or so scribes would work under one roof. While there is evidence of such ateliers in Paris and the Low Countries, it seems unlikely that the English book trade had developed to this stage; see Shonk 1985 and Christianson 1989.

most books in the Middle Ages were secondhand (Bühler 1960, 33). Chaucer gives some sense of the value of books when he says that to the Clerk of Oxenford, it

> . . . was levere have at his beddes heed   levere preferable to have
> Twenty bookes, clad in blak or reed,
> Of Aristotle and his philosophie,
> Than robes riche, or fithele, or gay sautrie. (*General Prologue* I [A] 293–96)

Chaucer does not say the clerk actually *had* twenty books, only that he desired them more than other forms of wealth, and in fact a library of twenty books was rare. A century later, this would still have been a large personal collection. When he died in 1493, Sir Roger Townshend left a diverse personal library of forty-four books, some printed and some manuscript, but he was a wealthy lawyer, and a collection of half a dozen law books would still have been considered quite respectable for most of his colleagues (Moreton 1991). Even the holdings of institutional libraries were small by modern standards. The library of Ramsey Abbey had 607 volumes; the cathedral and priory at Durham had 951, but Norwich Priory had only 49 books, and one or two hundred books was a respectable collection for either a monastery or a college (Ker 1964, xx–xxiii). Still smaller numbers of books were to be found in female religious houses.[4] The limited number of books in circulation is one reason medieval reading was often "intensive" rather than "extensive," with people reading the same books over and over again (Darnton 1986, drawing on Engelsing 1973).

Lay access to books was often indirect. Although by the fifteenth century literacy was coming to be the norm for people of a certain social status, recent research suggests that it was much more narrowly socially circumscribed than was once supposed. Even among the Lollards only about one man in five and one woman in thirty-three can be positively identified as literate (McSheffrey 1995b). Laypeople often heard books read aloud or paraphrased, as did Margery Kempe (excerpts 1.14 and 3.22), who, although the daughter of a mayor, probably could not read. Not that this mode of reading by hearing was necessarily perceived as a disadvantage: in a world in which most reading still took place aloud in groups (Coleman 1996), hearing books was often preferred to reading them oneself, even by the highly literate. After the Fourth Lateran Council (1215), there was a huge demand for works of religious instruction both in Latin and in the vernacular, for the use of priests and mendicant preachers (Pantin 1955, 189–243; Boyle 1985; Shaw 1985). In many cases these works took the form of cheap personal volumes, but there are also examples of huge and expensive miscellanies such as the mag-

---

4. For books that belonged to medieval English nunneries (or, in many cases, to individual nuns), see Bell 1995. Bell's study should not be interpreted too pessimistically, since it depends largely on marks of ownership within manuscripts and wills, thus excluding quite large numbers of books we know to have been in circulation among nuns (such as *Ancrene Wisse*).

nificent Vernon manuscript (Oxford, Bodleian Library MS Eng. Poet. a 1) and the closely related Simeon manuscript (London, British Library MS Addit. 22283). Each of these two late-fourteenth-century volumes weighs nearly fifty pounds, and each forms a small library in its own right, offering a range of religious texts, some suited for declaiming to large groups, others for reading alone or with intimates (Pearsall 1977, 140–43; Doyle 1974; Blake 1990). The visual display enhanced the authority of the religious message and had a powerful symbolic significance both for those who could not read the books and did not handle them directly and for the literate.[5]

Many people copied texts for themselves, and we have a number of plain collections whose casual appearance suggests they were made strictly for personal use. One example may be the copy of Eleanor Hull's religious translations from French (excerpt 3.21); another is a well-known miscellany of romances and religious works copied by the bibliophile Robert Thornton (Thompson 1994a). These personal books include a number of collections of songs and carols, almost never with music (Taylor 1991), and more miscellaneous collections, sometimes loosely called "commonplace books," whose contents might include recipes, medical information, historical notes, fragments of poetry, sermons, moral tags or commonplaces, or just about anything (Rigg 1968; Cameron 1980).

Some of the more prosperous laypeople simply commissioned professional scribes to copy the works they wanted. Letters survive from the scribe William Ebesham to Sir John Paston II (1442–79) specifying the work he has done making "the grete boke," an expensive collection of works on heraldry and chivalry, now identified as British Library MS Lansdowne 285 (Lester 1984, 36–37). Often, however, a patron relied on a network of religious advisers and dependents. One of the earliest known owners of a copy of Nicholas Love's *Mirror of the Blessed Life of Jesus Christ* (excerpt 3.10), for example, was Joan, countess of Kent, whose brother, Thomas de Holand, was one of the cofounders of Mount Grace, where Love was prior (Sargent 1992, xxviii). Thomas's sister, Margaret, duchess of Clarence, had her religious adviser, Symon Winter, a brother in the Bridgettine double house of Syon, compose a life of Saint Jerome for her (Keiser 1985; Tarvers 1992, 311–12). John Capgrave, prior of Lynn and author of several saints' lives (see excerpt 2.7), personally copied and corrected works for his patrons. In turn, wealthy patrons supplied religious with books; Margaret bought the brothers of Syon a Bible at Winter's request. A patron might develop this relation one step further, becoming in effect a publisher or promoter of a favored writer (Lucas 1982). Margaret encouraged others to read Symon's life of Jerome and to have copies made. The great fourteenth-century magnate Sir Thomas Berkeley not only supported the translator John Trevisa (see excerpt 2.2) but encouraged the distri-

---

5. For the powerful authority of the book as a physical object, see the forthcoming study by Richard Green, *A Crisis of Truth: Literature and Law in Ricardian England,* chap. 7; for the social conflict over literacy see Justice 1994, esp. chap. 1.

bution of his works, possibly even bringing copies to London scribes and circulating them among his friends (Hanna 1989b).

A handwritten book, in other words, was even more "a carrier of relationships" than a printed one, and circulated along lines of patronage, friendship, or kinship that it in turn reinforced.[6] Books were not only sufficiently valuable to be bequeathed, but were recognized to be especially suitable as legacies because of their religious content. Lord Scrope went so far as to commission books in his will so that they might be given away (Harris 1989, 164–65). The most striking example of a type of book that reinforces social bonds, however, is the common-profit book, a religious text loaned to an individual, for as long as he or she might need it, in exchange for prayers for the donor and on the condition the book be passed on (Scase 1992). One example is London, British Library MS Harley 2236, which includes *Pore Caityf* (see excerpt 3.6; for another example, see pages 360–61 below).

Even copying a book could be a social act, as it was with the Findern anthology, a fifteenth-century poetic anthology that belonged to the Findern family in Derbyshire, which was copied by a combination of professional scriveners and amateurs, at least two of them women (Beadle and Owen 1977). Rossell Hope Robbins wondered whether "young women of these neighbouring families, when visiting Findern, copied into the big book texts of poems which they enjoyed, from MSS. of their own or MSS. borrowed for the occasion" (1954, 628). Further investigation of the manuscript suggests his hypothesis may be correct (Harris 1983, 318, 327 n. 121). The anthology commemorated the social relationship of a small reading circle, which may also have been a small writing circle, since it is possible that many of the poems were composed by the women who copied them (McNamer 1991).

Booklets and the Beginnings of Speculative Publication

The medieval book trade, as has often been noted, was almost entirely "bespoke" (Pollard 1978b, 9; Blake 1989, 404); as the examples given above suggest, books were normally copied, just as texts were often composed, at the personal request of patrons. Producing a massive compendium such as the Auchinleck manuscript on the hopes of finding a buyer would have been too risky; it must therefore have been personally commissioned. There are, however, signs that by the fifteenth century and perhaps earlier the commercial book trade developing in London was beginning to rely on a predictable readership and to produce at least some work

---

6. The phrase "a carrier of relationships" is used by Natalie Davis (1975, 192) and discussed by Jennifer Summit (1995, 163). See the influential statement on the "sociology of the text" by D. F. McKenzie (1981, 82), and see McKenzie 1990 on the differences between the sociology of the manuscript and that of the printed text.

on speculation. Although bespoke copying had often been a commercial arrangement and the language of patronage continued to be influential well beyond the end of the Middle Ages, the move toward a more open market was underway.

The trend was greatly assisted by the production of small booklets, unbound quires usually devoted to a single work, which could be purchased cheaply and then brought together to form a larger volume. Such booklets appear in the thirteenth-century (Robinson 1980), and by the fifteenth century there is evidence that the market for booklets was expanding (Smith 1966, 234–41; Boffey and Thompson 1989, 288–90; Hanna 1996). The alliterative romance *The Awntyrs off Arthure at the Terne Wathelyne,* for example, was originally part of a collection from the third quarter of the fifteenth century that also contained works by Gower, Hoccleve, and Lydgate and prose reworkings of Lydgate's *Siege of Thebes* and *Troy Book* (see excerpt 1.7), and had been assembled from a number of booklets that were part of a stationer's regular stock (Smith 1966; Doyle 1982, 97); and single texts in booklet format were common (see excerpts 1.8 and 3.13).

There is also evidence of some standardization, both of the contents and the presentation of volumes. By the mid–fifteenth century a standard format had been developed for the layout of the pages of many luxury manuscripts, facilitating the work of the illuminators (Scott 1982, 364 n. 92). The illuminations themselves also appear to have been standardized in some cases (Harris 1989, 181; Lawton 1983). The low survival rate of medieval manuscripts makes it hard to be confident of circulation patterns, but certain items and combinations of items reappear so often in fifteenth-century manuscripts that they can scarcely reflect the personal taste of individual patrons. It is not just that certain works, like Love's *Mirror* (excerpt 3.10), were widely known and widely copied; certain combinations of texts turn up again and again.[7] The large miscellanies, such as Cambridge Ff. 2.38, that could provide a family with a range of reading, almost single-volume libraries, show the same combinations of pious romances, catechetical and devotional texts, and works of moral guidance and good manners (McSparran and Robinson 1979; Duffy 1992, 70).

All this suggests the development of commercial norms recognized both by those in the book trade and by their customers. The late medieval book trade had not yet become a mass market, but it was no longer entirely bespoke either.

Book Distribution and Social Control

The distribution of books in the later Middle Ages became more systematized as well. In the thirteenth century the church developed a system for distributing authorized religious texts, especially recent decrees, among the clergy. Archdeacons

---

7. The fifteen items that make up Pepys MS 1584 all reappear in Cambridge University Library Ff. 2.38 (Kreuzer 1938, 78–79), but this merely suggests a common source. It is the more general pattern of loose but recurring groupings (such as those in Cambridge University Library MS Ff. 2.38; the Auchinleck

were charged with keeping exemplars from which individual clerics could make personal copies, and the exemplars were periodically corrected. John Thoresby, archbishop of York, may have used this system to distribute the English verse translation of the Latin catechism he compiled in 1357, *The Lay Folks' Catechism* (see essay 4.2, page 336 above; Hughes 1988, 155, 170; Gillespie 1989, 317–18). If he did so, this might be considered one of the first examples of a major vernacular publication project, since it involved regulating not just oral delivery in the vernacular but the distribution of vernacular texts.[8] Eighty years earlier, when Archbishop Pecham had prepared the version of the catechism that served as Thoresby's model, the translation into English had been left to the individual cleric. By Thoresby's day vernacular writing, as an increasingly important supplement to vernacular preaching, had become an instrument of social control.

Just as the efforts of the religious authorities to enforce orthodoxy and combat Lollardy furthered the use of written English, so they furthered a more systematic distribution of English books. The numerous surviving copies of the *Northern Homily Cycle* (excerpt 2.1), made in the 1380s, may indicate what would be one of the earliest concerted efforts to influence the laity directly through the books they read rather than indirectly through the books used by the clergy who preached to them. The same is true of Love's *Mirror* (excerpt 3.10, c. 1409), a counter to Lollard demands for biblical translation. The large number of surviving manuscripts—fifty-six—and the fact that they are all more or less in the Central Midlands Standard, suggest that the copying was officially promoted.[9] The Lollards, for their part, developed networks for distributing books, with the poorer members often pooling their money to make purchases for small reading circles. It is not clear whether they actually ran scriptoria, but Lollard copying was sufficiently organized to permit a remarkable degree of control both over the texts, which were carefully corrected, and over the presentation (Hudson 1989). Book distribution was thus an instrument of religious education for both the church and its Lollard opponents, and the lines between the two sometimes became blurred. In roughly 1425, money from the estate of Richard Whittington, lord mayor of London, was used to found a library at the Guildhall, where theo-

---

manuscript; London, British Library MS Cotton Caligula A.II; and the two Thornton manuscripts, Lincoln Cathedral MS 91 and London, British Library MS Addit. 31042) that suggests the contents of late medieval miscellanies were partially standardized. This phenomenon has not yet been thoroughly examined, but Gisela Guddat-Figge's (1976) survey of manuscripts containing romances provides an invaluable starting point, and Murray Evans (1995) draws attention to many recurring patterns of decoration and layout. The limited availability of exemplars would also have led to recurring groupings. See Hanna 1996.

8. Thoresby was heavily influenced by the thinking of John Grandison, bishop of Exeter from 1327–69, who stressed the need to educate the secular clergy. At least part of his motivation was competition with the friars, who provided pastoral services of their own and were largely outside diocesan control (Hughes 1988, 147–9).

9. Sargent 1992, lxiii–lxv. As Sargent notes, however, some caution is in order regarding the extent of supervision, since the Central Midlands Standard had by this point attained such wide acceptance that its use does not necessarily imply direct supervision.

logical texts were made available to poor students (Scase 1992, 267–69). Similar libraries were established at Worcester and Bristol. One of the men appointed by Whittington's executors was the London tradesman John Colop, who commissioned on his own behalf a common-profit book (Cambridge University Library MS Ff.6.31) that contained a number of pieces arguing for the translation of Scripture (including *The Holi Prophete David Seith*, excerpt 2.5). One of Colop's associates was Bishop Reginald Pecock, whose enthusiasm for providing the laity with books was to lead to the condemnation and public burning of his works in 1457 (see excerpt 1.16 and Scase 1992). Ironically, Pecock saw his plans for widespread book distribution as a means of combating Lollardy.

The possibility of influencing people through the distribution of vernacular books was also being explored for political purposes. Owning a manuscript had always been a useful means of displaying wealth and cultural authority, just as presenting a patron with an expensive volume had been a standard way of appealing for support. The contents and iconographic programs of many expensive volumes were designed to subtly flatter the patron and pay tribute to the patron's authority (Alexander 1983; Turville-Petre 1988, 20–22). Under the Lancastrians, however, there are signs of a significant shift. To bolster the legitimacy of their rule, the Lancastrians actively promoted both living poets (notably Hoccleve and Lydgate) and Chaucer, who was transformed posthumously from a Ricardian court poet to the founding national poet (see essay 4.2, pages 347–49 above). Prince Henry commissioned handsome presentation copies of Lydgate and Hoccleve to cement friendships (Pearsall 1994, 396–97), and the same cultural policy may be at work in the production of the luxurious Chaucer manuscripts produced in the first two decades of the fifteenth century, such as the famous Ellesmere and Hengwrt copies of *The Canterbury Tales*. The Lancastrians were thus perhaps the first to assert their authority through books that belonged to others (see, e.g., Patterson 1993a [on London, British Library MS Royal 15 E.VI]).

One of the factors that made this possible was the wider use of the Central Midlands Standard that had developed in the London-Oxford-Cambridge triangle and in the royal Chancery (Fisher 1977; Richardson 1980; Sandved 1981; see essay 4.2, page 342). Dialectical variation does not die out, however, even in fifteenth-century texts, and scribes working in London retained traces of their native dialect. Even manuscripts copied largely in London Standard might sometimes include alliterative items in regional dialects. Chaucer's parson, a Southern man, may not have been able to deliver an alliterative poem ("I kan nat geeste 'rum, ram, ruf,' by lettre" [*The Canterbury Tales*, X (I) 43]), but some Southern readers were apparently capable of appreciating one. Alliterative poems continued to be copied throughout the fifteenth century both in the North and in the South of England, and *The Awyntyrs*, although in a North West Midlands dialect, was sold together with booklets from the Southeast and bears the signature of a London layman (Doyle 1982, 97; see also Hanna 1989a). By Caxton's day, however, despite his famous lament about the range of dialectal variation in England and the speed of language change (quoted in the introduction to Part One, page 12), the Central Midlands Standard was becoming authoritative, and dialectical variation in manuscripts was fading. The development of a written standard and the increased prestige of written English, now becoming available as a language of moral instruction and cultural achievement as never before, opened the way for more ambitious publication schemes.

The Manuscript Book Trade and the Making of the English Reader

Ian Watt's famous study of the social conditions that governed the development of the eighteenth-century novel shows how the spread of literacy promoted certain categories of writing, notably journalism and realistic fiction, bringing about a commercial market for writing and thus "the subjection of literature to the economic laws of *laissez faire*" (i.e., supply and demand) (1957, 60). More recent work takes such an analysis a step further, examining the ways in which reader and writer are linked together in mutual definition within a particular socioeconomic system. As Pierre Macherey puts it, "Readers are made by what makes the book"; that is, "the conditions that determine the production of the book also determine the forms of its communication" (1978, 70). The advantage of such a model is that it brings together a number of historical developments that were interconnected in their day but have often been considered separately by scholars.

Accounts of the development of English book production and English writing often base it on a single social development: the rise of the middle class (see, e.g., Bennet 1937, 19; Parkes 1973, 557), but the process is more complicated, and the taste for reading itself is a social phenomenon in need of explanation. The rise of the London book trade certainly reflected the increase in the urban population, the increased status and wealth of merchants, senior guildsmen, lawyers, and upper bureaucrats, and the increase in their pragmatic literacy (Thrupp 1948; Parkes 1973). Such a group is a "middle class" only in the sense that is neither peasantry nor aristocracy, but whatever term we choose for this group, its prosperity created a growing market for luxury goods, including books (Meale 1989, 201). What needs explanation, however, is why books in general and certain books in particular should have been so highly valued by this group. It would be a mistake to think of the market for manuscripts as "self-defining," a simple matter of meeting a pre-existing demand (*pace* McKenzie 1990, 94). For a book trade to flourish, it must have well-defined readerships, not just people who want to buy books but people who share with the writers and booksellers and with other readers certain expectations of what books should look like and what they should have inside them. Without such common norms, reading would lose much of its social prestige.

The demand for English books was certainly closely tied to social prestige. French would preserve its cultural cachet and was widely used among the aristocracy and some of the upper gentry into the fifteenth century (Riddy 1987, 12–13; Meale 1989, 207–9), but reading English books was also a mark of gentility. The ranking of the gentle rested "on a nice balancing of considerations of birth, lands, and type of service" (Thrupp 1948, 246), but it could also be affected by social polish, to which reading and book ownership contributed. Of course reading, especially devotional reading, was normally done in privacy or within an intimate circle, but it was a mark of social distinction nonetheless. Aristocratic women like Cecily Neville, duchess of York, Margaret Beaufort, mother of Henry VII, and Margaret of York, duchess of Burgundy were widely praised for their pious reading and became icons of women's devotion (Armstrong 1942; Meale 1996b; Riddy 1996b; Taylor 1996). By the fifteenth century, this image had expanded its social range, and we find images of prosperous gentlewomen at prayer with their primers (Barratt 1975; Duffy 1992, 213 and plate 82; Boffey 1996). These images are models to guide behavior as much as direct reports of actual behavior, but the one would soon lead to the other. Not all merchants or their wives were convinced that devotional or leisure reading was the necessary step toward social prestige (Thrupp 1948, 247), but enough were to produce a spate of books of manners and moral guidance (Keiser 1979, 158; 1987; Lerer 1993, 88–89).

These accounts of pious women readers like Cecily Neville do, however, raise important and difficult questions about the ways private or devotional reading was gendered. Were there objectively more women than men devotional readers, or is this merely a reflection of the preoccupations of modern scholarship? Were women readers depicted in the same way as men? It seems, to begin with, that religious authorities, as well as some fathers and husbands, made a greater effort to monitor or shape women's reading practice, leaving us with a wide selection of images and accounts of idealized women readers. Women were frequently regarded as more impressionable, so warnings against the dangers of bad reading are more often directed toward women (see, e.g., Caxton's *Book of the Knight of the Tower*, excerpt 2.16). In some cases, elaborate devotional practice may have been seen as more suitable for women, while oral entertainment in the hall or outer chambers became a form of homosocial bonding for men. Regulations for various male communities, such as the household squires of Edward IV (see the introduction to Part Two, pages 113–14) or the scholars of New College, specify that they read, recite, and sing together (Green 1980, 83; Coleman 1996, 136–38). The image of the Virgin as solitary bourgeois woman reader, on the other hand, offered an influential icon of the pious woman reader for which there was no full male equivalent.

None of this need mean that women were doing more reading than men.[10] Outside a few aristocratic or high-gentry households, they were probably doing less.

---

10. It has sometimes been suggested that aristocratic lay women were more enthusiastic devotional readers. Southern, for example, claims that it was the "conjunction of monastic piety and the religious impulses of great ladies which chiefly fashioned the private devotions of the Middle Ages" (1953, 37).

Certainly in the middle ranks of society, rates for male literacy were higher. But while book ownership and writing was a mark of cultural authority, book reading, like other forms of private behavior, was most fully displayed when it was female.[11] Hence we have images of male book owners but of female readers. When male readers are depicted, the descriptions are rarely as intimate. Although Froissart describes Richard II reading the book he presented to him, the account ends quickly, with the king's taking the book into his secret chamber. In comparison, the reading practices of various aristocratic women are described in great detail (Taylor 1995). But whether one was depicted as an owner or as a reader, being associated with books had become a mark of gentility.

The extension of the image of the pious lay reader across a broader social spectrum seems to have accompanied the standardization of the contents and format of commercially copied miscellanies discussed above. These two interconnected developments illustrate Macherey's principle that reader and book are constructed in the same social process, a middle-class reader and a middle-class market being formed together. In this respect, as in many others, the trade in manuscripts helped establish the conditions under which the printed-book trade could develop (Macherey 1978). The pattern of supply and demand changed dramatically with the introduction of print. Simply meeting the demand had been a major challenge for the manuscript book trade (Edwards and Meale 1993, 95), but a technology that produced several hundred copies at a time provided a new commercial drive for the formation of readerships.

Caxton depended heavily on a traditional patronage network to underwrite the cost of a print run and may even have run a scriptorium, but he also endeavored to expand his readership, deploying a complex set of strategies in his dedications and prefaces to "make" his readers.[12] In his prologue to the romance *Blanchardyn and Eglantine* he argues that gentlemen and gentlewomen should not confine themselves to "bokes of contemplacion" but should spend part of their time in the reading of chivalric material: "it is requesyte otherwhyle to rede in auncyent historyes of noble fayttes and valyaunt actes of armes and warre . . . in lyke wyse for gentyl yonge ladyes and damoysellys for to lerne to be stedfaste and constaunt in their part to theym that they ones have promysed and agreed to" (Blake 1973, 57–58). Here the formation of a readership is a deliberate commercial policy, and the central claim that reading is a prerequisite of gentility is explicit. In his prologue to the *Eneydos* (a translation that was to earn Caxton the scorn of

11. As Catherine MacKinnon notes, "Privacy is everything women as women have never been allowed to be or have; at the same time, the private is everything women have been equated with and defined in terms of men's ability to have" (1983, 656–57).

12. The traditional view of Caxton stresses his dependence on medieval patronage (Blake 1969, 1976, 1996). This has been reassessed by Lotte Hellinga (1982), Russell Rutter (1987), A.S.G. Edwards and Carol Meale (1993), and Jennifer Summit (1995). The suggestion that Caxton may have run a scriptorium is made by J.A.W. Bennett on the basis of Oxford MS Bodley 283, a copy of the Middle English *Mirroure of the Worlde* with illustrations by the artist known as the Caxton Master (Scott 1976, xi and 25).

the humanist Scottish poet Gavin Douglas, excerpt 3.16), he writes more elaborately of the difficulties involved in producing material that suits a mixed target
audience of gentlemen and clerks, each of whom makes different stylistic demands:
the former blaming him for "over curyous termes whiche coude not be
understande of comyn peple" and asking him "to use olde and homely termes,"
while the latter "desired me to wryte the moste curyous termes that I coude fynde."
After consulting an "olde boke" and finding the English in it "so rude and brood
that I coude not wele understande it," he rejects the gentlemen's plea on the
grounds that only provincials understand "homely termes," which vary from region to region and generation to generation, but also resists the clerks' desire for
"curyous termes," which only they understand, and settles instead on a middle
style whose propriety he asks "master John Skelton, late created poete laureate"
to "oversee" (see excerpt 3.15). Setting provinces against metropolis and rude
peasants against people of taste and education, Caxton again seeks to create a
market defined by gentility and education and to find a register of English that can
bring the diverse interests of that market together—to create a style that will sell:

> And thus bytwene playn, rude and curyous I stande abasshed. But in my
> judgemente, the comyn termes that be dayli used ben lyghter to be
> understonde than the olde and auncyent Englysshe. And for as moche as
> this present booke is not for a rude uplondyssh man to laboure therin ne
> rede it, but onely for a clerke and a noble gentylman, that feleth and
> understondeth in faytes of armes, in love, and in noble chyvalrye, therfor
> in a meane bytwene bothe I have reduced and translated this sayd booke in
> to our Englysshe, not over rude ne curyous, but in suche termes as shall be
> understanden by Goddys grace, accordynge to my copye. (Blake 1973, 80,
> punctuation modified)

4.4

HISTORICIZING POSTCOLONIAL CRITICISM: CULTURAL DIFFERENCE AND THE VERNACULAR

RUTH EVANS

You taught me language; and my profit on't
Is, I know how to curse.
                              —*The Tempest* (?1611; act I, sc. ii, 365–66)

The processes of colonialism and imperialism over the last half millennium have made English into a language of world domination. It may therefore require a certain mental effort to realize that English did not occupy a position of privilege, let alone have global status, in the later Middle Ages. Within medieval Europe the only vernacular with cultural authority across the whole continent was French, and Latin was the chief instrument of political power. Latin was the language of Roman colonization around the western Mediterranean and throughout western Europe. In the Middle Ages it was also the language through which the Catholic church attempted to impose a single religious formation on all Christendom, the language of a single universal theology that was then translated into specific moral guidance in vernacular preaching and instruction (Moore 1987).

But Latin also had immense cultural authority, providing a fundamental intellectual formation for the medieval world. To think in the rigorous logical categories of medieval scholasticism was to think in Latin. To read was either to read in Latin, as the medieval use of the term *litteratus* implies, or to read a vernacular text written in the Roman alphabet. But while the situation of medieval vernacular writers confronting the culturally authoritative tradition of Latinity is in some ways analogous to that of modern postcolonial writers confronting the cultural hegemony of English (and other colonial languages), this confrontation cannot be represented straightforwardly as English playing the David to Latin's Goliath. Although writers using English developed a number of strategies to excuse themselves for the selection of an inferior mode of communication, the construction of English by these writers was also a colonialist enterprise.

Colonization has a long history before the grand moments of territorial expansionism that mark the so-called early modern period. In medieval historiography the concept of *translatio* (transference) underwrote notions of empire via the "modernizing" narrative of conquest and displacement that was known as *translatio studii et imperii* (transferal of power from Rome and of learning from Athens or Rome to Christian "Europe," a topos current from at least the ninth century; Curtius 1990, 29). This discursive structure, which is essentially metaphoric, serves to define and reproduce cultural norms through translation and composition practices. The modern hegemony of Europe is thus subtended by a narrative of translation-as-empire that runs back through the Middle Ages to antiquity. As one postcolonial commentator observes, "[F]rom its beginnings the imperialist mission is . . . one of translation: the translation of the 'other' into the terms of the empire" (Cheyfitz 1991, 112). Some medieval vernacular translation (including Chaucer's) also conforms to this metaphoric structure: it "inserts itself into the ideological project of *translatio studii* as a new linguistic medium for carrying over the learning of the ancients" (Copeland 1991, 106). This process—albeit a complex and often unexpectedly subversive one—can be traced in the excerpts printed here, in their repeated meditations on the role of authority, ancient learning, and memory (see, e.g., Lydgate's *Troy Book*, excerpt 1.7, and Gower's *Confessio Amantis*, excerpt 2.11; see also the discussion in the section "Vernacular Theory and Translation" in essay 4.1).

One way we might approach vernacular prologues with postcolonial issues in mind is thus to consider their deployment of tropes of the transfer of power and learning (*translatio*). Translation in the Middle Ages, as in antiquity, was "a vehicle for expressing or playing out large questions of cultural difference" (Copeland 1991, 222). Translated texts play a highly significant role in transmitting the colonizer's ethos and in naturalizing the power relations between colonizer and colonized. In her book on colonial translation in eighteenth-century India, Tejaswini Niranjana notes the problematic role of translators' prefaces. Their positioning, she argues, "may suggest that they [the English translators] are aware of their marginality. But it is they who have drawn the margins, demarcated the text. The work from which they seem to exclude themselves is constituted by the traces of their historicity, and the gesture of exclusion they perform makes possible the presentation of the text as a unified and transparent whole" (Niranjana 1992, 49). These prefaces maintain the hegemonic Western project by effacing their own history, thus erasing the power relations in the transmission of texts. According to Niranjana, such prefaces uphold the essentially humanistic idea that translation facilitates cultural exchanges and offers a transparent window onto other cultures, while in fact producing "strategies of containment" of the colonized subject (1992, 3). It could similarly be argued that one impulse of Middle English vernacular writing, in appropriating the privileged discourse of the classical tradition, is toward the effacement of its specific historical situation by inserting itself into an apparently timeless structure.

However, while some genres of Middle English were confidently appropriating the trope of translation-as-empire, many other genres, particularly those which stood closest to traditions of Latinity—historiography, pastoral works, Bible translations and paraphrases, alchemical manuals—struggled to assert themselves against the weight of the privileged language. Like their modern postcolonial counterparts, medieval vernacular writers found ways to evade the all-encompassing authority of the colonial language. Writers such as Osbern Bokenham (excerpt 1.11), John Gower (excerpt 2.11), Margery Kempe (excerpt 1.14), and Julian of Norwich (excerpt 1.13) took existing Latin traditions and diverted their previous meanings. The prologues to their works exemplify a process speculatively described by Michel de Certeau:

> [T]he spectacular victory of Spanish colonization over the indigenous Indian cultures was diverted from its intended aims by the use made of it: even when they were subjected, indeed even when they accepted their subjection, the Indians often used the laws, practices, and representations that were imposed on them by force or by fascination to ends other than those of their conquerors; they made something else out of them; they subverted them from within—not by rejecting them or by transforming them (though that occurred as well), but by many different ways of using them in the service of rules, customs or convictions foreign to the colonization which they could not escape. They metaphorized the dominant order: they made it function in another register. (de Certeau 1984, 31–32)

The ways in which Middle English texts make Latin traditions "function in another register" is one of the main themes of this book (see especially the section "The Distinctiveness of Vernacular Theory" in essay 4.1). It is also important to record that the vernacular *can* challenge the official culture of Latinity by exposing that culture's ideological fictions, namely, by revealing the historical discontinuity that it is the project of imperialism to cover up (Copeland 1991, 106). For example, the authors of a number of the prologues edited here find ways of emphasizing their own historical situation, thereby revealing the fictions at work in the texts they translate or in the venerated traditions they appropriate.

Assessing the cultural and political work of Middle English vernacular prologues, both their reproduction of and resistance to cultural colonialization, is no easy matter. Writing in English has by no means always involved the aggressive displacements and usurpations noted by critics like Niranjana, who trace the underpinnings of the language's rise in the grand narrative of *translatio studii et imperii*. Yet the notion of "accessibility," so prominent in a substantial number of these medieval prologues and apparently so distinct from usurpation of a master language, bears closer examination. For example, Trevisa's "foreign policy," as set out in his *Epistle to Berkeley,* is to leave the names of "other" (oriental) places and people "in her owne kynde" (see excerpt 2.2b: 147–53). While this appears to represent cultural difference as much as possible on its own terms, Trevisa may in fact be doing just what Niranjana observes in prefaces by eighteenth-century colonial translators: inscribing the oriental subject as "naturally" subaltern by deploying a notion of translation itself as mimetic, simply reproducing what is "there." But in any case, Trevisa's maneuver signals an intention that can only be properly tested by looking at his translation of the *Polychronicon* as a whole. It would also be important to consider that translation in the light of relations of patronage. There is certainly more work to be done on how patronage shifts the *translatio imperii,* making it part of a socially situated and often highly localized set of power relations (as in the case, for example, of Trevisa and Berkeley) that neither simply aggrandize the patron or the author nor simply reproduce ideological containment.

The field of postcolonial studies has shown us the broader political implications of translation and the importance of the translator's immediate historical situation. As readers of medieval texts, we similarly need to consider the institutions that disseminated the translation-as-empire narrative in all its various and discontinuous forms: the church, medieval scholastic culture, the aristocracy and mercantile elites as patrons and sponsors of book production (see essay 4.3 above). Bible translation (see excerpts 1.15, 2.4, 2.5, 3.8) is one field in which readers can explore the emergence of what was later to become a major institution in transmitting European *Christianitas* to the colonies. Yet the tradition of vernacular Bibles (later helped of course by the Reformation and by printing) did not arise in the Middle Ages out of any single impulse toward Christian imperialism. As these excerpts show, it came out of competing and historically specific narratives about access and authority that were as much products as critiques of official church teaching.

We can also consider these vernacular texts in terms of the production of a particular historical understanding of "Europe." This is emphatically not to see the Middle Ages as the "tribal forebear of European historicity" (Beckwith 1992b, 79). That would mean thinking of its role in the history of colonialism as analogous to the role still too often ascribed to it in histories of the subject: as an innocent, one-dimensional period that predates the emergence of the modern (Aers 1992b). Rather, the Middle Ages are a historical locus that blurs the division between medievalism and modernity. Nor is this a call to write a history of colonial oppression that uses the Middle Ages to fill in the blanks. These prologues do not in any case furnish easily appropriated examples of colonial containment. It would be more productive to use them to understand something of the history of the larger discursive structures (especially *translatio*) that worked to exclude colonized subjects from history in the first place.

The "invention" of Europe in the Middle Ages depended on the understanding and deployment of a number of crucially formative categories as they intersected with each other and with the categories of masculine and feminine: for example,

Christianitas (Christendom) itself, Corpus Christi, and the Jew (Biddick 1993, 392–93); or the intersection of gender and ethnic identity present in Dante's *De vulgari eloquentia*. In Dante's "Europe" one country—Italy—is represented as culturally dominant because of its language's proximity to Latin. While Latin provides the "manly" norm, Italian vernacular dialects are branded "hirsute" or "effeminate": in other words, as approximations of the "barbarous" or "feminine" other (see the section "The Distinctiveness of Vernacular Theory" in essay 4.1). Here, Dante offers a version of what Patricia Parker has called (in the context of the early modern period) "that powerful mix of misogyny and orientalism conveyed from fifth-century Athens to Europe through the whole force of Roman tradition" (1996, 110).

That mix of misogyny and orientalism also informs English thinking on the vernacular. Although the excerpts printed here do not allow these issues to emerge in any simple way, they do suggest how representations of the barbarous (often Eastern or Jewish) other and the feminine operate to define and redefine the vernacular at the moment of its emergence. The *South English Legendary* (excerpt 2.15) and *The Croxton Play of the Sacrament* (excerpt 2.14) are important resources for examining this intersection, as are historiographical texts such as Mannyng's *Chronicle* (excerpt 1.1), *The Wars of Alexander* (excerpt 3.13), and Skelton's translation of Poggio Bracciolini's *Bibliotheca* (excerpt 3.15), and many vernacular theologies written for or by women, especially the *Pseudo-Augustinian Soliloquies* (excerpt 3.2) and Julian's *Revelation of Love* (excerpts 1.13 and 3.4). Such texts deploy notions of the "mother tongue" as a conscious strategy to defend the use of the "inferior" vernacular. To do so, they draw on the reevaluation of the feminine that marks some late medieval incarnational theologies, which appear to associate the flesh of Christ with Mary's female body and hence the female in general (Bynum 1987; Aers and Staley 1996).

One of the violent ironies of the brave new world of the Renaissance, as Shakespeare's Caliban recognizes, is that English as an educational tool was also an instrument of colonial rule. The passage from the end of our period (1520) to the moment of colonialism was short. English now has an almost uncontested position of high international visibility. In today's world of informatics English is the *lingua franca* of the Internet: of homepages and Web links. As modern readers confront the new technologies of reading and memorialization, we might ponder the complex history of the making of English and the technologies of its dissemination: manuscripts, book production, patronage, lay economic power, education, translation. The Middle Ages is not a point of origin here, but a historical moment in which structures of imperialism and resistance to those structures have marked forever the role of English in the international world today.

AN AFTERWORD
ON THE PROLOGUE

RUTH EVANS

But what do prefaces actually do? ... Oughtn't we some day to reconstitute their history and their typology? Do they form a genre? Can they be grouped according to the necessity of some common predicate, or are they otherwise and in themselves divided?

—Derrida (1981, 8)

This book argues for the existence of something called "Middle English literary theory," using evidence drawn mainly from prologues to vernacular works. What then of the status of these prologues? Is it especially significant that we have used these particular texts—almost a genre or set of genres in their own right—as evidence? How are they different—if at all—from the prefaces and introductions to modern books (including this book)? This essay considers these prologues not only as repositories of information about the English vernacular but as opaque entities, standing in a complex relation to the works they preface (and to which they explicitly direct the reader) and to the history of the vernacular of which they form a significant part.

Readers familiar with Chaucer's works will also be familiar, possibly without being conscious of the fact, with the genre (or even several genres) of the Middle English prologue. The prologues to Chaucer's works represent a particular honing and canonizing of the form, both as a distinctive generic type and as a form of literary theory. Often verging on the brink of taking on an existence separate from the works they introduce, in some cases they have become artworks in their own right. *The General Prologue to the Canterbury Tales* is now detached and taught as a discrete text. *The Wife of Bath's Prologue* overshadows the tale it is meant to preface. "This is a long preamble of a tale!" (*Canterbury Tales* III [D] 831) observes the Friar at the end of a prologue of over eight hundred lines to a tale of just over four hundred, a prologue that blurs the division between introduction and tale, affronting the audience's sense of discursive decorum but undeniably pleasing them with its fictional and titillating excess. If the prologue is intended to be an hors d'oeuvre to the main course, then by calling attention to the status of this prologue as excessive, the Friar makes us aware that Chaucer's Wife of Bath, easily sitting on her "amblere" (*Canterbury Tales, General Prologue* I [A] 469), comically disorganizes the prolocutory hierarchy of outside and inside, frame and picture. *The Clerk's Prologue,* on the other hand, ironizes prologue-making by having the clerk mime Petrarch's elaborate "prohemye" while at the same time rejecting its excentric nature as "a thing impertinent" (*Canterbury Tales* V [E] 54). From the evidence of Chaucer's practice alone, Middle English prologues are far from being a self-explanatory or self-effacing genre.

   Designed to stand outside the works they introduce, prologues offer frames for reading those works, frames that promise the reader a certain transparency of the ensuing text. A frame demarcates the boundary between outside and inside, showcasing a visual image as well as confining it. It is not intended as an object of study in its own right. Who, after all, goes to an art gallery to look at the frames? As Derrida says, "Prefaces, along with forewords, introductions, preludes, preliminaries, preambles, prologues, and prolegomena, have always been written, it seems, in view of their own self-effacement" (1981, 9). Mere supports for the texts they preface, prologues are ultimately meant to be kicked away. Yet on closer inspection, the apparently innocent question, "What do prefaces actually do?" invites reflection on their thoroughly contradictory nature. Written last but appearing first, and treated as integral to the works they are supposed to stand outside of, prefaces in fact continually overstep the line, disorganizing the categories of center and periphery, *theoria* and *praxis*.

   Like Chaucer's, the prologues edited here contribute to the problematizing of the traditional distinction between "text" and "preface." They participate in a long prolocutory tradition that has its origins in the classical period and in late antiquity. Yet Middle English vernacular prologues (as argued in essay 4.1), cannot be read simply as versions (or perversions) of the distinctive genres of formal Latin prologues (see, e.g., excerpt 1.11: 10–12 and note). Immensely varied, they include narratives, lyrics, letters, exhortations, and prayers, as well as formal discussions of a work's structure along academic lines (see the Introduction, pages xiv–xv). Nor are these vernacular prologues simply part of a generic tradition whose contours can be described and classified; they emerge out of a particular discursive matrix in which the prologue plays a historically specific role in differentiating theory from practice and in authorizing the text.

   An archaeology of the Middle English prologue might begin with its historical nomenclature. The most common English term among the texts represented here (and in Middle English in general) is "prologue" or "prologe." As several spellings testify, it comes via either Latin *prologus* or French *prologe* from the Greek (see Capgrave, excerpt 2.7: 43; Gower, *Confessio Amantis*, excerpt 2.11: 73; Glossary, s.v. *prolog*). Its earliest recorded appearance in English is in *Cursor Mundi* (excerpt

3.14: 93, c. 1300). Less common are the distinct but related forms "prohemy" from medieval Latin *prohemium* (Skelton, *Diodorus Siculus,* excerpt 3.15), and "proheymm" from the Old French *prohème* (Douglas, *Eneados,* excerpt 3.16: 69), both ultimately from the Greek for an opening or prelude. "Prohemy" and "proheymm" are elevated terms: Chaucer's use of "prohemye" in the *Clerk's Prologue* (*Canterbury Tales* V [E] 43) consciously evokes "heigh style." Both Skelton and Douglas may be imitating Chaucer; at any rate, they have dignified their respective epic histories with grand terms that also contribute to their texts' self-conscious status as translations. The term *prohemium* is found in the Latin inscriptions to two prologues here (*Knyghthode and Bataile,* excerpt 2.12, and Norton's *Ordinal of Alchemy,* excerpt 2.3), a reminder of vernacular proximity to the elite scholastic discourse from which "prohemy" is drawn. The Latin *prefacio,* used in the explicit to Walton's preface to his translation of Boethius (*Explicit prefacio translatoris,* excerpt 1.5: 73), is also on occasion Englished as "prefacyon." According to the *MED,* its earliest recorded use is in the text (not the prologue) of the later version (c. 1352) of the *Northern Homily Cycle* (excerpt 2.1), and it was used again in 1384 in a text traditionally ascribed to Wyclif. It also occurs in the *Speculum Devotorum* (excerpt 1.12). (These latter contexts are suggestive of the term's other, specialized liturgical meaning: "an introduction to the canon of the Mass," *MED: prefacioun* [*n.*]). Capgrave's is the only prologue here to use "preamble": "This is the preamble or elles the prologe of Seynt Gilbertis lif" (excerpt 2.7: 43). The doublet pairing with the more common "prologe" suggests a word that is less easily understood. "Preamble" (a going before) is not thought to appear in written English before the 1380s (in the Friar's remark in Chaucer's *Wife of Bath's Prologue* [III (D) 831], quoted above, page 371).

Most of these terms are first recorded in the fourteenth century. By no means all of them appear first, or exclusively, in Chaucer's prologues: the linguistic evidence points to an older—and very diverse—vernacular tradition. It seems that by the late fourteenth century the term "prologue" has come to be claimed for vernacular writing and to be considered an English word. The Latin loanwords "prohemy" and "prefacyon," on the other hand, may serve to situate the writings that they introduce explicitly within the scholastic tradition. Several Latin terms—*Prologus, Prefacio,* and *Prohemium*—are found in the rubrics, inscriptions, and margins of these texts, but these Latin descriptions may not all be authorial, and both the Latin and English terminology in any case appear fitfully because of the vagaries of manuscript transmission and preservation. A prologue may be titled a prologue in one manuscript and not in another (as in the case of the two manuscripts in which the introduction to the pseudo-Lydgatian *Nightingale* poem, excerpt 2.13, is extant: only the Corpus Christi manuscript includes the term "Proem").

Medieval prologues are in fact notoriously unstable. In the case of the *Confessio Amantis* (excerpt 2.11), a shift in authorial allegiance produces interesting effects of textual *mouvance*: the work has two prologues, one for Richard II, one for

Henry of Lancaster. Prologues were added or subtracted according to different political and social circumstances. The *Northern Homily Cycle* (excerpt 2.1), the later versions of which lack the prologue edited here, is a case in point: its emphasis on accessibility may have made it less acceptable at a later period when the clergy sought to curb, rather than encourage, the use of English for the Scriptures. The political work that a prologue may do cannot be known in advance.

Several prologues—perhaps significantly—do not name themselves at all, at least in the manuscript from which they have been edited here (e.g., Metham, *Amoryus and Cleopes,* excerpt 1.8; Ashby, *Active Policy of a Prince,* excerpt 1.9; Julian of Norwich, *A Revelation of Love,* excerpt 1.13; *Northern Homily Cycle,* excerpt 2.1). Their position is all. This may indicate the acceptance and even naturalization of a vernacular tradition of prologue-making, one that is independent of the Latin tradition. Some only announce their function as prologues at the end (see Pecock, *Donet,* excerpt 1.16: 126: "Here eendith the prolog of this book"). A number that do not call themselves prologues instead proclaim their extratextual and introductory function with versions of the formula "Here begins . . ." (Guy de Chauliac, *Cyrurgie,* excerpt 1.10: 1: "Here begynneth . . ."; *Spektakle,* excerpt 2.17: 1: "Heir begynnis . . ."; Caxton, *Reynard the Fox,* excerpt 3.17: 1: "Hyer begynneth th'ystorye of Reynard the foxe"; Brian Anslay's translation of de Pizan's *City of Ladies,* excerpt 3.24: 30–31: "Here begynneth the fyrste chapytre which telleth howe and by whome the Cyte of Ladyes was fyrst begon to buylde"). *A Talkyng* (excerpt 3.1) also refers to its prologue as a "bigynninge" (16). *The Cloud of Unknowing* (excerpt 3.3) uses both: "Here biginneth the prolog" (6). Bokenham (excerpt 1.11) only talks in general terms in his prologue about "begynnyng a werk" (2).

Formulaic as it is, the advertising of the prologue as itself the work's beginning not only makes these prologues integral to the works they introduce but may also emphasize the logical and chronological *ordinatio* of the individual work. Yet even when simply pointing to the locations of items in a manuscript book, prologues may suggest an aura of Latinity or in more complex ways enter into the politics of literary authorization (see, e.g., Kempe's two prologues, excerpt 1.14). Prologues are themselves various, are transmitted—or not—in varying ways, and serve a range of functions.

How do the Middle English writers gathered here conceptualize the relation of their prologues to the works they introduce? Fifteenth-century writers seem to be the most self-conscious and even playful about these relations. When, for example, Hoccleve in his *Complaint* (excerpt 1.6) announces, "Here endith my prolog and folwith my compleinte" (36), he seems to be marking a boundary between prologue and text, but in fact his "complaint" has already begun in his prologue. By rhetorically disorganizing the hierarchy of text and preface, Hoccleve can suggest the power of his grief. Lydgate conceives of the prologue to his *Troy Book* (excerpt 1.7) as a visible object: "I gan the prolog to beholde / Of Troye Boke" (99–100). This is the prologue as physical space, part of the book-as-city that makes Lydgate's poem coterminous with the city of Troy itself (compare Christine de Pizan's tactic in *The Book of the City of Ladies*, building a city from stories, excerpt 3.24). Such images allude to, and use strategically, long-standing traditions of memorial practices in which narratives are organized and recalled spatially, in architectural images. This gaze on the prologue also makes Lydgate himself into a conqueror of space, colonizing Guido's source text and surveying his achievement perspectivally. Here the prologue mimes the colonialist gesture of appropriation and displacement that signals the topos of translation-as-empire.

There are of course continuities between topoi in the prologues represented here and those in modern prologues: the humility topos (nowadays the disclaimer of authoritative mastery or the conventional statement about taking authorial responsibility for the faults that may remain); the dedication (to a patron or distinguished figure in the Middle Ages; nowadays to family, friends, or intellectual mentors); the acknowledgments (often in the medieval period to God or to spiritual advisers; nowadays to family, friends, and colleagues, and also, in the case of academic books, to grant-awarding bodies and institutions); the attempt to outline the work's structure and to explain the book's rationale to the reader. Notable among modern genre fiction is the idealized biography of the Harlequin (Mills and Boon) "authoress" that prefaces the Harlequin romance just as the troubadour's *vida* attends the Provençal love lyric. Both modern and Middle English prologues are sites of intense negotiation between authors and readers/ audiences, and they are instrumental in authorial self-fashioning. Yet there are important discontinuities: in an age of copyright, modern prefaces have to acknowledge debts and sources according to legal obligations that are consonant with the function of the "author" as a legal category. Middle English prologues have no such legal obligations. Their construction of authorship is rhetorical: a way of talking about intention that has not yet begun to locate that intention fully in the person of the author (see essay 4.1, pages 327–29).

The cultural and political work of prologues in transmitting the notion of translation-as-empire has already been discussed (see essay 4.4, pages 366–70). However, a way of extending that analysis is to go back to the etymologies of the various Middle English terms for a prologue: "before the Word" (from Greek *logos*), or, in the case of "preface," "before speaking" (from the Latin *fas*, "that which founds," from the verb *fari*, "to speak"). These etymologies suggest that the prologue is that which goes before the authoritative text, which stakes out for that text its cultural locus. These prologues have a status as what de Certeau calls "spatial stories," particularly as stories that have a role in delimitation: in authorizing the establishment and transgression of limits. De Certeau declares that a story's first function is to authorize or to found (1984, 123). This depends not on principles of law but on the principle of *fas:* "the mystical foundation." Drawing on the work of the anthropologist Georges Dumézil, de Certeau outlines a Roman ritual practice that exposes the "foreign policy" at the etymological heart of "pre-face":

> Occidental culture created its own ritual concerning *fas,* which was carried out in Rome by specialized priests called *fetiales.* It was practiced "before Rome undertook any action with regard to a foreign nation," such as a declaration of war, a military expedition, or an alliance. The ritual was a procession with three centrifugal stages, the first within Roman territory but near the frontier, the second on the frontier, the third in foreign territory. The ritual action was carried out before every civil or military action because it is designed to create the field necessary for political or military activities. . . . The *fas* ritual is a foundation. It "provides space" for the actions that will be undertaken; it "creates a field" which serves as their "base" and their "theater." . . . Like the Roman *fetiales,* stories "go in a procession" ahead of social practices in order to open a field for them. (de Certeau 1984, 124–25, quoting Georges Dumézil)

These Middle English prologues, then, can be thought of as sites where foundations are laid, which have a ritual quality, which mark out a sphere of operations for the text that follows them, and which act as prefaces to an essentially militaristic enterprise of conquering, perhaps of the conquering of intellectual spaces and social narratives.

Another aspect of the traditional prolocutory hierarchy of inside and outside is the gendering of that hierarchy, by which the text assumes primary status and the prologue is relegated to the merely secondary, inferior, and therefore (according to conventional cultural logic) feminine position. The prologue is the place where Middle English authors, translators, and compilers most often mime their protestations of humility (especially in the fifteenth century), as if recognizing a congruence between the conventional secondary status of the prologue and their own subordination to the vernacular. Yet the prologue is also the site of the most intense self-fashioning. The association between the secondariness of the prologue and the self-authorizing statement has interesting consequences for the notion of medieval authorship. It may appear odd to claim for prologues a feminine position, since they seem to be precisely where authority is most stamped (Minnis 1988), but the postures of humility they so often enact are also versions of later humanist concerns about the feminizing effects of eloquence (Parker 1996), suggesting the complexity of gendering issues at work throughout the history of the vernacular. Prologues, by virtue of their complex relationship to writing and textuality, are a genre that addresses supremely well the problematic of authority and translation in the medieval period.

Medieval prologues cannot have fulfilled, and did not fulfill, a universal function. They do not even clearly act as a medieval work's principal threshold. Michael Camille, for example, criticizes Alexandre Leupin's claim that the prose prologue of a work that falls outside our period, *The Life of St. Alexis,* preserved *inter alia* in the twelfth-century Hildesheim manuscript and otherwise known as the St. Albans Psalter, or the Psalter of Christina of Markyate, is "the first thresh-old of the work" (Leupin 1989, 40, cited in Camille 1996, 388). It is not the prologue that marks the first threshold, Camille remarks, but the image—the manuscript illumination—that precedes it. The miniature of Nebuchadnezzar's Dream that appears before the prologue (in the two manuscripts of Gower's *Confessio Amantis* from which the excerpt here [2.11] has been edited) marks a similar first threshold to that work, displacing the traditional janitorial, or "open-ing," function of the written prologue. In some cases, prologues may have operated as advertisements for the involvement of particular groups, such as the Gilbertines, in the composition of work (see Mannyng's *Chronicle,* excerpt 1.1; Capgrave's *Life of St. Gilbert,* excerpt 2.7). Less clear-cut but still important is the role of *The General Prologue to the Wycliffite Bible* (excerpt 1.15) in advertising the common interests and aims of a specific group of like-minded people. Although well outside our period, dramatic prologues (and epilogues) during the English Restoration became detachable comic "farces" alongside the main play, develop-ing their own lives and deploying spectacular effects—delivered from a seat on a donkey or by women dressed in men's clothes (Danchin 1994). It has been sug-gested that the function of the banns in medieval English drama (see *The Croxton Play of the Sacrament,* excerpt 2.14) was to announce the actual performance several days ahead, accompanied by showmanship and advertisement, including miming and even spectacular effects like stilt walking. Some guild returns include payments for horses involved in the "riding (proclamation) of the banns" (Moore 1993). The various medieval models for the riding of the banns suggest a ritual performance closely akin to the Roman *fas* ceremony described above: opening up a space for a "theater" of social practices, in this case, for the actual perfor-mance of the play that follows several days later. De Certeau's anthropological model suggests a blurring of the division between writing and social practices. Croxton's banns constitute both and mingle both, reminding us that these Middle English prologues are not inert texts but cultural performances with recognizable cultural effects.

Derrida's point is that prefaces in a postmodern age do not simply stand out-side their texts. The process of what he calls "dissemination"—the radical dispersal of meaning that entails the lack of fullness or presence—means that a prologue cannot perform the act of "fixing" the meaning of the ensuing text by offering a generalized and abstract key to that text (Derrida 1981, 5). The pro-logue itself is subject to those same processes of dissemination. It is itself a writing, just as the text it prefaces is a writing, and both escape fixing. In presenting these Middle English prologues as separate from their texts, we are suggesting that they might be read as both inside and outside, inessential and essential: not dispensable keys to those works, or even detachable texts, but simultaneously implicated in the writings they preface (as this volume has suggested all along) and yet also outside them. In that respect they perform what Derrida calls "work" or "practice," subverting the traditional distinction between *theoria* and *praxis* that attributes primacy to the text and installs the preface as secondary and inferior. The "work" of these prologues, therefore, and our "work" in presenting them as simultaneously a part of larger works and as separate from them, is a continuation of our argument that Middle English writers themselves are aware of their prologues not as programmatic keys but as mobile and open "writing."

ALTERNATIVE ARRANGEMENTS OF THE EXCERPTS

EXCERPTS BY DATE
(dates that are considered well established are printed in bold characters)

c. 1270–85 *South English Legendary* (2.15)
c. 1300 *Cursor Mundi* (3.14)
c. 1315 *Northern Homily Cycle* (2.1)
? 1330s–70s *A Talking of the Love of God* (3.1)
1338 Robert Mannyng, *Chronicle* (1.1)
c. 1345 Richard Rolle, *The English Psalter* (3.8)
c. 1350 *The Prick of Conscience* (3.7)
c. 1360–1450 *The Wars of Alexander* (3.13)
? 1370s–80s *The Cloud of Unknowing* (3.3)
1375–77 John Barbour, *The Bruce* (1.2)
c. 1380s *Pore Caityf* (3.6)
c. 1380s–1420s *The Knowing of Woman's Kind in Childing* (2.6)
1380s–1420s *The Holi Prophete David Seith* (2.5)
c. 1382–88 Julian of Norwich, *A Revelation of Love,* Short Text (1.13)
1384–87 Thomas Usk, *The Testament of Love* (1.4)
c. 1385 William Langland, *Piers Plowman,* C Text (3.19)
1387 John Trevisa, *Dialogue Between the Lord and the Clerk* (2.2)
1390s John Gower, *Confessio Amantis* (2.11)
c. 1390s *The General Prologue to the Wycliffite Bible* (1.15)
? 1390s–1420s *Pseudo-Augustinian Soliloquies* (3.2)
after 1393 Julian of Norwich, *A Revelation of Love,* Long Text (3.4)
? 1396, Geoffrey Chaucer, *Complaint of Venus* (1.3)
c. 1400 *Sermon of Dead Men* (3.11)
c. 1400–1440 Mechtild of Hackeborn, *The Book of Ghostly Grace* (3.20)
? 1401–7 *On Translating the Bible into English* (2.4)
1405 or **1410** *Dives and Pauper* (3.9)
c. 1409 Nicholas Love, *The Mirror of the Blessed Life of Jesus Christ* (3.10)
before 1410 John Walton, Translation of Boethius (1.5)
1412–20 John Lydgate, *Troy Book* (1.7)
c. 1415–25 *Speculum Devotorum* (1.12)
1420–40 *The Orchard of Syon* (3.5)
c. 1420–50 Guy de Chauliac, *Cyrurgie* (1.10, the "Paris" translation)
1420–50 *The Mirror of Our Lady* (3.12)
1421–22 Thomas Hoccleve, *The Complaint* (1.6)
1424–37 James I of Scotland, *The Kingis Quair* (3.23)
1430s Margery Kempe, *The Book of Margery Kempe* (1.14/3.22)

1440s Eleanor Hull, *A Commentary on the Penitential Psalms* (3.21)
1443–47 Osbern Bokenham, *Legendys of Hooly Wummen* (1.11)
1443–55 Reginald Pecock, *Donet, The Repressor of Over Much Blaming of the Clergy* (1.16)
1446 *The Nightingale* (2.13)
1448–49 John Metham, *Amoryus and Cleopes* (1.8)
c. 1450–1500 Robert Henryson, *The Fables* (3.18)
1451 John Capgrave, *Life of St. Gilbert* (2.7)
c. 1457–60 *Knyghthode and Bataile* (2.12)
c. 1461 *The Croxton Play of the Sacrament* (2.14)
1460s–70s George Ashby, *Active Policy of a Prince* (1.9)
c. 1477 Thomas Norton, *Ordinal of Alchemy* (2.3)
1481 William Caxton, *Reynard the Fox* (3.17)
1484 William Caxton, *Book of the Knight of the Tower* (2.16)
1488 John Skelton, Poggio Bracciolini's *Bibliotheca Historica of Diodorus Siculus* (3.15)
1489 William Caxton, Christine de Pizan's *Book of Fayttes of Armes and of Chyvalrye* (2.10)
1492 *Spektakle of Luf* (2.17)
c. 1510–19 *The Amesbury Letter* (2.9)
1513 Gavin Douglas, *Eneados* (3.16)
1517 Bishop Fox, *The Rule of Seynt Benet* (2.8)
1521 Henry Pepwell/Brian Anslay, Christine de Pizan's *Book of the City of Ladies* (3.24)

EXCERPTS BY GENRE
(many other arrangements could be made under this heading)

Histories, Chronicles, Romances

Robert Mannyng, *Chronicle* (1.1)
John Barbour, *The Bruce* (1.2)
John Lydgate, *Troy Book* (1.7)
John Metham, *Amoryus and Cleopes* (1.8)
The Wars of Alexander (3.13)
Cursor Mundi (3.14)
John Skelton, Poggio Bracciolini's *Bibliotheca Historica of Diodorus Siculus* (3.15)
Gavin Douglas, *Eneados* (3.16)

Saints' Lives, Lives of Christ, Passion Meditations

Osbern Bokenham, *Legendys of Hooly Wummen* (1.11)
Speculum Devotorum (1.12)
John Capgrave, *Life of St. Gilbert* (2.7)
South English Legendary (2.15)
A Talking of the Love of God (3.1)
Nicholas Love, *The Mirror of the Blessed Life of Jesus Christ* (3.10)

Visions, Allegories

Julian of Norwich, *A Revelation of Love* (1.13/3.4)
Margery Kempe, *The Book of Margery Kempe* (1.14/3.22)
John Gower, *Confessio Amantis* (2.11)
William Langland, *Piers Plowman,* C Text (3.19)
Mechtild of Hackeborn, *The Book of Ghostly Grace* (3.20)
James I of Scotland, *The Kingis Quair* (3.23)
Henry Pepwell/Brian Anslay, Christine de Pizan's *Book of the City of Ladies* (3.24)

Complaints and Lyrics

Geoffrey Chaucer, *Complaint of Venus* (1.3)
Thomas Hoccleve, *The Complaint* (1.6)
The Nightingale (2.13)

Drama, Debate, Polemic, Soliloquy

John Trevisa, *Dialogue* and *Epistle* (2.2)
On Translating the Bible into English (2.4)
The Holi Prophete David Seith (2.5)
The Croxton Play of the Sacrament (2.14)
Pseudo-Augustinian Soliloquies (3.2)

Fables

William Caxton, *Reynard the Fox* (3.17)
Robert Henryson, *Fables* (3.18)

Biblical Paraphrases, Commentaries

The General Prologue to the Wycliffite Bible (1.15)
Northern Homily Cycle (2.1)
Richard Rolle, *The English Psalter* (3.8)
Eleanor Hull, *A Commentary on the Penitential Psalms* (3.21)

Sermons, Religious Guides, Theological Treatises

Reginald Pecock, *Donet* (1.16a)
The Cloud of Unknowing (3.3) (guide to religious contemplation)
The Orchard of Syon (3.5)
Pore Caityf (3.6)
The Prick of Conscience (3.7)
Dives and Pauper (3.9)
Sermon of Dead Men (3.11)
The Mirror of Our Lady (3.12)

Guides to Study and Behavior

George Ashby, *Active Policy of a Prince* (1.9) (advice to princes)
Guy de Chauliac, *Cyrurgie* (1.10)
Thomas Norton, *Ordinal of Alchemy* (2.3) (guide to alchemy)
The Knowing of Woman's Kind in Childing (2.6) (gynecological guide)
Bishop Fox, *The Rule of Seynt Benet* (2.8) (religious rule for nuns)
The Amesbury Letter (2.9) (guide to nuns' vows)
William Caxton, Christine de Pizan's *Book of Fayttes of Armes and of Chyvalrye* (2.10)
    (guide to military strategy)
Knyghthode and Bataile (2.12) (guide to military strategy)
William Caxton, *Book of the Knight of the Tower* (2.16) (guide to female deportment)
Spektakle of Luf (2.17) (guide to male deportment)

EXCERPTS BY REGION
(texts that reached a broad national audience in England and/or Scotland are marked [N])

Scotland

John Barbour, *The Bruce* (1.2) (Aberdeen) [N]
Spektakle of Luf (2.17) (St. Andrew's)
Gavin Douglas, *Eneados* (3.16) [N]
Robert Henryson, *Fables* (3.18) (? Dumfermline) [N]
James I of Scotland, *The Kingis Quair* (3.23)

The North of England and North Midlands

Northern Homily Cycle (2.1) (?York) [N]
The Knowing of Woman's Kind in Childing (2.6)
The Prick of Conscience (3.7) [N]
Richard Rolle, *The English Psalter* (3.8) (Yorkshire) [N]
Nicholas Love, *The Mirror of the Blessed Life of Jesus Christ* (3.10) (Yorkshire, Mount
    Grace Charterhouse) [N]
? *The Wars of Alexander* (3.13)
Cursor Mundi (3.14) [N]
? Mechtild of Hackeborn, *The Book of Ghostly Grace* (3.20)

East Anglia

John Lydgate, *Troy Book* (1.7) (Suffolk, Bury St. Edmunds) [N]
John Metham, *Amoryus and Cleopes* (1.8) (Norfolk)
Osbern Bokenham, *Legendys of Hooly Wummen* (1.11) (Stoke Clare)
Julian of Norwich, *A Revelation of Love* (1.13/3.4) (Norwich)
Margery Kempe, *The Book of Margery Kempe* (1.14/3.22) (Norfolk, Lynn)
John Capgrave, *Life of St. Gilbert* (2.7) (Norfolk, Lynn)
The Croxton Play of the Sacrament (2.14) (Suffolk, Thetford, or Bury St. Edmonds)

Central, East, and South Midlands

Robert Mannyng, *Chronicle* (1.1) (Lincolnshire, Sixhills Priory)
Guy de Chauliac, *Cyrurgie* (1.10, the "Paris" Middle English translation)
The General Prologue to the Wycliffite Bible (1.15) (? near Oxford) [N]
On Translating the Bible into English (2.4) (? Oxford)
The Holi Prophete David Seith (2.5)
Pseudo-Augustinian Soliloquies (3.2)
The Cloud of Unknowing (3.3) [N]
Pore Caityf (3.6) (?) [N]
Eleanor Hull, *A Commentary on the Penitential Psalms* (3.21) (Hertfordshire, St. Albans)

London Area

Geoffrey Chaucer, *Complaint of Venus* (1.3) [N]
Thomas Usk, *The Testament of Love* (1.4)
Thomas Hoccleve, *The Complaint* (1.6)
George Ashby, *Active Policy of a Prince* (1.9)
Speculum Devotorum (Sheen Priory) (1.12)
Reginald Pecock, *Donet, Repressor* (1.16)
? William Caxton, Christine de Pizan's *Book of Fayttes of Armes and of Chyvalrye* (2.10) [N]
John Gower, *Confessio Amantis* (2.11) [N]
? *Knyghthode and Bataile* (2.12)
William Caxton, *Book of the Knight of the Tower* (2.16)
The Orchard of Syon (3.5) (Syon Abbey)
The Mirror of Our Lady (3.12)
John Skelton, Poggio Bracciolini's *Bibliotheca Historica of Diodorus Siculus* (3.15)
William Caxton, *Reynard the Fox* (3.17)
Henry Pepwell/Brian Anslay, Christine de Pizan's *Book of the City of Ladies* (3.24) [N]

West and Southwest Midlands, Southwest England

John Walton, Translation of Boethius (1.5) (Gloucestershire, Berkeley Castle) [N]
John Trevisa, *Dialogue* and *Epistle* (2.2) (Gloucestershire, Berkeley Castle) [N]
Thomas Norton, *Ordinal of Alchemy* (2.3) (Bristol) [N]
? *The Nightingale* (2.13)
South English Legendary (2.15) (? Worcester) [N]
A Talking of the Love of God (3.1)
Dives and Pauper (3.9) (perhaps Bristol) [N]
? *Sermon of Dead Men* (3.11)
William Langland, *Piers Plowman*, C Text (3.19) [N]

The South of England

The Amesbury Letter (2.9) (? Wiltshire)
Bishop Fox, *The Rule of Seynt Benet* (2.8) (Hampshire, Winchester)

WORKS BY PROFESSION OR BACKGROUND OF AUTHOR OR TRANSLATOR

Monks

John Lydgate, *Troy Book* (1.7) (Benedictine)
Anonymous, *Speculum Devotorum* (1.12) (Carthusian)
Anonymous, *The Cloud of Unknowing* (3.3) (? Carthusian)
Anonymous, *The Orchard of Syon* (3.5) (? Carthusian or secular priest)
Nicholas Love, *The Mirror of the Blessed Life of Jesus Christ* (3.10) (Carthusian, formerly ? Augustinian canon)
Anonymous, *The Mirror of Our Lady* (3.12) (? Carthusian or secular priest)
Mechtild of Hackeborn, *The Book of Ghostly Grace* (3.20) (? Carthusian)

Canons

Robert Mannyng, *Chronicle* (1.1) (Gilbertine)
John Walton, Translation of Boethius (1.5) (Augustinian)
Anonymous, *Northern Homily Cycle* (2.1) (? Augustinian)

Friars

Osbern Bokenham, *Legendys of Hooly Wummen* (1.11) (Augustinian)
John Capgrave, *Life of St. Gilbert* (2.7) (Augustinian)
Pore Caityf (3.6) (? Franciscan)
Dives and Pauper (3.9) (? Franciscan)

Hermits and Anchoresses

Julian of Norwich, *A Revelation of Love* (1.13/3.4)
Richard Rolle, *The English Psalter* (3.8)

Secular Clergy

John Barbour, *The Bruce* (1.2) (archdeacon of Aberdeen)
Reginald Pecock, *Donet* and *Repressor* (1.16) (bishop of St. Asaph's/Chichester)
John Trevisa, *Dialogue* and *Epistle* (2.2) (personal chaplain)
Anonymous, *Knyghthode and Bataile* (2.12) (? parson of Calais)
? Anonymous, *Sermon of Dead Men* (3.11)
Gavin Douglas, *Eneados* (3.16) (bishop of Dunkeld)

King

James I of Scotland, *The Kingis Quair* (3.23)

Royal and Municipal Administrators and Scribes

Geoffrey Chaucer, *Complaint of Venus* (1.3) (customs official, etc.)
Thomas Usk, *The Testament of Love* (1.4) (secretary to mayor of London, etc.)
Thomas Hoccleve, *The Complaint* (1.6) (clerk of the privy seal)

George Ashby, *Active Policy of a Prince* (1.9) (clerk of the signet, etc.)
Thomas Norton, *Ordinal of Alchemy* (2.3) (customs official)
John Skelton, Poggio Bracciolini's *Bibliotheca Historica of Diodorus Siculus* (3.15)

Gentry

John Gower, *Confessio Amantis* (2.11)
Eleanor Hull, *A Commentary on the Penitential Psalms* (3.21)
Brian Anslay, Christine de Pizan's *Book of the City of Ladies* (3.24)

Printers

William Caxton, Christine de Pizan's *Book of Fayttes of Armes and of Chyvalrye* (2.10);
    Book of the Knight of the Tower (2.16); *Reynard the Fox* (3.17)
Henry Pepwell, Christine de Pizan's *Book of the City of Ladies* (3.24)

Schoolmaster

Robert Henryson, *Fables* (3.18)

Urban Merchant

Margery Kempe, *The Book of Margery Kempe* (1.14/3.22)

Not Known

John Metham, *Amoryus and Cleopes* (1.8)
Guy de Chauliac, *Cyrurgie* (1.10, the "Paris" Middle English translation)
Anonymous, *The Knowing of Woman's Kind in Childing* (2.6)
Anonymous, *The Amesbury Letter* (2.9) (presumably a cleric)
Anonymous, *The Nightingale* (2.13)
Anonymous, *The Croxton Play of the Sacrament* (2.14) (presumably a cleric)
Anonymous, *South English Legendary* (2.15) (presumably a cleric)
Anonymous, *Spektakle of Luf* (2.17)
Anonymous, *A Talking of the Love of God* (3.1) (presumably a cleric)
Anonymous, *Pseudo-Augustinian Soliloquies* (3.2) (presumably a cleric)
Anonymous, *The Prick of Conscience* (3.7) (presumably a cleric)
Anonymous, *The Wars of Alexander* (3.13)
Anonymous, *Cursor Mundi* (3.14) (presumably a cleric)

AUTHORS WITH UNIVERSITY EDUCATIONS

Oxford

John Barbour, *The Bruce* (1.2) (also Paris and possibly Orléans)
John Lydgate, *Troy Book* (1.7)
? Anonymous, *The General Prologue to the Wycliffite Bible* (1.15)
Reginald Pecock, *Donet* and *Repressor* (1.16)

John Trevisa, *Dialogue* and *Epistle* (2.2)
? Anonymous, *On Translating the Bible into English* (2.4)
? Anonymous, *The Holi Prophete David Seith* (2.5)
Bishop Fox, *The Rule of Seynt Benet* (2.8)
Richard Rolle, *The English Psalter* (3.8)
John Skelton, Poggio Bracciolini's *Bibliotheca Historica of Diodorus Siculus* (3.15)
? William Langland, *Piers Plowman,* C Text (3.19)

Cambridge

Robert Mannyng, *Chronicle* (1.1)
Osbern Bokenham, *Legendys of Hooly Wummen* (1.11)
John Capgrave, *Life of St. Gilbert* (2.7)

Glasgow

Robert Henryson, *Fables* (3.18)

St. Andrew's

Gavin Douglas, *Eneados* (3.16)

EXCERPTS BY NAMED OR IMPLIED AUDIENCE OR PATRON OF WORK

Royal, Aristocratic, Court

John Barbour, *The Bruce* (1.2) (not specified)
Geoffrey Chaucer, *Complaint of Venus* (1.3) (unnamed prince/s or princess)
Thomas Hoccleve, *The Complaint* (1.6) (Joan, duchess of Westmoreland; Humphrey, duke of Gloucester)
John Lydgate, *Troy Book* (1.7) (Henry V)
John Walton, Translation of Boethius (1.5) (Elizabeth Berkeley)
George Ashby, *Active Policy of a Prince* (1.9) (Edward, prince of Wales)
John Trevisa, *Dialogue* and *Epistle* (2.2) (Thomas, Lord Berkeley)
John Gower, *Confessio Amantis* (2.11) (Richard II, Henry Bolingbroke)
Knyghthode and Bataile (2.12) (Henry VI)
The Nightingale (2.13) (Anne, duchess of Buckingham)
James I of Scotland, *The Kingis Quair* (3.23) (not specified)
Henry Pepwell/Brian Anslay, Christine de Pizan's *Book of the City of Ladies* (3.24) (Richard Grey, third earl of Kent)

Gentry

? Robert Mannyng, *Chronicle* (1.1) (Lincolnshire gentry and members of religious houses?)
John Metham, *Amoryus and Cleopes* (1.8) (Sir Miles and Lady Stapleton)
Osbern Bokenham, *Legendys of Hooly Wummen* (1.11) (various gentry women, Thomas Burgh)

William Caxton, Christine de Pizan's *Book of Fayttes of Armes and of Chyvalrye* (2.10)
William Caxton, *Book of the Knight of the Tower* (2.16)
Spektakle of Luf (2.17)
Dives and Pauper (3.9)
? *The Wars of Alexander* (3.13)

Female Religious

Speculum Devotorum (1.12) (nun of Syon)
John Capgrave, *Life of St. Gilbert* (2.7) (nuns of Sempringham)
Bishop Fox, *The Rule of Seynt Benet* (2.8) (nuns of Winchester diocese)
The Amesbury Letter (2.9) (two new sisters of the order)
A Talking of the Love of God (3.1) (an unnamed nun)
Pseudo-Augustinian Soliloquies (3.2) (unspecified nuns)
The Orchard of Syon (3.5) (nuns of Syon)
Richard Rolle, *The English Psalter* (3.8) (the anchoress Margaret Kirkeby)
The Mirror of Our Lady (3.12) (nuns of Syon)
Mechtild of Hackeborn, *The Book of Ghostly Grace* (3.20)

Male Religious

The Cloud of Unknowing (3.3) (an unnamed hermit)

Secular Women

The Knowing of Woman's Kind in Childing (2.6)

Medical Doctors and Surgeons

Guy de Chauliac, *Cyrurgie* (1.10)

National or General

Thomas Usk, *The Testament of Love* (1.4) (in practice, a small London group)
Julian of Norwich, *A Revelation of Love* (1.13/3.4) (in practice, a small East
    Anglian group)
The General Prologue to the Wycliffite Bible (1.15)
Reginald Pecock, *Donet* and *Repressor* (1.16) (in practice, small London and Oxford groups)
Thomas Norton, *Ordinal of Alchemy* (2.3) (in practice, educated practioners and patrons
    of alchemy)
South English Legendary (2.15)
Pore Caityf (3.6)
The Prick of Conscience (3.7)
Nicholas Love, *The Mirror of the Blessed Life of Jesus Christ* (3.10)
Sermon of Dead Men (3.11)
Cursor Mundi (3.14)
Gavin Douglas, *Eneados* (3.16)
William Caxton, *Reynard the Fox* (3.17)
William Langland, *Piers Plowman,* C Text (3.19)

Unspecified

The Book of Margery Kempe (1.14/3.22) (in practice included Carthusians of Mount
Grace Priory)
On Translating the Bible into English (2.4)
The Holi Prophete David Seith (2.5) (in practice included several London merchants)
The Croxton Play of the Sacrament (2.14)
John Skelton, Poggio Bracciolini's *Bibliotheca Historica of Diodorus Siculus* (3.15)
Robert Henryson, *Fables* (3.18)
Eleanor Hull, *A Commentary on the Penitential Psalms* (3.21)

EXCERPTS BY CIRCULATION: TEXTS SURVIVING PRIMARILY IN MANUSCRIPTS
(listed from largest to smallest number of surviving manuscripts)

Wycliffite Bible (1.15) **approx. 250** (mostly excerpts; *General Prologue* survives in **11**)
The Prick of Conscience (3.7) **approx. 127** (plus excerpts and a Latin translation)
South English Legendary (2.15) **62**
Nicholas Love, *The Mirror of the Blessed Life of Jesus Christ* (3.10) **56** (plus nine early
     printed editions)
William Langland, *Piers Plowman,* C Text (3.19) **52** (all three versions, **18** of C text, plus
     C16 printed editions)
Pore Caityf (3.6) **approx. 50** (mostly excerpts)
John Gower, *Confessio Amantis* (2.11) **46**
Richard Rolle, *The English Psalter* (3.8) **38**
Thomas Norton, *Ordinal of Alchemy* (2.3) **31** (plus several C16/17 printed editions)
John Lydgate, *Troy Book* (1.7) **23**
John Walton, Translation of Boethius (1.5) **22**
Northern Homily Cycle (2.1) **22** (two versions)
The Cloud of Unknowing (3.3) **17** (plus fragments and excerpts, plus two Latin versions)
Dives and Pauper (3.9) **11** (eight complete, plus three early printed editions)
On Translating the Bible into English (2.4) **9** (some postmedieval, plus two C16 editions)
Cursor Mundi (3.14) **9** (two versions, further fragmentary manuscripts)
Geoffrey Chaucer, *Complaint of Venus* (1.3) **8** (plus C16/17 printed editions)
Gavin Douglas, *Eneados* (3.16) **7** (C16 and C17, plus C16 printed edition)
Thomas Hoccleve, *The Complaint* (1.6) **5** (out of 11 MSS containing parts of the *Series*)
John Trevisa, *Dialogue* and *Epistle* (2.2) **5** (out of **14** of Trevisa's translation of Higden)
The Knowing of Woman's Kind in Childing (2.6) **5**
Robert Mannyng, *Chronicle* (1.1) **3** (plus partial C17 printed edition)
Knyghthode and Bataile (2.12) **3**
The Orchard of Syon (3.5) **3** (plus several sets of excerpts and C16 printed edition)
Speculum Devotorum (1.12) **2**
John Barbour, *The Bruce* (1.2) **2** (plus C16/17 printed editions)
Julian of Norwich, *A Revelation of Love* (1.13/3.4) **2** (**1** Short Text, **1** excerpt from Long
     Text, plus **2** C17 manuscripts and printed edition of Long Text)
John Capgrave, *Life of St. Gilbert* (2.7) **2** (one of them fragmentary)
The Nightingale (2.13) **2**
A Talking of the Love of God (3.1) **2**
Pseudo-Augustinian Soliloquies (3.2) **2**

Sermon of Dead Men (3.11) **2**

The Wars of Alexander (3.13) **2**

Mechtild of Hackeborn, *The Book of Ghostly Grace* (3.20) **2** (plus several excerpts)

Guy de Chauliac, *Cyrurgie* **1** (1.10, "Paris" Middle English translation; there are two others)

Reginald Pecock, *Donet* and *Repressor* (1.16) **1** each

Margery Kempe *The Book of Margery Kempe* (1.14/3.22) **1** (plus C16 printed edition of excerpts)

John Metham, *Amoryus and Cleopes* (1.8) **1**

George Ashby, *Active Policy of a Prince* (1.9) **1**

Osbern Bokenham, *Legendys of Hooly Wummen* (1.11) **1**

The Holi Prophete David Seith (2.5) **1**

The Amesbury Letter (2.9) **1**

The Croxton Play of the Sacrament (2.14) **1**

Spektakle of Luf (2.17) **1**

The Mirror of Our Lady (3.12) **1** (plus a C16 printed edition, seven surviving copies)

John Skelton, Poggio Bracciolini's *Bibliotheca Historica of Diodorus Siculus* (3.15) **1**

Robert Henryson, *Fables* (3.18) **1** (with several C16 printed editions)

Eleanor Hull, *A Commentary on the Penitential Psalms* (3.21) **1**

James I of Scotland, *The Kingis Quair* (3.23) **1**

EXCERPTS BY CIRCULATION: TEXTS SURVIVING IN PRINTED EDITIONS

Thomas Usk, *The Testament of Love* (1.4) (C16/17 editions of Chaucer's works, many surviving copies)

Bishop Fox, *The Rule of Seynt Benet* (2.8) (C16 edition, **2** copies)

William Caxton, Christine de Pizan's *Book of Fayttes of Armes and of Chyvalrye* (2.10) (1489 edition, **20** copies)

William Caxton, *Book of the Knight of the Tower* (2.16) (1484 edition, 6 full copies, 1 fragmentary)

William Caxton, *Reynard the Fox* (3.17) (1481 edition, 7 surviving copies; 1489 edition, **1** surviving copy)

Henry Pepwell/Brian Anslay, Christine de Pizan's *Book of the City of Ladies* (3.24) (few surviving copies)

ADAPTATIONS AND TRANSLATIONS: EXCERPT BY LANGUAGE OF SOURCE
(texts that are close translations or declare themselves translations are followed by [T])

Middle English

John Barbour, *The Bruce* (1.2) (lost chronicle of Robert le Roy)

Thomas Usk, *The Testament of Love* (1.4) (*Piers Plowman, Troilus and Criseyde,* ?Chaucer's *Boece*)

John Walton, Translation of Boethius (1.5) (Chaucer's *Boece*) [T] (ultimate source Latin)

A Talking of the Love of God (3.1) (*An Orison of God Almighty, The Wooing of Our Lord*)

Pore Caityf (3.6) (Richard Rolle, various works, and others in Anglo-Norman and Latin)

Anglo-Norman

Robert Mannyng, *Chronicle* (1.1) (Wace's *Roman de Brut;* Langtoft, *Chronicle*)
Northern Homily Cycle (2.1) (Robert of Greatham, *Miroir des evangiles*)
Pseudo-Augustinian Soliloquies (3.2) (unknown Anglo-Norman/French version of Latin) [T]
Prick of Conscience (3.7) (pseudo-Grosseteste, *Les peines de purgatorie*)

French

Chaucer, *Complaint of Venus* (1.3) (Oton de Graunson, 3 ballades) [T]
William Caxton, Christine de Pizan's *Book of Fayttes of Armes and of Chyvalrye* (2.10)
    (Christine de Pizan, military treatise) [T]
William Caxton, *Book of the Knight of the Tower* (2.16) (Geoffroy de la Tour-Landry,
    courtesy manual) [T]
Eleanor Hull, *A Commentary on the Penitential Psalms* (3.21) (lost French or Anglo-
    Norman commentary on Penitential Psalms) [T]
Henry Pepwell/Brian Anslay, Christine de Pizan's *Book of the City of Ladies* (3.24)
    (Christine de Pizan's *Livre de la cité des dames*) [T]

Dutch

William Caxton, *Reynard the Fox* (3.17) (Dutch *Roman de Renard* collection)

Latin

Thomas Usk, *The Testament of Love* (1.4) (Anselm, *De concordia*)
John Lydgate, *Troy Book* (1.7) (Guido delle Colonne, *Historia destructionis Troiae*) [T]
George Ashby, *Active Policy of a Prince* (1.9) (*Liber de dictis philosophorum*)
Guy de Chauliac, *Cyrurgie* (1.10) (the *Chirurgia magna*) [T]
Osbern Bokenham, *Legendys of Hooly Wummen* (1.11) (Jacobus de Voragine, *Legenda
    aurea,* and others)
Speculum Devotorum (1.12) (Johannes de Caulibus, *Meditationes vitae Christi,* and
    others) [T]
The General Prologue to the Wycliffite Bible (1.15) (Augustine, *De doctrina christiana*)
On Translating the Bible into English (2.4) (Richard Ullerston, *Determinatio*)
The Knowing of Woman's Kind in Childing (2.6) (*Trotula major*)
John Capgrave, *Life of St. Gilbert* (2.7) (unknown Latin *vita*)
Bishop Fox, *The Rule of Seynt Benet* (2.8) (Benedictine Rule) [T]
Knyghthode and Bataile (2.12) (Vegetius, *De re militari*) [T]
South English Legendary (2.15) (Jacobus de Voragine, *Legenda aurea,* and others)
The Orchard of Syon (3.5) (Latin translation of Catherine of Siena, *Dialogo*) [T]
The Prick of Conscience (3.7) (Honorius of Autun, *Elucidarium,* and many others)
Richard Rolle, *The English Psalter* (3.8) (Peter Lombard, commentary on the Psalms) [T]
Nicholas Love, *The Mirror of the Blessed Life of Jesus Christ* (3.10) (Johannes de Caulibus,
    Meditationes vitae Christi) [T]
Cursor Mundi (3.14) (Peter Comestor's *Historia scholastica* and others)
John Skelton, Poggio Bracciolini's *Bibliotheca Historica of Diodorus Siculus* (3.15)
(Poggio's Latin version of Diodorus Siculus's Greek history) [T]

Gavin Douglas, *Eneados* (3.16) (Virgil's *Aeneid*) [T]

Robert Henryson, *Fables* (3.18) (Gualterius Anglicus, fables collection)

Mechtild of Hackeborn, *The Book of Ghostly Grace* (3.20) (Mechtild's *Liber specialis gratiae*) [T]

Multiple, Unknown, or None

Thomas Hoccleve, *The Complaint* (1.6)

Julian of Norwich, *A Revelation of Love* (1.13/3.4)

Margery Kempe, *The Book of Margery Kempe* (1.14/3.22)

Reginald Pecock, *Donet* and *Repressor* (1.16) (scholastic theological texts)

John Trevisa, *Dialogue* and *Epistle* (2.2)

The Holi Prophete David Seith (2.5) (sermon on text from Bible)

The Amesbury Letter (2.9)

John Gower, *Confessio Amantis* (2.11) (multiple sources, including Ovid)

The Nightingale (2.13) (possibly John Pecham, *Philomena*)

Thomas Norton, *Ordinal of Alchemy* (2.3) (compendium from several alchemical treatises)

The Croxton Play of the Sacrament (2.14)

The Cloud of Unknowing (3.3)

Spektakle of Luf (2.17) (claims unknown Latin source)

Dives and Pauper (3.9) (includes many canon-law texts)

Sermon of Dead Men (3.11)

William Langland, *Piers Plowman,* C Text (3.19)

James I of Scotland, *The Kingis Quair* (3.23) (loose relationship with Boethius, *Consolation*)

GLOSSARY

THE LANGUAGE OF MIDDLE ENGLISH LITERARY THEORY

JOCELYN WOGAN-BROWNE

The Glossary continues the argument of this anthology as a whole by attempting to chart something of the intensely situated nature of Middle English literary theory and the themes and concerns of its discussions. In addition to terms for texts, their cultural prestige, and the activities and attitudes of their authors, the Glossary includes terms for the performance and reception of texts, the social locations and relations within which texts are embedded, and Middle English theories and models for reading them. For example, the term **conseytys** is included as a term for elaborate rhetorical figures (which it continues to be in sixteenth-century and later poetry). In this volume's texts, however, the term is more frequently used for audience understanding and responses, and these form the bulk of the entry for the word. The largely performative nature of medieval reading and its intense construction of reader response also produces a vigorous lexicon of the rhythms and occasions of reading and the complexities of interpretation and internalization (whether in the **hart**, the **reson**, **inward felyng**, or the collective **mend** and **remembrance** of cultural memory). Here terms (such as **conseyve, taaste, savoure**) whose metaphoric force has become inert in later literary discussions are often **refresched**. In an audiate culture (see the introduction to Part Two), verbs of **spekeynge** and **heeryng** are as important as those of **writing** and **enditing**, while the social matrices of Middle English literary production make audiences' and patrons' **desire** and **byddyng** as vital as authorial **entent**.

The Glossary thus includes much that would seem in some postmedieval literatures distinctly unliterary. But divisions between the literary and the nonliterary as created in early modern theorizing are often irrelevant or too narrow here: utility, instruction, and salvation are as important in these texts as aesthetic pleasure (whether of patrons and audiences or of authors). The problem of whether and how **wordes** and **writers** can impart **connyng** (knowledge) or embody **trouth**, and how **meanynge** and **sentence** can be **translat**, are persistent concerns, in which **litterature** overlaps with **historye, philosophie**, and theological **doctrine**. In addition to the lexis of pleasure (**joy, liking, plesance**, etc.) and of cognition and perception (**imagynacion, skylle, understandinge, wit, sight, fele, resceyve, conseyve**, etc.), that of spiritual **affeccion, comfort, recreacion, proffyte**, and **praysyng** has to be included, while the numerous topoi of authorial humility and inadequacy (**ignorance, humblesse, unabylnesse**, etc.) defer not only to predecessors among writers but to God, **auctor** of all creation. Not only are texts **undir correcion**, but writers, patrons, and audiences may be **amended** and their **mede** (reward) looked for from heaven as well as on earth. Even **sempyl men** must engage in active processes of interpretation in which they **take** the **text** of Holy Writ, with its **lettural** and **spiritual**, or **gastelye, sensce**, its **figuratiif spechis** and **holy wordes**, in **charite** (sometimes keeping, for their souls' sake, a wary eye on the **presumcion** with which some learned **expounnynge** is offered).

In such material, conceptual boundaries for what counts as literary terminology are not easily drawn or steadily maintained. Figurative representations, in particular, reach out widely into the language, and in some prologues almost every word could arguably count in this Glossary (Usk's magnificent demonstration of linguistic embodiedness for what can be written, thought, and understood in English is an example, as is Langland's discussion of ingesting the word of God [excerpts 1.4, 3.19]). Though long, the Glossary is still selective, and many other terms could arguably be included here. Fine, and doubtless inconsistent, lines have sometimes had to be drawn. The policy is to give as inclusive a representation as possible of the range of Middle English thinking about literature, particularly under the three main concerns addressed in Parts One to Three of this volume.

These considerations affect the Glossary in several practical ways. For each term, occurrences that can be deemed literary (in the extended ways referred to above) are normally cited and other uses excluded, but occasionally citations include less strictly literary senses (for example **translation,** where the cultural significance of the term in literature is supported by its long-established use in medieval saints' cults). Where a term's literary reference is established, it is lightly treated. So, for instance, **chapeter** is included, but not commented upon, whereas its neighbor **charite** (whose conceptual importance is considerable but less obviously part of a literary lexicon) is given more explication. Terms that do not occur in our texts are not included, even if, as in the case of the *Banna sanctorum* title for 2.15, they occur in other manuscripts of that text or if (as in the case of *banns,* 2.14) they are standardly used in discussion of medieval texts. Such terms are dealt with in the notes and headnotes to the excerpts. The Glossary seeks to give minimal definitions of as many words as possible: where more information is available, it is given in notes to excerpts. If terms occur in the same sense more than three times in any text, only the first three instances (followed by "etc.") are given.

Cross-references are always to the headword of an entry. Variant spellings are cross-referenced under *see* except where they would fall in the immediate neighborhood of the main entry. Where possible, cross-references are also supplied to sets of related terms under the rubric *see also.* These references are not exclusively to grammatically equivalent synonyms and may also include antonyms (as in **hony, soote: bitter, soure, sharp**). Since the boundaries of lexical sets fluctuate according to context, such cross-references should be regarded as invitations to consider the thematics of Middle English literary discussion rather than an exhaustive account of the cross-connections possible in this volume. Where variant spellings of a term occur, the headword is determined by alphabetical order, and the entry follows alphabetical order. Thus, for example, all entries for the noun **law(e)** will be found under **lagh,** since this spelling of the form is alphabetically the first to occur in our texts. Verb forms and adjectival forms are grouped together, but other grammatical forms are not. So, for instance, the adverb **lyghtely,** which has a relevant occurrence only with a *y* spelling in our texts, is placed under **ly-,** whereas the adjectival forms, which occur with both *i* and *y* spellings, are all grouped together under the form's first appearance at **light.** Similarly, past participles in **y-** or **i-** will be found under those letters if they are the only form of the verb to occur: where other forms of the same verb occur, however, past participles are placed under the relevant infinitive or other forms.

Only the senses in which words are used in our texts are given: for general accounts of terms included here, readers should see *MED* and *OED.* Equivalent terms from the vocabulary of Latin medieval literary theory are given as part of headword definitions where relevant. A selection of Latin terms occurring in our texts is listed separately at the end of the vernacular listings. Glossary citations are by part and excerpt number, followed by a colon and the line number (all in Arabic numerals). Superscript cardinal numbers refer to the total number of instances in a given line. Where only one of a number of occurrences is relevant, superscript ordinal numbers are used.

1., 2.,	first, second, third person
acc.	accusative
adj.	adjective
adv.	adverb
comp.	comparative
dat.	dative

etym.	etymologically
fig.	figuratively
fut.	future
gen.	genitive
gramm.	grammatical
imp.	imperative
impers.	impersonal
inf.	infinitive
lit.	literally
n.	noun
pa.	past tense
pass.	passive
perh.	perhaps
personif.	personification
pl.	plural
p.p.	past participle
pr.	present tense
pr.p.	present participle
refl.	reflexive
sg.	singular
s.o.	someone
s.th.	something
subj.	subjunctive
superl.	superlative
v.	verb (infinitive)
vbl.n.	verbal noun, gerund

MIDDLE ENGLISH TERMS

abidyngly *adv.* constantly (as reading mode) 3.10: 52. *See also* **bisily, easely, likyngly, moderatly: hast, swithenesse, tumultuosite.**

abilite *n.* ability (of author) 1.5: 6, **abylyte, my symple** ~ 2.9: 47. *See also* **unabylnesse, humblesse, unconnynge, unworthynesse.**

abredge *v.* abridge (of source material) 2.16: 70. *See also* **minisshyng.**

abyde *v.* abide, dwell (as capacity of written text) 2.9: 25, ~ **therupon** (mode of reading) 3.12: 122.

abydyng *adj.* lasting, sustained, ~ **meditacion** (as mode of reading) 3.2: 6. *See also* **abidyngly** (*adv.*).

accepte *imp.* accept (as authorial plea regarding literary work) 2.12: 85, 86, **acceptyng** (author's goodwill) 1.9: 69. See also **resceyve, take.**

actif *adj.* active voice (*gramm.*), ~ **for** ~ (in translation) 2.2: 143, ~ **for the passif** 2.2: 145–46.

addicioun *n.* amplification 1.9: 60. **addicionis** *pl.* 2.7: 45. *See also* **delatyng, puttyng [to].**

addressith *see* **adresse.**

adornne *v.* ornament rhetorically 1.8: 9. **adornyd** *p.p.* decorated (of illuminated book) 1.8: 34.

adresse *v.* direct (of author's plea to presiding goddess) 2.10: 42. **addressith** *pr.3.sg.* influences, **to vertue** ~ (of historical reading's effect on audience) 3.15: 60. *See also* **directe, dispose, dresse, rewlyd.**

advertysyn *v.* make manifest (at beginning of text) 1.11: 2.

affeccion *n.* emotion, affect (*affectio*), (of a reader) 3.10: 21, (of author) 2.10: 12, **affeccioun**

(response to images) 3.9: 4, **goostly ~** (reason for writing) 3.5: 8, **youre ~** (of reader preference) 3.5: 24, **affeccyoun** (of author) 1.11: 128, **excyte mennys ~** (purpose of writing) 1.11: 128, **affection, ~ and liking** preference (of audience) 3.4: 6. **affeccions** *pl.*, **inflawme his ~** (consequence of reading) 3.2: 8, **affecyons, sturre up the ~** (purpose of texts) 3.12: 145, 147, 149, etc. *See also* **felyng, stering.**

affectuouse *adj.* passionate, **~ thynkynge** (product of reading) 3.8: 49. *See also* **amorouse, lovely, lovesum, luffynge.**

aleye *n.* alley, *(fig.)* chapter or subsection of text 3.5: 19. **aleyes** *pl.* chapters 3.5: 35, **~ where ye wolen walk** (of readerly choices) 3.5: 21. *See also* **pathis, orcherd: frewte, herbis, wedis.**

allegis *pr.3.sg.* adduces in proof (of authorities) 2.17: 8. **allegit** *p.p.* (of literary examples) 2.17: 14, 19.

Almayne *adj. as n.* German (as language of biblical translation) 2.4: 5.

altyrris *pr.3.sg.* alters (of stylistic variation) 3.16: 33.

amende *v.* improve (text or author) 1.8: 142, 1.16: 45, 3.24: 25, (of audience) 3.12: 39, **amenden** 1.7: 210. **amende** *pr. subj.* **God ~** (of author's detractors) 1.16: 125. **amendyng** *pr.p.* (response to Bible) 2.5: 115. **amended** *p.p.* 2.2: 114, **amendyd** 1.5: 8. *See also* **correct, submitt.**

amendement *n.* improvement, **upon ~** to be amended (of book's reception by patron) 2.11: 90. *See also* **correccion, reproof.**

amorouse *adj.* loving, **~ and a wise entent** (reading mode) 3.2: 5 *See also* **affectuouse, lovely, lovesum, luffynge.**

antiquite *n.* antiquity, **bokys of ~** (venerated) old books 1.7: 80.

Apocalips *n.* Apocalypse, Book of Revelation 2.2: 106, 2.4: 25, 2.5: 5, **Apocalipse** 3.11: 8.

apperis *pr.3.pl.* are represented (of exemplary evils) 2.17: 42.

approvid *adj.* authorized (by senior churchmen) 1.16: 91, **approvyd, ~ wymmen** (of female visionaries) 1.12: 74.

argument *n.* argument (as logical category) 1.16: 38, 2.2: 40. **argumentis** *pl.* 2.2: 94.

artificyal *adj.* artistic, **procedyng ~** (as way of ordering literary work) 1.11: 83. *See also* **poetycal.**

assay *v.* experience 1.6: 50, carry out 2.3: 66, **assaye** *(fig.)* browse (in reading), **~ and serche** 3.5: 22–23. *See also* **taaste.**

assembled *p.p.* compiled 2.10: 21. *See also* **compacte, compile, gader, glene.**

assised *p.p.* composed (with sense of arranged, measured out) 2.11: 73. *See also* **foorme, ordire.**

asygne *v.* assign, **~ a place** (of dedicatee's acceptance of text) 2.13: 19.

attende *v.* pay attention (of audience) 1.11: 82, **~ to the circumstauncis** (attend to context) 1.16: 30.

auctor *n.* author *(auctor)* 1.11: 69, 2.17: 41, **~ of al wisdom and kunnynge** (of God) 2.5: 63, **auctour** 1.11: 13, 20, 32, etc., **~ of ful highe renoun** 1.7: 184, **the entent of the ~** 1.11: 23–24, **auctoure** 3.24: 81, **author, my ~** 3.18: 43, **myne ~** 3.16: 22, **mynne ~** 3.16: 29, **autour, ~ of Scripture** (human author through whom God's spirit works) 1.15: 4, 6. **au[c]tors** *pl.* authors, authorities, (as keepers of cultural memory 1.7: 101), **auctoures, ~ of gramer** 3.12: 71, **auctouris** 2.7: 24, **auctours** 2.3: 70, **dyvers ~** 3.24: 36, 88, 2.10: 19, **autoris, ~ of Hooly Scripture** 1.15: 52, **autouris, the first ~** (of patristic writers) 1.15: 54, **autours** 1.15: 49. *See also* **cause, endyter, faders, maister, poete, translatour, writer.**

auctorite *n.* authority *(auctoritate)* 2.5: 102, **auctoryte** 3.24: 57, **autorite** 1.15: 12, **~ of charite** (as principle of reading) 3.3: 20. **auctoritees** *pl.* 3.10: 15, **auctorytes** 2.9: 47.

aunters *see* **aventure.**

aureat *adj.* golden (of style) 1.7: 31. *See also* **sugred, soote.**

author *see* **auctor.**

aventure *n.* adventure (as autobiographical subject matter) 3.23: 68. **aventures** *pl.* adventures (as exemplary subject matter) 1.4: 34, **aunters** (as subject matter) 3.14: 14. *See also* **chaunces, dede, ferles, marvellys, wondres.**

avised *p.p.* counseled (function of literature) 2.11: 72. *See also* **counseil.**

avisement *n.* deliberation (in systematic reading) 2.2: 42, **avysement** 1.12: 61. *See also* **loking, stodyinge.**

bachelers *n.pl.* graduates in theology 1.14: 59. *See also* **auctor, clerk, doctour, lered, maister.**

balade *n.* formally rhymed verse 1.9: 1, 2.12: 60. **balades** *pl.* stanzaic poems 1.9: 33, 68, 2.16: 16. *See also* **layes, roundels, sange, vyrelayes.**

baston *n.* rhyming stanza 1.1: 51n. *See also* **couwee.**

begin *v.* begin (*incipit*), (composition or text) 3.18: 61, **begyn** 3.14: 59, **begynne** 1.5: 71, 1.7: 214, 1.10: 23, 2.7: 17, 3.14: 94 (reading) 3.2: 12 ~ **at the begynnyng** 3.2: 10, ~ **my presysyng** (of psalms) 3.21: 10, **biginnen** (reading instruction) 3.1: 5, **bygynne** 2.11: 180. **bigynne** *pr.1.sg.* 3.5: 33. **begynnes** *pr.3.sg.* 1.1: 30, **begynneth** 1.10: 1, 2.10: 1, 2.16: 1, 3.12: 1, 3.12: 61, 3.17: 1, 3.24: 30, (of reading) 3.6: 6, **begynnis** 2.17: 1, **begynnys** 3.16: 69, **begynnyth** 1.12: 1, **late** ~ (of Chaucer) 1.8: 127, **begynnythe** 1.14: 2, **biginneth** 3.3: 1, 6, **bigynnith** 1.16: 126, **bygynneth** 2.11: 175, ~ **at Yeres day** 2.15: 67. **begynne** *pr.2.pl.* (of reading) 3.12: 111. **begynnyng** *pr.p.* 1.11: 2. **began** *pa.3.sg.* ~ **ayeyne** (of exemplary reader) 3.10: 28. **begunne** *p.p. as adj.* ~ **matere** 1.11: 15. *See also* **blyn, ceesse, ende** (*v.*), **leve.**

beginnyng *n.* place in text, commencement (*incipit*) 3.3: 23, **begynnyng** 1.8: 82, 1.11: 2, 8, 3.14: 97, **begynnynge** (of Trinity as origin of text) 1.12: 89, **biginninge** 2.1: 115, **bigynninge** 3.1: 16, **bigynnyng** 1.15: 13, 44, 45, etc. **bygynnyng** 1.10: 13, 16. *See also* **myddel, ende** (*n.*), **endinge.**

bereth *pr.3.sg.* bears (*refl.*) **hit self** ~ **wyttenesse** (of book's format) 3.7: 21, **beryth,** ~ **wytnesse** shows (of proof text) 1.11: 61. **bering** *pr.p.* (morally responsible mode of possessing book) 3.3: 10.

besechen *v.* beseech (for eloquence) 1.5: 62. **beseche** *pr.1.sg.* (for skill) 1.8: 8, (for forgiveness) 1.8: 141, 1.9: 44, (tolerance of work) 1.11: 69, (prayers of audience) 1.11: 228, (God's help) 2.9: 52, (audience) 3.3: 8, 20, **beseke** (patrons) 1.8: 119. **besecheth** *pr.3.sg.* (dedicatee) 2.12: 85, **besechyth** (for indulgence) 1.8: 22. **besechinge** *pr.p.* (dedicatee) 2.13: 17, **besechyng** (author to patron) 1.5: 7, (author to God) 1.9: 56, 3.21: 10, **besechynge** (author to audience, for prayers) 3.12: 95, **beseking,** ~ **all ladyes and gentillwemen** (author to audience) 2.17: 39. *See also* **pray, requere.**

besynes *n.* labor (of versification) 1.8: 147, **besynesse** (of audience) 1.10: 9, **bisinesse** activity (of poet) 2.11: 70, **busynesse** 2.11: 137, **bysynes, ententyffe** ~ (of translator) purposeful industry 2.6: 11–12, **bysynesse** (of prose composition) 1.12: 19. *See also* **labour, occupacion, travail, wark.**

Bibel *n.* Bible 2.4: 6, **Bibile** 2.4: 2, **Bible** 1.15: 44, 85, 1.16: 129, **Byble** 1.12: 70, 2.4: 3, 2.16: 67, **Bybyl** 3.22: 35. *See also* **scripture, writ** (*n.*).

bille *n.* written petition 2.12: 52.

bisette *v.* arrange, fashion, ~ **my wordis** 1.16: 36. *See also* **devise, set.**

bisily *adv.* intently (reading mode) 3.10: 52, (*fig.*) of liturgical recitation 3.5: 1. *See also* **abidyngly, easely, likyngly, moderatly: hast, swithenesse, tumultuosite.**

bisinesse *see* **besynes.**

bitter *adj.* bitter (of reading) 3.5: 16, **bittir** 3.5: 39, **bittire** 3.5: 39, (of reader) 3.8: 11. *See also* **hard, scharpe, soure: soote.**

blaim *n.* blame, reproach (of texts and writers) 2.17: 40, **blame** 2.10: 10, **put in** ~ 1.11: 36, ~ **of bakbiters** 2.2: 138. **blames** *pl.* ~ **of women** (*blasmes des femmes:* literary topos, *see also* 2.16: 42, 54) 3.24: 61–62. *See also* **blamynge, detraccioun, diffames, inpugnacioun, slaundres.**

blame *v.* blame (of translation) 2.2: 115, 117, reproach, slander, dispraise (texts and authors) 3.12: 80, 82, **feyne and** ~ 2.11: 148. **blame** *pr. subj.* 1.1: 73, (of critics) 2.2: 117. **blameth** *pr.3.pl.* 2.2: 116. **blamed** *p.p.* 2.2: 116, 2.16: 55. *See also* **deprave, diffame, feyne.**

blamers *n.pl.* reproachers (unsuitable readers) 3.3: 29.

blamynge *vbl.n.* reproach (of women: literary topos) 3.24: 82. *See also* **blaim.**

blyn *v.* cease, stop (of narration or composition) 3.14: 69, **blynne** 2.2: 138. **blyn** *pr.1.sg.* 3.14:
93. *See also* **ceesse, ende** (*v.*), **leten, leve, rist: begin.**

bok *n.* book, work, volume 2.11: 25, 31, 60, etc., 3.7: 9, 21, 27, etc., **boke** 1.4: 8, 30, 63, etc.,
1.5: 28, 1.7: 199, 1.8: 29, 40, 1.12: 1, 10, 13, etc., 1.14: 1, 84, 93, etc., 2.3: 3, 90, 99, etc.,
2.10: 29, 3.2: 1, 16, 3.8: 10, 14, 26, etc., 3.9: 7, 3.10: 49, 3.11: 8, 14, 19, etc., 3.12: 1, 35,
66, etc., 3.14: 1, 74, 94, 3.17: 11, 3.20: 5, 3.22: 20, 3.23: 14, 29, 3.24: 9, 15, 39, etc. ~ **of
Clere and Noble Wimmen** 2.10: 36–37, ~ **of Convercions Naturalle** 2.3: 79, ~ **of Cristes
life** 3.10: 13, ~ **of hy contemplacyone** book of contemplative mysticism 3.22: 34, ~ **of
Matheolus** 3.24: 51, ~ **of perpetual memory** 1.4: 61, ~ **of the Testament of Love** 1.4: 100–
101, ~ **of ympnes** 3.8: 51, ~ **of ympnes of Crist** 3.8: 47, **first** ~ (of subdivision of a volume)
2.4: 7, **Hyltons** ~ 3.22: 35, **lytyl** ~ 1.8: 116, **Seynt Brydys** ~ 3.22: 35, **the** ~ *De animalibus*
1.4: 50, **Troye** ~ 1.7: 100, **book** 1.5: 10, 1.10: 35, 1.11: 9, 1.14: 107, 1.16: 1, 6, 7, etc., 2.7:
19, 2.10: 4, 17, 2.11: 112, 170, 177, 2.16: 1, 28, 53, etc., 3.3: 9, 31, 41, 3.5: 10, 3.9: 6, 28,
35, etc., subdivision of a volume 1.15: 12, 42, 43, etc., (*fig.*) visual imagery 3.9: 40, (sight
of God) 3.9: 41, 3.11: 13, ~ *of Consolacyion* 1.5: 10, ~ *of 83 Questioun* 1.16: 33, ~ **of
Fayttes of Armes and of Chyvalrye** 2.10: 1, ~ **of Liif** 3.11: 8, ~ **of moralite** 1.5: 38, ~ **of
peynture and of ymagerye** 3.9: 8, ~ **of revelaciouns** 3.5: 10, ~ **of the Byble** 2.16: 67, **his** ~
De questionibus armenorum 1.15: 45–46, **inward** ~ 1.16: 147, 149, 154, **inward preciose**
~ 1.16: 153, **litil** ~ 2.16: 58, **litil** ~ *Of knyghthode and bataile* 2.12: 46, *Litil* ~ **to be a
Declarative** *Little Book That Sets Everything Out* 1.16: 75–76, *Litil* ~ 1.16: 109, *The* ~ *of
Cristen Religioun* 1.16: 86, **booke** 1.10: 28, 1.14: 84, 97, 98, etc., 2.3: 17, 3.2: 64, 3.4: 1,
11, 3.17: 6, 3.20: 1, 2, 5, etc., **lytel** ~ 2.16: 48, ~ **of hyre felyngys and hire revelacyons** 1.14:
68, ~ **of Spyritualle Grace** 3.20: 7, 34–35, **the Frenche** ~ 3.2: 20, **buk** 1.2: 37, **lytill** ~ 2.17:
1, 21, 25, etc., **buke** 3.13: 17, 3.16: 63, 3.18: 59, 3.23: 52, subdivision of volume 3.16: 69.
boke *pl.* 3.9: 7, **bokes** 1.7: 129, 1.8: 146, 2.1: 68, 2.2: 18, 19, 20, etc., 2.8: 37, 2.10: 21,
2.11: 9, 44, 53, 3.6: 5, 3.8: 38, 3.10: 1, 3.12: 107, 136, 137, etc., 3.24: 34, 37, **Aristotils**
~ 2.2: 95, ~ **of cronicles** 2.2: 25, 28, 41, etc., ~ **of cronycles** 2.2: 20, ~ **of gostly fruyte** 3.12:
111, ~ **of hevynes and of drede** 3.12: 160–61, ~ **of interpretaciones** 2.7: 23, ~ . . . **of logik
and of philosophy** 2.2: 95, ~ **of yvel or occasyon to yvel** 3.12: 108, ~ **olde** 3.24: 7 **Denys** ~
2.2: 97, **holy** ~ 3.12: 98, **worldely** ~ 3.12: 105, **Ranulph of Chestres** ~ 2.2: 136, **Seynt
Gregories** ~ *Dialoges* 2.2: 102–3, **bokis** 1.16: 6, 41, 46, etc., 2.3: 63, 76, 100, etc., 2.8: 37,
bokis *gen.pl.* 1.16: 50, **ayens hise** ~ 1.16: 102–3, ~ **of Goddis lawe** 2.5: 130, **Englisch** ~
1.16: 46, **holy seintis** ~ 1.16: 103, **Latyn** ~ 1.16: 46, **profitable** ~ 1.16: 67, **bokys** 1.7: 80,
1.8: 130, 132, 2.13: 19, 3.22: 35, 41, 43, **amonge hyre** ~ (of patron's library) 2.13: 19, ~
of antiquite 1.7: 80, **holy** ~ 3.22: 46, **bookes** 1.6: 43, 1.9: 78, 1.10: 20, 2.16: 78, ~ **of
cirurgie** subdivisions of volumes on surgery 1.10: 34–35, **defaute of** ~ 1.10: 19, **bookis,
filosoferis** ~ 1.15: 58, **outward** ~ (of actual books, as opposed to metaphorical) 1.16: 148,
bookys, ~ **olde** 2.12: 57; **bukis** 3.16: 5. *See also* **merour, volume.**

booke *v.* put in a book 2.11: 139.

boystous *adj.* rough, unpolished (of lexis), 1.4: 6, 9, (of English) 3.2: 18. *See also* **laud, rewde.**

burel *adj.* unlearned, ~ **clerk** 2.11: 59.

byddyng *n.* command (of dedicatee) 1.7: 74, ~ **of the Holy Gost** (to discussion and composition) 1.14: 57. *See also* **comaundement, desir, heste, precept, requeist.**

cadence *n.* meter (*cursus*), **by crafte and** ~ through (poetic) art and the use of meter 1.7: 192,
use of rhetorical periods 3.1: 16.

calengid *p.p.* changed, translated (of truths of pagan philosophy) 1.15: 75. *See also* **chaunge,
drau, Englisshed, interpreted, save** (*imp.*), **set, translate, transmwe, turne.**

calle *pr.3.pl.* call, name (literary work) 3.14: 2. **called** *p.p.* 3.12: 2, 3.24: 42, **callit** 2.17: 1, 42, callyd 1.12: 20, 59. *See also* clepe, entitillit, het.

carnal *adj.* *(fig.)* overly literal or of limited understanding, ~ soulis 1.12: 78, ~ folke 1.12: 80. *See also* carnal, fleischli, lettural, naked: gastelye, spiritual.

carpe *v.* speak, ~ and to lestyn 3.13: 8. *See also* recyteth, reherce, reporte, say, schau, speke, spel, tel.

carpyng *vbl.n.* recitation 1.2: 10. *See also* saynge, tellynge: disours.

cause *n.* cause (*causa*), (of composition) 1.8: 29, 1.11: 21, ~ efficyent efficient cause (*causa efficiens*), (the author) 1.11: 10, 13, ~ materyal material cause (*causa materialis*), subject matter, sources 1.11: 11, ~ . . . seconde subject matter, sources 1.11: 16, ~ why purpose 1.11: 22, formal ~ formal cause (*causa formalis*), literary procedures and treatment 1.11: 12, 17, fourte [~] final cause, purpose 1.11: 12, fynal ~ final cause (*causa finalis*), purpose (of text) 1.11: 12, 21, thrydde [~] literary procedures and treatment 1.11: 12. causis *pl.* arguments 1.16: 9, 2.3: 73, causys, ~ two 1.11: 125, foure ~ (Aristotelian) causes of composition 1.11: 6, 27. *See also* auctor, endyter, maister, poete, translatour, writer: foorme, entent, mater.

ceesse *pr.1.sg.* cease, ~ of this prolog 3.5: 26, sese 1.8: 107. *See also* blyn, ende (*v.*), leten, leve: begynne.

cence *n.* sense, meaning, spirytuel ~ (used of allegorical meaning in Scripture) 3.21: 23, sensce, gostely ~ spiritual meaning 2.13: 28. *See also* meanynge, understandinge.

chaf *n.* chaff, *(fig.)* untruths of history 1.7: 103, author's inadequacy 1.11: 47. *See also* corn.

chalke *n.* chalk, *(fig.)* poor artistic technique, coles and ~ 1.4: 12.

chalky *adj.* chalky, rough, *(fig.)* of artistic representation 1.4: 13.

change *see* chaunge.

chapeter *n.* chapter (*capitulum*) 3.2: 11, chapetele 1.12: 62, 81, chapetre 2.5: 17, 94, chapiter 2.3: 146, 148, 152, etc., chapitere 2.3: 142, chapitre 1.16: 127, chapter 2.5: 5, chapytre 2.10: 2, 3.24: 30. chapetelys *pl.* 1.12: 11, chapiters 2.3: 139, chapitres 3.3: 41², 42, 3.5: 12, 21, 32, chapitris 1.16: 7, chapytres 3.24: 82.

charite *n.* charity, love (*caritas*), (as source of understanding Scripture) 1.15: 14, 25, (as completion of the law of the Old Testament) 1.15: 16, 17, (as principle of general understanding) 1.15: 27, (as revealed plainly in Scripture) 1.15: 29, (as concealed in Scripture) 1.15: 30², 33, etc., 2.5: 131, 132, 134, etc., charyte (as inspiration to composition) 1.13: 88, (as motive for teaching) 3.21: 44, 53, cheryte, ageyn ~ (of denial of dedicatee's request) 1.11: 194. *See also* love.

chaunces *n.pl.* adventures (as subject matter), bolde ~ 1.1: 65. *See also* aventure, dede, ferles, marvellys, wondres.

chaunge *v.* change (word order in nonliteral translation) 2.2: 145. change *pr. subj.* alter (text) 2.3: 171. changing *pr. p.* 2.3: 174, chaunging (in textual copying) 2.2: 147. chaunged *p.p.* 3.2: 17, ychaunged 2.2: 148. *See also* halff-chongyd, calengid, transmwe.

chese *v.* choose (of reader) 3.5: 20. chace *pa.3.sg.*, she ~ certayne parties (in reading) 3.10: 25.

chewe *see* schewe.

chosen *adj.* select, exquisite, ~ sange 3.8: 10.

clause *n.* clause (*clausula*) 3.12: 70, sentence 2.3: 102, sentence or subsection 1.11: 18². clauses *pl.* subsections of a chapter 3.24: 82.

cleer *adj.* clear (of style or meaning) ~ and pleyne 2.2: 142, clere 1.7: 43, 1.11: 16, 2.10: 29, *(fig.,* of composition) 1.7: 122, (of prose rather than verse) 2.2: 125, 2.10: 29, famous, illustrious 1.10: 4, Boke of ~ and Noble Wimmen 2.10: 36–37. *See also* commen, open, playn, rounde: derk.

clepe *pr.1.sg.* call, name (a book) 3.5: 11. cleped *p.p.* called, titled (of books), 1.4: 65, 1.10: 35, clepid 1.16: 4, 7, 8, etc., clepit 3.23: 15. *See also* calle, entitillit, het.

clerely *adv.* clearly, completely (of surveying reading choices) 3.5: 22, (of audience understanding), **clerely** (of texts) 3.24: 79.

clergie *n.* learning 1.16: 125, 3.10: 11, **clergy** 3.2: 90², 3.11: 9, **Clergye** (personified) learning 3.19: 1, 18, 40.

clerk *n.* cleric, scholar (*clericus*) 1.8: 136, 1.11: 1, 85, 1.16: 128, 136, 143, 2.1: 39, 2.11: 59, 3.6: 6, 3.18: 57, 3.23: 22, **clerke** 1.5: 44, 1.12: 20, 51, 2.3: 50, 153, 157, 2.4: 30, 3.10: 6, 3.11: 13, 17, **klerk** 2.1: 69. **clarkes** *pl.* 3.24: 78, **clerkes** 1.4: 26, 76, 1.10: 31, 2.2: 18, 2.16: 64, 3.10: 2, 3.12: 77, 3.24: 60, **clerkis** 1.15: 87, 1.16: 51, 122, 142, etc., 2.2: 117, 2.3: 4, 10, 35, etc., 2.4: 29, 2.5: 29, 43, 56, 3.5: 31, 3.18: 19, **clerkys** 1.8: 34, 1.14: 58, 65, 2.10: 25, 3.2: 88, 3.9: 7, 3.22: 2, 4, **klerkes** 2.1: 67. *See also* **auctor, bacheler, doctour, lered, maister.**

cloude *n.* cloud, ~ **of unconnyng** (*fig.*) ignorance (of author) 1.4: 74, **under** ~ (*fig.*) behind a cloud (used of truth in writing) 1.7: 138. **cloudis** *pl.* ~ [**of ygnoraunce**] (*fig.*) absence of compositional technique 1.7: 60. *See also* **enlumymne.**

cloudy *adj.* cloudy (*fig.*) obscure, unclear (of text) 1.4: 74, **clowdy** 1.4: 15, 2.3: 73.

code *see* **schewe.**

coles *see* **chalke.**

collacions *n.pl.* collations, refectory readings (*collatio*) 2.8: 17.

colour *n.* hue, appearance, (*fig.*) figure of speech (*color*), ~ **of rethorik** verbal ornament 1.7: 193–94, ~ **of trouthe** appearance of truth 3.15: 84. **coloures** *pl.* (*fig.*), **queynt knyttyng** ~ intricate unifying verbal ornament 1.4: 2, **colours, better** ~ (of more skilful ornament) 1.4: 14, ~ **ryche** 1.4: 11, **semelych** ~ (of appropriate stylistic ornament) 1.4: 8, ~ **of rethoryk** 1.11: 89. *See also* **enlumyne, peynten, sownde.**

comaunde *v.* command, **whiche al me may** ~ (of king's command of poet) 2.11: 118, ~ **scholde** (of [personified] Conscience's relation to Scripture) 3.19: 31. **comaunded** *pa.3.sg.* 1.7: 84, **comaundyd** (of God's interdiction of image making) 3.2: 56, **comawnded** (of God's injunction to write) 1.14: 73. **comawndyd** *p.p.* 1.14: 70.

comaundement *n.* command (of patron) 1.11: 182, **commandement** direction or commission (of patron) 2.11: 91. **commaundementes** *pl.,* ~ **of God** (subject of treatise) 3.6: 11, **Goddis** ~ 3.6: 19–20, **comaundementis, twey** ~ (Christ's) 1.15: 20, **comaundments, the Ten** ~ 3.8: 29. *See also* **byddyng, desir, heste, precept, requeist.**

comaundyng *vbl.n.* command (of patron) 2.11: 142. *See also* **comaundement.**

comfort *n.* comfort (purpose or result of reading, *confortatio*) 1.14: 3, 2.2: 140, **gastli** ~ (fruit of spiritually sustaining recitation) 3.8: 1, **comforte** 3.12: 117, 156, 162, **gostly** ~ 3.12: 31, **grace and** ~ 3.12: 99, **comforth** 3.13: 8, **gostelye** ~ 3.20: 3, **confort** 3.7: 19, **conforte** 1.12: 48, **goostly** ~ 2.9: 5, **cumfort, goostly** ~ 3.5: 10. *See also* **recreacion.**

comfortabyl *adj.* comforting, sustaining, ~ **tretys** 1.14: 2, **comfortabylle,** ~ **wordes** 1.13: 3, **confortable** 3.5: 57.

comforte *imp. pl.* let us take comfort (in interpreting text) 2.5: 61. **conforted** *p.p.* uplifted 3.5: 14, **counforted** 3.3: 39.

commandement *see* **comaundement.**

commen *adj.* common to all (of speech) 3.12: 72, **common** open to all (of vision) 1.13: 64, ~ **peplis langage** 1.16: 6–7, **commonn,** ~ **weill** common well-being 3.16: 40, **commoun** (of teaching within a vision) 1.13: 68, **in** ~ 3.14: 84, **commune** (of English langage) 2.8: 34, **commyn** (of learning to speak) 2.2: 3, ~ **peple** (of audience) 2.3: 58, **in** ~ 3.15: 18, **comon** (of speech) 2.3: 59, **comoun, the** ~ *Donet* (of grammar book in general use) 1.16: 2, ~ **peplis langage** 1.16: 13. *See also* **cleer, open, playn, rounde.**

commune *n.* the commons (of audience) 3.14: 78.

commune *v.* communicate 1.6: 58.

communynge *vbl.n.* communication 1.6: 57.

comonalte *n.* common people (of audience) 1.1: 61.

compacte *p.p.* compiled 3.15: 21. *See also* **gader.**

compellyng *vbl.n.* compulsion, ~ **of hys owyne consciens** (of reason for composition) 1.14: 143.

compellyth *pr.3.pl.* compel (to composition), **both thynges** ~ (of audience desire and Holy Spirit's prompting) 2.9: 22. **compellid** *p.p.,* ~ **by charite** 3.5: 8. *See also* **exciten, inflawme, kyndils, mevyde, quyken, stere.**

compendiosite *n.* comprehensiveness (of compilation) 1.10: 33.

compendious *adj.* (as in a *compendiloquium*) concise (of a narrative account) 1.7: 181.

compendyously *adv.* fully (of summarized doctrine) 1.11: 25.

compile *v.* compile (*compilo*) 1.7: 204, **compyle** 1.7: 88. **compiled** *p.p.* 2.3: 137, 3.6: 2, **compilede** 1.10: 2, **compilit** 3.23: 18, **compyled** 1.7: 105. *See also* **assembled, compacte, gader, glene.**

compiloure *n.* compiler 3.23: 16, **compylar** 2.17: 41.

complayntes *see* **compleinte.**

compleinte *n.* lament (genre of poetry, *planctus*) 1.6: 36, **compleynt** 1.3: 2, ~ **of Venus and Mars** 1.3: 12. **complayntes** *n.pl.* laments 3.24: 96.

compleyn *v.* complain (as response to poem) 3.16: 32, **compleyne** lament (in narrative verse) 1.8: 11. **compleynyd** *pa.3.sg.* (over lack of reading) 3.22: 38.

comprehend *v.* understand (Virgil's work) 3.16: 30, **comprehende, ful few clerkis can it** ~ 2.3: 158, 1.16: 116. **conprehendith** *pr.3.sg.* understands (of appropriately charitable reader) 1.15: 14. **comprehende** *p.p.* contained, ~ **alle that ys** (of salvation) 1.13: 76, **comprehendyd** (within words) 1.11: 6. *See also* **understand.**

comprise *v.* understand, take in 3.17: 14.

conclusioun *n.* ending (of text or book) 2.17: 21, **conclusyon** 1.8: 42, 2.14: 75, **conclusyoun** 1.11: 226. *See also* **ende** (*n.*), **endinge.**

confortable *see* **comfortabyl.**

connyng *n.* ability, skill, knowledge, learning, wisdom 1.5: 1, 2.10: 34, **sharpe sythes of** ~ (*fig.*) equipment for authoritative writing 1.4: 77, **connynge** 1.4: 87, 1.10: 39, 2.3: 86, **cunniynge** 2.5: 14, **cunnyng** 1.5: 22, 1.8: 47, 1.9: 102, 1.11: 14, 2.10: 53, 3.22: 42, **high** ~ (of clerics) 2.5: 127, **lytyl** ~ (of laymen) 2.5: 127–28; **cunnynge** 2.5: 13, 30, **konnyng** 1.9: 74, 86, **kunnyng** 1.8: 8, 1.15: 40, 1.16: 36, 96, 2.2: 26, ~ **of craftis** 3.11: 10, ~ **of Goddis lawe** 1.16: 1–2, ~ **of grammer** 1.16: 3, **kunnynge** 1.6: 60, 2.5: 18², 64, 3.5: 49, ~ **of filosoferis bookis** 1.15: 58, ~ **of Hooly Scripturis** 1.15: 59, **nakid** ~ intellectual knowledge 2.5: 18. **conynges** *pl.* knowledge 1.10: 22. *See also* **infformacion: unconnynge.**

connyng *adj.* knowledgeable 3.12: 75, **connynge** 3.12: 132, **kunnyng** 3.11: 9.

consayte *n.* understanding 3.24: 36. **consatis** *pl.* impulses, desires (of audiences) 3.16: 16, **conseytes,** ~ **or dowtys** (in reader response) 3.2: 87, **conseytys** conceits, fanciful expressions, ~ **off poetry** 1.8: 133. *See also* **affeccion, felyng, delite: mystakyng, imagynacion.**

conscripcion *n.* drawing up in writing (*conscriptio*) 3.15: 21.

conseyil *n.* counsel, advice, (over composition) 1.12: 23, 26, 31, **conseyle, be** ~ 1.12: 7, **counceil** 3.5: 22, **by** ~ (over choosing difficult reading) 3.5: 17, **counsayle, feendys** ~ (as source of erroneous readings) 3.2: 85–86, ~ **of clerkys** (for reading difficulties) 3.2: 88, (of patron) 3.24: 18, **cownsel** (as spur to composition) 1.14: 134. *See also* **counseil** (*v.*).

conseytes *see* **consayte.**

conseyve *v.* conceive, (*fig.*) form an idea, understand (author's purpose) 1.12: 42, ~ **mysly** misunderstand (text and authorial intention) 1.12: 53, (of response to text) 3.7: 7. **conceyving** *pr.p.* conceiving (books) 1.16: 52. **conceyved** *p.p.,* ~ . . . **wyth redyng** process of internalizing by reading 3.1: 7. *See also* **engendred, fele.**

considir *v.* consider, ~ **the matier** (assessing a work) 2.12: 68, **consydere,** ~ **how myche ye rede** 1.12: 64, **consydire** ponder, reflect upon 2.3: 17. **consyderyng** *pr.p.* (audience's desires)

2.9: 4, 20. **consederit** *p.p.*, red and ~ 2.17: 25–26, **consydred**, ~ the sentence 2.13: 31. *See also* **muse, perseyve, studie, thynkyn.**

consolacioun *n.* consolation (*consolatio*), (function of English poetry) 1.9: 31. *See also* **comfort.**

construccioun *n.* composition (*constructio*) 1.9: 59. **construcciouns** *pl.* compilations, accumulations 1.10: 22, 25. *See also* **formacioun, making: gader.**

contemplacion *n.* contemplation (*contemplatio*) (through reading) 3.15: 16, **hye** ~ (not for simple readers) 3.10: 11, ~ **of the godhede** 3.10: 18, (of all other humans through historiography) 3.15: 16, ~ **of the manhede of Criste** (for more profitable reading) 3.10: 17, **contemplacyon**, one of the partes of ~ (of devout reading) 3.12: 98, **contemplacyone** (fruit of hearing books and sermons books) 3.22: 47, **boke of hy** ~ 3.22: 34. *See also* **meditacion, revelation, schewynge, sight, thenkyng, visioun.**

contemplatyf *adj.* contemplative, ~ **lyf** (outcome of sustained successful psalter reading) 3.8: 6.

conveye *v.* accompany, (*fig.*) inspire (a text) 1.7: 33, represent 3.15: 15.

coppled *p.p.* linked (of couplets), ~ **a kowe** (of tail rhyme) 1.1: 50. *See also* **couwee.**

copyn *v.* copy, ~ **it owt** (of text) 1.14: 89. **copied** *p.p.* (of literary work) 1.16: 88, 2.3: 92.

corn *n.* grain, (*fig.*) historical truth 1.7: 102, useful literary work 1.11: 46, valuable truths of meaning 1.15: 69, **corne** moral meanings 3.18: 10. *See also* **kirnell, seed: chaf.**

correccion *n.* textual correction, improvement, **undyr** ~ (act of writing or composition) 1.8: 24, 121, **correccyon** (by the church) 3.12: 93, **correccioun** (by readers) 1.7: 212, (by authoritative colleagues) 1.10: 39. *See also* **amendement, reproof.**

correct *v.* correct, improve 3.18: 42, **correcte** 1.7: 30. *See also* **amende, submitt.**

counseil *pr. 1 sg.* counsel (to audience) 3.10: 30, **counsell** 3.12: 80, **cownsayle** 1.13: 52. *See also* **avised.**

couwee *adj.* tailed, **ryme** ~ tail-rhyme stanzas, verse with recurrent short lines 1.1: 47, 51, **kowe** 1.1: 50. *See also* **coppled: baston, enterlace, selcouth, strange.**

crafft *n.* poetic or compositional skill 1.8: 126, **craft**, ~ **of endytyng** art of composition 1.4: 5, **crafte**, ~ **of eloquence** rhetorical skill 1.5: 62, ~ **and cadence** compositional and metrical skill 1.7: 192, ~ **of a werkmen** of an artisan (in analogy to a writer) 1.4: 54. *See also* **science.**

craffty *adj.* skillful 1.8: 134, **crafty** 1.11: 85, 98, *as n.pl.* ~ **that con rimes make** (people) skilled in verse making 3.14: 50.

craftely *adv.* skillfully 1.5: 37, deceitfully (of disciplines using allegory), 3.15: 84, **crafty**, ~ **wrocht** skillfully made 3.16: 31.

creature *n.* creature, created being (as reader) 3.2: 86, (as source of text, persona of author) 1.14: 18, 20, 24, etc., 3.22: 1, 18, 22, etc., **creatures** *pl.*, **symples** ~ (of readers) 3.10: 9–10.

cronicles *n.* chronicles 2.2: 32, 35, 49, etc., **bokes of** ~ 2.2: 25, 28, 41, etc., **cronycles** 2.2: 136, ~ **of Fraunce and of Englond** 2.16: 68, **bokes of** ~ 2.2: 20.

cunnyng *see* **connyng.**

curiosite *n.* complexity (of composition) 1.3: 10.

curiosly *adv.* elaborately (of speech) 2.4: 33, **curyously** elegantly (of verse composition) 2.3: 57

curyous *adj.* complex (of subject) 1.5: 11. *See also* **queynt, strange.**

dalyawns *n.* love talk (as subject matter), **spechys and** ~ (of God to soul) 1.14: 44–45, 50, 3.22: 62, 66. *See also* **love.**

dalying *pr.p.* dallying (of devil's seduction of the soul) 3.22: 69. **dalyid** *pa.3.sg.* (of God's amorous speech to the soul) 1.14: 45, 3.22: 69.

dames *see* **tong.**

Danz *n.* Dom (*dominus*), honorific title of monastic dignitaries 1.1: 80.

Declarative *adj. as n.* explanation, *A Litel Book To Be a* ~ 1.16: 75–76.

declare *v.* explain, expound 1.16: 62, 2.10: 29, interpret 1.4: 22, relate, narrate 1.11: 121, 3.23: 46, **declaryn** 1.11: 99. **declare** *pr. 1 sg.* 1.8: 108. **declaryth** *pr.3.sg.* 1.11: 21, 81.

declaren *pr. 3 pl.* 2.10: 20. **declarit** *pa.3.sg.* 2.17: 35. **declared** *p.p.* revealed 1.7: 133, signified 2.13: 9, 10, 3.3: 24, **declaryd** 2.13: 29. *See also* **expounne, glosyde, opnyt, undo: say, schau, tel.**

declineson *n.* declension 3.21: 73.

dede *n.* deed, act of composition 2.2: 140, (of Troy) 1.7: 102n, **blessed ~** (of King Alfred's extempore translation of sermon) 2.4: 10, **lewde ~** (use of Latin to English speakers) 2.2: 84, **medeful ~** (of translation as meritorious activity) 2.2: 155. **dede** *pl.* **Cristes wordes and his ~** (as subject matter read at mass) 2.1: 94, **dedes** (of composition and other activities) 3.12: 96, (of saints) 2.15: 31, (of Christ's acts as subject matter) 2.1: 82, 84, 88, **gode ~** composition and other meritorious acts 2.2: 156, **good ~** (of scribal work as meritorious) 1.14: 121, **good ~ of good ladyes** (as exemplary subject matter) 2.16: 49, **Inglis ~** (as subject matter) 1.1: 28, **loore of ~** 2.2: 62, **of doynges and of ~** (as subject matter) 2.2: 22, **wordes equyvalent with the ~** 3.15: 85, **dedis, ~ of kynges** 1.1: 18, **dedys** (as subject matter) 1.8: 86, **knyghtys ~** 1.8: 45, **notabyl ~** 1.8: 79, **~ of stalwart folk** 1.2: 22, **wurthy ~** 1.8: 1. *See also* **fayttes, gestes.**

defaulte *n.* lack, fault (in text) 3.12: 84, 92, **defaute** (of eloquence) 1.5: 2, (of skill) 1.8: 47, (of books) 1.10: 19, **defawte** (of reading) 3.22: 38. **defautis** *pl.* (in writer's books) 1.16: 57.

delatyng *pr.p.* expanding, enlarging upon (*dilatio*), (with regard to source materials) 1.9: 81. *See also* **addicioun, puttyng [to].**

delectabill *adj.* delectable (as in *dilectatio*), (*fig.*) (of fables as carriers of meaning) 3.18: 16, **delectable** worthwhile or pleasurable, **doctryne ~** 3.15: 81, **ymagynacyonys . . . ~** (of some types of meditative reading) 1.12: 77, **delitabill** (reading) 1.2: 5, **delitable** 3.5: 38. *See also* **dilatabilte** (*n.*), **playsant, soote.**

delite *n.* delight (in reading and recitation) 3.8: 3, **delyte** 1.4: 49, 3.2: 9. *See also* **deynte, joy, liking, plesance, softnes: displesour.**

delyciousnesse *n.* pleasure (of texts heard), **swalowen the ~** 1.4: 1–2. *See also* **delectabill.**

delyten *v.* delight 3.15: 78. **delites** *pr.3.pl.* 3.8: 18. **delyted** *p.p.* delighted (in composition) 1.4: 48.

deminute *adj.* lacking (in rhetoric) 3.18: 41.

deprave *v.* disparage (literary work) 1.11: 198, 3.12: 84. **depraved** *pa.3.pl.* 3.12: 90. *See also* **blame, diffame, feyne.**

derk *adj.* dark, (*fig.*) obscure 2.3: 63, **over mykel and ~** 1.10: 38, **derke** 1.5: 42, **over litel and ~** 1.10: 27, **dirk, cloudis dym and ~** (*fig.*) of writer's ignorance 1.7: 60. *See also* **cleer.**

derkly *adv.* in veiled or figurative manner 1.15: 52. *See also* **openli, playnly.**

deryved *p.p.* derived (*etym.*) 2.7: 26.

descrybeth *pr.3.sg.* describes 3.15: 89. **discreveth** *pr.3.pl.* 2.2: 21. **discryved** *p.p.* 3.8: 39.

desir *n.* desire, **hevenly ~** (as produced by texts) 3.6: 18, **desire** (of patron) 1.7: 75, **~ of heven** (produced by psalter recitation) 3.8: 9, **desyr** (of dedicatee) 1.11: 195, **desyre** (of author) 1.13: 26, 44, 58, (of audience to enact reading) 3.12: 144, **cherytabyll ~** (of dedicatees) 2.9: 14, **~ of noblemen** (reason for composition) 2.10: 12. **desyres** *n.pl.* (of dedicatees) 2.9: 4, 20, 24. *See also* **byddyng, comaundement, heste, precept, requeist.**

desyre *v.* desire, **to ~ thyderwarde** (of longing for heaven produced by some genres of book) 3.12: 151, **what we ought to coveyte and ~** (as the lesson of reading historiography) 3.15: 4. **desire** *pr.1.sg.* (of patron) 2.2: 121. **desiren** *pr.3.sg.* (of audience, for God's word) 2.5: 154. **desired** *pa.2.sg.* (of text's addressee) 2.7: 14. *See also* **lyst, wille.**

detraccioun *n.* detraction 1.16: 76, 124. *See also* **blaim, blamynge, diffames, inpugnacioun, slaundres.**

detractouris *n.pl.* detractors 1.16: 111. *See also* **inpugners.**

devise *v.* fashion, compose 1.7: 142, **devyse** 1.11: 103. **devysid** *p.p.* composed 1.16: 119. *See also* **devyce** (*vbl.n.*), **ma(ke).**

devout *see* **reding, thynkynge.**

devyce *vbl.n.* devising 1.16: 87. *See also* **formacioun, setting.**

devyde *v.* divide, subdivide (into parts, chapters, etc.) 3.5: 12. **devydid** *p.p.* 3.5: 32, **devydit** 2.17: 3, **divised** 3.7: 22. *See also* **distincte.**

Dewche *n.* German (as scribe's language) 1.14: 86, **Duche** 1.14: 139. *See also* **Almayne.**

deynte *n.* esteem, pleasure (in reading) 1.7: 79, **in greet** ~ in high regard (of texts) 1.16: 113. *See also* **delite, joy, liking, plesance, softnes: displesour.**

dialog *n.* dialogue (as literary genre) 1.16: 4. *Dialoges* (title) *pl.* 2.2: 103.

dictis *n.pl.* sayings, maxims 2.17: 7, **dyttyes** 3.24: 88. *See also* **precept, proverb, sau, saynge, sentence.**

diffame *v.* slander, accuse (text or author) 1.16: 21. *See also* **blame, deprave, feyne.**

diffames *n.pl.* slanders 2.16: 40. *See also* **blaim, blamynge, detraccioun, inpugnacioun, slaundres.**

diffusely *adv.* in detail 2.7: 10. *See also* **poynt** (*v.*).

dilatabilte *n.* delectation (in reading) 3.8: 21. *See also* **delicyiousnesse, liking.**

diligence *n.* diligence (*diligentia*), (of author) 1.5: 5, 1.9: 69, 100, (of cultivation of meaning) 3.18: 9, ~ **do** exert oneself (in composition) 1.11: 133–34, **dyligence** 2.10: 23, **dylygence** 3.12: 100. *See also* **besynes, labour, payne.**

diligently *adv.* diligently (of readers) 1.15: 36, 3.17: 12, **dylygently** 1.12: 61, 62.

directe *v.* guide (plea to presiding deity for author's style) 1.7: 29. **dyrecte** *pr. 1 sg.* address 1.11: 203. **directe** *p.p.* directed (to patron) 1.3: 4. *See also* **adresse, dresse, dispose, rewlyd.**

dirk *see* **derk.**

disours *n.pl.* minstrels 1.1: 37. *See also* **harpours, mynstrell, seggers.**

displease *v.* displease (audience) 1.9: 85, 88. *See also* **displesour.**

displesour *n.* displeasure (of audience) 2.17: 40, **dyspleasaunce** (response to text) 3.24: 94. *See also* **plesance, reproof.**

dispose *v.* arrange, compose (as in *dispositio*) 1.16: 54, **dyspose**, ~ **you** *v. refl.* direct attention (of reader) 3.12: 112, 166. **disposed** *p.p.* inclined (of poet) 1.9: 40, (of men's use of seductive language) 2.16: 47, (of audience) 3.2: 29, **diposid** (of author) 1.16: 19, (of audience) 1.16: 43, 3.5: 20, **graciously** ~ of contemplative readers 3.3: 37, **dysposed** directed (of author's life) 3.24: 33. *See also* **adresse, directe, dresse, mysdisposed, undisposed, wel-disposid.**

distincte *p.p.* divided (into subsections, chapters, etc), ~ **wyth paraphes** marked with paraphs, divided into paragraphs 3.2: 11–12, **distyngid** 3.8: 32, **distyngwid** 3.3: 41. *See also* **poynte.**

dites *see* **dyte.**

divised *see* **dyvyde.**

doctour *n.* teacher, schoolman, theologian, authoritative exegete or source 1.15: 81, 3.19: 44, ~ **of Phisik** 1.10: 4, **docto[wr]** 3.22: 33, **doctur**, ~ **of dyvynytee** 1.12: 69. **doctoris** *pl.* 2.4: 1, **doctorys** 1.12: 67, 71, 72, etc., ~ **of Holy Chyrche** 1.12: 46–47, ~ **goynge therupon** (of textual commentaries or glosses) 1.12: 66, **doctouris** 1.16: 113, 2.7: 3, **deynous** ~ 3.11: 15, **haly** ~ 2.17: 7, **doctours** 2.2: 92, **haly** ~ 3.8: 66–67, **hooli** ~ 2.5: 85, **doctowrs**, ~ **of dyvynyte** 1.14: 58, **doctowrys**, ~ **therupon** (of textual commentaries or glosses) 3.22: 35. *See also* **auctor, bacheler, clerk, lered, maister.**

doctrine *n.* teaching, instruction (*doctrina*) 1.16: 87, etc., **doctryne** 1.4: 87, etc. **doctrinis** *pl.* 3.2: 88, **doctrynes** 2.16: 26. *See also* **ensample, ensygnementys, instruccioun, teching.**

Donet n. "Donatus," grammatical textbook 1.16: 2, 4, 5, etc.

doutouse *adj.* doubtful, unauthoritative (of elements in compilation) 1.10: 38.

draghes *see* **drau.**

drau *v.* draw, ~ **oute** translate 2.6: 12, **drawe** 3.12: 62, compose 2.1: 81. **draghes** *pr.3.pl.* expound 3.8: 38. **drawe** *p.p.* 3.7: 9, **drawe[n]**, ~ **togyder** synthesized 1.4: 9, **drawen** translated 3.12: 31, 79, **drawyn** 2.6: 18. *See also* **calengid, chaunge, declare, Englisshed, interpreted, save** (*imp.*), **set, translate, turne.**

drawyng *vbl. n.* translation 3.10: 14, 3.12: 79, 88, **drawynge,** ~ **oute** 3.10: 13.

drede *n.* fear (author's) 1.7: 12, 1.12: 30, 2.3: 171, (fruit of reading) 3.2: 2, (affective stimulus to be learnt by audience) 3.7: 1, 7, 15, etc., (of bad reputation in history writing) 3.15: 43, **affecyons of** ~ feelings of fear 3.12: 147, **maters of** ~ 3.12: 154–55, **bokes of hevynes and of** ~ 3.12: 160–61, **dreid** (as Virgil's subject matter) 3.16: 34.

dresse *imp.* address (patrons) 2.13: 13. **dresse** *pr. subj.* ~ **so your entente** direct your purpose (in reading) 3.12: 131, ~ **you in the redyng** conform your attitude in reading (to nature of subject matter) 3.12: 135–36. **dressed** *pa.1.sg.* ~ **my vysage** turned my countenance, gave attention (to particular reading matter) 3.24: 37. *See also* **adresse, directe, dispose, mysdisposed, undisposed, wel-disposid.**

dulleth *pr.3.sg.* dulls (effect of serious reading) 2.11: 21. **dulled** *p.p.* 1.7: 56, **dullid** bored 2.3: 73.

dylygente *adj.* diligent (of patron) 3.24: 19. *See also* **diligence** (*n.*).

dyrecte *see* **directe.**

dysporte *v. refl.* be entertained (by reading) 3.24: 38. **disporte** *pr.2.pl.* 3.5: 18. *See also* **gamen, myrthis, pastans, play, recreacion, salace, sport.**

dyte *n.* writing (*dictamen*) 3.18: 13. **dites** *n.pl.* poems 1.7: 48, 149. *See also* **poemys.**

dyvvyde *v.* divide (to form etymology) 2.7: 24. **devydit** *p.p.* divided (of oral or written division of book into parts) 2.17: 3, **divised** 3.7: 22, **dyvydyd** 1.12: 10.

dyvvyne *see* **pagyne.**

dyytyes *see* **dictis.**

easely *adv.* easily, in a relaxed manner (reading instruction) 3.2: 5, **esyliche** 3.1: 4. *See also* **likingly, moderatly, quyetnesse: hast, swithenesse, tumultuosite.**

easy *adj.* intelligible (of prose style) 2.2: 125, (of English) 2.8: 34. *See also* **light** *adj.*

Ebrew *adj. as n.* Hebrew 2.4: 2, 4, 3.21: 74, **Ebrewe** 2.7: 26, **Ebru** (as source language) 2.2: 77, 78[2], etc., 3.8: 27, **Hebrew** 2.7: 24.

edefie *v.* edify 1.15: 86. **edifiyng** *pr.p.* edifying 3.10: 9, **edifiynge** *as adj.* 3.10: 16.

edificacion *n.* edification (through reading or hearing read) 2.5: 12, 27, 3.10: 12, **edificacyon** 1.13: 57, **edyfycacyon** 3.12: 52, 86, 117, **edyfycacyone, gostly** ~ 3.12: 106.

edificatyf *adj.* edifying (of reading) 1.12: 37. *See also* **proffitable, spedeful.**

edifiying *vbl.n.* edifying, **goostli feeding and** ~ 1.16: 105–6, **leerning and** ~ 1.16: 118, **edyfyenge** 3.24: 53. *See also* **profityng.**

effectis *n.pl.* essentials, gist 2.3: 133.

efficyent *see* **cause.**

eloquence *n.* (*eloquentia*) art of writing with stylistic distinction, appropriateness, fluency 1.5: 2, 62, 1.7: 34, 195, 1.11: 93, 1.15: 48, 2.3: 179, 2.13: 30, 3.18: 37, rhetoric 3.15: 68.

eloquent *adj.* eloquent (of biblical writers) 1.15: 51[2].

embelysshing *pr.p.* embellishing, beautifying (the English language) 1.9: 30. **enbelshyd** *p.p.* (of style) 1.11: 89.

embrace *v.* undertake (literary work) 2.11: 97. *See also* **emprise, enterpryse.**

emprinted *p.p.* printed 2.8: 38. *See also* **impresse, prente, press, printer.**

emprise *n.* undertaking (of poem) 1.7: 97. *See also* **embrace, enterpryse.**

enbelshyd *see* **embelysshing.**

encomyne *n.* encomium (*encomium*) 3.15: 22.

end *v.* end, conclude (*explicit*), (of composition) 1.10: 23. **eendith** *pr. 3 sg.* 1.16: 126, **endeth** 2.16: 84, **endis** 2.17: 45, **endith** 1.3: 12, 1.4: 100, 1.6: 36, **endyth** 1.8: 151. **ended** *p.p.* 2.11: 81. *See also* **lede.**

ende *n.* place in text (*explicit*) 1.8: 78, 1.15: 42, 65, 3.2: 12, **make an** ~ 1.12: 35, conclusion 1.10: 18, **laste** ~ 1.12: 88, 2.7: 11, (of the Trinity as final purpose of composition) 1.12: 89. *See also* **beginnyng, endinge, myddel.**

endinge *n.* conclusion (of a literary composition) 2.1: 118, **endyng** 1.2: 39.

endite *v.* versify 1.5: 59, 2.3: 57, write, compose, **endyght** 1.8: 7, 98, **endyghte** 1.8: 87, **endyte** 1.4: 18, 1.11: 74, **do ~** compose or cause to be composed 3.24: 6, **endyten** 1.4: 26, 27. **endite** *pr.1.sg.* 1.5: 59, **endyght** 1.8: 29, 77, 98. **endyghte** *pr.3.sg., doht ~* 1.8: 111, **endytis** 3.16: 22. **endite** *pr.3.pl.* 2.11: 29, **endyte** 3.16: 48, **endyten** 1.4: 26, 27. **endytyd** *pa.1.sg.* 1.8: 114, 132. **endyte** *pa.3.sg.* 3.16: 48, **enditide** dictated 3.5: 3. **enditing** *pr.p.* 3.23: 44, **endyting** 1.3: 6, **endytyng, fayle ~** fall short in composing 1.8: 52. *See also* **laboure, ma(ke), werk, write.**

enditing *vbl.n.* writing, composition 1.9: 50, **endytyng** 1.4: 5, 1.8: 23, 120. *See also* **making, poetre, wark.**

endoctryned *pa.3.sg.* instructed 2.16: 28.

endyter *n.* poet, one who composes, writes, or translates 1.8: 59. *See also* **auctor, cause, maister, poete, translatour, writer.**

enforme *v.* instruct (function of books) 2.2: 64, **~ the understondynge** 3.12: 137, 163–64, **~ yourselfe** 3.12: 133. **enformed** *p.p.* 2.2: 59, **enformyd** 3.12: 87. *See also* **teche.**

engendred *pa.3.sg.* engendered, **~ in me a newe thought** 3.24: 58. *See also* **conseyve.**

Engliche *adj. as n.* the English language 2.4: 10, 13, 21, etc., **Englis** 2.1: 70, 3.7: 9, **Englisch** 2.7: 11, 22, 26, **Englishe** 3.10: 2, 14, **Englissh** 2.11: 30, **ryme in ~** 1.3: 9, **Englisshe** 2.2: 26, 31, 33, etc., **commune, playne, rounde ~** 2.8: 34, **oure ~** 1.9: 30, **fresshe, douce ~** 1.9: 32, **Englyische** 1.12: 22, 68, **Englysch** 2.6: 12, 18, **Englysche** 1.14: 138, 3.2: 18, **good ~** 1.14: 85–86, **Englysh** 2.13: 30, **Englyshe** 3.12: 4, 32, **Englyssh** 1.4: 24, **propre ~** 3.12: 63–64, **Englysshe** 1.4: 21, 3.12: 73, **Frenchemennes ~** 1.4: 21, **I[ng]eles** 3.14: 18, **Ingelis** 2.1: 63, **Inglis** 1.1: 49, 2.1: 97, 109, 3.8: 27, **myn ~** 1.1: 24, 34, **strange ~** 1.1: 40, 41, **this ~** this (version in) English 1.1: 70, **~ dedes** the deeds of the English 1.1: 28, **~ story** the history of the English 1.1: 31, **Inglisse** 2.1: 76, **Inglysch** 1.1: 7, **Ynglis** 3.8: 63, **propire ~** 3.8: 65, **straunge ~** 3.8: 62, **Ynglysh** 1.11: 122. *See also* **moder, langage, tong.**

Englis *adj.* English 3.14: 76, 77, 84, etc., **~ tong** 3.14: 88, **Englisch, ~ bokis** 1.16: 46, **Englische** 1.16: 29, **Englissh, ~ translacion** 2.2: 137, **Englisshe, ~ men** (as audiences and speakers) 2.2: 31, 34, 109, **~ preching** 2.2: 111, 112, **~ tonge** 2.2: 101, **~ translacioun** 2.2: 31, 65, 67, etc., **Englysche** 1.7: 85, 1.8: 30, **Englyshe, oure ~ tongue** 3.12: 62–63, **Englysshe, ~ tonge** 1.5: 29, 34, **Ingeles** 3.14: 75, **Ingelis, ~ tong** 2.1: 63.

Englisshed *p.p.* translated, made into English verse 1.9: 64, **Englisshede** 1.9: 48, **Englyshyd** translated 2.9: 40. *See also* **calengid, chaunge, drau, interpreted, save** (*imp.*), **set, translate, transmwe, turne.**

Englyschman *n.* 1.14: 78. **Englysshmen** *pl.* 1.4: 22, 24.

engyne *n.* talent, skill 2.3: 52, 3.16: 28.

enlumyne *v.* illuminate, (*fig.*) depict artistically, adorn 1.7: 59, **illumyne** enlighten 1.9: 109. **enlumyneth** *pr.3.sg.* adorn, make illustrious 1.7: 192. *See also* **peynten, sownde.**

enpryse[d] *see* **enterpryse.**

ensample *n.* something spoken or written to teach or persuade (*exemplum*) 2.5: 2, 79, 2.16: 52, 80, 82, precedent 1.4: 81, **ensaumple** 3.2: 93, 3.14: 27, **example** 1.7: 82, 2.9: 32, **exempill** 3.18: 47. **ensamples** *pl.* 2.16: 2, 26, **examples, ~ of scripture** 2.9: 47, **examplis** 2.17: 9, 14, 19, 3.15: 30, **exaunplys** (from Scripture) 1.11: 60, **exemplys** 3.16: 63. *See also* **doctrine, ensygnmentys, instruccioun, teching.**

ensampled *p.p.* instructed, provided with illustrative cases (by books) 2.11: 54, **essampled** 2.11: 14.

enspire *pr. subj.* inspire, **God . . . my spyrite ~** 1.5: 64. **enspired** *p.p.* 2.2: 104, **enspiirid** (authors by God) 1.15: 49. **inspyred** (by Holy Ghost) 1.14: 67. *See also* **inspiracion.**

ensygnementys *n.pl.* teaching, precepts 2.16: 2. *See also* **doctrine, ensample, instruccioun, teching.**

entencion *n.* meaning 2.10: 22, **entencioun** intention, purpose 1.7: 71, 96, 136, etc.

entende *v.* intend, mean 1.16: 143. **entend** *pr.1.sg.* 2.9: 37, **entende** 1.16: 72, 117, 2.3: 56, 2.9: 45, 2.10: 26, 3.2: 6. **entended** *p.p.* understood 3.12: 100.

entendible *adj.* intelligible 2.10: 27, 29. *See also* **lysable, understonding** (*adj.*).

entent *n.* import (*intentio*), (of subject matter) 1.5: 18, 1.9: 61, 2.14: 6, purpose (of a literary work) 1.11: 9, 3.8: 55, 3.10: 1, (of author) 1.11: 23, 1.12: 54, 55, 56, 1.16: 11, 71, 88, etc., 2.8: 25, 2.14: 6, 3.2: 14, 3.3: 3, (of reader) 3.2: 5, 3.3: 14, 3.10: 50, **entente** (of author) 1.9: 96, 3.24: 35, 40, (of reader) 3.12: 131, understanding 3.12: 79, (of audience) 3.24: 1, of work 3.17: 8. **ententis** *pl.* intentions (of author) 1.16: 96.

enterlace *n.* intricate rhyme 1.1: 48. *See also* **couwee, selcouth, strange.**

enterpryse *v.* undertake (elevated subject matter) 2.10: 3, **entrepryse** 2.10: 6, 16, ~ **alle jeopardies** undertake all hazards (of response to historical reading) 3.15: 41. **enpryse[d]** *p.p.* 2.10: 7. *See also* **embrace, emprise.**

entitillit *p.p.* entitled 2.17: 1, **entytled,** ~ **onto** named after 2.7: 2, **entytlyd** 1.11: 87, **intitillit** 2.17: 42. *See also* **calle, het, intytulacyon.**

entre *n.* introduction (to book or subject of discourse) 3.21: 2, **ontre** 3.7: 42. *See also* **prefacyon, proheymm, prolog.**

entrepryse *see* **enterpryse.**

envie *n.* envy (as motive for writing or for critical response) 1.16: 76, 124, **envye** 1.4: 78, 1.11: 196, 2.2: 138, 2.3: 82, 2.11: 146, (as devil's response to the copying of devout text) 1.14: 121. *See also* **blaim, blamynge, detraccioun, diffames, inpugnacioun, malice, pride, presumcion, slaundres.**

envoy *n.* envoy (concluding stanza addressed to dedicatee) 1.3: 1.

envyous *adj.* envious (nature of critical response) 2.3: 88, 3.8: 67.

epistil *n.* epistle 2.5: 83, **epistle** (*epistola*) (of Saint Paul) 1.16: 151, **pistil** 3.11: 7, **pistle** letter 1.16: 131, 134. **pistlis** *pl.* epistles 1.15: 51. *See also* **letere, scripture.**

erudicioun *n.* learning 1.9: 102. *See also* **connyng, lar.**

escriptures *n.pl.* writings 2.10: 13. *See also* **scripture.**

escuse *v.* excuse, ~ **the werke** 1.12: 55, ~ **the entent** 1.12: 55, **excuse** (literary work) 1.9: 65, (the author) 1.11: 223. **excuseth** *pr.3.sg.,* ~ **hirself** justifies herself (of author) 2.10: 3.

essampled *see* **ensampled.**

estudye *n.* study 3.15: 2. *See also* **stodie.**

esyliche *see* **easely.**

ete *imp.pl.* eat, ~ **thareof** (of reading) 3.5: 24. **etith** *pr.3.sg.* eats, ~ **this Scripture** (*fig.*) consumes 2.5: 165. *See also* **ete, fede, savoure, schewe, taaste.**

Evangelistes *n.pl.* Evangelists 3.10: 5, **Evangelius** 3.19: 20, **Evangelyst** 1.12: 45.

Evangelyis *n.pl.* evangelical letters 1.12: 47.

examplayre *n.* model of conduct, book containing such models 2.16: 65. *See also* **exemplary.**

examples, examplis, exempill, exemplys *see* **ensample.**

exciten *v.* excite, move (of texts) 1.4: 31, **exite,** ~ **and stere the mynde** 3.2: 2, **excyte,** ~ **mennys affeccyoun** (reason for writing) 1.11: 127. **exciting** *pr.p.* (desire in audience) 3.6: 18. **excyted** *p.p.* **our understandynge han** ~ 1.4: 93. *See also* **compellyth, inflawme, kyndils, mevyde, quyken, stere.**

excuse (*v.*) *see* **escuse.**

excuss *n.* apologia, justification 2.17: 21.

executed *p.p.* treated (of subject matter) 2.10: 23. *See also* **treate.**

exemplary *n.* exemplar (pattern of life initiated through literary means) 2.7: 20. *See also* **examplayre.**

exemplifyenge *pr.p.* telling exemplary stories (*exemplificatio*) 3.15: 3, **exemplifying** 2.12: 87.

exercise *n.* exercise (*exercitio*), **gostli** ~ spiritual reading and prayer 3.5: 50, **excercyse, gostly**

~ 3.12: 142. **exercyses** *pl.*, **gostly** ~ 3.10: 31.

exhorted *p.p.* exhorted (to literary production) 3.24: 21, **exorted** 2.10: 13. *See also* **byddyng**.

exortacion *n.* exhortation (*exhortatio*) (as genre of writing) 2.9: 37.

exposicioun *n.* a setting forth (*expositio*), a treatise 1.10: 11, 19, **opyn** ~ commentary, full exegesis 2.5: 85.

expounne *v.* expound (*exponere, tractare*) 1.15: 24, **expowne** 1.10: 10. **expounyth** *pr.3.sg.* 3.21: 27. **exponen** *pr.3.pl.* 1.12: 47. **expugnyd** *pa.3.sg.* expounded 1.8: 41. **expowned** *p.p.* 1.16: 139, 141. *See also* **declare, glosyde, opnyt, undo**.

expounnynge *vbl.n.* exposition 1.15: 54, **expounynge** 3.8: 66, **expowninge** interpretation 3.2: 89, **expownyng** 2.4: 15.

expressyn *v.* put into words 1.14: 54, 61, explain 1.14: 125. **expresse** *pr.1.sg.* declare 1.11: 33, 200. **expressede** *p.p.* 3.10: 5. *See also* **set, speke, tel**.

expugned *see* **expounne**.

fabill *n.* fiction (*fabula*) 1.2: 6, fable, short narrative 3.18: 18, 63. **fabillis** *pl.* 3.18: 43, **fabils** 3.18: 1, **fables, veyn** ~ idle tales 1.7: 136, ~ **and tryphlis** 3.15: 56. *See also* **poysy, story**.

fadyr *n.* father (used of dedicatee of text) 1.11: 203. **faders** *pl.* authorities 2.3: 80, 145, elders 3.15: 27. *See also* **auctor, patriarks**.

fand *see* **fynde**.

fantastyk *adj.* fantastical, the product of the imagination 1.8: 134.

fantasy *n.* preference (of reader) 3.16: 36, **fantasye** supposition 1.4: 20, product of creative imagination 3.23: 75. **fantasyes** *pl.* 1.4: 28.

farand *adj.* pleasant (of narration) 3.13: 2.

fayttes *n.pl.* exploits (as subject of literary treatment) 3.15: 65, **fayttis** 3.15: 5. *See also* **dede, gestes**.

febelnes *n.* weakness, lack of ability (in author) 3.5: 49. *See also* **humblesse, simplesse, unabylnesse, unconnynge**.

febil *adj.* feeble, **hys** ~ **proyss** (of Caxton as translator) 3.16: 51, **febille** (of author) 1.13: 86, **febull** (condition of audience, requiring composition) 2.6: 8.

fede *v.* feed, (*fig.*) reading or result of reading 1.4: 78, 3.10: 22, **worthy myndes to** ~ (of reading for noblemen) 3.24: 7, ~ **here soulis** (of reading Scripture) 2.5: 143. **feede**, ~ **you** *refl.* 3.5: 37. **fedde** *p.p.* 3.10: 10. *See also* **ete, savoure, schewe, taaste**.

fedynge *n.* feeding, (*fig.*) reading 3.5: 42, **feeding, goostli** ~ (*fig.*) purpose of writing 1.16: 105–6, **feedynge** ingestion, (*fig.*) internalizing (reading matter) 3.5: 40. *See also* **refeccions, sustenence**.

feele *v.* feel, respond (to reading matter) 3.2: 7, **fele**, ~ **comforte** (in hopeful reading matter) 3.12: 156, **understande and** ~ perceive (through reading and hearing) 3.17: 7, **that can** ~ **better** (of the spiritually mature) 3.12: 95, ~ **trewli** 3.10: 49, **feill** 3.16: 38. **feleth** *pr.3.sg.* ~ **more openly the trouth** 3.12: 116. **fele** *pr.2.pl.* **that** ~ **symplely in your owne wyttes** 3.12: 87. **feel** *pr.3.pl.* perceive 1.16: 21. **feelid** *p.p.* ~ **either undirstonden** (in reading) 1.15: 1–2. *See also* **conseyve, understand**.

feill *n.* understanding (on poet's part) 3.16: 37.

felawes *n.* fellowship, **for** ~ **sake** (reason for composition) 1.1: 81.

felawship *n.* company, **in** ~ (of audience for recitation) 1.1: 12.

felyng *n.* feeling, **inward** ~ (response to reading) 3.1: 4, **inward** ... ~ 3.1: 9, **symple** ~ (of author) 3.5: 9, **trewe** ~ (needed for composition) 3.5: 55. **felyngys** *pl.*, ~ **and revelacyons** (genre for composition) 1.14: 71–72, **a booke of hyre** ~ 1.14: 68, **wrytene hyre** ~ 1.14: 74, **wrytyn hyr** ~ 1.14: 69. *See also* **affeccion, stering: revelation, shewynge, sight**.

fenyeit *adj.* fictive 3.18: 1.

feyne *v.* tell fictions (in depreciation of a text) 2.11: 148. **feyned** *pa.3.sg.* 1.7: 145. **ifeyned** *p.p.* 1.7: 141. *See also* **blame, deprave, diffame**.

feynte *pr.subj.* be defective (of literary work) 2.12: 42.

feynynge *vbl.n.* fictionalizing (*fictio*) 1.7: 130. *See also* **fenyeit, lesinge.**

figuratiif *adj.* figurative, metaphorical 1.15: 84.

figure *n.* (*figura*) image 3.18: 7, **be ~** allegorically 3.18: 59, **fygour** 3.20: 35. **figuris** *n.pl.* 3.2: 70. *See also* **methaphoris, ymage.**

filosoferis *see* **phylosophyr.**

finders *n.pl.* inventors (of rhetorical or compositional productivity in writers) 1.9: 31. *See also* **fynd, invencion.**

fleischli *adv.* (*carnaliter*) carnally, (*fig.*) literally 2.5: 108, **fleschely** *as adj.*, unspiritual (of readers) 3.3: 29. *See also* **carnal, lettural, naked: spiritual.**

flour *n.* flower (*flos*), (*fig.*) rhetorical or stylistic embellishment, **~ of eloquence** 1.7: 194, **floure, ~ of rethorike** finest in rhetoric 1.5: 33, finest (of poets) 1.3: 11. **flouris** *pl.* (*flores*) (*fig.*) meaning 3.18: 10, **flours, motleyd wyth ~** (*fig.*) text using a variety of rhetorical figures 1.11: 92, **flowris** choice points of meaning or embellishment 2.3: 17. *See also* **colour, methaphoris, ymage.**

flourit *adj.* flowery, (*fig.*) ornate, **his ~ pen** (of style) 3.23: 24.

folowe *v.* follow, **~ worde by worde** 1.3: 10. **fologh** *pr.1.sg.*, **~ haly doctours** (of expounding text) 3.8: 66, **folow, ~ the lettere** (of translation) 3.8: 64, **~ the wit of the worde** 3.8: 65, **folowe, ~ the sentence** 3.12: 67. **folowes** *pr.3.sg.* matere that **~ aftyr** 1.13: 93, **foloweth** (of text succeeding prologue) 1.4: 100, **folowynge** *pr.p.* **the boke ~** 1.12: 1, 10, 14, etc., 3.12: 1, **kalendar ~** 3.5: 13, **medytacyonys ~** 1.12: 49–50, 60, 86, **the tabyl ~** 1.12: 9–10. **folowyd** *p.p.* (of using sources) 1.12: 67. *See also* **suwyng.**

foorme *n.* (literary) form (*forma*) 1.16: 52, 53, **forme** 2.7: 14, **~ of eloquence** in an eloquent style 2.3: 179, **~ of here levyng** (biographical genre) 1.14: 74, **~ of my writynge** (of style) 2.11: 141, **~ ordinat** form by which subject matter is ordered 1.11: 20, **~ of procedyng** (of ordering textual material) 1.11: 83. **formes** *pl.* versions 1.16: 93. *See also* **ordire, setting.**

formacioun *n.* making (of verse) 1.9: 32. *See also* **making, setting.**

formal *adj.* formal, **menyng ~** 1.9: 80, 1.11: 12, 17. *See also* **cause.**

formyd *p.p.* shaped (of letter forms) 1.14: 86.

four *see* **cause, understandinge.**

fraitur *n.* refectory (place for reading Benedictine Rule) 2.8: 16.

Frankis *adj. as n.* French 2.1: 74, **Frankys** 1.1: 10, **French** 1.4: 17, **Frenche** 1.4: 19, 25, 27, 3.14: 18, **Frensche** 1.7: 94, 2.4: 5, **Frensshe** 2.2: 99, 107.

French *adj.* French, **~ rimes** French songs 3.14: 79, **Frenche, the ~ booke** 3.2: 20, **~ man** *sg. as coll. pl.* 3.14: 81.

Frencheman *n.* Frenchman 1.4: 23. **Frenchemen** *n.pl.* Frenchmen 1.4: 20, **Frenchmen** 1.4: 27, **Frenchmennes** *gen.pl.*, **~ Englysshe** English writings of French poets 1.4: 21.

frendys *n.pl.* friends (address to audience of dramatic performance) 2.14: 65. *See also* **lordynges, soverayns.**

frewte *n.* fruit, (*fig.*) spiritual value (of text) 3.20: 30, **fruit** effect, value (of reading) 2.5: 130, 3.1: 10, **frute** (of text) 1.7: 181, (of inner meaning in fables) 3.18: 18, **fruyt** reading matter 3.5: 15², 23, 29, etc., spiritual value 3.10: 49, **fruyte** significance 3.23: 45, **bokes of gostly ~** books of spiritual worth 3.12: 111. *See also* **orcherd: herbis, hony, honycombe, lof, meate, mylk: savour, schewe, taaste.**

fructuouse *adj.* fruitful, **~ matire** (of subject matter) 3.10: 7–8.

fruytful *adj.* fruitful, **~ orcherd** (*fig.*, of valued text) 3.5: 11.

fute-hait *adj.* hot-foot, (*fig.*) fresh from the press 3.16: 52.

fygour *see* **figure.**

fynd *v.* find, discover (of readers' activities) 2.3: 173, 3.7: 37, 3.8: 45, **fynde** 1.7: 81, 1.8: 78, 146, 1.12: 15, 16, 37, 1.15: 62, 2.3: 7, 11, 75, etc., 2.5: 162, 163, 165, etc., 3.12: 79, 3.17:

14, (in a text or book) 1.8: 81, invent, discover (of writer's activity, as in *inventio*) 1.16: 44, 45, 54, etc., **fynden** (in reading) 3.1: 12, 16, **savour** ~ 3.1: 5, **swete fruit** ~ 3.1: 11. **fynd** *pr.1.sg.* 3.8: 65, **fynde** 2.7: 44, 2.12: 69, 3.2: 20. **find** *pr.2.sg. (polite) and pl.* 3.18: 40. **fyndith** *pr.3.sg.* 1.15: 61. **fynden** *pr.1.pl.* 2.4: 21. **fand** *pa.3.sg.* (written source material) 1.1: 6. **founden** *pa.3.pl.* 1.15: 79. **founde** *p.p.* 1.12: 39, 1.16: 44, 3.5: 34. *See also* **finders, invencion, inventif.**

gader *v.* gather, collect, ~ **the smale crommes** (*fig.*) harvest material 1.4: 82, (in reading) 3.2: 13, **gather**, ~ **in** 3.24: 35–36. **gathered** *pa.3.pl.* ~ **up** 1.4: 76. **gaderid** *p.p.* (*fig.*) compiled 3.5: 34, 45, **gadred** collected 2.10: 21. *See also* **assembled, garnyson, glene, compacte, compile, mowen.**

gaderyng *vbl.n.* audience (of a play) 2.14: 73, **gaderynge** (*compilatio*), ~ **delitable fruyt** (*fig.*) compiling 3.5: 38, **gadryng** 1.10: 19, 26, ~ **togedre** compilation 1.10: 1–2, 11, 19, **Gadrynge,** ~ *Togidre of Cirurgie* 1.10: 35–36.

galle *n.* poison (of content, as opposed to verse form, in Homer) 1.7: 151. *See also* **hard, purgyng, poisone, scharp, sour: hony, soote.**

gamen *n.* entertainment (through recitation) 1.1: 11. **gemmys** *n.pl.* (learned from Virgil) 3.16: 44. *See also* **dysporte, myrthis, pastans, play, recreacion, salace, sport.**

garnyson *n.* harvest, reward (of history writing in response to virtuous deeds) 3.15: 52. *See also* **corn: mede.**

gastelye *adj.* spiritual, (of revelation) 1.13: 51, **gastlic** (of teaching) 2.1: 41, 102, **gastly,** ~ **comfort** 3.8: 1, **goostly,** ~ **feele** (of response to reading in spirit) 3.2: 7, **gostely,** ~ **sensce** (of meaning) 2.13: 28, **gostelye,** ~ **comforth** 3.20: 3, **gostli** (blindness, linked with misunderstanding Scripture) 2.5: 43, ~ **exercise** (readings, devotions, etc.) 3.5: 50, ~ **orchard** (*fig.*) text 3.5: 54, **gostly** (of response to or visualization of text) 3.10: 29, (leading to reading) 3.22: 32, (of devotional exercises, readings, etc.) 3.10: 31, 3.12: 142, ~ **comforte** 3.12: 31 ~ **edyfycacyone** 3.12: 106, ~ **fruyte** (from books) 3.12: 111, ~ **lernynge** 3.5: 56. *See also* **comfort, fedynge, meate, orchard, recreacioun, understandinge: spiritual: carnal, fleischli, lettural, naked.**

gather *see* **gader.**

gemmys *see* **gamen.**

gestes *n.pl.* deeds (*gesta*) (as subject matter) 2.16: 68, 3.14: 63, 3.15: 20, ~ **principale** main events 3.14: 71, **jestes** narratives 1.4: 2. *See also* **dede, fayttes, historye, poysy, story.**

glas *n.* mirror (analogy for book) 2.17: 44, (of writing) 1.7: 122, **glasse** (*fig.*) book 2.7: 20. *See also* **merour, spectakle.**

glene *v.* glean, (*fig.*) gather materials 1.4: 87. *See also* **gader.**

gloses *n.pl.* commentaries 1.9: 79. *See also* **goynge.**

glosyde *pa.3.sg.* glossed, produced commentaries (upon texts) 1.12: 70. **glosid** *p.p.* 1.16: 139. *See also* **declare, expounne, opnyt, undo.**

Godspel *n.* Gospel 2.1: 104, **Goospelle** 2.9: 39, **Gospel** 1.12: 66, 2.2: 107, 109, 2.4: 12, 13, 20, 2.5: 4, 15, 81, etc., 3.6: 14, 3.10: 24, ~ **of Jon** 3.11: 3, ~ **of Joon** 2.5: 93, **Seynt Jone** ~ 2.2: 105–6, **Hooly** ~ **of Jhesu Crist** 1.15: 95, **Gospell** 2.9: 13, 3.10: 29, **Gospelle** 2.4: 23, 3.10: 5, 25. **Godspelles** *pl.* 2.1: 111, **Godspells** 2.1: 95.

Godspellers *n.pl.* Evangelists, **the faur** ~ 2.1: 87.

goynge *pr.p.* commenting (upon text), **doctorys** ~ **therupon** 1.12: 66.

grace *n.* grace, (of work's dedicatee) 2.13: 18, (of Calliope as muse) 1.7: 54, (of Mars as inspiration) 1.7: 32, (of God, needed by writer or work) 1.1: 71, 1.2: 38, 1.11: 232, 1.12: 35, 36, 1.16: 45, 2.1: 98, 119, 2.2: 127, 138, 3.3: 4, 3.5: 27–28, 3.20: 6, (in scriptural exposition) 1.15: 40, 54, 2.5: 78, 3.2: 91, (inexpressible in words) 1.14: 54, (impossible without the word of God) 2.5: 148, (source of subject matter) 2.3: 138, (for structuring work) 3.5:

11, (dispensed through text) 3.20: 35, (in visual representation) 1.13: 14, (for audience and author) 1.10: 7, 3.11: 27, 3.16: 66, 3.21: 97, (for opportunity of reading) 1.12: 9, 82, (for reading and copying) 1.14: 88, 109, 122, (in, or as the result of, reading) 1.12: 85, 1.15: 40, 3.1: 18, 3.2: 8, 3.3: 39, 3.8: 45, 3.12: 99, 115, (remedy for unwise reading) 3.5: 43. *See also* **inspiracion, stering.**

gramer *n.* grammar (*grammatica*) 3.12: 71, 76, **grammer** 1.16: 3.

grammaticaliche *adv.* grammatically (as mere correctness) 2.4: 34, **grammaticalliche** 2.4: 29.

Greek *adj. as n.* Greek (language) 2.4: 2, 3, **Grek** 2.6: 14, 3.8: 27, **Grue** 2.2: 77, 96, 97, etc., **Grwe** 1.8: 31, 37. **Grekys** *pl.* users of the Greek language 3.21: 73.

ground *n.* ground, (*fig.*) text for exposition 2.9: 38, **grounde** basis 1.12: 58, 65, atte ~ foundation (of reading) 3.6: 6, **grownd** 1.8: 42, **grownde** 2.3: 81. **groundis** *pl.* rules for interpreting Scripture 1.15: 46.

grounded *p.p. as adj.* with a basis, well-founded, ~ **lawes** (as product of literature) 3.15: 47.

groundid *p.p.* founded (on truth) 1.15: 8, (on oral report) 1.16: 133, (in Scripture) 1.16: 152, **growndid** (in Scripture) 3.4: 8, **growndyd**, ~ **in pete** (of audience request) 1.11: 193, **grunded, not al ~ upon truth** (of fiction) 3.18: 2.

halff-chongyd *adj.* part-translated (of highly Latinate diction) 1.8: 133. *See also* **calengid, chaunge, transmwe.**

hamelie *adj.* homely, ~ **language** 3.18: 36, **homely** (of style) 2.3: 60, ~ **resoun** (of quality of argument) 1.6: 61. *See also* **playn, rounde.**

hanging *pr.p.* incomplete (of subject matter not fully treated) 3.3: 24.

hard *adj.* hard (of subject) 1.5: 11, (of difficult writing or religious truths) 3.5: 16. *See also* **bitter, scharpe, soure.**

harkis *see* **herken.**

harpe *n.* harp (of Orpheus) 1.7: 49.

harpours *n.pl.* harpers (as professional entertainers) 1.1: 38. *See also* **disours, mynstrell, seggers.**

hart *n.* heart (as site of actors' intention) 2.14: 5, **hert** (as location of internalized text) 3.10: 42, (as organ or site of response to texts) 2.12: 83, 3.8: 11, 48, 52, (as site of author or narrator's intention or state of feeling) 1.7: 63, 3.3: 3, 3.21: 12, **haf in** ~ (of narrator) 2.1: 62, **holde in** ~ (of patron's wishes) 2.2: 134, **hald in** ~ (of ideal response for audience) 2.1: 113, **myn** ~ **is . . . glad** (author's response to commission) 2.11: 143, **set hir** ~ **stably** (of ideal female reader) 3.10: 44, **stableth the saule and the** ~ (as function of meditative reading) 3.10: 40, **herte** (as organ or site of response to texts) 1.4: 6, 1.15: 14, 1.16: 124, 2.11: 149, 2.16: 9, 3.1: 12, 3.9: 4, 3.20: 31, (as site of author or narrator's intention or state of feeling) 1.6: 7, 29, 1.7: 211, 1.10: 14, 1.11: 178, 2.11: 92, **hertys** (*gen. sg.*) **my** ~ **hole entencion** (of author's intent) 1.8: 141. **hartes** *pl.* (to be infused by liturgical meaning) 3.12: 48, **hertes** (humbled by fearful reading) 3.7: 6, (gladdened by psalter recitation) 3.8: 1, **hertis** (cheered by recitation after feasting) 3.13: 2, **hertys** (permeated and swelled by book as loaf by honey) 3.20: 36.

hartily *adv.* heartily, from the heart, (as audience's mode of gratitude for text) 3.4: 11, **hertely** (of pleading by author) 1.9: 65, (of welcome to audience) 2.14: 76, **hertly, preie ye ~ for hem** (of audience's response to proud clerks) 1.15: 89, *as adj.* heartfelt, ~ **lowe humblesse** (of author's humility) 1.7: 70. *See also* **herty.**

hast *n.* haste (frowned on in reading) 3.2: 4. *See also* **hastenesse.**

hastenesse *n.* hastiness (frowned on in reading) 3.2: 5, **hastynesse** 1.12: 61, 63. *See also* **hast, negligence, swithenesse, tumultuosite.**

hasty *adj.* hasty, ~ **to rede moche at ones** 3.12: 121.

hastynge *pr.p.* hastening, **not ~ to rede moche atones** 3.12: 45.

Hebrew *see* Ebrew.

heeryng *vbl.n.* (act of) hearing 3.17: 7, heryng 1.2: 9, 14, 1.4: 20, 2.2: 3, 2.7: 28, 3.9: 5, 3.22: 46², herynge (as university and clerical activity) 1.10: 32.

heir *v.* hear, ye sall ~ anone (to audience) 3.18: 63, her, ~ and hald in hart (of audience) 2.1: 113, here (narrative verse) 1.1: 58, (*fig.*, of reader) 1.4: 66, (of angelic praise) 3.8: 19, (as entertainment) 3.13: 1, (verse narratives) 3.14: 3, (various subject matters for various listeners) 3.14: 19, 21, 23, etc., (of reading Boethius) 3.23: 22, and yt lyke yow to ~ 2.14: 9, as ye aftyr shul ~ 1.11: 132, ~ it al over hear it through 3.3: 23, ~ it be red or spokin 3.3: 21, ~ or rede 3.7: 16, ~ speche (in language acquisition) 2.2: 4, ~ the dedis of kynges 1.1: 18, ~ . . . the nyghtyngale (*fig.*, attend to secular or sacred love discourse) 2.13: 24, 27, 53, rede or ~ 3.7: 2, 3, rede or to ~ 3.12: 111, 112, whoso lyste to ~ 1.11: 31, heryn (narrative) 1.11: 82, (visions and doctrines of damnation) 3.22: 54, 58, hure (narratives of battle) 2.15: 59, 61, 62. herde *inf. pass.* (of God) 3.12: 114. here *pr.1.sg.* (adventures) 3.14: 14. heerith *pr.3.sg.*, ~ and redith 2.5: 6, heres, that sees it and ~ it (visionary's revelation) 1.13: 61. heryn *pr.3.pl.* (God's word) 2.5: 4. herde *pa.1.sg.* ~ telle 1.12: 21. herde *pa.3.pl.* (narrative) 1.1: 53. herdest *pa. sg. subj.* (life of Christ) 3.10: 52. herde *p.p.* ~ speke 1.5: 25, 3.24: 44, sene and ~3.14.56. *See also* herken, lestyn, lythe, red.

herbis *n.pl.* herbs, (*fig.*) reading matter 3.5: 15², 23, etc. *See also* wedis: frewte, hony, honycombe, lof, meate, mylk: savour, schewe, taaste.

herer *n.* 1.4: 6, herere 1.15: 8, 9. heerers *pl.* 1.16: 43, 72, heere[r]s 1.16: 132, heres 3.8: 18, 3.12: 129. *See also* lysters, redare.

herken *v.* listen (to love songs) 3.13: 6. harkis *imp.* listen (to narrative) 3.16: 46. *See also* heir, lestyn, lythe, red.

hertely, hertly *see* hartily.

herty *adj.* heartfelt, of the heart ~ lust (of pleasure in study) 1.4: 58. *See also* hart.

heste *n.* command (of patron) 1.5: 4, my kinges ~ 2.11: 158, a book after his ~ 2.11: 170. *See also* byddyng, comaundement, desir, precept, requeist.

het *pr.3.sg.* is called ~ an ontre 3.7: 42. *See also* calle, entitillit, name (*v.*).

hevenesse *n.* boredom (in reading) 3.2: 13. *See also* noyen: light.

hid, hides *see* hyde.

historyal *adj.* historical 3.15: 31, 52, 58, etc., historyall 3.15: 72, hystoryal 3.15: 29. *See also* mater, processe.

historye *n.* history (*historia*) 3.17: 2, ystorye 3.17: 1. histories *pl.* 3.15: 1, historyes 2.16: 69, histouriis 2.17: 9. *See also* fayttes, gestes, poysy, story.

Holy Scripture *see* Scripture

hony *n.* honey, (*fig.*) verbal eloquence 1.7: 56, 150, honye, ~ of hevenlye Jerusalem (of spiritually nourishing text) 3.20: 15–16, 19, 21, huny, ~ til a bittire saule (of psalter) 3.8: 11. *See also* frewte, herbis, honycombe, lof, meate, mylk: savour, schewe, taaste.

honycombe *n.* honeycomb, (*fig.*) book 3.20: 16, 22. *See also* hony.

humble *adj.* humble, ~ herte (of author) 1.7: 211, ~ prayer (of author) 1.9: 51, ~ entent 1.11: 181, ~ oratour 2.12: 81, ~ reverence (of personified book) 2.13: 14.

humblesse *n.* humility (of author) 1.7: 70. *See also* ignorance, insuffishaunce, leudenesse, simplesse, unabylnesse, unconnynge, unworthynesse: suffisaunce.

humbly *adv.* humbly 2.10: 32. *See also* lowely, mekeli, symplely.

hure *see* heir.

hy *adj.* difficult, elevated, ~ revelacyons 3.22: 48–49, hye (of subject matter) 1.5: 11, 1.10: 10, 2.10: 3, 6.

hyde *v.* hide, ~ trouth 1.7: 138. hides *pr.3.sg.* (of talent) 2.1: 51, hid *p.p.* (of God's concealment of meaning in Scripture) 2.5: 36, hid *p.p. as adj.* hidden (truths within Scripture) 1.15: 2,

30, 31, etc., (of God's judgments) 3.3: 36, **hyd** 3.21: 97. *See also* **open, opnyt.**

ifeyned *see* **feyne.**

ignorance *n.* ignorance (of Latin Rule) 2.8: 24, **ignoraunce** (as cause of error in writing) 1.16: 16, (as reason for forbidding image making) 3.2: 55, **ygnoraunce** *n.* (of making poetry) 1.7: 61, 3.24: 84. *See also* **humblesse, insuffishaunce, leudenesse, simplesse, unabylnesse, unconnynge, unworthynesse: suffisaunce.**

ignorant *adj.* ignorant (of nuns, regarding Latin) 2.8: 18, **ignoraunt** uneducated 1.6: 60. *See also* **laud.**

illumyne *see* **enlumyne.**

imade *see* **ma(ke).**

imagynacion *n.* thought (*imaginationem*) 1.8: 140. **imagynacionys** *pl.* imaginings 1.8: 134, **ymagynacions** speculations 3.2: 87, **ymagynacyonys** pious imaginings (meditative exercise) 1.12: 77, 79, **ymagynationis** thoughts 2.17: 25.

impresse *v.* print 3.24: 13. *See also* **emprinted, prente.**

infformacion *n.* explanation (*informatio*) (of Greek text) 1.8: 41, **informacion** knowledge 3.15: 7, 83, **informacioun, ~ and lore** 2.2: 7, 24, 27, **informacyone** oral reporting 1.14: 146. *See also* **connyng, lore.**

inflawme *v.* inflame **~ his affecions** 3.2: 8. *See also* **compellyth, exciten, kyndils, mevyde, quyken, stere.**

inpugnacioun *n.* accusation 1.16: 74, 120. **inpugnaciouns** *pl.* 1.16: 102. *See also* **blaim, blamynge, detraccioun, diffames, slaundres.**

inpugners *n.pl.* accusers, faultfinders 1.16: 111, 120.

inspiracion *n.* inspiration (from God, for translation not to corrupt source) 1.5: 15, **inspiracioun** (from Holy Ghost) 2.2: 79, **inspiracyone** (of Holy Ghost) 1.14: 49. *See also* **enspire, grace, stering.**

instruccioun *n.* guidance (*instructio*) (from poets) 1.9: 41, **instrucioun** (from God) 1.9: 57, **instructyon** spiritual teaching 2.9: 5. *See also* **doctrine, ensample, ensygnementys, teching, lar.**

instructe *p.p. as adj.* learned 2.10: 26.

insuffishaunce *n.* lack (of knowledge or ability in author) 1.5: 1. *See also* **humblesse, ignorance, leudenesse, simplesse, unabylnesse, unconnynge, unworthynesse: suffisaunce.**

intential *adj.* intended, **~ substaunce** (meaning of text) 1.9: 66.

interpretacioun *n.* interpretation (*interpretatio*) (etymological) 2.7: 22. **interpretaciones** *pl.,* **bokes of ~** onomastic handbooks 2.7: 23.

interpreted *pa.3.sg.* acted as interpreter, translated 2.4: 10. *See also* **calengid, chaunge, drau, Englisshed, save** (*v.*), **set, translate, turne.**

interpretor *n.* translator 3.21: 74.

intitillit *see* **entitillit.**

intytulacyon *n.* formal list of titles (*intitulatio*) 3.24: 42. *See also* **tytyl.**

invencion *n.* discovery (*inventio*), (of rhetorical or compositional productivity) 3.15: 48. *See also* **finders, fynd, inventif.**

inventarie *n.* detailed list 1.10: 1, *Inventarie* (genre of work and title) 1.10: 35.

inventif *adj.* creative, inventive (rhetorically or poetically) 1.9: 39. *See also* **finders, fynd, invencion.**

jangelyn *pr. subj.* gabble (of learning without charity) 2.5: 12, **jangle** (of speech after Babel) 2.2: 9.

janglers *n.pl.* chatterers (as inadequate readers) 3.3: 29. *See also* **fleischli.**

jangling *vbl.n.* foolish talk 1.15: 87, evil talk 2.11: 157. *See also* **slaundres.**

jestes *see* **gestes.**

joy *n.* pleasure (from psalter reading) 3.8: 1, **joye** (in representation) 1.4: 14, (of patron's pleasure in reading) 1.7: 79–80, **take it with ... joye** (injunction to audience) 1.13: 58, **affeccions of ~** (stirred by reading) 3.12: 151. *See also* **delite, deynte, liking, plesance, softnes.**

joyous *adj.* joyous (of text for audience) 3.17: 16, **joyus** (capacity of Virgil as author) 3.16: 43.

jumpere *v.* jumble, put words together in a disorderly way 1.4: 23.

kalender *n.* table, chart 3.5: 13, 33, **in maner of a ~** 3.5: 26.

kirnell *n.* kernel (*fig.*) value, meaning 3.18: 16. **kernels** *pl.* (in analogy for Scripture as source of knowledge) 1.15: 70. *See also* **corn, nuttis, seed.**

klerk, klerkys *see* **clerk.**

knawynge *vbl.n.* knowledge (of affective knowing) 1.13: 18, **knowing** (figures of speech) 1.15: 84, (of Scripture) 1.15: 90, (of awareness of difficult doctrines) 3.5: 41, **knowyng** (of God, as object of reading) 3.2: 3, **knowynge** (of Latin) 1.4: 27. *See also* **connyng** (*n.*), **lore.**

knowe *v.* know (of philosophers) 1.4: 59, (text) 2.2: 49, 53, 56, (part of text) 3.7: 23, (through study) 3.24: 33, **hemself frust to ~** (function of English texts for laypeople) 3.7: 13, **~ and understande** (of nuns) 2.8: 26, **~ this matere** 2.7: 9, **~ what you read** (of nuns) 3.12: 45–46, **more pleyn to ~** (of prose) 2.2: 126, **profitable to ~** 3.5: 39–40. **knawen** *inf. pass.* **be ~** (God's will for text) 1.13: 93, **knowe** 2.2: 142. **knawes** *pr.3.sg.* **~ noght** (of critical reader) 3.8: 67. **knowe** *pr.2.pl.* **that ye ~** (to audience, of text's commissioner) 1.1: 80. **knawes** *pr.3.pl.* (Latin) 3.8: 63. **knoweth** *imp. pl.*, **tasteth hem and ~** 3.5: 41. **knawe** *subj. pl.* (of laymen) 2.1: 110. **iknowe** *p.p.* (of one universal language) 2.2: 16, (of English) 2.2: 30, 34, (of Latin) 2.2: 33, **knawenn** (of knowledge of God, as purpose of text) 1.13: 89, **knowe** (of translation) 2.2: 122, **knowun, ~ by clerkis** (of Latin) 1.16: 3, **yknowe** (of Latin) 2.2: 16.

knowlege *n.* knowledge (of Benedictine Rule) 2.8: 24, **no ~** (on part of nuns) 2.8: 18, **knowlegynge** (of recherché French terms) 1.4: 22. *See also* **connyng** (*n.*), **lore.**

knyttyng *pr.p. as adj.* unifying, linking (of figures of rhetoric) 1.4: 2. *See also* **colour.**

kowe *see* **couwee.**

kunnyng, kunnynge *see* **connyng.**

kynde *n.* nature (not knowable without writers) 1.7: 112, meaning, sense 3.2: 84, **her owne ~** (of proper nouns, as signifying only themselves) 2.2: 150. **kyndes** *pl.* genres **~ and maners of spekingis** (in Scripture) 1.15: 35. *See also* **maner, nature.**

kyndils *pr.3.pl.* kindles **~ thaire willes** (of psalter reciters) 3.8: 3–4. *See also* **compellyth, exciten, inflawme, mevyde, quyken, stere.**

labour *n.* labor (of author) 1.11: 14, 1.16: 50, 51, (of exegesis) 1.16: 154, **laboure** 1.16: 79, 2.9: 45, (of audience) 3.5: 52, (of Jerome) 3.12: 90. *See also* **besynes, occupacion, travail, wark.**

laboure *v.* labor (of author) 1.5: 41, 3.5: 47, 54, **~ in yourself inwardly** (of audience) 3.12: 153. **laboure** *pr.3.pl.* 1.8: 25. **laboure** *pr. subj.* 3.12: 65. **labouryng** *pr.p.* (of readers) **~ to knowe what you rede** 3.12: 45.

lagh *n.* law, **alde ~** Old Testament 3.14: 65, **law, elde ~** i.e., Old Testament 2.5: 103, **lawe** religion (Christian as opposed to Jewish) 1.15: 16², 17, etc., 2.14: 49, **alde ~** 3.14: 64, **elde ~** 2.5: 112, **Goddis ~** (of Bible) 2.5: 8, 10, 130, **newe ~** i.e., New Testament 2.5: 104, **~ of metre** metrical rules 1.5: 20.

langage *n.* language (*lingua*) 1.7: 93, 2.2: 6, 15, 2.4: 26, 27, 32, 2.6: 15, 3.2: 16, 3.12: 89, 3.14: 89, register, style 1.4: 25, 2.10: 27, fine style 1.5: 2, way of speaking 2.16: 37, **the common peplis ~** the vernacular 1.16: 7, **comoun peplis ~** the vernacular 1.16: 13, (*fig.*) birdsong 2.16: 8, **science of ~** rhetoric 2.10: 26, **langgage** 3.21: 74, **language** 1.11: 125, 3.12: 66, 72, 3.18: 36. **langages** *pl.* 2.4: 23, **langagis** 2.4: 22. *See also* **speche, tong: Engliche, Englis, Frankis, French, Lateyn, Latin.**

lange *n.* language 1.1: 63.

lar *n.* knowledge 2.1: 39, **lare** teaching 3.8: 39, **gastlic ~** 2.1: 41, 102, **halesome ~** 3.8: 15, **maner of ~** method of teaching (*modus tractandi*) 3.8: 57, **rihtwis ~** (of clerics' learning) 2.1: 35.

See also **connyng, teching.**

lastande *adj.* enduring, **a ~ werk** (of literary composition) 3.14: 60.

Lateyn *adj.* Latin, **~ word** 2.7: 26, Latin, **the ~ tonge** 2.8: 17, **~ bokis** 1.16: 46, **~ eretikes** 2.4: 22, **~ wordis** 3.8: 64, **~ declineson** 3.21: 72–73, **Latyne, ~ tong** 3.23: 44.

Latin *adj. as n.* the Latin language 2.1: 74, **Latine** 2.4: 4, **Latyn** 1.1: 10, 1.1: 25, 1.4: 17, 26, 1.7: 94, 1.12: 57, 1.16: 2, 3, 13, etc., 2.2: 16, 18, 20, etc., 2.4: 6, 2.6: 12, 14, 2.7: 18, 44, 2.17: 25, 3.7: 12, 3.8: 62, 63²ᵈ, 3.12: 63, 76, **Latyn, the ~** the Latin (i.e., Latin source or version) 1.1: 10, 1.7: 87, 2.2: 66, 84, 85, 3.8: 63¹ˢᵗ, 3.21: 75, (language of grammar teaching) 1.16: 2, **clerkis in ~** Latin scholars 1.16: 3, **we fynden in ~ mo heretikes** (of writers using Latin) 2.4: 21–22, **Latyne** 1.8: 30, 41, 133, 2.4: 3, 3.10: 2, 7, **Latyng, of ~** from Latin 3.18: 31. **Latyns** *pl.* Romans 2.4: 28.

laud *adj.* uneducated, unlearned 2.1: 38, **laued** 2.1: 36, 43, 65, etc., **lawed** 2.1: 100, **leude** 1.4: 13, 15, **leued** 1.13: 86, **lewde** ignorant 2.2: 61, 64, 89, etc., 2.3: 51, 3.24: 14, **lewed** 1.1: 46, 64, 69, **lettred or ~** 3.3: 33, 3.7: 11, 3.10: 3, **lewet, ~ and Englis** 3.14: 91, **lewid** 3.2: 65, 3.11: 15, **lewide** 1.6: 59, **lewyd** 3.9: 6, 40. **laued** *adj. as n.,* (as target audience) **lered and ~** 2.1: 77, **leude** (as stylistic "estate") 1.4: 16², **lewed** (as target audience) 1.1: 8, **lewyd, lernyd and . . . ~** 1.11: 146. **lewidest** *adj. superl.* least educated 3.11: 13. *See also* **boystous, rewde: laymen.**

law(e) *see* **lagh.**

lawriate *see* **poete.**

layd *p.p.* composed, **in myn Inglis ~** 1.1: 34.

layes *n.pl.* lays, songs 2.16: 16, **lays, lufe ~** love songs 3.13: 6. *See also* **balade, sange, roundels, vyrelayes.**

laymen *n.pl.* laymen, (as target audience) 1.16: 79, 118, 121, 2.3: 3, 5, 11, etc. *See also* **laud.**

lecture *n.* reading aloud (*lectura*) 3.15: 33. *See also* **poynte, pronounsyng, reding.**

lede *pr.1.sg.* lead, **~ owte** complete, finish 1.8: 43. *See also* **ende.**

leef *n.* leaf (*folium*) (one fold of book or manuscript with two writing sides, front and back) 1.14: 102, 125, 1.16: 104.

legende *n.* saint's life (*legenda*) 1.11: 81, 104, 176, lessons (from saints' lives) used in services 3.12: 31. **legendys** *pl.* 1.11: *title.*

lere *v.* learn 1.1: 4, **leyr** hear about, 3.16: 44. **leres** *pr.3.sg.* teaches 3.8: 29, **lerese** informs 3.8: 18. *See also* **lerne: heir.**

lered *adj.* learned 2.1: 35, 105, **lerned** 1.9: 39, 2.4: 30, 2.5: 75. **lered** *adj. as n.* (as target audience) **~ and laued** 2.1: 77, **lerid, not for the ~ bot for the lewed** 1.1: 8, **lernyd, ~ and eek on lewyd** 1.11: 146. *See also* **clerk, doctour, maister: laud, letteryd.**

lerne *v.* learn (from text) 3.17: 3, (by hearing) 2.2: 4, **~ and studye and understonde** 2.16: 59, **~ her Lordis lawe** 3.11: 16, **~ to rede** 2.16: 79, **rede, ~, and understond** 2.8: 10, **~ and practise** 1.9: 54. **lerneden** *pa.3.pl.* (of language acquisition) 1.4: 29. **lernede** *p.p.* taught 1.13: 51.

lernyng *vbl.n.* (act of) learning, teaching **commyn ~ of speche is by heryng** 2.2: 3, **lernyng** *n.* learning 1.9: 52, **~ and lore** (from Chaucer, Gower, and Lydgate's poetry) 1.9: 34, **gostly lernynge ~** spiritual learning 3.5: 57–58, **in ~** (to read) 2.16: 79.

lesing *n.* redemption, **~ of sayntis** (as literary subject matter) 3.13: 4.

lesinge *vbl.n.* fiction, lie 2.15: 62, **lesynge** fictionalizing 2.15: 60, figuration 3.15: 84. **lesynges** *pl.* lies (of seducers' discourse, to be countered by conduct books) 2.16: 39. *See also* **feynynge.**

lesson *n.* reading, something to be read (*lectio*) 3.11: 14, 22², 3.12: 127, **lessone** lesson 2.13: 51. **leszouns** *pl.* 2.1: 92. *See also* **lecture.**

lest *v.* endure, **~ ay furth in memory** (of written composition) 1.2: 18, **leste** (of liturgical calendar of saints) 2.15: 68.

lestyn *v.* listen, **to carpe and to ~** 3.13: 8, **listen** 1.1: 62, **listene, ~ and lere** 1.1: 4. *See also* **heir,**

herken, lysters, lythe, red.

leten *v.* cease (reading) 3.1: 5. *See also* **blyn, ceesse, leve, rist: begin.**

letere *n.* letter (*littera*) literal meaning 2.5: 119, ~ of Hooli Writ 2.5: 89, **letter** (of written mis-
sive) 3.2: 67, **lettere** literal meaning 2.5: 88, 102, 108, etc., 3.8: 64, the ~ . . . sleeth 2.5:
114, **lettre** 2.5: 8, 3.21: 24, 27, epistle 1.16: 131, to the ~ in the literal sense 1.15: 47, **lettyr**
alphabetic script 1.14: 86, 118. **letters** *pl.* 1.14: 86, (of written missives) 1.14: 98, **lettyrrys**
alphabetic characters 1.8: 32. *See also* **epistel, sperit.**

letteryd *adj.* learned 1.8: 34, **lettred**, educated ~ or lewed 3.3: 33, **lettyrde**, every whoman ~
2.6: 16. *See also* **lered: unlettyrd.**

lettural *adj.* literal (i.e., the first level of exegetical interpretation) 1.12: 70, 72. *See also* **carnal,
fleischli, naked: gastelye, spiritual.**

leude, leued *see* **laud.**

leudenesse *n.* ignorance 1.4: 15, **leude** ~ commendeth (of ignorant or unpracticed audiences)
1.4: 16, **leudnesse** crudeness ~ in travaile 1.4: 30, **lewydnesse** lack of learning 1.11: 209.
See also **humblesse, ignorance, insuffishaunce, simplesse, unabylnesse, unconnynge,
unworthynesse: suffisaunce.**

leve *pr.2.sg.* leave aside (of inappropriately selective reading) 3.4: 6. **leve** *pr.2.pl.* cease, stop
(focusing on author in favor of vision) 1.13: 53. *See also* **blyn, ceesse, leten.**

lewde, lewed, lewet, lewid, lewyd, lewidest *see* **laud.**

leyr *see* **lere.**

librarie *n.* library 1.16: 128, 136, 140.

lif *n.* biography (*vita*), (of saint) 2.7: 43, **life** (of Christ) 3.10: 25, 28, **Cristes** ~ 3.10: 4, 13, **liif**
(of saint and church doctor) 1.16: 100, **Book of** ~ 3.11: 8, **liyf**, ~ of Crist 2.5: 79, **lyf** (of
saint) 1.11: 75, 174, 2.7: 5, 13, 14, etc., (of counterexemplary women) 2.16: 54. **lyves** *pl.*
(of good women in conduct book) 2.16: 50. *See also* **felyng, tribulacyons.**

light *adj.* easy (*ornatus levis*), ~ **lange** (of simple style or narration) 1.1: 63, ~ **ryme** 1.1: 56,
lyght, ~ **doctrine** 3.10: 10–11, **not** ~ (to translate) 3.12: 62. **lightest** *adj. superl.* easiest, ~
in mannes mouth easiest to recite 1.1: 36, **lyghtest** (of English style in translation) 3.8: 62.
See also **hevenesse.**

light *v.* lighten, ~ **the spreit** (effect of poetry) 3.18: 21. *See also* **comfort.**

likand *adj.* agreeable (of subject matter both true and well presented) 1.2: 13. *See also* **plesand.**

liketh (1) *v. impers.* pleases (of audience and readers) 3.5: 24, **likes** 3.14: 20, **likis, rist quen us**
~ (of audience for recited narative) 3.13: 22, **likit** (of source author) 3.23: 43, **lyke** 2.14: 9,
3.5: 20, 38, **lyketh** (of author) 1.5: 41, (of reader) 3.2: 12, **lykis** 3.16: 8, **lykyth** 1.12: 13.
like *pr. subj.* 2.7: 9, 3.11: 22. **lykyd** *pa.3.sg.* pleased (of text) 2.7: 7, (to have read) 3.22:
45. (2) **lyke** *v.* ~ **of** take pleasure in (a text) 2.11: 28. **lyked** *pa.1.sg.* liked 3.24: 12. *See also*
lyst, please, quemes.

liking *vbl.n.* liking, pleasure (of audience) 3.4: 6, 3.10: 28, **likyng, more** ~ attractive (of contemplation of Christ's humanity) 3.10: 18, **lykyng, to fynde** ~ (principle for guiding
reading) 3.1: 3, **lykynge** (of audience) 1.13: 58, **mest** ~ 3.1: 6. *See also* **delite, deynte, joy,
plesance: displesour.**

likyngly *adv.* willingly, pleasurably (reading instruction) 3.10: 52. *See also* **abidyngly, bisily,
easely, moderatly.**

listen *see* **lestyn.**

litterature *n.* letters, **the motyf of** ~ 3.15: 45, **men of** ~ 3.15: 70.

lof *n.* loaf, (*fig.*) text 3.19: 34, **lofe** book 3.20: 22, **loofe** 3.20: 21, 22, 23. *See also* **hony,
honycombe, meate.**

logik *n.* logic (*logica*) (as branch of the quadrivium) 2.2: 95.

loke *v.* look (at a book) 2.7: 21, 19, 3.23: 31, 3.24: 17, ~ **in her lesson** to look over (their reading) 3.11: 22, (a work) 3.24: 39, **lokyn** 3.22: 32, **luke** 3.7: 41. **lokith** *pr.3.sg.*, ~ **in** 3.11: 14,

lokyst 3.9: 36. loke *pr.3.pl.* 2.7: 19, 21, loken, ~ on this book 3.11: 12, lokes consult (an encyclopedia) 2.1: 67. loke *imp. pl.* 3.12: 44. lokede *pa.1.sg.* 3.20: 31. lokede *pa.3.pl.* 3.20: 36. loked *p.p.* 3.24: 45, lokyd, ~ at 3.22: 33. *See also* red, se, studie.

loking *n.* perusal, ~ on her lesson 3.11: 22, ~ of other bokes (of consultation) 2.2: 42. *See also* avisement, stodyinge.

lord *n.* lord, (of patron as figure in text) 2.2: 132², (invoked by author) 2.3: 166, (of God as source of revelatory text) 3.22: 49, life of our ~ 3.10: 25, 37, ~ and clerk (of Boethius) 3.23: 22, ~ Cryst (as source of text's efficacy) 1.14: 9, (acts of Christ's life as subject matter) 3.10: 51, my liege ~ (of Richard II) 2.11: 130, my ~ Beaumont (as figure in text) 2.12: 54, 56, my ~ and mastyr (of patron) 1.8: 117, myn oghne ~ (of Henry of Lancaster) 2.11: 93, oure ~ 3.5: 9, 29, owere ~ (as determiner of time for composition) 1.14: 73, precept of ane ~ (command for composition) 3.18: 34, owre ~ 3.22: 20, 23, souverayn ~ (of God or king) 2.12: 75, (address to king) 2.12: 27, 80, yere of our ~ (time of events in text) 2.14: 58, (God's year as time of text) 1.14: 145, 2.16: 5, lorde, ~ Jesu (invoked for literary work) 1.9: 105, my ~ (of patron as figure in text) 3.24: 16, oure ~ (invoked for work's pleasure and usefulness) 1.12: 5, (for author's ability to complete work) 1.12: 35, (as ultimate source of revelatory text or vision) 1.13: 51, 98, yere of our ~ (of God's year, as time of text) 2.8: 40, (of king's year) 2.8: 41. lordes *gen.sg.*, my ~ byddyng (of patron) 1.7: 74. lordes *pl.* (in address to audience) my ~ leches 1.10: 30, ye ~ lewed (address to audience) 1.1: 69, lordis, approvid of my ~ (of audience of church superiors) 1.16: 91, lordys (as subject of work) 1.8: 21.

lordynges *n.pl.* gentlemen (address to audience) 1.1: 3. *See also* frendys, soverayns.

lore *n.* knowledge 1.9: 83, teaching (from a book) 2.16: 82, lernyng and ~ 1.9: 34, Cristen ~ 1.15: 41, Goddes ~ 1.9: 94, of informacioun and of ~ 2.2: 7, 24, 27, somwhat of lust, somewhat of ~ (as compositional compromise and ideal middle way) 2.11: 26. *See also* connyng, infformacion, techyng.

lovand *pr.p.* praising (in psalm recitation), voice of ~ 3.8: 52.

love *n.* love (as subject of book or treatise) 1.4: 63, 65, 101, 2.11: 82, 3.1: 1, 2, (as subject matter) 1.4: 75, 1.8: 19, affecyons of ~ (stimulated by reading) 3.12: 149, concorde and ~ (of cosmological subject matter) 2.3: 160, curtays ~ (God's motive for providing visionary subject matter) 1.13: 55, endles ~ 3.4: 12, inwarde ~ and devocyon (in reciters) 3.12: 58, for *Cristus* ~ (food of learning to be given for) 3.19: 10, large . . . connynge and ~ (of generous author, envied by Aristotle) 3.2: 86, ~ of Cristen lore (as motivation and effect of study) 1.15: 41, ~ of Englis lede (reason for translation) 3.14: 76, ~ of God (as effect of literary work) 3.2: 2–3, 10, ~ of oone (motive for writing) 2.3: 148n, ~ to God (in audience, as outcome of author's labors) 1.12: 8, ~ unlaufle (to be obliterated by proper reading) 2.13: 32, luf (as subject of treatise) 2.17: 2², 42, fyre of ~ (felt in psalm recitation) 3.8: 4, Goddis ~ (recalled in hymns) 3.8: 49, ~ of Jhesu (stimulated by reading) 3.10: 8, ~ of symple men (of author's goodwill toward audience) 1.1: 39, ~ of the lewed man 1.1: 64, lufe, ~ lays love songs 3.13: 6, (as subject matter) 3.16: 34. lovys *pl.* as subject matter 1.8: 11. *See also* charite, dalyawns.

love *v.* love, thys blyssyd virgyne to ~ (effect of reading or hearing saint's life) 1.11: 129, (of makers of verse and Christ) 3.14: 52, loven (God, as effect of literary work) 3.1: 3. love *pr.1.sg.* (of author's feeling for dedicatee) 1.11: 178. loves *pr.3.sg.*, God ~ (author) 1.13: 66. love *pr.2.pl.*, ~ to be enformyd 3.12: 87. loves *pr.3.pl.*, ~ God (of audience) 1.13: 68. love *pr. subj.* (of outcome of vision and/or its text) 1.13: 60. lovyde *pa.3.sg.* (of author's feeling for literary adviser) 1.12: 26. lovyd *pa.sg.subj.* 1.11: 183.

lovely *adj.* love-filled, ~ lokyng (of perusal of Book of Life) 3.11: 22. *See also* affectuouse, amorouse, lovesum, luffynge.

loverrys *n.pl.* lovers, (as audience for love story) 1.8: 11, lovers (as suitable readers) 3.4: 2.

lovesum *adj.* love-inspiring (of reading) 3.1: 17. *See also* affectuouse, amorouse, lovely, luffynge.

lovynge *vbl.n.* (1) praise (of Christ and God, in psalms and hymns) 3.8: 2, 47, **voice of** ~ 3.8: 50, **wordis of** ~ 3.8: 19. *See also* **praysyng.**

lovynge *vbl.n.* (2) loving ~ **of God** (as desired effect of visionary text) 1.13: 90.

lowely *adv.* humbly (of writer's submission to church) 3.12: 93, **lowly** (author's mode of soliciting favor for work) 1.11: 69. *See also* **humbly, mekeli, symplely.**

luf(e) *see* **love.**

luffynge *adj.* loving, amorous ~ **styrrynge** (as response to reading) 3.20: 32. *See also* **affectuouse, amorouse, lovely, lovesum.**

lust *n.* pleasure (effect of poetry, ideally coupled with instruction) 2.11: 26. *See also* **likand, lore, plesance.**

lusty *adj.* pleasurable (of poetry) 1.7: 62, fine (of rhetoric) 3.15: 68, 74.

lycour *n.* liquid, (of muse's help to author) 1.7: 55, **aureat** ~ (*fig.*) fine writing, verbal ornament 1.7: 31, **lykoure** (*fig.*) spiritually efficacious writing 3.20: 36.

lyght, lyghtest *see* **light** (*adj.*).

lyghtely *adv.* casually, **not** ~ (reading instruction) 3.12: 44. *See also* **abidyngly.**

lyke *see* **liketh.**

lykyng(e) *see* **liking.**

lymynyd *p.p.* illuminated (of a book) 1.8: 31.

lyne *n.* line (of verse), ~ **by** ~ 3.16: 31.

lysable *adj.* readable (as aim of translation) 3.2: 19. *See also* **cleer, entendible, playn.**

lyst *pr.3.sg.* (*impers.*) it pleases, **as Guydo** ~ **devise** (of author) 1.7: 142, **quha so** ~ 3.16: 44, **wych** ~ **attende** 1.11: 82, **lyste,** ~ **to rede** 3.15: 3, ~ **to rede and se** (of audience) 1.8: 76, ~ **to see hyt agen** (of reader and book) 1.12: 16, **yff thei** ~ (of readers) 1.8: 145, **who so** ~ **to here** 1.11: 31. *See also* **liketh, please, quemes.**

lysters *n.pl.* listeners 1.7: 64. *See also* **herer.**

lythe *v.* hear (of audience) 3.13: 4. *See also* **heir, herken, lestyn, lythe, red.**

ma *v.* make, compose 1.2: 37, **mak** make, compose, write (poetry) 3.18: 32, **make** 1.7: 88, 208, 1.8: 110, 1.11: 176, 1.16: 79, 98, 2.1: 119, 2.2: 118, 2.11: 30, 170, 2.16: 58, 65, (of an exhortation) 2.9: 37, ~ . . . **trusty** (of translation) 2.2: 128–29, ~ **a merour** (*fig.*) to compose 1.7: 120, ~ . . . **cleer and pleyne** (of translation) 2.2: 142, ~ **Englissh translacion** 2.2: 137, ~ **[of]** take as subject or theme 3.14: 51, ~ **remembrauns** commemorate in writing 1.8: 54, ~ **reporte** report 3.15: 67, ~ **a sermoun** compose 2.2: 82, **dyde doo** ~, had made, caused to be made 2.16: 69, **doo** ~ have composed, cause to be composed 2.16: 48, **rimes** ~ compose verses 3.14: 50, **makyne,** ~ **a booke** 1.14: 68. **make** *pr.1.sg.* (of book) 1.16: 6, (of discursive arguments) 1.16: 31². **maketh** *pr.3.sg.,* ~ **mencioun** commemorates 1.7: 87, ~ **no mencioun** 1.7: 162, **makith** makes (a translation) 2.2: 154, (of rendering a reader knowledgeable) 3.11: 8, **makyth,** ~ **remembrauns** commemorates 1.8: 68. **maken** *pr.3.pl.* 1.3: 11, **makith** 2.2: 18, ~ **mencion and mynde** commemorate 2.2: 21. **make** *imp.* (*refl.*) ~ **the in thi soule present** (meditative reading instruction) 3.10: 50. **mad** *pa.1.sg.* 1.1: 37, **made** 1.1: 45, 2.16: 67, 69, 3.12: 148. **made** *pa.3.sg.* 1.12: 20, 2.2: 104, 118, 2.16: 1, 16, 3.21: 5, ~ . . . **translate** caused [*s.o.*] to translate 2.2: 102. **made** *pa.3.pl.* 2.3: 63. **imade** *p.p.* made, composed 1.7: 100, 2.2: 114, constituted 1.10: 23, **mad** 3.1: 2, **made** 1.1: 47, 1.9: 63, 1.16: 75, 2.2: 88, 2.3: 3, 2.12: 57, 2.16: 78, 3.2: 1, 14, 3.12: 137, 145, formed 3.2: 34, 1.10: 17. *See also* **making** (*vbl.n.*): **endite, laboure, werk, write.**

magnifie *v.* praise (in a literary work) 1.9: 89.

maister *n.* master (*magister*), authority, **Guido** ~ 1.7: 202, **master** 1.9: 55, **mastyr** 1.8: 117, (Chaucer) 1.8: 128, **mayster,** ~ **Wace** (of author as literary authority) 1.1: 23, 25, 27, etc., **maystre** scholar 3.19: 22, **maystir** 2.7: 1, **maystur** 3.19: 5, 14, **maystyr** master (of arts, of theology), 2.7: 19, ~ **Nycholas of Lyre** 1.12: 69, ~ **of Storyis** Master of Histories (*Magister* *historiarum*) 1.12: 68, **meystre** teacher 3.21: 17. **maisteris** *pl.* (address to audience) 3.18: 29, **maisters**, ~ Gower, Chaucer and Lydgate 1.9: 28, **mastirs** teachers, authorities 2.3: 62, **mastrys** 2.6: 14. *See also* **clerk, doctour, lered: auctor, cause, poete, translatour, writer.**

maistresse *n.* mistress, (*fig.*) of music and rhetoric, (i.e., Venus) 1.7: 58, (*fig.*, of historiography) 3.15: 72, ~ **of trouthe** historiography 3.15: 59. *See also* **muse** (*n.*).

mak(e) *see* **ma.**

making *vbl.n.* making (of translations) 2.2: 90, **makyng** composition 1.1: 67, 1.5: 39, 1.7: 61, 65, 1.9: 41, **bokis** ~ 1.16: 50, 52, **makynge** 1.4: 48, 49, 1.5: 36, 1.9: 67. *See also* **enditing, labour, poetre, wark.**

malice *n.* malice (as motive for writing or criticism) 1.16: 77, 2.3: 91, 2.11: 150, **malyhs** 1.11: 199, **malys** 1.7: 139. *See also* **blaim, blamynge, detraccioun, diffames, envie, inpugnacioun, pride, presumcion, slaundres.**

maner *n.* manner, ~ **of lare** method of teaching (*modus tractandi*) 3.8: 57, ~ **of . . . praysynge** mode of praise 3.12: 9, 50, **on gud** ~ (of telling a story) 1.2: 8, ~ **of spekyng** mode of speech 3.12: 73, ~ **of spekeynge** mode of speaking 3.12: 110, ~ **of translatioun** reworking (periphrase for composition) 3.18: 32, **the thrid** ~ sense (of a word) 2.2: 57, **manere, in** ~ **poetyke** 2.10: 42. **maners** *pl.* **in thre** ~ 3.8: 59, ~ **of spekingis** modes of ambiguity (in Scripture) 1.15: 35. *See also* **kynde.**

maracle *n.* miracle (*miracula*) (act of God) 2.14: 53, **marycle** (literary genre) 2.14: 57, **myracle** (act of God) 1.11: 145, 2.14: 56. **myracles** *pl.* (deeds of martyrs) 2.4: 19, **myraclis**, ~ **and merveylis** (subject matter in Book of Life) 3.11: 11. *See also* **aventure, chaunces, dedis, ferles, marvellys, wondres.**

Martyrologe *n.* martyrology (*martyrologium*) (register of saints, often containing brief narrative histories) 2.8: 16.

marvellys *n.pl.* miraculous events (as subject matter of drama) 2.14: 7, **mervails,** marvels, **of** ~ **and of wondres** (as subject matter for chronicles) 2.2: 22, **merveylis, myraclis and** ~ (explained in Book of Life) 3.11: 11. *See also* **ferles, maracle, wondres.**

master, mastir *see* **maister.**

matarnall *adj.* maternal, ~ **toung** (the vernacular) 2.17: 27. *See also* **moder.**

mater *n.* subject matter (*materia*), 1.4: 23, 1.7: 204, 1.9: 110, 2.14: 6, 2.17: 26, 30, 3.3: 23, 26, 34, 3.14: 49, 3.17: 11, 3.23: 49, topic 3.2: 82, **historyal** ~ 3.15: 58, ~ **historyal** 3.15: 36, 66, **poysye** ~ material for poetry 1.4: 19, **as the** ~ **asketh** according to the demands of the subject matter 3.12: 67, **matere** 1.4: 12, 1.7: 198, 1.8: 10, 52, 76, 1.9: 62, 1.11: 15, 20, 73, 1.12: 14, 20, 43, 1.13: 93, 1.14: 114, 2.7: 9, 47, 2.10: 4, 9, 23, etc., 2.16: 83, 3.8: 54, 3.23: 54, **matier** 1.9: 103, 2.12: 68, **matiere** 2.11: 13, **matire** 1.5: 21, 3.10: 8, **matter** 1.4: 75, 3.12: 135, 154, 166, 3.24: 52, **as the** ~ **asketh** 3.12: 166, **matyre** 1.5: 9. **materis** *pl.* 3.18: 26, **maters** 2.3: 167, 2.10: 21, 3.1: 7, 8, 3.7: 4, 10, 38, 3.15: 6, 31, 33, etc., ~ **and histories** 3.15: 1, ~ **of drede** (of material designed to evoke fear) 3.12: 154, ~ **of hope** (of spiritually comforting material) 3.12: 156, ~ **to enforme the understondyng** 3.12: 163, **matires** 3.10: 15, **matters** 3.12: 158, 3.24: 35, 54, 56, ~ **to sturre up the affeccions** 3.12: 164, **worldley** ~ secular material 3.12: 105.

maystir, maystyr *see* **maister.**

meanynge *n.* meaning (of Latin liturgy) 3.12: 29, **meenyng** (authorial and/or textual) 1.16: 23, 26, 29, etc., (in interpretation) 1.16: 33, **menyng** (of authorial intention) 1.9: 84, 2.2: 128, 3.2: 83, (of patron's intention) 2.2: 135, (of text) 2.2: 147, **true** ~ **formal** 1.9: 80, **menynge** (of authorial intention) 1.13: 23, **trewe** ~ (of audience intention) 1.13: 62, **weiward** ~ 2.5: 91. *See also* **cence, sentence, understandinge, wit: mene** (*v.*).

meate *n.* food, prepared dish, (*fig.*) philosophical reading 1.4: 95, **mete** reading matter, food of learning 3.19: 18, penitential doctrine 3.19: 33, 43. **goostli** ~ spiritual food, Scripture 2.5: 148, 153, **hoolsum** ~ **of Hooli Writ** 2.5: 45, **my** ~ (attributed to Christ) the gospel 2.5: 159,

sadde ~ **of grete clergie** serious, learned reading 3.10: 11, **metis** *pl.* spiritually profitable reading 2.5: 168, 171, **goostli** ~ spiritual reading 2.5: 170, **medicinable** ~ healing reading 2.5: 172–73, **mene** ~ (*lit.*, simple dishes), plain and true doctrine 2.5: 168², **metus** patristic writings 3.19: 19, 22. *See also* **frewte, herbis, hony, honycombe, lof, mylk: savour, schewe, taaste.**

mede *n.* reward (for composition) 1.1: 67, 2.1: 121, 2.2: 155, 156, 3.1: 18 (of reader). *See also* **garnyson, recompense, rewarde.**

medeful *adj.* meritorious (of patron's intention) 2.2: 135, ~ **makyng** (of composition) 2.2: 140, ~ **dede** composition 2.2: 155.

meditacion *n.* meditative reading (*meditatio*) 3.1: 10, 3.2: 6, 3.10: 26, 39, **meditacyone** 1.14: 44, 3.22: 47, **medytacyon**, ~ **of the Passyon** (as literary genre) 1.12: 3. **meditacions** *pl.* soliloquies (literary genre) 3.2: 98, ~ **of Cristes life** 3.10: 4, **swete** ~ outcome of reading 3.2: 9, **meditacyons** soliloquies 3.2: 1, **medytacyonys** 1.12: 49, 51, 60, etc. *See also* **contemplacion, felyng, prayer, thenkyng.**

meeknesse *n.* meekness, humility (as mode of study) 1.15: 41, **good lyvynge and** ~ (needed for studying Scripture) 1.15: 84, **the wondirful highnesse and . . .** ~ (of style in Scripture) 1.15: 64–65. *See also* **humblesse, simplenes, simplesse.**

meenyng *see* **meanynge.**

mekeli *adv.* meekly, ~ **and charitabli** (how clerks should expound Scripture) 2.5: 11, (how laymen should inquire about Scripture) 2.5: 75, **mekely**, ~ **and devoutli** (of author's correction of heterodoxy) 1.16: 17. *See also* **humbly, lowely, symplely.**

mellodyus *adj.* melodious (of Orpheus's songs) 1.7: 48, **melodyouse** (of nightingale's song) 2.13: 54. *See also* **dites.**

melody *n.* melody, consonance of sound (of Virgil's style) 3.16: 35, **melodye** (of psalms) 3.21: 61. *See also* **sange.**

memorial *adj.* commemorative (of writing) 1.7: 123, **memoryal, in** ~ memorially, as a commemoration 3.15: 29–30.

memorial *n.* commemoration (purpose of text) 1.7: 98, 3.15: 65.

memorie *n.* memory, recording, commemoration (*memoria*) 3.16: 58, **memory** 1.2: 18, 1.8: 98, **worthy to** ~ 1.4: 55, **boke of perpetual** ~ 1.4: 61. *See also* **mend, remembrance: oblyvyon.**

mend *n.* mind, memory, **han** ~ (retrieve autobiographical source materials) 1.14: 131, **oblyvyon off** ~ (of loss of cultural memory) 1.8: 59, **mende, brynge to** ~ recall 1.8: 83, **steryn manys** ~ (function of images) 3.9: 2–3, **mynd** source (of authoritative text) 2.9: 27, power of intellect 2.14: 79, **mynde** cultural memory 1.7: 111, **kepe hyt in** ~ (function of table of contents) 1.12: 15–16, **come to** ~ **in spekyng** 2.16: 82–83, **delyten the** ~ (of poems) 3.15: 78, **exercice of my** ~ (in composition) 1.10: 29–30, **falle to my** ~ **in the writyng** 2.7: 46, **have it in** ~ (of treatise) 3.6: 4, **holde all thing in** ~ (function of compilations) 1.10: 21–22, **holde wel in** ~ (reading instruction) 1.15: 36, **holdeth in** ~ (a literal meaning of "eating" Scripture) 2.5: 166, **kepe hit in** ~ (function of translation) 2.2: 87, **mencion and** ~ 2.2: 21, **merour . . . to our** ~ 1.7: 120, ~ **of right menyng** (translator's concern) 2.2: 128, **set in** ~ (of image) 3.10: 19, **stere the** ~ (of reader) 3.2: 2. **mendys** *pl.* recollections 3.22: 62, **myndes, worthy** ~ **to fede** (function of reading for noblemen) 3.24: 7. *See also* **memorie, remembrance: oblyvyon.**

mene *adj.* lowly (of subject matter) 1.6: 58, plain (*fig.*) of reading matter 2.5: 167, 168.

mene *n.* interpreter 2.2: 14, **myddel or** ~ (of author's role in compiling when God controls beginning and outcome) 1.10: 16. *See also* **cause, myddel** (*n.*).

mene *v.* mean, intend 2.2: 15, 2.7: 22, interpret 2.14: 79, **what hit is to** ~ how it is to be interpreted 2.2: 85, **what the Latyn is to** ~ 2.2: 85–86. **meene** *pr.1.sg.* 1.13: 50. 86, **mene** 1.6: 58, 1.8: 61, 128, 1.13: 80, ~ **in mynde** 2.2: 134, 2.14: 79. **meenys** *pr.3.sg.* 1.13: 51, **meneth** 2.2: 147. **mente** *pa.1.sg.* 1.13: 86.

menehede *n.* moderation (in inclusion of material) 1.10: 33.

menyng *see* **meanynge.**

merke *n.* mark, target, **tac mi** ~ (*fig.*) take (as subject matter) 2.1: 84.

merour *n.* mirror (*speculum*), (*fig.*) encyclopedia, writings, 1.7: 120, **mirour** (of educated men's
  books) 2.1: 67, **myroure** (of text in praise of Virgin) 3.12: 38, **Myroure, Oure Ladyes** ~
  3.12: 2, 37, **myrowre** (of devotional treatise), **A** ~ **to Devout Peple** 1.12: *title*, 1.12: 59,
  myrrour, a perpetual ~ 1.4: 32, ~ **of glas** (simile for book) 2.17: 44, **myrroure** 3.12: 35, 40,
  44. *See also* **glas, spectakle.**

mervel *v.* marvel (of response to illuminated book) 1.8: 33. *See also* **marvellys** (*n.pl.*).

merwulus *adj.* marvelous (of workmanship) 1.8: 35.

mete, metis, metus *see* **meate.**

methaphoris *n.pl.* metaphors (*metaphorae*), figurative language 2.3: 64. *See also* **figure, flour,**
  ymage.

metir *n.* verse (*metrum*), **gay** ~ (of Latin elegiacs) 3.18: 58, ~ **suete** 3.23: 23, **metre, in** ~ (of verse
  translation) 1.5: 27, **lawe of** ~ metrical rules 1.5: 20. *See also* **rime, vers.**

mevyd *pa.3.sg.* moved 1.11: 175, **mevyde** (to composition) 1.12: 27, **movyd,** ~ **and exortyd**
  2.9: 34. **mevyd** *pa.3.pl.* 1.11: 126. **mevyd** *p.p.* (to scribal activity) 1.14: 141, **moeved** (by
  literature) 3.15: 46. *See also* **compellyth, exciten, inflawme, kyndils, quyken, stere.**

middel *adj.* middle (*mediocris*), ~ **weie** (of subject matter) 2.11: 24. *See also* **hye, meeknesse.**

minisshyng *n.* reduction (*diminutio*), dimunition (of source material) 1.9: 60. *See also* **abredge:**
  addicioun.

mirour *see* **merour.**

moder *n.* mother (with figurative overtones of affective and poetic generation) ~ **unto Orpheus**
  (i.e., Calliope) 1.7: 47, ~ **of philosophie** (i.e., historiography) 3.15: 59–60. **moders** *gen. sg.*
  ~ **tonge** the vernacular 2.8: 34. **moder** *n. as adj.,* ~ **tonge** 2.4: 7, ~ **tunge** 2.4: 6, **mother,** ~
  toung 3.18: 31. *See also* **matarnall, tong.**

moderatly *adv.* at a measured pace (of reading) 3.2: 5. *See also* **easely.**

moeved *see* **mevyd.**

moral *adj.* moral, ~ **doctryne** (as attribute of Virgil's writing) 3.16: 42, **morall** (of meaning in
  text) 3.18: 12, ~ **volume** work of morality 3.24: 80–81.

moralite *n.* moral subject matter (*moralitas*) 1.5: 38, **moralitee** morality (attribute of Boethius's
  writing) 3.23: 23.

moral[y]syd *p.p.* tropologically interpreted (as in *sensus moralis*) 2.13: 6.

movyd *see* **mevyd.**

mowen *p.p.* mown, (*fig.*) compiled or composed (of previous writers) 1.4: 77. *See also* **gader,**
  repers.

multiplicacion *n.* multiplication (of books) 3.6: 5.

multiplie *v.* increase (dignity of patrons through literary service) 1.9: 90, (of having books
  copies) 1.16: 79. **multipliers** *pl.* false coiners (as parallel for alchemical writers) 2.3: 13.

muse *n.* muse (*musa*) (of history) 1.7: 40. *See also* **maistresse.**

muse *v.* read carefully, study 1.5: 41, (of author) 1.11: 97. *See also* **consider, perseyve, studie,**
  thynkyn.

musicyens *n.pl.* musicians (as needing same muse as rhetoricians) 1.7: 58.

myddel *n.* middle section (of text) 1.10: 16, **myddil** middle place in text 1.15: 42, **myddyl** 1.12:
  87. *See also* **middel** (*adj.*).

mylk *n.* milk, (*fig.*) easy reading matter 3.10: 10. *See also* **frewte, herbis, hony, honycombe, lof,**
  meate, mylk: savour, schewe, taaste.

myn *v.* remember 3.14: 60. *See also* **remembre, renewe.**

mynde *see* **mend.**

mynstrell *n.* musician (accompanying dramatic performance) 2.14: 80. *See also* **disours,**
  harpours, seggers.

myracle *see* **maracle.**

myrrour *see* **merour.**

myrthis *n.pl.* entertainments (of Virgil's verse) 3.16: 46. *See also* **dysporte, gamen, pastans, play, recreacion, salace, sport.**

mysdisposed *p.p. as adj.* wrongly disposed (of readers) 1.16: 97. *See also* **adresse, dispose, dresse, undisposed, wel-disposid.**

mystaken *pr.3.pl.* misinterpret (words of Scripture) 2.5: 90. **mystake** *p.p.* 3.2: 82.

mystakyng *vbl.n.* mistaking, misinterpretation 2.5: 91, **folwyng the feendys counsayle by ~** (of Scripture) 3.2: 85–86, **mystakynge** (*fig.*) indigestion, **~ . . . of the hoolsum mete** (of Scripture) 2.5: 45.

mysundirstonders *n.pl.* literal readers (of Scripture) 2.5: 109.

naked *adj.* naked, **~ of doctryne** bereft of literary instruction 3.15: 71, **nakid** (*fig.*) literal, **~ kunnynge** (of knowledge without good works) 2.5: 18, **~ undirstondynge** literal interpretation 2.5: 22–23. *See also* **lettural.**

name *n.* name, literary reputation 1.7: 128, **unknowe shal be my ~** 2.3: 15, author's name 1.11: 33, 35, 200, 1.13: 2, title (of book) 3.20: 34, 3.23: 15, **unworthi to bere ony ~** 3.5: 6, **namme** reputation 3.16: 57. **names** *pl.* terms 1.1: 59, proper names (how to translate) 2.2: 148, 153, names (of writers) 3.24: 65. *See also* **renoun, termes.**

name *v.* identify (in interpretation) 2.7: 22. **name** *pr.1.sg.* (literary work) 3.12: 36. **namenede** *p.p.* **~ of God** named by God (of literary work) 3.20: 6.

naturally *adv.* with natural ability (of Chaucer's versification) 1.8: 130.

nature *n.* natural world (requires writers to be properly known) 1.7: 112. *See also* **kynde.**

negligence *n.* negligence (of reader) 1.12: 63, (of author) 3.18: 40, **neglygence** 3.12: 120. *See also* **hast, hastenesse: overhippis: unworthynesse.**

negligently *adv.* negligently (of reading) 1.12: 60.

noye *adj.* annoying, **irksome or ~ to rede hem** (of uncompendious information) 1.10: 21.

noyen *v.* annoy (readers) 1.10: 28. *See also* **displese.**

nuttis *gen. sg.* nut's, **~ schell** nutshell, (*fig.*) literary form 3.18: 15. *See also* **kirnell.**

oblyvyon *n.* oblivion, (prevented by writers) 1.8: 59, **oblyvyoun** (fate of inadequate writings) 1.11: 40, (fate of the inactive and unrecorded) 3.15: 63. *See also* **memorie, mend, remembrance.**

observance *n.* care (in composition) 1.9: 62, carrying out (of Benedictine Rule) 2.8: 9, 24, **observaunce** act of homage (to patron) 1.5: 70.

observe *v.* carry out (Benedictine Rule) 2.8: 12, (patron's will) 2.11: 160.

occupacion *n.* activity (of writing) 1.4: 15, 1.5: 67, **good ~ for Cristen laymen** (of reading) 1.16: 79, **occupacyon** (of composition) 1.12: 22. *See also* **besynes, labour, travail, wark.**

offringe *pr.p.* offering (of book to patron) 2.13: 14, **offrynge, ~ hymself** (of historiographic accounts, *personif.*) 3.15: 53.

ontre *see* **entre.**

open *adj.* open, available, **~ schewynge** (of exemplary liturgical recitation) 3.12: 54–55, **~ to other folkes knowlege** (of liturgy) 3.12: 53–54, **opene** clear (of argument) 1.16: 145, **opin** manifested, **charite is ~** (of meaning in text) 1.15: 29, **opun** available (of book) 3.11: 19, **opyn** clear (in Scripture) 1.15: 31, (of exposition) 2.5: 85, **~ preisers** (of audience) 3.3: 29. *See also* **cleer, commen, playn, rounde.**

open (*v.*) *see* **opnyt.**

openli *adv.* publicly 1.16: 89, **openly** fully, clearly (of nuns' performance of office) 3.12: 51[2], **expressyn more ~** 1.14: 125–26, **more ~ be schewed** more clearly to be declared (*prolep-*

sis) 1.14: 27, ~ . . . **and dystynctely** 3.12: 51, ~ **wer knowe** (of subject matter) 1.7: 91, ~ **sprad** (of audience's ears) 1.4: 1, **rede yt savourly and** ~ 3.12: 128–29, **opinly** 1.15: 44, **opunli,** ~ **schewede** 3.10: 41, **opynli** 2.5: 13, 14, 56, etc. *See also* **playnly, prevyly.**

opin (*adj.*) *see* **open** (*adj.*).

opinion *n.* opinion, judgment (of writer) 1.9: 101, **opinioun** position in argument 1.16: 70, **opynnyon** 3.2: 75, **opynyon** 3.2: 74, **opynyoun** reputation 2.7: 31, **opynyounn** belief (of narrator) 1.11: 156. **opyniouns** *pl.* 1.16: 68², 69, **opynyons** 3.2: 92, **opynyonys** 3.2: 85.

opnyt *pr.3.sg.* opens, begins (his book) 2.17: 35. **opene** *pr. subj.* open, reveal 2.5: 67, **opened** *pa.1.sg.* (of book) 3.24: 42, **openede** *p.p.* revealed 2.5: 68, (of book) 3.20: 28–29, 30, **oppynd** expounded 3.8: 45. *See also* **declare, expounne, glosyd, undo.**

opun, opyn (*adj.*) *see* **open** (*adj.*).

oratour *n.* petitioner (author in relation to patron) 2.12: 81, **oratoure** 2.12: 94.

orcherd *n.* orchard (*fig.*) literary work 3.5: 11², 14. *See also* **aleye, pathis: frewte, herbis, wedis.**

ordenaunce *n.* ordering (*ordinatio*), ~ **of this orcherd** (*fig.*) arrangement of text 3.5: 27.

ordeneelly *adv.* in the proper order (of prologue organization) 1.11: 3.

order *v.* order (of God's aid to author) 2.9: 32. *See also* **dispose.**

Ordinalle *n.* Ordinal (of church services), (*by extension*) book of regulation 2.3: 128, 130.

ordinat *see* **foorme.**

ordire *n.* ordering (of subject matter in a text, *dispositio*) 2.3: 127, **ordre** 1.11: 18, composition 3.24: 28, ~ **of wordes** (in translation) 2.2: 144, 145, **ordyr** 1.14: 115, **in** ~ narrated chronologically 1.14: 113, 131. *See also* **ordenaunce, reuwe, set: unordirede.**

ordirlye *adv.* in an orderly way (of text's organization) 2.3: 133.

orisoun *n.* petition, prayer (*orationem*) (to audience and/or patron) 1.9: 51, **orysun** (of author to Christ) 1.8: 138. *See also* **prayer.**

outward *see* **bok.**

over *adj. as adv.* excessively, ~ **litel** too abbreviated 1.10: 27, ~ **long** 1.16: 62, 70, ~ **mykel** verbose 1.10: 38, ~ **yong** (*fig.,* of author's training or experience) 3.23: 46.

over, ovyr *see* **red, studie.**

overgonn *p.p.* gone over, read in full 3.10: 28. *See also* **goyng, loke, red.**

overhippis *pr.3.sg.* skips over (in treating source material) 1.1: 26. *See also* **negligence.**

overryn *v.* run over, cover 3.14: 70. **overrynnys** *pr.3.sg.* 3.14: 96. *See also* **compendiosite.**

overse *v.* look over, ~ **theyr lesson** 3.12: 127. **oversayne** *p.p.* 2.3: 177. *See also* **loke, se.**

overthowartly *adv.* with mistakes (of recitation) 3.2: 33.

paas *n.* place (in reading), section of text 3.1: 6. *See also* **place, stedis.**

pagyne *n.* page, **dyvyne** ~ sacred reading (*divina pagina*) 3.8: 38.

parabols *n.pl.* parables 2.3: 64. *See also* **ensample.**

paraphes *n.pl.* paraph marks 3.2: 12. *See also* **distincte.**

parforme *v.* do, complete 1.12: 36, **performe** (with pun on writing as manual labor) 3.5: 54. **parformyd** *p.p.* 1.12: 5. *See also* **ende** (*v.*).

part *n.* part (*pars*), subsection of book or text 2.8: 14, 2.17: 4, 7, 9, etc., **ferth** ~ 3.7: 29, **frust** ~ 3.7: 23, **red therof a** ~ 2.12: 64, **parte** 2.9: 16, **of alle** ~ in every part 3.7: 37, **thryd** ~ 3.7: 27. **partes** *pl.* 3.7: 22, 36, **dyvyde names in** ~ (*etym.*) 2.7: 24. *See also* **parti.**

parti *n.* section (of text) 3.7: 39, **partie** 3.5: 32, **party** 3.5: 12, **partye** 3.5: 37, subdiscipline 1.10: 2. **parties** *pl.* 3.5: 12, 32, 3.10: 5, 14, 26, **partis** 2.17: 3. *See also* **part.**

particuler *adj.* partial, biased, **his writyng was** ~ 1.7: 180.

passif *n.* passive, ~ **for** ~ (in translation) 2.2: 143–44.

pastans *n.pl.* pastimes, entertainments 3.16: 47. *See also* **dysporte, gamen, myrthis, play, recreacion, salace, sport.**

pathis *n.pl.* paths, *(fig.)* reading choices 3.5: 36. *See also* **aleye, orcherd.**

patriarks *n.pl.* patriarchs (of Old Testament) 2.15: 35. *See also* **fadyr.**

patrown *n.* patron (of god of chivalry) 1.7: 7. *See also* **lord.**

pay *n.* pleasure (of patron) 1.7: 206. *See also* **pleasier, will** *(n.).*

payne *n.* trouble (of reading) 2.9: 54, of ~ with difficulty (of book search) 3.24: 80, **peine** effort in composition 1.9: 100, **peyne,** ~ **and wo** effect of obscure style 2.3: 65. *See also* **diligence, labour.**

peine, peyne *see* **payne.**

pen *n.* pen, **doo hyt wyth my** ~ (of providing advice and exposition) 2.9: 25, **his flourit** ~ *(fig.)* ornate literary style 3.23: 24, **penne** 1.7: 30, 1.14: 119, 2.3: 72.

percen *see* **perse.**

performe *see* **parforme.**

perse *v.* pierce *(fig.),* ~ **alle the prevytes** (of interpreting Scripture) 1.15: 25. **percen** *pr.3.pl.* (the heart of the listener) 1.4: 6. *See also* **synke.**

perseyve *pr.3.pl.* consider ~ **diligently** (words of Scripture) 1.15: 36. *See also* **consider, muse, studie, thynkyn.**

personally *adv.* in person, (of delivering text) 2.9: 24.

pertinent *adj.* appropriate, (of subject matter) 2.7: 46, **pertynente** 2.12: 69. *See also* **propire, semelych.**

peynten *pr.3.pl.* paint, *(fig.)* write ornately, ~ **with colours ryche** 1.4: 11. **peynte** *pr. subj.* paints, *(fig., of deceptive representation)* 2.12: 39. *See also* **colour, enlumyne, sownde.**

peynture *n.* painting, visual representation, *(fig.)* books of the unlearned, **ymagerye and** ~ 3.9: 7, 41, 42, **the boke of** ~ 3.9: 8. *See also* **purtreyture.**

philosophie *n.* philosophy *(philosophia),* (as subject not to be translated into English) 2.2: 92, characteristic of alchemy 2.3: 54, **moder of** ~ *(fig.)* history 3.15: 59–60, **philosophy** 2.2: 95, **naturall** ~ branch of philosophy concerned with study of the natural world 2.17: 33, **philosophye** (as source of doctrine of four causes in writing) 1.11: 28, **counsele of** ~ 3.23: 17.

Phylosophyr *n.* philosopher, **the** ~ (Aristotle) 1.11: 54. **filosoferis** *pl.* 1.15: 73, ~ **bookis** 1.15: 58, **filsoveris** 1.15: 78, 79, **philosofyrs** 1.11: 7, **philosophouris, sayngis of . . . ald** ~ 2.17: 8, **phylosophers** 1.4: 54, **naturel** ~ those who study nature or natural subjects 1.4: 50, **phylosphres** 3.24: 64.

pistil, pistle, pistlis *see* **epistle.**

place *n.* place (in a text) 1.15: 16, 62, 2.2: 143, 145, 146, 3.21: 21. **places** *pl.* 2.9: 36, 3.2: 17, 3.24: 80, **placis** 1.15: 3, 1.16: 31, 34, 2.3: 84, **placys** 1.8: 54, 87, 1.12: 73. *See also* **paas, stedis.**

place *(v.) see* **please.**

plante *v.* plant *(fig.)* stock a text with subject matter, compose 3.5: 28, **planten** (of meaning) 1.4: 7, **plaunte** 3.5:35. **plauntid** *p.p.* 3.5: 38. *See also* **set, ympe.**

plantynge *vbl.n.* planting *(fig., selecting or arranging material)* 3.5: 46. *See also* **setting.**

play *n.* play (dramatic text or performance) 2.14: 9, (as subject matter) 3.16: 34, **pley** delight 2.11: 173. **plays** *pl.* entertainment 3.16: 46. *See also* **dysporte, gamen, myrthis, pastans, recreacion, salace, sport.**

playn *adj.* plain (of style or expression) 2.3: 60, 2.10: 27, **playne** 2.3: 59, 97, ~, **rounde Englisshe** 2.8: 34, **pleyn** plain, clear, full (of meaning) 3.10: 8, **more** ~ **to knowe** (of prose as opposed to poetry) 2.2: 126, **pleyne** full *(perh.* plain), **prose** ~ 1.5: 27n, **cleer and** ~ 2.2: 142. **playnyst** *superl.* 2.3: 78. *See also* **cleer, commen, open, rounde.**

playnly *adv.* clearly, openly 2.9: 36, **pleynly** 1.7: 133, 1.11: 21, 3.10: 4, specifically 1.11: 30. *See also* **openli.**

playsant *pr.p. as adj.* pleasing, enjoyable (of text) 3.17: 16, **pleasaunt** 3.24: 39, **plesand** (of truth in representation) 1.2: 14, (of polished rhetoric) 3.18: 4. *See also* **likand, plesyng.**

please *v.* please (purpose of composition) 1.9: 87, 3.24: 27, **plese** 1.8: 27, **plesyn** (patron saint, by composition) 1.11: 134. **plesyth** *pr.3.sg.* (of God as auditor) 3.2: 30. **place** *pr. subj.* please, **and yt ~ yow** (said to audience) 2.14: 73, **please, if it ~ you** (to patron) 2.12: 58, **plesith** (of reader) 3.2: 11, (of God) 3.5: 54. *See also* **liketh, lyst, quemes.**

pleasier *n.* pleasure (of royal patron) 2.12: 67, **pleasure** (of audience) 2.9: 54, **wanton ~** (of poems) 3.15: 79. *See also* **pay, will.**

plesance *n.* pleasure (of audience) 1.2: 9, (in recitation) 1.2: 10, (of poetic masters) 1.9: 64, **Goddes ~** 1.9: 97, **~ of almyghty Jesu** 1.9: 103, (in romance reading) 3.16: 14, (ethic of pleasure in Virgil) 3.16: 19, **plesaunce** (of audience) 1.5: 72, (of patron) 1.7: 74, (of God) 1.9: 35, **plesauns** pleasantness (of author's greeting to patron) 1.8: 118. *See also* **delite, deynte, joy, liking, softnes: displesour.**

plesand *see* **playsant.**

pleseable *adj.* pleasing (of composition) 1.12: 6. *See also* **playsant.**

plesyng *pr.p. as adj.* pleasing (to the Trinity, of translation) 2.2: 129. *See also* **playsant.**

pleyd *p.p.* played, performed (of dramatic representation) 2.14: 70. *See also* **play** (*n.*).

pleynly *see* **playnly.**

plurel *adj.* plural, **in ~ nombre** (of translation crux) 3.21: 73–74.

plurie *adj. as n.* in the plural (*gramm.*), form of address (for Trinity) 3.2: 26, **plurye** 3.2: 22.

poemys *n.pl.* poems 3.15: 78. *See also* **dites, poetre, poysy.**

poesyes *see* **poysy.**

poete *n.* poet (*poeta*) 1.5: 34, 2.10: 36, **~ dyvyne** (Virgil) 3.16: 29, **~ lawriate** 3.18: 58, **poyet** 1.8: 136. **poetes** *pl.* 1.9: 29, 3.24: 39, 64. *See also* **auctor, cause, endyter, maister, translatour, writer.**

poetly *adj.* poetlike, poetic, **~ report** (of Boethius's narration) 3.23: 27.

poetre *n.* poetry, **ald ~** (of classical poetry) 3.18: 1, **poetry** 1.8: 133, 3.18: 13, **poetrye, Newe ~ Poetria nova** 1.11: 88. *See also* **poysy: enditing, making, wark.**

poetycal *adj.* poetical (of rhetorically ornate work) 1.11: 84. *See also* **artificyal.**

poetyke *adj.* poetic, **in manere ~** (of elevated prose prayer to classical goddess) 2.10: 42.

pointis *see* **poynt** (*n.*).

poisone *pr.3.pl. refl.* poison themselves (*fig.*, misinterpret Scripture) **~ hemself** 2.5: 44. *See also* **galle.**

polisshed *adj.* polished (of lexis) 2.10: 24, (of eloquence) 3.15: 74.

polite *adj.* polished (of rhetorical terms) 3.18: 3.

ponderose *adj.* weighty (in meaning) 2.3: 178. *See also* **unpeysed, wayenge.**

pourvennce *n.* providence, foresight (of authors) 1.9: 37.

poyet *see* **poete.**

poynt *n.* point (in a text) 1.16: 54, (in a translation) 2.2: 114, **~ to ~** (in reading) 2.12: 88, (in text content) 2.17: 40. **pointis** *pl.* points or arguments in a list 1.16: 76, **poyntes** (of reading) 3.1: 11, (of subject matter) 3.17: 2, 3, **poyntis** (of doctrine) 3.2: 80.

poynte *v.* punctuate (as in *punctatio*), phrase (in reading aloud) 3.12: 128. **poynted** *p.p.* 3.1: 17, 3.12: 128, **poyntyd** detailed 1.8: 35. *See also* **lecture, pronounsyng, reding.**

poysy *n.* poetry 1.7: 135. **poesyes** *pl.* poetry, **olde ~ derke** (of pagan, i.e., classical, poetry) 1.5: 42, **poyses** 2.3: 64, **poysies** 2.2: 104. *See also* **fabill, historye, poemys, poetre, story.**

poysye-mater *n.* subject matter for poetry 1.4: 19. *See also* **mater.**

practyk *n.* practice (*practica*), **~ off rymyng** 1.8: 129.

pray *v.* pray (for divine inspiration) 1.5: 63, (audience for patron) 1.8: 97, (audience for author) 1.8: 146, **praye** (audience for writing) 3.12: 96, **prey** (composer for scribe) 1.14: 108, **preye** (audience for author) 1.11: 229. **pray** *pr.1.sg.* (to learn from predecessors in poetry) 1.9: 52, (for mental steadiness and orthodoxy in writing) 1.9: 93, (author to reader) 2.6:

19, (for protection from slander) 2.11: 154, (to God for appropriate audiences) 3.4: 1, (author to audience for correction) 3.18: 39, **praye** (for integrity of text) 1.5: 14, (indulgence of writerly inadequacy) 1.10: 39, **preie** (author to prudent listeners) 1.7: 66, **preye** (author to inscribed audience) 1.11: 201, 1.13: 52, (author to God for understanding of Scripture) 2.5: 63, (author instructing audience) 3.3: 27, 3.9: 28. **prayeht** *pr.3.sg.* 3.21: 81. **pray** *imp. sg.* (to saints for outcome of composition) 2.12: 40. **pray** *imp. pl.* ~ **we** (performative injunction to audience) 2.1: 116, **prayes** pray (injunction to audience) 1.1: 71. **prayend** *pr.p.* (to God for patron) 2.11: 119, **prayeng** (for divine help in literary work) 1.10: 14, **prayenge** (printer to patron) 3.24: 24, **prayng** (author's request to audience) 2.3: 168, **preyng** (request for composition) 1.14: 100, 108, **preynge** 1.7: 209. **prayde** *p.p.* I have ~ (of instructions from author to readers) 1.12: 81. *See also* **besechen, requere.**

prayer *n.* prayer (*oratio*) (of author) 1.9: 51, 2.12: 44, (to presiding goddess) 2.10: 42, (for literary work) 2.12: 44, (fruit of reading) 3.2: 8, (of audience for translation's making) 3.10: 12, **prayere** (of audience for writer) 1.1: 68, (of audience) 1.12: 87, **preyer** (as part of prologue) 3.3: 1, **preyere** (request for composition) 1.1: 68, (fruit of reading) 3.1: 10. **prayeris** *n.pl.* (of audience) 3.5: 33, **prayers** (as genre) **meditacyons or** ~ 3.2: 1, **preyers** (audience for author) 2.3: 15. *See also* **meditacion, orisoun.**

prayse *v.* praise (in liturgical office) 3.12: 8, 13, 21, etc., **preyse** (in psalms) 3.21: 11. **prayse** *inf. pass.* be praised (of writing in English) 1.4: 15. **preyseth** *pr.3.sg.* (of discriminating audience) 2.11: 151. **prayse** *pr.2.pl.* 3.12: 51. **prayse** *pr.3.pl.* 3.12: 38, 50. **praysed** *p.p.* (for composing) 1.1: 45, (of English language) 3.14: 88, **preised** 2.11: 151, **ypreysed** (of translations) 2.2: 80.

praysyng *vbl.n.* (of recitation of office) 3.12: 25, 29, 52, **praysynge** praise 3.12: 23, sung office 3.12: 6, 10, 33, etc., **preising** (for usefulness of books) 1.16: 59, **preysyng** psalm singing 3.21: 3, 4, 10, ~ **of God with song** 3.21: 3, **preysynge** (of Trinity in explicit) 1.12: 90. **praysinges** *pl.* liturgical hours (of the Virgin) 3.12: 35, 39. *See also* **lovynge** (*vbl.n.*) (1).

preamble *n.* preamble, ~ **or elles the prologe** 2.7: 43. *See also* **entre, prefacyon, proheymm, prolog.**

precept *n.* command (for translation to be made) 3.18: 34. **preceptes** *pl.* (of Cato) 3.12: 119. *See also* **byddyng, comaundement, desir, heste, requeist: dictis, proverb, sau, saynge, sentence.**

preche *v.* preach 2.4: 9, 2.5: 31. **prechith** *pr.3.sg.* 2.5: 59. **prechyn** *pr.3.pl.* 2.5: 56, 3.22: 4. **preche** *imp. pl.* 2.5: 137. **prechid** *p.p.* 1.16: 89, **ypreched** 2.2: 108.

precheour *n.* preacher 2.1: 49. *See also* **clerk.**

preching *vbl.n.* preaching 1.16: 134, (of Saint Paul) 2.7: 37, **Englisshe** ~ 2.2: 111, **prechyng** 2.2: 112.

predycacyon *n.* preaching (*predicacio*) 3.21: 60. *See also* **sermon.**

preente *n.* imprint (of king's seal, analogy for images) 3.2: 67.

prefacyon preface (*prefacio*) 1.12: 1, 10, 13. *See also* **entre, preamble, proheymm, prolog.**

preisable *adj.* praiseworthy (of arguments in text) 1.16: 10.

prente *v.* print 3.24: 18, **prynte** 3.24: 21. *See also* **emprinted, impresse, press, printer.**

prentise *n.* apprentice (poet) 1.9: 55.

present *adj.* present, **this** ~ **boke** 2.10: 29, **this** ~ **book** 1.16: 87–88, 127, 2.10: 17, **this** ~ **dialog** 1.16: 3–4, **this** ~ **volume** 2.10: 22, **this** ~ **werke** 2.10: 8, open to spiritual reading (condition of soul) 3.10: 50, **presente, thys** ~ **boke** 3.12: 1.

presente *v.* present (book to patron) 2.12: 71, **presented** *p.p.* reported 2.14: 57.

press *n.* (printing) press 3.16: 52. *See also* **prente.**

presumcion *n.* presumption, ~ **of mannes witt** (of inadequate reading of Scripture) 2.5: 23, **presumpcion** (rejected as author's motive) 2.10: 11, **presumpcioun** 1.7: 72, **presumptioun, vane** ~ 3.18: 33. *See also* **envie, malice, pride.**

presumptuous *adj.* presumptuous (of critic) 3.12: 83.

prevyly *adv.* allegorically (how Scripture contains truths) 1.15: 68, **privelye** (of reading of nuns) 3.20: 4, **privyly** (of workings of literary envy) 1.11: 198. *See also* **prive, privete: openli.**

prey, preyer(e)(s) *see* **prayer.**

preye, preyng(e) *see* **pray.**

pride *n.* pride (as motive for writing or critical response) 1.7: 72, 1.16: 124, ~, **veynglorie, and boost** 2.5: 19, 23, ~ **of the word** motive for preaching 2.5: 32. *See also* **presumcion.**

printer *n.* printer 2.8: 39. *See also* **prente, press.**

prive *adj.* secret, private (of readers' inner conditions) 3.3: 3, 36, ~ **vertus** (articulated by psalms) 3.8: 12, **privy,** ~ **termes in French** 1.4: 25, **privye** (*as adv.*), **kept** ~ (of book) 3.20: 2. *See also* **prevyly** (*adv.*).

privete *n.* secrecy, ~ **of hir breste** (where women readers should metaphorically keep the gospel) 3.10: 30, **privyte** secret (of nature) 2.3: 173. **prevites** *n. pl.* secrets (of hidden meanings of Scripture) 2.5: 36, **prevyteis** 1.15: 52, **prevytes** 1.15: 25, **privytees** (of God) 1.4: 44, **privytyes, by** ~ (of author's modest gleaning from authoritative tradition) 1.4: 89.

probate *n.* written proof (*fig.*, of literary text) 3.15: 45.

procedyng *vbl.n.* ordering (of literary work), ~ **artifycial** artistic ordering 1.11: 83, **procedynge, honeste** ~ (of historiography) 3.15: 23.

proces *n.* account, exposition (*processus*) 1.16: 129, 130, 132, etc., **processe** narrative 1.11: 120, 2.9: 46, performance 2.14: 75, **historyal** ~ historical exposition or narration 3.15: 84–85, ~ **historyal** 3.15: 31, ~ **hystoryal** 3.15: 29. **processis** *pl.* course of arguments 1.16: 31. *See also* **ordire, ordenaunce, reherce, report, spel** (*n.*), **tellynge.**

procutoure *n.* steward, ~ **to laymen** (of author) 1.16: 118.

proffitable *adj.* profitable, useful, of value (of subject matter) 2.17: 26, 29, **proffytable** (of psalm singing) 3.21: 9, **profitabill** 3.18: 19, **profitable** 1.10: 17, 37, 1.15: 61, (of truths in texts) 1.16: 57, (of books) 1.16: 67, ~ **procutoure** (of author) useful intermediary 1.16: 118, (of translation) 2.2: 57, 155, (of Christ's words) 2.5: 101, (of devotional texts) 3.5: 16, 39, 3.10: 31, **profytabile** (of psalm translation for audiences) 3.8: 69, **profytable** (of composition) 1.12: 6, 37, **profytabyll** (for audience) 2.9: 54, **prophitable** 1.15: 58, 67, 74, **prouffitable** 3.17: 16. *See also* **edificatyf, spedeful: unprofitable.**

proffyte *n.* value, usefulness, ~ **of the commonn weill** general benefit (of Virgil) 3.16: 40, **profiit** benefit (of audience) 1.15: 76, **profit** value, usefulness, (of compilation) 1.10: 20, 26, **profite** (of authoritative writings) 1.16: 113, benefit (of readers) 1.16: 46, **in** ~ 1.16: 148, **profyt** 1.13: 53, **profyte** 1.12: 9, 62, 3.12: 31, 3.24: 53, 56, **profyth** 1.14: 8, **profytte** 1.13: 63, 65, **prouffyte** 3.15: 82, 3.17: 6. *See also* **deynte.**

profitabli *adv.* usefully (of permitted reading) 1.16: 114, **profitably** with benefit (of acquiring knowledge) 1.15: 62.

profityng *vbl.n.* benefit, usefulness (of texts) 1.16: 66.

profyte *v.* profit, benefit (by reading) 1.12: 9, 3.12: 31. **profyteth** *pr.3.sg.* 3.15: 90, **prouffyteth** 3.15: 79. **profytyd** *p.p.* 1.12: 32, 38.

proheymm *n.* prologue (*proemium*), 3.16: 69, **proym** 1.14: 125. *See also* **prolog.**

prolog *n.* prologue (*prologus*) 1.6: 36, 1.7: 99, 1.16: 8, 126, 3.5: 26, **prologe** 2.7: 43, 2.11: 73, 80, 177, 3.3: 1, 6, **prologue** 1.4: 100, 2.10: 2, 2.16: 4, 84, 3.12: 1, 61, 3.24: 29, **proloug** 3.14: 93, **prolouig** 2.17: 45. *See also* **entre, preamble, prefacyon, proheymm.**

pronounsyng *vbl.n.* pronunciation (of words in text) 2.4: 34. *See also* **poynte.**

prophecie *n.* prophecy 2.2: 108, 109, 2.5: 6, **prophecye** 3.21: 60.

prophet *n.* prophet 2.9: 17, **prophete** 2.5: 97, **the hooli** ~ 2.5: *title,* 2.5: 133. **prophetes** *pl.* 2.15: 35, **prophetis** 1.15: 21, 50.

prophitable *see* **proffitable.**

propire *adj.* proper, suitable (of English language) 3.8: 65, **propre** 3.12: 63. *See also* **pertinent, semelych.**

propryete *n.* meaning (in source text) 3.21: 76.

propyne *n.* pledge, offering (as in *propinare*), (*fig.*) verse 3.16: 52.

prose *n.* prose (*prosa*), ~ ner ryme 1.8: 45, **ryme other in** ~ 2.2: 124, 125², **in ~ for to abredge** 2.16: 70, ~ **pleyne** 1.5: 27n, **proyss** 3.16: 51.

proverb *n.* proverb (*sententia*) 3.16: 20, **proverbe** 2.11: 174. **proverbes** *pl.* 3.24: 88, **proverbys** 1.8: 130. *See also* **dictis, precept, sau, saynge, sentence.**

prouffitable *see* **proffitable.**

proym *see* **proheymm.**

proyss *see* **prose.**

prudent *adj.* prudent (of listeners) 1.7: 64.

prynte *see* **prente.**

psalme *n.* psalm (*psalmus*) 3.21: 2, 3, 5, **salm** 2.5: 52. **psalmes** *pl.* 3.8: 2, 7, 32, **psalmis** 3.21: 1, 6, **psalmys** 3.21: 61.

psalmystre *n.* psalm singer 3.21: 82.

Psaultier *n.* Psalter (*psalterium*) 2.12: 65, **Psautere** 3.8: 26, **Sauter** 2.2: 101, 120, 3.21: 61.

publischid *p.p.* published 1.16: 99. *See also* **rede, speke, write.**

purgynge *vbl.n.* purging (of penitential or difficult reading) 3.5: 16. *See also* **herbis, wedis: bitter, scharpe, soure.**

purpoos *n.* subject (of dramatic representation) 2.14: 9.

purtreyture *n.* portrayal, visual representation, (*fig.*) mode of writing 1.4: 13. *See also* **peynture.**

purveyde *pa.3.sg.* provided (intelligible meaning) 1.15: 8, **purveyed** (of God-given linguistic polysemy) 1.15: 10.

put *v.* put, ~ **in blame** 1.11: 36, ~ **it** (of mode of expression) 3.21: 73, ~ **it forth** produce (of literary work) 2.10: 8, ~ **it in to prente** 3.24: 18, ~ **in wryt** put in writing 1.2: 17, ~ **therto** add material in composition 2.7: 45, ~ **to** 1.9: 100, **putte** add 1.10: 36. **puttyng** *pr.p.* ~ **to** (of compilation of knowledge) 1.10: 23. **put** *p.p.,* ~ **to** added (to source material) 1.12: 7, 77, *as adj.* 3.10: 14, ~ **in exempill** 3.18: 47.

puttyng *vbl.n.* putting, ~ **to** adding (of compilation) 1.10: 23. *See also* **addicioun.**

quair *n.* quire (*quaternum*), booklet 3.23: *title,* **qu[ay]ere** 2.13: 13, **qwayre** 1.14: 125.

quekeneth *see* **quyken.**

quemes *pr.3.sg.* pleases (function of psalm singing) 3.8: 8. *See also* **liketh, lyst, please.**

questioun *n.* topic (*quaestio*), (in theology) 1.16: 34, issue (of translation) 2.2: 35. **questiouns** *pl.* 1.16: 33.

queynt *adj.* elaborate (of rhetorical figures) 1.4: 2, (of lexis) 1.4: 28. *See also* **curyous, strange.**

quiteth *pr. subj.* reward (of God, for patronage) 2.2: 156. *See also* **mede.**

quyck *adj.* living, (*fig.*) intelligible ~ **sentence** 2.3: 172.

quyetnesse *n.* quietness, **in ~** prescribed mode of reading 3.2: 4. *See also* **easely.**

quyken *v.* quicken, move (function of particular type of book) 3.12: 145. **quekeneth** *pr.3.sg.* (of scriptural meaning) 2.5: 109. *See also* **compellyth, exciten, inflawme, kyndils, mevyde, stere.**

qwayre *see* **quair.**

qweere *n.* choir (*chorus*), place for performing texts of the mass 3.20: 17.

rad(de) *see* **red.**

receptis *n.pl.* formulas 2.3: 91, 101, 102, **receytis** 2.3: 100.

receyved *see* **resceyve.**

recompense *n.* reward (for writing in English) 1.9: 47. *See also* **garnyson, mede, rewarde.**

recounted *pa.3.sg.* recounted 3.15: 55.

recreacion *n.* recreation, refreshment (from texts) **confortable ~** 3.5: 57, **recreacioun, goostly** ~ 3.5: 7. *See also* **comfort, dysporte, gamen, myrthis, pastans, play, salace, sport.**

recyteth *pr.3.sg.* recites, tells 2.10: 36. **recyten** *pr.3.pl.* 2.10: 37. *See also* **carpe, speke, spel, tel.**

red *v.* (1) read 2.7: 18, 3.8: 66, **rede** 1.7: 62, 80, 1.8: 96, 144, 150, 1.10: 21, 1.12: 13, 17, 41, etc., (of deciphering text) 1.14: 98, 143, 2.6: 16, 19, 2.9: 54, 2.11: 22, 2.12: 63, 65, 2.16: 69, 3.1: 18, 3.2: 6, 18, 3.3: 21, 3.7: 20, 27, 3.9: 8, 3.12: 45, 104, 105, etc., 3.14: 75, 3.15: 3, 3.23: 14, 3.24: 25, **come and ~ before me** 2.16: 67, **endyte and ~** 3.24: 6, **lerne to ~** 2.16: 58, 65, 79, **many tymes ~** 3.17: 11, **not ones to ~** 3.17: 13, **oftymes to ~** 3.17: 14, **~ the gospel** 2.4: 11, **~ many bokis** 2.3: 181, **~ and to prosede** continue reading 3.24: 51, **~ and to study** 3.12: 157–58, **~ and to synge** (liturgical) 3.5: 4, **~ and understonde** 2.2: 24, 38, 40, **~ and undyrstande** 2.6: 15, **~, lerne, and understond** 2.8: 10, **~ or here** 3.7: 2, **~ or se** 1.7: 209, **~ or to here** 3.12: 111, 112, **~ yt savourly** (of reading aloud) 3.12: 128–29, **~ where hym liketh,** 1.12: 14, **romance ~** 3.14: 4, **se and ~** 3.5: 12–13, **synge and ~** (liturgical) 3.12: 28, 34, **take hem tyme to ~** 3.3: 22, **storys to ~** 1.2: 5, **reden** 3.1: 4, **grace to ~ it** 1.14: 109, **redyn** 1.11: 39, 1.14: 110, (of deciphering text) 1.14: 87, 142, **~ in boke** 3.9: 7, **~ in ymagerye** 3.9: 7, **redyne** 1.14: 84, 88, 95, **reede** 3.20: 28. **radde** *inf. pass.* 3.2: 3, **red** 1.12: 60, 1.16: 114, **here it be ~ or spokin** 3.3: 21, **cause to be ~** 2.8: 14, **unable for to be ~** 1.14: 139, **redyn, herd ~** 3.22: 22. **redeth** *pr.3.sg.* 2.12: 88, 3.17: 12, **redis** 3.16: 14, **redith** 2.5: 6. **rede** *pr.1.pl.* 2.1: 93, 3.15: 5. **rede** *pr.2.pl.* 1.1: 68, 1.12: 64, 3.12: 46, 103, 118, etc. **rede** *pr.3.pl.* 1.1: 49, **here or ~** 3.7: 16, **reden** 1.15: 38, 3.1: 3, 18, **~ and stodien** 2.5: 158, **redin** 2.5: 1, **redys** 1.2: 21. **rede** *pr. subj.* 2.6: 20. **rede** *pr. subj. pl.* advise 2.11: 23, **daily ~** 2.8: 14, **~ or here** 3.7: 3. **rede** *imp.sg.* 3.3: 12, 3.9: 28. **rede** *imp. pl.* 1.8: 77, 2.5: 78. **red** *pa.3.sg.* 2.12: 64, 3.22: 20, 34, 41, etc., **~ it ovyr** 1.14: 111. **redde** *pa.3.pl.* 3.20: 4. **rad** *p.p.* read 1.16: 105, **red** 1.14: 98, 2.1: 96, 2.7: 13, 2.12: 52, 2.17: 25, **redde** 3.22: 45, 3.24: 81, **rede** 3.14: 79. (2) **redes** *pr.3.sg.* presents 1.1: 27. *See also* **loke, overse, se, seche: heir, herken, lestyn, lythe.**

redare *n.* reader 1.12: 61, **reder** 1.4: 66, 3.2: 2, **redere, ~ either to the herere** 1.15: 7–8, 9, [**redere**] 3.2: 6. **reders** *pl.* 1.10: 28, 1.16: 41, **heerers and ~** 1.16: 72–73, **heerers or ~** 1.16: 77, **~ or heerers** 1.16: 43.

reding *vbl.n.* (act of) reading (*lectio, lectura*) 2.8: 3, **oon ~ or tweyne** 2.3: 176, **redinge** 2.8: 16, **redyng** 3.1: 8, 3.2: 14, 3.12: 98, 131, 132, etc., 3.17: 13, **conceyved . . . with ~** understood by reading 3.1: 7, **over ~** 3.17: 14, 3.22: 4, **redynge** 1.12: 85, 3.2: 87, 3.12: 100, 101, 110², etc., 3.15: 33, 3.17: 7, (as God's speech to man) 3.12: 113, **herynge, ~, and worchyng** (as university and clerical activity) 1.10: 32, **redyngge** 3.9: 5, **reeding** 1.16: 80. **redingis** *pl.* (custom of) refectory reading 2.8: 17. *See also* **lecture, loke, se, spekeyenge, studye.**

reede *see* **red.**

refeccions *n.pl.* refection (*refectionem*), mealtime, (used for reading aloud in monastic houses) 2.8: 16. *See also* **ete, fede, savoure, schewe, taaste.**

refresched *p.p.* renewed, refreshed (of writing's service to the past) 1.7: 118.

regystred *p.p.* recorded (of historical writings) 3.15: 20.

reherce *v.* rehearse, recount 1.16: 129, 3.24: 65, **rehers** 3.13: 21, **reherse** utter 1.7: 35. **reherse** *pr.1.sg.* 3.2: 44. **rehersith** *pr.3.sg.* 2.4: 22. **rehersen** *pr.3.pl.* 2.4: 28. **rehersyng** *pr.p.* 2.13: 51, 3.22: 21. *See also* **carpe, reporte, say, schau, speke, spel, tel.**

rehersall *n.* recounting (of subject matter) 1.9: 81.

rekyn *imp. pl.* be still (of audience's tongues) 3.13: 21.

remembrance *n.* remembrance, (faculty of authorial remembering or cultural memory) **drawe into ~** (as audience response) 2.11: 76, **remembraunce** 1.3: 7, 1.6: 8, **our ~** 3.15: 26, **oute of ~** 3.15: 64, **remembrauns** reminder 1.8: 93, **make ~** commemorate, remind 1.8: 54, **bryng to ~** 1.8: 79, **makyth ~** 1.8: 68. *See also* **memorie, mend: oblyvyon.**

remembratife *n.* remembrance (of poets) 1.9: 38.

remembre *v.* remember, commemorate, **inwardly to ~** (dedicatee's request) 1.11: 192, **~ somme good ensample** (of audience for book) 2.16: 81–82, **~ the ourys of Cristys passoun** (of systematic meditative recollection) 2.13: 7, **verray knyghthod to ~** (as purpose of compo-

sition) 1.7: 76. **remembryd** *pa.1.sg. refl.* (as prelude to making book) 2.16: 29.
remembryng *pr.p.* (audience's desire) 2.9: 4, (as prelude to book making) 2.16: 10.
remembrid *p.p.* preserved as a cultural memory 1.7: 101. *See also* **myn, renewe.**

remembring *vbl.n.* retelling, **reportyng** and ~ 1.16: 132.

remnant *n.* part, section (of material or narrative) 3.13: 22. *See also* **part, parti.**

renewe *v.* bring to mind 1.5: 46, renew (through reading) 3.24: 4. *See also* **myn, remembre.**

renoun *n.* renown (of author) 1.7: 184. *See also* **name** (*n.*).

repers *n.pl.* reapers, (*fig.*) antecedent authors and commentators 1.4: 80.

report *n.* report, recounting 1.7: 128, (of reported example) 1.9: 58, **poetly** ~ 3.23: 27, **reporte** reputation 3.15: 44, **make** ~ 3.15: 67.

reporte *v.* report, recount 1.16: 129, 2.3: 84. **reported** *pa.1.sg.* referred to, relied upon 3.24: 85. **reporting** *pr.p.* 1.16: 131, 136. *See also* **reherce, tel.**

reporter *n.* reporter, narrator 1.16: 133.

reportyng *vbl.n.* reporting, ~ **and remembring** 1.16: 132, **reportynge** 3.15: 56.

repreif *v.* reprove (function of fables) 3.18: 6. *See also* **reproof** (*n.*).

representyst *pr.3.sg.* represents (function of image) 3.9: 44. **represent** *pr.3.pl.* 1.7: 129, **representis** 1.2: 22. **representynge** *pr.p.* 3.15: 85. **representyd** *p.p.* presented, performed 2.14: 10.

reprevable *adj.* blameworthy (of literal reading) 2.5: 89.

reproof *n.* reproof, correction (all books subject to) 1.10: 29. *See also* **amendement, correccion.**

requeist *n.* request (of dedicatee or audience) 3.18: 34, **request** 1.11: 182, 1.14: 142, **requeste** 2.8: 30. *See also* **byddyng, comaundement, desir, heste, precept.**

requere *pr.1.sg.* ask (of inscribed audience) 1.11: 202. **requere** *pr.1.pl.* 3.21: 92. **requyred** *pa.3.sg.* 3.24: 17. *See also* **besechen, pray.**

resceyve *pr. subj.* receive, **yit God . . . ~ here good wille** (of technically poor reader) 3.2: 34. **resseeyveth** *imp.* (to patron) 1.3: 1. **received** *p.p.* (of texts) 1.16: 56, **receyved** 1.16: 56, **resceyved** 3.5: 17.

reson *n.* sentence 3.12: 70, **resoun** argument 1.6: 61, 2.2: 68, 69, 73, etc., 3.23: 43, **a ~ for a worde** (in translation) a sentence for a word 2.2: 146, [faculty of] reason (of author) 1.6: 61, (of reader) 3.5: 19. **resounis** *gen. sg.* **inward writing of ~ doom** (of God's inscription of rationality in humans) 1.16: 147–48.

resonably *adv.* in a measured manner (of looking over text) 3.5: 23.

rethoricyens *n.pl.* practitioners of rhetoric 1.7: 57, **rethorycyens** 3.24: 65.

rethorik *n.* (the art of) rhetoric (*rhetorica*) 1.7: 194, **rethorike** 1.5: 33, 3.18: 38, **rethoryk** 1.11: 89, 95, **retoryk** 1.8: 132, **rhetore** 3.18: 3. *See also* **colour, termes.**

rethorikly *adv.* rhetorically, ~ **pykit** ornately adorned (of text) 3.23: 45.

reule *n.* religious rule (*regula*), (of Saint Gilbert) 2.7: 8, **rewle** (of Syon) 3.5: 2, 3.12: 108, **rule** (of Saint Benedict) 2.8: 9, 13, 14, etc. **reulis** *n.pl.* the Tyconian rules (of hermeneutics) 1.15: 43, 44, 83.

reuwe *n.* row, **bi** ~ in order (of sequence of saints in a legendary) 2.15: 66, **rewe** sequence (of words) 2.2: 145.

revelation *n.* revelation (*revelationem*) (literary genre), (from God to female visionary) 3.4: 4. **revelaciouns** *pl.* 3.5: 9, 10, **revelacyons** 1.14: 68, 3.22: 49, **revelacyonys** 1.12: 74, **revelations** 3.4: 12. *See also* **contemplacion, schewynge, sight, tribulacyons, visioun.**

rewarde *n.* reward (for composition) 1.16: 49. *See also* **garnyson, mede, recompense.**

rewde *adj.* unlettered 2.4: 31, **rude** rough, unpolished (of lexis) 1.4: 6, 9. ~ **endytyng** 1.8: 23, 120. *See also* **boystous, laud.**

rewe *see* **reuwe.**

rewlyd *p.p.* directed (of composition) 3.12: 96. *See also* **adresse, dispose, directe, dresse.**

rhetore *see* **rethoryk.**

right *adj.* correct 2.4: 34², 35, true 1.16: 32, 2.2: 128, *as n.* moral subject matter 3.14: 23, **riht** *(as adv.)* correctly 3.1: 17, **ryght**, ~ **understandyng** (in reading) 3.17: 14.

rime *n.* rhyme, verse 3.14: 17, ~ **and sange** 3.14: 51, **ryme** 1.1: 42, 56, 1.4: 2, 2.16: 70, **clere than** ~ (of prose compared with verse) 2.2: 125, **light** ~ 1.1: 56, **in** ~ **other in prose** 2.2: 123, ~ **couwee** 1.1: 47, ~ **in Englissh** 1.3: 9, 1.4: 2, **prose ner** ~ 1.8: 45. **rimes** *pl.* 3.14: 3, 50, **French** ~ 3.14: 79. *See also* **metir, rymes** *(v.),* **rymyng** *(vbl.n.),* **vers.**

rist *v.* rest, cease reciting 3.13: 22. *See also* **blyn.**

romance *n.* romance (narrative genre) 3.14: 4, **romans,** ~ **that he redis** 3.16: 14.

rounde *adj.* clear, ~ **Englisshe** 2.8: 34. *See also* **cleer, commen, open, playn.**

roundels *n.pl.* rondels, songs 2.16: 16. *See also* **balade, sange, vyrelayes.**

rude *see* **rewde.**

rule *see* **reule.**

runne *p.p.* run, ~ **abroad** made public 1.16: 88.

ryght *see* **right.**

rymes *pr.3.sg.* 1.1: 25. **rymyd** *pa.3.sg.* 1.8: 130. **rymed** *p.p.* (of prose) 3.1: 17. *See also* **rime** *(n.).*

rymyng *vbl.n.* versification 1.8: 122, 129, 147. *See also* **metir, vers.**

sad *adj.* sober, serious (of composition) 1.9: 59, (of subject matter) 3.18: 26, **sadde** mature 3.4: 4, ~ **mete** *(fig.)* serious or difficult subject matter 3.10: 11.

said(e) *see* **say.**

salace *n.* solace *(solatium)* (reason for composition) 1.10: 29, **solace** entertainment ~ **and gamen** 1.1: 11, 72, 82, **in maner of** ~ recreation 3.24: 45, **solas** (for audience) 1.14: 3, 41, 3.22: 9. *See also* **dysporte, gamen, myrthis, pastans, play, recreacioun, sport.**

salm *see* **psalme.**

sange *n.* melody, song 3.8: 6, 10, 18, etc., **rime and** ~ 3.14: 51, **songe** 2.13: 29, (of birds) 2.16: 7, 9. **sa[ng]es** *pl.* 3.14: 17, **songes** 2.16: 16, **newe** ~ fashionable (French courtly) songs 2.16: 17. *See also* **layes, melody, roundels, vyrelayes.**

sapour *n.* taste *(sapor),* *(fig.)* appetizingness of literary work 3.16: 54. *See also* **savour, taaste.**

sau *n.* speech, saying 2.1: 82. **saues** *pl.* sayings, narrations 2.1: 90, **sawes,** ~ **of wise men** 1.10: 34, (of Christ) 2.1: 88, **sawys** (of Virgil) 3.16: 41. *See also* **dictis, precept, proverb, sayngs, sentence.**

Sauter *see* **Psaultier.**

save *adj.* safe, ~ **guide** (of nature of text) 3.4: 13.

save *imp.* preserve, retain (plea to God regarding meaning in translation) 1.5: 23. *See also* **calengid, chaunge, drau, Englisshed, interpreted, set, turne.**

savour *n.* smell, taste *(sapor, sapientia),* *(fig.)* found in spiritual response by reader 3.1: 5, *(fig.)* reputation 2.7: 30, 31, 33, foretaste 2.7: 38, **savoure** 2.7: 35, 36, 37, etc. *See also* **sapour, taaste** *(n.).*

savoure *v.* *(sapere)* savor, enjoy, *(fig.)* read with spiritual affect 3.12: 48. **savouren** *pr.2.pl.* 3.5: 20. **savoureth** *imp. pl.* 3.5: 43. **savoure** *pr. subj.* 3.12: 130, **savoured** *pa.3.sg.* smelled *(fig.* of reputation) 2.7: 31. *See also* **ete, fede, schewe, taaste.**

savourly *adv.* with feeling (in reading) 3.12: 129. *See also* **affectuose.**

sawe *see* **se.**

sawes, sawys *see* **sau.**

Saxoun *n.* Anglo-Saxon (target language in translation) 2.2: 103.

say *v.* say, tell, narrate (of narrator) 2.1: 64, (of gospel) 2.1: 100, (of subject matter) 3.7: 38, (of critic's response) 3.8: 68², recite 3.12: 4, (narratorial comment) 3.23: 11, 3.24: 11 **soth to** ~ 3.14: 35, **that es to** ~ *(id est)* 3.20: 13, **that is to** ~ 3.12: 15, **thus to** ~ (of translated phrase) 3.12: 4, **saye, that es to** ~ *(id est)* 1.13: 45, **the sothe to** ~ 2.14: 11, **sayne, that is to** ~ 1.4: 62, **seie** (of audience theorization of authority) 1.16: 72, 132, ~ **and fele** 1.16: 138, **sey**

(reader addressing God) 3.2: 29, **as mech to** ~ 2.7: 25, **he wold** ~ (introducing paraphrase of source) 3.21: 70, ~ **lasse** translate fewer words 3.21: 75, **that is to** ~ 3.2: 21, **the sothe to** ~ 2.14: 33, **wyche is to** ~ 2.9: 18, **seye** 1.11: 202, recite (of audience) 1.12: 83, **that is to** ~ 3.5: 21, **seyn** 1.11: 138, **sothly for to** ~ 1.7: 75, **seyne, that is for to** ~ 1.11: 23, **this is to** ~ 3.23: 55. **say** *pr.1.sg.* (in performative narration) 1.1: 32, 1.2: 40, 3.10: 39, 3.14: 27, **saye** 1.13: 87, 3.2: 76, **seie** 1.7: 200, 1.16: 71, **sey** 1.11: 125, 3.3: 28, **seye** 3.21: 12. **sayeth** *pr.3.sg.* (of Scripture) 3.12: 7, 9, 10, etc., **says,** ~ **inwardlye** recites to him- or herself 2.1: 127, (of Creed) 3.16: 13, **saith** says (of authoritative book or its author) 2.10: 40, **sayth** 1.4: 48, 91, 3.2: 76, 3.12: 6, 89, 120, (of Holy Ghost in Scripture) 3.12: 6, **as who** ~ 1.4: 76, **saythe** 1.4: 50, **seith** (of human author of Scripture) 1.15: 5, (of authoritative book or its author) 1.15: 13, 15, 65, etc., 2.4: 16, 26, 2.5: 5, 17, 52, etc., 3.10: 17, 47, (of Christ) 1.15: 18, 2.5: 15, 34, 81, etc., 3.6: 8, 10, 14, (of God) 2.5: 116, recites (of the Paternoster, etc.) 3.2: 33, **as who** ~ so to speak 2.11: 50, **seyth** (of book or its author) 2.5: 102, 3.2: 89, (of Christ) 2.9: 13, **seythe** (of psalm title, *titulus*), **this tytyl** ~ 3.21: 1, (of book or its author) 3.21: 1, 3, 14, etc. **saies** *pr.3.pl.* (of Gospels) 2.1: 111, **sayen** (of ancient texts) 2.10: 35, **sayis** (of clerks) 3.18: 19, **says** recite 3.8: 2, **sey** (of textual authorities) 2.7: 24. **saide** *pa.1.sg.* (of narrator) 3.23: 50, **sayd** 3.8: 50, 3.16: 50, 3.24: 96, 114, **seid** 3.5: 31, **a sermon that I** ~ 2.7: 10, **seyde** 1.11: 174. **sayde** *pa.2.sg.* (of commissioner of work) 2.7: 13, **seide** (of patron) 2.2: 135. **said** *pa.3.sg.* (of source author) 3.18: 27, **seyde** (of God) 3.2: 24. **seiden** *pa.3.pl.* (of philosophers) 1.15: 74. **seying** *pr.p.* (of Gospel) 3.11: 3, (of God's dialogue with human soul) 3.22: 10, 58, 80. **iseide** *p.p.* dictated 2.2: 88, **said** told, narrated 1.2: 8, 2.17: 40, **saide** 1.9: 71, **sayd** (of sources) 1.1: 33, (of narrator) 2.10: 4, 2.16: 57, 63, 3.8: 50, **this wrytyng ys** ~ 1.8: 121, **sayde** 3.12: 166, **seid** said (in text or book) 1.15: 36, 1.16: 109, 115, 132, etc., 2.5: 135, delivered (of sermon) 2.7: 10, **that myght be bettir** ~ expressed 1.16: 115, **seide, it is** ~ 3.10: 6, **seyd** 1.11: 71, 201, **it is** ~ 2.13: 1, **seyde** (in translation) 3.2: 17, **it is** ~ 3.2: 22. *See also* **carpe, recyteth, reherce, reporte, schau, speke, spel, tel.**

saynge *vbl.n.* saying (as said in writing) 3.12: 77, **seynge** saying, dictum (Chist's) 2.9: 38. **sayenges** *pl.* accounts 2.16: 31, **sayngis,** sayings, maxims ~ 2.17: 7, speech 3.12: 81, **seyingis** (human *dicta*) 1.15: 95, ~ **of filosoveris** 1.15: 78. *See also* **dictis, precept, proverb, sau, sentence: carpyng, tellynge.**

says *see* **say.**

schapyne *p.p.* shaped (of letter forms) 1.14: 86.

scharpe *adj.* sharp, (*fig.*) of difficult reading material 3.5: 15. *See also* **bitter, hard, soure.**

schau *v.* show, make known, reveal, tell, declare 2.1: 49, 56, 62, **on Inglis** ~ 2.1: 109, **scheu** 2.1: 43, **schewe** 1.13: 55, 3.5: 27, 3.13: 15, **schewene** 1.14: 25, **schewyn** 3.22: 57, **shawe** 3.14: 63, 2.9: 46, 3.4: 9 (of Christ's revelation to readers), 3.14: 67, **shewe** 1.4: 28, expound 3.6: 16, 3.12: 22, ~ **by outwarde praysyng** 3.12: 25, ~ **hit forth** (of writer's capacity) 1.5: 40. **schawis** *pr.3.sg.* 2.17: 4, 7, 9, etc., **schawys** 1.2: 12, **schewys,** ~ **and techys** (of the church) 1.13: 13, **schewyth** 1.8: 27, 3.22: 82, **shewyth** 3.12: 49. **schawes** *pr.3.pl.* set forth (of books) 2.1: 87, **schewen** 2.11: 53, **shew** 2.3: 76. **shewe** *imp. pl.* reveal, tell, ~ **your synne** (injunction to audience) 2.14: 66. **schewed** *pa.3.sg.* 1.14: 59, 62, **schewede** 3.20: 8, **schewide** 3.5: 29, **schewyd** 1.14: 63, 3.22: 53, **shewyd,** ~ **ther lyves** (of confession) 2.14: 52. **schewing** *pr.p.* setting forth (of book) 3.23: 17, **schewyng** responding to or visualizing (text) 3.10: 29. **schewed** *p.p.* interpreted 1.1: 7, revealed 1.13: 1, 1.14: 27, 131, **schewede** 3.10: 41, 3.20: 5, 8, 35, **schewid** 2.5: 37, 3.5: 34, **schewyd** 1.13: 54, 59, 66, etc., **shewed** 1.1: 70, 3.12: 5, 10, 11, etc., **shewyd** 1.11: 145. *See also* **apperis, schewynge** (*vbl.n.*), **declare, se, teche: reherce, reporte, say, speke, spel, tel.**

schewe *v.* chew, (*fig.*) read (*ruminatio*) 3.19: 22. **chewe** *pr.3.pl.* ~ **not code** fail to chew the cud (of Bible reading without appropriate response) 2.5: 139. **chewe** *imp. pl.* 3.5: 24. *See also* **ete, fede, savoure, taaste.**

schewynge *n.* vision, revelation 1.13: 21, 24, 42, etc., **open** ~ disclosure, manifestation 3.12: 54–55. **shewings** *pl.* 3.4: 12. *See also* **schau** (*v.*), **contemplacion, felyng, revelation, sight, visioun.**

science *n.* knowledge (*scientia*) 1.4: 26, 1.7: 114, discipline 2.3: 55, 56, 143, etc., ~ **of langage** rhetoric 2.10: 26, **sciens** (of God's knowledge) 3.21: 97, **syens** art of composition 1.8: 25, discipline or branch of knowledge 1.8: 125. **sciences** *pl.* disciplines 2.10: 46, **sciencis** 1.15: 67. *See also* **crafft.**

scole *n.* university, schooling (*schola*), 1.11: 85, 1.15: 87, 2.2: 48, 95, 3.23: 46, ~ **of Christ** (of nunnery) 2.9: 2, 9, ~ *Storye Historia scholastica* 1.12: 68.

scolers *n.pl.* scholars 2.3: 65. *See also* **maister.**

scolid *p.p.* trained (at university) 1.16: 122.

scripture *n.* scripture (*scriptura*), writing, composition, 1.9: 47, 77, 1.11: 109, 3.2: 89, 3.8: 47, 3.10: 7, 3.21: 19, 3.22: 33, **Scripture** (*scriptura sancta*) the Bible 1.15: 2, 5, 6, 2.5: 166, 2.9: 14, 47, 3.19: 18, **Holi** ~ 1.16: 33, *The Just Aprising of* ~ 1.16: 150, **Holy** ~ 1.15: 38, 46–47, 2.9: 36, 3.4: 8, 3.12: 88, 3.22: 4, **Hooli** ~ 2.5: 69, 174, **Hooly** ~ 1.15: 4, 49, 52, etc., **Scripture** (*personification*) 3.19: 18, 31, 40, **Scrypture** the Bible 1.11: 60, **Holy** ~ 3.12: 4. **scriptures** *pl.* scriptures, writings 3.2: 87, **Scriptures** the Bible, **Holy** ~ 1.15: 24, 35, **scripturis** writings 3.2: 86, **Goddis** ~ 1.15: 15, **Scripturis** the Bible 1.15: 25, 29, 39, etc., **Holy** ~ 1.15: 36–37, **Hooly** ~ 1.15: 59, 65, 3.2: 86, **[s]cripturis** 2.5: 162, **scryptures** writings 3.12: 71. *See also* **Apocalips, Bibel, escriptures, Evangelistes, Godspel, epistle, word, writ, writing.**

se *v.* see, look at, read (a book) 1.7: 199, 209, 2.3: 3, 2.12: 61, see (as spectators) 2.14: 70, 3.5: 12, ~ **bothe fruyt and herbys** (*fig.*) look over useful reading matter 3.5: 14, ~ **and understonde** 3.12: 46, ~ **this boke** 3.12: 78, (of meaning in nuns' reading) 3.12: 29, **see** 1.8: 76, 1.16: 8, ~ **and studie** 2.5: 85, 3.17: 13, (of spectators) 2.14: 75, ~ **schortly** see in brief (of table of contents) 1.12: 9, 13, ~ **hyt agen** recur to textual matter 1.12: 16, **sen** (of book) 2.14: 74, **sene** 3.24: 43, **seyn, our to** ~ look over (books) 3.16: 5. **see** *imp. pl.* visualize (an image) 3.9: 21, 23. **sees** *pr.3.pl.* 2.1: 68. **sawe** *pa.1.sg.* understood 1.13: 92, 3.24: 42, saw (of matter seen in vision) 1.13: 50, 64, 65. **sawe** *pa.3.sg.* (of visionary) 3.20: 10, 18. **sawe** *pa. subj.* ~ **this book** 3.3: 31. *See also* **loke, rede.**

seche *v.* seek, scan (text) 1.11: 8, **sechen** 3.1: 9, **seeke** probe (text) 1.15: 24. **secheth** *pr.3.sg.* looks for (in a text) 3.1: 13, **fro poynt to poynt he** ~ 2.12: 88. *See also* **loke, red, expounne, perse.**

sechers *n.pl.* seekers (of truth) 1.4: 91.

sechyng *n.* seeking, searching out (in turning reading into prayer) 3.1: 8. *See also* **thenkyng.**

seed *n.* seed, (*fig.*) Scripture (as source of all meaning) 1.15: 69. *See also* **corn, kirnell.**

seeke *see* **seche.**

seggers *n.pl.* professional reciters 1.1: 38. *See also* **disours, harpours, mynstrell.**

selcouth *adj.* rare, strange (of terms) 1.1: 59, (of hidden meaning) 2.3: 173, **selcouthe** excellent ~ **rime** 3.14: 17. *See also* **strange.**

semely *adj. pl. as n.* seemly (of audience for dramatic representation) 2.14: 3. *See also* **worthi.**

semelych *adj.* appropriate (of rhetorical ornament) 1.4: 8. *See also* **pertinent, propire.**

sempyl *adj.* simple (of writer) 1.8: 22, **simple** unpretentious (of literary composition) 1.5: 70, unlearned (of lay audience) 3.6: 3, **symple** (of diction) 1.1: 35, (of audience) 1.1: 39, (of literary work) 1.11: 70, (of text) 1.12: 54, (of audience) 1.15: 85, 86, etc., ~ **processe** (of composition) 2.9: 45–46, ~ **abylyte** (of author) 2.9: 47, ~ **and lytyl** (of author) 2.10: 52, ~ **felyng** (of author) 3.5: 9, ~ **understandyng** (of audience) 3.10: 16, ~ **undurstandyng** 3.10: 3, ~ **soule** 3.10: 20, ~ **soules** 3.10: 16–17, **sympyl** (of author) 1.12: 42, 50, (of author's work) 1.8: 144, 1.12: 32, (of audience) 1.12: 56, ~ **meditacyonys** 1.12: 85. **symples** *pl.* (of audience) 3.10: 9. *See also* **simplesse, symplenes, light.**

sensce *see* **cence.**

sensyble *adj.* affective, ~ **understondynge** (*sapienia*) 3.15: 90. *See also* **feele, science.**

sentence *n.* meaning, import (*sententia*) 1.4: 3, 7, 1.5: 18, 32, 1.7: 187, 1.15: 8, 1.16: 130, 131, 133, etc., 2.5: 8, 10, 122, etc., 2.13: 31, 3.12: 65, **hent** ~ grasp the meaning 1.4: 10, **morall sweit** ~ 3.18: 12, **ponderose** ~ 2.3: 178, **quyck** ~ 2.3: 172, **the pleyn** ~ 3.10: 8, **the wordes and the** ~ 3.12: 66, **the** ~ **and not the wordes** 3.12: 67, **sentens** sentence, saying 2.9: 13, **sentensce** opinion 2.13: 24, **sentense** 1.15: 5, 7, 2.5: 145. **sentences** *pl.* sentences 3.6: 18, sayings 3.24: 36, **sentencis** meanings 3.16: 41. *See also* **meanynge, understandinge, wit.**

sentenciall *adj.* rich in meaning, wise 1.9: 78.

sermon *n.* sermon (*sermo*) 2.7: 10, 11, **sermoun** 1.15: 32, 70, 1.16: 130, 2.2: 82, 2.5: 132, **sermowne** 3.22: 6. *See also* **predycacyon.**

serve *v.* serve, (God, as result of reading) 2.16: 73.

service *n.* service (of patron by author) 1.5: 72, (of audience by author) 1.9: 90, (of royal patron by author) 2.11: 166, (of the Virgin in the liturgy) 3.12: 46, (*fig.*) presentation (of penitential texts for consumption) 3.19: 37, **servise** (liturgical) 3.5: 4, **servyce** 2.3: 131, 3.12: 27, 32, 3.19: 42, (of god of love) 2.16: 11, **servys** (of church) 3.8: 37, **servyse** (*fig.*) offices, devotions 2.12: 64.

sese *see* **ceesse.**

set *v.* set, ~ **yt awarke** (of reading) 3.12: 133, **to** ~ **you** (*refl.*) set yourself (in reading) 3.12: 155, **sett,** ~ **his wordis** (of writer) 1.16: 74, ~ **the actif for the passif** (in translation) 2.2: 145, ~ **a resoun for a worde** (in translation) 2.2: 146, **sette,** ~ **his wordis** (of arrangement of words) 2.4: 31, ~ **in Englisch** put into English 2.7: 11, ~ **worde for worde** (of translation) 2.2: 143, **plante it and** ~ **it** sow (*fig.*, arrange material) 3.5: 28–29, 35. **settith** *pr.3.sg.* ~ **owte** sets, arranges 2.3: 130, **settyth** 1.11: 18. **set** *pa.3.sg.* ~ **hir meditacion** concentrated (of reader) 3.10: 26, ~ **and bare it** (of reader's internalization of text) 3.10: 29. **iset** *p.p.* concentrated (of reader's mind) 3.1: 13, **set,** ~ **owte** placed, ordered (of subject matter) 2.3: 133, (of words) 3.12: 71, ~ **in a book** put in a book 2.16: 53, ~ **in mynde** (of internalized reading or audition) 3.10: 19, ~ **in ryme** 2.16: 70, **ymped in and** ~ grafted and set (*fig.* of eloquence) 1.7: 196, **sett** organized (of book) 1.14: 103, 1.16: 74, ~ **or plauntid** planted and arranged (*fig.* in a book) 3.5: 37, **sette** ordered, composed 1.12: 18, ~ **subtylly** subtly expressed 3.17: 12, **ysett** transposed 2.2: 150. *See also* **bisette, plante, gaderid, ympe; calengid, chaunge, drau, Englisshed, expressyn, ordire, save** (*imp.*), **translate, turne.**

setting *vbl.n.* final revision, **the device and** ~ **of this present book** 1.16: 87. **settynge** (*fig.*) sowing, **of** ~ **and of plantynge** (selecting and ordering material) 3.5: 45.

sey *see* **say.**

seyingis, seynge *see* **saynge.**

shew(e), shewed, shewyd *see* **schau.**

shewings *see* **schewynge.**

sight *n.* sight, vision, (perusal of texts) 1.16: 90, (of Trinity and God as Book of Life) 3.11: 2, 5, (of God's face as a feast of reading) 3.11: 24, **clere** ~ (needed for composition) 3.5: 55, **inward** ~ 3.1: 9, **syght** sight, vision (*visio*) 1.13: 21, 67, 3.22: 75, 76, 3.24: 57, view (of spectators) 2.14: 10, perception 3.12: 27, insight 3.12: 23, **bodylye** ~ physical vision 1.13: 17, **God** ~ 1.13: 98, **yeve** ~ (*fig.*) indicate 1.4: 16, **syghte** 3.9: 5. **sightis** *pl.* observations 2.3: 33, **syghtys, horybyl** ~ sights 3.22: 72. *See also* **contemplacion, revelation, schewynge, visioun.**

signified *pa.3.sg.* signified 1.16: 23, **sygnifyd** (of structural division in text) 3.8: 33.

sillable *n.* syllable (*syllaba*) 2.3: 174.

sillogisme *n.* syllogism (*syllogismus*) 3.18: 46.

similitude *n.* analogy (*similitudo*) 3.18: 47. **similitudis** *pl.* images 3.2: 56.

simple *see* **sempyl.**

simplesse *n.* simplicity (of writer) 1.9: 101, **symplesce** 2.11: 164. *See also* **symplenes: humblesse, ignorance, insuffishaunce, leudenesse, meeknesse, unabylnesse, unconnynge, unworthynesse: suffisaunce.**

skarsete *n.* scarcity (of rhymes in English) 1.3: 9.

skilefulli *adv.* reasonably (of reading Scripture) 2.5: 158.

skilfulle *adj.* reasonable, reasonably good (of translation) 2.2: 121.

skyl *n.* reason, cause (of composition) 1.11: 173, **skylle** skill (in composition) 1.7: 65.

skylle *v.* understand, make sense of 1.14: 85. *See also* **understand.**

slaundres *n.pl.* slanders (*blasme des femmes*), literary genre 3.24: 61. *See also* **blaim, blamynge, detraccioun, diffames, inpugnacioun.**

sleeth *see* **letere.**

slouthe *n.* sloth (avoided by composing poetry) 1.7: 83. *See* **ydelnesse: besynes.**

sofisticaly *adv.* sophistically (*sofistice*) 1.15: 72.

softe *adv.* softly (reading instruction) 3.1: 4. *See also* **easely.**

softelye *adv.* softly (of book's affect) 3.20: 36. *See also* **lyghtly.**

softnes *n.* pleasure (in affective reading) 3.8: 23, ~ **in saule** (fruit of psalter reading) 3.8: 52.

sofymys *n.pl.* sophistries 1.15: 71, 72.

solace, solas *see* **salace.**

songe *pa.3.pl.* sang (of birds), ~ **in theyr langage** 2.16: 7–8, **songene** (of instruments) resounded 3.10: 44. **songenn** *p.p.* sung 2.12: 28.

songe(s) (*n.*) *see* **sange.**

soote *adj.* sweet, (*fig.*) deceptive language 1.7: 150, **suete** good, delightful, **metir ~** 3.23: 23, **sweit, ~ rhetore** 3.18: 3, **ane morall ~ sentence** 3.18: 12, **swete** 2.7: 27, 29, **hony ~** inspiration of Calliope 1.7: 56, **so ~ a lykoure** (effect of text) 3.20: 35–36, ~ **fruit** (result of meditative reading) 3.1: 10, ~ **meditacions** (result of reading) 3.2: 9, ~ **melodye** (of psalms) 3.21: 61, ~ **smellyng** (of penitential reading) 3.21: 27, ~ **songe** 2.16: 9, ~ **taste** (in meditative reading) 3.10: 28–29. **swettere** *adj. comp.* 3.20: 37. **swettest** *superl.* most eloquent 1.15: 80.

sothe *n.* truth (in narrative) 1.7: 139, (in dramatic representation) 2.14: 11, 33. *See also* **suthfastnes, trouth.**

sothefast *adj.* true, ~ **pyth** (*fig.*) inner significance 1.7: 116, **suthfast** truthful (of narratives) 1.2: 7, 17, (of things narrated) 1.2: 40. *See also* **trewe.**

soun *n.* sound, (of heaven) 3.8: 6, (of psaltery) 3.8: 28, (*fig.*) reader's contemplation 3.8: 30, **sowne** (of birdsong) 2.16: 7. *See also* **sownde** (*v.*).

soure *adj.* sour (*fig.*) penitential or difficult reading 3.5: 39. *See also* **bitter, hard, scharpe.**

sovereyns *n.pl.* sirs (address to audience of dramatic production) 2.14: 9. *See also* **frendys, lordynges.**

sownde *v.* resound, (*fig.*) signify (of elaborating narrative with rhetorical figures) 1.7: 195. **soundith** *pr.3.sg.* means, signifies 2.7: 28, **sowneth** 2.9: 14, **sownyth** 3.21: 6.

Spaynesche (*adj.*) Spanish ~ **tunge** (as language of Bible translation) 2.4: 5.

speche *n.* language 1.4: 20, 2.2: 2², 3, 4, etc., 3.14: 85, discourse 2.1: 81, speech 2.2: 7, utterance 2.2: 135, talk 2.2: 139, **playne and comon ~** 2.3: 59, **symple ~** plain language 1.1: 35. **speches** *pl.* ways of speaking (i.e., languages) 2.2: 5, 13, **spechis, figuratiif ~** metaphoric discourses 1.15: 84, **Goddis ~** Scripture 1.15: 10, 23, **spechys, holy ~** words heard in contemplation 3.22: 48, 62, ~ **and dalyawns** 1.14: 44–45, 50. *See also* **langage, tong.**

spectakle *n.* mirror, (*fig.*) treatise, 2.17: 42, **spektakle** 2.17: 1. *See also* **glas, merour.**

spedeful *adj.* profitable (of meditative reading) 3.10: 18, **spedefull** 3.12: 104, 160, **spedful** 3.10: 15. *See also* **edificatyf, proffitable.**

speke *v.* speak, tell (in narrative or discourse), preach, expound 1.4: 75, 1.15: 50, 1.16: 69, 2.2: 50, 54, 56, etc., 2.5: 11, 2.7: 23, 2.10: 3, 17, 53, 2.11: 38, 2.13: 41, 2.15: 3, (of book or its author) 3.24: 44, expound 3.3: 22, (particular language) 3.14: 86, **herde ~** 1.5: 25, 3.24: 44, **so for to ~** so to speak (term of syllogistic argument) 2.2: 52, 56, **~ . . . curiosly** speak in an elaborate manner (of clerks) 2.4: 33, **~ . . . Latyn** (of patron) 2.2: 38, 40, **~ yt fourthe** 3.12: 132, **~ to** address 3.2: 27. **speke** *pr.1.sg.* 1.13: 96, 2.15: 3. **spekist** *pr.2.sg.* 2.2: 61. **spekes** *pr.3.sg.* (of text or author) 3.7: 40, **speketh** 2.16: 2, **spekis** 3.8: 57, 59, **spekith** (quoting Christ) 3.11: 3, (of book or its author) 1.16: 150, 3.11: 8, **~ sofisticaly** 1.15: 72, **spekyth** 3.2: 83, 3.12: 113, 114. **speke** *pr.1.pl.* 3.20: 11. **speke** *pr.3.pl.* 2.5: 11, **~ of** 3.12: 72, **bokes ~** 3.12: 136, **bokes that ~** 3.12: 107, **speketh, rethorycyens ~** 3.24: 65, **spekith** 3.3: 2, speak (languages) 2.2: 1, **speken** recite, compose (poetry) 1.4: 19. **speke** *pr.subj.* expound 3.3: 12, 21. **speke** *imp. sg.* 2.2: 38. **spekyng** *pr.p.* 2.16: 83. **spoke** *p.p.* 2.5: 116, **spoken** 2.5: 93, 2.9: 25, 3.24: 80, **spokin** 3.3: 21, **spokun** 1.16: 22, 24, **spokyn** expounded 3.3: 12. *See also* **carpe, recyteth, reherce, reporte, say, schau, spel, tel.**

speker *n.* speaker, preacher 1.16: 23.

spekeynge *vbl.n.* speaking, **redynge is a maner of ~** 3.12: 110, **speking** exposition 1.16: 26, **spekyng** speech **~ in Englysshe** 3.12: 73, **the ~ to God** address 3.2: 19, **right ~** correct speech 2.4: 34. **spekingis** *pl.* **kyndes and maners of ~** modes of speaking (in scriptural exegesis) 1.15: 35. *See also* **talkyng.**

spektakle *see* **spectakle.**

spel *n.* narration (of Gospel) 2.1: 91, **spelle** 2.1: 90. *See also* **Godspel.**

spel *v.* recite, tell, narrate 3.14: 92. *See also* **carpe, recyteth, reherce, reporte, say, schau, speke, tel.**

sperit *n.* spirit (of wisdom) 2.5: 78, **prive ~ of God** (as determiner of reading motives) 3.3: 36, **~ and liyf** (of gospel words) 2.5: 94, **the ~ quekeneth** 2.5: 109, **spirit, ~ of his mouth** [Christ's] words 2.5: 96, **~ of his lippis** 2.5: 97–98, **spreit, light the ~** (function of recreative reading) 3.18: 21, **spyrit** (locus of decisions about composition) 1.14: 136, 137, **spyrite, my ~ enspire** (in composition) 1.5: 64.

spiritual *adj.* **~ persons** (audience of a type of book) 3.12: 138, **spirytuel, ~ cence** spiritual sense 3.21: 23. *See also* **gastelye: carnal, fleischli, lettural, naked.**

sport *n.* play (i.e., recreative reading) 3.18: 20. **sportis** *pl.* (of Virgil's text) 3.16: 46. *See also* **dysporte, gamen, myrthis, pastans, play, recreacion, salace.**

stedis *n.pl.* places (in text) 3.8: 46, **stude** 3.1: 17. *See also* **paas, place.**

stere *v.* stir, move (reader) 3.2: 2, 9, 3.7: 15, **steryn** 3.9: 2, 4, **stire** 3.10: 22, **sturen** 3.1: 2, **sturre, ~ up the affeccyons** (purpose of some genres of books) 3.12: 145, 149, 150, etc. **steris** *pr.3.sg.* 3.16: 9, **stirith, charite ~** (of audience for author) 3.5: 53, **styrres, charyte ~ me** (to narration) 1.13: 88. **stered** *pa.3.sg.* (narrator) 1.14: 12. **stiryng** *pr.p.* 3.10: 8, **styrrande** 1.13: 4. **sterid** *p.p.* 2.5: 166, **steride** 3.2: 29, **steryd** moved 1.14: 21, 3.9: 5, (to translation) 1.11: 173, (regarding composition) 1.12: 18, **styred** 3.12: 38, **styrryd** 1.13: 63. *See also* **disposed: compellyth, exciten, inflawme, kyndils, mevyde, quyken.**

stering *vbl.n.* affective response (to devout reading and contemplation) 3.3: 36, **steryng** (prompting of author) 1.14: 13, **sterynge** 1.4: 64, **styrrynge** prompting (of author) 1.13: 43, 3.20: 32. **steringgys** *pl.* affective responses 1.14: 64. *See also* **affeccion, felyng, grace, inspiracion.**

steven *n.* voice (of nightingale) 2.13: 54, **stevyn** sound 2.14: 80.

stile *n.* style (of writing) 1.7: 29, 203, **style** 3.16: 33, composition 1.8: 110. *See also* **forme, middel** (*adj.*).

stire, stirith *see* **stere.**

stodie *n.* study (*studium*), reading (of Scripture) 1.15: 40, **studdy** 3.12: 83, **study** 1.4: 59, 92, 3.12: 132, 3.24: 49, **~ of naturall philosophy** 2.17: 33, **studye** 1.4: 55, scholarly reading 3.24: 34, **studye** (*studium generale*) university 1.10: 4. *See also* **estudye.**

stodyinge *n.* studying (of the Bible) 1.15: 84, **studiyng** 1.16: 154, 2.2: 42, **studying** 3.18: 25, 3.23: 51. *See also* **avisement, loking.**

story *n.* story, history (*historia,* potentially, though not always, opposed to fiction) 1.1: 78, 1.7: 91, 95, 112, etc., 1.8: 1, 23, 43, etc., 1.11: 100, 110, ~ **of Inglande** 1.1: 5, **a suthfast** ~ 1.2: 17, **the Inglis** ~ 1.1: 31, ~ **of Saynt Cecylle** 1.13: 41–42, *Scole Storye Historia scholastica* 1.12: 68. **stories** *pl.* 2.2: 105, **storyes** 3.2: 54, **storyis** 1.8: 50, 83, 98, etc., **Mayster of** ~ (of Peter Comestor) 1.12: 68, **storys** 1.2: 5, 7, **aulde** ~ 1.2: 21. *See also* **historye, poysy: fabill.**

strange *adj. as n.* elaborate or foreign rhyme 1.1: 57, **strangere** 1.1:48, **straunge** *adj.* unfamiliar (of a particular book) 3.24: 41, (of elaborate language) 1.4: 25, 3.8: 62, ~ **historyes** (of foreign chronicles) 2.16: 69, ~ **to other** *as pl.n.* strangers to one another (of human relations after Babel) 2.2: 2. *See also* **couwee, enterlace, selcouth.**

studdy, study, studye (*n.*) *see* **stodie.**

stude *see* **stedis.**

studie *v.* study 1.15: 34, 2.5: 7, 10, 31, **over** ~ 1.16: 128, **see and** ~ 2.5: 85, **study** 3.12: 160, **studye** 2.16: 59. **stodien** *pr.3.pl.* 2.5: 158. **study** *imp. pl.,* ~ **in this . . . myrroure** (of reading treatise) 3.12: 44. **studyed** *pa.1.sg.* 3.24: 37. *See also* **consider, muse, perseyve, thynkyn.**

studiose *adj.* immersed in the study of (Scripture) 1.15: 39.

sturen, sturre *see* **stere.**

style *see* **stile.**

styrrande, styrres *see* **stere.**

styrryng(e) *see* **stering.**

submitt *v.refl.* submit (of readers willing to accept correction of church) 3.4: 2, **submyt** *pr.1.sg.* (text to audience's correction) 1.10: 38, (author and works to correction of church) 3.12: 93. **submitting** *pr. p.* (translator to audience's correction) 3.18: 30. *See also* **amende, correct.**

substance *n.* substance, meaning (*substancia*) 1.9: 61, **intential** ~ intention 1.9: 66, **substaunce** 1.7: 189.

substancyallis *n.pl.* substantive meanings 2.9: 7.

subtell *adj.* subtle (of poetic composition) 3.18: 13, **subtile** (of alchemy) 2.3: 55, 156, **subtyl** (of audience) 1.11: 209, (of sharp practices against which reading protects) 3.17: 3, 7, 9, **subtyle** 1.5: 9, **subtyll** profound 3.24: 38.

subtilite *n.* subtlety (in composition) 1.3: 6. **subtyltees** *pl.* ~ **of wordes polisshed** 2.10: 24.

subtilye *adv.* subtly (of translators) 1.5: 26, **subtylly** (of expression in literary work) 3.17: 12.

suete *see* **soote.**

suetnes *n.* sweetness (of psalter) 3.8: 21, (gained in psalm saying) 3.21: 4, **swetnes** (fruit of reading) 3.1: 10, (of psalms) 3.8: 3, **swetnesse** (of reading) 3.2: 14. *See also* **hony: galle.**

suffice *v.* suffice (of author's intelligence) 1.2: 16. **suffisith** *pr.3.sg.* (of text for readers) 3.6: 1.

sufficiently *adv.* sufficiently, fully (of translation) 1.5: 28.

sufficyent *adj.* sufficient (of Christ as example) 2.9: 32.

suffisaunce *n.* capacity, ability (of author) **my litel** ~ 1.3: 4, **suffycyauns** 1.8: 65. *See also* **humblesse, ignorance, insuffishaunce, leudenesse, simplesse, unabylnesse, unconnynge, unworthynesse.**

suffrance *n.* mercy (of Christ, as judge of text) 1.9: 104. *See also* **support.**

sugred *adj.* sugared, (*fig.*) deceptive, ~ **wordes** 1.7: 150. *See also* **hony, soote: galle.**

sugrest *pr.2.sg.* sweeten, **[Calliope] . . . that** ~ **tongis** (with effect of improving style) 1.7: 57.

support *n.* indulgence (of audience) 1.7: 214, (of God) 1.9: 56, 98. *See also* **suffrance.**

supportacion *n.* indulgence (of audience) 1.8: 22, 120.

sure *adj.* sure, reliable, **gloses** ~ reliable commentaries 1.9: 79, (of literary work) 1.11: 67, (of history writing) ~ **garnyson** reliable harvest 3.15: 52.

sustenence *n.* food, sustenance (*fig.,* of moral meaning in poetry) 3.18: 11, **sustynaunce** (of God's word). *See also* **meate.**

suth *adj.* true (of subject matter) 1.2: 13. *See also* **sothefast, trewe, verreie.**

suthfastnes *n.* truthfulness (as source of pleasingness in narrative) 1.2: 11. *See also* **sothe, trouth.**

suwyng *pr.p.* ensuing (of text after prologue) 3.2: 1. *See also* **folowe.**

swalowen *pr.3.pl.* swallow (*fig.*, of texts heard) 1.4: 1. *See also* **ete, schewe.**

sweit, swete *see* **soote.**

swetely *adv.* sweetly, finely, ~ **Englisshed** 1.9: 64.

swetnes, swetnesse *see* **suetnes.**

swettere, swettest *see* **soote.**

swithenesse *n.* laboriousness (in reading) 3.2: 4. *See also* **hevenesse, tumultuosite.**

syens *see* **science.**

syght(e), syghtis, syghtys *see* **sight.**

sygnifyd *see* **signified.**

symple, sympyl *see* **sempyl.**

symplely *adv.* simply, humbly, sincerely (of audience) 3.12: 87, **symply,** ~ **endite** (of author) 1.5: 59. *See also* **humbly, lowely, mekeli.**

symplenes *n.* simpleness (disposition of reader) 3.12: 80, **symplenesse** 1.5: 71, ~ **and ygnoraunce** (of author of source material) 3.24: 83–84. *See also* **simplesse.**

symplesce *see* **simplesse.**

synge *v.* sing, perform (of liturgical texts) 3.20: 13, **to rede and to** ~ 3.5: 4, ~ **and rede** 3.12: 28, ~ **yt and rede yt** 3.12: 34. **synges** *pr.3.sg.* recites, says or ~ 3.8: 2, **syngeth** 2.13: 2, 3. **synge** *pr. subj.* 3.19: 27. **syngand** *pr.p.* singing, **voice of** ~ (of internalized psalms) 3.8: 18–19. *See also* **lovynge** *vbl.n.* (1), **praysyng, rede, say.**

synke *v.* sink, permeate (reader) 3.12: 48. *See also* **perse, savoure.**

sythes *n.pl.* scythes, (*fig.*) ~ **of connyng** scythes of knowledge (i.e., clerical learning used to harvest and produce further knowledge) 1.4: 77. *See also* **corn, garnyson, repers.**

taaste *n.* taste 1.6: 44, **tast** taste, savor (*fig.*, in affective reading) 3.1: 3, **taste** 3.10: 29. *See also* **sapour, savour.**

taaste *v.* taste, (*fig.*) experience 1.6: 50, read 3.5: 39, taste 3.5: 23. **tasteth** *imp. pl.* 3.5: 41. **tasted** *p.p.* drunk (at muse's well) 1.5: 57. *See also* **ete, fede, savoure, schewe.**

tabyl *n.* table (of contents) 1.12: 9, 12. *See also* **kalendar.**

take *v.* (1) take up (counsels of text) 1.15: 78, receive (as readers or audience) 2.5: 62, accept (request to patron) 2.13: 18, ~ **counsayle** (in interpreting text) 3.2: 88, ~ . . . **good ensaumple** (from books) 2.16: 52, ~ **that travail** (of work of translation) 2.2: 137, ~ **the witte of** understand 1.10: 10, ~ **hem tyme** *v. refl.* (for whole book) 3.3: 22, **tak[e]** take (subject matter) 3.14: 49. **tac** *pr.1.sg.* take (as subject) 2.1: 84, **take** (use as source material) 1.12: 70. **taketh** *pr.3.sg.* ~ **after mannes entent** accepts (God's reading of human devotions) 3.2: 32, **takis, plesance** ~ (in romances) 3.16: 14. **take** *pr.3.pl.* ~ **menyng upsodowne** misunderstand 3.2: 83–84, **takyn** interpret 2.5: 22. **take** *pr. subj.* ~ **not on thing** (instruction to audience) 3.4: 6. **take** *pr. subj. pl.* take, receive (of audience) 1.13: 28, 1.15: 78, ~ **ensaumple** 3.2: 93. **take** *imp.* 1.15: 91, ~ **every thing with other** (reading instruction to audience) 3.4: 7, **take** *p.p.* understood (of text) 1.16: 72, **taken** 3.5: 17, **taken** derived (from text) 1.16: 154, carried out (of meditative reading) 3.1: 11, interpreted 3.12: 69, 70, entrusted (of book) 3.24: 41, **takynn, trewlye** ~ properly understood 1.13: 94. **take** *v.* (2) pay attention, ~ **hede** (to text) 1.7: 64, (to different aspects of reading) 3.12: 103, ~ **lytel hede** (of inadequate attention to textual meaning) 1.4: 3, ~ **lytell heid** 3.12: 81. **taketh** *pr.3.sg.*, ~ **hede** attends 3.2: 23. **takyn** *pr.3.pl.*, ~ **hede** 2.5: 25. **take** *imp.* ~ **heid be the ymage** absorb, understand from 3.9: 11, 14–15, 20, etc. *See also* **accepte, embrace, understand.**

tale *n.* tale, narrative 1.11: 227, **have in** ~ have in the repertoire, be able to tell 3.14: 72, **sett no** ~ **of** take no account 2.13: 47, **tutilers of** ~ rumormongers 3.3: 30, **talle** 2.1: 89. **tales** *pl.*

2.15: 61. *See also* **fabill, tryphlis.**

talkyng *n.* discussion, meditation (*soliloquium*) 3.1: 1, 2. *See also* **contemplacion, thenkyng.**

tast *see* **taaste** (*n.*).

tauld *see* **tel.**

techare *n.* teacher, **soverayne ~** (of God) 1.13: 88, **~ of alle** 1.13: 95–96, **techere** (of author) 1.13: 85.

teche *v.* teach (as function of written works) 1.16: 65, 2.3: 58, 142, 164, (text and practice) 2.5: 2, (other people) 2.5: 155, (other nuns) 2.8: 13, (*fig.*, in the school of Christ) 2.9: 11, 3.12: 125, 126, 3.21: 45, 53, (of treatise) 3.6: 3. **teche** *pr. 1 sg.* (of author's own work) 1.16: 75. **techeth** *pr.3.sg.* 2.3: 152, **techis** (of church) 1.13: 97, **techith** 3.2: 81, **techys** (of church) 1.13: 13. **teche** *pr.3.pl.*, **do ~** (*periphrastic*) (of philosophers) 1.11: 7, **techeth** 3.3: 42. **taughte** *pa.3.sg.* (of Christ's teaching of Paternoster) 3.6: 17, (of Cato and his son) 3.12: 119. **taughten** *pa.3.pl.* (of apostles) 1.16: 146. **itaught** *p.p.* 2.2: 60, **taught** 2.2: 108, 2.16: 25. *See also* **enforme.**

teching *vbl.n.* teaching (of Scripture) 1.15: 15, (of the apostles) 1.16: 146, (of the learned) 3.4: 3, **book of Cristen ~** (Augustine's *De doctrina Christiana*) 1.15: 13, 42, 55, etc., **techynge** (of the church) 1.13: 15, 68, 100, (by God) 1.14: 45, (of daughters, by conduct book) 2.16: 3, **entre of the ~** (of psalm title) 3.21: 2, **~ of Seneke** 2.10: 40, **this visioun and this ~** 1.13: 56–57. **techingis** *pl.* (on the virtues) 1.15: 78. *See also* **doctrine, ensample, ensygnementys, instruccion, lar, visioun.**

tel *v.* tell, explain, narrate 3.12: 137, 3.14: 71, **tell** tell, narrate 2.14: 6, explain 3.8: 44, **telle** tell, narrate 1.1: 65, 1.13: 88, 91, 1.14: 52, 2.3: 45, 2.15: 36, 66, interpret 2.2: 14, expound 2.2: 147, enumerate 3.6: 11. **telle** *inf. pass.*, **here of ~** 3.14.14, **hure ~** 2.15: 59, **tellen** 2.11: 89, **tellyn** 1.14: 82. **tel** *pr.1.sg.* 3.14: 71, **telle** 1.1: 24. **telleth** *pr.3.sg.* (of chapter in text) 3.24: 30, **tellis** 1.1: 28, **~ forth** 1.1: 31, **the buke ~** 3.13: 17, **myn auctour ~** 3.18: 43, **tellith** (of book or author) 2.4: 8, **tellyth** explains 3.12: 13, 20. **tel** *pr.3.pl.* 3.12: 146, 147, **tell** 3.12: 72, **telle** 2.1: 89, 3.12: 150, 151. **tell** *imp. sg.* **~ on** 3.23: 77. **telle** *pa.1.sg.* **herd ~** 1.12: 21, 1.13: 41. **tauld** *p.p.* 3.18: 57, **tolde** 1.7: 134. *See also* **carpe, declare, reherce, reporte, say, schau, speke, spel.**

tellers *n.pl.* tellers, **tithing ~** gossips, tellers of news 3.3: 29–30.

tellynge *n.* narration 3.20: 8, 9. *See also* **carpyng, saynge.**

termes *n.pl.* terms 1.4: 21, 23, **privy ~** in Frenche 1.4: 25, **queynt ~** elaborate lexis 1.4: 28, **~ of sweit rhetore** 3.18: 3, **~ rude** 3.18: 36, **termys, ~ off retoryk** rhetorical figures 1.8: 132. *See also* **name.**

testament *n.* testament, will, covenant (*testamentum*), **~ of Love** 1.4: 65, 101, **a[i]thur ~** each Testament 3.14: 68, **Ald ~** Old Testament 3.8: 39, **Elde ~** 2.5: 105, **Newe ~** New Testament 2.5: 79, 114, **Old ~** 1.11: 61. *See also* **lagh.**

testimonial *n.* witness, **in ~** (of historiography) 3.15: 53. *See also* **proces.**

testymonye *n.* testimony, witness (capacity of literature) 3.15: 46. *See also* **witnesse.**

text *n.* text (*textus*) (of Scripture) 1.15: 85, 2.5: 1, 62, 78, **texte** source text 1.5: 17, **tixte** (of commentary, or interpolated psalter) 2.4: 15.

thenkyng *vbl.n.* thinking, **deplich ~** (in response to reading) 3.1: 5, **inward ~** 3.1: 7, **thynkynge, affectuouse ~** reflection (in psalms and response to them) 3.8: 49, **devout ~** (as response to text) 1.12: 57. *See also* **meditacion, sechyng, talkyng.**

thynkyn *v.* reflect (in devout meditation on images) 3.9: 3. **thynke** *imp.* 3.9: 9. *See also* **consider, muse, perceyve, studie.**

token *n.* token, **kynges ~ or letter** (*fig.*, analogy for religious images) 3.2: 67, **tokene, a ~ and a book** (of images) 3.9: 6, **tokynne** sign (of book's holy status) 3.20: 26. **tokens** *pl.* signs (of reader's adequacy or otherwise to the book) 3.3: 42.

tong *n.* tongue, language (*lingua*) 3.23: 44, **Englis ~** 3.14: 88, **Ingelis ~** 2.1: 63, **his fair Latyne ~** (of Boethius) 3.23: 44, **my ~** 3.23: 47, **tonge** 3.21: 69, 88, **Englisshe ~** 2.2: 101, **Englysshe**

~ 1.5: 29, 34, **Ingeles** ~ 3.14: 75, **Latin** ~ 2.8: 17, **moder** ~ 2.4: 7, **moders** ~ 2.8: 34, ~ **of prive vertus** voice of secret virtues (of psalter) 3.8: 12, **our dames** ~ 1.4: 29, **oure** ~ 1.7: 92, **whomen of oure** ~ (of women English speakers) 2.6: 15, **tongue, Englyshe** ~ 3.12: 62, **toung, mother** ~ 3.18: 31, **wulgar and matarnall** ~ 2.17: 26–27, **tunge** 2.11: 149, **Ebrewe** ~ 2.7: 26, **moder** ~ 2.4: 6, 7, **oure** ~ 2.7: 6, **Spaynesche** ~ 2.4: 5, **Frensche** ~ 2.4: 5. **tonges** *pl.* languages 2.2: 1, **tongis,** ~ **of rethoricyens** 1.7: 57, **rekyn your** ~ still your voices (injunction to audience) 3.13: 21, **tunges** 2.4: 33, 2.11: 155. *See also* **langage, speche.**

touche *v.* touch upon, deal with 2.11: 65, **to** ~ (*etym.* definition of psalter) 3.8: 27–28. **touchith** *pr.3.sg.* 1.15: 43, 44. **touched** *pa.3.sg.* 3.24: 54.

tracys *n.pl.* traces, **of my penne the** ~ writing, (*fig.*) composition 1.7: 30, (of source texts) 1.7: 185.

transformed *pa.3.pl.* transformed (as in *transformatio*), (of source material) 1.7: 135. *See also* **transmwe, treate.**

translacion *n.* translation (*translatio*) 1.5: 13, 1.8: 122, (to bishopric) 2.8: 41, **Englissh** ~ 2.2: 137, **translacioun** 1.7: 68, 2.2: 88, 114, 118, etc., 2.4: 4, 3.8: 64, **a bett Englissh** ~ 2.2: 154, **an Englisshe** ~ 2.2: 39, 65, 67, etc., **Englissh** ~ 2.2: 135–36, **Englisshe** ~ 2.2: 90, 111, 113, **skilfulle** ~ 2.2: 122, **the Englisshe** ~ 2.2: 31, ~ **cleer and pleyne** 2.2: 142, **translacyoun** 1.11: 124, **translation** 2.8: 37, **translatioun** 2.17: 29, **ane maner of** ~ 3.18: 32, **my sempill** ~ 2.17: 39. **translaciouns** *pl.* 2.2: 80, 119. *See also* **transumpcioun.**

translate *v.* translate 1.7: 85, **her lyf to** ~ 1.11: 174, **made . . .** ~ 2.2: 102, ~ **out of Latyn** 2.7: 44, (of Fortune's changes) 3.23: 56. **translat** *pa.1.sg.* 2.7: 6. **translated** *pa.3.sg.* 2.2: 78, (of precedents for translation) 2.2: 97, 100–101, 105, etc., **translatide, seint Jerom** ~ 2.4: 3. **translated** *pa.3.pl.* (out of Hebrew into Greek) 2.2: 76, **translatiden** 2.4: 1, 2. **translatyng** *pr.p.* 3.2: 16. **translat** *p.p.* 2.7: 14, **translate** 3.14: 74, 3.16: 48, ~ **into balade** (of Vegetius) 2.12: 59, **translated** 1.5: 28, ~ **into Englisshe** 2.2: 92, 99, ~ **out of Ebru** 2.2: 97, ~ **out of Latyn** 2.2: 25, 32, (of Benedictine Rule) 2.8: 33, **translatid,** ~ **out of Grue** 2.2: 96, ~ **into Spaynesche tunge, Frensche tunge, and Almayne** 2.4: 5, **translatyd** moved (of saint's relics) 1.11: 105, **translatyde** (out of Greek into Latin) 2.6: 14. *See also* **calengid, chaunge, drau, Englisshed, interpreted, save** (*imp.*)**, set, turne.**

translatour *n.* translator 2.17: 22. *See also* **auctor, cause, endyter, maister, poete, writer.**

transmwe *v.* change (*transumere*), transform (source material) 1.7: 186. *See also* **calengid, chaunge, halff-chongyd.**

transumpcioun *n.* alteration (*transumptio*), (of source material) 1.7: 137.

travail *n.* work, labor (of translation) 2.2: 137, **travaile** (of composition) 1.4: 30, **travayle** (of translator) 2.2: 140, (of philosophers) 1.4: 56, (*fig.*) ~ **of the almoygner** (of cultural custodianship and dispensing) 1.4: 83, **travell,** ~ **in vayne** (of imperfectly understood reading by nuns) 2.8: 5, **traveyle, my sympyl** ~ (author of work) 1.12: 32[1st]. *See also* **besynes, labour, occupacion, wark.**

travaile *v.* labor (in reading the Bible) 2.5: 87, (for royal patron) 2.11: 166, (in collecting material) 3.24: 35, **traveyle** 1.12: 32[2d]. **travayled** *pa.1.sg.* (narrator to audience) 1.1: 72. *See also* **werk.**

treate *v.* treat, deal with (*tractare*), (source material) 2.10: 9, 26, 39, **tret** 1.2: 39, **trete** 2.11: 84, **tretyn** 1.14: 10. **treateth** *pr.3.sg.* 3.24: 63, **trete** composes 1.5: 37. **treate** *pr.3.pl.* deal with, **bokes that** ~ 3.12: 163, **trete** 2.12: 56, **tretyn** take seriously (God's word) 2.5: 140. **treted** *p.p.* 1.10: 34. *See also* **executed.**

treitis *n.* treatise (*tractatus*) 2.17: 30, **tretees** 3.10: 2, **tretes** 3.7: 16, **tretice** 1.16: 75, 3.7: 2, **tretyhs** 1.11: 30, **this symple** ~ 1.11: 204, **tretys** 1.14: 10, 24, 141, 2.7: 17, 3.1: 1, 2, ~ **in cadence** 3.1: 16, **schort** ~ 1.14: 2, 128, **this lytyl** ~ 1.14: 10, **tretyse** 3.6: 1, 2. **treatyse** *pl.* 3.24: 61, **treatyses** 3.24: 64, **tretys** 2.6: 14.

tret *see* treate.

trewe *adj.* true, (of meaning of source text) 1.5: 18, (of author's purpose) 1.11: 198, (understanding of Scripture) 2.5: 21, 53, 62, etc., ~ **corn** (*fig.*) true meaning 1.7: 102, ~ **and opyn exposicioun** 2.5: 85, ~ **sentence** (of God's law) 2.5: 10, **trowe, trusty and** ~ (of translation) 2.2: 129, **true** (of meaning) 1.9: 80, ~ **thought** (of author or Christ) 2.12: 85. *See also* **suth, verreie.**

trewli *adv.* truly, **fele** ~ (of perceiving book's use) 3.10: 49.

tribulacyons *n.pl.* tribulations (*tribulationis*), (as subject matter for composition) 1.14: 130, ~ **and hire felingys** 1.14: 135. *See also* **felyng, lif.**

trouth *n.* (in narrative) 1.7: 95, 110, 132, (in exposition) 2.3: 97, (in reading) 3.12: 116, **trouthe** 1.7: 105, 138, 144, (as characteristic of historiography) 3.15: 59, **colour of** ~ (of apparent truth of poetry) 3.15: 84, **trowth** 2.3: 110, 136, **truth** 3.4: 9, 3.18: 2, **trwthe** 1.8: 109. **trouthis** *pl.* 1.16: 57. *See* also **sothe, suthfastnes.**

trowe, true *see* trewe.

tryphlis *n.pl.* idle tales 3.15: 56. *See also* **fabill.**

tumultuosite *n.* confusion (*tumultuositas*), **hast and in grete** ~ (reading modes to be avoided) 3.2: 4. *See also* **hastenesse, negligence, swithenesse.**

tung(e), tunges *see* tong.

turne *v.* translate 1.1: 56, ~ **and** ~ **agen** leaf through (books) 2.5: 129. **turne** *pr.1.sg.* ~ **ayeen** turn back to, resume treating 3.2: 98. **turnyth** *pr.3.pl.* alter (meaning) 3.2: 84. **turn** *pr. subj.* 1.1: 57, **turne** (turn to section of text) 1.16: 7. **turnynge** *pr.p.* ~ **ageyne** (to God) author's orientation in compiling 1.10: 13–14. **i-turnyd** *p.p.* translated 1.12: 22, **turnyd** 3.12: 64. *See also* **calengid, chaunge, drau, Englisshed, interpreted, save** (*imp.*), **set, translate, transmwe.**

tytyl *n.* title (*titulus*), (of individual psalms) 3.21: 1, 2², 6, etc. **tytyllys** *pl.* (of chapters) 1.12: 12. *See also* **intytulacyon.**

unable *adj.* incapable, unworthy (of interpreting Scripture) 2.5: 31, ~ **of blisse** (of inadequate readers) 2.5: 141.

unabylnesse *n.* inability 1.12: 40. *See also* **humblesse, ignorance, insuffishaunce, leudenesse, simplesse, unconnynge, unworthynesse: suffisaunce.**

unclene *adj.* unclean (*fig.*, nonruminant beasts), (of audiences who willfully ignore God's word) 2.5: 139, 141. *See also* **schewe.**

unconand *adj.* unlearned, uninformed (of audience) 3.8: 53, **unconna[n]d** 3.7: 11.

unconnynge *vbl.n.* ignorance, inability (in writer) 1.4: 74, **unkunnynge** 1.12: 30, 40. *See also* **humblesse, ignorance, insuffishaunce, leudenesse, simplesse, unabylnesse, unworthynesse: suffisaunce.**

understand *v.* understand (of audience) 2.1: 64, **Englis** ~ **kan** (of clerks and laypeople) 2.1: 70, ~ **Latin and Frankis** (not understandable by all) 2.1: 74, **understande** 2.4: 33, 2.8: 4, 3.12: 120, 3.14: 78, 3.24: 103, **knowe and** ~ (the Benedictine Rule) 2.8: 26, **laboure to** ~ 3.12: 118, ~ **and fele** 3.17: 7, **understonde** 2.2: 26, 31, 32, etc., 3.12: 124, 125, 128, etc., (of refectory reading) 3.12: 128, **lerne and** ~ 2.2: 45, **rede and** ~ 2.2: 24, 2.16: 65–66, **se and** ~ (of liturgy) 3.12: 46, **studye and** ~ 2.16: 59, **undirstond** (of audience) 2.3: 151, **undirstonde** (Scripture) 2.5: 69, **groundis to** ~ (of Scripture) 1.15: 46, **sumdel** ~ (of laymen and the Bible) 1.15: 85, **undurstand, no Latyn** ~ 3.7: 12, **undyrstande, rede and** ~ (of women and English) 2.6: 15, ~ **Latyn** 1.12: 57, **unneth can** ~ **Latyn** (of women in religion) 2.7: 18, **undyrstond,** ~ **the psalme** 3.21: 2, **undyrstondyn** 1.14: 2. **undirstondist** *pr.2.sg.* 1.15: 29, 30. **understondeth** *pr.3.sg.* ~ **otheres speche** 2.2: 8, 14, **understo[n]dth** 2.4: 30. **undirstonde** *pr.1.pl.* 1.15: 46. **understonde** *pr.2.pl.* 3.12: 123. **understandeth** *pr.3.pl.* 3.17:

15, **understandes** 3.14: 92, **understondeth**, ~ no Latyn 2.2: 44, **understondith**, ~ Latyn 2.2: 60, 63, ~ no Latyn 2.2: 59, **undirstonden** (of clerks) 2.5: 108, (of laypeople) 2.5: 124. **understande** *pr. subj.* 2.8: 4, 3.12: 119, **understonde**, ~ yt and savoure yt 3.12: 130, **undurstand** 3.7: 5. **understonden** *imp. sg.* 3.4: 8, **undyrstande** 1.12: 65. **undurstonde** *imp. pl.* 3.2: 15, **undyrstond** 3.21: 24, 57. **understude** *pa.1.sg.* 3.18: 38, **undyrstode** 1.13: 42, 99. **undirstond** *pa.3.sg.* meant 1.15: 3, **undyrstod** 1.14: 48. **understude** *pa.3.pl.* 3.18: 44. **understande** *p.p.* 3.17: 7, **redy to be** ~ (by women novices) 2.8: 34–35, **understond, knowe and** ~ 2.2: 122, **understonde** 2.2: 19, 24, 26, 2.11: 122, interpreted 3.12: 71, **knowe and** ~ 2.2: 126, 142, **understonden, better to be** ~ (of prose) 2.16: 71, **trewly** ~ 3.4: 8, **understondid** (of English dialects) 3.12: 73, **understondyd** (of meaning in translation) 3.12: 65, **undirstande** 3.10: 24, **undirstonden, feelid either** ~ 1.15: 1–2, ~ **in manye maners** (of biblical lexis) 1.15: 11, ~ **thus fleischli** (of literal interpretation) 2.5: 108, **undurstonden** signified 2.13: 8. *See also* **comprise, entende, fele, skylle.**

understandinge *n.* understanding, knowledge, **inwarde** ~ 3.12: 27, **understandyng** 1.4: 24, **comune** ~ 3.10: 9, **of symple** ~ (of audience) 3.10: 3, **ryght** ~ 3.17: 14, **very** ~ 3.17: 10–11, **understandynge** 1.4: 93, **myne** ~ 3.24: 83, **soo hyghe and grete** ~ (of clerks) 3.24: 78–79, **lyghte of** ~ the light of understanding 3.12: 115, **understondinge** 2.8: 18, ~ **of the heres** 3.12: 129, **understondyng** 1.4: 46, (of liturgy) 3.12: 164, **holesom** ~ 3.4: 3, **enforme the** ~ (purpose of some genres of book) 3.12: 163–64, **understondynge** 3.12: 137, **sensyble** ~ affective understanding (*sapientia*) 3.15: 90, **undirstandyng, fayrhed of** ~ (in psalms) 3.8: 14, **trewe** ~ (of Scripture) 2.5: 21, **undirstonding** 1.15: 40, **goostly** ~ spiritual understanding (opposed to literal understanding) 1.15: 47, (of writer's or speaker's intention) **the meenyng or the** ~ 1.16: 23, 26, 29, (of Scripture) **the veri** ~ 1.15: 38, **undirstondung** (of Scripture) 2.5: 53–54, **undirstondyng, fals** ~ (of Scripture) 2.5: 43–44, **goostli** ~ 2.5: 103, 110, **trewe** ~ 2.5: 62, 68, 76, (of God's law) 2.5: 51, **veri** ~ 2.5: 38–39, **undirstondynge, mystakynge and** ~ [mis]understanding 2.5: 45, **the nakid** ~ (of literal interpretation) 2.5: 22–23, **undurstandyng, symple** ~ 3.10: 3, **undyrstandynge, the letturall** ~ 1.12: 70, 72. **understondynges** *pl.* meanings 3.12: 68, **undirstondingis, iiii** ~ fourfold exegesis 1.15: 83, **wittis either** ~ intelligence or understanding 1.15: 68. *See also* **entente, feill, felyng: cence, meanynge, sentence, wit.**

understonding *adj.* comprehensible 1.4: 44, **understondynge** (*vbl.n. as adj.*) understanding, **hye and hardy** ~ **men** people of high and sustained comprehension (of audience) 1.10: 10. *See also* **entendible.**

undisposed *p.p. as adj.* ill-ordered, **mysguyded and** ~ (of readers whom historical reading can correct) 3.15: 53–54. *See also* **adresse, dispose, dresse, mysdisposed, wel-disposid.**

undo *v.* expound (*exponere*) 2.1: 97. *See also* **declare, expounne, glosyde, opnyt.**

unkunnynge *see* **unconnynge.**

unlettryd *adj.* unlearned, without Latin 3.2: 65, **unlettyrd** (*as n.*) women unable to read 2.6: 16. *See also* **laud.**

unorderide *adj.* (of books) unarranged, uncompiled and extracted 2.3: 132.

unpeysed *p.p. as adj.* unweighed (of injudicious praise or blame of literary work) 2.11: 152. *See also* **ponderose, wayenge.**

unprofitable *adj.* useless (of text changed in transmission) 2.3: 175.

unprovid *p.p.* unchallenged (of texts) 1.16: 104.

unsavery *adj.* unpleasant (of writing in English) 3.2: 18. *See also* **boystous, savour(e), taaste.**

unworth *adj.* worthless (reader's sense of self before God) 3.1: 14.

unworthi *adj.* unworthy, ~ **to bere ony name** (of author's anonymity) 3.5: 6. *See also* **semely, worthi.**

unworthynesse *n.* unworthiness (of author) 1.12: 19, 30, **unwurthynesse** 1.11: 34. *See also* **humblesse, ignorance, insuffishaunce, leudenesse, simplesse, unabylnesse, unconnynge: suffisaunce.**

unwritun *p.p.* unwritten 1.16: 66.

utteraunce *n.* utterance, **lusty ~** 3.15: 75.

verrefye *pr.3.pl.* verify, confirm (of books) 1.7: 165.

verreie *adj.* real, true, **~ trewe corn** (*fig.*) true significance 1.7: 102. *See also* **suth, trewe.**

vers *n.* verse 1.4: 11. *See also* **balade, endite, metir, making.**

visioun *n.* vision (*visio*) 1.13: 56, 3.20: 1, **visyoun** 1.13: 3, 56, **visyounn** 1.13: 1, **vysioun** 3.20: 10, 18. **visyonys** *pl.* 3.22: 70. *See also* **contemplacion, revelation, schewynge, sight, teching, tribulacyons.**

voice *n.* voice (*vox*) 3.8: 18, 50, 52, **~ spokun** (distinguished from speaker's intention) 1.16: 22, 24. *See also* **steven.**

volume *n.* volume, **this present ~** 2.10: 22, **ony morall ~** work of morality 3.24: 80–81. **volumes** *pl.* 1.10: 34. *See also* **bok, merour.**

vyrelayes *n.pl.* virelays (French *virelai,* type of song or short lyric piece) 2.16: 17. *See also* **balade, roundels, sange.**

vysyte *v.* visit, spend time with (a book) 3.24: 45, 51. **vysytynge** *pr.p.* 3.24: 55.

walke *v.* walk, (*fig.*) browse 3.5: 14, 21, **~ aboute** 3.5: 19. *See also* **aleye, orcherd, pathis.**

walkynge *vbl.n. as adj.* walking, **~ pathis** paths for walking (of reading choices) 3.5: 36.

wanton *adj.* wanton (of pleasures of poetry) 3.15: 79.

wark *n.* (poetic) work, literary composition 3.16: 31, **werc** (of labor in composition as form of worship) 2.1: 123, **werk** 1.8: 67, 135, 1.10: 15, 1.11: 2, 22, 27, etc., 2.1: 120, 2.7: 12, 2.11: 58, 2.12: 42, 57, 59, etc., (of reading and interpreting) 2.5: 3, (of contemplation) 3.3: 43, **a lastande ~** 3.14: 60, **crafty ~** 1.11: 98, **good ~** (effect of reading Scripture) 2.5: 167, **in ~** actively (of retained effect of reading) 2.5: 11, **this litil ~** (of text) 2.12: 81, **werke** 1.5: 3, 45, 1.12: 42, 54, 55, etc., 2.1: 83, 3.8: 62, 69, 3.12: 86, (of God as creator) 1.4: 54, (of alchemy) 2.3: 51, **soleyne ~** (of discipline of alchemy) 2.3: 62, **this present ~** 2.10: 8, **this simple ~** (as form of homage) 1.5: 70, **wirk** 1.7: 59, 70, **wirke** 1.7: 39, **work, his newe ~** (*Poetria nova*) 1.11: 86. **werkes** *pl.* 1.5: 50, 3.12: 93, **god ~** (audience response) 3.7: 8, **werkis** 2.3: 163, 3.15: 20, **good ~** (fruit of reading Scripture) 2.5: 19, **werkys** (of manuscript workmanship) 1.8: 35, **goode ~** 1.12: 89, (of Christ's deeds as example) 1.14: 7, (of effect of Christ as subject matter) 1.14: 11. *See also* **besynes, labour, occupacion, travail.**

wayenge *vbl.n.* weighing, evaluation (of literary texts) 3.24: 36. *See also* **ponderose, unpeysed.**

wedis *n.pl.* weeds (*fig.*) penitential or difficult spiritual reading 3.5: 39, 40, 42. *See also* **corn, frewte, herbis: bitter.**

wel-disposid *p.p. as adj.* well-disposed (of reader's attitude) 1.16: 55. *See also* **adresse, dispose, dresse, mysdisposed, undisposed.**

werbles *n. pl.* melodies 1.7: 49. *See also* **sange.**

werc, werk(e) (*n.*) *see* **wark.**

werk *v.* work, do, perform, **~ god werkes** (as audience response) 3.7: 8, **wirke** compose 2.1: 76, **worche** (of translation) 2.2: 128, (act in accordance with text) 3.6: 5, **~ youre wille** (to patron) 2.2: 134. **worche** *pr.3.pl.* (of texts' effect on audience) 3.5: 43. **wrocht** *p.p., crafty* **~** (of writing) 3.16: 31, **wroughte** (by God through authors of Scripture) 1.15: 6, **wrowght** worked (of gold lettering) 1.8: 32. *See also* **laboure, worchyng.**

will *n.* will, wish, desire (of author) 1.2: 15, (of audiences) 3.13: 14, **wille** (of patron) 2.2: 134, 141, (of author) 1.7: 213, (of reader) 3.3: 11, (of audience) 3.11: 10, **Goddys ~ and my desyre** (of author) 1.13: 57–58, **simple men and wymmen of gode ~** (audience) 3.6: 3–4, **good ~** (of audiences) 2.5: 1, (of poor reciters) 3.2: 35, **goode ~** (of author) 1.9: 69, (of audience) 1.13: 61, **gude ~** (of audience) 1.1: 76, **in ~** desiring (of author) 1.5: 72, **in a trewe ~** (desired state of audience) 3.3: 14, **wulle, good ~** (of scribe) 1.14: 89, **wyll** (of author) 3.24: 50. **willes** *pl.* (of audience) 3.8: 4, **willis** (of audience) 3.18: 42, **willys** (of all audiences and subjects) 3.16: 38. *See also* **desir, pay, pleasier.**

wille *pr.1.sg.* will, wish, want, ~ **no mede** (author's refusal of reward) 1.1: 67, **wole** 3.5: 18, ~ **and entende** 1.16: 72. **wille** *pr.2.pl.* (of audience) 1.1: 4, **wolen** (of readers' choice) 3.5: 14, 21. **wole** *pr. subj. pl.* (of readers' choice) 3.5: 21. **wold** *pa.2.sg.* (of addressee of work) 2.7: 7, **wolde** *pa.3.sg.* (of patron) 1.7: 90, (of author) 1.13: 9, 1.14: 38. **wolde** *pa.1.pl.* (of author) 2.8: 36. *See also* **desyre, lyst.**

wirke (*n.*) *see* **wark.**

wit *n.* wit, understanding (of difficult material) 2.11: 21, (of reader of Book of Life) 3.11: 10, (of mortal understanding) 3.11: 12, nonliteral meaning (in translation) 3.8: 65, **blynde of** ~ (for syllogistic argument) 2.2: 72, **floode of** ~ (of intelligence in texts) 1.4: 8, **my** ~ (of mental capacity of narrator) 1.6: 47, **simplesce of my** ~ (of author) 2.11: 164, **ther owne** ~ (of audience) 2.5: 77, **witt** knowledge, understanding 3.11: 26, (given to apostles for Scripture) 2.5: 68, (for seeing importance of translation) 2.2: 90, **menhede of my** ~ limitations (of author's understandng) 1.10: 37, **mannes** ~ (arrogance of, in reading Scripture) 2.5: 23, **symple men of** ~ (good audience of Scripture) 2.5: 124, **witte, defaute of** ~ 2.2: 47, **dyligence and** ~ (in composition) 2.10: 23, **man ys** ~ human understanding 1.13: 15–16, **wyt** (of author) 1.2: 16, 1.11: 103, **wytt** (of author) 1.9: 93, 1.12: 75, 1.14: 61, **wytte** (of author) **dul** ~ 1.4: 4, (lack in author) 1.5: 1, **dysgarnysshed of al** ~ **and reson** (of audience) 2.16: 24–25, **fresshe** ~ (of audience) 3.24: 28. **wittes** *pl.* **my** ~ **ben to smale** (of author) 2.11: 88, **wittis** (of audiences) 1.15: 68, 3.13: 14, (of author) 3.23: 70, (of narrator) 1.6: 53, ~ **of helthe** understanding of health (as fruit of compilation) 1.10: 10, **wyttes** 1.4: 18, 44, 93, (of audience) 3.12: 87, (of author) 1.5: 30, 1.14: 26, **wyttys** (in composing chivalric biography) 1.8: 48, (of potential audience) 1.11: 208, **bodyly** ~ (of author) 1.14: 53. *See also* **felyng, meanynge, sentence, understandinge.**

wit *v.* know, understand 2.1: 104, **wite** 1.6: 44 (of knowledge as dependent on experience), 1.16: 51, **witte** (of narrative's progress) 1.1: 54, **wytten** 1.1: 13. **wite** *imp.* 1.16: 6, **witte** 2.4: 30.

witnessith *pr.3.sg.* witnesses (of text or author), (of Saint Jerome) 1.16: 112, (of the apostle Peter) 3.11: 12. **witnesseth** *pr.3.pl.* (of saint's clerics and disciples) 3.5: 31, **wytnesseth** (of famous men against women) 3.24: 74, (of men against women) 3.24: 105. **wytnesse** *imp.* 1.5: 44. *See also* **probate, shewe, testimony.**

wlappingis *n.pl.* convolutions, ~ **of wordis** 1.15: 25.

wondres *n.pl.* wonders, **of mervails and of** ~ (as subject matter for chronicle) 2.2: 22. *See also* **dedis, ferles, marvellys.**

worche (*v.*) *see* **werk.**

worchyng *vbl.n.* working (at university study) 1.10: 32.

word *n.* word (*verba, vocabulum*) (in a composition or translation) 1.7: 35, 1.8: 24, 40, 1.14: 111, 3.22: 4, 7, (of Christ) 1.5: 147, (of Christ's utterance) 2.5: 116, (of God) 2.1: 39, 2.5: 4, 20, 144, etc., 3.22: 2, 4, 79, (of Scripture) phrase 2.5: 52, sentence 2.5: 57, **Goddis** ~ (as food of the soul) 2.5: 143, 153, **a** ~ **of Hebrew** 2.7: 24, **a Lateyn** ~ 2.7: 26, **pride of the** ~ 2.5: 32, ~ **unpeysed** (of injudicious literary judgment) 2.11: 152, **worde,** (not to have meaning altered in translation) 1.7: 187, **a resoun for a** ~ (of translation) 2.2: 146, **Godes** ~ 2.1: 39, **holy** ~ 3.22: 9–10, **reverence had to the** ~ 3.12: 115, **the wit of the** ~ the meaning of the sentence 3.8: 65, **trouth of the** ~ 3.12: 117, ~ **by** ~ (of a specific mode of translation) 1.3: 10, ~ **for** ~ (mode of translation) 1.5: 29, 2.2: 143, ~ **of falsenes** 2.4: 16. **word** *pl.* 1.14: 54, **wordes** 2.9: 6, 16, 34, etc., 3.12: 3, 6, 20, etc., 3.24: 54, 96, 114, (in quotation) 2.9: 40, 41, (of Christ) 2.1: 94, 2.9: 34, (of God) 1.15: 32, (of the mother tongue) 1.4: 29, (of monastic profession) 2.9: 6, 49, **chyding in** ~ 1.15: 87, **comfortabylle** ~ 1.13: 3, **dyverse** ~ 3.12: 70, **harde** ~ 2.9: 16, **kepe the . . .** ~ (in translation) 1.5: 19, **medicyne of** ~ 3.8: 14, moo ~ mosten be seyde (of need to paraphrase in translation) 3.2: 17, ordre of ~ 2.2: 144, 145, rude ~ and boystous 1.4: 6, 9, soo that the ~ be good 2.10: 41, some ~ mosten be chaunged (in process of translation) 3.2: 17, sugred ~ 1.7: 150, the sentence and not the ~ (to be followed in translation) 3.12: 67, ~ and names 2.2: 148, 153, ~ in Latyn 3.12: 63, ~ and the sentence 3.12: 66, ~ that have dyverse understandynges 3.12: 68, ~ equyvalent unto the dedes 3.15: 85, ~ polisshed 2.10: 24, ydel ~ 3.12: 109, wordis 1.15: 11², 1.16: 137², 3.2: 82, 3.21: 64, (as witnesses to authorial intention) 1.16: 39, (as objects of readers' attention) 1.16: 42, (of Christ) 2.5: 93, 95, 96, etc., (of Scripture) 1.15: 2, 1.16: 33, 2.5: 90, few ~ and playne 2.3: 97, groundid in the ~ 1.16: 152, Latyn ~ 3.8: 64, sett his ~ 1.16: 74, 2.4: 31, wlappingis of ~ convolutions of words (of involuted meaning) 1.15: 25, ~ and werkys 3.2: 78, 79, ~ and his writingis 1.16: 139, ~ of lovynge 3.8: 19, ~ of my writingis 1.16: 29, ~ of this prophecie 2.5: 6, wordris 1.16: 142, wordys 3.22: 38, (of encouragement to author) 1.12: 28, wurdys 1.11: 5, 26. *See also* sau, speche.

work (*n.*) *see* wark.

worthi *adj.* worthy (of argument) 2.2: 68, 81, (of cleric as author and source) 3.10: 6, worthy (of author) 2.10: 9, (of clerics and scholars as sources or authorities) 1.12: 20, 43, 51, etc., 1.14: 65, 3.23: 22, (of liturgical recitation) 3.12: 33, (of patron) 2.2: 132, (of sermons as God's word) 3.22: 7, (of subject matter for historiography) 3.15: 76, make me ~ (as authorial prayer) 3.21: 11, ~ myndes (of audience) 3.24: 7, ~ to memory worthy of being remembered (of philosophical writing) 1.4: 55, ~theyr hyer (*fig.*, of authors as workmen) 1.4: 80. *See also* semely, unworthi.

worthilich *adv.* worthily (of author's praising of God) 3.3: 5, worthyly (of writer and audience's praise for God) 3.21: 104.

worthines *n.* worthiness (of the Virgin as subject for portrayal) 3.12: 36, worthinesse (of royal dedicatee) 2.11: 138, worthynesse, to renewe all noble ~ (as aim of elite audience) 3.24: 4.

writ *n.* writing, scripture (*scriptura*), haly ~ holy writings 3.8: 37, Holi ~ 2.5: 1, 39, 51, Holy ~ 1.15: 34, 60, 85, etc., holy ~ 2.2: 76–77, 78, 82, etc., Hooli ~ 2.5: 21, 30, 31, etc., Hooly ~ 1.15: 60, 2.5: 62, 91, writt, holy ~ 3.10: 1, writte, holy ~ 2.2: 105, wryt, in ~ writing 1.2: 17. *See also* scripture, word.

write *v.* write, compose, copy 1.7: 89, 1.16: 15, 46, 65, etc., 2.9: 53, 2.11: 144, 171, 3.3: 21, 22, 31, entende to ~ 2.3: 56, speke and ~ 1.16: 69, writen 1.7: 35, writun 1.16: 12², wryght 1.8: 109, wryte 1.8: 86, 1.9: 94, 1.11: 73, 1.14: 136, 2.11: 70, 3.5: 9, 3.18: 37, ~ a bok 2.11: 25, 60, owt ~ copy 1.11: 120, wryten 1.14: 117, 135, 144, ~ Englysche ne Duche 1.14: 138–39, wrytin 1.14: 141, wrytyn 1.14: 89, 100, 109, ~ hyr felyngys 1.14: 69, ~ this boke 1.14: 104–5, wryt[yn] 2.9: 46, wrytyne 1.14: 70. wreton, *inf. pass.*, doo be ~ have (*s.th.*) written down 2.16: 48–49, write, doo ~ have it written down 2.16: 53, wryte, did it ~ caused to be written (of literary text) 1.1: 81, wryten have written, cause to be written, dede any ~ 1.14: 72, dede nothing ~ 1.14: 116, wrytene, don hem ~ and makyne 1.14: 67–68, to done ~ 1.14: 134. write *pr.1.sg.* 1.16: 71, 2.11: 148, wryght 1.8: 98, wryte 2.11: 28. writeth *pr.3.sg.* 2.5: 161, writis 3.16: 39, writith 1.15: 41, wrytis 3.16: 20. wryte *pr.1.pl.* 2.11: 13. write *pr.3.pl.* 1.7: 198, 2.3: 62, ~ under covert 2.3: 71, writen 1.7: 204, 1.16: 124, writeth 2.2: 18, wrye 1.8: 45, wryten 1.12: 45, 46. write *pr. subj.* 2.3: 60, 2.11: 20, 48, 3.3: 12. wroot *pa.1.sg.* 1.16: 39, wrote 1.1: 78, wher after I ~ translated 3.2: 16, ~ after followed (of source material) 3.2: 21. write *pa.3.sg.* dide ~ (*periphrastic*) wrote 2.3: 90. wrait *pa.3.sg.* 3.18: 59, wrate 3.18: 61, 3.20: 2, 10, wroot 1.15: 3, wroote 1.16: 73, wrot copied 1.14: 102, composed 1.14: 125, wrote 1.12: 43, 49, 2.2: 20, 2.3: 78, 3.10: 6, 3.20: 7, spake or ~ 1.16: 136–37. writen *pa.3.pl.* 1.4: 56, 2.4: 23, 2.11: 8, wrote 1.12: 47, 2.3: 72, wroten 1.16: 146. writyng *pr.p.* 2.7: 46. iwrite *p.p.* 2.2: 79, 88, wreton 3.17: 2, wretyn 1.14: 103, 113, 126, etc., ~ a qwayre 1.14: 125, 3.3: 12, wretyne 1.14: 81, evel ~ 1.14: 85, 114, 115, etc., write 1.16: 99, 2.11: 10, writen 1.16: 138, 147, 156, 2.4: 25, 3.2: 1, 15, 19, etc., 3.10: 1, 14, 23, etc., 3.12: 3, ~ in bookes 1.6: 43, ~ schorter 1.10: 27, ~ to longe 1.10: 28, ynke ~ (as mode of signification) 1.16: 22, 23–24. writtene 3.20: 6, wryten 1.4: 61, 3.24: 80, ~ and sayd 1.1: 33, wryttyn 2.6: 18, wrytyn 1.8: 24, w[rytyn] 2.9: 39, ywrite 2.2: 28, 106, 3.7: 41, ywriten 1.7: 93. writen *p.p. as adj.* al thes ~ 2.4: 25, bokis ~ 2.3: 100, pistle ~ 1.16: 134, ~ in the gospelle (of Christ's life) 3.10: 25, writun, bi me ~ 1.16: 12, proces of feith ~ 1.16: 129, wryten, ~ it fand found in written form (by *s.o.*) 1.1: 6, haf it ~ have in written form 1.1: 14, wrytyn 1.8: 31. *See also* drau, endite, laboure, ma(ke), unwritun, werk.

writer *n.* writer 1.16: 23, 40, writere 3.10: 15, wrytare 1.12: 87, wryter, the sempyl ~ 1.8: 22, ~ and endyter 1.8: 59, wrytere 3.20: 1, wrytyr scribe, copyist 1.14: 76. writers *pl.* 1.7: 111, wrytars 3.15: 1, wryters 3.15: 15, 20. *See also* auctor, cause, endyter, maister, poete, translatour.

writing *n.* writing, composition, copying 1.16: 98, 105, 119, etc., 2.2: 19, 3.23: 32, inward book and ~ 1.16: 154, inward ~ 1.16: 147, 149, *(fig.)* ~ buried in mannis soule 1.16: 153, writyng 1.7: 118, 123, 133, etc., 2.3: 61, 171, his ~ or in his speking 1.16: 26, scripture and ~ 3.10: 7, writynge, forme of my ~ 2.11: 141, wrytinge 2.11: 45, 58, wrytyng 1.8: 121, my sympyl ~ 1.8: 144, 1.14: 93, 99, wrytynge 3.12: 77, 3.24: 39. writingis *pl.* 1.16: 29, 32, 78, etc., writynges 1.4: 31, wrytynges 3.12: 93, treatyse and ~ 3.24: 61, wrytyngis 2.10: 35. *See also* enditing, poesys, scripture, tretis.

wrocht, wroughte, wrowght *see* werk.

wrytars, wryter(e), wryters, wrytyr *see* writer.

wryte(n)(e), wrytin, wrytis *see* write.

wrytinge, wrytyng(e)(s), wrytyngis *see* writing.

wulgar *adj.* vulgar, vernacular, ~ and matarnall toung 2.17: 26–27.

wurdys *see* word.

wytnesse *n.* witness, beryth ~ (of Old Testament) 1.11: 61, wyttenesse, hit self bereth ~ (of book's format, regarding structure of its text) 3.7: 21, to ~ (of God, regarding author's intention) 1.7: 69.

wytten *see* wit (*v.*).

ydelnesse *n.* idlenesss (avoided by composing poetry) 1.7: 83. *See* also slouthe.

ygnoraunce *see* ignorance.

ymage *n.* image (*imago*), visual representation (to be read devotionally) 3.9: 9, 11, 15, etc. 3.10: 19. ymages *n.pl.* images, visual representations (as books to the unlettered) 3.2: 56, (as *figurae*) 3.2: 62, ymagis 3.2: 62, ymagys 3.9: 1. *See also* figure, methaphoris.

ymagerye *n.* visual representation (as unlettered equivalent of books) ~ and peynture 3.9: 7, 8, (compared with priest's book) 3.9: 41, 42. *See also* purtreyture.

ymagynacions, ymagynacyonys, ymagynationis *see* imagynacion.

ympe *v.* graft (of past's truths added to present knowledge) 1.7: 116. ymped *p.p.* ~ in (of figures of rhetoric in narrative) 1.7: 196. *See also* plante, set.

ympis *n.pl.* grafts, *(fig.)* compilations, texts, ~ and trees 3.5: 34. *See also* orcherd, herbis, wedis.

ympne *n.* hymn (*hymnus*) 3.8: 47, 48. ympnes *pl.*, ~ of Crist psalter 3.8: 47, boke of ~ psalter 3.8: 51. *See also* sange, service, synge, synge.

ynke *n.* ink, red ~ *(fig.)* elaborate style 1.4: 12, ynke, the ~ writen signification (not identical with intention or meaning) 1.16: 22, 23–24.

ystorye *see* historye.

Select Latin Terms

advisamenta *adj. pl.* well-advised 1.9: 25.
Anglica *adj. pl.* English, ~ **metra** English verses 2.11: 4.
anglicatus *p.p.* rendered into English 1.9: 1.
Anglicus *adj.* of England, **Galfridus** ~ 1.11: 88.
anno *n.* year, ~ **domini** "in the year of our Lord" (time of text) 1.13: 2, 1.14: 126–27.

breviter *adv.* briefly, concisely 1.9: 27.

canam *pr. subj. sg.* sing 2.11: 2. **canit** *pr.3.sg.* 2.11: 3.
capitulo *n.* chapter or subheading 2.17: 6, 8, 10, etc., 3.22: 46, 3.24: 32.
clericus *n.* clerk 2.2: 28, 38, 45, etc., **clericum** 1.9: 2.
compilacio *n.* compilation 1.9: 10.
compilatus *p.p.* compiled 1.9: 1.
compositus *p.p.* composed 1.2: 1.
cronica *n.pl.* chronicles 1.9: 15.

depingit *pr.3.sg.* depicts 2.11: 106.
dialogus *n.* dialogue (as literary genre) 2.2: 131.
dividitur *fut. pass.3.sg.* will be divided (of arrangement of text and subject matter) 1.9: 11.
docebo *fut.1.sg.* teach 3.21: 55.
dominus *n.* lord (of patron) 2.2: 1, 35, 40, etc.

ebes *adj.* dull (of author's perception) 2.11: 1.
edicta *n.pl.* counsels ~ **et opiniones** (of philosophers) 1.9: 26.
Engisti *see* **lingua.**
epistola *n.* epistle (as literary genre) 2.2: 161.
experiencias *n.acc.pl.* retellings (of situation or plight) 1.9: 6.
explicit *fut.3.sg. or p.p. abbrev.* "here finishes" or "it is finished" (conventional signal of ending of a text or work) 1.5: 73, 2.2: 131, 161, 2.14: 81.
extractus *p.p.* extracted 1.9: 1.

gestis *n.pl.* deeds, events, (as subject matter) 1.2: 2.

historia *n.* history, narrative 1.1: 1.

incipit *fut.3.sg.* "here begins" (conventional signal of opening of text or work) 1.1: 1., 1.2: 1., 2.11: 7.
interpres *n.* interpreter 2.11: 6.

labor *n.* labor, **parva** ~ (as reason for inadequate composition) 2.11: 1.
legendo *pr.p.* reading (as form of remembrance) 1.9: 15.
libellus *n.* little book 1.9: 1.
liber *n.* book 1.2: 1, 1.14: 1. **librorum** *gen.pl.* books 1.9: 17
lingua *n.* language, ~ **mea** 3.21: 91, **materna** ~ mother tongue 1.1: 2, **Engisti** ~ Hengist's language, English 2.11: 3, **linguam,** ~ **meam** 3.21: 68.
loquar *v.* speak 2.11: 4.
loquelis *n.* speech 2.11: 5.

memin[iss]e *v.* remember 1.9: 14.
metra *n.pl.* verses, **Anglica** ~ 2.11: 4.
minimus *adj. as n.* least (of poets) 2.11: 2.
minora *adj. as n.* minor (themes) 2.11: 2.

opiniones *n.pl.* opinions, sayings 1.9: 26.
oro *pr.1.sg.* beg, pray 2.11: 3.
ossibus *n.pl.* bones, ~ **carens** boneless one, (*fig.*) tongue 2.11: 5.

philosophorum *n. gen.pl.* philosophers 1.9: 26.
prefacio *n.* preface, ~ **translatoris** translator's preface 1.5: *title*, 73.
proemium *n.* proem 2.12: 1, **prohemium** 2.3: *title*, 2.3: 1.
prologus *n.* prologue 1.1: 1, 1.11: *title*, 2.11: 7.

scola *n.* schooling 2.11: 1.
scripturam *n. acc.* Scripture, ~ **sacram** 1.9: 15.
sensus *n.* perception (as reason for wretched composition when dulled) 2.11: 1.
sp[e]culaciones *n.pl.* accounts 1.9: 15.
subscribuntur *pass. pl.* written below 1.9: 27.

torpor *n.* dullness 2.11: 1.
tractatu *n. dat. sg.* treatise 1.9: 27.
translatoris *n. gen. sg.* translator 1.5: 73.
transumpta *p.p.* translated 1.1: 1.

unicolor *adj.* single-colored, hypocritical (of the law) 2.11: 104. *See also* **colour** (Middle English).

vexillator *n.* banner-bearer (announcing dramatic performance) 2.14: 1, [**vexillator**] 2.14: 9.

vita *n.* life, biography, ~ **Christi** 1.12: 20.

ABBREVIATIONS

BJRL	Bulletin of the John Rylands Library
CCSL	Corpus Christianorum, Series Latina
EETS	Early English Text Society (Oxford and London: Oxford University Press, or various other places and publishers, especially in the early volumes; some volumes have been reprinted by Kraus Reprints, New York). EETS volumes are all designated "o.s." (ordinary series), "e.s." (extra series), or "s.s." (supplementary series)
MED	*Middle English Dictionary* (see Kurath, Kuhn, and Lewis 1956–)
OED	*Oxford English Dictionary* (see Simpson and Weiner 1989)
PMLA	Publications of the Modern Language Association of America
PG	*Patrologia Graeca* (see Migne 1857–62)
PL	*Patrologia Latina* (see Migne 1844–64)
SAC	Studies in the Age of Chaucer
STC	*A Short Title Catalogue of Books Printed in England, Scotland, and Ireland, and of English Books Printed Abroad, 1475–1640* (see Pollard and Redgrave 1976–86)

INDEX OF MANUSCRIPTS AND EARLY PRINTED BOOKS

Only manuscripts and early printed books consulted in editing the excerpts in this volume are listed here. Early printed books are designated by [**P**].

BIBLIOGRAPHY

Multiple items under a single name are listed chronologically (and alphabetically by title where more than one work per year is cited). Primary and secondary sources are listed together in alphabetical order by author's or editor's name.

Ackerknecht, Erwin H. 1968. *A Short History of Medicine*. New York: Ronald Press.

Aers, David. 1988. *Community, Gender, and Individual Identity: English Writing, 1360–1430*. London: Routledge.

———, ed. 1992a. *Culture and History, 1350–1600: Essays on English Communities, Identities, and Writing*. Hemel Hempstead: Harvester Wheatsheaf.

———. 1992b. "A Whisper in the Ear of Early Modernists; or, Reflections on Literary Critics Writing the 'History of the Subject.'" In Aers 1992a, 177–200.

Aers, David, and Lynn Staley. 1996. *Powers of the Holy: Religion, Politics, and Gender in Late Medieval English Culture*. University Park: Pennsylvania State University Press.

Agapitos, Panagiotis A., and Ole L. Smith. 1992. *The Study of Medieval Greek Romance: A Reassessment of Recent Work*. Copenhagen: University of Copenhagen Press.

Agutter, Alex. 1988. "Middle Scots as a Literary Language." In Jack 1988, 13–24.

Aitken, A. J. 1971. "Variation and Variety in Written Middle Scots." In *Edinburgh Studies in English and Scots*, ed. A. J. Aitken et al., 177–209. London: Longman.

Alexander, J.J.G. 1983. "Painting and Manuscript Illumination for Royal Patrons in the Later Middle Ages." In Scattergood and Sherborne 1983, 141–62.

Alford, John A. 1973. "Biblical *Imitatio* in the Writings of Richard Rolle." *Journal of English Literary History* 40:1–23.

———, ed. 1988. *A Companion to "Piers Plowman."* Berkeley and Los Angeles: University of California Press.

Allen, Hope Emily. 1910. *The Authorship of "The Prick of Conscience."* Studies in English and Comparative Literature. Radcliffe College Monographs 15. Boston: Ginn.

———. 1917. "The *Manuel des Pechiez* and the Scholastic Prologue." *Romanic Review* 8:434–62.

———, ed. 1931. *English Writings of Richard Rolle, Hermit of Hampole*. Oxford: Clarendon Press.

Allen, Judson Boyce. 1982. *The Ethical Poetic of the Later Middle Ages: A Decorum of Convenient Distinction*. Toronto: University of Toronto Press.

Allen, P. S., and H. M. Allen, eds. 1929. *Letters of Bishop Fox, 1486–1527*. Oxford: Clarendon Press.

Althusser, Louis. 1971. "Ideology and Ideological State Apparatuses (Notes Towards an Investigation)." In *Lenin and Philosophy*, trans. Ben Brewster, 121–73. London: New Left Books.

Ambrisco, Alan S., and Paul Strohm. 1995. "Succession and Sovereignty in Lydgate's Prologue to *The Troy Book*." *Chaucer Review* 30:40–57.

Amundsen, Darrel W. 1977. "Medical Deontology and Pestilential Disease in the Late Middle Ages." *Journal of the History of Medicine and the Allied Sciences* 32:403–21.

———. 1978. "Medieval Canon Law on Medical and Surgical Practice by the Clergy." *Bulletin of the History of Medicine* 52:22–44.

————. 1996. *Medicine, Society, and Faith in the Ancient and Medieval Worlds.* Baltimore: Johns Hopkins University Press.

Anderson, J.G.C. 1963. "The Eastern Frontier from Tiberius to Nero." In *The Cambridge Ancient History*, vol. 10, *The Augustan Empire, 44 B.C.–A.D. 70*, ed. S. A. Cook, F. E. Adcock, and M. P. Charlesworth, 743–80. Cambridge: Cambridge University Press.

Armstrong, C.A.J. 1942. "The Piety of Cicely, Duchess of York: A Study in Late Mediaeval Culture." In *For Hilaire Belloc: Essays in Honour of His 72nd Birthday*, ed. Douglas Woodruff, 73–94. New York: Greenwood Press.

Ascoli, Albert Russell. 1993. "The Unfinished Author: Dante's Rhetoric of Authority in *Convivio* and *De Vulgari Eloquentia*." In *The Cambridge Companion to Dante*, ed. Rachel Jacoff, 45–66. Cambridge: Cambridge University Press.

Ashley, Kathleen M. 1987. "Medieval Courtesy Literature and Dramatic Mirrors of Female Conduct." In *The Ideology of Conduct: Essays on Literature and the History of Sexuality*, ed. Nancy Armstrong and Leonard Tennenhouse, 25–38. London: Methuen.

Aston, Margaret. 1984. *Lollards and Reformers: Images and Literacy in Late Medieval Religion.* London: Hambledon.

————. 1988. *Laws Against Images.* Vol. 1 of *England's Iconoclasts.* Oxford: Clarendon Press.

————. 1993. *Faith and Fire: Popular and Unpopular Religion, 1350–1600.* London: Hambledon Press.

Ayto, John, and Alexandra Barratt, eds. 1984. *Aelred of Rievaulx's "De Institutione Inclusarum": Two English Versions.* EETS, o.s., 287.

Babington, Churchill, ed. 1860. *"The Repressor of Over Much Blaming of the Clergy" by Reginald Pecock, D.D., Sometime Lord Bishop of Chichester.* 2 vols. Rolls Series 19. London: Longman, Green, Longman, & Roberts.

Babington, Churchill, and Joseph Rawson Lumby, eds. 1865–86. *"Polychronicon Ranulphi Higden Monachi Cestrensis"; Together with the English Translation of John Trevisa and of an Unknown Writer of the Fifteenth Century.* 9 vols. Rolls Series 41. London: Longman, Green, Longman, Roberts, & Green.

Baird, Joseph L., and John R. Kane, eds. and trans. 1978. *Rossignol.* Kent, Ohio: Kent State University Press.

Baird-Lange, Lorrayne. 1985. "Trotula's Fourteenth-Century Reputation, Jankyn's Book, and Chaucer's Trot." In *Reconstructing Chaucer, SAC*, Proceedings, 1, 1984, ed. Paul Strohm and Thomas J. Heffernan, 245–56. Knoxville: New Chaucer Society, University of Tennessee Press.

Baker, Denise Nowakowski. 1994. *Julian of Norwich's "Showings": From Vision to Book.* Princeton: Princeton University Press.

Baker, Derek, ed. 1981. *Medieval Women: Essays Dedicated and Presented to Professor Rosalind M. T. Hill.* Studies in Church History. 1978. Reprint, Oxford: Basil Blackwell.

Banks, John P. 1959, ed. *"Speculum Devotorum:* An Edition with Commentary." Ph.D. diss., Fordham University.

Barnes, Geraldine. 1993. *Counsel and Strategy in Middle English Romance.* Cambridge: D. S. Brewer.

Barnes, Jonathan, ed. 1984. *The Complete Works of Aristotle.* Rev. ed. Princeton: Princeton University Press.

Barnum, Priscilla H., ed. 1976–80. *Dives and Pauper.* 2 vols. EETS, o.s., 275, 280. London: Oxford University Press.

Barr, Helen, ed. 1993. *The "Piers Plowman" Tradition: A Critical Edition of "Pierce the Plowman's Crede," "Richard the Redeles," "Mum and the Sothsegger" and "The Crowned King."* London: Everyman.

Barratt, Alexandra. 1975. "The Prymer and Its Influence on Fifteenth-Century English Passion Lyrics." *Medium Ævum* 44:264–79.

———. 1989. "Dame Eleanor Hull: A Fifteenth-Century Translator." In Ellis 1989, 87–101.

———, ed. 1992. *Women's Writing in Middle English*. London: Longman.

———, ed. 1995. *The Seven Psalms: A Commentary on the Penitential Psalms Translated from French into English by Dame Eleanor Hull*. EETS, o.s., 307.

Barthes, Roland. 1977. "The Death of the Author." In *Image–Music–Text,* trans. Stephen Heath, 142–48. New York: Hill & Wang.

Bartlett, Anne Clark. 1995. *Male Authors, Female Readers: Representation and Subjectivity in Middle English Devotional Literature*. Ithaca: Cornell University Press.

Bassnett-McGuire, Susan. 1991. *Translation Studies*. Rev. ed. New Accents. London: Routledge.

Baswell, Christopher. 1995. *Virgil in Medieval England: Figuring the "Aeneid" from the Twelfth Century to Chaucer*. Cambridge: Cambridge University Press.

———. 1997. "*Troy Book:* How Lydgate Translates Chaucer into Latin." In Beer 1997, 215–37.

Bateson, Mary, ed. 1899. *George Ashby's Poems*. EETS, e.s., 76.

Batt, Catherine, ed. 1996. *Essays on Thomas Hoccleve*. Westfield Publications in Medieval Studies 10. Turnhout: Brepols.

Baugh, Albert C., and Thomas Cable. 1993. *A History of the English Language*. 4th ed. Englewood Cliffs, N.J.: Prentice-Hall.

Bawcutt, Priscilla. 1976. *Gavin Douglas: A Critical Study*. Edinburgh: Edinburgh University Press.

Bawcutt, Priscilla, and Felicity Riddy, eds. 1987. *Longer Scottish Poems*. Vol. 1, *1375–1650*. Edinburgh: Scottish Academic Press.

Beadle, Richard. 1991. "Prolegomena to a Literary Geography of Later Medieval Norfolk." In *Regionalism in Late Medieval Manuscripts and Texts: Essays Celebrating the Publication of "A Linguistic Atlas of Late Medieval English,"* ed. Felicity Riddy, 89–108. Cambridge: D. S. Brewer.

Beadle, Richard, and A.E.B. Owen. 1977. *The Findern Manuscript: Cambridge University Library MS. Ff.1.6*. London: Scolar Press.

Beaton, Roderick. 1989. *The Medieval Greek Romance*. Cambridge: Cambridge University Press.

Beckett, Neil. 1993. "The Relations Between St. Bridget, Henry V, and Syon Abbey." In Hogg 1993, 2:125–50.

Beckwith, Sarah. 1992a. "Problems of Authority in Late Medieval English Mysticism: Language, Agency, and Authority in *The Book of Margery Kempe*." *Exemplaria* 4:171–99.

———. 1992b. "Ritual, Church, and Theatre: Medieval Dramas of the Sacramental Body." In Aers 1992a, 65–89.

———. 1993. *Christ's Body: Identity, Culture, and Society in Late Medieval Writing*. London: Routledge.

Beer, Frances, ed. 1978. *Julian of Norwich's "Revelations of Divine Love": The Shorter Version, ed. from BL Add. MS 37790*. Middle English Texts 8. Heidelberg: Carl Winter.

Beer, Jeanette. 1989. *Medieval Translators and Their Craft*. Studies in Medieval Culture 25. Kalamazoo, Mich.: Medieval Institute.

———, ed. 1997. *Translation Theory and Practice in the Middle Ages*. Studies in Medieval Culture 38. Kalamazoo, Mich.: Medieval Institute.

Beer, Jeanette, and Kenneth Lloyd-Jones, eds. 1995. *Translation and the Transmission of Culture Between 1300 and 1600*. Studies in Medieval Culture 35. Kalamazoo, Mich.: Medieval Institute.

Bell, David N. 1992. *The Libraries of the Cistercians, Gilbertines, and Premonstratensians.* London: British Library.

———. 1995. *What Nuns Read: Books and Libraries in Medieval English Nunneries.* Cistercian Studies Series 158. Kalamazoo, Mich.: Cistercian Publications.

Bell, Susan G. 1988. "Medieval Women Book Owners: Arbiters of Lay Piety and Ambassadors of Culture." *Signs: Journal of Women in Culture and Society* 7 (1982): 742–68. Reprinted in Erler and Kowaleski 1988.

Belsey, Catherine. 1988. "Literature, History, Politics." In *Modern Criticism and Theory: A Reader,* ed. David Lodge, 400–410. London: Longman.

Belyea, Barbara. 1981. "Caxton's Reading Public." *English Language Notes* 19:14–19.

Bennet, H. S. 1937. "The Author and His Public in the Fourteenth and Fifteenth Centuries." *Essays and Studies* 23:7–24.

Bennett, J.A.W., and G. V. Smithers, eds. 1974. *Early Middle English Verse and Prose.* 2d ed. Oxford: Clarendon Press.

Bennett, Michael J. 1992. "The Court of Richard II and the Promotion of Literature." In Hanawalt 1992, 3–20.

Benskin, Michael, and M. L. Samuels, eds. 1981. *So Meny People Longages and Tonges: Philological Essays in Scots and Mediaeval English Presented to Angus McIntosh.* Edinburgh: Middle English Dialect Project.

Benson, C. David. 1980. *The History of Troy in Middle English Literature: Guido delle Colonne's "Historia Destructionis Troiae" in Medieval England.* Cambridge: D. S. Brewer.

Benson, Larry D., ed. 1986. *King Arthur's Death: The Middle English Stanzaic "Morte Arthure" and Alliterative "Morte Arthure."* New York: Bobbs-Merrill; Exeter: University of Exeter Press.

———, ed. 1987. *The Riverside Chaucer.* 3d ed. Boston: Houghton Mifflin.

Benton, J. F. 1985. "Trotula, Women's Problems, and the Professionalization of Medicine in the Middle Ages." *Bulletin of the History of Medicine* 59:30–53.

Bergen, Henry, ed. 1906–35. *Lydgate's Troy Book.* 4 vols. EETS, e.s., 97, 103, 106, 126.

Berndt, Rolf. 1969. "The Linguistic Situation in England from the Norman Conquest to the Loss of Normandy (1066–1204)." In *Approaches to Historical Linguistics: An Anthology,* ed. Roger Lass, 369–91. New York: Holt, Rinehart & Winston.

———. 1976. "French and English in Thirteenth-Century England: An Investigation into the Linguistic Situation After the Loss of the Duchy of Normandy and Other Continental Dominions." In *Aspekte der anglistischen Forschungen in der DDR: Martin Lehnert zum 65. Geburtstag,* 129–50. Berlin: Akademie-Verlag.

Best, Thomas W. 1983. *Reynard the Fox.* Twayne World's Authors Series 673. Boston: Twayne.

Bestul, Thomas H., ed. 1987. *A Durham Book of Devotions.* Toronto Medieval Latin Texts 18. Toronto: Pontifical Institute of Mediaeval Studies.

Bevington, David M., ed. 1975. *Medieval Drama.* Boston: Houghton Mifflin.

Biddick, Kathleen. 1993. "Genders, Bodies, Borders: Technologies of the Visible." *Speculum* 68:389–418.

Bird, Ruth. 1949. *The Turbulent London of Richard II.* London: Longmans, Green.

Blake, Norman F. 1969. *Caxton and His World.* London: Deutsch.

———, ed. 1970. *The History of Reynard the Fox: Translated from the Dutch Original by William Caxton.* EETS, o.s., 263.

———, ed. 1973. *Caxton's Own Prose.* London: Deutsch.

———. 1976. *Caxton: England's First Publisher.* New York: Barnes & Noble.

———. 1986. "William Caxton." In Edwards 1986, 389–412.

———. 1989. "Manuscript to Print." In Griffiths and Pearsall 1989, 403–32.

———. 1990. "The Vernon Manuscript: Contents and Organisation." In Pearsall 1990, 45–59.

———. 1991. *William Caxton and English Literary Culture.* London: Hambledon.

———, ed. 1992. *The Cambridge History of the English Language*. Vol. 2. Cambridge: Cambridge University Press.

———. 1996. "William Caxton." In Seymour 1996a, 1–68.

Blamires, Alcuin, ed. (with Karen Pratt and C. W. Marx). 1992. *Woman Defamed and Woman Defended: An Anthology of Medieval Texts*. Oxford: Clarendon Press.

———. 1997. *The Case for Women in Medieval Culture*. Oxford: Clarendon Press.

Bloch, R. Howard. 1991. *Medieval Misogyny and the Invention of Western Romantic Love*. Chicago: University of Chicago Press.

Blume, Clemens, ed. 1930. *Johannis de Hovedene "Philomena": John Hoveden's "Nachtigallenlied."* Hymnologische Beiträge 4. Leipzig: O. R. Reisland.

Blumenfeld-Kosinski, Renate. 1994. "Jean le Fèvre's *Livre de Leesce*: Praise or Blame of Women?" *Speculum* 69:705–25.

Blunt, John Henry, ed. 1873. *The Myroure of Oure Ladye*. EETS, e.s., 19.

Blyth, Charles. 1987. *"The Knightly Stile": A Study of Gavin Douglas's "Aeneid."* New York: Garland.

Boas, Marcus, and Henricus Johannes Botschuyer, eds. 1952. *Disticha Catonis*. Amsterdam: North Holland

Boffey, Julia. 1985. *Manuscripts of English Courtly Love Lyrics in the Later Middle Ages*. Cambridge: D. S. Brewer.

———. 1991. "Chaucerian Prisoners: The Context of the *Kingis Quair*." In *Chaucer and Fifteenth-Century Poetry,* ed. Julia Boffey and Janet Cowan, 84–99. London: King's College.

———. 1996. "Women Authors and Women's Literacy in Fourteenth- and Fifteenth-Century England." 1993. Reprinted in Meale 1996c, 159–82.

Boffey, Julia, and John J. Thompson. 1989. "Anthologies and Miscellanies: Production and Choice of Texts." In Griffiths and Pearsall 1989, 279–315.

Boitani, Piero, and Anna Torti, eds. 1996. *Mediaevalitas: Reading in the Middle Ages,* J. A. W. Bennett Memorial Lectures, 9th ser., Perugia 1995. Cambridge: D. S. Brewer.

Bolton, Brenda. 1981. "*Vitae matrum:* A Further Aspect of the *Frauenfrage.*" 1978. Reprinted in Baker 1981, 253–74.

Bornstein, Diane, ed. 1977. *The Middle English Translation of Christine de Pisan's "Livre du corps de policie."* Middle English Texts 7. Heidelberg: Carl Winter.

———, ed. 1978. *Distaves and Dames: Renaissance Treatises For and About Women*. New York: Delmar, Scholars' Facsimiles & Reprints.

———. 1983. *The Lady in the Tower: Medieval Courtesy Literature for Women*. Hamden, Conn.: Archon.

Boureau, Alain, ed. 1989. *The Culture of Print: Power and the Uses of Print in Early Modern Europe*. Trans. Lydia G. Cochrane. Oxford: Polity Press.

Boyle, Leonard E. 1985. "The Fourth Lateran Council and Manuals of Popular Theology." In Heffernan 1985b, 30–60.

Bradley, Ritamary. 1993. "Julian of Norwich." Vol. 9, chap. 23, pt. 4, of Hartung and Severs 1967–.

Brady, Mary Teresa, ed. 1954a. "*The Pore Caitif:* Edited from MS Harley 2336 with Introduction and Notes." Ph.D. diss., Fordham University.

———. 1954b. "*The Pore Caitif:* An Introductory Study." *Traditio* 10:529–48.

———. 1957. "The Apostles and the Creed in Manuscripts of *The Pore Caitif.*" *Speculum* 32:323–25.

———. 1980. "Rolle's *Form of Living* and *The Pore Caitif.*" *Traditio* 36:426–35.

Bramley, H. R., ed. 1884. *The Psalter of the Psalms of David and Certain Canticles, with a Translation and Exposition in English by Richard Rolle of Hampole*. Oxford: Clarendon Press.

Braswell, Laurel. 1964. "The South English Legendary Collection: A Study in Middle English Religious Literature of the 13th and 14th Centuries." Ph.D. diss., University of Toronto.

———. 1986. "Utilitarian and Scientific Prose." In Edwards 1986, 337–87.

Bressie, Ramona. 1928–29. "The Date of Thomas Usk's *Testament of Love*." *Modern Philology* 26:17–29.

Brewer, Ebenezer Cobham. 1989. *Brewer's Dictionary of Phrase and Fable*. Ed. Ivor H. Evans. 14th ed. London: Cassell.

Bristol, Michael D. 1985. *Carnival and Theatre: Plebeian Culture and the Structure of Authority in Renaissance England*. London: Methuen.

Brockwell, Charles W., Jr. 1985. *Bishop Reginald Pecock and the Lancastrian Church: Securing the Foundations of Cultural Authority*. Lewiston, N.Y.: Edwin Mellen Press.

Brown, Carleton, and Rossell Hope Robbins. 1943. *The Index of Middle English Verse*. New York: Columbia University Press.

Brownlee, Marina S., Kevin Brownlee, and Stephen G. Nichols, eds. 1991. *The New Medievalism*. Baltimore: Johns Hopkins University Press.

Brownrigg, Linda, ed. 1990. *Medieval Book Production: Assessing the Evidence*. Proceedings of the Second Conference of the Seminar in the History of the Book to 1500, Oxford, July 1988. Los Altos Hills, Calif.: Anderson-Lovelace & Red Gull Press.

Bruns, Gerald L. 1980. "The Originality of the Texts in a Manuscript Culture." *Comparative Literature* 32:113–29.

Bühler, Curt F., ed. 1938. "A Lollard Tract: On Translating the Bible into English." *Medium Ævum* 7:167–83.

———. 1950. "The *Liber de Dictis Philosophorum* and Common Proverbs in George Ashby's Poems." *PMLA* 65.1:282–89.

———. 1960. *The Fifteenth-Century Book: The Scribes, the Painters, the Decorators*. Philadelphia: University of Pennsylvania Press.

Bullough, Vern L. 1966. *The Development of Medicine as a Profession: The Contribution of the Medieval University to Modern Medicine*. Basel: S. Karger.

———. 1971. "Chauliac, Guy de." In *Dictionary of Scientific Biography*, ed. Charles C. Gillespie, 3:218–19. New York: Charles Scribner's Sons.

Burke, Seán. 1995. *Authorship from Plato to the Postmodern: A Reader*. Edinburgh: Edinburgh University Press.

Burkitt, F. C., ed. 1967. *The Book of Rules of Tyconius*. Texts and Studies Series 3.1. Cambridge: Cambridge University Press. 1894. Reprint, Nedeln: Kraus.

Burnley, David, and Tajima Matsuji. 1994. *The Language of Middle English Literature*. Annotated Bibliographies of Old and Middle English Literature 1. Cambridge: D. S. Brewer.

Burnley, J. D. 1985. "Chaucer, Usk, and Geoffrey of Vinsauf." *Neophilologus* 69:284–93.

Burrow, John A. 1971. *Ricardian Poetry: Chaucer, Gower, Langland, and the "Gawain" Poet*. London: Routledge & Kegan Paul.

———. 1977. "Fantasy and Language in *The Cloud of Unknowing*." *Essays in Criticism* 27:283–98.

———. 1986. *The Ages of Man: A Study in Medieval Writing and Thought*. Oxford: Clarendon Press.

———. 1994. "Thomas Hoccleve." In Seymour 1994, 185–248.

———. 1997. "Hoccleve and the Middle French Poets." In Cooper and Mapstone 1997, 35–49.

Burrow, John A., and Thorlac Turville-Petre, eds. 1996. *A Book of Middle English*. 2d ed. Oxford: Basil Blackwell.

Byles, A.T.P., ed. 1937. *The Book of Fayttes of Armes and of Chyualrye*. EETS, o.s., 189. (Reprint 1971.)

Bynum, Caroline Walker. 1982. *Jesus as Mother: Studies in the Spirituality of the High Middle Ages*. Berkeley and Los Angeles: University of California Press.

———. 1987. *Holy Feast and Holy Fast: The Religious Significance of Food to Medieval Women*. Berkeley and Los Angeles: University of California Press.

Cadden, Joan. 1993. *The Meanings of Sex Difference in the Middle Ages: Medicine, Natural Philosophy, and Culture*. Cambridge: Cambridge University Press.

Caie, Graham D. 1976. "The Significance of the Early Chaucer Manuscript Glosses (with Special Reference to the 'Wife of Bath's Prologue')." *Chaucer Review* 10:350–60.

Calin, William. 1994. *The French Tradition and the Literature of Medieval England*. Toronto: University of Toronto Press.

Calkins, Robert G. 1983. *Illuminated Books of the Middle Ages*. Ithaca: Cornell University Press.

Cameron, Louis, ed. 1980. *The Commonplace Book of Robert Reynes of Acle: An Edition of Tanner MS 407*. New York: Garland.

Camille, Michael. 1989. *The Gothic Idol: Ideology and Image-Making in Medieval Art*. Cambridge: Cambridge University Press.

———. 1991. "Gothic Signs and the Surplus: The Kiss on the Cathedral." In *Contexts: Style and Values in Medieval Art and Literature*, Yale French Studies, Special Edition, ed. Daniel Poirion and Nancy Freeman Regalado, 151–70. New Haven, Conn.: Yale University Press.

———. 1996. "Philological Iconoclasm: Edition and Image in the *Vie de Saint Alexis*." In *Medievalism and the Modernist Temper*, ed. R. Howard Bloch and Stephen G. Nichols, 371–401. Baltimore: Johns Hopkins University Press.

Campbell, P.G.C. 1925. "Christine de Pisan en Angleterre." *Révue de littérature comparée* 5:659–70.

Canitz, A.E.C. 1990. "The Prologue to the *Eneados*: Gavin Douglas's Directions for Reading." *Studies in Scottish Literature* 25:1–22.

———. 1991. "From *Aeneid* to *Eneados*: Theory and Practice of Gavin Douglas's Translation." *Mediaevalia et Humanistica*, n.s., 17:81–99.

Cannon, Christopher. 1996. "The Myth of Origin and the Making of Chaucer's English." *Speculum* 71:646–75.

Caretta, Vincent. 1981. "*The Kingis Quair* and *The Consolation of Philosophy*." *Studies in Scottish Literature* 16:14–28.

Carley, J. P., and Colin Tite, eds. 1997. *Books and Collectors, 1200–1700*. London: British Library.

Carlson, David. 1993a. "Chaucer's Boethius and Thomas Usk's *Testament of Love*: Politics and Love in the Chaucerian Tradition." In *The Centre and Its Compass: Studies in Medieval Literature in Honor of Professor John Leyerle*, Studies in Medieval Culture 33, ed. Robert Taylor et al., 29–70. Kalamazoo, Mich.: Medieval Institute.

———. 1993b. *English Humanist Books: Writers and Patrons, Manuscript and Print, 1475–1525*. Toronto: University of Toronto Press.

———. 1995. "Chaucer, Humanism, and Printing: Conditions of Authorship in Fifteenth-Century England." *University of Toronto Quarterly* 64:274–88.

Carretta, Vincent. 1981. "*The Kingis Quair* and *The Consolation of Philosophy*." *Studies in Scottish Literature* 16:14–28.

Carruthers, Mary J. 1990. *The Book of Memory: A Study of Memory in Medieval Culture*. Cambridge: Cambridge University Press.

Cary, G. 1956. *The Medieval Alexander*, ed. D.J.A. Ross. Cambridge: Cambridge University Press. (Reprint 1967.)

Catto, Jeremy. 1985. "Religious Changes Under Henry V." In *Henry the Fifth: The Practice of Kingship,* ed. G. I. Harriss, 97–116. Oxford: Clarendon Press.

Cavanaugh, Susan H. 1984. "A Study of Books Privately Owned in England, 1300–1450." Ph.D. diss., University of Pennsylvania.

Cerquiglini, Bernard. 1989. *Éloge de la variante: Histoire critique de la philologie.* Paris: Éditions du Seuil.

Chambers, Raymond W. 1932. *On the Continuity of English Prose from Alfred to More and His School.* EETS, o.s., 191A. (Reprint 1966).

Chambers, Raymond W., and Marjorie Daunt, eds. 1931. *A Book of London English, 1384–1425.* Oxford: Clarendon Press.

Chazan, Robert, ed. 1980. *Church, State, and Jew in the Middle Ages.* New York: Behrman House.

Chesnutt, Michael. 1987. "Minstrel Reciters and the Enigma of the Middle English Romance." *Culture and History* 2:48–67.

Cheyfitz, Eric. 1991. *The Poetics of Imperialism: Translation and Colonization from "The Tempest" to "Tarzan."* New York: Oxford University Press.

Christianson, C. Paul. 1989. "Evidence for the Study of London's Late Medieval Manuscript-Book Trade." In Griffiths and Pearsall 1989, 87–108.

———. 1990. *A Directory of London Stationers and Book Artisans, 1350–1500.* New York: Bibliographical Society of America.

Cigman, Gloria, ed. 1989. *Lollard Sermons,* introd. Jeremy Griffiths. EETS, o.s., 294.

———. 1996. "'Comoun Mater and Hierr Witt': The Preacher's Task." In Ellis and Tixier 1996, 84–99.

Clanchy, M. T. 1983. *England and Its Rulers, 1066–1272: Foreign Lordship and National Identity.* Oxford: Clarendon Press.

———. 1993. *From Memory to Written Record: England 1066–1307.* 2d ed. Oxford: Clarendon Press.

Clark, John. 1978. "*The Cloud of Unknowing,* Walter Hilton and St. John of the Cross: A Comparison." *Downside Review* 96:61–78.

———. 1980. "Sources and Theology in *The Cloud of Unknowing.*" *Downside Review* 98:83–109.

Clark, John, and Cheryl Taylor, ed. 1987. *Walter Hilton's Latin Writings.* 2 vols. Analecta cartusiana 124. Salzburg: Universität Salzburg, Institut für Anglistik und Amerikanistik.

Coakley, John. 1991. "Friars as Confidants of Holy Women: Medieval Dominican Hagiography." In *Images of Sainthood in Medieval Europe,* ed. Renate Blumenfeld-Kosinski and Timea Szell, 222–46. Ithaca: Cornell University Press.

Cohen-Mushlin, Aliza. 1990. "The Twelfth-Century Scriptorium of Frankenthal." In Brownrigg 1990, 85–102.

Coldewey, John C. 1994. "The Non-Cycle Plays and the East Anglian Tradition." In *The Cambridge Companion to Medieval English Theatre,* ed. Richard Beadle, 189–210. Cambridge: Cambridge University Press.

Coldicott, Diana K. 1989. *Hampshire Nunneries.* Chichester: Phillimore.

Coldwell, D.F.C., ed. 1957–64. *Virgil's "Aeneid" Translated into Scottish Verse by Gavin Douglas.* 4 vols. Scottish Text Society 25, 27, 28, 30. Edinburgh: Blackwood.

Coleman, Janet. 1981. *Medieval Readers and Writers, 1350–1400.* English Literature in History. London: Hutchinson.

Coleman, Joyce. 1990. "The Solace of Hearing: Late Medieval Views on the Reading Aloud of Literature." *Scandinavian Yearbook of Folklore* 46:123–34.

———. 1996. *Public Reading and the Reading Public in Late Medieval England and France.* Cambridge: Cambridge University Press.

Coletti, Theresa. 1990. "Reading REED: History and the Records of Early English Drama." In Patterson 1990, 248–84.

———. 1991. "'Fragmentation and Redemption': Dramatic Records, History, and the Dream of Wholeness." *Envoi* 3:1–13.

Colish, Marcia L. 1983. *The Mirror of Language: A Study in the Medieval Theory of Knowledge.* Rev. ed. Lincoln: University of Nebraska Press.

Colledge, Edmund, and James Walsh, eds. 1978. *A Book of Showings to the Anchoress Julian of Norwich.* 2 vols. Studies and Texts 35. Toronto: Pontifical Institute of Mediaeval Studies.

Collins, Marie. 1985. "Will and the Penitents, B X 420–35." *Leeds Studies in English* 16:290–308.

Cooper, Helen, and Sally Mapstone, eds. 1997. *The Long Fifteenth Century: Essays for Douglas Gray.* Oxford: Clarendon Press.

Copeland, Rita. 1987. "Rhetoric and Vernacular Translation in the Middle Ages." *SAC* 9:41–75.

———. 1991. *Rhetoric, Hermeneutics, and Translation in the Middle Ages: Academic Traditions and Vernacular Texts.* Cambridge: Cambridge University Press.

———. 1993. "Rhetoric and the Politics of the Literal Sense in Medieval Literary Theory: Aquinas, Wyclif, and the Lollards." In *Interpretation: Medieval and Modern,* J.A.W. Bennett Memorial Lectures, 8th ser., Perugia, 1992, ed. Piero Boitani, 1–22. Cambridge: D. S. Brewer.

———. 1994. "Medieval Theory and Criticism." In *The Johns Hopkins Guide to Literary Theory and Criticism,* ed. Michael Groden and Martin Kreiswirth, 500–508. Baltimore: Johns Hopkins University Press.

———. 1996. "William Thorpe and His Lollard Community: Intellectual Labor and the Representation of Dissent." In Hanawalt and Wallace 1996, 199–221.

Coss, Peter. 1985. "Aspects of Cultural Diffusion in Medieval England: The Early Romances, Local Society, and Robin Hood." *Past and Present* 108:35–37.

Courtenay, William J. 1987. *Schools and Scholars in Fourteenth-Century England.* Princeton: Princeton University Press.

Craig, Hardin, ed. 1916. *The Works of John Metham.* EETS, o.s., 132.

Craigie, W. A., ed. 1923. *The Asloan Manuscript: A Miscellany in Prose and Verse Written by John Asloan in the Reign of James the Fifth.* Vol. 1. Scottish Text Society, n.s., 14. Edinburgh: Blackwood.

Crampton, Georgia Ronan, ed. 1994. *The "Shewings" of Julian of Norwich.* TEAMS. Middle English Texts Series. Kalamazoo, Mich.: Medieval Institute.

Crawford, Robert, ed. 1998. *The Scottish Invention of English Literature.* Cambridge: Cambridge University Press.

Crane, Mary Thomas. 1993. *Framing Authority: Sayings, Self, and Society in Sixteenth-Century England.* Princeton: Princeton University Press.

Crane, Susan. 1992. "The Writing Lesson of 1381." In Hanawalt 1992, 201–21.

Crittall, Elizabeth, and R. B. Pugh, eds. 1956. "The Religious Houses of Wiltshire." In *A History of Wiltshire,* vol. 3, Victoria History of the Counties of England, Institute of Historical Research, 150–397. London: Oxford University Press.

Cropp, Glynnis M. 1987. "*Le Livre de Boece de Consolacion:* From Translation to Glossed Text." In Minnis 1987, 63–88.

Crosby, Ruth. 1942. "Robert Mannyng of Brunne: A New Biography." *PMLA* 57:15–28.

Cunningham, Ian C. 1994. "The Asloan Manuscript." In *The Renaissance in Scotland: Studies in Literature, Religion, History, and Culture Offered to John Durkan,* ed. A. A. MacDonald, Michael Lynch, and Ian B. Cowan, 107–35. Leiden: E. J. Brill.

Curnow, Maureen, ed. 1975. "The *Livre de la cité des dames* of Christine de Pisan: A Critical Edition." Ph.D. diss., Vanderbilt University.

Curtius, Ernst Robert. 1990. *European Literature and the Latin Middle Ages*. Trans. Willard R. Trask. 1953. Reprint, with new epilogue, Princeton: Princeton University Press.

Cutts, Cecilia. 1944. "The Croxton Play: An Anti-Lollard Piece." *Modern Language Quarterly* 5:45–60.

Danchin, Pierre. 1994. "Le développement du spectaculaire sur le théâtre anglais (1660–1800): Le rôle des prologues et épilogues." *Medieval English Theatre* 16 (special issue, *Spectacle in Early Theatre: England and France*): 166–76.

d'Ardenne, S.R.T.O., ed. 1961. *The Liflade ant te Passiun of Seinte Iuliene*. EETS, o.s., 248.

Darnton, Robert. 1986. "First Steps Towards a History of Reading." *Australian Journal of French Studies* 23:5–30.

David, Alfred, and Helen Phillips, eds. Forthcoming. *Chaucer: The Minor Poems*. Vol. 2 of *The Variorum Chaucer*. Norman: University of Oklahoma Press.

Davis, Natalie Zemon. 1975. *Society and Culture in Early Modern France*. Stanford: Stanford University Press.

Davis, Norman, ed. 1970. *Non-Cycle Plays and Fragments*. EETS, suppl. ser., 1.

———, ed. 1971–76. *Paston Letters and Papers of the Fifteenth Century*. 2 vols. Oxford: Clarendon Press.

———, ed. 1979. *Non-Cycle Plays and the Winchester Dialogues*. Leeds: University of Leeds, School of English.

d'Avril, François, and Patricia Danz Stirneman. 1981. *Manuscrits enluminés d'origine insulaire VIIe–XXe siècle*. Paris: Bibliothèque Nationale.

Deanesly, Margaret. 1920. *The Lollard Bible and Other Medieval Biblical Versions*. Cambridge: Cambridge University Press.

Debus, Allen G. 1967. *[Elias Ashmole] Theatrum chemicum Britannicum*. New York and London: Johnson Reprint Co..

de Certeau, Michel. 1984. *The Practice of Everyday Life*. Trans. Steven Rendall. Berkeley and Los Angeles: University of California Press.

de Hamel, Christopher. 1994. *A History of Illuminated Manuscripts*. London: Phaidon.

Delany, Sheila. 1990. *Medieval Literary Politics: Shapes of Ideology*. Manchester: Manchester University Press.

———, trans. 1992. *A Legend of Holy Women: Osbern Bokenham: "Legends of Holy Women."* Notre Dame, Ind.: University of Notre Dame Press.

———. 1994. *The Naked Text: Chaucer's "Legend of Good Women."* Berkeley and Los Angeles: University of California Press.

———. 1996. "The Friar as Critic: Bokenham Reads Chaucer." In Boitani and Torti 1996, 63–79.

———. 1998. *Impolitic Bodies: Poetry, Saints, and Society in Fifteenth-Century England, the Work of Osbern Bokenham*. Oxford: Oxford University Press.

de Looze, Laurence. 1997. *Pseudo-Autobiography in the Fourteenth Century: Jaun Ruiz, Guillaume de Machaut, Jean Froissart, and Geoffrey Chaucer*. Gainesville: University Presses of Florida.

de Lubac, Henri. 1959–64. *Exégèse médiévale: Les quatre sens de l'écriture*. 4 vols. Paris: Aubier.

de Man, Paul. 1979. *Allegories of Reading: Figural Language in Rousseau, Nietzsche, Rilke, and Proust*. New Haven: Yale University Press.

———. 1986. *The Resistance to Theory*. With a foreword by Wlad Godzich. Minneapolis: University of Minnesota Press.

Denise, Mary. 1958. "*The Orcherd of Syon*: An Introduction." *Traditio* 14:269–93.

Derrida, Jacques. 1981. *Dissemination*. Trans. Barbara Johnson. Chicago: University of Chicago Press.

———. 1987. *The Post Card: From Socrates to Freud and Beyond.* Trans. Alan Bass. Chicago: University of Chicago Press.

Despres, Denise L. 1996. "Ecstatic Reading and Missionary Mysticism: *The Orcherd of Syon.*" In Voaden 1996b, 141–60.

d'Evelyn, Charlotte, ed. 1921. *Meditations on the Life and Passion of Christ.* EETS, o.s., 158.

———. 1959. *"The South English Legendary": Notes.* EETS, o.s., 244.

d'Evelyn, Charlotte, and Anna J. Mill, eds. 1956. *The South English Legendary.* 2 vols. EETS, o.s., 235, 236.

Dillon, Janette. 1996. "Holy Women and Their Confessors or Confessors and Their Holy Women? Margery Kempe and Continental Tradition." In Voaden 1996b, 115–40.

Dinshaw, Carolyn. 1989. *Chaucer's Sexual Poetics.* Madison: University of Wisconsin Press.

Diverres, A. H. 1984. "The Life of Saint Melor." In *Medieval French Textual Studies in Memory of T. B. W. Reid,* Anglo-Norman Text Society Occasional Publications Series 1, ed. Ian Short, 41–53. London: Anglo-Norman Text Society.

Dobell, William. 1924. *"Philomena": A Poem by John Peckham, O.F.M., Archbishop of Canterbury: The Latin Text with an English Version.* London: Burns, Oates & Washbourne.

Donoghue, Daniel. 1990. "Laȝamon's Ambivalence." *Speculum* 65:537–63.

Donovan, Claire. 1991. *The de Brailes Hours: Shaping the Book of Hours in Thirteenth-Century Oxford.* Toronto: University of Toronto Press.

Doubleday, H. A., et al., eds. 1900–14. *A History of Hampshire and the Isle of Wight.* 6 vols. Victoria History of the Counties of England. London: Constable & Co. (Reprint 1973.)

Doyle, A. I. 1974. "The Shaping of the Vernon and Simeon Manuscripts." In *Chaucer and Middle English Studies in Honour of Rossell Hope Robbins,* ed. Beryl Rowland, 328–41. London: Allen & Unwin.

———. 1982. "The Manuscripts." In Lawton 1982, 88–100.

———. 1983a. "English Books in and out of Court from Edward III to Henry VII." In Scattergood and Sherborne 1983, 163–81.

———. 1983b. "Retrospect and Prospect." In Pearsall 1983, 142–46.

———. 1987. *Introduction to the Vernon Manuscript: A Facsimile of Bodleian Library Oxford, MS. Eng Poet a.1.* Cambridge: D. S. Brewer.

———. 1989. "Publication by Members of the Religious Orders." In Griffiths and Pearsall 1989, 109–23.

———. 1990. "Book Production by the Monastic Orders in England (*c.* 1375–1530): Assessing the Evidence." In Brownrigg 1990, 1–19.

Doyle, A. I., and M. B. Parkes. 1978. "The Production of Copies of the *Canterbury Tales* and the *Confessio Amantis* in the early Fifteenth Century." In Parkes and Watson 1978, 163–210. (Reprinted in Parkes 1991, 201–48.)

Dragonetti, Roger. 1980. *La vie de la lettre au Moyen Âge (Le Conte du Graal).* Paris: Éditions du Seuil.

———. 1984. "Joufroi, Count of Poitiers and Lord of Cocaigne." *Yale French Studies* 67:95–119.

Dreves, G. M., Clemens Blume, and H. M. Banister, eds. 1886–1922. *Analecta Hymnica Medii Aevii.* 55 vols. Leipzig: Reisland.

Dronke, Peter. "Poetic Originality in *The Wars of Alexander.*" In Cooper and Mapstone 1997, 123–39.

Duffy, Eamon. 1992. *The Stripping of the Altars: Traditional Religion in England, c. 1400–c. 1580.* New Haven: Yale University Press.

Duggan, Hoyt N. 1994. *The Piers Plowman Electronic Archive.* http://jefferson.village.virginia.edu/piers/archive.goals.html

Duggan, Hoyt N., and Thorlac Turville-Petre, eds. 1989. *The Wars of Alexander.* EETS, s.s., 10.

Duncan, A.A.M., ed. 1997. John Barbour, *The Bruce: An Edition with Translation and Notes.* Edinburgh: Canongate.

Duncan, Edgar H. 1968. "The Literature of Alchemy and Chaucer's Canon's Yeoman's Tale: Framework, Theme, and Characters." *Speculum* 43:633–56.

Dundas, Alan, ed. 1991. *The Blood Libel Legend: A Casebook in Anti-Semitic Folklore.* Madison: University of Wisconsin Press.

Dutschke, C. W. (with the assistance of R. H. Rouse, Sara S. Hodson, et al.). 1989. *Guide to Medieval and Renaissance Manuscripts in the Huntington Library.* 2 vols. San Marino, Calif.: Huntington Library Publications.

Dutton, Anne. 1995. "Women's Use of Religious Literature in England, 1350–1500." Ph.D. diss., University of York.

Dyboski, R., and Z. M. Arend, eds. 1936. *"Knyghthode and Bataile": A XVth Century Verse Paraphrase of Flavius Vegetius Renatus' Treatise "De re Militari."* EETS, o.s., 201.

Dyer, Christopher. 1989. *Standards of Living in the Later Middle Ages: Social Change in England, c. 1200–1520.* Cambridge: Cambridge University Press.

Easting, Robert, ed. 1989. *Saint Patrick's Purgatory: Two Versions of "Owayne Miles" and "The Vision of William of Stranton."* EETS, o.s., 298.

Ebin, Lois. 1971–72. "John Barbour's *Bruce*: Poetry, History, and Propaganda." *Studies in Scottish Literature* 9:218–42.

———. 1985. *John Lydgate.* Boston: Twayne.

Echard, Siân. 1998. "With Carmen's Help: Latin Authorities in the *Confessio Amantis*." *Studies in Philology* 95:1–40.

Echard, Siân, and Claire Fanger, trans. 1991. *The Latin Verses in the "Confessio Amantis": An Annotated Translation.* East Lansing, Mich.: Colleagues Press.

Edwards, A.S.G. 1977. "The Influence of Lydgate's *Fall of Princes, c.* 1440–1559: A Survey." *Mediaeval Studies* 39:424–39.

———, ed. 1986. *Middle English Prose: A Critical Guide to Major Authors and Genres.* 1984. Reprint, New Brunswick, N.J.: Rutgers University Press.

———. 1994. "The Transmission and Audience of Osbern Bokenham's *Legendys of Hooly Wummen*." In Minnis 1994, 157–67.

Edwards, A.S.G., and Carol Meale. 1993. "The Marketing of Printed Books in Late Medieval England." *The Library,* 6th ser., 15:95–124.

Edwards, A.S.G., and Derek Pearsall. 1989. "The Manuscripts of the Major English Poetic Texts." In Griffiths and Pearsall 1989, 257–78.

Eisenstein, Elizabeth L. 1979. *The Printing Press as an Agent of Change: Communications and Cultural Transformations in Early-Modern Europe.* 2 vols. Cambridge: Cambridge University Press.

Elam, Diane. 1992. *Romancing the Postmodern.* London: Routledge.

Ellis, Roger. 1980. "A Literary Approach to the Middle English Mystics." In *The Medieval Mystical Tradition in England,* vol. 1, ed. Marion Glasscoe, 99–119. Exeter: University of Exeter Press.

———. 1982a. "The Choices of the Translator in the Late Middle English Period." In Glasscoe 1982, 18–48.

———. 1982b. "'Flores ad Fabricandum . . . Coronam': An Investigation into the Uses of the Revelations of St. Bridget of Sweden in Fifteenth-Century England." *Medium Ævum* 51:163–86.

———. 1984. *Syon Abbey: The Spirituality of the English Bridgettines.* Analecta cartusiana 68.2. Salzburg: Universität Salzburg, Institut für Anglistik und Amerikanistik.

———, ed. 1989. *The Medieval Translator: The Theory and Practice of Translation in the Middle Ages: Papers Read at a Conference Held 20–23 August 1987 at the University of Wales Conference Centre, Gregynog Hall.* Cambridge: D. S. Brewer.

———. 1990. "Margery Kempe's Scribes and the Miraculous Books." In *Langland, the Mystics, and the Medieval English Religious Tradition: Essays in Honour of S. S. Hussey,* ed. Helen Phillips, 161–76. Cambridge: D. S. Brewer.

———, ed. 1991a. *The Medieval Translator II.* London: Centre for Medieval Studies, Queen Mary & Westfield College.

———, ed. 1991b. *Translation in the Middle Ages. New Comparison* 12 (special issue).

Ellis, Roger, and Ruth Evans, eds. 1994. *The Medieval Translator IV.* Binghampton, N.Y.: Medieval and Renaissance Texts and Studies, and Exeter: University of Exeter Press.

Ellis, Roger, and René Tixier, eds. 1996. *The Medieval Translator V.* Turnhout: Brepols.

Emmerson, Richard K. 1988. "Dramatic Developments: Some Recent Scholarship on Medieval Drama." *Envoi* 1:23–40.

Enders, Jody. 1992. *Rhetoric and the Origins of Medieval Drama.* Ithaca: Cornell University Press.

Engelsing, Rolf. 1973. *Analphabetentum und Lektüre: Zur Socialgeschichte des Lesens in Deutschland zwischen feudaler und industrieller Gesellschaft.* Stuttgart: J. B. Metzler.

Erler, Mary, and Maryanne Kowaleski. 1988. *Women and Power in the Middle Ages.* Athens: University of Georgia Press.

Evans, Murray J. 1995. *Rereading Middle English Romance: Manuscript, Layout, Decoration, and the Rhetoric of Composite Structure.* Montreal: McGill-Queen's University Press.

Evans, Ruth. 1994. "Translating Past Cultures?" In Ellis and Evans 1994, 20–45.

Evans, Ruth, and Lesley Johnson. 1991. "The Assembly of Ladies: A Maze of Feminist Sign Reading?" In *Feminist Criticism: Theory and Practice,* ed. Susan Sellers, 171–96. Hemel Hempstead: Harvester Wheatsheaf.

Evans, Trena. 1998. "Framing the Reader in/of John Metham's Work." Paper given at "Frames and Framing in Medieval, Renaissance, and Baroque Culture," conference organized by the Medieval and Renaissance Seminar, University of Western Ontario, March 6–7.

Everett, Dorothy. 1922–23. "The Middle English Prose Psalter of Richard Rolle of Hampole." *Modern Language Review* 17:217–27, 337–50; 18:381–93.

Faber, Johann, ed. 1536. *D. Richardi Pampolitani Anglosaxonis Eremitae . . . in Psalterium Davidicum. . . .* Cologne: Ex officina Melchioris Novesiani.

Farmer, D. H. 1978. *The Oxford Dictionary of Saints.* Oxford: Clarendon Press.

Fein, Susanna Greer. 1997. "Twelve-Line Stanza Forms in Middle English and the Date of *Pearl.*" *Speculum* 72:367–98.

Ferrante, Joan M. 1982. "Was Vernacular Poetic Practice a Response to Latin Language Theory?" *Romance Philology* 35:586–600.

———. 1997. *To the Glory of Her Sex: Women's Role in the Composition of Medieval Texts.* Bloomington: Indiana University Press.

Ferster, Judith. 1996. *Fictions of Advice: The Literature and Politics of Counsel in Late Medieval England.* Philadelphia: University of Pennsylvania Press.

Finnegan, M. Jeremy. 1962. *Scholars and Mystics.* Chicago: H. Regnery Co.

Finnegan, Ruth. 1977. *Oral Poetry: Its Nature, Significance, and Social Context.* Cambridge: Cambridge University Press.

Fisher, John H. 1964. *John Gower, Moral Philosopher and Friend of Chaucer.* New York: New York University Press.

———. 1977. "Chancery and the Emergence of Standard Written English in the Fifteenth Century." *Speculum* 52:870–99.

———. 1979. "Chancery Standard and Modern Written English." *Journal of the Society of Archivists* 6:136–44.

———. 1984. "Caxton and Chancery English." In Yeager 1984, 161–85.

———. 1988. "*Piers Plowman* and the Chancery Tradition." In Kennedy, Waldron, and Wittig 1988, 267–78.

———. 1992a. *The Importance of Chaucer*. Carbondale: Southern Illinois University Press.

———. 1992b. "A Language Policy for Lancastrian England." *PMLA* 107:1168–80.

———. 1996. *The Emergence of Standard English*. Lexington: University Press of Kentucky.

———, ed. (with Malcolm Richardson and Jane L. Fisher). 1984. *An Anthology of Chancery English*. Knoxville: University of Tennessee Press.

Fletcher, Alan J. 1994. "A Hive of Industry or a Hornet's Nest? MS Sidney Sussex 74 and Its Scribes." In Minnis 1994, 131–55.

Flutre, Louis-Fernand. 1962. *Tables des noms propres avec toutes leur variantes figurant dans les romans du Moyen Âge écrits en français ou en provençal et actuellement publiés ou analyses*. Poitiers: Centre d'Études Supérieres de la Civilisation Médiévale.

Foreville, Raymonde, and Gillian Keir, eds. and trans. 1987. *The Book of St. Gilbert*. Oxford: Clarendon Press.

Forshall, Josiah, and Frederic Madden, eds. 1850. *The Holy Bible, Containing the Old and New Testaments, with the Apocryphal Books, in the Earliest English Versions made from the Latin Vulgate by John Wycliffe and his Followers*. 4 vols. Oxford: Oxford University Press.

Foster, Frances A., ed. 1926. *A Stanzaic Life of Christ Compiled from Higden's "Polychronicon" and the "Legenda Aurea."* EETS, o.s., 166.

Foucault, Michel. 1977. *Language, Counter-Memory, Practice*. Ed. Daniel Bouchard; trans. Daniel Bouchard and Sherry Simon. Oxford: Basil Blackwell.

———. 1979. "What Is an Author?" Trans. Josué V. Harari. In *Textual Strategies: Perspectives in Post-Structuralist Criticism*, ed. Josué V. Harari, 141–60. Ithaca: Cornell University Press.

Fowler, David C. 1960. "John Trevisa and the English Bible." *Modern Philology* 58:81–98.

———. 1994. "John Trevisa." In Seymour 1994, 65–126.

———. 1995. *The Life and Times of John Trevisa, Medieval Scholar*. Seattle: University of Washington Press.

Fox, Alastair. 1989. *Politics and Literature in the Reigns of Henry VII and Henry VIII*. Oxford: Basil Blackwell.

Fox, Denton, ed. 1981. *The Poems of Robert Henryson*. Oxford: Clarendon Press.

———. 1984. "The Coherence of Henryson's Work." In Yeager 1984, 275–81.

Fradenburg, Louise. 1984. "Henryson Scholarship: The Recent Decades." In Yeager 1984, 65–92.

———. 1991. *City, Marriage, and Tournament: The Arts of Rule in Late Medieval Scotland*. Madison: University of Wisconsin Press.

Francis, W. Nelson, ed. 1942. *The Book of Vices and Virtues*. EETS, o.s., 217.

Frantzen, Allen J. 1990. *Desire for Origins: New Language, Old English, and Teaching the Tradition*. New Brunswick, N.J.: Rutgers University Press.

Fredeman, Jane Cowan. 1972. "John Capgrave's Life of St. Gilbert of Sempringham." *Bulletin of the John Rylands Library of Manchester* 55:112–45.

Freeman, Michelle A. 1979. *The Poetics of "Translatio studii" and "Conjointure": Chrétien de Troyes' "Cligés."* French Forum Monographs 12. Lexington, Ky.: French Forum.

Fristedt, S. L., ed. 1953. *The Wycliffe Bible*. Pt. 1. Stockholm Studies in English 4. Stockholm: Almqvist & Wiksell.

Furnivall, F. J., ed. 1866. *The Book of Quinte Essence*. EETS, o.s., 16.

———, ed. 1868. *The Babees Book*. EETS, o.s., 32.

———, ed. 1887. *The Story of England by Robert Manning of Brunne*. Rolls Series 87. 2 vols. London: Longman.

———, ed. 1897. *Hoccleve's Works: "The Regement of Princes" and Fourteen Minor Poems*. EETS, e.s., 72. (Reprint 1975.)

Furnivall, F. J., and I. Gollancz, eds. 1970. *Hoccleve's Works: The Minor Poems.* 1892, 1925. Reprint, rev. Jerome Mitchell and A. I. Doyle, EETS, e.s., 61, 73.

Gallo, Ernest, ed. 1971. *The "Poetria Nova" and Its Sources in Early Rhetorical Doctrine.* The Hague: Mouton.

Gallop, Jane. 1982. "Encore Encore." In *Feminism and Psychoanalysis: The Daughter's Seduction,* 43–55. London: Macmillan.

Geary, Patrick. 1978. *Furta Sacra: Thefts of Relics in the Central Middle Ages.* Princeton: Princeton University Press.

Gibson, Gail McMurray. 1989. *The Theater of Devotion: East Anglian Drama and Society in the Late Middle Ages.* Chicago: University of Chicago Press.

Gilchrist, Roberta. 1994. *Gender and Material Culture: The Archaeology of Religious Women.* London: Routledge.

Gillespie, Vincent. 1980. "*Doctrina* and *Predicacio*: The Design and Function of Some Pastoral Manuals." *Leeds Studies in English,* n.s., 11:36–50.

———. 1982. "Mystic's Foot: Rolle and Affectivity." In Glasscoe 1982, 199–230.

———. 1984. "'Lukynge in Haly Bukes': *Lectio* in Some Late Medieval Spiritual Miscellanies." In Hogg 1984, 1–27.

———. 1987. "Strange Images of Death: The Passion in Later Medieval English Devotional and Mystical Writing." In *Zeit, Tod, und Ewigkeit in der Renaissance Literatur,* vol. 3, Analecta cartusiana 117, ed. James Hogg, 111–59. Salzburg: Universität Salzburg, Institut für Anglistik und Amerikanistik.

———. 1989. "Vernacular Books of Religion." In Griffiths and Pearsall 1989, 317–44.

———. 1994. "Thy Will Be Done: *Piers Plowman* and the *Pater Noster*." In Minnis 1994, 95–120.

Glasscoe, Marion, ed. 1982. *The Medieval Mystical Tradition in England.* Vol. 2. Exeter: University of Exeter Press.

———, ed. 1984. *The Medieval Mystical Tradition in England,* Vol. 3. Cambridge: D. S. Brewer. (Reprint 1988.)

———, ed. 1987. *The Medieval Mystical Tradition in England.* Vol. 4. Cambridge: D. S. Brewer.

———. 1989. "Visions and Revisions: A Further Look at the Manuscripts of Julian of Norwich." *Studies in Bibliography* 42:103–20.

———, ed. 1993. *Julian of Norwich, A Revelation of Love.* 1976. Reprint, Exeter: University of Exeter Press.

Glauning, Otto, ed. 1900. *Lydgate's Minor Poems: The Two Nightingale Poems.* EETS, e.s., 80.

Goering, Joseph. 1992. *William de Montibus (c. 1140–1213): The Schools and the Literature of Pastoral Care.* Studies and Texts 108. Toronto: Pontifical Institute of Mediaeval Studies.

Golding, Brian. 1995. *Gilbert of Sempringham and the Gilbertine Order, c. 1130–c. 1300.* Oxford: Clarendon Press.

Goldstein, R. James. 1986. "Freedom Is a Noble Thing! The Ideological Project of John Barbour's *Bruce*." In *Scottish Language and Literature, Medieval and Renaissance, Fourth International Conference 1984—Proceedings,* ed. Dietrich Strauss and Horst W. Drescher, 193–206. Frankfurt: Peter Lang.

Goodman, Anthony. 1981. "The Piety of John Brunham's Daughter, of Lynn." 1978. Reprinted in Baker 1981, 347–58.

Gordon, Benjamin Lee. 1959. *Medieval and Renaissance Medicine.* New York: Philosophical Library.

Görlach, Manfred. 1974. *The Textual Tradition of the South English Legendary.* Leeds Texts and Monographs, n.s., 6. Leeds: Leeds Studies in English.

Gottfried, Robert S. 1986. *Doctors and Medicine in Medieval England, 1340–1530*. Princeton: Princeton University Press.

Grady, Frank. 1995. "The Lancastrian Gower and the Limits of Exemplarity." *Speculum* 70:552–75.

———. 1996. "Chaucer Reading Langland: *The House of Fame*." *SAC* 18:3–23.

Grant, Edward, ed. 1974. *A Source Book in Medieval Science*. Cambridge, Mass.: Harvard University Press.

Grantley, Darryl. 1983. "Producing Miracles." In *Aspects of Early English Drama*, ed. Paula Neuss, 78–91. Cambridge: D. S. Brewer.

Gray, Douglas. 1979. *Robert Henryson*. Medieval and Renaissance Authors. Leiden: E. J. Brill.

———. 1996. "Robert Henryson." In Seymour 1996a, 147–72.

Greatrex, J. 1990. "On Ministering to 'Certayne Devoute and Religiouse Women': Bishop Fox and the Benedictine Nuns of Winchester Diocese on the Eve of the Dissolution." In *Women in the Church*, Studies in Church History 27, ed. W. J. Shiels and D. Wood, 223–35. Oxford: Clarendon Press.

Green, Monica H. 1989. "Women's Medical Practice and Health Care in Medieval Europe." *Signs: Journal of Women in Culture and Society* 14:434–73.

———. 1992. "Obstetric and Gynecological Texts in Middle English." *SAC* 14:53–88.

Green, Richard Firth. 1980. *Poets and Princepleasers: Literature and the English Court in the Late Middle Ages*. Toronto: University of Toronto Press.

———. 1983. "Women in Chaucer's Audience." *Chaucer Review* 18:146–54.

———. Forthcoming. *A Crisis of Truth: Literature and Law in Ricardian England*. Philadelphia: University of Pennsylvania Press.

Green, V.H.H. 1945. *Bishop Reginald Pecock: A Study in Ecclesiastical History and Thought*. Cambridge: Cambridge University Press.

Greenberg, Cheryl. 1982. "John Shirley and the English Book Trade." *The Library*, 6th ser., 4:369–80.

Greenblatt, Stephen. 1997. "What Is the History of Literature?" *Critical Inquiry* 23:460–81.

Greentree, Rosemary. 1993. *Reader, Teller, and Teacher: The Narrator of Robert Henryson's "Moral Fables."* Scottish Studies 15. Frankfurt am Main: Peter Lang.

Greet, William Cabell, ed. 1927. *The Reule of Crysten Religioun*. EETS, o.s., 171.

Griffin, Nathaniel Edward. 1970. *Guido de Columnis, "Historia Destructionis Troiae."* 1936. Reprint, Medieval Academy Publications 26, Cambridge, Mass.: Medieval Academy.

Griffiths, Jeremy. 1992. "A Newly Identified Manuscript Inscribed by John Shirley." *The Library*, 6th ser., 14:83–93.

Griffiths, Jeremy, and Derek Pearsall, eds. 1989. *Book Production and Publishing in Britain, 1375–1475*. Cambridge: Cambridge University Press.

Griffiths, Ralph A. 1981. *The Reign of Henry VI and the Exercise of Royal Authority, 1422–1461*. Berkeley and Los Angeles: University of California Press.

Grigsby, J. L. 1963. "A New Source of the *Livre du Chevalier de la Tour Landry*." *Romania* 83:171–208.

Grundmann, Herbert. 1958. "Litteratus-illitteratus: Der Wandel einer Bildungsnorm vom Altertum zum Mittelalter." *Archiv für Kulturgeschichte* 40:1–65.

Guddat-Figge, Gisela. 1976. *Catalogue of Manuscripts Containing Middle English Romances*. Munich: W. Fink.

Gullick, Michael. 1995. "How Fast Did Scribes Write? Evidence from Romanesque Manuscripts." In *Making the Medieval Book: Techniques of Book Production*, Proceedings of the Fourth Conference of the Seminar in the History of the Book to 1500, Oxford, July 1992, ed. Linda Brownrigg, 39–58. Los Altos Hills, Calif.: Anderson-Lovelace & Red Gull Press.

Hadfield, Andrew. 1994. *Literature, Politics, and National Identity: Reformation to Renaissance*. Cambridge: Cambridge University Press.

Hahn, Thomas. 1998. "Early Middle English." In Wallace 1998, 61–91.

Halligan, Theresa A., ed. 1979. *The Booke of Gostlye Grace of Mechtild of Hackeborn*. Studies and Texts 46. Toronto: Pontifical Institute of Mediaeval Studies.

Hanawalt, Barbara A., ed. 1992. *Chaucer's England: Literature in Historical Context*. Minneapolis: University of Minnesota Press.

Hanawalt, Barbara A., and David Wallace, eds. 1996. *Bodies and Disciplines: Intersections of Literature and History in Fifteenth-Century England*. Minneapolis: University of Minnesota Press.

Hanna, Ralph, III. 1989a. "The Scribe of Huntington HM 114." *Studies in Bibliography* 42:120–33.

———. 1989b. "Sir Thomas Berkeley and His Patronage," *Speculum* 64:878–916.

———. 1994. "William Langland." In Seymour 1994, 127–84.

———. 1996. "Miscellaneity and Vernacularity: Conditions of Literary Production in Late Medieval England." In Nichols and Wenzel 1996, 37–52.

Hardman, Phillipa. 1978. "A Mediaeval 'Library *in Parvo.*'" *Medium Ævum* 47:262–73.

Harriss, G. L. 1960. "The Stuggle for Calais: An Aspect of the Rivalry Between Lancaster and York." *English Historical Review* 75:30–53.

Harris, Kate. 1983. "The Origins and Make-Up of Cambridge University Library MS Ff.1.6." *Transactions of the Cambridge Bibliographical Society* 8:299–333.

———. 1989. "Patrons, Buyers, and Owners: The Evidence for Ownership, and the Role of Book Owners in Book Production and the Book Trade." In Griffiths and Pearsall 1989, 163–99.

Harthan, John. 1982. *Books of Hours and Their Owners*. 1977. Reprint, London: Thames & Hudson.

Hartung, Albert E., and J. Burke Severs, eds. 1967–. *A Manual of the Writings in Middle English, 1050–1500*. 9 vols. to date. New Haven: Connecticut Academy of Arts and Sciences. (Vols. 1 and 2 ed. Severs; vols. 3–9 ed. Hartung.)

Harvey, E. Ruth, ed. 1984. *The Court of Sapience*. Toronto: University of Toronto Press.

Haug, Walter. 1996. *Vernacular Literary Theory in the Middle Ages: The German Evidence*. Trans. Joanna M. Catling. Cambridge: Cambridge University Press.

Hearne, T., ed. 1725. *Peter Langtoft's Chronicle (as Illustrated and Improv'd by Robert of Brunne) From the Death of Cadwalader to the End of King Edward the First's Reign*. 2 vols. Oxford: Printed at the Theater.

Heffernan, Thomas J. 1975. "A Middle English Poem on Lovedays." *Chaucer Review* 10:172–85.

———. 1985a. "The Authorship of the *Northern Homily Cycle:* The Liturgical Affiliation of the Sunday Gospel Pericopes as a Test." *Traditio* 41:289–309.

———, ed. 1985b. *The Popular Literature of Medieval England*. Knoxville: University of Tennessee Press.

———. 1990. "Orthodoxies *Redux:* The *Northern Homily Cycle* in the Vernon Manuscript and Its Textual Affiliations." In Pearsall 1990, 75–87.

Helgerson, Richard. 1992. *Forms of Nationhood: The Elizabethan Writing of England*. Chicago: University of Chicago Press.

Hellinga, Lotte. 1982. *Caxton in Focus: The Beginning of Printing in England*. London: British Library.

Hindman, Sandra, ed. 1991. *Printing the Written Word: The Social History of Books, Circa 1450–1520*. Ithaca: Cornell University Press.

Hirsh, John C. 1975. "Author and Scribe in *The Book of Margery Kempe*." *Medium Ævum* 44:145–50.

Hitchcock, Elsie Vaughan, ed. 1921. *"The Donet"* [. . .] *collated with "The Poore Mennis Myrrour."* EETS, o.s., 156.

———, ed. 1924. *The Folewer to the Donet*. EETS, o.s., 164.

Hodgson, Phyllis, ed. 1944. *"The Cloud of Unknowing" and "The Book of Privy Counselling."* EETS, o.s., 218.

———. 1964. *"The Orcherd of Syon* and the English Mystical Tradition." *Proceedings of the British Academy* 50:229–49.

Hodgson, Phyllis, and Gabriel Liegey, eds. 1966. *The Orcherd of Syon.* EETS, o.s., 258.

Hogg, James, ed. 1973–74. *The Speculum Devotorum of an Anonymous Carthusian of Sheen.* Analecta cartusiana 12–13. Salzburg: Universität Salzburg, Institut für Anglistik und Amerikanistik.

———, ed. 1984. *Spätmittelalterliche geistliche Literatur in der Nationalsprache.* Analecta cartusiana 106. Salzburg: Universität Salzburg, Institut für Anglistik und Amerikanistik.

———, ed. 1993. *Studies in St. Birgitta and the Brigittine Order.* 2 vols. Spiritualität Heute und Gestern, 19. Analecta cartusiana 35.10. Salzburg: Universität Salzburg, Institut für Anglistik und Amerikanistik.

Holmyard, E. J., ed. 1928. *The "Ordinall of Alchimy" by Thomas Norton of Birstoll; Being a Facsimile Reproduction from "Theatrum Chemicum Britannicum" with Annotations by Elias Ashmole.* London: Arnold.

Homan, Richard. 1986–87. "Devotional Themes in the Violence and Humour of the *Play of the Sacrament.*" *Comparative Drama* 20:327–41.

Horrall, Sarah M., gen. ed. 1978–90. *The Southern Version of "Cursor Mundi."* 4 vols. of 5 published, various eds. Ottawa: University of Ottawa Press. (Vol. 5 forthcoming.)

Horstmann, Carl, ed. 1887. *The Early South-English Legendary.* EETS, o.s., 87.

———. 1893. *"The Life of St. Katharine of Alexandria," by John Capgrave.* EETS, o.s., 100.

Howarth, Lisa J. 1996. "The Practice of Midwifery in Late Medieval England." Master's diss., Centre for Medieval Studies, University of York, England.

Hudson, Anne, ed. 1978. *Selections from English Wycliffite Writings.* Cambridge: Cambridge University Press. (Reprinted 1997, Medieval Academy Reprints for Teaching 38. Toronto: University of Toronto Press).

———. 1985. *Lollards and Their Books.* London: Hambledon.

———. 1986. "Wycliffite Prose." In Edwards 1986, 249–70.

———. 1988. *The Premature Reformation: Wycliffite Texts and Lollard History.* Oxford: Clarendon Press.

———. 1989. "Lollard Book Production." In Griffiths and Pearsall 1989, 125–42.

Hudson, Anne, and H. L. Spencer. 1984. "Old Author, New Work: The Sermons of MS Longleat 4." *Medium Ævum* 53:220–38.

Hughes, Jonathan. 1988. *Pastors and Visionaries: Religion and Secular Life in Late Medieval Yorkshire.* Woodbridge, Suffolk: Boydell.

Hull, Suzanne W. 1982. *Chaste, Silent, and Obedient: English Books for Women, 1475–1640.* San Marino, Calif.: Huntington Library Publications.

Hunt, R. W. 1980. "The Introduction to the *Artes* in the Twelfth Century." In *The History of Grammar in the Middle Ages: Collected Papers,* Amsterdam Studies in the Theory and History of Linguistic Science 5, ed. G. L. Bursill-Hall, 117–44. Amsterdam: John Benjamins.

Hunt, Simon. 1994. "An Edition of Tracts in Favour of Scriptural Translation and of Some Texts Connected with Lollard Vernacular Biblical Scholarship." Ph.D. diss., Oxford University.

Hunt, Tony. 1991. *Teaching and Learning Latin in Thirteenth-Century England.* 3 vols. Cambridge: D. S. Brewer.

Hutchinson, Ann M. 1989. "Devotional Reading in the Monastery and in the Late Medieval Household." In Sargent 1989, 215–27.

———. 1993. "*The Myrroure of Oure Ladye*: A Medieval Guide for Contemplatives." In Hogg 1993, 215–27.

———. 1995. "What the Nuns Read: Literary Evidence from the English Bridgettine House, Sion Abbey." *Mediaeval Studies* 57:205–22.

Hyams, Paul. 1974. "The Jewish Minority in Mediaeval England." *Journal of Jewish Studies* 25:270–93.

Irvine, Martin. 1994. *The Making of Textual Culture: "Grammatica" and Literary Theory, 305–1100.* Cambridge: Cambridge University Press.

Jack, R.D.S., ed. 1988. *The History of Scottish Literature.* Vol. 1, *Origins to 1660.* Aberdeen: Aberdeen University Press.

Jacob, E. F. 1968. "Reynold Pecock, Bishop of Chichester." In *Essays in Later Medieval History,* ed. E. F. Jacob, 1–34. Manchester: Manchester University Press.

Jacobus, Mary. 1986. *Reading Women: Essays in Feminist Criticism.* London: Methuen.

Jager, Eric. 1996. "The Book of the Heart: Reading and Writing the Medieval Subject." *Speculum* 71:1–26.

James, Clair F. 1993. "*The Kingis Quair*: The Plight of the Courtly Lover." In *New Readings of Late Medieval Love Poems,* ed. David Chamberlain, 95–118. Lanham, Md.: University Press of America.

Jankofsky, K. P., ed. 1992. *The South English Legendary: A Critical Assessment.* Tübingen: Franke Verlag.

Jansen, Sharon L. 1991. *Political Protest and Prophecy Under Henry VIII.* Woodbridge, Suffolk: Boydell.

Jardine, Lisa. 1993. *Erasmus, Man of Letters: The Construction of Charisma in Print.* Princeton: Princeton University Press.

Jeffrey, David L., and Brian J. Levy. 1990. *The Anglo-Norman Lyric: An Anthology.* Studies and Texts 93. Toronto: Pontifical Institute of Mediaeval Studies.

Johnson, Ian R. 1987. "Walton's Sapient Orpheus." In Minnis 1987, 139–68.

———. 1989. "Prologue and Practice: Middle English Lives of Christ." In Ellis 1989, 69–85.

———. 1990. "The Late-Medieval Theory and Practice of Translation in the Middle Ages with Special Reference to Some Middle English Lives of Christ." Ph.D. diss., University of Bristol.

———. 1994a. "Tales of a True Translator: Medieval Literary Theory, Anecdote and Autobiography in Osbern Bokenham's *Legendys of Hooly Wummen.*" In Ellis and Evans 1994, 104–24.

———. 1994b. "'This Brigous Questioun': Translating Free Will and Predestination in Walton's *Boethius* and Chaucer's *Troilus and Criseyde.*" *Carmina Philosophiae* 3:1–21.

———. 1996. "New Evidence for the Authorship of Walton's Boethius." *Notes and Queries,* n.s., 43, no. 1:19–21.

———. 1997. "Vernacular Valorizing: Functions and Fashionings of Literary Theory in Middle English Translation of Authority." In Beer 1997, 239–54.

Johnson, Lesley. 1995. "Etymologies, Genealogies, and Nationalities (Again)." In *Concepts of National Identity in the Middle Ages,* Leeds Texts and Monographs, n.s., 14, ed. Simon Forde, Lesley Johnson, and Alan V. Murray, 125–36. Leeds: University of Leeds, School of English.

Johnson, Lesley, and Jocelyn Wogan-Browne. 1998. "National History, World History, Women's History: Writers and Readers of English in Post-Conquest England." In Wallace 1998, 92–121.

Johnson, Lynn Staley. See Staley and Staley Johnson.

Jolliffe, P. S. 1974. *A Checklist of Middle English Prose Writings of Spiritual Guidance.* Subsidia Mediaevalia 2. Toronto: Pontifical Institute of Mediaeval Studies.

Jones, Michael K., and Malcolm G. Underwood. 1992. *The King's Mother: Lady Margaret Beaufort, Countess of Richmond and Derby*. Cambridge: Cambridge University Press.

Jones, Richard Foster. 1966. *The Triumph of the English Language*. Stanford: Stanford University Press.

Justice, Steven. 1994. *Writing and Rebellion: England in 1381*. Berkeley and Los Angeles: University of California Press.

Kane, George, ed. 1960. *Piers Plowman: The A Version*. London: Athlone.

Kane, George, and E. Talbot Donaldson. 1975. *Piers Plowman: The B Version: Will's Visions of Piers Plowman: Do-Well, Do-Better, and Do-Best*. London: Athlone Press.

Kantorowicz, Ernst. 1944. "The 'King's Advent.'" *Art Bulletin* 26:207–31.

Kaske, R. E. (with Arthur Groos and Michael Twomey). 1988. *Medieval Christian Literary Imagery: A Guide to Interpretation*. Toronto Medieval Bibliographies 11. Toronto: University of Toronto Press.

Kauffmann, Claus Michael. 1975. *Romanesque Manuscripts, 1066–1190: A Survey of Manuscripts Illuminated in the British Isles*. Vol. 3. London: Harvey Miller.

Keil, Gundolf, ed. 1976. *Chirurgia Magna Guidonis de Gauliaco*. Facsimile ed. Darmstadt: Wissenschaftliche Buchgesellschaft. (Orig. pub. Loudin, 1585.)

Keiser, George R. 1979. "Lincoln Cathedral Library MS. 91: Life and Milieu of the Scribe." *Studies in Bibliography* 32:158–79.

———. 1985. "Patronage and Piety in Fifteenth-Century England: Margaret, Duchess of Clarence, Symon Wynter, and Beineke MS 317." *Yale University Library Gazette* 60:32–46.

———. 1987. "The Mystics and the Early English Printers: The Economics of Devotionalism." In Glasscoe 1987, 9–26.

———. 1995. "Serving the Needs of Readers: Textual Division in Some Late-Medieval English Texts." In *New Science out of Old Books: Studies in Manuscripts and Early Printed Books in Honour of A. I. Doyle*, ed. Richard Beadle and A. J. Piper, 207–26. Aldershot: Scolar Press.

Kekewich, Margaret. 1990. "George Ashby's *The Active Policy of a Prince*: An Additional Source." *Review of English Studies*, n.s., 41:533–35.

Kelly, Douglas. 1978. "*Translatio Studii*: Translatio, Adaptation, and Allegory in Medieval French Literature." *Philological Quarterly* 57:287–310.

Kelly, L. G. 1979. *The True Interpreter: A History of Translation Theory and Practice in the West*. Oxford: Basil Blackwell.

Kennedy, Angus J. 1984. *Christine de Pizan: A Bibliographical Guide*. London: Grant & Cutler.

———. 1994. *Christine de Pizan: A Bibliographical Guide*. Supplement 1. London: Grant & Cutler.

Kennedy, Edward Donald. 1989. "Chronicles and Other Historical Writing." Vol. 8, chap. 21, of Hartung and Severs 1967– .

Kennedy, Edward Donald, R. Waldron, and J. S. Wittig, eds. 1988. *Medieval English Studies Presented to George Kane*. Cambridge: D. S. Brewer.

Ker, N. R. 1960. *English Manuscripts in the Century After the Norman Conquest*. Oxford: Clarendon Press.

———. 1964. *Medieval Libraries of Great Britain*. 2d ed. London: Royal Historical Society.

———. 1969–83. *Medieval Manuscripts in British Libraries*. 3 vols. Oxford: Clarendon Press. (Vol. 1, *London*, 1969; vol. 2, *Abbotsford-Keele*, 1977; vol. 3, *Lampeter-Oxford*, 1983.)

Kerby-Fulton, Kathryn. 1990. *Reformist Apocalypticism and "Piers Plowman."* Cambridge: Cambridge University Press.

Kerby-Fulton, Kathryn, and Steven Justice, eds. 1997. *Written Work: Langland, Labor, and Authorship*. Philadelphia: University of Pennsylvania Press.

Kieckhefer, Richard. 1989. *Magic in the Middle Ages*. Cambridge: Cambridge University Press.

King, John N. 1982. *English Reformation Literature: The Tudor Origins of the Protestant Tradition*. Princeton: Princeton University Press.

Kinsman, Robert S. 1979. *John Skelton, Early Tudor Laureate: An Annotated Bibliography, c. 1488–1977*. Boston: G. K. Hall.

Kipling, Gordon. 1977. "Triumphal Drama: Form in English Civil Pageantry. *Renaissance Drama*, n.s., 8:41–45.

———. 1984. "The Idea of the Civic Triumph: Drama, Liturgy, and the Royal Entry in the Low Countries." *Dutch Crossing* 22:60–83.

———, ed. 1990. *The Receyt of the Ladie Kateryne*. EETS, o.s., 296.

———. 1998. *Enter the King: Theatre, Liturgy, and Ritual in the Medieval Civic Triumph*. Oxford: Clarendon Press.

Kliman, Bernice W. 1973. "The Idea of Chivalry in John Barbour's *Bruce*." *Mediaeval Studies* 35:477–508.

———. 1975. "Speech as a Mirror of *Sapientia* and *Fortitudo* in Barbour's *Bruce*. *Medium Ævum* 44:151–61.

Knight, Stephen. 1986. "The Social Function of the Middle English Romances." In *Medieval Literature: Criticism, Ideology and History*, ed. David Aers. Brighton: Harvester, 99–122.

Knowles, David. 1950. *The Religious Orders in England*. Vol. 2. Cambridge: Cambridge University Press.

Knowles, David, and R. Neville Hadcock. 1971. *Medieval Religious Houses, England and Wales*. 1953. Reprint, London: Longman.

Koht, Halvdan. 1943. "Medieval Liberty Poems." *American Historical Review* 48:281–90.

Koerner, Konrad. 1980. "Medieval Linguistic Thought: A Comprehensive Bibliography." In Koerner, Niederehe, and Robins 1980, 265–98.

Koerner, Konrad, Hans-J. Niederehe, and R. H. Robins, eds. 1980. *Studies in Medieval Linguistic Thought, Dedicated to Geoffrey L. Bursill-Hall*. Amsterdam Sources in the Theory and History of Linguistic Science. Amsterdam: John Benjamins.

Kölbing, E. 1892. "Ein Fragment von Robert Manning's Chronik." *Englische Studien* 17:166–71.

Kratzmann, Gregory. 1980. *Anglo-Scottish Literary Relations, 1439–1500*. Cambridge: Cambridge University Press.

Krochalis, Jeanne E. 1988. "The Books and Reading of Henry V and His Circle." *Chaucer Review* 23:50–77.

Krueger, Roberta L. 1985. "Love, Honor, and the Exchange of Women in *Yvain*: Some Remarks on the Female Reader." *Romance Notes* 25:302–17.

———. 1993. "Intergeneric Combination and the Anxiety of Gender in *Le Livre du Chevalier de la Tour Landry pour l'Enseignement de Ses Filles*." *L'Esprit Créateur* 33:61–72.

Kreuzer, James R. 1938. "The Twelve Profits of Anger." *PMLA* 53:78–85.

Kuczynski, Michael P. 1995. *Prophetic Song: The Psalms as Moral Discourse in Late Medieval England*. Philadelphia: University of Pennsylvania Press.

Kuhn, Sherman M. 1968. Review of *The Middle English Translation of Guy de Chauliac's "Anatomy," with Guy's Essay on the History of Medicine*, ed. Björn Wallner. *Speculum* 43:552–56.

Kurath, Hans, Sherman M. Kuhn, and Robert E. Lewis, eds. 1956–. *Middle English Dictionary*. Ann Arbor: University of Michigan Press.

Laennec, Christine Moneera. 1988. "Christine 'Antygrafe': Authorship and Self in the Prose Works of Christine de Pizan with an Edition of B.N. Ms. 603, *Le Livre des Fais d'Armes et de Chevallerie*." 2 Vols. Ph.D. diss., Yale University. Abstract in *Dissertation Abstracts International* 50 (1990): 3581A.

Lagorio, Valerie, and Michael Sargent (with Ritamary Bradley). 1993. "English Mystical Writings." Vol. 9, chap. 23, of Hartung and Severs 1967–.

Laidlaw, J. C. 1982. "Christine de Pisan, the Earl of Salisbury, and Henry IV." *French Studies* 36:129–43.

Lander, J. R. 1980. *Government and Community: England, 1450–1509.* Cambridge, Mass.: Harvard University Press.

Langmuir, Gavin I. 1990a. *Toward a Definition of Antisemitism.* Berkeley and Los Angeles: University of California Press.

———. 1990b. *History, Religion and Anti-Semitism.* London: I. B. Tauris.

Lawler, Traugolt. 1983. "On the Properties of John Trevisa's Major Translations." *Viator* 14:267–88.

Lawton, David. 1981. "The Middle English Alliterative *Alexander A* and *C:* Form and Style in Translation from Latin Prose." *Studia Neophilologica* 53:259–69.

———, ed. 1982. *Middle English Alliterative Poetry and Its Literary Background.* Cambridge: D. S. Brewer.

———. 1987. "Dullness and the Fifteenth Century." *English Literary History* 54:761–99.

———. 1992. "Voice, Authority, and Blasphemy in the Book of Margery Kempe." In *Margery Kempe: A Book of Essays,* ed. Sandra J. McEntire, 93–116. New York: Garland.

Lawton, Lesley. 1983. "The Illustration of Late Medieval Secular Texts, with Special Reference to Lydgate's *Troy Book.*" In Pearsall 1983, 41–69.

Leclercq, Jean. 1961. *The Love of Learning and the Desire for God: A Study of Monastic Culture.* Trans. Catharine Misrahi. New York: Fordham University Press.

Le Goff, Jacques. 1984. *The Birth of Purgatory.* Trans. Arthur Goldhammer. Chicago: University of Chicago Press.

Lentricchia, Frank. 1980. *After the New Criticism.* Chicago: University of Chicago Press.

Lerer, Seth. 1993. *Chaucer and His Readers: Imagining the Author in Late-Medieval England.* Princeton: Princeton University Press.

———. 1996. "'Representyd Now in Yower Syght': The Culture of Spectatorship in Late Fifteenth-Century England." In Hanawalt and Wallace 1996, 29–62.

Lester, G. A. 1984. *Sir John Paston's "Grete Boke": A Descriptive Catalogue with an Introduction, of British Library MS Lansdowne 285.* Cambridge: D. S. Brewer.

———. 1988. *The Earliest English Translation of Vegetius' "De re Militari."* Middle English Texts 21. Heidelberg: Carl Winter.

Leupin, Alexandre. 1989. *Barbarolexis: Medieval Writing and Sexuality.* Trans. Kate M. Cooper. Cambridge, Mass.: Harvard University Press.

Lewis, Gertrud, and Jack Lewis, trans. 1989. *Gertrud the Great of Helfta: Spiritual Exercises.* Cistercian Fathers Series 49. Kalamazoo, Mich.: Cistercian Publications.

Lewis, Robert E., and Angus McIntosh. 1982. *A Descriptive Guide to the Manuscripts of the "Prick of Conscience."* Medium Ævum Monographs, n.s., 12. Oxford: Society for the Study of Mediaeval Languages and Literature.

Lewis, Suzanne. 1991. "The English Gothic Illuminated Apocalypse, Lectio Divina, and the Art of Memory." *Word and Image* 7:1–32.

———. 1995. *Reading Images: Narrative Discourse and Reception in the Thirteenth-Century Illustrated Apocalypse.* Cambridge: Cambridge University Press.

Lindberg, Conrad, ed. 1959–97. *MS Bodley 959: Genesis-Baruch 3.20 in the Earlier Version of the Wycliffite Bible.* 8 vols. Stockholm Studies in English 6, 8, 10, 13, 20, 29, 81, 87. Stockholm: Almqvist & Wiksell. (Vols. 6, 7, and 8 have the title *The Earlier Version of the Wycliffite Bible.*)

———. 1970. "The Manuscripts and Versions of the Wycliffite Bible: A Preliminary Survey." *Studia Neophilogica* 42:333–47.

Liszka, Thomas R. 1985. "The First 'A' Redaction of the *South English Legendary:* Information from the 'Prologue.'" *Modern Philology* 82:407–13.

———. 1992. "Manuscript 6 (Lambeth Palace 223) and the Early *South English Legendary.*" In Jankofsky 1992, 91–101.

Lochrie, Karma. 1986. "*The Book of Margery Kempe:* The Marginal Woman's Quest for Literary Authority." *Journal of Medieval and Renaissance Studies* 16:33–55.

———. 1991. *Margery Kempe and Translations of the Flesh.* Philadelphia: University of Pennsylvania Press.

Lodge, R. A. 1991. "Language Attitudes and Linguistic Norms in France and England in the Thirteenth Century." In *Thirteenth-Century England,* ed. P. R. Coss and S. D. Lloyd, 4:73–83. Woodbridge, Suffolk: Boydell.

Loomis, Laura Hibbard. 1942. "The Auchinleck Manuscript and a Possible London Bookshop of 1330–1340." *PMLA* 57:595–627.

Louth, Andrew. 1981. *The Origins of the Christian Mystical Tradition from Plato to Denys the Areopagite.* Oxford: Clarendon Press.

———. 1989. *Denys the Areopagite.* London: Chapman.

Lucas, Peter J. 1982. "The Growth and Development of English Literary Patronage in the Later Middle Ages and Early Renaissance." *The Library,* 6th ser., 4:219–48.

———, ed. 1983. *John Capgrave's "Abbreuiacion of Chronicles."* EETS, o.s., 285.

Luibheid, Colm, trans. 1987. *Pseudo-Dionysius: The Complete Works.* Classics of Western Spirituality. New York: Paulist Press.

Lusignan, Serge. 1986. *Parler vulgairement: Les intellectuels et la langue française aux XIIIe et XIVe siècles.* Paris: Vrin.

———, 1997. "Written French and Latin at the Court of France at the End of the Middle Ages." In Beer 1997, 185–98.

Lyall, Roderick J. 1988. "Vernacular Prose Before the Reformation." In Jack 1988, 163–81.

Lyall, Roderick J., and Felicity Riddy, eds. 1981. *Proceedings of the Third International Conference on Scottish Language and Literature (Medieval and Renaissance).* Stirling/Glasgow: The Authors and Editors.

Lyotard, Jean-François. 1971. *Discours, Figure.* Paris: Klincksieck.

Macaulay, G. C., ed. 1900–1901. *The English Works of John Gower.* 2 vols. EETS, e.s., 81, 82.

Machan, Tim William. 1985. *Techniques of Translation: Chaucer's "Boece."* Norman, Okla.: Pilgrim Books.

———, ed. 1991. *Medieval Literature: Texts and Interpretation.* Medieval and Renaissance Texts and Studies 79. Binghampton, N.Y.: Center for Medieval and Early Renaissance Studies.

———. 1994. "Language Contact in *Piers Plowman.*" *Speculum* 69:359–85.

Macherey, Pierre. 1978. *A Theory of Literary Production.* Trans. Geoffrey Wall. London: Routledge.

MacKinnon, Catharine A. 1983. "Feminism, Marxism, Method, and the State: Toward Feminist Jurisprudence." *Signs: Journal of Women in Culture and Society* 8:635–58.

Maddern, Philippa C. 1992. *Violence and Social Order: East Anglia, 1422–1442.* Oxford: Clarendon Press.

Maltman, Sister Nicholas. 1974. "Meaning and Art in the Croxton Play of the Sacrament." *English Literary History* 41:149–64.

Manion, Margaret M., and Bernard James Muir, eds. 1991. *Medieval Texts and Images: Studies of Manuscripts from the Middle Ages.* Philadelphia: Harwood Academic Press.

Mann, Jill. 1979. "Eating and Drinking in 'Piers Plowman.'" *Essays and Studies,* n.s., 32:26–43.

———. 1990. *Apologies to Women.* Cambridge: Cambridge University Press.

Manzalaoui, M. A., ed. 1977. *"Secretum Secretorum": Nine English Versions.* EETS, o.s., 276.

Mapstone, Sally. 1997. "Kingship and the *Kingis Quair.*" In Cooper and Mapstone 1997, 51–69.

Margherita, Gayle. 1994. *The Romance of Origins: Language and Sexual Difference in Middle English Literature.* Philadelphia: University of Pennsylvania Press.

Marotti, Arthur F. 1991. "Patronage, Poetry, and Print." *Yearbook of English Studies* 21:1–20.

Maskell, William. 1970. *Monumenta Ritualia Ecclesiae Anglicanae.* 3 vols. 2d ed. Farnborough: Gregg International.

McCann, Justin, ed. and trans. 1952. *The Rule of St. Benedict in Latin and English.* London: Burns & Oates.

McCarthy, Adrian James. 1981. *Book to a Mother: An Edition with Commentary.* Salzburg Studies in English: Elizabethan and Renaissance Studies 92: Studies in the English Mystics I. Salzburg: Institut für Anglistik und Amerikanistik.

McCash, June Hall, ed. 1996. *The Cultural Patronage of Medieval Women.* Athens: University of Georgia Press.

McClure, J. Derrick, and Michael R. G. Spiller, eds. 1989. *Bryght Lanternis: Essays on the Language and Literature of Medieval and Renaissance Scotland.* Aberdeen: Aberdeen University Press.

McDiarmid, Matthew P., ed. 1973. *The Kingis Quair of James Stewart.* Totawa, N.J.: Rowman & Littlefield.

McDiarmid, Matthew P., and James A. C. Stevenson, eds. 1980–85. *Barbour's Bruce: A Fredome Is a Noble Thing!* 3 vols. Edinburgh: Scottish Text Society. (Vol. 1, 1985; vol. 2, 1980; vol. 3, 1981.)

McEntire, Sandra J. 1990. *The Doctrine of Compunction in Medieval England: Holy Tears.* Lewiston, N.Y.: Edwin Mellen Press.

———, ed. 1992. *Margery Kempe: A Book of Essays.* Garland Medieval Casebooks 4. New York: Garland.

———, ed. 1998. *Julian of Norwich: A Book of Essays.* Garland Medieval Casebooks 21. New York: Garland.

McGinn, Bernard. 1991. *The Foundations of Mysticism: Origins to the Fifth Century.* Vol. 1 of *The Presence of God: A History of Western Christian Mysticism.* New York: Crossroads.

McKenzie, D. F. 1981. "Typography and Meaning: The Case of William Congreve." In *Buch und Buchhandel in Europa im Achtzehnten Jahrhundert, Fünftes Wolfenbütteler Symposium 1977,* ed. Giles Barber and Bernhard Fabian, 81–126. Hamburg: Hauswedell.

———. 1990. "Speech–Manuscript–Print." In *New Directions in Textual Studies,* ed. David Oliphant and Robert Bradford, 87–109. Austin: University of Texas at Austin, Harry Ransom Research Center.

McKitterick, Rosamond. 1990. "Carolingian Book Production: Some Problems." *The Library,* 6th ser., 12:1–33.

McLuhan, Marshall. 1962. *The Gutenberg Galaxy: The Making of Typographic Man.* Toronto: University of Toronto Press.

McNamer, Sarah. 1991. "Female Authors, Provincial Setting: The Re-Versing of Courtly Love in the Findern Manuscript." *Viator* 22:279–310.

McSheffrey, Shannon. 1995a. *Gender and Heresy: Women and Men in Lollard Communities, 1420–1530.* Philadelphia: University of Pennsylvania Press.

———. 1995b. "Literacy and the Gender Gap in the Late Middle Ages: Women and Reading in Lollard Communities." In Smith and Taylor 1995, 1:157–70.

McSparran, Frances, and P. R. Robinson, eds. 1979. *Cambridge University Library MS. Ff.2.38.* London: Scolar Press.

McVaugh, Michael R., ed. 1997. *Guigonis de Caulhiaco (Guy de Chauliac) Inventarium sive Chirurgia Magna.* Vol. 1. Leiden: E. J. Brill.

Meale, Carol M. 1989. "Patrons, Buyers, and Owners: Book Production and Social Status." In Griffiths and Pearsall 1989, 201–38.

———. 1990. "'The Miracles of Our Lady': Context and Interpretation." In Pearsall 1990, 115–36.

———. 1992. "Caxton, de Worde, and the Publication of Romance in Late Medieval England." *The Library,* 6th ser., 14:283–98.

———. 1994a. "'Gode Men / Wiues Maydnes and Alle Men': Romance and Its Audiences." In Meale 1994b, 209–25.

———, ed. 1994b. *Readings in Medieval English Romance.* Cambridge: D. S. Brewer.

———. 1996a. "'. . . Alle the Bokes That I Have of Latyn, Englisch, and Frensch': Laywomen and Their Books in Late Medieval England." 1993. Reprinted in Meale 1996c, 128–58.

———. 1996b. "Reading Women's Culture in Fifteenth-Century England: The Case of Alice Chaucer." In Boitani and Torti 1996, 81–101.

———, ed. 1996c. *Women and Literature in Britain, 1150–1500.* 1993. Reprint, Cambridge: Cambridge University Press.

Medcalf, Stephen. 1989. "Transposition: Thomas Usk's *Testament of Love.*" In Ellis 1989, 181–95.

———. 1997. "The World and Heart of Thomas Usk." In *Essays on Ricardian Literature in Honour of J. A. Burrow,* ed. Alastair J. Minnis, Charlotte C. Morse, and Thorlac Turville-Petre, 222–51. Oxford: Clarendon Press.

Meech, Sanford Brown, and Hope Emily Allen, eds. 1940. *The Book of Margery Kempe.* EETS, o.s., 212.

Meek, Mary Elizabeth. 1974. *"Historia Destructionis Troiae," Guide delle Colonne.* Bloomington: Indiana University Press.

Middleton, Anne. 1978. "The Idea of Public Poetry in the Reign of Richard II." *Speculum* 53:94–114.

———. 1990. "William Langland's 'Kynde Name': Authorial Signature and Social Identity in Late Fourteenth-Century England." In Patterson 1990, 15–82.

———. 1992. "Medieval Studies." In *Redrawing the Boundaries: The Transformation of English and American Literary Studies,* ed. Stephen Greenblatt and Giles Gunn, 15–40. New York: MLA of America.

———. 1998. "Thomas Usk's 'Perdurable Letters': The *Testament of Love* from Script to Print." *Studies in Bibliography* 51:63–116.

Migne, J.-P., ed. 1844–64. *Patrologiae Cursus Completus: Series Latina.* 221 vols. Paris: J.-P. Migne.

———, ed. 1857–62. *Patrologiae Cursus Completus: Series Graeca.* 166 vols. Paris: J.-P. Migne.

Miller, Robert P., ed. 1977. *Chaucer: Sources and Backgrounds.* New York: Oxford University Press.

Millett, Bella. 1983. *"Hali Meiðhad, Sawles Warde* and the Continuity of Old English Prose." In *Five Hundred Years of Words and Sounds: A Festschrift for Eric Dobson,* ed. E. G. Stanley and Douglas Gray, 100–108. Oxford: Clarendon Press.

———. 1996. "Women in No Man's Land: English Recluses and the Development of Vernacular Literature in the Twelfth and Thirteenth Centuries." 1993. Reprinted in Meale 1996c, 86–103.

Millett, Bella, and Jocelyn Wogan-Browne, eds. and trans. 1992. *Medieval English Prose for Women: Selections from the Katherine Group and "Ancrene Wisse."* 1990. Reprint, Oxford: Clarendon Press.

Minnis, Alastair J. 1980. "John Gower, *Sapiens* in Ethics and Politics." *Medium Ævum* 49:207–29.

——. 1981. "The Influence of Academic Prologue on the Prologues and Literary Attitudes of Late-Medieval English Writers." *Mediaeval Studies* 43:342–83.

——. 1982a. *Chaucer and Pagan Antiquity.* Cambridge: D. S. Brewer.

——. 1982b. "The Sources of *The Cloud of Unknowing*: A Reconsideration." In Glasscoe 1982, 63–75.

——, ed. 1983. *Gower's "Confessio Amantis": Responses and Reassessments.* Cambridge: D. S. Brewer.

——. 1986. "*The Cloud of Unknowing* and Walter Hilton's *Scale of Perfection.*" In Edwards 1986, 61–82.

——, ed. 1987. *The Medieval Boethius: Studies in the Vernacular Translations of "De Consolatione Philosophiae."* Cambridge: D. S. Brewer.

——. 1988. *Medieval Theory of Authorship: Scholastic Literary Attitudes in the Later Middle Ages.* 2d ed. Aldershot: Wildwood.

——, ed. 1994. *Late-Medieval Religious Texts and Their Transmission: Essays in Honour of A. I. Doyle.* York Manuscripts Conferences: Proceedings Series, 3. Cambridge: D. S. Brewer.

——. 1997. "The Author's Two Bodies? Authority and Fallibility in Late-Medieval Textual Theory." In *Of the Making of Books: Medieval Manuscripts, Their Scribes and Readers: Essays Presented to M. B. Parkes,* ed. P. R. Robinson and Rivkah Zim, 259–79. Aldershot: Scolar Press.

—— (with Ian Scott). Forthcoming. Section on medieval vernacular literary theory and translation. *The Cambridge History of Literary Criticism.* Vol. 2, *The Middle Ages,* ed. Alastair J. Minnis. Cambridge: Cambridge University Press.

Minnis, Alastair J., and A. B. Scott (with the assistance of David Wallace). 1988. *Medieval Literary Theory and Criticism, c. 1100–c. 1375: The Commentary-Tradition.* Oxford: Clarendon Press.

Mitchell, Jerome. 1968. *Thomas Hoccleve: A Study in Early Fifteenth-Century English Poetic.* Urbana: University of Illinois Press.

Moffat, Douglas. 1994. "Sin, Conquest, Servitude: English Self-Image in the Chronicles of the Early Fourteenth Century." In *The Work of Work: Servitude, Slavery, and Labour in Medieval England,* ed. Allen J. Frantzen and Douglas Moffat, 146–68. Glasgow: Cruithne.

——. 1995. "The Intonational Basis of Layamon's Verse." In *Prosody and Poetics in the Early Middle Ages: Essays in Honour of C. B. Hieatt,* ed. M. J. Toswell, 133–46. Toronto: University of Toronto Press.

Montfaucon, Bernard de, ed. 1835–39. *Johannis Chrysostomi: Opera Omnia.* 13 vols. Paris: Gaume.

Moore, Bruce. 1993. "The Banns in Medieval English Drama." *Leeds Studies in English,* n.s., 24:91–122.

Moore, Robert. 1987. *The Formation of a Persecuting Society.* Oxford: Basil Blackwell.

Moore, Samuel. 1912–13. "Patrons of Letters in Norfolk and Suffolk, c.1450." *PMLA* 27:188–207; 28:79–105.

Moreton, C. E. 1991. "The 'Library' of a Late-Fifteenth-Century Lawyer." *The Library,* 6th ser., 13:338–46.

Morgan, Margery M. 1952a. "*A Talking of the Love of God* and the Continuity of Stylistic Tradition in Middle English Prose Meditations." *Review of English Studies,* n.s., 3:97–116.

——. 1952b. "A Treatise in Cadence." *Modern Language Review* 47:156–64.

Morgan, Nigel. 1988. *Early Gothic Manuscripts: 1250–1285.* Vol. 2 of *A Survey of Manuscripts Illuminated in the British Isles.* London: Harvey Miller.

Morison, J. L., ed. 1909. *Reginald Pecock's "Book of Faith": A Fifteenth-Century Theological Tractate.* Glasgow: J. Maclehouse & Sons.

Morris, Richard, ed. 1973. *"The Pricke of Conscience (Stimulus Conscientiae)": A Northumbrian Poem by Richard Rolle of Hampole*. 1863. Reprint, New York: AMS.

———, ed. 1874–93. *Cursor Mundi: A Northumbrian Poem of the Fourteenth Century*. 7 vols. EETS, o.s., 57, 59, 62, 66, 68, 99, 101. (Reprint 1961–62.)

Munro, J. J., ed. 1910. *John Capgrave's Lives of St. Augustine and St. Gilbert of Sempringham, and a Sermon*. EETS, o.s., 140.

Murphy, James J. 1974. *Rhetoric in the Middle Ages: A History of Rhetorical Theory from St. Augustine to the Renaissance*. Berkeley and Los Angeles: University of California Press.

Mutzenbecher, Almut, ed. 1975. *Sancti Aurelii Augustins: De Diversis Questionibus Octaginta Tribus*. Turnhout: Brepols.

Myers, A. R., ed. 1969. *English Historical Documents*. London: Eyre & Spottiswoode.

Nairn, J. A. 1906. *The "De Sacerdotia" of John Chrysostom*. Cambridge: Cambridge University Press.

Nelson, Venetia, ed. 1981. *A Myrour to Lewde Men and Women: A Prose Version of the "Speculum Vitae."* Middle English Texts 14. Heidelberg: Carl Winter.

Nevanlinna, Saara, ed. 1972–84. *The Northern Homily Cycle: The Expanded Version in MSS Harley 4196 and Cotton Tiberius E.VII*. 3 vols. Mémoires de la Société Néophilologique de Helsinki. Helsinki: Société Néophilologique.

Newlyn, Evelyn S. 1991. "Luve, Lichery, and Evill Women: The Satiric Tradition in the Bannatyne Manuscript." *Studies in Scottish Literature* 26:283–93.

———. 1992. "The Political Dimensions of Desire and Sexuality in Poems of the Bannatyne Manuscript." In *Selected Essays on Scottish Language and Literature: A Festschrift in Honour of Allan H. MacLaine*, ed. Steven R. McKenna, 75–96. Lewiston, N.Y.: Edwin Mellen Press.

Newman, Barbara. 1995. *From Virile Woman to WomanChrist: Studies in Medieval Religion and Literature*. Philadelphia: University of Pennsylvania Press.

Nicaise, E., ed. 1890. *La Grande Chirurgie de Guy de Chauliac*. Paris: Ancienne Librairie Germer Baillière et cie.

Nicholls, Jonathan. 1985. *The Matter of Courtesy: Medieval Courtesy Books and the Gawain-Poet*. Cambridge: D. S. Brewer.

Nichols, Ann E. 1988–89. "The Croxton Play of the Sacrament: A Rereading." *Comparative Drama* 22:117–37.

Nichols, Stephen G., and Siegfried Wenzel, eds. 1996. *The Whole Book: Cultural Perspectives on the Medieval Miscellany*. Ann Arbor: University of Michigan Press.

Nicholson, Peter, ed. 1991. *Gower's "Confessio Amantis": A Critical Anthology*. Publications of the John Gower Society 3. Cambridge: D. S. Brewer.

Nierenstein, M., and P. F. Chapman. 1932. "Enquiry into the Authorship of *The Ordinall of Alchimy*." *Isis* 18:290–321.

Niranjana, Tejaswini. 1992. *Siting Translation: History, Post-Structuralism, and the Colonial Context*. Berkeley and Los Angeles: University of California Press.

Noffke, Suzanne, trans. 1980. *Catherine of Siena: "The Dialogue."* Classics of Western Spirituality. New York: Paulist Press.

Nolan, Barbara. 1992. *Chaucer and the Tradition of the "Roman Antique."* Cambridge: Cambridge University Press.

Norton-Smith, John, ed. 1966. *John Lydgate: Poems*. Oxford: Clarendon Press.

———, ed. 1971. *James I of Scotland, "The Kingis Quair."* Oxford: Clarendon Press.

———. 1979. Introduction to *Oxford Bodleian Fairfax MS. 16*. Facsimile ed. London: Scolar Press.

O'Boyle, Cornelius. 1994. "Surgical Texts and Social Contexts: Physicians and Surgeons in Paris, c. 1270 to 1430." In *Practical Medicine from Salerno to the Black Death*, ed. Luis García-Ballester et al., 156–85. Cambridge: Cambridge University Press.

Obrist, Barbara. 1982. *Les débuts de l'imagerie alchimique (XIV–XV siècles)*. Paris: Le Sycomore, in association with Centre Nationale de la Recherche Scientifique.

Offord, M. Y., ed. 1971. *The Book of the Knight of the Tower*. Trans. William Caxton. EETS, s.s., 2.

Ogden, Margaret S., ed. 1971. *The "Chirurgie" of Guy de Chauliac*. EETS, o.s., 265.

Ogilvie-Thomson, S. J., ed. 1988. *Richard Rolle: Prose and Verse*. EETS, o.s., 293.

Oguru, Shoichi, Richard Beadle, and Michael G. Sargent, eds., 1997. *Nicholas Love at Waseda: Proceedings of the International Conference 20–22 July 1995*. Cambridge: D. S. Brewer.

Olson, Glending. 1979. "Making and Poetry in the Age of Chaucer." *Comparative Literature* 31:272–90.

———. 1982. *Literature as Recreation in the Later Middle Ages*. Ithaca: Cornell University Press.

Orme, Nicholas. 1989. *Education and Society in Medieval and Renaissance England*. London: Hambledon Press.

Page, Christopher. 1989. *The Owl and the Nightingale: Musical Life and Ideas in France, 1100–1300*. London: Dent.

Page, Stephen. 1996. "John Metham's *Amoryus and Cleopes*: Intertextuality and Innovation in a Chaucerian Poem." *Chaucer Review* 311:201–8.

Pantin, William A. 1931–33. *Documents Illustrating the Activities of the General and Provincial Chapters of the English Black Monks, 1215–1540*. Vols. 1 and 2. Camden Third Series, 45, 47. London: Royal Historical Society.

———. 1955. *The English Church in the Fourteenth Century: Based on the Birkbeck Lectures, 1948*. Cambridge: Cambridge University Press.

Park, Katharine. 1992. "Medicine and Society in Medieval Europe, 500–1500." In *Medicine in Society*, ed. Andrew Wear, 59–90. Cambridge: Cambridge University Press.

Parker, Patricia. 1996. "Virile Style." In *Premodern Sexualities*, ed. Louise Fradenburg and Carla Freccero, 99–116. London: Routledge.

Parkes, M. B. 1973. "The Literacy of the Laity." In *Literature and Western Civilization*, vol. 2, *The Mediaeval World*, ed. David Daiches and Anthony Thorlby, 555–78. London: Aldus.

———. 1976. "The Influence of the Concepts of *Ordinatio* and *Compilatio* on the Development of the Book." In *Medieval Learning and Literature: Essays Presented to Richard William Hunt*, ed. J.J.G. Alexander and M. T. Gibson, 115–41. Oxford: Clarendon Press. (Reprinted in Parkes 1991, 35–70.)

———. 1991. *Scribes, Scripts, and Readers: Studies in the Communication, Presentation, and Dissemination of Medieval Texts*. London: Hambledon Press.

Parkes, M. B., and Andrew G. Watson, eds. 1978. *Medieval Scribes, Manuscripts, and Libraries: Essays Presented to N. R. Ker*. London: Scolar Press.

Parr, Johnstone. 1952. "Astronomical Dating for Some of Lydgate's Poems." *PMLA* 67:251–58.

Parrey, Yvonne. 1994. "'Devoted Disciples of Christ': Early Sixteenth-Century Religious Life in the Nunnery at Amesbury." *Historical Research: The Bulletin of the Institute of Historical Research* 67, no. 164: 240–48.

Partner, Nancy F. 1991. "Reading *The Book of Margery Kempe*." *Exemplaria* 3:29–66.

Patterson, Lee. 1987. *Negotiating the Past: The Historical Understanding of Medieval Literature*. Madison: University of Wisconsin Press.

———, ed. 1990. *Literary Practice and Social Change in Britain, 1380–1530*. Berkeley and Los Angeles: University of California Press.

———. 1992. "Court Politics and the Invention of Literature: The Case of Sir John Clanvowe." In Aers 1992a, 7–41.

———. 1993a. "Making Identities in Fifteenth-Century England: Henry V and John Lydgate." In *New Historical Literary Study: Essays on Reproducing Texts, Representing History,* ed. Jeffrey N. Cox and Larry J. Reynolds, 69–107. Princeton: Princeton University Press.

———. 1993b. "Perpetual Motion: Alchemy and the Technology of the Self." *SAC* 15:25–57.

Pearsall, Derek. 1970. *John Lydgate*. Charlottesville: University of Virginia Press.

———. 1975. "John Capgrave's *Life of St. Katherine* and Popular Romance Style." *Medievalia et Humanistica,* n.s., 6:121–37.

———. 1977. *Old and Middle English Poetry*. London: Routledge & Kegan Paul.

———, ed. 1978. *"Piers Plowman" by William Langland: An Edition of the C-Text*. York Medieval Texts, 2d ser. London: Edward Arnold.

———, ed. 1983. *Manuscripts and Readers in Fifteenth-Century England: The Literary Implications of Manuscript Study: Essays from the 1981 Conference at the University of York*. Cambridge: D. S. Brewer.

———. 1985. "Middle English Romance and Its Audience." In *Historical and Editorial Studies in Medieval and Early Modern English for Johan Gerritsen,* ed. Mary-Jo Arn and Hanneke Wirtjes, 37–47. Gröningen: Wolters-Noordhoff.

———, ed. 1990. *Studies in the Vernon Manuscript*. Cambridge: D. S. Brewer.

———. 1992. *The Life of Geoffrey Chaucer: A Critical Biography*. Oxford: Basil Blackwell.

———. 1994. "Hoccleve's *Regement of Princes:* The Poetics of Royal Representation." *Speculum* 69:386–410.

———. 1997. *John Lydgate (1371–1449): A Bio-Bibliography*. English Literary Studies Monograph Series 71. Victoria, B.C.: University of Victoria.

Pearsall, Derek, and Ian C. Cunningham. 1977. *The Auchinleck Manuscript, National Library of Scotland Advocates' MS. 19. 2. 1*. London: Scolar Press.

Peck, Russell A., ed. 1980. *Confessio Amantis*. Medieval Academy of America Texts 9. Toronto: University of Toronto Press.

Perry, A. J., ed. 1925. *Trevisa's "Dialogus Inter Militem et Clericum."* EETS, o.s., 167.

Peterson, Ingrid. 1986. *William of Nassington: Canon, Mystic, and Poet of the "Speculum Vitae."* New York: Peter Lang.

Pfeffer, Wendy. 1985. *The Change of Philomel: The Nightingale in Medieval Literature*. New York: Peter Lang.

Phillips, Helen. 1993. "Chaucer's French Translations." *Nottingham Medieval Studies* 37:65–82.

———. 1994. *"The Complaint of Venus:* Chaucer and de Graunson." In Ellis and Evans 1994, 86–103.

———. 1997. "Frames and Narratives in Chaucerian Poetry." In Cooper and Mapstone 1997, 71–97.

Piaget, Arthur, ed. 1941. *Oton de Grandson: Sa vie et ses poésies*. Mémoires et documents publiés par la Société de la Suisse Romande. Ser. 3, vol. 1. Lausanne: Payot.

Pickering, O. S. 1973. "The *Temporale* Narratives of the *South English Legendary.*" *Anglia* 91:425–55.

———. 1996. "The South English Legendary: Teaching or Preaching?" *Poetica* 45:1–14.

Pinti, Daniel J. 1995. "The Vernacular Gloss(ed) in Gavin Douglas's *Eneados.*" *Exemplaria* 7:443–64.

Pollard, A. W., and G. R. Redgrave. 1976–86. *A Short Title Catalogue of Books Printed in England, Scotland, and Ireland, and of English Books Printed Abroad, 1475–1640*. 2d ed., revised and enlarged. Begun by W. A. Jackson and F. S. Ferguson, completed by Katherine F. Pantzer. 3 vols. London: Bibliographical Society.

Pollard, Graham. 1964. "The University and the Book Trade in Mediaeval Oxford." *Miscellanea Medievalia* 3:336–44.

———. 1978a. "The *Pecia* System in the Medieval Universities." In Parkes and Watson 1978, 145–61.

———. 1978b. "The Rise of the Wholesale Trade." *Publishing History* 4:9–48.

Porter, Mary Louise, ed. 1929. "Richard Rolle's Latin Commentary on the Psalms." Ph.D. diss., Cornell University.

Powell, Marianne. 1983. *Fabula Docet: Studies in the Background and Interpretation of Henryson's "Morall Fabillis."* Odense University Studies in English 4. Odense: Odense University Press.

Powell, Sue. 1994. "The Transmission and Circulation of *The Lay Folks' Catechism.*" In Minnis 1994, 67–84.

Power, Eileen, ed. and trans. 1928. *The Goodman of Paris.* London: Routledge.

Purdon, Liam O., and Julian N. Wasserman. 1994. "Chivalry and Feudal Obligation in Barbour's *Bruce.*" In *The Rusted Hauberk: Feudal Ideals of Order and Their Decline,* ed. Liam O. Purdon and Cindy L. Vitto, 77–95. Gainesville: University Presses of Florida.

Quilligan, Maureen. 1991. *The Allegory of Female Authority: Christine de Pizan's "Cité des Dames."* Ithaca: Cornell University Press.

Quinn, William. 1981. "Memory and the Matrix of Unity in *The Kingis Quair.*" *Chaucer Review* 15:332–55.

Raby, F.J.E. 1935. "A Middle English Paraphrase of John of Hovedon's *Philomena* and the Text of His *Viola.*" *Modern Language Review* 30:339–43.

———, ed. 1939. *Poems of John Hovedon.* Surtees Society 154. Durham: Andrews & Quaritch.

———. 1953. *A History of Christian-Latin Poetry from the Beginnings to the Close of the Middle Ages.* Oxford: Clarendon Press.

Rafael, Vicente L. 1988. *Contracting Colonialism: Translation and Christian Conversion in Tagalog Society Under Early Spanish Rule.* Ithaca: Cornell University Press.

Ramsey, Lee C. 1983. *Chivalric Romances: Popular Literature in Medieval England.* Bloomington: Indiana University Press.

Raymo, Robert R. 1986. "Works of Religious and Philosophical Instruction." Vol. 7, chap. 20, of Hartung and Severs 1967–.

Reidy, John, ed. 1975. *Thomas Norton's "Ordinal of Alchemy."* EETS, o.s., 272.

Relihan, Robert J. 1978. "*Les peines de purgatorie*: The Anglo-Norman and Latin Manuscript Traditions." *Manuscripta* 22:158–68.

Renoir, Alain. 1967. *The Poetry of John Lydgate.* Cambridge, Mass.: Harvard University Press.

Reynolds, Suzanne. 1996. *Medieval Reading: Grammar, Rhetoric, and the Classical Text.* Cambridge: Cambridge University Press.

Rhodes, J. T. 1993. "Religious Instruction at Syon in the Early Sixteenth Century." In Hogg 1993, 151–69.

Rice, Joanne A. 1987. *Middle English Romance: An Annotated Bibliography, 1955–1985.* New York: Garland.

Richards, Earl Jeffrey, trans. 1982. *The Book of the City of Ladies,* by Christine de Pizan. New York: Persea.

Richardson, Malcolm. 1980. "Henry V, the English Chancery, and Chancery English." *Speculum* 55:726–50.

Riddy, Felicity. 1987. *Sir Thomas Malory.* Leiden: Brill.

———. 1996a. "Mother Knows Best: Reading Social Change in a Courtesy Text." *Speculum* 71:66–86.

———. 1996b. "'Women Talking About the Things of God': A Late Medieval Sub-Culture." 1993. Reprinted in Meale 1996c, 104–27.

————. 1997. "Abject Odious': Feminine and Masculine in Henryson's *Testament of Cresseid.*" In Cooper and Mapstone 1997, 229–48.

Ridley, Florence H. 1984. "Studies in Douglas and Dunbar: The Present Situation." In Yeager 1984, 93–117.

Rigg, A. G. 1968. *A Glastonbury Miscellany of the Fifteenth Century: A Descriptive Index of Trinity College, Cambridge, MS. O.9.38.* London: Oxford University Press.

————. 1970. "Hoccleve's *Complaint* and Isidore of Seville." *Speculum* 45:564–74.

————. 1992. *A History of Anglo-Latin Literature, 1066–1422.* Cambridge: Cambridge University Press.

Rissanen, Matti et al., eds. 1992. *History of Englishes: New Methods and Interpretations in Historical Linguistics.* Topics in English Linguistics 10. Berlin: Mouton de Gruyter.

Robbins, Rossell Hope. 1954. "The Findern Anthology." *PMLA* 69:610–42.

————, ed. 1955. *Secular Lyrics of the Fourteenth and Fifteenth Centuries.* 2d ed. Oxford: Clarendon Press.

Robbins, Rossell Hope, and John L. Cutler. 1965. *Supplement to the Index of Middle English Verse.* Lexington: University of Kentucky Press.

Robertson, D. W., Jr., trans. 1958. *Augustine's "On Christian Doctrine."* Indianapolis: Bobbs-Merrill.

————. 1962. *A Preface to Chaucer: Studies in Medieval Perspectives.* Princeton: Princeton University Press.

Robertson, D. W., Jr., and Bernard Huppé. 1963. *Fruyt and Chaf: Studies in Chaucer's Allegories.* Princeton: Princeton University Press.

Robinson, Pamela R. 1980. "'The Booklet': A Self-Contained Unit in Composite Manuscripts." *Codicologica* 3:46–69.

Rogers, Nicholas John. 1982. "Books of Hours Produced in the Low Countries for the English Market in the Fifteenth Century." Master's diss., Cambridge University.

————. 1987. "Fitzwilliam Museum MS 3-1979: A Bury St. Edmunds Book of Hours and the Origins of the Bury Style." In *England in the Fifteenth Century: Proceedings of the 1986 Harlaxton Symposium,* ed. Daniel Williams, 229–43. Woodbridge, Suffolk: Boydell & Brewer.

Rosenthal, Joel T. 1982. "Aristocratic Cultural Patronage and Book Bequests, 1350–1500." *Bulletin of the John Rylands Library* 64:522–48.

————, ed. 1990. *Medieval Women and the Sources of Medieval History.* Athens: University of Georgia Press.

Rothwell, William. 1976. "The Role of French in Thirteenth-Century England." *Bulletin of the John Rylands Library* 58:445–66.

————. 1983. "Language and Government in Medieval England." *Zeitschrift für Französische Sprache und Literatur* 93:258–70.

————. 1993a. "The 'Faus Franceis d'Angleterre': Later Anglo-Norman." In *Anglo-Norman Anniversary Essays,* Anglo-Norman Text Society Occasional Publications Series 2, ed. Ian Short, 309–26. London: Anglo-Norman Text Society.

————. 1993b. "The Legacy of Anglo-French: Faux Amis in French and English." *Zeitschrift für Romanische Philologie* 109:16–46.

————. 1994. "The Trilingual England of Geoffrey Chaucer." *SAC* 16:45–67.

Rouse, Richard H., and Mary A. Rouse, eds. 1991. *Registrum Angliae de Libris Doctorum et Auctorum Veterum.* London: British Library in association with the British Academy.

Rowland, Beryl, ed. 1981. *Medieval Woman's Guide to Health: The First English Gynaecological Handbook.* Kent, Ohio: Kent State University Press.

Rubin, Miri. 1991. *Corpus Christi: The Eucharist in Late Medieval Culture.* Cambridge: Cambridge University Press.

Rudd, Gillian. 1994. *Managing Language in "Piers Plowman."* Piers Plowman Studies 9. Cambridge: D. S. Brewer.

Runnalls, Graham. 1994. "Were They Listening or Watching? Text and Spectacle at the 1510 Chateaudun Passion Play." *Medieval English Theatre* 16:25–36.

Rusch, William G. 1977. *The Later Latin Fathers.* London: Duckworth.

Russell, George, and George Kane, eds. 1997. *Piers Plowman: The C Version.* London: Athlone; Berkeley and Los Angeles: University of California Press.

Rutter, Russell. 1987. "William Caxton and Literary Patronage." *Studies in Philology* 84:440–70.

Saenger, Paul. 1982. "Silent Reading: Its Impact on Late Medieval Script and Society." *Viator* 13:367–414.

———. 1997. *Space Between Words: The Origins of Silent Reading.* Stanford: Stanford University Press.

Salter, Elizabeth. 1974. *Nicholas Love's "Myrrour of the Blessed Lyf of Jesu Christ."* Analecta cartusiana 10. Salzburg: Universität Salzburg, Institut für Anglistik und Amerikanistik.

———. 1983. *Fourteenth-Century Poetry: Contexts and Readings.* Oxford: Clarendon Press.

Salter, F. M., and H.L.R. Edwards, eds. 1956–57. *The "Bibliotheca Historica" of Diodorus Siculus, Translated by John Skelton.* 2 vols. EETS, o.s., 233, 239.

Samson, Annie. 1986. "The *South English Legendary:* Constructing a Context." In *Thirteenth-Century England,* ed. P. R. Coss and S. D. Lloyd, 185–95. Woodbridge, Suffolk: Boydell.

Samuels, M. L. 1963. "Some Applications of Middle English Dialectology." *English Studies* 44:81–94. (Reprinted 1969 in *Approaches to English Historical Linguistics,* ed. Roger Lass, 404–18. New York: Holt, Rhinehart & Winston.)

———. 1981. "Spelling and Dialect in the Late and Post–Middle English Periods." In Benskin and Samuels 1981, 43–54.

Sanderlin, George. 1942. "Usk's *Testament of Love* and St. Anselm." *Speculum* 17:69–73.

Sandler, Lucy Freeman. 1986. *Gothic Manuscripts, 1285-1385.* (I. *Text and Illustrations*; II. *Catalogue*). Vol. 5 of *A Survey of Manuscripts Illuminated in the British Isles,* ed. J.J.G. Alexander. London. Harvey Miller.

Sandved, Arthur O. 1981. "Prolegomena to the Renewed Study of the Rise of Standard English." In Benskin and Samuels 1981, 31–42.

Sargent, Michael. 1976. "The Transmission by the English Carthusians of Some Late Medieval Spiritual Writings." *Journal of Ecclesiastical History* 27:225–40.

———. 1983. "Walter Hilton's *Scale of Perfection:* The London Manuscript Group Reconsidered." *Medium Ævum* 52:189–216.

———. 1984. "Bonaventure English: A Survey of the Middle English Prose Translations of Early Franciscan Literature." In Hogg 1984, 145–76.

———, ed. 1989. *De Cella in Seculum: Religious and Secular Life and Devotion in Late Medieval England.* Woodbridge, Suffolk: Boydell.

———, ed. 1992. *Nicholas Love's "Mirrour of the Blessed Lyf of Jesus Christ Oure Lord."* Garland Medieval Texts 18. New York: Garland.

———. 1995. "Versions of the Life of Christ: Nicholas Love's *Mirror* and Related Works." *Poetica* 42 (for 1994): 39–70.

Saussure, Ferdinand de. 1983. *Course in General Linguistics.* Ed. Charles Balley and Albert Sechehaye, with Albert Riedlinger; trans. Roy Harris. London: Duckworth.

Savage, Anne. 1993. "*Piers Plowman:* The Translation of Scripture and Food for the Soul." *English Studies* 74:209–21.

———. 1994. "The Translation of the Feminine: Untranslatable Dimensions of the Anchoritic Works." In Ellis and Evans 1994, 181–99.

Savage, Anne, and Nicholas Watson, trans. 1991. *Anchoritic Spirituality: "Ancrene Wisse" and Associated Works*. Classics of Western Spirituality. New York: Paulist Press.

Scanlon, Larry. 1990. "The King's Two Voices: Narrative and Power in Hoccleve's *Regement of Princes*." In Patterson 1990, 216–47.

———. 1994. *Narrative, Authority, and Power: The Medieval Exemplum and the Chaucerian Tradition*. Cambridge: Cambridge University Press.

Scase, Wendy. 1992. "Reginald Pecock, John Carpenter, and John Colop's 'Common-Profit' Books: Aspects of Book Ownership and Circulation in Fifteenth-Century London." *Medium Ævum* 61:261–74.

———. 1996. "Reginald Pecock." In Seymour 1996a, 69–146.

———. Forthcoming. "King-making: Literature and Royal Propaganda in Lancastrian England." Paper given at University of Pennsylvania, March 1998.

Scattergood, John. 1990. "The Date and Composition of George Ashby's Poems." *Leeds Studies in English*, n.s., 21:167–76.

———. 1994. "Chaucer's *Complaint of Venus* and the 'Curiosite' of Graunson." *Essays in Criticism* 44:171–89.

Scattergood, John, and J. W. Sherborne, eds. 1983. *English Court Culture in the Later Middle Ages*. New York: St. Martin's Press.

Scheps, Walter, and J. Anna Looney. 1986. *Middle Scots Poets: A Reference Guide to James I of Scotland, Robert Henryson, William Dunbar, and Gavin Douglas*. Boston: G. K. Hall.

Schibanoff, Susan. 1988. "The New Reader and Female Textuality in Two Early Commentaries on Chaucer." *SAC* 10:71–108.

———. 1994. "Taking the Gold out of Egypt: The Art of Reading As a Woman." In *Feminist Readings in Middle English Literature*, ed. Ruth Evans and Lesley Johnson, 221–45. London: Routledge. (Orig. pub. in *Gender and Reading: Essays on Readers, Texts, and Contexts,* ed. Elizabeth A. Flynn and Patrocinio P. Schweickart, 83–106. Baltimore: Johns Hopkins University Press, 1986.)

Schirmer, Walter F. 1961. *John Lydgate: A Study in the Culture of the XVth Century*. Trans. Ann E. Keep. London: Methuen.

Schmidt, A.V.C., ed. 1995a. *Piers Plowman: A Parallel-Text Edition of the A, B, C, and Z Versions*. London: Longman.

———. 1995b. *The Vision of Piers Plowman: A Critical Edition of the B-Text Based on Trinity College Cambridge* MS *B.15.17*. 2d ed. London: Dent.

Schmitt, F. S., ed. 1946–61. *S. Anselmi opera omnia*. 6 vols. Edinburgh: Nelson.

Science, Mark, ed. 1927. *Boethius "De Consolacione Philosophiae" Translated by John Walton Canon of Oseney*. EETS, o.s., 170.

Scott, Kathleen L. (see also Smith, Kathleen L.). 1976. *The Caxton Master and His Patrons*. With a preface by J.A.W. Bennett. Cambridge Bibliographical Society Monographs 8. Cambridge: Bibliographical Society.

———. 1982. "Lydgate's Lives of Saints Edmund and Fremund: A Newly Located Manuscript in Arundel Castle." *Viator* 13:335–66.

Serjeantson, Mary S., ed. 1938. *"Legendys of Hooly Wummen" by Osbern Bokenham*. EETS, o.s., 206.

Severs, J. Burke. See Hartung and Severs.

Seymour, M. C., ed. 1981. *Selections from Hoccleve*. Oxford: Clarendon Press.

———. 1993. "The Manuscripts of *The Legend of Good Women*." *Scriptorium* 47:73–90.

———, ed. 1994. *Authors of the Middle Ages: English Writers of the Late Middle Ages*. Vol. 1 (chaps. 1–4). Aldershot: Variorum. (Chaps. orig. pub. as four separate vols., 1993–94.)

———. 1995. *A Catalogue of Chaucer Manuscripts*. Pt. 1, *Works Before the Canterbury Tales*. Aldershot: Scolar Press.

————, ed. 1996a. *Authors of the Middle Ages: English Writers of the Late Middle Ages*. Vol. 3 (chaps. 7–11). Aldershot: Variorum. (Chaps. orig. pub. as five separate vols., 1995–96.)

————. 1996b. "John Capgrave." In Seymour 1996a, 195–256.

Seznec, Jean. 1953. *The Survival of the Pagan Gods: The Mythological Tradition and Its Place in Renaissance Humanism and Art*. Trans. Barbara F. Sessions. New York: Pantheon Books.

Shapiro, Marianne. 1990. *"De Vulgari Eloquentia": Dante's Book of Exile*. Lincoln: University of Nebraska Press.

Shaw, Judith. 1985. "The Influence of Canonical and Episcopal Reform on Popular Books of Instruction." In Heffernan 1985b, 44–60.

Shippey, T. A. 1970. "Listening for the Nightingale." *Comparative Literature* 22:46–60.

Shoaf, R. A., ed. 1998. *Thomas Usk, the Testament of Love*. TEAMS. Middle English Texts Series. Kalamazoo, Mich.: Medieval Institute.

Shonk, Timothy A. 1985. "A Study of the Auchinleck Manuscript: Bookmen and Bookmaking in the Early Fourteenth Century." *Speculum* 60:71–91.

Short, Ian. 1980. "On Bilingualism in Anglo-Norman England." *Romance Philology* 33:467–79.

Simmons, T. F., and H. E. Nolloth, eds. 1901. *The Lay Folks' Catechism*. EETS, o.s., 118.

Simpson, James. 1986. "From Reason to Affective Knowledge: Modes of Thought and Poetic Form in *Piers Plowman*." *Medium Ævum* 55:1–23.

————. 1990. *Piers Plowman: An Introduction to the B-Text*. London: Longman.

————. 1995. *Sciences and the Self in Medieval Poetry: Alain of Lille's "Anticlaudianus" and John Gower's "Confessio Amantis."* Cambridge: Cambridge University Press.

Simpson, John A., and E.S.C. Weiner, eds. 1989. *The Oxford English Dictionary*. 2d ed. 20 vols. First edited by James A. H. Murray, Henry Bradley, W. A. Craigie, and C. T. Onions. Combined with *A Supplement to the Oxford English Dictionary*, ed. R. W. Burchfield. Oxford: Clarendon Press.

Sinclair, K. V. 1992. "The Anglo-Norman Patrons of Robert the Chaplain and Robert of Greatham." *Forum for Modern Language Studies* 27:193–208.

Singerman, Jerome E. 1986. *Under Clouds of Poesy: Poetry and Truth in French and English Reworkings of the "Aeneid."* New York: Garland.

Siraisi, Nancy G. 1990. *Medieval and Early Renaissance Medicine: An Introduction to Knowledge and Practice*. Chicago: University of Chicago Press.

Skeat, Walter W., ed. 1897. *The Complete Works of Geoffrey Chaucer*. Vol. 7, *Chaucerian and Other Pieces*. Oxford: Clarendon Press.

————, ed. 1968. *The Bruce by John Barbour*. 2 vols. 1870–89. Reprint, vol. 1: EETS, e.s., 11, 55; vol. 2: EETS, e.s., 21, 29.

Small, John, ed. 1973. *English Metrical Homilies from Manuscripts of the Fourteenth Century*. 1862. Reprint, New York: AMS Press.

Smalley, Beryl. 1983. *The Study of the Bible in the Middle Ages*. 3d ed. Oxford: Blackwell.

Smedick, Lois K. 1975. "*Cursus* in Middle English: *A Talkyng of the Love of God* Reconsidered." *Mediaeval Studies* 37:387–406.

Smith, Jeremy. 1992. "A Linguistic Atlas of Early Middle English: Tradition and Typology." In Rissanen et al. 1992, 582–91.

Smith, Kathleen L. 1966. "A Fifteenth-Century Vernacular Manuscript Reconstructed." *Bodleian Library Record* 7, no. 5:234–41.

Smith, Lesley, and Jane H. M. Taylor, eds. 1995. *Selected Proceedings of the St. Hilda's Conference, 1993*. Vol. 1, *Women, the Book, and the Godly*; vol. 2, *Women, the Book, and the Worldly*. Cambridge: D. S. Brewer.

Solterer, Helen. 1991. "Figures of Female Militancy in Medieval France." *Signs: Journals of Women in Culture and Society* 16:522–49.

Somerset, Fiona. 1998. *Clerical Discourse and Lay Audience in Late Medieval England*. Cambridge: Cambridge University Press.

Southern, Richard W. 1953. *The Making of the Middle Ages*. New Haven: Yale University Press.

———. 1990. *Saint Anselm: A Portrait in a Landscape*. Cambridge: Cambridge University Press.

Spearing, A. C. 1984. "Lydgate's Canterbury Tale: *The Siege of Thebes* and Fifteenth-Century Chaucerianism." In Yeager 1984, 333–64.

Speed, Diane. 1994. "The Construction of the Nation in Medieval English Romance." In Meale 1994b, 135–57.

Spence, Sarah. 1996. *Texts and the Self in the Twelfth Century*. Cambridge: Cambridge University Press.

Spencer, Helen Leith. 1993. *English Preaching in the Late Middle Ages*. Oxford: Clarendon Press.

Sponsler, Claire. 1992. "The Culture of the Spectator: Conformity and Resistance to Medieval Performances." *Theatre Journal* 44:15–29.

Staley, Lynn. 1994. *Margery Kempe's Dissenting Fictions*. University Park: Pennsylvania State University Press.

———, ed. 1996. *The Book of Margery Kempe*. TEAMS. Middle English Texts Series. Kalamazoo, Mich.: Medieval Institute.

Staley Johnson, Lynn.1991. "The Trope of the Scribe and the Question of Literary Authority in the Works of Julian of Norwich and Margery Kempe." *Speculum* 66:820–38.

Staub, Susan C. 1990. "Recent Studies in Skelton (1970–1988)." *English Literary Renaissance* 20:505–16.

Stepsis, R. P., ed. 1967. "An Edition of Part II of Robert Mannyng of Brunne's *Chronicle of England*." Ph.D. diss., Harvard University.

Stevens, Mark. 1992. "John Skelton's Inflated Reputation as an Enricher of English Vocabulary." *Language Quarterly* 30:20–27.

Stevens, Martin. 1987. *Four Middle English Mystery Cycles: Textual, Contextual, and Critical Interpretations*. Princeton: Princeton University Press.

St.-Jacques, Raymond C. 1989. "The *Middle English Glossed Prose Psalter* and Its French Source." In Beer 1989, 135–54.

Stock, Brian. 1983. *The Implications of Literacy: Written Language and Models of Interpretation in the Eleventh and Twelfth Centuries*. Princeton: Princeton University Press.

———. 1990. *Listening for the Text: On the Uses of the Past*. Baltimore: Johns Hopkins University Press.

Stone, Louise W. 1947. "Jean de Howden: Poète anglo-normand du XIIIe siècle." *Romania* 69:496–519.

Strang, Barbara M. H. 1970. *A History of English*. London: Methuen.

Strohm, Paul. 1977. "Chaucer's Audience." *Literature and History* 6:26–41.

———. 1979. "Form and Social Statement in *Confessio Amantis* and *The Canterbury Tales*." *SAC* 1:17–40.

———. 1982. "Chaucer's Fifteenth-Century Audience and the Narrowing of the 'Chaucer Tradition.'" *SAC* 4:3–32.

———. 1983. "Chaucer's Audience(s): Fictional, Implied, Intended, Actual." *Chaucer Review* 18:137–64.

———. 1989. *Social Chaucer*. Cambridge, Mass.: Harvard University Press.

———. 1990. "Politics and Poetics: Usk and Chaucer in the 1380s." In Patterson 1990, 83–112.

———. 1992. *Hochon's Arrow: The Social Imagination of Fourteenth-Century Texts*. Princeton: Princeton University Press.

———. 1996a. "Afterword: What Happens at Intersections?" In Hanawalt and Wallace 1996, 223–32.

———. 1996b. "The Trouble with Richard: The Reburial of Richard II and Lancastrian Symbolic Strategy." *Speculum* 71:87–111.

———. 1997. *Sir John Oldcastle: Another Ill-Framed Knight.* The William Matthews Lectures, 1997. London: Birkbeck College.

Sturges, Robert S. 1985. "A Middle English Version of the Pseudo-Augustinian *Soliloquies*." *Manuscripta* 29:73–79.

———. 1995. "Medieval Authorship and the Polyphonic Text." In *Bakhtin and Medieval Voices,* ed. Thomas J. Farrell, 122–37. Gainesville: University Press of Florida.

Sullens, Idelle, ed. 1983. *Handlyng Synne.* Binghamton, N.Y.: Medieval and Renaissance Texts and Studies.

———, ed. 1996. *Robert Mannyng of Brunne: "The Chronicle."* Binghamton, N.Y.: Medieval and Renaissance Texts and Studies.

Summit, Jennifer. 1995. "William Caxton, Margaret Beaufort, and the Romance of Female Patronage." In Smith and Taylor 1995, 2:151–65.

Sutton, Anne F., and Lydia Visser-Fuchs, 1997. "The Cult of Angels in Late Fifteenth-Century England: An Hours of the Guardian Angel Presented to Elizabeth Woodville." In *Women and the Book: Assessing the Visual Evidence,* ed. Lesley Smith and Jane H. M. Taylor, 230–65. London and Toronto: British Library and University of Toronto Press.

Swanson, R. N. 1991. "The Origins of *The Lay Folks' Catechism*." *Medium Ævum* 60:92–100.

Swinburn, L. M. 1917. *The Lanterne of Light.* EETS, o.s., 151.

Talbert, Ernest W., and S. Harrison Thomson. 1970. "Wyclif and His Followers." Vol. 2, chap. 3, of Hartung and Severs 1967–.

Tanner, Norman P. 1984. *The Church in Late Medieval Norwich, 1370–1532.* Studies and Texts 66. Toronto: Pontifical Institute of Mediaeval Studies.

Tarvers, Josephine K. 1992. "'Thys Ys My Mystrys Boke': English Women as Readers and Writers in Late Medieval England." In *The Uses of Manuscripts in Literary Studies: Essays in Memory of Judson Boyce Allen,* Studies in Medieval Culture 31, ed. Charlotte Cook Morse, Penelope Reed Doob, and Marjorie Curry Woods, 305–27. Kalamazoo, Mich.: Medieval Institute.

Taylor, Andrew. 1991. "The Myth of the Minstrel Manuscript." *Speculum* 66:43–73.

———. 1992. "Fragmentation, Corruption, and Minstrel Narration: The Question of the Middle English Romances." *Yearbook of English Studies* 22:38–62.

———. 1995. "Reading the Body in *Le Livre de Seyntz Medecines*." In *The Body in Medieval Art, History, and Literature,* Essays in Medieval Studies 11, ed. Allen J. Frantzen and David. A. Robertson, 103–18. Chicago: Illinois Medieval Association.

———. 1996. "Into His Secret Chamber: Reading and Privacy in Late Medieval England." In *The Practice and Representation of Reading in England,* ed. James Raven, Helen Small, and Naomi Tadmor, 41–61. Cambridge: Cambridge University Press.

———. 1997. "Anne of Bohemia and the Making of Chaucer." *SAC* 19:95–119.

Teague, Frances. 1991. "Christine de Pizan's *Book of War*." In *The Reception of Christine de Pizan from the Fifteenth Through the Nineteenth Centuries: Visitors to the City,* ed. Glenda McLeod, 25–41. Lewiston, N.Y.: Edward Mellen Press.

Thiolier, Jean Claude, ed. 1989. *Edition critique et commentée de Pierre de Langtoft: Le règne d'Édouard 1er.* Vol. 1. Créteil: Centre d'Etudes Littéraires et Iconographiques du Moyen Age (C.E.L.I.M.A.), Université de Paris XII.

Thomas, Keith. 1973. *Religion and the Decline of Magic: Studies in Popular Beliefs in Sixteenth- and Seventeenth-Century England.* Harmondsworth, Middlesex: Penguin.

Thompson, John J. 1983. "The Compiler in Action: Robert Thornton and the 'Thornton Romances' in Lincoln Cathedral MS 91." In Pearsall 1983, 113–24.

———. 1994a. "Another Look at the Religious Texts in Lincoln Cathedral Library, MS 91." In Minnis 1994, 169–88.

———. 1994b. "The *Cursor Mundi*, the 'Inglis Tong,' and Romance." In Meale 1994b, 99–120.

———. 1997. "The *Cursor Mundi* and Its French Tradition." In *Individuality and Achievement in Middle English Poetry*, ed. Oliver Pickering, 19–37. Cambridge: D. S. Brewer.

Thomson, S. Harrison. 1940. *The Writings of Robert Grosseteste, Bishop of Lincoln, 1235–1253*. Cambridge: Cambridge University Press.

Thorndike, Lynn. 1934. *A History of Magic and Experimental Science*. Vols. 3 and 4, *Fourteenth and Fifteenth Centuries*. New York: Columbia University Press.

Thrupp, Sylvia L. 1948. *The Merchant Class of Medieval London (1300–1500)*. Chicago: University of Chicago Press. (Reprint 1962, Ann Arbor: University of Michigan Press.)

Tolkien, J.R.R. 1929. "*Ancrene Wisse* and *Hali Meiðhad*." *Essays and Studies* 14:104–26.

Torti, Anna. 1989. "From 'History' to 'Tragedy': The Story of Troilus and Criseyde in Lydgate's *Troy Book* and Henryson's *Testament of Cresseid*." In *The European Tragedy of Troilus*, ed. Piero Boitani, 171–97. Oxford: Clarendon Press.

Tout, Thomas F. 1920–33. *Chapters in the Administrative History of Medieval England*. 6 vols. Manchester: Manchester University Press.

Trigg, Stephanie, ed. 1990. *Wynnere and Wastoure*. EETS, o.s., 297.

Turville-Petre, Thorlac. 1977. *The Alliterative Revival*. Cambridge: Cambridge University Press.

———. 1988. "Politics and Poetry in the Early Fourteenth Century: The Case of Robert Manning's *Chronicle*." *Review of English Studies*, n.s., 39:1–28.

———, ed. 1989. *Alliterative Poetry of the Later Middle Ages: An Anthology*. London: Routledge.

———. 1996. *England the Nation: Language, Literature, and National Identity, 1290–1340*. Oxford: Clarendon Press.

van Bavel, T. J., and R. Canning, eds. 1996. *The Rule of St. Augustine: Masculine and Feminine Versions*. London: Darton, Longman & Todd.

van Buuren, Catherine. 1996. "John Asloan and His Manuscript: An Edinburgh Notary and Scribe in the Days of James III, IV, and V (c. 1470–c. 1530)." In *Stewart Style, 1513–1542: Essays on the Court of James V*, ed. Janet Hadley Williams, 75–96. East Linton, East Lothian: Tuckwell.

van Buuren-Veenenbos, Catherine, ed. 1982. *The Buke of the Sevyne Sagis*. Leiden: Leiden University Press.

Vessey, Mark. 1994. "Erasmus' Jerome: The Publishing of a Christian Author." *Erasmus of Rotterdam Society Yearbook* 14:62–99.

Vinaver, Eugene. 1971. *Sir Thomas Malory: Works*. Oxford: Oxford University Press.

Voaden, Rosalynn. 1995. "God's Almighty Hand: Women Co-Writing the Book" In Smith and Taylor 1995, 1:55–66.

———. 1996a. "The Company She Keeps: Mechtild of Hackeborn in Late Medieval Devotional Compilations." In Voaden 1996b, 51–70.

———, ed. 1996b. *Prophets Abroad: The Reception of Continental Holy Women in Late Medieval England*. Cambridge: D. S. Brewer.

———. 1996c. "Women's Words, Men's Language: *Discretio Spirituum* as Discourse in the Writing of Medieval Women Visionaries." In Ellis and Tixier 1996, 64–83.

Voigts, Linda Ehrsam. 1985. "Handlist of Middle English in Harvard Manuscripts." *Harvard Library Bulletin* 33:17–67.

———. 1989. "Scientific and Medical Books." In Griffiths and Pearsall 1989, 345–402.

———. 1996. "What's the Word? Bilingualism in Late-Medieval England." *Speculum* 71:813–26.

von Nolcken, Christina. 1986. "Julian of Norwich." In Edwards 1986, 97–108.

Waldron, R. 1988. "John Trevisa and the Use of English." *Proceedings of the British Academy* 74:171–202.

———. 1996. "Trevisa's Original Prefaces on Translation: A Critical Edition." In Kennedy, Waldron, and Wittig 1988, 285–99. Reprinted in Burrow and Turville-Petre 1996, 215–22.

Wallace, David. 1984. "Mystics and Followers in Siena and East Anglia: A Study in Taxonomy, Class, and Cultural Mediation." In Glasscoe 1984, 169–91.

———, ed. 1998. *The Cambridge History of Medieval English Literature: Writing in Medieval Britain, 1066–1547*. Cambridge: Cambridge University Press.

Wallner, Björn, ed. 1964. *The Middle English Translation of Guy de Chauliac's "Anatomy," with Guy's Essay on the History of Medicine*. Lund: C.W.K. Gleerup.

———. 1965. "Drawings of Surgical Instruments in MS Bibl. Nat. Angl. 25." *English Studies* 46:182–86.

———, ed. 1969. *The Middle English Translation of Guy de Chauliac's "Treatise on the Fractures and Dislocations."* Bk. 5 of *The Great Surgery: Edited from MS. New York Academy of Medicine 12 and Related MSS*. Lund: C.W.K. Gleerup.

———, ed. 1971. *A Middle English Version of the Introduction to Guy de Chauliac's "Chirurgia Magna."* Lund: C.W.K. Gleerup.

———, ed. 1979. *The Middle English Translation of Guy de Chauliac's "Treatise on Wounds."* Bk. 3 of *The Great Surgery: Edited from MS. New York Academy of Medicine 12 and Related MSS*. Stockholm: Almqvist & Wiksell.

———, ed. 1982–84. *The Middle English Translation of Guy de Chauliac's "Treatise on Ulcers."* Bk. 4 of *The Great Surgery: Edited from MS. New York Academy of Medicine 12 and Related MSS*. Stockholm: Almqvist & Wiksell.

———, ed. 1988. *The Middle English Translation of Guy de Chauliac's "Treatise on 'Apostemes.'"* Bk. 2 of *The Great Surgery: Edited from MS. New York Academy of Medicine 12 and Related MSS*. Lund: Lund University Press.

———, ed. 1995–96. *An Interpolated Middle English Version of "The Anatomy" of Guy de Chauliac*. Lund: Lund University Press.

Ward, Benedicta. 1983. "Inward Feeling and Deep Thinking: The Prayers and Meditations of St. Anselm Revisited." *Anselm Studies* 1:177–83.

Ward, Jennifer. 1992. *English Noblewomen in the Later Middle Ages*. London: Longman.

Warner, George F., ed. 1889. *The Buke of John Mandeuille, Being the Travels of John Mandeville, Knight, 1322–56*. London: Roxburgh Club.

———, ed. 1926. *The Libelle of Englyshe Polycye: A Poem on the Use of Sea-Power, 1436*. Oxford: Clarendon Press.

Warren, Ann K. 1985. *Anchorites and Their Patrons in Medieval England*. Berkeley and Los Angeles: University of California Press.

Watkin, A. 1941. "Some Manuscripts in the Downside Abbey Library." *Downside Review* 59:75–83.

Watson, Andrew G., ed. 1987. *Supplement: N. R. Ker, Medieval Libraries of Great Britain: A List of Surviving Books*. London: Royal Historical Society.

Watson, George, ed. 1974. *The New Cambridge Bibliography of English Literature*. Vol. 1, *600–1660*. Cambridge: Cambridge University Press.

Watson, Nicholas. 1991. *Richard Rolle and the Invention of Authority*. Cambridge: Cambridge University Press.

———. 1993. "The Composition of Julian of Norwich's *Revelation of Love*." *Speculum* 68:637–83.

———. 1994. "Outdoing Chaucer: Lydgate's *Troy Book* and Henryson's *Testament of Cresseid* as Competitive Imitations of *Troilus and Criseyde*." In *Shifts and Transpositions in Medieval Narrative: A Festschrift for Dr. Elspeth Kennedy*, ed. Karen Pratt, 89–108. Cambridge: D. S. Brewer.

———. 1995a. "Censorship and Cultural Change in Late-Medieval England: Vernacular Theology, the Oxford Translation Debate, and Arundel's Constitutions of 1409." *Speculum* 70:822–64.

———, ed. 1995b. *Richard Rolle, "Emendatio vitae," "Orationes ad honorem nominis Ihesu."* Toronto Medieval Latin Texts 21. Toronto: Pontifical Institute of Mediaeval Studies.

———. 1996. "Melting into God the English Way: Deification in the Middle English Version of Marguerite Porete's *Mirouer des Simples Ames Anienties.*" In Voaden 1996b, 19–50.

———. 1997a. "Conceptions of the Word: The Mother Tongue and the Incarnation of God." *New Medieval Literatures* 1:85–124.

———. 1997b. "Visions of Inclusion: Universal Salvation and Vernacular Theology in Pre-Reformation England." *Journal of Medieval and Early Modern Studies* 27:145–87.

———. 1998. "The Middle English Mystics." In Wallace 1998, 539–65.

Watt, Diane. 1994. "Nationalism in Barbour's *Bruce.*" *Parergon* 12, no. 1: 89–107.

———. 1997. *Secretaries of God: Women Prophets in Late Medieval and Early Modern England.* Cambridge: D. S. Brewer.

Watt, Ian. 1957. *The Rise of the Novel: Studies in Defoe, Richardson, and Fielding.* London: Chatto & Windus.

Watts, John. 1996. *Henry VI and the Politics of Kingship.* Cambridge: Cambridge University Press.

Webber, Teresa. 1992. *Scribes and Scholars at Salisbury Cathedral: C. 1075–1125.* Oxford: Clarendon Press.

Welliver, Warman. 1981. *Dante in Hell: The "De Vulgari Eloquentia": Introduction, Text, Translation, Commentary.* Ravenna: Longo Editore.

Westra, M. Salvina, ed. 1950. *A Talking of the Love of God.* The Hague: Nijhoff.

Willard, Charity Canon. 1970. "Christine de Pisan's Treatise on the Art of Medieval Warfare." In *Essays in Honor of Louis Francis Solano,* University of North Carolina Studies in the Romance Languages and Literature 92, ed. Raymond J. Cormier and U. T. Holmes 1970, 179–91. Chapel Hill: University of North Carolina Press.

———. 1984. *Christine de Pizan: Her Life and Works.* New York: Persea.

Williams, Glanmor. 1979. *Religion, Language, and Nationality in Wales: Historical Essays.* Cardiff: University of Wales Press.

Williams, Jeni. 1997. *Interpreting Nightingales: Gender, Class, and Histories.* Sheffield: Sheffield Academic Press.

Wilmart, André. 1971. *Auteurs spirituels et textes dévots du Moyen Âge Latin.* 1932. Reprint, Paris: Études Augustiniennes.

Wilsher, Bridget Anne. 1956. "An Edition of *Speculum Devotorum,* a Fifteenth-Century English Meditation on the Life and Passion of Jesus Christ." 2 vols. Master's thesis, University of London.

Wilson, C. Anne. 1991. *Food and Drink in Britain: From the Stone Age to Recent Times.* Chicago: Academy Chicago Publishers. (Orig. pub. London: Constable, 1973.)

Wilson, Grace G. 1990. "Barbour's *Bruce* and Harry's *Wallace:* Complements, Compensations, and Conventions." *Studies in Scottish Literature* 25:189–201.

Wilson, R. M. 1943. "English and French in England, 1100–1300." *History* 28:37–66.

———. 1970. *The Lost Literature of Medieval England.* 2d ed. London: Methuen.

Wimsatt, James I. 1991. *Chaucer and His French Contemporaries: Natural Music in the Fourteenth Century.* Toronto: University of Toronto Press.

Windeatt, B. A. 1977. "Julian of Norwich and Her Audience." *Review of English Studies,* n.s., 28:1–17.

Winstead, Karen A. 1991. "Piety, Politics, and Social Commitment in Capgrave's *Life of St. Katherine.*" *Medievalia et Humanistica,* n.s., 17:59–80.

———. 1996. "John Capgrave and the Chaucer Tradition." *Chaucer Review* 30:389–400.

Withington, Robert. 1918. *English Pageantry.* 2 vols. Cambridge, Mass.: Harvard University Press.

Wogan-Browne, Jocelyn. 1994a. "The Apple's Message: Some Post-Conquest Hagiographic Accounts of Textual Transmission." In Minnis 1994, 39–54.

———. 1994b. "Wreaths of Time: The Female Translator in Anglo-Norman Hagiography." In Ellis and Evans 1994, 46–65.

Woodforde, Christopher. 1950. *The Norwich School of Glass-Painting in the Fifteenth Century.* London: Oxford University Press.

Wormald, Francis, and C. E. Wright, eds. 1958. *The English Library Before 1700.* London: Athlone Press.

Wright, Laura. 1992. "Macaronic Writing in a London Archive, 1380–1480." In Rissanen et al. 1992, 582–91.

———. 1996. *Sources of London English.* Oxford: Clarendon Press.

Wright, T., ed. 1868. *The Knight de la Tour Landry: A Book for Daughters.* EETS, o.s., 33.

Yeager, Robert F., ed. 1984. *Fifteenth-Century Studies: Recent Essays.* Hamden, Conn.: Archon.

———. 1990. *John Gower's Poetic: The Search for a New Arion.* Publications of the John Gower Society 2. Cambridge: D. S. Brewer.

Zumthor, Paul. 1972a. *Essai de poétique médiévale.* Paris: Éditions du Seuil.

———. 1972b. "Jonglerie et Langage." *Poétique* 11:321–36.

———. 1979. "From Hi(story) to Poem, or the Paths of Pun: The Grands Rhétoriqueurs of Fifteenth-Century France." *New Literary History* 10:231–63.

———. 1992. *Toward a Medieval Poetics.* Trans. Philipp Bennett. Minneapolis: University of Minnesota Press. (Translation of Zumthor 1972a.)

INDEX

Names are normally entered under their modern spelling. Page references to excerpts are in bold. The index covers proper names and selected themes; Middle English literary terms are covered in the Glossary. The index does not include listings under Alternative Arrangements.

ABOUT THE EDITORS

JOCELYN WOGAN-BROWNE teaches at the University of Liverpool, U.K., and researches Middle English and Anglo-Norman literature, especially texts for or by twelfth- and thirteenth-century women. As well as many articles—including a study of Anglo-Norman women and hagiography in Carol Meale's volume *Women and Literature in Britain, 1150–1500* (Cambridge: Cambridge University Press)—her publications include *Middle English Prose for Women: Selections from the Katherine Group and "Ancrene Wisse"* (with Bella Millett) (Oxford: Clarendon Press, 1992); *Virgin Lives and Holy Deaths: Two Exemplary Biographies for Anglo-Norman Women* (with Glyn S. Burgess) (London: Everyman, 1996), which includes the first translation of Clemence of Barking's *Life of St. Catherine*; *Concordance to Ancrene Wisse* (with Jennifer Potts and Lorna Stevenson) (Cambridge: D. S. Brewer); and *Voicing Medieval Women*, a two-volume tape anthology in Middle English, French, Provençal, Anglo-Norman, and Old Norse (Chaucer Studio, 1996). She is currently finishing her book, *Authorized Virgins: Saints' Lives and the Literary Culture of Women in Britain, c. 1150–c. 1300*, for Oxford University Press, and is working on a *Concordance to the Katherine Group and the Wooing Group* for D. S. Brewer (with Lorna Stevenson), and a study of women and the Bible in Anglo-Norman England, as part of a larger project on the French culture of women in medieval England to 1450, including Anglo-French and Flemish connections.

NICHOLAS WATSON teaches at the University of Western Ontario, Canada, and researches religious writing from the twelfth to the fifteenth centuries, especially in Middle English and Latin. Besides articles in essay collections and such journals as *Journal of Medieval and Early Modern Studies* and *New Medieval Literatures*—including "The Composition of Julian of Norwich's *Revelation of Love* (1993) and "Censorship and Cultural Change in Late-Medieval England" (1995), both published in *Speculum*—his publications include *Richard Rolle and the Invention of Authority* (Cambridge: Cambridge University Press, 1991); *Anchoritic Spirituality: "Ancrene Wisse" and Associated Works* (with Anne Savage), Classics of Western Spirituality (New York: Paulist Press, 1991); and *Richard Rolle: Emendatio vitae, Orationes ad honorem nominis Ihesu* (Toronto: Pontifical Institute, 1995). He is currently working on a parallel-text edition of Julian of Norwich's *Revelation of Love* for Penn State Press (with Jacqueline Jenkins); an edition and study of John of Morigny's ritual magic text, the *Liber visionum*, for Alan Sutton (with Claire Fanger); and a book called *Balaam's Ass: Vernacular Theology in Medieval England*, an attempt to rethink the history of religious writing in Middle English in relation to the complex history of medieval attitudes to the vernacular.

ANDREW TAYLOR teaches at the University of Saskatchewan, Canada, and researches Middle English, Anglo-Norman, French, and Latin literature from the twelfth to the sixteenth centuries, especially in relation to minstrelsy, oral performance, and private reading. Besides articles in essay collections and in such journals as *Speculum* and *Exemplaria*—including "Anne of Bohemia and the Making of Chaucer," in *Studies in the Age of Chaucer* (1997), and "Into His Secret Chamber: Reading and Privacy in Late Medieval England," in James Raven's collection *The Practice and Representation of Reading in England* (Cambridge University Press, 1996)—his publications include *The Tongue of the Fathers: Gender and Ideology in Twelfth-Century Latin* (with David Townsend) (Philadelphia: University of Pennsylvania Press, 1998), to which he also contributed an article on Peter Abelard. He is currently working on *The Edge of the Book: Three Medieval Manuscripts and Their Readers*, which explores the challenges of reading medieval manuscripts in an age of digital reproduction.

RUTH EVANS teaches at the University of Cardiff, Wales/Cymru, U.K., and researches medieval translation, Middle English cycle drama, and critical theory. As well as writing review articles on literary theory and medieval studies for journals such as *Southern Review*, *Textual Practice*, and the *Journal of Gender Studies*, she has published numerous articles, including "When a Body Meets a Body: Fergus and Mary in the York Cycle," in the first issue of *New Medieval Literatures* (1997) and "Gender, Sexuality, and Space in the York Cycle," in Sarah Stanbury and Virgina Raguin's collection *Women's Spaces* (Philadelphia: University of Pennsylvania Press, 1998). She is also the editor of *Simone de Beauvoir, The Second Sex: New Interdisciplinary Essays* (Manchester: Manchester University Press, 1997); co-editor of *Feminist Readings in Middle English Literature: The Wife of Bath and All Her Sect* (with Lesley Johnson) (London: Routledge, 1994); and co-editor of *The Medieval Translator*, vol. 4 (with Roger Ellis) (Exeter: Exeter University Press, 1994), to which she also contributed an article on medieval translation theory and postcolonialism. She is currently preparing an edition of early fifteenth-century vernacular sermons with Lollard connections for the series Middle English Texts, and writing a book on Chaucer for Macmillan.